| | | | |
|---|---|---|---|
| 80 03 27 | 81 05 09 | | |
| 80 03 20 | 91 09 05 | | |
| 81 03 27 | 91 08 29 | | |
| 81 03 20 | 94 08 22 | | |
| 81 11 29 | 94 08 08 | | |
| | 94 09 02 | | |
| 81 11 26 | 94 09 29 | | |
| 83 01 13 | | | |
| | | | |
| 83 01 12 | | | |
| 85 11 01 | | | |
| 85 10 30 | | | |
| 86 05 06 | | | |
| 86 02 09 | | | |
| 91 01 09 | | | |

# AMERICAN MARKETING ASSOCIATION

## AVAILABLE PROCEEDINGS

| Series No. | Title | Price Member | Nonmember |
|---|---|---|---|
| 33 | **RELEVANCE IN MARKETING**<br>**MARKETING IN MOTION**<br>Combined Proceedings of the 1971 Spring & Fall Conferences | 17.95 | 23.95 |
| 35 | **INCREASING MARKETING PRODUCTIVITY**<br>**CONCEPTUAL & METHODOLOGICAL FOUNDATIONS OF MKTG**<br>Combined Proceedings of the 1973 Spring & Fall Conferences | 17.95 | 23.95 |
| 36 | **NEW MARKETING FOR SOCIAL AND ECONOMIC PROGRESS**<br>**MARKETING'S CONTRIBUTION TO THE FIRM AND TO SOCIETY**<br>Combined Proceedings of the 1974 Spring & Fall Conferences | 17.95 | 23.95 |
| 37 | **MARKETING IN TURBULENT TIMES**<br>**MARKETING: THE CHALLENGES AND THE OPPORTUNITIES**<br>Combined Proceedings of the 1975 Spring & Fall Conferences | 17.95 | 23.95 |
| 38 | **MARKETING LOOKS OUTWARD**<br>Proceedings of the 1976 Spring Business Conference | 10.00 | 15.00 |
| 41 | **CONTEMPORARY MARKETING THOUGHT**<br>Proceedings of the 1977 Educators Conference | 15.00 | 20.00 |

Proceedings not listed here are out of print. Reproduced copies may be ordered from Xerox University Microfilms, Inc. Ann Arbor, Michigan 48106.

# Contemporary Marketing Thought

# 1977 Educators' Proceedings

## Series #41

Edited by: **Barnett A. Greenberg**
Georgia State University

and

**Danny N. Bellenger**
Georgia State University

American **Marketing** Association

222 S. Riverside Plaza          Chicago, IL 60606          (312) 648-0536

Cover design by Mary Jo Galluppi

**Library of Congress Cataloging in Publication Data**

Contemporary marketing thought.

  (Series - American Marketing Association; 41)

    1. Marketing—Congresses.  I. Greenberg, Barnett, 1944—
II. Bellenger, Danny, 1946—  III. American Marketing
Association.  IV. Series: American Marketing Association.
Series; 41.
HF5415.C54753     658.8      77-24923
ISBN 0-87757-098-1

This Proceeding was prepared from camera-ready
copy supplied by the authors.

TABLE OF CONTENTS

# PREFACE

The American Marketing Association 1977 Marketing Educators' Conference was held in Hartford, Connecticut, August 7-10. The conference had no specific theme leading us to a title for the Proceedings of "Contemporary Marketing Thought". This title seems appropriate in that the program was structured in a manner which would encourage discussion of topical issues.

The Proceedings contains 107 papers and 54 abstracts. Although most of the papers were competitive entries, a number were invited. This approach afforded the program chairman an opportunity to direct discussion in certain key areas of marketing thought. A novel feature of the 1977 program was the round-table session. These sessions were added to the program to encourage interaction among the conference attendees. Papers from the roundtables were submitted in abstract form for the Proceedings. Finally, John Keene's presidential address at last year's conference is published in this year's Proceedings.

We would like to thank everyone involved in the conference including the Program Chairman, Track Chairmen, the Session Chairmen, and especially the authors. Everyone has been most helpful in cooperating with us to insure maximum participation in the Proceedings.

The Educators' Proceedings are being prepublished for the second consecutive year. Under this relatively new arrangement, the Association is able to produce its Proceedings at a significantly reduced cost, but the time and effort devoted to the Proceedings by many individuals is significantly greater than in past years. Our assistants here at Georgia State University bore the brunt of the effort and we commended them for their devotion and reliability in meeting deadlines which appeared at times to be unreasonable. Both Ruth Otte and Brneda Franz have made an invaluable contribution to the Association in this regard.

We are grateful to the various officers of the AMA who provided invaluable support to our efforts. Specifically, we express our appreciation to Pat Dunn, Keith Cox, and Ron Shawver. We would also like to thank AMA staff members Peggy Simpson and Joan Perrell. It is our hope that the 1977 Proceedings will uphold the tradition of quality as a contribution to the marketing literature which has made the Educators' Conference such an important component of marketing scholarship today.

Barnett A. Greenberg
Danny N. Bellenger
Co-Editors

School of Business Administration
Georgia State University
Atlanta, Georgia

xi

FUTURE MARKETING EDUCATION: RUBBISH OR CHERISH? [1]

John G. Keane, Managing Change, Incorporated
President, American Marketing Association

August 19, 1975, the Eastman Kodak Company treated most of us attending last year's conference to an evening in its marketing education center. That splendid facility and its activity bespeak the philosophy of company founder and eminent educator, George Eastman. Said Eastman, "'...The progress of the world depends almost entirely on education.'" [17] Today, progress in the marketing world critically depends upon marketing education. But is it progressing satisfactorily?

Professor Twedt, in the current issue of Marketing News, presented relevant trend statistics. His analysis indicates that: [22]

The number of marketing degrees annually conferred peaked around 18 thousand in 1972.

From a high of 18 percent in 1972, marketing's share of total business degrees annually declined to 15 percent in 1975 (latest available year).

While the number of business degrees annually awarded continues to climb, the number of marketing degrees continues to decline. Marketing's challenges surely were never more formidable. But business students and business employers lately are tending to favor other business disciplines over marketing. Marketing educators beware: your market may be ebbing!

Therefore, it is with caring and concern that I address you. My title, "Future Marketing Education: Rubbish or Cherish?", is not intended as a coy or curt pun. Rather, it is intended to focus attention on the marketing education needs of business where most marketing graduates go.

Before outlining remedial suggestions for you to consider you should know their basis. They stem from:

- my recurring contact with this Association's academic and business members,
- my recent correspondence with a diverse group of university marketing department heads and corporate marketing department heads,
- plus my continual monitoring of the business environment and consulting with a wide variety of companies and marketing operations.

Knowing my reference points may help you judge the merit of my suggestions.

SUGGESTIONS

My suggestions deal with directions for marketing education to either initiate or expand. There are seven. Perhaps several of them will strike a responsive cord.

1. Externalize Curriculum Focus

Those of you attending our June international marketing conference may recall its theme, "Marketing Looks Outward." That theme aptly reflects the conceptual, definitional, functional and geographic elasticizing of traditional marketing thought and practice.

Perhaps three incidents occurring just within the past

---

[1]Speech to the Marketing Educator's Conference, "Marketing: 1776-1976 and Beyond", American Marketing Association, Hyatt Regency Memphis Hotel, Memphis Tennessee, August 9, 1976.

month will illustrate mounting externalities confronting marketing. In July, "Three of Fifth Avenue's most fashionable stores -- Bergdorf Goodman, Bonwit Teller, and Saks Fifth Avenue -- offered $5.2 million Friday to settle a series of consumer civil lawsuits alleging a conspiracy to overprice women's clothing from 1964 to 1974."[9] Such class action suits go beyond pricing to ultimately influence store merchandising, company image, advertising, customer relations and other areas of marketing more than ever before. Two days later, Business Week carried an age discrimination story. Its lead paragraph captures what is at stake: "The Labor Department will soon slap American Motors Corporation with a potentially costly age discrimination suit. The principal charge: in reshaping its marketing department, AMC forced out several hundred employees including managers and salesmen, simply because they were considered too old."[1]

Let us shift our attention to the recently completed 21st Summer Olympiad. While television viewers absorbed themselves with the superb performances of Nadia Comaneci and Bruce Jenner, commercial sponsors of the games concerned themselves with the increasing geopolitical strife and its future sponsorship implications. Would future international turmoil curb or curtail their promotion opportunities during the 1980 Olympics?

These three instances evidence the intensifying need for macro marketing education. Beyond providing a cluster of skills, the overriding challenge is to induce an outside-in perspective. Effective response to the evolving marketing environment depends ever more on developing external sensitivity than on skills development.

2. Address Contemporary Reality

R. L. Crandall, Senior Vice President of Marketing for American Airlines says, "...The greatest fault I find with new graduates of all disciplines is the lack of appreciation for the pragmatic requirements."[6] Last March, a New York Times marketing position advertisement had this headline: "The Quaker Oats Company is Seeking a Marketing Research Manager with Marketing Savvy." Note the phrase "marketing savvy" suggestive of a real-world feel. The company's desire for a marketing realist is reinforced in the body of the advertisement where it reads: "In short, we are seeking a researcher who evidences the desire and talent to participate in the marketing leadership of Quaker's grocery products group."[21]

To underscore the need for reality, I cite four (of many) examples of real-world marketing that I have seen scant mention of in the marketing literature and curricula. One example is so-called "stock dusting." Euphemistically labeled, this practice, known well to health care and other sales force personnel consists of rearranging their brands at the expense of competitors for shelf advantage.

Another example is the advertising/promotion strategy and tactic termed "four-walling." The promotion planners at Hollywood film companies use it well. Four-walling refers to local market advertising blitzkreigs -- especially television -- to boost the box office of such movies as "Exorcist," "Jaws," and less prominent efforts desperate for the Hollywood hype.

The use of blind typists in transcribing audio-recorded focus groups combines social responsibility with more accurate transcription because of the enhanced voice discriminatory power the blind typically possess. Better transcripts, analysis and resultant marketing decisions are the

1

likely result.

You may counter with, "These are fringe examples and don't rate space in any already topic-tight marketing curriculum". If so, then you might be interested in what three quite recent marketing MBA's (two from Harvard and the other from Northwestern) reported where they work, Kraft Foods, in research and marketing. Commenting to Senior Vice President of Marketing, H. K. Ridgway, on the needs of future marketing education, they listed nine areas they collectively agreed were under-addressed in their respective university curricula. The nine areas are:

> "demographic trends and implications,
> lifestyle and attitudinal analysis,
> study of competitive action and reaction,
> retailing structure and management sophistication,
> legal contraints: pricing laws, Robinson-Patman, trademarks, etc.,
> raw materials systems: commodities, manpower, energy,
> more analysis on trade and consumer promotions (compared to volume already done on consumer advertising),
> advertising specifics, not just advertising's general role in the marketing mix: more on media efficiency and editorial climate,
> and [under financial analysis] product line efficiency: product mix studies, product proliferation."[15]

I choose only to report -- not to judge -- the beforementioned list of areas in which these three MBA's felt their training relative to the real world was deficient.

What does seem to be indicated from a number of directions is more reality-based marketing education. Along these lines, I am suggesting that we do not confuse rationality with reality ... that we seek **practically over sophistication** ... that we gear teaching toward trending needs over traditional approaches and, above all, that we stress relevance over rigor. On this last point, Professor Buzzell of Harvard states: "I think the field has made great progress in the past 10-15 years in achieving more rigorous, intellectually demanding courses. Now, I think, this rigor needs to be maintained but in the context of much greater relevance. We need to study, teach and write about problems of greater significance than (for example) brand switching in the tooth paste category."[4]

3. Expand Academic-Business Exchangeability

Several years ago, a Florida State University Assistant Professor of Criminology, Dr. George L. Kirkham, wanted to understand law enforcement firsthand. He explained his motivation this way, "For some years, first as a student and later as a Professor of Criminology, I was troubled by the fact that most of us who write books and articles on the police have never been policemen ourselves. I decided to take up this challenge..."[12] So after formal Police Academy training, he became a policeman and member of the 800-person Jacksonville-Duval County Police Force.

Within a few short months, Dr. Kirkland experienced adrenal in-pumping personal fear, the need for split-second critical decisions, the angry mob, etc., and the gap between theory and practice. For instance, as a beat cop he saw criminals in the cold act rather than after the fact as he had as a professor. It dramatically changed his views and teachings. Observed Dr. Kirkland after six months of "street lessons:" "Those few steps have given me a profoundly new understanding and appreciation of our policy, and have left me with the humbling realization that possession of a Ph.D. does not give a man a corner on knowledge, or place him in the lofty position where he cannot take lessons from those less educated than himself."[13]

The point is obvious. There is no substitute for having personally experienced marketing situations taught. The

factors of timing, budget, personalities, weather and other uncertainties are far less orderly, predictable and controllable than marketing theorists might imply. Experiments, clinical observations and consulting are quite worthwhile. Assuming the marketing roles taught is far better.

Analogously, there is an opportunity under-realized because of lack of academic and business marketing exchange programs. In my experience, the fault lies more with business than academe. Caught up in their day-to-day activites businesses too often short-shrift the educational well from which they drink. Giving money is commendable. Sharing data helps. But business should greatly expand the amount and quality of data shared with academics. Competitive disclosure is too often used as an "out" when the strategic corporate risk isn't all that significant. Dwarfing both giving money and data is for business to offer its experienced managers to work side-by-side with dedicated faculties to enhance the relevance of marketing education such as IBM does with its commendable external professor program. Conversely, business would benefit itself by improving the quantity and particularly the quality of summer and sabbatical openings in marketing.

My final comment on this point is to stress the **desirability** of expanded student **internship programs**. **One senior marketing** executive, William P. Stiritz, Vice President and Director of Ralston Purina Grocery Products opts for "more emphasis on combination school and work programs where the student would be required to spend 15 to 20 hours weekly on a paid job with an area firm."[18] I agree. Yet, the distressing part of such an academic-business coop program is that, in general, neither group seems to work at this opportunity with sustained zeal. Shortsightedly, it remains under-developed. Perhaps our association should undertake a program to foster well-integrated marketing student internship programs among businesses.

4. Interdisciplinize the Marketing Curriculum

From his vantage point, James W. Button, Senior Vice President-Merchandising for Sears, Roebuck and Co., anticipates a broadened marketing curriculum in the future. He says, "As to specifics, I can see increased need for training in quantitative methods in the behavioral sciences, international economics and financial management and accounting on top of a well-grounded program of marketing, economics and business management."[3]

Along with many others I've encountered, Mr. Button sees the coming business environment inevitably requiring a broader student perspective. One need but recall recent events to understand why. For instance, in late 1975, Mexico was confronted with remarketing its tourist trade to a prime market segment. The U.S. Jewish community, alienated by Mexican support of the United Nations' resolution equating Zionism with racism, effectively boycotted and severely depressed Mexico's tourism trade. Several months later, news of Lockheed's and others' alleged foreign payoffs triggered resounding debate about contrasting business cultures and ethics in marketing. Currently, ponder the Concorde. The marketing outcome of this Anglo-French Concorde airplane is inextricably woven into historical U.S. diplomatic, military and trade ties with both countries, environmentalism, OPEC, nationalism, egocentrism and a host of other traditional non-marketing factors.

Somehow, under these cirucmstances, the old definitions of marketing confined to moving goods and services seem inadequate. The new complexities prompt a new definition -- at least from me. It contains the traditional notions but recast in light of the trending marketing environment. Also, you'll note some departures in concept and wording. Here is my definition of marketing:

> Marketing is an interdisciplinary, flexible process.
> This process begins as a state of mind and may trans-

late into any legitimate activities required to satisfy the interests of business, consumers, government and others. Such interests span goods, services, institutions, ideas and people. Marketing's aim and justification are to help satisfy these interests at a profit ... usually, but not necessarily, monetary in nature... in socially responsive and responsible ways.

Among the definitional departures are substitution of the word interests for the classical reference word, demand. There is also the definitional allowance for marketing's profit aim to be non-monetary in nature, as for instance when the Archdiocese of New York spend $100,000 in advertising to attract men to the priesthood in 1973. Too, the interdisciplinary nature of marketing is made explicit in this definition.

Circuitously, this returns me to the point that futurizing marketing education is tied to interdisciplinizing the marketing curriculum. For instance, I contend that perhaps the number one influence on contemporary marketing is political which is fast becoming geopolitical. Should not marketing studies then formally reflect this plus ethics and other disciplines vitally impacting marketing?

For those troubled by this suggested blurring of functional departments in favor of a more interdisciplinary, cooperative approach, it is well to realize how extensively it is already occurring. Lawyers, doctors and theologians are currently cooperating on an exceedingly sensitive task, that of redefining death. Archeologists and astrophysicists are jointly studying how ancient civilizations kept time. Psychologists and architects are successfully teaming up to design "communication territories" within offices. Dare marketing do less?

## 5. Develop Organizational Appreciation and Sensitivity

"How many times have we seen a young, aggressive MBA call for radical revisions in the systems without any understanding of the environment in which he is working or the overall implications of the changes for which he's pressing?" This is the rhetorical question posed by Charles R. Stuart, Jr., Vice President-Marketing Services, Bank of America. [19] Such comments imply the need for MBAs going into business to understand more about the corporate organizational environment. (For a partial insight into the MBA-business mutual adjustment challenges, refer to the "Wise Guy MBA" articles appearing in Dun's in 1972).[2]

Specifically, a better MBA-organizational fit would likely occur if students were schooled in corporate structure, communications, politics and company perspective. Each deserves a brief comment.

Knowing structure concerns fundamental knowledge of how and why corporations are organized as they are and operate as they do. This knowledge facilitates the understanding of and practice of the marketing function within the total corporate environment, enhancing marketing effectiveness in the process.

Another area for academic emphasis is communications. On this point, Bank of America's Stuart registers a rather common business complaint: "We frequently encounter bright, well-educated young people who have difficulty with both verbal and written communication. ...Although this problem has its origins long before the marketing student reaches college, there is still a need for the university to continue instruction in language and communications skills."[20] Of what benefit are non-communicated or miscommunicated marketing ideas and practices? Lack of communication ability hampers both marketing graduates and organizations they join.

Stanford Professor Thomas W. Harrell with his wife,

Margaret, has been studying the business career progress of Stanford MBAs for over 15 years. He concludes: "In order of importance the qualities making for success are oral persuasiveness, social boldness, self confidence, energy and sociability."[11] Because communications is part of virtually all marketing efforts, how can its importance be over-emphasized? Surely marketing curriculum planners know this and business' disatisfactions well. If so, then the question is what are they doing about it?

The third aspect of developing organizational appreciation and sensitivity concerns politics. Organizational politics is a fact of life within a company and with outside companies such as customers and suppliers. Politics may nudge a division president to prematurely release a new product to get volume on the books before year end "to look **good** at corporate." Politics may push an advertising agency research supervisor to be more favorably disposed than he or she wishes in interpreting research results on an expensive campaign to a client. Personally, I have seen politics operate to alter a sales forecast technically well done because higher management preferred optimism over realism. Politics is inevitably human nature in action. Virtually no marketing organization is devoid of politics.

The fourth area is organizational perspective. Understanding organizational structure, its strategic goals, politics and management style along with utilizing communications skills escalates a marketing graduate's ability to operate effectively. It would be well for teachers to balance technical competence with organizational perspective in the marketing (or any other business) curriculum. Ultimately, the contribution of marketing and the **acceptance of marketers would be accordingly enhanced.**

In emphasizing what is most important in educating tomorrow's business manager, UCLA Graduate School of management Dean, Harold M. Williams, summarizes the need to promote students with an organizational appreciation: "The process of managing is largely one that takes place in group context. Yet everything we experience in education is individually based. We are graded as individuals, often in competition with each other. The very nature of the educational process tends to create in the student a sense of being alone. The process does little to educate the student to understand his role as a participant in a group or how to relate to a group."[23] As a former businessman, Dean Williams makes a provocative point.

## 6. Stress Ends Over Means

Twenty-six years ago, Albert Einstein said: "Perfection of means and confusion of goals seem -- in my opinion -- to characterize our age."[8] Currently, could we not legitimately question whether or not certain areas of marketing education are "perfection of means" oriented?

Unintendedly, methodological means seem to have overpowered marketing ends. Course titles such as "Quantitative Analysis," "Distribution Logistics," "Research Survey Methods," and "Marketing Models," suggest technique or means orientation. In contrast, marketing courses labeled "Strategic Planning," "Sales Management," and "New Product Development", nominally at least suggest an ends orientation.

Does not esoteric jargon also tend to reinforce a means orientation in marketing teaching materials? Designed to facilitate, so-called researchese paradoxically tends to frustrate and alienate many who seek and would seize the ideas conveyed. Like the car thief who crossed the horn instead of the ignition wires, we may cause the very thing we seek to avoid! Why not just say "The product lost money" rather than "Deterministically the product experienced a negative budget variance"? For a humorous vent to pent-up frustrations caused by researchese, please read an article by Ruth Zanes published in Marketing Review in January, 1976 titled: "Cognitive Associations Related to Implicit Theories of Factors Affecting **Resistance** to Marketing Research -- Or Tell it Like it Is."[24]

I share with this scholarly group the apparently heretical notion that some university curricula overdo the quantitative approach. Realistically, we can't validly quantify all marketing-related behavior for decision making. Nor need we. Many important, if not vital, decisions in other fields are based on so-called soft data. Nobel and Pulitzer Prize committees decide winners of these coveted distinctions without models or mathematical data. Our highest court, the Supreme Court, decides momentous issues of enormous implications usually on the basis of **unquantified** legal precedents and evidence.

The point here is a basic one. Arcane language and preoccupation with methods may detail or divert student priorities and energies from the necessary attention to marketing ends. The search for excellence too often subverts excellence.

James L. Schoor, Senior Vice President-Marketing at Holiday Inns, thinks the obstacle is more basic than a means-ends confusion. He minces no words on "What University Market**ing Education Needs to Accomplish Most." He earnestly** directs: "Tell those teachers to teach kids how to think." ..."There are three separate processes here, and I'd teach each one independently from the others: I'd have four separate courses, each a prerequisite for the others. The first might be titled, 'So What's the Problem?'; the second, 'What Could We Do About it?'; the third, 'What Should We Do About it?'; and the fourth, simply, 'Thinking.'"[16]

Apparently anticipating some rebuttal to this viewpoint, Schoor goes on to state, "When they tell you they hope they already teach these kids these things, you can tell them for me that not one in ten graduates we see really knows 'how to think.'"[16]

Mr. Schoor's forceful assertion and suggestions are provocative ones forcing us to think. One is reminded of Professor Marvel in the legendary movie, "Wizard of Oz." Remember? Professor Marvel claimed he had a Th.D, standing for Doctor of Thinkology. Perhaps Professor Marvel was not all spoof!

Another viewpoint put forth is that business school compartmentalization of functions into production, finance, marketing, etc., also manifests a means orientation but lays the blame on business because of its functional departmentalization. Faculty members Burt Nanus and Robert Coffee at the University of Southern California question this kind of functional division because it imparts a fallacious perspective. Their argument runs, "A firm is surely not in business to do accounting [or marketing, etc.]; it is in business to satisfy certain of society's needs and only if it does that well, will it be able to survive. Surely then, one might ask whether graduate business schools should not be at least as concerned about ends as they are about means."[14]

The total implication of these comments regarding future marketing education seems clear. It would do well for those planning and practicing marketing education to stress marketing ends over methodological means.

7. Rebalance Teacher Reward System

I do not question the desirability of a balanced marketing educator reward system of research, publishing and teaching. The three can deliver complimentary benefits. Some observers say that the best researchers are the best teachers. (Of course, those claiming this tend to be those teachers who are most research-oriented!) Nevertheless, I wonder if certain sectors of the teaching community are not over-doing research and publishing at the expense of teach-ing. Within these sectors, I am perplexed by what may suggest misrepresentation and misplaced emphasis regarding the research-publishing-teaching reward system.

Some universities seem to have a preach-practice gap. Examples of the preach-practice gap regarding teacher rewards are university presidents who preach a teaching gospel to state legislators and practice a publishing gospel back on the campus. There may be an external-internal dualism wherein deans and marketing department heads verbalize to external publics a reward emphasis on teaching but internally reward the researcher-publisher. If not a questionable practice, it seems to create confusion among new teachers when senior faculty impose publishing standards on younger colleagues not demanded of themselves, before or now.

When pronounced, does not the **emphasis** on publishing at least partially supplant teaching as an end? Is not the by-product of such an imbalanced reward system tenuous and/ or irrelevant research? As you, I have read my share of research articles in academic journals mounted on assumptive and methodological quicksand. Reference-ladened articles with elegant data manipulations and silken-smooth prose can't overcome data deficiencies/insufficiencies, dubious assumptions and insignificant issues. Just think of the time and energy here which could be directly channeled into improved teaching and more meaningful research. What an opportunity **lost!**

A person with first-rate credentials in both academe and business, Dr. Henry Claycamp, International Harvester's Vice President-Marketing, hits the issue squarely: "In my opinion, the greatest cause of irrelevant academic research is the 'publish or perish' dictum in many institutions. Since the reward structure in many institutions is geared to quantity rather than quality, there is great pressure to study even the most trivial problems..."[5] Other disciplines are similarly suffering and similarly concluding. For instance, the Mathematical Association of America's 1973 convention panel on "What to Publish" concluded: "The active, talented mathematicians, both the beginners and the established ones, complain about the flood of junk in the journals; their estimates of how much of it should have been published vary from a generous 50% to a stringent 2%. The less active, less motivated members of the community complain (in my opinion, rightly so) about the great pressure that is used on them to publish, publish, publish."[10]

To illustrate how pandemic the publishing syndrome has become, I cite Peking University in the People's Republic of China. "There are 2,200 teachers for the 4,300 students, but only 700 faculty are engaged in teaching, another aftermath of the Cultural Revolution. The majority are working on textbooks and other materials so that higher education will be properly oriented to the Mao point of view."[7]

Because publishing pressure is widespread and apparently accepted, this does not devalue its potential threat to quality marketing education. A marketing professor's controlling obligation and justification and to profess -- to teach or instruct so that students learn. No matter how cogently appealing the counter argument is, when research and publishing begin to upstage the teaching function, does not the quality of teaching inevitably suffer? That is why it seems that the reward system in some institutions requires rebalancing so that promotion, pay and prestige flow directly from superior teaching performance with research and publishing trailing considerations -- then critically judged on their contributory relevance. The point here is to put research and publishing into a more realistic perspective, for both are necessary for self-renewing and enhancing the marketing discipline. Increased quality should be our controlling pursuit.

4

## PARTING THOUGHTS

In many respects marketing educators form the cutting edge of business and social improvements. As beacon and backbone of the marketing discipline, your contributions have been extraordinary.

Because they have been, I've chosen not to dwell on past contributions. There wouldn't be time. Instead I've chosen to suggest some areas for future success -- and from a business perspective, I am as optimistic about this prospect as I am grateful for this privilege to address you.

My parting thoughts reduce to the following four, capsule points.

Optimum marketing education depends upon both understanding principles _and_ undertaking their real world practice. One without the other weakens the contribution of both.

Skillful marketing practitioners require much more than technical skills. Complementary understanding of such environment factors as corporate structure and priorities, communications, organization politics and business ethics loom as of controlling importance for successful managers.

Continuing development of the marketing discipline greatly depends upon its accelerated interaction and combination with other disciplines.

As marketing education ascends the strenuous 1970s, let us retain clearly that distinction between teaching and learning which Maria Montessori pioneered. Teaching is the means. Learning is the end. Teaching is teacher-based whereas learning is student-based. The emphasis may be easily misplaced.

To the extent these contentions are applied, future marketing education will perhaps be cherished and the following graduate lament avoided:

"I'm well educated, 'tis easy to see;
The world's at my feet, for I have my A.B..
M.A. will come next, then of course, Ph.D.
But I'd **chuck it all for a good J.O.B.**"

(Author unknown)

## REFERENCES

1. "American Motors: Too Much Young Blood?" Business Week, 2440 (July 12, 1976), 83.

2. Bernstein, Leonard S. "Advice to the Wise-Guy MBA." Dun's Review, 99,5 (May, 1972), 89-94 and Leech, Robert E. "A 'Wise Guy MBA' Answers Back." Dun's Review, 100,1, 79-80.

3. Button, James W. Personal correspondence with the author, April 5, 1976.

4. Buzzell, Robert D. Personal correspondence with the author, May 6, 1976.

5. Claycamp, Henry J. "Research in Marketing: Legitimate and Otherwise." Address to the **Chicago Chapter, Ameri**can Marketing Association (January, 1976), 8.

6. Crandall, R.L. Personal correspondence with the author, March 12, 1976.

7. Dedman, Emmett. China Journal. Chicago: Rand McNally and Company, 1973, 42.

8. Einstein, Albert. Out of My Later Years. Greenwood, 1950.

9. "Fifth Avenue Big 3 Set Settlement," Chicago Tribune, 192 (July 10, 1976), 2, 2

10. Halmos, P.R. "What to Publish?" The American Mathematical Monthly, 82 (January, 1975), 15.

11. Harrell, Thomas W. and Margaret S. "Stanford MBA's Ten Years Out." Alumni Bulletin (Fall, 1975), 14.

12. Kirkham, George L. "A Professor's 'Street Lessons.'" FBI Law Enforcement Bulletin (March, 1974), 2.

13. op. cit., 9.

14. Nanus, Burt and Robert E. Coffee. "Future-Oriented Business Education." California Management Review, 14, 4 (Summer, 1973), 29.

15. Ridgway, H.K. Personal correspondence with the author, April 1, 1976.

16. Schoor, James L. Personal correspondence with the author, March 4, 1976.

17. Solbert, O.M. George Eastman. Rochester: The George Eastman House, Inc., 1953, 19.

18. Stiritz, William P. Personal correspondence with the author, March 3, 1976.

19. Stuart, Charles R., Jr. Personal correspondence with the author, April 5, 1976.

20. op. cit.

21. "The Quaker Oats Company is Seeking a Marketing Research Manager with Marketing Savvy." The New York Times, 43144 (March 7, 1976), 3, 25 (advertisement).

22. Twedt, Dik W. "Business Degrees Show Steady Increase, But Marketing Education's Share Shrinks." Marketing News, 10 (July 30, 1976), 1.

23. Williams, Harold M. "View from the Business Schools." DuPont Context, 1 (1974), 11.

24. Zanes, Ruth L. "Cognitive Associations Related to Implicit Theories of Factors Affecting Resistence to Marketing Research -- or 'Tell It Like It Is.'" Marketing Review, (January, 1976) 18-19.

# SOME MULTIVARIATE ASPECTS OF BRAND IMAGE MEASUREMENT

Paul E. Green, University of Pennsylvania
Michael T. Devita, Robinson Associates, Inc.

## ABSTRACT

This paper describes some practical applications of principal components analysis and preference mapping to the analysis of ratings data. Operational measures of discriminating attributes and image stability are described and illustrated with data on media buyers' evaluations of eight women's service magazines.

## INTRODUCTION

The collection and analysis of brand or vendor image ratings is one of the most frequently undertaken activities in marketing research. One commonly followed procedure involves developing a set of attributes that are thought to be important in product choice and also capable of discriminating among brands [3]. Focused group interviews, repertory grids, or other such means are often employed to obtain the desired set of attributes [2].

Following this, consumers who are familiar with the brands under study are asked to rate each brand on each attribute. Variations on this simple theme crop up in seemingly diverse activities, such as concept testing, attitude measurement, corporate image measurement, and the like.

The purpose of this note is to suggest and illustrate ways to analyze image measurement data that utilize various multivariate tools. In the process of doing this, operational characterizations of:
- Brand image stability
- Discriminating attributes

are also presented that would seem to have applicability across various marketing contexts.

In brief, we propose to show how a set of brand ratings data can be analyzed from a multivariate viewpoint to provide descriptive measures related to brand (or vendor) image measurement. However, it should be borne in mind that the example is strictly illustrative and not necessarily representative of typical data sets in this field. Specifically, our samples of respondents and variables are both quite small, as judged by the usual type of field study.

## AN ILLUSTRATIVE DATA SET

For purposes of illustration, consider Table 1, in which appear the names of eight women's service magazines and nine attributes that are often used to characterize magazine images. A group of 56 media buyers from various advertising agencies in the New York area were interviewed regarding their perceptions and preferences for each of the magazines with respect to space buying for their clients' advertising.[1] In particular, respondent ratings were obtained for each of the eight magazines on each of the nine

attributes in Table 1 according to a 7-point scale, ranging from 1 (little of the attribute) to 7 (much of the attribute). As mentioned earlier, this type of data collection is quite typical of brand image studies.[2]

TABLE 1

MAGAZINES AND ATTRIBUTES USED IN RATING STUDY

| Magazines* | Attributes |
|---|---|
| American Home | Large Audience |
| Better Homes and Gardens | Stimulating Content |
| Family Circle | Good Reproduction Quality |
| Good Housekeeping | Upscale Audience |
| Ladies Home Journal | Good Ideas |
| McCalls | Authoritative |
| Redbook | Innovative |
| Woman's Day | Good Client Acceptance |
| | Good Discounts |

*While the plotting codes for magazines are A, B, ..., H, these letters represent a random permutation of the above magazine order (so as to preserve confidentiality).

Since each of the 56 respondents rates each magazine on each attribute, ratings across magazines (within attribute) will not be independent. (This suggests the need to incorporate a covariance measure.) Moreover, so as to remove possible mean response biases all magazine ratings, within attribute, can be expressed as deviations from the respondent's mean rating over all eight magazines on that attribute. Thus, for each attribute separately, we can compute an 8×8 matrix of covariances obtained from each 56×8 row-centered input matrix. There will be, of course, nine such covariance matrices, one for each attribute.[3]

With this preliminary out of the way, the following questions can be raised:
1. How discriminating is each attribute across all magazines and respondents? Furthermore, how much agreement is observed across individuals in their ratings of magazines on the attribute in question?
2. How stable is each magazine's image; that is, how much agreement is observed across individuals in their attribute ratings on the magazine in question?
3. What is the average respondent's image of the magazines on each attribute scale?

Operational representations of the data that relate to each of these questions are taken up next as we present the results of the pilot application.

---

[1] The actual study was of considerably larger scope than described here (see [5] for more details). As noted in Table 1, magazine identification has been replaced by the coded letters A, B, ..., H, to preserve confidentiality.

---

[2] As observed from Table 1, all of the attributes in this illustrative study are phrased monotonically in the sense of the more the better; this type of phrasing is in keeping with the projection (vector) model used later in analyzing the data.

[3] It is also possible to seek respondents' judgments of attribute importance. However, this extension of the methodology is not pursued here, although analytical procedures would be similar to those employed in the present study.

Attribute Discrimination

The question of how discriminating each attribute is across magazines and respondents is answered quite simply by computing a covariance matrix for each of the nine attributes and examining the total variance of each of these matrices (i.e., the trace of each matrix). Table 2 shows the basic idea from an intuitive standpoint, with hypothetical data on a 1-9 rating scale.

TABLE 2

RESPONDENT DIFFERENCES IN MAGAZINE RATINGS
UNDER DIFFERENT ATTRIBUTES

| Respondent | 1 | 2 | 3 | 4 | 5 | 6 | 7 | 8 | Σ | SS | Var. |
|---|---|---|---|---|---|---|---|---|---|---|---|
| | | | | Attribute 1 | | | | | | | |
| 1 | -3 | 3 | 2 | 3 | -3 | -2 | 2 | -2 | 0 | 52 | 6.5 |
| 2 | 1 | -1 | 0 | 0 | -1 | 0 | -1 | 2 | 0 | 8 | 1.0 |
| 3 | 0 | 0 | 0 | 0 | 0 | 0 | 0 | 0 | 0 | 0 | 0 |
| | | | | | | | | | | Total | 7.5 |
| | | | | Attribute 2 | | | | | | | |
| 1 | -4 | 4 | 3 | 2 | 0 | -1 | -4 | 0 | 0 | 62 | 7.75 |
| 2 | -4 | 4 | 3 | 3 | -3 | 2 | -3 | -2 | 0 | 76 | 9.50 |
| 3 | -3 | 3 | 2 | 4 | -2 | -4 | 3 | -3 | 0 | 76 | 9.50 |
| | | | | | | | | | | Total | 26.75 |
| | | | | Attribute 3 | | | | | | | |
| 1 | -3 | 3 | 2 | 2 | 0 | 1 | -1 | -4 | 0 | 44 | 5.5 |
| 2 | -3 | 3 | 2 | 2 | 0 | 1 | -1 | -4 | 0 | 44 | 5.5 |
| 3 | -2 | 2 | 2 | 2 | 0 | 1 | -1 | -4 | 0 | 34 | 4.25 |
| | | | | | | | | | | Total | 15.25 |

Suppose each of the first three respondents rating the eight magazines on attribute 1 exhibited a mean rating of 5. Respondent 1's profile of deviation scores exhibits a sum of squares (SS) of 52 and a variance (Var) of 6.5, while respondent 3 displays a variance of 0; that is, he gave the same rating of 5 to each magazine on attribute 1. Respondent 2's variance is 1.0, which is also small. If we sum up the variances across the three respondents we get a total variance of 7.5 for attribute 1.

If we examine the same respondents' ratings of all magazines on attribute 2, however, we observe that the total variance of 26.75 is higher than that of attribute 1. The larger the total variance, then, the more discriminating is the attribute in the sense that ratings across magazines (and/or across respondents) are more variable (leading to the larger total variance measure). Of course, in the data of the illustrative problem we sum all 56 respondents to get a total variance for each of the nine attributes.

If we compute the 8×8 covariance matrix (across individuals) it turns out that the total variance (sum of the diagonal elements of this matrix) is the same as that obtained from the 56×56 covariance matrix that could be computed (across magazines). Since we shall be using the 8×8 covariance matrix later, we compute the smaller order (8×8) covariance matrix. Nine such matrices are computed and nine total variances (sum of the diagonal elements of each covariance matrix) are obtained, one for each attribute.

These nine attribute variances can also be summed and each separate attribute variance expressed, relatively, as a percentage of the grand total. Panel I of Figure 1 shows a plot of the relative size of each attribute's variance (across magazines and respondents). As noted, attributes differ considerably in their discriminating power. For example, the attribute Large Audience shows a high dispersion across magazines/respondents while Good Reproduction Quality does not.

An attribute can be discriminating across magazines but not

highly variable in its profile across respondents. As an example, if we consider attribute 3 in Table 2 we note that the first two respondents display identical rating patterns; even respondent 3's pattern is quite close to that of the first two. To the extent that all respondents exhibit very similar patterns (as illustrated by attribute 3 in Table 2), the first principal component of the covariance matrix for that attribute will account for a large percentage of the attribute's total variance. Hence, we can measure the agreement across respondents by factor analyzing each covariance matrix separately and finding the variance accounted for (VAF) by the first principal component for each attribute. Note that this measure utilizes covariances across respondents in order to see if a common point of view can be found.

FIGURE 1

ATTRIBUTE VARIANCES AND CONTRIBUTIONS OF
FIRST PRINCIPAL COMPONENT

I.   Attribute Variance Expressed as
Per cent of Grand Total

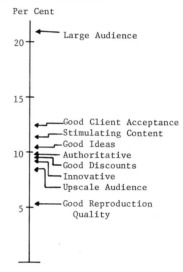

II.   Per Cent of Variance Accounted for by
First Principal Component

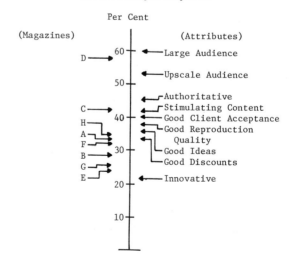

Panel II of Figure 1 shows this summary for the nine attributes of the pilot study. Again, we observe large differences in performance across the nine attributes. The attribute Large Audience shows high uniformity across respondents in the sense that the first principal component accounts for 60 per cent of the variance in the data for that attribute. Thus, not only is Large Audience an attribute that exhibits high discrimination across magazines, but it also displays high uniformity across respondents in the sense that <u>all</u> respondents rate the magazines in pretty much the same way.

On the other hand the attribute Innovative shows low agreement across respondent raters. That is, respondents differ enough in their perceptions of magazine innovativeness that the first principal component accounts for only 22 per cent of the variance in that attribute's ratings data.

Magazine Image Stability

As might be surmised at this point, a partially analogous set of computations can be carried out for the eight magazines. In this case each of the eight input matrices is of the order 56×9 and consists of the 56 respondents' row-centered ratings of the magazine of interest on the nine attributes. While a row variance could be computed to measure how variable a respondent's ratings of the magazine are across the nine attributes, it is difficult to give a useful substantive interpretation to this measure. That is, a respondent <u>could</u> believe that a magazine rates 4 on each of the nine attributes and be highly reliable in responding this way on a test-retest basis. Accordingly, we do not compute a measure of magazine "discrimination" (across attributes and respondents), largely because it has no analogous meaning to that of discriminating attribute (as displayed in Panel I of Figure 1).

However, we <u>can</u> consider the second part of the computations, namely, finding how stable a magazine's profile is across respondents. Again, principal components analysis can be applied to each of the eight 9×9 covariance matrices of interest. To the extent that respondents agree on the magazine's rating profile, the first principal component will account for a high percentage of the total variance and we can say that the magazine's image is stable across respondents.

Panel II of Figure 1 shows the counterpart results for magazines. The stability of the magazines' images differs rather considerably across respondents. For example, in the case of magazine D variance accounted for is almost 60 per cent, indicating a highly stable image. In contrast, magazine E shows a variance accounted for of only 23 per cent.

A Multidimensional Representation
of Magazines and Attributes

In most marketing studies the researcher is also interested in the third question stated earlier: how are the magazines perceived <u>simultaneously</u> on the nine attributes? This is a problem in multidimensional scaling and involves analyzing a 9×8 input matrix of <u>averaged</u> <u>ratings</u> for each of the eight magazines on each of the nine attributes.[4]

One rather popular model that would appear applicable to the present data is the vector or projection model [1] which J. D. Carroll calls MDPREF, denoting <u>M</u>ulti<u>D</u>imensional Scaling of <u>Pref</u>erence data. In this model each input datum

---

[4]Again, we center the input matrix by row and deal with deviation-from-row-mean data. Also, we could, if desired, apply the projection model to subsets of respondents (in the tradition of market segmentation analysis).

is viewed as the scalar product of a vector for the attribute and a vector for the magazine in a common multidimensional space. Conventionally, we let each attribute vector be of unit length and project the magazines, as stimulus points, onto it.

FIGURE 2

TWO-DIMENSIONAL REPRESENTATION OF MAGAZINES
AND ATTRIBUTES VIA THE PROJECTION MODEL

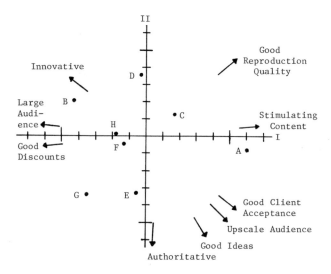

Figure 2 shows the summary map for the illustrative problem. Here, for ease of graphical representation is shown a two-dimensional spatial configuration that represents a rather good (84 per cent of total variance accounted for) fit to the average ratings. A scale value for each magazine can be found by projecting each magazine onto the attribute vector of interest. For example, in the case of the attribute, Large Audience, the magazines project in the order (most to least) of B, G, H, ..., A. However, in the case of the attribute, Stimulating Content, we see that magazine A is perceived to have the highest rating.

Figure 2 illustrates how the projection model provides a convenient summary of the full set of 9×8 = 72 averaged ratings. That is, by projecting the magazine points onto each attribute vector, in turn, one can estimate the averaged ratings on that attribute.[5] That is, one could construct a 9×8 table from these projections that would approximate the input data quite closely, since 84 per cent of the total variance was accounted for. Moreover, the cosine of the angle separating each pair of attribute vectors provides a measure of the estimated product moment correlation between attributes.[6] For example, the estimated correlation between Large Audience and Good Discounts is 0.98, since the angle separating them is only 12 degrees. On the other hand, the estimated correlation between Large Audience and Stimulating Content is −0.98,

---

[5]It should be mentioned that one could also allow the goodness of fit of each attribute to be represented by the squared distance of its vector's terminus from the origin. In Figure 2, however, we use unit length. Hence, we can find large point projection separations on (say) Good Reproduction Quality even though from a relative standpoint (see Figure 1) this attribute does not exhibit high discriminating ability across persons/magazines.

[6]We say "estimated" correlation because only a two-dimensional solution is involved (albeit one accounting for 84 per cent of the variance).

since the angle separating them is 168 degrees. In a similar manner we could find the estimated correlation between any pair of attribute vectors. This information could be useful in selecting specific attributes for further study.

The projection model provides a convenient summary (and estimation) of a large amount of numerical data as well as providing ancillary information regarding the estimated correlations of various attribute pairs and the relative positions of the various magazines (points) in the space.

## DISCUSSION

This note has attempted to show how multivariate tools can be employed in characterizing various aspects of brand or vendor ratings data. In particular, operationalizations of:

- attribute discrimination and stability
- brand image stability

were illustrated. Standard techniques, such as principal components and preference mapping were used to carry out the analyses. It is appropriate to discuss some of the limitations of this analysis and point out possible alternative approaches. We can then discuss potential areas of application.

### Limitations

The focus of this approach has been on data description rather than significance testing. It is possible, of course, to introduce tests for differences among covariance matrices and at other places in the methodology as well. However, with the typically large samples found in marketing research one wonders whether these refinements are useful. It will often be the case with large samples that if operationally useful differences are found, they will also be statistically significant (although the converse may not hold). At any rate, this paper has focused on descriptive (rather than inferential) procedures.

In our view, a more compelling limitation of the methodology is the absence of discussion on test-retest replication and cross-validation. In practice, it would be useful to have respondents rate brands on a test-retest basis so that a measure of individual reliability (as well as individual response bias) could be developed in terms of reliability coefficients. Also, one might want to perform split-half analyses--or, other types of cross-validation--in regard to any of the steps described here.

In addition to the preceding extensions the researcher might emphasize subgroup analysis (in the spirit of market segmentation) to a greater extent than described here. This is particularly appropriate in the case of developing multidimensional scaling maps, as illustrated in Figure 2. All that is required is some preliminary clustering of respondents prior to developing separate MDPREF configurations, a topic that is discussed in detail in [2].

Finally, since the original data matrix is a three-way array of brands by attributes by respondents, other methods, such as three-mode factor analysis or canonical decomposition analysis [1] might be employed. The approach described here is much simpler and emphasizes techniques that are more easily communicated to nontechnical personnel. Still, it should be pointed out that more elegant procedures exist for analyzing this general type of data.

### Potential Applications

Operational characterizations of attribute discrimination, and attribute and brand stability (over respondents) would seem to be most useful in cases where a sequence of image studies is being conducted over time. However, even when image tracking is not under consideration, the methodology could be useful at the pretest level. For example, in the present application one might want to consider discarding attributes like Good Reproduction Quality prior to conducting the main study.

If image tracking is planned, then the stability of a brand's image can be operationally characterized in ways described earlier. For example, one could examine whether the brand's image becomes more (or less) consistent across consumers after a particular promotional campaign. Alternatively, one could examine the multidimensional space to see if the brand "moves up" in its projections on desired attributes.

Many of the preceding comments are still speculative, however. Relatively few applications of the suggested methodology have been made, either in the context of image measurement or in other problem areas, such as new concept evaluation. Some of this work is now in progress.

## REFERENCES

1. Carroll, J. Douglas. "Individual Differences and Multidimensional Scaling," in R. N. Shepard, A. K. Romney, S. B. Nerlove, eds., Multidimensional Scaling: Theory and Applications in the Behavioral Sciences, Vol. I. New York: Seminar Press, 1972.

2. Green, Paul E. and Donald S. Tull. Research for Marketing Decisions, Third Edition. Englewood Cliffs, N.J.: Prentice-Hall, Inc., 1975, Chapters 13, 15 and 18.

3. Myers, James H. and Mark I. Alpert. "Determinant Buying Attitudes: Meaning and Measurement," Journal of Marketing, 32 (October 1968), 13-20.

4. Sherif, M. and C. I. Hovland. Social Judgment: Assimilation and Contrast Effects in Communication and Attitude Change. New Haven, Conn.: Yale University Press, 1961.

5. Wind, Yoram and Stephen E. Silver. "Segmenting Media Buyers," Journal of Advertising Research, 13 (December 1973), 33-8.

# A MODEL FOR STRATEGIC POSITIONING IN RETAILING

Peter Doyle, Bradford University, U.K.
Alok Sharma, University of South Carolina

## ABSTRACT

This paper describes the importance of positioning strategies in retailing, tests some hypotheses about how consumers evaluate stores and illustrates a methodology for
monitoring store positioning. The study also suggests
inadequate research has led to a striking divergence
between the formal strategies of certain major stores and
their current positions.

## INTRODUCTION

During the 1970's new forms of competition and sharp
changes in the environment within which retailers operate
have brought positioning strategy into the forefront of
retail planning. This paper has two main objectives.
First, to review the importance of store positioning strategies. Second, to describe and illustrate a methodology
for measuring how stores are perceived and for evaluating
the effects of repositioning. The results suggest that
inadequate research has led to a striking divergence between the formal strategy of certain major stores and their
current positions. The findings also give no support to
two hypotheses prominent in retailing: that different
socio-economic groups perceive stores differently [e.g. 17,
23] or that store managers systemmatically differ from consumers in the dimensions and weights they use to evaluate
stores [e.g. 18, 20, 21].

## POSITIONING IN A CHANGING ENVIRONMENT

Positioning is central to store performance because it is
the main determinent of both the shoppers' choice of store
and how management allocates resources. Shoppers choose
among competing stores on the basis of how they are perceived along dimensions regarded as important to them [12].
Previous studies have emphasised consumer perceptions of
merchandise quality, prices, assortment, styling and locational convenience as common dimensions [16]. An effective positioning strategy employs a marketing approach that
profitably distinguishes the store from its rivals along
these dimensions.

In retailing, the necessity of reconciling conflicting
marketing and financial objectives implies management must
make difficult trade-offs in defining a clear positioning
strategy. A store cannot be "better" than others along all
dimensions important to shoppers. For example, if it
decides to compete along the price dimension then the need
to achieve return on asset goals requires high investment
turnover and low operating expenses which imply sacrifices
along the merchandise quality, service and assortment dimensions [9]. These trade-offs have two important implications: (1) certain positions in the perceptual space are
unattainable, and (2) repositioning to gain new customers
will also mean losing some existing ones.

Positioning is not a static concept. An effective position
is one attuned to current consumer wants and competitive
policies. As wants change and new competition emerges,
repositioning is necessary. Several developments have
occurred in recent years to erode existing positions including:

1. Changes in consumer tastes, notably towards fashions
and higher quality merchandise [1].

2. New demographic patterns, particularly the slowing of
suburban growth, housebuilding and automobile ownership [2].

3. The prospects of slower overall economic growth [3].

4. Increasing intra- and inter-type competition among
stores [9].

5. New forms of market segmentation and speciality stores
[26].

6. Innovations in retailing institutions (e.g. catalogue
stores, phone selling, superstores) accelerating the decline
of older forms of retailing [10].

The value of repositioning research can be seen by comparing two types of experience. One is that of retailers
which monitor change and gradually reposition alongside.
Sears and J. C. Penney, for example, have both been upgrading and adding fashion lines in a successful response
to emerging spending patterns and competition from discounters. The other experience is of retailers which have
not planned for change and been eventually forced by declining profits into dramatic and costly repositioning
attempts. One example is Woolworth, which failed to adapt
to the long decline in the competitive position of the
variety store. In 1974 it announced a radically new positioning strategy:

> Woolworth's merchandise would be broadened and
> up-graded to position the stores in the "market
> void that exists between discount stores and the
> higher priced full-line department stores".
> This gap, management claimed, had been created
> by the upgrading policies of Sears, Penney and
> Ward, which shoppers now thought of as trad-
> itional department stores [8, p. 2].

Later we question this repositioning strategy and the
assumption upon which it was made. Even when these
rescues work, however, their suddenness means greater dis-
orientation of existing customers and severe problems of
developing consistent merchandising policies. Gradual
change based on periodic positioning research offers a more
successful alternative.

## PRINCIPLES OF POSITIONING RESEARCH

Previous studies suggest two problems have to be overcome
in positioning research. First, managers are biased in
how they perceive stores [18, 20, 21]. This source of
invalidity must be avoided in the design of the study to
measure how customers evaluate stores. Second, consumers
themselves have different viewpoints depending upon their
socioeconomic backgrounds and shopping behavior [17, 23].
Averaging can be misleading and the research should
identify and meaningfully group these different points-of-
view. Modern multidimensional scaling methods offer an
attractive approach to both these problems [12].

To audit its position, the store must answer three questions: (1) What is its current position and how favorably
is it viewed by consumers? (2) Is this position likely to
be as effective in the future? (3) What actions should be

taken if a repositioning is required? These entail a
research program which can:

1. Identify the number and nature of the major perceptual
dimensions used by shoppers.
2. Determine how competing stores are evaluated along
these dimensions. What are their major similarities and
differences?
3. Establish how consumer preferences are distributed in
the perceptual space. What types of stores are most preferred by shoppers? Are any "gaps" to be filled?
4. Discover any customer segments. Are there important
groups of shoppers with discrete viewpoints?
5. Forecast shopping and competitive trends in segments
relative to the store's present position and future opportunities.
6. Evaluate the impact on profits of alternative positioning strategies open to the store.

## A POSITIONING METHODOLOGY

Multidimensional scaling methods were used in a pilot
positioning study of the following 11 stores in Columbia,
South Carolina:

Sears. America's largest retailer. The group
has one medium-sized department store in
Columbia. This is an older store in a downtown off-center location.

J. C. Penney. The second largest general
merchandiser in the U.S. In Columbia it has
one downtown department store and one in the
main suburban shopping mall.

Woolworth. With 5,000 stores, it is trying
to reposition from being the leading limited-
price variety store to a broader department store
merchandiser. It has four stores in Columbia.

K-Mart. A rapidly expanding subsidiary of
Kresge with over 900 stores. It has four
large discount department stores in Columbia's
suburban shopping centers.

Woolco. A Woolworth subsidiary, currently with 350
stores, designed to emulate K-Mart's success. It
has two stores in Columbia.

Belk. A group of traditional full-service
department stores located mainly in South
Eastern U.S. It has two stores in Columbia,
one downtown and one suburban.

Berry's. A local concern with four large stores
and a turnover of $6 million. Three stores
specialize in women's fashions, one in men's.

Davison's. One of the six regional department store divisions of the Macy Group. It
has one large downtown store in Columbia.

Sam Solomon. A successful discount department
store group in the Southeast. It emphasizes
attractive displays, jewelry and watches.
It has one modern store in Columbia's leading shopping mall.

Tapps. A local group of three full-service
department stores: one downtown and two in
suburban shopping centers. They emphasize
softlines and fashions.

J. B. White. A division of Merchandise Stores
Inc. with two department stores in Columbia.

They emphasize medium and higher-price
fashion goods.

The stores were chosen on the basis of an initial screening
to identify those most familiar to local shoppers. Questionnaires were mailed to a representative sample of 196
households, 145 were returned and of those 98 were complete.
An identical questionnaire was completed by all eleven
store managers. Information was elicited on pairwise
similarity judgments, ratings along seven commonly used
store merchandising dimensions, preferences and socioeconomic and shopping patterns.

Store Positions

Carroll and Chang's INDSCAL [5] is an attractive technique
for identifying how shoppers and managers viewed these
stores. The initial input were consumer's ratings on 7-
point scales of each pair of stores according to overall
similarity. In view of recent questions concerning the
reliability of multidimensional scaling techniques [19, 25]
it was decided to measure the reliability of the results.
Respondents were randomly allocated to two sets and each
half was separately analyzed. The two maps fortunately
proved virtually identical. A canonical correlation between the two three-dimensional stimulus maps gave coefficients of 0.999, 0.985 and 0.916.

TABLE 1

SUMMARY STATISTICS FROM INDSCAL ANALYSIS OF
SIMILARITIES DATA FOR TWO TO FIVE DIMENSIONS

| Number of Dimensions | % Variance accounted for by INDSCAL | Average Correlation Coefficient across subjects |
|---|---|---|
| 5 | .767 | .874 |
| 4 | .763 | .871 |
| 3 | .760 | .870 |
| 2 | .700 | .828 |

Correlation between axes:

1 and 2 : -.06
1 and 3 : -.53
2 and 3 : +.14

The number of dimensions chosen to represent the positioning solution depends upon judgment of the trade-off between interpretability and fit [11, 14]. Table 1 shows
the INDSCAL solution for two to five dimensions. Three
appear to offer both high explained variance and the possibility of visual interpretation. While interpretation
of these axes is not always necessary it is often appealing. Interpretation should reflect both perceptual and
evaluative aspects of choice. To develop interpretative
data on perceptual aspects, respondents rated the stores
in terms of seven merchandise and other features. These
property vectors were then fitted into the INDSCAL space
using the "max r" option on Carroll and Chang's PROFIT
program [7]. Table 2 gives the direction cosines and the
correlation coefficient for the best-fitting vector. The
number adjacent to the correlation coefficient indicates
the predictive value of each dimension (as described below).
If the product of this value and the correlation coefficient is formed, an intuitive ordering of properties by

importance is obtained. Thus the perceived quality of the merchandise, prices, level of service, and variety rate highest. These labels are applied to the dimensions.

TABLE 2

RESULTS OF MAX "R" LINEAR REGRESSION

| PROPERTY VECTOR | CORRELATION COEFFICIENT (AND VALUE) | DIRECTION COSINE | | |
|---|---|---|---|---|
| | | AXIS 1 | AXIS 2 | AXIS 3 |
| Quality | .980 (1.9) | .660 | .740 | .123 |
| Variety | .740 (0.8) | -.449 | .453 | .769 |
| Prices | .932 (1.0) | .973 | -.156 | .173 |
| Location | .587 (0.6) | .643 | -.070 | -.761 |
| Service | .962 (0.5) | .957 | -.192 | .214 |
| Layout | .910 (0.02) | .740 | .671 | .017 |
| Reputation | .945 | .835 | .542 | .092 |

FIGURE 1

PERCEPTUAL SPACE FROM INDSCAL ANALYSIS

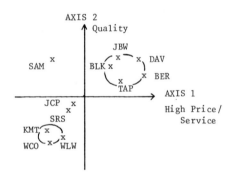

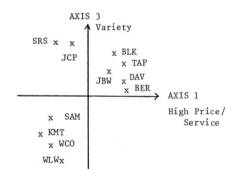

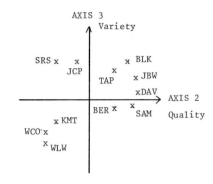

BER - Berry's; BLK - Belk; DAV - Davison's; JBW - J. B. White; JCP - J. C. Penney; KMT - K-Mart; SAM - Sam Solomon; SRS - Sears; TAP - Tapps; WCO - Woolco; WLW - Woolworth.

Interpretation of Figure 1 is interesting. The five traditional department stores form a closely defined group characterized by favorable perceptions in terms of quality of merchandise, and level of service, with average or above average merchandise variety. But, not surprisingly, prices are seen as relatively high. Three stores form a tightly-knit discount group — K-Mart, Woolworth and Woolco. These are seen to have low prices but to be poor in terms of quality and variety. These weaknesses increasingly concern the larger discounters [24]. In contrast to Woolworth's assumptions, the gap between the discounters and higher priced department stores (at least in Columbia) still appears to be squarely filled by Sears and J. C. Penney.

The most attractive position by far is held by Sam Solomon with the almost ideal image of being as highly regarded for quality as the traditional department stores but having prices perceived as close to the discounters. This at least rationalizes the stores considerable successes in the Southeast. None of the traditional department stores appears to have a significant advantage over the others. Woolworth has conspicuously failed to achieve the position of their 1974 strategy statement. A question which has worried industry analysts is also exhibited. Woolworth and Woolco are seen as so similar that they risk canibalizing each other's business (especially since they are often located in the same shopping centers).

Individual Differences and Management Perceptions

The results offered little support to the hypotheses of sharply different consumer viewpoints or that managers as a group have sharply different perceptions from shoppers. For individual shoppers the INDSCAL weights showed both remarkably uniform goodness-of-fit and dimension weights. To examine this further, weights were forced into groups by Johnson's hierarchical clustering program. Three centroids were distinguished and these were resubmitted to INDSCAL along with the 11 store managers' similarity ratings. The stimulus map remained relatively unchanged; the subject space is shown in Figure 2 for the first two dimensions.

This illustrates both hypotheses. First, consumers themselves are highly homogeneous even where cluster analysis is used to maximize variance between potential groups. Second, managers themselves show considerable heterogeneity but do not show any viewpoint which as a group distinguishes them from shoppers. In fact, shoppers appear to be around the average management viewpoint. Thus the results support Isaacson's findings that "when managers try to predict image patterns they can do a fairly good job of it" [15] rather than those of May [18] and Oxenfeldt [20] who suggest managers systemmatically bias their perceptions.

FIGURE 2

INDSCAL RESPONDENT SPACE:
3 CUSTOMER CLUSTERS AND 11 STORE MANAGERS

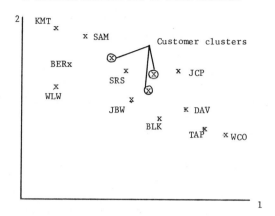

### Analyzing Individual Preferences

So far only perceptions have been analyzed. Further insights into store positions and alternative repositioning strategies can be gained from including respondent preferences.

FIGURE 3

PREFMAP: PREFERENCE VECTORS FOR STORE
MANAGERS AND SHOPPERS

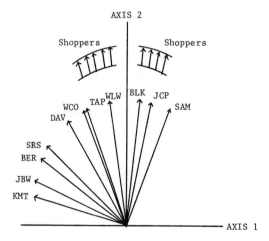

Two levels of analysis were employed. The first used PREFMAP (6) to represent subjects' preferences as vectors in the perceptual space generated from the initial INDSCAL analysis. Figure 3 shows the pattern of consumer preferences with those of the 11 store managers as inliers. Preferences are shown to be clustered towards the higher quality stores, with a trade-off towards lower prices. As with perceptions there is no evidence to support either distinct customer preference segments or managers as a group having different preference judgments from their customers.

The second stage tried to decompose preferences into actionable components. Respondents were asked to rate

hypothetical department stores differing (high or low) on each of the six merchandising properties described earlier ("overall reputation" was omitted as being a result rather than a component of action). To test all combinations (i.e. $2^6 = 64$) would have involved asking respondents to rate a prohibitively large number. Instead the orthogonal design (22) shown in Figure 4 was used which allowed the main effects of each of the variables to be tested using only 12 of the 64 combinations. The results are shown in Table 3.

FIGURE 4

ORTHOGONAL EXPERIMENTAL DESIGN FOR
EVALUATING CONSUMER PREFERENCES

| | Q | V | P | C | S | L |
|---|---|---|---|---|---|---|
| 1 | + | − | + | − | − | − |
| 2 | + | + | − | + | − | − |
| 3 | − | + | + | − | + | − |
| 4 | + | − | + | + | − | + |
| 5 | + | + | − | + | + | − |
| 6 | + | + | + | − | + | + |
| 7 | − | + | + | + | − | + |
| 8 | − | − | + | + | + | − |
| 9 | − | − | − | + | + | + |
| 10 | + | − | − | − | + | + |
| 11 | − | + | − | − | − | + |
| 12 | − | − | − | − | − | − |

Q – Quality; V – Variety; P – Prices; C – Convenience;
S – Service; L – Layout.

TABLE 3

REGRESSION OF PREFERENCES AGAINST STORE CHARACTERISTICS
(ORTHOGONAL MAIN EFFECTS DESIGN)

| | b | t |
|---|---|---|
| CONSTANT | 2.0 | 11.57 |
| QUALITY | 1.89 | 14.52 |
| VARIETY | 0.81 | 6.20 |
| PRICES | −1.03 | −7.86 |
| CONVENIENCE | .65 | 5.00 |
| SERVICE | .54 | 4.16 |
| LAYOUT | .02 | .16 |

$R^2 = .38$

13

Care must be taken in interpreting these figures since the
independent variables are only dummies and an absence of
interactions is assumed. Nevertheless they do highlight
the trade-offs involved in positioning. For example, the
model confirms what some department stores have recently
learned the hard way [e.g. 4], i.e., the strategy of sacrificing quality to cut prices can have a significantly net
negative effect on preferences. On the other hand, if a
discount store can upgrade its quality image, its preference rating in the model jumps from 0.42 to 2.31, significantly differentiating it from competitors. This is the
policy K-Mart is attempting and what Sam Solomon appears to
have achieved. With the perceptual maps, these models
provide insightful diagnostics for planning the repositioning strategies which inevitably accompany successful management in a changing environment.

SUMMARY

Positioning is the central dimension of retail competition
in today's changing markets. Inability to adapt to the
evolving competitive environment has been the major cause
of retail failures. Successful long-term growth requires
stores to systemmatically plan for change. Research into
how the store is perceived relative to competition is
basic to such planning. This paper showed how modern
multidimensional scaling methods provide an effective
approach to this problem. It also showed how multivariate
methods can be used as diagnostics to compare alternative
repositioning strategies.

REFERENCES

1.  Business Week: August 18th, 1975. "J. C. Penney:
    Getting More from the Same Space", 80 - 88.

2.  Business Week: December 8th, 1975. "Sears' Identity
    Crisis", 52 - 58.

3.  Business Week: December 20th 1976. "How OPEC's High
    Prices Strangle World Growth", 44 - 49.

4.  Business Week: August 30th, 1975. "Department Store
    Developments", 20 - 21.

5.  Carroll, J. D. and J. J. Chang, "Analysis of Individ-
    ual Differences in Multidimensional Scaling Via an
    N-way Generalization of Eckart-Young Decomposition",
    Psychometrika, 35 (May 1970), 283 - 319.

6.  Carroll, J. D. and J. J. Chang, "Relating Preference
    Data to Multidimensional Scaling Solutions Via a
    Generalization of Coombs' Unfolding Model", Bell
    Telephone Laboratories, Murray Hill, NJ., 1967.

7.  Carroll, J. D. and J. J. Chang, "How to Use PROFIT, A
    Computer Program for Property Fitting by Optimizing
    Nonlinear or Linear Correlation", Bell Telephone
    Laboratories, Murray Hill, NJ., 1970.

8.  Chain Store Age: December 1974, "Woolworth's Strategy
    for the late 1970's and the 1980's".

9.  Davidson, W. R., A. F. Doody and D. J. Sweeney.
    Retailing Management New York: Ronald Press, 1975

10. Davidson, W. R., A. D. Bates and S. J. Bass. "The
    Retail Life Cycle", Harvard Business Review, 54,
    (November 1976), 89 - 96.

11. Degerman, R. L. "The Geometric Representation of Some
    Simple Structures", in Multidimensional Scaling:
    Theory and Applications in the Behavioral Sciences,

Vol 1, R. N. Shepard, A. K. Romney and S. B. Nerlove,
eds. New York: Seminar Press, 1972. 194 - 212.

12. Doyle, P. and I. Fenwick. "Shopping Habits in
    Grocery Chains", Journal of Retailing. 50 (Winter
    1974 - 75), 39 - 52.

13. Doyle, P. and P. Hutchinson. "Individual Differences
    in Family Decision-Making", Journal of the Market
    Research Society, 15 (October 1973), 193 - 206.

14. Green, P. "Marketing Applications of MDS: Assessment
    and Outlook", Journal of Marketing, 39 (January 1975),
    24 - 31.

15. Isaacson, H. L. Store Choice (Unpublished D.B.A. Diss-
    ertation, Cambridge, Mass: Harvard University, 1964).

16. Lindquist, J. D. "Meaning of Image", Journal of
    Retailing, 50 (Winter 1974 - 75), 29 - 38.

17. Martineau, P. "The Personality of the Retail Store"
    Harvard Business Review, 36 (January 1958), 47 - 55.

18. May, E. G. Department Store Images: Basic Findings.
    Cambridge, Mass: Marketing Science Institute, October
    1972.

19. Neidell, L. A. "Procedures for Obtaining Similarities
    Data", Journal of Marketing Research, 9 (August 1972),
    335 - 7.

20. Oxenfeldt, A. R. "Developing a Favorable Price-Quality
    Image", Journal of Retailing, 50 (Winter 1974-75),
    8 - 14.

21. Pathak, D. S., W. J. Crissy and R. W. Sweitzer.
    "Customer Image versus the Retailers' Anticipated
    Image", Journal of Retailing, 50 (Winter 1974-75)
    21 - 28.

22. Plackett, R. L. and J. P. Burman. "The Design of
    Optimum Multifactorial Experiments". Biometrika, 33
    (1940), 305 - 325.

23. Rich, S. U. and B. D. Portis. "The Imageries of
    Department Stores", Journal of Marketing, 28 (April
    1964), 10 - 15.

24. Standard and Poor's Industry Surveys. "Retailing:
    Department, Mail Order, Variety and Drug Chains"
    (March 1976).

25. Summers, J. O. and D. B. Mackay. "On the Validity
    and Reliability of Direct Similarity Judgments",
    Journal of Marketing Research, 13 (August 1976)
    289 - 95.

26. Tillman, R. "Rise of the Conglomerchant", Harvard
    Business Review, 49 (November 1971), 44 - 51.

# MARKET SEGMENTATION:  SOME UNRESOLVED ISSUES

P. C. Burger, State University of New York at Binghamton
A. Venkatesh, State University of New York at Binghamton

## ABSTRACT

Market Segmentation has been developed as an empirical concept. Methods involving measurement and analysis have been devised by a large number of researchers. This paper develops a typology of the segmentation concepts and suggests means for more effective use of segmentation in model building and management decision making.

## INTRODUCTION

Market segmentation is a multidimensional concept in need of a closer scrutiny at the theoretical and applied level. Although a well researched area from an empirical viewpoint, little has been done to develop a perspective of segmentation which is needed to help researchers and decision-makers organize and use the basic idea to its full potential. To date, the work by Frank, Massy, and Wind [3] can be considered an important contribution to the field more for its comprehensive integration of empirical research and treatment of some problem areas rather than for presenting a unified scheme. Its strength as well as its weakness lies in limiting itself to empirical findings. Another work which helps organize the area is a collection of readings by Engel, Fiorillo and Cawley [2]. This paper proposes to build on the previous works to impose an additional degree of order to the use of segments in marketing research.

A question arises as to whether any search for a more unified scheme of segmentation is doomed to failure from the very beginning because of the nature of marketing phenomena which are essentially dynamic. These include shifting segments, changing tastes and needs of consumers, and non-measurable marketing factors beyond the grasp of the manager and the researcher. It is our view that there is an abundance of technology which enhances empirical research in certain areas of segmentation. However, what the field of marketing research needs is more effective theoretical perspective regarding segmentation. In this paper our objective is to present a multidimensional conceptualization of segmentation and to examine some basic issues which confront the manager and researcher. The paper examines managerial and researcher points of view regarding segmentation, categorizes segmentation into typologies and interfaces model building and research technology with the typologies.

## MULTIDIMENSIONAL CONCEPTUALIZATION

In our study, we make a distinction between the (a) Philosophy of Market Segmentation, (b) Logic of Market Segmentation, (c) Meaning of Market Segmentation, (d) Rationale of Market Segmentation, (e) Strategy of Market Segmentation, (f) Process of Market Segmentation, (h) Problem of Market Segmentation. An appreciation of this distinction is important both for manager and research. The purpose of the conceptualization is to help the manager and researcher develop an informed perspective about segmentation in relation to their organizational roles. Table 1 summarizes these issues.

The _meaning_ of market segmentation is its most simplistic dimension in that a marketer is required to divide his market into smaller groups of individuals or, conversely, aggregate individuals up to groups.

## TABLE 1

### MULTIDIMENSIONAL CONCEPTUALIZATION

| Dimension Description | Explanation | Implication for Manager | Implication for Researcher |
|---|---|---|---|
| 1. Meaning of Segmentation | Division of Market into Smaller Segments | Conveys the most elementary meaning of segmentation | Conveys the most elementary meaning segmentation |
| 2. Philosophy of Segmentation | Incorporates marketing concept | Useful to manager for implementing marketing concept | Of limited use to researcher |
| 3. Logic of Segmentation | No market is either completely homogeneous or completely heterogeneous | Useful in understanding the markets and consumers | Useful in developing research objectives and determining the desired degree of homogeneity within a segment |
| 4. Rationale of Segmentation | Segmentation is carried out in the best interests of the consumers and the company | Segmentation provides best marketing opportunities and facilitates best use of resources | Researcher can develop an understanding of why segmentation is important |
| 5. Strategy of Segmentation | As a planning tool | Manager is concerned with competitive issues, developing integrated plans within organizational concept | Researcher must work to provide methods to help decide whether strategy is cost effective |
| 6. Process of Segmentation | The dynamics of segmentation | Of limited use to the manager | Researcher's understanding of the process critical in developing a suitable approach to the research design |
| 7. Method of Segmentation | Procedure for identifying segmentation | Of limited use to the manager | Possibly the most important dimension for the researcher |
| 8. Problem of Segmentation | Identifying the various issues | Of equal interest to manager and researcher in developing overall prospective of a market | |

15

The underlying philosophy of market segmentation is derived from the marketing concept. The marketing concept directs marketers to recognize customers' needs and match the needs with relevant products and services. Market segmentation is thus a philosophy of action that incorporates marketing concept.

The logic of market segmentation is that no market, however defined, is entirely homogeneous or entirely heterogeneous. On the other hand, it contains elements both of homogeneity and heterogeneity. Segmentation follows the well-known "unity in diversity" logic and is operationalized by increasing within group homogeneity and between group heterogeneity.

The rationale of market segmentation is to, (a) provide additional marketing opportunities for the marketer, in order to (b) facilitate the best use of marketer's resources. Ideally, segmentation is carried out in the best interests of the consumers, the company, and the community.

The strategy of market segmentations is the overall decision to divide or not to divide markets into sub-groups and to develop distinct marketing programs for one or more of the sub-groups chosen as target segments such that the emergent segments are maximally useful for the manager.

The process of market segmentation is either aggregative or disaggregative. It is difficult to specify segmentation uniquely in terms of process, because both empirical evidence and conceptualization of the concept suggest either possibility.

The method of market segmentation includes one of the three, (a) Discrimination, (b) Classification and (c) Dissection, each having its own specific purpose.

The problem of market segmentation is embodied in the question of how to form segments that make sense both to the manager and the researcher. In the words of Claycamp and Massy, the problem may generally be stated as, (a) defining mutually exclusive market segments, (b) measuring response elasticities on a segment by segment basis, (c) handling constraints in the segmentation strategy.

## THE MANAGER'S VIEW OF SEGMENTATION

Segmentation of a market can only be considered useful from the manager's viewpoint if it leads to improved efficiency of the marketing function. This improved efficiency can take the form of increased sales at the same input cost or lower costs to achieve the same marketing result. Marketing texts [5, 7] advocate the use of segmentation but provide little operational advice as to what issues should the manager be concerned with in understanding and developing segmentation strategies.

An examination of the Wall Street Journal, Fortune and other publications reporting on the success or failure of actural practice suggests that the practice of segmented strategies has not been uniformly successful. Decisions which may have involved ineffective segmentation include:

- Small cars are not selling well. These cars were aimed at the second car purchase of families and first cars for lower income individuals.
- Low price "first" houses for young families.
- Air travel. Various discount structures lowered rather than increased revenue. A major ad campaign for a leading airline aimed at the business traveler resulted in an increase in consumer complaints.
- The highest price microwave ovens are selling much more than low price units.

Similarly, more successful segmentation can be found:

- Media planners have used the segmented approach for several years.
- Site locations for retail clothing stores has been done using a segmented approach quite effectively.
- Movies have been quite successful using a segmented approach to story lines and promotion.
- Travel agencies have developed tour packages appealing to various homogeneous segments which have proved quite viable.
- News magazines and related communications media have been developed which appeal to specific segments while broad appeal media have become less important.

The manager can successfully use segmentation if he can more efficiently reach a particular group of individuals who are users of his product. Thus, if young unmarried are the target market, the manager would prefer to sell his product in stores catering to that group, advertise in media which are read by that group, design his product to fit that group's needs and price the product in a range that the group can afford. The degree to which the above can be done determines the effectiveness of the segmentation approach. If none of the options above exist, a segmented approach may not be possible.

## THE RESEARCHER'S CONCERN

### Process

The segmentation process can be viewed both as aggregative and disaggregative. According to Wendell Smith [9] "in the language of the economist, segmentation is disaggregative in its effect and tends to bring about recognition of several demand schedules, where only one was recognized before." However, Frank et al. [3, p. 203] observe "First of all, the models (theoretical models discussed earlier by the authors) tell us that segmentation should be viewed as a process of aggregation rather than disaggregation....the fundamental problem of market segmentation can be characterized as that of finding the point where the marginal reduction of profile by the level of aggregation, is just balanced by the marginal reduction in research and administrative costs made possible by the constraint...the concept that segment is a process of aggregation implies building up to a viable segmentation strategy rather than tearing apart to find one." According to the authors, the implication of whether the segmentation process is aggregative or disaggregative for the manager is that it affects the implementation of the segmentation strategy.

However, from a researcher's point of view, the implication should be cast in terms of truth or falseness of inferences about relationships between variables. This is especially important if these relationships are used for predicting consumer behaviors, i.e. better segmentation should lead to improved levels of behavioral prediction. Misspecification of segments can cause ecological invalidity. For example, if data on macro-segments indicate a high positive correlation between age and use of a product, it may not follow that such a relationship exists at the level of individuals. Ecological variables are descriptive properties of groups and ecological correlations are correlations between such group data. Ecological correlations cannot be used to infer correlations between properties of individuals. Such inference is known as ecological fallacy [8]. In the aggregative method of segmentation, there is less chance for this to occur because individual correlations are inferred from individual data.

### Method

The statistical method of market segmentation involves three broad typologies: (a) Classification, (b) Discrimination, (c) Dissection. Each of them is shown in Table 2. The column headings relate the key attributes of the segmentation type. The purpose of the segmentation can

TABLE 2

A RESEARCHER'S APPROACH TO METHODS AND MODELS OF SEGMENTATION

| Method | Purpose | Example-Research Problems | Analytical Method | Appropriate Sampling Procedure | Model Type |
|--------|---------|---------------------------|-------------------|--------------------------------|------------|
| Discrimination | Evaluate Differences Between Known Populations | Identify Buyers of Given Brand | Multiple Discriminant Analysis or Econometric Analysis | Stratified Random Sampling | Behavioral Analytic |
| Classification | Populations Unknown-Identify them | Defining Media or Psychographic Groups | 'Q' Factor Analysis Cluster Analysis plus AID | Multi-Stage Cluster Sampling | Descriptive Behavioral |
| Dissection[1] | Assume Single Population but Multiple Categories or Subgroups. How to Set Up These Categories | Identify Benefit Use Groups For Durables | Multiple Classification Analysis or Cross Tabulation Analysis | Judgment or Quota Sampling | Behavioral Forecasting |

fall into three groups based on the degree of prior knowledge possessed by the researcher. If the groups are very well defined in the sense that some choice or use behavior which is unique is observed such as buying one brand or contracting one disease, then discrimination procedures are appropriate. Classification can be used when very weak notions of groups exists. Dissection can be used when a single population exists which contains gradation or categories of behavior.

The column heading "research problems" suggests situations in which a researcher might effectively use that type of segmentation. The analytical method most appropriate is shown in the next column. The type of segmentation has implication for the type of sampling method used to collect data. If the inappropriate sampling method is undertaken, inadequate cell sizes for required statistical techniques may result. The last column is to discriminate between the specification level of the underlying consumer model which is being tested. If the underlying model is merely verbal or descriptive, then classification may be implied (searching for the right segments). However, if specific forecasts of behavior or attitudes are to be done, the consumer model might be quite specific to a population requiring dissection.

Discrimination

Given a sample of members from each of K known populations and values on p variables for each member in each population the researcher is required to set up a method which (a) discriminates between the populations, (b) assigns a new member to the correct population (establishes validity) and (c) discovers the relative strengths of the variables in the overall discrimination process. Discrimination can be undertaken if different consumer models[2] (parameters) hold for various segments.

The use of multivariate linear discriminant and econometric analysis in segmentation research appears to be becoming more common. The basic problems facing the researcher in applying these analyses are several, (a) the difficulty in obtaining large enough samples of high quality, (b) the selection of relevant variables, (c) the non-metricity of some of the characteristics of the individuals. The first difficulty is the general difficulty in marketing research requiring careful samples. The second difficulty invokes the spectre of model misspecification. The last point re-

fers to the nature of data which in marketing is more often ordinal without being continuous/normal. The success of the linear discriminant technique depends on the metricity and error distributions of the data.

Linhart [6] has proposed a procedure which he calls "nonparametric discriminant analysis" for imperfect data. The advantages of this procedure are (a) there is no need to calculate variances and covariances, (b) discrete variables can be used together or without continuous variables and (c) no assumptions are made about their frequency distribution.

Balakrishnan and Sanghvi [1] have proposed a scheme that computes "distance between populations on the basis of attribute data". The indices are similar to Mahalanobis $D^2$ but are based on "multinomial distribution" rather than "normally distributed quantitative characteristics." These latter techniques can relax some of the assumptions imposed by the traditional normal function estimators.

Classification

Given a sample of members who may or may not have originated from the same population and values on p variables for each member, the researcher is required to set up a method of deciding whether the members fall into different populations, and if so, to define such populations.

When the researcher has weak prior knowledge of group existence and wishes to "search" a known aggregate population, classification can be useful. Such work is typical, for example, when performing psychographic analysis related to fashion adoption and media viewing habits. The usual method is to perform a cluster sample to maximize the variance within the sample and to maximize representation across a large number of variables. Then 'Q' factor analysis, Automatic Interaction Detector or some other related technique is used to search the data to develop the natural groupings. Such groupings can be called descriptive because they are representative of what individuals are rather than what they do. Examples of this kind of research abound in the literature. Classification should only be performed where there is a common behavioral model across segments. Thus, inter-segment differences are assumed to be due to the degree to which the segments possess various characteristics. From the management point of view, there is no guarantee that management relevant segments will emerge from classification.

Dissection

Given a sample of members from a single population and the values for each member, on p variables, the researcher is required to dissect the population into groups with pre-

---

[1]Dissection is a term used by Kendall [4] as a concept related to Discrimination and Classification.

[2]The cause-effect relationships may differ from segment to segment.

determined properties. In marketing literature classification and discriminant schemes are more frequently discussed. There is little formal development of dissection schemes although the operations performed by the researcher or the practitioner in most cases can be interpreted as dissection.

For example, a common way of segmenting the market is on the basis of usage rate (heavy, medium, low). Conventionally, in marketing research one views the three samples based on usage rate as emanating from three populations and then sets up a procedure to discriminate between them on the basis of some demographic and personality variables. An alternative approach is not to treat them as different populations but as three categories within the same population. This has both managerial and research implications.

Dissection is a method of reducing a given population into categories. Dissection can take place either independently of discrimination or as a subsequent step to discrimination whether or not the latter yields discriminable segments. The basic feature of dissection is the ability to categorize a macro-segment or a micro-segment on some meaningful basis. Dissection groups can be specified to make them maximally management relevant although there is no guarantee that meaningful segment differences will emerge from the statistical analysis.

Although, in a statistical sense, hypothesized segments may not be discriminable, a researcher may still like to divide the market into segments based on certain categories. Examples include dividing a population into heavy, medium and light users based on differences in income groupings, education levels and other variables. In such a method of dissection, the technique may be used to establish cut-off points which make marketing sense. By examining segments based on independent variable values, useful behavioral differences may be found which will be of value to the manager and researcher. The simple technique of Multiple Classification Analysis or Cross-Tabulation can be used for dissection. These techniques have the property that they do not place excessive demands on sample size or metricity of data.

## THE REFINED SEGMENTATION APPROACH

While Kotler [5] suggests that measurability, accessability and substantiability are requirements for segmentation, a more specific scheme for assessing the potential for undertaking the necessary research and management strategies for segmentation is needed. Thus, we are proposing a refined structure for segmentation. The closer that an actual situation approximates the refined structure, the better the chance that the segmentation approach will be successful.

The first condition for successful segmentation appears to be the degree to which specific groups exist within a larger population. A meaningful group can be defined as two or more persons who seem to behave according to same underlying consumer model. If there is a non-zero probability that such a group exists and if the group can be found using one or another techniques and the group can be reached through marketing techniques, segmentation can be useful.

A second condition needed to guarantee that segmentation can be undertaken is that consumer behavior variables can be developed which will capture data needed to find the segment. The literature tells us that demographics, lifestyle, usage, attitudes, communications and other behaviors are possible segment identification variables.

The third criterion is that the segment definition is useful for prediction of behaviors appropriate to the product category, e.g., brand usage, brand choice, etc. In other words, the unique behavior of the segment can be predicted in terms of input condiitons and output behaviors. In addition, the effect of time and the changing dynamics of the segment can be tracked.

The fourth condition which must be satisfied is that an analytic technique exists which allows the researcher to determine if a consumer belongs to a segment. The literature tells us that a number of techniques are available ranging from cross tabulations to multidimensional scaling. These techniques are only useful to the extent that they can yield a segment definition which is valid and reliable. As the discussion of these techniques in the preceding section shows, the techniques are highly specific to certain conditions.

## REFERENCES

1.  Balakrishnan, V. and Sanghvi, L.D. "Distance Between Populations on the Basis of Attribute Data," Biometrics, Vol. 26, 1968, 859-65.

2.  Engel, James, Henry F. Fiorillo, and Murray A. Cayley. "Market Segmentation." New York: Holt, Rinehart, and Winston, Inc. 1972.

3.  Frank, Ronald E., William F. Massey, and Yoram Wind. "Market Segmentation." Englewood Cliffs, N.J.: Prentice Hall Inc., 1972.

4.  M. G. Kendall. "Discrimination and Classification," in P. R. Krishnaiah, ed., 'Multivariate Analysis' New York: Academic Press, 1966.

5.  Kolter, Philip. "Marketing Management: Analysis, Planning and Control," 3d Ed. Englewood Cliffs, N.J.: Prentice Hall, Inc. 1976.

6.  Linhart, H. "Techniques for Discriminant Analysis with Discrete Variables," Metrika, Vol. 2, 1959, 129-139.

7.  McCarthy, E. Jerome. "Basic Marketing: A Managerial Approach," 4th ed. Homewood, Ill.: Richard D. Irwin, Inc., 1971.

8.  Selvin, H. "Durkheim's 'Suicide' and Problems of Empirical Research," Journal of Sociology, Vol. 63, May 1958, 607-620.

9.  Smith, Wendell R. "Product Differentiation and Market Segmentation as Alternative Marketing Strategies," Journal of Marketing, Vol. XXI, July, 1956, 3-8.

EFFECTS OF BLACK MODELS IN TELEVISION ADVERTISING
ON PRODUCT CHOICE BEHAVIOR

Paul J. Solomon, University of Mississippi
Ronald F. Bush, University of Mississippi

## ABSTRACT

A laboratory experiment regarding black models in television advertising is reported. The subject's race (black
or white), the products advertised (wine and bath soap),
and the model's race (black or white) were the independent
variables, while the dependent variable was product choice
of the subjects. One hundred and seventy-nine whites and
114 blacks evaluated the advertisements. The results suggest that although white subjects respond similarly to
television advertisements showing either black or white
models, black subjects respond more positively to advertisements featuring black models.

## INTRODUCTION

Since 1967 businesses have increasingly directed their
attention to the large and growing black market segment.
This increased interest can be explained in economic terms
because black consumers represent 11 percent of the population and spend approximately 77 billion dollars yearly
with expectations that this amount will rise to 120 billion
in 1980 [13]. Other explanations, however, lie in the
various forms of social pressures applied to business firms
and advertisers by CORE and NAACP in the mid 1960's. Due
to the growing importance of the black market the black
consumer has been the subject of many research studies such
as consumption differences between blacks and whites [1];
motivations of the black consumer [4, 6]; and the effects
of the black models in advertising [16].

One possible problem which business firms face is that of
appealing to the black market segments by utilizing black
models in ads without alienating the dominant white market.
Though several studies have been reported on the effects
of black models in advertising the findings of these studies, unfortunately, have not been consistent. For example,
Barban [2]; Guest [14]; Schlinger and Plummer [21] and
Szybillo and Jacoby [24] found white subjects responded in
a positive manner to all black (ads containing all black
models) or integrated ads (ads containing at least one
black model). Cagley and Cardozo [9]; Muse [18]; and Block
[5], however, received negative responses in at least one
situation by white subjects to black models. Barban and
Cundiff [3]; Tolley and Goett [26]; and Bush, Gwinner, and
Solomon [7] found neither positive nor negative reactions
but neutral reactions by white subjects to black models.

Black subjects, on the other hand, have been more consistent in their responses to models of their own race. Barban and Cundiff [3]; Barban [2]; Tolley and Goett [26];
Choudhury and Schmid [10]; and Szybillo and Jacoby [25]
found that black subjects responded in a positive manner
to black models. Neutral responses by black subjects have
been reported by Schlinger and Plummer [21] and Solomon,
Bush and Hair [22]. Gould, Sigband and Zoerner [15] did
find that young black subjects (i.e. age 14-29) responded
negatively to the concept of integrated advertising.

Since the black model literature is replete with inconsistencies, it is logical that one should examine other plausible hypotheses to explain the results. For example, it
would seem reasonable to assume that any findings related
to attitudes of subjects toward blacks would be geographic
specific. The studies on this subject have been done
throughout the United States. New York, Minnesota,

Illinois, California, Arizona, Florida, Missouri, and Texas
have all been used as experimental areas. There is no consistency regarding the results of these experiments with
respect to geographic locale. One, for example, would
expect the Southern states to react more negatively than
Northern states. This assumption may not be warranted
based on the findings of former research. One major study
which found negative reactions to blacks was done in Minnesota [9]; whereas studies done in Florida [14] and Mississippi [22] found no negative white responses to black
models.

The year in which the study was undertaken must also be
considered as an important variable since general attitudes
toward blacks have likely changed. The relevant research
was done between 1963 and 1976; here, once again, the
studies' inconsistencies are not reconciled based upon the
time in which they were undertaken.

The subjects used in research can also effect the results
of a study as well as the validity of generalizing from the
findings [20]. The subjects used to study the reaction to
black models in advertisements has been quite diverse.
College students have been widely used as samples in this
area of research but adult populations have been sampled
more often. This variable does offer some promise with
respect to understanding the contradictions in the literature. Gould et. al. [15] found young blacks (i.e. below
age 29) to have negative affects directed toward integrated
advertising. Cagley and Cardozo's [9] study used college
students where they found highly prejudiced whites negatively predisposed toward blacks in advertisements. Thus,
it appears that age may be a meaningful variable in understanding the inconsistent black model literature. Szybillo
and Jacoby [24] further point out that college aged adults
should serve as one set of interesting subjects in this
particular area of research because: (a) Little research
has tested both young black and white subject reactions.
(b) The black college educated population has grown in
economic impact [27]. (c) Advertising can give minority
consumers impressions about a manufacturer's hiring practices [24].

The measurement devices used to measure dependent variables
in previous research may help to account for some of the
inconsistencies in the black model literature. A form of
the semantic differential (developed by Barban and Cundiff
[3]) was used most often as a key dependent variable to
measure responses to black models. This instrument was
followed, in order of frequency of use, by rankings, unaided recall, open-ended questions and observed behavior.

One explanation for the inconsistencies in the literature
is that black and white subjects' responses to black models
are product related. For example, Muse's [18] results
indicated that white subjects responded negatively toward
an advertisement using black models to promote a "personal
care" product. On the other hand, a study by Bush et. al.
[7] did not confirm the personal care product hypothesis.
In the present study, therefore, a personal care product--
bath soap--was utilized as an independent variable in order
to test further the "personal care product hypothesis."

Products that are consumed in the presence of others (socially consumed products) have also been the focus of several
marketing investigations. Black model advertisements for
an alcoholic beverage--a socially consumed product--

19

received negative evaluations from white consumers [9]. Differing results were obtained by Muse [18] who found that white subjects evaluated equally alcoholic beverage advertisements showing black and white models. In contrast, black subjects in the Barban [2] study indicated a preference for alcoholic beverage advertisements using black models. Wine was used as the independent variable to test the "social consumption hypothesis" in the present study.

Prints or slides, depicting print media, have been most often used to study the effect of black models. Schlinger and Plummer [21] have been the only researchers to utilize television, a perplexing situation in view of the fact that television has been the most widely used medium for black models. The present study employed television as its medium.

The authors' purpose in the present study was to measure the behavioral responses of both white and black subjects to television advertisements utilizing black and white models to promote a personal care as well as a socially consumed product.

### HYPOTHESES

H₁ There are no differences in white consumers' behavioral response to television advertisements that depict either a black or a white model using a personal care product--bath soap.

H₂ There are no differences in white consumers' behavioral response to television advertisements that depict either a black or a white model as a user of a socially consumed product--wine.

H₃ There are no differences in black consumers' behavioral response to television advertisements that depict either a black or a white model using a personal care product--bath soap.

H₄ There are no differences in black consumers' behavioral response to television advertisements that depict either a black or a white model as a user of a socially consumed product--wine.

### METHOD

#### Subjects

The subjects were 179 white and 114 black college students attending universities in a Southern state. In order to avoid the problem of the volunteer subject [20] and to strengthen the cover story, classes of core business topics (i.e. Introductory classes in Accounting, Business, Management, and Marketing) were used. While it is possible for systematic bias to exist based on the class meeting time, the professor, the subject matter, or other extraneous factors, it was felt the above items should have little effect upon a person's product choice behavior. Beyond this, the intact groups were randomly assigned to the experimental treatments.

#### Experimental Design

The laboratory experiment utilized a 2 X 2 X 2 design. A series of 2 X 2 comparisons utilizing the chi-square test for categorial variables was made to test the hypotheses. For all comparisons the .05 level of significance was used. The subjects' race (black or white), the products advertised (wine or bath soap), and the model's race (black or white) were the independent variables while the dependent variable was the product choice selection of the subjects (Figure 1).

### FIGURE 1

### RESEARCH DESIGN TO MEASURE EFFECTS OF MODELS' RACE ON PRODUCT CHOICE

| Treatment Conditions | | Race of Subject | |
|---|---|---|---|
| Product Type | Models' Race | Black | White |
| Personal Care Product | Black Model Bath Soap Ad | n=30 | n=50 |
| | White Model Bath Soap Ad | n=30 | n=57 |
| Socially Consumed Product | Black Model Wine Ad | n=37 | n=36 |
| | White Model Wine Ad | n=16 | n=35 |

#### Independent Variables

The independent variable of subjects' race was treated as a classification variable (black versus white). The other two independent variables--product type and models' race--were manipulated in the experimental treatments. There were four possible experiment treatments: (1) a white model, bath soap condition; (2) a black soap model, bath soap condition; (3) a white model, wine condition; and (4) a black model, wine condition. Subjects were exposed to only one experimental treatment.

The four experimental treatments were advertisements for the two products (bath soap and wine). These advertisements were made especially for the experiment. The two sets of commercials were written by a professional television commercial copy writer and filmed at a commercial studio. Everything possible was done to insure that the advertisements were identical. They: used the same wording; were the same length (60 seconds); were filmed in identical settings; had the same musical scores; and their photographic quality was identical. They differed only by the race of the professional model used in the advertisement.

#### Dependent Variable

The dependent variable was the actual product choice of the subject. This behavioral measure was designed to be as similar to naturalistic instore behavior as possible. To accomplish this the product selection room was designed in a store-like manner with three separate display areas. Each of the different display areas contained similar displays of three different brand name products of that particular product category. For example, one display area contained three brands of cookies, while another area contained three brands of another product, and the third area contained three brands of either bath soap or wine depending upon the experimental treatment being administered. All products in the display area had approximately the same prices and market shares in the region of the study. The subjects were allowed to select only one brand from each of the three display areas. The displays, multiple brand choice, and the limited selection situations were all created in an effort to simulate, as much as possible, the real-world shopping environment. While each subject selected a total of three products, only one selection was the dependent variable--the product category corresponding to the experimental treatment condition.

## Procedure

One class at a time was brought into a television viewing room. Each class was told by the experimenter that the study they were about to participate in was concerned with the failure of a television show that appeared for the first time the previous television season. The subjects were then told they would see a video-taped segment of the show for the purpose of deciding why the show had failed. For helping in this effort, the subjects were told they would receive several free gifts. The video-taped show was played in its entirety. After viewing the television show the subjects completed a bogus questionnaire concerning the subjects' various opinions about the program. There were no questions on the questionnaire concerning the experimental treatment. This was done to avoid pre-test sensitization of the subjects. When the individual subjects completed their questionnaires, they were ushered into an adjoining room where they selected their free gifts for participating in the study. Upon selecting their gifts, they were free to leave.

## Debriefing

The cover story and bogus questionnaire were utilized to conceal the true intent of the study. The degree to which these deceptions were successful was measured in a post-experimental debriefing questionnaire. The results of the debriefing questionnaire indicated that the deception was successful as none of the subjects identified the real intent of the experiment. It is interesting to note that, while a few subjects thought the experiment had something to do with "product selection," not one subject said anything concerning the race of the models. Because of the deception necessary to implement the study, all subjects were thoroughly debriefed within two weeks of the experiment.

## ANALYSIS

Hypotheses 1, 2 and 3 were not statistically significant (see Table 1). For hypothesis 1, the white subjects' responses to the personal care product (bath soap) advertisements were the same regardless of whether the model was white or black. White subjects responded in a similar fashion to the socially consumed product (wine) advertisements (hypothesis 2). That is, the black and white model elicited similar product choice behavior from the white respondents. Regarding hypothesis 3, black consumers responded no differently to black and white models portrayed as users of a personal care product--bath soap.

Hypothesis 4, however, was statistically significant. Twelve percent of the black subjects selected the wine (socially consumed product) advertised by a white model, whereas 49 percent selected the wine advertised by a black model as their product choice ($x^2$=4.77, p < .05, $\underline{df}$=1). The black model portrayed as a user of wine elicited significantly greater product choice behavior from black consumers than the white model.

A further analysis was based upon the variables of age and sex. No difference was indicated between the ways males and females respond to models of a different race. Likewise, age played an insignificant role in determining responses to the models.

## DISCUSSION

Advertisers have been concerned with the effects of black models in advertisements. Former research suggests that consumers' responses to black models are not consistent. This experiment is an extension of the previous literature in that it examines the effects of variables such as

TABLE 1

THE EFFECTS OF MODELS' RACE ON THE BEHAVIOR OF BLACK AND WHITE SUBJECTS

| Subjects' Race | Experimental Treatment Received | (number) | Product Selected Advertised | Non-advertised |
|---|---|---|---|---|
| H₁ White | Black Model, Soap Condition | (50) | 14% | 86% |
| | White Model, Soap Condition | (57) | 12% | 88% |
| H₂ White | Black Model, Wine Condition | (36) | 28% | 72% |
| | White Model, Wine Condition | (35) | 23% | 77% |
| H₃ Black | Black Model, Soap Condition | (30) | 7% | 93% |
| | White Model, Soap Condition | (30) | 20% | 80% |
| ***H₄ Black | Black Model, Wine Condition | (37) | 49% | 51% |
| | White Model, Wine Condition | (16) | 12% | 88% |

***Significantly different at .05 level.

product type (socially consumed and personal care products); broadcast medium (television); response measure (product choice behavior); and race of the subjects as well as the race of the advertisements' models.

The white subjects included in this study responded similarly to white and black television models. The behavioral process of selecting products from a simulated store shelf was not affected by the race of the model. This finding is in agreement with Barban [2]; Guest [14]; Schlinger and Plummer [21]; Bush et. al. [7]; and Szybillo and Jacoby [24] as these researchers found white subjects respond positively to blacks in advertisements. Barban and Cundiff [3] and Tolley and Goett [26] have reported neutral attitudes by white subjects toward black models. If the slight attitudinal differences reported in previous studies exist in the general population, the findings of this study suggest that these slightly different attitudes probably do not manifest themselves in negative short-term behavior patterns.

The negative white reactions to black models found by Cagley and Cardozo [9] are in disagreement with the reported findings. Also, white reactions to black models were not product specific in the present study. This is in contrast to Muses' [18] hypothesis that black model, personal care product advertisements receive negative responses by white subjects. However, it is in agreement with Bush et. al. [7] who found in a field experiment that white consumers respond positively to black model, personal care product promotions.

Black subjects who saw the wine advertisements responded in a significantly different manner to the white and black models. The black model elicited greater product choice behavior than the white model among the black subjects. Thus, for a socially consumed product--wine--a model similar in racial characteristics to the subjects' (black) was more influential with respect to behavioral change than a model of a differing race (white). This result is consistent with the literature in that it has often been suggested that black models in advertising are effective in influencing black consumers. (For example, see Barban and Cundiff [3]; Tolley and Goett [26]; Choudhury and Schmid [10]; and Szybillo and Jacoby [24].)

Black subjects selected the advertised personal care product--bath soap--the same whether the advertisement they were exposed to contained a black or a white model. This result is similar to studies done by Schlinger and Plummer [21] and Solomon, Bush, and Hair [22] but is in contrast to most other studies done on black subjects. Basically, it has been assumed that black consumers respond positively to all advertisements that contain black models. This research indicates that black subjects' responses may be product specific. That is, black consumers may respond more favorably to black models advertising "socially conspicuous" products.

The results of this study are based upon two sets of advertisements for two products using black and white models. It is likely that other products using different advertisements would provide different results. Confounding factors such as the social deference of the models (Guest [14]); the level of integration of the models (Szybillo and Jacoby [24]); and the attractiveness of various physical characteristics of the models (Block [5]) were not included to enhance the internal validity of the research. Furthermore, the results are based upon simulated in-store behavior rather than real life in-store behavior. These factors may, of course, affect the results.

The findings of this study should serve to aid advertisers in future decisions regarding the use of black models. Apparently, advertisers need not be overly concerned about alienating at least college educated white consumers, because they respond equally well to black or white models in television advertising. On the other hand, at least for some products, black models may help attract a larger share of the young black market segment.

## REFERENCES

1. Alexis, M. "Some Negro-White Differences in Consumption," American Journal of Economics and Sociology, 1, (1962), 11-28.

2. Barban, A. "The Dilemma of Integrated Advertising," The Journal of Business of the University of Chicago, 42, (1969), 477-496.

3. Barban, M., and E. W. Cundiff. "Negro and White Responses to Advertising Stimuli," Journal of Marketing Research, 1, (1964), 53-56.

4. Bauer, R. B. and S. M. Cunningham. "The Negro Market," Journal of Advertising Research, 10, (1970), 3-13.

5. Block, C. E. "White Blacklash to Negro Ads: Fact or Fantasy?" Journalism Quarterly, 49, (1972), 258-262.

6. Bullock, H. A. "Consumer Motivations in Black and White--I." Harvard Business Review, 39, (1961), 89-104; "Consumer Motivations in Black and White--II." Harvard Business Review, 39, (1961), 110-124.

7. Bush, R. F., R. F. Gwinner and P. J. Solomon. "White Consumer Sales Response to Black Models," Journal of Marketing, 38 (1974), 25-29.

8. Bush, R. F., P. J. Solomon and J. F. Hair, Jr. "The Changing Role of Black Models in TV Ads," Journal of Advertising Research, 17 (1977), 21-25.

9. Cagley, J. W. and R. N. Cardozo. "White Response to Integrated Advertising," Journal of Advertising Research, 10 (1970), 35-39.

10. Choudhury, P. L. and L. S. Schmid. "Black Models in Advertising to Blacks," Journal of Advertising Research, 14 (1974), 19-22.

11. Cox, K. K. "Social Effects of Integrated Advertising," Journal of Advertising Research, 10 (1970), 41-44.

12. Engel, J. F., D. T. Kollat and R. D. Blackwell. Consumer Behavior, 2nd ed. New York: Holt, Rinehart and Winston, Inc., 1973, 270-274.

13. The Gibson Report. "Marketing to Minorities Outlook Good in the Year Ahead." New York: D. Parke Gibson International, Inc., 1976, 16.

14. Guest, L. "How Negro Models Affect Company Image." Journal of Advertising Research, 10 (1970), 29-33.

15. Gould, J. W., N. B. Sigband and C. E. Zoerner, Jr. "Black Consumer Reactions to Integrated Advertisements: An Exploratory Study," Journal of Marketing, 3 (1970), 20-26.

16. Journal of Advertising Research, special issue, 10, 1970.

17. Kassarjian, H. H. "The Negro and American Advertising," Journal of Marketing Research, 6 (1960), 29-39.

18. Muse, William V. "Product-related Response to Use of Black Models in Advertising," Journal of Marketing Research, 7 (1971), 107-109.

19. Pinson, C. and E. L. Roberto. "Do attitude Changes Precede Behavioral Change? Journal of Advertising Research, 13 (1973), 33-38.

20. Rosenthal, R. and R. L. Rosnow. "The Volunteer Subject," Artifact in Behavioral Research, eds. Robert Rosenthal and Ralph Rosnow. New York and London: Academic Press, 1969, 61-110.

21. Schlinger, M. J. and J. T. Plummer. "Advertising in Black and White," Journal of Marketing Research, 9, (1972), 11-17.

22. Solomon, P. J., R. F. Bush and J. F. Hair, Jr. "White and Black Consumer Sales Response to Black Models," Journal of Marketing Research, 13 (1976), 431-434.

23. Stafford, J. E., A. E. Birdwell and C. E. Van Tassel. "Integrated Advertising--White Blacklash?" Journal of Advertising Research, 10 (1970), 15-27.

24. Szybillo, G. J. and J. Jacoby. "Effects of Different Levels of Integration on Advertising Preference and Intention to Purchase," Journal of Applied Psychology, 59, (1974), 274-280.

25. Szybillo, G. J., J. Jacoby and J. Busato. "Effects of Integrated Advertising on Perceived Corporate Hiring Policy." Proceedings of the 81st Annual Convention of the American Psychological Assoc., 8 (1973), 819-820.

26. Tolley, B. and J. T. Goett. "Reactions to Blacks in Newspaper Ads," Journal of Advertising Research, 11 (1971), 11-17.

27. Wattenberg, B. J. and R. M. Scammon. "Black Progress and Liberal Rhetoric," Commentary, 55 (1973), 35-44.

# THE EMOTIONAL VALUE OF DIFFERENT COLOR COMBINATIONS

Charles M. Schaninger, University of Ottawa

## ABSTRACT

Preference orderings for eight different print-background color combinations were obtained for three different emotional themes in a laboratory setting, for a sample of male and female subjects. Different combinations of colors were associated with specific emotional themes. Consistent results were found with a word association test also given. A relatively high degree of inter-subject consistency was found, although there were a number of interesting sex differences in both the preference orderings and word associations.

## INTRODUCTION

It is widely assumed that certain colors have emotional value: e.g., red: blood, fire, excitement, sex, passion, anger; yellow: sunlight, comfortable warmth, cheerfulness; blue and green: calm, cool, refreshing; etc. [6, 10] yet very few studies in this area have been reported. Most modern texts in the area of advertising or promotion emphasize that the use of color has been demonstrated to be more effective than black and white ads, in attention value, in readership, and in actual sales effectiveness [3, 10]. Most of these authors also suggest that color may be used to create different moods in advertisements, or contribute to the emotional context of a package design's perceptual impact [5]. Valiente [12] suggests that the combination of colors in an advertisement is now as important as the use of color or the number of colors in ads. He suggests that advertisers should test different color combinations to obtain one that will maximize attention, interest, and purchase. Most current texts and articles have drawn upon research findings reported before 1940, citing the results of studies by Burtt [1], Luckiesh [7] and Dorcus [2]. Generally, these studies demonstrate that there are consistent associations between colors and emotions, although most were based on either word associations or subjective ratings.

Bright colors such as red, yellow, and orange have high attention value and exciting emotional connotations, while colors such as blue, green, and violet tend to be lower in attention value and have either tranquilizing or subduing emotional connotations [3, 6, 7, 10]. Burtt [1] found that men preferred blue and disliked yellow, with red and green erratically preferred. If the desired emotional appeal was to emphasize tranquility, calmness, or coolness to males, blue would seem to be highly appropriate and red highly inappropriate, although the affective values of these colors conflict with their attention values.

This study focuses on the use of different print/background color combinations for emotional appeals. It was felt that certain color combinations would be differentially effective for differing emotional themes. Combinations of red and black or red and yellow were hypothesized to be effective for an exciting, romantic, adventurous theme; combinations of blue on green and yellow on blue for a calm, cool, restful theme; and combinations of red and yellow for a warm, glowing, sunny theme.

## METHODS

This experiment consisted of a word-color association test, and of a preference ordering of eight different print-background color combinations for each of three different emotional themes.

Thirty-eight subjects, nineteen males and nineteen females were randomly selected from the introductory psychology course of a large private eastern university.

The word association test consisted of a list of 38 words typical of those used in previous research, and included most of the words used in the three emotional themes described below. Subjects were asked to write down, next to each word any color, colors, or combination of colors which they associated with that word.

Three sets of eight posterboards also served as stimuli. The posterboard dimensions were eleven by fourteen inches. Fifty-six point gothic press-on letters were used to print the messages on each poster. The colors of the lettering and posterboard backgrounds for the eight color combinations were: red on black, black on white, blue on green, blue on yellow, black on red, yellow on red, yellow on blue, and red on yellow. Three advertising themes are depicted below as they appeared on the eight posterboards:

| FOR AN EXCITING ROMANTIC VACATION VISIT ADVENTURE VILLAGE | FOR A WARM, GLOWING VACATION VISIT SUNSHINE VALLEY | FOR A CALM COOL VACATION VISIT RESTFUL MOUNTAIN LAKE |
|---|---|---|

Each line was properly centered and spaced on the posterboards, and each of these themes was printed for all eight color combinations. These specific themes and locational placements were chosen after pilot testing several alternatives on a small pilot sample. The basic theme of a vacation was used to obtain an emotionally ambivalent product. The hypothetical resort names were chosen to avoid any associations with existing resorts.

Subjects were tested in groups of three, with all subjects receiving the word association test first. They were then randomly given one of the three sets of eight posterboards (shuffled to control for order effects). They were instructed to read the message and to examine all eight posterboards, and then to arrange them in the order of preference for each specific color combination. They were then told to record their preferences on a sheet provided, giving their first choice a rank of one and their last choice a rank of eight. If they regarded two posters as equal in preference, they were instructed to give both that rank equal to the average of what the two posters would have received had they not been equal:

> "For example, if the fourth and fifth posters were decided upon as equal, give them both a rank of four and one half, and give the next poster after these a six."

After completing the first set, subjects then arranged, in turn, each of the other two reshuffled sets in order of preference and scored them. Post experimental debriefing revealed that the subjects did notice the messages on each set of posters and took that into account in their preference rankings.

## RESULTS

The results of the word association test were basically consistent with previous research, although there were some sex differences. Both males and females tended to associate red with love, warmth, passion, excitement,

TABLE 1

PROPORTIONS OF MALES AND FEMALES FOR TEN WORD ASSOCIATION

| | Proportion | | | | Proportion | | |
|---|---|---|---|---|---|---|---|
| | males | females | Z | | males | females | Z |
| Love/White | .26 | .53 | 1.72* | Hate/Black | .42 | .74 | 2.08** |
| Romantic/White | .16 | .37 | 1.52 | Hate/Red | .68 | .42 | -1.69* |
| Calm/White | .26 | .53 | 1.72* | Excitment/Red | .74 | .95 | 1.86* |
| Laziness/Yellow | .32 | .53 | 1.35 | War/Red | .89 | .68 | -1.65* |
| Warmth/Yellow | .26 | .63 | 2.46** | War/Black | .53 | .74 | 1.38 |

*p < .10          **p < .05

TABLE 2

MEAN RANKS OF EIGHT COLOR COMBINATIONS, BY THEME AND BY SEX

| | Black on Red | Black on White | Blue on Green | Blue on Yellow | Red on Black | Red on Yellow | Yellow on Blue | Yellow on Red | $X_r^2$ | W |
|---|---|---|---|---|---|---|---|---|---|---|
| | | | | Exciting-Romantic Theme | | | | | | |
| Males | 4.16 | 6.89 | 5.50 | 4.58 | 3.84 | 3.92 | 3.95 | 3.16 | 30.8*** | .23*** |
| Females | 4.11 | 7.29 | 3.68 | 4.29 | 5.18 | 3.92 | 4.24 | 3.29 | 34.8*** | .26*** |
| Mann-Whitney U | 178 | 134.5 | 90** | 163 | 143 | 179 | 166.5 | 168.5 | | |
| | | | | Calm-Cool Theme | | | | | | |
| Males | 5.82 | 4.84 | 1.68 | 3.13 | 6.24 | 5.45 | 2.82 | 6.03 | 65.6*** | .49*** |
| Females | 5.68 | 4.58 | 1.63 | 3.53 | 6.58 | 5.76 | 2.63 | 5.61 | 67.2*** | .51*** |
| Mann-Whitney U | 177.5 | 167.5 | 167.5 | 155 | 151.5 | 172.5 | 171 | 160.5 | | |
| | | | | Warm-Glowing Theme | | | | | | |
| Males | 4.45 | 6.71 | 5.95 | 4.16 | 5.11 | 2.74 | 4.71 | 2.18 | 50.6*** | .38*** |
| Females | 5.24 | 6.53 | 4.34 | 3.24 | 6.11 | 2.39 | 5.18 | 2.97 | 50.9*** | .38*** |
| Mann-Whitney U | 136 | 149 | 96.5** | 113* | 130 | 152 | 149.5 | 128.5 | | |
| $X_r^2$ Males | 6.6* | 10.3** | 24.7*** | 7.2* | 4.3 | 13.3** | 7.6* | 19.5*** | | |
| $X_r^2$ Females | 3.0 | 9.8** | 14.9*** | 4.1 | 3.9 | 16.0*** | 11.6** | 8.0* | | |
| $X_r^2$ Total | 8.3* | 19.4*** | 39.0*** | 7.6* | 7.9* | 29.1*** | 18.8*** | 26.0*** | | |

*P < .05          **p < .01          ***p < .001

adventure, sex, and immorality; to associate blue (and to a lesser degree green) with calm, cool, comfortable, tranquility, and lakes; and to associate red, orange, and yellow with warmth, sunshine, and glowing. Table 1 presents the proportions of males and females indicating a particular word association for ten selected word associations. Only those word associations demonstrating sex difference tendencies are presented. These proportions were tested for sex differences using a two tailed z test. Females were more likely than males to associate white with the words love, romantic, and calm; to associate yellow with laziness and warmth; to associate black with hate and war; and less likely to associate red with hate or war.

Table 2 presents the mean rankings for the eight color combinations, broken down by emotional theme and by sex, with appropriate statistical tests. Friedman two-way analyses of variance, $(X_r^2)$ were calculated for each of the three emotional themes for both males and females, to test the hypotheses that the eight color combinations received significantly different rankings. Similarly $X_r^2$ figures were calculated for each color combination across the three themes, to test the hypotheses that each theme received significantly different rankings. To examine sex differences in the mean rankings, the Mann-Whitney U test was applied to each color combination for each theme. Kendall W coefficients of concordance were calculated for each theme to examine the overall degree of consistency between subjects in the rankings.

The eight color combinations received significantly different rankings for all three emotional themes for both males and females, although the differences in rankings were less pronounced for the exciting-romantic theme.

Combinations of yellow and red tended to be most preferred, and black on white least preferred for the exciting-romantic theme; blue on green tended to be preferred by females, and red on black by males.

For the calm-cool theme, blue on green and yellow on blue tended to be most preferred with combinations of yellow and red and of red and black least preferred.

Combinations of red and yellow tended to be most preferred for the warm-glowing theme, with black on white and red on black least preferred. Females tended to prefer blue on either yellow or green more than did males.

Each of the eight color combinations received significantly different rankings across the three themes, although the results were weak for combinations of red and black and for blue on yellow.

There were a few significant sex differences in mean rankings, for the exciting-romantic theme and the warm-glowing theme, and others approached significance. The Mann-Whitney U test is sensitive to differences in central tendency, but not to other distributional differences.

## TABLE 3

### CROSS TABULATIONS OF PREFERENCE RANKING BY SEX FOR FIVE COLOR COMBINATIONS, EXCITING-ROMANTIC THEME

| Preference Ranking | Black on Red | | Blue on Green | | Blue on Yellow | | Red on Black | | Yellow on Red | |
|---|---|---|---|---|---|---|---|---|---|---|
| | male | female | male | female | male | female | male | female | male | female |
| 1-2 | 4 | 6 | 2 | 5 | 6 | 3 | 9 | 4 | 6 | 10 |
| 3-4 | 8 | 4 | 4 | 7 | 0 | 8 | 4 | 3 | 10 | 3 |
| 5-6 | 4 | 7 | 4½ | 6 | 12½ | 5½ | 0 | 4 | 3 | 4 |
| 7-8 | 3 | 2 | 8½ | 1 | ½ | 2½ | 6 | 8 | 0 | 2 |
| $x^2$ | 2.75 | | 8.24** | | 13.06*** | | 6.35* | | 6.91* | |

*$p < .10$   **$p < .05$   ***$p < .01$

An examination of the raw data revealed some tendencies toward bimodal distributions and other modal differences, particularly for the exciting romantic theme. Table 3 presents cross classifications of rankings by sex for four color combinations. The red on black color combination particularly reflects both a bimodal tendency and significant sex differences. Subjects tend to rank this color combination as either highly preferred or highly disliked; more males tended to prefer it, and more females to dislike it. More females tended to respond favorably to blue on green, blue on yellow, and yellow on red than did males.

The Kendall W coefficients of concordance demonstrated a significant degree of intersubject consistency among the rankings for all three themes. Rankings for the exciting romantic theme were less consistent than for the other two themes, in part reflecting the bimodal tendencies observed for the red on black color combination.

## CONCLUSIONS

The results of this study were generally consistent with those of previous research--certain colors and combinations of colors were differentially associated with emotional themes. Combinations of yellow and red tended to be preferred for the exciting-romantic theme; combinations of blue on green and yellow on blue were preferred for the calm-cool-restful theme; combinations of yellow and red were preferred for the warm-glowing-sunny theme. These results indicate that specific color combinations may be more effective for advertising products with such themes than the traditional black on white background combination. Similar implications can be made for advertising.

Generally, a relatively high degree of inter subject consistency in preference rankings for the eight color combinations was found, supporting the generalizability of the findings. There were a number of sex differences in both the rankings and in the word associations, particularly for the exciting-romantic theme. Females were more likely to associate romance and love with white than males, less likely to associate red with hate or war, and more likely to associate black with hate or war. This may explain the tendency of females to be more likely to rank the red on black color combination as least preferred for the exciting-romantic theme. The bimodal tendency for this particular color combination, as well as the sex difference parallels the findings of Morrison and Sherman [9]. They found that women were more likely than men to notice suggestiveness of copy, and found a bimodal reaction among women in noticing nudity in ads. These results indicate that women may be more perceptually sensitive to sex-related advertising, but that they are more likely to institute defense reactions to such suggestiveness. Further research on sex differences in color preferences for products associated with sex or romance may provide useful information for package designs or advertising color combinations. Perhaps other color combinations not used in this study (e.g., pink and black, red and white) may be differentially preferred by females.

Psychophysical measures of attention value, arousal, or anxiety may prove useful for further investigation of such non-traditional color combinations for advertising or package design for different emotional themes. Various psychophysical measures such as polygraph (GSR, vertical/horizontal thumb pressure, heartbeat, etc.), or pupillary dilation measures [4, 5], or aniseikonic lens measures [8, 11] may prove useful in measuring arousal or anxiety, in conjunction with eye camera measures of attention value.

The results of this study were based on reported preference orderings and on word associations. Before any realistic practical implications can be drawn, behavioral validation measures are necessary, using actual choice behavior in buying situations as criteria for assessing the effectiveness of particular color combinations for advertising or package design. Furthermore, it should be noted that these results were based on college student responses, and may not be fully generalizable to older age groups.

## REFERENCES

1. Burtt, H.E. Psychology of Advertising. Boston: Houghton-Mifflin, 1938.

2. Dorcus, R.M. "Habitual Word Associations to Colors as a Possible Factor in Advertising". Journal of Applied Psychology, 16 (1932), 227-287.

3. Engel, J.F., H.G. Wales, and M.R. Warshaw. Promotional Strategy. Rev. ed. Homewood, Illinois: Irwin, 1971.

4. Greeno, D.W. "Physiological Correlates of Verbally Stated Preference and Signal Value". American Marketing Association Combined Proceedings, 33 (1971), 454-459.

5. Horowithz, I.A. and R.S. Kaye. "Perception and Advertising". Journal of Advertising Research, 15 (1975), 15-21.

6. Lucas, D.B. and S.H. Britt. Advertising Psychology and Research. New York: McGraw-Hill, 1950.

7. Luckiesh, M. Light and Color in Advertising and Merchandising. New York: Van Nostrand, 1923.

8.  MaGee, M. and S. Fisher.  "Aniseikonic Perception of Injured Areas of One's Own Body".  <u>Perceptual</u> <u>and</u> <u>Motor</u> <u>Skills</u>, 33 (1971), 47-50.

9.  Morrison, J. and R.C. Sherman.  "Who Responds to Sex in Advertising?".  <u>Journal</u> <u>of</u> <u>Advertising</u> <u>Research</u>, 12 (1972), 15-19.

10. Sandage, C.H. and V. Fryburger.  <u>Advertising</u> <u>Theory</u> <u>and</u> <u>Practice</u>.  (9th ed.) Homewood, Illinois:  Irwin, 1975.

11. Schaninger, C.M. "The Use of Aniseikonic Lenses to Measure Perceived Risk and Product Preference, and to Measure Anxiety as a Personality Trait".  Unpublished Doctoral Dissertation, University of Rochester, 1975.

12. Valiente, R. "Mechanical Correlates of Ad Recognition".  <u>Journal</u> <u>of</u> <u>Advertising</u> <u>Research</u>, 13 (1973), 13-18.

# ON THE RELATIONSHIP OF CONSUMER BEHAVIOR AND THE SENSE OF TOUCH

Lyndon E. Dawson, Jr., Louisiana Tech University
Charles O. Bettinger, III, Northeast Louisiana University

## ABSTRACT

The senses are important variables in analyzing human behavior. To date little formal analysis has been undertaken concerning the causal effects of the sense of touch as applied to consumer behavior and marketing situations. Packaging, closed display counters or other barriers may act as either a stimulus or deterrent in the formulation of positive consumer attitudes toward a product offering.

Utilizing a semantic differential scale, this paper explores the self-reported differences in attitudes concerning touch among four test groups of consumers toward selected products exhibited in a simulated retail store display. Results of the investigation reveal that the ability to touch and handle various products has a positive impact on consumer attitudes toward those items.

## INTRODUCTION

The greatest sense in our body is our touch sense. It is probably the chief sense in the process of sleeping and waking; it gives us our knowledge of depth or thickness and form. We feel, we love and hate, are touchy and are touched, through the touch corpuscles (membranes) of our skin [16].

The sense of touch plays a significant role in consumer attitudes toward products and therefore should influence tactical decisions related to marketing strategy. For example, many products now displayed behind counters or in packages may possess greater appeal if they are within the customers' reach. Formal research conducted on the sense of touch has generally centered on its physiological and psychological implications [4, 6, 7, 10] and an extensive review of the literature reveals few previous applications to a marketing situation.

One previous study by Olson and Jacoby [12] determined that product attributes which cannot be changed without changing the (intrinsic) physical characteristics of the product itself are generally perceived to be better indicators of brand quality than are those product-related characteristics (extrinsic) that are not a part of the physical product. In another exploratory examination, Szybillo and Jacoby [15] found that intrinsic physical product cue differences (primarily tactile) were stronger determinants of consumer perceived quality judgments than were extrinsic cue differences of price or store image. Perceptions of a product as a result of the intrinsic sense of touch therefore may have broad marketing implications for product distribution, packaging, and display. The following investigation is, perhaps, one of the first attempts to present a description of the influence of consumers' touch sense as it affects the packaging, display, and product image aspects of marketing. The specific research hypothesis for investigation is that there is no difference in consumer attitudes concerning both touched and untouched test products.

## SENSE OF TOUCH

The sense of touch is experienced not only as a physical sensation but affectively through human emotions [11, pg. 4]. Consumers receive information about the external environment through a number of sensitivities. Receptors, or free nerve endings act as detectors; then this information is carried to the central nervous system to create sensations.

A given stimulus, for instance, can feel pleasant or unpleasant depending upon its usefulness as determined by internal signals [2, pg. 1103].

Among humans, even the youngest child can be shown to prefer and even seek out certain patterns of peripheral stimulation, and to delight in certain shapes and textures [17]. Thus, everyday objects communicate certain sensations via the sense of touch.

This language of objects is used pervasively in marketing. Rarely, if ever, does a verbal description achieve the same effect as an exhibit of merchandise; no merchant would attempt to influence his customers through the display and arrangement of things if it were not for the fact that the success of such nonverbal methods can be measured in dollars and cents [14]. The fact that objects on display are bought would indicate that the desired effect is often achieved. The effect that objects achieve in terms of their communicative value are dependent not only upon arrangement but also upon variations of materials, shape, and surface. Any material evokes tactile and thermal images of smoothness, roughness, hardness, softness, coldness, and warmth. These tactile images often produce sharp and immediate physical and emotional reactions. Consumer discrimination of size, shape, locus, intensity, or duration can be utilized in product recognition as well as image formulation.

The mechanism through which individuals touch, the skin, is the largest human organ and constitutes 16 to 18 percent of total body weight [8, pg. 464]. In addition to being the largest organ, the various elements comprising the skin have a large representation in the brain [11, pg. 6]. As a sensory system, the skin is an important organ of the body and, along with other senses, may be extensively utilized by consumers in the formulation of purchase judgments.

## METHOD

In order to answer the question of whether the sense of touch affects consumer attitudes, six products and 120 consumer subjects were utilized in a laboratory experiment. Briefly, the investigation consisted of four groups of consumers who touched and did not touch a series of six products at a simulated retail store display and who rated the identified products by means of a semantic differential type questionnaire [3, 1].

Important to the research was the manner in which the products were displayed. Products were all displayed in a room (known to test subjects as a marketing laboratory) containing a simulated retail store with both open-top counter display and closed display with products visable to the prospective customers. Test groups of consumers were exposed to one of four simulated type displays as follows:

Products were displayed in packages which were sold to consumer subjects who were not able to feel the merchandise.

Products were displayed in actual packages with test subjects encouraged to touch the goods.

Products were removed from packages and displayed with the consumer unable to touch them.

Products were removed from packages with subjects encouraged to examine the displayed products.

27

Several factors carried considerable weight in choosing the products to be rated. First, it was considered desirable for the merchandise to be familiar to all subjects participating in the study. Second, products were chosen for experimental analysis which were in fact actually displayed in packages, cases, or behind counters of local retail stores in the metropolitan area. The six tested products included a pair of terrycloth Dearfoam house shoes, a brown Career Club shirt, a Timex watch, a pair of rabbit fur lined leather gloves for men, a wooden box purse for women, and a blue Career Club knit shirt. Consumer subjects participating in the investigation ranged from fifteen to eighteen years in age and were divided into four equal sized test groups. Each group was exposed to one of the four above mentioned types of display.

Students were utilized as subjects for two reasons. Not only has student opinion been found to approximate closely those of the general population [5, 9] but this particular type of study did not require a specific age group. If the purpose of the study had been to ascertain attitudes concerning children's toys, participating subjects would have consisted of either a group of children or a group of parents. In this particular investigation, however, attitudes common to people as a whole were being sought.

The rating instrument, a six-page printed questionnaire with semantic scale range of one to nine was distributed to each participating subject. Each page of the instrument was identical and contained fifteen semantic differential bipolar-type adjectives. The fifteen pairs of tested adjectives were those which received the highest "loadings" in Osgood's test [13, pg. 48] of the semantic differential technique. Thus, for an evaluative factor, the following six adjective pairs were used: awful/nice, bad/good, worthless/valuable, ugly/beautiful, sad/happy, and pleasant/unpleasant. In addition to the above factors, three adjective pairs for an activity factor were used and were: dull/sharp, slow/fast, and old/young. The four adjective pairs comprising a potency factor were: delicate/rugged, soft/loud, weak/strong, and smooth/rough. Osgood's scale of semantic factors was used as the test instrument because it has been repeatedly tested, is easy to understand, and has been found appropriate for many marketing research situations. In addition to the above evaluative, activity, and potency factors, a miscellaneous factor containing two adjective pairs was used. These adjective pairs, high quality/low quality and same/different, were not taken from Osgood's text but were added because of their appropriateness for the type of products in the experiment.

Six products were then presented, individually to the four groups of participating subjects, taking one consumer at a time. An identifying number was displayed next to each of the products and corresponded to the number on each page of the questionnaire. Order of product presentation differed with each tested consumer group.

Test group 1 was composed of consumers who were not allowed to touch the packaged products. The consumer subjects were not informed that the items could not be touched but were prevented from doing so by a wooden counter-type barrier. Test group 2 consisted of consumers who filed by the display and closely examined the merchandise contained in the packages. Barriers in front of the display were removed for this group of test subjects. Test group 3 was composed of consumers who were instructed to pass by and look at the merchandise which had been removed from the packages but who were not allowed to touch the merchandise. Finally, test group 4 consisted of consumer subjects who were asked to view and closely examine the products which had been removed from the packages. All of the subjects in group 4 touched the items and examined them closely.

Each consumer in every group was instructed to walk past the display, look at the item presented and described by a salesclerk, and fill out the questionnaire. Each time a

new product was described the test group of consumers was again asked to repeat the procedure. Such a procedure was necessary to approximate store display conditions. Simply passing the product from hand to hand was considered as an alternative but was ruled out because such a method is not a true life situation and more importantly, as part of the experiment, two of the four groups of subjects were not supposed to touch the merchandise.

Devised to determine if the sense of touch plays a significant role in consumers' attitudes toward various products, the investigation was conducted twice in order to confirm the findings. The experiment was constructed in a way that could be tested statistically utilizing the Z test and the following hypotheses:

$H_0$ = There is no significant difference in consumer attitude toward products among the four experimental groups of consumers.

$H_1$ = There is a significant difference in consumer attitude toward test products among the four experimental groups of consumers.

ANALYSIS AND CONCLUSIONS

In order to investigate the importance of the sense of touch in product packaging and display, a laboratory experiment was devised utilizing four test groups of consumers who touched and did not touch a series of products in a simulated retail store display.

The first step in attempting to quantify the data collected from the questionnaire was the computation of an arithmetic mean for each tested product [13, pg. 161]. Did the experimental groups of consumers exhibit a difference in attitude concerning the sense of touch among the tested products? Test results reveal no apparent significant attitude differences from product to product. Attitude mean results of each experiment, classified by consumer subject group, did appear, however and are shown in Table 1.

TABLE 1

ADJECTIVE MEAN SCORES OF CONSUMER IMPRESSIONS
REGARDING SIX PRODUCTS WHICH WERE TOUCHED
OR NOT TOUCHED IN EXPERIMENTS 1 AND 2

| Adjectives | Arithmetic Mean | | | |
| --- | --- | --- | --- | --- |
| | Group 1 | Group 2 | Group 3 | Group 4 |
| Good/Bad | 7.7 (7.5) | 7.1 (7.5) | 6.4 (7.4) | 7.6 (7.5) |
| Nice/Awful | 7.5 (7.6) | 6.9 (7.1) | 6.2 (6.9) | 7.6 (7.2) |
| Valuable/ Worthless | 6.7 (6.6) | 6.4 (6.1) | 5.9 (6.2) | 6.4 (6.4) |
| Happy/Sad | 6.3 (6.4) | 5.8 (5.7) | 5.3 (5.7) | 6.2 (6.1) |
| Beautiful/Ugly | 6.8 (7.0) | 6.5 (5.6) | 5.7 (5.7) | 6.9 (6.5) |
| Pleasant/ Unpleasant | 7.2 (7.6) | 6.5 (6.6) | 6.0 (6.8) | 7.1 (6.8) |
| Rugged/Delicate | 3.6 (3.7) | 3.8 (3.8) | 4.4 (4.1) | 3.3 (3.4) |
| Loud/Soft | 3.6 (3.7) | 4.1 (3.3) | 4.1 (3.4) | 3.3 (3.3) |
| Strong/Weak | 6.1 (6.2) | 5.7 (5.8) | 4.7 (5.6) | 6.0 (5.9) |
| Rough/Smooth | 3.5 (3.3) | 4.0 (3.2) | 4.2 (2.7) | 3.1 (2.9) |
| Sharp/Dull | 6.5 (6.1) | 5.9 (5.8) | 5.9 (5.8) | 6.5 (6.3) |
| Fast/Slow | 5.8 (5.6) | 5.4 (5.2) | 5.0 (5.1) | 5.5 (5.6) |
| Young/Old | 7.0 (6.9) | 6.6 (6.4) | 5.7 (7.0) | 7.1 (6.9) |
| High Quality/ Low Quality | 6.7 (6.7) | 6.0 (6.4) | 5.3 (6.4) | 6.9 (6.5) |
| Different/Same | 5.3 (5.6) | 5.2 (5.0) | 5.0 (5.3) | 5.1 (4.6) |
| Average Mean | 6.0 (6.0) | 5.7 (5.6) | 5.3 (5.6) | 5.9 (5.7) |

( ) Denotes second experiment.

28

Type (1), (2), and (3) test results conclude that among all four groups of subjects the evaluative factor had more positive scores than the activity, potency, or miscellaneous dimensions. Consumer group 3 registered the lowest average mean ranking. Merchandise was displayed out of the packages to this test group and the products could not be touched by the subjects.

The most significant changes between mean rankings occurred between consumer groups 3 and 4 in the first experiment, perhaps indicating that when displayed out of packages, consumers want to touch and examine the product. The identical experiment on a replicated trial did not produce the same results, however. Comparing consumer test groups 2 and 4 (those who touched packages and who touched merchandise), a number of findings indicate that if subjects examined a product, an examination of it without a barrier of cellophane or other wrapping was desired.

In order to obtain experimental Z values for a normal curve, the variance, the standard error of the mean, and the standard error of the difference between means were calculated, and are presented in Table 2. Using a one-tailed test, the Z values, to be considered significant, must exceed 1.65, using an alpha level of .05. Test results reveal that a number of Z values exceeded 1.65 in both experiments. Significant values: Experiment 1. The largest number of significant Z values occurred between groups 3 and 4, followed by groups 2 and 4. Overall, the consumer evaluative factor had more significance than the activity, potency or miscellaneous factors. The potency factor had only one significant Z value score and the activity factor showed only three significant Z values between experimental consumer groups 3 and 4. Significant values: Experiment 2. The largest number of significant Z values in experiment two occurred between subject groups 2 and 4, followed by three significant Z values between test groups 3 and 4. The evaluative and activity dimensions of the bipolar semantic differential test both contain several Z values of significance whereas the potency dimension had none at all.

Results of both experiments indicate the presence of some definite trends. For example, greatest differences between consumers occurred between test groups 2 and 4 and between test groups 3 and 4. In experiment two, only three Z values above 1.65 were found for test groups 3 and 4, indicating only a slight degree of significance at the .05 level of confidence. Experimental differences between groups 2 and 4 however, are worth noting. For subject group 2, the product remained in the package while being touched. In subject group 4, the product was not in a package while being touched. Four significant Z values were present between the two groups in experiment one, and experiment two revealed five significant Z values generated from consumer rankings. The comparison between consumer test groups 2 and 4 thus appear valid over a wide range of descriptive stimuli.

The question, of course, is what accounts for the difference in findings between subject groups 2 and 4. Based on the experimental findings, consumers do not like to examine products that are separated from them by any type of artificial barrier such as cellophane, watch cases, plastic, and other forms of packaging. Test results also indicate that if purchase behavior results in close examination and comparison of a product then the consumer desires to be able to touch and handle the article.

TABLE 2

EXPERIMENTAL Z VALUES DERIVED FROM CONSUMER JUDGEMENTS CONCERNING THE SENSE OF
TOUCH FOR SIX TESTED PRODUCTS (EXPERIMENTS 1 AND (2))*

| Adjective | Z Values | | | | | |
|---|---|---|---|---|---|---|
| | Groups 1 & 2 | Groups 1 & 3 | Groups 1 & 4 | Groups 2 & 3 | Groups 2 & 4 | Groups 3 & 4 |
| Evaluative Factor: | | | | | | |
| Good/Bad | | | | | 1.66 | 4.16 ( .46) |
| Awful/Nice | | | .39 | | 2.05 ( .40) | 4.73 (1.15) |
| Valuable/ Worthless | | | | | (1.16) | 1.84 ( .83) |
| Sad/Happy | | | | | 1.35 (1.68) | 3.86 (1.72) |
| Ugly/ Beautiful | | | .37 | ( .32) | 1.17 (3.14) | 3.90 (2.88) |
| Unpleasant/ Pleasant | | | | ( .76) | 1.78 ( .80) | 3.79 |
| Potency Factor: | | | | | | |
| Delicate/Rugged | .53 (.35) | 2.38 (1.44) | | 1.56 ( .99) | | |
| Soft/Loud | 1.35 | 1.59 | | | | |
| Weak/Strong | | | | | .89 ( .39) | 4.46 (1.24) |
| Smooth/Rough | 1.40 | 2.28 | | .54 | | ( .81) |
| Activity Factor: | | | | | | |
| Dull/Sharp | | | (.71) | ( .31) | 1.16 (1.68) | 3.25 (1.36) |
| Fast/Slow | | | | | .37 (1.88) | 2.29 (2.35) |
| Young/Old | | | .37 | (2.16) | 1.51 (1.87) | 4.88 |
| Miscellaneous: | | | | | | |
| Low Quality/ High Quality | | | .66 | | 2.40 ( .33) | 5.06 ( .35) |
| Same/Different | | | | (1.05) | | .32 |

*Significant values (1.65 or above) underlined.
( ) Denotes second experiment.

On the basis of the number of significant Z value findings, the null hypothesis of this investigation therefore can be rejected and $H_1$ accepted. In other words, the number of significant Z values in the present investigation is too large to attribute all of them to chance or sampling error. The null hypothesis cannot, however, be rejected for all subject groups, but only for differences between perceptions of groups 2 and 4 and groups 3 and 4.

Many consumers exhibit tendencies to open boxes, packages, and other containers that have been placed in their hands. Consumers have an even stronger tendency merely to touch items while shopping. The touching of an item evokes certain images of shape and texture that are reinforcing to the shopper. Thus, the shopper's attitude toward certain products may be strengthened by the tactile experience of touching an item. The results of this investigation indicate that the desire of consumers to touch and handle the product should be a strong marketing consideration. Both economic and ecological implications are requiring marketers to seek new forms of packaging and display. While further research concerning the importance of the consumers sense of touch is needed, new emphasis must be placed upon this factor as a marketing tool.

## REFERENCES

1. Brinton, James E. "Deriving an Attitude Scale from Semantic Differential Data," Public Opinion Quarterly, 25, No. 2 (1961), 289-295.

2. Cabanac, Michel. "Physiological Role of Pleasure," Science, 173 (September 17, 1971), 1103-1107.

3. Collins, Barry E., Charles A. Diesler, and Norman Miller. Attitude Change: A Critical Analysis of Theoretical Approaches. New York: John Wiley & Sons, Inc., 1969.

4. Crutchfield, R. S., and D. Krech. Theory and Problems in Social Psychology. New York: McGraw-Hill, 1948.

5. Enis, Ben M., Keith K. Cox, and James E. Stafford, "Students as Subjects in Consumer Behavior Experiments," 9 (February, 1972), 72-74.

6. Geldard, Frank A. "Adventures in Tactile Literacy," The American Psychologist. (September, 1956), 115-117.

7. Gibson, Eleanor and James Gibson. "The Senses as Information Seeking Systems," Times Literature Supplement, 71 (June 23, 1972), 711-712.

8. Hennessy, John R. "Cutaneous Sensitivity Communications," Human Factors, 8, No. 5 (October, 1966) 463-469.

9. Khera, Inder P. and James D. Benson, "Are Students Really Poor Substitutes for Businessmen in Behavioral Research," Journal of Marketing Research, 7 (November, 1970).

10. Klopfer, Peter H. "Sensory Physiology and Esthetics," American Scientist, 58 (July-August, 1970), 399-403.

11. Montagu, Ashley. Touching: The Human Significance of the Skin. New York: Columbia University Press, 1971.

12. Olson, Jerry C., and Jacob Jacoby, "Cue Utilization in the Quality Perception Process," Proceedings. Third Annual Conference, Association for Consumer Research, 1972, 167-179.

13. Osgood, Charles E. and James G. Snider, (eds.) Semantic Differential Technique. New York: Aldine Publishing Company, 1969.

14. Ruesch, Jurgen and Weldon Kees. Nonverbal Communication. Los Angeles: University of California Press, 1970.

15. Szybillo, George J., and J. Jacoby. "Intrinsic Versus Extrinsic Cues as Determinants of Perceived Product Quality," Journal of Applied Psychology, 59 (February, 1974), 74-78.

16. Taylor, J. Lionel. The Stages of Human Life, 1921.

17. Taylor, John G. "Neural Connexions and the Life-Cycle of the Senses," Times Literature Supplement, 71 (June 23, 1972), 721-722.

# CPA ATTITUDES TOWARD MARKETING COMMUNICATIONS

Ronald Stiff, University of Baltimore
Gary Siegel, University of Illinois, Chicago Circle

## ABSTRACT

A number of legal, social, and professional trends lead to the expectation of increased marketing effort by professionals. An analysis of CPAs in a variety of work environments confirms the hypothesis that professionals who are in closer direct competition with para-professionals will have more favorable attitudes toward the use of marketing communications. It is concluded, however, that increased use of impersonal marketing communications by CPAs is likely to be quite gradual.

## INTRODUCTION

The opportunities and pressures for professionals to adopt formal marketing and advertising activities appear to be increasing [1,5]. Professionals have traditionally preferred to communicate their skills through direct and word-of-mouth communications, ignoring or minimizing -- sometimes even prohibiting -- formal written communications and advertising. Opponents of this traditional view, including consumerists and federal regulatory agencies, view the limitations of impersonal channels of communication as violating freedom of speech or as a restraint of trade. Indeed, in a recent FTC complaint against the American Dental Association, it was charged that the dental group's ban on advertising results in price fixing, retards the development of new ways to provide dental care and eliminates competition [8].

Several completed and ongoing legal actions have cleared barriers to professionals' greater use of advertising. Even the legal profession, recognizing this trend, has loosened the ban on advertising [6,7]. Bloom and Stiff, however, have questioned whether professionals will actually exercise the right to advertise even if given the opportunity to do so [1,5].

Central to the process of beginning or increasing an advertising program is the attitudes of professionals toward advertising. This research[1] is an analysis of the attitudes held by Certified Public Accountants (CPAs) in a variety of work environments toward advertising and toward public designation of areas of specialized practice.

## WORK ENVIRONMENT AND ATTITUDES TOWARD ADVERTISING

Stiff has hypothesized that marketing practices will achieve greater or lesser degrees of acceptance as a function of a professional's work environment [5]. He assumed that para-professionals would be the first group to begin or increase marketing efforts. This expectation has been demonstrated by the recent action of makers of dentures in California. Traditionally, dentists were the only group to fit patients for dentures. Recently, however, denture makers advertised the fact that people in need of dentures can avoid the trip to the dentist and have the denture makers both fit and make the dentures, and save money to boot.

---

The authors express appreciation to the Illinois CPA ociety for their cooperation with the research effort and or their partial support of the study. We are especially rateful to the CPAs who responded to the questionnaire.

In the accounting profession there are also professionals and para-professionals. The professionals are CPAs: accountants who have passed a uniform, national examination covering auditing, accounting theory and practice, business law and federal income tax law. The para-professionals are non-CPA accountants.

CPAs are protected by accountancy law in all 50 states to perform the audit function. Non-CPAs, the para-professionals, however, can and do engage in all other aspects of accounting. These non-CPAs, performing services such as bookkeeping and tax preparation, engage in advertising programs while CPAs are forbidden by their Code of Ethics to advertise or to formally designate their areas of specialization.

CPAs may be employed in public accounting, private industry, education or government. Only in public accounting, however, is the CPA's monopoly to perform the audit function relevant. And it is primarily in public accounting that CPAs face competition from their non-CPA competitors. Within public accounting CPAs work in large international accounting firms, multi-office national or regional firms, local firms (two-to-50 partners) or solo practice. The pressure to market is felt most strongly by solo practitioners who are the most likely group to face competition from non-CPAs. Similarly, researchers have shown that lawyers in solo practice are more likely than lawyers in firms to face competition from people outside the profession: they compete with savings and loan associations for real estate closings; with banks on trusts and wills; and with accountants on tax matters [2,4].

Therefore, we expect that solo practitioners will have more positive attitudes toward advertising than CPAs in firms. Also we expect CPAs in firms to favor those forms of advertising which emphasize and maintain organizational rather than individual reputations. This will strengthen the firms and minimize the perceived threat to professionalism of advertising personal skills.

Finally, if professionals follow the principle of client orientation they can be expected to adopt more consumer oriented forms of communications. Specifically, a consumer orientation would lead to preference of more public forms of media. Mitigating against client orientation is the tradition of public media communications being viewed as non-professional.

## RESEARCH DESIGN

The research reported in this paper is part of a larger study conducted on Illinois CPAs. Questionnaires were mailed to a computer-generated random sample of 1208 Illinois CPAs engaged in the practice of public accounting. This represents 25 per cent of all public accounting practitioners who are members of the Illinois CPA Society. CPAs working in industry, education and government were not included in this study.

The research was designed to determine: the extent of existing specialization in the practice of public accounting, the attitudes of CPAs toward formal designation of areas of specialization, attitudes toward advertising and the media through which specialties should be designated, and the causal factors of particular attitudes being held by various segments of CPAs.

## FINDINGS

CPAs indicate that despite the profession's ban on advertising and specialty designation, de facto recognition of functional specialties is pervasive in accounting practice. Over 70 per cent of the respondents: define themselves as specialists, work in firms having distinct departments devoted to a functional specialty, have colleagues who are specialists, and perceive the accounting profession as characterized by a high degree of specialization [3].

When asked whether this de facto recognition of specialties should be formally recognized by the profession through a change in the Code of Ethics which would allow for public designation of specialties, only 50 per cent responded in the affirmative. Discriminant analysis revealed that the dichotomy in opinion appears to exist because of uncertainties over the socioeconomic consequences of such a policy change [3].

The important factor for purposes of this study is how such designation is viewed. Table 1 indicates that 53 per cent of the CPAs in solo practice and in local firms believe that designation of specialties is, indeed, a form of advertising. However, only 30 per cent of CPAs in Big 8 firms (the eight largest international accounting firms) agree. Apparently CPAs in solo practice and local firms are not as constrained by labels and appearances as their international firm counterparts.

Table 1 also reveals that solo practitioners and Big 8 CPAs are the most positively inclined toward advertising. This may reflect the fact that Big 8 firms offer a full range of accounting services and want that fact to be repeatedly communicated, and that solo practitioners, who include in their definition of advertising designation of specialties, want the distinction to be made between themselves and their non-CPA competitors.

## TABLE 1

RESPONDENTS' VIEWS ON ADVERTISING AND THE RELATION OF ADVERTISING TO SPECIALTY DESIGNATION BY WORK ENVIRONMENT

Per Cent Respondents in Each Work Environment Responding Positively to the Following:

| Type of Work Environment | Should CPAs Be Allowed to Advertise?[a] | Is Specialty Designation a Form of Advertising?[a] | N |
|---|---|---|---|
| Big 8 Firms........... | 27% | 30% | (221) |
| Other International Firms........... | 19 | 40 | ( 48) |
| National Firms........ | 20 | 40 | ( 20) |
| Regional Firms........ | 18 | 43 | ( 43) |
| Local Firms........... | 17 | 55 | (224) |
| Solo Practice......... | 31 | 53 | ( 88) |
| All Respondents....... | 23 | 44 | (644) |

[a]Significant differences exist between work environments at the .05 level by Chi-square test for each question.

Another indication of the unabashed views of solo practitioners on advertising is the position taken by the North Shore Chapter of the Illinois CPA Society. The North Shore Chapter, controlled by a group of vocal solo practitioners and CPAs in small local firms, has called for a program of institutional advertising whereby the public would be informed of the services offered by CPAs and of the differences between CPAs and non-CPAs. This proposal has not been acted upon due to the tremendous cost of such an advertising campaign.

On the assumption that specialties are to be designated as they are in the medical, legal, and engineering professions, CPAs were asked what media should be used to communicate this information. Table 2 indicates that CPAs prefer the traditional less public media such as business cards and shy away from highly visible forms of designation such as press releases. Indeed, if we rank the four alternatives in terms of public visibility, CPAs overwhelmingly favor designation on the least public vehicle: business cards. This is followed by their preference for designation on the firm's stationery. Business cards and company stationery, of course, may be distributed to selected audiences.

## TABLE 2

RESPONDENTS' POSITIONS ON WHERE FUNCTIONAL SPECIALIST STATUS SHOULD BE DESIGNATED BY WORK ENVIRONMENT.

Per Cent Respondents in Each Work Environment Believing Functional Specialization Should be Designated:

| Type of Work Environment | On Firm Stationery[a] | On Business Cards[b] | In Yellow Pages[a] | In Press Releases[a] | N |
|---|---|---|---|---|---|
| Big 8 Firms...... | 60% | 85% | 54% | 37% | (212) |
| Other International Firms.. | 64 | 83 | 54 | 28 | ( 47) |
| National Firms... | 56 | 90 | 56 | 25 | ( 20) |
| Regional Firms... | 63 | 84 | 56 | 35 | ( 43) |
| Local Firms...... | 69 | 87 | 46 | 26 | (208) |
| Solo Practice.... | 83 | 89 | 71 | 49 | ( 78) |
| All Respondents.. | 67 | 86 | 54 | 34 | (608) |

[a]Significant differences exist between work environments at the .05 level by Chi-square test.

[b]There is not a significant difference between respondents on this proposed form of specialty designation.

Ranking third in public visibility and in CPAs' preferences for designation is the Yellow Pages. If specialty designation were to be made via this media, all potential users of accounting services would be exposed to the specialized functions performed by CPAs. Press releases, the most publicly visible form of designating specialties, is the only alternative unacceptable to CPAs. If specialties were to be designated in press releases, all readers of the financial pages of newspapers would be exposed to this information.

We note also in Table 2 that solo practitioners favor, to a greater extent than other groups of CPAs, all suggested media for designating specialties.

## CONCLUSIONS

A significant number of CPAs have favorable attitudes toward advertising. The expectation that solo practitioners would have more positive attitudes toward advertising than CPAs in firms was supported by the data. This reflects the fact that solo practitioners are more likely to face competition from non-CPAs than are CPAs in firms and that they want the public to be reminded that they as CPAs are superior to their non-CPA competitors.

32

In addition to views on advertising, solo practitioners favor all forms of suggested media to designate areas of functional specialization to a greater extent than do CPAs in firms. Again, this is likely to be due to the solo practitioners' desire to have themselves differentiated from para-professionals who advertise the fact that they offer similar accounting services.

Regarding the media through which specialty designations are to be made, the data reveal that CPAs favor a relatively personal approach to informing the public of their specialized activities. The more publicly visible the suggested means of communicating specialized activities, the less likely are CPAs to favor it. This may reflect the fact that CPAs want to avoid the costly and aggressive public information campaigns that the numerous firms might wage.

Recent opinion of federal regulatory agencies, the actions of consumerists, and the thinking of leaders in the accounting profession suggests that more public forms of marketing communications can be expected. However, there are two strong forces discouraging the use of these marketing tools.

First, solo practitioners, who are most prone to advertise have less resources than their counterparts in firms. Second, solos are also likely to feel strong professional pressures against advertising generated by the feelings of powerful members of their professional association. Hence, we conclude that increased use of impersonal marketing communications by CPAs is likely to be a gradual process at best.

## REFERENCES

1. Bloom, Paul N., "Advertising in the Professions: The Critical Issues." Journal of Marketing, (forthcoming).

2. Carlin, Jerome E., Lawyers on Their Own. New Brunswick: Rutgers University Press, 1962.

3. Siegel, Gary, Attitude Study: Specialization and Sectionalization in the Accounting Profession. Chicago: Illinois CPA Society, 1976.

4. Smigel, Erwin O., The Wall Street Lawyer: Professional Organization Man? Glencoe: The Free Press, 1964.

5. Stiff, Ronald, "The Changing Role of Professional Service Marketing." Proceedings. 1976 Educator's Conference of the American Marketing Association. Chicago: American Marketing Association, 1976, 283-286.

6. Wall Street Journal, "ABA Eases Rules That Barred Lawyers From Disseminating Information on Fees." February 18, 1976, p. 13.

7. Wall Street Journal, "Easing of Advertising Ban on Lawyers and Law Firms is Proposed by ABA Unit." December 8, 1975, p. 13.

8. Wall Street Journal, "Dental Group is Target of FTC in Drive Against Codes it Says Limit Competition." January 17, 1977, p. 14.

# SEGMENTING CHARITABLE GIVERS:
## AN APPLICATION OF TOBIT

C. Samuel Craig, Cornell University
Terry Deutscher, The Ohio State University
John M. McCann, Cornell University

## ABSTRACT

Using a sample of 800 males, a study is made of three types of charitable giving behavior - religious giving, community giving, and political giving. Donor profiles are developed for each segment using demographic predictors. Similar results are obtained using ordinarily least squares and TOBIT analysis, but the coefficients are consistently higher for the TOBIT regressions.

## INTRODUCTION[1]

Kotler and Levy's [6] call to broaden the concept of marketing has sparked considerable interest in extending the domain of marketing beyond so-called traditional areas. Several texts [5, 11] and numerous articles have looked at the problems and opportunities nonprofit organizations face in applying marketing principles and practices. Attempts to apply marketing to nonprofit organizations have centered primarily on identification of marketing mix elements in nonprofit sectors and examples of successful marketing strategies in those contexts. Attention has also been given to how specific nonprofit organizations could benefit from a marketing approach to their operations.

This identification of macro concepts and approaches suited to nonprofit marketing has been an essential first step. What remains to be done is to examine unique aspects of nonprofit marketing to establish a basis for micro level strategies. The purpose of this paper is to examine one phenomenon that is unique to nonprofit marketing efforts, charitable giving. The specific questions to be answered are: (1) What are the characteristics of the charitable giver? and (2) are there defined segments in the giving market? The paper is divided into four major sections. First, salient literature on giving behavior is reviewed. Then, the sample composition and method of analysis are discussed. The analysis and results form the third major section. Finally, conclusions are drawn from the present research and suggestions for future research are made.

## LITERATURE

The need to understand why people give has long been recognized. In the late 1950's the American Association of Fund Raising [2] identified five motives for giving: (1) security, (2) fear, (3) recognition, (4) immortality and (5) belonging. In the mid-1960's Dichter [4] identified additional giving motives, which had strong Freudian overtones. Dichter's list has one motive in common with the above list, fear. He adds the following reasons for giving (or not giving): (1) to play God, (2) to avoid embarrassment, (3) to obtain psychological satisfaction by pleasing a parent figure, and (4) to acquire power. While these motives are interesting and no doubt play a role in

---

[1]The authors would like to acknowledge the helpful suggestions of a reviewer concerning the method of analysis.

giving behavior, they do not in and of themselves provide a sufficient basis for a marketing strategy. Perhaps two of the greatest shortcomings that characterize most of this early research are first, it appears to assume that the motives for giving are constant across different types of charities, and second, it ignores the question of who gives.

Levy [7] helps clarify the motives behind giving behavior by advancing a hierarchy of giving priorities. Within each he suggests motives that apply. The most important organization in the hierarchy of giving loyalties is the church. Next come socially purposeful groups such as fraternal organizations and schools. Third are emotionally related organizations such as health groups, orphanages, or old people's homes. Finally, there are obligatory commitments such as United Fund or Community Chest. Within each element of the hierarchy Levy discusses motives for giving which loosely fall into the categories of emotional, rational and social. This giving hierarchy goes beyond earlier works in that it provides some indication of the relative importance of various organizations. However, it too does not provide an adequate basis for a marketing strategy.

Insights into what is important for a fund raising organization's marketing strategy are provided by Shapiro [12]. He indicates that regardless of the type of organization attempting to raise funds, the most important aspect of its marketing strategy is "resource attraction." He goes on to point out that the problem of resource attraction "is a dual one of segmenting the donor 'market' into homogeneous groups and of determining which appeal or 'product' position will be most effective for that segment." He then proceeds to identify broad market segments. For example, with university giving he identifies segments such as alumni, parents of students, and businesses.

The problem of segmentation has also been looked at by Mindak and Bybee [8]. They were concerned with segmenting potential givers for the March of Dimes fund raising on an intuitive basis. They begin by assuming that the target market for the campaign is parents. This is refined somewhat with data that indicate a geographic bias in past giving. They then go on to perform an empirical test of alternative appeals. However, no attempt was made to relate the appeals to actual giving behavior.

Thus, most of the early research on giving behavior has focused on the motives behind giving. The most recent literature has suggested market segmentation as a promising approach for strategy development by fund raising agencies. This paper follows from these suggestions by examining the characteristics of givers to different types of organizations.

## METHOD

### Approach

There are two general approaches that can be used to develop an understanding of giving behavior. First, one can identify a specific institution and examine the giving behavior of individuals in different roles (e.g., alumnus, parent member, etc.). This is a particularly useful approach for individual fund raising organizations.

Records are maintained on past donations and research can be conducted on the different donor groups. Such analysis provides insight as to the motives for giving and market potential of the various groups. A second approach is to look at a group of individuals and examine their giving behavior across organizations. If successful, this approach allows an organization to focus on the most appropriate target audience. More importantly it provides increased understanding of the phenomenon of charitable giving.

The approach taken in this paper is the latter one, examining the giving behavior of a group of individuals. Three distinct types of giving behavior are examined: (1) religious, (2) community and (3) political giving. The task is to determine whether different factors are related to the different types of giving behavior. If different factors emerge, it strongly suggests that distinct market segments do exist.

Sample Composition

For this study the giving behavior of 800 adult males was examined. The data are a random subset of the total sample for a large national survey conducted by Axiom Market Research Bureau in 1974. The dependent variable used in the analysis was self-report of the amount of money given to a particular organization during a one year period. As Table 1 indicates, the percent of people giving to any one organization varies considerably. Giving to a church or synagogue was most common (59 percent). Specific community organizations received donations from between 17 and 43 percent of the individuals, while political parties received donations from less than 10 percent.

TABLE 1

CHARITABLE GIVING BY ORGANIZATIONS: ADULT MALES

| Organization | Percent of Individuals Giving |
|---|---|
| Church or Synagogue | 58.9 |
| United Fund or Community Chest | 43.4 |
| Red Cross | 22.1 |
| Health Organizations | 22.0 |
| Hospitals and Orphanages | 17.0 |
| Political Parties | 9.7 |

Source: Compiled from Target Group Index 1974, Axiom Market Research Bureau, Vol. P-36.

Since the phenomenon of interest is charitable giving per se rather than giving to specific organizations, certain categories were combined. The following types of giving behavior served as the dependent variables: (1) religious giving (church or synagogue), (2) community giving (United Fund, Community Chest, Red Cross, Health Organizations, Hospitals and Orphanages) and (3) Political giving. The independent variables were demographics and socioeconomic characteristics.

Method of Analysis

Multiple regression analysis is an appropriate means of testing hypotheses about predictors of giving for the different segments. However, the distribution of the dependent variable, amount given, creates an interesting problem for ordinary least squares (OLS) regression. For each type of charity, a significant fraction of the sample did not give. This fraction ranges from 41.1% (non-givers to religious organizations) to 90.3% (non-givers to political organizations).

Tobin [13] pointed out the problem that is encountered when OLS is used on limited dependent variables. A fundamental assumption underlying the use of OLS is that the regression error terms are randomly distributed. When a substantial fraction of the observations on the dependent variable fall at a limit (zero in the case of charitable donations) the assumption is violated. According to the model, both negative and positive deviations must be possible from any expected value of the dependent variable. However, negative deviations from an expected value of zero giving would imply that a respondent gave less than nothing. Since data were collected only on amounts given to charities, the value of the dependent variable cannot be less than zero, and the OLS assumptions cannot be satisfied.

To determine the extent of the distortion when OLS is used, the OLS coefficients were compared with the coefficients obtained using the model proposed by Tobin [13]. These results are presented and discussed subsequently. First, however, Tobin's model (TOBIT) will be explained very briefly.

Tobin positioned his model as a hybrid of OLS and probit analysis (a model which is appropriate for explaining probabilities of dichotomous responses, such as purchase vs. non-purchase). The TOBIT model is constructed as follows:

Let W be the dependent variable of interest, limited at the lower bound L. Let Y be an unconstrained variable which is related to W. Let the hypothesized predictors of W be $(X_1, X_2, ..., X_m)$.

Then the model can be formulated as:

$$Y_i = \beta_0 + \beta_1 X_1 + \beta_2 X_2 + ... \beta_m X_m + \mu_i \qquad (1)$$

$$W_i = Y_i \quad \text{if } Y_i \geq L \qquad (2)$$
$$= L \quad \text{if } Y_i < L$$

Since least squares estimation is inappropriate, the model is estimated with the method of maximum likelihood. The solution of the estimation problem cannot be obtained analytically, so it is necessary to apply an iterative technique such as Newton's method [3].

As Amemiya has observed, the TOBIT model is potentially a useful one, but it has not been widely applied in the past [1]. Widespread use has perhaps been hampered by the lack of suitable computer programs. This problem has recently been remedied by the work of Nelson in constructing a general algorithm for models with limited dependent variables [10]. As a result of his efforts, a program is now available through the National Bureau of Economic Research [9].

ANALYSIS AND RESULTS

Before the examination of the variables associated with the different types of giving, the data were used to examine the relationship among the three types of giving themselves. Then giving behavior was examined in terms of the demographic characteristics associated with the different types of giving behavior, using both TOBIT and OLS.

Relationships Between Types of Giving

One of the principal objectives of this paper is to examine giving behavior across different types of charities. The greater the differences which exist, the more important it would be to develop distinctive strategies for the various charities. A simple way to look at relationships between different types of giving is to consider these two questions:

1) Does giving to one type of organization affect the likelihood of giving to another?

2) Is the amount given to one type of institution related to the amounts given to others?

These questions are answered in Table 2, parts a) through d). The first three parts of the table are simple cross-tabulations which test whether one type of giving (regardless of amount) is related to another. From part a) of the Table, it is clear that givers to religious organizations are much more likely than non-givers to make donations to community charities. In fact, 78% of religious givers (406 of the 522 givers to churches or synagogues) also give to community organizations, while only 37% of the non-givers to religious organizations (103/278) give to community organizations. Not surprisingly, this relationship is a statistically significant one.

TABLE 2

RELATIONSHIPS BETWEEN TYPES OF GIVING

a) Religious giving vs. community giving

| | | Community Giving | | Marginal Total |
| | | Non-giver | Giver | |
|---|---|---|---|---|
| Religious Giving | Non-giver | 175 | 103 | 278 |
| | Giver | 116 | 406 | 522 |
| | Marginal Total | 291 | 509 | |

Chi-square = 130.0, p < .01

b) Religious giving vs. political giving

| | | Political Giving | | Marginal Total |
| | | Non-giver | Giver | |
|---|---|---|---|---|
| Religious Giving | Non-giver | 263 | 15 | 278 |
| | Giver | 455 | 67 | 522 |
| | Marginal Total | 718 | 82 | |

Chi-square = 10.91, p < .01

c) Community giving vs. political giving

| | | Political Giving | | Marginal Total |
| | | Non-giver | Giver | |
|---|---|---|---|---|
| Community Giving | Non-giver | 284 | 7 | 291 |
| | Giver | 434 | 75 | 509 |
| | Marginal Total | 718 | 82 | |

Chi-square = 30.59, p < .01

d) Product-moment correlations of amounts given[a]

| | Political Giving | Religious Giving |
|---|---|---|
| Religious Giving | 0.114 | |
| Community Giving | 0.138 | 0.343 |

[a] All correlations are significant, p < .01.

The relationships tested in the contingency Tables in parts b) and c) of Table 2 are also statistically significant although the interdependence is not as pronounced as the one in part a). Almost 13% of religious givers (67/522) also gave to political organizations, while less than 6% (15/278) of religious non-givers gave to these organizations (part b)). From part c), a similar conclusion follows -- most of the people who gave to political organizations also gave to community charities.

Part d) of Table 2 considers the relationship between amounts donated to the different institutions. Given the conclusions from the first three parts of the Table, it is not surprising that all three correlation coefficients are significant at the .01 level. Again in this situation, the two relationships involving political giving appear not to be as strong as the religious/community giving affiliation, whose correlation (0.343) is almost three times each of the other two.

Demographic Characteristics

To determine what characteristics are associated with the different types of giving, three separate OLS multiple regressions were run along with three separate TOBIT analyses. The dollar contribution to each of the three types of organizations served as the dependent measure. The independent measures were: age, education, income, interviewer's assessment of socio-economic status, number of televisions, amount spent on clothing, and a composite variable which measured extent of involvement in various community activities. The results of these analyses are discussed by type of giving (see Table 3).

Religious Giving. Individuals who make large contributions to churches or synagogues tend to be older, have higher incomes, higher socio-economic status, and spend more on clothing than those who make smaller contributions. Overall, these variables explained 16 percent of the variance in religious giving. Results from both models are consistent.

Community Giving. Similar factors are associated with the amount given to various community organizations. Age and income are again related to contribution levels. In addition the number of televisions owned is positively related to the dependent variables. The composite variable created to indicate the extent to which individuals were involved in community activities is also significant. Those who are more active in community affairs give larger contributions. In the OLS analysis, the seven-variable equation accounts for 16 percent of the variance in community giving. Again, the OLS and TOBIT results are similar, although the TOBIT coefficients are higher.

Political Giving. A somewhat limited set of variables is associated with political giving and the results are not consistent between OLS and TOBIT. The TOBIT coefficients are much larger. Both age and the extent to which individuals are involved in community activities are related in both analyses to the amount contributed to political organizations. Amount spent on clothing was also significant, but only in the OLS analysis. Overall, the seven variables explain only 3 percent of the variance in political giving behavior in the OLS analysis.

Psychographic Characteristics

Analysis of giving behavior was also attempted with a number of personality and buying behavior variables (e.g., conservativeness, egocentricity, tendency to be cautious in shopping, tendency to experiment). It was necessary to rely on self-reported ratings on each characteristic. By and large, these variables were not significant determinants of giving behavior, and they accounted for a very small portion of the variation in the dependent variables.

DISCUSSION AND CONCLUSIONS

At the outset of this paper, two questions were posed: 1) What are the characteristics of the charitable giver? and 2) Are there defined segments in the giving market? Obviously, the greater the differences found on the second question, the more rigorous the qualifications that must be imposed in answering the first. If substantial differences exist across types of giving, then it is not at all appropriate to talk about "the" charitable giver.

The analysis of this data base indicates that for the second question, a qualified "yes" is appropriate. There do appear to be some important differences between different types of charitable giving. However, these differences are not so large that they indicate totally different behavior from one segment to the next. So, in response to the first question, it does appear that there are some important common features as well as some differences.

The initial analysis demonstrated that there were significant relationships between giving to one type of charity and to another, both in terms of probability of giving and

TABLE 3

DEMOGRAPHIC CHARACTERISTICS OF GIVERS

| Predictors | Religious | | Community | | Political | |
|---|---|---|---|---|---|---|
| | OLS | TOBIT | OLS | TOBIT | OLS | TOBIT |
| Age (years)[a] | $1.04^d$ $(.16)^b$ | $1.34^d$ $(.23)$ | $.62^d$ $(.13)$ | $.94^d$ $(.18)$ | $.07^c$ $(.04)$ | $.53^c$ $(.25)$ |
| Education (years) | 1.28 $(1.70)$ | 1.20 $(2.42)$ | 2.10 $(1.36)$ | 3.13 $(1.89)$ | .47 $(.39)$ | 5.18 $(2.66)$ |
| Income (000)[a] | $4.76^d$ $(1.26)$ | $6.67^d$ $(1.83)$ | $4.83^d$ $(1.01)$ | $8.24^d$ $(1.48)$ | .15 $(.29)$ | 1.26 $(2.10)$ |
| SES (6 point scale) | $9.97^d$ $(2.80)$ | $14.81^d$ $(4.01)$ | 3.50 $(2.23)$ | 5.32 $(3.15)$ | .54 $(.64)$ | 4.72 $(4.43)$ |
| Amount Spent on Clothing | 4.21 $(1.48)$ | $5.08^c$ $(2.13)$ | 2.04 $(1.18)$ | 2.93 $(1.64)$ | $.69^c$ $(.34)$ | 2.80 $(2.33)$ |
| Extent of Community Activity (10 point scale)[a] | 2.21 $(1.69)$ | 3.12 $(2.42)$ | $3.05^c$ $(1.34)$ | $4.16^c$ $(1.88)$ | $.98^d$ $(.38)$ | $6.69^d$ $(2.35)$ |
| Number of Televisions owned | .49 $(3.20)$ | 0.51 $(4.56)$ | $7.14^d$ $(2.55)$ | $11.31^d$ $(3.56)$ | .61 $(.73)$ | .38 $(5.09)$ |
| Adjusted $R^2$ (OLS results) | .16 | | .16 | | .03 | |
| F (OLS results) | $19.8^d$ | | $19.6^d$ | | $3.85^d$ | |

[a] One-tailed hypothesis tests were used for this variable.

[b] Standard error of the estimate.

[c] $p < .05$

[d] $p < .01$

[e] Coefficients in a TOBIT model can be tested either by examining the ratio of the coefficient to its standard error, or by the likelihood-ratio method (See [13, p. 34]).

amount donated. The relationship between religious giving and community giving appeared to be the strongest. What implications might this conclusion have for development of marketing strategy for a charitable organization in the community? Suppose the organization were relatively new in the area or that it had rather low penetration in terms of percentage of households donating. If it were seen as appropriate by the religious community, the charitable organization might do well to establish informal links with the local churches. Perhaps opinion leaders in these religious organizations could be induced to serve as volunteers for the community charity. It would seem, at any rate, that the greatest elasticity (in terms of increases in donations in return for increases in fund-raising effort) might apply within the religious community. A similar analysis could be appropriate for more established charities -- with one major difference. These institutions might already be benefiting from the support of a significant percentage of the local church and synagogue membership. Then, strategy could shift toward getting increased support from present donors rather than broadening the donor base.

In general, the importance of some demographic characteristics seemed to be consistent for all three types of giving that were studied. Age was an important predictor in all six equations (OLS and TOBIT for each type of giving). It is also interesting to note that education was not significant in any of the equations.

However, some differences across segments also emerged. If anything, the extent of these differences is probably masked by these data, rather than overemphasized. Since the data are self-reported behavior, any tendencies of a respondent to bias his true behavior (by either under or over-reporting), likely apply in fairly similar fashion to each type of giving. For that reason, differences across giving situations might be under-emphasized in the analysis.

Nonetheless some important differences did occur. Extent of community activity was a significant predictor of both political and community giving, but not religious donations. In the latter case, socioeconomic status and clothing expenditures were significant, but they were not important in explaining community or religious donation levels. It is also interesting to note that television ownership was significantly related to community giving, although not to the other types of charities. Perhaps this result is a manifestation of greater interest in local activities, or more simply, just a result of the fact that the community charities, in contrast with the others, employ at-home solicitation. Owners of television sets (or multiple sets) are probably more likely to be at home in the evenings.

As the literature review indicated earlier in this paper, there has been little research in the past which has attempted to study different types of charitable giving. From this particular paper, a few noteworthy directions for further study emerge. First, it would be of interest to investigate the accuracy of reported giving behavior by comparing self-reports with organizational records of giving. Second, much more could be learned about political giving if a better data base were used -- perhaps one collected during a time of high political interest so that there would be a larger sample of donors. Finally, efforts to obtain good measures of consumer personality characteristics and motivations should be undertaken. The failure of the psychographic measures to account for giving behavior in this study should inspire further effort in this area.

In conclusion, much remains to be learned about charitable giving. This study seems to indicate that progress in understanding the phenomenon might need to occur on several fronts. Because of the similarities between types of giving, a planner for a charity could certainly learn from considering what his counterparts in other charitable organizations are doing in the marketing area. However, before applying that knowledge to his own situation, he would be well advised to consider the differences in giving behavior that exist among different segments of the population.

It is also appropriate to draw some methodological conclusions from this analysis. When dealing with a dependent variable which has a lower (or upper) limit where many of the respondents are located (e.g., in situations considering purchase data where many respondents might have spent nothing on a particular brand or category), TOBIT is the model of choice. In this situation, comparison of TOBIT results with OLS produced two observations. Significance of the coefficients was usually not materially different in the two analyses. However, the magnitudes of the TOBIT coefficients were much greater, especially in the case of political giving. This was the situation where the fraction of respondents at the lower limit was greatest (over 90%), so the violation of OLS assumptions was most serious.

The TOBIT model has much to offer to marketing researchers. It has not realized widespread acceptance in the past, probably because it was not readily available in a computer package. Since this problem has now been remedied, the model should become an important tool for marketing analysis.

REFERENCES

1. Amemiya, Takeshi. "Regression Analysis When The Dependent Variable Is Truncated Normal," Econometrica, 41(November 1973), 997-1016.

2. The Bulletin of the American Association of Fund-Raising Counsel, 4 (April 15, 1958), p. 3.

3. Crockett, J.B. and H. Chernoff. "Gradient Methods of Maximization," Pacific Journal of Mathematics, 5 (1955), 33-50.

4. Dichter, Ernest. Handbook of Consumer Motivation, New York: McGraw-Hill, 1964.

5. Kotler, Philip. Marketing for Nonprofit Organizations, Englewood Cliffs, New Jersey: Prentice-Hall, 1975.

6. Kotler, Philip and Sidney J. Levy. "Broadening the Concept of Marketing," Journal of Marketing, 33 (January 1969), 10-15.

7. Levy, Sidney J. "Humanized Appeals in Fund-Raising," Public Relations Journal, (July 1965), 17-18.

8. Mindak, William A. and H. Malcolm Bybee. "Marketing's Application to Fund Raising," Journal of Marketing, 35 (July 1971), 13-18.

9. National Bureau of Economic Research, Inc. TROLL Experimental Programs: Quantitative and Limited Dependent Variable Models, NBER Computer Research Center, Cambridge, Mass., July 1976.

10. Nelson, Forrest D. "On a General Computer Algorithm for the Analysis of Models with Limited Dependent Variables," Annals of Economic and Social Measurement, 5 (Fall 1976), 493-510.

11. Rathmell, John M. Marketing in the Service Sector, Cambridge, Mass.: Winthrop Publishers, 1974.

12. Shapiro, Benson P. "Marketing for Nonprofit Organizations," Harvard Business Review, 51 (September 1973), 123-32.

13. Tobin, James. "Estimation of Relationships for Limited Dependent Variables," Econometrica, 26 (1958), 24-36.

THE PROMOTION OF MEDICAL AND LEGAL SERVICES: AN EXPERIMENTAL STUDY

Philip G. Kuehl, University of Maryland
Gary T. Ford, University of Maryland

## ABSTRACT

The marketing and promotion of professional services is a highly visible societal issue that reflects legal, consumerist, economic, and marketing perspectives. Results from this experimental study show that the availability of alternative forms of consumer information--personal and nonpersonal sources--affect behavioral intention and attitudinal measures more than practitioner attribute and professional fee level factors for physicians and lawyers.

## INTRODUCTION

In the near future, it appears that a highly visible issue in contemporary society--the promotion of professional services--will begin to have a substantial impact on marketing thought and practice. Three general factors contribute support for this conclusion.

First, the legal dimensions of this issue have been crystallized through a series of publicized actions involving such professional groups as physicians, dentists, lawyers, engineers, pharmacists, accountants, and opthalmologists, optometrists, and opticians [3,11,12,13]. In all of these professions, either the Federal Trade Commission (FTC) or state agencies have filed suits challenging or are investigating prohibitions against the use of paid advertising and/or the withholding of pricing and fee schedule information from the public.

Second, since the consumer has traditionally supported public policymaking activities such as "truth-in" legislation, which lead to greater information disclosure and which strengthened consumers' abilities to make better informed choices, it is likely that in the future consumerists will support most public policies that require or encourage the promotion of professional services.

Third, the economic consequences of promotional bans in the professions is beginning to be investigated by marketing scholars. For instance, Bloom [3] has hypothesized potential market structure implications of professional service marketing and advertising efforts in terms of its effects on: (1) industry-profession structure (i.e., barriers to entry, economic concentration, and degree of product differentiation); (2) market conduct (i.e., competitive behavior through "price" advertising); and (3) market performance (i.e., the efficient use of society's resources resulting in better services at lower market prices). While these theoretical views provide useful insights about the potential effects of professional marketing and advertising efforts, only two studies [2,4]--examining the prescription eyeglass and prescription drug industries--have examined the economic aspects of the issue in empirical terms.

In summary, there are many indications that interest in the marketing and promotion of professional services is increasing at the present time. Unfortunately, as Bloom states [3, p. 13], ". . . there is a serious lack of empirical evidence available . . ." for evaluating the perspectives expressed by scholars writing on this subject area. The basic objective of this study is to provide empirical input for this emerging professional dialogue. This objective is accomplished by providing experimental findings on marketplace effects--measured by consumer behavioral intentions and attitudes--of promotional efforts in the medical and legal professions.

The following discussion highlights briefly the conceptual context for the research design and includes a description of the specific objectives guiding the research. Second, the study methodology is presented and the experimental procedures are described. Next, the study findings are reported and fourth, the implications of these findings are presented in the final section of this paper.

## CONCEPTUAL CONTEXT

### General Perspectives

An evaluation of the legal, consumerism, and economic issues discussed in the preceding section suggests that the "information availability" or "information dissemination" issue is a dominant theme in all of these perspectives. However, as previously noted, very few studies examining this issue have been reported in the marketing literature. Therefore, it appeared that empirical insights on likely marketplace effects of increased consumer information should be one of the major thrusts of this study.

In one of the few published studies relevant to professional service marekting, Feldman and Spencer [6] examined the effect of alternative information sources (i.e., nonpersonal sources--the telephone directory, personal/professional sources, and personal/nonprofessional sources) on the selection of a physician by 182 new residents in a midwestern metropolitan area. In general, study findings suggest a majority of the new residents in their cross-sectional sample select a physician within the first month (and more than 90 percent select a physician within four months) of their residency.

In another study, Ratchford and Andreasen [10] examined consumer perceptions of service provider decisions in order to determine the importance, complexity, subjectivity, and information availability in seven different areas (i.e., selection of a hairdresser, plumber, general practitioner, etc.). Their study, which asked consumers ". . . to imagine they had just moved to a new community where they had never lived before. . . ." [10, p. 336], found that selection of a physician was regarded as an important, complex, fairly subjective decision about which relatively little information was available.

Findings from the Feldman et al. and Ratchford et al studies were instrumental in shaping the design of the present study in two ways. First, their studies indicate that the selection of a physician is an important decision that new residents attempt to make fairly soon after moving to a new community. In addition, the Ratchford and Andreasen study implies that information relevant to the selection of a physician would be welcome by the new residents. Therefore, the inclusion of an experimental variable to assess alternative effects associated with the source of information about a physician appeared to be a relevant and important variable in the study.

Second, the Ratchford and Andreasen "scenario" approach that asked respondents to place themselves in the hypothetical situation of being new residents appeared to reasonably sound. Such an approach, while containing the traditional external validity problems associated with laboratory experiments, does allow examination of the behavioral intention and attitudinal impact of the major independent variables used in the study, while avoiding the potential situational effects of professional service information-seeking under conditions of immediate emergency or extreme dissatisfaction with currently used practitioners.

In addition to drawing on the research findings and techniques of previous studies, this research effort was guided by some recent activities of the FTC and the courts. The FTC, as highlighted previously, alleges that professional society "codes of ethics," which prohibit advertising and other promotional activities by their members regarding qualifications and fee schedules, represent violations of First Amendment guarantees of free speech [7]. Furthermore, the fee-setting practices of professional societies, which censure members who charge below the set fees, have been found by the Virginia Supreme Court to be an illegal restraint of trade in violation of the Sherman Act [8]. Based on these occurrences, it is not unlikely that developments in professional service marketing practices will occur in the promotion of the qualifications of individual or group practitioners and/or through price competition among providers. Therefore, the present study was designed to provide some preliminary evidence on the two issues of promotion of fee differences and professional qualifications differences as well as on the previously discussed issue of the source of information.

Specific Variables

Consistent with the preceding general conceptual framework for the study, it is possible to identify specific independent and dependent variables for the study. The three major independent variables chosen for the study include: (1) information source effects, (2) practitioner attribute effects, and (3) price effects for professional services. In addition, these effects were replicated in the study design to produce effects for physicians and lawyers.

The information source effect for the study recognizes the dominant personal source (e.g., either professional or nonprofessional) information seeking patterns found by Feldman and Spencer [6], by manipulating the source of information in a direct mail campaign sponsored by a lawyer or physician. A direct mail approach was used because it is likely that professionals' initial trials with promotion will focus on relatively low-cost media selection policies that provide good precision in terms of geographic coverage.

The three levels of the information source effect developed for this study were:

(1) Information Source Effect $(IS_n)$

$IS_L$ - Direct mail promotional campaign for a physician and lawyer (i.e., nonpersonal information source).

$IS_{LR}$ - Direct mail promotional campaign supplemented with a recommendation from a friend--in support of a (new) physician and lawyer (i.e., nonpersonal and personal/nonprofessional sources).

$IS_{LRR}$- Direct mail promotional campaign supplemented with a recommendation from a friend and a professional referral from another physician and lawyer--in support of a (new) physician and lawyer (i.e., nonpersonal, personal/nonprofessional, and personal/professional sources).

The types of promotional themes and appeals to be used in the direct mail campaign are the second set of independent variables used in the study. To obtain three levels of practitioner characteristics of physicians and lawyers, which provide a basis to identify promotable attributes, the researchers conducted a pilot study among a subsample of the overall respondent group used for the study sample-- none of the pilot study respondents were included in the experiments itself. These respondents were asked to identify, describe, and evaluate the relative importance of various types of physician and lawyer attributes. The results of this analysis enabled the research team to develop the following three levels of practitioner attributes for the study:

(2) Practitioner Attribute Effect $(PA_n)$

$PA_F$ - Basic functional attributes of medical and legal practitioners (i.e., office hours, location, answering and referral service, payment and credit procedures, etc.).

$PA_S$ - Attributes reflecting the types and quality of the professional services offered (i.e., (1) house call availability, hospital affiliation, years in practice, etc. for physicians; and (2) range of professional services, years in practice, community and professional affiliation, etc. for lawyers).

$PA_O$ - Other descriptive attributes of medical and legal practitioners (i.e., age, professional school, teaching positions and experience, professional awards, etc.).

The final independent variable used in the study was a price effect. The use of this variable encompasses general concern about professional service fee structures and levels among many groups of consumers and, in addition, reflects traditional emphasis in the marketing literature on price-quality relationships. As a result, the price variable was defined as an important variable--separate from other professional attributes--in the study.

(3) Professional Fee Level Effect $(PFL_n)$

$PFL_H$ - Price of the physician and lawyer fees "somewhat above" the level commonly charged by other practitioners in the area (i.e., high fee).

$PFL_A$ - Price of the physician and lawyer fees "comparable to" the level commonly charged by other practitioners in the area (i.e., average fee).

$PFL_L$ - Price of the physician and lawyer fees "somewhat below" the level commonly charged by other practitioners in the area (i.e., low fee).

Two major dependent variables, both commonly used in behavioral experiments, were used in the study. Since the actual marketplace effect (i.e., changes in the behavioral patterns of consumers) is one of the major issues in the legal, economic, and consumerist viewpoints on the issue of professional service marketing, it is important that a variable reflecting consumer choice behavior be included in the study as one of the two dependent variables.

(1) Purchase Probability Scale. The measurement of respondents' estimates of the probability or likelihood that they would use the professional services of the medical and legal practitioners described in the experiment (i.e., a seven-point scale ranging from "certain, practically certain" to "almost no chance, no chance").

Since the promotion of professional services is likely to influence the cognitive structures of consumers as well, an attitude measure is the second dependent variable included in the experiment.

(2) Attitude Scale. The physician and lawyer were each evaluated on seven point semantic differentials evaluating (a) professionalism, (b) trustworthiness, (c) competency and (d) qualifications.

## Project Objectives

The preceding discussion of the descriptive and conceptual dimensions provides a basis for stating the two major objectives addressed in this experimental study:

(1) To examine the impact of information source, practitioner attribute characteristics, and professional service pricing levels of medical and legal practitioners on the behavioral intentions of the study respondents; and

(2) To examine the impact of information source, practitioner attribute characteristics, and professional pricing levels of medical and legal practitioners on the attitudes of the study respondents.

### METHODOLOGY

Figure 1 summarizes how the three experimental variables were structured within a replicated (i.e., for physicians and lawyers) Latin Square design [1, pp. 168-79] to provide data on the behavioral intention and attitudinal scales used in the study. Although Latin Square designs allow the the researcher to gather data about three main effects in an efficient manner they do not allow measurement of interaction effects. Since the present research represents one of the first attempts to perform a controlled experiment using these independent variables, the authors chose not to measure interactions. The authors believe that future research should build on the results reported herein, perhaps by using complete factorial designs.

### FIGURE 1
### 3 x 3 LATIN SQUARE DESIGN FOR PHYSICIANS AND LAWYERS

The convenience sample consisted of individuals from a broad sociodemographic range in the Baltimore, Maryland area who were enrolled in adult education courses sponsored by Baltimore County. All of the respondents were adult heads of households (68.3 percent were male and 31.7 percent were female) and over three-quarters (77.8 percent) were employed on a full-time basis. Nearly one-half (49.2 percent) of the sample respondents were college graduates or had "some college" and 35.0 percent had annual household incomes in excess of $19,000, while 41.2 percent represented households with annual incomes of $12,000 to $18,999.

The following procedures were used in the implementation of the study design:

(1) All respondents were given a brief, descriptive scenario in which their families, as a result of a job promotion, had recently moved to a new city. Furthermore, it was stated that one of their first concerns was to establish relationships with a new family doctor and personal lawyer. Finally, depending upon the cell assignment of the respondent, the scenario contained statements describing one of the three levels of the information source effect

variable (i.e., the direct mail promotion, personal/nonprofessional recommendation, and personal/professional recommendation).

(2) After reading the scenario, respondents were required to read the direct mail promotional letter (on an appropriate letterhead) for the hypothetical doctor and lawyer, which contained the practitioner attribute and professional fee pricing variables for their respective cell.

(3) Finally, without referring back to the scenario or direct mail materials, the subjects responded to the behavioral intentions, attitudinal, and sociodemographic scales contained in the study questionnaire.

(4) All subjects were debriefed regarding the purpose of the study after all experiments were completed.

A total of 108 respondents were recruited for the study—12 being randomly assigned to the nine (9) cells in Figure 1. After editing data by deleting all incomplete returns (8) and deleting respondents with frequent interaction with legal and medical practioners (18) and then randomly deleting some respondents to equalize cell sizes at seven per cell, a total of 63 subjects were included for further analysis.

### RESULTS

The effect of the 3 x 3 Latin Square experimental design on the behavioral intentions and attitudinal measures for the physician and lawyer described in the study scenario are presented in the following discussion.

Objective 1: Experimental Effects on Behavioral Intentions

Table 1 and Table 2 show results from the 3-Way Analysis of Variance (ANOVA) conducted on the behavioral intention scale data for the physician and lawyer, respectively. As these data show, the significant source of variation on the behavioral intention dependent variable was the "information source" effect, which produced an F-Ratio of 9.63 (significant at $\alpha = .01$) for the physician and 3.96 (significant at $\alpha = .05$) for the lawyer.

### TABLE 1
### 3-WAY ANOVA RESULTS FOR BEHAVIORIAL INTENTIONS TOWARD THE PHYSICIAN

| Source of Variation | Sum of Squares | Degrees of Freedom | Squares | F/ Ratio |
|---|---|---|---|---|
| Practitioner Attribute Effect | 1.75 | 2 | .88 | 1.57 |
| Information Source Effect | 10.78 | 2 | 5.39 | 9.63[a] |
| Professional Fee Level Effect | .21 | 2 | .11 | .20 |
| Error | 31.28 | 56 | | |
| TOTAL | 44.02 | 62 | | |

[a]Significant at $\alpha = .01$.

TABLE 2
THREE-WAY ANOVA RESULTS FOR BEHAVIORAL
INTENTIONS TOWARD THE LAWYER

| Source of Variation | Sum of Squares | Degrees of Freedom | Mean Squares | F/ Ratio |
|---|---|---|---|---|
| Practitioner Attribute Effect | 1.26 | 2 | .63 | 1.19 |
| Information Source Effect | 4.20 | 2 | 2.10 | 3.96[a] |
| Professional Fee Level Effect | .14 | 2 | .07 | .13 |
| Error | 34.57 | 56 | .53 | |
| TOTAL | 40.17 | 60 | | |

[a]Significant at $\alpha = .05$

Further insights on the thrust of these findings is provided by the data in Table 3, which show the direction of the behavioral intention mean values. These data show that a consistent and increasing behavioral intention probability across the three levels of the information source independent variable (i.e., from nonpersonal to nonpersonal/ personal sources) was found for both the physician and lawyer. In examining this table, it should be noted that lower mean values connote higher behaviorial intention probabilities.

TABLE 3

SUMMARY OF INFORMATION SOURCE EFFECT MEAN
VALUES BY PHYSICIAN AND LAWYER

| Profession | Information Source Effect Mean Values | | |
|---|---|---|---|
| | Letter, Recommendation and Referral | Letter and Recommendation | Letter |
| Physician[a] | 3.52 | 3.62 | 5.10 |
| Lawyer[b] | 3.95 | 4.43 | 5.05 |

[a]Significant at $\alpha = .01$.

[b]Significant at $\alpha = .05$.

The pattern of results found for the behavioral intention data suggest three major interpretations. First, the data illustrate the exposure to alternative sources of information significantly affect the behavioral intentions of consumers. However, the content (i.e., promotional appeals represented by practitioner attributes and fee level information) did not produce such an effect on behavioral intentions. Such a finding supports the view that consumers are sensitive to alternative sources of information and public policymaking processes, which promote the easy accessibility of marketplace information, should be encouraged (i.e., an important policy variable is consumer accessibility to alternative sources of information in the marketplace).

Second, while the study design does not permit the analysis of interaction effects between nonpersonal and personal

sources of information, these results are generally consistent with the findings of Spencer and Feldman [6]. In other words, it appears that the traditional usage and influence of personal information sources (if available from nonprofessional and professional sources) dominate physician and lawyer consumer decion-making processes—a characteristic found in other service-oriented product categories [10].

Third, the lack of significant behavioral intentions for the professional fee level and practitioner attribute effects provides useful insights. For instance, nonsignificant findings for the price level variable might indicate that, in fact, consumers are not highly price sensitive for medical and legal services—which are highly important and personal in nature. Price sensitivity, of course, might dramatically change in situational contexts other than the "new resident" scenario used in this study. The emerging tendency of third-party payment mechanisms also provides a probable explanation for the lack of price level significance for medical services in this study. Finally, a general tendency among many consumers to use lawyers on a relatively infrequent basis (compared with such services as provided by physicians, dentists, etc.) may account for the lack of sensitivity to the price variable for this professional class.

The inability of the practitioner attribute variable to affect behavioral intentions probably reflects a lack of firm attribute choice criteria for medical and legal practitioners among many consumers. In other words, consumers may not be able to assess which alternative set of practitioner attributes correctly reflects the availability of "quality service at a reasonable price." Such a situation may foreshadow the need for increased consumer education efforts by individual practitioners, professional societies, and governmental agencies (i.e., adult and continuing education programs, etc.) to ensure that consumers are equipped to effectively evaluate their service need structures and alternative market offerings.

Objective 2. Experimental Effects on Attitudinal Characteristis.

Results related to the attitudinal measures obtained in the experiment are summarized in Table 4. In general, the pattern of these results is similar to the behavioral intentions data in that the "information source" effect produced the only significant results in all cases. Furthermore, the direction of the mean scores for all significant relationships across the three levels of this source of variation was identical to the behavioral intention data in all cases except the "trustworthiness" attribute (i.e., the "information source" effect was the only significant independent variable and attitude scores were progressively more favorable from the nonpersonal source to nonpersonal and nonprofessional-professional sources of information). As in Table 3, the lower mean value connotes a more favorable attitudinal perception.

Two major implications evolve from the findings in Table 4. First, as expected, recognition in the community and among peer groups (combined with the direct mail promotion) did produce favorable attitudes regarding the "professionalism" of the physician and lawyer described in the study. However, favorable "professionalism" attitudes do not appear to carry over to attitudes towards the "qualifications" of two practitioners. In essence, then, a positive recognition of a practitioner's "professional" standing in the community appears to be a separate issue from the "qualifications" of both practitioners in the eyes of the consumer—even though the practitioner attribute effect (i.e., which contained information of professional credentials and qualifications) did not cause any attitudinal shifts. This situation reinforces the view that broad-scale education programs may be necessary if consumers are to have confidence in their ability to effectively judge the

| Attitudinal Attribute | Professional Category | Significant Effect | Information Source Effect Means | | |
| --- | --- | --- | --- | --- | --- |
| | | | Letter, Recommendation, and Referral | Letter and Recommendation | Letter |
| Professionalism | Physician | Information Source[a] | 2.33 | 2.76 | 3.90 |
| | Lawyer | Information Source[b] | 2.33 | 2.67 | 3.67 |
| Trustworthiness | Physician | Information Source[c] | 2.95 | 2.86 | 3.86 |
| | Lawyer | NS | -- | -- | -- |
| Competency | Physician | NS | -- | -- | -- |
| | Lawyer | Information Source[c] | 2.76 | 3.19 | 4.05 |
| Qualifications | Physician | NS | -- | -- | -- |
| | Lawyer | NS | -- | -- | -- |

[a]Significant at $\alpha = .01$.    [b]Significant at $\alpha = .05$.    [c]Significant at $\alpha = .10$.

qualifications of professional service providers.

Second, the results on the "trustworthiness" and "competency" scales show different attitudinal perceptions between the two practitioners. While the "qualifications" of both practitioners were not affected by any of the experimental variables, physicians were viewed as more "trustworthy" and lawyers as more "competent" as a result of the "information source" effect. For physicians, it appears that attitudes about "professionalism" and "trustworthiness" are related (i.e., professionalism in the community and among peers is prima facie evidence of "trustworthiness")--a situation that is not the case for lawyers (i.e., the "trustworthiness" of lawyers may be regarded by consumers as a distinct characteristic that is apart from "professionalism" in legal services). Finally, the competency of the lawyer increased across the three levels of the information source effect, suggesting that meaningful interpersonal input from the community and peers is a surrogate indication of a lawyer's ability to perform needed legal services.

## SUMMARY IMPLICATIONS

Findings from this experimental study provide some important implications for marketing scholars and practitioners interested in the promotion of professional services.

### Policy Implications

Study results are consistent with findings of previous researchers [6, 10] that consumer decision processes for medical and legal services are complex and that consumers place greater reliance on personal rather than nonpersonal information sources. The finding that consumers did not exhibit high behavioral intention probabilities or extremely favorable attitudinal structures from using nonpersonal sources provides preliminary evidence that promotional efforts by medical and legal practioners will not cause rapid, substantial changes in economic structure [3]. This general implication has further significance for all practitioners who desire to maintain their present client base and attract new client groups. Since interpersonal communication patterns and contact are uncontrollable variables in the promotional mix, it might be difficult for established practitioners to maintain or increase the size of their present client group or for new practitioners to attract a viable client base (if few consumers or practitioners are able to personally recommend a new practitioner) without nonpersonal information sources. Therefore, practitioners in this situation may want to participate in ongoing forums that provide opportunities for interpersonal communication (i.e., speaking before community groups, participation in panel discussions, etc.).

Second, results indicate the likelihood that consumers are not highly qualified to assess information on practitioner attributes and fee levels and to relate such input to their need structures. Therefore, significant effects found for information sources vis-a-vis attribute and price level information content suggest that consumer education programs are needed before nonpersonal sources will be cost-effective and relied upon by many consumers. Through such educational efforts, consumer sensitivity to alternative sources of information can be used to provide a basis for "rational and informed choice" behavior in the marketplace, which includes efficient promotional efforts of individual practitioners as well as traditional reliance on interpersonal information sources.

The final general implication evolving from the present analysis and interpretation is marketing-oriented. Professional service providers must be encouraged to embrace the basic philosophy of the discipline that is commonly labeled the "marketing concept." Second, professionals must recognize the marketing tools and techniques that are allied with this concept (i.e., segmented need structures related to effective use of pricing, service (product), distribution (location), and promotional variables) must be used to create a total marketing program [9]. In this way, marketing thought and practice will have contributed to mutually satisfying and beneficial relationships between practitioners and their clients.

### Future Research Implications

The authors recognize that the empirical findings generated in this study provide only preliminary insights into the general subject area of professional service marketing. The following suggestions for future research would help to overcome the inherent limitations of the present study (i.e., a scenario approach using hypothetical practitioners in a laboratory environment) and provide a basis for an emerging research tradition in the area of professional service marketing.

Future research efforts, for instance, might incorporate several new configurations of the independent variables used in this study. First, alternative media sources (i.e., broadcast and print mass media) could be used in addition to the direct mail promotions employed in this study. A second opportunity to extend the present research concerns the types of promotional appeals presented through the alternative media sources. For example, explicit fee structure and pricing information could be presented and actual fee comparisons could be made in a "comparative advertising" context. Similarly, alternative promotional appeals contained in non-price practitioner attributes could be examined in future research (i.e., refining attribute typology generated for this study). As already noted, future researchers might use factorial designs to measure the combined effects of these independent variables.

In terms of dependent variables to be used in future research, attitudinal measures could be expanded to include perceived risk scales associated with consumer decision-making processes in the professions. Secondly, consumer attitudes toward alternative (1) information sources and (2) promotional content could be measured.

The final set of recommendations for future research is more general in nature. First, the marketing of other professional services (i.e., dentists, engineers, accountants, etc.) should be incorporated into future experimental research. Additionally, other marketing variables in the professional marketing mix could be incorporated into empirical research. This work could contribute to generalized strategic planning models for the marketing function that are applicable to the professional environment of professional service providers.

In any event, the evolving present and likely future visibility of professional service marketing support continued conceptual and empirical work by marketing academicians and practitioners in this subject area. It is hoped that this study makes a preliminary contribution to such understanding and stimulates other marketers to conduct additional research on the marketing of professional services.

## REFERENCES

1.  Banks, Seymour. _Experimentation in Marketing_. New York: McGraw-Hill Book Company, 1965.

2.  Benham, Lee. "The Effect of Advertising on the Price of Eyeglasses," _Journal of Law and Economics_, 15 (October 1972), 337-352.

3.  Bloom, Paul N. "Advertising in the Professions: The Critical Issues," _Journal of Marketing_, 41 (July 1977), forthcoming.

4.  Cady, John F. _Drugs on the Market_. Lexington, Mass.: Lexington Books, 1975.

5.  Engel, James F., David T. Kollat, and Roger D. Blackwell. _Consumer Behavior_, 2nd ed. New York: Holt, Rinehart and Winston, Inc., 1973, 632-635.

6.  Feldman, Sidney and Merlin Spencer. "The Effect of Personal Influence in the Selection of Consumer Services," in _1975 Combined Proceedings_, Edward M. Mazze, ed. Chicago: American Marketing Association, 1975, 597-600.

7.  "Giving Advertisers a Right to Free Speech," _Business Week_ (February 2, 1976), 21-22.

8.  Goldfarb v. Virginia State Bar, US, 44L Ed. 2nd 572 (1975).

9.  Kotler, Philip and Richard A. Connor, Jr. "Marketing Professional Services," _Journal of Marketing_, 41 (January 1977), 71-76.

10. Ratchford, Brian T. and Alan R. Andreasen. "A Study of Consumer Perceptions of Decisions," in _Advances in Consumer Behavior: Volume I_, Scott Ward and Peter L. Wright, eds. Boston: Association for Consumer Research, 1972, 283-286.

11. Sheredan, Bart. "Will an HMO Grab Your Patients?" _Medical Economics_ (September 17, 1973), 220.

12. Sprague, W. Douglas. "The Advertising Dilemma," _CPA Journal_ (January 1977), 27-30.

13. Stiff, Ronald. "The Changing Role of Professional Service Marketing," in _Marketing: 1776-1976 and Beyond_, Kenneth L. Bernhardt, ed. Chicago: American Marketing Association, 1976, 283-286.

REVISING THE UNDERGRADUATE
MARKETING CURRICULUM:  THE VIEWS
OF PRACTITIONERS AND EDUCATORS

Danny N. Bellenger, Georgia State University
Kenneth L. Bernhardt, Georgia State University

## ABSTRACT

The study reported in this paper investigates the views of
marketing practitioners and marketing educators with respect to the orientation, structure, and course content of
the undergraduate marketing program.  The survey results
show interesting areas of both agreement and disagreement.
A suggested curriculum, based on these findings, is presented in the implications section of the paper.

## INTRODUCTION

A number of studies recently have indicated that the
courses offered in the marketing curriculum by colleges
and universities with marketing majors have been undergoing a process of change [4, 10].  Sometimes individual
courses are initiated, revised or deleted, and in other
circumstances the whole curriculum is revised.  This paper
describes the process undertaken at one university to determine what courses should be offered in an undergraduate
marketing program.

The ideal program is one which is compatible with the objectives of the students, the faculty, and the business
community which hires marketing graduates.  Several recent
articles have described ways in which individual universities have been able to balance off the needs of each of
these groups in developing their marketing programs [1, 7].
Many marketing programs, however, are not closely aligned
with what educators or businessmen think should be offered.
At the 1972 AMA Conference, David Hardin argued that marketing educators were offering courses that provided students with strong backgrounds in quantitative methods and
advanced management planning concepts, but were not preparing them for the needs they would have in their initial
job [5].  Dyer and Shimp reported that the views of marketing department chairmen differed considerably from those
of members of Sales & Marketing Executives with regard to
the need for personal selling and sales management in the
marketing curriculum [3].  Although there appears to be a
significant demand for the sales oriented courses by marketing practitioners hiring graduates of undergraduate
marketing programs, there is evidence that this demand is
ignored.  For example, Coyle reports that fewer courses in
personal selling and sales management were offered in 1973
than in 1968 [2].

There is also evidence that many undergraduate marketing
programs do not offer a number of courses which marketing
educators think should be offered in an up-to-date marketing curriculum [6].  Other evidence indicates that at many
schools there is a difference between course offerings and
the program of courses desired by recent graduates and
marketing executives [2].

While there have been many publications concerning the
content of marketing courses and the marketing program,
very few of the articles have used empirical data to support the recommendations.  There have been a few studies,
however, which examined recent graduates [8, 9, 2] or marketing executives [2].

In addition to determining the specific courses that
should be included in an up-to-date marketing curriculum,

it is important to determine what orientation, philosophy,
and structure the undergraduate marketing curriculum should
reflect.  The purpose of this paper is to examine the attitudes of both marketing practitioners and marketing educators with regard to the orientation and structure of the
marketing program as well as their attitudes toward the importance of individual courses.  Because previous research
reported no difference in the perceptions of the value of
various marketing courses by recent graduates and marketing
practitioners [2], it was decided that it was not necessary
to separately examine the attitudes of recent graduates.

In developing a recommended undergraduate marketing curriculum, the authors will discuss courses in terms of whether
or not they should be required, and whether or not it is
important to offer the courses as electives in the program.
Hise's study of 135 undergraduate marketing programs indicated that a mean of 4.4 marketing courses are required and
a mean of 10.4 marketing courses are offered [6].  A program approximating these constraints is developed from the
findings of the research presented here.

## THE STUDY

### Sample

Data for the study were secured by a mail survey during the
Winter Quarter 1976-77.  It should be noted that the views
of marketing educators and marketing practitioners as determined from this survey were but one informational input
into the curriculum revision process.  The other inputs
were, however, more narrowly directed to the school in
question.

For the survey, approximately 500 questionnaires were
mailed to the marketing educators who are members of the
Southern Marketing Association, the regional marketing
association in which the school is located.  Usable responses from 225 faculty (45% response rate) were returned by
the cut off date.  Another 2,000 questionnaires were mailed
to marketing practitioners in the region where the university is located.  Usable responses were received from 227
members of this group (11.4% response rate) by the cut off
date.  This difference in response rate might be taken to
indicate a relative lack of interest in this topic among
marketing practitioners.  Although this group may not be
representative of all marketing practitioners, their inputs
are nevertheless important because they are probably representative of the subset of practitioners who have the
greatest interest in marketing education.

### Questions

Several sets of questions were included in the questionnaire.  Two of the more interesting and useful sets related
to (1) orientation and structure of the curriculum and
(2) whether or not each of 29 different courses should be
included in the undergraduate marketing program.  Relative
to orientation and structure, the respondents were asked to
indicate their level of agreement with the twelve statements shown in Table 1.  They were then asked to evaluate
the 29 course titles shown in Table 2 on the following
scale:

(1) Definitely Should be Required
(2) Probably Should be Required
(3) Definitely Should be Offered as an Elective
(4) Probably Should be Offered as an Elective
(5) Shouldn't Be Offered
(6) Not Sure

In order to rank the courses for comparison purposes the percentage of responses in categories (1) and (2) were first combined (see Table 2) and then the percentage of responses in categories (1), (2), and (3) were combined (see Table 3).

The differences between the two groups on the Likert-type statements were tested for statistical significance using Chi Square. The similarity in terms of the ranking of the desired courses by the marketing educators and marketing practitioners were evaluated using Spearman's rank-order correlation.

Table 1 shows the level of agreement with a series of statements relating to program orientation and structure. Several points of interest can be seen:

(1) More marketing practitioners are inclined toward preparation for the first job than are marketing educators.

(2) More marketing practitioners than educators stress that courses should emphasize practice rather than theory.

(3) More members of both groups are inclined to stress actual rather than "ideal" business decision making processes. This view is more prevalent among practitioners.

TABLE 1
THE ORIENTATION AND STRUCTURE OF THE
UNDERGRADUATE MARKETING MAJOR

| Statement | Marketing Educators | | | Marketing Practitioners | | |
|---|---|---|---|---|---|---|
| | Agree | Neutral | Disagree | Agree | Neutral | Disagree |
| 1. Courses should stress material helpful to the student in their first job rather than preparing them for the job they will hold later in their career.*** | 35.9% | 24.0% | 40.1% | 57.8% | 15.9% | 26.3% |
| 2. Courses should emphasize practice rather than theory.*** | 38.1 | 34.4 | 27.4 | 64.9 | 22.9 | 12.2 |
| 3. Students should be taught "ideal" business decision making processes rather than actual business decision making processes.*** | 17.7 | 28.2 | 54.1 | 15.7 | 10.4 | 73.9 |
| 4. The program should turn out good strategic planners.*** | 46.1 | 35.5 | 18.4 | 66.7 | 23.7 | 9.6 |
| 5. Curriculum needs to be comprised primarily of courses on specific functional areas such as advertising, retailing, and selling rather than more general courses such as consumer behavior and marketing strategies.* | 39.1 | 20.0 | 40.9 | 46.8 | 21.9 | 31.2 |
| 6. In a good program the student has a large number of electives rather than primarily required courses.** | 33.2 | 32.7 | 34.1 | 36.4 | 21.3 | 42.3 |
| 7. A marketing major should allow the student to have a specific concentration within the major such as advertising, sales, or retailing.*** | 47.0 | 16.0 | 37.0 | 63.2 | 15.1 | 21.7 |
| 8. A good marketing program requires that all majors take a course that gives them field experience.*** | 48.2 | 26.4 | 25.5 | 79.0 | 13.6 | 7.4 |
| 9. The program should have a strong quantitative emphasis rather than being behavioral.*** | 4.3 | 48.8 | 46.9 | 30.1 | 42.1 | 27.8 |
| 10. The marketing major should have an emphasis on environmental and social issues. | 39.0 | 38.1 | 22.9 | 34.2 | 39.3 | 26.5 |
| 11. Marketing education overly emphasizes the marketing problems of large companies.*** | 66.8 | 18.6 | 14.5 | 38.9 | 31.9 | 29.3 |
| 12. Marketing education should place more emphasis on marketing for nonprofit organizations.*** | 42.0 | 33.3 | 24.7 | 13.3 | 29.9 | 56.8 |

Note: Astericks are used to indicate that a statistically significant difference exists between the two groups' level of agreement with the statement based on a Chi Square test as follows:

* $p < .10$

** $p < .05$

*** $p < .01$

TABLE 2
WHAT COURSES SHOULD BE REQUIRED?

| | Marketing Educators | | Marketing Practitioners | |
| --- | --- | --- | --- | --- |
| | Rank | Percent | Rank | Percent |
| Principles of Marketing | 1 | 99.1* | 1 | 98.1 |
| Marketing Management | 2 | 87.1 | 2 | 73.6 |
| Marketing Research and Information Systems | 3 | 81.0 | 4 | 63.0 |
| Consumer Behavior | 4 | 70.5 | 6 | 60.1 |
| Quantitative Methods in Marketing | 5 | 37.9 | 11 | 46.8 |
| Marketing Problems | 6 | 36.5 | 3 | 66.0 |
| Marketing Strategy | 7 | 36.5 | 9 | 56.8 |
| Advertising | 8 | 30.3 | 8 | 58.5 |
| Sales Management | 9 | 23.9 | 10 | 49.1 |
| Distribution Channels | 10 | 22.5 | 18 | 29.4 |
| Physical Distribution | 11 | 21.0 | 17 | 31.9 |
| Internship in Marketing | 12 | 19.3 | 12 | 43.3 |
| Marketing Planning | 13 | 17.3 | 7 | 59.5 |
| Retailing | 14 | 16.8 | 16 | 35.2 |
| Principles of Selling | 15 | 15.5 | 5 | 60.8 |
| Social Issues in Marketing | 16 | 12.0 | 25 | 13.5 |
| Product Development and Management | 17 | 11.5 | 14 | 36.2 |
| Marketing Theory | 18 | 11.4 | 13 | 41.9 |
| Pricing | 19 | 10.1 | 15 | 35.6 |
| Industrial Marketing | 20 | 9.7 | 20 | 23.6 |
| Advertising Campaigns | 21 | 9.2 | 19 | 29.1 |
| International Marketing | 22 | 8.7 | 27 | 7.7 |
| Transportation | 23 | 6.4 | 23 | 15.2 |
| Advanced Marketing Research | 24 | 6.1 | 24 | 14.2 |
| Marketing for Nonprofit Organizations | 25 | 3.3 | 29 | 3.7 |
| Purchasing | 26 | 2.3 | 21 | 23.4 |
| Marketing to the Government | 27 | 1.0 | 28 | 5.6 |
| History of Marketing Thought | 28 | .9 | 26 | 13.1 |
| Marketing to Ethnic Groups | 29 | .9 | 21 | 23.4 |

*Percentage of respondents indicating that the course should be either definitely or probably required.

(4) Good strategic planners are desired by both groups, although to a somewhat greater degree by marketing practitioners.

(5) More practitioners are inclined toward the functional based curriculum while the educators are almost evenly divided on this issue.

(6) A few more practitioners prefer a structured curriculum than is the case with educators. Both groups were divided on the question of whether the program should be primarily required courses or electives.

(7) The largest percentage of both groups favors concentrations within the major. The view is more widely held among practitioners, however.

(8) Both groups are inclined toward a course giving field experience although the view is held by a larger percentage of practitioners.

(9) A quantitative emphasis is desired by a larger percentage of practitioners than educators. This may, however, be due to a differing perception of the term "quantitative."

(10) There is some support for an emphasis on environmental and social issues among both groups. This was the only orientation question on which the difference between the two groups was not statistically significant at the .10 level or greater.

(11) Many more marketing educators feel that the problem of large companies are overly emphasized than is the case among marketing practitioners.

(12) More marketing educators favor greater emphasis on marketing for nonprofit organizations than do marketing practitioners.

Table 2 shows the percentage of each group that indicated a given course should be either definitely or probably required. Among the educators, Principles of Marketing,

TABLE 3
WHAT COURSES SHOULD BE
INCLUDED IN THE PROGRAM?

| | Marketing Educators | | Marketing Practitioners | |
|---|---|---|---|---|
| | Rank | Percent | Rank | Percent |
| Principles of Marketing | 1 | 99.6* | 1 | 99.6* |
| Marketing Research and Information Systems | 2 | 98.1 | 4 | 90.0 |
| Consumer Behavior | 3 | 94.6 | 10 | 83.3 |
| Marketing Management | 4 | 92.2 | 2 | 92.2 |
| Advertising | 5 | 86.3 | 3 | 91.7 |
| Sales Management | 6 | 82.6 | 7 | 86.6 |
| Retailing | 7 | 78.4 | 11 | 80.8 |
| Quantitative Methods in Marketing | 8 | 68.0 | 12 | 76.2 |
| Physical Distribution | 9 | 67.1 | 15 | 70.8 |
| Marketing Problems | 10 | 65.4 | 5 | 88.8 |
| Industrial Marketing | 11 | 62.0 | 16 | 70.0 |
| Distribution Channels | 12 | 60.6 | 18 | 68.3 |
| Marketing Strategy | 13 | 58.5 | 8 | 85.0 |
| International Marketing | 14 | 56.0 | 24 | 52.7 |
| Principles of Selling | 15 | 53.9 | 6 | 87.1 |
| Internship in Marketing | 16 | 50.2 | 20 | 67.0 |
| Advanced Marketing Research | 17 | 43.5 | 21 | 65.5 |
| Marketing Planning | 18 | 42.5 | 9 | 84.4 |
| Product Development and Management | 19 | 41.8 | 13 | 76.0 |
| Advertising Campaigns | 20 | 37.9 | 14 | 72.4 |
| Social Issues in Marketing | 21 | 35.6 | 26 | 41.7 |
| Transportation | 22 | 33.0 | 23 | 52.7 |
| Marketing for Nonprofit Organizations | 23 | 31.9 | 29 | 27.9 |
| Pricing | 24 | 30.7 | 19 | 67.8 |
| Purchasing | 25 | 26.3 | 22 | 55.9 |
| Marketing Theory | 26 | 25.2 | 17 | 68.5 |
| Marketing to the Government | 27 | 14.2 | 27 | 38.7 |
| History of Marketing Thought | 28 | 8.2 | 28 | 32.4 |
| Marketing to Ethnic Groups | 29 | 7.8 | 25 | 42.8 |

*Percentage of respondents indicating that the course should be either definitely required, probably required, or definitely offered as an elective.

Marketing Research and Information Systems, and Consumer Behavior are the top choices, all of which were favored by at least 70 percent of the respondents. The percentage drops off significantly for the other courses. It is interesting to note that practitioners want many more things required than educators. This perhaps indicates a lack of appreciation of resource constraints faced by colleges and universities.

Although they want more courses required, the marketing practitioners seem to favor a ranking of required courses similar to that of the educators (Spearman rank order correlation = .89). The Marketing Strategy course favored by a high percentage of practitioners, is probably in most cases a Marketing Management type course. The only major difference is in the percentage that would require Principles of Selling. Many more practitioners (60.8%, fifth ranked) favor this as a required course than do educators (15.5%, fifteenth ranked).

Table 3 shows the percentage of each group that indicated that a given course should be either definitely required, probably required, or definitely offered as an elective. This could be interpreted as the percentage that indicates a given course should definitely be included in the undergraduate marketing program. Although there were some differences, again the rankings of the two groups were similar (Spearman rank order correlation = .80). The marketing practitioners had a greater preference for Principles of Selling and Marketing Planning and the educators were more favorable toward Consumer Behavior and International Marketing.

Beyond the four required courses noted earlier Advertising, Sales Management, Retailing, Quantitative Methods in Marketing, Physical Distribution, Industrial Marketing, Distribution Channels and Principles of Selling appear to be good candidates for inclusion in the program, with the majority of both groups indicating they should be offered. Again, courses like Marketing Problems, Marketing Strategy, and Marketing Planning could be considered in the Marketing Management category.

International Marketing, Internship in Marketing, Advanced Marketing Research, Product Development and Management, and Advertising Campaigns should be given consideration for inclusion in the program depending on resources and the nature and size of the school. The other topics on the list do not appear to justify inclusion as separate courses and might be incorporated into other courses instead.

## IMPLICATIONS

Several implications can be drawn from the findings of this survey. These implications are, of course, a single input which should be blended with several others in the revision process, but they do offer an interesting starting point.

On a general level a program should be pragmatic with strong emphasis on actual business practices, it should allow for concentration in a specific area of marketing, and offer a blend of required and elective courses. A program should offer the students an opportunity to gain field experience and should expose them to environmental and social issues in a marketing context.

Specific course offerings might look as follows:

Required Courses:   Principles of Marketing
Marketing Management
Marketing Research and Information
 Systems
Consumer Behavior

Elective Courses:   Advertising
Sales Management
Retailing
Quantitative Methods in Marketing
Physical Distribution
Industrial Marketing
Distribution Channels
Principles of Selling

Others might be added to the elective list if skills and resources permit. In order to achieve the notion of concentrations in specific areas of marketing, the electives could be formed into tracks such as Sales, Retailing, and Advertising.

Hopefully, in terms of both a starting point and an approach, this paper will provide some useful inputs for those undertaking curriculum revisions.

## REFERENCES

1. Berry, Leonard L. "Marketing Education for Today and Tomorrow: Developing a Marketing Curriculum from Scratch." 1975 Southern Marketing Association Proceedings, ed. by Henry W. Nash and Donald P. Robin, 1976, 67-69.

2. Coyle, Charles A. "How Marketing Executives and Marketing Graduates Value Marketing Courses." Collegiate News and Views, 29 (Fall 1975), 1-3.

3. Dyer, Robert F. and Terence A. Shimp. "An Attitudinal Analysis of Marketing Educators and Executives: Suggestions for Curriculum Design." 1975 Combined Proceedings, ed. by Edward M. Mazze, American Marketing Association, 1975, 614-617.

4. Enis, Ben M. and Sam V. Smith. "The Marketing Curriculum of the 70's: Period of the Pendulum or New Plane of Performance?" in Kenneth L. Bernhardt, ed., Marketing: 1776-1976 and Beyond, American Marketing Association, 1976, 25-28.

5. Hardin, David K. "Marketing Freedom Periled." The Marketing News, 7 (1972), 5.

6. Hise, Richard T. "The Marketing Curriculum: Does It Reflect the Recommendations of Marketing Educators?" Collegiate News and Views, 29 (Spring 1975), 11-16.

7. Hugstad, Paul S. and William E. Bell. "Curriculum Adaptation: A Model and Case." 1975 Combined Proceedings, ed. by Edward M. Mazze, American Marketing Association, 1975, 618-622.

8. Loudenback, Lynn J. "The Recent Graduate: A Source for Curriculum Evaluation." Collegiate News and Views, 27 (Fall 1973), 10-15.

9. _____. "The Relevance of the Concepts We Teach to Marketing Careers." 1971 Combined Proceedings, ed. by Fred C. Allvine, American Marketing Association, 1972, 10-15.

10. Mahmoud, Shah and Creighton Frampton. "Changes in Marketing Curricula in American Assembly of Collegiate Schools of Business 1943-1974." 1974 Southern Marketing Association Proceedings, ed. by Barnett A. Greenberg, 1975, 191-192.

POSITIVISM AND NORMATIVISM:
A CROSSROAD OF VALUES IN MARKETING EDUCATION

Marc G. Weinberger, University of Massachusetts

## ABSTRACT

The consequences of positivism in the marketing curriculum are presented in the context of the increasing external conflict facing marketers. The widespread discussion given to including social issues in marketing courses in the early 1970s has apparently not widely materialized in the form of new courses or in changes in course content. The discipline is presented as being at a crossroads in terms of its philosophical foundation and the role of social issues in its curriculum.

## INTRODUCTION

Traditionally, marketing educators and practitioners have averted conflict within their discipline by being uncritical of themselves. Kotler [1, p. 42] has noted, "It [marketing] has the distinction of being singularly uncontroversial within its ranks, while being endlessly controversial outside of its ranks." It is the purpose of this essay to break from this mold and critically examine the ethical foundations of marketing education, and the directions which it might pursue in the future.

## UNDERLYING PHILOSOPHIES

The two conceptual schemas examined here are positivism and normativism. Each of these philosophies has important implications for the direction that marketing education has taken and will take in the future and for the implicit value systems embraced by marketers.

### Positivism/Behaviorism

Positivism [16] emerged in the early 19th century with the French philosopher Comte. According to him all problems of nature and life are in principle capable of being solved by means of observation and experiment. German positivists in the late 19th and early 20th century represented their view as "monistic." According to the monistic philosophy anything non-material which transcends matter was simply denied. That which could not be verified or studied with the methods of physical science was not worthy. The most recent version of positivism is known as neo-positivism and originated in the 1930s. Without entering into great detail, all positivistic currents limit the concept of "science" to empirical science excluding philosophy and theology. Greatest preference is given to the sciences of nature which are considered to be the genuine sciences because they do not accept anything that is not verified experimentally. Sciences of man and culture are considered rank sciences. In the investigation of any phenomenon, mathematical logic as represented in the scientific method is the modus operandi.

### Normativism

The origins of normativism [16] are less certain than positivism but it provides a distinct alternative to the positivistic perspective. Science according to normativism is made up of physical, philosophical and theological circles of knowledge [16] each an integral link to the other. The rules for embodying knowledge under the umbrella of science are less rigid than the scientific method and empirical verification which the positivists require.

The results of the positive and normative philosophies become critical when they are extended into the arena of ethical consideration. Because it excludes philosophy and theology as science, positivism shuns value judgments about the ethics or broader morality of an action. Newman [14, p. 65], an avowed normativist, stated:

> I observe, then, that if you drop any science out of the circle of knowledge, you cannot keep its place vacant for it; that science is forgotten; the other sciences close up or, in other words, they exceed their proper bounds, and intrude where they have no right.

Positivism arbitrarily drops elements out from the circles of knowledge to which Newman refers. It is precisely the philosophical and the theological circles of knowledge which the normativists include as elements of science but which are subverted by positivism. Thus, the ethical normative perspective calls for a prescription of what is acceptable based upon the interaction of the three circles of knowledge that represent science (physical, theology, philosophy). The positive view rejects the humanistic elements of man as not being subject to empirical verification.

## THE PHILOSOPHIES AND EDUCATION

The positivistic approach in the university has been the preeminent contemporary approach to the study of the hard sciences as well as psychology, economics, education, and business [18]. This approach to university education began to emerge between 1920 and 1940, and in the period following World War II achieved preeminence. Under such a paradigm the university's mission was one of producing value free research. Collective normative judgments represented subjective preference and were not subject to scientific verification. Instruction was to consist of more than personal preference, it was to be objective, verified knowledge that was value free. In the conduct of his classroom and research the instructor was to hold to intellectual standards in terms of acquisition, analysis, and discussion of appropriate bodies of knowledge.

The ethical philosophy underlying marketing in the period since World War II has also been dominated by positivism. In the 1950s the managerial study of marketing was the predominant theme consisting largely of description and operational techniques to handle problems. The marketing concept emerged as the key to providing a harmony between customer satisfaction and profitability through integrated consumer-oriented planning. In this closed system the individual consumer, not the marketer, provides the normative value judgments by way of his economic vote. Though the marketing concept has endured as a central tenet, the marketing discipline began to become increasingly cognizant of its eclectic nature. More and more the work of mathematics, economics, sociology, psychology, anthropology and other positivistically oriented branches of the university came to bear on marketing. Marketing educators in the 1960s become more aware of themselves as scientists in the mold of those who they saw as providing vital inputs to their discipline. Greater reliance on the measurable and controllable behavioral experiment, increased use of computer technology, mathematics and the behavioral sciences have all been hallmarks of the more eclectic marketing. The reflection of these interests came in the form of more varied courses in computer technology, the development of courses in consumer behavior and the development of more sophisticated research and experimental design courses in the marketing curriculum. Beginning with the marketing concept and through the development of more diverse tool courses, the period through the late 1960s was solidly positivistic.

This positivistic view transcended each and every course taught ranging from consumer behavior through personal selling. In consumer behavior we attempted to describe and predict perception, attitudes, personality and learning based upon empirical findings. Where possible we attempted to teach how these findings could be utilized in marketing strategy. In market research we spoke about methodologies of data collection and analysis, and the sanctimony of the scientific method. In advertising we discussed the process of building a communications bridge upon consumer research by using techniques of media selection and copy strategy to influence consumers in directions compatible with an advertiser's goals. In product strategy, issues of management, organization, positioning, segmentation, deletion were considered.

The positivistic value system which was the foundation of marketing education and which paralleled all of our instruction avoided value judgment. The user of the information which the education presents attaches his own morality to its proper use. The oughts of society are ultimately determined by the empirical success of strategy as reflected in the high frequency consumer purchase behavior.

The empirical measurement of profit provided the framework for the normative value judgment. In such a context morality and ethics were tertiary. The perspective of the positivistically oriented curriculum is illustrated in Figure 1.

FIGURE 1

|  | POSITIVISTIC VIEW | NORMATIVE VIEW |
|---|---|---|
| Overall View | Education should be value free and all that is known should be presented to students. | Education must be taught in an ethical and moral framework. |
| Assumption | Based on an exclusively empirical view of science. | Based on a blend of empirical, theological, and philosophical views of science. |
| Need to Teach Values | Each man will attach his own morality to his action. | The morality of each man exists in the context of broader moral universe and this must be part of what is taught. |
| Marketing Concept | Profitability is the ultimate goal with customer satisfaction as a by-product. | Societal satisfaction is the ultimate goal with profit as a residual. |
| Consumer Behavior | Uncover and teach the elements of behavior and information processing to better predict and control behavior. | Uncover and teach the elements of behavior and information processing in the context of whether marketers should as well as can gain control of specific behaviors. |
| Marketing Research | The scientific method is the mode of investigation. Methodologies should be taught based on their empirically verified ability to work. | The scientific method is just one mode of investigation. Methodologies should be taught based upon their verified ability to work as well as their ability to infringe on the consumer's rights in data collection and application. |
| Promotion | Teaching of communication elements, processes, and techniques based upon their ability to gain increased compliance of the target market. | Teaching of communication elements, processes, and techniques based upon their ability to work as well as their desirability and the likelihood that their effectiveness is based upon a subversion of the consumer's judgemental processes. |
| Product Strategy | Education aimed at teaching strategies of product development, product management, and deletion which best enhance the firm's competitive stance. | Education aimed at teaching strategies of product development, product management, and deletion within the context of resource, safety, legal, environmental and moral imperatives. |
| Pricing Strategy | Teaching of verified tactics that aid in pricing to achieve maximal profits. | Teaching of verified tactics within the context of the moral impact of price changes. Possible subversion of the consumer's judgmental processes as well as the ability of price to achieve satisfactory profits. |
| Social Issues | If taught at all should be value free. Should be examined as a body of knowledge. | Must be studied as an integral element of the curriculum to provide students with a moral perspective of their discipline. |

## Change in the Late 1960s

The late 1960s marked an important point for the university as a whole and marketing education specifically. Here was a time when our institutions as well as marketing practice came under increased external pressure from social critics, consumerists, environmentalists, government agencies, and others advocating change in specific marketing behaviors. Among some of the charges made against marketers were of the production of shoddy, unsafe or unnutritious products, wasteful products and product packaging, misleading and distasteful advertising, pollution, improper appeals to vulnerable consumer groups, improper selling tactics, deceptive pricing, unethical methods of obtaining market research and subsequent misuse of findings. The list of charges seemed endless. For the most part this criticism of marketing behavior emerged from outside the discipline. It is safe to say that marketers were unprepared for this deluge of criticism and thus the initial reaction was defensive. Corrective behaviors were less a part of a conscious overall effort to alter the ethical and moral marketing behavior and more a patchwork of programs designed to repair problems arising from a stream of crises.

This hostility that marketers were faced with came as an enigma to many. After all, marketing education and marketers had preached and believed in the gospel of the marketing concept. Despite the post-war acceptance of the concept, marketing continued to come under increased external pressure. Bell and Emory [3] questioned whether the marketing concept will lead to mutually compatible goals for marketing and society. In the past, they stated, we have assumed the customer satisfaction and societal good are one in the same; however, the societal response against marketing indicated perhaps that such an assumption is not valid. Peter Drucker [5] went so far as to call consumerism the shame of the marketing concept.

The point is that the rules of marketing changed in the late 1960s and marketing educators had not provided their students with the proper tools to deal with the rule change.

If one examines the problem from the positive/normative perspective the question of why the challenge to marketing emerged is quickly resolved. In essence marketing education itself is a culprit for the attack that took place and that is still taking place on the marketing discipline. The attack is simply a natural result of the positivistic philosophy which has been the underpinning of the post-war marketing curriculum. It has been stated by Martindale [13] that positivism is not unethical but nonethical. This author takes exception to this notion for when an attempt is made to avoid an ethical framework, that decision itself is a normative judgment. In essence positivist education implicitly assigns its own norm by virtue of the absence of ethical and moral guidance offered to the individual. Boulding [4] has commented on the inevitable opportunity in our economic system for the individual to sacrifice moral principles for personal gain. "The institutions of exchange provide neither the policy nor the integration by which moral values can be sustained."

Gelb and Brien [7] suggested that the universities share the burden of guilt for business executives failing to fully recognize the need for "social responsibility" in business action. Hawkins and Cocanougher [8] extended this argument of burden a step further in a study conducted with groups of business and non-business majors to determine whether their exposure to coursework in each field contributed to the ethical perspective which was held. Results indicate that:

... there may be a relationship between educational environment and development of standards of ethics. The existence of such an influential relationship suggests that the academic community should carefully evaluate its responsibility both to future business executives and the consuming public in regards to standards of business behavior. [8]

Essentially, a relationship is posited here in which the morality and ethics inherent in the education received by marketers is reflected in their eventual behavior in the marketplace. Positivism in marketing education effectively dropped the two circles of knowledge, theology and philosophy, out of the realm of relevance in the name of methodologies, techniques, and narrowly defined managerial concepts. Essentially, marketing educators lost sight of the fact that its ultimate goal is connected with a definite purpose which refers to the well-being and perfection of man. "In the realm of economics the norms are often too much determined by the interest of certain groups ..." [16, p. 206]. Van Laer [16, p. 207] notes that the special operative sciences such as marketing,

... should be guided by higher norms of goodness and beauty, deduced from a knowledge of man as an individual and as a social being which is not onesided but takes all of man's aspects into consideration.

The positivistic philosophy fails on this account. The ethical and moral structure which Boulding indicates our business leaders lack, was never provided by our educational system.

Marketers and marketing educators were caught by surprise by the outcry against marketing. As indicated in Figure 1, the more societal orientation that critics called for is embodied in the normative perspective which was not widely used. In a 1969 study [15] it was noted that social issues related to marketing were not covered extensively. Two movements in marketing emerged in the late 1960s. On one hand a call for extending the traditional marketing methods to non-traditional arenas was made [11]. Simultaneously change in the treatment of social issues (ethics, morality, consumerism, ecology, business responsibility, etc.) in the marketing curriculum was called for [7, 12].

The broadening movement largely was embodied in applications to health care, education, religion, etc. and resulted in little alteration in university coursework. The critical movement for helping marketers adapt to the criticism facing the behavior of marketing practitioners was potentially the emergence of a greater social issue orientation in the marketing curriculum. Kangun [10] conducted a study in 1971 surveying schools of their anticipated emphasis of social issues within the context of existing courses. This did not necessarily involve the creation of new course titles. In introductory undergraduate, advanced undergraduate and in graduate marketing courses approximately 62%, 75%, and 76% of respondents respectively indicated that they would not include significant coverage of social issues in the future. A study by Gaedeke [6] indicated that in 1971 only 35 percent of the 84 accredited AACSB schools offered or planned to offer a separate course related to social issues between 1971 and 1973. The remaining two-thirds of the schools were either not planning or uncertain about their plans to offer a separate social issue course. Though the percentage in the Kangun and Gaedeke studies indicated that there was an upturn in social issue considerations and courses, the numbers were still small. A follow-up survey by Hise [9, p. 13] stated, "A number of schools have indicated that marketing curricula include or expect to include a course emphasizing social issues and responsibility. However, such is apparently not the case in practice for fewer than ten schools [sample size of 135] indicated the availability of a course of this type." Rather, the traditional marketing management, distribution, research, behavior, and promotion courses dominated the offerings surveyed. Evidently between the Gaedeke study in 1971 and the Hise study in 1973 the percentage of schools offering separate socially oriented courses diminished markedly.

Another possible indicator of the infusion of social issues into marketing is its treatment in textbooks. Issues such as legal factors have long been a stand-by treated in separate chapters in marketing texts and this remains in most introductory texts. If any change at all can be noted it would be in some of the contemporary principles texts of a social issues chapter in the text. Texts devoted solely to the discussion of environments or social issues have apparently fallen on hard times. Though the text is a poor measure of treatment of subject matter by instructors, we can conclude that the average marketing student probably has more exposure to the societal issues facing marketing than did his counterpart ten years ago. To date, however, the visible signs do not indicate a pronounced trend in the curriculum toward significant consideration of social issues within the context of the marketing curriculum.

The Future

Results of the Kangun [10], Gaedeke [6] and Hise [9] studies do not indicate a broad adoption of the social issue orientation into the marketing curriculum. The question which arises is whether the conditions that caused public criticism of marketing behavior in the late 1960s and early 1970s have changed. The indications are that they have not; consumerism, environmentalism, government regulation, legal wrangling, and a call for more sensitive concern for the ethical and moral issues have not disappeared. Wilson [16, p. 32] states that, "the moral question is an issue to which professions should continue to respond if there is to be an improvement in the moral stance of business and increased legitimate commitment of moral issues themselves within the institution of business." Andrews [2] calls upon the professional schools to help define the new social problems and to help create the concepts necessary to solving them.

The scenario of conflict and reaction has been a mode that marketers have been accustomed to in recent years. The future is one which is in part controlled by marketing educators. Figure 1 clearly distinguishes the differences which the positive and normative philosophies have for the way in which the marketing curriculum is presented. To date the positivistic perspective has not provided the framework necessary for marketing practitioners to operate in harmony with the broad environments. Indications are that little visible effort to develop social issues within the marketing curriculum has been made. It appears that marketing education is at a crossroad of whether to proceed with the traditional positive curriculum or with the more value laden normative perspective must be made.

PRESCRIPTION FOR THE FUTURE

The unavoidable philosophical perspective of the future for marketing educators is for a normative value system.

Without direction from educators, practitioners cannot be expected to gain the broader moral and social perspective which is being demanded of them and which is becoming increasingly necessary to survive in the exchange system. Marketers are part of a social and human system which must be consciously guided toward the paths of appropriate ethical and moral behavior. If a new attractive package is to be developed which visually appears to have more product than a competitor's, then the marketer of today and the future must look beyond whether consumers like the package and purchase it. The rightness of a marketing decision can no longer be based solely upon the positivistic notion of high frequency behavior. Rather the questions of should the package design be used or should special labels indicating similar content to other packages be included must be asked. The consequences in terms of possible legislation or consumer discontent are the realities for those who neglect the normative perspective.

The direction which marketing education is currently taking is clouded. Adoption of separate social issues courses never achieve widespread acceptance and their numbers are apparently diminishing. High percentages of programs give little or no treatment to social issues.

To adequately deal with the social imperatives of the future marketers it seems must move on two fronts. First, coursework dealing with the social issues that will face them as practitioners must be developed. Indications are that only a half hearted attempt was made to accomplish this in the past. Secondly, to be truly effective, the social issues of ethics and the morality of action must become embodied in each course we teach. Currently textbooks tend to devote a chapter or two to social issues. More parallelism between the teaching of principles, findings, tactics and strategy; and ethics and morality must occur. Thus, the marketing educator has a dual responsibility to simultaneously teach how new products are developed as well as whether new products should be developed.

CONCLUSION

The special operative sciences in particular will always have to pay attention to the norms of ethics. It is not sufficient to know that a particular way of acting is useful or desirable for the attainment of this or that purpose. Man has to see also whether or not this way of acting conflicts with the demands of human nature and fosters his integral and ultimate welfare. In other words, these sciences must always take ethical considerations into account. [16, p. ]92]

If marketing educators are to fully equip their students with the ability to operate in the business environment and reduce conflict some conscious decisions about the positive or normative philosophies underlying their instruction and curriculum must be made. The direction that marketing education will take is at a crucial crossroad.

REFERENCES

1. "A Marketing Man Takes Marketers to Task," Business Week (July 28, 1975), 42-3.

2. Andrews, Kenneth R. "Toward Professionalism in Business Management," Harvard Business Review, 47 (March-April 1969).

3. Bell, Martin L. and C. William Emory. "The Faltering Marketing Concept," Journal of Marketing, 35 (October 1971), 37-42.

4.  Boulding, Kenneth. Beyond Economics. Ann Arbor, Michigan: University of Michigan Press, 1969.

5.  Drucker, Peter F. "The Shame of Marketing," Marketing/Communications (August 1969), 60.

6.  Gaedeke, Ralph M. "Social Issues in Marketing Curricula, A Status Report," Collegiate News and Views, 16 (1973), 13-6.

7.  Gelb, Betsy D. and Richard H. Brien. "Survival and Social Responsibility: Themes for Marketing Education and Management," Journal of Marketing, 35 (April 1971), 3-9.

8.  Hawkins, Del I. and A. Benton Cocanougher. "Student Evaluations of the Ethics of Marketing Practices: The Role of Marketing Education," Journal of Marketing, 36 (April 1972), 61-4.

9.  Hise, Richard T. "The Marketing Curriculum: Does It Reflect the Recommendations of Marketing Educators?" Collegiate News and Views, 18 (Spring 1975), 11-6.

10. Kangun, Norman, "Societal Issues in the Marketing Curriculum: An Optimistic Assessment," Journal of Marketing, 37 (April 1973), 60-63.

11. Kotler, Philip and Sidney J. Levy. "Broadening the Concept of Marketing," Journal of Marketing, 33 (January 1969), 5.

12. Lazer, William. "Marketing Education: Commitments for the 1970s," Journal of Marketing, 34 (July 1970), 7-11.

13. Martindale, Don. "Social Disorganization: The Conclict of the Normative and Empirical Approaches," in Howard Becker and Alvin Boskoff, eds., Modern Sociological Theory. New York: Holt-Dryden, 1957, 340-67.

14. Newman, John H. The Idea of a University. New York: Longmans, Green and Company, 1947.

15. Scott, Richard M. and Norton E. Marks. "Contemporary Changes in Basic Marketing," Collegiate News and Views, 13 (March 1970), 15-8.

16. Van Laer, P. Henry. Philosophy of Science, Part 2, Pittsburgh, Pennsylvania: DuQuesne University Press, 1962.

17. Wilson, James A. "Morality and the Contemporary Business System," Journal of Contemporary Business (Summer 1975), 31-57.

18. Young, Stanley. "Behaviorism--A Critique," working draft, University of Massachusetts, Amherst, 1975.

# REFLECTIONS ON CREATIVITY AND RELEVANCE OF CONSUMER RESEARCH

Yoram Wind, University of Pennsylvania

## ABSTRACT

An examination of the current status of the consumer research literature suggests a need for: (a) greater creativity in methodology and theory and (b) increased relevance of the research—moving from a product (researcher) oriented research to a marketing (user) oriented research. Some suggestions for increased creativity and relevance are offered.

## INTRODUCTION

With few exceptions, the typical reaction of marketing practitioners to the academic research on consumer behavior is negative. Irrelevant, academic, ivory tower, and impractical are often descriptors used by industry based marketing managers and researchers to describe their disenchantment with consumer research. Only a small fraction of the subscribers to the Journal of Consumer Research are from industry, and most likely the majority of those are the "academically oriented" marketing researchers—those who frequent the AMA and ACR professional conferences.

At the same time, research on consumer behavior and especially (but not only) commercial studies of consumer behavior have not escaped criticism concerning their lack of creativity. Consider, for example, the frequent and not always justified use of Likert type attitude scales as the major attitude measurement instrument or the numerous studies on value expectancy models.

Are these criticisms of the lack of creativity and relevance in consumer research justified? The answer is obviously not a simple "yes" or "no." The objectives of this paper are to offer my personal assessment of the degree of creativity and relevance of consumer research and to suggest some ways to improve these two key ingredients of research on consumer behavior.

## CREATIVITY IN CONSUMER RESEARCH

In exploring the degree of creativity in research on consumer behavior, it is necessary to distinguish between creativity in methodology and in concepts and theory.

### Creativity in Methodology

An examination of the consumer research literature reveals a high level of methodological innovativeness and creativity. The most notable methodological developments are those borrowed and adapted from mathematical psychology. Consider, for example, multidimensional scaling procedures for the measurement of consumers' perceptions and preferences (e.g., [5,8,4]), conjoint measurement (e.g., [9,10]), and other approaches to the study of consumer choice processes (such as Bettman's decision nets [2] and Jacoby's information experiments [13]). More recently there have been proposed a number of complex measurement procedures which simplify the respondent task, provide richer insight into consumer behavior, and improve our ability to predict consumers' responses to new stimuli. One such innovative design incorporates conjoint measurement, multinomial logit analysis, an orthogonal array, and BIB design [6].

Methodological innovations in the study of consumer behavior have had a significant impact on the direction of re-search on consumer behavior. The innovative applications of measurement models, which were borrowed primarily from mathematical psychology, and the developments of innovative designs for research on consumer behavior, did enrich not only the consumer behavior and marketing disciplines but also the other behavioral sciences.

In contrast to these and other innovative methodological developments and applications, the majority of consumer research would have to be characterized, unfortunately, as nonimaginative. Most industrial studies of consumer behavior rely on relatively standardized surveys which are analyzed quite superficially with the aid of cross tabs. Even more serious is the focus of many of the published consumer research studies which tend to employ some "fad" analytical procedures (such as multiple regression analysis, factor analysis, or MDS) without any attempt to offer new methodological insights or improve the current procedures (so as to increase their relevance to the problem under study).

There is nothing wrong in the straightforward utilization of established multivariate statistical techniques in the study of consumer behavior. One would hope, however, that at least the published studies would demonstrate a higher degree of creativity, especially when the use of these techniques often requires a set of assumptions which are not always consistent with our knowledge of consumer behavior. Over the last decade the technical sophistication of most consumer researchers has improved considerably, and the analytical techniques, in the majority of cases, are employed correctly. Yet, one would hope that there is more to research than the correct utilization of some canned multivariate statistical computer program. Nor is it creativity for the sake of creativity that should guide the researcher. Consumer research should not rely only on designs utilized in the past, but rather attempt to explore new and creative designs. This requires a fresh look at, and specification of, the consumer behavior problem under study. The researcher should ask himself, "What research designs can be utilized to best achieve the study's objectives?" Consideration should be given, for example, to experimental vs. nonexperimental designs, longitudinal vs. cross sectional studies, unobtrusive vs. obtrusive measures, projective vs. direct approaches, open ended vs. structured tasks, etc.

Once an overall design is decided upon, attention should be given to the stimulus definition and respondent task. Consider, for example, the numerous studies reporting on consumers' lifestyle and psychographics (including studies which fall under the label of need or attitude segmentation studies). The bulk of these studies is based on the selection of a large set of items (typically ranging from 60-300 items) which are rated by a sample of respondents on a 5-, 6-, or 7-point Likert type scale ranging from "describes me completely" to "does not describe me at all" or from "strongly agree" to "strongly disagree." The resulting data are then usually submitted to some factor analysis program which provides both the factor loading structure and the factor scores, which in turn are often used in subsequent multiple regression or discriminant analysis aimed at relating the lifestyle data to some purchase behavior.

This procedure has, of course, a number of advantages. The data collection procedure is very simple (it can be self-administered), the selection of items is usually done by stealing seemingly "relevant" items from previous studies and other sources, and the data analysis stage is straightforward requiring little methodological skills. Once such a procedure has been established, there seems to be little value in publishing or attempting to publish papers based on this procedure (unless, of course, one were to use projectable samples which can provide generalizable substantive findings on patterns of lifestyle or psychographics). It is surprising, therefore, that so many researchers have continued to conduct such studies, with no or little attempt to improve the procedure. Such improvements can and should encompass all aspects of the study and include:[1]

The selection of items—Instead of an ad hoc selection of items, the selection of items following the design of an appropriate lifestyle model.

The respondent task—Instead of the conventional rating scale, the design of more creative data collection procedures utilizing any number of approaches such as those attempted in personality impressions and other psychological studies.

The analytical procedure involved—Instead of the conventional factor analysis which often results in a very large number of factors, one can consider procedures such as higher order factor analysis [19] or other appropriate approaches depending on the nature of the data collected.

Methodological creativity cannot and should not be limited to the development of a research design and plan of analysis. A strong need for methodological creativity exists also at the analysis stage. Consider, for example, the following study which was conducted to assess the differences between working and nonworking wives with respect to preference and purchase patterns of certain food items. Surprisingly, the initial results showed no significant differences between the two segments. The analysis could have stopped here (with most likely a publishable article on the results). Yet, the no-difference finding required an explanation. One possible explanation was that each of the segments was quite heterogeneous. To test this, the working women were further segmented based on their occupation (professional, white collar, and blue collar), and the nonworking wives were segmented based on their degree of involvement with activities outside the house. Not surprisingly, there were significant differences among the subsegments of each of the two basic segments. Furthermore, the professional segment had characteristics very similar to the nonworking but actively involved outside the house segment; while the nonworking wives had characteristics very similar to the white and blue collar worker segments.

Creativity in Concepts and Theory

Most of the concepts and hypotheses tested in consumer behavior studies are borrowed from the behavioral sciences (especially social psychology). Whereas borrowing in itself can be quite useful, it is quite discouraging to note that little attention has been given by consumer researchers to the modification of concepts or hypotheses, or to the development of new ones consistent with the idiosyncratic characteristics of consumer behavior.

Some of the concepts, models, and theories proposed in the consumer behavior literature are insightful and innovative. The Howard [11] and Nicosia [15] models of consumer decision processes were developed in the early 60s and are innovative and insightful (especially in contrast to the consumer flow models of the late 60s and early 70s). Similarly, there are a number of creative consumer behavior applications of concepts and areas of study borrowed from the

behavioral sciences—such as the study of time [12], gift giving behavior [1], and socioeconomic incongruency [16], to mention just a few. Yet, most of the published consumer research studies focus on concepts and hypotheses which are neither insightful nor of any practical relevance. Consider, for example, the explosion of value expectancy studies and the numerous studies in search of a relationship between some personality traits and purchase behavior. Lacking are consumer behavior models which take into account the idiosyncratic characteristics of consumer processes (e.g., shopping, purchase, consumption, and disposal processes), the needs of the users of consumer behavior knowledge (the marketing and public policy decision makers who need information on consumer responses to various stimuli) and the relevant behavioral science concepts and theories.

To illustrate the difference between a creative and the more conventional approach to consumer concepts, let's consider the area of personality. The conventional approach to personality in consumer behavior has been to attempt to establish the statistical link between some general personality test and some form of consumer behavior. A more creative approach would call for the development of a consumption related personality inventory designed to explain those general (or product category dependent) personality traits which relate to the consumer behavior process. Such a consumer related personality inventory could try to identify types of shoppers (e.g., impulsive vs. planners), dominant purchase criteria (e.g., economy vs. convenience), preference for variety (e.g., size of desired product portfolios), and other relevant dimensions of the consumer shopping, purchase, consumption, and disposal processes.

THE QUESTION OF RELEVANCE

While assessing the relevance of consumer research, two points of view should be considered: (a) the view of the marketing practitioner or public policy decision maker who is concerned with the application of the methodology and/or findings and concepts of consumer research to his specific needs, i.e., the transferability of methodology and the testability of concepts and hypotheses, and (b) the views of students of consumer behavior and the marketing practitioners and public policy decision makers who are interested in substantive findings and knowledge about consumer behavior, i.e., the availability of generalized principles of behavior.

The methodology currently (and potentially) employed in consumer research can easily be transferred to the commercial study of consumer behavior. Consider, for example, the utilization of the tradeoff (conjoint analysis) model and algorithms which, since their introduction to the marketing profession in the early 70s [7,9,14], have been employed in over 200 commercial studies.

In contrast to the transferability of consumer research methodology, the concepts and findings from consumer research studies have limited generalizability (primarily due to nonrepresentative samples).[2] The most one can hope for, therefore, is the utilization of these concepts and findings as hypotheses which should be tested in subsequent commercial studies.

The consumer behavior discipline has failed in developing a body of substantive findings. This shortcoming can be corrected if attention is given over the next decade to the need for accumulating a substantive body of knowledge of consumer behavior. The need for substantive knowledge of consumer behavior is quite evident if one considers, for example, the way consumer related public policy decisions

---

[1]For a discussion of some of the limitations of the typical lifestyle studies and suggestions for alternative approaches, see Wind and Green [18].

[2]For a discussion of the nonrepresentative sample issue in consumer research, see Ferber [3].

are made. In making these decisions, there is quite a reliance on the "economic man" model, which could lead to erroneous decisions. It is imperative, therefore, that predictive models be developed and a substantive body of
knowledge be established to assess the likely impact of
various public policy decisions on the economic activities
of consumers—their choice behavior and welfare (as perceived by them, not the regulators). The lack of a substantive body of knowledge limits considerably the relevance of research on consumer behavior to the other behavioral science disciplines. The link between consumer behavior and the other disciplines has been predominantly
one-sided—borrowing from the other disciplines, but little
impact of consumer research on the development of the
lending disciplines. To the extent that such impact has
existed, it has been primarily in the methodological domain.

More serious, however, is the fact that a significant part
of the current research on consumer behavior ignores the
needs of the "real world." Most consumer research is "producer (researcher) oriented" as opposed to "marketing (user) oriented." This orientation has led to overemphasis of
methodological niceties and a tendency to ignore or over-
simplify many key aspects of consumer behavior. This oversimplification is often justified on the grounds that it
leads to more manageable research designs. Its main feature
is, however, that it does not require the development of
new concepts and research procedures. The cost of this
oversimplification is not only the lack of more innovative
approaches to consumer research, but also the considerable
reduction in the value of the studies to their potential
users (e.g., marketing managers or public policy decision
makers).

To illustrate the difference between most of the current
research on consumer behavior and the potentially more
relevant, real-world oriented research, consider some of
the following implications of a real-world orientation to
research on consumer behavior:

> The unit of analysis—The shift from an individual to
> the buying center. Given this shift how, for example,
> should one analyze incongruent preferences within the
> buying center, or segment the given market?[3]

> The object of analysis—The shift from a focus on a
> single product or brand to product assortment. The
> conceptual and methodological implications of this
> shift are numerous. Conceptually, one should consider
> the order of acquisition of items within an assortment
> and the positioning (and centrality) of various prod-
> ucts and brands within a specific assortment. These
> new concepts require the design of new respondent task
> definitions, stimulus sets, and analytical procedures.

> The time dimension—The shift from static to dynamic
> analysis. Although the desire for dynamic consumer
> behavior models has long been recognized (e.g., [15]),
> most of the research on consumer behavior has taken a
> static view relying predominantly on cross sectional
> data.

> The domain of interest—A real-world orientation calls
> for two major shifts in the domain examined in consum-
> er studies: (a) a shift from almost exclusive focus
> on the purchase decision process and act to a broader
> focus on purchase, usage, maintenance (when appropri-
> ate), and product disposal, and (b) the shift from a
> primary focus on consumer characteristics to the link
> between marketing controllable variables (e.g., prod-
> uct features, price, etc.) and consumer characteristics
> and behavior. This may suggest greater focus on con-

---

For a discussion of some of the conceptual and methodological problems associated with the buying center, see [17].

ditional analysis, and further developmental work on
multidimensional psychophysics studies.

## CONCLUDING REMARKS

Many of you may disagree with my pessimistic evaluation of
the state of creativity and relevance of consumer research.
A few exceptionally creative, insightful, and relevant
studies can occasionally be found in the consumer research
literature,[4] and even in some "higher risk" commercial projects. Yet, the discipline, despite tremendous methodological developments and sophistication, has demonstrated, in
the majority of its published and unpublished commercial
studies, a relatively low level of creativity and relevance. This lack of creativity and relevance is also evident in most of the standard consumer behavior texts. Most
of these texts are organized around various behavioral science concepts (e.g., perception, motivation, social class,
etc.), devote little attention to concepts unique to consumer behavior, report on almost no conclusive substantive
findings, and, with the exception of a few forced applications of some concepts and findings to marketing strategy
variables, they provide little insight into the relevance
of consumer behavior research to the various marketing decisions of firms and public policy decision makers.

The need for greater creativity and relevance in research
on consumer behavior is quite evident and should be viewed
as the major challenge to consumer researchers. Devoting
greater attention to the creativity and relevance issue is
essential to the continued growth and viability of the consumer research discipline, and its relevance to the various
users of this research.

## REFERENCES

1. Belk, R. W. "It's the Thought that Counts: A Signed
   Digraph Analysis of Gift-Giving," Journal of Consumer
   Research, 3 (December 1976), 155-162.

2. Bettman, J. R. "Toward a Statistics for Consumer Decision Net Models," Journal of Consumer Research, 1
   (June 1974), 71-80.

3. Ferber, R. "Research by Convenience," Journal of Consumer Research, 4 (June 1977).

4. Green, P. E. "Marketing Applications of MDS: Assessment and Outlook," Journal of Marketing, 39 (January
   1975), 24-31.

5. Green, P. E. and F. J. Carmone. Multidimensional
   Scaling and Related Techniques in Marketing Analysis.
   Boston, Mass.: Allyn & Bacon, Inc., 1970.

6. _____. "A BIB/Logit Approach to Conjoint Analysis," Wharton School Working Paper, April 1977.

7. Green, P. E. and V. R. Rao. "Conjoint Measurement for
   Quantifying Judgmental Data," Journal of Marketing Research, 8 (August 1971), 355-363.

8. _____. Applied Multidimensional Scaling: A
   Comparison of Approaches and Algorithms. New York:
   Holt, Rinehart & Winston, Inc., 1972.

9. Green, P. E. and Y. Wind. Multi-Attribute Decisions
   in Marketing: A Measurement Approach. Hinsdale, Ill.:
   The Dryden Press, 1973.

---

[4]The specific studies mentioned in this paper are not intended to present an exhaustive list of creative studies,
but rather illustrate this type of creative research.

10. Green, P. E. and Y. Wind. "New Way to Measure Consumers' Judgment," <u>Harvard Business Review</u>, 53 (July-August 1975), 107-117.

11. Howard, J. A. <u>Marketing Management: Analysis and Planning</u>. Homewood, Ill.: Richard D. Irwin, 1963, 31-114.

12. Jacoby, J., G. J. Szybillo, and C. K. Berning. "Time and Consumer Behavior: An Interdisciplinary Overview," <u>Journal of Consumer Research</u>, 2 (March 1976), 320-339.

13. Jacoby, J., G. J. Szybillo, and J. Busato-Schach. "Information Acquisition Behavior in Brand Choice Situations," <u>Journal of Consumer Research</u>, 3 (March 1977), 209-216.

14. Johnson, R. M. "Trade-Off Analysis of Consumer Values," <u>Journal of Marketing Research</u>, 11 (May 1974), 121-127.

15. Nicosia, F. M. <u>Consumer Decision Processes: Marketing and Advertising Implications</u>. Englewood Cliffs, N.J.: Prentice-Hall, 1966.

16. Wind, Y. "Incongruency of Socioeconomic Variables and Buying Behavior," in P. R. McDonald, ed., <u>Marketing Involvement in Society and the Economy</u>. Proceedings of the American Marketing Association, August 1969, 362-367.

17. _____. "Organizational Buying Center: A Research Agenda," in Gerald Zaltman and Thomas V. Bonoma, eds., <u>Organizational Buying Behavior</u>. Chicago: AMA, in press.

18. Wind, Y. and P. E. Green. "Some Conceptual Measurement and Analytical Problems in Life Style Research," in William Wells, ed., <u>Life Style and Psychographics</u>. Chicago: AMA, 1974.

19. Wind, Y., P. E. Green, and A. Jain. "Higher Order Factor Analysis in the Classification of Psychographic Variables," <u>Journal of the Market Research Society</u>, 15 (1973), 224-232.

# TRANSACTIONS AMONG BUYING AND SELLING CENTERS

Arch G. Woodside, University of South Carolina
James L. Taylor, University of South Carolina
S. Travis Pritchett, University of South Carolina
William M. Morgenroth, University of South Carolina

## ABSTRACT

Two criticisms of most of the research on buyer behavior
are reviewed. Analysis of the interaction process within
and between naturally occurring buying and selling centers
and one insurance selling center suggest useful theoretical
and practical field research implications on marketing
transactions.

## INTRODUCTION

While Kotler [12] has proposed that the essence of marketing is the transaction, that is, the exchange of values
between two parties, Capon, Holbrook, and Hulbert [3],
Rogers [18], and Howard [11] have criticized buyer behavior and diffusion research for lacking a process orientation. Transactions in buyer behavior imply a process
of exchanging values between two or more parties. Most research into transactions has focused on the purchase outcome, e.g., Evans [6], and not the interaction process.

The psychological orientation in buyer behavior has been a
second major criticism since the emphasis has been placed
on the individual instead of the group as the basic unit
of analysis. Howard [11] has stressed the role of the
group in shaping buyer behavior in his review of Liu and
Duff's [13] principle of the "strength in weak ties," that
is, a certain amount of heterophilydyadic relationships
between unlike people is necessary for a new product to be
purchased.

Wind [26] has offered a particularly useful criticism of
the psychological orientation in buyer behavior. He notes
that the relevant unit of analysis typically is the buying
center and not the individual, and although one person or
persons will have key responsibility for each of the center's buying decisions, one cannot neglect the influence
of the interests and objectives of other group members on
this person's behavior. Wind provides a reward-balance
model of buyer behavior to direct attention to the buying
center:

The buyer (P) must maintain balance between his perceived
relationships with the other members of the group (O) and
the object of these relationships (X). The buyer (P)-the
purchasing agent in the industrial buying center or the
housewife in the household buying center-is the person
designated by the group as responsible for most purchases
[27].

Purchase considerations of most products and services new
to the household or firm are likely to involve joint decisions made by buying centers. The substantial likelihood
of conflict among members of the buying center in purchasing products new to the household or firm has been hypothesized by Sheth [19, 20]. Conflict is likely to occur
since the expectations and choice criteria used to evaluate the products are likely to be different among purchasing agents, engineers, users and financial officers, or
wives, husbands, children, and grandparents. Conflict is
likely to be resolved using one or more of four processes:

1. Problem solving - actively search for more information, deliberate more on available information, and seek
out other suppliers' (or stores) not seriously considered
before.

2. Persuasion - attempt to influence a dissenting member
by pointing out the importance of overall corporate (household) objectives and how his or her criterion is not likely
to attain these objectives.

3. Bargaining - changing the differences in relative importance of the buying goals or objectives of the individuals involved.

4. Politicking and back stabbing - name calling, forming
secret alliances, and delay tactics [19].

Capon et al. [3] were able to locate only one interactive,
verbal, field observational study [16, 17, 25] in their
review of selling processes and buyer behavior. Nearly
all selling process studies may be classified as nonverbal
or verbal but one-way in perspective with examinations of
two-way exchange processes not performed [3]. Thus, the
study of behavior between members of a buying center and a
selling center suffer from the same lack of process orientation as the study of behavior within buying centers.
The work of Varela [21] on designs of complex persuasion is
a noteworthy exception.

Varela [21] provides excerpts of transcripts of transactions between buying and selling centers to demonstrate
applications of social psychological theories to actual
business settings. As a consultant to a textile manufacturer, Varela applied assimilation-contrast theory [10],
cognitive dissonance [7], psychological reactance [1], distraction [22], and foot-in-the-door strategies [8] to
design flexible procedures to influence the direction and
outcome of buying-selling exchanges.

Some research exists on transactions within selling centers
particularly in the field of retailing. Lombard [14] provides detailed observations of transactions of salesgirls
with each other and salesgirls with sales managers in a
department store. The following is one example from
Lombard [14, p. 65]:

$S_5$, for example, busy with one customer, called $S_6$ to take
care of a second customer of hers who was getting impa-
tient. $S_1$ spoke to $S_5$ about her troubles with a male customer: "You see, he wanted a blue shirt, and I told him
five or six times we didn't have blue. I showed him the
green, and he kept saying, 'Well, why can't I see the blue?
Show me the blue in some other size!' He just couldn't
understand that we didn't have the blue. Gosh, he was ter-
rible!" "Calm yourself, $S_1$," said $S_5$. "I am calm!" $S_1$
insisted fiercely. "I bet he comes back again," said $S_5$.
"Oh, sure he will," agreed $S_1$ "but you won't catch me waiting on him!" A little later $S_1$ came up to the wrapping
desk again to find $S_5$ wrapping a purchase for the man.

"Well, I sold a shirt to him," $S_5$ told her. "What did he
say?" $S_1$ asked.

"He wanted to know if we had the shirt in blue," $S_5$ told
her. "I said, 'Didn't the other salesclerk tell you we
didn't have it?' He said, I don't know whether she looked.
I wanted to be sure.'"

Lombard was able to develop patterns in the person's "log-
ics," behavior, and outcomes of the transactions between
sales managers and salesclerks, salesclerks and salesclerks,

and salesclerks and customers based on direct observations of the transactions and environments in the department store.

The verbal interactions and production activities of cashiers and bundlers in eight supermarkets were examined by Clark [4] and reviewed by Homans [9]. Relationships and verbal interactions within and between buying and selling centers in restaurants were placed in a sociological perspective by Whyte [24].

Whyte observed that handling of the customer relationship is crucial for the adjustment of the restaurant personnel, and a large part of that problem can be stated in strictly quantitative interaction terms.

Who originates action for whom and how often? In a large and busy restaurant a waitress may take orders from fifty to one hundred customers a day (and perhaps several times for each meal) in addition to the orders (much less frequent) she receives from her supervisor. When we add to this problem of adjusting to service workers, bartenders, and perhaps checkers, we can readily see the possibilities of emotional tension - and, in our study, we did see a number of girls break down and cry under the strain [24].

Whyte observed that the skillful waitress, who maintained her emotional equilibrium, did not simply respond to the initiative of customers. "In various obvious and subtle ways she took the play away from customers, got them responding to her, and fitted them into the pattern of her work"[24]. The skills of the waitress and dining room supervisor as well as status, sex, and layout and equipment affected the nature and outcomes of the transactions.

Whyte [24] provided diagrams of the persons, positions, and direction of orders in restaurants at five levels of complexity. His work was a forerunner of structural role analysis. In structural role analysis, the concept of role is represented in graph theoretic terms and structural role theory is the particular _persons_ making up the organization or some subsystem of it (e.g., buying). The second set of elements is _positions_ which people occupy in the organization [a position is any means of designating a particular location or status in a social system]. The third set of elements is the _tasks_ which constitute the operational units of any workflow through the organization[2]. Calder [2] identifies five types of persons in applying structural role theory to buying centers: (1) buyers who have formal authority for contacting suppliers, (2) influencers who affect decisions by providing information and evaluative criteria, (3) deciders who choose among alternatives, (4) users who work with the purchased products and services, and (5) gatekeepers who control the flow of information to and from the buying center. Several of these persons may be the same individual within the buying center, e.g., the housewife may be the buyer and gatekeeper for household cereal purchases.

Structural role analysis may also be applied to selling centers to identify the persons, positions, and tasks related to selling the product. Application of structural role theory to marketing transactions could be used to identify patterns of exchanges between all persons involved in the negotiations.

The positions and most likely occurring contacts within and between buying and selling centers are shown for the household in Figure 1 and the firm in Figure 2. The figures are drawn with the assumption of first-time purchase consideration or an extensive problem solving situation [11] for the buying centers. The figures include the hypothesis that the transactions will likely include four or more persons in the selling centers and four or more persons in the buying centers being directly involved in some aspects of the negotiations. The research reviewed supports the general hypothesis that the salesperson

interacts with other salespersons for advice, approval, and to exchange values in general. The salesmanager likely interacts directly with the salesperson to provide advice, and more importantly, verbal support before and after negotiations with the buying center.

Notice in Figure 2 that the purchasing agent is unlikely to contact purchasing agents in other firms, the equivalent of friends in Figure 1, see Webster [23] and Martilla [15] for support of this hypothesis. The technical assistant in Figure 1 may be represented by an appraiser for an automobile or underwriter of a life insurance policy, i.e., the specific position would vary according to the product bought. A separate order processor is shown only in Figure 2 since the salesperson is likely to perform order processing tasks himself (herself) with the household buying center.

FIGURE 1
BUYING AND SELLING CENTERS FOR THE HOUSEHOLD

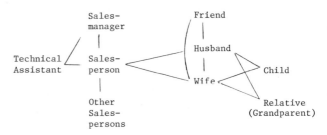

FIGURE 2
BUYING AND SELLING CENTERS FOR THE FIRM

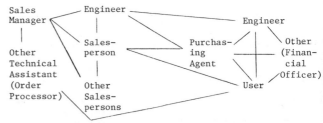

Cyert, Simon, and Trow [5] provide an example of a case study of a buying center and multiple selling centers on the feasibility of using electronic data-processing equipment. Their narrative illustrates multiple tasks performed by many persons in the buying center and two common processes: communication and problem solving processess. The findings indicate the presence of gatekeepers acts as information filters to secure a large influence over the decisions reached by the decider. Also, the search for alternative suppliers and products terminates when a satisfactory solution has been discovered even though the field of possibilities has not been exhausted. ("Hence, we have reason to suppose that changes in the search process or its outcome will actually have major effects on the final decision" [5]).

Cyert et al. [5] were quick to point out that they did not wish to try to transform one swallow into a summer by generalizing too far from a single example of a decision process. They did illustrate some of the processes involved in business decision making and indicated the sort of theory of the choice mechanism that is needed to accomodate these processes. For computer equipment for an industrial buying center, their research suggests that "search processes and information gathering processes constitute significant parts of decision making and must be incorporated in a theory of decisions if it is to be adequate [5].

The following research includes examples of additional case studies of transactions among household buying and selling centers. The purpose of such research is to identify the persons, positions, tasks, content and direction of the interactions, and outcomes of the transactions. The eventual goals of such research include the development of valid theory, recommendations to centers for more skillful buying and selling, and recommendations for social policy makers for increasing the efficiency and value received from marketing transactions.

## RESEARCH ON HOUSEHOLD BUYING CENTERS AND INSURANCE SELLING CENTERS

The national, regional, and local headquarters of an insurance company agreed to participate in an observation study of the selling center in a southeastern city of the United States in 1977. The salesmanager and five sales agents agreed to permit tape recordings of their interactions in the office including informal meetings and weekly sales meetings.

Interviews were conducted with three sales agents in their automobiles before and after sales calls with buying centers. Meetings between the sales agent(s) and the buying center were tape recorded with the permission of the buying center. A total of 47 meetings involving 37 buying centers were tape recorded. A member of one of 38 buying centers refused to have the meeting tape recorded. Five meetings of five different buying centers were tape recorded without the presence of a member of the selling center (these five meetings included interviews by the observer of the buying center).

The research findings are limited to being case reports of buying and selling transactions and the results are offered only as suggestive of useful insights to a basic unit of analysis in marketing - the transaction.

### Results

Analysis of the tape recordings and observations revealed a number of specific findings within and between the centers. The salesmanager originated the majority of the exchanges during sales meetings. The contents of the interactions during the sales meetings included (1) comparisons of salespersons' performances with prior developed objectives, (2) persuasive appeals by the salesmanager to meet 10 qualified prospects per week, (3) case examples of sales successes with buying centers, (4) contests rules and salespersons success examples, and (5) the need and methods of servicing accounts. Over 80% of the time of the sales meetings involved verbal communication from the salesmanager to the salespersons.

Meetings between members of the buying center and the selling center were in the buying centers' home (34 of 47) or office (13 of 47). The majority of both types of meetings included one salesperson while nine meetings included two salespersons.

Meetings between buying and selling centers resulting in purchases (sales) were characterized by a greater number of questions to the buying center from the salesperson which may have produced greater effort and commitment to the transactions by the buying center members. Both wives and husbands participated actively in 85% of meetings with the salespersons in the homes. Meetings resulting in sales outcomes usually involved a confirmation of salesperson attempts to (1) reduce buyer reactance, (2) change basic premises held by members of the buying center, (3) provoke buyer reactance to produce assimilation of a new attitude, (4) use foot-in-the-door techniques to achieve compliance by receiving cooperation in answering questions, (5) achieve multiple commitments from the buying center, and in five cases, (6) inoculate against future counterpersuasions.

The substantial majority (over 90%) of all meetings with buying centers suggested little search for information from alternative insurance companies before purchase. The majority of buying centers purchasing an insurance policy from the salespersons in the study did so without meeting with other salespersons. The communication process during the meetings of the buying and selling centers always included a communication from the salesperson within four exchanges between the husband (H), wife (W), and salesman (S) would include the following sequence of speakers: S-H-W-S-H-S-W-H-S. The following excerpts are taken from the transcripts of a meeting with a particularly successful sales agent and a buying center. (The names and several demographics are fictitious.)

### Case of Mr. & Mrs. Charles C. Buyers and Ivan Salesman

The husband in this family had been insured by the cooperating company through his parents. Neither the wife nor the husband had insurance with the company that they had purchased themselves. Since the husband's parents had been clients of the salesman (Ivan), the salesman decided to approach the prospects to discuss a policy of their own.

Ivan Salesman is a 34 year old black male who is married and has two children. His children are girls aged one and four years old. Ivan has been a salesman with the cooperating company for four years.

Educational experience includes a Bachelor of Science degree from Rutgers University. Ivan's major field of study at Rutgers was business management. After graduating from college, Ivan joined the U.S. Army and was commissioned as an aviation and armory officer. He remained in the Army for nine years and served two tours in Viet Nam. The rank of Captain was obtained. After leaving the Army, Ivan was employed by the cooperating company. He has been working for this company since that time.

Mr. and Mrs. Buyers are a white upper-lower social class couple with no children. Mr. Buyers is 26 years old and his wife is 25. Mr. Buyers is employed as a steel worker but has ambitions of becoming a professional bowler. Mrs. Buyers works in the customer complaint department of a South Carolina insurance company. They are presently renting a two bedroom apartment in the Northeast part of Columbia, South Carolina.

S: How long you guys been married?
W: It'll be two years this month.
H: The 26th.
S: Let me tell you, the Buyers family has been insured with The Protection Life Company for quite a while. And, unfortunately, we've had a succession of agents kind of switch over on you, and we're sorry that that's happened. I've been with Protection Life about 5 years now. Are you familiar with Protection Life?
W: More or less.
S: OK. Protection is a company out of Madisonville and they've been in busines since 1905. And they're one of the largest corporations in S.C. They own such things as Roadway Mall and WAC-TV and a lot of other pretty good size...[salesman establishes credibility].
W: I didn't know that.
S: You didn't know that? They try to keep some of those things not too much before the public notice, but they are a good, strong, substantial company. And the people that have been policy holders of theirs for years, they like to take good care of them. So, they assigned the Buyers family to me, so that's why I called C.C. and asked him if I could come out and sit down with you and go over what you presently have and maybe talk about some things you might want to accomplish in the future. OK? And to do that I've got a little questionnaire that takes a few minutes to answer [solicits compliance with small request].

Now we might discuss some things that are somewhat confidential. If you'd care not to divulge something say so, OK? But it's basic stuff. For instance, Linda where do you work?

W: S.C. Farm Owner's Insurance.

S: You work for an insurance department? Uh oh. Big trouble already.

W: I work in the Complaint Department.

S: What is that gentleman's name? I met a gentleman up there not too long ago.

W: Which department?

S: Mr. Sam Kay. Kahn.

W: Mr. Conners?

S: Conners. Yeah. Fine gentleman [salesman establishes common ground between prospects and himself].

S: C.C. you work where?

H: Boyd and Loy Corporation.

S: What exactly do you do?

H: I'm a steel worker, of sorts, I guess.

S: OK, and how long have you been there?

H: A year in June.

S: You like it or...

H: It's hard work, but it's ok. It's different.

S: Let me ask you this, you're a pretty young fellow, and you've got your whole career ahead of you and everything. What do you envision for yourself in about 5 years.

H: I would like to think that I'd be a professional bowler within 5 years.

S: Oh, good. How's it coming? You have a specific program geared towards that end? Do you have any advice?

H: Really, I know several pros and they've given me different ideas and suggestions on how to get there, but I haven't sat down and mapped out a plan. But hopefully within the next 3 years that's what I will be doing.

S: That's interesting. I wish you all the luck in the world, and I'm going to follow your progress very attentively. My wife is a big bowling fan. I used to bowl when I was smaller. I used to do a lot of pin setting [salesman establishes similarity].

———

S: What we try to do is — we ask you to let us sit down with you at least once a year to review your program so we're never more than a year away from the solution to the problem [solicits commitment]. We hope that you'll continue to improve your program year by year as you go along — always within; in fact, under what you consider you can do at the particular time. I'd much rather you under do a little bit than to burden yourself. The priority for you is to live and enjoy life and all those good things. But your insurance program, of course, saves you from what? Catastrophe, being wiped out financially, and just living a life of misery [dissonance creation]. So this is what your insurance program is supposed to do. OK. What other coverage do you have, C.C.? Do you have any other coverage?

H: I thought that my mother and father had taken out a policy.

S: They do. They have one on you. They're paying the premiums on it. I discussed that with her. Almost all parents have a little coverage on their children and she's paid for it and I say just let it lie. That's her wish so I would continue to do that but I think you should consider that separate and apart from your own personal program.

W: Yeah, that's hers.

S: So this is your extent of coverage. Linda, what do you have?

W: Nothing.

S: You don't have a thing?

W: Well, what I've got at work.

S: OK. Let me explain something to you - you may have a little more than you think. As a state employee you have at least a year's slary, plus $3,000 in your Blue-Cross-Blue Shield program. So that gives you 9,300 a year [establishes expertise]. C.C., right now you've got about 10,000 coverage and roughly, Linda, you've

got about 10. I think a young family on the start — my basic recommendation is to accomplish just what you want to accomplish, to provide either partner with a readjustment sum and to pay off any final expenses. I think you both need somewhere in the neighborhood of $25,000 each. I don't think that's unrealistic for today's society. Of course, as you grow, you're going to have a need for additional coverage. We have some real good programs where - we have what we call family type program policies where we cover both partners for a like amount. In this instance, I think something around 15,000 at least is needed.

Now, you indicated that you were saving a little bit of money in the credit union. I don't want to disrupt your life style or whatever. Approximately what are you saving in the credit union?

W: About 200.

S: 200 a month? OK. One suggestion you might do — you're putting that away for your house payment. Most house payments — I don't want to shock you, but 200 is not going to be enough.

H: We've been looking.

W: That's what I know.

S: Let me take a look at something....Let me show you something. This is what we call our Protection Life savings type program. This comes in amounts from 20,000 to 5 million. But, for instance, this is 50,000. The reason I showed you this is that it would provide 25,000 coverage for each one; but we can scale this down to the amount you need. I just use this as an illustrative program. This would be $25,000 on Linda and $25,00 on yourself; if you paid that annually, you'd have to deposit 646.50 per year through the program. The first year it's just a small cash value; that means just like savings with the credit union - that's the amount you can take out, if you need it. Now, this is a little bit unusual. Most insurance companies don't give you any cash value the first year. This is a new policy; it's a little bit unusual. You deposit the $646.50 the first year; the first year you have a $100 cash increase in policy. So the net cost to you in the first year is $546.50. That's pretty expensive the first year, but let's look at what happens after that. Let's look at the second year. You deposit 646.50; the cash value increases the second year $600.00, so the cost of insurance for both of you is only 46.50 for that whole year. That means if you decided to stop the policy, that all it would have cost you for that year was 46.50 [Traditional persuasion].

———

S: Now, what you could do so it wouldn't disrupt your life style is just reduce the amount to the credit union to 160 and take that extra money and put it in your checking account. So you really don't disrupt your life style. You don't have to take it from your disposable income. It will be a different type of savings.

H: I could stop it any time? And give you a call and say, "Hey, I need the money."

S: All you have to do is call the bank and say don't honor the draft and it could be the same minute.

H: I do need more coverage than just that one thing.

S: You do. I think it's imperative that you have some additional coverage on your wife.

W: It bothers me that I don't have anything on me, because $10,000 wouldn't be a drop in the bucket for me. Of course, it would be worse on me, because he makes a heck of a lot more money than I do.

H: The reason I'm not worried about that is because if anything ever did happen to her, I could live on what I make and I wouldn't see a need.

W: Unless we had a bunch of kids [wife helps salesman by exerting social pressure].

S: Let me point this out to you. You're not only buying for right now. As I indicated, your needs won't decrease - they're going to increase as you go along [Dissonance creation].

H: Right.

S: You'll have more obligations. This is why I recommend that you do something substantial now. Really, I think you can get by on a 15,000 right now. But, you'll find out, that these years are going to fly by, so fast and we're going to sit here, maybe not in this apartment, but at this same table and you're going to say, Ivan, I wish I'd bought 50 that night. Because you're going to need the coverage later on and it's going to be terribly expensive and I'm going to say, well, I wanted you to live within your means but I wanted you to at least get that program started. I've seen both ends of the spectrum [expertise]. I've seen those that have bought it and got by pretty good and then I've seen some that made a decision of trying to save 10 dollars a month and that cut off $10,000 in protection and so I come back with a check for 10 instead of 20. I feel terrible, she feels terrible [dissonance creation]. And that's why we try to ascertain what's comfortable for you and then you go from there.

H: Insurance is one of the worse things I could buy..as far as having to make a decision, it's hard for me on that. I can go out and buy me a new bowling ball right now.

S: We're talking about what, about $8 a week? You tell me what family doesn't take $8 and look in your wallet at the end of the week and...

H: I know one that does -- this one right here.

S: This is a good investment in your family's future [creates cognitive dissonance]. I think this is important to you.

H: Well, I'll go along with you about that...(Pause)... about that right now.

S: Who's the one in the family that takes care of the money?

H: Me.

S: You? OK. Would you give me a check to Protection Life for $36.75 [solicits commitment]?

H: Right now?

S: I need to get some information from your wife while you're doing that.

H: Boy, you cut me short this time.

S: Well, let me point this out to you. I need to have that in my hands in case I walk out the door and something happens. You can postdate it whenever you want to [solicits commitment].

H: I get paid tomorrow.

W: We wouldn't be covered in this tomorrow.

S: Yes ma'am. That's why I get that check, because the policy is in force as soon as he writes out that check.

H: No matter what the date is on the check.

S: That's right. As long as I have it in my possession. You may pay one month and then decide to stop it, then you made a $36 mistake. We all make a lot of those. But I'd hate to be the one who made a $25,000 mistake. We don't make too many of those and get away with it. [dissonance creation].

H: What date do I have it withdrawn?

W: Whenever you want it: it's up to you.

S: What is your social security number? [salesperson fills out the application and Mr. Buyers writes the check].

----

S: Once the policy is issued, I'll come back, and we'll sit down and we'll go over the policy provisions and everything about it. At that particular time, if you don't like anything in the policy, if you're dissatisfied in any way, I'll give you your money back. No hasty decision - don't want you to feel like that. I think you realize the importance of what we covered. I think we're getting an adequate amount and I think it's something that you can work within your budget...Tomorrow you might say,"I don't know if I made the right decision." Well, you're not out anything. Wait 'til you get the policy back. We'll sit down. We'll go over it and you'll see that it's good coverage by law and by contract. You ask anybody in the insurance commissioner's office. Ask them about Protection Life

[salesman attempts to reduce post purchase regret by validating decision].

S: Let me mention a couple of things and I'll get out of your hair. Number 1: I hope this will be the start of a long and enjoyable relationship. I'll do those things to keep you informed of any age changes, any new rules, etc. If anything, God forbid, should happen to either one of you, I will do whatever is required to help get your lives straightened out. And that's the last time I will say anything about that. I promise to come by and do all those things and renew your program every year. In return, this is what I ask [cultivates the long term relationship]. I ask you to at least be a little bit loyal to me. You'll probably be bothered with every insurance guy in the world coming by and wanting to talk to you. You won't have all that time to sit down and spend a lot of evenings with insurance people. If they come by, tell them, look, I've got a pretty good agent, named Ivan Salesman. If you've got any ideas you think I could use, give him a call. I'll look it over for you and if I'll be able to see something of value to it, I'll get back in touch with you and let you know and I'll give you an impartial answer. I think that way you save a lot of time and effort, problems and everything else. Then you won't be jumping into hasty decsions, getting all confused by every guy that comes. There are 1800 companies. If you'd let 1800 different people come in here and explain things to you, you'd go whacky. The minute I don't do my job, fire me. Say, you're fired and go on out and get yourselves another agent. So I have to earn the right to continue doing business with you.

H: I have no complaints from the last 4 years.

S: Anytime anything comes up, that you don't understand or you don't agree with me, call me. That's why I've got my home number and my office number there. Call me; I'm at your service.


CONCLUSIONS

The need for studying transactions between buying and selling centers in field settings is advocated. Analysis of the interaction process within and between buying and selling centers represents the natural ground for the development of theory. That is, an inductive approach to the formulation of a positive theory of buyer - seller interactions is suggested. Useful implications can be made directly to management and buying centers of cooperating firms and households in research into marketing transactions.


REFERENCES

1. Brehm, J.W. A Theory of Psychological Reactance. New York: Academic Press, 1966.

2. Calder, Bobby J. "Structural Role Analysis of Organizational Buying: A Preliminary Investigation," in Arch G. Woodside, Jagdish N. Sheth, and Peter D. Bennett, eds., Consumer and Industrial Buying Behavior. New York: Elsevier North-Holland, 1977.

3. Capon, Noel, Morris B. Holbrook, and James M. Hulbert. "Selling Processes and Buyer Behavior: Theoretical Implications of Recent Research" in Arch G. Woodside, Jagdish N. Sheth, and Peter D. Bennett, eds., Consumer and Industrial Buying Behavior. New York: Elsevier North-Holland, 1977.

4. Clark, J.V. "A Preliminary Investigation of Some Unconscious Assumptions Affecting Labor Efficiency in Eight Supermarkets," D.B.A. Thesis. Boston: Harvard University, 1958.

5. Cyert, Richard M., Hubert A. Simon, and Donald B. Trow, "Observation of a Business Decision," _Journal of Business_, 29 (April 1956), 237-48.

6. Evans, Franklin B. "Selling as a Dyadic Relationship: A New Approach,: _American Behavioral Scientist_, 6 (May 1963), 76-9.

7. Festinger, Leon. _A Theory of Cognitive Dissonance_. Evanston, Ill: Row, Peterson, 1957.

8. Freedman, J.L. and S. Fraser. "Compliance without Pressure: The Foot-in-the-Door Technique." _Journal of Personality and Social Psychology_, 4 (1966), 195-202.

9. Homans, George Casper. _Social Behavior: Its Elementary Forms_. New York: Harcourt Brace Jovanovich,1974.

10. Hovland, C.I., O.J. Harvey and M. Sherif. "Assimilation and Contrast in Reaction to Communication and Attitude Change." _Journal of Abnormal and Social Psychology_, 55 (1957), 244-52.

11. Howard, John A. _Consumer Behavior: Application of Theory_. New York: McGraw-Hill, 1977.

12. Kotler, Philip. _Marketing Management_. Englewood Cliffs, N.J.: Prentice-Hall, 1976.

13. Liu, W.T. and R.W. Duff. "The Strength of Weak Ties," _Public Opinion Quarterly_, 36 (Fall 1972), 361-6.

14. Lombard, George F.F. _Behavior in a Selling Group_. Boston: Harvard University, 1955.

15. Martilla, John A. "Word-of-Mouth Commuication in the Industrial Adoption Process," _Journal of Marketing Research_, 8 (May 1971), 173-8.

16. Olshavsky, Richard W. "Customer-Salesman Bargaining Behavior in Retail Transactions," _Journal of Marketing Research_, 10 (May 1973), 208-12.

17. Pennington, Allen L. "Customer-Salesman Bargaining Behavior in Retail Transactions," _Journal of Marketing Research_, 5 (August 1968), 255-62.

18. Rogers, E.M. "New Product Adoption and Diffusion," in Robert Ferber, ed., _Synthesis of Selected Aspects of Consumer Behavior_. Washington, D.C.: U.S. Government Printing Office for the National Science Foundation, 1977.

19. Sheth, Jagdish N. "A Model of Industrial Buyer Behavior," _Journal of Marketing_, 37 (October 1973), 50-56.

20. Sheth, Jagdish N. "A Theory of Family Buying Decisions," in Jagdish N. Sheth, ed., _Models of Buyer Behavior_. New York: Harper and Row, 1974.

21. Varela, Jacobo A. _Psychological Solutions to Social Problems_. New York: Academic Press, 1971.

22. Venkatesan, M. and G.A. Haaland, "The Effect of Distraction on the Influence of Persuasive Marketing Communications,: in Johan Arndt, ed., _Insights into Consumer Behavior_. Boston: Allyn and Bacon, 1968.

23. Webster, Frederick E. "Informal Communication in Industrial Markets," _Journal of Marketing Research_, 7 (May 1970), 186-9.

24. Whyte, William Foote. "The Social Structure of the Restaurant,: _American Journal of Sociology_, 54 (1949), 302-10.

25. Willett, Ronald P. and Allen Pennington, "Customer and Salesman: The Anatomy of Choice in a Retail Setting: _Proceedings_. Fall Conference, American Marketing Assoication, 1966, 598-616.

26. Wind, Yoram. "A Reward Balance Model of Buying Behavior in Organizations," in George Fisk,_New Essays in Marketing Theory_. Boston: Allyn and Bacon,1971.

# CHILDREN'S REACTIONS TO PREMIUMS - AN EXPERIMENTAL APPROACH

John H. Hallaq, University of Idaho

## ABSTRACT

Third, fourth, fifth, and sixth graders in two schools
were shown two sets of cereals with two sets of premiums
to determine if their selections of cereals could be influenced. "Large" premiums seem to have an impact on this behavior, but not "small" premiums. In both cases, the children showed a remarkable ability in pricing the premiums.
No significant differences in overpricing or underpricing
were discovered among the four classes. Boys, however,
showed a narrow premium preference compared to the girls
who demonstrated a much wider selection.

## INTRODUCTION

The Federal Trade Commission and the Premium Advertising
Association of America have been embroiled in the last
three or four years over the issue of premiums used in the
sale of products to children. The FTC hypothesized that
children will exert pressure on their parents to purchase
the product advertised not for its own sake but for the
premium, thus resulting in a social and/or economic cost
to society. The PAAA argued that it was "unfair" to single
out a method of promotion which is no less legitimate than
any other marketing tool. It released survey results
which indicate that over 90 percent of those who purchase
premiums rated them as good or better than expected [4].
While Donohue [2] reports that about as many children
bought cereal for the prize inside as for the cereal itself, and while other researchers have concluded that survey and experimental research evidence show that premiums
stimulate sales [7, 8, 9], two other reports [10, 11] suggest that a premium in a commercial does not significantly
enhance children's evaluations of the product; while the
results of several studies suggest that television commercials leave their imprint on children and tend to influence their desires to obtain the advertised product [3, 6,
12]. Banks [1] reports that in 1973 the Federal Communication Commission received over 55,000 letters commenting
or complaining about TV, the medium most commonly used for
the promotion of both cereals and their premiums, but only
34 of these were complaints about advertising to children
(it is this author's opinion that today with so many parents up in arms against TV programs to children, the results will be significantly different). Such conflicting
evidence led Griffin to suggest that, "Government officials and self-regulators are making daily judgments about
what is fair to children without enough reliable data to
guide them" [5, p. 15]. As a consequence, this author became interested in attempting to determine whether or not
some such conclusions can be empirically demonstrated
through the use of a field experiment. (It is interesting
to note that the Wall Street Journal reported in December
1976 that the FTC has reached the conclusion that research
on the effects of premiums was in conflict. Instead of
issuing guidelines, the agency is expected to deal with
any premium abuses case by case.) To this purpose the
field experiment described below was designed to gather
information which would help test a number of hypotheses
relevant to the premium issue.

## RESEARCH METHODOLOGY

The data was collected using a combination of a field experiment and a short questionnaire. Third, fourth, fifth,
and sixth graders in two different agricultural communities at about the same proximity from a university town

were selected. In the first school, 119 students were
taken, one by one, to eliminate peer group bias, to a room
where each was shown four brands of sugar-coated cereals:
Sugar Pops, Cocoa Puffs, Trix, Honey Comb. Four small
premiums: a game, iron-on patch, bike reflector, panda
bear poster, usually found inside such cereals, were placed
in front of each box and the child was asked to choose the
brand of cereal he or she would like to have. Since we
had access to four classes and four brands of cereals were
used, it was possible to rotate the four premiums to effect
a Latin Square design.

In the second experiment, 99 children in the other school
were similarly treated but with a different set of cereals
and premiums. Four brands of what may be called "adults'
cereals": Wheaties, Total, Special K and Spoon Size
Shredded Wheat were selected. In both cases the two sets
of brands of cereals selected represented the most popular
brands in that region. Four large premiums: play do,
puzzle, doll, and racing car usually sent for, for a price,
were placed beside each box and the selection of each
child was recorded. The car and the doll were selected for
their sexist connotations and the other two were considered
to be relatively asexual.

After the individual selections were completed, the children in each class were given a very simple and short questionnaire to fill out. The children were asked to record
their sex, age, whether or not they ate cereals more than
once a week, and the number of hours they watched TV on
Saturday morning until noon. The four premiums used in
each case were now placed on a table in front of the class
without the cereal boxes. Each child was asked to indicate on the questionnaire the premium he or she would like
to have and the price he or she would be willing to pay
for it. The scale used for the small premiums was 5, 10,
15, and 20 cents. These premiums had an average market
price of 10 cents. In the case of the large premiums, the
scale included prices of 39, 59, 79, 99 cents, and $1.19.
Actual retail prices were 39 cents for the play do, 59
cents for the puzzle, 97 cents for the doll, and $1.19 for
the car.

### Hypotheses

A number of hypotheses were established to test the influence of premiums or other behavior relevant to their use
in promoting products to children.

1. Main hypothesis: Use of premiums will influence the
   selection of a brand of cereal.
2. Children will tend to overprice the premium they would
   like to have, which may result in an economic and/or
   social cost.
3. Overpricing will decrease by age (class).

## RESULTS

### The Main Hypothesis

This hypothesis is testable under both sets of conditions
in which two types of premiums were used. Even though a
Latin Square design was used in both instances to record
selections made by the children, it would be more valid to
use a nonparametric test rather than analysis of variance
which assumes interval scaling. It is more realistic to
assume nominal scaling and use a less powerful test such
as the $X^2$ statistic. Tables 1 and 2 show the results

obtained for each set of premiums, both in absolute and percentage form.

### TABLE 1

SUGAR-COATED CEREALS SELECTED WITH PREMIUMS COMPARED TO
EXPECTED SELECTIONS BASED ON REGIONAL MARKET
SHARE OF EACH BRAND

| Sugar Pops | Cocoa Puffs | Trix | Honey Comb | Total |
|---|---|---|---|---|
| 17 (21) | 40 (43) | 27 (31) | 35 (24) | 119 |
| 15% (18%) | 34% (36%) | 23% (26%) | 27% (21%) | 100% |

$$X^2 = \frac{(17-21)^2}{21} + \frac{(40-43)^2}{43} + \frac{(27-31)^2}{31} + \frac{(35-24)^2}{24} = 6.5*$$

*significant at 0.10.

These findings do not show sufficiently large differences in selections with premiums compared with selections observed in the market place based on regional market shares. Therefore, the findings are not consistent with the hypothesis that premiums influence brand selection.

### TABLE 2

"ADULT" CEREALS SELECTED WITH PREMIUMS COMPARED TO
EXPECTED SELECTIONS BASED ON REGIONAL
MARKET SHARE OF EACH BRAND

| Wheaties | Total | Special K | Spoon Size Shredded Wheat | Total |
|---|---|---|---|---|
| 19 (35) | 18 (12) | 33 (29) | 29 (23) | 99 |
| 19% (35%) | 18% (12%) | 33% (29%) | 29% (24%) | 100% |

$$X^2 = \frac{(19-35)^2}{35} + \frac{(18-12)^2}{12} + \frac{(33-29)^2}{29} + \frac{(29-23)^2}{23} = 12.3*$$

*significant at 0.01.

On the other hand, the findings, using larger premiums, do show a definite impact of these premiums on brand selection. The results, therefore, are highly consistent with this hypothesis. The two conflicting results may demonstrate how each situational analysis can result in significantly different conclusions relating to the premiums issue.

The Second Hypothesis

Although the small premiums are not purchased for cash, one wonders if their inclusion may influence the child's decision to obtain these premiums. Since each child was asked to indicate the premium he or she would like, one can argue that the price indicated for that premium would be the highest price a child was willing to pay for any of the four premiums used in the experiment. The analysis shows that the children were willing to pay an average price of 12.7 cents with a standard deviation of 4.6, compared to the retail price of 10.0 cents, which shows a rather remarkable and insightful price consciousness by these children, despite the fact that the difference is statistically significant. Furthermore, since the average price is a maximum price and since these premiums do not involve a direct out-of-pocket cost, we assume they are of no critical concern to the FTC.

Prices of the large premiums are more critical to the premium controversy. These premiums exemplify those that children may pressure their parents to buy for them by asking parents to order the premiums for an out-of-pocket amount of cash. Furthermore, since prices show a wide range, one may speculate that it will be easier to influence a child to overprice the premium desired.

The reader will recall that the average market price of the premiums used in the experiment was 78.5 cents. Each child selected the premium he or she would have liked to have and indicated the price he or she was willing to pay for it. Data analysis shows that the average price these children were willing to pay was 69 cents, well below the market price. This would lead to the rejection of the second hypothesis.

Since a wide price range did exist, an interesting analysis would be to compare actual prices and the prices children were willing to pay for each of the four premiums. This is shown in Table 3.

### TABLE 3

ACTUAL PRICES AND PRICES INDICATED BY CHILDREN

| Prices Willing To Pay | Actual Prices | | | |
|---|---|---|---|---|
| | Play Do 39¢ | Puzzle 59¢ | Doll 97¢ | Car $1.19 |
| 39¢ | 10 | 8 | 7 | 10 |
| 59¢ | 2 | 1 | 1 | 19 |
| 79¢ | 3 | 1 | 2 | 9 |
| 99¢ | 2 | 1 | 6 | 6 |
| $1.19 | 1 | 1 | 1 | 8 |

This table clearly shows a tendency to underprice the premiums. The true price and the most frequently selected price coincide rather well in the case of the first premium, and to a lesser degree in the case of the third. The other two were well underpriced.

The Third Hypothesis

Cross classification of prices children were willing to pay for each premium with class (a good proxy for age at this level of education) can be used to test this hypothesis. The results of this analysis are shown in Tables 4 and 5.

### TABLE 4

PRICES CHILDREN WERE WILLING TO PAY FOR THE SMALL PREMIUMS

| Class | Price of Premium | | | | |
|---|---|---|---|---|---|
| | 5¢ | 10¢ | 15¢ | 20¢ | Total |
| 3rd & 4th | 18 (16) | 6 (8) | 11 (13) | 17 (15) | 52 |
| 5th & 6th | 17 (19) | 12 (10) | 19 (17) | 17 (19) | 65 |
| | 35 | 18 | 30 | 34 | 117 |

$X^2 = 2.4$ – not significant.

The classes were combined into two categories to permit the use of an $X^2$-test (using four-class categories resulted in several cells with value less than five). Accordingly, this hypothesis cannot be accepted in the case of the small premiums. Although a few more children in the higher grades tended to offer somewhat higher prices than the average price of 12.7 cents, the differences were not large enough to be statistically significant.

TABLE 5

PRICES CHILDREN WERE WILLING TO PAY FOR THE LARGE PREMIUMS

| Class | Price of Premiums | | | | | Total |
|---|---|---|---|---|---|---|
| | 39¢ | 59¢ | 79¢ | 99¢ | $1.19 | |
| 3rd & 4th | 15 (16) | 7 (10) | 7 (7) | 9 (7) | 7 (5) | 45 |
| 5th & 6th | 20 (19) | 16 (13) | 8 (8) | 6 (8) | 4 (6) | 54 |
| | 35 | 23 | 15 | 15 | 11 | 99 |

$X^2 = 4.0$ - not significant.

To test this hypothesis for the large premiums, the classes were also combined for the reason given earlier. Although the results were not significant, they do show a greater variation than was observed in the prices of the smaller premiums. This phenomenon should have been anticipated because of the wide price range of the larger premiums. Nevertheless, one has to reject the hypothesis that overpricing will decrease by age (class).

## OTHER RESULTS

A number of other results obtained from the questionnaire may be appropriate for discussion. The children from both schools had an almost equal number of males and females. It is interesting to note, however, that more girls tended to favor the puzzle and the play do premiums. It is surprising that 83 percent of the boys selected the racing car compared to 33 percent of the girls selecting the doll. This would seem to indicate a much broader interest among the girls. It is also rather amusing that 14 percent of the girls selected the car and two percent of the boys selected the doll. In both schools the number of students in the four classes was quite uniform, and about 78 percent of the children indicated they ate cereal more than once a week. Although all children averaged a little better than three hours watching TV on Saturday mornings, a slight tendency toward fewer hours was observed among older children. Both boys and girls showed similar behavior with respect to the number of hours spent watching TV on Saturday mornings and with respect to the frequency of cereal consumption. When pricing the large premiums, more girls tended to indicate lower prices (39 cents: 22 percent boys to 47 percent girls) and more boys were willing to pay the higher price ($1.19: 17 percent boys to 8 percent girls). However, this may be a function of the narrow selection indicated by the boys and the wider selection shown by the girls.

## DISCUSSION

The results of this experiment amplify the premium controversy and lead one to the conclusion that it would be difficult to generate policies or guidelines on the use of premiums that would fit many situations. In the case of "small" premiums, no effect was discovered in changing selections of brands of cereals, yet they did in the case of "large" premiums. Nevertheless, in the case of large premiums normally sent for, for a price, children were not willing to pay the retail value of these premiums. In fact, as a rule, most of these premiums can be purchased at lower than their retail value anyway since most of them are self-liquidating and, hence, their purchase in the past has resulted in the high degree of satisfaction reported in the introduction. The only reservation one may have from a social point of view would be to argue that children may be influenced to buy products they do not really "need." This same concern has been expressed by social critics with

respect to the influence of advertising on consumers, but this issue is beyond the confines of this experiment. Somewhat surprisingly, was the fact that children in the third through the sixth grades showed no discernible differences with respect to the issues raised in this experiment.

## LIMITATIONS

One must recognize, as in many other situations, that the findings of this study are limited and the design suffers from a number of shortcomings. The findings, at best, apply to agricultural communities which are influenced by a university community existing in their proximity. Furthermore, as an example, the design could have been improved with a larger sample which would have taken into account a number of different combinations such as using the large premiums with the sugar-coated cereals. Furthermore, lack of funding, for instance, did not permit obtaining more reliable responses by giving away the premiums selected. As a result of these and other limitations, the conclusions must be tainted with a degree of caution.

## REFERENCES

1. Banks, Seymore. "Public Policy on Ads to Children," Journal of Advertising Research, 15 (August 1975), 7-14.

2. Donohue, Thomas R. "Effect of Commercials on Black Children," Journal of Advertising Research, 15 (December 1975), 41-47.

3. Froderes, James S. "Advertising, Buying Patterns and Children," Journal of Advertising Research, 13 (February 1973), 34-36.

4. "FTC Proposes Kid's Premium Ad Ban Guide," Washington Report. July 3, 1974.

5. Griffin, Emilie. "What's Fair to Children? The Policy Need for New Research on Children's Perceptions of Advertising Content," Journal of Advertising, 5 (Spring 1976), 14-18.

6. Goldberg, Marvin E. and Gerald J. Gorn. "Children's Reactions to Television Advertising: An Experimental Approach," Journal of Consumer Research, 1 (September 1974), 69-75.

7. Razran, G. "Conditioning Away Social Bias by the Luncheon Technique," Psychological Bulletin, 35 (November 1938), 693.

8. Schwartz, B. "The Social Psychology of the Gift," American Journal of Sociology, 73 (July 1967), 1-11.

9. Seipel, Carl-Magnus, "Premiums--Forgotten by Theory," Journal of Marketing, 35 (April 1971), 26-34.

10. Shimp, T. and Robert Dyer. "The Harmful Effects of Premium-Oriented Commercials: An Extended Interpretation," in Kenneth R. Bernhard, ed., Marketing: 1776-1976 and Beyond. Chicago: American Marketing Association, 1976, 368-372.

11. Shimp, T., Robert Dyer, and Salvatore Divita. "Advertising of Children's Premiums on Television: An Experimental Evaluation of the F.T.C.'s Proposed Guide," unpublished paper, George Washington University and Kent State University, April 1975.

12. Ward, Scott, "Children's Reactions to Commercials," Journal of Advertising Research, 12 (1972), 37.

# MASS MEDIA AND INTERPERSONAL INFLUENCES
## ON ADOLESCENT CONSUMER LEARNING

George P. Moschis, Georgia State University
Gilbert A. Churchill, Jr., University of Wisconsin

## ABSTRACT

This study examines the influences of mass media, family, and peers on adolescents' acquisition of materialistic values and motivations for consumption. The findings suggest that adolescents learn from the media and their peers the "expressive" elements of consumption while from their parents they seem to learn the "rational" aspects. While some social processes might contribute to the child's learning the expressive aspects of consumption from television commercials, announcement of the availability of products and demonstration of their social uses in advertisements would appear to contribute to the formation of materialistic attitudes and to social "non-rational" motivations for consumption.

## INTRODUCTION

The learning of consumer skills by young people has become an area of increasing interest to public policy makers, marketing practitioners, consumer educators, and students of socialization and consumer behavior [12]. Primary forces behand the development of this interest have been the various contemporary issues relating to public policy information. Major concerns at the 1971 FTC hearing, for example, were the effects of marketing practices on consumer learning and, generally, the processes by which young people develop consumer skills, knowledge, and attitudes [1].

Although there is a growing interest in consumer socialization (i.e., the processes by which young people acquire consumer-related cognitions and behaviors), little information is available to answer the increasing number of public policy questions regarding consumer learning. One main issue is the effect of television and other sources of consumer information on the development of young people's consumer behavior, values, and attitudes. Advertising critics, for example, argue that advertising strongly influences youths and results in undesirable socialization (e.g., materialistic values; nonrational, impulse-oriented choices). On the other hand, defenders of advertising practices argue that the main sources of such cognitions and behaviors are parents and peers. According to Ward, these and similar differences of opinion seem to exist partly because research has not focused on the influence of various sources of information on consumer socialization [12].

This study examines the influence of mass media, family, and peers on the acquisition of (1) materialistic values, (2) economic motivations for consumption, and (3) social motivations for consumption by adolescents. Adolescence is a crucial period for socialization; at that time, the mass media, parents, and peers all serve as significant sources of information shaping the person's consumer-related patterns of thinking and behaving [3,5,6,9].

## BACKGROUND AND HYPOTHESES

Research into the acquisition of thought and action patterns that comprise consumer behavior is based mainly on two models of human learning: the cognitive development model and the social learning model. The cognitive development approach essentially views learning as a cognitive-psychological process of adjustment to one's environment, with age used as a proxy variable for cognitive development. The social learning model, on the other hand, focuses on sources of influence--commonly known as "socialization agents" which transmit attitudes, motivations, and values to the learner. Learning is assumed to be taking place during the person's interaction with socialization agents in various social settings [4,5,6].

In this study, consumer learning is viewed mainly as a social process, with special emphasis on three socialization agents: family, mass media, and peers. Age, social class, and sex are treated as control variables that locate the adolescent in his social environment [6]. To the extent the adolescent interacts with the three socialization agents, the person is expected to be learning the different consumer values and cognitions of interest in this research.

### Family

As an agent of socialization, the family would seem to play a significant role in influencing how the child acquires consumer skills. Early sociologists speculated that young people learn basic "rational" aspects of consumption from their parents [8,9]. Recent research findings appear to support this contention. For example, research by Moore and Stephens shows that overt parent-child communication about consumption predicts fairly well the adolescent's knowledge of prices of selected products [5]. Similarly, Ward and Wackman found that parental "general goals" included teaching their children about price-quality relationships [14]. These findings suggest the following hypothesis:

$H_1$ There is a positive relationship between the frequency of intrafamily communication about consumption and the degree to which the adolescent holds economic motivations for consumption.

### Mass Media

The influence of mass media may come from either programming or advertising. A programming influence would be operating, for example, if the young person aspired to have the material blessings of certain television characters [11]. However, of the two, advertising is believed to exert the major influence on consumer learning [8].

Bandura argues that people learn through observation and imitation of television advertising how to attach social meaning to material goods, i.e., the "expressive" or "adaptive" elements of consumption [2]. Bandura's speculation about the learning of conspicuous consumption suggests the following hypotheses:

$H_2$ The amount of television viewing correlates positively with the strength of the adolescent's social motivations for consumption.

$H_3$ The amount of television viewing correlates positively with the strength of the adolescent's attitudes toward materialism.

Although Bandura tends to subscribe to the hypodermic model of communication effects [4], recent research suggests that learning social and materialistic orientations toward consumption may be a second-order consequence of more fundamental aspects of social learning. For example, one study found no relationship between materialism and exposure to television, but it found significant relationships between materialism and social utility reasons for watching commercials (e.g., watching commercials to form impressions of what kinds of people buy certain brands and to make associations between products and various life styles [13]). Thus, learning may also occur as a function of the quality of television use (gratifications sought in advertisements and programs), which may be conditioned by social processes.

$H_4$   Social utility reasons for viewing television advertisements correlate positively with the strength of the adolescent's attitudes toward materialism.

$H_5$   Social utility reasons for viewing television advertisements correlate positively with the strength of the adolescent's social motivations for consumption.

$H_6$   Social utility reasons for viewing television programs correlate positively with the adolescent's attitudes toward materialism.

$H_7$   Social utility reasons for viewing television programs correlate positively with the strength of the adolescent's social motivations for consumption.

Peers

Adloescent peer groups are particularly significant sources of influence [3]. Reisman and Rosenborough [9], as well as Parson and his colleagues [8], speculate that children learn from peers "expressive elements of consumption" ("styles and moods of consumption"). These speculations suggest the following hypothesis:

$H_8$   The frequency of peer communication about consumption is positively related to the degree of social motivations for consumption held by adolescents.


METHODOLOGY

The sample for this study consisted of 806 adolescents from 13 schools in seven towns and cities in urban, suburban, semi-rural, and rural Wisconsin. Some of the schools were chosen on a convenience basis and some on a random basis. Cooperation was requested from school officials at middle schools and senior high schools, and questionnaires were delivered to those who agreed to participate. These self-administered questionnaires were filled out by the students during regular class sessions and took approximately 30-45 minutes to complete. Most of the classes chosen by school officials to participate in the survey were consumer-related courses such as home economics and consumer education. Because of this, the sample contained a disproportionate number of females, almost two-thirds. The sample was well balanced, though, with respect to age group, geographical location, and social class.

The variables were constructed by summing appropriate items to form scales and using coefficient alpha to assess the reliability of the scales [6,7]. The Appendix lists the items which form each of the scales. Reliability coefficients for the scales used in this research ranged from .60 to .85, above the .50 to .60 reliability coefficients often recommended for constructs in the early stages of research [7, p. 226].

Materialism was operationally defined in this research as an "orientation emphasizing possession and money for personal happiness and social progress [13, p. 426]. It was measured by soliciting responses to six items. A typical item of this scale was, "It is really true that money can buy happiness," possible responses ranging from strongly agree to strongly disagree on a five-point Likert scale.

Economic motivations for consumption were operationally defined as a cognitive orientation concerning the importance of products' functional and economic features. This variable was measured on a zero to 25-point index

by summing responses to five products (bicycle, watch, camera, pocket calculator, and hair dryer) possessing various degrees of such properties. Respondents were asked to check whether they thought it was important to know five different items when buying each one of the products. A typical item of information was "guarantees on different brands."

Social motivations for consumption were operationally defined as a cognitive orientation emphasizing conspicuous consumption and its importance to self-expression. The measurement consisted of summing responses to consumption situations with various degrees of social visibility. Respondents were asked to indicate whether they thought it was important to know four different items before buying the above five products. A typical item of information was "what friends think of different brands of products."

Family communication about consumption was defined as overt interaction between parent and adolescent concerning goods and services. It was measured by summing responses to 12 items. A typical item on this scale was "My parents and I talk about buying things," with responses measured on a five-point, very often-never scale.

Amount of television viewing was measured by asking respondents how frequently they watched specific program categories. These program categories were national and local news, sport events, movies, variety shows, cartoons, police and adventure shows. Responses to program content were measured on a five-point, every day-never scale and summed to form the television viewing index.

Social utility reasons for viewing television advertisements were operationally defined as motivations to watch television commercials as a means of gathering information about life styles and behaviors associated with uses of specific consumer products. The measurement consisted of the summed responses to 10 items indicating whether the respondent viewed commercials for that reason. A typical item was, "I watch television commercials to find out what kinds of people use certain products." Positive responses were summed to form a zero to 10-point scale.

Social utility reasons for viewing television programs were operationally defined as motivations to watch television shows as a means of gathering information about life styles and behaviors associated with the use of specific products. The measurement technique and items were similar to those used in measuring the previous variable.

Peer communication about consumption was operationally defined as overt peer-adolescent interactions concerning goods and services. It was measured by summing the responses to six items such as "My friends and I talk about buying things," using a five-point, very often-never scale.


ANALYSIS AND RESULTS

Before testing the hypothesized relationships between sources of consumer learning information and the dependent variables, the effects of the antecedent variables (age, sex, and social class) were assessed using analysis of variance. Those antecedent variables that were found to be significantly related to the dependent variables were included in the analysis as control variables [6].

Family

On the basis of sociological theories and some recent empirical findings in the area of consumer learning, it was hypothesized that overt parent-to-adolescent communication about consumption would correlate positively with the adolescents' economic motivations for consumption (Hypothesis 1). Table 1 shows zero-order and partial correlations between parent-adolescent communication about consumption and adolescents' economic motivations for consumption. The resulting correlation coefficient of .082 was large enough to support the first hypothesis (p < .020). This statistically significant relationship also remained after removing the effects of sex and age. In fact, the resulting partial correlation coefficient for the hypothesized relationship increased slightly (r = .094, p < .007).

TABLE 1

RELATIONSHIPS BETWEEN ECONOMIC MOTIVATIONS FOR CONSUMPTION AND SELECTED EXPLANATORY VARIABLES[a]

| Independent Variables | Economic Motivations for Consumption | Sig. Level |
|---|---|---|
| Family Communication about Consumption | .094 (.082) | .007 |
| Social Class | .119 (.119) | .001 |
| Age | .107 (.119) | .002 |

[a]Table entries are partial correlation coefficients. Zero-order correlations are shown in parentheses.

Mass Media

A positive statistical relationship (r = .147, p < .001) was found between the amount of television viewing and the strength of social motivations for consumption. The correlation between the two variables was reduced (r = .079, p < .025) when the effects of other independent variables were held constant (Table 2). These data provided support for Hypothesis 2.

TABLE 2

RELATIONSHIPS BETWEEN SOCIAL MOTIVATIONS FOR CONSUMPTION AND SELECTED EXPLANATORY VARIABLES[a]

| Independent Variables | Social Motivations for Consumption | Sig. Level |
|---|---|---|
| Amount of Television Viewing | .079 (.147) | .025 |
| Peer Communication about Consumption | .127 (.142) | .000 |
| Social Utility for Watching TV Shows | .038 (.154) | .277 |
| Social Utility for Watching TV Ads | .121 (.194) | .001 |
| Social Class | .007 (−.008) | .845 |
| Sex | −.129 (−.096) | .000 |

[a]Table entries are partial correlation coefficients. Zero-order correlations are shown in parentheses.

While the zero-order correlation between attitudes toward materialism and the amount of television viewing was statistically significant (r = .134, p < .001), the partial correlation between the two variables was not strong enough to support Hypothesis 3 (Table 3). However, the significant relationships (1) between materialism and social utility reasons for watching television programs (r = .085, p < .016) and (2) between materialism and social utility reasons for watching television commercials (r = .135, p < .001) support Hypotheses 4 and 6, respectively. These findings suggest that the learning of materialistic attitudes may not be a function of the

TABLE 3

RELATIONSHIPS BETWEEN MATERIALISM AND SELECTED EXPLANATORY VARIABLES[a]

| Independent Variables | Materialism | Sig. Level |
|---|---|---|
| Amount of Television Viewing | .054 (.134) | .127 |
| Social Utility for Watching TV Shows | .085 (.179) | .016 |
| Social Utility for Watching TV Ads | .135 (.207) | .000 |
| Sex | −.195 (−.168) | .000 |

[a]Table entries are partial correlation coefficients. Zero-order correlations are shown in parentheses.

adolescent's mere exposure to television; rather, these cognitive orientations may develop as a result of the adolescent's social utility motivations for television viewing.

Somewhat similar results emerged regarding social motivations for consumption. While the zero-order correlation between social motivations for consumption and social utility reasons for watching television programs is statistically significant, the partial correlation between the two variables is not strong enough (r = <.038, p < .277) to support Hypothesis 7 (Table 2). However, the partial correlation between social motivations for consumption and social utility reasons for watching television commercials is statistically significant (r = .121, p < .001) and supports Hypothesis 5. These results suggest that social motivations for consumption may not only be a function of the adolescent's frequency of interaction with (exposure to) television, but may also be a function of the child's motivations for watching television commercials.

Peers

On the basis of sociological theories, it was hypothesized that the frequency of the adolescent's communication with his peers would correlate positively with his degree of social motivations for consumption. The resulting correlation between the two variables was .142 (p < .001), while the partial correlation was .127 (p < .001) (Table 2). Thus, the data appear to support Hypothesis 8, which suggests that adolescents may acquire social motivations for consumption from their peers.

DISCUSSION AND IMPLICATIONS

The family appears to be important in teaching adolescents "rational" aspects of consumption. The data indicate a significant positive relationship between the amount of intrafamily communication about consumption and the extent to which adolescents hold economic motivations for consumption. The findings appear to be consistent with speculations of some sociologists with respect to the kinds of consumer behaviors young people learn from their parents [8, 9].

This research also supports the contention of Bandura and others that young people learn from television the "expressive" or "adaptive" elements of consumption [2, 8]. However, the learning of these skills may not develop through imitation and observation alone, as Bandura argues. Rather, social processes (e.g., communications with peers) seem to condition adolescents' perceptions and interests in goods and services, which in turn seem to cause them to pay more attention to television programs and commercials in order to learn about social uses of products.

TABLE 4

CORRELATION MATRIX

| | 1 | 2 | 3 | 4 | 5 | 6 | 7 | 8 | 9 | 10 | 11 |
|---|---|---|---|---|---|---|---|---|---|---|---|
| 1. Family Communication | 1.00 | | | | | | | | | | |
| 2. Television Viewing | .22 | 1.00 | | | | | | | | | |
| 3. Social Utility: TV Shows | .18 | .28 | 1.00 | | | | | | | | |
| 4. Social Utility: TV Ads | .12 | .29 | .54 | 1.00 | | | | | | | |
| 5. Peer Communication | .33 | .06 | .17 | .13 | 1.00 | | | | | | |
| 6. Age | -.11 | .08 | -.16 | -.21 | .13 | 1.00 | | | | | |
| 7. Social Class | .01 | -.30 | -.03 | -.11 | .10 | .09 | 1.00 | | | | |
| 8. Sex | .07 | -.04 | .10 | .09 | .13 | -.05 | .03 | 1.00 | | | |
| 9. Materialistic Values | .05 | .13 | .18 | .21 | .13 | -.02 | .01 | -.17 | 1.00 | | |
| 10. Economic Motivations | .08 | -.07 | .06 | -.05 | .10 | .12 | .12 | .05 | -.05 | 1.00 | |
| 11. Social Motivations | .04 | .15 | .15 | .19 | .14 | -.02 | -.01 | -.10 | .14 | .24 | 1.00 |

Peers appear to be an important socialization agent. The findings suggest that adolescents' communication with their peers about consumption matters may focus on the social importance of goods and services and it may be a second-order consequence of learning from parents rather than from television. For example, the correlation between intrafamily communication about consumption and communication with peers was relatively high (r = .33), while television viewing was weakly associated with peer communication about consumption (r = .06) (Table 4). These findings suggest that interpersonal interaction with peers about consumption matters may make the adolescent aware of goods and services in the marketplace and of the buying processes. This greater awareness of the consumer environment apparently contributes to active interaction about consumption matters with other socialization agents such as the mass media, which results in additional learning. For example, the correlations between the frequency of the adolescent's interaction with his peers and social utility reasons for viewing television programs and commercials were significant (r = .13, p < .001 and r = .17, p < .001, respectively) (Table 4).

While interpersonal social processes (e.g., communication with peers) might cuase the adolescents to view television commercials for social utility reasons, the mere availability and demonstration of social uses of products in advertisements would appear to contribute to the formation of materialistic attitudes and to social motivations for consumption. The amount of television viewing also seems to contribute to the strength of social motivations for consumption. Such learning may be the effect of programming and/or advertising.

The results of this study suggest some directions that might be taken in future research. Perhaps one of the most demanding needs is for understanding the development of social motivations for using the mass media. This research suggests that the learning of expressive elements of consumption is mainly a function of social utility reasons for watching television programs and advertisements. However, how such motivations develop is not quite clear. It would be interesting to know whether social reasons for media use develop as a function of the child's interaction with the various socialization agents (especially with family and peers) or whether these processes develop as a function of specific social and cultural characteristics, as some research suggests [12].

APPENDIX

Item Composition of the Scales

1. Materialism

    a.  It is really true that money can buy happiness.
    b.  My dream in life is to be able to own expensive things.
    c.  People judge others by the things they own.
    d.  I buy some things that I secretly hope will impress other people.
    e.  Money is the most important thing to consider in choosing a job.
    f.  I think others judge me as a person by the kinds of products and brands I use.

2. Economic Motivations for Consumption

    a.  Guarantees on different brands.
    b.  Name of the company that makes the product.
    c.  Whether any brands are on sale.
    d.  Kinds of materials different brands are made of.
    e.  Quality of store selling a particular brand.

3. Social Motivations for Consumption

    a.  What friends think of different brands or products.
    b.  What kinds of people buy certain brands or products.
    c.  What others think of people who use certain brands or products.
    d.  What brands or products to buy to make good impressions on others.

4. Family Communication about Consumption

    a.  My parents tell me what things I should or shouldn't buy.
    b.  My parents want to know what I do with my money.
    c.  I help my parents buy things for the family.
    d.  My parents complain when they don't like something I bought for myself.
    e.  My parents ask me what I think about things they buy for themselves.
    f.  My parents and I talk about things we see or hear advertised.
    g.  I ask my parents for advice about buying things.
    h.  My parents tell me why they buy some things for themselves.
    i.  I go shopping with my parents.
    j.  My parents tell me I should decide about things I should or shouldn't buy.
    k.  My parents and I talk about buying things.
    l.  My parents tell me what they do with their money.

5. Social Utility Reasons for Viewing Television Advertisements

    a.  To get ideas on how to be successful.
    b.  To find out what kinds of people use certain products.
    c.  To find out what kinds of products to buy to feel like those people I wish I were.
    d.  To learn what things to buy to make good impressions on others.
    e.  To dream of the good life.
    f.  To find out what qualities people like in others.
    g.  To find out how others solve the same problems I have.
    h.  To give me something to talk about with others.
    i.  To learn about the "in" things to buy.

    j.  To tell others something they don't already know about new ideas or products.

6. Peer Communication About Consumption

    a.  I ask my friends for advice about buying things.
    b.  My friends and I talk about buying things.
    c.  My friends and I talk about things we see or hear advertised.
    d.  My friends ask me for advice about buying things.
    e.  My friends tell me about things I should or shouldn't buy.
    f.  I go shopping with my friends.

REFERENCES

1. Action for Children's Television.  Testimony before
   the Federal Trade Commission, November 10, 1971.

2. Bandura, Albert.  "Modeling Influences on Children,"
   Testimony to the Federal Trade Commission, November,
   1971.

3. Campbell, Earnest Q.  "Adolescent Socialization,"
   in David A. Goslin, ed., Handbook of Socialization
   Theory and Research.  Chicago:  Rand McNally, 1969.

4. McLeod, Jack M. and J. Garret, Jr.  "The Socialization
   Prospective and Communication Behavior," in G. Kline
   and P. Tichenor, eds., Current Perspectives in Mass
   Communication Research.  Beverly Hills, California:
   Sage, 1972.

5. Moore, Roy L. and Lowndes F. Stephens.  "Some
   Communication and Demographic Determinants of Adolescent Consumer Learning," Journal of Consumer Research,
   2 (September 1975), 80-92.

6. Moschis, George P.  "Acquisition of the Consumer Role
   by Adolescents," Unpublished Ph.D. Dissertation,
   University of Wisconsin-Madison, 1976.

7. Nunnally, Jim C.  Psychometric Theory.  New York:
   McGraw-Hill Book Co., 1967.

8. Parsons, T., R. F. Bales, and E. A. Shils.  Working
   Papers in the Theory of Action.  Glencoe, Ill.:
   The Free Press, 1953.

9. Reisman, David and Howard Roseborough.  "Careers and
   Consumer Behavior," in Lincoln Clark, ed., Consumer
   Behavior, Vol. II, The Life Cycle and Consumer
   Behavior.  New York:  New York University Press,
   1955.

10. Robertson, Thomas S.  "The Impact of Television
    Advertising on Children," Wharton Quarterly, 6
    (Summer 1972), 38-41.

11. Vener, Arthur M. and Charles R. Hommer.  Adolescent
    Orientation to Clothing, Technical Bulletin 270.
    East Lansing, Michigan:  Agricultural Experiment
    Station, Michigan State University, 1959.

12. Ward, Scott L.  "Consumer Socialization," Journal of
    Consumer Research, 1 (September 1974), 1-14.

13. Ward, Scott and Daniel B. Wackman.  "Family and Media
    Influences on Adolescent Consumer Learning,"
    American Behavioral Scientist, 14 (January-February
    1971), 415-27.

14. Ward, Scott L. and Daniel B. Wackman.  "Effects of
    Television Advertising on Consumer Socialization,"
    Working Paper, Cambridge, Mass.:  Marketing Science
    Institute, 1973.

# THE CREDIBILITY OF MEDIA ADVERTISING
# FOR THE ELDERLY

Warren A. French, University of Georgia
Melvin R. Crask, University of Georgia

## ABSTRACT

Ads directed to the old age market can have a noticeable impact on purchase behavior. The elderly's choice of both products and stores appears to be influenced more by ad messages than by the ad media. The format of the ad, though, may be just as important as the actual appeals. Also, the senior citizen's approach to retirement living appears to be more strongly related to the use of advertised information than does the actual age of the retiree.

## INTRODUCTION

To justify the isolation of senior citizens as a profitable market segment, it is worthwhile to quote some statistics. First, people over 65 number more than 22 million, or more than 10% of the U.S. population [7]. This number is expected to increase by one-third in the next 25 years [14]. Second, only about two percent of the elderly are institutionalized [5], leaving the vast majority as "relatively free choice" consumers. Of this group approximately 84% have incomes above the poverty line [16].

Survey reports have shown that the elderly's product purchases are different than those of younger adults [11]. If the size of the market and its differentiated buying behavior (the first two criteria for successful segmentation) have been established, attention must be turned to the third criterion for successful segmentation [9]--that of reaching the segment. Though a more detailed categorization of product purchases is certainly needed, attention should be directed to the means of influencing the buying behavior of senior citizens.

So far, very little research has been directed to the topic. Phillips and Sternthal have attempted to deduce a relation between influenceability and old age [15] from empirical studies in psychology. They note that people with a high internal, as compared to external, locus of control appear to be more resistant to persuasion [2]. Since elderly people in the aggregate have been typified by high levels of internal locus of control [18], Phillips and Sternthal believe that the old age-influenceability inference certainly merits testing. Such testing, in a marketing context would concern not only the effectiveness of ads but the choice of commerical media as well.

The media used to influence behavior cannot be divorced from the actual promotional appeals, given the nature of information processing during old age. In a recent review of the literature Layton documents the diminished sensory and nervous system capabilities associated with aging [10]. Because of these diminished capacities, especially sight and hearing, questions about choice of appropriate media naturally arise. It is these questions, in null hypothesis form, concerning appropriate media and appeals that are addressed in the pilot study reported here.

## HYPOTHESES

$H_1$ There is no identifiable pattern in senior citizens' use of commercial media.

A recent Canadian study found high usage rates among senior citizens for television, radio and newspapers [1].

A similar study in the United States showed greater media usage as people entered into their retirement years [6]. The hypothesis posed in this study relates not only to the absolute use of media but also to potential meaningful differences in the use of television vs. radio vs. newspapers.

$H_2$ Senior citizens perceive no different in the credibility of ads carried by different media.

Past research has shown that newspapers are thought by the elderly to be more credible than either television or radio [19]. This second hypothesis was posited to test if such a credibility relation holds not for information in general but for advertisements presented by each of the media. Accordingly, opinions were elicited on both the credibility of advertisements and the relative credibility of commercial messages carried by each of the three media.

$H_3$ Ads in commercial media have little impact on senior citizens' buying behavior.

This hypothesis is presented to test two contrasting points of view. One is that the increased cautiousness associated with old age [4] would negate much of the influence of advertisements. The second point of view is that advertisements may be an important source of shopping information [8] for at least some senior citizens. Survey questions related to this hypothesis covered the influence of advertisements as well as ad recognition rates for specific commercial themes.

$H_4$ Senior citizens exhibit no common preference for appeals stressing salient benefits of a given store.

Senior citizens are often portrayed as a homogeneous market [3]. The initial phase of this study included a focus group interview in which six factors related to store patronage were uncovered. A preference rating using a paired comparison format was constructed to discover if agreement (implying homogenity) existed among the sample respondents about the relative merit of those six factors as potential advertising appeals.

$H_5$ There is no difference as to the age level of senior citizens and a.) media usage, b.) perceived advertising credibility, c.) impact of advertising, or d.) preference ratings of store appeals.

Neugarten has observed that there are differences in behavior between the young-old (under 75) and the old-old [12]. Her observation is tested here as it relates to the variables mentioned in the first four hypotheses. This fifth hypothesis focuses on the potential for a greater degree of homogeneity of opinion and behavior to exist among the old-old than with the young-old.

$H_6$ There is no difference between relatively active and relatively passive senior citizens and a.) media usage, b.) perceived advertising credibility, c.) impact of advertising, or d.) preference ratings of store appeals.

Both active and passive approaches to retirement living have been observed and documented [13]. Combining the many stereotypes of active and passive living from the studies of Neugarten [13] and Reichard [17], nine self-descriptions were presented to the sample members. The sample members were asked to pick the description closest to their own self perception. Their answers (six descriptive stereotypes were designated passive, the other three active) were matched against the variables tested in the first four hypotheses.

## METHOD

Comments from nine senior citizens gathered in a group setting on the topics of media usage and advertising appeals led to the construction of a questionnaire. The survey instrument contained 12 items related to the six hypotheses posited for testing. A list of senior citizens (65 and over) was then compiled from the records of legal and social agencies in the test city--one with a population of approximately 70,000 people.

Five interviewers, all of whom participated in the group interview, contacted as many of the people on the list as possible [21]. All interviews were on a one-to-one basis in the homes of the respondents. 89 completed interview forms were judged acceptable, i.e., all the questions were understood by the respondents and all questions were answered.

## RESULTS

The first null hypothesis was rejected since a significant difference was found in the elderly's use of commercial media. The sampled respondents watched television more frequently than they read newspapers or listened to radio. There was no meaningful difference between radio and newspaper usage, but there were significant differences between the use of those two media and the higher usage rate of television; t values show respective chance probability levels of .001 between television and newspapers and .02 between television and radio.

The second hypothesis, which dealt with the relative credibility of advertisements in the three media, could not be rejected. 52% of the respondents perceived no difference in credibility. Of the remainder 22% judged T.V. ads most credible, 19% chose newspaper ads and the remaining seven percent put their trust in radio ads. In reply to a summary question 64% of the sample answered that media ads in general were truthful.

The third hypothesis stated that ads have little impact on senior citizens. That hypothesis can be rejected by the data. A majority of the respondents [72%] said that ads were an important source of information for them. 55% noted that media ads influenced their choice of products while 45% stated that ads influenced their choice of stores.

The exact type of ad to direct at elderly consumers has been the subject of some dispute. Marketers have previously been cautioned that ads aimed solely at the old age market may cause resentment among the target audience rather than sales [20]. To gauge the relative impact of ads on senior citizens, brand associations were asked for six well advertised commercial themes.

Two of the themes are directed primarily at the old age market.

"Can give you back your smile" - DENTUCREME
"For thorough relief"         - HALEY'S M O

Two other themes have featured senior citizens in their ads but have also used younger people.

"It's the next best thing to being there" - LONG DISTANCE
"And leave the driving to us"             - GREYHOUND

The final two themes are promoted to a general market with little reference to the elderly.

"It's the real thing" - COCA COLA
"We do it all for you" - McDONALD'S

The degrees of recognition are presented in TABLE 1. The ads directed primarily at the elderly market had by far the lowest theme recall rate of the three sets. The differences between degrees of recall and sets of ads show a significant difference at the .001 level of chance.

### TABLE 1

### THEME RECALL FOR DIFFERENT AD SETS[a]

| Degree of[b] Recognition | Old Target Audience | Old & Young Target Audience | General Target Audience |
|---|---|---|---|
| Both brands | 1 | 14 | 10 |
| One brand & one product | 2 | 6 | 2 |
| Both products | 6 | 21 | 31 |
| One product only | 6 | 12 | 1 |
| No recognition | 74 | 36 | 45 |

[a] Chi square value of 44.9 is significant at the .001 level.
[b] The data are not adjusted to reflect differences in advertising budgets for the six themes.

Store advertising appeals are the subject of the fourth hypothesis. That null hypothesis was rejected since the sample showed marked preferences for some appeals over others. The matrix presented in TABLE 2 contains the cross comparisons of store appeals and the probabilities of chance differences. The six appeals are listed in order of preference reading top or bottom or left to right. Low price and convenient location stood out in the respondents' opinions as the two dominant benefits that could be offered by a retail store.

The fifth hypothesis has four sections, each relating to a variable tested in the first four hypotheses. In three of those four cases no statistically meaningful relations between the age of the respondents and the tested variables were found. Only one aspect of the aggregate variable - impact of advertising - gives grounds for rejecting part of the hypothesis. That one aspect concerns the young-old's (accounting for 53% of the sample) greater reliance on advertising as a basis for choosing a place to shop. 68% of those senior citizens under 75 are influenced by store advertising, but only 24% of old-old admit that influence. The probability of such a difference occurring by chance is less than .001 according to a chi square analysis.

The sixth and final hypothesis tests the difference between active and passive approaches to retirement living as matched against the variables treated in the first four hypotheses. The activity-passivity classification variable proved to be a more accurate differentiator of senior citizens' feelings about media ads than did the young-old, old-old variable. 66% of the sample described themselves as active. Of those self perceived actives 75% thought that ads in general are truthful while only 43% of those characterized as passives agreed with that opinion. This difference is significant at the .02 level of chance.

TABLE 2

DIFFERENCES BETWEEN PREFERENCES FOR STORE APPEALS

| | Low Prices | Convenient Location | Friendly Employees | Senior Citizen Discount | Wide Product Selection | Home Delivery |
|---|---|---|---|---|---|---|
| Low prices | – | t = 1.57 (0.120)[a] | t = 3.66 (0.001) | t = 3.83 (0.001) | t = 5.68 (0.001) | t = 6.76 (0.001) |
| Convenient location | – | – | t = 2.28 (0.025) | t = 2.19 (0.031) | t = 4.98 (0.001) | t = 7.39 (0.001) |
| Friendly employees | – | – | – | t = 3.74 (0.001) | t = 2.36 (0.020) | t = 0.13 (0.900) |
| Senior citizen discount | – | – | – | – | t = 1.61 (0.112) | t = 3.92 (0.001) |
| Wide product selection | – | – | – | – | – | t = 1.90 (0.060) |
| Home delivery | – | – | – | – | – | – |

[a] Levels of chance probability are shown in parentheses.

Other significant differences occurred as to whether ads are considered important sources of information and whether ads influenced store choices. In both cases a majority of the actives answered "yes" while a majority of the passives responded "no". The respective chance probabilities gauging the differences in those two answers are .008 and .002.

Three other discrepencies between the actives' and the passives' responses were judged statistically significant. Actives recalled the themes as ads aiming to both a young and old market to a greater degree than did the passives (p=.02). In rating store appeals actives were impressed more by a wide product selection while the passives were more attracted by the senior citizen discount. The chance probabilities associated with those two differences are .001 and .04.

## CONCLUSIONS

Generalizing the results of a survey with a limited sample should always be undertaken with caution. Any inferences made here are more appropriate for lines of future research rather than for an immediate plan of promotional strategy. With this caveat in mind, the following preliminary conclusions are drawn.

Television appears to be an effective way of reaching the old age market. Only 20% of the respondents didn't watch television, and of those who did all watched programs in the evening. In turn, radios were turned on primarily in the morning. These statistics, though, reveal nothing new. What is worth attention is the high credibility which the sample attributed to ads carried by all three media.

The cautiousness-low persuasibility theory of old age purchase behavior is questioned by these survey results. Ads for both products and stores are considered as important sources of information. In addition, the discriminating judgments about store appeals bear out the sampled respondents' ability to recognize and rate preferences.

In a similar vein the respondents' inability to recognize ad themes directed specifically to old age people with old age problems does not contradict the previously stated notion that some old age orientated ads may be considered insulting. Only one specific complaint, however, was mentioned by as much as 10% of the respondents. That complaint centered on using sex appeals in advertisements. Perhaps, the price and convenient location appeals which had ranked highly for the sample could provide a sound initial base for an ad campaign to the senior citizen market.

The activity-passivity distinctions might hold the clue for the most fruitful path of future research. Treating the old age market as homogeneous in its reactions to marketing stimuli would be naive. An interesting research tract might first focus on the various attitudinal mannerisms characterizing different approaches to retirement living. Then these approaches could be cross-classified with the many aspects of purchase behavior.

Problems and disputes over senior citizens' consumption patterns may dissipate if old age were abandoned as a construct and replaced by different modes of behavior adopted by people in their retirement years. The nine categories synthesized from the research of Reichard and Neugarten furnish a starting place. Refining the descriptions of such modes of behavior and then matching them to consumption patterns makes more sense than to pursue further studies using an aggregate variable, i.e., old age which can mask many causes of variance in purchase activities.

## REFERENCES

1. Adams, Michael and Richard Groen, "Media Habits and Preferences of the Elderly", Journal of Leisurability, 2 (April, 1975), pp. 25-30.

2. Biondi, John and A.P. MacDonald, "Internal-External Control and Response to Influence Attempts", Journal of Personality, 39 (September, 1971), pp. 407-419.

3. Block, Joyanne E., "The Aged Consumer and the Market Place: A Critical Review", Marquette Business Review, 18 (Summer, 1974), pp. 73-81.

4. Botwinik, Jack, Aging and Behavior, New York: Springer Publishing Company, Inc. 1973, pp. 105 & 117.

5.  Butler, Robert N., quoted in "Youthful America's Showing Its Age: Longevity, Birth Rate Create Elderly Crisis", <u>The Miami Herald</u>, (September 26, ]976), pp. 1g and 12g.

6.  Chaffee, S. and D. Wilson, "Adult Life Cycle Changes in Mass Media Use", in Charles K. Atkin, "Mass Media and the Aging" in Herbert J. Oyer and E. Jane Oyer (eds.) <u>Aging and Communication</u>, Baltimore: University Park Press, 1976.

7.  <u>Economic Report of the President 1976</u>, Washington, D.C.: U.S. Department of Commerce, Bureau of the Census, U.S. Government Printing Office, 1976, p. 195.

8.  Hwang, John Chung-san, <u>Information Seeking and Opinion Leadership Among Older Americans</u>, Dissertation Abstracts International, Vol. 32 Sec. A, 1972, p. 5257A.

9.  Kotler, Philip, <u>Marketing Management 2nd ed.</u>, Englewood Cliffs, N.J.: Prentice-Hall, Inc., 1972, pp. 167-168.

10. Layton, Barry, "Perceptual Noise and Aging", <u>Psychological Bulletin</u>, 82 (6, 1975), pp. 875-883.

11. Loudon, David L., "Senior Citizens: An Underdeveloped Market Segment", <u>Proceedings of the Southern Marketing Association</u>, 1976, pp. 124-126.

12. Neugarten, Bernice L., "Age Groups in American Society and the Rise of the Young Old", <u>Annals of American Academy of Political & Social Sciences</u>, 1974, pp. 187-198.

13. Neugarten, Bernice L., Robert J. Havighurst and Sheldon S. Tobin, "Personality and Patterns of Aging", in Bernice L. Neugarten (ed.) <u>Middle Age and Aging</u>, Chicago: The University of Chicago Press, 1968, pp. 173-177.

14. "New Study Points to Growth in Job Opportunities in Work with the Elderly", <u>United States Department of Labor News</u>, Washington, D.C.: Bureau of Labor Statistics, (January 11, 1977), p. 1.

15. Phillips, Lynn W. and Brian Sternthol, "Aging and Information Processing: A Perspective on the Aged Consumer", <u>Working Paper from the Graduate School of Management, Northwestern University</u>, (August 1976), p. 16.

16. "Poverty by Age, Sex and Race", <u>The World Almanac & Book of Facts</u>, New York: Newspaper Enterprise Association, Inc., 1976, p. 206.

17. Reichard, Suzanne, "Consumption of Five Patterns", in Suzanne Reichard, Florine Livson and Paul G. Petersen (eds.) <u>Aging and Personality</u>, New York: John Wiley & Sons, 1962, pp. 162-164.

18. Ryckman, R. and M. Malikiosi, "Relationship Between Locus of Control and Chronological Age", <u>Psychological Reports</u>, 36 (April, 1975), pp. 655-658.

19. Steiner, Gary, "The People Look at Television", New York: Alfred Knopf, Inc. 1963.

20. "The Power of the Aging in the Marketplace", <u>Business Week</u>, (November 20, 1971), pp. 52-58.

21. The authors wish to thank H.C. Barksdale, Ms. M. Heaton, J. McDonald, S. Ritter, and C. Woodliff for their help in constructing and administering the research instrument.

MARKETING EDUCATION IN THE 1980s:  STRATEGY CONSIDERATIONS FOR A MATURE PRODUCT LINE*

Ben M. Enis, University of Houston

## ABSTRACT

Marketing education is a product.  Ironically, marketing professors are rather poor marketers.  This paper suggests that marketing educators could profit from practicing what we preach:  customer (student) oriented marketing of our product line.

## INTRODUCTION

"I am interested in the future" inventor Charles Kettering once remarked, "because I am going to spend my life there." His comment provides an all-too-rare glimpse of the obvious.  It is appropriate in 1977 that we discuss Marketing Education in the 1980s.

In his call for papers, Conference Chairman Alan Andreasen stated, "particular attention will be given to papers that are not in effect journal articles but which use the conference format as an opportunity to present higher risk papers that can significantly advance the field."  This paper is "higher risk" in the sense that it advances speculations and propositions that may be neither popular nor readily accepted.  Whether or not they "significantly advance the field" is arguable.

## MARKETING EDUCATORS AS MARKETERS

Our purpose today is to discuss Marketing Education in the 1980s from the viewpoint of a professional marketer.  Our primary expertise is as analysts of marketing management.  We teach and we practice the discipline of marketing more as professionals than as scholars, more as technicians than philosophers.  Let us use that expertise to focus upon how we can market the product "marketing education" more effectively and/or efficiently in the 1980s.

Despite current criticism, the marketing concept perhaps remains our dominant philosophy.  Theodore Levitt phrased it most concisely: "find a need and fill it."  E. Jerome McCarthy gave us its most widely accepted operationalization:  the 4 Ps (product, promotion, place, and price).  These are useful frameworks for contemplating marketing.  But I think that the 1980s will require a somewhat more comprehensive perspective.  So I would add my own framework:  seeking customers, matching their desires with organizational products, programming the marketing mix to fulfill those desires, and consummating the exchange process.

This set of marketing functions has served me fairly well in teaching and in consulting.  This framework can be applied to the product "marketing education."

## SEEKING CUSTOMERS:  TARGET MARKET SEGMENTS

Marketing begins with the search for customers.  Table 1 provides a basis for the discussion.  Perhaps the key point

is that students are viewed as customers.  Students are not raw materials to be manufactured, nor are they adversaries to be defeated, nor children to be guided.  They are valuable customers, to be served to mutual advantage.  But they are not ultimate consumers.  Ours is an industrial-type product.  Marketing education is purchased by students not only for consumption (the sheer joy of learning), but for resale to our ultimate consumers:  employers.

A second point is that market segmentation strategy is required.  We will in the 1980s face different market segments which will require different marketing mixes.  Product differentiation strategies, and totally new products, will be required.  Third, we had better think about marketing--not selling--to our non-consumer public segments.

## MATCHING CUSTOMERS' DESIRES AND MARKETING'S PRODUCTS

The matching function addresses environmental (demand) and organizational (supply) constraints upon the ability of the product to fulfill customers' demands.  Table 2 summarizes the issues.

We need to stress two points with respect to demand.  First, our competition is more vigorous, and at more levels.  We compete not only with other "brands" (universities), but other institutions offering similar products (junior and community colleges, vocational schools).  At an even broader level, other products may offer similar generic satisfactions:  the desire for knowledge may be satisfied by libraries, and that for job training by apprenticeships.  And we must not forget that our product competes with all other products for its share of the consumer's fixed budget.

The second point to recognize on the demand side is that the environment is less friendly to higher education than used to be the case.  Education is no longer the fondest dream of the middle class.  And we generally do not yet view policymakers and the public-at-large as potential customers--those with whom we might consummate mutually advantageous exchanges.

On the supply side, our personnel problems result from two major constraints.  First, educators, from presidents to professorial recruits, are "production-oriented."  Everyone must publish, and the rewards for publication (production) greatly exceed those for marketing (teaching) at most institutions.  Research in teaching(methods, class formats, and student evaluation)is seldom encouraged.

Second, most of us are scholars in the discipline, but are politicians at faculty meetings.  I could not imagine members of the American Marketing Association voting on the merits of, say, the Howard-Sheth model of consumer behavior; we try to test it by scientific procedures.  But in matters of curriculum design, faculty hiring, etc., we abandon our scientific orientation to wheel and deal like wardheeling politicians.  The result is resistance to the innovativeness and flexibility that characterize successful marketing-oriented companies.

Also on the supply side, we must recognize the fact that capital and physical assets are going to be more difficult for universities to acquire, and therefore will be

---

* This paper was prepared as stimulus for a panel discussion.  Panel members Bernard J. LaLonde, David J. Luck, E. Jerome McCarthy and Yoram Wind commented on drafts.  Ideas expressed profited from their suggestions, but cannot be blamed upon them.

## TABLE 1
### SEEKING CUSTOMERS FOR MARKETING EDUCATION

| Customer Segments | Current Status | Trends and Opportunities |
|---|---|---|
| **1. Consumers** | | |
| 18-22 year olds | basic desire: degree; naive, dis-interested, compliant | market no longer growing; potential conversion could be improved |
| older students | desire: knowledge (and degree); more aware, motivated, demanding | large potential; requires broader, more flexible product line |
| marketing managers | desire: training; pragmatic, motivated, pressed for time | very large potential; considered "moonlighting" to serve; requires different products |
| **2. Other Publics** | | |
| University administrators | desire: national eminence; liberal arts backgrounds; little formal knowledge of marketing | considerable potential; some indication of interests; requires careful "marketing" |
| professors | desire: academic excellence; little knowledge; provincial | increasingly important segment in allocation of institutional resources |
| managers | desire: problem-solving; technical backgrounds; narrow perspective; naive, optimistic, creative | all of these segments need a broader perspective of the role of marketing in society |
| public policymakers (legislation & donors) | desire: power; pragmatic; intuitive people-skills; little knowledge of marketing and economic action; short-run oriented | |
| social observers | desire: influence; abstract thinkers; hostile toward marketing; critically-oriented | |

## TABLE 2
### MATCHING CUSTOMER'S DESIRES AND MARKETING'S PRODUCTS

| Factors | Current Status | Trends and Opportunities |
|---|---|---|
| **1. Environmental (Demand)** | | |
| competitors | many at various levels (brand, product, generic, budget) | especially non-consumer publics will intensify: JC's and community colleges; vocational schools (public & private); apprenticeships; TV and libraries (two-way computers?) |
| public opinion | at best, uneasy; at worst, hostile | probably will get worse, especially if we continue to take an adversary rather than an exchange approach to education |
| policy-makers | suspicious at present; not basically "anti-education" | depends upon public opinion; competitor's actions, and our strategies will be crucial determinants of success |
| **2. Institutional (Supply)** | | |
| people | "production-oriented"; democratic rather than scientific decision processes | tenure: harder to get, harder to dislodge; incredible pressures upon junior faculty; increased unionization |
| capital | tight; budgets carefully constructed and minutely scrutinized | more results-oriented; requests to be justified in terms of "university objectives," e. g. better teaching |
| physical assets | often inadequate, especially for innovation | probably will get worse; less support for secretarial help, travel, computer, grading; fewer new facilities, less new equipment |

more carefully managed. Of course, we are not the only marketers experiencing such difficulties today. All marketing managers should define their tasks in terms of managing rather than stimulating or enlarging consumer demand. Thus, the "matching" function will become more important in marketing management generally, and in the management of marketing education specifically, than has been the case to date.

## PROGRAMMING FOR MARKETING EDUCATION

Programming involves the conception, development, testing, and integration of the marketing mix of product, promotion, distribution, and price. Table 3 summarizes issues here for marketing education.

With regard to the product variable, the need to carefully examine our product line is apparent. It is in many cases not sufficiently diverse for the nontraditional student segment, and part of the line intended for the traditional customer is outdated. Today's customer is job-oriented. The jobs, at the undergraduate level, are largely in personal selling and retailing. At the graduate level, there are opportunities in product management, marketing research, and advertising, as well as retailing and sales management. Many schools no longer offer such courses. On the other hand, colleagues who continue to teach these courses feel vindicated: "you see, the old standbys are coming back."

I think both groups are mistaken. We should not simply blow the dust off old products. Personal selling is more than "shine your shoes and smile;" retailing is more than descriptions of store layout and computation of markups. New courses, incorporating advances in behavioral, quantitative, and managerial knowledge, and oriented toward job opportunities, are required--at both undergraduate and graduate levels.

Some of our courses are obsolete or at least obsolescent. For example, most of us no longer "market" quantitative methods, at least to undergraduates, as a separate course. It is not that we feel that quantitative methods are not important, but that they should be introduced as appropriate in other courses. Perhaps the subject matter of consumer behavior should also be treated in this way. That is, appropriate behavioral material should be integrated into such courses as personal selling, retailing, and advertising. This argument could also be advanced for other pertinent material often relegated to separate courses which many students do not take: international marketing, marketing in society, the marketing of services. Systematic thinking here is analogous to a product portfolio (integrated curriculum)--rather than an individual product item (isolated course)--approach to product decisions.

Our attitude toward promotion is downright embarrassing. We simply ignore this element of the marketing mix. College catalogs are dismal promotion pieces. The "sales office" is staffed by graduate students and secretaries. We vie to escape from counseling students.

Our record in distributing marketing education is no better. Lecturing, our dominant distribution method, is a practice left over from the universities of the middle ages--when books were scarce. We do not like to teach at night, or on the weekends. And we even make the customers park the farthest distance from the marketplace, while we (the sellers) grab the choice parking locations next to the building.

The entire marketing discipline needs a broader interpretation of price. To the consumer, price represents value given up for benefits received. This involves not only monetary outlays, but also time and energy expended, frustration and aggravation endured, and opportunities foregone. We know that the monetary costs of a college

TABLE 3
PROGRAMMING FOR MARKETING EDUCATION

| Mix Elements | Current Status | Trends and Opportunities |
|---|---|---|
| 1. Product | life cycle of many courses in decline stage; line fragmented and proliferated; professorial posture: provincial | review of courses from "consumer" perspective, overhaul if necessary; curriculum integration within segments; new product lines for new segments |
| 2. Promotion | almost non-existent; image diffuse to poor; professorial posture: indifference | sensitivity to importance; use of principles course as recruiting device; emphasis on job opportunities |
| 3. Distribution | archaic; distribution system largely unchanged since the middle ages; professorial posture: resistant to change | sensitivity; willingness to experiment with materials, methods, timing |
| 4. Price | very high opportunity costs; rising out-of-pocket costs; professorial posture: ignorance | sensitivity; perhaps "mass distribution" to achieve economics of scale |

education are rising, and that the expected monetary benefits, relative to jobs which do not require a college
education, are diminishing.  We should at least attempt
to reduce the frustrations associated with a college education.  When I was in school, faculty and students had
segregated washrooms.  This type of discrimination no
longer exists at most schools, but many others linger.  We
really should not treat our customers this way.

## CONSUMMATING THE EDUCATIONAL EXCHANGE

The tasks of marketing management are not completed once
the marketing program has been developed.  The exchange
transaction must be consummated, and then product use and
evaluation by the customer should be monitored, as shown
in Table 4.

The "marketplace" for most educational exchanges is the
classroom--a standardized, impersonal, dull setting for
the purchase of knowledge.  We could do better here.  In
addition, there is increasing opportunity for individual
instruction and student counseling, but we are novices in
this area.  We would not award a degree in marketing to a
person who had five years of selling experience, but no
formal education.  But we, who have never studied counseling and guidance techniques, consider ourselves experts
in professor-student interaction.  And we devote almost no
attention at all to other possible marketplaces.

The area of student "consumption" of education disturbs
me most.  We measure learning by the surrogate of testing.
My own view is that testing inhibits learning.  How many
times have you hear a colleague say, "I taught them that,
but they did not learn it"?   Can you imagine a salesperson telling the boss, "I sold it to them, but they did not
buy it"?   We need to develop more effective measures of
what the student has actually consumed, rather than what
the professor thinks has been sold.  We might even raise
the broader question of whether grading is necessary at
all.  We seem to do pretty well without it in executive
development programs.

Finally, and perhaps more importantly, I think we ignore
the long-term satisfaction of our customers.  And this is
a great mistake.  A "satisfied customer" can be very, very
valuable to an education institution, in terms of word-of-
mouth advertising, as a source of jobs for future students, contributions of money and time, and sharing those
real-world experiences that so enrich our classroom presentations.

## CONCLUSION

In closing, there are at least three broader issues that
constrain marketing strategy development for the product
marketing education.  First, we have talked about the
marketing of marketing education.  We have ignored "production", i.e., research in the field of marketing.  We
know that both teaching and research are necessary, but
have not addressed the problems of attaining a proper
balance.

Second, customer orientation can be carried too far.  As
British statemen Benjamin Disraeli once remarked, "we
serve the peoples' interests, not their desires."  But how
do we design curricula that are both palatable to students in the short-run, and supportive of their life
styles and livelihoods in the long-run?  Third, teaching
has traditionally been a profession acknowledged to be
rich in intrinsic, and poor in extrinsic, rewards.  More
and more of us seem to be focusing on activities which
result in extrinsic rewards, e.g., publishing, and minimizing personally satisfying but low-payoff tasks like
student counseling.  Again, the question is one of proper
balance.

In summary, this paper's purpose is to pique curiosity
and provoke controversy about marketing eduction.  We
need to explore such issues, and we have the professional
expertise to do so.  I personally am an optimist.  I see
these issues as opportunities rather than obstacles.  But
we should think about them now.  To ignore the future by
pleading the press of current affairs is rather like not
taking the time to put gasoline in your car.  We really
cannot afford not to prepare now for marketing education
in the 1980s.

TABLE 4
CONSUMMATING THE EDUCATIONAL EXCHANGE

| Steps | Current Status | Trends and Opportunities |
|---|---|---|
| 1. "Purchase" | | |
| classroom | standardized, impersonal, dull | better use of new technologies, more effect-ive presentation |
| other "market-places" (e.g., correspondence, company premises, television) | tolerated; not encouraged | active pursuit of "sales" in these new formats |
| individual instruction | limited; professorial choice | better understanding of human interaction |
| 2. Use & Evaluation | | |
| "consumption" (learning) | measured by surrogate | development of effective measures of student learning rather than instructor expertise |
| satisfaction | ignored | development of procedures to monitor graduates, update skills, etc. |

AN INVESTIGATION OF SOME DATA COLLECTION ISSUES
IN CONJOINT MEASUREMENT[1]

Franklin Acito, Indiana University

ABSTRACT

A number of marketing applications of conjoint measurement
have been reported. However, relatively little attention
has been directed at the problems involved in the design
of instruments for collecting data required in conjoint
analysis. A number of data collection issues are raised
and investigated in this pilot study and suggestions for
future conjoint measurement applications are made.

INTRODUCTION

Since its introduction in the marketing literature in 1971,
[7] conjoint analysis has been applied in a wide variety
of situations, including the measurement of preferences for
air travel alternatives [4], retail discount cards [8], and
health care organizations [1] to name but a few. Several
algorithms have been developed to derive additive utility
functions from ranked data [10, 12, 15] and extensions of
the basic additive model have been made. [6] Despite this
high level of interest and activity, relatively little work
has been published to date concerning the reliability and
validity of conjoint measurement. A similar situation
seems to exist with regard to multidimensional scaling,
although two recent studies [9, 16] have addressed these
issues.

There has been some effort made to assess the reliability
of conjoint measurement, its predictive validity, the fit
of the additive model versus more complex models, and the
robustness of several algorithms under varying data conditions. [1, 2, 5, 13]. However, it is felt that testing
and refinement of data collection procedures have not kept
pace with the development of powerful and sophisticated
computer techniques for analysis of the data. Therefore,
the present study focuses on the data collection phase of
conjoint analysis. The data collection phase normally
involves forming factorial combinations of attributes
which are then presented to respondents as alternatives.
Respondents are asked to consider the alternatives and to
rank, rate or otherwise react to them. Normally only a
fraction of the total possible number of alternatives are
presented to respondents since realistic problems the
total number of combinations can easily number in the hun-
dreds. Respondents must still consider a fairly large
number of alternatives even when fractional factorial
designs are used. Since the alternatives may differ only
in very minor ways from one another, the possibility of
error and noise in the resultant respondent evaluations
may be high.

This study was conducted to investigate the following data
collection issues. First, it appears reasonable to ask
whether or not a respondent would rank multiattribute alternatives in the same or a similar manner on several
occasions. As noted before test-retest reliability has
been investigated previously in this context [1, 13], but
the present study goes beyond other studies by investigating the reliability over several retests. The second

issue concerns the order in which factors are listed on
each alternative concept. Factors which appear first or
last on each card, for example, might receive disproportionate attention from respondents. The third issue
concerns the appropriateness of the additive model. There
are ways to deal with interaction effects from an analytical standpoint [6], but the extent to which randomness in
the data causes deviations from the additive model needs
to be investigated. The fourth issue stems from problems
in analyzing conjoint measurement data when respondents
rank the alternative concepts using a lexicographic or
other hierarchical rule. This can lead to estimates of
utility weights for attributes which are not unique. This
problem has been recognized by previous authors [1, 13, 14],
but the question to be considered here is whether the lexicographic ordering stems from real preferences by respondents or is rather an artifact of the data collection
process.

DESCRIPTION OF STUDY

To explore the four issues described above, a study was
conducted in which respondents were asked to rank a set of
alternatives on several occasions. The alternatives were
variations of instant picture cameras, of which several
types and brands are now on the market. Each of three
attributes of the cameras was offered at three levels for
a total of 27 possible camera concepts. Table 1 shows the
attributes and levels used. The attributes were selected
to roughly correspond to real alternatives now offered on
the market. Respondents were told to assume that the
cameras were alike in all other features, including performance, cost of film, and so on.

TABLE 1

ATTRIBUTES OF INSTANT CAMERAS USED IN STUDY

| ATTRIBUTE | LEVEL | | |
| | 1 | 2 | 3 |
|---|---|---|---|
| A  Picture Size | 2 1/2" x 3 1/2" | 3" x 3" | 4" x 3" |
| B  Type | Camera does not fold up for storage. After snapping picture, a crank is turned to eject the print. | Camera does not fold up for stor- age. After snapping picture, print is automati- cally ejected from the camera. | Camera folds up for stor- age. After snapping picture, print is automatical ly ejected from the camera. |
| C  Price | $55 | $70 | $85 |

[1]Computer assistance for this project was provided by
Indiana University-Purdue University at Indianapolis Office
of Computer Services.

Respondents were presented with a packet containing six
sets of the 27 camera concepts and asked to rank the 27
concepts in order of preference on six consecutive days.
Each of the six sets of 27 camera concepts was based on
the attributes shown in Table 1, but the order in which
the attributes appeared on the cards varied across sets.
All six possible permutations of the order of the three
attributes (ABC) were formed: ABC, ACB, BCA, BAC, CAB,
CBA. The order in which the respondents were given the
cards was also varied so that on the first day, for example, some respondents would have 27 cards with the factors in order ABC, others would have ACB, etc. Respondents were instructed not to attempt to memorize the order
of the cards or to look back at their previous responses.
Identification numbers on the cards were varied randomly
across the six sets so that checking previous rank orders
was made difficult.

Respondents in the study were 19 undergraduate university
students. While the sample is small, it was felt that the
issues of interest could nonetheless be investigated in a
satisfactory manner.

## RESULTS

### Reliability of Rankings

To examine the consistency of the rank order of the 27
camera alternatives for each respondent, the Spearman rank
correlation coefficient was used. Correlations were computed between each of the six successive orderings, for a
total of five coefficients per person. The mean and median
correlations are shown in Table 2. The median is probably
a better measure of central tendency because the distribution of the correlations is highly skewed. Correlations
for individual respondents were as low as .51, but, in
general, as can be seen in Table 2, the correlations were
high. It should also be noted that the correlations
shifted upward as the ranking task was repeated. This is
not unexpected, as respondents were undoubtedly "learning"
on successive replications. All of the observed correlations were significant at the .01 level.

TABLE 2

SPEARMAN RANK CORRELATIONS BETWEEN SUCCESSIVE REPLICATIONS

| | Correlations between replications | | | | |
|---|---|---|---|---|---|
| | 1+2 | 2+3 | 3+4 | 4+5 | 5+6 |
| Median | .89 | .95 | .97 | .99 | 1.0 |
| Mean | .86 | .93 | .95 | .96 | .97 |

A second measure of the reliability of the rankings was
computed with Kendall's coefficient of concordance, W.
[3] W reflects the extent to which each individual's six
sets of rankings were consistent. W ranged from .85 to
1.0, with a mean of .93. Using the appropriate chi-square
test, it was found that observed W were significant beyond
the .01 level for all of the 19 respondents.

These results indicate that respondents can evaluate the
27 camera concepts in a consistent and reliable manner.
Since the time between successive replications of the task
was short (one day), the observed correlation coefficients
can be considered an "upper limit."

### Order Effects

The next issue considered was the effect of position or
order of an attribute on its measured importance. To
determine the importance of the attributes, each individual's preference rankings for each of the six replications was submitted to MONANOVA [12], a commonly used
conjoint measurement algorithm. The relative importance
of each attribute was determined by computing the difference between each attribute at its most and least favorable levels. Which levels were most favorable varied
across respondents. For example, some felt that the 3" x
3" picture size was least favorable, while others felt
that the 2 1/2" x 3 1/2" picture was least favorable.
Table 3 shows how the importance of factors varied as the
order in which factors were listed was varied.

TABLE 3

IMPORTANCE OF ATTRIBUTES VERSUS ORDER OF PRESENTATION

Number of times each factor found to be most important

| Factor found to be most important* | Order of Presentation | | | | | |
|---|---|---|---|---|---|---|
| | BAC | ACB | ABC | CBA | CAB | BCA |
| A | 0 | 1 | 1 | 0 | 0 | 1 |
| B | 13 | 11 | 10 | 10 | 7 | 10 |
| C | 6 | 7 | 8 | 9 | 12 | 8 |

*Factor A: Size of Picture
Factor B: Type of Camera
Factor C: Price

Inspection of Table 3 suggests a tendency for attributes
appearing first on a card describing a camera alternative
to be given greater importance. A statistical test of
this issue was performed using Cochran's Q. [3] Ordinary
chi-square analysis is inappropriate because the successive observations are not independent. The analysis was
carried out for the "B" factor only, with the null hypothesis being that the number of times "B" was ranked first
in importance was independent of the order of presentation
of the attribute. Cases where "B" was most important were
assigned zero. Q is distributed chi-square, with k-1
degrees of freedom. The value of Q was computed to be
12.56, which indicates significance at the .05 level.
Thus, the null hypothesis of no difference in the importance of "B" across the six groups must be rejected. This
suggests that the order in which attributes were listed on
cards affected the way in which respondents evaluated the
cards.

### Appropriateness of the Additive Model

Many conjoint measurement algorithms assume that the overall utility for an alternative is simply the sum of the
utility values for each component attribute. It is difficult in practice to determine whether or not this additive
model is appropriate. One approach to determining the
adequacy of the additive rule is based on a set of axioms
which the data must satisfy for the additive rule. While
no complete axiomatic testing is attempted here, a test of
perhaps the most basic axiom can be easily performed. This
axiom is that of independence of the factors. Factor A is
said to be independent of factors B and C if the rank ordering (in terms of preference in the present case) of the
levels of Factor A is the same for all levels of factors B
and C. [11] This, of course, is not sufficient to prove
additivity, but it is a necessary condition.

Independence of factors A, B, and C was checked for each respondent's rank ordering on the first replication of the task. Of the 513 checks made (3 factors x 9 checks per factor x 19 respondents), 76 violations of independence were found. This would seem to suggest that the additive model might not be appropriate for this data.

For purposes of comparison, the independence of factors A, B, and C was also checked for each respondent's ordering based on the sum of his ranks for the six replications. Kendall has suggested that if W, the coefficient of concordance, is significant, then the best estimate of the true rankings of the set of objects is given by the order of the sum of the ranks. [3] This procedure has also been used by others investigating conjoint measurement axioms. [5] Of the 513 checks made for the sum-of-ranks model, only 20 violations of independence were observed.

The above results suggest that the observed violations of independence on the first day's rankings were probably caused by randomness in the rankings. Table 4 provides additional evidence for this interpretation. In Table 4 the number of violations of independence is shown to vary with the importance of the attributes. The fact that many more violations were observed for the least important attribute than for the most important attribute is again suggestive of noise rather than lack of independence of the factors. The reasoning here would be that the respondent pays less attention to the less important attributes (or finds the ranking more difficult) and thus is more likely to make random responses. A previous study [5] has reported more violations of independence for less important attributes.

TABLE 4

VIOLATIONS OF THE INDEPENDENCE ASSUMPTION
BY IMPORTANCE OF THE ATTRIBUTE

| | Number of Violations | |
| | Rankings from first replication | Rankings from sum-of-ranks model |
| --- | --- | --- |
| Most Important Attribute | 8 | 0 |
| Intermediate Attribute | 28 | 3 |
| Least Important Attribute | 40 | 17 |
| Total Number of Violations | 76 | 20 |

Another approach to this issue is to examine Kruskal's stress value, which is an indication of the goodness of fit of the additive model. Stress values of over 10% are felt to be indicative of noise and/or interaction effects in the ranked data. The average stress value for the first replication of the ranking was 11.1%. The average value for the sum-of-ranks data based on all six replications was 1.9%. Using a correlated t-test, this difference was found to be significant beyond the .01 level. Again, these results suggest the presence of noise in the first day's ranking.

Lexicographic Processing

In analyzing conjoint measurement data with MONANOVA (or any of several other algorithms such as LINMAP [15] or Johnson's non-metric regression [10]), a problem can arise

if the alternatives with an attribute at a certain level are ranked higher (or lower) than all alternatives with that attribute at other levels. This can occur if the respondent finds a level of one attribute that is critically important and refuses to "trade off" for other levels of this same attribute. Lexicographic and other hierarchical information processing strategies can also lead to this situation. Under these data conditions, estimates of utility values are not unique.

Evidence of lexicographic processing of the alternative camera concepts was found in the present study. Furthermore, as Table 5 shows, there was an increased tendency by respondents to use at least a partially lexicographic strategy over replications of the ranking task (except for a slight reversal on the last replication).

TABLE 5

EXTENT OF LEXICOGRAPHIC PROCESSING BY RESPONDENTS

| | REPLICATION | | | | | |
| | 1 | 2 | 3 | 4 | 5 | 6 |
| --- | --- | --- | --- | --- | --- | --- |
| Number of Respondents Using Lexicographic Strategy | 6 | 10 | 10 | 10 | 14 | 12 |

On an overall basis, using the sum-of-ranks model, 11 of the respondents were classified as using a non-lexicographic strategy, and 8 were classified as lexicographic. The average value of W, the coefficient of concordance, for the non-lexicographic respondents was .90, while the average value for those classified as lexicographic was .98. (This difference is significant beyond the .01 level using the t-test). This suggests that respondents using the lexicographic strategy were significantly more consistent in ranking the camera alternatives.

DISCUSSION

The results of this study can be integrated and summarized as follows. First, successive rank orderings of 27 multi-attribute alternatives were found to be far more consistent than one would expect by chance. But, comparisons of the first replication with the results using the sum-of-ranks model suggest a fair amount of noise or randomness in the former. This noise produced higher stress values and more violations of the assumption that the factors were independent. Second, a possible source of bias in applications of conjoint measurement was found in the significant differences due to the order in which attributes appeared on the alternative cards. Third, a tendency by respondents to use a lexicographic ordering procedure was found to increase with successive replications. Respondents using the lexicographic strategy were also found to be more consistent in their rankings, as measured by Kendall's coefficient of concordance. Although no causal direction can be established by these results, it is possible that respondents use the lexicographic ordering strategy as a means of dealing with the data collection problem rather than as a reflection of their actual decision making process. When respondents realized that they could relieve some of the tedium involved in ranking the 27 cards by adopting a lexicographic strategy, they adopted it.

Although the sample used in this study was small, and of

a specialized nature (students), several suggestions for future conjoint measurement applications can be offered. First, to avoid order bias, a randomizing scheme may be necessary wherein the order in which attributes appear on the alternatives is varied, either across respondents or possibly for the same respondent. Varying the order of attributes for each respondent might cause confusion and make evaluation of the concepts quite difficult. The order bias would be expected to decrease if the attributes used are critical to respondents. On the other hand, many conjoint measurement applications use seven or more attributes. As the number of attributes is increased, it would seem that the possibility of some order bias would also increase.

A second suggestion would be that if interaction effects are expected, more powerful data collection techniques should be used. Some sort of redundancy could be built into the data collection procedure such as requiring respondents to react to the same stimulus several times during the interview. Otherwise, noise in the data, especially for attributes that are relatively unimportant, could suggest interaction effects where none actually exist.

A third suggestion concerns the tendency for respondents to use a lexicographic ranking strategy. One way to avoid this is to not force respondents to rank alternatives but rather to react to them singly (by rating) or in pairs (by paired comparisons). Neither of these techniques will prevent lexicographic ordering, but they should reduce the chance that lexicographic ordering is adopted merely as a response to the data collection task.

If rating data is collected, and one is willing to accept it as being approximately interval scaled, then the entire problem of non-unique utility values can be avoided by using metric ANOVA to analyze the data. This strategy was suggested by Carmone et al. [2], but for another reason (saving computer time).

The overall findings of this study suggest caution in future applications of conjoint analysis. The technique has a number of attractive features, but a number of problems remain. Further efforts at discovering these problems and generating and testing solutions seem necessary to strengthen its usefulness.

## REFERENCES

. Acito, Franklin. "Consumer Preferences for Health Care Services: An Exploratory Investigation," unpublished doctoral dissertation, State University of New York at Buffalo, 1976.

. Carmone, Frank J., Paul E. Green and Arun K. Jain, "The Robustness of Conjoint Analysis: Some Monte Carlo Results," Working Paper No. 268, School of Management, State University of New York at Buffalo, May, 1976.

. Churchill, Gilbert A., Jr. Marketing Research: Methodological Foundations. Hinsdale, Ill.: Dryden Press, 1976.

. Davidson, J. D., "Forecasting Traffic on STOL," Operational Research Quarterly, 24 (1973), 561-569.

. Fischer, Gregory W., "Multidimensional Utility Models for Risky and Riskless Choice," Organizational Behavior and Human Performance, 17 (October 1976), 127-146.

. Green, Paul E. and Michael T. Devita, "An Interaction Model of Consumer Utility," Journal of Consumer Research, 2 (September 1975), 146-153.

7. Green, Paul E. and Vithala R. Rao, "Conjoint Measurement for Quantifying Judgmental Data," Journal of Marketing Research, 8 (August 1971), 355-363.

8. Green, Paul E. and Yoram Wind. Multiattribute Decision Making: A Measurement Approach. Hinsdale, Ill.: Dryden Press, 1973.

9. Jain, Arun K. and Christian Pinson, "The Effect of Order of Presentation of Similarity Judgments on Multidimensional Scaling Results: An Empirical Examination," Journal of Marketing Research, 13 (November 1976), 435-439.

10. Johnson, Richard M., "A Simple Method for Pairwise Monotone Regression," Psychometrika, 40 (June 1975), 163-168.

11. Krantz, David H. and Amos Tversky, "Conjoint-Measurement Analysis of Composition Rules in Psychology," Psychological Review, 78 (March 1971), 151-169.

12. Kruskal, Joseph B., "Analysis of Factorial Experiments by Estimating Monotone Transformation of the Data," Journal of the Royal Statistical Society, Series B, 27 (March 1965), 251-263.

13. Parker, Barnett R. and V. Srinivasan, "A Consumer Preference Approach to the Planning of Rural Health-Care Facilities," Operations Research, 24 (September-October 1976), 991-1025.

14. Rao, Vithala and Samuel Craig, "Consumer Evaluation of Product Information by Source: An Application of Conjoint Measurement," Working Paper, Cornell University, 1975.

15. Srinivasan, V. and Allan D. Shocker, "Linear Programming Techniques for Multidimensional Analysis of Preferences," Psychometrika, 38 (September 1973), 337-369.

16. Summers, John O. and David B. MacKay, "On the Validity and Reliability of Direct Similarity Judgments," Journal of Marketing Research, 13 (August 1976), 289-295.

# THE APPLICATION OF ADDITIVE CONJOINT ANALYSIS IN MARKETING RESEARCH: ASSUMPTIONS, ADVANTAGES, AND LIMITATIONS

Terry C. Wilson, Central Michigan University
Brian F. Harris, Michigan State University

## ABSTRACT

Conjoint measurement is a recent addition to the arsenal of marketing research techniques. A review of how the technique has been used in marketing is presented. Particular emphasis is given to explicating some critical assumptions underlying the technique which must be recognized by researchers in assessing the advantages and limitations of its application.

## INTRODUCTION

The past two decades have witnessed a vast expansion in the analytical techniques available to marketing researchers [20, 29]. A recent addition to the arsenal of techniques is conjoint measurement. The purpose of this paper is to review the technique as it has been applied in marketing with particular emphasis on explicating some of the critical assumptions that must be recognized in evaluating the advantages and limitations of its use. Such a review facilitates improved application and more valid interpretation of the technique and provides a focal point for future discussion.

The first published composition on conjoint measurement is attributed to Luce and Tukey [24], although aspects of the background were developed by Fisher in the 1930s. After the initial conceptualization of the technique, the literature in the field of mathematical psychology was extended by Tversky [31, 32], Lingoes [23], Krantz and Tversky [21], Young [33], and Johnson [16, 19]. These references provide the theoretical underpinnings of the technique.

## CONJOINT MEASUREMENT AND CONJOINT ANALYSIS: A CLARIFICATION

There is much interchanging in the literature of certain terms which provides an ideal setting for confusion and ambiguity. The definition of conjoint measurement in its originally used context applies to the measurement models of conjoint variables [24]. The terms conjoint analysis and conjoint scaling also appear in the literature. In this paper, conjoint analysis refers to the measurement of the values of jointly occurring variables through quantification of respondent value systems. An example of jointly occurring variables can be taken from the expectancy/value type models, one of which is the Fishbein model of attitudes. The jointly occurring variables are $a_i$ (desirability) and $B_i$ (belief), the measurement of which has traditionally been separated in the marketing literature. In other words, they are measured separately with different scales. Conjoint measurement is a method of measuring $a_iB_i$ as one unit and then searching for a combination rule that best fits $a_iB_i$ when they are decomposed into separate entities; that is to say, conjoint measurement provides a systematic search procedure to test whether $a_i$ and $B_i$ are best predicted by a multiplicative, additive, or quadratic function. Berner [2] has performed such an analysis for the expectancy theory in work motivation which is a closely analogous case.

Conjoint analysis, in contrast to conjoint measurement, heuristically searches for an intervally scaled utility function that best fits the rank ordered responses on a specified list of attributes. The utility function can thus be examined for rank order of attribute levels for each respondent. Conjoint scaling is an anomaly referring to the similarity between conjoint and non-metric multidimensional scaling algorithms.

The first reference to conjoint measurement in the consumer research literature was made by Green and Rao [11] whose article noted that the original work of Luce and Tukey was the foundation for the type of analysis employed. Conjoint analysis is also referred to in some literature as trade-off analysis [18]. The reason for the latter designation is that both methods were being developed simultaneously but independent of each other. The trade-off terminology simply refers to a specific method of obtaining respondent data. There is, however, no other difference between the two terms. There is no evidence that any method of data collection is more valid than any other or gives rise to different results [16, 17].

## THE MODEL ASSUMPTIONS

The assumptions of conjoint analysis have been previously specified in various pieces of the theoretical literature, although they have not been outlined specifically for application of the technique. It is essential that they be recognized as the technique has undergone relatively minor investigations thus far with respect to its robustness.

First, in order to delimit a workable scope, the basic model of interest in this paper is assumed to be additive. The major use of the additive model is the measurement of the joint effects of a set of independent variables on the ordering of a dependent variable, analogous to the main effects model in analysis of variance. The general model can be expressed as:

$$U(X) = U_1x_1 + U_2x_2 + \ldots U_nx_n \tag{1}$$

where:
$U(X)$ = the overall worth (utility) of a set of attributes
$U_1x_1$ thru $U_nx_n$ = the part worths (utilities) for each level

Second, the respondent is assumed to have completely ordered all of the orthogonal combinations of attribute levels. Orthogonal (nonredundant) combinations imply that the efficient use of fractional factorials can be appropriate especially when there are many attributes with many levels which would induce respondent fatigue and non-involvement [9]. In their original conceptualization, Luce and Tukey assumed only nominally measured data, but the more restrictive case of ordered data is much easier to handle as a measurement model than the nominal case [6].

In the event of obtaining ordered data, there is a third assumption called the cancellation axiom which must be satisfied [6, 24]. This axiom, coming from mathematical psychology, has a simple counterpart in the economics literature which is more familiar to marketers. This assumption states that indifference curves do not cross unless a consumer has inconsistent tastes, which is an inadmissable contradiction [28]. One method of evaluating respondent consistency, i.e., the cancellation axiom, in a conjoint analysis context is to test the rank orders produced by the respondent and by the conjoint algorithm using Kendall's tau statistic [5]. As a rule of thumb, a tau value of less than .70 would denote too great an inconsistency on the part of the respondent to be included in the analysis [1]. Admittedly, this is not a scientifically derived number, but it does indicate that a reasonably close fit does exist.

A fourth implicit assumption is noted in mathematical psychology as solvability which is analogous to the assumption in economics which states that indifference curves are everywhere dense. In other words, an indifference curve passes through each point in a commodity space, an assumption which is, of course, not technically true, especially in the case of indivisible goods [26]. However, given that a consumer develops a relevant range of utilities for a commodity space, and that the commodity space is a function of product attributes rather than separate and individual products, this assumption will be met to such a sufficiently high degree of approximation that it will be unlikely to develop as an empirical problem.

A fifth and final assumption is that the product attributes are independent; that is to say, the additive model precludes any interaction effects among attributes being present. It should be noted that mathematically the multiplicative model is a trivial derivation of the additive model since numbers have the same rank order as their logarithms and when logarithms (antilogs) are taken of multiplicative (additive) utilities they become additive (multiplicative) utilities [18].

## DESIRABLE DIMENSIONS OF A MARKET SITUATION

Given the above assumptions, it is useful to outline the desirable characteristics of a market situation whereby conjoint analysis becomes an appropriate technique. Following is a list of such desirable dimensions.
1. Product (or service) is realistically decomposable into a set of basic attributes leading to the decision process. This is primarily a reductionist viewpoint. For example, the purchase of a durable good such as an automobile would be decomposable. People use explicit criteria to purchase such an item such as price, seating capacity, and warranty. On the other hand, an impulse or fad purchase would most likely not be required to meet such explicit criteria.
2. Product (or service) choice tends to be a more economically rational, high stake decision process. It generally follows that the choice tends to be high cost and high individual involvement, and that there is substantial time devoted to making the decision. Again, the above example of a durable good would fit these criteria.
3. There is one decision maker. Although this statement needs no explanation, it can pose difficulties. In an industrial setting it can usually be determined whether the decision is made by an individual or a committee. But it also is possible, as it is with consumer purchase decisions, that one person may make the decision but only after considerable external influence. A case in point is the purchase of a consumer durable. The family unit may not make the decision, but it is reasonable to conclude that the decision maker was influenced by family members. Specifically, then, the problem is that a respondent may be able to provide attribute rank orders, but these rank orders may not be the ones actually used in the final decision process. One possibility is for husband and wife to respond to the measurement instrument together. Another possibility is that each individual may revise the rank order after input by other family members. Rank order revision, however, has no present empirical verification.
4. Product (or service) is chosen according to highly specific, non-subjective attributes. In other words, attribute level specification is perceptively homogeneous across consumers. Specificity and objectivity are factors to be considered in the choice of attribute levels, but it is flexible almost to the point of being arbitrary. For example, attribute levels that mean totally different things to different people are unacceptable. Seating capacity in

an automobile might be denoted as four. To some people, this may mean four adults; to others it may mean two adults and two children. The solution is to state the levels more specifically, such as adult seating capacity. In many instances it is possible to argue either way concerning the homogeneous meaning of words. The solution is an _a priori_ consideration of attribute levels.
5. In the event of many attribute level combinations, the factorial combinations of the basic attribute levels must be believable. The alternatives must be realistic or non-involvement by the respondents confounds any research results. For instance, an automobile with seating capacity of six adults that gets forty mpg, and costs $2,000 is ludicrous in today's marketplace. The attribute levels must be within a range considered relevant for present consumers.

As is true with most methodologies, it is difficult to imagine a product that would fit exactly all of the model assumptions detailed above. It is desirable to satisfy as many of the above dimensions as possible and to recognize the limitations of the research with respect to the other dimensions.

## COMPUTER ALGORITHMS

It is not within the scope of this paper to delineate all of the technical aspects of the available algorithms, but merely to indicate those that are generally available. All algorithms noted here are non-metric decomposition methods similar to the techniques of non-metric scaling [10]. As is the case with many multivariate algorithms, each of the programs has its own special technical pecularities. These unique properties may be important for mathematical purposes, but tend not to be revealed in empirical work [12]. Common algorithms include MONANOVA [22], CCM [3], POLYCON [33], CM-I [23], LINMAP [30], NMRG [19], ORDMET [25], and PREFMAP [4].

## DATA COLLECTION

Thus far, the data collection procedures for conjoint analysis in market settings have generally involved one of two methods. The first is referred to as the trade-off method and the second as the full profile or concept evaluation method. Under similar conditions similar results will be obtained using either method [16, 17].

### The Trade-Off Method

The trade-off method requires rank ordering by a respondent of preferences in all levels of two attributes. An example will clarify exactly what a trade-off matrix attempts to do. A respondent might be shown a matrix like the following pertaining to automobiles and be asked to fill in the respective alternatives by rank ordering each. Note that one axis is a ratio scale (price) and the other is a nominal

|  | Purchase Price | | |
|---|---|---|---|
|  | $3,000 | $3,500 | $4,000 |
| U.S. Manufacturer |  |  |  |
| Foreign Manufacturer |  |  |  |

(origin). These axes could be any combination of levels of measure because the respondent is able to rank order any combination of levels. The attributes can be determined from a comprehensive list by use of a technique such as factor analysis, or from previous research [15]. Attribute levels must be believable, i.e., levels within a relevant range for consumers, and each combination of levels must be realistic.

Now, let us suppose that given the above matrix the respondent has hypothetically rank ordered the alternatives as follows:

|  | Purchase Price | | |
| --- | --- | --- | --- |
|  | $3,000 | $3,500 | $4,000 |
| U.S. Manufacturer | 1 | 2 | 4 |
| Foreign Manufacturer | 3 | 5 | 6 |

By simple inspection, it can be ascertained that this respondent prefers an auto that is manufactured in the U.S. as opposed to a foreign manufacturer and lower prices to higher prices, other things being equal. By a joint examination of the attributes in the above matrix, more information can be obtained. For instance, while this consumer's second choice is a $3,500 auto manufactured in the U.S., it would be more desirable to switch to a foreign manufacturer than pay another increment in price. This conclusion assumes that the consumer trade-off is with only these two attributes with the ceteris paribus assumption holding. Thus, the relative influence of the factor level can be ascertained, and, through investigation of other attributes such as warranty, seating capacity, etc., the respondent's value system for an automobile purchase can be reconstructed. Such reconstruction would be done by allowing an algorithm such as NMRG to restructure as closely as possible all combinations of rank ordered factor levels and by assigning appropriate utility values to each level. Through knowledge of the utilities of each level, the rank order of preference of a given combination of levels for that respondent could be made.

The Full Profile Method

The above data collection procedure is quite different from the procedure described initially by Green and Rao [11] whose approach has been referred to as the full profile or **concept evaluation** method which is closer to the functional form investigations in psychology [2]. With this procedure respondents are asked to rank order product concepts which differ simultaneously with respect to several attributes. An example might be: "An automobile manufactured in the U.S., for a price of $3,500, with a 2 year warranty, and a dealer that is a 20-minute drive from your home." The above statement would be in an array of statements that varied with respect to the relevant attributes, i.e., country of origin, price, length of warranty, and dealer location. The assortment of choices can be written, verbal, or pictorial. In the event of a totally new product concept, the actual experimental product could be used. When the number of options requiring rank order is large a sort board can be efficiently utilized.

Differences Between The Two Methods

An examination of the two methods described above reveals differences which would concern researchers under varying circumstances. The trade-off method is laborious for the respondent and requires the respondent to abstract each comparison due to the ceteris paribus assumption. On the other hand, the full profile method specifies a concept fully and thus promotes a higher probability of commonality of perception. Still, the greater inherent realism in the full profile method is limited by the fact that respondents cannot easily interpret profiles including more than five to seven attributes [18]. A drawback in this method is the cost, especially for the more reliable pictorial method where scale drawings are a necessity and where mock models are often needed. Both methods call for a great deal of respondent training with each requiring an interview of approximately 1½ hours. The problem of too many factor level combinations for rank ordering by respondents is solved through various orthogonal designs, e.g., Latin square, fractional factorials [9].

## APPLICATIONS IN THE LITERATURE

A limited number of examples of conjoint analysis have made their way into the literature. A wider range of applications has been noted in such areas as consumer non-durables, financial services, industrial goods, automobiles and transportation but are generally unavailable for academic perusal [11].

The original marketing publication [11] paved the way for a range of applications by suggesting suitable areas and developing the groundwork for using the technique, including the model, its assumptions, and the available algorithms. Green, Wind, and Jain [14] applied the additive conjoint model to consumer menu preferences using MONANOVA and Fiedler used the NMRG program to study condominium design and pricing [8]. A study by Green, Carmone, and Wind [10] on the worth of discount cards to housewives introduced the possibility of combining the use of conjoint analysis with multidimensional scaling. A natural complementarity exists between the two techniques as the criteria (axes) must be subjectively evaluated for most scaling procedures, while in conjoint analysis the axes are prespecified. The ideal is a matching of subjective and prespecified criteria but this depends largely upon the care taken to prespecify the correct attributes.

In a study for Air Canada, Davidson [7] applied the NMRG algorithm to determine the utility function of respondents for alternative transportation modes (car, bus, train, conventional air, and STOL aircraft). Thirteen independent attributes were identified and specified in twenty-one trade-off matrices. The objective of the study was to build a model that would forecast and evaluate the different modes and the effect of different marketing strategies on the STOL market share.

Johnson [18] used the NMRG algorithm to analyze trade-offs in automobile brand choice. The study was used to explicate the practical considerations concerning the assumptions, computations, and validity of conjoint analysis. It was noted that sufficient data was not available to validate the procedure through comparison of program generated results with actual variables in the marketplace. Green and Wind [13] applied MONANOVA in examining the market for a new spot remover. The use of orthogonal designs to overcome the practical limitations of cost and respondent fatigue was demonstrated. Finally, Parker and Srinivasan [27] used LINMAP to investigate the problem of locating rural health care facilities according to consumer preferences, community considerations, and cost/benefit constraints.

## LIMITATIONS AND ADVANTAGES
## OF CONJOINT ANALYSIS

Clearly, the above applications indicate the initial spectrum of possibilities using conjoint analysis, although, admittedly, there are limitations. For instance, it is difficult to obtain an interview of 1½ hours with industry personnel. Because the technique is cross sectional in nature, it would be desirable to repeat such interviews at selected intervals and this may again be difficult to do. It is also obvious that utilities change over time and at different rates for different situations. In general, it is believed that sample sizes of from 200 to 500 are required, and this too could present problems. It is also possible that in industrial settings, where the product specifications are explicit but numerous (greater than ten or twelve), the technique would not be efficient. It is also worthy to note that no error theory is available for conjoint analysis; that is to say, there are no significance tests as such for the utilities or the general model. Another problem that is difficult to overcome is that of non-involvement by respondents. The mental task of explicitly comparing multidimensional statements is quite rigorous. Many respondents may find the task involves too much thinking and therefore requires a substantial incentive to participate.

The distinct and unique advantage of the technique is, of course, its potential ability to construct consumers' valu systems given the satisfaction of the assumptions. People are generally unable to explicate utility values either because they do not know them or they feel they must adhere to socially acceptable norms. Conjoint analysis implicitly constructs the utilities within each respondent's system. However, the assumptions and limitations underlying the technique must be recognized in its marketing research application.

## REFERENCES

1. American Telephone and Telegraph, Marketing Department/Research Section. "Dataspeed 40 Market Study, Morristown, New Jersey, January, 1974, pp. 7-14.

2. Berner, John G. "Conjoint Measurement Analysis of the Multiplicative Composition Rule Contained in Expectancy Theory." Unpublished Ph.D. dissertation, Michigan State University, 1976.

3. Carroll, Douglas J. "Categorical Conjoint Measurement" Ann Arbor, Michigan, Meeting of Mathematical Psychology, August, 1969.

4. Carroll, Douglas J. and Chang, J. J. "Relating Preference Data to Multidimensional Scaling Solutions Via A Generalization of Coombs' Unfolding Model," Bell Telephone Laboratories, Murray Hill, N. J.

5. Conover, W. J. Practical Nonparametric Statistics. New York: Wiley, 1971, pp. 249-253.

6. Coombs, Clyde H.; Dawes, Robyn M.; and Tversky, Amos. Mathematical Psychology: An Elementary Introduction. Englewood Cliffs, New Jersey: Prentice-Hall, 1970, Chapters 3 and 5.

7. Davidson, J. D. "Forecasting Traffic on STOL." Operational Research Quarterly, 24 (Dec., 1973), pp. 561-69.

8. Fiedler, John A. "Condominium Design and Pricing: A Case Study in Consumer Trade-Off Analysis." Proceedings: 3rd Annual Conference For Consumer Research. University of Chicago, 1972, pp. 279-293.

9. Green, Paul E. "On the Design of Choice Experiments Involving Multifactor Alternatives." Journal of Consumer Research, 1 (Sept., 1974), pp. 61-68.

10. Green, Paul E.; Carmone, Frank J.; and Wind, Yoram. "Subjective Evaluation Models and Conjoint Measurement" Behavioral Science, 17 (1972), pp. 288-99.

11. Green, Paul E. and Rao, Vithala R. "Conjoint Measurement for Quantifying Judgmental Data." Journal of Marketing Research, 8 (Aug., 1971), pp. 355-63.

12. Green, Paul E. and Tull, Donald S. Research For Marketing Decisions, 3rd ed., Englewood Cliffs, New Jersey: Prentice-Hall, 1975.

13. Green, Paul E., and Wind, Yoram. "New Way to Measure Consumer's Judgments." Harvard Business Review, (July-August, 1975), pp. 107-17.

14. Green, Paul E.; Wind, Yoram; and Jain, Arun K. "Consumer Menu Preference: An Application of Additive Conjoint Measurement." Proceedings: 3rd Annual Conference For Consumer Research. University of Chicago, 1972, pp. 304-315.

15. Harrell, Gilbert D., and Bennett, Peter D. "An Evaluation of the Expectancy Value Model of Attitude Measurement for Physician Prescribing Behavior." Journal of Marketing Research, (Aug., 1974), pp. 269-278.

16. Johnson, Richard M. "Pairwise Nonmetric Multidimensional Scaling," Psychometrika, (1973(a)), 38, pp. 11-18.

17. Johnson, Richard M. "Varieties of Conjoint Measurement." Research Paper, Market Facts, Inc., (August, 1973(b)).

18. Johnson, Richard M. "Trade-Off Analysis of Consumer Values." Journal of Marketing Research, 11 (May, 1974), pp. 121-27.

19. Johnson, Richard M. "A Simple Method for Pairwise Monotone Regression." Psychometrika, 40 (June, 1975), pp. 163-68.

20. Kinnear, Thomas C. and Taylor, James R. "Multivariate Methods in Marketing Research: A Further Attempt at Classification." Journal of Marketing Research, (October, 1971), pp. 56-59.

21. Krantz, David H., and Tversky, Amos. "Conjoint-Measurement Analysis of Composition Rules in Psychology." Psychological Review, 78 (1971), pp. 151-69.

22. Kruskal, Joseph B. "Analysis of Factorial Experiments by Estimating Monotone Transformations of the Data." Journal of the Royal Statistical Society, Series 8, 27, (March, 1965), pp. 251-63.

23. Lingoes, James C. "An IBM-7090 Program for Guttman-Lingoes Conjoint Measurement-I." Behavioral Science, 12 (1967), p. 501.

24. Luce, R. Duncan, and Tukey, John W. "Simultaneous Conjoint Measurement: A New Type of Fundamental Measurement." Journal of Mathematical Psychology, 1 (1964), pp. 1-27.

25. McClelland, Gary H. and Coombs, Clyde H. "ORDMET: A General Algorithm for Constructing all Numerical Solutions to Ordered Metric Structures." Psychometrika, 40 (September, 1975), pp. 269-90.

26. Nicholson, Walter. Microeconomic Theory. Hinsdale, Illinois: Dryden Press, 1972, Chapter 9.

27. Parker, Barnett R., and Srinivasan V. "A Consumer Preference Approach to the Planning of Rural Primary Health Care Facilities." Research Paper No. 271, Graduate School of Business, Stanford University (July, 1975).

28. Scott, Robert Haney. The Pricing System. San Francisco: Holden-Day, Inc., 1973, Chapters 2 and 6.

29. Sheth, Jagdish N. "The Multivariate Revolution in Marketing Research." Journal of Marketing Research, 35 (January, 1971), pp. 13-19.

30. Srinivasan V. and Allan D. Shocker. "Linear Programming Techniques for Multidimensional Analysis of Preferences." Psychometrika, 38, (September, 1973).

31. Tversky, Amos. "Utility Theory and Additivity Analysis of Risky Choices." Journal of Experimental Psychology, 75, (1967a), pp. 27-36.

32. Tversky, Amos. "A General Theory of Polynomial Conjoint Measurement." Journal of Mathematical Psychology, 4 (1967b), pp. 1-20.

33. Young, Forest W. "A Model for Polynomial Conjoint Analysis Algorithms." Multidimensional Scaling. Edited by Roger N. Shepard, A. Kimball Romney, and Sara Beth Nerlove. New York: Seminar Press, Volume I, 1972, pp. 69-104.

# AN INVESTIGATION OF THE EFFECTS OF SPECIFIC USAGE
## SITUATIONS ON THE PREDICTION OF CONSUMER CHOICE BEHAVIOR

Eric N. Berkowitz, University of Minnesota
James L. Ginter, The Ohio State University
W. Wayne Talarzyk, The Ohio State University

## ABSTRACT

This paper initially focuses on the effects of situation specific attribute ratings on the prediction of consumer choice behavior. In order to investigate this issue, the multi-attribute model is employed. A second phase of the analysis addresses the effects of proportion of use within a specific usage situation on attribute ratings and subsequent prediction of brand choice. A data base of 368 purchasers of selected new automobiles is used to test the research question.

Results from the use of situational specific attribute importance ratings with the multi-attribute model were found to be positive when proportion of usage within a given situation category was incorporated into the analysis. Conclusions included the position that specific usage situations should prove to be a fruitful arena for additional research efforts aimed toward increasing the probability of accurately predicting brand choice behavior.

## INTRODUCTION

Recent research on consumer decision making has focused on the possible effects of situations on behavior. Ward and Robertson argued that, "situational variables may account for considerably more variance than actor-related variables" [13, p. 26]. Engel, Kollat, and Blackwell [7] noted that both situational and individual factors must be considered in order to explain consumer choices. Subsequent research efforts [1, 11] have also indicated that consideration of specific usage situation may improve understanding and prediction of choice behavior. Yet investigations of situational effects have been limited, as Belk observed: "Growing recognition of limitations in the ability of individual consumer characteristics to explain variation in buyer behavior has prompted a number of appeals to examine situational influences on behavior... nevertheless these suggestions...have gone largely unheeded" [4, p. 157].

Situational elements have been a difficult concept to operationalize in attempting to predict consumer choice. Several researchers have developed comprehensive taxonomies of situational characteristics. These systems have been reviewed by Belk [4]. At present, however, most studies of situational effects have occurred in the laboratory with hypothetical choices [2,3,5,10,12]. These studies have given support to a situational influence on behavior, and offer tentative support to consideration of situation in consumer behavior models [7,9].

This paper specifically examines the effect of inclusion of situation specific variables on the prediction of past choice. Comparison of the effects of situation specific attribute ratings to general ratings (not specific to individual situations) on the accuracy of choice prediction is operationalized with the multi-attribute model. Situations have been defined in this study as use situations for a related product class. In addition, the effect of consideration of product usage level on predictive accuracy is investigated. To date, little attention has been paid to proportions of use on situation-specific attribute ratings.

Recent purchasers of a selected new automobile comprised the data base for examination of these questions. The following form of the multi-attribute model is used in the analysis:

$$A_{jk} = \sum_{i=1}^{n} I_{ik} B_{ijk} \qquad (1)$$

where, $i$ = automobile attribute
$j$ = brand of automobile
$k$ = respondent

and, $A_{jk}$ = respondent k's attitude score for automobile j
$I_{ik}$ = the importance weight given attribute i by respondent k
$B_{ijk}$ = respondent k's belief concerning the extent to which automobile j provides attribute i

Accuracy of prediction of brand of automobile purchased was employed in comparing general and situation specific attribute ratings. While this measure of affect is clearly an indirect one, previous work discussed in the methodology section of this paper suggest that it is a suitable criterion variable for comparison of alternative model forms.

## RESEARCH OBJECTIVES

The focus of this research is upon two principal issues:
a) the effect of situation-specific attribute ratings on the prediction of brand owned.
b) the effect of proportion of use on attribute ratings and subsequent prediction of brand owned.

## DATA DESCRIPTION

A mail questionnaire was sent to 600 individuals who had purchased a selected new automobile. The four brands shown in Table 1 were chosen because of their differences on product attributes and similarity of price in comparison with the total automobile market. The nine attributes also presented in Table 1, were selected for inclusion on the basis of prior research studies by the authors.

Names of purchasers of these automobiles were obtained from dealer and court records. Prior to the mailing of the questionnaire, prospective subjects were contacted by telephone and asked for their cooperation in the survey. A total of 368 respondents returned questionnaires which were usable for the analysis. The car ownership composition of these responses was: Plymouth Duster - 29.6%, Volkswagon Dasher - 25%, Audi Fox - 15%, and Oldsmobile Cutlass - 30.4%.

Data were collected on brand owned, attribute importances and specific use situations (Table 1). These usage situations were selected on the basis of prior research by the authors and consultation with marketing personnel within the cooperating automobile firm. Belief measures were collected for all four brands on each of the nine attributes. Question forms for collection of importance and belief information were: (1) importance - How important is it to you that a car satisfy you on the characteristic

90

listed below? (Table 1), and (2) beliefs - Indicate how much each of the following cars has of each of the following characteristics. Scale values for the importances and beliefs ranged from one (very unimportant or low) to six (very important or high).

After additional questions, importances were gathered on three of the specific usage situations for parsimony in the data gathering. Listed in Table 1 there were (1) driving back and forth to work, (2) shopping and errands, and, (3) use as a pleasure vehicle. Situation-specific attribute importances were collected by asking: importance - How important is it for you that a car satisfy you on the characteristics (Table 1) listed below in the specific situation? Scale values for the situation-specific attributes were similar to those for the general attribute importances. Belief data were not collected for the specific situations. It was felt that beliefs would be stable regardless of the usage situation. For example, there is little reason to assume if a person believed a car to have a high degree of style or workmanship, overall, that his belief rating would be different in a back and forth to work, or shopping situation.

Thus, in the general importance attributes, respondents were asked to evaluate their importance on an overall basis. The situation-specific measurement, however, required the respondents to rate the importance of these attributes with respect to each particular usage situation. The importance of an attribute may vary depending on the usage situation. For example, trunk space may be even more important than in the general situation.

Information with respect to proportion of car usage in each situation listed in Table 1 was also gathered by asking: During an average week, how many hours is your new car used for each particular situation? Respondents placed hours used beside each situation.

The number of respondents varied in each analysis due to missing data. Four aggregate situation usage groups were used in the analysis. These were: (1) driving back and forth to work (n=147), (2) shopping and family errands (n=29), (3) pleasure (n=41), and (4) other (n=140). The other category consisted of those respondents that reported using the car most for (1) driving by son or daughter, (2) driving around town by husband and wife, and (3) other miscellaneous uses. Subjects were classified into usage situations groups on the basis of their highest usage in any one of the four situations. The following analysis focused on the back and forth to work group because it consisted of the largest usage segment.

TABLE 1

DATA DESCRIPTION

| BRANDS | ATTRIBUTES | USE SITUATIONS |
|---|---|---|
| Oldsmobile Cutlass | Style and Appearance | Driving Around Town by Husband and Wife |
| Volkswagon Rabbit | Reputation of Manufacturer | For Shopping and Family Errands |
| | Miles per Gallon | |
| Audi Fox | Overall Quality of Workmanship | By Son or Daughter |
| Plymouth Duster | Riding Comfort | As a Pleasure Vehicle |
| | Value for Money | |
| | Durability | Transportation Back and Forth to Work |
| | Overall Safety | |
| | Trunk Space | Other (Specify) |

## METHODOLOGY OF ANALYSIS

The following procedure was employed to investigate the effects of (a) general versus situation-specific information and (b) proportion of use in the most frequent situation, on choice prediction with the multi-attribute model. This approach examined the relationship between affect as measured by the multi-attribute model and another measure of affect, brand ownership. It should be noted that the dependent measure, brand owned, may not be directly related to the level of affect at the time of the study. This means that the ability of any form of the model to predict ownership may be less than its ability to predict affect at the time of data collection. The absolute level of predictive accuracy of each form of the model (general vs. situation-specific attribute importances) is not important to this study, however, since the models are compared in terms of their relative accuracy. Craig and Ginter [6] found that although the two types of dependent measures led to different absolute levels of accuracy for a model form, the relative accuracy of alternative model forms was consistent.

Predictive accuracy of brand owned was computed with all nine attributes for all subjects. For each respondent brand owned was predicted as that brand with the highest attitude score. Respondents whose highest attitude scores were equal for two or more brands were dropped from the computation of percentage correct predicted. While other methods of handling tie scores could have been used, it was felt that this indication of percentage of correct unambiguous predictions would be of most value in both diagnostic and managerial settings. In addition, this approach provides an accurate measure of the predictive power of the model.

Five steps were followed in examining the effect of general versus situation-specific attribute importances on the prediction of brand choice. Initially, the accuracy of the model was determined for the back and forth to work group using the general attribute importances. As defined, the general importances are those obtained without reference to a specific situation. Next, the situation-specific attribute importances were employed in the model. The third step consisted of a further subdivision of the back and forth to work group. These respondents were segmented into "heavy" and "light" users. The groups were defined as:

"HEAVY" users - respondents who specify using their car for back and forth to work at least 70% of the total time it's in use.

"LIGHT" users - those individuals who specify using their car for back and forth to work less than 70% of the time, but more than in any other specific usage situation.

In the remainder of the paper, these groups will be referred to as "heavy" and "light" users.

As stated, respondents classified into the back and forth to work group were utilized for this analysis. Segmenting of the back and forth to work group into heavy and light users, however, was considered necessary. Conceptually, it was hypothesized that if an individual was a "heavy" user of a car for any particular situation, it would be quite likely that attributes which he considers important for his dominant use will be almost the total base by which his purchase decision is made. An example may better clarify this reasoning and justification for dividing the group into "heavy" and "light" users.

If a person purchased a car only for back and forth to work purposes, one would not expect a difference in his general or his specific usage situation attribute importances. However, if an individual used his automobile 60% of its time for going back and forth to work, and the remainder for pleasure, or shopping, his specific usage situations ratings may be different than his general ratings. In the general importance ratings, the respondent would take into consideration not only back and forth to work aspects, but also attributes that may be important for other situations.

Step 4 analyzed the predictive accuracy of the model with regard to brand owned (with general and specific usage situation importances), for the "heavy" and "light" back and forth to work group. The last stage consisted of an investigation of the absolute mean differences of the attribute importance ratings for the general and specific usage situations. This was done for the entire back and forth to work group and for the "heavy" and "light" users separately.

In summary, the analysis may be outlined as:
(1) Determine predictive accuracy of brand owned for the back and forth to work group with general attribute importances.
(2) Compute predictive accuracy of brand owned for the back and forth to work group with the situation-specific attribute importances.
(3) Divide back and forth to work users into "heavy" and "light" groups according to specified criterion.
(4) Calculate predictive accuracy of model on brand owned for "heavy" and "light" back and forth to work users
    (a) with general attribute importance ratings.
    (b) with situation-specific attribute ratings.
(5) Examine mean absolute differences of attribute importance ratings for the back and forth to work group, and then "heavy" and "light" users.

## RESULTS

As stated, the first step of the analysis investigated the accuracy of predicting brand owned for the back and forth to work group using the general attribute importance ratings. 81.5% of the respondents' brands owned were correctly predicted (Table 2). In the second stage, situation-specific attribute importance ratings were used in the model. This approach led to a lower predictive accuracy of 77.0% (Table 2) of the back and forth to work group's car ownership. This result appeared incongruous with the hypothesized effect of situation-specific attribute importances of the prediction of choice behavior. Consequently, further analysis was conducted with respect to the degree of use within the specific situation (back and forth to work).

### TABLE 2

ACCURACY OF BRAND CHOICE PREDICTION
FOR BACK AND FORTH TO WORK GROUP

BACK AND FORTH TO WORK GROUP

| | |
|---|---|
| General Attributes | 81.5%<br>n=108 |
| Situation-Specific Attributes | 77.0%<br>n=113 |

Step 3 consisted of segmenting the back and forth to work users by degree of automobile usage with this situation. Subjects were classified into "heavy" and "light" users by the pre-defined criterion (70% of total usage in this situation). Subsequently, choice predictions were calculated for each group. Table 3 displays the model's predictive accuracy of brand owned for the heavy and light users.

### TABLE 3

COMPARISON OF PREDICTIVE ACCURACY FOR HEAVY
AND LIGHT USERS IN BACK AND FORTH TO WORK SITUATIONS

| General Attribute Importances | n | % correct |
|---|---|---|
| Heavy | 22 | 86.4% |
| Light | 86 | 80.2% |
| Situation Specific Importances | | |
| Heavy | 23 | 87.0% |
| Light | 90 | 74.4% |

Utilizing general attribute importances with the "heavy" group resulted in 86.4% correct predictions of brand owned (Table 3). This is an increase in predictive accuracy from 81.5% (Table 2) when the back and forth to work group was not subdivided by degree of use. Predictive accuracy of brand owned for the "light" group was slightly lower (80.2%) with general attribute importances than when the back and forth to work group was not segmented.

Employing the situation-specific attribute importances for the "heavy" users increased the predictive accuracy of the model to 87.0% (Table 3), from 77.0% (Table 2) when the back and forth to work group was not subdivided. Again lower predictive accuracy of brand owned resulted for the "light" users (74.4%). As hypothesized with the situation-specific attribute importance ratings, prediction was lower for the light users of the back and forth to work group. Light users (as previously defined), while using a car more in one situation than others, still consider these other situations when rating attribute importances. Inclusion of other uses in attribute ratings confounds the predictive accuracy of brand owned. The direction of the results, while positive, are not totally conclusive.

### TABLE 4

"Z" VALUES OF ABSOLUTE MEAN DIFFERENCES
OF ATTRIBUTE IMPORTANCE RATINGS BETWEEN
THE GENERAL AND BACK AND FORTH TO WORK SITUATION

| Attributes | Back and Forth to Work Group | "Heavy" Users | "Light" Users |
|---|---|---|---|
| Style and Appearance | 13.09 | 5.57 | 11.83 |
| Reputation of Manufacturer | 9.80 | 4.25 | 8.90 |
| Miles Per Gallon | 7.67 | 4.18 | 6.47 |
| Quality of Workmanship | 8.18 | 3.21 | 7.53 |
| Riding Comfort | 9.20 | 4.71 | 7.95 |
| Value for Money | 9.55 | 5.30 | 8.15 |
| Durability | 8.54 | 3.58 | 7.82 |
| Overall Safety | 7.44 | 3.95 | 6.31 |
| Trunk Space | 12.73 | 5.71 | 11.38 |

$"Z"_{.95} = 1.64$

In the final phase of analysis, examination of the differences of attribute ratings between the general and situation-specific attribute importances reveals that all mean absolute differences were statistically significant (shown in Table 4). This result supports the hypothesis that while "light" users drive their cars more for back and forth to work than any other situation, the other uses enter into their general attribute importance ratings. Consequently, a difference would be expected to exist between the general and situation specific attribute ratings for the "light" users. This result, however, was not hypothesized to exist for the "heavy" users in the back and forth to work group. Yet, while all mean differences for the other groups ("light" and all) are clearly significant, the "z" value for each attribute in the heavy group is less than the light group. As noted, the proportional usage cut-off for heavy users was at least 70% of the time in the back and forth to work use situation. Raising the criterion for classification to the "heavy" group may reduce the significant mean differences between the general and situation-specific attribute importance ratings in Table 4.

## CONCLUSIONS

Investigation of the use of situation-specific attribute importance ratings in the prediction of brand owned led to positive results. It was found that situation-specific attribute ratings, alone, however are not sufficient for increasing the predictive accuracy of past choice. Rather, proportion of usage within a situation appears to be an important factor. Initially in this analysis, the general attribute importance ratings led to better predictive accuracy of brand owned for respondents classified by the dominant use of their car (back and forth to work). Yet when this group was further divided into "heavy" and "light" users, there was a positive increase in the predictive accuracy of brand owned for the "heavy" users. Results support the conceptual hypothesis proposed in this paper that individuals who use a car almost totally in one situation appear to consider the important attributes in that situation as the overriding elements in the purchase decision. Lighter, though predominant, users of a car in a particular situation may still consider other use situations in their purchase decisions. Thus, their general and situation-specific attribute importance ratings are different.

While significant mean differences were found in the importance ratings of the general and situation-specific contexts for "heavy" and "light" users, differences were greater for the light users. These results, while not directly supportive of the conceptual hypothesis, are in the right direction. The significant mean differences of the attribute importance ratings for the "heavy" group may depend on the classification criterion for "heavy" users. As will be recalled, in this study respondents who used a car at least 70% of the time of its total use for back and forth to work purposes were considered "heavy" users. Segmenting on a higher proportion of use would probably aid in eliminating the significant differences between the general and situation-specific attribute importance ratings.

One cautionary note should be made with regard to situations and product use. Durable good purchases (in this instance, automobiles) require one choice for use in all situations. Therefore, the dependent variable does not vary by situation. This is not true for many other product classes (nondurable, perhaps) i.e., each choice may be relevant to only one situation (e.g., fast food purchases). Therefore, the concept of proportion of use has limited application, depending on the product class.

## IMPLICATIONS FOR FUTURE RESEARCH

This study has four implications for future research. First, the classification of respondents by usage situation and proportion of use indicates the possibility of increasing accuracy in predicting consumer choice. Inclusion of situational elements may lead to further refinements in models of the consumer decision process. Specifically, the employment of situation-specific information along with usage data would significantly enhance the diagnosis of a consumer's attitudes. Secondly, methods must be considered by which measures of proportion of use in situations may be obtained. These methods may lead to highly accurate classification of heavy and light users on these situations. In addition, it will be necessary to determine how to best operationalize a definition of heavy and light usage in a particular situation for a product class. This approach should be both quantifiable and managerially useful. Finally, the application of situation-specific data to predict brand choice should be investigated for other consumer durable products.

## REFERENCES

1. Belk, R.W., "Situational Influence in Consumer Behavior," Faculty Working Papers, College of Commerce and Business Administration, University of Illinois, #195, 1974a.

2. _____, "An Exploratory Assessment of Situational Effects in Buyer Behavior," Journal of Marketing Research, 11 (May, 1974b), pp. 156-163.

3. _____, "Application and Analysis of the Behavior Differential Inventory for Assessing Situational Effects in Consumer Behavior," in Scott Ward and Peter Wright (eds.), Advances in Consumer Research, Vol. 1, Urbana: Association for Consumer Research.

4. _____, "Situational Variables and Consumer Behavior," Journal of Consumer Research, 2 (Dec. 1975), pp. 157-164.

5. Bishop, D.W. and P.A. Witt, "Sources of Behavioral Variance During Leisure Time," Journal of Personality and Social Psychology, 16 (October, 1970), pp. 352-360.

6. Craig, C.S., and J.L. Ginter, "An Investigation of the Effect of the Dependent Measure and Attribute Selection on the Predictive Power of the Multi-Attribute Attitude Model," Proceedings, Fall Conference, American Marketing Association, 1974.

7. Engel, J.F., D.T. Kollat, and R.D. Blackwell, Consumer Behavior, Second Edition, New York: Holt, Rinehart, and Winston, Inc., 1972.

8. _____, "Personality Measures and Market Segmentation," Business Horizons, 12 (June, 1969), pp. 61-70.

9. Hansen, F., Consumer Choice Behavior, New York: The Free Press, 1972.

10. Lutz, R.J. and P.K. Kakkar, "The Psychological Situation as a Determinant of Consumer Behavior," in Mary Jane Schlinger (ed.), Advances in Consumer Research, Vol. 2, Chicago: Association for Consumer Research, 1974, pp. 439-454.

11.  Miller, Kenneth, "A Situational Multi-Attribute
     Attitude Model," in Mary Jane Schlinger (ed.),
     Advances in Consumer Research, Vol. 2, Chicago:
     Association for Consumer Research, 1974, pp. 455-464.

12.  Sandell, R.G., "The Effects of Attitudinal and
     Situational Factors on Reported Choice Behavior,"
     Journal of Marketing Research, 4 (Aug. 1968),
     pp. 405-408.

13.  Ward, S. and T.S. Robertson, "Consumer Behavior
     Research:  Promise and Prospects," in Scott Ward
     and Thomas S. Robertson, Consumer Behavior:
     Theoretical Sources,  Englewood Cliffs:  Prentice
     Hall, 1973, pp. 3-42.

# THE CONSUMER INVOLVEMENT MATRIX: SOME PRELIMINARY FINDINGS

Michael L. Rothschild, University of Wisconsin-Madison
Michael J. Houston, University of Wisconsin-Madison

## ABSTRACT

This paper presents a measure of consumer involvement based largely on social judgment theory. A matrix-like notion of involvement where the vertical dimension represents the size of the consumer's set of evaluative criteria and the horizontal dimension represents ranges of tolerable attribute levels is developed. The ratio of the vertical to horizontal dimensions represents involvement. Preliminary tests of validity are reported.

## INTRODUCTION

The heterogeneity of the consumer market place has provided the impetus for a continuous search for variables that moderate consumer behavior and, thus, account for differences between and within individuals. Early efforts centered on descriptive differences between individuals (e.g., demographics). The between-individuals perspective continued with an examination of personality differences (see [7] for a summary). More recently, attention has centered on variables that might account for differences within individuals. Situational influences [1, 6] and product differences [2] have been a focus of these efforts. To a large extent, these efforts have been eclectic, never really dealing with variables that might simultaneously account for both between- and within-individual differences. The purpose of this paper is to report some preliminary findings on a variable that can potentially deal with a multitude of between- and within-individual differences.

## INVOLVEMENT AS A MODERATING VARIABLE

A concept that has been recognized as having considerable explanatory potential [3] but has received only theoretical lip-service and rather shallow empirical treatment is "involvement." Although the concept is not a new one, the exact meaning of involvement is somewhat elusive. As a starting point, though, involvement refers to a "general level of interest in an attitude object" [3].

Various approaches to the study of involvement have been taken in consumer research. Krugman [8] was the first to link involvement with consumer behavior when he posited that the learning of television advertising is a passive phenomenon and is due to the low involvement of the individual towards both the product class and television. Hupfer and Gardner [5] confirmed the low-involvement nature of a variety of consumer goods vis à vis various social issues. Krugman [9] further distinguished between media in terms of involvement. The print media are high involvement because the medium is passive, requiring an active consumer to receive information. Broadcast media are low involvement because they take the active role allowing the consumer to passively receive information.

More recent consumer research [12, 14] links involvement with the hierarchy of effects [10]. For example, Rothschild [12] hypothesizes three types of involvement in terms of the hierarchy of effects:

. zero order involvement -- an individual behaves without first developing an attitude;
. higher-order loyal involvement -- behavior is the result of continued loyalty to a brand, i.e., a deeply rooted attitude;

3. higher-order information-seeking involvement -- behavior is a result of active information-seeking and evaluation.

While Rothschild's work does account for between- and within-individual differences, it, like Krugman's work, does not allow for a priori determination of the level of involvement. The next section reviews social judgment theory as a neglected but important contribution to the study of involvement in marketing.

## SOCIAL JUDGMENT THEORY

While involvement appears to be an interesting concern of consumer researchers, it has received very little attention in the context of perhaps the most penetrating social psychological theory of involvement, social judgment theory. Social judgment theory, as developed by Sherif and his colleagues [16, 17, 18], is a theory of attitude development and attitude change. A central issue treated in the theory is the impact of persuasive communications on attitude change. Message impact is a function of the discrepancy between the perceived position of the message and the recipient's own position.

Social judgment theory relies on psychological notions to define an individual's position on a specific issue. Three concepts are used to reflect an individual's attitude structure. For any issue which could be defined as having a spectrum of positions, an individual would have a range of acceptable positions (latitude of acceptance) which include an ideal or most acceptable position, a range of objectionable positions (latitude of rejection) which include a most objectionable position, and a range of neither acceptable nor objectionable positions (latitude of noncommitment).

Assimilation and contrast processes characterize the effect of a message. If the content of the message falls within the individual's latitude of acceptance or noncommitment, it is perceived as more acceptable than it actually is (assimilation). Falling within the latitude of rejection, the message is distorted in a negative direction (contrast).

The major concern of this paper, however, is the treatment of involvement within social judgment theory. The theory uses attitude structure as defined by latitudes of acceptance, rejection, and noncommitment to reflect the degree of personal involvement of an individual toward the issue at hand. Generally, high involvement is indicated by narrow latitudes of acceptance and noncommitment, and a wide latitude of rejection, suggesting the individual is highly committed to a particular position on the issue. Low involvement, on the other hand, is indicated by wide latitudes of acceptance and noncommitment with a rather narrow latitude of rejection. The next section presents a measure of consumer involvement based on the postulates of social judgment theory.

## THE CONSUMER INVOLVEMENT MATRIX

The proposed measure of consumer involvement is based on two constructs: Sherif's latitude of acceptance and the size of the choice criteria set (number of attributes used) of an individual in decision-making. These two constructs, when combined, provide a matrix-like measure of consumer involvement.

While Sherif's work measures overall attitude towards an issue or object, the proposed measure examines the latitude of acceptance for each salient attribute of the issue or object, since much choice behavior occurs for objects possessing multiple attributes as choice criteria. For each attribute there is a range of possible values that a particular choice object can possess; for each attribute there will be a range of acceptable values, with one value being the most preferred or "ideal point." With few exceptions [e.g., 11], no previous work has examined individuals and their treatment of choice criteria from this perspective.

As discussed above, social judgment theory states that highly involved individuals have wide latitudes of rejection, while individuals with low involvement have narrow latitudes of rejection. The measure reported here transforms this notion so that a highly involved individual will have a narrow latitude of acceptance and an individual with low involvement will have a wide latitude of acceptance. Sherif shows that his model holds for objects and issues; the proposed measure deals with attributes within objects or issues.

The second dimension of the involvement matrix concerns the number of attributes used by the individual in making a decision. A considerable amount of research exists [19] to show that individuals attach importance to some attributes while paying virtually no attention to others in making a choice. Between-individuals differences exist in terms of the number of attributes that are salient for a given set of choice objects. Within-individual differences in the number of salient attributes occur across product categories. It has been postulated that the greater the involvement of an individual, the greater will be the number of salient attributes for evaluation purposes [20]. Therefore, one can posit that the more involved an individual is with a product relative to other individuals/products, the greater will be the number of attributes employed to make the choice.

Combining the two involvement dimensions, a matrix-like representation of an individual's involvement with an issue or product can now be derived. The horizontal axis of the matrix represents the width of the latitudes of acceptance across attributes, while the vertical axis represents the size of the set of salient choice criteria. High involvement would be indicated by a rather long, narrow matrix (see Figure 1) where several attributes with generally narrow latitudes of acceptance are used. Low involvement, on the other hand, would be indicated by a short, wide matrix (Figure 1) where a small number of attributes with generally wide latitudes of acceptance are used.

FIGURE 1

MATRIX REPRESENTATION OF INVOLVEMENT

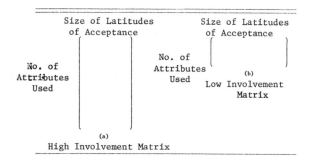

It is important to note that it is the shape rather than the size of the matrix that indicates involvement. A large/small set of choice criteria is offset by wide/narrow latitudes of acceptance. As the matrix moves toward a vertically rectangular shape, it reflects increasing levels of involvement, while as it moves toward a horizontally rectangular shape, it reflects diminishing levels of involvement. Thus, it is the ratio of the vertical size of the matrix to the horizontal size that indicates the shape of the matrix and provides a direct measure of involvement.

There are a number of ways by which the consumer involvement matrix can contribute to the understanding of consumer behavior and the formulation of marketing strategy. First, the matrix captures both between- and within-individual differences in involvement. Second, it provides a single-score measure that reflects the varying complexities of attitude structure possessed by high and low involvement individuals. Third, it may prove useful as a moderating variable in explaining the complexities of other consumer processes such as information processing.

Managerially, the matrix provides a framework within which a firm can assess its products with respect to the attribute-by-attribute demands of its consumers. For example, discrepancies from consumer ideal points in the firm's offering can be determined for each attribute. A number of differences between consumers can also be captured beyond the basic row-column dimensions, e.g., ideal points, ranges of tolerance around the ideal point for individuals with different and identical points. A number of other explanatory and managerial features of the matrix are discussed elsewhere [4, 13].

A PRELIMINARY TEST

Design of the Study

To provide some initial tests of the validity of the involvement matrix, data were collected from a convenience sample of ninety residents of the Madison, Wisconsin area in September, 1976. The context of the study was the attitude structure of individuals for making political voting decisions.

Subjects were asked to complete an involvement matrix for making a choice in a political race in each of two types of elections: the presidential election (to intuitively represent a high-involvement situation), and a state assembly election (to intuitively represent a low involvement situation). Latitudes of acceptance were measured for each of eleven attributes (see Table 1) using a nine-point scale of the type presented in Figure 2. Subjects first indicated ideal points by placing a box about the corresponding number on the scale. Other tolerable attribute levels were indicated by circling the corresponding numbers. The size of the latitude of acceptance for an attribute was simply the total number of circled and squared points on the scale. On a separate set of scales, subjects indicated if they would use an attribute and, if so, how important it would be in choosing a candidate. The following ratio was computed as a measure of the shape of an individual's involvement matrix for each election:

Number of attributes subject indicated would be put to some use
/
Total number of acceptable scale points on attributes included in numerator
/
Total number of scale points on attributes included in numerator

For example, if an individual indicated usage of five attributes and a latitude of acceptance of three levels

TABLE 1

ATTRIBUTES INCLUDED IN STUDY AND CORRELATIONS BETWEEN
IMPORTANCE AND LATITUDES OF ACCEPTANCE FOR
EACH ELECTION

| Attributes | Correlations | |
| --- | --- | --- |
| | Presidential Elections | State Assembly Electns. |
| Experience in Politics | $-.17^a$ | $-.47^a$ |
| Honesty | $.04^a$ | $.00^a$ |
| Liberal/Conservative Stance | $-.29^a$ | $-.35$ |
| Defense Spending Stance | $-.10^a$ | $-.48$ |
| Personal Appearance | $-.61$ | $-.32$ |
| Amnesty Stance | $-.36$ | $-.41$ |
| Conservation Stance | $-.21$ | $-.22$ |
| Equal Rights Stance | $-.54$ | $-.30$ |
| Religion | $-.53$ | $-.44$ |
| Local vs. Federal Control Stance | $-.32$ | $-.43$ |
| Abortion Stance | $-.46$ | $-.37$ |

$^a$Insignificant

of each of the five attributes, an involvement score of $5/((5\times3)/(5\times9)) = 15$ would be computed. An individual exhibiting a higher level of involvement would be one who used, say, 7 attributes and accepted a total of 11 cells of those attributes (involvement score = $7/(11/63) = 40$).

FIGURE 2

EXAMPLE OF SCALE USED FOR ATTRIBUTES

| EXPERIENCE IN POLITICS: | No Experience | Very Little Experience | Some Experience | | Quite a Bit of Experience | | A Great Deal of Exp. |
| --- | --- | --- | --- | --- | --- | --- | --- |
| | 1 | 2 | 3 | 4 | 5 | 6 | 7 | 8 | 9 |

Tests of Validity and Findings

Several tests were conducted to provide some preliminary evidence of the validity of the involvement matrix. First, since importance is related to involvement [5], significant negative correlations between the importance of an attribute and its latitude of acceptance should obtain. The results of such an analysis are provided in Table 1. Overall, the results are consistent with expectations. Twenty of twenty-two correlation coefficients are negative; nineteen of these are significant ($p < .05$).

To supplement this analysis, intra-individual correlations of attribute importance and latitude of acceptance were computed across attributes for each race. An r-to-z transformation was performed for each race and transformed back to r. Correlation coefficients of $-.34$ and $-.26$ resulted for the presidential and state assembly elections, respectively. While these values are not high, they are in the expected direction and, given the discrete nature of the data, provide reasonable supporting evidence. The difference in the strengths of these values is probably due to more consistent strengths of conviction across individuals in the higher-involvement presidential race. Krugman [9] reports other evidence supporting such a contention.

While the above analyses indicate preliminary support for the link between involvement and latitudes of acceptance, a more critical issue is the validation of the shape of the overall matrix as an index of involvement. Since on an a priori basis it was determined that the presidential

election was a high-involvement situation relative to the state assembly election, a higher ratio of the vertical to horizontal dimensions of the matrix should occur for the presidential race. Such was the case as a median ratio of 34.7 was observed for the high-involvement presidential race and a median ratio of 26.2 was observed for the low-involvement state assembly race. A sign test [15] for the direction of movement showed that the ratio was generally higher for the presidential race ($z = 4.20$, $p < .001$). A McNemar test for the significance of changes [15] also confirmed the higher-involvement shape of the matrix for the presidential race ($x^2 = 17.7$, $p < .001$). Generally, the results of these analyses provide preliminary evidence of the validity of the overall matrix as well as its individual components.

SUMMARY

This paper has presented a measure of consumer involvement based in large part on social judgment theory. A matrix-like notion of involvement was developed where the vertical dimension is represented by the size of the choice criterion set of a consumer and the horizontal dimension is represented by ranges of tolerable attribute levels. The shape of the matrix, i.e., the ratio of the row-to-column dimensions, represents level of involvement. Preliminary tests of validity in a political context appeared to provide sufficient support to suggest the measure is worthy of further consideration.

REFERENCES

1. Belk, Russell W. "Situational Variables and Consumer Behavior," Journal of Consumer Research, 2 (December 1975), 157-64.

2. Blattberg, Robert C., Peter Peacock, and Subrata K. Sen. "Purchasing Strategies Across Product Categories," Journal of Consumer Research, 3 (December 1976), 143-54.

3. Day, George S. "Theories of Attitude Structure and Change," in S. Ward and T. S. Robertson, eds., Consumer Behavior: Theoretical Sources. Englewood Cliffs: Prentice-Hall, Inc., 1973.

4. Houston, Michael J. and Michael L. Rothschild. "Involvement as a Moderating Variable in Consumer Information Processing," in progress.

5. Hupfer, Nancy T. and David M. Gardner. "Differential Involvement with Products and Issues: An Exploratory Study," Proceedings of the Association for Consumer Research, 1971.

6. Kakkar, Pradeep and Richard J. Lutz. "Toward a Taxonomy of Consumption Situations," Working Paper No. 27, UCLA, 1975.

7. Kassarjian, Harold H. "Personality and Consumer Behavior: A Review," Journal of Marketing Research, 8 (November 1971), 409-18.

8. Krugman, Herbert E. "The Impact of Television Advertising: Learning Without Involvement," Public Opinion Quarterly, 29 (Fall 1965), 349-56.

9. _____. "The Measurement of Advertising Involvement," Public Opinion Quarterly, 30 (Winter 1966-67), 583-96.

10. Lavidge, Robert J. and Gary A. Steiner. "A Model for Predicting Measurements of Advertising Effectiveness," Journal of Marketing, 25 (October 1961), 59-62.

11. Monroe, Kent B. "Measuring Price Thresholds by
    Psychophysics and Latitudes of Acceptance," Journal
    of Marketing Research, 8 (November 1971), 460-4.

12. Rothschild, Michael L. "The Effects of Political
    Advertising on the Voting Behavior of a Low Involve-
    ment Electorate," Unpublished Ph.D. Dissertation,
    Stanford University, 1974.

13. _____. "Advertising Strategies for High and Low
    Involvement Situations," Paper presented at the
    American Marketing Association Attitude Research
    Conference, Las Vegas, March 1977.

14. _____ and Michael L. Ray. "Involvement and
    Political Advertising Effect: An Exploratory
    Experiment," Communications Research, 3 (July 1974),
    264-85.

15. Siegel, Sidney. Nonparametric Statistics. New York:
    McGraw-Hill, Inc., 1956.

16. Sherif, Muzafer and C. Hovland. "Judgmental
    Phenomena and Scales of Attitude Measurement: Place-
    ment of Items with Individual Choice of Number of
    Categories," Journal of Abnormal and Social Psychol-
    ogy, 48 (1953), 135-41.

17. _____ and C. Sherif. Attitude, Ego-Involvement
    and Change. New York: John Wiley and Sons, Inc.,
    1967,

18. Sherif, Carolyn, M. Sherif, and R. W. Nebergall.
    Attitude and Attitude Change. Philadelphia:
    Saunders, 1965,

19. Wilkie, William L. and Edgar A. Pessemier. "Issues
    in Marketing's Use of Multi-Attribute Attitude
    Models," Journal of Marketing Research, 10
    (November 1973), 428-41.

20. Wright, Peter and Barton Weitz. "Time Horizon
    Effects on Product Evaluation Strategies," Journal
    of Marketing Research, 14 (May 1977), in press.

# CONSUMER GIFT BUYING BEHAVIOR: AN EXPLORATORY ANALYSIS

Adrian B. Ryans, Stanford University

## ABSTRACT

A large proportion of the purchases in many product classes are made for gift purposes. To date there has been little empirical research on gift purchasing behavior that might provide guidance to marketing managers responsible for gift-oriented products. The empirical research reported in this study demonstrates, for several small electrical appliance product classes, that there are important differences on several dimensions of consumer purchasing behavior between those customers purchasing the products for personal use and those purchasing them as gifts. These differences do have important implications for manufacturers and retailers of gift-oriented products.

## INTRODUCTION

In many product classes a significant proportion of the purchases are made, not for personal use, but for gift purposes. Gifts represent well over 50 per cent of the purchases made in some small electrical appliance product classes. Despite the importance of gift purchasing in certain product classes, it is only recently that consumer behavior researchers have begun to study this area intensively. Lowes, Turner and Wills [9] reviewed the role gifts play in both primitive and contemporary Western societies and presented some descriptive data from three studies of gift giving, primarily involving Christmas gifts, in Great Britain. Caron and Ward [3] investigated children's Christmas gifts ideas and the gifts actually received by the children, but they did not examine the process by which the parents purchased the gifts. Belk [2] recently reported a model of gift selection based on cognitive consistency theory, which allowed him to make predictions about the amount of satisfaction the selection brings the giver and the conditions under which giver tastes dominate recipient tastes in gift selection. While these studies do contribute to our understanding of gift giving and the gift selection process, there are, at this point in time, few research findings to guide the marketing manager in developing a marketing strategy for a gift oriented product. In particular there is no reported empirical research on how gift buying behavior differs from personal use buying behavior. The objective of this paper is to present a comparison of consumer gift buying behavior and personal use buying behavior within the same product classes.

In considering gift buying behavior it seems reasonable to distinguish two categories of gift purchases: inhome gifts, where the giver and recipient are members of the same household and outhome gifts, where the giver and recipient are members of different households.[1] One major reason for making this distinction is that the close interaction between members of the same household is more likely to result in the recipient being involved in the gift buying decision. This involvement may have an influence on some aspects of gift buying behavior, such as length of search, and the importance of various types of information sources. Furthermore, anthropological and sociological findings also suggest the dichotomy might be useful. Schwartz [13, pp. 3-6] has discussed the rule of

approximate reciprocity in many gift giving situations in which the pair involved exchange gifts of approximately equal value, so that one member of the pair does not become greatly indebted to the other. Lowes, Turner and Wills [9, pp. 218] point out that gifts between husbands and wives and others with close kinship ties (which will often be inhome gifts) are more likely to be "pure" gifts, where factors other than reciprocity are likely to dominate the gift selection. This reasoning suggests that the focus of this study should not simply be on gift versus personal use, but also on the two categories of gifts: inhome and outhome. This split also has the added practical benefit that it is likely to be relevant to marketing managers. Many companies have been categorizing gifts in this manner in their data gathering activities for a number of years.[2]

## THE HYPOTHESES

As Schwartz has pointed out, the gift imposes an identity upon the giver as well as the recipient [13]. In addition to the particular product selected as the gift, one might hypothesize that the giver would believe his image would be improved by [1] a well-known quality brand name [2] purchased in a quality store. The first part of the hypothesis is difficult to define operationally due to the probability of highly idiosyncratic, difficult to quantify, perceptions of the relative quality of brands. However, the second part lends itself more readily to empirical testing. The importance of the gift being purchased in a store with a quality image will probably be enhanced where there is a reasonably high probability that the recipient might have to return the gift to the store to be exchanged, serviced, etc. There is a reasonable probability of this happening for product classes like small electrical appliances. Given the types of retail outlets where small electrical appliances are purchased, the type of outlet in Canada with the most consistent quality image is the department store. Thus we have (stated in terms of the alternate hypothesis):

H1: Gift purchases are more likely to be made in stores with quality images, such as department stores. There is no basis for hypothesizing whether or not this difference will be more pronounced for inhome or outhome gifts.

If the rule of approximate reciprocity is indeed an important factor in many gift giving situations we would expect the giver to set an approximate price to be paid before beginning his search for the gift since this is the most obvious measure of value. We would argue that this is less likely to occur where the person is buying the product for personal use. Given our earlier discussion about the importance of distinguishing between inhome and outhome gifts and the belief that the rule of approximate reciprocity would be more influential in the outhome gift situation we hypothesize:

H2: Gift purchasers are more likely than personal use purchasers to set an approximate price to be paid before beginning the search for the product, and this tendency will be more pronounced in the case of outhome gifts.

---

[1]This dichotomy has previously proved useful in another context [12].

[2]For example gifts are categorized in this manner in the General Electric consumer panel described in [11].

The length of the prepurchase information seeking process is a factor of major importance to marketing managers responsible for making marketing communications decisions. Thus any substantial differences in this length between gift and non-gift purchases would be important. It is likely that some gift purchases are made under significant time constraints. Furthermore it is probably reasonable to assume that people generally have a much more clearly defined picture of their own needs than they do of somebody else's. If the need is less clearly defined, it is probably easier to find a brand or model that fills this need once the product class has been selected. In general, we would expect that the need is less clearly defined in the case of gift purchases, and especially so in the case of an outhome gift. Thus we have:

H3: The time interval between deciding to purchase a particular product and the selection and purchase of the chosen brand and model will be smaller for outhome gifts than for personal use purchases. Inhome gifts will occupy an intermediate position.

Another hypothesis that flows from the assumption that people have a more clearly defined picture of their own needs than somebody else's relates to the relative reliance on the importance of instore and outstore information sources. We would expect that people with less definite ideas of the particular features they desire in a product to find less value in extensive outstore information seeking, i.e. looking at consumer magazines, talking to their peers, looking at ads, etc. Also, because they go to stores with less clearly defined needs and less outstore information, we would expect them to be more influenced by point of purchase information sources, such as retail displays and retail salespersons. Combining these two lines of reasoning we have:

H4: Gift purchasers will report attaching more importance to instore information sources relative to the importance of all information sources in selecting the brand and model purchased. There is no basis for hypothesizing whether or not this difference will be more pronounced for inhome or outhome gifts.

To test these hypotheses adequately it may be necessary to control on other variables, such as product class and income which could conceivably be correlated with both the dependent and independent variables.

## THE STUDY

In order to test the hypotheses a study was conducted in the summer of 1974. The study was confined to one product category to reduce the probability that the empirical results would be obfuscated by product category differences. Small electrical appliances were selected as the product category for the study for two reasons. First, in order to generate a sufficiently large sample size for the study, it was necessary to have a product category in which a reasonable proportion of the population would have made a recent purchase. Second, it was desirable to have a product category which would provide a reasonable split between inhome gifts, outhome gifts and personal use purchases. In a 1974 study conducted for the National Housewares Manufacturers Association [14], 66% of the respondents reported that they bought small electrical appliances as gifts. After reviewing shipments and sales data from government and trade sources, the following high volume small electrical appliance product classes were included in the study: irons, toasters, electric coffeemakers, electric kettles, blenders, handmixers, electric frying pans and hairdryers/hairstylers.

A questionnaire was mailed to a random sample of 1400 English-speaking members of the Consumer Mail Panel of Market Facts of Canada. Respondents were questioned about their most recent purchase in the selected product classes and whether it was an inhome gift, outhome gift, or for personal use. By the cut-off date (three weeks after the questionnaires were mailed) 1058 questionnaires had been received, giving a response rate of 75%. A total of 487 respondents had completed most of the questionnaire and had made a purchase in the chosen product classes within the previous 12 months. One-third of these purchases had been made within the previous three months and over two-thirds had been made in the previous six months. These 487 respondents comprise the sample used in the analyses. Of the reported purchases, 18% were inhome gifts, 19% were outhome gifts and 63% were personal use purchases.

## THE ANALYSIS

The manner in which the variables used in testing the hypotheses were operationally defined is described in Table 1. Also included in Table 1 are the definitions of a number of variables that might possibly be correlated with both the dependent and the independent variable mentioned in the hypotheses and, unless controlled for, could confound the results. The fourth dependent variable, the index of relative importance of instore information sources, requires further explanation. The numerator of the index was computed by summing the reported importance of retail salespersons and retail store displays in helping the respondent select the brand and model she finally chose. A score of 0 was given if the respondent reported no usage of the source, 1 if the source was used but rated as not important, 2 if it was rated slightly important, 3 if it was rated quite important and 4 if it was rated extremely important. The denominator was developed in an analogous manner using all information sources for which data was gathered: retail salespersons, retail store displays, discussions with friends and relatives, newspaper or magazine articles, radio commercials, television commercials, consumer magazine articles, and mail-order or store catalogues. While the index was relatively crude, it was believed to be sufficiently good for the purposes of this exploratory analysis.

The first hypothesis, which was concerned with the reason for the appliance purchase and the type of store where the purchase was made, was tested by developing a linear probability function with whether or not the appliance was purchased in a department store as the dependent variable [6, pp. 248-50]. In this case it clearly seemed important to control for the size of the city in which the respondent lived, since people living in rural areas or in smaller cities would have much poorer access to department stores than those living in large cities. Income was considered to be a second possible confounding variable and was included in the preliminary analysis. This analysis indicated that income did not contribute significantly to explained variance and that its exclusion did not result in any major change in any of the coefficients of the other independent variables. Therefore the income variables were omitted from this analysis. The results are reported in the first column in Table 2.

All the coefficients are significant at least at the .1 level, if the usual assumptions about the form of the error term are made. As anticipated, respondents living in rural areas or in small cities were less likely to purchase the product at a department store. In this case we can reject the null hypothesis associated with H1 and can conclude that both inhome and outhome gift purchasers are more likely to make their purchase for these types of product classes in department stores. The Table 2 results suggest that after controlling on the city size variables the probability of the purchase being made at a department store was about .10 higher, if the product was being purchased as a gift. Thus while a personal use purchaser with a mean score on the city size variables has a probability of .40 of making his purchase of the appliance at a department store, inhome and outhome gift purchasers have probabilities of .49 and .50, respectively, an increase of approxi-

TABLE 1

DEFINITION OF THE VARIABLES INCLUDED IN THE ANALYSES

| DESCRIPTION OF VARIABLE | VARIABLE NAME | DEFINITION |
|---|---|---|

A. Dependent Variables

| | | |
|---|---|---|
| Type of store where purchase made | DEPT | Appliance purchased in department store = 1, otherwise = 0 |
| Length of search | SEARCH | Length of search in days |
| Price met by respondent | PRICE | Yes = 1, No = 0 |
| Index of relative importance of instore information sources | INDEX | $\sum_{i=1}^{2} IN_i I_i / (\sum_{i=1}^{2} IN_i I_i + \sum_{i=1}^{6} OUT_i I_i)$ |

where $IN_i = 1$ if the ith instore information source used, otherwise $= 0$, $OUT_i = 1$, if ith outstore information source used, otherwise $= 0$, and $I_i =$ respondent's rating of the importance of the ith source (ranging from 1 (not important) to 4 (extremely important)).

B. Independent and Control Variables

| | | |
|---|---|---|
| Reason for purchase[a] | INHOME | Inhome gift = 1, otherwise = 0 |
| | OUTHOME | Outhome gift = 1, otherwise = 0 |
| Income | INC 1 | Income < $6000 = 1, otherwise = 0 |
| | INC 2 | Income $6000-8999 = 1, otherwise = 0 |
| | INC 3 | Income $9000-12999 = 1, otherwise = 0 |
| Buying experience for this appliance | BOUGHT | Number of times this type of appliance purchased in previous 5 years |
| Used this type of appliance in previous year | USE | Yes = 1, No = 0 |
| Bought product by mail order | MAIL | Bought, by mail = 1, otherwise = 1    1 |
| Price of appliance | PRICE | Price in dollars |
| Product Class[b] | DRYER | Hair dryer or hairstyler = 1, otherwise = 0 |
| | TOASTER | Toaster = 1, otherwise = 0 |
| | COFFEE | Coffeemaker = 1, otherwise = 0 |
| | KETTLE | Electric kettle = 1, otherwise = 0 |
| | BLENDER | Blender = 1, otherwise = 0 |
| | HANDMIX | Hand mixer = 1, otherwise = 0 |
| | FRYPAN | Frying pan = 1, otherwise = 0 |
| City size | FARM | Respondent lives on farm = 1, otherwise = 0 |
| | SMLCITY | Respondent lives in city with population < 100,000 = 1, otherwise = 0 |

[a]When both INHOME and OUTHOME equal 0, purchase was made for personal use.

[b]When all product class dummy variables equal 0, an electric iron was purchased.

mately 25%.[3]

The dependent variable in the second hypothesis was whether or not the respondent had set a price before beginning the search process. In considering possible control variables to be included in the analysis to test this hypothesis, family income was the only variable that seemed potentially important. One might assume that respondents from high income families would be less likely to set the price to be paid before shopping. A preliminary regression analysis indicated that income did not contribute to the explained variance, and the hypothesis was therefore simply tested using a chi square analysis. The cross-tabulation of whether or not a price was set prior to the

[3]The use of a linear probability function in this situation is not ideal, since the assumption of homoscedasticity is untenable [6, pp. 249], resulting in unbiased but inefficient estimates. Therefore a linear logit binary choice model was also estimated using the procedure outlined in Theil [15, pp. 632-35]. The probabilities implied by the logit model of the purchase being made in a department store for personal use, inhome gift and outhome gift purchase were virtually identical to the results reported here.

search process versus the reason for purchase is presented in Table 3. As can be seen from the chi-square statistics reports beneath the table, there was no significant difference in the proportion of respondents setting a price in advance between personal use purchases and inhome gift purchases. However, there was a significant difference between personal use purchases and outhome gift purchases. This difference was in the predicted direction and the magnitude of the difference was of practical significance.

The reported length of time between the decision to buy a particular appliance and the actual purchase corresponded very closely to those reported by Udell in his study of buying behavior for small electrical appliances [16]. Over 87% of the respondents reported that the purchases were made within one month, and 52% reported that the purchase was within one week. The corresponding figures from the Udell study were 83% and 50% respectively. In order to test the hypothesis that the length of search for gift purchases would be less than that for personal use purchases, it was again necessary to control on other variables that would probably be related to both the dependent and independent variables. The Newman and Staelin study [10] on differences in buyer decision times for purchases of major appliances and automobiles suggested a number of possible control variables. Product class, previous buying experience for this particular appliance, income and the

TABLE 2

ORDINARY LEAST SQUARES ESTIMATES OF THE REGRESSION COEFFICIENTS
FOR THE MODELS USED TO TEST HYPOTHESES 1, 3 and 4

Dependent Variable

| Independent Variable | (1) Type of Store | (2) Length of Search | (3) Square Root of Length of Search | (4) Information Importance Index |
|---|---|---|---|---|
| INHOME | $0.09^{c,g}$ | -2.71 | 0.12 | $0.08^{b}$ |
| OUTHOME | $0.10^{b}$ | $-11.16^{b}$ | $-0.65^{b}$ | -0.01 |
| FARM | $-0.26^{a}$ | ---- | ---- | ---- |
| SMLCITY | $-0.19^{a}$ | ---- | ---- | ---- |
| INC1 | $---^{h}$ | 3.13 | 0.42 | ---- |
| INC2 | ---- | $18.06^{c}$ | $0.97^{e}$ | ---- |
| INC3 | ---- | $9.46^{f}$ | $0.54^{f}$ | ---- |
| PRICE | ---- | 0.21 | $0.03^{f}$ | ---- |
| BOUGHT | ---- | -1.33 | -0.14 | ---- |
| USE | ---- | $9.16^{f}$ | $0.78^{c}$ | ---- |
| MAIL | ---- | $22.79^{c}$ | $1.57^{d}$ | $-0.23^{d}$ |
| TOASTER | ---- | 0.89 | 0.35 | ---- |
| COFFEE | ---- | $41.26^{d}$ | $1.96^{d}$ | ---- |
| KETTLE | ---- | -5.28 | -0.21 | ---- |
| BLENDER | ---- | $26.93^{d}$ | $2.19^{d}$ | ---- |
| HANDMIX | ---- | 5.82 | 0.48 | ---- |
| FRYPAN | ---- | 0.85 | 0.14 | ---- |
| DRYER | ---- | 10.80 | $1.13^{c}$ | ---- |
| CONSTANT | 0.49 | 7.04 | 2.23 | 0.39 |
| | | | | |
| n | 468 | 431 | 431 | 401 |
| $R^2$ | 0.05 | 0.10 | 0.13 | 0.03 |
| $\bar{R}^2$ (adjusted $R^2$) | 0.04 | 0.07 | 0.10 | 0.03 |

[a] $p < .01$ (one-tailed test)

[b] $p < .05$ (one-tailed test)

[c] $p < .10$ (one-tailed test)

[d] $p < .01$ (two-tailed test)

[e] $p < .05$ (two-tailed test)

[f] $p < .10$ (two-tailed test)

[g] One-tailed tests were used where directional hypotheses were made, otherwise all tests are two-tailed.

[h] Not included in model

cost of the product seemed appropriate for the present study. Familiarity with the product class, measured by whether or not the respondent had used the appliance in the previous 12 months and whether or not the product was purchased by mail order, was also considered to be a potentially important control variable and these two measures of familiarity and were included.

The initial regression analysis was performed using length of search in days as the dependent variable. An examination of the residuals from this analysis suggested heteroscedasticity. A second regression analysis was conducted using the square root of the length of search as the dependent variable. Heteroscedasticity did not seem to be

a serious problem with this specification. Conceptually this transformation implies that the difference in length of search between inhome gift (or outhome gift) and personal use purchase will be larger the longer the average length of search suggested by the values taken by the other independent variables. The results of both analyses are reported in the second and third columns of Table 2. The results indicate that the null hypothesis that outhome gift purchasers do not take significantly less time to make their purchase than do people shopping for personal use can be rejected. However, the analogous hypothesis for inhome gift purchasers cannot be rejected. The results of the analysis also indicate that the middle income respondents, those with total family income of between

TABLE 3

CROSSTABULATION OF WHETHER OR NOT PRICE
SET IN ADVANCE WITH REASON FOR PURCHASE

|  | Personal Use | Inhome Gift | Outhome Gift |
|---|---|---|---|
| Price set in advance | 147 (49%) | 49 (56%) | 61 (65%) |
| Price not set in advance | 156 (51%) | 39 (44%) | 33 (35%) |
|  | 303 | 88 | 94 |

$\chi^2$ (personal use with inhome gift) = 1.12(n.s.)

$\chi^2$ (personal use with outhome gift) = 6.72 (p<.01)

$6,000 and $13,000, took considerably longer than high income respondents to make their purchase.[4] This is in keeping with the earlier findings of Katona and Mueller [8, pp. 54-56]. In the analysis using the square root of length of search as the dependent variable, this difference was significant at the .05 level for the group with incomes between $6,000 and $9,000 a year. The length of search for coffee-makers, blenders and hairdryers and hairstylers was significantly longer than that for electric irons. These results make intuitive sense. The variety of types of coffeemakers available is likely to make the selection process more complex and lengthy. Blenders are also a product class with a variety of features available on the different brands and models. At the time of the study, hairstylers was a relatively new product class, which would again probably require more information seeking than would be the case for the other product classes which are all relatively mature products. The only regression coefficient that does not make intuitive sense is the one for use experience. Although no directional hypothesis was made for this coefficient, it might be expected that greater product familiarity through usage experience would result in a shorter duration of this search. However, the results of this analysis suggest that this is not the case.

The dependent variable for H4 was the ratio of the importance the respondent claimed to have attached to instore information sources. It was felt that most potential control variables for inclusion in the regression equation to test this hypothesis, such as income, use experience, buying experience, price and product class, would tend to have similar relationships with both the numerator and the denominator of the index, thus obviating the need to include them in the regression equation. The one exception to this was felt to be the dummy variable representing whether or not the purchase was made by mail, since presumably people purchasing by mail would be less likely (or unable) to use instore information sources, possibly because of their living in rural areas.

The results of the regression analysis are reported in the fourth column of Table 2. As anticipated, the coefficient of the mail order dummy variable term was large, negative and highly significant. The coefficient for inhome gifts was positive and significant, suggesting that the null hypothesis that there is no difference in the relative

_____
[4] With respect to another dimension of the consumer search process, Udell [14] made a similar finding. His research indicated that middle income purchasers of small electrical appliances were more likely to visit the store, where they finally purchased the appliance, more than once than were either high-income or low-income respondents.

importance of instore information sources for inhome gifts and personal use purchases can be rejected. The coefficient for outhome gifts, however, was not in the predicted direction but was not significantly different from zero.

DISCUSSION

In general, the results of the analyses reported above provide greater support for the hypotheses in the case of outhome gifts than inhome gifts. Relative to purchases of small electrical appliances for personal use, outhome gift purchases of these products are more likely to be made in department stores, the length of search is likely to be significantly shorter, and a price is more likely to be set before the search process begins. For inhome gifts we can conclude that, relative to personal use purchases, they are more likely to be purchased in department stores, and respondents are more likely to report that a greater proportion of their information, after weighting sources by reported importance, was provided by instore information sources.

The explained variance in the various regression analyses was uniformly low, although roughly comparable to those reported in other market segmentation studies [5]. While this indicates that there is a large amount of variation within each segment, it does not mean, as Bass, Tigert and Lonsdale [1] have pointed out, that the results are necessarily of no managerial significance.

While the results of this study are strictly only generalizable to small electrical appliances, they may also apply to many other product categories. These results, if supported by further research, have a number of important implications for manufacturers and retailers of gift-oriented products. Since gift purchases are more likely to be made in department stores than are purchases of similar products for personal use, it is important for a manufacturer of a gift-oriented small electrical appliance brand to obtain distribution in department stores. The fact that the length of search is significantly shorter for outhome gift purchases than for personal use purchases has important marketing communications implications. The shorter duration of search implies that a marketer with a product targeted at the outhome gift segment has less time to communicate his brand message to the purchaser than is the case for a product targeted at personal use purchasers. This may influence the media he uses and the timing of his messages. Given that outhome gift purchasers are more likely to set a price before beginning the search process, and if this price is adhered to in the subsequent purchase, then it would be important for a marketer who is targeting his product line at the outhome gift market and who wants to appeal to most of the market to have models available at the various price points in the market.

Inhome gift purchasers also report attaching relatively more importance to instore information sources than do personal use purchasers. This would seem to imply that a manufacturer or retailer who targets his product at the gift market should make use of instore displays and promotions since these seem to be an effective information source for the inhome gift segment.

One caveat is in order with respect to the last implication discussed above. It is not clear at all given the nature of this descriptive study which is cause and which is effect. It could very well be that at times of the year when small electrical appliances are heavily purchased as gifts that manufacturers and retailers currently emphasize instore displays and promotions relative to outstore communication approaches.

## CONCLUSIONS

This exploratory study has demonstrated for several small electrical appliance product classes that there are important differences on several dimensions of consumer purchasing behavior between purchasing these products for either inhome or outhome gifts. These differences appear to have important implications for marketing managers involved with these types of products. It remains to be seen whether similar differences will be found in future research on other types of products. If so, it would appear that the purpose for the purchase may be a managerially relevant basis on which to segment the market for products that are purchased both for personal use and as gifts.

## REFERENCES

1. Bass, Frank M, Douglas J. Tigert and Ronald T. Lonsdale, "Market Segmentation: Group Versus Individual Behavior." Journal of Marketing Research, 5 (August 1968), 264-70.

2. Belk, Russel W. "It's the Thought that Counts: A Signed Digraph Analysis of Gift-Giving," Journal of Consumer Research, 3 (December 1976), 155-62.

3. Caron, Andre and Scott Ward. "Gift Decisions by Kids and Parents" Journal of Advertising Research, 15 (August, 1975), 15-20.

4. Engel, James F., David T. Kollat and Roger D. Blackwell. Consumer Behavior (2nd edition) New York: Holt, Rinehart and Winston, Inc. 1973.

5. Frank, Ronald E. "Market Segmentation Research: Findings and Implications," in Frank M. Bass, Charles W. King, and Edgar A. Pessemier, Application of the Sciences in Marketing Management, New York: John Wiley & Sons, Inc., 1967.

6. Goldberger, Arthur S. Econometric Theory. New York: John Wiley & Sons, Inc., 1964.

7. Katona, George. The Mass Consumption Society. New York: McGraw-Hill, 1964.

8. Katona, George and Eva Mueller. "A Study of Purchase Decisions," in Lincoln H. Clark (ed.) Consumer Behavior: The Dynamics of Consumer Reaction, New York: New York University Press, 1965.

9. Lowes, Bryan, John Turner and Gordon Wills. "Patterns of Gift Giving and Their Marketing Implications," British Journal of Marketing, 2 (Autumn 1968), 217-29.

10. Newman, Joseph W. and Richard Staelin, "Multivariate Analysis of Differences in Buyer Decision Time," Journal of Marketing Research, 8 (May 1971), 192-98.

11. Pratt, Robert W. Jr. "Continuous Information Systems: One Approach to Meeting Changing Management Needs," Attitude Research in Transition. Edited by Russel I. Haley. Chicago: American Marketing Association, 1972.

12. Ryans, Adrian B., and Terry Deutscher. "Product Class Experience, Dimensionality and Reliability: Their Relationship in a Nonmetric Scaling Study," Advances in Consumer Research, Volume 2. Edited by Mary Jane Schlinger. Association for Consumer Research, 1975.

13. Schwartz, Barry. "The Social Psychology of the Gift," American Journal of Sociology, 73 (July, 1967) pp. 1-11.

14. Survey of Attitudes and Purchase Habits of Consumers of Housewares Products. Chicago: National Housewares Manufacturers Association, 1975.

15. Theil, Henri. Principles of Econometrics. New York: John Wiley & Sons, Inc. 1971.

16. Udell, John G. "Prepurchase Behavior of Buyers of Small Electrical Appliances," Journal of Marketing, 30 (October 1966), 50-52.

# MARKET SEGMENTATION BY GASOLINE CONSUMPTION INTENTIONS

William H. Cunningham, The University of Texas at Austin
Robert A. Peterson, The University of Texas at Austin

## ABSTRACT

This study focuses on the gasoline consumption intentions of a sample of nearly 1,900 adult consumers from three Southwestern states based upon their responses to price increases in gasoline and their associated willingness to conserve gasoline. Cluster analysis was used to segment respondents into two distinct groups based upon their willingness to conserve gasoline in response to increases in the price of gasoline. The segments were shown to have substantially different patterns of consumption intentions as well as different demographic characteristics.

## INTRODUCTION

Recent disruptions in delivery of and price increases for fuels have combined to create dramatic changes in consumer behavior. For instance, it is apparent that consumers are adopting more energy conserving practices, and purchasing more energy efficient goods [3, 4]. They are pressed from two directions in this matter: the one, economic; the other, political. Ever increasing fuel prices have created a situation in which energy can no longer simply be taken for granted. Likewise, political pressures to reduce U.S. dependence on foreign energy sources are manifested in programs to approach, if not secure, "energy independence," in large part through conservation.

At the present time there exists no consistent, national energy policy. Moreover, there even appears to be a paucity of empirical knowledge concerning energy-related attitudes and behavior, especially regarding consumers. Despite the importance of the issue, little research has been conducted. That research which has been conducted often has tended to be contradictory. For example, while Kilkeary [6] and Warren [13] found middle-income consumers to be the most energy conscious and conservative, Grier [5], Perlman and Warren [9], and Talarzyk, Wayne and Omura [11] report more energy conservation among higher income groups. Similarly, although Stearns [10] obtained a relationship between education and energy conservation practice, Murray, et. al [7] reported no relationship between the two.

### Purpose

The purpose of this research was to provide a preliminary basis for understanding consumer attitudes and behavior relating to a specific form of fuel--gasoline. Ultimately, the type of information provided here may help federal and state governments establish the nation's energy policies.

This present paper reports the results of segmenting a sample of consumers on the basis of their gasoline consumption intentions. Gasoline was chosen as the focal energy source because of its broad impact upon most consumers, and the recent widespread awareness concerning its relatively short future supply [2]. A segmentation approach was selected due to the belief that more meaningful (i.e., relevant, actionable) findings would result from an analysis of group, as opposed to individual, attitudes and behavior, especially from a policy perspective.

## PROCEDURE

### Sample Determination

Study data were obtained from a questionnaire mailed to nearly 10,000 consumers living in five cities in three southwestern states. The respective cities were Austin and El Paso, Texas, Flagstaff and Prescott, Arizona and Albuquerque, New Mexico. While cities were not randomly selected, they ranged in size from 10,000 to nearly one million and were deemed representative of the population in those states investigated. Consumers were randomly drawn from customer lists of an energy company servicing more than 90 percent of the households in the cities sampled. A response rate of 24 percent was obtained from the mail survey. The data were collected in October 1975, shortly after the largest gasoline price increases in history [14].

For the present research the effective sample size was 1873. Due to the cluster analysis technique employed, it was necessary to eliminate respondents with any missing data on the segmentation variables. While this resulted in culling out a relatively large number of respondents, a preliminary analysis of respondents used and not used in this study revealed no systematic differences on demographic or attitudinal characteristics.

### Segment Determination

In one section of the questionnaire respondents were asked to indicate:

> "What would be your reaction to the following percentage increases in the price of gasoline?"

Respondents were then presented with nine percentage price increases, ranging from 5 to 150 percent. For each percentage increase they were requested to indicate, on a six point scale, whether their reaction would be:

| | |
|---|---|
| no reduction in the use of gasoline . . . | (coded "6") |
| slight reduction . . . | (coded "5") |
| moderate reduction . . . | (coded "4") |
| substantial reduction . . . | (coded "3") |
| maximum possible reduction . . . | (coded "2") |
| would no longer use gasoline . . . | (coded "1") |

While the first four categories are relatively straightforward, the last two may require a brief explanation. "Maximum possible reduction" implied that the respondent would still use gasoline but only in as small amounts as possible. In contrast "would no longer use gasoline" implied that the respondent would cease purchasing gasoline altogether. Given the geographic areas studied, the latter response seemed highly unlikely (due to a lack of alternative transportation modes).

Responses to these nine items (the percentage price increases) served as the basis of the segmentation procedure. Respondents were initially subjected to a cluster analysis.[1] Statistical testing of cluster (group

---

[1]More precisely, the procedure consisted of a two-stage clustering routine. This routine employed a Euclidean distance measure, unstandardized variables, a sum-of-squares error criterion, a random starting point, and unrestricted cluster membership and inter-cluster movement.

or segment) error terms ultimately led to the selection of five as being the most appropriate number of segments as well as the most clearly distinguishable segments.

Once segments had been determined, two further analyses were undertaken. First, individual segments were characterized with regard to their gasoline consumption intentions. This was done by investigating segment profiles on the nine percentage price increase items. Second, to determine if it was possible to discriminate among the segments, gasoline purchasing behavior demographic characteristics, and energy-related attitudes were compared across segments by means of analysis of variance.

RESULTS

Gasoline Consumption Intentions

Application of the cluster analysis resulted in five distinct groups or segments of respondents with regard to gasoline consumption intentions. The respective sizes of these groups were:

| Group (segment) | Size | Percent of Total |
|---|---|---|
| 1 | 283 | 15.1 |
| 2 | 257 | 13.7 |
| 3 | 643 | 34.3 |
| 4 | 564 | 30.1 |
| 5 | 126 | 6.8 |
| Total | 1873 | 100.0% |

The "size-structure" of the groups was, as commonly found in traditional market structuring situations--one or two large or dominant segments, one relatively small segment.

Figure 1 presents a graphical display of mean consumption intentions for each percentage increase in price for each segment. For comparison purposes total sample responses are reported as well. To assist in interpretation, the data have been presented in a traditional demand curve format.

In general, the curves are as would be expected: as the price of gasoline increased, intended consumption decreased. However, even a cursory inspection of the figure will reveal two major distinctions among the five segments. Not only did the segments differ with respect to the level of intention, as could be expected given the segmentation technique used; they also differed in the shape of the respective intention curves. More specifically, investigation of the intention curves shows:

> In no instance do the curves overlap. Group 5 was always the most resistant to changing its gasoline consumption while Group 2 was always the most likely to change its gasoline consumption as price increased.

With the exception of Group 5, intended gasoline consumption decreased rapidly as price increased from 5 to 50 percent. Above a 50 percent price increase intended consumption decreased relatively more slowly. Indeed, for Groups 2, 3, and 4 the curves are basically "flat" above a 100 percent

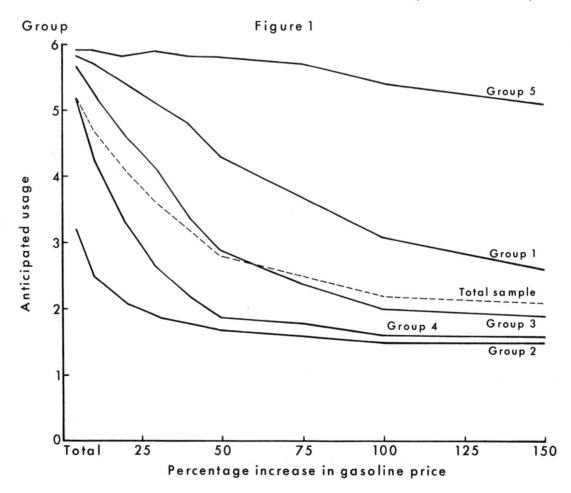

Figure 1

price increase.[2]

Only in Groups 2 and 3 did any consumers indicate they would no longer use gasoline should the price increase reach 150 percent.[3] At the other extreme, Group 5 respondents indicated that, regardless of price increases, they did not intend to reduce their gasoline consumption.

Based upon the notion that the intention curves can be treated as analogous to demand curves, an attempt was made to quantify the "intention elasticity" of each segment. By taking appropriate logarithmic transformations of the data, and applying regression techniques, a crude price-responsiveness index, based upon the respective slope coefficients, was constructed for each segment. After standardizing the slope coefficient it was ultimately possible to arrive at a percentage index representing the relative intention elasticity or "price responsiveness" of each segment. This resulted in the following scale of elasticity, where the larger the percentage, the greater the relative responsiveness to percentage price increases:

| Group (segment) | Responsiveness Index |
|---|---|
| 1 | 24% |
| 2 | 12% |
| 3 | 31% |
| 4 | 28% |
| 5 | 5% |

These values support the data presented in Figure 1; group 5 was by far the least responsive to price increases while Group 3 was most responsive according to this measure.

Other Segment Characteristics

To better understand gasoline consumption intentions, selected behavioral, demographic and attitudinal variables were compared across segments. This was done to determine if relationships existed between these variables and gasoline consumption intentions.

At one point in the questionnaire respondents were queried about "last month's" consumption of gasoline. Table 1 presents the average dollar amount reportedly spent by each segment. Analysis of variance indicated mean differences were not statistically significant. Also contained in the table is the percentage of total gasoline dollars expended by each segment as well as the relative size of the segment. Corresponding percentages are not statistically different for each segment, reinforcing the lack of gasoline consumption differences.

Table 2 shows selected demographic characteristics of the groups. Significant differences were obtained for income, social class and race. The average incomes of Groups 1 and 5 were greater than the average income of Group 2. Similarly, Groups 1 and 5 differed significantly in that the average social class "index score" of Group 1

---

[2]It is important to point out that the data were collected after the large increases in the price of gasoline had taken place. These increases occured in the 1973-August 1975 period. From 1975 to 1976 the average price of gasoline rose less than one cent [8].

[3]Obviously, however, responses relating to a complete cessation of gasoline consumption are somewhat suspect, and must be considered in this regard.

was greater than that of either Group 2 or 4.[4] Other demographic characteristics failed to distinguish significantly among the groups.

TABLE 1

CONSUMPTION OF GASOLINE BY GROUP

| Group | Prior Month's Average Dollar Expenditure $ | Percentage of Total Dollars Spent % | Percentage of Total Sample % |
|---|---|---|---|
| 1 | 33.96 | 15.4 | 15.1 |
| 2 | 29.67 | 13.4 | 13.7 |
| 3 | 31.50 | 34.2 | 34.3 |
| 4 | 32.82 | 30.3 | 30.1 |
| 5 | 31.78 | 6.7 | 6.8 |

TABLE 2

SELECTED GROUP DEMOGRAPHIC CHARACTERISTICS

| Group | Average Yearly[a] Income in Dollars $ | Average Age | Average Social[a,b] Class Index | Percent White % | Percent Married % |
|---|---|---|---|---|---|
| 1 | 16,400 | 38.4 | 77 | 90 | 88 |
| 2 | 11,200 | 40.5 | 60 | 79 | 80 |
| 3 | 13,900 | 38.0 | 69 | 88 | 83 |
| 4 | 12,500 | 41.1 | 65 | 80 | 80 |
| 5 | 14,600 | 37.8 | 68 | 92 | 78 |

[a] $p < .0001$

[b] See Footnote 3 for description of index.

Finally, selected energy-related attitudes of the groups were compared. Although attitudinal data were collected by means of Likert scales, to facilitate inter-group and inter-item comparisons results are reported on percentage agreement scales ranging from strongly agree (100%) to strongly disagree (0%). Results from this analysis are presented in Table 3. When differences did occur among the groups they were primarily between Groups 1 and 2, with Group 2 tending to believe the energy problem is artificial.

DISCUSSION AND CONCLUSIONS

The present research appears to contradict the study of Willenborg and Pitts which found that the "price mechanism was relatively ineffective in reducing consumption of gasoline when prices increased gradually over time" [14]. However, the contradictions may be more superficial than real; in that, the present study was done after the price increases that Willenbord and Pitts studied had taken place and because the present research focused on a segmentation approach to the problem. Investigating the issue of understanding and predicting energy attitudes and behavior from

---

[4]The social class variable consisted of combining income, education, and occupation into a single index according to a scheme proposed by the U.S. Bureau of the Census [8]. The higher the index, the higher the social class.

TABLE 3

SELECTED GROUP ENERGY ATTITUDES

| Statement | Percentage Agreement Score[a] | | | | |
| --- | --- | --- | --- | --- | --- |
| | Group 1 | Group 2 | Group 3 | Group 4 | Group 5 |
| The United States currently has an energy problem.[b] | 85 | 77 | 83 | 78 | 79 |
| Our energy problem exists only because we are being charged high prices for energy.[b] | 22 | 44 | 29 | 37 | 30 |
| The petroleum companies are responsible for the energy problem.[b] | 40 | 60 | 51 | 57 | 49 |
| The petroleum companies have done all they could to solve the energy problem. | 26 | 21 | 22 | 20 | 26 |
| The petroleum companies did not cause the energy problem, but have taken advantage of it to raise prices. | 68 | 69 | 65 | 66 | 65 |
| There will be no energy shortage in the U.S. as long as we are willing to pay a high price for energy. | 37 | 46 | 39 | 40 | 43 |
| I feel the energy problem will cause major difficulties for the U.S. during the next 5 years. | 80 | 82 | 80 | 80 | 78 |
| The energy problem has put a substantial strain on my budget.[b] | 62 | 83 | 72 | 78 | 67 |

[a]The higher the percentage score, the greater group agreement with the statement.

[b]p < .001

an individual (as opposed to group) perspective, or stopping with a correlational (compensatory) analysis of the total sample, could result in inconclusive or even misleading findings.

It is probably necessary to approach problems of this nature from some sort of "demand curve decomposition" perspective. The methodology employed here executes such a decomposition. While the method is not unique to this research (see [1] for example), its full potential has not been reached in public policy research.

Second, the research yielded numerous specific insights into gasoline consumption intentions and related char-

acteristics of a particular sample of consumers. Perhaps, the most intribuing conclusion from the research relates to the complex interrelations among the variables investigated. The finding of an insensitive, unresponsive segment such as Group 5 has great importance for gasoline-related decision making. Going one step further, it is imperative to consider the affects of any public policy gasoline decision on a segment such as Group 2, probably a segment injured most by past increases in the price of gasoline because of its low economic status.

The important point is that for social policy reasons or for simply maximizing conservation efforts, government, through its powers of taxation and income credits, can generate different conservation efforts in particular market segments. As an example, referring again to Figure 1, the total sample is very responsive to price increases up to 50 percent. Price increases above this do not yield very substantial conservation efforts. This pattern seems to also exist for the subjects in Groups 3 and 4 and to a lesser extent in Groups 1 and 2. However, it is clear that a tax on fuel will have virtually no impact on Group 5 and relatively little impact on Group 1. In contrast, Group 2 seems to be willing to make most of its total conservation efforts as a result of a price increase of 25 percent while further price increases result in virtually a perfectly inelastic intention curve. While there may in fact be differences between intentions and behavior, results of the nature presented here can prove useful in numerous ways. For instance, through such research evidence it may be possible to anticipate consumer behavior prior to certain policy formulations.

REFERENCES

[1] Boggis, J. G. and I. Held. "Cluster Analysis--A New Tool in Electric Usage Studies," Journal of the Market Research Society, 13 (January), pp. 49-66.

[2] Cunningham, William H. and Sally Lopreato. Consumers' Energy Attitudes and Behavior. Prager, September 1977 (in press).

[3] Curtin, Richard T., "Consumer Adaptation to Energy Shortages," University of Michigan Survey Research Center, 1974.

[4] Doner, W. B., "Consumer Study--Energy Crisis Attitudes and Awareness," Lansing: Michigan Department of Commerce.

[5] Grief, Eunice S., "Changing Patterns of Energy Consumption and Costs in U.S. Households." Paper presented at Allied Social Science Association Meeting, Atalntic City, New Jersey, 1976.

[6] Kilkeary, Rovena. "The Energy Crisis and Decision-making in the Family," Paper prepared for National Science Foundation. Washington, D.C.: National Technical Information Service, 1975.

[7] Murray, James; Michael J. Minor; Norman M. Bradburn; Robert F. Cotterman; Martin Frankel; and Alan E. Pisarski. "Evolution of Public Response to the Energy Crisis," Science, 184 (1974), pp. 257-263.

[8] "Gasoline Prices," Oil and Gas Journal, January 3, 1977, p. 109.

[9] Perlman, Robert and Roland L. Warren. Energy-Saving by Housholds of Different Incomes in Three Metropolitan Areas, Waltham, Massachusetts: Brandels University Florence Heller Graduate School of Advanced Studies in Social Welfare, 1975.

[10]  Sterns, Mary D.  The Social Impacts of the Energy
      Shortage:  Behavioral and Attitude Shifts,
      Washington, D.C.:  U.S. Department of Transportation,
      1975.

[11]  Talarzyk, W. Wayne and Glenn S. Omura.  "Consumer
      Attitudes Toward and Perceptions of the Energy
      Crisis," New Marketing for Social and Economic
      Progress and Marketing Contributions to the Firm
      and to the Society edited by Ronald C. Curhan,
      American Marketing Association 1974 Combined
      Proceedings.

[12]  U.S. Bureau of the Census.  U.S. Census of
      Population: 1960.  Subject Reports Socioeconomic
      Status, Final Report PC (2)-5C, Washington, D.C.:
      U.S. Government Printing Office, 1967.

[13]  Warren, Donald I., Individual and Community Effects
      on Response to the Energy Crisis in Winter, 1974:
      An Analysis of Survey Findings from Eight Detroit
      Area Communities, Ann Arbor:  University of Michigan
      Institute of Labor and Industrial Relations,
      Program in Community Effectiveness, 1974.

[14]  Willenborg, John F. and Robert E. Pitts.  "Gasoline
      Prices:  Their Effect on Consumer Behavior and
      Attitudes," Journal of Marketing 41 (January),
      p. 31.

# INFORMATION SEEKING BEHAVIOR IN
## CONSUMER DURABLE PURCHASES

Noel Capon, University of California, Los Angeles
Marian Burke, University of California, Los Angeles

## ABSTRACT

Information acquisition behavior was measured in three simulated consumer durable purchase decisions. Findings quite
different from those previously reported with consumer non-
durables were observed. The results suggest that while the
"more is better" philosophy currently guiding policy decisions for consumer information provision is a step in the
right direction, the form of information provision and the
availability of specific types of information are critically
important dimensions which should enter into policy formulation.

## INTRODUCTION

In recent years there has been an increasing tendency on
the part of government to modify the consumer information
environment by requiring that specific types of information
be made available to consumers (e.g., Truth in Packaging,
Truth in Lending, Nutrient Labeling). This legislative
thrust has spurred consumer researchers to investigate
consumer information processing behavior. To the extent
that greater understanding of consumer information processing is obtained, policy makers should be able to make decisions, guided by research findings, which are more appropriate than those dominated by the "more is better" axiom
which appears to be the basis of current legislation.

Process-oriented consumer information processing research
to date has been limited in focus, largely in frequently
purchased non-durable goods [5,6,12,14,15,19] (dry cereal
is particularly popular as a product class), while relatively little published research on consumer durable products has been reported [16,17,20].[1] This is a serious
ommision, since the consumer decision process is likely to
be different for consumer durables than for frequently
purchased non-durables, and the associated information
processing activity might be expected to be similarly different. Specifically, one might expect non-durable purchases to reflect routinized response behavior or limited
problem solving while durable purchase would tend towards
limited and extended problem solving [9]. Such differences
have not, however, deterred Jacoby and his colleagues from
generalizing from their research on non-durables to the
spectrum of consumer products [12]. Thus, on the basis of
research findings that less than 10% of total available
information is selected by consumers in choice decision
tasks, and noting that in earlier survey studies on durables, claimed information use was low [1,8,22], he argues
for a relaxation of government regulation to require industry to provide information to consumers. It would appear that information processing research on consumer durables is necessary before such policy recommendations can
be made for products in that category.

This paper is concerned with the nature of consumer information processing in consumer durable purchase. A set of
hypotheses specific to consumer durables is developed and
tested, and comparison of the consumer durable findings
with those from previous studies on non-durables is made.
The methodology employed is the information monitoring
approach developed by Jacoby and others [5,6,11,12,13,16,
17], in which the subject-controlled information acquisi-

tion process is captured and preserved for analysis.[2]

## DEVELOPMENT OF HYPOTHESES

Jacoby has developed a model for investigating information
processing behavior in which three elements in information
processing, depth of search (amount of information employed), sequence of search (order of selection of information)
and information content (type of information selected) are
viewed as being influenced by two sets of variables [12].
These variables are individual difference variables and environmental variables, the latter encompassing task related
items. In this study three specific task related variables,
perceived risk of purchase, number of information items
available, and availability of an external memory aid, are
examined for their influence on depth of search, sequence
of search, and information content chosen. All hypotheses
are formally stated in Table 1.

### TABLE 1

### HYPOTHESES

Depth of Search

H1  The greater the perceived risk of purchase, the greater
the depth of search.

H2  The greater the amount of information made available,
the greater the depth of search.

H3  The presence of an external memory aid leads to a reduced depth of search.

Sequence of Search

H4  The greater the perceived risk of purchase, the greater
the use of attribute (CPA) processing.

H5  The greater the amount of information available, the
greater the use of attribute (CPA) processing.

H6  The availability of an external memory aid leads to
decreased use of attribute (CPA) processing.

Information Content

H7  The greater the perceived risk of purchase, the less
use of brand name in the decision process.

H8  The greater the perceived risk of purchase, the greater
the use of a consumer testing agency rating in the
decision process.

H9  The use of price information is invariant with the
degree of perceived risk.

---

[1]There are a number of unpublished studies in this
area [18,21].

[2]Bettman has recently reviewed the information monitoring and other methodologies available for studying
consumer information processing [3].

## Depth of Search

Specific hypotheses concerning depth of search are formulated with respect to each of the three task related variables. First, the concept of perceived risk has been closely related to information use [2,7] and it was hypothesized in line with recent findings [10] that the higher the perceived risk, the greater the depth of search (Hypothesis 1). Second, it was anticipated that depth of search would vary with the amount of information made available, the greater the information availability, the greater the depth of search (Hypothesis 2). Third, in any task which involves acquisition of information and subsequent decision some degree of cognitive strain is involved. Availability of external memory devices are a means of reducing such strain [4], and to the extent that they are available, other aspects of information processing may be affected. Specifically, since information items and summaries of information can be remembered more effectively with an aid, presence of a memory aid was expected to lead to decreased depth of search (Hypothesis 3).

## Sequence of Search

Bettman and Jacoby [6] have identified three broad patterns of information acquisition, Choice by Processing Brands (CPB), Choice by Processing Attributes (CPA) and Choice by Feedback Processing (CFP). Consumers employing CPB tend to select one brand and gather information on several dimensions of that brand. They then move on to other brands, repeating the process, but without necessarily choosing information on the same dimensions as for earlier brands. Consumers whose strategy is best described as first selecting a dimension, determining the specific attributes for several brands on that dimension and then moving onto other dimensions are identified as using a CPA strategy. Finally, CFP strategies involve alternating sequences of brand and attribute processing, a hybrid strategy in which subjects seem to use direct feedback from information acquired during search.[3]

Since information processing strategies employed have been shown to be strongly affected by the structure of the information presented, rather than being individual difference characteristics [5], it was anticipated that the type of processing might be affected by the task related variables of this study. Specifically, it was postulated that the more complex the choice setting, and the greater the potential for cognitive strain, the greater would be the use of strategies which involved attribute processing for reducing the number of alternatives. Thus, a CPA strategy was expected to be employed more the greater the perceived risk of purchase, (Hypothesis 4), the greater the amount of information available (Hypothesis 5), and to the extent that a memory aid was not present (Hypothesis 6).

## Information Content

Three major dimensions of information content were considered, brand name, a consumer testing agency rating, and price. First, research on consumer non-durables has shown that consumers place great reliance on brand name as an aid to choice [14]. However, in consumer durables where risk of purchase is generally higher, and there are many more measurable characteristics on which a choice can be

---

[3]Each of these categories contains a number of subclasses, in particular pure brand and pure attribute processing, but they were not utilized in this study.

made, brand name might be expected to be less important. Further, with consumer durables, consumers might be expected to engage in more information acquisition the higher the risk (Hypothesis 1) and conversely place less reliance on brand name (Hypothesis 7). However, the more risky the purchase, the more likely it may be that consumers would choose summary information from an independent source such as a consumer testing agency (Hypothesis 8). Choice of price information was not expected to vary by product class (Hypothesis 9), nor was the choice of these items of information content expected to be affected by the other task variables.

## METHOD

### Subjects:

The subjects were 24 women selected from the Los Angeles area, specifically from the membership of the Santa Monica Chapter of the American Association of University Women and from administrative personnel in the Graduate School of Management, UCLA. Most of the subjects had a college degree and had family incomes in excess of $15,000 They were paid $7.50 for their participation.

### Apparatus

The consumer information environments were simulated by use of a series of information display boards. Each board, one per product class, was designed so that 6 brands and either 14 or 27 information items could be displayed, each brand being represented by a horizontal row of either 14 or 27 information items.

In each cell of the matrices, hooks were screwed into the board. On each hook were hung twenty identical pieces of paper, each of which represented information on that particular brand, on that particular dimension, the actual information being on the reverse side of the paper.

### Choice of Product Classes

Three product classes were chosen to represent three different levels of perceived risk. From a master list of consumer durable products rated by students in an introductory marketing class at California State University at Northridge; (7 point scale, 1 = very risky); a steam iron ($\mu = 4.95$, $\sigma = 1.73$), a toaster oven ($\mu = 4.41$, $\sigma = 1.73$) and a microwave oven ($\mu = 2.89$, $\sigma = 1.60$) were chosen to represent low, medium and high perceived risk respectively. The steam iron and toaster oven were each significantly different from the microwave oven at $p < .01$ ($t = 6.51$ and 5.16 respectively), but were different from each other only at $\rho < .10$ ($t = 1.75$).

### Development of Information Display Boards

The information items for each brand of a product class were determined by a four stage process. First, exhaustive lists of dimensions which might be used to describe the product classes were gathered from Consumer Reports, Consumer Research Magazine, advertisements in local and national newspapers, mail order catalogues, labels, packages, and in-store displays. Second, an informed judge selected twenty-seven dimensions for each product class by a process of combining dimensions and eliminating those of least information value. Third, the brands were selected from those available in the Los Angeles area, which also appeared in the consumer magazines. Finally, the specific brand/dimension information items were developed, each piece of information being actually available in the Los Angeles area, from where the subject sample was drawn.

TABLE 2

INFORMATION DIMENSIONS EMPLOYED FOR 3 PRODUCT CLASSES

### MICROWAVE OVEN

**

| | |
|---|---|
| Hold a 20 lb. turkey? | Warranty terms-magnetron |
| Provision for catching spills? | Number of watts |
| Consumer Reports rating | Reduced power setting? |
| Model number | Amount of noise |
| *Brand name | Defrosting capability? |
| Maximum time setting | Speed of cooking |
| Cooking utensil restrictions | Evenness of cooking |
| Accuracy of timer for short | Browning capability |
| settings | Need for service |
| Adequacy of recipe book | Safety considerations |
| Usable oven volume | Exterior dimensions |
| *List price | Amount of radiation |
| Warranty terms-parts and | leakage |
| labor | Complies with Federal |
| End of cooking alarm? | Bureau of Radiological |
| Interior light? | Health Standards? |

### TOASTER OVEN

**

| | |
|---|---|
| Continuous clean interior? | Underwriters laboratory |
| *Consumer Reports rating | certification? |
| Crumb tray? | Adjustable baking rack? |
| Warranty terms | Evenness of broiling |
| Toast selector? | Ease/method of convert- |
| *List price | ing from baking to |
| Model number | broiling |
| Mft. name & address | Temperature of door |
| Thermostat settings | handles during cooking |
| Pilot light? | Glass window in door? |
| Vertical clearance for | Size-exterior dimensions |
| baking | Weight |
| Power consumption | Removeable door? |
| *Brand name | Ease of removing doors |
| Cord Length | Size-interior dimensions |
| | Shock hazard |
| | Evenness of baking |

### STEAM IRON

**

| | |
|---|---|
| *List price | Rate of steaming |
| Time to cool from high | Tank size |
| setting to lower setting | Length of time iron will |
| Number of settings | steam with one fill of |
| Number of watts | water |
| Number of shots of steam | Tendency to spew |
| over life | Effectiveness of spray |
| Number of vents | Burst of steam feature? |
| *Brand name | Effectiveness of self- |
| Model number | cleaning feature |
| Weight | Type of soleplate |
| Evenness of temperature | Type of water level |
| distribution | indicator |
| Need for distilled water | Electrical hazards |
| *Consumer Reports rating | Electricity consumption |
| Underwriters Laboratory | Warranty terms |
| Certificate | Soleplate termperature |
| Safety heel rest? | indicator? |

*Items Employed in Testing Hypothesis 7, 8 and 9
**Items in this column employed in the 14 item condition

The twenty-seven dimensions were randomly arranged on the display boards, with the exception that brand name, price, and a consumer testing agency rating were placed, randomly, among the first fourteen items. This procedure ensured that this most critical information was available to all subjects, both those that received information on all dimensions, and those that were given only fourteen, and further, allowed for testing of the information content

hypotheses. Lists of dimensions as they appeared are shown in Table 2.

### Experimental Conditions

The product class manipulation was performed by having one information board per product class. The variation in number of available information items was obtained by presenting either the complete boards (27 items) or boards with the right hand side covered up and 14 items accessible. Finally, in the external memory aid condition, subjects were given a pad of paper and a pen to use in their choice process if they wished to do so. Each subject made a choice in each product class, the number of information items per board and existence of a memory aid held constant across all three choices for any one subject.

### Procedure

Subjects were run in groups of one, two or three. On arrival they were told that they were to imagine that they were shopping in turn for three new products, a steam iron, a toaster oven, and a microwave oven, and that they had to make a decision of which brand to buy. They were told to act as if they were actually purchasing a brand in that product class.

The information board was explained to them and they were told that they could take information from anywhere in the matrix, in any order they liked, as much or as little as they liked, and were to stop only when they had made a decision. Each piece of information selected was to be placed on a spike and once viewed was not to be looked at again; rather they should take an identical piece of information a second time if they wished to see that information item again. When it was clear that a subject understood the task, she completed some questionnaires, including one which measured perceived risk of purchase of a number of consumer durable products. After each decision subjects completed a short questionnaire relating to the decision. When decisions on all three product classes had been made, demographic information was obtained and subjects were debriefed. The order of decisions made was randomized across subjects.

### Analysis

Depth of Search. Depth of search was operationalized as the number of information items chosen. Hypotheses 1, 2, and 3 were tested by means of a 2 x 2 x 3 repeated measures ANOVA (amount of information available x availability of a memory aid x product risk; product risk was the repeated dimension).

Sequence of Search. The classification scheme developed by Bettman and Kakkar [5] from Bettman and Jacoby [6] was used to categorize each of the decision processes as CPA, CPB, CFP, or Other. As this scheme has been generally used in assessing the strategies consumers use in experiments involving non-durables, a comparison of durable versus non-durable results was made possible. The scheme rests on an analysis of transitions from one piece of information chosen to the next where:

SB = Total number of same brand transitions/n-1
SA = Total number of same attribute transitions/n-1
 n = Total number of information items chosen

These indices together with their normalized counterparts (a same brand index (SBI) and a same attribute index (SAI)), obtained by taking into account the numbers of information items, brands, and attributes considered in each process, were used to develop classificatory rules for each process type. The classifactory categories and methods for assignment are shown in Table 3.

## TABLE 3

### CLASSIFICATION SYSTEM FOR SEQUENCE OF SEARCH

| | Criteria |
|---|---|
| Choice by Processing Attri- butes (CPA) | SA >.5, SAI >.6  SA-SB >.3 |
| Choice by Processing Brands (CPB) | SB >.5, SBI >.6  SB-SA >.3 |
| Choice by Feedback Processing (CFP) | \|SB-SB\| >.2, SB >.3, SA>.3 SBI >.4, SAI >.4, and presence of alternating brand and attribute processing |
| Other (O) Pattern | All sequences not meeting above criteria |

To test Hypothesis 4, 5 and 6, each CPA strategy was first coded as "1" and each CPB, CFP, or other strategy as "0". Since product risk was a repeated dimension, the Cochrane test was then employed for hypothesis 4, while a simple chi-square test was used for hypotheses 5 and 6.

Information Content. The number of times the information items brand name, consumer testing agency rating, and price were chosen was determined for each condition and then combined across availability of memory aid. Hypotheses 7, 8, and 9 were tested using a 2 x 3 x 3 repeated measures ANOVA (amount of information available x product risk x information content dimension (brand name, consumer testing agency rating, price); product risk and information content dimensions were repeated dimensions).

## RESULTS

### Manipulation Check

A manipulation check was performed on the perceived risk dimension, but fewer significant differences were found than in the pretest. Specifically, the marginally significant difference between the steam iron and toaster oven was no longer identified. Nevertheless, on the basis of the pretest results and since the means were in the right direction, the analysis proceeded with three levels of risk.

One way ANOVA produced an $F_{2,69}$ = 12.03 ($p<.01$); microwave oven ($\mu=1.75$, $\sigma=1.11$), toaster oven ($\mu=3.5$, $\sigma=1.74$) and steam iron ($\mu=3.88$, $\sigma=1.85$). A Newman-Keuls analysis confirmed the significant differences between the microwave oven and both the toaster oven and steam iron at $p<.01$ ($q_{2,69}$ = 5.35; $q_{3,69}$ = 6.50 respectively).

### Depth of Search

Overall depth of search was high, averaging 37.2% of available information and reaching as high as 84.6% for one individual subject. A summary of the significant results from the 2 x 2 x 3 repeated measures ANOVA used to test hypotheses 1, 2 and 3 is shown in Table 4. A significant main effect ($p<.01$) for degree of product risk was obtained in the right direction to provide good support for hypothesis 1. In particular a Newman-Keuls comparison of treatment means revealed that the effect was due to significantly greater depth of search for the microwave oven than for the toaster oven ($p <.01$) and the steam iron ($p <.05$).

## TABLE 4

### ANALYSIS OF VARIANCE SUMMARY: TOTAL QUANTITY OF INFORMATION ITEMS SELECTED

| Source of Variation | Degrees of Freedom | SS | MS | F |
|---|---|---|---|---|
| **Between Subjects** | | | | |
| Amount of Information | 1 | 2616.06 | 26.6.06 | 2.823 |
| Availability of Memory Aid | 1 | 3528 | 3528 | 3.807[a] |
| Error between | 20 | 18533 | 926.65 | |
| **Within Subjects** | | | | |
| Degree of Product Risk | 2 | 1492.19 | 746.09 | 6.094[b] |
| Error within | 40 | 4896.67 | 122.42 | |

[a] $p<.10$    [b] $p<.01$

Hypothesis 2, depth of search is positively related to the amount of information available, was rejected for lack of a significant effect. The marginally significant main effect ($p <.10$) for availability of memory aid, in the right direction, provided limited support for Hypothesis 3, a memory aid leads to decreased information use. All of the means displayed the monotonic relationships hypothesized.[4]

### Sequence of Search

Information acquisition strategies were classified according to the four category scheme described in Table 4. Overall, fifty-one sequences (71%) were CPA strategies, six sequences (8%) were CFP strategies, three sequences (4%) were CPB strategies, and eleven sequences (17%) were classified as Other. Tests of the effect of product risk (Hypothesis 4) and presence of an external memory aid (Hypothesis 6) on information acquisition strategies all produced non-significant results, leading to rejection of both hypotheses. (Hypothesis 4, T = 1.8 , df = 2; Hypothesis 6, $x^2$= .07, df = 1).

A marginally significant main effect ($x^2$ = 3.29, df = 1, $p<.10$) was obtained for information availability but in the wrong direction and Hypothesis 5 was therefore also rejected. The interpretation of this result is that less CPA strategies and more CFP and Other strategies were used the greater the availability of information.

### Information Content

In Table 5 is displayed a summary of the 2 x 3 x 3 repeated measures ANOVA, showing just the significant results. Support for Hypotheses 7 and 8 would have been obtained had there been a significant right direction, interaction effect between product risk and information content dimension. Such an effect was not found and the hypotheses were rejected.

---

[4] For hypothesis 1: Iron ($\bar{x}$ = 33.8, s = 20.9, n = 24), Toaster Oven ($\bar{x}$ = 33.3, s = 22.3, n = 24), Microwave ($\bar{x}$ = 43.2, s = 21.9, n = 24). For hypothesis 2: 27-information items ($\bar{x}$ = 42.8, s = 26.9, n = 24); 14 Information items ($\bar{x}$ = 30.1, s = 13.21, n = 24). For hypothesis 3: with a memory aid ($\bar{x}$ = 29.8, s = 14.1, n = 36), without a memory aid ($\bar{x}$ = 43.8, s = 26.0, n = 36).

By the same token, support was gained for Hypothesis 9, the use of price information is invariant with the degree of perceived risk. The marginal means are shown in Footnote 5.

TABLE 5

ANALYSIS OF VARIANCE SUMMARY
QUANTITY OF SELECTED INFORMATION CONTENT ITEMS CHOSEN

| Source of Variation | Degrees of Freedom | SS | MS | F |
|---|---|---|---|---|
| Within Subjects | | | | |
| Information Type | 2 | 79.148 | 39.148 | 3.292[a] |
| Information Type x | | 63.229 | 31.615 | 2.630[b] |
| amount of information | 2 | 63.229 | 31.615 | |
| Error within | 44 | 528.93 | 12.02 | |

[a] $p < .05$ [b] $p < .10$

A weak interaction effect ($p < .10$) between information content type and amount of information available was identified, subjects in the 14 item condition used consumer testing agency ratings more frequently than those in the 27 item condition, the reverse being true for brand name and price. Finally, a significant main effect ($p < .05$) was found for information content type, a Neuman-Keuls analysis identifying that consumer rating information was chosen more frequently than brand name ($p < .01$) and price ($p < .05$).

Additional Analysis

The finding that availability of information did not affect depth of search (Hypothesis 2) was quite unexpected, and an additional analysis was performed to investigate whether the number of information dimensions chosen was affected by information availability. The test was performed by means of a 2 x 2 x 3 repeated measures ANOVA (amount of information available x availability of a memory aid x product risk; product risk was the repeated dimension). The results, presented in Table 6, indicate that a main effect for information was present, more information dimensions being sought, the greater the number available.[6] Detailed analysis of individual information choice revealed that only one information dimension, out of eighty-one, was never chosen.

---

[5]For hypothesis 7: Use of Brand Name, Iron ($\bar{x}$ = 2.7, s = 2.6, n = 24), Toaster Oven ($\bar{x}$ = 3.4, s = 2.8, n = 24), Microwave Oven ($\bar{x}$ = 3.3, s = 2.8, n = 24). For Hypothesis 8: Use of Consumer Reports Rating, Iron ($\bar{x}$ = 4.8, s = 2.4, n = 24), Toaster Oven ($\bar{x}$ = 4.4, s = 2.6, n = 24), Microwave Oven ($\bar{x}$ = 4.6, s = 2.4, n = 24). For Hypothesis 9: Use of Price Information, Iron ($\bar{x}$ = 3.3, s = 2.3, n = 24), Toaster Oven ($\bar{x}$ = 3.8, s = 2.6, n = 24), Toaster Oven ($\bar{x}$ = 3.8, s = 2.6, n = 24), Microwave Oven ($\bar{x}$ = 3.8, s = 2.6, n = 24).

[6]For the 27-item condition, $\bar{x}$ = 13.5, s = 5.1, n = 36; for the 14-item condition, $\bar{x}$ = 8.6, s = 2.9, n = 36.

TABLE 6

ANALYSIS OF VARIANCE SUMMARY
NUMBER OF INFORMATION DIMENSIONS SELECTED

| Source of Variation | Degrees of Freedom | SS | MS | F |
|---|---|---|---|---|
| Between Subjects | | | | |
| Number of Dimensions | 1 | 435.125 | 435.125 | 15.133[a] |
| Memory Aid | 1 | 78.125 | 78.125 | 2.717 NS |
| Interaction | 1 | 17.014 | 17.014 | .592 NS |
| Error Between | 20 | 28.753 | 28.753 | |

[a] $p < .01$

DISCUSSION

Two of the most striking findings involve comparison of the overall results of this study with previous research on consumer non-durables. Thus depth of search, which averaged 38.2% of available information in this study, is considerably higher than the less than 10% figure typically found in research on consumer non-durables. This finding suggests strongly that Jacoby's argument, based on depth of search findings, for a generalized reduced requirement of industry to provide information to consumers, may be ill-founded. This difference between non-durables and durables suggests that perceived risk of purchase is a critical dimension across which depth of search varies, an inference which is supported by the evidence in favor of Hypothesis 1, in which greater perceived risk of purchase within the durable category led to increased depth of search.

An interesting and related finding was that increased information availability did not lead to increased depth of search at the levels of information manipulated. However, the more dimensions of information made available, the greater were the number of information dimensions employed. This finding, together with the usage of all but one dimension argues in favor of the "more is better" philosophy and suggests that consumers themselves are able to perform the selection function from a wide range of dimensions, an intuitively more appealing prospect than having some third party select a limited number of information items to be made available to consumers. Consumers' ability to manage the complex nature of the task is further supported by the finding that availability of a memory aid tends to lead to decreased information usage. During debriefing, many subjects stated that they would normally take notes during the process of purchasing items of this nature.

That the "more is better" philosophy is an insufficient prescription for consumer information programs is provided from the results of a second comparison with non-durable research, that concerned with the information processing strategies employed. In this study CPA processing (71%) was favored overwhelmingly more than all other strategies, CPB strategies being employed in only 4% of all sequences. This result is strikingly different from information monitoring research on consumer non-durables in which Jacoby and Bettman [6] found 50% CPB processing and Bettman and Kakkar found 42%. This finding provides further evidence that consumers are able to reduce the complexity of their task, by modifying their processing strategy, given that information is available in a form which allows CPA processing to be made without high cost. Further, there was some evidence to suggest that more elaborate strategies, CFP and Other, were used as task complexity was increased

114

by increasing the number of information dimensions.

A final comparison with results from non-durable research is in the use of summary information items. Research on consumer non-durables has shown that consumers employ summary information items as an aid to decision making, and that in particular brand name is extremely important as an information chunk. In this study the importance of information chunks was supported, but consumer rating information was chosen more often than brand name. Consumers thus preferred an independent information chunk to one related to the manufacturer. Indeed, the fact that the consumer rating information was chosen more often under the 14 item condition than the 27 item condition, and that the reverse was true for brand name and price, suggests that brand name may be treated less as an information chunk and more as a simple information item in consumer durable decisions.

## CONCLUSION

The results of this study showed that information processing for consumer durable purchase decisions is much different from non-durable purchase decisions on the dimensions of depth of search, sequence of search and critical information chunks selected. Consumers appear to act rationally in selecting more information the greater the degree of risk and in being more selective in choosing information, the more is made available. While these findings argue for a "more is better" philosophy in information provision, the findings on information sequence highlight the critical importance of making information available in a form which allows CPA processing. Finally, the heavy selection of an independent testing agency report argues for policy decisions either to support existing independent rating services, or to release government information on products currently tested, and/or develop a comprehensive government testing service.

Two caveats are necessary. First, the sample of subjects were of high education and income levels and the study should therefore be replicated employing other consumer groups before completely general statements can be made (this research is now in process). Second, the operationalization of the consumer information environments approached an ideal situation in which extensive information was available for consumers and CPA processing was no more costly than CPB processing. Thus, despite attempts to ensure that subjects acted as they would in an actual purchase situation, the operationalization may be less a reflection of actual purchasing behavior than that of purchasing behavior in some ideal information environment which may be striven for.

## REFERENCES

1. Arndt, Johan. Consumer Search Behavior, Oslo, Norway: University Press, 1972.

2. Bauer, Raymond A. "Consumer Behavior as Risk Taking," in R.S. Hancock, ed., Dynamic Marketing for a Changing World, Chicago: American Marketing Association, 1970, 389-398.

3. Bettman, James R. "Data Collection and Analysis Approaches for Studying Consumer Information Processing," in William Perreault, ed., Advances in Consumer Research, Volume 4, Association for Consumer Research, 1977, in press.

4. Bettman, James R. An Information Processing Theory of Consumer Choice, Reading, Mass: Addison-Wesley, forthcoming.

5. Bettman, James R., and Pradeep Kakkar. "Effects of Information Presentation on Consumer Information Acquisition Strategies," Journal of Consumer Research, 3 (March 1977), 233.240.

6. Bettman, James R. and Jacob Jacoby. "Patterns of Processing in Consumer Information Acquisition," in Beverlee B. Anderson, ed., Advances in Consumer Research, Volume 3, Chicago: Association for Consumer Research, 1976, 315-320.

7. Cox, Donald F. "The Influence of Cognitive Needs and Styles on Information Handling in Making Product Evaluations," in Donald F. Cox, ed., Risk Taking and Information Handling in Consumer Behavior, Boston: Harvard University Press, 1967, 370,393.

8. Dommermuth, William P. "Shopping Matrix and Marketing Strategy," Journal of Marketing Research, 2 (May 1965), 128-132.

9. Howard, John A and Jagdish N. Sheth. The Theory of Buyer Behavior, New York: John Wiley, 1969.

10. Jacoby, Jacob. "Perspectives on a Consumer Information Processing Research Program," Communication Research, 2 (July 1975), 203-215.

11. Jacoby, Jacob. "The Emerging Behavioral Process Technology in Consumer Psychology," Purdue Papers in Consumer Psychology, No. 169, 1976.

12. Jacoby, Jacob, Robert W. Chestnut and William A. Fisher. "Simulating Non Durable Purchase: Individual Differences and Information Acquisition Behavior," Purdue Papers in Consumer Psychology, No. 153, 1976.

13. Jacoby, Jacob, Robert W. Chestnut, Karl C. Weill and William Fisher. "Pre-purchase Information Acquisition: Description of a Process Methodology, Research Paradigm, and Pilot Investigation," in Beverlee B. Anderson, ed., Advances in Consumer Research, Volume 3, Chicago: Association for Consumer Research, 1976, 306-314.

14. Jacoby, Jacob, George J. Szybilio, and Jacqueline Busato-Schach. "Information Acquisition Behavior in Brand Choice Situations." Purdue Papers in Consumer Psychology, No. 140, 1976.

15. Lussier, Denis, A. and Richard W. Olshavsky, "An Information Processing Approach to Individual Brand Choice Behavior," Paper Presented at the ORSA/TIMS Joint National Meeting, San Juan, Puerto Rico, October 1974.

16. Payne, John W. "Heuristic Search Processes in Decision Making," in Beverlee B. Anderson, ed., Advances in Consumer Research, Volume 3. Chicago: Association for Consumer Research, 1976a, 321-327.

17. Payne, John W. "Task Complexity and Contingent Processing in Decision Making: An Information Search and Protocol Analysis," Organizational Behavior and Human Performance, 1976b.

18. Russ, Frederick A. "Consumer Evaluation of Alternative Product Models," Unpublished Doctoral Dissertation, Carnegie-Mellon University, 1971.

19. Russo, J. Edward and Barbara A. Dosher. "Dimensional Evaluation: A Heuristic For Binary Choice," Unpublished Doctoral Dissertation, Carnegie-Mellon University, 1971.

20. Russo, Edward and Larry D. Rosen. "An Eye Fixation Analysis of Multi-Alternative Choice," Memory and Cognition, 3 (May 1975), 267-276.

21. Svenson, Ola. "Coded think aloud protocols obtained when making a choice to purchase one of seven hypothetically offered houses: some examples," Unpublished Paper, University of Stockholm, 1974.

22. Udell, Jon, C. "Prepurchase behavior of buyers of small electrical appliances," Journal of Marketing, 30 (October 1966), 50-52.

# IS MARKETING EDUCATION MISSING THE BOAT?
## OR.....
## WHAT SHOULD BUSINESS SCHOOLS BE TEACHING THEIR MARKETING STUDENTS TO BETTER PREPARE THEM FOR MARKETING WORK?

LeRoy Joseph, American Can Company
Donald J. Keller, General Foods Corporation
Ian MacFarlane, MacFarlane & Company, Inc.
David A. Teaze, Union Carbide Corporation
Karl van Leer, Boise Cascade Manufactured Housing Division

### ABSTRACT

A distinguished panel of marketing executives discusses business schools' marketing curricula and suggests those aspects of greatest interest to major companies involved in industrial and consumer product marketing. Generally, preferences are for practical training to equip students for marketing positions.

### INTRODUCTION

Mr. MacFarlane

Many of you in the audience know my views on marketing curricula, especially insofar as industrial marketing is concerned, and I will say only briefly that I believe marketing curricula need to be

-- much more practical in preparing students for marketing jobs

-- less research theory and model oriented

-- providing greater emphasis in the study of actual marketing situations, by emphasizing field trips, guest lectures, training for job placement and how to find good marketing jobs, intern and work-study programs, and so forth

-- providing more courses and even majors in industrial marketing, with courses that thoroughly explore the marketing aspects of pricing, physical distribution, transportation, purchasing, product management, and the many other ingredients that we frequently describe as comprising the marketing mix.

Without belaboring my own views on the subject, I would like to introduce a distinguished panel of four marketing executives representing major companies, including

-- LeRoy Joseph, Vice President and General Manager, Meat & Special Products, American Can Company, Greenwich, Connecticut

-- Donald J. Keller, Group Vice President, General Foods Corporation, White Plains, New York; Mr. Keller's present position includes responsibility for Food Products, Beverage and Breakfast Foods, Pet Foods, and the W. Atlee Burpee Company, a subsidiary of General Foods

-- David A Teaze, Associate Director of Marketing, Chemicals and Plastics, Union Carbide Corporation, New York, New York

-- Karl van Leer, General Manager, Boise Cascade Manufactured Housing Division, Leisure Homes East, Lexington, Massachusetts.

These gentlemen will speak in alphabetical order for approximately 12 minutes each, which should allow us at least 30 minutes for group discussion.

Mr. Joseph

In preparing marketing students for more effective marketing work, business schools have, in my opinion, a need for greater emphasis in five major areas:

1. The quality of the teacher or professor should be evaluated as to experience and expertise in the business community; we find that teachers who have had actual business experience are much more effective than those who have not.

2. The Case Method, which is used to excellent advantage by most business schools, is excellent and should be broadened to dwell heavily on futures instead of the past and the present; several of the case studies that I have been involved with deal with fact and history only and do not do an adequate job of training students to think about the future consequences of present situations.

3. Procurement is an extremely important part of every business operation, and in my opinion, attention to industrial, commercial, and business procurement in general has been lacking; particular attention should be paid to both short term and long term implications of major raw materials, especially those in which a shortage or potential shortage clearly exists.

4. The pricing concept, stressing value, market relationships, cost/price flexibility, and supply implications should be given much more consideration.

5. Employee relations, which covers a broad spectrum, is probably the most important part of the curriculum in any post-graduate business course; the role of management development, compensation, and labor relations will change so drastically over the next ten to 15 years that many businesses will find their executives poorly prepared for the revolution that will occur in employee relations; while not only related to marketing, employee relations training is extremely important and needs further emphasis in business schools.

**Mr. Keller**

General Foods is an active and successful recruiter of graduate business school students, and we maintain a relationship with a number of different schools. We do, it seems to me, have a point of view that would be of interest to the audience.

In thinking about what we like graduate business schools to teach marketing students, we believe it is best to concentrate on practical, readily usable skills such as

-- strategic planning: development of long-term objectives, business, and functional strategies

-- marketing from the consumer point of view

-- brand marketing strategies

-- brand positioning

-- the role and development of copy strategy

-- basic business knowledge in accounting and finance.

Many of our managers prefer more extensive use of cases and none of our managers perceives a need for more theory or teaching of mathmatical models.

Several of our marketing managers also have stressed that additional emphasis is needed on marketing research, including actual project-related experiences like questionnare design, field interviewing, and data analysis using statistical techniques. In addition, our marketing managers see a need for marketing curricula to include more emphasis on sales, including an understanding of distribution channels, and they also stress the need for more pertinent courses dealing with new product development.

Finally, our marketing managers have made many suggestions that students should learn more about alternative marketing career choices, including product management versus advertising agency opportunities and consumer versus industrial marketing career choices and opportunities.

**Mr. Teaze**

In considering "What should business schools be teaching their marketing students to better prepare them for marketing work?", my comments focus on college and university business school preparation for careers in industrial marketing. Although the differences in marketing industrial versus consumer products must be stressed, there are many similarities as well. Challenging courses in industrial marketing should be offered more widely. Until fairly recently, consumer product marketing courses were more readily available, and more research has been done in the consumer field.

With the rapid growth in competition among organizations marketing industrial products, companies in these businesses are not only turning more toward the academic field for consulting services, but they are also encouraging business schools to strengthen their industrial marketing curricula. Specific needs include

-- greater exposure to pricing industrial products

-- selection of channels of distribution

-- the psychology of industrial purchasing

-- marketing research related to industrial products

-- strategic commercial planning

-- implementation methods for industrial marketing plans and programs

-- the legal aspects of industrial marketing, especially pitfalls and dangers.

**Mr. van Leer**

I have been looking forward to this participation in the AMA Educators' Conference because the subject of marketing curricula is one that needs to be discussed. The business schools are not doing a good job preparing young people for work, and a typical interview with a recent college graduate usually leaves me honestly wondering what he got for $6,000 per year. I have discussed this very matter with various deans of good business schools, and I am concerned. My suggestions may be summarized in three areas:

1. The student should be taught to sell himself or herself well in an interview. I am utterly amazed at the number of business school graduates I interview who profess to have an interest in marketing but do a very poor job of selling themselves. If they cannot do that well, what are they going to do for me with our products? In the senior year, business schools should have a full credit course or two taught by outside personnel people on the subject of how to get a job. The course should not be taught by last year's graduate who could not find a job but is a friend of the Dean.

2. When I went to the undergraduate Agricultural College at Cornell, it was necessary that students spend at least one or two summers working on a farm. It was and is Cornell's contention that if a degree was to be awarded in agriculture, the recipient had to have some basic knowledge of agriculture that can only be learned by working on the farm. Business schools should do likewise by having meaningful programs that include

   -- summer work

   -- taking off a year and working

   -- co-op programs where students can work a semester and go to school a semester

   -- other practical methods, such as intern programs and the like.

3. Students should do some field work that involves them with an on-going business; the market research work, for example, can be done for a real company on a real product; theory is great, but why not practice it at the local supermarket, or with a local manufacturer?

**Mr. MacFarlane**

The panel is well aware that the audience is comprised largely of marketing educators from fine colleges and graduate schools of business administration throughout the country. The panel is also aware of some of the problems of marketing education and is prepared to discuss questions and those problems with the audience at this time.  I would like to thank each distinguished panelist for taking the time to be away from the important jobs they have in their companies, but I also believe that part of the reason each of them is here is that he expects to learn something from the audience and from his fellow panel members.  We are now ready for what I hope will be an active and lively series of questions and discussion. Prior to each question, please give your name and school or organization.

# DISTRIBUTED LAG MODELS OF CUMULATIVE ADVERTISING EFFECT AND REPEAT PURCHASE BEHAVIOR

Darral G. Clarke, Brigham Young University

## ABSTRACT

Distributed lag models of advertising effect have been popular for a number of years: they seem to fit the data in most instances and the $R^2$'s are almost always high. But the effect of advertising on purchase behavior is different for first purchase and subsequent repeat purchase. Recent evidence would indicate that the communication effects of advertising are of rather short duration, while the duration of repeat purchase behavior may be long. Whether or not one wishes to attribute repeat purchase behavior to advertising, ignoring this dual underlying structure leads to serious biases using present estimation procedures.

## INTRODUCTION

Few thoughtful researchers would dispute the statement that almost all sales time series are aggregates of first purchase sales and sales due to repurchase. It is likely that the advertising influence on first purchase is different than for repurchase. In the former, the information role of advertising is dominant whereas, in the latter, the rest of the marketing mix and product satisfaction may dominate or equal the importance of advertising. In particular the duration of these two behaviors is likely to be different.

In a survey of nearly seventy sales-advertising applications of distributed lag models [2] only two papers utilized methodologies which could possibly separate advertising effect from routine repeat purchase. The model used by Clarke [1] is a distributed lag type model augmented by autocorrelated disturbances in an attempt to compensate for time dependent non-advertising influences. Houston and Weiss [5] utilize a similar model estimated with a more powerful algorithm than Clarke's and attribute the observed autocorrelation to repeat purchase behavior. While each of these papers attempts to deal with the problem, it will be shown that neither of them succeeds to a significant degree.

## MODELS

The distributed lag model with autocorrelated disturbances utilized by both Clarke, and Houston and Weiss is essentially the same.[1]

$$y_t = a_o + \lambda y_{t-1} + ax_t + u_t \tag{1}$$

where

$y_t$ = sales at time t

$x_t$ = advertising at time t

$u_t =$ Model 1a: $u_t$ independent normally distributed random disturbance

Model 1b: $\begin{cases} u_t = \rho u_{t-1} + \varepsilon_t \\ \varepsilon_t = \text{independent normally distributed} \\ \quad\text{random disturbance.} \end{cases}$

---

[1]Clarke's model is a partial adjustment model and was not formulated to reflect cumulative advertising effects.

In the Clarke paper and the subsequent paper by Clarke and McCann [3], autocorrelation was included in the model to compensate for its tendency to affect the estimate of $\lambda$. Houston and Weiss go a step further and speculate that the autocorrelation parameter, $\rho$ is an estimate of the carryover represented by repeat purchase. In a reply to the Houston and Weiss paper, Clarke and McCann [4] recognize the importance of Houston and Weiss' more powerful autocorrelated disturbance model in decreasing the estimate of $\lambda$, subsequently reducing the estimate of the duration of the cumulative advertising effect.

This paper explores whether the autocorrelation term $\rho$ measures repeat purchase and also investigates the dependence between $\hat{\rho}$ and $\hat{\lambda}$. An experiment is performed in which a model with explicit functions for both repeat purchase and cumulative advertising effect was defined as follows:

Cumulative advertising effect model

$$y_{1t} = \lambda_1 y_{1t-1} + ax_t, \tag{2}$$

Repeat purchase model

$$y_{2t} = \lambda_2 \dot{y}_{t-1}, \tag{3}$$

where $\dot{y}_t$ is a four month moving average of $y_t^2$

Total Sales

$$y_t = y_{1t} + y_{2t}. \tag{4}$$

Using this model, data are generated in which the carryover effects of advertising communication and repeat purchase are known. The dual underlying processes are necessary because of the probable different duration of the effects. The communication effects of advertising are probably about 3 to 9 months in duration [see, 2] while repurchase could possibly last for years. This composite sales history (4) is then hoped to be representative of the type of data confounding encountered in the real world.

What sort of estimates result when this underlying structure is ignored and a single distributed lag model such as (1) is misspecified? In particular

1) How well does $\hat{\lambda}$ estimate $\lambda_1$, the actual cumulative advertising effect?
2) How close does $\hat{\rho}$ come to estimating $\lambda_2$, the repeat purchase factor?
3) How does the value of $\lambda_2$ affect the estimates of $\lambda_1$ and "a" in the cumulative advertising model?

---

[2]A four month moving average was used for a number of reasons. First, it was desired that the repeat purchase process be quite smooth and not drastically affected by current, advertising influenced sales. It is possible that the results would be somewhat sensitive to the length of this moving average. Although not examined specifically, it would be expected that longer moving averages would not affect the results very much. A shorter moving average such as one or two months would become more closely tied to the cumulative advertising function. The more interesting and relevant case seemed to be when the two processes were different in length.

As a first step, an attempt was made to apply the model to Palda's [7] much worked Lydia Pinkham data and see if the autocorrelation parameter could be estimating repeat purchase as Houston and Weiss hypothesized. Of course $\lambda_1$ and $\lambda_2$ are not known in the Palda data and furthermore, model (2-4) may not be the underlying process. If, however, the advertising time series is taken as an input and sales data are generated for various values of $\lambda_1$ and $\lambda_2$, how well do models 1a and 1b recover the underlying structure? The estimation procedure used for model 1a was OLS and the Cochran-Orcutt procedure of the TSP package developed at MIT was used to estimate Model 1b.

Table 1 displays OLS estimates of $\lambda$ and "a" when $\lambda_1$ varies from 0.4 to 0.7, and $\lambda_2$ varies from 0.75 to 0.90. The coefficient of advertising ("a") is held constant at 0.15. The inadequacy of the OLS estimates to recover the proper parameter estimates is readily apparent.

### TABLE 1

OLS Estimates of Advertising Effect
Pinkham Simulation

$$y_t = a_o + ax_t + \lambda y_{t-1}$$

| | | Estimated Value of $\lambda$ $\lambda_1$ | | | | | Estimated Value of "a" $\lambda_1$ | | |
|---|---|---|---|---|---|---|---|---|---|
| | | .4 | .5 | .6 | .7 | | .4 | .5 | .6 | .7 |
| | .75 | .837 | .859 | .900 | .949 | .75 | .094 | .097 | .100 | .100 |
| $\lambda_2$ | .80 | .849 | .871 | .908 | .915 | .80 | .099 | .102 | .105 | .104 |
| | .85 | .807 | .849 | .895 | .906 | .85 | .104 | .107 | .109 | .109 |
| | .90 | .883 | .923 | .936 | .938 | .90 | .108 | .112 | .114 | .114 |

In this table the important comparison is $\lambda$ with $\lambda_1$

In this table the true value of a = .15

Although the estimated $\lambda$ increases monotonically with increasing $\lambda_1$ (as it should) its value is grossly inflated. As $\lambda_2$ increases, the estimate of $\lambda$ generally increases, but is actually lowest when $\lambda_2 = .85$. The OLS estimate of $\lambda$ is a poor and inconsistently biased estimate of the cumulative effect of advertising when repeat purchase behavior is present. (The bias in this example varies from 23 to 38 standard errors.)

Similarly, "a" is consistently underestimated, as would be expected, since $\lambda_1$ is overestimated. It is interesting, however, that this underestimate is remarkably stable under various values of $\lambda_1$ and $\lambda_2$. For each $\lambda_1$ the difference between the high and low estimates of "a" (for different $\lambda_2$) is within 2 standard errors. From the high to the low estimate "a" is barely over two standard errors. The estimate of "a" is thus significantly biased downwards (from 9 to 39 standard errors) with little absolute variance with $\lambda_1$ and $\lambda_2$. Although this is not surprising since OLS has no means of accounting for the repeat purchase component of the model (3), it is disturbing since many published distributed lag applications utilize OLS.

Table 2 presents the Cochran-Orcutt estimates of the distributed lag model with autocorrelated disturbances (model 1b). The estimates of $\lambda$ in Table 2 are closer to $\lambda_1$ in about 50% of the equations than were the OLS estimates, but $\lambda$ is still a biased estimate of $\lambda_1$ (the bias varies from 2.7 to 86 standard errors!). The bias is generally increasing with $\lambda_1$ and $\lambda_2$. The estimates of the coefficient of advertising "a" are remarkably similar to the OLS estimates. There is a more pronounced increase in "a" with increasing $\lambda_2$ as the autocorrelation term reduces the estimate of $\lambda$ and simultaneously allows "a" to increase.

### TABLE 2

Autoregression Model Estimates of Advertising Effect
Pinkham Simulation

$$y_t = a_o + ax_t + \lambda y_{t-1} + u_t$$

$$u_t = \rho u_{t-1}$$

| | | Estimated Value of $\lambda$ $\lambda_1$ | | | | | Estimated Value of "a" $\lambda_1$ | | |
|---|---|---|---|---|---|---|---|---|---|
| | | .4 | .5 | .6 | .7 | | .4 | .5 | .6 | .7 |
| | .75 | .489 | .623 | .785 | .940 | .75 | .097 | .099 | .103 | .104 |
| $\lambda_2$ | .80 | .515 | .646 | .891 | .952 | .80 | .104 | .107 | .108 | .111 |
| | .85 | .530 | .670 | .925 | .948 | .85 | .111 | .114 | .114 | .117 |
| | .90 | .523 | .938 | .956 | .959 | .90 | .116 | .118 | .120 | .122 |

Estimated Value of $\rho$

| | | $\lambda_1$ | | | |
|---|---|---|---|---|---|
| | | .4 | .5 | .6 | .7 |
| | .75 | .914 | .895 | .710 | .067 |
| $\lambda_2$ | .80 | .916 | .856 | .161 | .039 |
| | .85 | .895 | .781 | .001 | .009 |
| | .90 | .947 | .106 | -.060 | -.053 |

But what of Houston and Weiss's hypothesis that $\hat{\rho}$ measures repeat purchase behavior? This simulation is not the actual situation they were studying, of course. It is probably a much simpler process than the actual one, but the estimates of $\rho$ in Table 2 challenge the imagination to think they measure anything. $\hat{\rho}$ certainly bears little resemblance to $\lambda_2$, the repeat purchase carryover term in the model. As $\lambda_1$ and $\lambda_2$ increase, $\hat{\rho}$ decreases and as $\lambda_1$ and $\lambda_2$ both become large there is an apparent confounding. If $\lambda_1$ and $\lambda_2$ are vastly different in magnitude, this procedure may perhaps yield acceptable results (note that the $\lambda_1 = .4$ column improves as $\lambda_2$ increases).

It must be noted that the Lydia Pinkham advertising time series itself might contain an autocorrelation function which would compound the processes measured by $\hat{\rho}$ and thus $\hat{\rho}$ couldn't estimate $\lambda_2$. It is also possible that there is a more complex mathematical expression which connects $\lambda_2$ and $\rho$. One thing is certain in this example, however, the autocorrelation coefficient is at best an obscure and unreliable estimate of repeat purchase behavior.

It is to be expected that most advertising histories exhibit some kind of pattern so this compounding of advertising time series autocorrelation function and repeat purchase patterns is to be expected as the rule rather than the exception.

### RANDOM ADVERTISING INPUT

To explore the reliability of the OLS and Cochran-Orcutt estimates of the cumulative effects of advertising, if there is no contamination by an advertising autocorrelation function, a time series of random numbers with no autocorrelation was generated as "advertising" input to model (2-4). A "sales" time series was generated by model (2-4) with no random error for the same values of $\lambda_1$, $\lambda_2$ and "a" used in the previous example and the results are presented in Tables 3 and 4.

In Table 3 the OLS estimates of $\lambda$ and "a" are presented. Clearly $\lambda$ is still a poor estimate of $\lambda_1$, the parameter which defines the duration interval of the cumulative advertising effect. One anomaly of the OLS estimates of the Pinkham experiment is removed: the $\lambda$ estimates increase monotonically with $\lambda_1$ and $\lambda_2$.

## TABLE 3

### OLS Estimates of Advertising Effect
### Random "Advertising" Input

$$y_t = a_o + ax_t + \lambda y_{t-1}$$

| | Estimate of $\lambda$ $\lambda_1$ | | | | | Estimate of "a" $\lambda_1$ | | | |
|---|---|---|---|---|---|---|---|---|---|
| $\lambda_2$ | .4 | .5 | .6 | .7 | $\lambda_2$ | .4 | .5 | .6 | .7 |
| .75 | .846 | .860 | .888 | .929 | .75 | .116 | .116 | .115 | .114 |
| .80 | .871 | .888 | .917 | .946 | .80 | .124 | .123 | .123 | .121 |
| .85 | .885 | .909 | .936 | .951 | .85 | .132 | .131 | .130 | .128 |
| .90 | .915 | .941 | .955 | .961 | .90 | .141 | .140 | .138 | .135 |

It must be noted however, that the estimates of $\lambda$ differ from $\lambda_1$ by more than they did in the Pinkham example. The estimate of the coefficient of advertising "a" is larger than in the Pinkham example and shows more sensitivity to $\lambda_2$ than to $\lambda_1$. This is a disturbing property since it is the repeat purchase parameter which has more effect on the estimate of advertising effectiveness than does the parameter in the cumulative advertising effect model.

In Table 4 the Cochran-Orcutt estimates of model 1b are presented. Here things are really strange. $\lambda$ is seen to be a U-shaped function of $\lambda_2$ when $\lambda_1$ = .4 or .5 with the everpresent overestimation of $\lambda_1$. Except for $\lambda_2$ = 0.75, the performance is reasonably predictable and the estimates are significantly better than the OLS estimates. Again Cochran-Orcutt is unreliable when $\lambda_1$ and $\lambda_2$ are of the same magnitude. The estimate of "a" is more sensitive to $\lambda_2$ than it is to $\lambda_1$.

## TABLE 4

### Autoregression Model Estimates of Advertising Effect
### Random "Advertising" Input

$$y_t = a_o + ax_t + \lambda y_{t-1} + u_t$$

$$u_t = \rho u_{t-1}$$

| | Estimate of $\lambda$ $\lambda_1$ | | | | | Estimate of "a" $\lambda_1$ | | | |
|---|---|---|---|---|---|---|---|---|---|
| $\lambda_2$ | .4 | .5 | .6 | .7 | $\lambda_2$ | .4 | .5 | .6 | .7 |
| .75 | .869 | .880 | .898 | .925 | .75 | .118 | .115 | .115 | .117 |
| .80 | .498 | .634 | .906 | .943 | .80 | .117 | .119 | .128 | .124 |
| .85 | .530 | .665 | .931 | .956 | .85 | .126 | .128 | .135 | .132 |
| .90 | .542 | .931 | .958 | .967 | .90 | .133 | .151 | .141 | .139 |

| | Estimate of $\rho$ $\lambda_1$ | | | |
|---|---|---|---|---|
| $\lambda_2$ | .4 | .5 | .6 | .7 |
| .75 | .084 | .007 | .053 | .413 |
| .80 | .934 | .934 | .357 | .244 |
| .85 | .950 | .949 | .258 | .127 |
| .90 | .985 | .415 | .085 | .062 |

The performance of $\hat{\rho}$ as an estimate of $\lambda_2$ (or anything else) is again very disappointing. There is no consistent pattern and the likelihood that any functional relationship at all exists between $\lambda_2$ and $\hat{\rho}$ is doubtful.

## SUMMARY

The ability of two distributed lag model estimation procedures to estimate the cumulative effects of advertising in a situation in which repeat purchase is present has been explored. Both OLS and Cochran-Orcutt estimates of such a situation were seen to be biased and susceptible to effect confusion, particularly when the duration of the two

processes are somewhat comparable. The Cochran-Orcutt procedure was unstable in the random advertising experiment when $\lambda_2$, the repeat purchase process, is not appreciably larger than $\lambda_1$, the cumulative advertising effect process. The problem is that $\hat{\lambda}$ is a poor estimate of $\lambda_1$.

For those who philosophically separate repeat purchase behavior from cumulative advertising effect, since the former is due to product satisfaction and the marketing mix as a whole, and the later is due to communication effects of advertising alone, the results are disturbing. They probably indicate that distributed lag models of cumulative advertising effect are seriously biased upwards, even more than was previously suggested [2].

Those who philosophically wish to attribute repeat purchase behavior to advertising are faced with a similar problem: $\hat{\lambda}$ is not a good estimate of either $\lambda_1$ or $\lambda_2$, neither is it a reasonable estimate for some average of them since it does not necessarily lie between them. Perhaps a function exists connecting $\lambda_1$, $\lambda_2$ and $\hat{\lambda}$ in some meaningful way. I haven't investigated it since it appears unlikely and I belong to the other philosophical camp.

The actual repurchase process for most products is surely at least as complex as that represented by equation 3. If these common distributed lag models do so poorly in reproducing this simple process, how much more poorly do they express more complex processes? Regardless of what philosophical leaning a researcher has, isn't it time to stop performing distributed lag analysis on aggregate sales-advertising data and begin to produce models of greater insight, reflecting a more sophisticated expression of the phenomena involved?

## REFERENCES

1. Clarke, Darral G., "Sales-Advertising Cross-Elasticities and Advertising Competition," _Journal of Marketing Research_, Vol. X (August 1973).

2. _____, "Econometric Measurement of the Duration of Advertisng Effect on Sales," _Journal of Marketing Research_, Vol. XIII (Nov. 1976).

3. _____, and John M. McCann, "Measuring the Cumulative Effects of Advertising: A Reappraisal, _Proceedings_, American Marketing Association, 1973.

4. _____, _____, "Cumulative Advertising Effects: The Role of Serial Correlation; A Reply, _Decision Sciences_, (January, 1977).

5. Houston, Franklin S. and Doyle L. Weiss, "Cumulative Advertising Effects: The Role of Serial Correlation," _Decision Sciences_, Vol. 6 (July, 1975).

6. Palda, Kristian, _The Measurement of Cumulative Advertising Effects_, Englewood Cliffs: Prentice Hall (1964).

# AGGREGATED AND DISAGGREGATED CUMULATIVE ADVERTISING MODELS

Franklin S. Houston, Temple University

## ABSTRACT

This paper illustrates that proper modeling will result in comparable parameter estimates for cumulative advertising models at differing levels of aggregation.

## INTRODUCTION

In the November 1976 issue of the Journal of Marketing Research, Darral Clarke examined numerous econometric studies to determine the duration of cumulative advertising. He concludes that the implied duration of cumulative advertising has been confounded by the level of aggregation found in the data base. This study addresses the question of what is the impact of temporal aggregation on the parameter estimates of cumulative advertising models.

To best investigate these issues, one must study situations where advertising is felt to develop a cumulative impact and compare and contrast results drawn from analyses done on differing data intervals. The following report describes such a comparison of aggregated and disaggregated lag models with the data base being common for both levels of aggregation.

## INTERPRETING THE COEFFICIENT OF THE LAGGED DEPENDENT VARIABLE

In 1964, Palda [2] suggested the following model to represent the cumulative impact of advertising. The advertising effect was hypothesized to decay geometrically:

$$Y_t = bX_t + \lambda bX_{t-1} + \lambda^2 b X_{t-2} + \ldots , \qquad (1)$$

where

$Y_t$ represents sales in period t,

$X_t$ represents advertising expenditures in period t, and

$$0 < \lambda < 1.$$

The reduced form of equation (1) is

$$Y_t = \lambda Y_{t-1} + bX_t . \qquad (2)$$

The interpretation of equation (2) is that b represents the current impact of advertising expenditures and $\lambda$ represents the decay of advertising over time.

In regard to the interpretation of the $\lambda$, Clarke [1, p. 347] notes that with some alternative model forms "the meaning of $\lambda$ is not clear at all . . ." and seems to be "a function of other marketing mix elements, product loyalty, and other factors...". There are several reasons why it is difficult to avoid this confusion in interpreting $\lambda$. First, advertising plays a role in forming product loyalty, and the effects of advertising need not be isolated for

most management applications. Loyalty is the result of a successful marketing program, and $\lambda$ can be argued to represent both a measurement of this loyalty as well as the carry-over or cumulative impact of a marketing program.

Secondly, it is difficult to include all important elements in an examination of historical data, and we can at best hope that the impact of other variables is well-behaved.

## THE DATA BASE

To best look at cumulative advertising alone, would require a product which does not involve repeat purchasing (no product loyalty) and has a fixed marketing program, i.e. no shifts in price, distribution, product quality. The subsequent analysis is based on a promotional campaign promoting a concept over broadcast media and meets such criteria.

The promotional program was conducted by the American Civil Liberties Union of St. Louis and attempted to make the citizens of the St. Louis community more aware of their right to privacy. Paid advertisements were used to promote this concept, and at the conclusion of the commercial a telephone number was given and an announcer urged the viewer/listener to call the number for a booklet on the topic. The data base studied is the dollar cost of these commercials and the number of phone calls received. The observations cover a period of seventy-two days not all of which received ad exposures.

Several caveats should be made about this data base. First, other forms of promotion existed, including several billboards, a newspaper advertisement, and general non-paid news coverage. It is not felt that these other activities represent any major and systematic impact on the number of calls generated. A second point is to note that while this study reports on the relationship between phone calls and advertising expenditure, the purpose of the campaign went beyond a simple attempt to distribute booklets.

## CUMULATIVE ADVERTISING MODELS

The first model examined postulates a lagged dependent variable:

$$Y_t = \lambda Y_{t-1} + b X_t + d W_t + \varepsilon_t , \qquad (3$$

where

$Y_t$ represents the number of requests on day t,

$X_t$ is the cost for the broadcast time aired on day t, and

$W_t$ is zero on weekdays and one (1) on weekends.

The latter variable is necessary because the agency was not able to staff the telephone regularly on weekends while promotions continued and presumably the responses continued during these days.[2]

[1] The author would like to thank Ms. Joyce Armstrong, director of the ACLU in St. Louis, as well as Mr. Robert Benjamin and other participants of the ACLU Privacy Project for making this data available. The University of Missouri - St. Louis provided funding to help compile the data base used in this study.

[2] This suggests more involved analysis of this data set, and further study is being carried out.

As discussed in Clarke [1], this equation form can come from several hypotheses. Examination of table 1 shows that the parameter estimates are consistent with any of these underlying theories.

We might, as an alternative, employ the test used in Clarke [1, pgs. 352-3] for testing interval bias, i.e. the current effects/serially correlated model:

$$Y_t = \rho Y_t + b X_t - b \lambda X_{t-1} + \varepsilon_t. \tag{4}$$

Estimating this equation using ordinary least squares requires that the following form be estimated:

$$Y_t = A X_t + B X_{t-1} + C Y_{t-1} + \varepsilon_t. \tag{5}$$

Table 1 shows that the estimate for C is positive and therefore inconsistent with the model hypothesized in equation (4). Thus the data can not be explained by the "current effects" model suggested by Clarke.

Since the lagged advertising parameter is estimated to be positive and significantly different from zero, it can be argued that these parameter estimates are consistent with the "nonmonotonic declining cumulative effect [1, p. 352]." That is, the data are consistent with an hypothesized koyck geometric decay, but the decay does not begin until the second period:[3]

$$Y_t = \lambda Y_{t-1} + b_1 X_t + (b_2 - \lambda b_1) X_{t-1} + \varepsilon_t. \tag{6}$$

If we assume that our structural model is a geometric decay which starts in the second period, then the advertising effect will last at least 2½ days.[4]

## AGGREGATING THE DATA BASE

The most logical aggregation for this data base is to aggregate into ten one-week periods. This still provides enough observations to allow for estimation and also means that the weekend dummy variable can be omitted from the models (thus preserving degrees of freedom).

Table 2 contains estimates for distributed lag models using the weekly data base. The results suggest that an immediate decay best describes the data rather than a weekly model similar to equation (6). If the assumed model is:

$$Y_t = \lambda Y_{t-1} + b X_t + \varepsilon_t,$$

then the lower bound of the advertising interval duration can be calculated by:

$$\frac{\log(.1)}{\log(\lambda)} .$$

In this instance that lower bound is estimated to be two weeks.

---

[3]This equation is similar to equation (6) in [1]. The further implication of this equation form is that the parameter estimate associated with the lagged advertising could have been equal to zero or negative without disproving the existence of a geometric decay.

[4]This estimate comes from equation (5) in [1] with the exception that the inequality in equation (5) is incorrect. The error appears to result from a failure to recognize that division by $\log \lambda$ will necessarily mean dividing by a negative number which reverses the sign of the inequality.

## RATIONALIZING THE MODELS

The weekly and daily models appear to give contradictory results. The first thing which should be noticed about the estimates of the advertising duration is that they are not contradictory. The estimate derived from the daily data implies that to experience 90% of the advertising impact we will need to wait at least 2½ days. The weekly model implies a wait of at least 2 weeks. While little comfort comes from these divergent estimates, they are not contradictory.

The second issue to recognize is that the two models are not comparable. If equation (6) were summed the resultant equation would be:

$$\sum_{i=0}^{6} Y_{t+i} = \lambda \sum_{i=0}^{6} Y_{t-1+i} + b_1 \sum_{i=0}^{6} X_{t+1}$$
$$+ (b_2 - \lambda b_1) \sum_{i=0}^{6} X_{t-1+i}$$
$$+ \text{Error}, \tag{7}$$

where t and i are measuring days. This equation is not the weekly model estimated above, however. This model says our lagged values are lagged by one day! The weekly model estimated above employed weekly lags. Thus, we have had different models as well as different degrees of aggregation.

Unfortunately, we should expect to encounter difficulty in estimating this model since the two advertising terms will be highly collinear, as will the two sales terms. This latter would suggest that we could explain Monday through Sunday sales well by looking at Sunday through Saturday sales for the same week.

The inverse of the above problem is somewhat different. Instead we might ask whether an aggregate model (such as Palda's) reflects what we would find upon disaggregating. This problem could be addressed with our current data quite easily.

The weekly model,

$$\sum_{i=0}^{6} Y_{t+i} = \lambda \sum_{i=0}^{6} Y_{t-7+i} + b \sum_{i=0}^{6} X_{t+i} \tag{8}$$

when disaggregated would look like:

$$Y_t = \lambda Y_{t-7} + b X_t. \tag{9}$$

If we believed that the nonmonotonic function similar to (6) is appropriate, then our daily model could be:

$$Y_t = \lambda Y_{t-7} + b_1 X_t + (b_2 - \lambda b_1) X_{t-1}. \tag{10}$$

The weekly equivalent of this would be:

$$\sum_{i=0}^{6} Y_{t+i} = \lambda \sum_{i=0}^{6} Y_{t-7+i} + b_1 \sum_{i=0}^{6} X_{t+i}$$
$$+ (b_2 - \lambda b_1) \sum_{i=0}^{6} X_{t+1-1}, \tag{11}$$

or

$$\sum_{i=0}^{6} Y_{t+1} = \lambda \sum_{i=0}^{6} Y_{t-7+1} + [b_1(1-\lambda) + b_2] \sum_{i=0}^{5} X_{t+i}$$
$$+ b_1 X_{t+6} + (b_2 - \lambda b_1) X_{t-1}. \tag{12}$$

Assuming (10) to be the true daily model would still result in the weekly model (8) as an approximation to equation (12).

Examination of table 3 shows that the $\lambda$ (.354) resulting from estimating equation (10) is quite similar to the estimate derived from the weekly estimate (.322). It should be noticed that while the aggregation levels differed, the parameters to be estimated remained the same   The $\lambda$ from a weekly model, equation (11), is the same $\lambda$ that would be found in a daily model, equation (10). Similarly, the two advertising coefficients (.206 and .154) from table 3 sum to be approximately equal to the advertising coefficient from the weekly estimation (.375).

In comparing the results for the two aggregation levels we have found similar results. What is critical to note is that even though we were using different levels of aggregation the underlying models were comparable.

## SUMMARY

If the researcher properly models the advertising relationship, he/she should not expect to find differences between models at differing levels of aggregation.[5] Comparisons made between different levels of aggregation generally result in comparisons being made between different model forms. Unfortunately, researchers let the data base guide the type of model being developed. A number of different models were hypothesized and estimated above. The data set studied is of interest because of the unique role played by advertising, but the statistical techniques can not determine which of the models is most appropriate. Judgment will have to guide the researcher in drawing conclusions from this data set.

## TABLE 1

### PARAMETER ESTIMATES USING DAILY OBSERVATIONS

The OLS Parameter Estimates of
the Coefficients Associated with
the Designated Variables

|  | Intercept | $Y_{t-1}$ | $X_t$ | $X_{t-1}$ | $W_t$ | No. of Observations |
|---|---|---|---|---|---|---|
| Equation (3) | 14.183 (4.32)[ac] | .365 (4.23)[c] | .211 (4.84)[c] | –[b] | -26.10 (-5.37)[c] | 71 |
| Equation (5)/(6) | 13.760 (4.29) | .307 (3.47) | .158 (3.23) | .103 (2.11) | -27.340 (-5.72) | 71 |

a. Ratio of coefficient to the standard error.
b. Not included in the model.
c. Significant at the .05 level.

## TABLE 2

### PARAMETER ESTIMATES USING AGGREGATED (WEEKLY) OBSERVATIONS

The OLS Parameter Estimates of
the Coefficients Associated with
the Designated Variables

|  | Intercept | $Y_{t-1}$ | $X_t$ | $X_{t-1}$ | Number of Observations |
|---|---|---|---|---|---|
| Equation (3) | -d | .322 (6.97)[ac] | .375 (16.83)[c] | -d | 9 |
| Equation (5)/(6) | 3.940 (.19) | .322 (3.72)[c] | .372 (12.70)[c] | -.012 (.23) | 9 |

a. Ratio of coefficient to the standard error
b. Not included in the model.
c. Significant at the .05 level.
d. Deleted.

## TABLE 3

### PARAMETER ESTIMATES USING DAILY OBSERVATION WITH A WEEK LAG

The OLS Parameter Estimates of
the Coefficients Associated with
the Designated Variables

|  | Intercept | $Y_{t-7}$ | $X_t$ | $X_{t-1}$ | $W_t$ | No. of Observations |
|---|---|---|---|---|---|---|
| Equation (10) | 5.901 (1.39)[a,b] | .354 (4.57)[b] | .206 (4.57)[b] | .154 (3.42)[b] | -20.144 (-3.76)[b] | 65 |

a. Ratio of coefficient to standard error.
b. Significant at .05 level.

## REFERENCES

1. Clarke, Darral G., "Econometric Measurement of the Duration of Advertising Effect on Sales," _Journal of Marketing Research_, 13 (November, 1976), 345-57

2. Palda, Kristian S., _The Measurement of Cumulative Advertising Effects_, Englewood Cliffs: Prentice-Hall, 1964.

[5]This discussion has not examined the problems arising from assumptions about the error terms.

# THE TIME-VARYING EFFECTIVENESS OF ADVERTISING

Gary M. Erickson, Stanford University

## ABSTRACT

A model is presented that permits the use of linear regression to estimate the variance over time of the effectiveness of advertising. An analysis using the model shows advertising effectiveness rising to a peak late in the product life, rather than declining monotonically over the life of the product.

## INTRODUCTION

There has been much speculation as to the varying effectiveness of advertising as a product passes through its life cycle [2-6, 10, 12, 13]. Most authors agree that advertising effectiveness is large initially and decreases subsequently. Mickwitz [10], however, has advanced the argument that the decline may not be monotonic. He suggested that advertising may become important again in the late maturity, after the competition in other marketing variables (price, product differentiation, etc.) has been pursued to the limit.

## EMPIRICAL RESEARCH

Empirical investigations into the question of the variance of advertising effectiveness over time have been few. Beckwith [1] used various methods, including assuming polynomial relationships with respect to time, to study the variation over time of the coefficient of advertising in a Koyck scheme.[1] He analyzed the Lydia Pinkham data.[2] Beckwith determined that advertising effectiveness declined in the initial part of the data period and then increased in later years. It appears that the changes could be attributed to changes in copy forced by FTC requirements; Beckwith did not attempt to adjust for the copy changes to examine any life-cycle-related variation.

Parsons [12] investigated the variation of the coefficients of advertising and lagged sales in a Koyck scheme, using data on the Sapolio household cleanser. He assumed exponential time relationships (forcing monotonicity) and concluded that the advertising elasticity declined over time and that the carryover effect increased.

Winer [17] used a model that interprets coefficients in a linear model as having two components - permanent and transitory. The permanent component is assumed to change according to a random walk with a continuous state space, the amount of change being normally distributed with mean 0 and a known covariance structure. The transitory component is assumed to be normally distributed with mean 0 and a known covariance structure. He analyzed the Lydia Pinkham data, using a Koyck scheme. Winer determined that the advertising effect initially grew and later declined,

---

[1]A Koyck scheme is defined by the following relationship:
$$Y_t = \alpha + \beta X_t + \lambda \beta X_{t-1} + \lambda^2 \beta X_{t-2} + \ldots + \mu_t$$
This leads to
$$Y_t = \alpha(1-\lambda) + \beta X_t + \lambda Y_{t-1} + [\mu_t - \lambda \mu_{t-1}]$$
See [9], [11].

[2]First analyzed in a Koyck setting by Palda [11].

Wildt [16] used a method called "moving window regression" which starts with the first (r+s) observations of a data set, where r is the number of parameters to be estimated and s is some positive increment, estimates via ordinary least squares, drops observation 1 and adds observation (r+s+1), estimates again, and so forth until the last observation is used. This provides a "moving window" look at the estimated coefficients. Wildt found a general increase in the carryover effect over time, no apparent trend for the advertising coefficient, and mixed results for the coefficient of promotion.

## MODEL

The following basic model is assumed for the present study:

$$S_t = \alpha(t) + \beta(t)A_t + \lambda\beta(t-1)A_{t-1} + \lambda^2\beta(t-2)A_{t-2} + \ldots + \mu_t \tag{1}$$

where $S_t \equiv$ sales in period t

$A_t \equiv$ advertising in period t

Notice that the parameters $\alpha$ and $\beta$ are allowed to be functions of time. Using the Koyck transformation [9,11] leads to

$$S_t = \alpha(t) - \lambda\alpha(t-1) + \beta(t)A_t + \lambda S_{t-1} + \nu_t \tag{2}$$

where

$$\nu_t \equiv \mu_t - \lambda\mu_{t-1} \tag{3}$$

Further, assume that, for a general $\tau$

$$\alpha(\tau) = \alpha_0 + \alpha_1\tau + \ldots + \alpha_a\tau^a \tag{4}$$

$$\beta(\tau) = \beta_0 + \beta_1\tau + \ldots + \beta_b\tau^b \tag{5}$$

allowing the parameters to vary as polynomials over time. These assumptions lead to

$$S_t = \alpha_0^* + \alpha_1^* t + \ldots + \alpha_a^* t^a + \beta_0 A_t + \beta_1 t A_t + \ldots + \beta_b t^b A_t + \lambda S_{t-1} + \nu_t \tag{6}$$

where

$$\alpha_j^* \equiv \alpha_j - \lambda \sum_{k=j}^{a} (-1)^{k-j} \binom{k}{j} \alpha_k \tag{7}$$

It can be readily shown that

$\alpha_a = 0$ if and only if $\alpha_a^* = 0$

$\alpha_a = \alpha_{a-1} = 0$ if and only if $\alpha_a^* = \alpha_{a-1}^* = 0$

.

.

.

so that the estimates of $\alpha_j^*$ can be used directly to test for the significance from 0 of members of important subsets of the $\alpha_j$.

The focus of the present study is on the time-varying effectiveness of advertising. Other empirical studies have allowed the coefficient of lagged sales to vary as well. There had been no previous theoretical justification for this in the literature, and the results of the empirical studies have been mixed, not allowing any general conclusions that would improve the theory. In addition, allowing $\lambda$ to vary in the present study would have created a much more complex model. As a result, $\lambda$ was not allowed to vary.

A general n-period delay in the onset of the decaying advertising effect can be incorporated in the model. Consider:

$$S_t = \alpha(t) + \beta_0(t)A_t + \ldots + \beta_n(t)A_{t-n} + \beta_n(t-1)A_{t-n-1} + \lambda^2\beta_n(t-2)A_{t-n-2}$$

$$+ \ldots + \mu_t \qquad (8)$$

The Koyck transformation produces

$$S_t = \alpha(t) - \lambda\alpha(t-1) + \beta_0(t)A_t + [\beta_1(t) - \lambda\beta_0(t-1)]A_{t-1}$$

$$+ \ldots + [\beta_n(t) - \lambda\beta_{n-1}(t-1)]A_{t-n} + \lambda S_{t-1} + \nu_t \qquad (9)$$

Let

$$\alpha(\tau) = \alpha_0 + \alpha_1\tau + \ldots + \alpha_a\tau^a \qquad (10)$$

$$\beta_i(\tau) = \beta_{i0} + \beta_{i1}\tau + \ldots + \beta_{ib}\tau^b \text{ for } i = 0,1,\ldots,n \qquad (11)$$

These lead to

$$S_t = \alpha_0^* + \alpha_1^*t + \ldots + \alpha_a^*t^a + \beta_{00}A_t + \beta_{01}tA_t + \ldots + \beta_{0b}t^bA_t$$

$$+ \beta_{10}^*A_{t-1} + \beta_{11}^*tA_{t-1} + \ldots + \beta_{1b}^*t^bA_{t-1}$$

$$+ \ldots + \beta_{n0}^*A_{t-n} + \beta_{n1}^*tA_{t-n} + \ldots + \beta_{nb}^*t^bA_{t-n} + \lambda S_{t-1} + \nu_t \qquad (12)$$

where $\alpha_j^*$ are defined in (7) and

$$\beta_{ij}^* \equiv \beta_{ij} - \lambda \sum_{k=j}^{b} (-1)^{k-j}\binom{k}{j}\beta_{i-1,k} \text{ for } i = 1,\ldots,n \qquad (13)$$

The assumption of polynomial time-variance of the parameters in (4), (5), (10) and (11) offers the following advantages:

(a) standard linear regression procedures can be used

(b) maximum flexibility is allowed in the shape of the time-variation while requiring that the variation be "systematic"--this is important in this early phase of the study of the time-variation of effectiveness of marketing variables, since the shapes of the time paths are not known

(c) no time-variation of a particular parameter is a special case--a polynomial of degree 0.

Of course, the polynomial assumptions will only approximate reality, and, because of this misspecification, biased estimation results. However, the reality is unknown, except that, in many situations, there exists some time-variation. It is hoped that the flexible procedure proposed herein will offer the opportunity to approach the real situation in general and/or in a particular analysis, and as a result will involve minimal bias.

An important consideration is that the model involves variables directly related to time: equation (6), for example,

includes the following variables: $t,\ldots,t^a,tA_t,\ldots,t^bA_t$. As a result, omitting important variables will almost surely bias the estimates. Consider, for example, a price variable $P_t$. If $P_t$ has a time-varying parameter

$$\gamma(\tau) = \gamma_0 + \gamma_1\tau + \ldots + \gamma_c\tau^c$$

leaving $P_t$ out of the analysis also necessarily leaves out the variables $tP_t,\ldots,t^cP_t$. The variables will likely covary with the time-related variables included in the analysis. Hence, biased estimation results (for non-zero $\gamma_0$, $\ldots,\gamma_c$) (see [7], pp. 168-9). Even if $\gamma(\tau)$ is constant, and therefore only the variable $P_t$ is left out, biased estimation will result if $P_t$ generally increases (or decreases) over time, since then $P_t$ will covary with the time-related variables. It becomes quite clear that it is important to include all relevant variables in any application of the model.

## DATA

It was decided that the model be applied to the Sapolio household cleanser data, initially analyzed in a time-variance framework by Parsons [12]. This data base was selected because it spans a large part of the life cycle of the product. It appears to include all of the mature stage, the initial portion of the decline period, and perhaps the latter part of the growth stage. Additionally, Parsons' forcing of monotonicity on the time-variance of the advertising elasticity was thought to be too restrictive.

The advertising data (in dollars) were deflated before analysis by the general price index [15], as was done by Parsons in his study. Data on other marketing policy variables was not available.

## RESULTS

The data were analyzed using a data management and analysis package written for use on the HP 2000F time-shared system. Matrix inversion was accomplished using the Gauss-Jordan method.

A major problem with the model is the presence of highly covariant time-related variables, causing less efficient estimation. To dampen the potentially harmful effects, the following steps were taken in the estimation of (6):

(a) the origin of the time variable t was centered (making 1900=0)

(b) initially, a step-wise approach, stopping when the latest variable added was not significant at the .05 level, was used on the time-related variables $(t, t^2, \ldots, tA_t,\ldots)$, with $S_{t-1}$ and $A_t$ always included, to determine the degrees needed for the polynomials $\alpha(\tau)$ and $\beta(\tau)$--then the **appropriate full model was estimate**

(c) The maximum degree allowed for each polynomial was 3.

Besides the basic linear model, a double-log version of (6 was also estimated.[3] The double-log model offers the convenience that $\beta(\tau)$ is the (time-varying) elasticity of advertising.

Linear Model

The step-wise procedure produced only one time-related

_____

[3]This assumes the following underlying model:
$$S_t = e^{\alpha(t)}A_t^{\beta(t)}A_{t-1}^{\lambda\beta(t-1)}\ldots e^{\mu_t}$$

variable, $t^3A_t$. The intercept term was found not to vary "significantly". The full model was then estimated with the following results (with the t-values in parentheses):

$$\hat{S}_t = 19,994 + \underset{(1.56)}{.063126A_t} + \underset{(0.87)}{.0029936tA_t} - \underset{(-1.32)}{.00034960t^2A_t}$$

$$- \underset{(-1.92)}{.000036391t^3A_t} + \underset{(6.45)}{.81099S_{t-1}} \qquad (14)$$

$$R^2 = .965, \bar{R}^2 = .958$$

To test for the existence of a delay of one period in the onset of the decay, (12) was estimated assuming a=0 and b=3:

$$\hat{S}_t = 15,136 - \underset{(-0.22)}{.017239A_t} + \underset{(2.72)}{.036293tA_t} + \underset{(1.91)}{.0017634t^2A_t} - \underset{(-2.68)}{.00028261t^3A_t}$$

$$+ \underset{(0.44)}{.030503A_{t-1}} - \underset{(-2.65)}{.036492tA_{t-1}} - \underset{(-2.31)}{.0021289t^2A_{t-1}} + \underset{(2.62)}{.00027411t^3A_{t-1}}$$

$$+ \underset{(7.63)}{.93332S_{t-1}} \qquad (15)$$

$$R^2 = .977, \bar{R}^2 = .967$$

The F value for testing for a significant incremental contribution to the regression of the variables $A_{t-1}$, $tA_{t-1}$, $t^2A_{t-1}$, $t^3A_{t-1}$ was not significant at the .05 level. Therefore, there was no basis for including a delay of one period in the model, and (6) was assumed to be the appropriate model.

To check for autocorrelation of the error terms, both the Durbin h and Durbin-Watson d statistics were calculated for the estimated model (14).[4] Durbin h (asymptotically a normal (0,1) random variate) was 1.83 (not significant at the .05 level), and Durbin-Watson d was $1.50 < D_u(.95,5,30) = 1.83$. A visual check of the residuals plotted against time revealed a marked autocorrelation effect. It was apparent that significant autocorrelation was present. This is a potentially serious problem with lagged sales included as an exogenous variable; inconsistent estimates result (see [7], p. 307). Hence it was decided to use the Cochrane-Orcutt iterative technique [7, pp. 262-3][5] to estimate and account for the autocorrelation. This yielded the following results:

$$\hat{S} = 87,470 + \underset{(2.69)}{.12304A_t} + \underset{(2.57)}{.017348tA_t} - \underset{(-0.53)}{.00024181t^2A_t} - \underset{(-2.30)}{.00012216t^3A_t}$$

$$+ \underset{(1.49)}{2.8015S_{t-1}} \qquad (16)$$

$$\hat{\rho} = .709$$

The cubic polynomial

$$\hat{\beta}(t) = \hat{\beta}_0 + \hat{\beta}_1 t + \hat{\beta}_2 t^2 + \hat{\beta}_3 t^3 \quad \text{for } t = -15, \ldots, 15 \text{ (t=0 corre-}$$

sponds to the year 1900)

---

[4] The h statistic is really only appropriate asymptotically (the present study has only 30 observations), and the d statistic is biased towards nonsignificance due to the presence of the lagged sales variable. A Monte Carlo study by Kenkel [8] indicates that for a sample of the size in this study, the best available test is probably one in which the null hypothesis of no autocorrelation is rejected if $d < D_u$, the upper value of the "inconclusive" range of the Durbin-Watson statistic.

[5] Note that t-values calculated for this technique are valid asymptotically.

where the estimates are from (16), is depicted in Figure 1, together with the sales and (deflated) advertising curves. Notice the initial decline and the subsequent increase, followed by another decline. The second peak occurred in 1906, coinciding with the beginning of the sales decline of the product.

FIGURE 1

Sales, Advertising and Advertising Effectiveness (Linear Model)

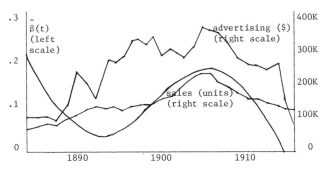

An analysis of the residuals plotted against advertising revealed a "bow" shape; that is, estimates exceeded actuals for low and high values of advertising and actuals exceeded estimates for middling values. The double-log transformation is an appropriate one for correcting this problem.

Double-Log Model

The step-wise procedure yielded one time-related variable, $t^2\ln A_t$, and again the intercept showed no "significant" variation. The full-model regression yielded:

$$\hat{\ln S}_t = 1.9044 + \underset{(0.80)}{.0423761\ln A_t} - \underset{(-0.38)}{.00013249t\ln A_t} - \underset{(-1.27)}{.000049841t^2\ln A_t}$$

$$+ \underset{(6.13)}{.801001\ln S_{t-1}} \qquad (17)$$

$$R^2 = .966, \bar{R}^2 = .961$$

To test for the incremental contribution of advertising lagged one period, the following regression was run:

$$\hat{\ln S}_t = 2.9084 - \underset{(-0.73)}{.105691\ln A_t} - \underset{(-0.79)}{.0054367t\ln A_t} + \underset{(1.29)}{.0012931t^2\ln A_t}$$

$$+ \underset{(0.22)}{.0297401\ln A_{t-1}} + \underset{(0.79)}{.0055969t\ln A_{t-1}} - \underset{(-1.37)}{.0013750t^2\ln A_{t-1}}$$

$$+ \underset{(6.31)}{.841821\ln S_{t-1}} \qquad (18)$$

$$R^2 = .972, \bar{R}^2 = .963$$

The calculated F value was not significant at the .05 level, and again (6) was assumed to be the proper model.

Durbin h was 1.06, not significant at the .05 level, but Durbin-Watson d was $1.72 < D_u(.95,4,30) = 1.74$. A visual examination of the residuals revealed a significant autocorrelation effect. Hence, it was again decided to estimate and account for autocorrelation via Cochrane-Orcutt:

$$\hat{\ln S}_t = 7.8626 + \underset{(2.05)}{.107931\ln A_t} + \underset{(1.80)}{.0012613t\ln A_t} - \underset{(-2.19)}{.00017750t^2\ln A_t}$$

$$+ \underset{(1.23)}{.239421\ln S_{t-1}} \qquad (19)$$

$$\hat{\rho} = .680$$

The estimated quadratic

$$\hat{\beta}(t)=\hat{\beta}_0+\hat{\beta}_1 t+\hat{\beta}_2 t^2 \quad \text{for } t=15,\ldots,15 \quad (t=0 \text{ corresponds}$$

to the year 1900)

where the estimates are from (19), is shown in Figure 2, along with the sales and advertising curves. The initial decline found in the linear model was not in evidence for the double-log model, but the rise to a peak in late maturity remained, 1904 being the peak year for this model.

FIGURE 2

Sales, Advertising and Advertising
Effectiveness (Double-Log Model)

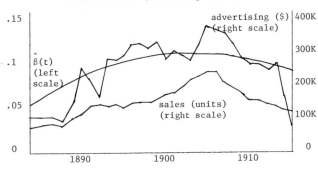

DISCUSSION

According to Tull [14], the era of decline for the Sapolio product began about 1905, when powdered cleansers were introduced (the Sapolio cleanser was in cake form). That year was also the peak sales year for Sapolio. As discussed above, both the linear and double-log models revealed a peak in advertising effectiveness just about that time (1906 for the linear and 1904 for the double-log model).

The result indicates the emergence (probably re-emergence) of advertising as an important marketing variable in the late maturity and early decline stages of the product life cycle. This is valuable knowledge for the marketing manager, since heavy advertising can be used to maintain product sales at a high level for a time late in the product life. It may be profitable to advertise heavily in this time period even though this may not be so in the prime of the product life.

CONCLUSION

The analysis of the Sapolio data confirmed the speculation by Mickwitz that advertising effectiveness does not decline monotonically throughout the product life cycle; for the Sapolio household cleanser, at least, the effectiveness of advertising rose to a peak late in the life of the product.

The analysis did not confirm the initial high effectiveness and subsequent decline as a product approaches maturity. This is probably due to the fact that the data begins 16 years after the Sapolio product was first introduced in 1869. If the early part of the data set is indeed contained in the growth stage of the product life cycle, the bulk of the growth period is still not captured.

Confirmation of the results found in this study is of course necessary. Also needed are analyses of data that come from the initial years of product life, the stages of introduction and growth into the market, to get a clear

picture as to whether the theory is correct in asserting that advertising effectiveness starts out high and declines over the early portion of product life.

REFERENCES

1. Beckwith, Neil E., "Regression Estimation of the Time Varying Effectiveness of Advertising," unpublished paper, 1972.

2. Buzzell, Robert D., "Competitive Behavior and Product Life Cycles," World Congress Proceedings, American Marketing Association, 1966, 46-68.

3. Clifford, Donald D., Jr., "Leverage in the Product Life Cycle," Dun's Review and Modern Industry, May 1965, 62-70.

4. Cox, William E., Jr., "Product Life Cycles as Marketing Models," The Journal of Business, Vol. 40, No. 4 (October 1967), 375-82.

5. Dean, Joel, "Pricing Policies for New Products," Harvard Business Review, Vol. 28, No. 6 (November 1950), 45-53.

6. Forrester, Jay W., "Advertising: A Problem in Industrial Dynamics," Harvard Business Review, Vol. 37, No. 2 (March-April 1959), 100-10.

7. Johnston, J., Econometric Methods, 2nd edition, New York: McGraw-Hill Book Company, 1972.

8. Kenkel, James L., "Some Small Sample Properties of Durbin's Tests for Serial Correlation in Regression Models Containing Lagged Dependent Variables," Econometrica, Vol. 42, No. 4 (July 1974), 763-9.

9. Koyck, L. M., Distributed Lags and Investment Analysis, Amsterdam: North-Holland Publishing Company, 1954, Ch. II.

10. Mickwitz, Gosta, Marketing and Competition - The Various Forms of Competition at the Successive Stages of Production and Distribution, Helsingfors: Central-tryckenet, 1959, 87-9.

11. Palda, Kristian S., The Measurement of Cumulative Advertising Effects, Englewood Cliffs, N. J.: Prentice-Hall, Inc., 1964.

12. Parsons, Leonard J., "The Product Life Cycle and Time Varying Advertising Elasticities," Journal of Marketing Research, XII, No. 4 (November 1975), 476-80.

13. Smallwood, John E., "The Product Life Cycle: A Key t Strategic Marketing Planning," MSU Business Topics, Vol. 21, No. 1 (Winter 1973), 29-35.

14. Tull, Donald S., "A Re-Examination of the Causes of the Decline in Sales of Sapolio," The Journal of Business, Vol. 28, No. 2 (April 1955), 128-37.

15. U. S. Department of Commerce, Bureau of the Census, Historical Statistics of the United States, 1789-1945 Washington, D.C.: Government Printing Office, 1949.

16. Wildt, Albert E., "The Empirical Investigation of Time Dependent Parameter Variation in Marketing Models," Educators' Proceedings, Series #39, American Marketing Association, 1976, 466-72.

17. Winer, Russell S., "A Time-Varying Parameter of the Sales-Advertising Relationship," Educators' Proceedings, Series #39, American Marketing Association, 1976, 461-5.

# CONSISTENT MULTIPLICATIVE MARKET SHARE MODELS

Timothy W. McGuire, Carnegie-Mellon University
Doyle L. Weiss, University of British Columbia
Frank S. Houston, Temple University

## ABSTRACT

This report reviews or summarizes many of the contributions to building, estimating, and comparing structural
market share models which have appeared in the marketing,
economics, and statistics literature.  Treatment of
multiplicative, or log-linear, formulations and a comparison of these models with linear models is emphasized.

## INTRODUCTION

The building, estimation, and comparison of structural
models describing the influence of managerial decision
variables on the sales or market shares of brands in a
product class has been one of the principal "research
streams" in the marketing literature.  While many developments in the areas of economics and statistics have
at times been incorporated into marketing analyses, we
know of no systematic survey of the relevant contributions.  Although an exhaustive review is not possible
here, we have tried to include principal contributions
and provide references to other material not covered.

We restrict our attention to market share models,
although we note that models of brand sales conditional
on industry sales are logically equivalent to share
models.  Following is one possible categorization of
contributions to the analysis of market shares.

I.  Modeling
   A.  Logical consistency
      1.  Sum constraint (predicted shares must
         sum to 100%)
      2.  Bound constraint (predicted shares
         must be between 0 and 100%)
   B.  Economic consistency [22, p. 513]
      1.  Homogeneity (market share functions
         must be homogeneous of degree 0 in
         prices and income; i.e., market shares
         must not be affected by equi-pro-
         portionate changes in income and all
         prices)
      2.  Slutsky symmetry conditions (the cross-
         substitution effects must be equal for
         all pairs of brands  X  and  Y ; i.e.,
         the rate of change in the quantity of
         brand  X  demanded with respect to the
         price of brand  Y  must equal the rate
         of change of the quantity of  Y  with
         respect to the price of  X [7, p. 36].
      3.  Additivity (same as the sum constraint
         above)
   C.  Stochastic Specification

II.  Empirical analysis
   A.  Estimation
   B.  Model comparison

The remainder of this report is organized as follows.  In
the next section we cite the important developments for
logically consistent modeling.  We then discuss economic

consistency in the context of the multinomial logit model,
which is the most general logically consistent multiplicative
model amenable to least squares estimation which has been
formulated to date.  The next section treats econometric
issues:  error structure specification, estimation, and
model comparison.  Following a description of the data
base, empirical results for the product class consisting
of mayonnaise and other mayonnaise-like salad dressings
and spreads are presented and discussed.  The report concludes with a discussion of managerial implications.

## LOGICAL CONSISTENCY

### Sum Constraint

Kuehn [12] developed the first logically consistent
structural model of product class sales of which we are
aware.  Kuehn, McGuire, and Weiss [13] fitted a version
of this model to data, as did Weiss [25,26], who also
estimated a number of logically inconsistent linear and
log-linear models for comparison; however, none of these
studies took account of the implications of the sum constraint on the error structure.

McGuire et al. [14] examined the implications of the sum
constraint on specification of the mean function and error
structure in linear models and suggested an asymptotically
efficient estimator for the mean function parameters.  An
error in their paper, which persists in the study of Naert
and Bultez [16], was corrected in McGuire and Weiss [15].

### Bound Constraint

Although the models of Kuehn [12], Kuehn, McGuire, and
Weiss [13], and Weiss [26] satisfy both the sum and
bound constraints, they are intrinsically nonlinear.
The nonlinearity results from specification of the
attractiveness of a brand as the weighted sum of two
terms, each of which is in the form of a gravity, or
attraction, type model.  The attendant estimation
difficulties undoubtedly explain the failure of the
model to gain wider appeal.  Nakanishi [17] made an
important contribution to the marketing literature by
showing one method of transforming a gravity model
into a general linear model amenable to estimation by
multiple regression techniques.  For the first time,
a multiplicative market share model which satisfies
both logical consistency conditions and which can be
estimated by least squares had been specified.  The
price of this linearity is that all of the weight must be
placed on one or the other of the two components of
attractiveness in the Kuehn model.  Nakanishi's gravity
model is a special case of the multinomial extension of
the linear logit model developed by Theil [23] and applied
to market share relations by Bultez and Naert [4].

The multinomial logit model developed by Theil [23] can be written generally as

$$\frac{s_{it}}{s_{jt}} = e^{\alpha_i - \alpha_j} \prod_{h=1}^{H} z_{ht}^{\beta_{hi} - \beta_{hj}} \prod_{\ell=1}^{L} \left(\frac{x_{\ell it}}{x_{\ell jt}}\right)^{\gamma_\ell} e^{u_{it} - u_{jt}},$$

$$i,j = 1,\ldots,M, \quad t = 1,\ldots,T. \quad (1)$$

Summing both sides over $i=1,\ldots,M$ while holding $j$ fixed, applying the sum constraint $\sum_{i=1}^{M} s_{it} = 1$, and taking the reciprocals of both sides gives the alternative equivalent formulation

$$s_{jt} = \frac{e^{\alpha_j} \prod_{h=1}^{H} z_{ht}^{\beta_{hj}} \prod_{\ell=1}^{L} x_{\ell jt}^{\gamma_\ell} e^{u_{jt}}}{\sum_{i=1}^{M} e^{\alpha_i} \prod_{h=1}^{H} z_{ht}^{\beta_{hi}} \prod_{\ell=1}^{L} x_{\ell it}^{\gamma_\ell} e^{u_{it}}}, \quad j=1,\ldots,M, \quad t=1,\ldots,T. \quad (2)$$

This model might be applied to shares within a product class as follows. Let $s_{jt}$ be the share of brand $j$ in time period $t$ (measured as a fraction rather than as a percent), $M$ be the number of brands in the market (where perhaps brand $M$ is an "all other brands" category), $z_{ht}$, $h=1,\ldots,M$, be the price of brand $h$ in period $t$ (also denoted $P_{ht}$ below), $z_{M+1,t}$ be income in period $t$ (also denoted $\mu_t$ below), and $z_{M+2,t}$ be a price index for all goods other than those in the product class under investigation (i.e., for marketing studies $z_{M+2,t}$ is a general price index).

Additionally, $z_{M+2+h,t}$, $h=1,\ldots,M$, might be advertising expenditures on brand h in period t, and other $z_{ht}$'s could represent other marketing variables.

Also, $x_{1jt}$, $j=1,\ldots,M$, could be brand j's market share in the previous time period, thereby allowing a lag in the response of consumers to marketing and other factors.

Economic theory requires demand generally to be a function of all prices and income [7]. By making the bold assumption that all goods not in the product class being studied can be treated as a composite good, the model suggested above satisfies this condition. The homogeneity requirement for economic consistency requires $\sum_{h=1}^{M+2} \beta_{hj}$ to be a constant for all $j$, assuming that other variables, if any, are in real rather than nominal terms. If in the example above advertising expenditures are measured in current dollars, then homogeneity requires $\sum_{h=1}^{2M+2} \beta_{hj}$ to be constant for all $j$.

The Slutsky symmetry conditions cannot be satisfied by the general multimonial logit model. It has been shown by Arrow [20, p. 631n] that the most general model in the class of multinomial logit models which meets the economic consistency conditions is

$$(s_{it}/s_{jt}) = (a_i^*/a_j^*)\mu_t^{b_i - b_j} P_{it}^{-b_i} P_{jt}^{b_j} e^{u_{it} - u_{jt}}. \quad (3)$$

This model is known in the economics literature as the "indirect addilog model" [9,20]. The own-price elasticities ($\varepsilon_{iit}$), cross-price elasticities ($\varepsilon_{ijt}$), and income elasticities ($\eta_{it}$) of quantities ($q_{it}$), not shares ($s_{it}$), for this model are

$$\varepsilon_{iit} \equiv \text{percentage change in } q_{it}$$
$$\div \text{percentage change in } P_{it}$$
$$= -(b_i + 1) + b_i w_{it}, \quad \text{all } i,t, \quad (4)$$

$$\varepsilon_{ijt} \equiv \text{percentage change in } q_{it}$$
$$\div \text{percentage change in } P_{jt}$$
$$= b_j w_{jt}, \quad \text{all } i \neq j, t, \quad (5)$$

$$\eta_{it} \equiv \text{percentage change in } q_{it}$$
$$\div \text{percentage change in } \mu_t$$
$$= b_i + 1 - \sum_{j=1}^{M} b_j w_{jt}, \quad \text{all } i,t, \quad (6)$$

where the $w_{it}$'s are expenditure shares defined by

$$w_{it} = P_{it} q_{it} / \mu_t. \quad (7)$$

One property of this class of models is that cross-elasticities of demand tend to be near zero, since they are the product of an own elasticity, which is likely to be small in magnitude, with an expenditure share, which is likely to be near zero for most product classes of interest. Since cross-elasticities are undoubtedly larger than implied by these models, the models are not wholly adequate.

An alternative approach is to assume that the marginal rates of substitution between each pair of brands in the product class depend only on goods in that product class. This assumption, which is known in the economics literature as "the utility tree hypothesis," should be applicable in many marketing investigations. A comprehensive review of its implications for consumer behavior can be found in Pollak [21]. Among other things, Pollak concludes, "If the utility function is a tree, then the demand for a good can be written as a function of the prices of all goods in its branch [product class] and total expenditure on these goods" [21, p. 432]. As a result, $\mu_t$ in (7) would be defined as total expenditures for goods in the product class.

One difficulty with the utility tree hypothesis is, as Pollak [21, p.427n] notes, that "...total expenditure on food cannot be taken as exogenous." Pending further research, we propose that this problem be resolved by using market shares within the product class to calculate elasticities and measuring $\mu_t$ as total income and including a general price index term in the model for the purpose of estimation.

The indirect addilog model is the special case of the multinomial logit model (1) where $z_{ht} = P_{ht}$ ($h=1,\ldots,M$), $z_{M+1,t} = \mu_t$, $\alpha_i = \ell n \alpha_i^*$, $\beta_{hi} = \{-b_i, i=h; 0, i \neq h\}$, $\beta_{M+1,i} = b_i$, $H=M+1$, and $L=0$. This is the form of the "extended model" estimated by Bultez and Naert [4, pp. 532-33].

When all the $b_i$ parameters in the indirect addilog model are constrained to be equal (say to $b$), the model reduces to the special case used by Nakanishi [17] and later Bultez and Naert [4, pp. 530-31],

$$s_{it}/s_{jt} = (a_i/a_j)(P_{it}/P_{jt})^{-b} e^{u_{it}-u_{jt}} . \qquad (8)$$

Alternatively, (8) can be viewed as the special case of (1) in which $a_i = e^{\alpha_i}$, $H=0$, $L=1$, $x_{1it} = P_{it}$, and $\gamma_1 = -b$ .

## PARAMETER ESTIMATION AND MODEL TESTING

### Linearization of the Multinomial Logit Model

The general multinomial logit model and specializations of it can be transformed into a model which is linear in the mean function parameters by taking the natural logarithms of both sides of (1). As shown by McGuire et al. [14], if a product class contains $M$ brands (including the "all other" category, if any) whose (fractional) shares sum to unity, there are (at most) only $M-1$ independent share relations. We choose to look at the equations for $s_i/s_M$, $i=1,\ldots,M-1$. Hence we shall be fitting the system of $M-1$ equations

$$y_{it} = \alpha'_i + \sum_{h=1}^{M} \beta'_{hi} x_{ht} + u'_{it} ,$$

$$i=1,\ldots,M-1, \qquad t=1,\ldots,T, \qquad (9)$$

where $y_{it} \equiv \ln(s_{it}/s_{Mt})$ , $x_{ht} \equiv \ln(z_{ht}/z_{Mt}) \equiv \ln(P_{ht}/P_{Mt})$ for $h=1,\ldots,M-1$, $x_{Mt} \equiv \mu_t$, $\alpha'_i = \alpha_i - \alpha_M$ , $\beta'_{hi} = \beta_{hi} - \beta_{hM}$ , and $u'_{it} = u_{it} - u_{Mt}$

Nakanishi [17] suggested an equivalent alternative specification which has been used subsequently by Naert and Bultez [16], Nakanishi and Cooper [18], and Bultez and Naert [4]. Nakanishi derived his result for the restricted class of multinomial logit models with no $z_{ht}$ variables, i.e., with no variables having exponents with double subscripts, one of which is equation-specific [17, Appendix, p. 343]. While his technique is valid for the general class of multinomial logit models, the estimates of the doubly-subscripted exponents must be interpreted with care, as demonstrated below.

Since the denominator of (2) is independent of the equation subscript $j$ , denote its logarithm by $K$ . Then, taking natural logarithms of both sides of (2) and using a tilde over a variable to denote its logarithm gives

$$\tilde{s}_{jt} = \alpha_j + \sum_{h=1}^{H} \beta_{hj} \tilde{z}_{ht} + \sum_{\ell=1}^{L} \gamma_\ell \tilde{x}_{\ell jt} + u_{jt} ,$$

$$j=1,\ldots,M, \quad t=1,\ldots,T . \qquad (10)$$

Summing both sides of (10) over $j$ and dividing by $M$ ,

$$\tilde{\bar{s}}_{.t} = \bar{\alpha}_. + \sum_{h=1}^{H} \bar{\beta}_{h.} \tilde{z}_{ht} + \sum_{\ell=1}^{L} \gamma_\ell \tilde{\bar{x}}_{\ell.t} + \bar{u}_{.t} , \qquad (11)$$

where $\tilde{\bar{s}}_{.t}$ and $\tilde{\bar{x}}_{\ell.t}$ are the respective geometric means (over $j$) of the $\tilde{s}_{jt}$ and $\tilde{x}_{\ell jt}$ and $\bar{\alpha}_.$ , $\bar{\beta}_{h.}$ , and $\bar{u}_{.t}$ are the respective arithmetic means of the $\alpha_j$ , $\beta_{hj}$ , and $u_{jt}$. Subtracting (11) from (10),

$$\tilde{s}_{jt} - \tilde{\bar{s}}_{.t} = \alpha_j - \bar{\alpha}_. + \sum_{h=1}^{H} (\beta_{hj} - \bar{\beta}_{h.}) \tilde{z}_{ht}$$

$$+ \sum_{\ell=1}^{L} \gamma_\ell (\tilde{x}_{\ell jt} - \tilde{\bar{x}}_{\ell.t}) + u_{jt} - \bar{u}_{.t}, \quad j=1,\ldots,M,$$

$$t=1,\ldots,T . \qquad (12)$$

This generalization of Nakanishi's result shows that the estimated coefficient of $\tilde{z}_{ht}$ is an estimate of $\beta_{hj} - \bar{\beta}_{h.}$ , not of $\beta_{hj}$ . Thus, for example, the correct interpretation of estimates of the "extended model" of Bultez and Naert [4, pg. 532] is as follows. In their model, $\beta_{hj} \equiv b_{jp}$ (p for price) if $j=h$ and $\beta_{hj} \equiv 0$ for $j \neq h$ , $h=1,2,3$ . Thus, $\beta_{hj} - \bar{\beta}_{h.} = (2/3)\beta_{hh} = (2/3)b_{hp}$. Hence, for example, when they report an iterated generalized least squares (IGLS) estimate of $b_{1p}$ of -3.372,

this is really an estimate of $(2/3)b_{1p}$ . The correct IGLS estimate of $b_{1p}$ is $(3/2)\hat{b}_{1p} = (3/2)(-3.372) = -5.058$.

Subtracting the generalized Nakanishi specification (12) with $j=M$ from (12) for $j=1,\ldots,M-1$ gives (9), since all mean and geometric mean terms cancel out. Hence the generalized Nakanishi formulation (12) and our formulation (9) are indeed equivalent.

### Error Structure Specification

Bultez and Naert [4, pp. 530-31] specify the covariance structure of the errors as

$$Eu_{it}u_{js} = \begin{cases} \sigma_{ij}, & s=t, \\ 0, & s \neq t ; \end{cases} \qquad (13)$$

this is analogous to the structure for linear market share models suggested by McGuire et al. [14].

Nakanishi and Cooper have proposed a structure which accounts not only for such serially uncorrelated specification error but also for sampling error, which could arise from many sources including the use of panel data. Although we shall be using panel data in this study, we believe that sampling error is unimportant relative to specification error, and consequently we ignore this source of error.

If the disturbances may not be independent over time, the method suggested by Parks [19] and corrected by Berndt and Savin [3] might be explored. We note also that many econometricians and statisticians are working in the area of estimation of time-dependent systems; we do not review the contributions in this area in this report.

### Estimation

Space limitations do not allow us to describe the estimation procedure in detail. We note simply that by "stacking" the observations (relative to brand M), first for brand 1, then for brand 2, and so forth through brand M, the model is in the form of a multivariate regression model. Joint generalized least squares estimation of this class of models has been treated in many places (see, e.g., Johnston [10, pp. 238-41], Theil [24, pp. 299-311]), and applications of this technique can be found in Beckwith [1], Houston and Weiss [8], and Parks [20]. This procedure yields asymptotically efficient and normal estimators of the mean function parameters. By applying this procedure iteratively, maximum likelihood estimators can be obtained. Such maximum likelihood estimates of parameters for the various models of this paper were obtained using a modified Gauss-Newton procedure programmed by Berndt [2].

## Model Comparisons

We shall be testing both nested and non-nested hypotheses in nonlinear models. Nonlinearities are introduced into the linear expenditure system (estimated for comparison purposes) by various constraints on the parameters (Stone [22]). In addition, estimation of the covariance matrix introduces nonlinearities into both the linear expenditure system and the multinomial logit models. Within either class of models, nested hypotheses are tested by invoking the asymptotic properties of minus twice the natural logarithm of the likelihood ratio statistic.

In the remainder of this section we outline the method we use to compare non-nested models. While the comparisons involve choosing the model with the higher value of the likelihood function, this procedure should not be confused with the asymptotic tests mentioned in the previous paragraph. Whereas the tests of nested hypotheses described above are based on statistics with known asymptotic distributions, comparisons of non-nested models simply amount to betting on the model with the higher posterior odds (or, with a symmetric loss function, likelihood (Gaver and Geisel [6]).

We present below a method for comparing the model

$$\underline{y}_t = \underline{g}^{(1)} [X_t^{(1)}, \underline{\beta}^{(1)}] + \underline{\varepsilon}_t^{(1)}, \qquad t=1,\dots,T \qquad (14)$$

(hereinafter model 1) with the model

$$\underline{h}(\underline{y}_t) = \underline{g}^{(2)} [X_t^{(2)}, \underline{\beta}^{(2)}] + \underline{\varepsilon}_t^{(2)}, \qquad t=1,\dots,T \qquad (15)$$

(hereinafter model 2), where $\underline{\beta}^{(j)}$ is a $p_j$-component vector of unknown parameters, $j=1,2$; $X_t^{(j)}$ is an $(M-1) \times p_j$ matrix of explanatory variables, $j=1,2$; $\underline{y}_t$ is an $(M-1)$-component vector of observations on the dependent variable, $t=1,\dots,T$; $\underline{h}(\underline{y}_t)$ is an $(M-1)$-component vector-valued function of $\underline{y}_t$, $t=1,\dots,T$, and $\underline{\varepsilon}_t^{(j)}$ is an $(M-1)$-component vector of multivariate normal random variables with mean vector zero and covariance matrix $\Sigma^{(j)}$, $j=1,2$, distributed independently over time. The likelihood ratio statistic is

$$\lambda = (|\hat{\Sigma}^{(1)}|/|\hat{\Sigma}^{(2)}|)^{-T/2} \{abs(det[J])\}^{-1}, \qquad (16)$$

where $abs(det[J])$ is the absolute value of the determinant of the Jacobian matrix $J$. For time-independent models it can be shown that

$$abs(det[J]) = abs \prod_{t=1}^{T} det \left[ \frac{\partial \underline{h}(\underline{y}_t)}{\partial \underline{y}_t} \right]. \qquad (17)$$

Model 1 is selected as the better model if $\lambda > 1$ while model 2 is selected if $\lambda < 1$.

A difficulty arises when the number of unknown parameters is not the same in the two models. In this case the above model comparison procedure is strongly biased in favor of the model with the larger number of parameters. Although the proper treatment of this problem is an unsolved statistical problem, a heuristic way of allowing for this bias is to adjust for degrees of freedom in a manner analogous to the adjustment made in linear models with scalar covariance matrices. Accordingly, our comparisons across model classes are based on the statistic

$$\lambda^* = \left\{ \left[\frac{(m-1)T-p_2}{(m-1)T-p_1}\right] \left[\frac{|\hat{\Sigma}^{(1)}|}{|\hat{\Sigma}^{(2)}|}\right] \right\}^{-T/2} \left\{abs(det[J])\right\}^{-1}. \quad (18)$$

The absolute value of the Jacobian for transforming from logit to linear dependent variables can be shown to be

$$det [J] = \left[ \prod_{s=1}^{T} \prod_{i=1}^{M} y_{is} \right]^{-1}. \qquad (19)$$

Extensive reviews of classical and Bayesian model comparison techniques can be found in Gaver and Geisel [6] and Dhrymes et al. [5].

## RESULTS AND DISCUSSION

### Data Base

The data supporting this analysis have been aggregated from four years of individual family purchase histories collected by the Chicago Tribune's Family Survey Bureau. The product class is mayonnaise and other mayonnaise-like dressings and spreads. We analyze data for three "brands": Hellmann's Mayonnaise, Kraft Miracle Whip, and "all others". The data cover the period 1960 through 1963 and represent purchases by approximately 900 panel families.

Bimonthly estimates of income for the sample period were derived from quarterly estimates of unadjusted National Income from the Survey of Current Business. The income series was assumed linear and the bimonthly estimates were interpolated from the quarterly data.[1] The estimated models do not include a general price index variable; we are currently estimating models containing such a variable.

### Multinomial Logit Models

Parameter estimates for the following three logically and economically consistent multinomial logit models are presented in Table 1.

1. Model (3) in log-linear form
2. Model (8) in log-linear form [model (3) with $b_i = b$, $i = 1,2,3$]
3. Model (8) with equal intercepts [$a_i = a_j$, all $i$ and $j$]

Interest in the equality of intercept terms results because such terms reflect product quality and the accumulated effects of such slowly changing variables as distribution, brand loyalty, advertising capital, etc.

Any nested pair of these models can be compared using the likelihood ratio statistic

$$\lambda = |\hat{\Sigma}^{(1)}|^{-T/2} / |\hat{\Sigma}^{(2)}|^{-T/2}, \qquad (20)$$

[1] The linear assumption appears good. The squared correlation between national income and a time trend variable for the sample period is .9904.

132

TABLE 1

Estimated Parameters and Related Statistics

| Multinomial Logit Models | $a'_1$ | $a'_2$ | $b_1$ | $b_2$ | $b_3$ | $-2 \ln\mathcal{L}$ [#] |
|---|---|---|---|---|---|---|
| 1. | 23.94 (4.96) | 14.02 (3.70) | 3.69 (9.88) | 2.63 (8.32) | 1.16 (2.45) | 89.38 |
| 2. | .16 (1.30) | .07 (2.20) | 3.20 (9.20) | - | - | 109.92 |
| 3. | - | - | 2.94 (27.9) | | | 115.0 |

$a'_1 = \ln(a^*_1/a^*_3)$, i=1,2

| General Linear Models | $a_1$ | $a_2$ | $b_{11}$ | $b_{12}$ | $b_{13}$ | $b_{21}$ | $b_{22}$ | $b_{23}$ | $-2 \ln\mathcal{L}$ |
|---|---|---|---|---|---|---|---|---|---|
| 1. Eq. (21) | .615 (4.80) | .591 (3.96) | -28.78 (9.63) | 12.34 (5.83) | 1.05 (.182) | 15.1 (4.33) | -41.3 (6.10) | 10.7 (1.60) | - 79.28 |
| 2. Eq. (22) | .605 (6.84) | - | -28.74 (9.81) | 12.62 (2.41) | 1.35 (.264) | 15.0 (4.41) | -41.7 (7.02) | 10.3 (1.79) | - 79.26 |

[#] $-2 \ln\mathcal{L}$ - twice the value of the log-likelihood function.

where $\Sigma$ is a 2x2 matrix with (i,j)-th element $\sigma_{ij}$ [see (13)]. The statistic $-2\ln(\lambda)$ is asymptotically distributed as $\chi^2(p_2-p_1)$, where $p_2$ is the dimension-ality under the null hypothesis. The null hypothesis (model 1) is rejected in favor of the alternative hypoth-esis (model 2) if the calculated value of $-2\ln(\lambda)$ ex-ceeds the critical value of $\chi^2(p_2-p_1)$ at the chosen significance level.[2]

All legitimate pairwise comparisons of the 3 multinomial logit models are shown in Table 2. Note that the models are nested; model 3 is a special case of model 2, which in turn is a constrained version of model 1. Examination of Table 2 reveals that all models are significantly worse than model 1 (the most general economically consistent specification of the multinomial logit model) at the 0.0001 level.

Linear Models

In addition to the multinomial logit models, two logically consistent but economically inconsistent versions of the general linear model (Stone [22], Parks [20]) were fitted to the data to provide comparisons with the logit forms.

$$s_{it} = a_i + b_{i1}P_{1t} + b_{i2}P_{2t} + b_{i3}P_{3t} + u_{it}, \quad i=1,2. \quad (21)$$

$$s_{it} = a + b_{i1}P_{1t} + b_{i2}P_{2t} + b_{i3}P_{3t} + u_{it}, \quad i=1,2. \quad (22)$$

Estimates of the parameters of these models are presented in Table 1, while nested pairs are compared in Table 2. Again, the last column of Table 2 indicates that the more general specification (21) is the better of these two linear models.

[2]See Kendall and Stuart [11], pages 85-88.

Comparison of Linear and Logit Models

The best linear and multinomial logit models can be compared using the statistic $\lambda^*$ defined in (18). From (19), $\ln|J| = 85.7$, so $\lambda^* = -2.25$. Since $\ln \lambda^* < 0$, it follows that $\lambda^* < 1$. Thus the model in the denominator of $\lambda^*$, the logit model, is chosen over the general linear model in this application if this comparison is the sole basis for choice.

TABLE 2

Tests of Nested Hypotheses About the Multinomial Logit and Linear Models

| Row Model (R) (null hypothesis) | Column Model (C) (alternative hypothesis) | |
|---|---|---|
| | 2 | 1 |
| **Logit Models** | | |
| 3. $-2 \ln(\lambda_R/\lambda_C)$ | 5.08 | 25.6 |
| $df_R - df_C$ | 2 | 4 |
| significance level | .075 | .00003 |
| 2. $-2 \ln(\lambda_R/\lambda_C)$ | | 20.5 |
| $df_R - df_C$ | | 2 |
| significance level | | .00005 |
| **Linear Models** | | |
| 1. $-2 \ln(\lambda_R/\lambda_C)$ | .02 | |
| $df_R - df_C$ | 1 | |
| significance level | .89 | |

## MANAGERIAL IMPLICATIONS

Own- and cross-price elasticities for the three brands studied have been calculated according to (4) and (5) using estimated coefficients for the best logit and linear models and are presented in Table 3. That brand 3 is an "all other" classification may obscure some of the implications, but the general conclusions seem sensible. Hellmann's appears to be the most volatile brand in the product class with respect to price changes. Its own price elasticity is approximately 30% greater than those of the remaining brands, and its cross-elasticities with brands 2 and 3 are the largest in the product class.

### TABLE 3

Own- and Cross-
Elasticities for the most General
Consistent Logit Model (3), Period 24

| Row Brand | Column Brand 1 | 2 | 3 |
|---|---|---|---|
| 1. Hellmann's | -3.46 | .970 | .348 |
| 2. Kraft Miracle Whip | 1.22 | -2.66 | .348 |
| 3. All Other | 1.22 | .970 | -2.51 |

### REFERENCES

1. Beckwith, Neil E. "Multivariate Analysis of Sales Responses of Competing Brands to Advertising," Journal of Marketing Research, 9 (May 1972), 168-76.

2. Berndt, E. R. "Notes on a Computational Algorithm for Estimating Parameters in a System of Linear or Nonlinear Equations by Method of Least Squares", unpublished working paper, Economics Department, University of British Columbia.

3. Berndt, Ernst R. and N. Eugene Savin. "Estimation and Hypothesis Testing in Singular Equation Systems with Autoregressive Disturbances," Econometrica, 43 (September-November 1975), 937-57.

4. Bultez, Alain V. and Philippe A. Naert. "Consistent Sum-Constrained Models," Journal of the American Statistical Association, 70 (September 1975), 529-35.

5. Dhrymes, Phoebus J. et al. "Criteria for Evaluation of Econometric Models," Annals of Economic and Social Measurement, 1 (July 1972), 291-324.

6. Gaver, Kenneth M. and Martin S. Geisel. "Discriminating Among Alternative Models: Bayesian and Non-Bayesian Methods," in Paul Zarembka, ed., Frontiers in Econometrics. New York: Academic Press, 1974, 49-77.

7. Henderson, James M. and Richard E. Quandt. Microeconomic Theory: A Mathematical Approach, 2nd Edition. New York: McGraw-Hill, 1971.

8. Houston, Franklin S. and Doyle L. Weiss. "An Analysis of Competitive Market Behavior," Journal of Marketing Research, 11 (May 1974), 151-55.

9. Houthakker, H.S. "Additive Preferences," Econometrica, 28 (April 1960), 244-57.

10. Johnston, J. Econometric Methods, 2nd Edition, New York: McGraw-Hill Book Company, 1972.

11. Kendall, M. C. and A. Stuart. The Advanced Theory of Statistics, Vol. 3, Second Edition. London: Charles Griffin and Company, Ltd., 1968.

12. Kuehn, Alfred A. "A Model for Budgeting Advertising," in Frank M. Bass et al., ed., Mathematical Models and Methods in Marketing. Homewood, Illinois: Richard D. Irwin, Inc., 1961, 315-48.

13. Kuehn, Alfred A., Timothy W. McGuire and Doyle L. Weiss. "Measuring the Effectiveness of Advertising," in R. M. Hass, ed., Science, Technology and Marketing. Chicago: American Marketing Association, 1966, 185-94.

14. McGuire, Timothy W., John U. Farley, Robert E. Lucas, Jr. and L. Winston Ring. "Estimation and Inference for Linear Models in Which Subsets of the Dependent Variable are Constrained," Journal of the American Statistical Association, 63 (December 1968), 1201-13.

15. McGuire, Timothy W. and Doyle L. Weiss. "Logically Consistent Market Share Models II," Journal of Marketing Research, 13 (August 1976), 296-302.

16. Naert, Philippe A. and Alain Bultez. "Logically Consistent Market Share Models," Journal of Marketing Research, 10 (August 1973), 334-40.

17. Nakanishi, Masao. "Measurement of Sales Promotion Effect at the Retail Level--A New Approach." Proceedings. Fall Conference, American Marketing Association, 1972, 338-43.

18. Nakanishi, Masao and Lee G. Cooper. "Parameter Estimation for a Multiplicative Competitive Interaction Model--Least Squares Approach," Journal of Marketing Research, 11 (August 1974), 303-11.

19. Parks, R. W. "Efficient Estimation of a System of Regression Equations When Disturbances are Both Serially and Contemporaneously Correlated," Journal of the American Statistical Association, 62 (June 1967), 500-509.

20. Parks, R. W. "Systems of Demand Equations: An Empirical Comparison of Alternative Functional Forms," Econometrica, 37 (October 1969), 629-50.

21. Pollak, Robert A. "Conditional Demand Functions and the Implications of Separable Utility," The Southern Economic Journal, 37 (April 1971), 423-33.

22. Stone, Richard. "Linear Expenditure Systems and Demand Analysis: An Application to the Pattern of British Demand," The Economic Journal, 64 (September 1954), 511-27.

23. Theil, Henri. "A Multinomial Extension of the Linear Logit Model," International Economic Review, 10 (October 1969), 251-59.

24. Theil, Henri. Principles of Econometrics. New York: John Wiley and Sons, Inc., 1971.

25. Weiss, Doyle L. An Analysis of Market Share Behavior for a Branded Consumer Product. Unpublished Ph.D. Dissertation, Graduate School of Industrial Administration, Carnegie Institute of Technology, June, 1966.

26. Weiss, Doyle L. "An Analysis of the Demand Structure for Branded Consumer Products," Journal of Applied Economics, 1 (January 1969), 37-49.

# A COMPARISON OF QUALITATIVE RESPONSE
# MODELS OF CONSUMER CHOICE

Vithala R. Rao, University of Illinois
Hans S. Solgaard, Cornell University

## ABSTRACT

Several choice models applicable to qualitative response data collected in marketing research are reviewed in this paper. Following a discussion of a general model, four binary choice models are compared in terms of underlying choice processes and methods of estimation. Availability of computer algorithms for analysis and areas of application in marketing are also discussed.

## INTRODUCTION

Development and testing of models to describe consumer choice has been a major concern in marketing and consumer behavior research [6, 16, 29]. The criterion variable-- consumer choice--had been operationalized in many ways in the literature. Measures employed include amount bought or consumed of a product or brand, brand chosen, intention to buy a brand, preference toward a brand, and probability of brand switching. Usually, however, only one measure[1] is used at a time for model construction.

From a technical viewpoint, measures of consumer choice belong to the three basic scales of measurement, namely, interval, ordinal or categorical. Methods of analysis associated with these measures have respectively been multiple regression, ordinal regression, and two-group or multiple discriminant analysis [8, 12].

The focus of this paper is on models when the consumer choice is measured on a categorical scale. This scale represents a variety of consumer choice situations such as buying or not buying a brand, viewing or not viewing television, buying a gift or not, an industrial buyer seeing a salesman or not, etc. In addition, the scale can also represent particular choices made within a set of alternatives such as brands of a product category, prime time television programs, television news programs, and suppliers of an industrial product.

Even when the measure of consumer choice is not categorical, it can easily be converted to that scale by a suitable regrouping (or collapsing) of the original scale. For example, consumers can be classified as heavy or light on the basis of amount of reported consumption measured on an interval scale. Such a conversion offers a potential advantage of reducing the errors associated with data collection. In addition, the concept of finally using a categorical scale would make it easier to collect such data in the first place (as opposed to later conversion).

Despite the apparent niceties of the qualitative response variable (i.e., categorical scaled data), much of the model building of consumer choice has largely concentrated on measures of interval or ordinal scale. When the data are categorical, researchers usually utilize chi-square (contingency) analysis or multivariate discriminant analysis. An application of the multivariate probit model for purchasing decisions of farmers can be found in [17]. It is only recently that other models, namely, logit and loglinear, are proposed and used in marketing research [11]. The emphasis of this application is on contingency table analysis in contrast to model building of consumer choice, per se. These two models are relatively simple and quite well-known, but not much used in marketing prior to this application.

During the last five years or so, there has been a renewed interest in the analysis and modeling of qualitative dependent variables among econometricians. The interest apparently arose due to the need to look at consumption data such as the transportation mode choices and the inadequacy of using ordinary least squares analysis on a qualitative dependent variable owing to heteroskedasticity [10]. This recent effort gave rise to extensions of techniques such as the probit and logistic models and associated computer algorithms.

Against this background, the objective of this paper is to review some alternative models of consumer choice applicable to qualitative responses. Specifically, we will consider four models: (1) discriminant model, (2) linear probability model, (3) multivariate probit model, and (4) multivariate logit model. For sake of simplicity, we will only consider binary choice situations in some parts of the discussion.

The remainder of this paper is organized into five additional sections. In the next and second section, we present the notation and the general problem of modeling consumer choice using qualitative response data and one particular case leading to the above-mentioned four models. The third section describes briefly the methods of estimation for four binary choice models. The problem of measuring the effect of changes in the independent variables (e.g., characteristics of consumers or choice alternatives) on the probability of choosing an alternative for each model is considered in the fourth section. A brief review[2] of the computer programs available for analysis of data according to these models is presented in the fifth section. We conclude the final section with a discussion of potential applications in marketing and some research issues with these models.

## A GENERAL MODEL FOR QUALITATIVE RESPONSES

The problem of modeling qualitative responses of consumer choice from the econometric perspective has been reviewed by McFadden [20, 22]. When the choice is binary, the work by Cox [4] is relevant. Other references from a theoretical point of view include [14, 24, 26, 30]. While we do not wish to trace through the historical origins of the subject, mention should be made of the pioneering work on probit analysis by Finney [7]. Some applications in areas other than marketing are found in [5, 13, 27, 32, 33]. In the sequel, we will adapt much of this literature as it relates to the problem of modeling qualitative responses of consumer choice in marketing.

To see the relevance of the problem to marketing and consumer research, consider the following situation. Imagine

---

[1]While canonical correlation is an appropriate method for models with multiple measures, its use has been insignificant owing to the difficulty of interpreting results.

[2]Empirical comparisons and testing based on real-life market survey data are under progress. These will be presented at the conference session.

observing a sample of consumers choosing one of many brands in a product category under a set of different choice situations or scenarios during a given period of time. Assume further that it is possible to observe at least one choice for each consumer under each situation in this period. (Of course, many of these replications may be only one.) The data observed, namely, the brand chosen,[3] are then the responses for each consumer and are qualitative. The response is related to the characteristics of consumers, characteristics of brands, and the characteristics of the situation. The problem of modeling the qualitative responses deals with the specification of the form of the function (f) relating the various characteristics to the probability of response for each brand. The methods of estimation are concerned with the determination of the parameters of f as dependent on the availability of replications of observations and the number of brands. We will assume that there exists no order[4] in the responses (i.e., brands are not ordered).

## Notation

We will adopt the following notation to present the model in a formal manner. For simplicity, we will consider the case of one choice situation.

$m$ = number of consumers
$n$ = number of brands
$R_i$ = number of replications observed under the situation for the ith consumer; $i = 1, 2, \ldots, m$; $(R_i \geq 1)$
$J$ = set of possible responses for any replication (i.e., set of n brands)
$r$ = number of attributes of the brands
$s$ = number of characteristics of the consumer
$XB_j$ = r-dimensional vector of attributes for the jth brand; $(j = 1, 2, \ldots, n)$
$XC_i$ = s-dimensional vector of characteristics for the ith consumer; $(i = 1, 2, \ldots, m)$
$\beta$ = r-dimensional parameter vector associated with the brand attributes
$\gamma$ = s-dimensional parameter vector associated with consumer characteristics
$F_{ij}$ = observed frequency with which brand j is chosen across all replications by the ith consumer $(i = 1, 2, \ldots, m; j = 1, 2, \ldots, n)$
$P_{ij}$ = observed probability of choice of the jth brand $(P_{ij} = F_{ij}/R_i; i = 1, 2, \ldots, m; j = 1, 2, \ldots, n)$
$Y_i$ = n-dimensional vector of probabilities $(P_{i1}, P_{i2}, \ldots, P_{in})$ of choice of the n brands for the ith consumer; $i = 1, 2, \ldots, m$. (If there is only one replication, then $Y_i$ will contain n-1 zeroes and one unity.)
$\alpha$ = a constant parameter

## Models

The theory of qualitative responses postulates the existence of an indicator variable, denoted by I, which takes on different values across various brands for a given consumer. In general, it is assumed to be a function of variables XB and XC. Much of the modeling work involves specification of the functional form for I. A convenient starting point is the linear model such as:

$$I = \alpha + \beta'XB + \gamma'XC \qquad (1)$$

This form can be easily extended to include within-set interactions among the attributes of brands or characteristics of consumers as well as between set interactions. Generally, however, such specification should be guided by

the substantive nature of the choice being modeled.

Further, the consumer is assumed to have threshold values on the indicator scale which lead to the choices of various brands. Assumption of a particular probability distribution for the threshold values would then generate a set of theoretical choice probabilities $(\pi_{i1}, \pi_{i2}, \ldots \pi_{in})$ for the ith person which are functions of parameters associated with brands and/or persons. The observed frequencies $(F_{i1}, F_{i2}, \ldots, F_{in})$ can then be assumed to arise from a multinominal distribution with these theoretical probabilities. The parameters can be estimated using maximum likelihood methods or least squares methods.

This approach is indeed complicated for the general case. Several simplifications occur, however, for special cases. In particular, we will consider the binary choice case (i.e., n=2) to compare the above-mentioned four models for the situation of one replication. This situation is highly appropriate in marketing where much of the analysis deals with cross-sectional data. Such data come closest to the case of one replication. Further, the binary choice analysis can be repeated to model the choices with respect to each brand in the choice set.

Case n=2. Here, there are only two choice alternatives. Therefore, we can reduce the vector variable Y to a scalar variable by considering only the probabilities for one of the two brands. Such reduction would preserve all of the information in the data for the case of one replication. Further, the reduced variable is either 1 or 0.

The index can be written simply in terms of the consumer specific variables. Thus, the model would become:

$$I = \alpha + \gamma'XC. \qquad (2)$$

Let $I_i^*$ denote the threshold value specific to the ith consumer. The four models--discriminant model, linear probability model, multivariate probit model, and multivariate logistic model--would result from different assumptions on the probability distributions for the threshold values, $I^*$. These are shown in Table 1. The reader should note that different assumptions are also involved with respect to the threshold values across consumers. We have shown an extremely simplified conceptualization of the discriminant model in order to keep the assumptions to a minimum. The general two-group discriminant analysis model would follow when we assume multivariate normal distribution for the consumer-specific variables (XB) and equal covariance matrix for the two groups of consumers respectively choosing the two brands. See multivariate texts by Anderson [1], Morrison [23] or Press [25] for a discussion of these. In order to adapt this analysis to the modeling of qualitative responses, we indeed need additional knowledge[5] on the prior belonging of the consumer to the groups or nonbuyers of the brand.

## ESTIMATION OF PARAMETERS FOR FOUR BINARY CHOICE MODELS

Table 2 reviews various methods of estimation appropriate to the case of single replication (i.e., when y is either 0 or 1) for the four binary choice models under comparison. It also shows the major problems with the procedure and properties of estimates. The methods are based on variations of least squares method or maximum likelihood procedure. Two additional comments may be in order. First, the maximum likelihood method can be employed for any probability distribution prespecified for the underlying choice process of the consumer. Second, we have only covered one method of estimating the parameters of the discriminant model; for others, see [1, 23, 25].

---

[3]Other data such as amount bought could also be treated using these models by appropriate discretization.

[4]The problem of modeling responses that are either sequentially obtained or ordered in any manner is more complicated and is beyond the scope of this paper.

[5]In fact, possibilities exist for combining a discriminant analysis model with logit analysis for purposes of estimation; see [2].

TABLE 1

SOME ASSUMPTIONS AND PROBABILITY OF
CHOICE FOR FOUR BINARY CHOICE MODELS

| Model | Assumed Probability Distribution for Threshold Value | Probability of Choosing Brand 1 for Consumer i |
|---|---|---|
| Discriminant Model[6] | Single point distribution with whole mass at $I_i$ | 0 if $I_c \geq I_i$<br>1 if $I_c < I$. |
| Linear Probability Model | Uniform distribution in the interval (a, b) | Varies linearly with $I_i$ in the interval (a, b)<br>0 if $I_i \leq a$<br>$(I_i-a)/(b-a)$ if $a<I_i<b$<br>1 if $I_i \geq b$ |
| Multivariate Probit Model | Normal probability distribution; $\Phi(\cdot)$ is the cumulative density function. | $\Phi(I_i)$ |
| Multivariate Logit Model | Logistic probability function; $f(x)=exp(-x)/\{1+exp(-x)\}^2$ | $\{1 + exp(-I_i)\}^{-1}$ |

[6] See text for elaboration.

TABLE 2

ESTIMATION METHODS AND PROPERTIES OF
ESTIMATES FOR FOUR BINARY CHOICE MODELS

| Model | Estimation Method | Major Problems with the Method | Properties of Estimates |
|---|---|---|---|
| Discriminant Model[7] | Weighted least squares, usually a two-step procedure. | 1. Prediction of y could lie out (0,1) interval.<br>2. Extreme values of y predictions could be biased.<br>3. Estimates are sensitive to specification error. | Unbiased, consistent |
| Linear Probability Model | Quadratic programming to minimize squared error subject to inequality constraints (e.g., Dantzig-Cottle Algorithm) | 1. Very costly to implement<br>2. Extreme value bias exists<br>3. Sensitive to specification error. | Consistent, not unbiased, but estimates tend to be distributed tightly about true values. |
| Multivariate Probit Model | Maximum likelihood method; involves solution of nonlinear equations using iterative methods (e.g., Newton-Raphson method). | 1. Very costly to implement<br>2. Need fairly large samples | Consistent, not unbiased, efficient. |
| Multivariate Logit Model | Same as for Multivariate Probit Model | Same as for Multivariate Probit Model | Same as for Multivariate Probit Model |

[7] This is not the same method used in standard packages for discriminant analysis.

When the replications are more than one, several other methods could be employed. One of these [3] involves converting the observed probability into its logit, i.e., log [P/(1-P)], expanding it as a Taylor series in terms of the parameters to be estimated and using least squares method of estimation. Some modifications to this method are possible in order to improve its accuracy [4, 32]. Empirical comparisons of various methods discussed in this section as applied to Monte Carlo and real data can be found in [5, 24].

RESPONSE EFFECTS OF CHANGES IN INDEPENDENT VARIABLES

We will briefly consider the effect of changes in consumer characteristics on the theoretical probability of choosing the brand according to each model. These measures are useful in forecasting the demand for a brand due to changes in consumer characteristics and also in the development of strategies to influence choice. Additionally, knowledge of the response coefficients could be valuable in testing the accuracy of alternative formulations of the choice process.

Simply stated, these are $\partial \pi_i / \partial XC_k$ where $\pi_i$ is the theoretical probability of choosing one brand (in the binary situation) and $XC_k$ is the kth measured characteristic of the ith consumer. It is computed using the relationship:

$$\frac{\partial \pi_i}{\partial XC_k} = \frac{\partial \pi_i}{\partial I_i} \cdot \frac{\partial I_i}{\partial XC_k} \tag{3}$$

where $I_i$ is the indicator for the ith consumer. The response coefficients computed using equation (3) are summarized below for each model. Of course, to be correct, one needs to take into account the fact that probability cannot exceed unity for the discriminant model.

| Model | Response Coefficient |
|---|---|
| Discriminant Model | $\gamma_k$ |
| Linear Probability Model | $\{\begin{matrix} \gamma_k/(b-a) \text{ if } I_i \epsilon [a,b] \\ 0 \text{ otherwise} \end{matrix}$ |
| Multivariate Probit Model | $\phi(I_i) \cdot \gamma_k$ where $\phi(\cdot)$ is the unit normal density function |
| Multivariate Logit Model | $\pi_i(1-\pi_i)\gamma_k$ where $\pi_i$ is the theoretical value of probability at $I_i$. |

While the value of the response coefficient is uniformly the same for the discriminant model and the linear probability model (except for the end zones), it depends upon the location of the indicator variable for the probit and logit models. In the absence of the knowledge of the true underlying model, it is difficult to choose between these coefficients in practice. Empirical evidence and accuracy of predictive testing are some ways to resolve this issue. In fact, Haberman [14, p. 311] claims

> ...that no empirical evidence exists that the normal distribution provides more accurate models than the logistic distribution. Theoretical arguments have been advanced which favor one or the other distribution, but none of them appears convincing, at least to the author.

COMPUTATIONAL ALGORITHMS

Several computer programs exist for implementing these models.[8] We will briefly describe four of these: (a) Generalized Chi-Square Analysis of Categorical data using a weighted least squares program which has the acronym GENCAT [18]; (b) Multiple Logistic Program due to Duncan

---

[8]These do not include the quadratic programming algorithms applicable to the linear probability model.

and Walker [15, 32]; (c) Multivariate dichotomous variable program [24]; and (d) Conditional logit multinominal estimation program called XLOGIT [22, 34]. Our comments on these will be necessarily very brief.

(a) GENCAT Program. This program implements the analysis of multivariate categorical data. It enables estimation of functions to describe observed proportions in terms of several descriptor variables using a weighted least squares method. It also computes several statistics for testing hypotheses on the functional forms of the relationships.

(b) Multiple Logistic Program. This program implements the method developed by Duncan and Walker for estimating the probability of occurrence of an event from dichotomous or polychotomous data. A recursive technique is used in estimating the multiple logistic risk function in accordance with maximum likelihood methods. The program also computes the linear discriminant function for obtaining initial estimates in the iterative process.

(c) Multivariate Dichotomous Variable Program. This program implements log-linear and logistic models for up to four jointly dependent dichotomous variables using maximum likelihood methods. Its special features include ability to study the bivariate interactions of the exogenous explanatory variables.

(d) XLOGIT Program. This program implements the estimation of the conditional logit multinomial model using maximum likelihood procedures. Estimation is carried out by standard unconstrained maximization procedures. While we have not described the theory of this procedure in this paper, the program can be employed for estimating the binary choice models.

CONCLUSIONS

It should be clear from the foregoing discussion that there exists a significant body of knowledge on the qualitative response models and that it pertains almost exclusively to areas other than marketing. Researchers in marketing and consumer behavior could possibly benefit from a close scrutiny of the theory and analysis methods currently available in the literature.

While we have largely concentrated on the binary choice models, theory and estimation methodology extend to the polytomous qualitative variable. Multiple response variables can also be studied in this framework.

Obviously, these models need to be subjected to validation and testing. Opportunities exist for predictive testing using behavioral experimental techniques. The resolution as to which model to use and which method of estimation can only result from extensive application and research on the underlying choice process.

Nevertheless, various applications are possible in marketing and consumer areas. We will briefly touch upon three directions: (i) direct applications of the binary choice models reviewed; (ii) application to the decision processes of one consumer toward a set of brands or concepts; and (iii) study of longitudinal choice behavior.

Direct applications of binary choice models include a study of choice behavior toward brands, services, television programs, shopping centers, stores and the like. Emphasis here would be to fit models to cross-sectional data and estimate response coefficients to changes in characteristics of the population of consumers. Further, future demand can also be estimated. Differences among prespecified segments can be studied by fitting models to samples of consumers in each segment. Another application would be to study the response/nonresponse behavior in survey research.

The general model can be applied to describe the choice process of one consumer toward a set of brands or product concepts. This is the case when m=1. Such a situation is prototypical of the data collected in concept testing studies using such methods as conjoint measurement. The response here would be "no" or "yes" with respect to buying the brand represented by the concept (or some other criterion). In this case, the model would be $I=\alpha+\beta'XB$. The model can be fitted to data for each consumer, thereby enabling an examination of individual differences in the response coefficients for changes in the brand attributes. Rao and Winter [28] present an application of this approach to the issue of product design and market segmentation. The general qualitative response models can be employed to extend current approaches to modeling comparative and categorical judgmental data [31].

The methodology can also be used to analyze panel data. The problem here would be to estimate the transition probabilities from one time period to the next using these models and compare them to known stochastic models [2, 19].

REFERENCES

1. Anderson, T. W. Introduction to Multivariate Statistical Analysis. New York: Wiley, 1958.

2. Bass, Frank M. "The Theory of Stochastic Preference," Journal of Marketing Research, 11 (February, 1974), 1-20.

3. Berkson, J. "A Statistically Precise and Relatively Simple Method of Estimating the Bioassay with Quantal Response," Journal of the American Statistical Association, 48 (1953), 565-99.

4. Cox, D. R. Analysis of Binary Data. London: Methuen, 1970.

5. Domencich, Thomas A. and Daniel McFadden. Urban Travel Demand: A Behavioral Analysis. Amsterdam and New York: North Holland/American Elsevier, 1975.

6. Engel, James F., David T. Kollat and Roger D. Blackwell. Consumer Behavior (Second edition). New York: Holt, Rinehart and Winston, Inc., 1973.

7. Finney, D. J. Statistical Methods in Biological Assay. London: Cambridge University Press, 1964.

8. Frank, Ronald E., William F. Massy and Yoram Wind. Market Segmentation. Englewood Cliffs, N.J.: Prentice-Hall, Inc., 1972.

9. Gladhart, Peter M. and Tim D. Mount. "Program Description for Multivariate Probit Analysis," Ithaca, N.Y.: Cornell University, September, 1972.

10. Goldberger, Arthur S. Econometric Theory. New York: John Wiley and Sons, Inc., 1964.

11. Green, Paul E., Frank J. Carmone and David P. Wachpress. "On the Analysis of Qualitative Data in Marketing Research," Journal of Marketing Research, 14 (February, 1977), 52-9.

12. Green, Paul E. and Donald S. Tull. Research for Marketing Decisions (Third edition). Englewood Cliffs, N.J.: Prentice-Hall, Inc., 1973.

13. Gunderson, Morley. "Retention of Trainees: A Study with Dichotomous Dependent Variables," Journal of Econometrics, 2 (1974), 79-93.

14. Haberman, Shelby J. The Analysis of Frequency Data. Chicago and London: The University of Chicago Press, 1974.

15. Halperin, M., W. Blackwelder and J. Verter. "Estimation of the Multivariate Logistic Risk Function: A Comparison of the Discriminant Function and Maximum Likelihood Approaches," Journal of Chronic Diseases, 24 (1971), 125-58.

16. Howard, John A. and Jagdish N. Sheth. The Theory of Buyer Behavior. New York: John Wiley and Sons, 1969.

17. Kau, Paul and Lowell Hill, "A Threshold Model of Purchasing Decisions," Journal of Marketing Research, 9 (August, 1972), 264-70.

18. Landis, J. Richard, William M. Standish and Gary G. Koch. "A Computer Program for the Generalized Chi-Square Analysis of Categorical Data Using Weighted Least Squares to Compute Wald Statistics (GENCAT)," Biostatistics Technical Report No. 8. Ann Arbor: University of Michigan, February, 1976.

19. MacRae, Elizabeth C. "Estimation of Time-Varying Markov Processes with Aggregate Data," Econometrica, 45 (January, 1977), 183-98.

20. McFadden, Daniel. "Quantal Choice Analysis: A Survey," Annals of Economic and Social Measurement, 5, No. 4 (1976), 363-90.

21. McFadden, Daniel. "A Comment on Discriminant Analysis 'Versus' Logit Analysis," Annals of Economic and Social Measurement, 5, No. 4 (1976), 511-23.

22. McFadden, Daniel. "Conditional Logit Analysis of Qualitative Choice Behavior," in Paul Zarembka, ed., Frontiers in Econometrics. New York: Academic Press, 1974.

23. Morrison, Donald F. Multivariate Statistical Methods (Second edition). New York: McGraw-Hill, Inc., 1976.

24. Nerlove, Marc and S. James Press. "Univariate and Multivariate Log-Linear and Logistic Models," Santa Monica: Rand Report No. R-1306-EDA/NIH, December, 1973.

25. Press, James S. Applied Multivariate Analysis. New York: Holt, Rinehart and Winston, Inc., 1972.

26. Quandt, Richard. "Probabilistic Theory of Consumer Behavior," Quarterly Journal of Economics, 70 (1956), 507-536.

27. Quandt, Richard. The Demand for Travel. London: D. C. Heath, 1970.

28. Rao, Vithala R. and Frederick W. Winter. "An Application of the Multivariate Probit Model for Market Segmentation and Product Design," Working Paper #388, Faculty Working Papers, College of Commerce and Business Administration, University of Illinois, Urbana-Champaign, March, 1977.

29. Sheth, Jagdish N., ed. Models of Buyer Behavior: Conceptual, Quantitative and Empirical. New York: Harper and Row Publishers, Inc., 1974.

30. Theil, Henri. Statistical Decomposition Analysis. New York: North Holland/American Elsevier, 1972.

31. Torgerson, Warren S. Theory and Methods of Scaling. New York: Wiley and Sons, 1967.

32. Walker, Strother H. and David B. Duncan. "Estimation of the Probability of an Event as a Function of Several Independent Variables," _Biometrika_, 54 (1967), 167-79.

33. Westin, Richard B. "Predictions from Binary Choice Models," _Journal of Econometrics_, 2 (1974), 1-16.

34. Wills, Hugh. "XLOGIT Programmer's Guide, 2.1," Working Paper #7411, Travel Demand Forecasting Project, Institute of Transportation and Traffic Engineering, University of California, Berkeley, August, 1974; Revised, January, 1975.

# APPLYING THE MARKETING CONCEPT TO MARKETING EDUCATION

Derek F. Abell, Harvard University

## ABSTRACT

This paper provides 1) a typology of marketing courses and suggests important dimensions along which they may be classified; 2) an analysis of the needs of major segments, notably undergraduate, graduate and executive education and 3) a definition of important program objectives. This framework is used to address the question raised in the initial "call for papers," namely "what marketing graduates don't learn in college that they need to learn." Directions are suggested to correct deficiencies at each educational level, and to align curricula to meet the highly segmented needs of the marketplace.

## INTRODUCTION

The "call for papers" for this track of the conference strongly suggested by implication that as marketing educators we often fail to meet customer needs. The statement in the October 8th edition of Marketing News was provocative. "One topic of particular interest is what marketing graduates don't learn in college that they need to learn."

To address this issue, it is important, as in all marketing problems, to be concerned with three major issues:

1. What is the nature of the 'product' (or service in this case) and along which attribute dimensions is it differentiated?

2. Who are the customers and how is the customer market segmented?

3. What are the program objectives?

## PRODUCT (SERVICE) DIMENSIONS

Based on a review of a variety of undergraduate and graduate catalogues, as well as direct acquaintance with numerous executive education courses in marketing, three dimensions appear to be important in the development of a typology of course offerings. These are: a) course content, b) their strategic as opposed to administrative focus and c) pedagogical approach.

### Course Content

It appears that courses can be divided into six basic categories on the basis of content:

'Resource' Courses are those courses which develop the skills, disciplines, or knowledge which underpin and support the marketing management function. Included in this category are courses such as Consumer Behavior, Marketing Research, Quantitative Methods in Marketing, Marketing Models, Forecasting, Micro-Economics, etc.

Functional Courses are those courses oriented to individual elements of the marketing mix. Included in this category are courses such as Advertising, Sales Management, Product Policy and New Products, Pricing, Distribution Strategy, etc.

Core Marketing Management Courses are those courses which are oriented to the total marketing management function. These include such courses as Principles of Marketing, "Marketing 101", Marketing Management, etc.

Sector Courses are those courses which focus on marketing problems and concepts germane to particular sectors of the economy. Included in this category are such courses as Industrial Marketing, Services Marketing, Agribusiness and Agribusiness Marketing, Marketing in Non-Profit Organizations, and International Marketing (a geographic sector).

Macro-Marketing Courses are those courses which deal with the impact of marketing on society and the corollary problem of society's impact on marketing via government ownership, public policy pressures, regulation, structural reorganization, etc. Included here are courses dealing with such subjects as consumerism, anti-trust and "ethics in marketing."

Field Courses are those courses which bring the student into contact with real world 'live' projects. Such courses provide an opportunity to apply concepts, theory, and skills learned elsewhere. In particular they provide an opportunity to learn the severe difficulties and realities of collecting, organizing, analyzing, and acting on the limited data which is available to most organizations.

### Strategic Versus Administrative Focus

Courses in any of the above six categories may be taught with either a "strategic" or "administrative" focus. This dichotomy, although it is not meant to imply complete mutual exclusivity, may be clarified with the aid of some examples. A Sales Management course for example might emphasize the relationship between marketing strategy and sales strategy, decisions to use pooled selling, or the design of compensation and reward policies (a strategic focus); another course with exactly the same title might emphasize account management issues, administration of the compensation plan, and territory assignment issues (an administrative focus). Likewise a Marketing Principles course might deal with total marketing mix decisions, channel and communications policies (a strategic focus); or it might deal with the way in which the marketing manager interacts with a large number of other functional managers inside and outside the firm to administer (as opposed to design) marketing programs. A course of this type would deal with such issues as the relationship between the controller's department and marketing and the provision of relevant cost data for marketing decisions; the process of new product planning and introduction; administration (as opposed to selection) of channels of distribution; and day to day decisions relating to changes in marketing activity in the course of the budget year. It is relatively easy to think of administrative analogs for strategic courses classified in any of the other major course categories. Even so called resource courses may be taught with either a strategic or administrative focus. A strategic course in Marketing Research for example might focus heavily on the design of the data requirements to satisfy various classes of strategic decision. An 'administrative' version of the same course would focus more heavily on the implementation and administration of the marketing research function and the day to day practical issues involved in doing useful and relevant research.

### Pedagogical Approaches

Pedagogy is perhaps the most difficult dimension of the product to describe. Educators themselves have unfortunately adopted misleading labelling practices. The most common mistake in this report is to dichotomize 'case' or 'readings' courses as if the first focused on problems but not concepts, and the second on concepts and theory but not problems. A more viable classification scheme might be based on the extent to which the course emphasizes a process orientation as opposed to a theoretical orientation.

A 'process' orientation, one major variant of which is the case method,[1] forces the students' attention on the process of making marketing decisions, doing consumer analysis, doing competitive analysis, developing the financial implications of marketing decisions, etc. In so doing, theory and concepts are used to organize and structure otherwise difficult to understand problems. The students, as a result, become proficient in applying theory, and selectively educated to theory and concepts which appear relevant to decision making. Course outlines for such courses are usually divided into sections dealing with different decision areas within the major course topic. The benefits of such an approach are captured in the old Japanese moto:

"If you give a man a fish he can eat for a day. If you teach a man how to fish he can eat for a thousand years."

There are disadvantages, however. Although theory and concepts are used extensively as crutches to organization and problem solving, every individual situation studied takes on the appearance of being relatively unique. A course taught by the case method alone, for example, may (depending how the cases are used) run the risk of finely honing the students' process skills at the expense of developing any overall theories and typologies of products, markets, customers, competitive styles, etc. The student (and later the practitioner) is forced to reinvent the wheel in terms of developing appropriate theory for each new problem that he confronts.

A theoretical orientation focuses the student's attention on the theories and concepts themselves, and in some cases on the empirical research which led to the theory development. Course outlines for such courses are usually subdivided into sections organized around classes of theory or concepts. A Marketing Principles course, for example, might have sections dealing with segmentation, product life cycles, communications theory, etc. The benefits and disadvantages of this approach are well known. Even if an attempt is made to combine theory with process through the selective use of, for example, cases, students often do not develop enough process skill to creatively structure marketing problems and solve them.

## CUSTOMER AND MARKET SEGMENTATION

As in all marketing problems, an eclectic approach is needed to segment the market in ways which are relevant and useful. As a fundamental cut the market may be divided into three major segments, one of which is sub-segmented: a) undergraduate; b) MBA concentrators, MBA nonconcentrators; c) longer executive programs (i.e., more than one to two days). The needs of these three segments are substantially different for two major reasons:

1. students are differently prepared at entry;

2. different expectations and opportunities confront each group at exit.

_____

[1]Other 'process' oriented approaches include "experimential" methods, simulation games, etc.

Undergraduate

In general, undergraduates have little or no real world experience of marketing or business on which to draw for context. By contrast, however, they usually have a reasonably well developed habit of studying and learning and (hopefully) a good working knowledge of underlying skills such as math and scientific methodology.

In terms of exit requirements, few undergraduates develop in college clear ambitions to work forever in either defined industry sectors, or particular functions within marketing. Even those for whom an undergraduate education is a terminal degree often change career paths several times in their twenties and thirties. On the other hand most undergraduates feel, rightly, that after so many years of education they ought to be prepared to do a job! This pressure has unfortunately been responsible for the proliferation of 'vocational' undergraduate education without firm intellectual underpinnings.

MBA

The MBA is in a very different situation at entry and at exit from the undergraduate. Many are prepared by virtue of some on-the-job experience as well as academic training. In terms of exit, there is, usually, during the second half of such a program, a growing interest in either a sector of the economy, a particular type of organization, or function. MBA concentrators in particular, have presumably selected marketing as a career path and maybe even an industry or marketing function of major interest.

Executive Education

There are obviously many important subsegments within executive ranks depending on position, experience, and academic background. It is the author's belief, however, that certain generalizations are possible.

At entry:

1. Many executives have had no formal marketing education prior to such a program. We are still some way from reaching the "bottom of the barrel" in terms of educating "first timers" as opposed to reeducating MBAs, etc.

2. Virtually all have substantial on-the-job experience and a 'context' to which educational programs can be related.

3. Many have difficulty in establishing efficient and effective work study routines and habits. For many, it is the first time 'back to school' after ten to fifteen years.

4. Many have difficulty with math and the scientific method in general. "Pushing the numbers" causes more difficulty than nearly any other subject.

5. The ability to think in abstract terms and to conceptualize problems is not as highly developed as for the MBA.

6. Shrewdness, well developed judgment, commitment to one viewpoint, and personal experience, often drive out rigorous analysis, creative thinking, and recognition of the pros and cons of different alternatives.

At exit:

1. Most, if not all, executives have a high likelihood of returning to the industry from which they have come.

2. Many executives have a high likelihood of returning to the function from which they have come, at least initially.

3. Many are attending with a view to moving to higher ranks, often with broader responsibilities, in the foreseeable future.

4. All executives will have to struggle, the day the program ends, with how to apply what they have learned to their own particular situation. The transition from classroom to practice is cruel and immediate.

## SETTING PROGRAM OBJECTIVES

The matching of the product (service) with customer needs has to be performed with three major sets of objectives in mind:

1. Objectives which promise immediate, short-run benefits in terms of improved capability to do a particular job. This can take the form of specific knowledge, skills or attitudes. However, it seems difficult to justify any curriculum offering which does not address at least one of these dimensions.

2. Objectives which promise longer run returns in the sense of preparing the individual for jobs which he might hold five to ten years after graduation. Given the increasing opportunity for continuing education, it seems hard to justify courses which provide training whose pay off is much longer.

3. Objectives aimed at motivating the student during the actual educational process. Attention to such objectives is essential if students are to learn to be excited by marketing, to recognize its enormous contribution to development, and to understand the opportunities it presents.

It is apparent that these three groups of objectives may be in conflict. Trade-offs between them are often required. The most exciting and motivating marketing decisions, for example, are often those which lie closest to the president, and involve broad questions of corporate strategy. How much time should be devoted to such problems by an undergraduate preparing for his first job, or a sales executive preparing to take over a new territory?

## "WHAT MARKETING GRADUATES DON'T LEARN THAT THEY NEED TO LEARN"

We may now return to the question which was originally posed. Although the primary intention of this paper has been to provide the marketing educator with a way to think about the problem and the important dimensions involved, it would be remiss not to comment on current practice and apparent gaps. It must be borne in mind, however, that much of this paper is more in the form of hypotheses than conclusions. It reflects inevitably the author's own biases and personal experience. It is the responsibility of every reader to confirm or reject the hypotheses in his own situation. In many cases this will require much research, testing, and monitoring of courses and their impact. Little, if any, such measures are available today. Until they are we are all forced to speculate.

### Undergraduate Education

The foregoing analysis might suggest that undergraduate marketing education needs to be concentrated on 1) "resource" courses; 2) macro-marketing courses and; 3) a core marketing management course, with some exposure to the "real world" of marketing via field project experience. Concentration on particular industry sectors or particular functions within marketing seems harder to justify given the limited time available and the uncertain shape of future job demands.

Most undergraduates on graduation will be performing administrative as opposed to strategic decision making roles. This suggests, in general, administrative decisions should be stressed at least as much as strategic decisions in any courses which have a decision making orientation. Developing student motivation and interest in marketing is, however, vital. At least one segment of a basic marketing course should put the student in the role of top management, and impart the sense of excitement which such decisions entail.

Pedagogically, a balance has to be struck between process and theoretical education. Process is important as a motivational device. However, undergraduates may have more reason, and more time, to study theory and concepts for their own sake than say MBAs or practicing executives.

As far as setting objectives is concerned, the short-run should probably dominate the long-run. This does not imply developing specific, narrowly defined vocational skills. On the contrary, it argues for the development of broadly applicable resource skills and the ability to apply them to a wide variety of administrative as opposed to strategic tasks. The holder of an undergraduate degree should be able to do things -- lots of things. He should be an intellectual generalist -- not a vocational specialist.

### MBA Nonconcentrators

Marketing education for nonconcentrators needs to expose students to marketing rather than educate them for marketing jobs. Resource courses, functional courses, and field project courses are of less importance than: 1) core marketing management courses and 2) macro-marketing courses. Concentration in an industry sector is, however, often justified by well defined career plans or job ambitions.

Few nonconcentrators will be involved in marketing administration. The major need is to understand broad marketing strategies and their relationship to the total activities of the firm.

Pedagogically, courses which deal with marketing theory for its own sake should be kept to a minimum. Process oriented education with the objective of developing analytical and process skills should be encouraged.

As far as objectives are concerned, preparation for the long-run should dominate the short-run. The education should be such that it can "last a life time." Few nonconcentrators, after all, will ever have another formal exposure to marketing.

### MBA Concentrators

The MBA concentrator needs balance in all dimensions. In terms of course content this is often achieved. In terms of other dimensions it is often not achieved. In particular, most if not all MBA marketing curricula give insufficient attention to administration as opposed to strategic decision making. Graduates are often ready to take over the marketing manager or president's job, but much less well prepared to administer a sales force, to coordinate a new product development activity, to conduct market research, to work with channels of distribution, or to organize a new products committee.

Secondly, an unhealthy polarization seems to have occurred in schools of business between those schools emphasizing process education (often extensively case method) and those emphasizing theory. For the concentrator, both are important. Which schools can sincerely claim to do an outstanding job in each?

As far as objectives are concerned, both the long-run and short-run are important. However, the MBA concentrator has the luxury of time to be able to develop specific job entry expertise as well as foundations for the longer run.

Specifically these short-run objectives may translate into courses in specific functions or industry sectors, or into field projects which are likely to be germane to the first job after graduation.

Executive Education

The overriding variable in executive education is time. Executives usually have only a few weeks to devote to education. Time has to be allocated with a much higher degree of efficiency when the passage of time is measured in weeks, and not as it is by MBAs and undergraduates, in years.

Often this means that generalized resource skills must be developed in short two or three day specialized seminars. Longer executive programs can then be concentrated on broad marketing management and macro-marketing materials. In many cases, a useful format is to develop general skills in the first part of such a program and to tailor the second part to specific industry sectors and/or functional needs. It is hard to justify teaching a case dealing with potato chips to a sales manager for heavy electrical apparatus. Looked at in reverse, sales managers have every reason to expect that marketing education will help them to perform the sales management function better.

Both strategy and administration are important aspects of education for marketing executives. Their expertise is often towards the latter, but it is experience often derived without the benefit of formal concepts and theory to guide action.

In terms of pedagogy, executives have to be motivated by the promise that the education will improve their on-the-job performance. This argues strongly against theory and concepts for their own sake (in contrast to the under-graduate's needs). It argues strongly for process orientation education which focuses on the application of concepts and theory to relevant problems. The executive cannot, however, be assumed to learn like the MBA. Often, unless the instructor highlights concepts and how they can be usefully applied, the end result of a series of case studies is lots of excitement but lots of confusion and little generalized learning. A much higher degree of 'hand holding', conceptualization by the instructor, and firm guidance in the form of providing a clear model of how analyses should be conducted, is required than for MBAs.

In terms of objectives, the short to medium run is of paramount importance. Executives need to be able to perform their current and next immediate job assignment demonstrably better than they could without the benefit of marketing education. This objective sometimes conflicts with the objective of providing high motivation. Many lower echelon marketing executives are fascinated by broad strategic marketing and corporate strategy problems. It provides a vicarious opportunity to escape from the daily routine of their jobs to the excitement of the Board Room. Even though a certain amount of such education is essential, as marketing educators we concentrate solely on that objective at our peril, except in truly top management programs. For the rest, such motivation has to be tempered by a realistic appraisal of more immediate career development needs.

In summary, it would appear that as educators we have the tools, and even some of the knowledge, to practice what we preach to others. Experience suggests, however, that we still have a way to go in terms of implementing the marketing concept in our own profession.

REFERENCES

1. Salmon, Walter J. et al. "Cases and Concepts -- The Twain Do Meet," American Marketing Association Proceedings, September 1966.

MEETING THE NEEDS OF THE PART TIME
MBA MARKETING STUDENT:
A FEEDBACK SYSTEM:

J. Donald Weinrauch, Tennessee Technological University

## ABSTRACT

For many MBA programs the older, fully employed and part-time students are providing promise for growth and expansion during the next decade. Marketing curricula and teaching approaches should thus cater to this viable student market. To apply the marketing concept within the graduate marketing courses, a formal feedback system was created and used to gauge the mature student's learning needs and desires.

## INTRODUCTION

Graduate business schools are currently experiencing some exciting but volatile times. The present conditions of economic uncertainty in our spaceship earth economy have had a tremendous impact on graduate business schools. Such occurrences as evening and weekend classes, concentrated week long courses, correspondent graduate classes, extension courses, joint MBA program with other disciplines, and classes on commuter trains have become common phenomena.

Given the economic conditions, business managers and professionals from other fields are encountering some career frustrations. Job security, mobility, earlier retirements, unemployment, underemployment, mid-career crisis, and slow promotions are some of the major career concerns. Hence, for many MBA programs, older, part-time students from diverse backgrounds are the major groups that provide promise for growth and expansion during the next decade.

In teaching the part-time MBA student, marketing curricula and teaching approaches should adjust as needed to the changing MBA student markets. It is becoming quite difficult, however, to develop meaningful MBA courses to meet the needs of each individual student. It is also a tedious project to anticipate and fulfill the ever changing manpower needs of the business community. In sum, graduate marketing professors face a major challenge for developing curricula and for planning teaching strategy.

Many techniques are presently being utilized to pinpoint both the needs of students and the business community. Some of them are:

- Surveying companies for preferences on course content and overall curriculum.
- Examining other MBA programs.
- Using formal and informal methods of feedback from alumni.
- Course evaluation questionnaires at the end of the course.
- Providing "talk-ins" with executives of the local business community.
- Keeping up with the literature on collegiate graduate education.
- Developing a dean's community advisory council of executives.
- Employing faculty curriculum committees.

Albeit these above techniques furnish some valuable input and should be continued, they do have two major limitations. One problem with many of these methods is the time constraint. For example, a survey may become obsolete by the time the study is conceived and the actual results implemented. The second limitation is the credibility factor. Are the responses of the business people pertinent to the needs of the full-time executives/part-time MBA students? Faculty members and business executives, participating in course development and its content, may be thinking of their own self-interests. However, do the mid-managers who are part-time MBA students really need the type of instruction that was recommended by non-students? It is possible that the current feedback methods are sometimes more self-serving to the organization than to the students. Therefore, it is also necessary to be sensitive to the needs and desires of the actual students of the MBA program.

## AN ADDITIONAL FEEDBACK TECHNIQUE: STUDENT PROFILE FORMS

Other feedback approaches are needed to apply the marketing concept within the classroom. To overcome some of the forementioned short-comings of traditional input for developing and teaching the marketing graduate courses, a comprehensive six-page student profile form was developed. (See the appendix for examining the entire instrument.)

During the past three years, the student profile form was used for an elective marketing course that was entitled, "Marketing Problems and Analysis". Originally, the course was designed as a case problem course that students would take after a graduate core survey marketing course. To gauge students' interests, needs, and wants, the profile form which was distributed the first class period attempted to obtain vital information on:

- student demographic data
- business background
- motivations for taking the course
- preferred teaching methodology
- degree of student interest in various marketing topics
- degree of perceived significance of marketing topics to both the student's own professional development and to the community.

## IDENTIFYING THE MARKET CHARACTERISTICS

In the first two pages the graduate students were asked to provide their place of employment, job title, brief job description, other pertinent experiences, educational background, professional certificates, and previous undergraduate and graduate marketing courses completed. It was found that many of the students had excellent business experience in marketing while others clearly lacked the educational and/or practical background in marketing. It was surprising, for example, to find that a few of the students had Ph.D.'s in other fields, such as engineering or mathematics. Whenever necessary, it was thus possible to recognize and use their highly specialized skills.

Throughout the semester these two pages were also used to acknowledge the students' organizations and positions. It made for an informal atmosphere and the students appreciated the idea of knowing what organizations were represented in the classroom. (In a few cases a student who was looking for another position would contact a fellow student about his or her organization.) The student data in this section also proved valuable when discussing cases. For example, when discussing the role of a product manager, it was often possible to allude to a student in the class who had actual product management experience. There was excellent interface with the cases and the students' own practical experiences. In summary, by knowing the students' backgrounds, it was easier to structure the course and appeal to individual strengths while still eliminating some of their deficiences in marketing. Also, by making minor adaptations in structuring the course, the students truly appreciated the instructor's attempts to meet their learning interests and needs.

## MOTIVATIONS AND LEARNING OBJECTIVES

The profile form had questions relating to the primary reason for enrolling in the elective course. Since most of the students were in the thirty to fifty-five age bracket, it was surprising to observe the tremendous interest in various available marketing careers. Many of them were indeed experiencing the "mid-career crisis". Without the profile form this topic would have never been covered. A number of students also stated that their jobs required a high degree of interaction with both marketing personnel and the marketing functions. Hence, these students expressed a desire to examine the normative and proper roles that might exist between various business functions. They wanted to acquire more empathy for their marketing counterparts. The question served a useful purpose in trying to meet the immediate needs of the majority of the older students.

The students were also asked to specify their desired learning objectives. Since this was an open-end question they had some latitude in expressing their own goals for the semester. Even though it was not possible to attain all of the objectives for each student, some were personally directed to secondary sources for meeting specific personal goals. This part of the survey also helped in formulating some behavioral learning objectives to coincide with the students' objectives.

## IMPROVING TEACHING STRATEGY

The form contained a question pertaining to preferred teaching methodology (e.g., role playing, lectures, and cases). Besides the usual request for cases, lectures, group discussions, and questions and answers, a number of students wanted films and guest speakers from industry. Again their responses were somewhat surprising since most of them do come in daily contact with marketing executives. Based on these responses, speakers from major firms gave presentations.

Another teaching-related question dealt with a request for the students to provide any innovative ideas that might be different from the traditional classroom environment. Based on their suggestions, classes were sometimes held in the students' own work environments. These organizational facilities proved to be excellent for they had modern visual aids and other amenities that are usually not available in the academic environment. In summary, the students had many helpful ideas. Without the questionnaire, many of their pedagogical suggestions would not have been recognized nor attempted.

## PLANNING AND DEVELOPING COURSE CONTENT

To help in defining the specific topics that might be emphasized during the semester, the profile form had three closed-ended questions. (See the appendix for examining the three questions.) This part of the profile form attempted to fulfill student interest on specific marketing topics while also covering topics the students felt were important to their own professional development and/or to the business community.

A separate list of definitions of the topics was also administered. This helped the students in understanding various marketing topics.

Despite the length of this section (it consisted of three pages), it facilitated the planning of weekly topics that would be covered during the course. Without these three questions, students could have been instructed on superfluous topics. For example, since the subject of marketing for non-profit organizations was popular in the literature, it was assumed that this area might be of interest to the students. However, after summarizing the students' preferences during the first class period, it was found that there was little perceived importance or interest in this subject. Hence, it was not covered in the class. Alternatively, during another semester there were two ministers, two directors of non-profit organizations, and some other students who were interested in the application of marketing to social and religious causes. To partially meet their learning needs and interests, a formal debate was organized. The subject dealt with the ethics and feasibility of applying marketing concepts to social causes and/or non-profit organizations. The teaching approach would never have been carried out without the feedback system.

## ADDITIONAL FEEDBACK TECHNIQUES

It should be noted that other feedback techniques were used during the rest of the semester. There were random student critiques of certain class periods, weekly activity reports, quarterly student evaluations, a suggestion box available at all times, random sample of student-teacher personal interviews and formal talk-ins with selected groups of MBA students. All of these feedback techniques helped in improving this MBA marketing course. They also aided other marketing professors in considering new graduate marketing courses while reevaluating current MBA courses.

## EVALUATION OF STUDENT PROFILE TECHNIQUE

Advantages: The purpose of the student profile questionnaire form was to obtain student input on needs, interests and preferences. The form furnished an excellent guideline for designing the course content and employing a variety of teaching methods. Also, these mature students were better served in their own professions. Another advantage is that the process insures us that the topics covered were worthwhile and beneficial to the students. Like any other MBA program there is a limit on the number of elective graduate business courses that can be offered in any one field. Thus, it is imperative to avoid innocuous topics and maximize learning efforts.

Disadvantages: There are a few disadvantages in structuring a graduate marketing course on student feedback. One might argue that the students do not know enough in the field or are not mature enough to design a course. This might be a major criticism of using the profile form. However, the students are more mature and have more experiences than the typical full-time student to partially off-set this problem. Also, there is still some flexibility and control in the feedback system to allow some judgement on instruction by the marketing professor.

Another disadvantage is that it is difficult for the professor to plan for the course until the results have been compiled. Consequently, this approach requires the professor to work extra hard in the first few weeks to develop and organize the course. Another limitation is that the professor must be willing to adjust to the students' desires. A teacher may have to forego a favorite topic or teaching technique. Lastly, the form does take 30 to 45 minutes to complete. As a result, part of the first class period is used for answering questions.

Differences: Unlike many other feedback techniques, the marketing professor is able to survey the specific needs of the current students. Also, a profile form helps one to identify contemporary educational needs and keep up with the information explosion. Other feedback techniques may be more time consuming and slower. Lastly, each class had its own teaching preferences, backgrounds, business contacts, and access to resources. Consequently, for instructional purposes market segmentation by class is adopted. The MBA students of a particular class made initial contacts for speakers, outside facilities, and audio and visual aids. This feedback mechanism then serves as a vehicle in identifying and implementing specific pedagogical ideas for each class which has its own unique characteristics.

## CONCLUSIONS AND IMPLICATIONS

The student profile form and other feedback techniques that were mentioned in this article can help marketing professors in meeting the needs and goals of the students. The entire process can assist business professors in making the marketing concept operational within the classroom.

The student profile form described in this article could be used by marketing professors in almost any graduate marketing course. Depending upon individual circumstances, addition and deletion of questions may be appropriate. It should also be noted that the concept of student profile forms can be used for the full-time MBA students. The application of it does, of course, depend on such circumstances as the maturity and previous business experience of the full-time students. With some further modifications, marketing professors could also use a student profile form in some undergraduate courses.

In conclusion, it is axiomatic that graduate business schools cannot afford to ignore older, part-time students' desires for they are the future market for many schools. Hopefully, the feedback technique that was incorporated in this course allowed the arteries to remain open and is another fruitful addition in listening to a viable and vibrant student segment.

## APPENDIX

### STUDENT PROFILE FORM

Name:_____
Place of Employment:_____
Job Title:_____
Brief Job Description:_____
Business Address and Phone Number:_____
Home Address and Phone Number:_____
Business Background:_____
Educational Background: (List Degrees held and your major and minor fields; also, mention any professional certificates that you hold, e.g., C.P.A.)

Please list all previous Marketing courses (State

if they are graduate or undergraduate courses.)
9. Primary reason for taking this course.
10. Learning Objectives (e.g., in general terms, what are some of the things you would like to accomplish from this course).

An example: To learn some of the more important terms in the field of marketing.
11. The teaching methodology that you prefer. (e.g. Lectures, cases, etc., or a combination of...).
12. The following marketing areas and/or topics are sometimes covered in a graduate course in marketing. Please indicate the degree of interest that you have in these subjects: (The categories that were placed above the topics for this question were: "Considerable Interest", "Somewhat of Interest", "Negligible Interest", and "Not Sure"...the student had the opportunity to then check the degree of interest which applied for each topic on the original profile form.)

a. Sales Management ___ ___ ___ ___
b. Salesmanship ___ ___ ___ ___
c. Advertising ___ ___ ___ ___
d. Sales Promotion ___ ___ ___ ___
e. Public Relations ___ ___ ___ ___
f. Publicity ___ ___ ___ ___
g. Retailing ___ ___ ___ ___
h. Wholesaling ___ ___ ___ ___
i. Purchasing ___ ___ ___ ___
j. International Marketing ___ ___ ___ ___
k. Physical Distribution ___ ___ ___ ___
l. Marketing Research ___ ___ ___ ___
m. Quantitative Marketing ___ ___ ___ ___
n. Consumer Behavior
   (incl. Buyer Behavior) ___ ___ ___ ___
o. History of Marketing ___ ___ ___ ___
p. Channels of Distribution ___ ___ ___ ___
q. Marketing Theory ___ ___ ___ ___
r. Small Business Marketing ___ ___ ___ ___
s. Industrial Marketing ___ ___ ___ ___
t. Pricing ___ ___ ___ ___
u. Legal Marketing
   (Laws, Regulations, etc.) ___ ___ ___ ___
v. Marketing of Public Services ___ ___ ___ ___
w. Other

13. Please indicate how important the following subjects are to your own professional development: (The categories that were placed above the topics for this question were: "Highly Important", "Somewhat Important", "Not at all Important", and "Not Sure"...the student had the opportunity to then check the degree of importance which applied for each topic on the original profile form.)

a. Sales Management ___ ___ ___ ___
b. Salesmanship ___ ___ ___ ___
c. Advertising ___ ___ ___ ___
d. Sales Promotion ___ ___ ___ ___
e. Public Relations ___ ___ ___ ___
f. Publicity ___ ___ ___ ___
g. Retailing ___ ___ ___ ___
h. Wholesaling ___ ___ ___ ___
i. Purchasing ___ ___ ___ ___
j. International Marketing ___ ___ ___ ___
k. Physical Distribution ___ ___ ___ ___
l. Marketing Research ___ ___ ___ ___
m. Quantitative Marketing ___ ___ ___ ___
n. Consumer Behavior
   (incl. Buyer Behavior) ___ ___ ___ ___
o. History of Marketing ___ ___ ___ ___
p. Channels of Distribution ___ ___ ___ ___
q. Marketing Theory ___ ___ ___ ___
r. Small Business Marketing ___ ___ ___ ___

s. Industrial Marketing     __ __ __ __
t. Pricing
u. Legal Marketing     __ __ __ __
v. Marketing of Public Service     __ __ __ __
w. Other

14. Please indicate how important the following subjects are to the business community in general: (The categories that were placed above the topics for this question were: "Highly Important", "Somewhat Important", "Not at all Important", and "Not Sure"...the student had the opportunity to then check the degree of importance which applied for each topic on the original profile form.)

a. Sales Management     __ __ __ __
b. Salesmanship
c. Advertising     __ __ __ __
d. Sales Promotion
e. Public Relations     __ __ __ __
f. Publicity
g. Retailing     __ __ __ __
h. Wholesaling
i. Purchasing     __ __ __ __
j. International Marketing
k. Physical Distribution     __ __ __ __
l. Marketing Research
m. Quantitative Marketing     __ __ __ __
n. Consumer Behavior
    (incl. Buyer Behavior)     __ __ __ __
o. History of Marketing
p. Channels of Distribution     __ __ __ __
q. Marketing Theory
r. Small Business Marketing     __ __ __ __
s. Industrial Marketing
t. Pricing     __ __ __ __
u. Legal Marketing
v. Marketing of Public Services     __ __ __ __
w. Other

15. Can you think of anything that might be somewhat different from the traditional classroom environment which could make the course more informative and interesting. (e.g. Teaching Methodology, facilities, use of equipment, etc.)

16. Other comments you think helpful to the instructor in meeting your expectations from the course.

17. What is Marketing?

# THE MARKETING PRINCIPLES COURSE: CORRESPONDENCE
## WITH STUDENT INTERESTS, ATTENDANCE TO DIVERSE SEGMENTS

F. Robert Dwyer, University of Arizona

## ABSTRACT

Marketing's declining share of all business degrees is a significant problem requiring the immediate attention of marketing educators. More effective recruiting of top quality marketing majors demands a greater understanding of the interests of students in the principles course. This study examines student importance ratings for various subject areas in the principles course and identifies diverse student segments. In light of the findings, significant course modifications have been implemented in subsequent sections in order to achieve congruence between student interests and teaching objectives. In addition, segmentation teaching strategies have been employed to increase subject area relevance to previously uninterested students.

## INTRODUCTION

Several years ago, as a student in my first marketing class, I can recall several accounting majors expressing frustration over the assigned case analysis and arguing that a break-even analysis was impossible because selling price information had not been provided. The instructor tried in vain to assure them that price determination was, indeed, part of the problem. Finally, he sighed, drew a large T on the board and asked the students what they saw. "Nothing," they replied, swallowing the bait. Like a swift touché he snapped, "Take a T-account away from an accountant and he's blind--there's a desk, blackboard, walls ...."

In light of the recent calls to aggressively recruit top quality marketing majors [1], the story illustrates the complexities of "marketing marketing" to students with diverse orientations and backgrounds. The purpose of this article is to identify the interests of students pursuing different fields of study, and suggest curriculum changes to more effectively market marketing.

## BACKGROUND

The problem of attracting top quality students to studies and careers in marketing was recognized as early as 1964. At the AMA Educator's Conference of that year, McCarthy [5] and Meloan [6] warned that marketing departments must project an aggressive and attractive image to students or they will choose other fields of study. It was only after two successive years showing declines in marketing education's share of all business degrees that Uhr and Roundtree [9] sought to assess the image of marketing. Their survey of 33 members of a professional business fraternity showed only 11.5 percent having an "unfavorable" image of marketing. However, the unfavorable group's distribution included higher proportions of accounting majors and students with high grade point averages and two or more academic honors. In addition, these authors found that the marketing educator has only one or two opportunities to interest and favorably impress students who hold marketing in an unfavorable light.

In spite of these calls to action, available evidence indicates that marketing education is still losing ground. Sedt [8] reports six consecutive years of decline of marketing's share of all business degrees.

At least two alternatives are available for halting and reversing this unfavorable trend. The first alternative was proposed in 1964 and echoed by Enis [2] more recently. In the basic marketing course increased emphasis must be placed on recruiting top quality marketing majors. Certainly, the first step in problem solving is recognition of that problem and the remedial action imperatives.

The second alternative has relevance for those educators who have already attended to the first one. The thrust here is to refine and improve the marketing of marketing efforts that have already received emphasis. This requires a thorough understanding of the needs of students as well as a current grasp of the course objectives.

To contrast the two approaches, strategy one focuses on increasing the amount of emphasis placed on attracting marketing majors in the principles course. The second approach, the subject of this article, is to improve the effectiveness of educators already striving to recruit first rate marketing majors.

## IMPLEMENTING THE MARKETING CONCEPT

Marketing scholars, of all people, should be aware of the required flexibility of organizational objectives in light of the diverse and dynamic nature of consumer needs. Too often, however, in the marketing principles classroom, teaching objectives are merely unstructured, implicit goals given little consideration beyond those times when exams or lecture notes are developed. Initially notes are developed prior to face-to-face contact with students. The problem is magnified when, in the absence of formal student feedback, these lecture notes and exams get routinely recycled each year with little or no modification.

Implicit in the above criticism is the view that traditional end-of-quarter/semester course evaluations are of limited value in addressing these problems. The nature of their drawback is twofold. First, although it is generally assumed that student ratings provide instructors with valuable information for course redesign, the research provides no conclusive evidence that teachers use this information effectively to improve their courses or their ratings [4]. An exception is Whipple's [10] account of instructors who used evaluations to improve turn-around time on graded papers and avoid side-tracks in class lectures. However, while Whipple's research proves traditional evaluations have the capacity to facilitate impact on class format, his account also leads into the second shortcoming.

The major weakness of most course evaluations has been a narrow focus restricted to what might be called "packaging" issues. Traditional evaluations attempt to measure student (consumer) satisfaction with the instructor's personality, approachability, and apparent knowledge in the field; with the difficulty of the course work; with the fairness of examinations; and with the readability of the text.

These "packaging" issues are by no means unimportant. Instructors can benefit from these evaluations by changing their style of presentation--usually to include more showmanship. Also, office hours may be extended or shortened; text books re-used or dumped; examinations altered; and, increasingly, faculty promoted or terminated. In fact, a 1971 AMA sponsored survey of 224 marketing professors at

AACSB schools showed that 45 percent were positively inclined toward faculty evaluation by students, as compared to 28 percent against such evaluations [3]. However, while these types of measures continue to be taken and used in greater extents, attention must be paid to an area in a critical state of neglect--namely, marketing principles curriculum evaluation.

## Student Needs

It has been generally assumed that students enroll in the marketing principles course--per requirement or otherwise-- with a primary concern for making themselves more employable. If this assumption is correct (though it has seldom been questioned), educators can expect student interests to be tempered by their perceptions of the needs of prospective employers. In addition to student career interests, pretest data for this research and Painter and Granzin [7] suggest that students expect the basic marketing class to have significance for their future academic pursuits and for their general education experience.

It would be of considerable value for the marketing educator to know which subject areas in marketing students perceive as having the greatest importance. Analysis of this type of curriculum evaluation could focus on the identification of discrepancies between student and instructor importance ratings on various subject areas. Also, the identification of differences across student types is possible. This study will examine interest differences of accounting students, because of their apparently unique need for closure; non-accounting business students, because of their relatively large numbers in the principles course; and students in non-business fields.

## Implications of Evaluation Data

Should discrepancies exist between student importance ratings and the instructor's valuation of the corresponding teaching objectives, two options are available for pursuing congruence. The instructor's first option is the employment of more creative approaches to specific subject areas in order to increase the students' perceived relevance of those areas. Alternatively, the instructor can re-examine and modify teaching objectives in light of the student feedback. Also, the presence of interest differences across student types may suggest segmentation teaching strategies.

## METHODOLOGY

In the marketing principles teaching situation under study, curriculum and enrollment factors led to the development of a topical outline probably similar to that used by most instructors. Moreover, a personal concern for decision-making and communication skills--problem recognition, data use and development, logical report writing, etc.--led to the cultivation of such skills through the use of a limited number of case studies, short problems, and a three-person team research paper.

At the conclusion of the quarter students were asked to complete a questionnaire that covered items in the topical outline and the list of sought decision-making and communication skills. Opposite each subject/skill area students were asked to consider its personal importance to them. Rather than using an overall importance rating, that might mask the diverse goals of students from various backgrounds, three situation-specific importance scores were obtained. As mentioned earlier, previous research [7] and pretest focus groups had indicated potential benefits from the marketing principles course in terms of its relevance to: (1) future career opportunities, (2) future academic pursuits, and (3) present and future roles as citizens and consumers. For each subject/skill area, then,

students were asked to consider and score its importance to them in terms of its likely relevance to each of the importance categories described above. Importance was scored on a five-point itemized rating scale (1 = Not at all important; 5 = Extremely important). Background data on grade point average, field of study, class, and sex were also obtained. Fifty-three of 61 students completed the questionnaires, which had been distributed toward the end of the last class period.

It should be noted that end-of-quarter ratings may be somewhat contaminated by the instructor's and text's enthusiasm (or lack thereof) in different topical areas. However, a curriculum evaluation by naive students, familiar with perhaps little more than a two-sentence course description, would surely yield nonsense.

## FINDINGS

The data presented in Table 1 reveal the average importance scores for all 53 respondents. The numbers in parentheses correspond to the rank of that subject/skill area in that importance category. For example, "Product management through the product life cycle" is ranked 17th with a mean score of 3.56 on its importance for future career opportunities. The subject ranks 13th in terms of its mean importance to future academic pursuits, 3.26. Finally, as far as its relevance to students' roles as consumers and citizens, the product life cycle received an average score of 2.88; good enough to rank it 18th in this importance category. It is worthwhile to note that as a whole, students are more interested in developing analytical, problem solving skills than understanding key marketing concepts or subject areas.

Also, the rankings suggest a high correlation between the importance scores in the career dimension and the scores in the academic importance category. This correlation is really not surprising since for most students career interests and goals determine academic pursuits.

## Segmentation Analysis

The purpose of the segmentation analysis was to examine the notion that students from different academic programs have diverse interests in the topics of the marketing principles class. The first stage of this analysis was to explore the existence of diverse segments from a multivariate perspective. More specifically, the possibility of using importance scores on a set of subject/skill areas to correctly assign students to their field of study was tested. While space limitations prohibit a detailed review of this multivariate analysis, a summary of procedures is presented below. Analysis of single subject/skill area differences across segments follows.

In order to reduce the large number of variables and determine the underlying dimensions of the data, for each importance category, a factor analysis of the subject/skill area scores was performed. The subject/skill areas loading on each of the seven factors identified were nearly identical for the career importance and academic importance variables. This further supports the notion of high correlation between the two importance scores. Hence, future attention focuses primarily on the career opportunities scores.

Meanwhile, the factor analysis of the subject/skill area scores in the consumer/citizen role category resulted in slightly different factors. Beyond what could be acclaimed as the re-discovery of the 4-P's, the factor analyses served well to identify variables for inclusion in a stepwise discriminant analysis--a procedure that attempts to correctly predict an individual's group membership on the basis of his or her scores on a number of interval scaled predictor variables.

TABLE 1

SUBJECT/SKILL IMPORTANCE SCORE RANKINGS AND MEANS

| | Career Importance | | Academic Importance | | Consumer/ Citizen Importance | |
|---|---|---|---|---|---|---|
| | Rank | Mean | Rank | Mean | Rank | Mean |
| Problem recognition/definition | (1) | 4.14 | (1) | 3.96 | (5) | 3.34 |
| Data use and development | (2) | 3.98 | (2) | 3.81 | (11) | 3.02 |
| Alternative evaluation | (3) | 3.95 | (4) | 3.79 | (3) | 3.37 |
| Logical, concise report writing | (4) | 3.89 | (2) | 3.81 | (13) | 3.00 |
| Pricing tools I: break-even, marginal analysis | (5) | 3.80 | (7) | 3.50 | (29) | 2.53 |
| Concept integration | (6) | 3.79 | (5) | 3.77 | (8) | 3.12 |
| Cooperation & division of labor in group efforts | (7) | 3.77 | (17) | 3.22 | (17) | 2.89 |
| Familiarity with secondary data sources | (8) | 3.72 | (6) | 3.71 | (11) | 3.02 |
| Research techniques of forecasting | (9) | 3.69 | (8) | 3.46 | (26) | 2.57 |
| Consumer decision-making | (9) | 3.69 | (12) | 3.28 | (1) | 3.63 |
| Demand, supply, competition factors in pricing | (11) | 3.64 | (10) | 3.37 | (6) | 3.34 |
| Determining the promotion budget | (11) | 3.64 | (26) | 3.08 | (36) | 2.16 |
| Consumer motivation | (13) | 3.64 | (14) | 3.25 | (2) | 3.59 |
| Pricing tools II: flexible break-even, demand estimation | (14) | 3.62 | (9) | 3.38 | (33) | 2.40 |
| Role of marketing research in the decision process | (15) | 3.60 | (14) | 3.25 | (21) | 2.71 |
| Pricing strategies: skimming, penetration, price-lining, etc. | (16) | 3.58 | (16) | 3.23 | (15) | 2.98 |
| Product management through product life cycle | (17) | 3.56 | (13) | 3.26 | (18) | 2.88 |
| Research techniques of experimentation | (18) | 3.54 | (11) | 3.30 | (31) | 2.51 |
| The marketing environment-political, legal, economic, social | (19) | 3.51 | (19) | 3.17 | (4) | 3.50 |
| Evaluation of advertising | (20) | 3.50 | (25) | 3.10 | (10) | 3.06 |
| New product development | (21) | 3.49 | (28) | 3.03 | (9) | 3.11 |
| Market structure-mktg. implications | (22) | 3.45 | (22) | 3.13 | (16) | 2.94 |
| Organizational buying behavior | (23) | 3.41 | (27) | 3.07 | (14) | 2.98 |
| Distribution channels & utility delivery | (24) | 3.41 | (21) | 3.14 | (23) | 2.67 |
| Manufacturer's options for channel control | (25) | 3.40 | (30) | 3.00 | (29) | 2.53 |
| Branding strategies and their rationale | (26) | 3.37 | (29) | 3.01 | (7) | 3.19 |
| Cost trade-offs in logistics | (27) | 3.36 | (24) | 3.10 | (34) | 2.25 |
| Research techniques of observation | (28) | 3.35 | (20) | 3.15 | (19) | 2.75 |
| Promotion mix and communication objectives and imperatives | (29) | 3.31 | (33) | 2.93 | (27) | 2.58 |
| Management of personal selling | (30) | 3.27 | (32) | 2.93 | (29) | 2.49 |
| Techniques of survey research | (31) | 3.26 | (18) | 3.17 | (26) | 2.57 |
| Channel characters: roles and goals | (32) | 3.20 | (23) | 3.12 | (28) | 2.56 |
| Shadow pricing in non-dollar transaction situations | (33) | 3.15 | (36) | 2.76 | (24) | 2.59 |
| Trends in distribution | (34) | 3.10 | (30) | 3.00 | (19) | 2.75 |
| Evaluation of alternatives by decision trees | (35) | 2.94 | (34) | 2.90 | (37) | 2.13 |
| Innovation diffusion | (36) | 2.90 | (35) | 2.81 | (22) | 2.67 |
| Origin of marketing | (37) | 2.13 | (37) | 2.23 | (35) | 2.17 |

this case the groups are students' fields of study, llapsed to: accounting, other business, and non-business jors. Eighteen variables for potential inclusion were lected by judgmental sample of one to three subject/ skill areas, which loaded heavily (i.e. were highly correlated with the factor), from each of the first five factors obtained from the career importance and consumer/citizen role importance factor analyses.

The step-wise discriminant analysis was performed on 40 of the 53 cases. Three of the cases had either missing values on two or more variables or chose not to indicate their field of study. Ten cases were withheld for subsequent model validation. With each group's prior probability established by the sample's proportion of cases falling into each group, nine of 18 variables proved sufficient to correctly classify 92.5 percent of these 40 students. This yields a chi-square value of 63.01 which is significant at $p < .001$.

In the validation sample, the two standardized discriminant scores were calculated for each case and compared to the classification functions from the model building sample. Seven out of these ten cases were correctly classified. The likelihood of achieving this level of success by chance alone is given by:

$$P \ (r=7 \ / \ n=10, \ p=.45) = .102 \tag{1}$$

This is evidence enough to conclude that the interests of students in accounting are quite homogeneous, as are the interests of other business and non-business students. Furthermore, the interests across these three student groups are significantly different.

The second stage of analysis is required to explore the interest differences across segments in more detail. Attention must shift from multivariate to univariate analysis. Table 2 presents importance means for the three student segments for each subject/skill area yielding a significant F-statistic in a oneway analysis of variance. For example, in the "Consumer decision making" subject area, on average, accountants scored it 2.92 on importance to their career opportunities; other business students rated it 3.88 in importance and non-business students scored it 4.17. The regression approach to testing for equality among group means (ANOVA) yielded an F-statistic of 5.31, which is significant at $p < .01$.

It is worthwhile to note that all the statistically significant differences occur within the career opportunities importance category. Also, accountants give the marketing principles course its lowest overall importance score and with amazing consistency rate almost all subject/skill areas lower than the other two segments. Non-accounting business majors express primary interests in decision-making and management areas. Non-business students show above average interest in advertising and behavioral areas.

Finally, while multiple univariate tests on the data tend to reduce the effective alpha-level, the identification of 18 student segment mean differences across 37 subject/skill areas cannot be attributed to mere chance.

## DISCUSSION

This type of evaluation and segmentation analysis is meaningless unless it can be employed to improve the marketing principles course offering. In the teaching-evaluating situation of this study, aggregate importance ratings of each subject/skill area have been examined for congruence with their corresponding teaching objectives. Overall, there is reasonably consistent agreement. Two discrepant areas, however, are "Evaluation of alternatives by decision trees" and "Shadow-pricing in non-dollar transaction situations."

### Pursuit of Congruence

When presented with discrepancies, the instructor has two strategies for achieving balance. Notice that the options pivot on the two elements of the marketing concept: (1) satisfaction of consumer needs, and (2) the achievement of organizational objectives.

The instructor's first alternative is the employment of more creative approaches to specific subject areas in order to increase the students' perceived relevance of those areas. In addition to increased showmanship; meaningful examples, short cases, involvement exercises, and computer games are possible tactics for this strategy.

The second alternative involves the re-examination and modification of teaching objectives in light of the student feedback. If, for example, students showed a greater concern for exploring organizational buyer behavior, the instructor may wish to devote additional time and teaching resources to that marketing subject. However, since teaching is often a zero-sum game, additional resources for one area may mean fewer resources for another. Reallocation, therefore, requires the existence of slack or feasible tradeoffs.

It is important to note that these two options will rarely be equally attractive in discrepant situations. Obviously, instructors often have, and should have, teaching objectives on which they will not compromise. In the event of a student consensus that break-even analysis is relatively unimportant, it would likely be inadvisable to lessen its significance among course objectives. The instructor in this case must strive for a more germane approach to the subject.

Returning to the two discrepant areas previously identified, in light of student-instructor shared high valuation of "Alternative evaluation," it is disappointing that students are not convinced of the relevance of the decision tree approach. Rather than compromise on this objective, efforts have been made in subsequent sections of the principles course to wield more colorful and realistic examples. (Perhaps the new product go/no-go situation, the ice cream vendor heading for the beach, and the drill/don't drill oil well examples have been a bit overworked.) Increased discussion time has been devoted to the technique's strengths, weaknesses and possible alternatives for identifying the best course of action.

In an effort to remedy the "Shadow-pricing" discrepancy, students have been assigned an additional reading. It is hoped that, in conjunction with the previous quarter's lecture/discussion, Dilley's "Case of Nebulous Numbers" [1] will bring home the point that when the marketing concept is broadened to non-business activities new measures must substitute for sales and profits in performance evaluation.

### Implications of Student Segments

The potential for taking truly substantive action in appreciation of the segmentation analysis rests in the hands of curriculum committees and college administrators. The evidence indicates the presence of substantial interest differences across students pursuing accounting, other business and non-business degrees. Certainly, should special marketing courses be offered, the accounting section, for example, could press on with more rigor in pricing and forecasting without substantial sacrifice on other objectives. The non-business section, meanwhile, could progress more slowly through quantitative aspects of research and pricing without detracting from critical areas of consumer behavior and promotion strategies.

Likely responses to this proposed curriculum change are that, in addition to scheduling problems, students benefit from having other students from a broad range of backgrounds in the classroom to present contrasting viewpoints. This may have some validity, but it has yet to be demonstrated. Furthermore, unless the class format is organized around a remarkably high amount of meaningful student contribution, it is generally the instructor who plays the "Devil's Advocate" (or some role less formidable in presenting diverse perspectives.

TABLE 2

SUBJECT/SKILL AREA IMPORTANCE SCORE MEANS STATISTICALLY DIFFERENT
ACROSS STUDENT SEGMENTS

| Subject/Skill Area | Accounting (n = 13) | Other Business (n = 26) | Non-Business (n = 12) | F-Statistic |
|---|---|---|---|---|
| The marketing environment | 3.31 | 3.81 | 3.18 | $2.88^e$ |
| Consumer motivation | 3.00 | 3.77 | 4.08 | $3.78^d$ |
| Consumer decision-making | 2.92 | 3.88 | 4.17 | $5.31^b$ |
| Role of marketing research | 3.23 | 4.00 | 3.50 | $2.65^e$ |
| Research techniques: Experimentation | 3.15 | 3.81 | 3.42 | $2.76^e$ |
| New product development | 2.62 | 4.00 | 3.42 | $7.73^a$ |
| Product management over the product life cycle | 2.54 | 4.00 | 3.58 | $7.17^a$ |
| Branding strategies and their rationale | 2.46 | 3.65 | 3.67 | $4.91^c$ |
| Market structure – marketing implications | 2.85 | 3.65 | 3.75 | $3.07^e$ |
| Demand, supply, competition factors in pricing | 3.00 | 4.00 | 3.58 | $3.68^d$ |
| Distribution channels and utility delivery | 2.77 | 3.65 | 3.67 | $3.23^d$ |
| Promotion mix and communication objectives and imperatives | 2.54 | 3.65 | 3.40 | $4.51^c$ |
| Management of personal selling | 2.15 | 3.58 | 3.83 | $9.34^a$ |
| Evaluation of advertising | 2.46 | 3.72 | 4.08 | $7.18^a$ |
| Problem recognition | 3.54 | 4.44 | 4.33 | $6.13^a$ |
| Concept integration | 3.15 | 4.16 | 3.82 | $4.27^c$ |
| Data use and development | 3.46 | 4.28 | 3.82 | $4.33^c$ |
| Familiarity with secondary data | 3.23 | 4.08 | 3.58 | $3.58^d$ |
| Research techniques of observation[f] | 3.00 | 2.85 | 2.18 | $2.30^{(n.s.)}$ |
| Research techniques of experimentation[f] | 2.77 | 2.35 | 2.27 | $1.33^{(n.s.)}$ |
| Promotion mix and communication objectives and imperatives | 2.62 | 2.72 | 2.33 | $.45^{(n.s.)}$ |
| Problem recognition[f] | 3.31 | 3.36 | 3.64 | $.33^{(n.s.)}$ |
| Marketing principles overall | 3.17 | 3.96 | 3.73 | $2.68^e$ |

[a] $p < .005$

[b] $p < .01$

[c] $p < .02$

[d] $p < .05$

[e] $p < .1$

[f] Indicates variable measures importance in role as consumer/citizen.

*Indicates variable showing no statistical significance by itself, yet selected for inclusion in the discriminant function discussed earlier.

While this issue is wrestled with in the offices of deans and department chairmen, instructors must make concerted efforts to implement segmentation strategies on the intra-course level. This study's findings have resulted in a considerable increase in the number and nature of pre-facing remarks for various marketing subject areas. For example, in recognition of their apparent need for closure or structure, accounting students are encouraged to "bite the bullet" in consumer behavior discussions that they may eventually "see the light." Also, problem sets and examination questions have been broadened to include, for example, market research issues in a public school setting, more retailing problem situations, as well as traditional product management situations.

## CONCLUSION

This article has argued that successful efforts to market marketing require an increased understanding of student needs in relationship to teaching objectives. The identification and prioritization of student interests in the marketing principles course have facilitated their comparison with instructor valuations. Discrepancies have led to significant modifications in subsequent sections of the principles course.

Moreover, the identification of student segments suggests the desirability of separate basic marketing courses for accounting, other business, and non-business students. While administrators and committees attend to this issue, instructors must make conscious efforts to serve each of the unique segments harbored in their introductory marketing courses.

## REFERENCES

1. Dilley, Steven C. "Case of Nebulous Numbers," Harvard Business Review 52 (November-December, 1974), p. 42-52.

2. Enis, Ben M. "Marketing Principles Course's Principal Principle Should be to Market Marketing," Marketing News, Vol. 10, No. 3 (July 30, 1976), p. 1+.

3. _____. "Some Thoughts and a Little Data on the Formal Evaluation of Teaching Effectiveness in Market-ing," in Combined Proceedings, Fred C. Alvine, ed. Chicago: American Marketing Association, 1971, p. 94-7.

4. Kulik, James A. and Chen-Lin C. Kulik. "Student Ratings of Instruction," Teaching of Psychology, Vol.1, No. 2 (December, 1974), p. 51-7.

5. McCarthy, Jerome. "Has Marketing Really Lost Share?," in Reflections on Progress in Marketing, L. George Smith, ed. Chicago: American Marketing Association, 1964, p. 498-99.

6. Meloan, Taylor W. "Marketing Education in Transition," in Reflections on Progress in Marketing, L. George Smith, ed. Chicago: American Marketing Association, 1964, p. 505.

7. Painter, John J. and Kent L. Grangin. "An Investi-gation of Determinants of Student Course Ratings," in Combined Proceedings, Boris W. Becker, ed. Chicago: American Marketing Association, 1972, p. 90-4.

8. Twedt, Dik. "Business Degrees Show Steady Increase, But Marketing Education's Share Shrinks," Marketing News, Vol. 10, No. 3 (July, 1976), p. 1+.

9. Uhr, Ernest B. and W. Daniel Roundtree. "Who Likes Marketing: Educational Differences Between Students with Favorable and Unfavorable Images of Marketing," in Combined Proceedings, Boris W. Becker, ed. Chicago: American Marketing Association, 1972, p. 153-7.

10. Whipple, Thomas. "Using Student Evaluations to Improve Graduate Marketing Courses and Instruction," in Combined Proceedings, Thomas V. Greer, ed. Chicago: American Marketing Association, 1973, p. 52-8.

# VALENCE FOR REWARDS AS A FUNCTION OF SATISFACTION AMONG INDUSTRIAL SALESMEN

Neil M. Ford, University of Wisconsin-Madison
Orville C. Walker, Jr., University of Minnesota-Minneapolis
Gilbert A. Churchill, Jr., University of Wisconsin-Madison

## ABSTRACT

Although a considerable amount of research exists in industrial psychology pertaining to the motivation of employees, very little research exists pertaining to the motivation of the field salesforce. In particular, this article explores three particular questions concerning the valence (strength) of rewards as viewed by actual sales people. These are: (1) Is there any consistent relationship between the salesman's satisfaction with his current rewards and his valence for future rewards? (2) Does a salesman's satisfaction or dissatisfaction with the amount of a particular reward he is currently receiving affect his valence for more of that reward? (3) Does a salesman's satisfaction with one kind of reward influence his valence for other kinds of rewards? The paper presents answers to these questions and discusses their implications for management.

## INTRODUCTION

In many ways, the practice of sales management resembles the practice of medicine by tribal witch doctors. Sales managers must often rely on large doses of folklore, tradition, intuition and personal experience in deciding how to motivate and direct the performance of their salesforces. While many firms spend thousands to learn why their customers behave the way they do, too few have conducted any formal research to help improve the motivation and performance of the salespeople who deal with those customers. Unfortunately, sales managers have also been unable to turn to marketing academicians for any information or guidance. There is little published theory and even less empirical research concerning the variables that influence one salesperson to perform better than another.

## CONCEPTUAL FOUNDATION

To improve understanding and encourage research in the area of salesmen's behavior, the authors have developed a conceptual model of sales motivation and performance [18]. One of the major components of this model describes the determinants of a salesman's motivation to perform his job. As outlined in Diagram 1, motivation is defined as the amount of effort the salesman desires to expend on each of the various activities or tasks associated with his job, such as calling on potential new accounts, planning sales presentations, filling out reports and so forth. The model assumes that expending effort on each of these activities will lead to some level of achievement on one or more dimensions of job performance, such as total sales volume, new account sales, quota attainment, etc. It is further assumed that the salesman's level of performance on at least some of these dimensions will be evaluated by his superiors and be rewarded with one or more rewards, such as increased pay, recognition, or advancement.

The model suggests, then, that a salesman's motivation to expend effort on any specific task (i) depends on three psychological variables.

(1) Expectancy--($E_{ij}$)--the salesman's estimate of the probability that expending a given amount of effort on task (i) will lead to an improved level of performance on some performance dimension (j). Expectancies are the salesman's perceptions of the linkages between job activities and the various dimensions of job performance.

(2) Instrumentality--($I_{jk}$)--the salesman's estimate of the probability that achieving an improved level of performance on some performance dimension (j) will lead to increased attainment of a particular reward (k). Instrumentalities are the salesman's perceptions of the linkages between specific types and levels of job performance and the kinds and amounts of rewards he is likely to receive.

(3) Valence for Rewards--($V_k$)--the salesman's perception of the desirability of receiving increased amounts of each of the variety of rewards he might attain as a result of improved performance.

The model also indicates that each of these three motivational variables is, in turn, influenced by a variety of environmental, organizational, and personal factors. In general, though, a salesman's motivation level for some activity (i) is a function of his expectancies times his instrumentalities times his valences, i.e.,

$$F_i = \sum_{j=1}^{P} E_{ij} \times ( \sum_{k=1}^{r} I_{jk} \times V_k)$$

## OBJECTIVES

This paper focuses on one aspect of the "valence for rewards" variable, specifically, the relationship between a salesman's current level of satisfaction and his valences for rewards.

(1) Is there any consistent relationship between a salesman's satisfaction with his current rewards and his valence for future rewards?

(2) Does a salesman's satisfaction or dissatisfaction with the amount of a particular reward he is currently receiving affect his valence for more of that reward?

(3) Does a salesman's satisfaction with one kind of reward influence his valences for other kinds of rewards?

The basic issue underlying these questions is whether a salesman's satisfaction with the rewards he is currently receiving has any impact on his valence for more of those rewards, or on his desire for different kinds of rewards.

## EXISTING THEORY AND RESEARCH

### The Marketing Literature

While the relationship between satisfaction and valence for rewards has seldom been explicitly studied by marketing researchers, the issue has often been alluded to in

FIGURE 1

THE MOTIVATION COMPONENT

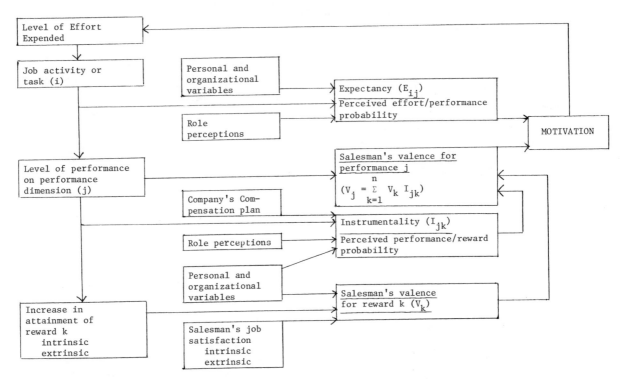

the marketing and sales management literature, particularly in discussions of financial compensation. Some sales executives assume that the promise of more pay will continue to motivate salespeople regardless of how much they earn or how satisfied they are with their current pay [12; 17, p. 111]. Other authors suggest that there is a point beyond which offering more pay produces diminishing returns in terms of motivation and effort [6]. As one executive said, "When a man has gotten his kids through college and he's earning a comfortable salary ... he has very little incentive to earn another thousand bucks or two ..." [16, p. 51].

The Psychology Literature

The psychological theories most relevant for explaining the relationship between satisfaction and valence for rewards are the need hierarchy theories of Maslow and Alderfer [1,2,13,14,15]. Maslow's theory classifies all human needs into five categories: 1) physiological needs; 2) safety/security needs; 3) needs for belonging and love; 4) esteem needs (i.e., both self-esteem and recognition or respect from others); and 5) self-actualization needs (i.e., self-fulfillment, personal growth, and the realization of one's potential). Alderfer's model is similar except that it contains only three levels: 1) existence needs; 2) relatedness (social) needs; and 3) growth (personal fulfillment needs).

Both Maslow and Alderfer argue that human needs exist in a hierarchy of prepotency such that the lowest order needs are inherently more important than the higher order needs. Thus, before higher order needs can become important for motivating an individual, that person's lowest order physiological needs must first be satisfied. Once those physiological needs are satisfied, their strength decreases and the next higher level needs become the most important motivators of behavior. This process of "need

satisfaction/ decreased importance/increased importance of the next highest need" repeats itself until the highest level of the need hierarchy is reached. Both Maslow and Alderfer argue, though, that at the top of the hierarchy, the relationship between satisfaction and importance reverses itself. In other words, increased satisfaction of self-actualization or growth needs serves to increase the strength of those needs for an individual.

Relatively little research has been done concerning the effects of satisfaction on the importance of the highest order self-actualization and growth needs. Further, the research that does exist does not entirely support the idea that increased satisfaction of such needs leads to an increase in their importance. These needs do appear to be insatiable, though, in the sense that high levels of satisfaction do not reduce the amount of importance that people attach to personal growth and fulfillment [10, p. 34; 7, 11].

There is obviously a close correspondence between the need categories Maslow and Alderfer have identified and the kinds of rewards used to motivate workers. For example, pay is most relevant for satisfying a worker's lowest order existence and safety needs. Promotion, recognition and respect correspond most closely to the middle level social needs. Finally, opportunities for personal growth and accomplishment are rewards that closely match the worker's needs for self-actualization [11].

This correspondence between needs and rewards, however, i probably not perfect since it is possible for a single reward to satisfy more than one need. Pay, for example, may help satisfy a worker's social and esteem needs as well as his existence needs. The relationship between needs and rewards is close enough, though, that it is possible to think of a "hierarchy of rewards" which corresponds to the need hierarchies outlined above.

Instead of a five-level or a three-level hierarchy of human needs, the existing research suggests that there is only a two-level hierarchy, with existence and safety needs in the lower category and social and fulfillment needs at the higher level. There is substantial evidence to support the view that lower order existence and security needs must be satisfied before higher order social and growth needs will become important, and that the satisfaction of lower order needs reduces their importance to the individual [1,5,8,11]. On the other hand, there is very little evidence to suggest that a consistent hierarchy of higher order needs exists above the safety/security level. Most people seem to be motivated by more than one higher level need simultaneously [10, p. 34; 11].

### RESEARCH PROPOSITIONS

In light of the existing research, we will also assume that salesmen have a two-stage need hierarchy. Thus, we can group the seven types of rewards examined in this study into two classes corresponding to the two need categories. Low order rewards are defined as those which primarily satisfy the lower order existence and safety needs; i.e., pay and security. High order needs are those which satisfy the higher order social and fulfillment needs. Promotion, recognition, respect, sense of accomplishment and opportunities for personal growth are all classified as high order rewards.

Given the theories of Maslow and Alderfer and the existing research in psychology, the following research propositions are suggested concerning the effects of satisfaction on salesmen's valences for low order and high order rewards.

Proposition #1: Salesmen who are relatively satisfied with their current attainment of low order rewards will have a lower valence for more of those rewards than salesmen who are dissatisfied with the amount of low order rewards they are currently receiving.

Proposition #2: Salesmen who are relatively satisfied with their current attainment of low order rewards will have a higher valence for high order rewards than salesmen who are dissatisfied with the low order rewards they are currently receiving.

Proposition #3: Salesmen who are relatively satisfied with their current attainment of high order rewards will have a higher valence for more of those rewards than salesmen who are dissatisfied with the high order rewards they are currently receiving.

### RESEARCH METHODS

Data Collection and Response Rates

The results obtained in this paper were obtained from a sample of two large companies employing 481 salespeople. Information was obtained from salesmen via mail questionnaires. Due to the large number of questions involved and the variety of kinds of information sought, each salesman received two separate questionnaires about three weeks apart. An introductory letter from the top sales executive in each company and follow-up letters from the researchers were used to encourage response.

Completed sets of questionnaires were received from 227 of the 481 salesmen, for a response rate of 47 percent. It should be noted, however, that an additional 202 salesmen (about 40 percent of the sample) returned either the first or the second questionnaire, but not both. While the responses of these individuals could not be used in

this study, a comparison of their responses and their demographic characteristics with those of the salesmen who completed both questionnaires did not reveal any systematic differences.

Data Collection Instruments

Each salesman's valence for rewards was measured by asking him to indicate the amount of additional satisfaction he would receive from a specified increase in each of a number of rewards. The rewards were company-specific and were chosen on the basis of preliminary personal interviews with small groups of salesmen and sales managers from each firm. In company "A," salesmen indicated their valences for 13 different rewards, while in company "B," nine rewards were presented to the respondents. For purposes of analysis, these specific rewards were grouped into the following seven reward categories.

1) A 10 percent increase in pay/financial compensation.

2) A 10 percent increase in job security.

3) Promotion--a higher level job; a better territory; larger account responsibility.

4) Recognition--selection for some form of "sales club," or other form of formal recognition.

5) A 10 percent increase in the amount of liking and respect received from other people the salesman has contact with on the job.

6) A 10 percent increase in opportunities for personal growth and development.

7) A 10 percent increase in the salesman's feelings of worthwhile accomplishment on the job.

Each salesman was asked to rank all of the rewards listed on the questionnaire according to the relative amount of satisfaction he would receive from each. They were then told to place their highest ranked reward at the 100° mark on a 100 point "thermometer" scale and to position all of the remaining rewards on the scale according to the satisfaction each would provide relative to their most desired reward. This procedure produced a set of quantitative valence scores from each salesman in a form that approximates ratio scale data.

Each salesman's current satisfaction level was measured with an instrument that was developed specifically for industrial salesmen. The 95-item instrument provided satisfaction scores for each of seven job components: 1) the job itself; 2) fellow workers; 3) supervision; 4) company policies and support; 5) pay; 6) promotion; and 7) customers. A more detailed description of this instrument, including an evaluation of its reliability and validity, has been published elsewhere [3].

The "pay" and "promotion" component satisfaction scores were used in this study as measures of each salesman's satisfaction with his current financial rewards and promotional opportunities. Five relevant items from the "job" component were used as a measure of the salesman's satisfaction with his own sense of accomplishment, and eight items from the same component provided a measure of satisfaction with opportunities for personal growth. Unfortunately, the satisfaction scale included only one or two items relevant to security, recognition and liking and respect. Since such small numbers of items are unlikely to constitute valid measures by themselves, we were unable to determine salesmen's current satisfaction with those rewards in this study.

### RESEARCH RESULTS

Since measures were obtained only for salesmen's satisfaction with their pay, promotional opportunities, sense of accomplishment and personal growth, the analysis in this section concentrates on the relationship between satisfaction and valence for only those four rewards. Pay will be considered representative of low order rewards, while promotion, sense of accomplishment and personal growth will be evaluated as high order rewards. An examination of these four rewards should provide an adequate test of our theoretical propositions since they were ranked as the four most important rewards by the salesmen in both companies in the sample [4].

Table 1 and Figure 1 show the relationships between salesmen's current satisfaction with each type of reward and their valence for more of that reward. These data indicate a strong negative relationship between satisfaction with pay and valence for more pay. This relationship is statistically significant at the p < .01 level and it supports proposition #1.

It is interesting to note in Figure 1 that the relationship between satisfaction and valence is similar for salesmen from both companies, even though their absolute valences for pay are quite different.

When the three high order rewards are examined individually, as they are in Table 1, the predicted positive relationship between satisfaction and valence is not present at a statistically significant level. There is a tendency, though, for valences to be somewhat higher among satisfied salesmen for all three of these rewards. However, when salesmen's valences for the three high order rewards are combined and viewed as a function of their overall satisfaction with those rewards, the positive relationship between satisfaction and valence becomes statistically significant at the p < .10 level. This relationship, shown in Table 2, supports proposition #3. Taken together, the measurement of the three higher order rewards is more reliable than when they are examined individually. It is also more conceptually correct to examine the relationship between satisfaction and aggregate higher order rewards since the theories of Maslow, and particularly Alderfer, focus on broad need categories.

Figure 2 shows graphically the relationship between total satisfaction with high order rewards and overall valence. While an overall positive relationship exists, it is

largely due to company A even though the absolute valences for such rewards are lower than in company B.

Finally, the effect of satisfaction with low order rewards (i.e., pay) on salesmen's valences for higher order rewards is shown in Table 3. These data do not show the kind of positive relationship predicted by proposition #2. The relationship is in the predicted direction among salesmen in company B, but is is in the opposite direction among respondents from company A. One possible explanation for this phenomenon may be the strong dissatisfaction with pay (and the high valence for more pay) among the salesmen of company A who averaged $4,500 less per year than salesmen in company B. Also, there had been a sharp decline in the percentage of salesmen reaching quota and qualifying for bonuses in company A during the year preceding this study, due to increases in quotas of as much as 25% over the year before. While Table 3 compares those salesmen who are relatively satisfied with those who are relatively unsatisfied, the range of pay satisfaction scores in our sample may be strongly skewed toward the low end of the scale; particularly among the salesmen from company A who may not have reached a sufficient absolute level of satisfaction for higher order rewards to become very attractive or motivating.

## DISCUSSION AND CONCLUSIONS

The results of this study are not inconsistent with the conventional wisdom that salesmen are strongly motivated by money. Pay received the highest average valence score from the salesmen in our sample [4]. However, this study also supports the need hierarchy theories of Maslow and Alderfer. The salesmen in the sample who felt most satisfied with their current financial compensation had the lowest valences for earning increased pay. This suggests that it is possible to pay salesmen too much in the sense that the marginal effort produced by each additional dollar of pay will probably decline after a salesman has achieved a level of pay that he finds "satisfactory."

TABLE 1

VALENCE FOR REWARDS AS A FUNCTION OF CURRENT SATISFACTION WITH THOSE REWARDS

| Reward | Company | Satisfaction Level | | | F Ratios (a) |
| | | Lowest Quartile | Middle Half | Highest Quartile | |
|---|---|---|---|---|---|
| LOW ORDER REWARDS: | | | | | |
| Pay | A | 93.2 | 91.4 | 87.1 | |
| | B | 86.6 | 80.2 | 74.9 | |
| | Total | 90.8 | 87.5 | 83.6 | 5.28*** |
| HIGH ORDER REWARDS: | | | | | |
| Promotion | A | 64.5 | 64.2 | 67.0 | |
| | B | 78.9 | 73.7 | 73.9 | |
| | Total | 67.3 | 67.7 | 70.1 | .18 |
| Personal Growth | A | 75.3 | 71.5 | 74.7 | |
| | B | 84.2 | 89.0 | 90.7 | |
| | Total | 78.8 | 77.6 | 82.7 | 1.33 |
| Sense of Accomplishment | A | 74.9 | 72.8 | 81.9 | |
| | B | 85.3 | 84.2 | 84.6 | |
| | Total | 78.5 | 76.6 | 82.8 | .73 |

a) Degrees of freedom - 2,224.
* = p = < .10;  ** = p = < .05;  *** = p = < .01

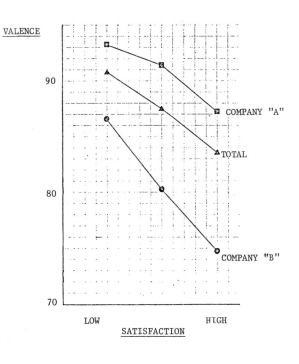

FIGURE 1

VALENCE FOR PAY AS A FUNCTION OF SATISFACTION WITH PAY

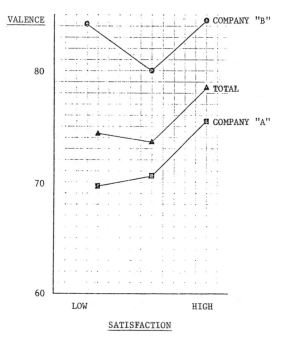

FIGURE 2

VALENCE FOR HIGHER ORDER REWARDS AS A FUNCTION OF
SATISFACTION WITH HIGHER ORDER REWARDS

TABLE 2

OVERALL VALENCE FOR HIGHER ORDER REWARDS AS A FUNCTION OF
CURRENT OVERALL SATISFACTION WITH HIGHER ORDER REWARDS

| | | Overall Satisfaction with Higher Order Rewards | | | | |
|---|---|---|---|---|---|---|
| Rewards | Company | Lowest Quartile | Middle Half | Highest Quartile | F ratio | (a) |
| Overall Valence for Higher Order Rewards | A | 69.7 | 70.5 | 75.4 | | |
| | B | 84.1 | 80.0 | 84.4 | | |
| | Total | 74.3 | 73.7 | 78.4 | 2.19* | |

(a) Degrees of freedom = 2,224.
* = p <.10;  ** = <.05;  *** = <.01

TABLE 3

OVERALL VALENCE FOR HIGHER ORDER REWARDS AS A FUNCTION OF CURRENT
SAFISFACTION WITH PAY

| | | Pay Satisfaction Level | | | | |
|---|---|---|---|---|---|---|
| Rewards | Company | Lowest Quartile | Middle Half | Highest Quartile | F Ratio | (a) |
| Average Valence for Higher Order Rewards | A | 70.6 | 70.6 | 73.9 | | |
| | B | 85.2 | 81.6 | 79.5 | | |
| | Total | 75.7 | 74.5 | 75.5 | .10 | |

(a) Degrees of freedom = 2,224.

The administrative problem, of course, is that different salesmen may define a "satisfactory" pay level quite differently. Satisfaction with pay not only reflects the amount a salesman is earning, but also the amount of financial obligations he has, his alternative employment opportunities, and other personal characteristics [4]. Thus, a given compensation plan may be very effective for motivating the salesmen in one company but not another. This suggests the need for intracompany studies of salesmen's valences as a basis for designing compensation systems. Similarly, a salesman's satisfaction with his pay, and his valence for more pay, may change over time as his environment and personal characteristics change. Managements should survey their salesmen's valences for rewards periodically and, if necessary, adjust the compensation system to meet changing valences with the salesforce.

While the salesmen in the sample had relatively high valences for pay, they also valued higher order rewards, such as opportunities for accomplishment and personal growth. These rewards were considered second in importance by the total sample, and in company B, they were valued even more highly than pay. In addition, when high order rewards were examined as a group, we found a positive relationship between salesmen's satisfaction with high order rewards and their valence for more of those rewards. This underlines the desirability of placing greater emphasis on such rewards for motivating its salesforce. It would seem wise to offer a variety of promotional opportunities (particularly within the salesforce) and opportunities for career and personal development as rewards for good performance.

Unfortunately, few firms have developed formal mechanisms for rewarding salesmen with the kinds of self-fulfillment they desire. Part of the reason for this is probably that such rewards are difficult to control and administer. After all, a sense of accomplishment or personal growth really refers to the salesman's perceptions or emotional feelings about the value of his work. He experiences them for himself. They are not given to him by management in the same way that he is given a paycheck.

On the other hand, however, management does have some control over the content of the salesman's job, and over the opportunities the salesman has to achieve high order rewards. These opportunities can be directly linked to a salesman's performance and used as part of the firm's reward system. For example, a company could develop "advanced sales training" or "career development" programs that would be attended by only a few select, high performing salesmen each year. Similarly, selected salesmen could be given an active role in training other salesmen or they could be used as a "panel of advisers" in the formulation of some company policies. The critical point, though, is that such opportunities for personal development must be directly tied to good job performance in order to be effective as motivational tools.

Finally, a word of caution. Due to the limited number of firms in our sample, these findings must necessarily be considered tentative. Hopefully, they will help stimulate further research in the area of salesforce motivation--an area that has been neglected for too long.

REFERENCES

1. Alderfer, C. P. "An Empirical Test of a New Theory of Human Needs," Organizational Behavior and Human Performance, 4 (1969), 142-175.

2. _____. Existence, Relatedness and Growth: Human Needs in Organizational Settings. New York: The Free Press, 1972.

3. Churchill, G. A., Jr., N. M. Ford, and O. C. Walker, Jr. "Measuring the Job Satisfaction of Industrial Salesmen," Journal of Marketing Research, 11 (August 1974), 254-260.

4. _____. "Motivating the Industrial Salesforce: The Attractiveness of Alternative Rewards," Report No. 76-115, Cambridge, Mass.: The Marketing Science Institute, October 1976.

5. Dachler, H. P., and C. L. Hulin. "A Reconsideration of the Relationship Between Satisfaction and Judged Importance of Environmental and Job Characteristics," Organizational Behavior and Human Performance, 4 (1969), 252-266.

6. Darmon, R. Y. "Salesmen's Response to Financial Incentives," Journal of Marketing Research, 38 (July 1974), 39-46.

7. Deci, E. L. "Effects of Externally Mediated Rewards on Intrinsic Motivation," Journal of Personality and Social Psychology, 18 (1971), 150-115.

8. Keys, A., J. Brozek, A. Henschel, O. Mickelsen, and H. Taylor. The Biology of Human Starvation. Minneapolis: The University of Minnesota Press, 1950. 2 Vols.

9. Lawler, E. E., II. Pay and Organizational Effectiveness: A Psychological View. New York: McGraw-Hill, 1971.

10. _____. Motivation in Work Organizations. Monterey, Calif.: Brooks/Cole Publishing Company, 1973.

11. Lawler, E. E., II, and J. L. Suttle. "A Causal Correlation Test of the Need Hierarchy Concept," Organizational Behavior and Human Performance, 7 (1972), 265-287.

12. Leahy, J. K. "Total Motivation Equals Top Performance," Sales Management, (April 30, 1973), 265-287.

13. Maslow, A. H. "A Theory of Human Motivation," Psychological Review, 50 (1943), 370-396.

14. _____. Toward a Psychology of Being, 2nd edition. Princeton, N.J.: Van Nostrand, Reinhold, 1968.

15. _____. Motivation and Personality, 2nd edition. New York: Harper and Row, 1970.

16. Sales Management. "Re-Motivating Older Salesmen," (May 19, 1961), 51-56.

17. Smyth, R. C. "Financial Incentives for Salesmen," Harvard Business Review, (January-February, 1968), 109-117.

18. Walker, O. C., Jr., G. A. Churchill, Jr., and N. M. Ford. "Motivation and Performance in Industrial Settings: Existing Knowledge and Needed Research," Journal of Marketing Research, forthcoming.

# BEHAVIORAL EFFECTS OF MANAGERIAL SATISFACTION AND MOTIVATION IN THE RETAIL ORGANIZATION

Richard L. Oliver, University of Kentucky
Arthur P. Brief, University of Iowa

## ABSTRACT

In contrast to an emerging body of research on industrial salesmen, the behavioral analysis of retail sales and managerial personnel has not been systematically developed. This paper seeks to expand the small body of retail personnel research through an analysis of the behavioral consequences of manageral satisfaction and motivation. Specifically, two models borrowed from industrial psychology incorporating intervening variables were used to examine the effects of overall job satisfaction and motivational perceptions in a predictive study of subsequent turnover and performance. The sample consisted of 88 department managers in a multistore, multiline midwestern retailing corporation. The results showed that satisfaction appeared to play a role in turnover decisions, that motivation was sequentially related to performance, but that little overlap between satisfaction and motivation effects was evident. Implications of these findings for retail management are discussed.

## INTRODUCTION

A new wave of interest in the field of applied marketing management has spurred recent research on the behavior of industrial salesmen and, to a lesser extent, retail personnel. This new focus has been evidenced by a number of studies relating to the determinants of salesmen's satisfaction and performance [e.g. 3, 6, 8, 22, 26] in an apparant response to earlier calls for new thinking and research in the area [11, 27]. A concomitant research tradition has also been slowly emerging in the area of retail management where studies investigating various aspects of the sales manager's job have appeared in the *Journal of Retailing* [e.g. 5, 10, 15, 21]. Unfortunately, interest in the latter area has been frustrated because the manager's job is typically more ambiguous and his performance less objective than that of the industrial salesman. Accordingly, the purpose of this paper is to suggest an empirical base for applying a number of behavioral principles now being used in the sales literature to the retail manager's satisfaction and performance and to address the notion of a theoretical link between the two constructs.

### Theories of Satisfaction and Performance

Practitioners and academicians alike have been in dispute for years over the causal interrelationship between job satisfaction and performance. Lately, reviewers [9, 29, 31] are generally agreed that neither the time honored satisfaction → performance theory nor the more recent performance → satisfaction interpretation is entirely accurate. Rather, the relationship is thought to be time dependent with intervening variables operating as shown below:

satisfaction (1) → intervening → performance (1) →
               variables

    intervening → satisfaction (2)...
    variables

In the scheme below, those variables intervening between satisfaction (1) and performance (1) are thought to be motivation constructs while those between performance (1) and satisfaction (2) are believed to be related to the attainment of intrinsic and extrinsic rewards. Because of the intervening variables and the temporal nature of the hypothesized causal relationships, no necessary correlation between satisfaction and performance at any one point in time may be evident. In fact, reported correlations are typically nonsignificant [1, 30].

While the suggested multi-stage scheme is intuitively appealing, a test of such a model would require a longitudinal design and a complicated analysis. In contrast, the approach to be taken here is more modest in that it views satisfaction as an attitude [17] with known behavioral effects and performance as a behavior with theoretically based attitudinal determinants where the cross-dependency between the constructs may exist but is not specified. The behavioral effects of satisfaction and suggested attitudinal determinants of performance are discussed below.

### Consequences of Job Satisfaction

A number of reviews of the behavioral effects of job dissatisfaction among employees emphatically suggest that the primary effect is voluntary resignation [1, 18, 25, 28, 30]. Recently, theorists have hypothesized that satisfaction does not affect turnover directly but does so only through its effect on the worker's commitment to his organization [24]. Low commitment, therefore, may be a more direct antecedent of resignation. Moreover, this interpretation allows one to insert a theoretically based behavioral tendency construct between satisfaction, an attitude, and turnover behavior. Hence, the satisfaction → turnover relation will be viewed in this paper as a causal chain with organizational commitment intervening between the two variables.

### Determinants of Performance

Industrial researchers have had varying levels of success using a job motivation scheme attributed to Vroom [30] to predict worker productivity [20]. Recently, this conceptual structure has been successfully applied to the performance of salesmen [19, 22] and retail managers [16] while others have adapted it to broader sales personnel schemata [31]. Although the theory shares an isomorphism with current multiattribute attitude models [14], it is not generally known in marketing circles and is briefly reviewed below.

The focus of Vroom's [30] theory is on the worker's force to perform which has been interpreted by most writers as effort or motivation [20]. Motivation, in turn, is viewed as a function of various worker expectancies regarding (a) the degree to which effort will result in performing at some specified level (expectancy) and (b) the degree to which performance at the specified level is related to the attainment of intrinsic and/or extrinsic rewards (instrumentality). Vroom requires that the individual instrumentalities be weighted by the worker's "anticipated satisfaction" to be derived from each reward (valence). Although the combinatorial rules used for combining these variables are the subject of debate [20], most researchers follow Vroom's recommendation that the weighted instrumentalities be summed to provide an aggregate instrumentality score. This aggregate is then multiplied by the effort → performance probability or expectancy score to arrive at an estimate of the worker's motivational state. Motivation, in turn, is thought to influence future productivity.

Jacoby's [14] comparison of expectancy theory to the attitude models deriving from the work of Fishbein [7] suggests that an intervening variable approach similar to that employed in the satisfaction → turnover relationship may provide a profitable perspective. It is argued that, in much the same way that one's attitudinal predisposition toward a brand is related to purchase only through intention to buy, so must one's proclivity to produce be translated first into a conscious intention to strive for high sales levels. This intention, in turn, is expected to be more highly correlated with performance than the motivation score. Thus, the relation between motivation and performance can also be viewed as a sequential chain of events where one's intention to perform is an intervening variable.

Hypotheses

Two major hypotheses were investigated in this study. The first states that voluntary resignation is a function of low organizational commitment which, in turn, is determined by overall job dissatisfaction while the second posits that job performance is a function of a behavioral intention to perform well which, in turn, is determined by a highly motivated state. Note that although no specific hypotheses are made about the relation between the satisfaction constructs and the performance antecedents, the data will permit one to address a possible relation or overlap between the satisfaction and motivation measures in the research setting.

METHOD

Sample

All sales managers (n = 114) employed in the eight outlets of a midwestern multiline retailer were asked to complete a job attitudes questionnaire immediately preceding the fall merchandise season. Each manager supervised the sales personnel assigned to a merchandise group and had full responsibility for training and motivating the personnel in his department. Moreover, many managers engaged in direct selling activities at their discretion.

Returns were received from 105 managers (92%) including 52 males and 53 females. Of these respondents, 17 were involved in job status changes during the fall season which precluded an analysis of their performance data. Consequently, the final sample consisted of 88 managers.

Design

The design of the study was predictive in nature. All attitudinal data were collected before the six month performance period under study.

Measures

Job satisfaction and organizational commitment were measured on multi-item scales developed by Brayfield and Rothe [2] and Porter, el. al., [24] respectively. The satisfaction instrument has been used in prior studies of retail managerial personnel [5] while the commitment scale, due to its recent development, has had limited field testing. Nonetheless, internal consistency reliability estimates of .88 and .87 were obtained for the two instruments. The criterion of turnover during the fall season was scored in dummy variable format; managers who resigned their position were assigned a score of one while those who did not were scored zero. In all resignation cases, the manager completed at least four months of the six month performance period.

The operationalization procedures used to measure the motivation components are currently the subject of controversey among industrial researchers. Mitchell [20] has summarized much of this literature and his suggestions have been incorporated into the present study where applicable.

In the first stage of the research, a list of job outcomes similar to those used in [22] was examined by executive and supervisory personnel who had had retail management experience. Based on this administrative feedback, the list of outcomes was amended until a final set of 25 was agreed upon. The manager sample was then asked to rate the valence of these outcomes on attractiveness scales ranging from extremely unattractive (-3) to extremely attractive (+3). Importance was not used as a measure of valence because of the ambiguity surrounding the meaning of importance as a concept.

The instrumentality of performance for the attainment of outcomes was measured with reference to the performance criterion, department goal attainment. Managers were asked to scale their "chances in 10" of receiving each of the outcomes if they exceeded their departmental sales goal. Negative instrumentalities (corresponding to a blocking effect) were not used because it was inconceivable that exceeding one's goal would have a negative impact on any of the outcomes. Expectancy was measured in terms of the "chances in 100" that the manager's efforts would permit him to exceed his goal. Specifically, each manager was asked to allocate 100 percentage points to the three categories of meeting, exceeding, and falling short of one's goal. Finally, the motivation (M) score was calculated in the following manner: M = [Σ(instrumentality x valence)] x expectancy.

The performance criterion used in this study was the percent of the manager's departmental sales goal achieved in the merchandise season following administration of the questionnaire. The authors acknowledge that no one-dimensional criterion adequately reflects the totality of the sales manager's job nor can one control for the large number of exogenous variables which influence department sales. The goal attainment criterion was selected because management believed that the goal setting process adequately reflected differences in the seasonality and current demand for the various merchandise lines. Moreover, the different tasks which constitute the manager's job and which may be viewed as performance subcriteria (e.g., merchandise presentation and display, inventory control, staffing) were believed to be reflected in the numerator of the goal attainment criterion, department sales. Nonetheless, the degree to which the criterion used here did not accurately reflect the managers' efforts constitutes a limitation of the study.

Analysis

Simple correlations were first calculated between all variables. Multiple regression was later applied to the relevant dependent variables with all suggested antecedent variables in the regression equations. This technique will allow one to determine if inclusion of the intervening variables attenuates the simple effects of satisfaction and motivation on the respective behavioral criteria.

## RESULTS

Correlations between all variables appear in Table 1 where it is evident that all hypothesized linkages were supported at the zero order level. Specifically, job satisfaction was highly correlated with commitment to the organization which, in turn, was negatively correlated with turnover. Moreover, satisfaction was also correlated with turnover at a level higher in magnitude than that with commitment. In a similar manner, motivation was highly correlated with intention to perform which, in turn, was significantly correlated with goal attainment. The relation between motivation and goal attainment, however, was not significant indicating that a sequential chain of events may be plausible in this case.

### TABLE 1
### INTERCORRELATIONS BETWEEN VARIABLES

|  | 1 | 2 | 3 | 4 | 5 |
|---|---|---|---|---|---|
| 1. Job Satisfaction | -- | | | | |
| 2. Organizational Commitment | .58** | -- | | | |
| 3. Turnover | -.36** | -.28** | -- | | |
| 4. Motivation | .20 | .18 | -.01 | | |
| 5. Intention | .25* | .24* | -.07 | .45** | -- |
| 6. Goal Attainment | -.01 | -.15 | .01 | .18 | .29** |

$^*$ $p \leq .05$

$^{**}$ $p \leq .01$

It is also interesting to note that satisfaction and motivation were marginally correlated and that both satisfaction and commitment were correlated with intention to perform. Goal attainment, however, was not related to satisfaction nor was turnover related to motivation. Thus, it appears that the behavioral criteria were related only to the antecedents suggested in the literature.

Table 2 shows the results obtained when the two intervening variables and two dependent variables were regressed on all suggested antecedents. In accord with results obtained in non-sales environments, commitment to the organization was related only to satisfaction while intention to perform was significantly related only to motivation indicating that little overlap between satisfaction and motivation constructs is evident at this point.

At the behavioral criterion level, turnover was significantly related only to satisfaction when all other antecedents were also in the equation. Surprisingly the contribution of organizational commitment was suppressed relative to that of satisfaction. Apparently the causal chain sequence suggested in the literature was not operative in this study in that satisfaction appeared to affect both commitment and turnover directly.

### TABLE 2
### MULTIPLE REGRESSION COEFFICIENTS

| Antecedent Variables | Dependent Variables | | | |
|---|---|---|---|---|
| | Commit-ment | Turn-over | Inten-tion | % of goal |
| Job Satisfaction | .57** | -.31* | .17 | .06 |
| Motivation | .07 | .07 | .42** | .08 |
| Organizational Commitment | -- | -.11 | -- | -.27* |
| Intention | -- | .00 | -- | .30* |
| $R^2$ | .35** | .14* | .23** | .14* |

$^*$ $p \leq .05$

$^{**}$ $p \leq .01$

The regression of goal attainment on all independent and intervening variables revealed that the suggested chain of events, motivation → intention → performance, may be accurate as the coefficient attributed to intention was significant while that due to motivation was not. Interestingly, the organizational commitment variable made a significant but negative contribution to the equation. While it is not clear why commitment and performance were negatively related in this study, it appears as though commitment may be acting as a suppressor variable [4] for the intention measure in that it partials out a portion of the shared variance in intention which is attributable to commitment but not goal attainment. Thus, it is the authors' opinion that this significant regression weight is a statistical artifact as opposed to a meaningful relationship.

In summary, little overlap was evident between satisfaction and motivation constructs when viewed from the perspective of the affected behavioral criteria. While modest relationships were observed between satisfaction and motivation and organizational commitment and intention to perform, these constructs were shown to be specifically related to the hypothesized criteria when entered jointly into the various regression equations. Only in the case of the goal attainment criterion was the contribution of a satisfaction-related construct evident.

## DISCUSSION AND IMPLICATIONS

The results reported here suggest that the motivational antecedents of job performance and job satisfaction in retail management may require separate organizational emphasis. Although a modest degree of association was observed between satisfaction and motivation, the results clearly show that satisfaction measured before the performance period under study was not related to performance in that time period. In a similar manner motivation was unrelated to turnover, a known consequence of job dissatisfaction. Thus, it appears that the more recent interpretations of the satisfaction → performance linkage incorporating intervening variables and long time intervals of effect may be more appropriate than earlier views of a direct satisfaction → performance relationship.

The implications of these findings are straightforward. Retail executives are advised to continue their emphasis on fostering job satisfaction among retail management. In this regard, it is clear that satisfaction is a known deterent to voluntary termination. However, the effect of job satisfaction on performance is more tenuous and much less direct. Because of this, a sound motivation program should also be implemented in the retail setting in an effort to influence the sales manager's intention to strive for high departmental goals apart from his or her desire to remain with the organization.

This interpretation suggests that a modified two factor approach to retail management [12, 23] may be warranted whereby satisfaction programs are instituted to insure that retail management is committed to the organization and motivational programs are introduced as an adjunct to or in coordination with various morale-boosting strategies. The retail organization's personnel executive may wish to closely observe the interdependency between these programs as it has been suggested that satisfaction is a necessary but not sufficient condition for motivation to occur. Although this view is not accepted by all [13], it may be a worthy area of study.

The retail personnel manager is also advised to attempt to refine the methods and measures used to implement and test these programs. A number of issues have been raised by Mitchell [20] which bear on the use of expectancy models of work motivation. Still others, including Walker, Churchill, and Ford [31], are working on an integrated structure of motivation and satisfaction effects. Future researchers and practitioners alike could benefit from these efforts.

## REFERENCES

1. Brayfield, Arthur H. and Walter H. Crockett. "Employee Attitudes and Employee Performance," Psychological Bulletin, 52 (September 1955), 396-424.

2. Brayfield, Arthur H. and Harold F. Rothe. "An Index of Job Satisfaction," Journal of Applied Psychology, 35 (June 1951), 307-11.

3. Churchill, Gilbert A., Jr., Neil M. Ford, and Orville C. Walker, Jr. "Organizational Climate and Job Satisfaction in the Salesforce," Journal of Marketing Research, 13 (November 1976), 323-32.

4. Darlington, Richard B. "Multiple Regression in Psychological Research and Practice," Psychological Bulletin, 69 (March 1968), 161-82.

5. Dermer, Jerry D. "Budgetary Motivation of Retail Store Managers and Buyers," Journal of Retailing, 50 (Fall 1974), 23-32, 76.

6. Donnelly, James H., Jr., and John M. Ivancevich. "Role Clarity and the Salesman," Journal of Marketing, 39 (January 1975), 71-4.

7. Fishbein, Martin and Icek Ajzen. Belief, Attitude, Intention and Behavior. Reading, Massachusetts: Addison-Wesley, 1975.

8. Futrell, Charles M., John E. Swan, and John T. Todd. "Job Performance Related to Management Control Systems for Pharmaceutical Salesmen," Journal of Marketing Research, 13 (February 1976), 25-33.

9. Greene, Charles N. "The Satisfaction-Performance Controversy," Business Horizons, 15 (September 1972), 31-41.

10. Harvey, Reed A. and Robert D. Smith. "Need Satisfaction in Retail Management: An Empirical Study," Journal of Retailing, 48 (Fall 1972), 89-95.

11. Hauk, James G. "Research in Personnel Selling," in George Schwartz, ed., Science in Marketing. New York: John Wiley & Sons, 1965.

12. Herzberg, Frederick, Bernard Mausner, and Barbara Block Snyderman. The Motivation to Work, second edition. John Wiley & Sons, 1959.

13. House, Robert J. and Lawrence A. Wigdor. "Herzberg's Dual-Factor Theory of Job Satisfaction and Motivation: A Review of the Evidence and A Criticism," Personnel Psychology, 20 (Summer 1967), 369-89.

14. Jacoby, Jacob. "Consumer and Industrial Psychology: Prospects for Theory Corroboration and Mutual Contribution," in Marvin D. Dunnette, ed. Handbook of Industrial and Organizational Psychology. Chicago: Rand McNally, 1976.

15. Kanuk, Leslie. "Leadership Effectiveness of Department Managers in a Department Store Chain: A Contingency Analysis," Journal of Retailing, 52 (Spring 1976), 9-16, 93.

16. Lawler, Edward E., III and J. Lloyd Suttle. "Expectancy Theory and Job Behavior" Organizational Behavior and Human Performance, 9 (June 1973), 482-503.

17. Locke, Edwin A. "What is Job Satisfaction?" Organizational Behavior and Human Performance, 4 (May 1969), 309-36.

18. March, James G. and Herbert A. Simon. Organizations. New York: John Wiley & Sons, 1958.

19. Matsui, Tomao and Toshitake Terai. "A Cross-Cultural Study of the Validity of the Expectancy Theory of Work Motivation," Journal of Applied Psychology, 60 (April 1975), 263-5.

20. Mitchell, Terence R. "Expectancy Models of Job Satisfaction, Occupational Preference and Effort: A Theoretical, Methodological, and Empirical Appraisal," Psychological Bulletin, 81 (December 1974), 1053-1077.

21. Muczyk, Jan P., T. H. Mattheiss, and Myron Gable. "Predicting Success of Store Managers," Journal of Retailing, 50 (Summer 1974), 43-49, 104.

22. Oliver, Richard L. "Expectancy Theory Predictions of Salesmen's Performance," Journal of Marketing Research, 11 (August 1974), 243-53.

23. Olsen, Robert M. "The Liberating Motivational Climate - An Essential for Sales Effectiveness," in Thomas R. Wotruba and Robert Olsen, eds., Readings in Sales Management. New York: Holt, Rinehart and Winston, 1971.

24. Porter, Lyman W., William J. Crampon, and Frank J. Smith. "Organizational Commitment and Managerial Turnover: A Longitudinal Study," Technical Report No. 13. Irvine, California: University of California, 1972.

25. Porter, Lyman W. and Richard M. Steers. "Organizational, Work, and Personal Factors in Employee Turnover and Absenteeism," Psychological Bulletin, 80 (August 1973), 151-76.

26. Pruden, Henry O. and Richard M. Reese. "Inter-organization Role-Set Relations and the Performance and Satisfaction of Industrial Salesmen," <u>Administrative Science Quarterly</u>, 17 (December 1972), 601-9.

27. Rathmell, John M. <u>A Bibliography on Personal Selling</u>. Chicago: American Marketing Association, 1966.

28. Ronan, W. W. "Individual and Situational Variables Relating to Job Satisfaction," <u>Journal of Applied Psychology Monograph</u>, 54 (February 1970), 1-31.

29. Schwab, Donald P. and Larry L. Cummings. "Theories of Performance and Satisfaction: A Review," <u>Industrial Relations</u>, 9 (October 1970), 408-30.

30. Vroom, Victor H. <u>Work and Motivation</u>. New York: John Wiley & Sons, 1964.

31. Walker, Orville C., Jr., Gilbert A. Churchill, Jr. and Neil M. Ford. "Measuring and Improving Salesmen's Motivation and Performance," Paper presented at the American Marketing Association Industrial Marketing Conference, Los Angeles, California, June 1976.

# A DYNAMIC SALES FORCE MANAGEMENT SYSTEM

René Y. Darmon, McGill University

## ABSTRACT

This paper attempts to model a sales force system by means of an absorbing Markov chain. Elements enter the system as soon as they are considered for a sales position and move from state to state as their status in the sales force changes. Each element in the system ends up being absorbed either by being promoted outside the sales force or by leaving the system for voluntary or involuntary reasons. This simple framework is shown to be useful in a number of decisions related to the sales force management function.

## INTRODUCTION

As evidenced by the high failure rate of sales managers [5], sales management is a complex and difficult process. At least two types of reasons may account for this fact. First, decisions in one specific area of sales force management generally affect many other interrelated aspects of the selling organization; for instance, salesmen's remuneration levels also affect sales force morale and motivation, turnover rate, ability to recruit able sales people etc.; recruiting salesmen from one specific source has obvious implications for training as well as for supervision, compensation, or management styles decisions; and so on. Second, many sales force decisions have important lagged effects; hiring salesmen now will have long run effects on the competence level of the sales force for the next few years; the effect of a salesmen's training or retraining session can be either positive or negative for months or even years after it has taken place.

The implications of these omnipresent interactions and carryover effects are clear. Sales force decisions should be taken in light of their long run effects on the whole sales force. They underscore the need for a dynamic systems approach. Unfortunately, however, very few sales systems have been reported in the sales management literature so far. Following the concept of a decision calculus [2], such systems should be simple enough to be understood by sales managers and to survive to the paucity of relevant data which plagues many sales organizations. On the other hand, they should still be robust and complete enough to have predictive and normative value. Some limited applications of this concept have given promising results in a sales force context. [See for instance 3 and 4].

This paper attempts to model a sales force as a dynamic and complex system within the relatively simple structure of an absorbing Markov chain. It shows how, with relatively small data requirements, this simple structure can aid a sales manager in several areas. Possible applications are outlined. Section 2 outlines the proposed model; Section 3 discusses how sales managers can control and use the system; finally, sample applications in different areas are sketched in Section 4.

## MODEL

As shown in Figure 1, a sales force can be characterized by its number of salesmen and sales trainees as well as by the competence level of each individual in the system. Given a certain size and competence level, a sales force generates sales and profits through sales activities.

Most sales management tasks are designed to build a sales force of the size and quality that will result in optimal sales and profit performances. Decisions about sales force size, salesmen's recruiting, selection, training, supervision, and retraining procedures directly affect one or several characteristics of the sales force system (as shown on Figure 1).

A sales force is not a static system. Even in two consecutive months, a large sales organization may not be comprised of exactly the same individuals. Some applicants become sales trainees; trainees become salesmen. Salesmen and trainees may leave the sales force as the result of the evaluation procedures of sales managers ( promotion, dismissals), or for other reasons (new position in other companies, death, retirement, etc.) Attrition is probably affected by a salesman's competence level. For instance, attrition rate is generally higher among better performing salesmen because they are more likely to be promoted within the organization or to be hired away by competitors [7].

The system outlined in Figure 1 could be represented as an absorbing Markov chain. An absorbing Markov chain is a Markov chain with at least one absorbing state, i.e. a state which once entered cannot be left, and which can be reached from every nonabsorbing state [1]. Absorbing Markov chains have already been used in a sales force management context by Schuchman [6] and by Thompson and McNeal [8]. But, unlike these two studies, this application suggests a description of the sales force at a macro level. At any one period, individuals are in different states of the sales force (candidates for a sales position, sales trainees, junior salesmen, senior salesmen, etc.). In addition, they move from one state to other states over time, as their status in the sales force changes.

The transition of individuals from one state i to another state j occurs with the transition probability $P_{ij}$ over a certain period. A period of time can be defined as a month, a quarter, or even a year. For any individual in the system, the three following absorbing states are defined:

$A_1$ = individual promoted during the most recent period

$A_2$ = individual dismissed during the most recent period

$A_3$ = individual resigned during the most recent peirod.

In the same way, nonabsorbing states are defined as follows:

C = candidate for a sales position - no history with the sales force

$T_1..T_k$ = sales trainee in the 1, 2, ... kth stage of the training program (assuming a k-period training program)

$S_1..S_m$ = salesmen in the 1, 2, ... mth competence group during the most recent period (it is assumed that present salesmen can be classified by management into m groups according to their competence level -- the definition of the m groups being also left to management's judgment).

All probabilities $P_{ij}$ can be determined from historical personnel data of the sales force, and, whenever necessary, they can be supplemented, corrected, and adjusted according to sales managers' judgments. As an example, let us assume that a sales training program is one-period long and that salesmen can be properly classified into three performance groups: below average ($S_1$), average ($S_2$), and

FIGURE I

SALES FORCE MANAGEMENT SYSTEM

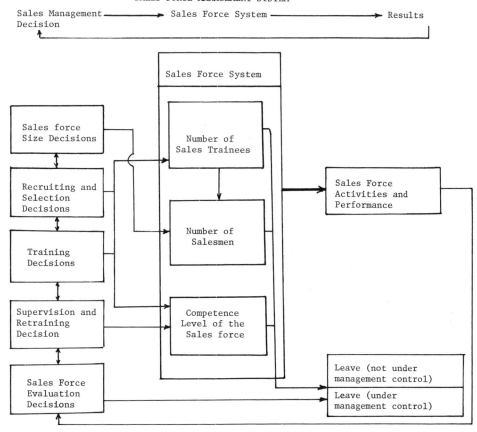

above average performance ($S_3$). The computed transition matix could be:

$$
P = \begin{array}{c} A_1 \\ A_2 \\ A_3 \\ C \\ T_1 \\ S_1 \\ S_2 \\ S_3 \end{array}
\begin{array}{cccccccc}
A_1 & A_2 & A_3 & C & T_1 & S_1 & S_2 & S_3 \\
1 & 0 & 0 & 0 & 0 & 0 & 0 & 0 \\
0 & 1 & 0 & 0 & 0 & 0 & 0 & 0 \\
0 & 0 & 1 & 0 & 0 & 0 & 0 & 0 \\
0 & .40 & .20 & 0 & .40 & 0 & 0 & 0 \\
0 & .05 & .05 & 0 & 0 & .30 & .55 & .05 \\
0 & .10 & .05 & 0 & 0 & .80 & .05 & 0 \\
.05 & 0 & .05 & 0 & 0 & .05 & .80 & .05 \\
.07 & 0 & .10 & 0 & 0 & 0 & .03 & .80
\end{array}
$$

In this example, an individual being screened and evaluated as a candidate for the sales force has probabilities of .4 of not being accepted, of .2 of withdrawing, and of .4 of becoming a sales trainee in the following period; and so on. Given that at some point in time a sales force is composed of a certain number of individuals in different states, it is possible using this probability transition matrix to determine what will be the composition of the sales force n periods from now.

## MANAGERIAL CONTROL OVER THE SYSTEM

This simple description of the system may have several managerial applications. Managers have some control over the system through the manipulation of some specific probabilities and definitions. The main controllable variables of the system are:

1.  The number k of training stages determining the length of the training program; through k, a sales manager controls the distribution of the salesmen entering the system in the various competence level categories $P_{Tk,Sl}$, $l = 1 \ldots m$. Sales force competence can be raised through initial training.

2.  The column vector $P_{i,A2}$, $i = 1 \ldots n$, which can be characterized as a selectivity vector; this vector represents the proportion of individuals at each stage in the system that the sales manager wants to fire. Through proper screening and supervision procedures, sales management can get rid of the elements with lower potential in the system and control the competence level of the sales force.

3.  The number of candidates for a sales position $V_{C,t}$ to be generated, in conjunction with the preceding probabilities, affects the size and competence level of the resulting sales force; to some extent, this element is also under management's control.

4. Through supervision and retraining decisions, sales management can have a positive effect on the proportion $P_{Si,Sj}$ of salesmen moving from one competence level category to another.

5. Finally, managers can, to some extent, affect the attrition probabilities $P_{i,A3}$, $i = 1 \ldots n$, by raising the general compensation level, providing an appropriate organizational climate, etc.

All these decisions, which may have some positive effects are subject to at least three types of constraints. First, are cost constraints; for instance, costs are associated with longer training programs, more selective sales force policies, higher compensation, more frequent retraining sessions, etc. Such cost must be warranted by the additional gross profits they can generate and should be taken explicitly into account. Second, time also acts as a constraint. Hiring a sales trainee now can only have an effect on sales several periods after. Third, the present state of the system is a binding constraint. Depending on the present state of the system, more or less time will be required to reach a desired objective.

The sales manager's decision variables as well as his constraints can be taken explicitly into account by the proposed model. A simple look at the probability transition matrix may well reveal the flows of salesmen in the sales force through time. This should enable management to spot possible problem areas and to analyze sales force turnover. However, Markovian analysis may be even more useful as a decision tool in cases where a sales manager has to assess the long run as well as the short run effects of important sales force decisions and policies.

From a practical point of view, this model is being tested for future implementation on a computer time-sharing system for a pharmaceutical product firm. To use this system, a manager will supply (or update) computer files with relevant data on each salesman's history with the company. From these data, probability transition matrices can be derived by salesmen category (according to previous experience, profile, etc.) These data can be supplemented, corrected, or adjusted with managerial judgments. In the same way, cost data may be supplied by accounting people or as judgmental inputs. Thus, the system is being designed to be used in a conversational way for a variety of problems. Some of them are outlined in the next section.

## SAMPLE APPLICATION

### Where Salesmen Should Come From

From what sources should a company recruit its salesmen? For instance, a company can hire experienced salesmen from similar industries; or it can hire potential sales people from other departments of its own organization; or hire inexperienced college graduates for its sales force; or it may use any other type of relevant sources. Generally, hiring experienced salesmen may cost more in terms of immediate expenses because higher compensation has to be given to senior salesmen. However, higher sales volume and shorter training periods may (or may not) offset these additional expenses.

On the other hand, hiring college graduates may require larger training expenses, higher turnover and higher sales opportunity costs; however, college graduates may not require as high a compensation level in the short run and may turn out to be better salesmen in the long run. All salesmen's sources have their own advantages and limitations, and very often it is not apparent which one has the highest long run expected value for a company.

This problem can be analyzed using the framework outlined above by finding the expected value per time period of keeping one active salesman over time from each source. Of course, the higher the expected value, the better the source. A numerical example is given in Tables I and II for two possible sources: experienced salesmen and college graduates.

Tables I and II show that keeping one salesman in the sales force requires an average of .38 candidates to be generated each period when this salesman is selected among experienced salesmen, and 1.35 when he is selected among college graduates. In the first case, .15 sales trainees per active salesman are constantly required in the system, while .62 sales trainees per active salesman in the various stages of the training program are required in the second case. The remaining steady state figures can be given a probabilistic interpretation. They may be considered as the probabilities that a salesmen from a given source will fall in each competence category in the long run. In the reported example, an experienced salesman has respectively .34, .51, and .15 probabilities of turning out to be below average, average, or above average performer; a salesman from college source has .55, .36, and .09 probabilities of falling in each of the aboved mentioned categories.

Simple computations give an expected contribution to profits of \$9,820 per period for an experienced salesman, and of \$8,395 per period for college graduates. This suggests that experienced salesmen are a more profitable source of salesmen than college graduates for this company. (Note that, in practice, the fixed costs involved for each source, especially those associated with training programs, should also be taken into account). In this application, a sales manager could query the system to evaluate the profitability of each type of recruit and to carry sensitivity analysis of these values to various estimates.

### Other Possible Applications

Sales managers can use the framework outlined above in a number of ways. As shown in Figure 2, these areas of possible applications encompass all stages of the sales management process: analysis, planning, and control.

At the analysis stage, using the system can bring additional insight into the present structure of the sales force (diagnosis) and into the long run effects of present policies (prognosis). At the planning stage, many policies in the areas of recruiting, training and retraining can be tested for their immediate and long run effects. Thus, the system can be used to simulate the sales force's short and long run reactions to contemplated new policies or actions. For instance, a sales manager could query the system to find out the number of sales force applicants he should seek and the size of the training program he should set up in order to reach or to maintain a certain sales force size. By changing the length of the training program and assessing the effect on salesmen's long run efficiency, a sales manager could estimate the optimal length, taking into account the costs and the benefits involved at each level. In another application, the system evaluates possible actions a sales manager could take as a result of top salesmen being hired away by competitors, or being promoted. For each alternative course of action (such as, hiring and training a new salesman, promoting salesmen from within, retaining salesmen with higher compensation, etc.), the system can estimate the costs and time involved to regain overall sales force efficiency; this would give a manager precious indications as to what course of action to follow. In yet further applications, a sales manager would question the system about the costs and benefits involved in hiring and training salesmen in various numbers, and retaining only the best salesmen for a given sales force size. Finally, the system can be

TABLE I

EVALUATION OF THE EXPECTED PROFIT GENERATED OVER EACH PERIOD IN THE
LONG RUN BY AN EXPERIENCED SALESMAN

| Original State | New State | | | | | | | | Revenue from one individual $ | Cost associated with one individual $ |
|---|---|---|---|---|---|---|---|---|---|---|
| | $A_1$ | $A_2$ | $A_3$ | C | $T_1$ | $S_1$ | $S_2$ | $S_3$ | | |
| $A_1$ | 1 | 0 | 0 | 0 | 0 | 0 | 0 | 0 | 0 | 0 |
| $A_2$ | 0 | 1 | 0 | 0 | 0 | 0 | 0 | 0 | 0 | 5,000 |
| $A_3$ | 0 | 0 | 1 | 0 | 0 | 0 | 0 | 0 | 0 | 0 |
| C | 0 | .40 | .20 | 0 | .40 | 0 | 0 | 0 | 0 | 1,000 |
| $T_1$ | 0 | .05 | .05 | 0 | 0 | .30 | .55 | .05 | 0 | 8,000 |
| $S_1$ | 0 | .10 | .05 | 0 | 0 | .80 | .05 | 0 | 40,000 | 35,000 |
| $S_2$ | .05 | 0 | .05 | 0 | 0 | .05 | .80 | .05 | 100,000 | 85,000 |
| $S_3$ | .07 | 0 | .10 | 0 | 0 | 0 | .03 | .80 | 150,000 | 130,000 |
| Steady State | .04 | .19 | .14 | .38 | .15 | .34 | .51 | .15 | | |
| | | | | | | | 1.00 | | | |
| Expected Contribution to profits of one salesman | $9,820 | | | | | | | | | |

TABLE II

EVALUATION OF THE EXPECTED PROFIT GENERATED OVER EACH PERIOD IN
THE LONG RUN BY A COLLEGE GRADUATE SALESMAN

| Original State | New State | | | | | | | | | | Revenue from one individual $ | Cost associated with one individual $ |
|---|---|---|---|---|---|---|---|---|---|---|---|---|
| | $A_1$ | $A_2$ | $A_3$ | C | $T_1$ | $T_2$ | $T_3$ | $S_1$ | $S_2$ | $S_3$ | | |
| $A_1$ | 1 | 0 | 0 | 0 | 0 | 0 | 0 | 0 | 0 | 0 | 0 | 0 |
| $A_2$ | 0 | 1 | 0 | 0 | 0 | 0 | 0 | 0 | 0 | 0 | 0 | 2,000 |
| $A_3$ | 0 | 0 | 1 | 0 | 0 | 0 | 0 | 0 | 0 | 0 | 0 | 0 |
| C | 0 | .50 | .30 | 0 | .20 | 0 | 0 | 0 | 0 | 0 | 0 | 500 |
| $T_1$ | 0 | .10 | .20 | 0 | 0 | .70 | 0 | 0 | 0 | 0 | 0 | 5,000 |
| $T_2$ | 0 | .10 | .05 | 0 | 0 | 0 | .85 | 0 | 0 | 0 | 0 | 8,000 |
| $T_3$ | 0 | .05 | .05 | 0 | 0 | 0 | 0 | .60 | .29 | .01 | 5,000 | 10,000 |
| $S_1$ | 0 | .10 | .05 | 0 | 0 | 0 | 0 | .80 | .05 | 0 | 40,000 | 32,000 |
| $S_2$ | .05 | 0 | .05 | 0 | 0 | 0 | 0 | .05 | .80 | .05 | 100,000 | 80,000 |
| $S_3$ | .07 | 0 | .10 | 0 | 0 | 0 | 0 | 0 | .03 | .80 | 150,000 | 120,000 |
| Steady State | .03 | .78 | .53 | 1.35 | .27 | .19 | .16 | .55 | .36 | .09 | | |
| | | | | | | | | 1.0 | | | | |
| Expected Contribution to profit of one Salesman | $8,395 | | | | | | | | | | | |

FIGURE 2

POSSIBLE AREAS OF MODEL APPLICATION

| Sales Management's Task | Possible Areas of Model Application |
|---|---|
| ANALYSIS<br>a) Diagnosis | - Sales force turnover analysis<br>- Sales force competence level analysis |
| b) Prognosis | - Future size, competence level of the sales force with present recruiting, screening and sales personnel management policies<br>- Salesmen's career path analysis |
| PLANNING | A. Test of Various Recruiting Policies<br>   - Number of candidates to be recruited<br>   - Salesmen's sources to use<br><br>B. Test of Various Training Programs<br>   - Length of the training program<br>   - How long to keep each trainee in the program<br>   - Various training methods<br><br>C. Test of Various Sales Personnel Management Policies<br>   - What proportion of sales candidates to hire<br>   - What proportion of trainees to keep as salesmen<br>   - What proportion of salesmen to keep at various competence levels<br><br>D. Test of Various Retraining Policies<br>   - Frequency and length of retraining sessions<br>   - For which categories of salesmen |
| CONTROL | - How selected sales management policies match objectives.<br><br>- Reasons for gap between sales force management objectives and sales force results. |

used in the control stage to assess how sales force policies and practices help achieve sales force objectives.

## SUMMARY AND CONCLUSIONS

In this paper, an attempt was made to model a sales force system by means of an absorbing Markov chain. Elements enter the sales force system as soon as they are considered for a sales position; then, they move from state to state as their status in the sales force changes; finally, each element in the system ends up being absorbed, either by being promoted or by leaving the system voluntarily or involuntarily. This simple framework has been shown to be extremely useful in a number of decisions covering the whole management process of analysis, planning and control of a sales force.

In order to implement such a procedure, data requirements are minimal. Basically, they call for analysis of historical sales personnel data, which could be replaced or supplemented by managers' judgmental inputs. In the latter case, this approach is consistent with the decision calculus concept. This simple one-line computerized mathematical procedure permits a manager to extend his reasoning and make sure that basic judgments are consistent with their short and long run implications [2].

REFERENCES

1. Kemeny, John C., Arthur Schliefer, Jr., J. Laurie Snell, and Gerald L. Thompson. *Finite Mathematics with Business Applications*, 2nd ed., Englewood Cliffs: N.J.: Prentice-Hall, 1972, 224-229.

2. Little, John D.C. "Models and Managers: The Concept of a Decision Calculus." *Management Science*, 16 (April 1970), 466-485.

3. Lodish, Leonard M. "Call Plan: An Interactive Salesman's Call Planning System." *Management Science*, 18 (December 1971), 25-40.

4. _____. "Sales Territory Alignment to Maximize Profit." *Journal of Marketing Research*, 12 (February 1975), 30-36.

5. Mazze, Edward M. *Personal Selling: Choice Against Chance*. Saint Paul: West Publishing Company, 1976, 42-43.

6. Schuchman, Abraham. "The Planning and Control of Personal Selling Effort Directed at New Account Acquisition: A Markovian Analysis." in *New Research in Marketing*. Berkeley, Calif.: The Institute of Business and Economic Research, 1966, 45-56.

7. Smyth, Richard C. "Financial Incentives for Salesmen." *Harvard Business Review*, (January-February 1968), 112-113.

8. Thompson, William W. and James U. McNeal. "Sales Planning and Control Using Absorbing Markov Chains." *Journal of Marketing Research*, 4 (February 1967), 62-66.

# THE CONSEQUENCES OF MEASUREMENT ERROR

Franklin S. Houston, Temple University
Doyle L. Weiss, University of British Columbia

## ABSTRACT

Measurement error is examined in two multivariate regression analyses previously reported by Weiss [8] and Palda [7]. The consequences of such errors are that the parameter estimate associated with the variable in question is biased toward zero. It is important to notice, however, that in the multivariate case, the remaining parameter estimates will show distinct biases which cannot be predetermined.

## INTRODUCTION

One of the major stumbling blocks confronting marketing in the development and application of analytic methods is the problem of measurement. King [5] argues that, ".... the measurement function.... may prove to be the "Achilles' heel" of the analytic movement in marketing". King appears to feel that while theory construction and testing methodology are undergoing strong development, the state of the "measurement function" can be characterized as being "weak with slow progress forecast".

King's remarks were mainly directed at "behavioral" research and the problems associated with defining operational units of measurement for such elusive variables as "youth appeal" [4] and "feel physically tense"[2]. As such, he was not concerned with measurement problems for such well defined variables as unit price and expenditures for advertising. The recent results published by Clarke and McCann[1] would indicate, however, that King's remarks are equally applicable to the associated problem of "observation error".

The purpose of this paper is to re-examine two previous studies into the effects of advertising expenditures on sales in light of the problems introduced by measurement error. The analysis extends the usual treatment of "error in the variables" [3] by extending the analysis to several variables.

## THE PREVIOUS STUDIES

The two previous studies chosen for examination are those by Weiss [8] and Palda [7]. The study by Weiss examined the relationship between market share and price and advertising expenditures. Although the results of this analysis were in general strong, the advertising variable did not play a major role in determining market share. The model used in Weiss' analysis is:

$$S_{B,t} = a_o + a_1 \, (P_{B,t} / \bar{P}_t) + a_2 \, (A_{B,t} / \bar{A}_t) + a_3 Q_1 + a_4 Q_2 \qquad (1)$$

where:

$P_{B,t}$    is the average price per ounce (weighted by volume) for brand B in period t,

$A_{B,t}$    is thousands of dollars spent on advertising

$\bar{P}_t$    is the average price (weighted by volume) for all three brands in period t,

$\bar{A}_t$    is $\sum\limits_{B} A_{B,t} / 3$,

$Q_1$    is 1 when B is 2 and 0 otherwise, and

$Q_2$    is 1 when B is 1 and 0 otherwise.

In addition to the additive form of (1), a multiplicative (or log-linear) version is also examined for possible measurement biases.

Palda's now classic study of cumulative advertising effects has again been called into question. This time by Clarke and McCann [1]. A comparison of Palda's results with results obtained from spectral analysis showed Palda's coefficient of current advertising (.537) to be 17% lower than the Clarke and McCann estimate. In addition, Palda's coefficient of lagged sales (.628) indicates a longer carry over than the one year which Clarke and McCann obtained with spectral analysis.

Of the models analyzed by Palda, the KOYL 2 (Y-LESS) model was selected for re-examination since it, like the Weiss models, contains four independent variables. That model is

$$S_t = b_0 + b_1 S_{t-1} + b_2 \log A_t + b_3 D_t + b_4 T_t \qquad (2)$$

where:

$S_t$    is sales (in thousands of dollars) for period t,

$A_t$    is advertising expenditures (in thousands of dollars) for period t,

$D_t$    is 1 for the years 1908-25 and 0 otherwise, and

$T_t$    is trend, counting 1-53 for the years 1908-60.

A variation of the above model which used advertising rather than the log of advertising, is also examined.

## THE CONSEQUENCES OF ERROR IN VARIABLES

The following analysis assumes the biases in all of the models to be the result of measurement error in the advertising variables. This error is assumed to be random error, resulting in a well-defined bias for the ordinary least squares' estimates of the advertising coefficients. The origin of this bias and the bias of the remaining coefficients is examined below.

Let the initial model be restated as:

$$Y = X_1 \beta_1 + X_2 \beta_2, \qquad (3)$$

with this being assumed an exact linear relationship. This relationship cannot be directly observed, however, because of the measurement problem. The variables are:

1) the dependent variable, assumed to be measured with error, is defined as the true value of the sales (or market share) variable plus an error term, i.e.:

$$Y^* = Y + U, \qquad (4)$$

where:

$Y*$ is the observed value of the sales (or market share variable),

$Y$ is the true value of the sales (or market share), and

$U$ is the error term.

The measurement is $Y*$ with $U$ representing the error of this measurement. Conventional assumptions are made about this error ($U$).

$$E(U) = 0, E(U_i U_j) = \sigma_U^2 \text{ for } i = j, \text{ and } 0 \text{ for } i \neq j. \quad (5)$$

2) a <u>single</u> independent variable, assumed to be measured with error,

$$X_1^* = X_1 + \varepsilon, \quad (6)$$

where

$X_1^*$ is the observed value of the independent variable; advertising expenditures,

$X_1$ is the true value of the independent variable, advertising expenditures, and

$\varepsilon$ is the error term.

The measurement is $X_1^*$ with $\varepsilon$ representing the error of this measurement. Again, conventional assumptions are made with respect to this error.

$$E(\varepsilon) = 0, E(\varepsilon_i \varepsilon_j) = \sigma_\varepsilon^2 \text{ for } i = j \text{ and } 0 \text{ for } i \neq j, \quad (7)$$

3) $X_2$, a <u>set</u> of independent variables assumed to be measured without error.

The final equation form, using the measured variables is:

$$Y* = (X_1^* - \varepsilon)\beta_1 + X_2\beta_2 + U$$

or:

$$Y* = X_1^*\beta_1 + X_2\beta_2 + U - \varepsilon\beta_1. \quad (8)$$

## ORDINARY LEAST SQUARES ESTIMATION

Goldberger [2] and Levy [4] demonstrated[1] that estimation by ordinary least squares can produce inconsistent estimates of the parameters. For convenience, this demonstration is reproduced below.

The OLS parameter estimates are:

$$\hat{\beta} = (X*'X*)^{-1} X*'Y*$$

where:

$X*$ is the T x K matrix of observed independent variables, containing the <u>single</u> variable measured with error in the first column (for convenience).

$Y*$ is the T x 1 set of dependent variable observations,

---

[1]Goldberger's analysis (2, pp. 282-84) examines the single independent variable case, while Levy (4) extends this to three independent variables. Levy's analysis still, however, assumes error in one variable.

Substitution for $Y*$ provides:

$$\hat{\beta} = (X*'X*)^{-1} X*'(X* + U - \varepsilon\beta), \quad (10)$$

where:

$U$ is the T x 1 vector of $U_i$, and

$\varepsilon$ is the T x K matrix of independent variable error terms,

$$\varepsilon = \begin{bmatrix} \varepsilon_{11} & 0 & 0 \dots & 0 \\ \varepsilon_{12} & 0 & 0 & 0 \\ \vdots & \vdots & \vdots & \\ \varepsilon_{1T} & 0 & 0 \dots & 0 \end{bmatrix}$$

Thus:

$$\hat{\beta} = \beta + (X*'X*)^{-1}X*'U - (X*'X*)^{-1}X*'\varepsilon\beta \quad (11)$$

Examination of the probability limits for this equation demonstrates the inconsistency of the OLS estimator.

An initial result necessary in evaluating the OLS estimator concerns the relationship between the observed independent variables and their errors:

$$\text{plim} \frac{X*'\varepsilon}{T} = \text{plim} \frac{X'\varepsilon}{T} + \text{plim} \frac{\varepsilon'\varepsilon}{T} = \text{zero} + \Omega \quad (12)$$

where:

$$\Omega = \begin{bmatrix} \sigma_\varepsilon^2 & 0 & 0 \dots & 0 \\ 0 & 0 & 0 \dots & 0 \\ \vdots & \vdots & \vdots & \\ 0 & 0 & 0 \dots & 0 \end{bmatrix}$$

Assume that no relationship exists between the "true" independent variable ($X$) and the dependent variable's error term ($U$). Similarly, assume no relationship exists between the error terms for the dependent variable ($U$) and the independent variable's error ($\varepsilon$); thus the first right hand term of (11) is zero. That is, since

$$\text{plim} \frac{X*'U}{T} = \text{plim} \frac{X'U}{T} + \text{plim} \frac{\varepsilon'U}{T} = \text{ZERO} \quad (13)$$

then:

$$\text{plim} \frac{X*'X*)^{-1}X*'U}{T} = \text{ZERO} \quad (14)$$

As a result, the "new" covariance matrix takes the form:

$$\text{plim} \frac{X*'X*}{T} = \text{plim} \frac{X'X}{T} + \frac{2\varepsilon'X}{T} + \frac{\varepsilon'\varepsilon}{T} = \Sigma + \text{ZERO} + \Omega \quad (15)$$

This result, in addition to the earlier result, (12) yields the final form:

$$\text{plim } \hat{\beta} = \beta - (\Sigma + \Omega)^{-1}\Omega\beta. \quad (16)$$

## EXAMINATION OF THE ESTIMATOR BIAS

The above expression (16) shows the general nature of bias which will enter into the parameter estimates if measurement error exists in all the independent variables. Although knowledge of measurement error's covariance is required to determine the nature of this bias, Levy [4] demonstrated that <u>if only a single</u> variable is measured with error, the parameter estimate for this variable will be biased towards zero. No generalization can be made about the direction of bias introduced into the remaining parameter estimates.

In the present analysis concern is with four independent variables. As a result, the development of the form of the measurement bias will be in that context. Consider:

$$\text{plim } \hat{\beta} = \beta - (\Sigma + \Omega)^{-1}\Omega\beta \tag{17}$$

where:

$$\hat{\beta} = (\hat{\beta}_1 \ldots \hat{\beta}_4)', \quad \beta = (\beta_1 \ldots \beta_4)'$$
$$\Omega\beta = (\sigma_\epsilon^2\beta_1 \, 0 \, 00)', \text{ and}$$

$$(\Sigma+\Omega)^{-1} = \begin{bmatrix} \sigma_1^2 + \sigma_\epsilon^2 & \sigma_{21} & \sigma_{31} & \sigma_{41} \\ \sigma_{12} & \sigma_2 & \sigma_{32} & \sigma_{42} \\ \sigma_{13} & \sigma_{23} & \sigma_3 & \sigma_{43} \\ \sigma_{14} & \sigma_{24} & \sigma_{34} & \sigma_4^2 \end{bmatrix}$$

Evaluation of the inverse and the $\Omega\beta$ expressions requires only that the expressions for the first column of this inverse be known since the remaining elements are multiplied by zeros, and disappear.

Let $|\Sigma + \Omega| = \theta$. Since this term is positive it will not alter the direction of any relationships. The inverse elements for $(\Sigma + \Omega)$ can be expressed by the following:

ELEMENT 1/1

$$[\sigma_2^2\sigma_3^2\sigma_4^2 + 2\sigma_{23}\sigma_{34}\sigma_{24}] - [\sigma_{24}^2\sigma_3^2 + \sigma_{23}^2\sigma_4^2 + \sigma_{34}^2\sigma_2^2]$$
$$= \sigma_2^2\sigma_3^2\sigma_4^2[1 + 2(\tau_{23}\tau_{34}\tau_{24}) - (\tau_{24}^2 + \tau_{34}^2 + \tau_{23}^2)]. \tag{18}$$

ELEMENT 1/2

$$-[(\sigma_{12}\sigma_3^2\sigma_4^2 + \sigma_{13}\sigma_{34}\sigma_{24} + \sigma_{14}\sigma_{23}\sigma_{34})$$
$$-(\sigma_{24}\sigma_{14}\sigma_3^2 + \sigma_{34}^2\sigma_{12} + \sigma_{13}\sigma_{23}\sigma_4^2)] =$$
$$-\sigma_1\sigma_2\sigma_3^2\sigma_4^2[\tau_{12}(1-\tau_{34}^2) + \tau_{13}(\tau_{34}\tau_{24} - \tau_{23})$$
$$+\tau_{14}(\tau_{23}\tau_{34} - \tau_{24})]. \tag{19}$$

ELEMENT 1/3

$$(\sigma_{12}\sigma_{23}\sigma_4^2 + \sigma_{14}\sigma_{34}\sigma_2^2 + \sigma_{13}\sigma_{24}^2)$$
$$-(\sigma_{14}\sigma_{23}\sigma_{24} + \sigma_{12}\sigma_{24}\sigma_{34} + \sigma_{13}\sigma_2^2\sigma_4^2) =$$
$$\sigma_1\sigma_2^2\sigma_3\sigma_4^2[\tau_{13}(\tau_{24}^2-1) + \tau_{12}(\tau_{23}-\tau_{24}\tau_{34})$$
$$+\tau_{14}(\tau_{34}-\tau_{23}\tau_{24})]. \tag{20}$$

ELEMENT 1/4

$$-\{[\sigma_{12}\sigma_{23}\sigma_{34} + \sigma_{13}\sigma_{24}\sigma_{23} + \sigma_{14}\sigma_2^2\sigma_3^2]$$
$$-[\sigma_{14}\sigma_{23}^2 + \sigma_{12}\sigma_{24}\sigma_3^2 + \sigma_{13}\sigma_{34}\sigma_3^2] =$$
$$-\sigma_1\sigma_2^2\sigma_3^2\sigma_4[(1-\tau_{23}^2)\tau_{14} + \tau_{12}(\tau_{23}\tau_{34}-\tau_{24})$$
$$+\tau_{13}(\tau_{24}\tau_{23}-\tau_{34})], \tag{21}$$

where: $\tau_{ij} = \sigma_{ij}/\sigma_i\sigma_j$.

Element 1/1 can be reduced to the following expression by substitution:

$$[(1-\tau_{34}^2)(1-R_{2,34}^2)] \, \sigma_2^2\sigma_3^2\sigma_4^2, \tag{22}$$

where:

$$R_{2\cdot34}^2 = (\tau_{23}^2\tau_{24}^2 - 2\tau_{23}\tau_{24}\tau_{34})/(1-\tau_{34}^2),$$

thus assuming that this element is necessarily positive.

Let $\gamma_{ij}$ be the i/j element of the inverse of $(\Sigma+\Omega)$. The expression for the probability limit of the first parameter estimate is:

$$\text{plim } (\hat{\beta}_1) = \beta_1 - \frac{\gamma_{11}}{\theta} \cdot \sigma_\epsilon^2\beta_1, \tag{23}$$

where $\theta = |\Sigma + \Omega|$.

Since $\gamma_{11}$, $\theta$, $\sigma_\epsilon^2$ are each positive, the estimate of $\beta_1$ is necessarily biased towards zero independent of the sign of $\beta_1$.

Thus, if advertising is assumed to be the only variable with measurement error, it will have a downward bias. The value estimated for the advertising coefficient can be said to be a lower limit on the "true" value of this parameter.

An upper bound can be similarly estimated. The original relationship is:

$$Y^* = X^*_1\beta_1 + X_2\beta_2 + U - \beta_1\epsilon. \tag{24}$$

By treating the advertising variable as the dependent variable the following expression is formed:

$$X^*_1 = 1/\beta_1 Y^* - \frac{1}{\beta_1}X_2\beta_2 - \frac{1}{\beta_1}U + \epsilon. \tag{25}$$

The upper bound is determined by taking the reciprocal of the dependent variable's coefficient (i.e., calculate $\beta_1$ from [25]).

Of additional interest to this analysis is the effect of this measurement error on the other parameter estimates. While no generalization can be made as to the direction the bias will have, specific situations can be examined. The relationship for the other parameter estimates is:

$$\text{plim } (\hat{\beta}_i) = \beta_i - \frac{\gamma_{1i}}{\theta}\sigma_\epsilon^2\beta_1. \tag{26}$$

Since the signs of all but the elements of the inverse are known, once these elements are calculated, the direction of the bias will be known. Table one lists the variables, the sign of the element of the inverse, and the direction of the bias for the Weiss and Palda models.

IMPLICATIONS

The results imply that the Weiss models are much stronger than the initial results would suggest. The advertising parameter for the additive model was estimated to be .0154 and can be interpreted as the lower bound of the true parameter value. The price coefficient was similarly biased toward zero, while the two dummy variables were biased away from zero. Had the "true" advertising measurement been available, the price and advertising variables would have played a more meaningful role in the analysis.

The results for the Palda model are of even greater interest since Clarke and McCann have suggested bias in Palda's
results.[2]    The estimate of the advertising parameter is
biased toward zero and the coefficient of lagged sales is
biased away from zero (over-estimated), thus supporting
Clarke and McCann's contention.

## CONCLUSION

The above development demonstrates that parameters of
independent variables measured with error are necessarily
underestimated (i.e., biased toward zero) by ordinary least
squares.   The remaining parameter estimates will be biased
in some unspecified direction.   Fortunately, the direction
of these biases are easily determined.  Finally, the
"measurement error" problem has been extended from the
single independent variable case (discussed by Goldberger
[3]), to the more generalizable case of three (by Levy
[6]) and four independent variables.

### TABLE 1
### DIRECTION OF BIAS AND
### SIGN OF INVERSE ELEMENT
### FOR WEISS AND PALDA MODELS

#### WEISS ADDITIVE MODEL

| Variable | Inverse Element | Bias |
|---|---|---|
| Price | $\gamma > 0$ | $(\hat{\beta}-\beta) > 0$ |
| $Q_1$ (dummy) | $\gamma < 0$ | $(\hat{\beta}-\beta) > 0$ |
| $Q_2$ (dummy) | $\gamma < 0$ | $(\hat{\beta}-\beta) > 0$ |

#### WEISS LOG LINEAR MODEL

| Variable | Inverse Element | Bias |
|---|---|---|
| Price | $\gamma > 0$ | $(\hat{\beta}-\beta) > 0$ |
| $Q_1$ (dummy) | $\gamma < 0$ | $(\hat{\beta}-\beta) > 0$ |
| $Q_2$ (dummy) | $\gamma < 0$ | $(\hat{\beta}-\beta) > 0$ |

#### PALDA KOYL (Y-LESS) MODEL
#### WITH LOG OF ADVERTISING

| Variable | Inverse Element | Bias |
|---|---|---|
| Lagged Share | $\gamma < 0$ | $(\hat{\beta}-\beta) > 0$ |
| D (dummy) | $\gamma > 0$ | $(\hat{\beta}-\beta) < 0$ |
| Trend | $\gamma < 0$ | $(\hat{\beta}-\beta) > 0$ |

#### PALDA KOYL (Y-LESS) MODEL
#### WITHOUT LOG OF ADVERTISING

| Variable | Inverse Element | Bias |
|---|---|---|
| Lagged Share | $\gamma < 0$ | $(\hat{\beta}-\beta) > 0$ |
| D (dummy) | $\gamma > 0$ | $(\hat{\beta}-\beta) < 0$ |
| Trend | $\gamma < 0$ | $(\hat{\beta}-\beta) > 0$ |

### TABLE 2
### UPPER AND LOWER BOUNDS
### ON THE ADVERTISING
### PARAMETER ESTIMATES

| Model | Upper Bound | Lower Bound |
|---|---|---|
| Weiss Additive | 2.754 | .0154 |
| Weiss Log-Linear | .253 | .0723 |
| Palda w. Log Advertising | 4167. | 1314. |
| Palda w/o Log Advertising | 2.353 | .541 |

### REFERENCES

1.  Clarke, Darrall G. and John M. McCann, "Measuring the
    Cumulative Effects of Advertising: A Reappraisal",
    Krannert Graduate School of Industrial Administration,
    Purdue University, Working Paper No. 140 (May, 1973),
    West Lafayette, Indiana;  also Proceedings, Fall
    Conference, American Marketing Association, 1973.

2.  Frank, Ronald E. and Charles E. Strain, "A Segmen-
    tation Design Using Consumer Panel Data", Journal of
    Marketing Research, IX, (November, 1972), pp. 385-390.

3.  Goldberger, Arthur S., Econometric Theory, New York:
    John Wiley and Sons, Inc., 1964.

4.  Green, Paul E., Yoram Wind, and Arum K. Jain,
    "Analyzing Free Response Data in Marketing Research",
    Journal of Marketing Research X, (February, 1973),
    pp. 45-52.

5.  King, Charles W., Jr., "Mathematical Models in
    Marketing: Status and Forecast", Attitude Research in
    Transition, Proceedings of meeting sponsored by
    ATTITUDE RESEARCH COMMITTEE, AMERICAN MARKETING ASSOC.,
    Marketing Research Techniques, Series No. 15.

6.  Levy, Maurice, Inventory Disequilibrium and the Effects
    of Monetary and Fiscal Policy, unpublished Ph.D.
    Thesis, University of Chicago, 1972.

7.  Palda, Kristian S., "The Measurement of Cumulative
    Advertising Effects", Journal of Business, 38 (April,
    1965).

8.  Weiss, Doyle L., "The Determinants of Market Share",
    Journal of Marketing Research, 5 (August, 1968)
    pp. 290-295.

[2]It should be pointed out that Clarke and McCann
compare their results to the KOYK model, which incorporates lagged sales, advertising and three dummy
variables.  The parameter estimates for lagged sales
and advertising in the KOYK and variation used above
are similar.

$$S_t = -388.67 + .684 S_{t-1} + .541 A_t + 485.D + 11.T$$

$$(.082) \quad (.143) \quad (103.) \quad (3.)$$

# RELATIONSHIPS BETWEEN THE PURCHASE TIMING
## PROCESS AND THE CHOICE PROCESS

Abel P. Jeuland, The University of Chicago

### ABSTRACT

In order to model multibrand markets, one needs to incorporate both a submodel of the purchase timing process and a submodel of the choice process. The former deals with describing the occurrence over time of purchase occasions of the product class. In other words, purchase timing is concerned with describing the rate of purchase of the product class, some consumers being light buyers and others being heavier buyers. The choice model deals with describing how a choice is made on a given purchase occasion. The present article investigates some issues related to the question of the association between the two processes. Whether there is dependence or independence between the purchase timing process and the multibrand choice process has important implications for combining them in order to obtain a complete model of the market.

### INTRODUCTION

In this paper the author investigates conditions under which it is reasonable to compound a stochastic submodel of purchase timing with a stochastic submodel of the choice process so as to obtain a model of multibrand purchase behavior. The important condition is whether the two subprocesses are independent, and the method used must depend on this independence. If the condition of independence is satisfied, one can study the joint distribution over the population of the rate of purchase R and the frequency of buying brand $i, \Theta_i$, by simply studying the marginal distributions of R and $\Theta_i$ independently. The joint distribution will be simply the product of the two distributions

$$f_{R,\Theta_i}(r, \theta_i) = f_R(r) \cdot f_{\Theta_i}(\theta_i) . \qquad (1)$$

On the other hand, if R and $\Theta_i$ are not independent, it is impossible to study them independently. In other words, knowledge of the marginal distributions of R and $\Theta_i$ is insufficient to deduce the joint distribution. One needs the marginal distribution of one of the random variables and also the conditional distribution of the other random variable with respect to the first:

$$f_{R,\Theta_i}(r, \theta_i) = f_R(r) \cdot h_{\Theta_i}(\theta_i|r) = f_{\Theta_i}(\theta_i) \cdot g_R(r|\theta_i) . \qquad (2)$$

Notably, all models of purchase behavior incorporating both processes (3, 4) have assumed that they are independent.

### MARKET SHARES IN THE LIGHT, MEDIUM
### AND HEAVY-BUYERS SEGMENTS

An indication of what relationship exists between the choice and purchase timing processes can be obtained by segmenting the market on the basis of the rate of purchase and looking at the distribution of market shares within each segment.

Let us consider a population of individuals who are each described by a mean rate of purchase per period of time (denoted as R) and a probability of choosing the brand under study on a given purchase occasion (denoted as $\Theta_i$). By definition, the market share m of a brand is the percentage of sales going to the brand. With the sales volume defined as the number of purchase occasions, the sales of the brand contributed by the customers whose mean rate of

purchase is R = r and whose probability of choice of the brand is $\Theta_i = \theta_i$ and $r \cdot \theta_i$. So

$$m_i = \frac{\sum_{\theta_i} \sum_r r \cdot \theta_i \cdot P(r, \theta_i)}{\sum_r r \cdot P(r)} = \frac{E(R \cdot \Theta_i)}{E(R)} \qquad (3)$$

where the E denotes the expected value over the population. From (3), it is evident that if the choice process and the purchase timing process are independent,

$$m_i = E\Theta_i = \theta_i \qquad (4)$$

But, if there is a relationship between R and $\Theta_i$, (3) leads to

$$m_i = E\Theta_i + \rho_i \frac{\sigma_i \sigma_R}{E(R)} = \theta_i + \rho_i \frac{\sigma_i \sigma_R}{r} \qquad (5)$$

where $\rho_i$ denotes the correlations between $\Theta_i$ and R and $\sigma_{\Theta_i}$ and $\sigma_R$ their standard deviations respectively; r and $\theta_i$ are the mean values of the random variables R and $\Theta_i$.

The data used in this study come from a French panel of 1,961 consumers for the period 1971-1972. Figures 1a, 1b, and 1c show the monthly market shares of six brands of cooking oil in each of three segments, each segment defined on the basis of the rate of purchase as light, medium, and heavy segments: segment 1 includes the people who bought 30 times or less during the two-year period, segment 3, the people who bought more than 60 times, and segment 2, the remainder. Table 1 and Figure 2 give the total monthly demand for each segment.

The graph of brand 3 does not suggest any pattern. The curves corresponding to brand 4 show that the heavy segment curve is in general below the two other curves, thus indicating a negative correlation. The relationships for brands 10 and 11 are clearer. In both cases there is a positive correlation. The opposite situation is found for brands 20 and 21. The correlations were in fact computed between the frequencies of purchase $\Theta_i$ and the two-year rate of purchase R, and are given in Table 2. Although some correlations are significant, absolute values are all below .10 so that no major discrepancies would be expected if one assumes the independence of the choice process and the purchase timing process.

### NUMBER OF BRANDS BOUGHT BY THE LIGHT,
### MEDIUM AND HEAVY SEGMENTS

Another important notion involves the connection between the choice process and the purchase timing process. In particular, Ehrenberg tried to differentiate heavy and light buyers on the basis of the number of brands bought [1]. He wrote: ". . .heavy product usage goes together with the purchasing of more than one brand. . . . The average number of brands bought increases as we move from light buyers up the scale to heavy buyers. This is a typical finding in most product-fields. . ." [1, p.183]. Tables 3 and 4 reproduce some of his findings.

However, one should be cautious about these findings. The reason is that buying more brands is a mere consequence of

FIGURE 1 - A

MARKET SHARES OF BRANDS 3 AND 4 IN EACH OF
THE THREE (3) SEGMENTS (LIGHT, MEDIUM,
HEAVY BUYER) DURING 1971-1972.

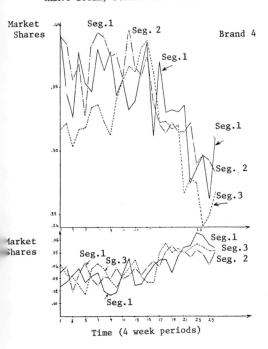

FIGURE 1 - C

MARKET SHARES OF BRANDS 20 AND 21 IN EACH OF
THE THREE (3) SEGMENTS (LIGHT, MEDIUM, HEAVY
BUYER) DURING 1971-1972.

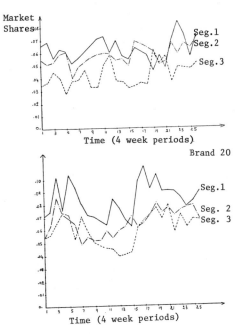

FIGURE 1 - B

MARKET SHARES OF BRANDS 10 AND 11 IN EACH OF
THE THREE (3) SEGMENTS (LIGHT, MEDIUM,
HEAVY BUYER) DURING 1971-1972.

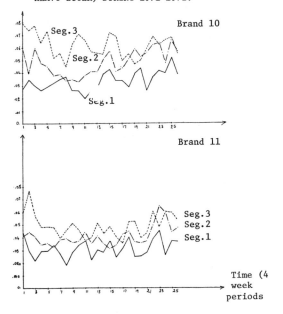

TABLE 1

TOTAL DEMAND EXPRESSED IN NUMBER OF
PURCHASE OCCASIONS FOR EACH OF THE THREE SEGMENTS

| Time Periods (period length= 4 weeks) | Light Buyers $\leq 30$ Purchases | Medium Buyers $31\leq$ No. of Purchases$\leq 60$ | Heavy Buyers $\geq 61$ Purchases |
|---|---|---|---|
| 1 | 763 | 1086 | 823 |
| 2 | 701 | 1088 | 819 |
| 3 | 739 | 1142 | 830 |
| 4 | 737 | 1179 | 854 |
| 5 | 803 | 1223 | 864 |
| 6 | 853 | 1172 | 854 |
| 7 | 757 | 1186 | 834 |
| 8 | 657 | 992 | 783 |
| 9 | 657 | 965 | 739 |
| 10 | 793 | 1117 | 868 |
| 11 | 771 | 1182 | 875 |
| 12 | 700 | 1087 | 850 |
| 13 | 659 | 1060 | 836 |
| 14 | 665 | 1055 | 830 |
| 15 | 752 | 1106 | 826 |
| 16 | 724 | 1049 | 821 |
| 17 | 724 | 1084 | 847 |
| 18 | 714 | 1111 | 822 |
| 19 | 752 | 1123 | 816 |
| 20 | 731 | 1115 | 861 |
| 21 | 628 | 969 | 739 |
| 22 | 689 | 969 | 705 |
| 23 | 775 | 1109 | 808 |
| 24 | 755 | 1078 | 826 |
| 25 | 634 | 1012 | 819 |
| 26 | 622 | 1006 | 801 |

177

FIGURE 2

MONTHLY NUMBER OF PURCHASE OCCASIONS

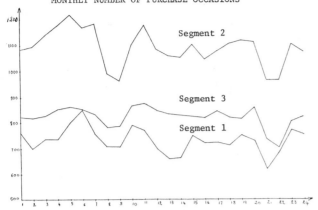

Total Demand for Each Segment (1 = {$\leq$ 30 purchases},
2 ={$\geq$ 31 and $\leq$ 60}, 3 ={$\geq$ 61}).

TABLE 2

COOKING OIL - CORRELATIONS $r_1$ BETWEEN )$_i$ , i = 2,...,35[+]
AND R AND CORRESPONDING STANDARDIZED Z TRANSFORMS[++]

|  | $r_1$ | $z_1$ |  | $r_1$ | $z_1$ |
|---|---|---|---|---|---|
| i=2 | .0723 | 3.207** | i=19 | −.0399 | −1.765 |
| i=3 | .0128 | .5648 | i=20 | −.0543 | −2.407* |
| i=4 | −.0166 | −.735 | i=21 | −.0332 | −1.470 |
| i=5 | .0968 | 4.298** | i=22 | −.0429 | −1.784 |
| i=6 | −.0296 | −1.310 | i=23 | −.0052 | −.2303 |
| i=7 | −.00098 | −.0434 | i=24 | −.0253 | −1.122 |
| i=8 | −.0164 | −.727 | i=25 | −.0206 | −.9111 |
| i=9 | .0667 | 2.955** | i=26 | −.0337 | −1.493 |
| i=10 | .0829 | 3.677** | i=27 | .05613 | 2.4865* |
| i=11 | .0438 | 1.934 | i=28 | .04786 | 2.1192* |
| i=12 | .0130 | .5756 | i=29 | −.00735 | −.3252 |
| i=13 | .0305 | 1.349 | i=30 | −.0213 | −.9427 |
| i=14 | −.0104 | −.459 | i=31 | −.0108 | −.4763 |
| i=15 | −.0589 | −2.609** | i=32 | −.0173 | −.7639 |
| i=16 | −.0377 | −1.670 | i=33 | .05555 | 2.4604* |
| i=17 | −.0334 | −1.480 | i=34 | .00185 | .081 |
| i=18 | −.0569 | −2.522* | i=35 | −.0441 | −1.952 |

[+]There are 35 brands in the cooking oil product class.
Brand 1 is not included in the analysis because it was
bought by only one of the 1,961 panel members.
[++]R. Fisher r to z transform; $Z_1 = 1/2 \text{Log}[(1+r_1)/(1-r_1)] N^{-3}$
N=1961 (cf Hays, p. 662).
*Significant at the .05 level ($|Z| > 1.96$)
**Significant at the .01 level($|Z| > 2.58$)

TABLE 3

EHRENBERG'S EMPIRICAL FINDINGS - THE PERCENTAGE OF BUYERS
OF THE PRODUCT-FIELD WHO BUY 1, 2, 3, etc. BRANDS
IN THE YEAR

| No. of Brands bought in 48 weeks | Buyers of the product field* | | | |
|---|---|---|---|---|
|  | All % | Light % | Medium % | Heavy % |
| 1 | 33 | 46 | 21 | 14 |
| 2 | 27 | 29 | 24 | 22 |
| 3 | 15 | 13 | 19 | 21 |
| 4+ | 24 | 12 | 36 | 43 |
| Average | 2.5 | 1.9 | 3.0 | 3.6 |

TABLE 4

THE AVERAGE NUMBER OF BRANDS BOUGHT IN PERIODS
OF VARIOUS LENGTHS

| Average No. of Brands Bought | Buyers of the product-field* | | | |
|---|---|---|---|---|
|  | All | Light | Medium | Heavy |
| in 48 weeks | 2.5 | 1.9 | 3.0 | 3.6 |
| in 12 weeks | 1.7 | 1.3 | 1.7 | 2.3 |
| in 4 weeks | 1.4 | 1.1 | 1.3 | 1.7 |
| in 1 week | 1.1 | 1.0 | 1.0 | 1.2 |

*Light buyers --- 1-12 purchases in the year (55%)
 Medium buyers -- 13-25 purchases in the year (25%)
 Heavy buyers --- 26+ purchases in the year (21%)

the sample size; i.e., if two customers have the same probabilities of purchase but one buys more often than the other, the expected value of the number of brands bought by
the latter is smaller. This can be easily illustrated in
the two-brand case. If customer 1 buys $n_1$ times and customer 2 buys $n_2 > n_1$ times, the mean number of brands
bought for customer 1 is

$$\theta^{n_1} + (1 - \theta)^{n_1} + 2(1 - \theta^{n_1} - (1 - \theta)^{n_1}) = 2 - \theta^{n_1} - (1 - \theta)^{n_1}$$

and, for customer 2, $2 - \theta^{n_2} - (1 - \theta)^{n_2}$. The function
$2 - \theta^n - (1 - \theta)^n$ is a monotone decreasing function of n
as illustrated in Table 5 below for several $\theta$'s.

TABLE 5

MEAN NUMBER OF BRANDS BOUGHT UNDER THE BINOMIAL
ASSUMPTION (B(n,0).

| 0 | n=2 | n=5 | n=10 |
|---|---|---|---|
| .1 | 1.180 | 1.410 | 1.651 |
| .2 | 1.320 | 1.672 | 1.893 |
| .3 | 1.420 | 1.830 | 1.972 |
| .4 | 1.480 | o.921 | 1.994 |
| .5 | 1.500 | 1.938 | 1.998 |

As shown by the above table, the differences in apparent
heterogeneity appear to be substantial. This should be
kept in mind as one compares the numbers 1.9, 3.0, 3.6 of
mean numbers of brands bought in each segment (see Ehrenberg's tables which follow). The problem in investigating
the matter further is that the distribution of the number
of brands bought if brand choice is multinomial is not
available in a statistically tractable form.

ANALYSIS OF HOW CUSTOMERS SPREAD
THEIR PURCHASES OVER SEVERAL BRANDS

The above discussion prompted a search for an approach
which could statistically test the question of how people
distribute their purchases among several brands. The

entropy of a distribution as a measure of the spread of such distribution is a logical candidate (5, p. 3). In the case of a discrete distribution defined by the set of probabilities $P_i$ of the categories i, i = 1 ... n, the entropy is

$$H(\vec{P}) = -\sum_i P_i \cdot \text{Log } P_i \quad . \tag{6}$$

However, there is a difficulty in using H. Because of the Log function, it is not easy to find an unbiased estimate of H under the multinomial assumption. If one replaces the $P_i$'s by their maximum likelihood estimates

$P_i = \dfrac{x_i}{n}$ ($x_i$ denotes the number of purchases of brand i and n the number of purchases of the product class), the estimate of H,

$\hat{H} = -\sum_i \dfrac{x_i}{n} \cdot \text{Log } \dfrac{x_i}{n}$ is a biased estimate of H as shown by

the examples in Table 6, where six brands are considered. Only one case was computed for n = 30, because of large computing time cost: with six brands, there are a large number of possible arrangements of 30 purchases! Clearly, a naive reading of Table 6 leads to the conclusion that heavy buyers buy more brands, or spread their probability vectors more than do light buyers. The problem is that the bias of $\hat{H}$ is a monotone function of the number of purchases.

TABLE 6

EXPECTED VALUE OF H AND ACTUAL ENTROPY VALUE FOR n=10 AND n=20 PURCHASES (n=30 for one case) WHEN SIX BRANDS ARE AVAILABLE

|  | n=10 | n=20 | n=30 | Actual Entropy |
|---|---|---|---|---|
| case 1* | .5819 | .6811 |  | .8223 |
| case 2 | .5603 | .6472 |  | .7777 |
| case 3 | .8230 | .9087 |  | 1.0366 |
| case 4 | .8695 | .9542 |  | 1.0820 |
| case 5 | .7244 | .8119 |  | .9404 |
| case 6 | 1.2187 | 1.3569 | 1.4067 | 1.4991 |
| case 7 | 1.2627 | 1.4004 |  | 1.5401 |
| case 8 | 1.3170 | 1.4686 |  | 1.6094 |
| case 9 | 1.4852 | 1.6453 |  | 1.7820 |

*Cases 1 through 0 of the above table are defined by the vector $\vec{P} = P_1, P_2, \ldots, P_6$) since 6 brands only are considered.
The nine vectors are:

VECTOR OF CHOICE PROBABILITIES $\vec{P}$

|  | Brand 1 | Brand 2 | Brand 3 | Brand 4 | Brand 5 | Brand 6 |
|---|---|---|---|---|---|---|
| case 1 | .8 | .04 | .04 | .04 | .04 | .04 |
| case 2 | .8 | .1 | .025 | .025 | .025 | .025 |
| case 3 | .6 | .3 | .025 | .025 | .025 | .025 |
| case 4 | .5 | .4 | .025 | .025 | .025 | .025 |
| case 5 | .7 | .2 | .025 | .025 | .025 | .025 |
| case 6 | .4 | .3 | .1 | .07 | .07 | .06 |
| case 7 | .4 | .2 | .2 | .1 | .05 | .05 |
| case 8 | .4 | .2 | .1 | .1 | .1 | .1 |
| case 9 | .2 | .2 | .15 | .15 | .15 | .15 |

In order to find an alternative to the function $- P_i \text{ Log } (P_i)$, the first objective would be to avoid the use of a transcendental function like Log. One logical method is to try to replace the Log function by its series expansion:

$\text{Log } P = \text{Log}(1 - (1-P)) = -(1-P) - \dfrac{1}{2}(1-P)^2 - \dfrac{1}{3}(1-P)^3 - \ldots.$

By choosing the first term only, the entropy function becomes

$$F = \sum_i P_i(1 - P_i) = 1 - \sum_i P_i^2 \tag{7}$$

which is an algebraic function, and as such much more tractable. It is interesting to notice that $\sum_i P_i^2$ has been used in studies of industrial concentration. Theil [5] calls this function the Hirschman-Herfindahl Index of industrial concentration since it was proposed by each of those two authors in 1945 and 1950 respectively. One should also remark that the above approach can be generalized to any function of higher degree than two. The degree of the polynomial in P is a function of the number of terms used in the series expansion of the log function.

The function in (7) has its maximum value at $P_i = \dfrac{1}{n}$, i = 1, ..., n, like the entropy function. It is also concave like the entropy function. This can be easily seen when the new function is rewritten

$1 - \left\lVert \vec{P} \right\rVert^2$ where $\left\lVert \cdot \right\rVert^2$ denotes the Euclidean squared distance. It is well known that

$\left\lVert \cdot \right\rVert^2$ is a convex function.

$\left\lVert \vec{x} + \vec{y} \right\rVert \leq \left\lVert \vec{x} \right\rVert + \left\lVert \vec{y} \right\rVert$ (Triangular Inequality)

which implies $\left\lVert \vec{x} + \vec{y} \right\rVert^2 \leq \left\lVert \vec{x} \right\rVert^2 + \left\lVert \vec{y} \right\rVert^2$ and also $\left\lVert \vec{x} + (1 - \lambda)\vec{y} \right\rVert^2 \leq \lambda^2 \left\lVert \vec{x} \right\rVert^2 + (1 - \lambda)^2 \left\lVert \vec{y} \right\rVert^2 \leq \lambda \left\lVert \vec{x} \right\rVert^2 + (1 - \lambda) \left\lVert \vec{y} \right\rVert^2$ if $\lambda \epsilon (0, 1)$. So $F(P) = 1 - \left\lVert \vec{P} \right\rVert^2$ is concave. The concavity of $H = -\sum P_i \text{ Log } P_i$ comes from the fact that the function $x \text{Log} x$ is convex as illustrated in Figure 3. The very close relationship between H and F can be seen by observing the two-brand case (cf. Figure 4). The major advantage of the function F is that an unbiased estimate can be easily obtained. If $X_i$ denotes the random variable number of purchase occasions when brand i is chosen, an unbiased estimate of

FIGURE 3

CONVEXITY OF THE FUNCTION xLOGx

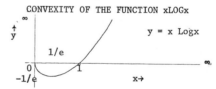

COMPARISON OF THE FUNCTIONS H AND F IN THE TWO-BRAND CASE

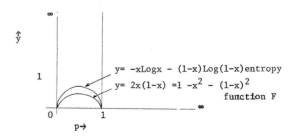

179

$P_i^2$ is $\dfrac{X_i(X_i - 1)}{n(n - 1)}$ because $EX_i^2 - EX_i = \text{var } X_i + (EX_i)^2$

$- EX_i = nP_i(1 - P_i) + n^2P_i^2 - nP_i$ under the multinomial assumption. The unbiased estimate of $1 - \vec{P}^2$ is then:

$$F = 1 - \frac{1}{n(n - 1)} \sum_i X_i(X_i - 1) = 1 - \frac{1}{n(n - 1)} \left( \sum_i X_i^2 - n \right) \quad . (8)$$

Applied to the cooking oil data, the correlation between F and n, the rate of purchase was found to be insignificant: the F-test value is only 2.37 for a .05 significance value of 3.84 (sample size = 1,961). On the contrary, a .01 significance was found between $\hat{H}$ and n, since the F-test value was 12.73. Clearly, this result is influenced by the bias mentioned earlier. One should also keep in mind that the multinomial assumption is only approximately true when applied to the entire population. This would suggest that care should be taken in interpreting results based on the previous F-test comparisons.

## CONCLUSION

This paper has illustrated some issues pertinent to the relationships between the choice process and the purchase timing process. There may appear significant differences between light buyers and heavy buyers as far as specific brands are concerned. However, Ehrenberg's assertions that heavy buyers have "a need for variety" [1, p. 183]. because of buying more brands does not necessarily mean that they have a vector of choice probabilities more spread over the set of brands of the product class than the light buyers do.

The above results are limited to one product class, and thus more cases are needed to justify the conclusion that heavier buyers do not very significantly differ from light buyers as far as brand choice is concerned. This result, if generalizable, has important implications for modeling purchase behavior, as discussed in the introduction.

## REFERENCES

1. Ehrenberg, A. S. C. Repeat-Buying: Theory and Applications. Amsterdam: North-Holland Publishing, 1972.

2. Hays, William L. Statistics for the Social Sciences. Holt, Rinehart and Winston, 1973.

3. Herniter, Jerome D. "A Probabilistic Market Model of Purchase Timing and Brand Selection," Management Science, 18 (December 1971).

4. Jeuland, Abel P. "A Multibrand Stochastic Model Incorporating the Purchase Timing and Brand Choice Processes," Working Paper, University of Chicago (September 1976).

5. Theil, Henri. Statistical Decomposition Analysis. North-Holland Publishing Company, 1972.

# THE ADVERTISING-SALES RELATIONSHIP:
## WHEN IS A SIMULTANEOUS SPECIFICATION NECESSARY?

Johny K. Johansson, University of Washington

## ABSTRACT

The need for a simultaneous specification of the advertising-sales relationship is analyzed. It is shown that a precise understanding of actual causal lags relative to observation period is required for a correct model specification. Generalizing, simultaneous models are seen as appropriate when common disturbances affect the endogeneous variables. The particular problems involved in using a decision variable (advertising) as an endogeneous variable are then surveyed and it is shown how misspecification of the firm's advertising decision making process leads to incorrect model specification. Possible tests for simultaneity and guidelines for re-specification are indicated.

## INTRODUCTION

Recent research into the advertising-sales relationship has argued for the use of a simultaneous equation framework [2, 3, 12]. Not only are the sales seen as determined partly by advertising, but the advertising itself is seen as determined by a product's sales. One reason for this interdependence between sales and advertising is that advertising is often decided upon with reference to sales--the simplest example being the determination of an advertising budget as a percentage of sales. However, since there has been--and continues to be--a considerable amount of research in a non-simultaneous mode, one might ask under what conditions simultaneous specifications do become necessary. The present paper attempts to answer that question in some depth.

## CAUSAL FEEDBACK LOOPS

The most common justification for a simultaneous approach is based on causal feedback loops. These can be incorporated into a simple specification of a simultaneous advertising-sales model that will do for our purposes:

$$S_{it} = f_1 (A_{it}, \underline{X}_{is}) \tag{1}$$

$$A_{it} = f_2 (S_{it}, \underline{X}_{ia}), \quad i=1,\ldots,n; \ t=1,\ldots,T, \tag{2}$$

where $S_{it}$ denotes grand i's sales at t, $A_{it}$ the brand's advertising at t, and $\underline{X}_{is}$, $\underline{X}_{ia}$ denote vectors of various predetermined variables in the sales and the advertising equation, respectively. Sales could be replaced by market share without any difficulty (although if all brands were estimated some constraint on the sum of the total market shares would have to be incorporated). Advertising could be measured in dollars, or relative share, without any essential loss of generality. The predetermined variable vectors would contain assumed exogeneous variables.[1]

The version competing with the simultaneous specification would be the recursive model

$$S_t = f_3 (A_{it}, \underline{X}_{is}) \tag{3}$$

$$A_{it} = f_4 (S_{i,t-1}, \underline{X}_{ia}), \tag{4}$$

where it is assumed that advertising is based on last period's sales rather than the present period's. Alternatively, a recursive version would be obtained if sales were excluded completely from the right hand side of (4), or--another version--if sales were not made a function of present but only last period's advertising while advertising in the current period was made dependent upon present sales. Clearly, these alternative specifications will be appropriate depending upon the particular substantive understanding upon which the model is formulated. One particular alternative is the single equation

$$S_{it} = f_5 (A_{it}, \underline{X}_{is}), \tag{5}$$

where it is assumed that interest centers solely on the determination of sales, with advertising determined without reference to sales, and thus exogeneous. If advertising were to be treated as an endogeneous variables, its equation

$$A_{it} = f_6 (\underline{X}_{ia}) \tag{6}$$

could be evaluated separately from (5).

It is clear that the recursive specification (3) and (4) as well as the single equation version (5) and (6) are special cases of the simultaneous specification (1) and (2). Thus, when the predetermined variables in (2) include lagged sales, and the coefficient for current sales goes to zero, the resulting model is (3, 4). When no sales variable enters in (2), the equations (5, 6) result.[2] These correspondencies have been clearly established by Basmann [1].

Conversely, however, one can conceptualize the simultaneous specification as a limiting case of the recursive system where the time lags in the causal loop between sales and advertising go to zero. This view has been espoused primarily by Wold [16] but also by Bentzel and Hansen [5], and, more recently, Fisher has provided a rigorous analysis developing the conditions under which this limit argument is correct [10]. Since his discussion throws some interesting light on the question of choice of specification, a brief review of Fisher's approach follows.

Fisher assumes that the interactions between the endogeneous variables--sales and advertising in our case--work themselves out within some short but non-zero "reaction" interval. The observations of the process, however, are on variable averages over a longer period, called the "observation" interval. He then asks what will happen to the relationships between the endogeneous variables in the

---

[1] For identification purposes the predetermined variables in $\underline{X}_{is}$ and $\underline{X}_{ia}$ would generally not all be the same.

---

[2] The recursive specification (3,4) can sometimes be estimated using separate least squares for each equation and then becomes very much similar to (5, 6). With lagged endogeneous variables on the right hand side, however, this is not always the case--hence, we will refer to single equations only when exogeneous variables appear alone on the right hand side. The model consisting of (5) and (6) together, in fact constitutes a recursive specification.

limit as the reaction interval goes to zero, but the observation interval stays fixed. The main question is whether in fact the limiting model of this basically recursive process will be correctly specified as a simultaneous system.

Fisher shows [10, p. 78] that in the case the model is linear in all equations, the conditions sufficient and necessary to the limiting specification being simultaneous are simple to state.[3] If the matrix of coefficients for the endogeneous variables in all the equations is denoted by M (a 2 by 2 matrix in our case, containing the advertising and sales coefficients from the two equations (1) and (2)), the characteristic values of M, denoted $h_j$, j=1, 2, will have to satisfy

$$|h_j| \leq 1, \; h_j \neq 1, \tag{7}$$

where $|h_j|$ denotes the modulus of $h_j$. This condition is necessary and sufficient even if M has multiple roots.

These conditions are conceptually very attractive, since they simply amount to a constraint on the dynamics of the causal process. In brief, when the conditions (7) are fulfilled, the lags in the causal loops give rise to a set of difference equations which are dynamically stable. Thus, the limiting case of the reaction interval going towards zero while the observation interval remains at a longer period will be modelled correctly as a simultaneous system whenever the model is linear and the interaction between sales and advertising is non-explosive.

The conditions (7) can be seen as a test of appropriateness of a simultaneous specification derived for the case where the causal system is seen as "really" recursive, but where observation periods are too long to account for the separate loops. The test involves the comparison of the estimated coefficients in M relative to the condition expressed in (7). If (7) is not satisfied, there are two possibilities. Either at least one equation of the submodel is incorrectly specified, or sampling problems ("bad data") have led to strange parameter values. The second possibility would generally lead to large variances and thus instability in the parameter estimates. If the parameter estimates seem stable, the problem lies with misspecification in the equations. Unfortunately, even though Fisher's approach allows the model to be tested using (7), the remedy for misspecification is not indicated by the test results. The solution will generally have to be found in a reconsideration of the underlying theory.

When the advertising-sales data are yearly, it would often be the case that the simultaneity comes about because of the type of "smearing" or "bunching" of the causal loops that Fisher deals with. Thus, one would generally assume that some of the advertising effect occurs within the month, perhaps even week--newspaper advertising, or local spot TV could be examples of this, especially with respect to frequently purchased products. The feedback to advertising from observed sales figures could likewise occur within some months, and new advertising efforts be carried out within the year. If the simultaneous specification is derived on the basis of this type of reasoning, then clearly the estimated model should be tested against the conditions in (7).

In other cases the data on advertising and sales refer to shorter time intervals, however. Among the simultaneous

specifications reported in the literature, bimonthly data are common (see for example [2, 12]). In such cases the use of the simultaneous approach implies that not only are sales influenced by advertising within the two months, but that the sales during those two months in turn affect those same months' advertising. Is it realistic to assume that the sales feedback to the advertising budget decision process is really that fast? Perhaps the use of panel data can yield such quick information, but is it then possible to set the new budget allocation, and implement the media strategy within those two months?

In most cases one would probably have to say that the answer to both those questions is a "No." This answer would seem to imply that the simultaneous specifications in cases such as these ought to be replaced by the recursive specification of the type depicted in (3, 4), perhaps extending the lag of $S_{i,t-1}$ even longer if advertising budgets and media choices have to be set far in advance. The simultaneous specification could still be valid and necessary, however. To see why, we need to extend the concept of simultaneity to include the _full_ set of possible causal relations. In order to accomplish this, it will be necessary to develop in some detail the statistical properties of simultaneous systems.

## COMMON DISTURBANCES

One statistical problem with the specification in (1, 2) is that the residual variation in the equations cannot be seen as independent of the current endogenous variable introduced on the right hand side. Let the statistical model be given by

$$S_{it} = b_0 + b_a A_{it} + \sum_{j=1}^{m_s} b_j X_{jis} + e_{its} \tag{8}$$

$$A_{it} = c_0 + c_s S_{it} + \sum_{j=1}^{m_a} c_j X_{jia} + e_{ita}, \tag{9}$$

where $m_s$ and $m_a$ denote the number of predetermined variables in the sales and advertising equation, respectively, and the e denotes the errors in the equations. To get unbiased estimated of $b_a$ and $c_s$ using ordinary least square requires expectations E to be such that

$$E(A_{it}, e_{its}) = E(S_{it}, e_{ita}) = 0. \tag{10}$$

But substituting $A_{it}$ from (9) into (8) we see that the error term in (8) really comprises the sum $(e_{its} + b_a e_{ita})$, so $S_{it}$ depends on both disturbances. Similarly, a substitution in (9) will produce corresponding results there. In other words, the specified simultaneity implies that advertising and sales are influenced by the same disturbances.

Turning the last statement around, it is easily seen that the simultaneity occurs precisely because the same disturbances affect both equations. It is this problem that the recursive formulation (3, 4) resolves by making the advertising in (4) _not_ a function of $S_{it}$ and thus not (necessarily) of $e_{its}$.

Now we can get back to the simultaneous specification of the advertising-sales relationship for bimonthly data. Let us assume that the model rather than being simultaneous as in (1, 2) is better seen as the recursive (3, 4), because the feedback to advertising takes more than two months. What could make a simultaneous specification still necessary?

The answer lies with the specification of the error terms in (3, 4). Let us denote them $u_{its}$ and $u_{ita}$ for the two equations. These disturbances refer to the current time period and represent at least partly the random effects

---

[3]Note, that linearity here--as usual in econometric models--refers to models linear in the parameters. Whether or not the models are nonlinear in the variables--the more common case--matters little since simple transformation can usually be used to induce linearity.

of omitted variables. If the excluded variables affecting current sales will also affect current advertising, then there will be a correlation between $u_{its}$ and $u_{ita}$. This correlation means that the coefficient for advertising in the sales equation will be biased and inconsistent--a simultaneous equation bias, prohibiting the use of ordinary least squares for estimation of the sales equation. Furthermore, if there are reasons to believe that the correlation between the errors is strong, the omitted variables should either be introduced explicitly, or, where that is prohibited by lack of data, the sales variable $S_{it}$ should be introduced on the right hand side of the advertising euqation, making for the simultaneous specification in (1, 2). This would provide one rationale in the bimonthly case for the simultaneous model of sales and advertising.

It should be noted that omitted variables provide only one possible rationalization of the error term approach. Another hinges on measurement error in the endogenous variables. Such errors could affect both sales and advertising, and cross sectional data would seem to be especially prone to exhibit such reasons for simultaneity. Thus as one can often reasonably assume that advertising-sales data across brands are affected by the same general disturbances--general economic and market conditions, factors affecting the firms' position, such as price controls, etc.--any analysis that uses across-brands data might have to be specified as a simultaneous system. This argument would also hold for survey research into individuals' exposure to advertisements and behavior towards the particular brand, when there is reason to believe that the responses to the questions are interdependent, a not too uncommon characteristic [6 7].

So far we have seen simultaneous models as limiting phenomena of basically recursive models, and also as ecompassing the interdependency induced by disturbances common to the observations on the endogenous variables.[4] An interesting special case of the latter occurs when one endogenous variable--in our case advertising--is a decision variable for the firm handling brand i. Let us turn to that case and its implications next.

### ADVERTISING AS A DECISION VARIABLE

There are at least two complications that arise when the fact that the endogeneous variable advertising is under the control if the i'th firm is taken into account. First, t is clear that the advertising equation should be specified as firm i's decision rule. Thus, if the analysis is carried out by analysts within the firm, there should be little reason to expect misspecification. Outside of the firm one usually has to estimate the parameters of the decision rule from past data. To the extent one can reasonably assume that current sales enter the rule--which depends upon one's a priori knowledge of the firm--the simultaneous specification in (1, 2) is correct. If sales do not enter (or enter with a lag) a simultaneous specification will be incorrect.

The second complication is somewhat more difficult to handle. We can sometimes treat equation (1) as a "production

function," with sales as "output" and advertising as one of the "inputs." From such a viewpoint it follows naturally that when input levels are chosen some attention is given to outputs (this is in fact the rationale underlying the simultaneous specification as we have seen). But we can go further. In some cases the desired sales level is set first and then advertising budgeted so that the target sales will be reached--the "objective-task" method of budgeting. In such a case, the model in (1, 2) is clearly incorrect. Rather, the advertising equation should specify current sales (or, if desired sales refer to future sales, expected sales) as the main determinant of advertising. The sales equation should be modelled on the basis of one's understanding of what decision process led to the setting of a particular desired or target level of sales. In most cases the variables determining desired sales would be exogeneous to the system--that target would perhaps be laid down by higher-echelon executives--and thus the advertising-sales would be best modelled as a recursive system, with sales affecting advertising but no feedback.

For most cases, this is too simpleminded a picture, however. It is clear that advertising is assumed to have some effect upon sales otherwise there would be no use in setting advertising at a level different from zero (provided sales enter the firm's objectives). To be able to set the appropriate advertising level requires not only the target sales figure, but also the precise effect of advertising upon these sales, as they are determined in the marketplace. Therefore, it will be necessary to make sales a function of current advertising, in addition to the advertising being a function of (desired) sales. We are back to the full simultaneous specification (1, 2).

Or are we? We have not yet discussed the possible time lags involved. Several cases are possible, each with its own particular specification. For example, if the desired sales are specified for two months, if advertising is set for those two months, and if the advertising effect is felt during those two months, a simultaneous specification will be all right (assuming we have bimonthly data).[5] On the other hand, if observation intervals are different, or if the desired sales cover a longer period, of if the advertising budgets and allocations will have to be set for longer periods, the particular lag structure has to be explicitly set down and the consequences for simultaneity assessed using the previously developed framework. It is clear that in many cases the appropriate model will be recursive rather than simultaneous.

We have so far dealt with the problem of advertising decision making when it is reasonable to assume that the firm is setting its budget according to an objective-task approach. But this is of course only one alternative. Another possibility, given that the firm feels reasonably confident about the estimates of the sales equation it can derive from past history, is that the firm sets advertising so as to maximize sales or even profits. Maximizing sales is generally a feasible alternative only when the sales equation is concave so that the finite maximum advertising level can be solved for, or when there are constraints that inhibit the possible advertising variability. Since both sales and profit maximization leads to a similar estimation complication--although certainly not to the same advertising levels--we will illustrate the issue with respect to a profit maximizing case.

Assume that we as analysts think the sales function is quadratic:

---

[4]Again, when the observation interval is greater than the reaction interval, the latter being greater than zero, multaneous specifications are necessary. Also, there might cases where the causal loops in fact are instantaneous, for the advertising-sales relationship that would usually not be the case. Finally, it should be reiterated that common disturbances represents *statistically* all the er cases, even though *conceptually* it is here seen as a arate case.

---

[5]Notice that throughout we are not concerned with lagged effects of advertising--only when the effect starts. For the lagged effects we can often introduce lagged endogeneous variables on the right hand side in (1).

$$S_{it} = b_0 + b_{1a}A_{it} - b_{2a}A^2_{it} + \sum_{j=1}^{m_s} b_j X_{jis} + e_{its}, \qquad (11)$$

where the parameters have been estimated (or are known) using some, not necessarily simultaneous, specification. We assume that management considers its knowledge of the sales function sufficient as a basis for decision making, where the objective is to maximize expected profits. With the only source of uncertainty assumed to be the equation error, whose expectation is zero, we can write expected profits as

$$E(P_{it}) = E(mS_{it} - A_{it}),$$

$$= mE(S_{it}) - A_{it}$$

$$= m(b_0 + b_{1a}A_{it} - b_{2a}A^2_{it} + \sum_{j=1}^{m_s} b_j X_{jis}) - A_{it}, \qquad (12)$$

where m denotes the profit margin (price minus non-advertising costs). If we treat the X's as fixed and given, the first order condition for profit maximization leads to an optimal advertising level which is equal to

$$A^*_{it} = (mb_{1a} - 1)/2mb_{2a}. \qquad (13)$$

Unless it is assumed that the decision maker is less than capable, it is clear that any equation relating the advertising to a host of other variables, including current and lagged sales, is basically misspecified. Rather, if the objective in decisions on advertising is known, such a second equation comprises something like the expression (13). Note that in general the first-order condition will also contain dependencies upon some other predetermined variables, including previous advertising levels; see, e.g., multiplicative models.

Furthermore, it can be useful to test one's specification using those relationships. Thus, if we use (1, 2) as an initial specification, where (2) in effect models the decision rule, one should ask whether the estimated coefficient values are compatible with some acceptable firm objective. In fact, the modelling of the decision rule should start with an acceptable definition of what the firm is trying to accomplish with its advertising, and only then proceed to derive a decision rule that will make sense considering the objectives. After the estimates of the coefficients are obtained one can use them to predict the choice of $A^*_{it}$ and compare with the actual values observed— a simple statistic to use would be the R-square.

## CONCLUDING COMMENT

As we have seen, simultaneity is not an either/or proposition in the specification of advertising-sales models. Whether or not a simultaneous system is necessary depends on the periodicity of the feedback loops versus the observation period, on the degree to which the endogeneous variables are affected by the same unobserved variables, and to what extent the decisions on advertising spending anticipate future sales. As the paper has shown, there are also ·some possibilities of using the estimated coefficients to test for simultaneity. Whether or not the "true" model is finally identified in any particular application is still a moot question, but some of the considerations presented should serve to reduce the risk of misspecification.

## REFERENCES

1. Basmann, R. L., "A Note on the Statistical Testability of 'Explicit Causal Chains' Against the Class of 'Interdependent' Models," Journal of the American Statistical Association, Vol. 60, No. 312, December, 1965, pp. 1080-1093.

2. Bass, Frank M., "A Simultaneous Equation Regression Study of Advertising and Sales of Cigarettes," Journal of Marketing Research, Vol. VI, August, 1969, pp. 291-300.

3. Bass, Frank M. and Leonard J. Parsons, "Simultaneous-Equation Regression Analysis of Sales and Advertising," Applied Economics, Vol. 1, April, 1969, pp. 103-124.

4. Beckwith, Neil E., "Multivariate Analysis of Sales Responses of Competing Brands to Advertising," Journal of Marketing Research, Vol. 9, May, 1972, pp. 168-176.

5. Bentzel, R., and B. Hansen, "On Recursiveness and Interdependency in Economic Models, Review of Economic Studies, Vol. 22, pp. 153-168.

6. Bradburn, Norman M. and Seymor Sudman, Toward a General Theory of Response Effects in Surveys, Chicago: National Opinion Research Center, University of Chicago, 1973.

7. Bucklin, Louis P., and James M. Carman, The Design of Consumer Research Panels: Conception and Administration of the Berkeley Food Panel, Berkeley: University of California, Institute of Business and Economic Research 1967.

8. Clarke, Darral G., "Sales-Advertising Cross-Elasticities and Advertising Competition," Journal of Marketing Research, Vol. X, August, 1973, pp. 250-261.

# COMMENTS ON THE SOCIOLOGY OF MARKETING RESEARCH

Johan Arndt, Norwegian School of Economics and Business Administration

## ABSTRACT

The basic argument of this article is that scientific activity is a social process. Research in marketing has mainly been inspired by the research paradigms in Logical Empiricism or Positivism emphasizing reductionism, search for empirical regularities, and quantification. Results of this are a narrow methodological repertoire, conceptual poverty, and a conceptualization of marketing as mainly a seller's technology.

## INTRODUCTION

Marketing is concerned with the exchange and communication processes in the resolving of economic needs in society. Hence, it is somewhat ironic that the marketing discipline for such a long time has managed to remain in almost "splendid isolation" from the fundamental (and sometimes devastating) debate in many behavioral sciences questioning the goals, ideals, values, and methods of the discipline.

An exception to the rule is the stimulating debate on the broadening of marketing, following in the wake of the pioneering article by Kotler and Levy [11]. A result of this debate is the functional and generic redefinition of marketing to apply to all situations involving exchange of values between two or more parties.

Of perhaps equal value are the efforts of Zaltman and his colleagues [17, 18] and Hunt [8] to introduce into the marketing literature the rigorous thinking methodology from the philosophy of science generally referred to as metatheory. The subject matter of metatheory is not the substance of the theories within the discipline of interest, but rather the process of theorization and conceptualization. So far, the metatheoretic work in marketing has mainly been of a normative nature as the contributions have aimed at formulating and applying "quality control" criteria for the evaluation of theories and concepts.

However, there is also a descriptive metatheoretic research tradition, sometimes referred to as sociology of science, which is concerned with how scientific standards, norms, and values develop, and with the interrelations of science and society.

This paper is an attempt to contribute to a descriptive metascientific tradition in marketing. The discussion takes the view that scientific activity is essentially a social process. Specifically, the paper outlines a theoretical framework for studying the behavioral influences on research in marketing (and other behavioral sciences) and discusses the relations between the set of influences and the predominant research paradigms in marketing.

This paper is organized as follows:

- On the notion of science as a process

- A behavioral view of the research process

- Scientific orientations

- Empiricism as a research orientation

- Marketing as a positivistic discipline

- The road ahead

## ON THE NOTION OF SCIENCE AS A NOTION

The discussion in this section and the following one is partly inspired by the general ideas in sociology of science, see for instance [9], and partly by the work of Törnebohm and his colleagues at the Institute of the Theory of Science at the University of Gothenburg [5, 16]. A central notion in the latter school of thought is the conceptualization of science as a sequence of partly cumulative and partly non-cumulative transformations of knowledge (K), problems (P), and instruments (I).

By knowledge is meant generalized "certified" knowledge portraying an aspect of reality. An aspect is a selected group of characteristics or the phenomena in some sphere of the "real world". Problems arise from the discrepancies between what is known and what is unknown or from the uncertainties of applying generalized knowledge to concrete situations. Instruments or methods refer both to what Kornhauser and Lazarsfeld [10] call "master techniques" (such as overall research design, models, etc.), and "servant techniques" (such as questionnaire construction, statistical methods, hard-ware instruments, etc.).

Figure 1 depicts this view of the process of research.

### FIGURE 1

### A GENERAL MODEL OF THE PROCESS OF RESEARCH

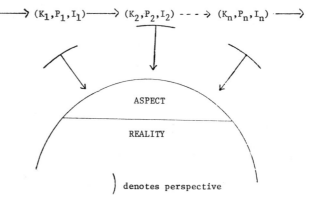

$$\longrightarrow (K_1, P_1, I_1) \longrightarrow (K_2, P_2, I_2) \dashrightarrow (K_n, P_n, I_n) \longrightarrow$$

ASPECT

REALITY

) denotes perspective

Adapted from Tornebohm [16]

Figure 1 may be interpreted as follows: The aspect of interest (in this case, some aspect of market processes) is mapped by applying the initial KPI (knowledge, problems, and instruments) to it. In this process, the KPI complex is filtered through what is termed the perspective of the research, referring to the fact that there are alternative ways of approaching the aspect, and that the researcher is selective in his choice of approach. The aspects studied are not given once and for all. New knowledge may widen the boundaries, as may have happened in marketing after the broadening of marketing debate.

The transitions, from instance from complex $(K_1P_1I_1)$ to $(K_2P_2I_2)$ occur when the problems $P_1$ are solved so as to increase the knowledge from $K_1$ to $K_2$. In the problem solving process, new instruments may be created or borrowed and adapted from other disciplines, hereby changing $I_1$ to $I_2$.

In marketing, it appears that much of the progress in knowledge occurs by what may be characterized as "development by accumulation". In the terms of historian of science Kuhn [12], marketing research is presently essentially a "normal science" based on shared paradigms and an orderly theory-building in a cumulative fashion. By paradigm is meant generally accepted examples of actual scientific practice including theories, concepts, and applications as well as methods, providing models from which spring particular coherent traditions of scientific research [12, p 10]. In marketing, perhaps the marketing

and the broadened marketing concepts are what come closest to a paradigm in this sense.

However, as shown by Kuhn for the natural sciences, there are sometimes important exceptions to the orderly and marginal pattern of scientific progress, as some disciplines have been found to pass through periods of "development by revolution" or discontinuous leaps forward. Such abolitions of existing paradigms may occur when disciplines enter crisis situations in which the existing knowledge is inadequate to explain and to cope with the problems in their part of reality. There are indications that such a situation is imminent for marketing [1].

## A BEHAVIORAL VIEW OF THE RESEARCH PROCESS

To some extent, a behavioral and social view of the research process challenges the myth of the autonomy and open-mindedness of the researcher. However, impressive evidence against this stereotype image of the researcher is marshalled by Barber [2] who examined "irrational" resistance to scientific discovery in the natural sciences

FIGURE 2
A CONCEPTUAL SCHEME OF SOCIAL INFLUENCES ON RESEARCH

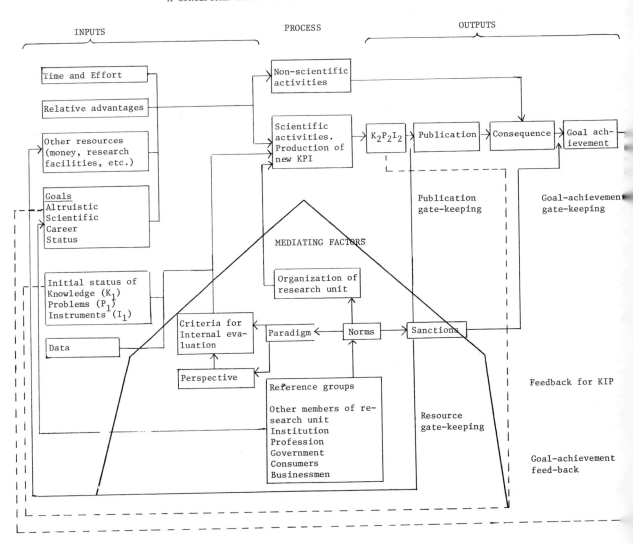

An example from the behavioral sciences, though extreme, may be found in the _Time_ issue of December 6, 1976, which reported the charges against the late distinguished British psychologist Burt who allegedly produced fake data and misused his position as a journal editor to favor contributions attacking his professional enemies.

Figure 2 shows a conceptual framework for the behavioral and social influences on research - or rather on the researcher. For expositional reasons, the discussion which follows assumes that the researcher mainly works alone on his project. However, the argumentation can easily be extended so as also to include operations of research teams. Owing to the limitations imposed by the length of the paper, the discussion will be brief.

A key idea in the framework in Figure 2 is the notion that research is motivated and purposeful, as the researcher is viewed as being engaged in scientific activities to reach certain goals. In some cases, the researcher may be motivated by the proverbial goal intrinsic to the science of "pushing back the frontiers of knowledge". In other cases, the goals may be extrinsic to science as the research may be instrumental to attaining other goals such as helping others, or more selfishly, to advance the researcher's own career and/or status. Goals may also be attained by non-scientific activities such as good teaching, administrative abilities, fund raising skills, professional affairs, management consulting, etc.

Other determinants than goals of the transformation of $K_1 P_1 I_1$ to $K_2 P_2 I_2$ are the inputs time and effort invested, the relative advantages or skills of the researcher, and other resources available such as money, computer facilities, assistants, etc.

After the new $K_2 P_2 I_2$ combination has been "produced", a next step is the publication of the results. Since research output in the form of journal articles, conference proceedings contributions, and books tend to be a major factor in career development, goal achievement is linked to publication by the variable consequences of publication.

A set of mediating social factors is shown at the bottom of Figure 2, which identifies several interest or reference groups whose norms serve as anchoring points for the researcher in developing his research paradigms, perspective and criteria for internal evaluation. For researchers of a "localite" orientation, other members of the research unit or the institution may be the most influential reference groups. More "cosmopolite" researchers may be oriented toward consumers or consumer organizations, or more frequently, governmental agencies. A particularly dominant reference group is marketing practitioners, who demand actionable results helpful in planning and implementing marketing operations. The fact that most marketing researchers are also professors in professional schools actually training managers adds to the salience of the group. Finally, there is the influence of the collective of researchers or the profession. Though this group appears to have internalized the practitioners' norms to a great extent, the group also harbors pure science norms prescribing more emphasis on theory-building and more rigorous methodology. Many marketing researchers appear to be caught in the conflicting cross-pressures between the demands from marketing practitioners and the profession, referred by Robertson and Ward [14] as the pay-off dilemma.

As suggested in Figure 2, the reference groups influence the research process also directly through various sanctions made possible by the strategic location of the group. First, colleagues serving on review or tenure boards may serve in a goal-achievement gate-keeping capacity. It may be that the custom of evaluating researcher performance on a short-term basis contributes to the growing flow of marginal, but programmable research in marketing. Second, fellow researchers may have a publication gate-keeping role as referees for journals and conference contributions or as editors for the book publishers. Third, there is resource gate-keeping performed by reference groups empowered to administer research funds. The growth of the project grant system may also contribute to force a short-term orientation on researchers.

The main function of the mediating influences in the research process is to reduce uncertainty for the researcher by providing standards for "what is good research". A net result of this is more continuity and orderly progression in the discipline, but also more conformity and less creativity. For the cost of heresy is high. As iconoclast economist Galbraith warns:

> The good scholar is the man who sticks tightly to his last, declines any concern with the truth or error of the system of which his work is a part. And such concern, since it involves the difficult task of offering more satisfactory alternatives, can usually be attacked as deficient in methodology or proof [6, p. 8].

## SCIENTIFIC ORIENTATIONS

This section draws on an analytical framework proposed by Galtung [7]. According to this view, a common goal of all scientific activities is to establish what is called sentences (or theses) dichotomizing their "world space" by including some "world points" and excluding others. Hence, data-sentences are verbal reports defining the empirical world by including what is observed and excluding what is non-observed. Theory-sentences (hypotheses), on the other hand, define the foreseen world, including aspects which are foreseen according to the underlying theory. Finally, there are so-called value-sentences, which refer to the preferred world including what is accepted and excluding what is rejected.

In scientific activity, sentences may be compared with other sentences of the same type. For instance, reliability tests imply comparisons of data-sentences. However, an essential characteristic of science is the comparison of sentences of different kinds. To define fundamentally different scientific schools or research orientations, Galtung has formulated the "science triangle" in Figure 3 for the three pairwise comparisons possible:

FIGURE 3
THE SCIENCE TRIANGLE FOR BILATERAL SCIENTIFIC ACTIVITY

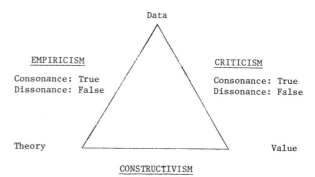

Adapted from Galtung [7]

Empiricism, which is the type of scientific activity most prevalent in marketing, consists of comparing data-sentences with theory-sentences. If there is dissonance, the data-sentences are given priority so that consonance is established by producing new theory-sentences.

Criticism is the type of scientific activity where data-sentences are compared with value-sentences. An analogy is a court of law where the police and the testimonies provide the data-sentences, the law the value-sentences, and judge, actorate and denfensorate struggle over the validity of either. By the tenets of this school of research, consonance is created by producing new data-sentences (by changing reality).

Constructivism implies confronting theory-sentences with value-sentences to see to what extent the foreseen world is also the preferred world. The conclusion is in terms of adequate-inadequate. In case of dissonance, theory- and value-sentences are about equal in priority, and both may be changed.

Since the research orientation termed Empiricism seems to have inspired most of the thinking in marketing, the nature of this metascientific tradition will be briefly commented on.

## EMPIRICISM AS A RESEARCH ORIENTATION

The type of Empiricism providing the methodological platform for most marketing research is the so-called Logical Empiricism or Positivism. This school of thought, whose origin is attributed to the philosopher Auguste Comte, has articulated an ideal of science for the natural sciences as well as for the behavioral sciences. This ideal regulates the relationship between the researcher, the research process, and the environment.

As observed by Radnitzky [13], the common denominator of the various schools within Logical Empiricism is that they view science as being monistic, reductionistic, and physicalistic.

In principle, all scientific disciplines are believed to be a part of a higher-order, basic discipline (monism). Hence, the idea of "unified science" is a central theme. A corollary of this view is that the hypothetico-deductive method of the unified science is elevated into being the only acceptable scientific approach.

Among the present scientific disciplines, physics seems to be closest to the ideal of Logical Empiricism (physicalism). Because of the unquestionable advances of the natural sciences in general and physics in particular, their goals of prediction and control and their criteria for "good science" can then be transferred to the apparently less developed and less prestigeous behavioral disciplines. According to this logic, behavioral concepts may be treated in the same way as physical entities, for instance by isolating bits of behavior from the rest of which they are constituent parts (reductionism). Such bits of behavior may furthermore be treated as "things", for instance manipulated in the experimental laboratory and measured by ratio or interval scales.

Human behavior, like phenomena in nature, is believed to be governed by invariant laws. According to Galtung [7], ideally the tenability of an hypothesis should be invariant of variations in time, space, consciousness of the subjects (who formulate the sentences), and consciousness of the objects (whom the sentences are about). The goal of science is to uncover these empirical regularies to obtain a basis for prediction and control. The laws should be expressed in such a way that they are non-ambiguous and satisfy the aesthetic demand for an harmonious system, and are preferably formulated in mathematical terms. Objective and reproducible observations and measurement by detached outsiders to the process increase the chance of detecting the laws of behavior.

## MARKETING AS A POSITIVISTIC DISCIPLINE

In a way, marketing gives the impression of being academically other-directed lacking the autonomy and professional integrity of a mature discipline. In the past, marketing seems to have obtained its goals and research priorities mainly from the dominant reference group marketing practitioners. Its methodology, on the other hand, seems to have been mainly transferred from the more prestigeous and developed behavioral sciences such as psychology, social psychology, and sociology, which in turn to a great extent emulate the natural sciences.

An examination of leading marketing journals such as Journal of Advertising Research, Journal of Consumer Research, Journal of Marketing, and Journal of Marketing Research and the conference proceedings of the American Marketing Association gives ample evidence of the predominance of positivistic research paradigms in Marketing. The important and timely metatheoretic work of Hunt and Zaltman and his associates further corroborates this impression.

The adherence to the positivistic research orientation has had a pervasive impact on marketing thought. First, undeniable contributions of Logical Empiricism are the rigorous application of logic and logical analysis to the scientific process and its attempt to check the impact of subjective biases and prejudices. A chief limitation of this research tradition in marketing and the behavioral sciences so far, however, is the sometimes mindless and anti-intellectual complying of a notion of what physics is. This uncritical imitation has resulted in preoccupation with method, in particular with measurement and quantification, at the cost of theory building and even validation of the concepts used. To some extent, positivistic science is ritualistic in its reliance on the safe distance between researcher and respondent, quantified measurements of isolated aspects of behavior, and the use of high-powered statistical tools and the computer. The reductionism produces collections of facts and hypotheses which often are trivial and inconsequential and which may be compared to a randomly scattered collection of pieces of furniture lacking an overall design or common theme.

Few of the important hypotheses or concepts currently used in marketing appear to have originated in our discipline. Possible exceptions are "channels of distribution" "marketing mix", and "market segmentation".

The absence of coherent theoretical schemes limits marketing to being an inside-out management technology, centering on a set of techniques applicable to certain problems. Such a micro-perspective cannot help automatically conceptualizing marketing as a one-way control process, in which "sellers are doing something to buyers" [1].

Since marketing research is data-centered, and since data are only defined for the past, and never for the future, it follows that most marketing research is past-oriented, supporting and legitimizing past and current practices. The research tends to focus on describing the status quo of systems. Hence, marketing research becomes conservative and passive. Its results can to some extent be used to bring about adaptive changes in marketing systems, but never real radical changes in the structure of the systems

## THE ROAD AHEAD

A first requirement for substantial progress in marketing is the firm resolve of a sizable part of the leading researchers in the area to let the subject area break out of its present strait-jacket limiting scientific activity to narrow "normal science" research and problem-solving. Instead, an all-out effort should be made to develop marketing into a behavioral science, concerned with the social instruments through which members of society receive their standard of living. This means that the conceptualization of marketing must use a macro or societal perspective rather than the narrower perspective of the individual firm or organization. One proposal for redefining marketing views marketing as: (1) the social process consisting of (2) the conception, planning, and implementation of (3) the total set of activities undertaken as exchanges by (4) individuals or organized groups of individuals being actors in the system, (5) in order to bring about the satisfaction of consumer needs for economic goods and services, and (6) the social and environmental effects of the activities undertaken [1].

As earlier pointed out, the subject in most marketing studies has been marketing managers (tellingly referred to as "marketers"), while the other actor set most frequently studied, consumers, has been treated as the object. Symptomatically, most studies of consumers have been descriptive, while marketing manager studies have been normative, as they have aimed at formulating criteria for optimal manipulations of the marketing mix. Exceptions to this rule are the descriptive studies of channel relationships [15], and studies of business practices such as Churchill, Ford and Ozanne [4].

When a behavioral science of marketing develops, the contents may be of value also to user groups other than marketing managers. In principle, all actor groups in the marketing system may be studied both descriptively and normatively from the perspective of all actor groups, as suggested in Figure 4.

FIGURE 4
A TAXONOMY FOR MARKETING STUDIES
(in cells: D=Descriptive study
N=Normative study)

| | | Subject | | |
|---|---|---|---|---|
| | | Marketing Managers | Consumers | Government |
| Object | Marketing Managers | D / N | D / N | D / N |
| | Consumers | D / N | D / N | D / N |
| | Government | D / N | D / N | D / N |

While not all combinations indicated by the cells are of equal value, it appears that marketing research has been limited to only a few of the potential approaches to the subject matter. In the future, intriguing research opportunities may, for instance, be found in "marketing manager behavior" as seen from a government, see [3] or from a consumer perspective. Even "government behavior" relating to marketing may be thinkable research area.

## CONCLUDING COMMENTS

Paradoxically, while much marketing management thinking is future-oriented, marketing research has tended to be

past oriented, concerned with the status quo.

A partial explanation for this may be found in the social and behavioral nature of marketing research, as other research. Such a view challenges the myths of the autonomy of the scientist and the value-free, independent research.

The prevailing research orientation in marketing is identified as Logical Empiricism or Positivism, emphasizing reductionism, quantification, and data- rather than theory-orientation. An outcome of adopting this orientation is an empirical over-feeing of marketing combined with theoretical malnutrition.

The road to progress for marketing leads through developing marketing into a behavioral science adoptiong a societal perspective. Such a behavioral science is likely to contain knowledge useful also to user groups other than marketing managers.

## REFERENCES

1. Arndt, Johan. "The Marketing Thinking of Tomorrow," in George Fisk, Johan Arndt, and Kjell Grønhaug, eds., New Frontiers for Marketing, forthcoming.

2. Barber, Bernard. "Resistance by Scientists to Scientific Discovery." Science, 134 (September 1961), 596-602.

3. Bloom, Paul N. and Nikhilesh Dholakia. "Marketer Behavior and Public Policy: Some Unexplored Territory," Journal of Marketing, 37 (October 1973), 63-77.

4. Churchill, Gilbert A., Jr., Neil M. Ford, and Urban B. Ozanne. "An Analysis of Price Aggressiveness in Gasoline Marketing," Journal of Marketing Research, 7 (February 1970), 36-42.

5. Danielsson, A. and H. Törnebohm. On Complex Systems with Human Components. Stockholm: Forsvarets Forskningsanstalt, Planeringsbyran, 1968.

6. Galbraith, John K. Economics and the Public Purpose. Boston: Houghton Mifflin Company, 1973.

7. Galtung, Johan. "Empiricism, Criticism, Constructivism: Three Approaches to Scientific Activity." Paper presented at the Third World Future Research Conference in Bucharest, September 3-10, 1972.

8. Hunt, Shelby D. Marketing Theory: Conceptual Foundations of Research in Marketing. Columbus, Ohio: Grid, 1976.

9. Kaplan, Norman. "Sociology of Science," in Robert E.L. Faris, ed., Handbook of Modern Sociology. Chicago: Rand McNally and Company, 1964, 852-81.

10. Kornhauser, Arthur and Paul F. Lazarsfeld. "The Analysis of Consumer Actions," in Paul F. Lazarsfeld and Morris Rosenberg, eds., The Language of Social Research. New York: The Free Press, 1955, 392-404.

11. Kotler, Philip and Sidney J. Levy. "Broadening the Concept of Marketing," Journal of Marketing, 33 (January 1969), 10-5.

12. Kuhn, Thomas S. The Structure of Scientific Revolutions. Chicago: University of Chicago Press, 1962.

13. Radnitzky, Gerard. Contemporary Schools of Metascience. Gothenburg: Akademiförlaget, 1970.

14. Robertson, Thomas S. and Scott Ward. "Toward the De-
    velopment of Consumer Behavior Theory," in Boris W.
    Becker and Helmut Becker, eds., Combined Proceedings
    1972. Chicago: American Marketing Association, 1973,
    57-64.

15. Stern, Louis W., ed. Distribution Channels: Behav-
    ioral Dimensions. Boston: Houghton Miffling Company,
    1969.

16. Törnebohm, Håkan. "Funderinger over forskning i
    fysiken." Unpublished paper. Gothenburg: Institu-
    tionen for vetenskapsteori, 1971.

17. Zaltman, Gerald, Reinhard Angelmar, and Christian
    Pinson. "Metatheory in Consumer Behavior Research,"
    in David M. Gardner, ed., Proceedings of the 2nd
    Annual Conference of the Association for Consumer
    Research. College Park, Maryland: Association for
    Consumer Research, 1971, 476-97.

18. Zaltman, Gerald, Christian R.A. Pinson, and Reinhard
    Angelmar. Metatheory and Consumer Research.
    New York: Holt, Rinehart and Winston, 1973.

# THE ROLE OF ROLE PLAYING
## IN EXPERIMENTS ABOUT CONSUMER BEHAVIOR

Alan Sawyer, The Ohio State University

## ABSTRACT

The advantages and disadvantages of role playing in experimentation are discussed. The conclusions about the
use of role playing as a substitute for real experiments
are quite negative. Some areas in which role playing
might be useful are proposed.

## INTRODUCTION

The goal of this paper is to discuss role playing in experiments about consumer behavior. There are several potential advantages to the use of role playing. Conversely,
there are also some serious disadvantages. After a presentation of these issues, there will be an attempt to delineate a proper role of role playing in consumer behavior
research.

## TYPES OF ROLE PLAYING

The type of role playing discussed in this paper involves
situations in which a subject is presented with a description of a scenario and then asked to predict the behavior
of the actor in that scenario. The scenario description
is the means by which various independent variables are
manipulated. The subject is told that he or someone else
will be given a shock, see an advertisement, or whatever
and then asked to predict what behavior would follow.
This discussion does not include the several areas of research in which role playing is an independent variable.
For example, role playing has been effectively used as
means to obtain attitude change [e.g., 8] and role behavior has been studied in such areas as socialization [14]
and family decision making [7]. Nor is the use of role
playing in non-experimental projective measurement such as
TAT tests discussed.

Within the broad category of role playing in experimentation, there are two distinguishing factors. First of all,
subjects may be asked to role play either themselves or
others. Subjects are probably better able to accurately
predict their own behavior than that of others. However,
they are also less likely to be able to free themselves
from any hesitations to admit behavior that is either socially undesirable or somewhat embarrassing. Role playing
subjects may be more willing to project such types of behavior to others and perhaps will express their own feelings in their projections.

A second factor involves how much information is given to
the subjects about the experimental hypotheses and any deception. Some researchers including Kelman [13] have argued that, even if a researcher chooses not to completely
debrief subjects about the exact nature of experimental
hypotheses and accompanying deception, role playing subjects can at least be forewarned that the experiment is
not real, that they are to pretend they are subjects, and
that some parts of the description may include deception.
For example, in an Asch-like study of conformity [3], ful-
ly-debriefed role playing would involve telling subjects
that they were to pretend that they were in an experiment,
that the experiment was studying the effects of others'
opinions on the subject's opinion, and that some of the
other subjects were actually confederates of the experimenter and that the expressed opinions of the confederates

were not their real opinions. A forewarned-only role playing situation might tell subjects that they were to pretend they were subjects in an experiment, that they would
be asked their opinions after other people gave their
opinions, and that some of the things described to them
might be deceptions designed to fool the subjects.

## ADVANTAGES OF ROLE PLAYING

Role playing is an ethically-superior alternative to deception. The prime force behind the arguments for role
playing have concerned the moral distaste of deception.
Kelman [13, p.5] argues that "serious ethical issues are
raised by deception per se and the kind of use of human
beings that it implies. . . . Yet we seem to forget that
the experimenters-subject relationship -- whatever else it
is -- is a real interhuman relationship, in which we have
responsibility toward the subject as another human being
whose dignity we must preserve. . . ."

Role playing is superior to deception in producing data
free from artifacts from adopted subject roles or reactive
response styles. Some researchers suspect that deception
is less than complete and that the mixture of fully deceived, partially deceived, and different subject roles
for the incompletely deceived subjects biases the data
[e.g., 1,26,27]. The data from role playing may be more
realistic and less biased [5,24]. Role playing may be especially helpful in eliminating a negative subject role in
which a subject tries to act contrary to the way he believes the experimenter would like him to behave [29].

Role playing is very flexible and permits easy, expense-
free manipulations of independent variables. The convenience of role playing manipulations is its most appealing
advantage. By merely describing a situation and its various parameters, including the levels of key independent
variables, the researcher can manipulate all aspects of
the experiment. Hansen [10] points out that role playing
is especially helpful in studying choice behavior. With
role playing, one does not feel confined to studying inexpensive products due to high costs of actually offering a
choice of relatively expensive products. A related advantage is that the experimenter does not have to be concerned
with the real life timing of a choice; role playing allows
the study of one or more choices without waiting until the
subject is actually shopping for a particular product.

Role playing permits a more complete control over the effects of past events on subject's current behavior. By
using descriptions of another person's history and internal
states and motivations, Hansen [10] tries to force a subject to discard his own feelings and beliefs and to instead use those of the described person. This may be particularly helpful in controlling beliefs and evaluations in
cognitive structures. The use of a cooperative, role playing subject also permits possible statistical control by
allowing more facile measurement of variables that are
possible causes of behavior. For example, a researcher
could more easily monitor a subject's thinking and motivation by periodically asking "what would you be thinking
now?" or "why would you do that?". A pretest might provide less bias for role playing subjects than naive ones.

Role playing subjects are more likely than naive subjects to adopt subject roles which will artificially affect their behavior. There are many roles that may be adopted by subjects in an experiment. These roles include the good or cooperative role, the negative role, the faithful role, and the apprehensive role [22,29]. Although role playing may reduce the frequency of the negative role, it probably also increases the incidence of the good role [17] and the apprehensive role [20]. The good subject tries to decipher the experimenter's hypothesis and then acts according to how he believes he is expected to behave, whereas the apprehensive subject behaves in a manner in which he thinks he will be most positively evaluated by observers. Even if he knows he is acting as a collaborator of the researcher, it is highly doubtful that the subject will be unbiased. It seems likely that a subject will tend to act as a good subject - either consciously or unconsciously. The past evidence of the transference of experimenter bias from one researcher to another may be evidence of the ease of adoption of behavior consistent with the experimenter's hypothesis [21]. Even more of a problem is the high possibility of the adoption of the apprehensive role where subjects would hesitate to admit to researchers (or perhaps even to themselves) that they would do something that would be negatively evaluated. If the two roles conflict, it is likely that the apprehensive role will dominate behavior [25]. For example, in an Asch study of conformity, how many role players would admit that they would conform to the opinions of others in what is essentially an easy judgement task? As Miller suggests in his review of role playing [16], asking a subject to suspend judgement about an experimental hypothesis or how he should behave "is tantamount to suggesting that subjects suspend their breathing [p. 623]."

Role playing subjects are often unable to predict what they would do in a given situation. Freedman [9] emphasizes this warning. "No amount of discussion of other aspects of role playing can conceal the fact that this procedure provides information about what people think they would do, not necessarily what they would do. And experimental results are not always easy to predict; people do not always behave the way they or we expect them to [p. 110]." Available empirical evidence suggests that, although forewarned role players may sometimes produce results similar to those of naive subjects, fully debriefed role playing subjects are less likely to match the results [11]. Willis and Willis [30] found that fully debriefed subjects were able to produce results similar to those of a deceived group; these results concerned a fairly obvious main effect. However, the role players did not predict a more subtle interaction effect found with the naive subjects.

Several researchers have argued that equivalent results between deceived and non-deceived subjects may be produced by non-equivalent processes [16]. There may be different causes with the same results. For example, a naive subject's behavior may be more likely to be relatively more influenced by the assumed causal variables than by experimental artifacts.

A role playing situation does not result in sufficient subject involvement to behave as naive subjects would. Aronson and Carlsmith [2] use the term "experimental realism" to describe a research procedure and variable manipulation that involves subjects in such realistic fashion that they behave in a spontaneous, natural manner. Without experimental realism, subjects have time and self-presence to probe the experimental situation for clues as to its purpose. The mere fact that subsequent behavior is the result of conscious and deliberate thinking about what they would do, are expected to, or should do may mean that they act differently or for different reasons.

Freedman [9] outlines four ways of utilizing role playing as a means of conducting experimental research. These four uses of role playing include: (1) as a straight substitute for experimental research, (2) in tandem with experimental research in the hopes that, if eventual results of the two methods prove comparable, role playing can be a substitute, (3) only when experimental research proves impossible or unfeasible, and (4) to test the plausibility of alternative explanations of results of experimental research.

The advantages and disadvantages discussed above apply to the first two uses of role playing. Given a choice of experimental (non-role playing) research and role playing, one cannot rationalize the use of role playing as a straight substitute. The convenience, ease, and low cost of variable manipulation and the ethical advantage of less or no deception are very tempting. However, role playing will always be only subjects' opinions about what they think they will do and not their actual behavior or what they will, in fact, do. Miller [16] concludes that role playing is evitably "second rate" data since one would always have to check the validity of the role playing results by running an actual experiment. This necessity would negate any ethical value of not gathering the actual data.

Employing role playing along with research with naive subjects in the hopes of eventually pinpointing theoretical areas or research situations in which role playing is a satisfactory substitute may have some promise. However, the bulk of the published opinions and results lend doubt that such research areas will exist. Role playing is more likely to be less biased when (1) subjects are asked to forecast their own behavior, (2) when the likely alternative behaviors do not include anything socially embarrassing or undesirable, (3) when the experiment involves circumstances that are somewhat familiar to subjects so they have some basis for their projections, (4) when the salient features of the research situation are simple enough to be readily communicated to subjects, and (5) when hypotheses are limited to fairly obvious main effects and do not include subtle interactions. Although the above list of requirements is arguable, there should be high agreement that research situations meeting even a subset of those characteristics are quite rare and, if found, probably not very interesting.

It is perhaps tautological to say that role playing is acceptable if other research strategies are not available. However, it might be useful to identify some research situations in which experimental research either should not be done or is highly unlikely because of high costs or other problems. One such situation involves tests of the effect of variables which ethically should not be manipulated. For example, the persuasive effects of extremely high levels of fear could not ethically be studied experimentally unless the opportunity for a quasi-experiment was presented by a natural occurrence of a high fear situation. Other instances where extreme manipulations of subject states would not be proper could be mentioned. Another instance where experimentation is not very feasible involves the above mentioned area of choice among highly expensive alternatives or choices that are very infrequent. (Of course, opinions about the feasibility of a manipulation of something such as an infrequently encountered product choice may differ. Aronson and Carlsmith [2] seem to argue that such "infeasible" manipulations merely provide a greater challenge to the ingenuity of the investigator). Finally, role playing of how others would behave may have to be considered if the appropriate subject population is not available. Again, it can be seen that role playing is hardly a good solution. For example, in a study of how salesmen and purchasing agents bargain, an accessible population such as students may have to be used to role play the behavior [19]. If the key aspect is not the types of participants but the process, perhaps a better solution would be to try to reduce the bargaining problem to a set of variables that can be meaningfully manipulated in an actual experiment with the available subject pool [e.g., 15]. Moreover, if there are truly unique characteristics of the particular population to which the results are to be generalized, then the role players can not successfully provide duplicate behavior.

A final use of role playing is to test the plausability of alternative explanations of experimental results. These alternative explanations might be theoretically or methodologically based. The only known example of the first type was by Bem [4] who cleverly used role playing to test his theory that some experimental results of forced compliance could be explained by his self-perception theory as well as by cognitive dissonance. Despite some later arguments [12], Bem proved that similar results could be generated by role playing subjects simply on the basis of self-judgements, and without any need to refer to unobservable states of dissonance. Bem's results supported the plausibility of his explanation, and, although, they did not refute the dissonance explanation, the results did prove that they were not, as claimed by some dissonance advocates, counter-intuitional to subjects.

A second type of alternative explanation might include demand characteristics. To check the plausibility of demand bias, Orne [17] suggests the use of a "non-experiment" in which role players predict the behavior of real subjects on the basis of descriptions of the experimental procedures and variable manipulations - including any suspected demand cues. If the data of the role players who do not actually experience the experimental treatment but are told the suspected experimental procedures and the data of real subjects are comparable, there is some support for the demand bias explanation. As with the Bem results, however, comparable data does not disprove the alleged cause-and-effect relationship; it merely demonstrates the possibility of an alternative explanation [see 23].

Another use of role playing to test an alternative, methodological-based explanation of a set of results is the use of subject simulators to test a researcher's ability to detect subjects whose behavior is not real and only presented. This type of role playing, also suggested by Orne [17], utilizes confederate subjects who attempt to fool the researchers. Perhaps subject simulators could also be used to test the sensitivity of such techniques as "catch scales" in personality testing and other measurement tasks [6].

In summary, role playing seems to be acceptable only in the last of the four suggested uses. This use, by far the least utilized, may lend credibility to alternative explanations of a given set of experimental results. The use of role playing as a substitute for real experimental behavior data from naive subjects is not recommended and is considered advisable only when the alternative of non-role playing is not available. In these latter situations, one can never have full confidence in the validity of role playing data.

However, it seems a shame to discard a technique that allows such easy and low cost variation of independent variables. Perhaps one solution to this dilemma would be the use of role playing to generate hypotheses and to pretest experimental variations. Certainly, subjects' insights into why they would behave in a certain way or predictions of a behavior unanticipated by a researcher would be valuable inputs into the research process. Ray [18] has suggested a research scheme where laboratory experimentation weeds out ideas not powerful enough to have an effect even in the lab before more expensive field experimentation is done. Perhaps, role playing could be used prior to lab experiments in a manner similar to that

advocated for lab experiments by Ray. A potential drawback to this research hierarchy would be contingent on the validity of the implicit assumption that role players would be more sensitive to the contemplated independent variables than naive subjects. Future research comparing role playing with actual lab experiments can provide some information about this necessary assumption.

## SUMMARY AND CONCLUSIONS

Several issues about the use of role playing in experimentation have been discussed. Most of the conclusions about the efficacy of role playing were quite negative. However, the last recommendation about the use of role playing to generate hypotheses and to pretest ideas before their tests in laboratory experiments should perhaps be employed more in consumer research.

## REFERENCES

1. Agyris, C. "Some Unintended Consequences of Rigorous Research," Psychological Bulletin, 70 (September 1968), 185-97.

2. Aronson, E. and J.M. Carlsmith. "Experimentation in Social Psychology," in G. Lindzey and E. Aronson, The Handbook of Social Psychology, Vol. II. Reading: Addison Wesley, 1968, 1-79.

3. Asch, S.E. "Effects of Group Pressure Upon the Modification and Distortion of Judgements." In H. Guetzkow, ed., Groups, Leadership, and Men, Pittsburgh: Carnegie Press, 1951.

4. Bem, D.J. "Self-Perception: An Alternative Interpretation of Cognitive Dissonance Phenomena," Psychological Review, 74 (May 1967), 183-200.

5. Brown, R. "Models of Attitude Change," in R. Brown et al. eds., New Directions in Psychology, Vol. 1, New York: Holt Rinehart, 1962.

6. Cronbach, L. Essentials of Psychological Testing, New York: Harper and Row, 1970.

7. Davis, H.L. "Decision Making Within the Household." Journal of Consumer Research 2 (March 1976), 241-60.

8. Elms, A.C. "Role Playing, Incentive and Dissonance." Psychological Bulletin, 68 (1967), 132-48.

9. Freedman, J.L. "Role Playing: Psychology by Consensus." Journal of Personality and Social Psychology, 13 (October 1969), 107-14.

10. Hansen, F. Consumer Choice Behavior: A Cognitive Theory. New York: Free Press, 1972.

11. Horowitz, I.A. and B.H. Rothschild. "Conformity as a Function of Deception and Role Playing," Journal of Personality and Social Psychology, 14 (March 1970), 224-26.

12. Jones, R.A., Linder, D.E., Kiesler, C.A., Zanna, M., and J.W. Brehm. "Internal States or External Stimuli: Observers' Attitude Judgements and the Dissonance." Journal of Experimental Social Psychology, 4 (1968), 247-69.

13. Kelman, H.C. "Human Uses of Human Subjects: The Problem of Deception in Social Psychological Experiments," Psychological Bulletin, 67 (January 1967), 1-11.

14.  Maccoby, E.E.  "Role-Taking in Childhood and its Con-
     sequences for Social Learning," Child Development, 30
     (1959), 239-52.

15.  Mathews, H.L., Wilson, D.T., and J.F. Monoky.  "Bar-
     gaining Behavior in a Buyer-Seller Dyad."  Journal of
     Marketing Research 9 (February 1972), 103-5.

16.  Miller. A.G.  "Role-Playing:  An Alternative to De-
     ception?  A Review of the Evidence," American Psycho-
     logist, 27 (July 1972), 623-36.

17.  Orne, M.T.  "Demand Characteristics and the Concept
     of Quasi-Controls," in Robert Rosenthal and Ralph L.
     Rosnow, eds., Artifact in Behavioral Research.  New
     York:  Academic Press, 1969, 143-79.

18.  Ray, M.L.  "The Present and Potential Linkages Be-
     tween the Micro-theoretical Notions of Behavioral
     Science and the Problems of Advertising:  A Proposal
     for a Research System," in Harry Davis and Alvin
     Silk, eds.,  The Behavioral and Management Sciences
     in Marketing.  New York:  Ronald, in press.

19.  Rosenberg, L.J. and L.W. Stern.  "Conflict Management
     in the Distribution Channel," Journal of Marketing
     Research 8 (November 1971), 437-42.

20.  Rosenberg, M.J.  "The Conditions and Consequences of
     Evaluation Apprehension," in R. Rosenthal and R. L.
     Rosnow, eds., Artifact in Behavioral Research, New
     York:  Academic Press, 1969, 280-349.

21.  Rosenthal, R.  "Interpersonal Expectations:  Effects
     of the Experimenter's Hypothesis."  in R. Rosenthal
     and R.L. Rosnow, eds., Artifact in Behavioral Re-
     search, New York:  Academic Press, 1969, 181-277.

22.  Sawyer, A.G.  "Demand Artifacts in Laboratory Experi-
     ments in Consumer Research," Journal of Consumer Re-
     search, 1 (March 1975), 20-30 (a).

23.  Sawyer, A.G.  "Detecting Demand Characteristics in
     Laboratory Experiments in Consumer Research:  The
     Case of Repetition-Affect Research," in M.J. Schling-
     er, ed., Advances in Consumer Research, 2 (1975),
     713-24 (b).

24.  Schultz, D.P.  "The Human Subject in Psychological
     Research," Psychological Bulletin 72 (1969), 214-28.

25.  Sigall, H., E. Aronson, and T. Van Hoose.  "The Co-
     operative Subject:  Myth or Reality?," Journal of
     Experimental Social Psychology, 6 (January 1970),
     1-10.

26.  Stricker, L.G.  "The True Deceiver." Psychological
     Bulletin, 68 (1967), 13-20.

27.  Tybout, A.M. and G. Zaltman.  "Ethics in Marketing
     Research: Their Practical Relevance," Journal of
     Marketing Research 11 (November 1974), 357-68.

28.  Venkatesan, M.  "Experimental Study of Consumer Be-
     havior Conformity and Independence," Journal of Mar-
     keting Research, 3 (November 1966), 384-87.

29.  Weber, S.J. and T. Cook.  "Subject Effects in Labor-
     atory Research:  An Examination of Subject Roles, De-
     mand Characteristics, and Valid Inference," Psycho-
     logical Bulletin, 77 (April 1972), 273-95.

30.  Willis, R.H. and Y.A. Willis.  "Role Playing vs. De-
     Ception:  An Experimental Comparison," Journal of
     Personality and Social Psychology, 16 (November 1970),
     472-77.

QUALITATIVE KNOWING AND
CONSUMER RESEARCH

Bobby J. Calder, Northwestern University

## INTRODUCTION

This paper examines consumer behavior research from a
philosophical point of view. Two types of knowledge about
consumers are discussed. One type is scientific knowledge,
and this is the type to which most academic studies aspire.
The other is qualitative knowing, i.e., the intuitive,
everyday understanding of consumer behavior.

## BACKGROUND

Most philosophical analyses of consumer behavior [e.g.,3],
discuss the field in terms of scientific knowledge. That
is, they deal with theory construction, the relationship
of constructs to empirical indicants, the criteria of
scientific evidence, etc. It is argued in this paper that
such discussions need to be expanded to include knowledge
based on qualitative knowing. The usual assumption that
the role of scientific knowledge is to replace everyday
knowledge is potentially misleading. The development of
consumer behavior as a field might be facilitated by a
broader view of the role of qualitative knowing.

## DISCUSSION

At a minimum it is necessary to recognize that scientific
constructs originate with qualitative knowing. The basis
of science is the creativity of the individual. Scientific
concepts arise out of qualitative knowing. It is argued
that it is important to recognize this process in consumer
behavior research, and the notion of "grounded" theory
[2] is discussed.

Perhaps even more important is the possibility of confusing
scientific knowledge and qualitative knowing. It is possible that some of the concepts used in consumer behavior
are not scientific at all, but are rather everyday concepts
that have been reified in an attempt to seem scientific.
It is argued that it is important to distinguish constructs
in consumer behavior which are not truly scientific. A
similar argument has recently been applied to commercial
marketing research [1].

Finally, it is important to realize that scientific know-
edge does not exist in a vacuum. Scientific knowledge is
not interpretable without assuming the validity of most
everyday knowledge. This implies that qualitative knowing,
far from being supplanted by scientific knowledge, can provide an important check on scientific knowledge.

Implications for the development of consumer behavior research are drawn from these observations.

## REFERENCES

. Calder, B. "Focus Groups and the Nature of Qualitative
Marketing Research." Journal of Marketing Research,
(August 1977), in press.

. Glaser, B. and A. Strauss. The Discovery of Grounded
Theory. Chicago: Aldine, 1967.

. Zaltman, G., C. Pinson, and R. Angelmar. Metatheory
and Consumer Research. New York: Holt, Rinehart &
Winston, 1973.

# GOVERNMENT POLICIES: BARRIERS OR STIMULI TO NEW PRODUCT AND INNOVATION?*

Alok K. Chakrabarti,·Drexel University
William E. Souder, University of Pittsburgh

## ABSTRACT

Government policies have significant influence on the success of new products. Both the positive and negative effects of federal regulations on new products have been discussed here. Based on the empirical data from a number of companies, this paper points out that the contextual conditions have to be investigated to understand how a specific regulation will affect a particular company.

## INTRODUCTION

There has been a growing amount of concern for the lack of technological innovation (as manifested primarily by the number of new products and processes) in the U.S. The results of a study conducted by the National Science Board indicated that the U.S.'s lead in technology is eroding over the last decade, compared to the countries like the U.S.S.R., West Germany, and Japan. [1] In a recent survey conducted by Business Week, [2] it was observed that a "disproportionate part of the R&D budget has been diverted to the unproductive areas of government regulations. A substantial part of corporate efforts are now involved with compliance rather than with new products." General Motors, for example, is reputed to be spending about 20 percent of its R&D to meet federal safety and emission standards. Government regulations have been seen as a deterrent and barrier to innovation in the industry. On the other hand, there has been another school of thought which wants to utilize government policies and regulations as stimuli and leverage points for promoting innovation. In this paper we propose to examine the role of federal interventions in the innovation process and their consequence. Both schools of thought will be touched upon.

## GOVERNMENT INFLUENCE

Government policies and regulations, do indeed, affect the success of innovative efforts in corporate organizations. Arthur D. Little, Inc. and the Industrial Research Institute, Inc., in their study on barriers to innovation [3] found that there are several government-related factors which significantly affect the innovation process. More specifically, they found these to be very important: uncertainties in private sector about federal regulatory policies and future rulings; uncertainties about state and local government practices; lack of precise data on effects of regulation and independent regulatory agencies' scope and practices on innovativeness of traditionally regulated industries; uncertainty in the private sector about current and prospective rulings on multicorporate prototype test facilities. Another detailed study of more than one hundred projects in six firms indicated that the following three factors were significantly related to commercial success [4]: degree of certainty about federal regulatory policies or future rulings; anti-trust complications in marketing; and consumer and environmental safeguards prescribed by the government.

*Portions of this study were funded by grants from the Office of Policy Research Analysis, National Science Foundation, and the Carl Foundation to the Technology Management Studies Group at the University of Pittsburgh

The A. D. Little and IRI study recommended various courses of action by the government to stimulate and nurture innovation in the American economy. Their suggestions involved among other:

rationalization of federal and state/local regulatory policies

streamlining and upgrading federal agency staffing with more competent personnel to improve the ability for standard setting

forums for interchange of ideas between the private and public sectors

using the leverage of federal agency procurement programs to affect market fragmentation for certain types of programs

market creation for certain products by formulating performance specification and thus creating need for the products

The involvement of the federal government with the innovation process is exemplified through its experimental programs at the National Science Foundation, Department of Commerce, etc. The Experimental Technology Incentive Program at the Department of Commerce is actively involved in initiating and monitoring experimental programs centered around changes in government regulations, such as procurement regulations, etc.

All of this raises a fundamental question: Is government a barrier or stimulus to innovation? From our empirical observations, it seems that the contingent conditions should be considered before answering this type of question. A particular regulation may adversely affect one industry, but it may be favored by other industry. Within the same industry, a regulation can have adverse effect on one company, while benefiting another. The same can be true for different divisions or product groups within the same corporation.

## A SURVEY OF NON-REGULATED FIRMS

Souder [5] surveyed twenty-nine innovative projects at seven companies in the "non-regulated" industries, which were not under the domain of the regulatory agencies, such as the Federal Communications Commission, Federal Trade Commission, etc. They operated purely within the private sector. None of their products were sold to the government, and they were free to set their prices and carry on their business without direct regulation by the federal agencies. In other words, the study was focused on companies where the direct federal involvement in their innovation/new product decision-making was minimal. Hence, one would expect the federal agencies to have little influence.

Yet, surprisingly, there were very significant federal governmental influences, as shown by Table 1. The federal government influenced the innovation process in two ways. In fifteen of these projects, it effectively provided a market opportunity. In another fourteen of these projects the federal government effectively retarded the commercial success of the new products. Federal intervention can vary from directly influencing the product specifications

### TABLE 1

| Nature of Government Intervention | Number of Products Successful | Number of Products Failed | Total |
|---|---|---|---|
| Number of Cases government provided market opportunity | 12 | 3 | 15 |
| Number of Cases government retarded the products | 2 | 12 | 14 |
| Total | 14 | 15 | 29 |

$$x^2 = 12.52 \qquad p \leq .001$$
Relationship between gov. intervention & product success.

to indirectly affecting its products through environmental regulations. These actions in turn can affect the vendors in providing new market opportunity. For example, the stricter auto emission standards necessitated the catalytic converter. For automobile manufacturers it was a disruptive event. But for primary material manufacturers, it offered an opportunity for developing an alloy which will have high corrosion resistance at high temperatures. The pollution control regulations offered increased market opportunity to the manufacturer of industrial waste treatment products. Our sample companies were manufacturers of chemicals, plastics, primary metals, fabricated products. Some of the products were novel and not mere designs of existing products.

In the first category of positive influence, the federal government had recently imposed some restrictions, performance specifications and requirements. For example, the auto safety requirements opened up market opportunities for a line of products which did not have much market potential before. On the other hand, the government virtually took away the market for certain products, such as the ban on saccharin did. In twelve of the fourteen cases where the government actions adversely affected the new products, the actions were taken during the development of the products. The results shown in Table 1 are very striking when one considers the fact that the companies involved here are in "non-regulated" industry.

Table 2 provided additional insights. Interestingly, as Table 2 shows, the companies foresaw government intervention in a statistically significant number of projects. In most of the incentive cases, the companies had sufficient awareness of the federal intervention so that they could have new products ready to be marketed when the market opportunity opened up!

### TABLE 2

| | |
|---|---|
| Number of Cases Government Action Foreseen | 22 |
| Number of Cases Government Action Not Foreseen | 7 |
| Total | 29 |

Significant at $p \leq .05$
Anticipation of government action

Finally, Table 3 shows that there was a statistically significant relationship between whether or not the firms tried to influence government actions, and the outcome of their innovations. This table shows the implications for a dynamic interaction between the government and the business. Active involvement of the firms in the process of regulatory policy formulation has direct impact on product success. While some firms recognized this, others did not. In this context, one ought to consider the various legal and ethical mechanisms available to the corporate managers. Lobbying is a commonly used mechanism for large corporations who have Washington lobbyists. Trade associations and other business groups periodically interact with government agencies and the legislators to present their case.

Moreover, the important point to be considered here is the participation of many firms in the development of product performance standards. Some companies take very active roles in participating in the standards development process. Some of them have developed such high reputations that many government agencies and professional bodies pay great attention to their work. This latter mechanism needs careful planning and dedication to maintain professional technical integrity by the management. It cannot be achieved over night. But we observed that it is an effective strategy for the long term operation of a company.

### TABLE 3

| Corporate Action | Number of Products Successful | Number of Products Failed | Total |
|---|---|---|---|
| Number of Cases Company tried to influence | 10 | 3 | 13 |
| Number of Cases Company did not try to influence | 4 | 12 | 16 |
| Total | 14 | 15 | 29 |

$$x^2 = 7.92 \qquad p \leq .01$$
Relationship between company action and product success

In summary, the following was found:

Government looms large and is highly influential, even in the least expected places--the non-regulated industries.

Government influence is indeed decisive in the sense that when it provides market opportunity via regulations, such as OSHA, product safety standards, some new products needed to comply with these regulations will succeed. When the regulation prohibits certain type of products, they will fail.

In about 80 percent of the innovative new products, the government actions were anticipated by the firms. There were relatively few "surprise" actions by the government.

The firms which attempted (in various ways to influence the government actions clearly improved the chances of success of their new products; those which did not, experienced high failure rate.

### SOME SPECIFIC CASES

Here, we shall examine three cases from our studies. (Identities have been disguised.)

Case A -- Strict emission regulations have affected the automobile industry quite adversely. A significant amount of resources are being spent on devices which will help control the emissions. Catalytic converters are now universally adopted by many automobile models. For the specialty steel manufacturer, the catalytic converter opens a new market and new opportunity. One of the companies we visited, saw this opportunity and successfully developed a product which is intended to replace stainless steel, the usual material of construction. Over the past couple of years, the prospect for such indigenous material has improved as the price of stainless steel sky rocketed due to the shortage of chromium in the international market.

Case B -- Antitrust regulations, we were told by many respondents, prevent the free flow of ideas as well as collaborative efforts. However, in reality we found examples of collaborative efforts between companies in their new product program. Company A developed a rust-proofing technique and coating materials. Since Company A is not a primary metal manufacturer, it could not profitably market their product to the automotive manufacturer who is interested in rust prevention of automotive bodies. Company A was led to Company B, a steel manufacturer, to perfect the technique and the customer agreed to buy from Company B on the condition that the technology will be shared through licensing with other steel companies. The auto company did not want to be dependent on a sole source. Thus this case exemplifies the inter-company collaborative efforts in the new product area which succeeded.

Case C -- Company Z anticipated the trend towards the need for cleaner emission from internal combustion engines. As a leading manufacturer in the industry, Company Z embarked on a project to develop an engine which will have less pollutants in its emissions than the conventional engines. By 1972-73 the company was ready to market the special engine which would conform to the State of California environmental regulations. Around that time the Environmental Protection Agency was willing to enforce the strict emission control regulations. The company had a very real competitive edge with its new product. However, the federal government, through an executive order, postponed the enforcement of the strict environmental rules. Company Z lost its competitive edge generated through prudent foresight and active technical programs. However, the federal decision about relaxation (or more appropriately, postponement) of enforcement of the strict environmental regulations, favorably affected Company Y. Among many industrial and consumer products, Company Y manufactures industrial gas filtration products. By 1972-73, Company Y was in the process of developing some products which will be useful for plants where the gaseous effluents are heavily contaminated with solid particles. Potential customers demanded the product right at that time, as they themselves were obliged to comply with federal pollution standards. It was premature for Company Y to deliver the product at that time, as it needed more time to develop and perfect the product. The executive decision at Washington accorded an opportunity to work on the product since the time pressure was removed.

## CONCLUSIONS

Specifically, federal regulations can affect a company's product program in many ways:

By regulating the product specifications, the government can severely affect the potential market. For instance, restrictions on aerosol manufacture adversely affected the market of the propellant manufacturers.

Regulations can force a manufacturer to redesign an existing product, which it would not have otherwise done. These are compliance type of activities, which have been termed a "waste" by many industrial corporations.

Regulations can open up new product opportunities. New demand is created for a product due to the need to comply with the government regulations.

Government, as the largest customer, has the procurement leverage which has been used to affect market aggregation.

Specifications and product requirements prescribed by the government can be used as guidelines for product development.

The likelihood of changing the product specifications by federal agencies injects uncertainty in the product development process. Arbitrariness involved in interpretation of the regulation and its enforcement by incumbents in regulatory agencies adds another dimension of uncertainty.

Government regulations may prevent a particular company from getting into certain product lines. For example, a meat packer signed a consent degree with the Department of Justice in the twenties which affected its product line in the sixties. Through negotiation, the restrictions were removed and the company was allowed to expand its product program.

Fiscal policies as well as tax policies are very powerful tools at the hand of the government to influence corporate behavior.

At the macro-social level, we have to understand the role of the government in initiating and controlling the economic activities in the country. This role is evolved through our political process, shaped and implemented by the various political institutions. A prudent corporate manager will have to understand this role and will have to adapt his corporate behavior accordingly.

More specifically, there is a great need for maintaining a dynamic interaction with government agencies. Companies should recognize that there are ethical and legal ways of participation in the policy-formulation process in our society. Although traditional lobbying through regular lobbyists may not be feasible for many companies, yet there are groups such as trade associations and chambers of commerce through which one can participate. Secondly, there is a great need for awareness of laws and regulations and the possible changes in these regulations. It needs careful analysis and understanding of trends in current socio-political events to predict the changes. Lastly and not the least, the managers must be adaptable and flexible to adjust the corporate strategy to conform to societal needs.

## REFERENCES

1. Clauser, Henry M. "United States R&D Lead is Eroding" Research Management, May 1976.

2. Business Week Editorial, June 28, 1976, p. 120.

3. Little, A. D. and Industrial Research Institute. "Barriers to Innovation" Report to the National Science Foundation, Washington, D.C., 1973.

4. Rubenstein, A. H., A. K. Chakrabarti, R. D. O'Keefe, W. E. Souder, and H. C. Young. "Factors Influencing Innovation Success at Project Level." Research Management, May 1976.

5. Souder, W. E. "A Preliminary Survey of the Impact of Federal Intervention on Innovation." Unpublished paper, September 1975.

MARKETING IMPLICATIONS OF THE PROPOSED
BALANCED GROWTH AND ECONOMIC PLANNING ACT

Iqbal Mathur, Southern Illinois University
Rajendra Srivastava, University of Pittsburgh
Subhash C. Jain, University of Connecticut

## ABSTRACT

In early 1975, a bill sponsored by Senators Humphrey and
Javits, titled "Balanced Growth and Economic Planning Act,"
was introduced in the U.S. Senate. The purpose of the proposed act is to provide for accumulation and dissemination of economic information and to ensure the preparation
of a long-term balanced economic growth plan for the U.S.
This proposed act has numerous connotations for marketing-
related activities. The act and its marketing implications are of great potential interest to the marketing
manager. In this paper the proposed act, and its associated agencies and their primary duties are briefly
reviewed. The act calls for greater control over economic
resources and selective growth of segments of the economy.
From a marketing perspective, the proposed act influences
resource allocation, representation of consumer interests,
forecasting, collective advertising, long-range marketing
strategies and international marketing. The paper highlights the proposed act-marketing management interaction.

## INTRODUCTION

The influence of governmental policies and decisions on the
U.S. economy is a major factor that marketing managers
can ill afford to ignore. Marketing decision-makers have
to continually adapt to legislative and regulatory activity and must try to incorporate forecasts of such activity
into their planning process [3]. The dynamic nature of
the technological, economic, social and consumer environments creates unstability for maintaining healthy competition among business firms and preserving consumer interests.
This instability leads to uncertainty and (sometimes)
unwarranted restraints for business marketing activities.
The proposed Balanced Growth and Economic Planning (BGEP)
Act of 1975 would add another very significant dimension
to governmental influence on business firms as it shifts
the focus of government regulation based on the hitherto
exposed concept of growth resulting from free enterprise
activities to planned growth. Indeed it may produce
governmental intervention in the economy on a massive
scale [10].

It is, therefore, necessary to appraise the proposed BGEP
Act as its impact on the macro-environment (economy,
technology, public policy) directly influences the constraints within which marketing managers must function.
Of special interest is the term "balanced growth."
Balanced by whom? For whom? Balanced growth implies a
governing objective or set of objectives. This necessarily involves a value judgement by the policy makers on
Capitol Hill and has generated much debate and discussion
(see, for example, [5], [11] and [12]). The proposed BGEP
Act generates issues that are of great relevance to
marketers. The purpose of this paper is two-fold: to
briefly discuss the proposed BGEP and discuss its implications for marketing activities and to stimulate additional debate and research on this topic by marketers.

## THE PROPOSED BALANCED GROWTH AND ECONOMIC PLANNING ACT

The proposed BGEP Act is aimed at reviving and maintaining
the economic health of the country by calling for a comprehensive system of national economic planning. Such
proposals have been encountered whenever the nation
has encountered economic difficulties, but generally interest diminishes with the resolution of problems. Consequently, no single agency has been charged with the total
planning responsibility for national economics [7]. The
most recent push for such an agency took place in early
1975, a direct result of the recent recession, in the form
of Senate Bill 1795. Originally drafted by the Initiative
Committee for National Economic Planning, Inc. [8], it
gained support from Senators Humphrey (D - Minnesota)
and Javits (R - New York) and was introduced by the
former on May 21, 1975. Subsequently, due to its widespread anticipated impact on business firms, it has
generated considerable debate and discussion (see, for
example, [2], [5], [6], [10], [11] and [12]). A slightly
different version of the Bill, titled "Full Employment
and Balanced Growth Act of 1977," or the Humphrey-Hawkins
Bill, was introduced in the Senate this year [1]. While
the present discussion focuses on the BGEP Act, it is
reasonable to assume that it is a prototype of national
planning proposals.

The purpose of Senate Bill 1795 appears to be two-fold:
(1) to provide for the accumulation and dissemination
of economic information, and (2) to ensure the
(continuing) preparation of a long-term "balanced
economic growth plan" for the nation. It proposes the
creation of new agencies at the level of Federal Government for oganizing the planning effort [14]. It is not
feasible within the space limitation of this paper to
fully discuss the BGEP Act; the various agencies and
their primary duties tnat it calls for are listed in
Exhibit 1. A detailed explanation of the provisions
of the Act as well as pro and con arguments for economic
planning are detailed elsewhere [9].

The plan is to be formulated by the Economic Planning
Board. The Board is to seek active participation of
the private sector and the various levels of the public
sector in the formulation of the plan. The Council for
Economic Planning than reviews the plan and transmits
the approved plan to the President. The President then
presents the plan to the Congress for final approval.

Though the interpretations of the plan (and the planning
process) vary even amongst the sponsors of the Bill,
rather than debate the intricacies of the Bill, we will
focus our attention on issues relevant to marketers.
From the provisions of the Bill, it is apparent that
it calls for [14]:

A. At the national level: planned growth characterized by:

   (1) Greater control over resources, industrial
       structure, etc.
   (2) Selective growth of segments of the economy
       such as medical care, energy, housing, etc.,
       based on the values of a select decision-
       making minority and tempered by political
       and social arguments rather than purely
       economic ones.
   (3) A thrust on long-term planning to achieve
       social objectives rather than crisis manage-
       ment.

B.  At the international level:

   (1) Planning of domestic economy in keeping with
       stability in international trade and relations.

In order to study the impact of the above issues on marketing activities, it becomes necessary to examine the nature
of the relationships between business and the government.

## GOVERNMENTAL INFLUENCE ON MARKETING DECISIONS

Business firms have long recognized the value of designing
strategies that take into account the effects of proposed
or expected government actions.  This is because besides
the function of regulation, the government also happens
to be a major source of information and is the largest
single consumer of goods and services.  In general,
marketers tend to use the lobbying process to inform and
often influence the legislative bodies and agencies of
the executive branch in their decision making processes.
They also use the channels provided by the legal structure
(the courts) to contest the legality and interpretation
of legislation.  By and large, however, marketers adapt
to legislation and regulation permeated by the government
to promote competition, to avoid the ills of monopoly, to
serve consumer interests, etc.  There is very little
"self-regulation" by the private sector and its relationship with the public policy makers tends to be antagonis-
tic.  The result has been a whole series of anti-trust
and consumer protection laws that sometimes do more harm
than good.

The implementation of the proposed BGEP Act will add a
new flavor to governmental activity.  This is because in
addition to measures aimed at preventing the lessening
of competition, there will be an additional thrust towards
the control of scarce resources, the selective growth of
"socially desirable" segments of the economy, etc.  This
is to be done with active participation from the private
as well as the public sector.  One may envision that
under such a framework of long-term planning, lobbying
activities will become much more important and, perhaps,
for the first time industry can see governmental agencies
as collaborators.  Specifically, the notion of BGEP, if
implemented, will affect several major areas of concern
to marketers.  These are briefly discussed in the following section.

## THE PROPOSED BGEP ACT AND MARKETING ACTIVITIES

### Use of Scarce Resources

Traditionally, the system of free enterprise has sponsored
the ideal of unlimited growth, and consumption for the
sake of growth.  Recent shortages of energy, paper, lead,
etc., are understandably viewed by marketers with mixed
feelings since not only do they require changes in
marketing strategy, but also affect changes in lifestyles
--towards conservatism.  So far these scarcities have been
handled on a competitive basis, thereby maintaining and
further fueling inflation.  The implementation of the
BGEP Act, however, may lead to (1) guidelines that require
more efficient use of scarce resources, and (2) allocation
of scarce resources based on sociopolitical priorities.
Thus the marketing of goods or services that require the
use of scarce resources is likely to be subject to
pressures from the consumer (due to lower demand for
wasteful and nature polluting products and services),
as well as from regulators (due to allocations based on
priorities of resources necessary for production).  This
means that the marketing of such goods or services will
require marketing strategies aimed at both consumers and
regulators.

### Representation of Consumer Interests

The implementation of BGEP may limit the ability of
individuals to act as they choose in economic matters.
Consumer soverignity reigns in a free economy but the
government makes decisions for the consumer in a planned
economy [6].  Since the democratic process is less than
perfect, the government cannot accurately represent
consumer decisions.  Already, in several instances the
government has restricted consumer choice (for example,
the mandatory installation of safety belts) [3], and the
BGEP proposal promises further restrictions.  This time
the restrictions may arise not only due to guidelines
stating what features a product may or may not have, but
also due to control of materials the product may be made
of.

Obviously the restriction of consumer choice affects
marketing strategy as marketers may more often have to
see the governmental agencies as decision-makers rather
than the consumers themselves.

### Forecasting

One of the provisions of Senate Bill 1795 (the proposed
BGEP Act) is the accumulation and dissemination of
economic information.  In the past such information has
been available to big businesses who had the ability
and the resources to process it in order to meet their
planning requirements.  It is doubtful that any new
concentrated effort to collect and disseminate information is going to benefit the smaller manufacturers and
service agencies.  However, the availability of precise
economic information, if not lost in the maze of
bureaucracy, is apt to lead to greater predictability
which is a boon to marketing managers for purposes such
as the forecasting of market demand, etc.  If one agrees
that the proposed BGEP Act will lead to greater availability of valid information, then it becomes pertinent
for the competent marketing manager to process such
information efficiently for competitive reasons.

### Selective Growth of Markets

The proposal calls for "meeting (of) essential national
needs in transportation, energy, agriculture, raw
materials, housing..." [14].  This implies the selective
growth of industries based on priorities established by
the planning agencies.  Such subsidization of essential
industries is nothing new (for example, the support
rendered to the aircraft industry and to companies
involved in defense production) in the marketplace, but
its practice on a larger scale will result in much
scrambling, lobbying and chaos.  Of course, the outcomes
are debateable and indeed the end results may be beneficial.  But for the marketing manager it promises
further headaches as he must:  (1) keep track of what is
happening in Washington, and (2) devise strategies to
influence (appropriately) the planning process to get his
piece of the pie.  Again one may debate the productivity
or indeed the need of such activity.

### Collective Advertising

The notion of "balanced growth and economic planning"
as discussed earlier leads to the selective growth of
segments of the economy based on sociopolitical considerations.  Since marketers can influence the planning
agencies either directly (through lobbying) or indirectly
(via public sentiment), collective advertising by companies within an industry should become relatively more
important for their continued profitability or existence.
Thus the BGEP  proposal asks for greater cooperation
between companies within an industry and may lead to
collusion.  This is in direct contrast to the purposes
of much of the anti-trust legislation and could

complicate the legal aspects of the marketing manager's job.

## Collaborative Strategies

The Bill specifically calls for collaboration by the private sector with the planning agencies in the planning process. Since the planning process could be influenced by skewed forecasts of demand, resource reserves, etc., the market manager must learn to effectively play the political game.

It is feasible that the planning agencies will have difficulty remaining independent of the businesses due to the nature of the collaborative efforts. Previous experience (in France) shows that "planning by consultation and negotiation drives the planners into such close alliance with business interests that the (planning) board becomes a champion of the firms it finds easiest to deal with" [2]. This illustrates the benefit of successful "collaboration" with planning agencies.

Collaboration with other business firms to promote issues of common interest or for exchange of support becomes relevant. Such clandestine activities are likely to be effectively reduced by suitable checks and balances.

In spite of all the negative connotations of collaborative strategies, the proposed BGEP Act provides the marketing managers an opportunity to cooperative with the governmental planning agencies, and with other corporations. André van Dam notes the advantages of such cooperative efforts for the survival and prosperity of businesses [4].

## Long-Range Marketing Strategies

Long-range planning at the national level will foster similar planning efforts at the industry and company levels, particularly if the mechanisms for involving the private sector in the planning process are successful. Though long-range forecasting can be inaccurate, one can hardly argue that it will be totally useless. At the very least, the planning process will alert marketing managers to relevant issues that may guide the course in the future. However, the implication here is that the successful marketer will have to plan his activities based on long-range goals rather than on crisis management -- research evidence shows that firms that utilize formal long-range planning have historically outperformed comparable firms that do not [13].

## International Marketing

André van Dam in his appraisal of the new international economic order points out growing importance of underdeveloped nations due to their: (1) control over scarce resources (for example, oil, copper), and (2) growth of purchasing power [4]. The proposed BGEP Act specifically recognizes this trend by requiring that the economic objectives be established paying particular attention to stable international relations and international trade [14]. Thus to maintain balance of trade, and hence a healthy national economy, it becomes necessary that marketers pay attention to the growing international markets. In addition, in order to reduce dependence on foreign resources marketers must draw "demand away from products and services which are materials -- wasteful and energy-intensive" and research, develop and market" new products to absorb the released purchasing power in the domestic market"[4]. This is by no means an easy task. However, cooperation between the governmental planning agencies and the private sector as endorsed by the proposed BGEP Act will provide a starting point.

It is, therefore, important for marketing managers to develop strategies (in cooperation with the governmental planning agencies) directed at foreign consumption and reduction of dependence on foreign resources.

## CONCLUDING REMARKS

The implications of the proposed Balanced Growth and Economic Planning Act for marketing activities were discussed. It was pointed out that Senate Bill 1795, if passed and implemented, would have diverse effects on marketing strategies. Briefly, marketers will find it increasingly important to: (1) present their interests to the planning agencies, something that would require greater concentration on lobbying and collective advertising, (2) utilize the information accumulated and disseminated by the planning agencies for their own long-term planning, and (3) collaborate with the government and other companies with common interests.

As pointed out, the proposed BGEP Act appears to encourage activities that are against the purposes of much of the existing anti-trust legislation and could indeed complicate the legal aspects of marketing strategies. In addition, there is considerable debate regarding the interpretations of the Bill and its weakness in areas of implementation and enforcement. Our interest was not to conduct a definitive evaluation of the "balanced growth and economic planning" proposal, but merely to illustrate its widespread influence on marketing activities. It is our hope that some of the issues brought up will generate further research -- not only in relation to the specific Bill considered in this article but in the general areas of public policy, planning and marketing.

## EXHIBIT 1

PLANNING AGENCIES: PROPOSED BY SENATE BILL 1795

A. **Executive Agencies**

　　1. Economic Planning Board (within the Executive Office of the President).
　　　Primary duties:
　　　(1) Prepare and submit to the Council on Economic Planning a "proposed balanced economic growth plan."
　　　(2) Evaluate and measure the achievement of the plan.
　　　(3) Review the major programs and activities of the Federal Government for consistency with the approved plan.
　　　(4) Coordinate the long-range planning activities of the departments and agencies of the Federal Government.
　　2. Division of Economic Information (within the Economic Planning Board).
　　　Primary duties:
　　　(1) "Secure information, data, estimates, and statistics directly from various departments, agencies, and establishments of the executive branch of Government."
　　　(2) Disseminate "economic data, statistics, and information in such form and manner as will provide a basis on which state and local governments, private enterprise, and the Federal Government can make informed economic decisions and participate effectively in the planning process."
　　3. Council on Economic Planning (within the Economic Planning Board).
　　　Primary duties:
　　　(1) Review and revise the balanced economic

growth plan submitted to it by the Economic
Planning Board.
(2) Submit the final plan to the President.
(3) Review progress in the implementation of the
plan.
4. Advisory Committee on Economic Planning (advisory
to the Economic Planning Board).
Primary duty:
(1) Furnish advice to the Economic Planning Board
"on the views and opinions of broad segments
of the public in matters involved in the
formulation and implementation of the balanced
economic growth plan."

B. New Congressional Agency

1. Division of Balanced Growth and Economic Planning
(within the Congressional Budget Office).
Primary duties:
(1) Perform long-term economic analysis.
(2) Assist the Joint Economic Committee of the
Congress in reviewing the "proposed balanced
economic growth plan" prepared by the Economic Planning Board and submitted to the
Congress by the President.

## REFERENCES

1. Alexander, Tom, "The Deceptive Allure of National
Planning," Fortune (March 1977), pp. 148-156.

2. American Enterprise Institute. The Economic Planning
Proposal (Washington, D.C.: American Enterprise
Institute, 1975).

3. Cravens, D. W.; G. E. Hills and R. B. Woodruff.
Marketing Decision Making: Concepts and Strategy
(Homewood, Illinois: Richard D. Irwin, Inc.,
1976), Chapter 6.

4. van Dam, André, "Marketing in the New Economic
Order," Journal of Marketing, Vol. 41 (January 1977),
pp. 19-23.

5. Friedman, J., "A Planned Economy in the U.S.?"
New York Times (May 18, 1975), p. 53.

6. Friedman, J., "National Economic Planning," Newsweek
(July 14, 1975), p. 18.

7. Grannon, J. P., "Perplexed Economists Hunt for Ways
to Cure U.S. Economy Woes," The Wall Street Journal
(May 9, 1975), p. 1.

8. Initiative Committee for National Economic Planning.
The Case for Planning (White Plains, New York: The
Initiative Committee for National Economic Planning,
1975).

9. Jain, Subhash C. and Iqbal Mathur, "National Economic Planning," Working Paper, Graduate School of
Business, University of Pittsburgh, 1977.

10. Olsen, L. H., "The Pitfalls of Economic Planning."
Paper presented at the Planning Executives Institutes
Conference, Washington, D.C., November 13, 1975.

11. Sharpe, M. E., "The Planning Bill," Challenge,
Vol. 18 (May/June 1975), pp. 3-8.

12. Stein, H., "Better Planning of Less," The Wall
Street Journal (May 14, 1975), p. 14.

13. Thune, S. S. and R. J. House, "Where Long-Range
Planning Pays Off," Business Horizons, Vol. 13
(August 1970), pp. 81-87.

14. U.S. Congress. Balanced Growth and Economic Planning
Act of 1975, H.R. S 1795.

# LIABILITY OF ADVERTISING AGENCIES
# FOR DECEPTIVE ADVERTISING

Gene W. Murdock, University of South Dakota

## ABSTRACT

Deceptive advertising has defied effective regulation. As consumer activists search for new methods of countering deceptive advertising, advertising agencies are certain to face increased scrutiny for their part in creating deceptive ads. This paper examines the legal basis for holding advertising agencies liable for deceptive ads and looks into future areas of potential advertising agency liability.

## THE AGENCY/ADVERTISER RELATIONSHIP

Historically, consumer ire and litigation precipitated by deceptive advertising have focused on manufacturers rather than advertising agencies. However, increasing dissatisfaction with the slow, "after-the-fact" remedies of government and self-regulatory mechanisms is encouraging the deceived consumer to seek new solutions to the problem of deceptive advertising. One solution is to hold advertising agencies responsible for the content of their creative efforts. The rationale is much the same as that used to hold accountants liable for errors or omissions on financial statements bearing their approval. From the consumer's standpoint this solution is attractive because it should discourage deceptive advertising at its point of creation (the trade-off being the possible loss of information). This paper investigates the potential liability of advertising agencies for deceptive advertising from the agency's point of view.

Because of the titles, agent and agency, and the fact that advertising agencies are commonly remunerated by commission, there is the implication that advertising agencies are agents at law.

> However, although agencies work on behalf of, and enter into agreements for the ultimate benefit of, their clients, as a result of the history of the creation of advertising agencies it was acknowledged many years ago that the commonest practice was for agencies to enter into agreements, with suppliers, media owners and other associated bodies, on their own authority and for them to accept full responsibility for such agreements. By so doing they were acting as principals at law [11 p. 1],

The distinction is important. An agent by law is an individual or firm empowered to enter into contracts on behalf of its principal. Thus, the principal, not the agent, becomes liable for any rights or duties under the contract. The mere engagement of an advertiser of an advertising agency does not give rise to a legal agency relationship. Therefore, the agency must exercise great care in the fulfillment of its functions with suppliers, media, and personnel. Unless specifically authorized to do so, by contract or operation of circumstances, the agency rather than the advertiser will stand liable for any contracts entered into with third parties. This fact has become painfully apparent to agencies whose clients contract for a final, desperate advertising campaign which, having failed, has caused them to go into bankruptcy without paying for the advertising. The agency then becomes liable for all the costs incurred. If the agency meets all of the following criteria, it may leave the advertiser solely liable on contracts made to third parties:

1. The advertiser gives his authority for the agency to so contract, or has acted in a manner that would lead the supplier to reasonably believe that the agency has such authority
2. The agency properly acts within the authority given to it expressly or by implication from the conduct of the principal
3. The agency discloses the identity of its principal to the supplier
4. There is no agreement, express or implied, between the agency and supplier to fix the liability solely upon the agency[1].

Conversely, if the agency violates any of the above criteria it can be held liable on the contract. The agency must also be wary (especially in television commercials) because its liability may be affected by union arrangements applicable to suppliers such as actors, musicians, directors, and others who provide specialized service. In general, the forms of liability discussed above pertain to contracts (or contractual liability) primarily with suppliers. However, advertising agencies also become involved with competitors, the public, and the government. Because of this, tortious liability and even criminal liability must be considered.

The most important torts from the agency's point of view are libel, infringement of copyright or trademark, improperly disparaging or defaming a competitor's goods or business, defamation, invasion of privacy, and piracy of another's creative ideas [1]. Additionally, breach of warranties found in advertisements and product liability are expanding sources of actions against agencies. Criminal liability arises when an action, possibly initiated by an individual, leads to prosecution as a violation of a state or federal law (such as lottery laws).

Traditionally, the major risk has fallen upon the advertiser rather than the media or the agency. However, it is always open to the injured party to sue all parties connected with the tort and a number of people may be held separately liable for the same tort. Thus, while most injured parties have chosen to go against the advertiser, they could just as easily bring action against the agency. The FTC has shown an increased tendency to attack the agency. The following cases will illustrate the agency's increasing vulnerability.

## CURRENT CASES

Although it is not clear just when an advertising agency will be held jointly liable along with the advertiser, there is no doubt that it can be done. An early and much publicized case involving both deceptive advertising and the liability of advertising agencies was the Colgate case in 1965 [4]. This case involved the use of a deceptive television mock-up for advertising shaving cream. The FTC said:

While the advertiser , as principal, is unques-
tionably responsible for the advertisements
broadcast on its behalf, it would be strange
indeed if  the agency , as the moving party
in originating, preparing and publishing the
commercials, and having full knowledge not only
that the claim was false but that the "proof"
offered to the public to support it was a sham,
should be relieved from responsibility [1].

The United States Court of Appeals in affirming the commission noted that it could "see no reason why advertising
agencies, which are now big business, should be able to
shirk from at least prima facie responsibility for conduct in which they participate" [1].  Thus, while an advertising agency is not held to as strict a form of liability as the advertiser (in which knowledge of falsity
and intent are immaterial) an agency which is directly
involved in the creation of the offending ad can be held
liable.  This concept was reinforced in Merck and Co. v.
FTC in 1968.  The FTC in this case involving Sucrets
throat lozenges stated that:

> the agency was at least equally responsible with
> its principal for the deception found to be im-
> plicit in the advertising under consideration.
> Moreover, we believe that the agency should
> have been aware of the deceptive capacity of
> such advertising.  Although the agency contends,
> in this connection, that it relied on information
> furnished by Merck, the deception found to exist
> stems not only from the falsity of this information
> but from the use made of it by the agency...

> Nor is it a defense to the agency that the adver-
> tising was approved by Merck's legal and med-
> ical departments.  The agency, more so than its
> principal, should have known whether the adver-
> tisements had the capacity to mislead or deceive
> the public.  This is an area in which the
> agency has expertise.  Its responsibility for
> creating deceptive advertising cannot be shifted
> to the principal who is liable in any event [5].

These two cases firmly established the FTC's power to
hold an agency equally liable with the advertiser.  Additionally, in the Geritol case Parkson Advertising Agency
Inc. was fined $356,000 in January 1973 [7].  The Geritol
case is significant because it established that an advertising agency, as well as the advertiser, is subject to
penalties for violating a cease and desist order.  In
deciding the amount of the penalties, the court took into
account three factors;

1. The financial ability of the companies
   (Parkson's financial statement was held
   not to be a true determination of the
   company's financial worth).
2. The degree of harm caused by the violations.
3. The company's good or bad faith or serious
   intent to comply [7].

A 1974 General Motors case involving an ad agency in an
agreed-to consent decree detailed the responsibilities of
the agency in its effort to comply with the substantiation of the ad.

> The agency can produce the claims in question
> only if it or its client possesses a basis for
> the claim consisting of scientific tests that
> substantiate the claim.  As an alternative, the
> agency may possess a written opinion by a qualified
> person (including an employee of the client)
> that scientific tests exist to substantiate the
> representation.  This opinion must also disclose
> the nature of the tests.  Furthermore, the

> advertising agency must neither know nor
> have reason to know that the tests do not,
> in fact, substantiate the representation  8 .

A Standard Oil case in 1975 again named the advertising
agency in the cease and desist order.  The agency was
deeply involved in designing the ad.  Batten, Barten,
Durstine, and Osborn (BBD&O) conducted a survey to determine what direction the advertising would take.  They
found that pollution was a major concern and appropriately devised a commercial to "show" how F-310 fought pollution.  The playing on the anxieties of consumers about
pollution and the deceptive demonstration, which caught
pollution in plastic bags, led to action by the FTC.
BBD&O attempted to defend on the basis that it lacked the
research facilities to check Standard's claims for technical correctness.  But the commission ruled that the claims
went so far beyond any reasonable interpretation of the
test results that BBD&O must have known of the deception.
Additionally, the FTC pointed out that BBD&O had been
involved in the development of the ads from the very beginning [9].

From these cases it can be deduced that advertising agencies are in a vulnerable position and need to protect
themselves.  In addition to liability insurance a good
way for an ad agency to protect itself is through knowledge of what the FTC will look at to determine if an ad
is deceptive.  Reviewing the previous important cases in
deceptive advertising (see appendix) is one way to obtain
this knowledge.

In protecting itself from liability to suppliers, competitors, and the public, the advertising agency needs to
rely on well-written contracts, good judgment, and common
sense.  There will always be "calculated legal risks"
with which the advertiser must become voluntarily involved.  Advertising agencies must take risks to get the
competitive edge, but they must also look forward to a
future filled with more regulation and public attention.
Even the utmost honesty cannot always assure legality,
and the best policy is an insurance policy.


LIABILITY OF AGENCIES AND MEDIA IN THE FUTURE

There are at least three areas of potential concern for
both advertising agencies and media.  First is the increasing desire for a right of private action under
Section 5 of the FTC Act.  Currently the public can bring
actions to recover monetary damages for actual injuries
resulting from reliance on deceptive advertising, but
individuals cannot stop the deceptive practices themselves.  However, the FTC's lack of effectiveness in
regulating deceptive advertising has motivated authors in
recent law reviews to call for a private right of action
to supplement the FTC enforcement [ 2, 3 ].  If such a
right were acknowledged by the courts, individuals could
use the words of the FTC Act to seek injunctions against
deceptive advertising and ask the court to assess appropriate civil and criminal penalties.  This concept is not
new and has been tried several times, always unsuccess-
fully [2] .  The right of private action has both a historical and legal base and may become a reality unless
the FTC can become more effective in enforcing its
standards.

Secondly, as the scope of product liability has expanded
to the point where privity and negligence are considered
only after "ability to pay", advertising agencies and
media are almost certain to become defendants in product
liability actions.  Although no cases to date have named
an advertising agency as a defendant in a products liability action, the probability increases as agencies perform more sophisticated and varied services for their
clients [6].  Additionally, the concept of express war-

ranty and the requirement that the injured consumer must show reasonable reliance on the advertisement will be easier to meet as ads become more rational and informative. The push for informative, comparative advertising is increasing the liability of agencies and media. Here again there is both the legal and historical basis for holding advertising agencies liable for false product claims, which lead to injury or breach of warranty [6]. There is a similarity between the accountant and the advertiser. Both the accountant's and the agency's work are designed to do the same thing where third parties are concerned: convincing the third party to enter into a relationship with their clients.

One of the most important cases in the area of product liability (for both media and ad agencies) is Hanberry v. Hearst [6]. Mrs. Hanberry purchased a pair of shoes which caused her to fall and sustain severe injuries. She sued the retailer, wholesaler, and Hearst Corporation (publisher of Good Housekeeping) stating that she had relied upon the Good Housekeeping seal in selecting the shoes. She recovered damages from all and the court issued a statement which should encourage agencies to be extremely careful in wording their product claims:

> The basic question presented on this appeal is whether one who endorses a product for his own economic gain, and for the purpose of encouraging and inducing the public to buy it, may be liable to a purchaser who, relying on the endorsement, buys the product and is injured because it is defective and not as represented in the endorsement. We conclude such liability may exist....In arriving at this conclusion, we are influenced more by public policy than by whether such cause of action can be comfortably fitted into one of the law's traditional categories of liability [6].

So, although no successful product liability claim has been filed against an advertising agency, it appears to be only a matter of time until the broad reach of the strict product liability doctrine encompasses ad agencies.

The last potential area of increased liability is based on an acknowledged purpose of advertising: to produce action. In the future agencies and media may be forced to consider what their liabilities will be if they produce "too much" or the "wrong kind" of advertising. For example, in August 1975, the California Supreme Court affirmed a lower court's verdict and awarded a $300,000 judgment to an accident victim's estate [10]. The victim was killed when two teenagers racing to follow a disc jockey's car and win a radio station's prize caused the victim's car to roll over a center divider. The court held that the radio station (KHJ in Los Angeles) was liable. This greatly broadens the liability of companies whose promotional advertising leads to injuries. The decision also has implications for "while-they-last" sales and "limited-seating" sports events. Naturally, advertising agencies will have to assure that any copy they create does not intend to influence the audience toward reckless action that might bring harm to others. Advertising directed toward children requires extreme care in this respect. The future does not hold any promise of decreased liability for the ad agency, advertiser, or media.

## SUMMARY AND CONCLUSIONS

A substantial review of the FTC's actions concerning deceptive advertising reveals that advertising agencies are certainly not free from liability for deception. Liability itself has been discussed in its different forms and an attempt was made to discuss some of the current cases involving liability of advertising agencies for deceptive advertisements. Lastly, a brief look at three possible future areas of agency liability painted a picture of increased susceptibility to both FTC and private actions.

This is not a complete coverage of advertising agencies' liabilities. Several important areas have been ignored to concentrate on deceptive advertising. A comprehensive coverage of ad agency liability would have to include topics such as defamation, copyright and trademark infringement, agency-employee relations, cooperative advertising, trade secrets, lotteries, privacy, and warranties. Perhaps it is enough to say that the courts have been increasingly liberal in their awards (as have juries) and that ability to pay more than "rightness" or "wrongness" seems to be the criteria to determine liability.

### APPENDIX

| Year | Court Case or Reference | Significance |
|---|---|---|
| 1919 | Sears, Roebuck & Co. v. FTC 258 Fed. (7th Cir.): First test case. FTC decision was upheld not because of subsequent damage caused the consumer, but by the fact that smaller competitors could be injured. | |
| 1931 | FTC v. Raladam Co. 283 U.S. 643: Court held that FTC could not prohibit false advertising if there was no evidence of injury to a competitor. Led to Wheeler-Lea Amendment. | |
| 1934 | FTC v. R. F. Keppel & Bro., Inc. 291 U.S. 304: Repudiated Raladam by holding that unfair competitive practices were not limited to those likely to have anticompetitive consequences violative of the antitrust laws; nor were unfair practices in commerce confined simply to competitive behavior. | |
| 1937 | FTC v. Standard Education Society 302 U.S. 112: FTC was to protect trusting as well as the suspicious. | |
| 1938 | Wheeler-Lea Amendment 52 Stat. 111: "Unfair methods of competition in commerce, and unfair or deceptive acts of practices in commerce, are declared unlawful." And to Sec. 12 was added an explicit prohibition of "false advertisements" for the purpose of inducing or which is likely to induce purchase of food, drugs, devices, or cosmetics". | |
| 1942 | Aronberg v. FTC 132 F.2d 165, 167 (7th Cir.): Law is made to protect the public, which includes the ignorant, the unthinking and the credulous. | |
| 1943 | Bockenstette v. FTC 134 F.2d 369 (10th Cir.): Literal truth is not a defense if an ad contains implicit misrepresentations. | |
| 1944 | Charles of the Ritz Distrib, Corp. v. FTC 143 F.2d 676 (2d Cir.): Tendency to mislead is all that is necessary. Deception need not be empirically established. | |
| 1944 | Gelb V. FTC 144 F.2d 580 (2d Cir.): Low intelligence level (ignorant man standard) reached extreme with one woman indicating some people might be misled by the word permanent in a hair coloring ad. | |
| 1946 | Jacob Siegel Co. v. FTC 327 U.S. 608: Courts tend to uphold FTC decisions unless it can be shown that the commission acted arbitrarily, abused its discretion, or failed to make an allowable judgment in its choice of remedies. | |

1946    Carlay V. FTC 153 F.2d 493 (7th Cir.): Legitimized puffery, the exaggerated use of superlatives to describe goods or services.

1950    P. Lorillard Co. v. FTC 186 F.2d 52 (4th Cir.): "To tell less than the whole truth is a well known method of deception; and he who deceives by resorting to such method cannot excuse the deception by relying upon the truthfulness per se of the partial truth by which it has been accomplished."

1953    Rhodes Pharmaceutical Co. v. FTC 208 F.2d 382 (7th Cir.): If an ad has two meanings, one of which is false, the ad is false.

1955    Doris Savitch, 50 FTC 828 (1954): Aff'd per curiam, 218 F.2d 817 (2d Cir.) Any vulnerable segment of the audience such as children or women who fear they might be pregnant, will require a different interpretation of the ignorant man standard.

1959    FTC v. Colgate-Palmolive Co. 380 U.S. 374, 85 S. Ct. 1035, 13 L. Ed.2d 967,: Mock-ups which fail to show simulated demonstrations on T.V. in a truthful manner are deceptive. Advertising agencies can be held liable even though they did not know the advertisements were illegal. Deception must be a material influence on the buying decision.

1963    Heinz v. Kirchner 63 FTC 1282: FTC indicated that it no longer intended to protect the blithely ignorant.

1968    Merck & Co. v. FTC 392 F.2d 921 (6th Cir.): Advertising agency is liable for deceptive ads by virtue of its knowledge and expertise.

1971    ITT Continental Baking Co. 36 Fed. Reg 18,552: First final corrective advertising order was issued. Effect of advertising on "special audiences" such as children.

1971    Bristol-Myers Co. CCH 19,765 FTC File No. 712-3035: FTC decides that the costs of prosecution outweigh the benefits from stopping the deception in some cases. Dry Ban case.

1971    Warner-Lambert Pharmaceutical Co. CCH 19,838, FTC File No. 692-3248: FTC ordered that 25% of all advertising for Listerine for one year must contain disclosure of previous false advertising.

1971    Sugar Association, Inc. CCH 19,857, FTC File No. 712-3635: First time FTC included in a proposed order compulsory corrective advertising.

1972    Ocean Spray Cranberries, Inc. CCH 19,981, FTC Dkt. 8840: Clarifies difference between affirmative disclosure and corrective advertising. Requires Ocean Spray to institute corrective advertising.

1972    National Petroleum Refiners Assn. v. FTC CCH 73,910 DC-D.C., (April): One of the most important cases affecting the power of the FTC. Repudiated any concept that the FTC has the authority to promulgate trade regulation rules that have the effect of substantiative law.

1972    Pfizer, Inc. FTC docket N. 8819, July 11, 1972: Establishes the principle that substantiation for ads exists even if the claim is true and the product ultimately performs as advertised.

1972    Firestone Tire & Rubber Co. CCH 20,112, FTC Dkt. 8818 (Sept.): In examining the evidence and in preparing a statement, the FTC reviews a number of criteria that have been set out concerning deceptive advertising. Also established the commission's authority to issue corrective advertising orders and suggested areas for empirical research concerning corrective advertising.

1973    U.S. v. J. B. Williams Co., Inc. and Parkson Advertising Agency, Inc. CCH 74,330 (D.C. D. N.Y., January); Unusual imposition of extensive civil penalties on violation of a cease desist order. Court reviewed the propriety of a motion for summary judgment (Geritol and its advertising agency were not entitled to trial by jury). Court also held that it didn't have to decide if the ads were deceptive, only if they fell within the prohibitions of a valid FTC order. In justifying the penalties, the court said that although Parkson was an affiliate of Williams, both were subject to the FTC order.

1973    National Petroleum Refiners Assoc. v. FTC, 482 F.2d 672: Reversed district court decision and recognized FTC's authority to prescribe rules that substantively affect the conduct of business on the basis of broad standards of unfair methods of competition or unfair or deceptive acts or practices.

1973    American Motors, Chrysler, etc. CCH 20,168, FTC File No. 732-3055 (January): The FTC announced that future ad substantiation requests will concentrate on major themes and will require a "plain language" version of the technical data submitted.

1973    ITT Continental Baking Co. CCH 20,464, FTC Dkt. 8860 (October): This is the final order in a highly publicized case. A charge of false advertising of Hostess Snack Cakes was dismissed while a cease and desist order was issued to stop advertising Wonder Bread as more nutritious than other foods. Failed to resolve "uniqueness claim" and "unfairness" to children issue, but dealt with both.

1973    Coca-Cola Co. CCH 20,470 FTC Dkt. 8839 (October): Examined the issue of implied representations in advertising, as distinct from express representations.

1974    GAC Corp. et al., CCH 20,554, FTC File No. 722-3087 (March): The FTC instituted restitution, or the offering of refunds to those who may have been misled by unfair or deceptive practices. In this case it involved returning more than $17 million and redevelopment of one of the subdivisions so the lots would be usable by the purchasers. Restitution is limited to those cases where a clear determination can be made to the extent of monetary damage.

1974    U.S. v. J. B. Williams Co., Inc. and Parkson Advertising Agency, Inc., CCH 75,041 (CA-2, May 1974): Court of Appeals held that an advertiser subject to a reviewed and final order of the commission to cease and desist from deception is entitled to a plenary trial, including a jury, on the question of whether the order has been violated by a "new" commercial and on the question of damages assessed for violation of the FTC order.

1974    Joseph's Furniture Co., Inc., et al., CCH 20,596 (May): FTC order would give the customer right to use binding arbitration to settle a dispute with a company. The Arbitrator would be appointed by the Better Business Bureau.

1974 True-View Plastics, Inc., et al., CCH 20,712, FTC File No. 752-3030 (September): Attempts to distinguish between bait and switch and trading up. Required True-View to keep records to show relationship between cost of advertising and sales of advertised products in an attempt to measure bait and switch.

1974 General Motors Corp., et al., CCH 20,747, FTC Dkt. 8907 (November): Representations of superior handling in an automobile ad must be documented. Spelled out ad agencies responsibilities for substantiation.

1974 General Foods Corp., CCH 20,718, FTC File No. 732-3402 (September): The FTC can require a firm to maintain records that support advertising claims for a period of time after the dissemination of these claims.

1974 Standard Oil of California and Batten, Barten, Durstine and Osborn, CCH 20,789, FTC DKT. 8827 (November): Where advertisers rely even partially on serious consumer concerns (such as in the area of pollution) to advance their own interests, they must exercise an extra measure of caution.

1974 Warner-Lambert Co., CCH 20,776, FTC Dkt. 8891 (November): First time a corrective advertising provision was issued in a cease and desist order (previous provisions have been issued as part of consent decrees). Listerine was so established as a cold remedy the judge said only corrective advertising would help.

1975 Great Atlantic and Pacific Tea Co., Inc., CCH 20,826, FTC Dkt. 8916 (January): Advertising products and failing to have them available in all stores covered by the advertisements or failure to have them at the prices advertised is both (a) unfair, misleading and deceptive, and (b) an unfair method of competition; and (c) the existence of a "raincheck" or substitution policy does not cure the unavailability of advertised products.

1975 Fedders Corp., CCH 20,825, FTC Dkt. 8932 (January): The FTC rejected the defenses of "insubstantiality" and "abandonment" in this particular case. That is, it is not a defense to argue that the offending ads constituted only a small percentage of the total advertising expenditures or that you have ceased to issue the ads.

1975 Horizon Corp., CCH 20,845, FTC Dkt. 9017 (March): First actions to be filed under the new powers granted the FTC in Title II of the Magnuson-Moss Act. These powers include the right to seek relief to redress injury to consumers, or other persons, partnerships or corporations, in the form of restitution and refunds for past, present, and future consumers.

## REFERENCES

1. Barton, Roger, ed. Handbook of Advertising Management. New York: McGraw-Hill Book Company, 1970, 32-1 to 32-80.

2. Carpenter, David W. "Implied Civil Remedies for Consumers under the FTC Act," Boston Law Review, 43(July 1974), 606-23.

3. Castleman, James A. "Advertising, Product Safety, and a Private Right of Action Under the Federal Trade Commission Act," Hofstra Law Review, 2 (Summer 1974), 669-91.

4. 380 U.S. 374, 85 S. Ct. 1035, 13 L.Ed.2d 904.

5. "Final Order (8635)," FTC News Summary, April 27, 1966; Merck & Co. v. FTC, 392 F.2d 921 (6th Cir. 1968).

6. Werber, Stephen J. and William L. Trombetta. "Product Liability: The Potential Liability of the Advertising Agency," Cleveland State Law Review, 24 (1975), 413-21.

7. Werner, Ray O. ed. "Legal Developments in Marketing," Journal of Marketing, 37(July 1973), 83.

8. _____. "Legal Developments in Marketing," Journal of Marketing, 39(April 1975), 88-89.

9. _____. "Legal Developments in Marketing," Journal of Marketing, 39(July 1975), 88-89.

10. "When a Giveaway Backfires," Business Week, (November 24, 1975), 82.

11. Woolley, Diana. Advertising Law Handbook. London: Business Books Limited, 1973.

# MANAGING THE ACADEMIC DEPARTMENT

Leonard L. Berry, Georgia State University
Thomas V. Greer, University of Maryland
Gerald E. Hills, University of Tennessee
William B. Locander, University of Houston

## ABSTRACT

Presented in this paper are the independent views of two marketing department chairmen and two marketing department faculty on three questions pertaining to the management of the academic marketing department. The questions concern the roles, managerial style and personal attributes of the "effective" chairman.

## INTRODUCTION

The role of the department chairman[1] in an academic institution, never an easy role, has become increasingly challenging in the era of retrenchment and belt-tightening now characterizing higher education. Although this difficult job is becoming more difficult all the time, marketing department chairmen are exposed to few formal opportunities for developing their administrative and leadership skills.

This paper, and the dialogue session of which it is a part, is meant to be a step forward in addressing this problem. What follows are the independently developed answers of four panelists to three common questions:

1. What are the principal roles of the marketing department chairman? What should chairmen do?

2. What is the best managerial style for a chairman? How should chairmen do what they are supposed to do?

3. Who should be a chairman? What types of people make good chairmen? What qualities are most desirable?

Leonard Berry and Thomas Greer, two of the panelists, are presently chairmen of academic marketing departments. Gerald Hills and William Locander, the other two panelists, are presently faculty members in academic marketing departments. For each question, the responses of the chairmen panelists are presented before the responses of the faculty panelists to facilitate comparison.

## WHAT ARE THE PRINCIPAL ROLES OF THE MARKETING DEPARTMENT CHAIRMAN?[2]

Berry

Although a department chairman has a number of important roles, I would suggest that none is more important, and more often overlooked, than the role of faculty development, the role of developing human potential so that organizational goals and individual faculty member goals can be simultaneously fulfilled.

The faculty role is a knowledge development and dissemination role which means that faculty must continue to grow and develop in a way and at a pace that fosters optimum performance from the institution's standpoint. Viewed this way, faculty development becomes not a peripheral concern for the chairman but, rather, a central concern in which such non-glamorous decisions as travel budget allocations and course assignments are made within the framework of this question: what will this mean to this faculty member's personal development?

The faculty development role for the chairman divides into a number of sub-roles including those of consultant, model, facilitator and recruiter.

Concerning the consultant role, a chairman needs to be prepared to provide individualized assistance in whatever area a faculty member might need advice and counsel so long as the chairman is competent to do so. Hence, the chairman, in effect, serves as a publications consultant to one faculty member and a teaching consultant to another while trying to persuade a third faculty member to believe in himself.

Concerning the model role, department chairmen are limited in their ability to help others in areas where they themselves are weak or inactive. To be in the best position to help a poor teacher improve, the chairman needs not only to regularly teach but to teach well. To be in the best position to ask for quality research from a faculty member more inclined towards quantity research, the chairman needs not only to do research and publish, but to do quality work that is cited and reprinted, research that means something.

Concerning the facilitator role, the chairman is regularly exposed to opportunities to put people together who can benefit from one another, opportunities to be the impetus or smooth the way for an advantageous relationship between one faculty member and another or between a faculty member and an opportunity within the profession.

---

[1] In this paper, the terms "chairman," and "chairmen" and "he" are used strictly for convenience of presentation. The use of these terms is not meant to infer that women are, or should, be excluded from this particular academic position.

[2] The role of the chairman is to some extent situational in the sense that it will be shaped by such factors as authority granted the chairman, size and diversity of the department, experience and caliber of the faculty, and whether the chairmanship is a permanent or rotating position. The comments of all panelists to this question assume a situation where the chairman has considerable decision-making authority, is responsible only for marketing faculty, is working with faculty of a caliber that research/publication activity is expected behavior, and is in a non-rotating position.

Concerning the <u>recruiter</u> role, faculty development is enhanced when the search for new faculty focuses on individuals who will be good teachers for other faculty, as well as for the students. Success in this role requires finding faculty who have attractive personal qualities as well as attractive academic credentials, finding good people not just people with good resumes.

## Greer

There are many roles a chairman can play to good effect. Since time resources are limited, I feel that a major block of the chairman's administrative time should be devoted to careful decisions on course selection, scheduling, and staffing assignments. Thoughtful decisions in this area must take into account long-run department plans, relative emphasis on graduate and undergraduate curricula, purposes of course offerings (e.g., "service" courses versus courses for majors only), supply and assortment of teaching manpower, and student demand. Although the casual observer of the process may think of this flow of decisions as perfunctory, easy, or routine, I do not. Such decisions affect the heart of the teaching mission of the school, and on my campus influence the studies of thousands of students every year. It is also well worth noting that these decisions commit enormous blocks of faculty time. Careful scheduling of each individual professor can husband the remaining time into viable blocks for research, while a helter-skelter approach can leave some faculty members with a fragmented, underutilized work week. Secondly, assignment of faculty to courses can stimulate or stifle research streams. Consideration of current faculty research interests in making course assignments can create an atmosphere in which research and teaching nurture each other instead of competing with each other.

It goes without saying that the chairman should be a good faculty recruiter. Also, although students are plentiful, he should be a student recruiter. Even if quantity is satisfactory, one can always work on quality!

A chairman should function as a spokesman to the administration for the faculty group he represents. However, he must temper this role carefully. It is not appropriate for him to become a spokesman on every small topic that interests one faculty member. After all, the individual faculty member can also speak with committee chairmen, deans, chancellors, and presidents whenever they wish. The chairman must assume the role of spokesman selectively, in view of the other demands on his time, and pursue especially those matters that would tend to benefit the entire department. Only secondly can his time and energy be devoted to pursuing the interests of individual faculty members, and then only if the advantage of the individual will not harm the good of the group. The chairman must be able on occasion to say "No" to a request to assume the role of spokesman. Bringing home the bacon is legitimate, but it can't be the chairman's overriding goal, and often he must take a global view of the purposes and needs of the entire college. That is, he must be a good team player in relations with the other departments and the college administrators.

Whether one likes it or not, a chairman is in some ways a supervisor, a representative of the institutional chain of command. Therefore, he must evaluate faculty annually for purposes of promotions and tenure. This involves crucial appraisals of research and publications, teaching and service. In all justice, distinctions among faculty performances must be identified, not avoided.

The chairman should make sincere efforts to aid the development of the individual faculty member. Thoughts on this role are expanded upon later.

## Hills

The department chairman is faced with wearing many "hats" even when we ignore the chairman's personal responsibilities to teaching, research and public service [1, 2, 5]. The chairman occupies the roles of planner, coordinator and delegater, motivator and facilitator, and evaluator. The chairman is also a constant "environmentalist," acting as the department's link to other administrative levels in the college and university as well as to the department's many constituencies or publics [4]. The chairman must monitor changes in the organizational and the external environment of potential significance to the department's goals and priorities. Finally, the chairman must recognize all available scarce resources as such and work to maximize output from available resources and also attract additional resources. The department chairman generally should be output, not activity, oriented.

In sum, the department chairman would ideally be a visionary genius, able to move mountains (and faculty) with few, if any, discretionary resources. The effectiveness of the chairman, being more realistic, must hinge on specialization in a few areas of highest priority, although not ignoring the larger "picture." The specific priorities presumably would be somewhat unique to each university; but the following roles of the chairman are seemingly critical in any environment:

1.  <u>Efficient Administrator</u>. This role must be a "given" in filling the position of department chairman; otherwise the individual will become inundated with day-to-day routine (such as correspondence and budget matters), and will not have the time for the more critical roles that should receive priority. It is a necessary but not sufficient role of the chairman.

2.  <u>Motivator/Facilitator</u>. Perhaps the most critical role of the chairman is one of an enthusiastic, positive motivator. It is also one of the most difficult roles, given the independent, freedom-oriented nature of most faculty. If the faculty member feels coerced, the effort is likely doomed. Most faculty members hold the self-concept of high performers in their various activities; thus attempts at negative motivation may be counterproductive. The chairman must instead consciously identify the sources of faculty job satisfaction (and their relative importance) as the basis for developing individually directed motivational efforts. Few faculty are motivated entirely by economics; thus, given tight budgets, the potential for building high morale as a base for building high productivity will come largely from the non-economic realm. Part of motivating, of course, also includes removing impediments (e.g., resource availability or bureaucracy) that make faculty productivity difficult.

3.  <u>Coordinating Resources to Achieve Niches of Excellence</u>. Related to the motivational role (and in a sense preceding it) is the role of leader and coordinator. This is again an extremely difficult role for the chairman to occupy. Indeed, the most successful chairman is probably viewed by the faculty as, at most, a coordinator and not a strong leader. Most university faculty, as suggested above, prefer to be their <u>own</u> leader and many question even the appropriateness of departmental "leadership" in the conventional sense. For the chairman to be effective, the faculty must willingly provide the chairman with authority; that is, authority must flow upward in the university, not downward, even granting that some universities have a more established authority structure than others.

The department cannot be "everything to everybody," so a
department is inevitably faced with assigning priorities to
its constituencies with attendant differential emphases on
the amount and quality of teaching, research and service.
In the chairman's role as leader it is essential to use
creativity to foster synergistic productivity (between faculty) to develop organized excellence in selected "niches."
But again, this is possible only through positive encour-
agement by the chairman and uncoerced participation by the
faculty. More generally, coordination of departmental
activities with the view that faculty time is the single
most valuable resource is an important part of the leadership role. This outlook, among other things, involves the
chairman in supporting some degree of faculty specialization and working to remove inflexible, bureaucratic constraints and dysfunctional reporting functions from above.

Locander

A department chairman must be a manager of academic effort.
That is, he must be able to manage his department members
so that they contribute in the ways which match their
skills. It is likely that any one department is going to
have individuals whose talents vary on a number of dimensions: teaching-research, qualitative-quantitative, ten-
ured-nontenured, committed-not committed, service oriented-
not service oriented. In order to manage effectively, the
chairman must first understand his department members and
then meld each person into the group's efforts so that
their talents are well used and weaknesses are overcome.
The key to any department's internal growth is personal
development. The chairman has to encourage the non-writer
to match up with a writer to start publishing. The leader
might be matched with the "detail person" for a key committee. The "nationally eminent" member could be selected
to serve on committees with more national visibility while
those more internally oriented do a job of equal value on
an internal issue.

The department chairman is also a manager of resources.
He must balance teaching schedules and work loads so that
sufficient time can be given to teaching, research and
service. By balancing resources, I mean allowing members
to contribute their major effort in areas where they wish,
but not to the exclusion of other areas. One member might
teach a 9 hr. load and publish moderately--while another
might be on a 3 or 6 hr. load and be a strong publisher.

The department chairman has to serve as middleman between
his faculty and the Dean, a role which is dependent on the
type of system in which the chairman operates. Nevertheless, the chairman must act as a buffer/communication link
between the Dean and his faculty. Usually this means representing the department's wishes to the Dean and acting
as a communicator back to the department. The chairman's
relationship with the Dean is extremely important to the
department's ability to get resources. Part of the middleman role has to do with another role--rewarder. Depending
on the type of merit system the college has implemented,
the chairman has to, in some way, present the case for
each of his members which ultimately brings about year-end
rewards.

The role of planner is very important to the department.
The chairman must recognize college goals and then interpret them in terms of his department. He has to ask himself the same 3 questions that any manager has to ask:
(1) Where is the department now? (2) Where do we want to
be in 1, 2, 5 yrs.? and (3) With our people and resources,
how do we get there?

## WHAT IS THE BEST
## MANAGERIAL STYLE FOR A CHAIRMAN?

Berry

My observation is that personal honesty, openness, willingness to delegate and a sense of the future are crucial.
Honesty is important because the chairman should set an
example for others, because the academic grapevine is such
that uneven treatment of individual faculty will not remain
a secret, and because responsible, truthful feedback to faculty is more likely to lead to improved performance than
irresponsible, non-truthful feedback.

Openness is important because without it the rumor mill and
hallway gossip flourish. Although the chairman must be
very protective of personal information concerning individual faculty members, virtually all other matters are the
faculty's business and should be treated openly and can-
didly.

Willingness to delegate is important because faculty are
not going to optimumly develop and grow if not given "a
piece of the action" and because a spirit of community and
teamwork and sharing is not going to occur in any department dominated by one individual.

A sense of the future is important because the chairman
must take many actions in the present that have important
implications for the future. Whether designing a faculty
evaluation system or determining course assignments for
next semester or giving feedback to a non-tenured faculty
member who may not make tenure, the chairman needs to routinely consider the futurity of his present actions.

Greer

In order to minimize friction generated by the supervisory
aspects of the position, the chairman should adopt a managerial style of a counselor as much as possible. Very
little aid from the chairman may be appropriate in developing a faculty member who is an established full professor.
However, even in his case serving as a sounding board for
ideas and plans is useful. Aid can be extensive and perhaps detailed in the case of a younger faculty member. At
the minimum, the chairman should assist each faculty member
in setting specific goals for each academic year.

The chairman should be accessible. This means making large
blocks of time available to the faculty and spending much
time at the office. He must be basically familiar with the
progress of their work. To the extent that his personality
allows, he should convey an attitude of receptiveness,
openness, and personal interest in faculty members. The
chairman should always remember that the faculty members
are his colleagues and he is their colleague. In designing
and perfecting, or merely trying to find his managerial
style, he should ask himself how he would like to be dealt
with if he were not the chairman.

Hills

"The most successful chairman in dealing with his department thinks and acts in terms of 'we' far more than 'I'.
He looks upon himself as a peer with his department members. . ." [3]   The management style of the chairman must
reflect this quotation; that is, that the chairman is still
first a faculty member and secondly a democratic administrator. Although the chairman should not be just a vote
taker, responding to the wishes of the faculty, neither can
the chairman authoritatively direct the faculty at every
turn. This may make the chairmanship position less satisfying unless the persons occupying it can find job satisfaction within themselves. This is because the unobtrusive, interactive management style that is required tends
to result in the faculty crediting themselves for much that
the chairman has at least partially accomplished.

Locander

A department chairman's managerial style should be parti-
cipative. That is, within the limits of college goals and
allotted resources, a chairman should attempt to create a
group concensus of where the department should be going and
how to get there. It should be noted that the chairman can
frequently use his maturity and experience to guide the
group to goals and courses of action. This style of management requires more of the "cards on the table" approach
with open discussion of issues. This is favored over "back
room" decision making with little member participation.
Leadership comes into play when the chairman creates an
environment within the department so that there is a sense
of attainable goals and most faculty are working on some
committee to achieve these goals. Managing academics
almost requires a low key leadership style because most
academics are highly individualistic and don't always see
themselves as members of an organizational structure.

The chairman must also be a credible figure, not only
within the department, but also the college. In fulfilling
his role as a middleman, the chairman must have the support
of his faculty, the Dean, and the faculty at large. In
order to remain credible, many times the chairman of a department has to adopt a "college model" in making decisions.
That is, he must recognize the needs of other departments
and not work solely for optimizing his department's position or rewards.

WHO SHOULD BE A CHAIRMAN?

Berry

A department chairmanship is not for everyone. The chairman must be an administrator and a leader, perceptive,
mentally tough, academically savvy, and personally unself-
ish. Anyone contemplating a chairmanship should undergo
a self-appraisal on these criteria.

Much of the chairman's job is minutia, or record-keeping
details. The ability to self-organize, to classify and
categorize, and to delegate to an administrative assistant
or secretary is crucial to a chairman's effectiveness and
productivity. But so is the ability to lead, to be a cata-
lyst, to plan and to strategize, to involve others in the
making of progress, to share, to inspire.

Also crucial is the chairman's perceptiveness and sensitivity. The ability to pick up non-verbal signals from
others, to empathize, to handle delicate matters delicately
is perhaps as important as any single trait for a department chairman.

Mental toughness is necessary because the chairman makes
decisions on a daily basis that directly affect the circumstances, fortunes and future of individual faculty.
Criticism is inevitable and a chairman has to be able to
take the "heat." An individual who wants to be "loved" is
probably better off letting someone else be chairman.

Academic savvy is important because unless a chairman
understands how academic careers are built, and ruined,
and how the university really works, not how it appears to
work, he is not able to properly counsel individual faculty or properly represent the departmental interest inside
the university system.

Finally, personal unselfishness is vital because the chairman must necessarily spend a very significant amount of
time on activity that will never be reflected in an academic vita. Said another way, much time that a chairman
might spend on publishing is instead spent on other
people's careers, on making up course schedules, on preparing documentation for tenure/promotion decisions, on
reading every other faculty member's teaching evaluations,

on budget planning, etc. This is not to say that the chairman can't or shouldn't publish but, rather to suggest that
there are many more claims on a chairman's time than is the
case with a regular faculty member.

Greer

A chairman is a member of a community of scholars. In my
opinion, only a productive scholar should become a chairman.
Unfortunately, on becoming a chairman, one can expect that
one's scholarly productivity will decrease if one takes the
chairmanship seriously. One should be a full professor or
very senior associate professor.

One could specify many other qualities desirable in a chairman, such as being tactful yet persuasive, or flexible yet
forceful. He should have a good sense of humor and should
be resilient. He should be a good planner and enjoy planning, and yet be resourceful in adapting to change. He
should like people and the marketing profession enough to
participate in the appropriate local, regional, and national
organizations. It is very hard to put into a list of characteristics, but the chairman must exhibit leadership.

Hills

Desirable qualities for the chairman to possess include
(1) a positive, enthusiastic orientation, (2) a democratic,
non-authoritarian personality, (3) highly effective communication skills, and (4) a respected record as an academician. Given the earlier discussion, these qualities should
require very little elaboration. One exception may be the
dimension of academic respectability. The authority held
by the chairman, conveyed upward by the faculty, comes from
respect, not just personal friendship. Indeed, the latter
may be dysfunctional whereas serving as a respected model
for the faculty is very constructive.

Locander

Who should be a chairman and who shouldn't? A good chairman has to be able to recognize areas where the department
needs to develop and open up these issues to discussion.
This could range from doing more research, to redesigning
the undergraduate program, to building bridges with the
local community businessmen. This is where the leadership
factor is very important. Likewise, a chairman should be
recognized as having a good record in the research, teaching and service areas. That is, he should be able to help
his faculty in each of these areas.

There are two traits where "a little goes a long way" in
being a chairman: authoritarianism and the "political men-
tality." In managing an academic department, an authoritarian figure tends to reduce the openness of the group and
stifle creativity. Most academics need some direction of
their energies, but not much. A dictatorial system frequently brings about negative reaction on the part of department members.

The "politico" should not be a department head. These are
the people who see the system as almost "issueless" because
the level of one's political clout determines the outcome.
Unfortunately, many times the political game replaces the
real game of addressing the pertinent issues and getting
the job done well.

REFERENCES

1. Brann, James and Thomas A. Emmet, eds. The Academic
   Department or Division Chairman: A Complex Role.
   Detroit: Balamp Publishing, 1972.

2. Delahanty, James. "What Do Faculty Want In A Departmental Chairman?" in Brann and Emmett, op. cit., 221-226.

3. Gils, Kenneth. "The Chairman: A Wearer of Many Hats." The Clearing House, 48 (December, 1973), 248.

4. Kotler, Philip. Marketing for Nonprofit Organizations. Englewood Cliffs, N. J.: Prentice-Hall, 1975.

5. Peterson, Marvin W. "The Academic Department: Perspectives from Theory and Research," in John C. Smart and James R. Montgomery eds. Examining Departmental Management. San Francisco: Jossey-Boss, Inc. (Summer, 1976) 21-38.

# A COGNITIVE APPROACH TO MODEL-BUILDING AND EVALUATION

Dipankar Chakravarti, Carnegie-Mellon University
Andrew Mitchell, Carnegie-Mellon University
Richard Staelin, Carnegie-Mellon University

## ABSTRACT

In this paper we suggest that in order to improve model-building and implementation procedures for decision calculus type models, research is needed to understand the cognitive abilities of managers. We demonstrate that managerial judgment is critical in estimating the parameters of these types of models and then use a quasi-experimental design to explore managers' abilities to estimate the parameters of a simplified model. The results indicate that a manager's experience in a limited region of a non-linear response function does not enable him to accurately predict decision outcomes or parameters in the unfamiliar regions.

## INTRODUCTION

Little [11] introduced decision calculus in 1970, as a "model-based set of procedures for processing data and judgments" to assist managerial decision-making. The concept emphasizes the following six design criteria to facilitate model implementation and usage: 1) simplicity, 2) robustness, 3) ease of control, 4) adaptability, 5) completeness and 6) interactive capability.

According to Montgomery and Weinberg [12], decision calculus models are best implemented in a four-step iterative process. First, the model-designer determines the manager's implicit model of the process which is in turn translated into a formal structure. Procedures are then developed for model parameterization. Finally, an interactive usage program is designed. The first three steps generally require the greatest time and attention in implementation [12].

Marketing models using the decision calculus approach have been frequently appearing in the literature.[1] These models have been implemented in industry [12] and are also used extensively as instructional material in many graduate business programs [6,18].

## A COGNITIVE APPROACH TO MODEL-BUILDING

### Overview

Although we agree with the basic decision calculus philosophy and believe that on-line computer models are beneficial to marketing management,[2] we feel that a better understanding of the cognitive abilities of managers is required to improve both the model building and implementation process. We believe that both of these processes should be designed to draw upon a manager's cognitive strengths and

---

[1]Since Little's [11] pioneering article in 1970, over a dozen decision calculus models have appeared in Management Science, Operations Research and the Journal of Marketing Research. These models range from applications to specific aspects of marketing decision-making such as advertising budgeting, media planning and salesman call-planning to overall marketing mix planning models.

[2]For a review of applications of management science models in marketing, see Montgomery and Weinberg [18].

---

circumvent his weaknesses.

Research in cognitive psychology has found man generally susceptible to severe errors of judgment. Slovic [14], summarizing much of this research has noted that:

> "...the belief that man can behave optimally when it is worthwhile for him to do so, gains little support from these studies. The sources of judgmental bias are cognitive and not motivational."

This implies that an on-line computer model might be of great value to a manager since it does not have the same limitations of accurately processing information according to some pre-specified rule. A number of studies have investigated this hypothesis in data synthesis situations and have generally found that mechanical models will outperform an individual who is using raw judgments [5,8,13]. This improvement in human decisions by replacing raw judgments with a simple model of those judgments has been termed 'bootstrapping' [9].

At the same time, evidence of man's limited judgmental processes suggests possible problems with a manager's ability to infer the structure of the process generating data and to estimate the parameters of this process. Consequently, before the bootstrapping phenomenon can be taken advantage of, the manager must correctly specify both the model and its parameters.

In summary, a computer model can be a valuable aid in helping a manager process information. However, its value in decision making depends on whether the structure of the model and its parameters are valid. In this paper we concentrate almost entirely on the problems of parameter estimation. It should be noted, however, that inferring the structure of the model is probably the more difficult cognitive task.

### Parameterization

Numerous procedures have been suggested for parameterizing models, including: market tests, statistical techniques, managerial judgment and tracking. Although most proponents of the decision calculus approach have emphasized data based forms of parameterization (e.g., market tests and statistical techniques), they are generally inappropriate for at least some of the required parameters. For instance, making a model robust generally requires that some of the estimated parameters must lie outside the general operating range of the corporation. Consequently statistical techniques cannot be relied upon to estimate these parameters and management may be very reluctant to conduct market tests at these levels [1]. Also, the criteria of simplicity and completeness generally require that some parameters that can only be estimated by a manager need to be included in the model (Little [11], Urban [17]).

Therefore, some parameters of most decision calculus models must be estimated by managerial judgment and/or tracking. Although some model builders have suggested that only managerial judgment should be used (Gensch and Welam [7]), most decision calculus proponents advocate a combination of managerial judgment and tracking, i.e., managerial judgments be "validated" and adjusted, when necessary, by replicating past history. Unfortunately, as we show next, it is possible for many sets of parameter values to provide excellent fits to past data. Consequently, good tracking does not guarantee good parameter estimation.

## Over-parameterization

In order to obtain both simplicity and completeness, many decision calculus models are over-parameterized (e.g., under-identified). This means that many sets of parameter values will frequently provide an excellent fit to the data.

To demonstrate the above problem, consider a firm having a ten-period advertising expense and market share history shown in Table 1A (Rows 2 & 3). Table 1B shows five different sets of managerial estimates required to parameterize a simplified version of ADBUDG [11].[3] Table 1A (Rows 4-8) shows five replications of past history using the parameter estimates in Table 1B. Comparison of the five sets of results with the history shows few discernible differences between the replications and the actual data.[4]

Thus past data replication may narrow down plausible parameter sets, but probably will be ineffective for an unambiguous choice of the 'true' set. Moreover, it should be noted that the above analysis has simplified the normal parameter estimation problem by ignoring all the special indices such as advertising effectiveness, seasonality, non-advertising effects, etc., which are free to vary from period to period in the ADBUDG model.

Another way to pick the 'true' parameter set is to compare future predictions with a manager's expectations. Unfortunately, decision calculus models are normally designed to be 'robust', i.e., they do not produce results with absurd normative implications even for extreme managerial inputs. Consequently, robustness tends to lower the sensitivity of predicted outcomes to model input variations and produces reasonable outcomes even from grossly erroneous inputs.

In summary, then, some of the parameters of a decision calculus model can be estimated only through managerial

### TABLE 1A

'ACTUAL' VERSUS MODEL-PREDICTED MARKET SHARES AND CORRESPONDING OPTIMAL ADVERTISING DECISION USING PARAMETERS SHOWN IN TABLE 1B

| 1 | PERIOD NUMBER | | 1 | 2 | 3 | 4 | 5 | 6 | 7 | 8 | 9 | 10 | 11 |
|---|---|---|---|---|---|---|---|---|---|---|---|---|---|
| 2 | ADVT. EXPENSE ($ '000) | | 350 | 375 | 400 | 425 | 450 | 475 | 500 | 525 | 550 | 575 | PREDICTED OPTIMAL ADVT. |
| 3 | ACTUAL MARKET SHARE (%) | | 4.60 | 4.55 | 4.61 | 4.88 | 4.96 | 5.17 | 5.32 | 5.63 | 5.67 | 5.77 | DECISION ($ '000) BY MODEL |
| 4 | MARKET SHARES (%) | 1 | 4.58 | 4.57 | 4.70 | 4.86 | 5.03 | 5.19 | 5.34 | 5.47 | 5.60 | 5.70 | 567 |
| 5 | PREDICTED BY MODEL, | 2 | 4.58 | 4.53 | 4.64 | 4.81 | 4.99 | 5.18 | 5.35 | 5.51 | 5.66 | 5.79 | 567 |
| 6 | USING PARAMETER | 3 | 4.63 | 4.62 | 4.73 | 4.88 | 5.19 | 5.34 | 5.48 | 5.75 | 5.75 | 655 |
| 7 | SET NUMBER: | 4 | 4.56 | 4.54 | 4.67 | 4.85 | 5.04 | 5.23 | 5.41 | 5.58 | 5.74 | 5.89 | 715 |
| 8 | (TABLE 1B) | 5 | 4.64 | 4.57 | 4.66 | 4.85 | 5.06 | 5.27 | 5.46 | 5.63 | 5.77 | 5.88 | 0 |

NOTES
1. Initial (period zero) market share = 5.00%
2. Optimal Advertising decision figures rounded off to nearest thousand dollars.
3. The optimal advertising decision is based on a one-period time horizon.

### TABLE 1B

MANAGERIAL ESTIMATES USED TO GENERATE MODEL PARAMETER SETS FOR PREDICTED DATA IN TABLE 1A

| PERIOD ZERO ESTIMATES OF | PARAMETER SET NUMBER | | | | |
|---|---|---|---|---|---|
| | 1 | 2 | 3 | 4 | 5 |
| 1 LONG RUN MINIMUM SHARE (%) | 1.00 | 0.25 | 1.00 | 1.00 | 0.50 |
| 2 SHARE IN PRD.1 IF ADVT. IS CUT TO ZERO DOLLARS (%) | 2.50 | 2.50 | 2.50 | 2.50 | 4.00 |
| 3 ADVT. REQD. IN PRD.1 TO MAINTAIN SHARE ($ '000) | 430 | 430 | 430 | 430 | 400 |
| 4 SHARE IN PRD.1 IF ADVT. IS 15% OVER MAINTENANCE. (%) | 5.25 | 5.25 | 5.25 | 5.30 | 5.20 |
| 5 SATURATION SHARE FOR PRD.1 (%) | 6.25 | 6.25 | 7.50 | 7.50 | 5.30 |

[3]In this paper we have used ADBUDG since we feel that it is a good example of the decision calculus concept. However we believe that the points we make hold for most decision calculus models.

[4]The data are hypothetical. Monotonically increasing advertising allocations were chosen to ensure a smooth market share curve over time, a situation in which discrepant trends are relatively easy to discern. In fact, the 'actual' data were generated by adding a random noise $N(0,0.05)$ to one of the predicted sets. There thus is a 'true' parameter set, which we leave to the reader to ascertain. Industry sales and the contribution margin were held constant at 20 million units and $2.00 per unit respectively.

judgment and cannot be validated by tracking. These, most certainly, will include parameters that lie outside the general operating range of the corporation.

The question then is: "How sensitive is the model to these parameter estimates?" There is some indication that the ADBUDG model, for instance, may be relatively insensitive to these parameter estimates (Weinberg, et al. [18] if used only for predicting the outcomes of decisions within the normal operating range. Obviously, as predictions are made for control variable values outside the normal operating range, the quality of these predictions will become more dependent on these parameters. If the model is used to determine the optimal decision, these parameter estimates may, in fact, become quite critical. In Table 1A, we show that the different sets of parameters, which all gave good fits to the data, yield optimum advertising decisions for the next period ranging from $0 to $715,000. We take this to be strong evidence that 'valid' parameters can have substantially different managerial implications.

The previous discussion has demonstrated the importance of managerial judgment in estimating parameters of decision calculus models. That erroneous parameter estimates may generate outcomes that conform quite closely to expectations and past data is a particularly troublesome fact. Behavioral evidence suggests that people tend to believe their estimates more strongly than they should. For example, Alpert and Raiffa [2] as well as Kahneman and Tversky [10,15,16] found that subjects place far too narrow confidence bands on their estimates. These findings suggest that the methodology of tracking may create undue managerial confidence in both the structure and the estimated parameters of the model. Unfortunately, the predictive validity of these models in operational ranges gives no indication of the model's structural validity and very little indication of the predictive validity of the parameter estimates outside operational ranges.

In conclusion, behavioral evidence leads us to doubt the decision calculus or the Gensch-Welam [7] assumptions that credit managers with exceptional faculties or heuristics for judgment and estimation. Such assumptions, to the best of our knowledge, are speculative and lack evidence of generalizability. Since the proposed utility of these models is founded on such assumptions, we undertake to investigate the extent to which these assumptions hold and in the process gain some insights as to how model-building may be improved.

## RESEARCH OBJECTIVES

The preceding discussion has raised the issues that we propose to examine. We address ourselves explicitly to the following four questions:

1. Does accumulation of experience enable managers to judgmentally estimate decision outcomes with accuracy? This question is addressed in two parts:
   a) Are managers intrinsically good judgmental estimators?
   b) Do they learn with time and are their estimation errors dependent on specific circumstances and/or decision variability?
2. Can managers estimate market response over the entire possible range of values of a decision variable and does model usage significantly aid this ability, if it exists?
3. Does a model combining several managerial estimates to predict future operational performance do any better than a direct managerial 'gut-feel' estimate of the performance variable? In other words, does 'bootstrapping' work for a manager using decision calculus?
4. Apart from estimation, does a model-based framework improve the optimality of a manager's decision over what he would do independent of the model?

## EXPERIMENTAL METHODOLOGY

### Basic Philosophy

We used a market response model that for this experiment represents 'truth'. Our subjects made advertising decisions and the model was then used to generate deterministic outcome data. We were thus able to measure subjects' abilities to determine truth from the data that they saw, both with and without the aid of exposure to an explicit structural model.

The model presented to the subjects was in fact the 'true' model. By giving them this model, we circumvented the need for subjects to come up with the correct explicit model. Consequently, our experiment is concerned with the managers' estimation ability and the impact of the structural model in terms of making better decisions. In other words, we specifically address managerial ability to correctly parameterize structural truth with judgmental estimates based on data. This task is simpler than in the real world.

### Subjects

Subjects were twenty-eight senior and middle managers from a national consumer products company. Twenty-five percent of the group was in marketing operations, the remaining had varied functional backgrounds. All subjects had previous exposure to marketing concepts. The experiment was incorporated as a management game in a two-week training program for the subjects at Carnegie-Mellon University.

### The Simulation Model

The model simulating 'truth' in our experiment was an adaptation of ADBUDG [11], which featured a non-competitive S-shaped market-share response function. Competitive advertising effects were modelled through a separate industry sales response function which together with the market-share function determined a firm's sales performance. Details of the mathematical relationships are given in [4].

### Procedure

Subjects were randomly assigned to one of ten competing firms in each of three hypothetical pharmaceutical industries and told to manage marketing activities of the firm.[5] Each subject was instructed to focus exclusively on the impact of advertising on one-period sales, market-share and profits, and to de-emphasize other marketing variables.

In each industry, firms were of three size categories (two big firms; four each of medium and small firms) as measured by starting market shares (20%; 10%; and 5% respectively). Response function parameters were different across firm categories so that firms not only had different initial shares but also different S-shaped response functions and starting positions at different distances from the optimal expenditure level. The reader is referred to [4] for specific parameter values.

The actual experimentation was done in three parts. In the first part, subjects made six sequential advertising decisions. After each decision, they also submitted an estimate of expected market share associated with their decision. Subjects studied the outcome of each decision before they made the next one. After six decisions, a questionnaire was used to elicit the following nine parameter estimates:

— Long run minimum share if the firm stopped advertising altogether in future;
— Market share next period if advertising allocation was a) cut to zero, b) cut by 50%, c) cut by 15%, d) increased by 15%, e) increased by 50%, and f) increased to 'saturation' levels;
— Long run maximum share if the firm kept advertising at 'saturation' levels in the future.

In the second part of the experiment, a random subset of the subjects was exposed to the structural form of the model generating the data. The treatment consisted of: a) an adaptation of Little's ADBUDG exposition, which was discussed in detail in a 90-minute classroom session; and b) a parameterization exercise in which subjects were allowed to try a maximum of nine trial estimate sets to parameterize the model.[6] This composite treatment was given over three days.[7]

The final part of the experiment was a rerun of the first, with firms restored to initial conditions. Once again,

_____

[5] As we had only 28 subjects, one of the industries was two firms short. We used dummy competitors to fill in. The same procedure was used to handle subject attrition that occurred later.

[6] Subjects varied in utilization of parameterization opportunities, but all made at least five attempts. Inconsistencies and intransitivities were pointed out and interpretive guidance was given if requested. No other monitoring was done and subjects used the parameterization opportunity exactly as they desired.

[7] Eight subjects left the experiment due to sudden corporate committments. We completed the experiment with twenty subjects. Pre-treatment data from these subjects was not discarded but was used as control group data.

sequential advertising decisions accompanied by market-share estimates were obtained from both treatment and control subjects. The questionnaire was again used to elicit the same parameter estimates as before. Subjects then filled out task evaluations before being de-briefed.

## ANALYSIS

### Basic Validity Checks

Using managers as experimental subjects satisfied one of the basic requirements for mundane realism [3]. To check for deficiencies in experimental realism, we examined subjects' parameter estimates (which were in terms of market share) in the first and third parts of our experiment. We would expect transitive increases in estimates for advertising levels over the current level, and corresponding transitive decreases for levels below the current allocation. Only in six out of 384 estimates was such transitivity not noticed, which indicates that subjects were not engaged in thoughtless guessing during the parameter estimation phases of the experiment.

We also checked to see whether subjects showed any learning during the experiment. As reported in the results section, we found that our measure of managerial estimation accuracy improved linearly with time during our experiment. This implies that subjects did learn to estimate market share outcomes better as they repeated the task. We take this to indicate that the managers took the task seriously.

### Methodology

Analysis of covariance in a multiple regression framework was used for data analysis. Due to space limitations we will not present a detailed description of our analyses in the body of this paper, instead we will attempt to give the reader a verbal overview of the results. The interested reader is referred to [4] for a detailed description of the variables and models used in the analysis.

## RESULTS

### Learning with Time

Learning was measured in terms of an increase in accuracy of the subjects' estimates of the market share resulting from their advertising decision. In this analysis, the ratio of the absolute deviation of the subjects' predicted market share from the actual market share to the actual market share was used as the dependent variable. We hypothesized that learning would be affected additively by the number of times the subject had previously made an advertising decision (t); the extent to which he changed his advertising decision from the present level $|\overset{o}{A}|$; and the firm size (F). Time (t) and changes in advertising level $|\overset{o}{A}|$ were found to be the only statistically significant variables.

The relationship between accuracy and t implies, as mentioned earlier, that managers learned to estimate market share outcomes better as they repeated the task. Moreover, the results indicate that managers are more likely to have large forecast errors (in terms of market share) when they significantly alter their advertising budget compared to when they make smaller changes. In other words, they have difficulty predicting outcomes of decisions that are not near their current position.

### Accuracy of Parameter Estimates

The nine parameter estimates obtained after the first and third parts of the experiment were also examined for accuracy. The error measure of these estimates was defined as

the ratio of deviation from actual to actual. We postulated that this error would be influenced additively by 1) the firm size (F); 2) whether it was the first or second time a manager made a prediction (B); 3) whether or not the manager was exposed to the model (M); 4) whether or not the manager was part of the control group (G); 5) the particular parameter being estimated (V); and 6) a behavioral measure (D) which attempted to measure the cognitive difficulty of the task. (D) was determined by measuring the distance between the firm's current market share and the true value of the parameter being estimated and dividing by the latter.

Of the effects hypothesized, three were found to be statistically significant--these being firm size (F); the identity of the specific parameter being estimated (V); and the variable (D). Figure 1 displays the first two factor effects graphically. The effects of (V) and (D) must be interpreted jointly. First, the significant coefficient on (D) indicates that the greater the normalized distance between the true parameter and the manager's current position, the bigger the size of the percentage estimation error. Moreover, since the coefficient is positive, parameters greater than the current position are underestimated and those less than the current position are overestimated. In other words, the estimates tend to be closer to the current position than they should be. This is akin to the anchoring phenomenon reported by Slovic [14].

### FIGURE 1

NORMALIZED ESTIMATION ERRORS AS A FUNCTION OF PARAMETER IDENTITY (V) AND FIRM SIZE (F)

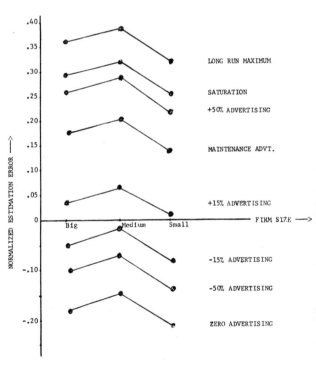

The effect of (V), (i.e., the identity of the parameter being estimated), after controlling for (D), is shown in Figure 1. The results show that managers tend to overestimate the effects of advertising increases and underestimate the effects of advertising cuts, making their best estimates of parameters close to their current position.

It should be noted that the effects of (V) and (D) act in opposite directions thus tending to cancel each other out.

However, in our experiment, this cancellation was not complete, (D)'s effects dominating in the case of parameters associated with advertising cuts, and (V)'s effects dominating for parameters associated with increases in advertising. Consequently, the aggregate effects of (V) and (D) show managers making larger errors estimating parameters away from their current position, their best estimates being when both (V) and (D) effects are small (i.e., for very small changes around their current position).

The insignificance of our before and after measure (B) and the variable associated with exposure to the model (M) suggests that managers do not seem to improve in terms of the accuracy of their parameter estimates even after exposure to the model and/or the decision experience. We believe these results have direct implications in terms of decision calculus models since it is normally assumed that managers can learn to estimate parameters better, especially as they gain exposure to the model and parameter estimation.

'Bootstrapping' with Decision Calculus

Model parameters were estimated from five of the nine[8] estimates elicited from subjects after the first and third parts of the experiment respectively. These parameters were then used to generate model-predicted market shares for the advertising decisions that subjects made in the third part of the experiment. Error measures associated with these predictions as well as the managers' 'gut-feel' estimates were computed similar to our previous accuracy measures. We then postulated an analysis of variance model where the errors were a function of 1) firm size (F), 2) exposure to the model (M), 3) group effect (G), and the estimation method used (E) (i.e., 'gut-feel' or model based).

Analysis of variance showed significant effects of all factors except the method used to generate the prediction. This reinforces the hypothesis that if model inputs are not reliable (i.e., the parameter estimates are poor), the use of the true model using these poor parameter estimates does no better than managers' gut-feel estimates in predicting future outcomes. Thus we find no evidence of 'bootstrapping' with respect to being able to predict next period's market share.

Treatment Effects on Decision Optimality

Regardless of the quality of parameter estimates or the inability of the model to improve the managers' estimation of future market share outcomes, it is still possible that model usage could improve the managers' decisions by imposing structure or by providing better understanding of the 'rules of the game'. To study such effects we defined an optimality index equal to the ratio of the profit contribution associated with each advertising decision to the corresponding optimal single-period contribution for each subject in each pre and post treatment decision. This criterion variable was modeled as an additive function of 1) firm size (F); 2) whether the decision was made before or after presentation of the model (B); 3) exposure to the model (M); 4) group effect (G); and 5) a behavioral factor which measured how far away the firm was from the optimal advertising decision before the decision was made.

---

[8] We used estimates of long-run minimum share; zero advertising share; maintenance advertising; 15% increase advertising and share for saturation advertising to generate model parameters.

[9] Our measure is in terms of single-period decision optimality. This criterion was prescribed to our subjects in the interests of simplicity, and hence our evaluation is in terms of the same criterion.

Analysis of covariance indicated three statistically significant variables, these being firm size (F); exposure to the model (M) and $|\Delta|$. Exposure to the model seemed to help managers make better decisions (as measured by the optimality index), although the estimated effect was only a 2.6% improvement. However, the most important effect was again a measure of task complexity; in this case how far the firm was from its optimal advertising level before making the decision.

CONCLUSIONS AND IMPLICATIONS

Summary of Results

While our subjects demonstrated learning effects as measured by the decrease in size of market share estimation errors over time, we also found that the more a manager varies his decision from current operational levels, the greater the forecast error he makes in predicting decision outcomes. In addition, we found extremely clear direction and magnitude biases in the errors made by managers while estimating parameters associated with decision outcomes over the entire possible range of values of a decision variable. Together, these results provide strong evidence for the hypothesis that experience in limited regions of a non-linear market-response function does not enable accurate estimation of decision outcomes in unfamiliar response regions. Specific knowledge of the structure of the response function does little to correct these biases.

We found no evidence of 'bootstrapping' in our experiment with respect to estimation of market share outcomes, showing that if the model inputs are erroneous, model usage does not generate any improvement over a manager's gut-feel estimation ability. This lends credence to the hypothesis that without valid implicit models, the explicit structure provided by decision calculus does not help the manager to any significant extent.

We noted a statistically significant effect of model usage on managerial decision-making as measured by profit optimization. However, the effect was dominated by that of the distance between the optimal advertising budget and the current budget. This result tends to confirm the notion that managers' ability to make 'optimal' decisions tends to be influenced more by the current situation than by the use of model-based procedures.

Implications for Model Builders

Our results imply that managerial judgments of parameter estimates are reliable only within limited operation ranges. Outside of these ranges the parameter estimates tend to have large error and are subject to biases. Therefore, models based on judgmental parameter estimates are probably invalid outside the operating range. We take this to imply that decision calculus models which are used to identify 'optimal' marketing strategies should be used with caution since they need to evaluate the entire feasible range of decision possibilities.

Our results also indicate that managers tend to make 'good' predictions of the outcome of decisions within the normal operating range and that the use of a model did not improve these predictions. Therefore, if models are valid only within this range there is some question as to the value of decision calculus models to a marketing manager. This conclusion is reinforced in that the group of managers using a model only made slightly better decisions than the group without the model.

Finally since in real world situations 'truth' is never known and decision calculus models tend to a) be able to reproduce past data and b) produce 'reasonable' future predictions no matter what the value of the decision variable, we believe managers may be lulled into thinking the model is providing them with the best course of action. Clearly this may not be the case.

## REFERENCES

1. Ackoff, R.I. and J.R. Emshoff. "Advertising Research at Anheuser-Busch, Inc. (1963-68)." Sloan Management Review. (Winter 1975).

2. Alpert, M. and H. Raiffa. "A Progress Report on the Training of Probability Assessors." Unpublished manuscript Harvard University, quoted by Slovic [14].

3. Aronson, Eliot and J.M. Carlsmith. "Experimentation in Social Psychology." Handbook of Social Psychology. (Vol. II. Addison-Wesley 1968).

4. Chakravarti, D., A.A. Mitchell, and R. Staelin. "The Decision Calculus Approach to Modelling Marketing Phenomena: A Quasi Experimental Investigation." Unpublished paper. Carnegie-Mellon University, (January 1977).

5. Dawes, R.M. "A Case Study of Graduate Admissions: Applications of Three Principles of Human Decision-Making." American Psychologist. (1971, 26).

6. Day, G.S., et al. "Cases in Computer and Model-Assisted Marketing." Hewlett-Packard, Inc. (Cupertino, Calif. 1973).

7. Gensch, D.H. and U. P. Welam. "An Optimum Budget Allocation Model for Dynamic Interacting Market Segments." Management Science. (October 1973).

8. Goldberg, L.R. "Man Versus Models of Man: A Rationale Plus Some Evidence for a Method of Improving on Clinical Inferences." Psychological Bulletin. (1970, Vol. 73, No. 6).

9. Huber, J. "Bootstrapping of Data and Decisions." Journal of Consumer Research, Vol. 2. (December 1975).

10. Kahneman, D. and A. Tversky. "Anchoring and Calibration in the Assessment of Uncertain Quantities." Oregon Research Institute Bulletin. (1972, Vol. 12, No. 5).

11. Little, J. D. C. "Models and Managers. The Concept of a Decision Calculus." Management Science. (April 1970).

12. Montgomery, D.B. and C.B. Weinberg. "Modelling Marketing Phenomena--A Managerial Perspective." Journal of Contemporary Business. (Autumn 1973).

13. Sawyer, J. "Measurement and Prediction, Clinical and Statistical." Psychological Bulletin. (1966, Vol. 66, No. 3).

14. Slovic, P. "From Shakespeare to Simon: Speculation and Some Evidence of Man's Ability to Process Information." Oregon Research Institute Bulletin. (Vol. 12, No. 12, April 1972).

15. Tversky, A. and D. Kahneman. "Judgements Under Uncertainty. Heuristics and Biases." Science. (September 1974, Vol. 185).

16. _____. "Intuitive Prediction." Oregon Research Institute Bulletin. (1972, Vol. 12, No. 4).

17. Urban, G.L. "An Emergent Process of Building Models for Management Decision-Makers." Working Paper 591/72 Massachusetts Institute of Technology. (March 1972).

18. Weinberg, C.B., D.B. Montgomery, and G.S. Day. "Teaching Notes for Cases in Computer and Model-Assisted Marketing." Technical Report No. 50, Graduate School of Business, Stanford University. (May 1976).

STRATEGIC MARKETING PLANNING: A COMPARISON AND CRITICAL
EXAMINATION OF TWO CONTEMPORARY APPROACHES[1]

Noel Capon, University of California at Los Angeles
Joan Robertson Spogli, University of California at Los Angeles

## ABSTRACT

This paper examines two contemporary approaches to strategic planning, that of the Profit Impact of Market Strategy
(PIMS) project and the developments of the Boston Consulting Group (BCG). The two approaches were found to exhibit
similarities but also a number of differences. Despite
some limitations, both approaches offer management guidelines for strategic level decision making, but rather than
being competitive appear to complement each other.

## INTRODUCTION

During the past few years two new approaches to strategy
formulation, the Profit Impact of Market Strategy (PIMS)
project and the developments of the Boston Consulting Group
(BCG) have had increasing impact on corporations both in
the USA and abroad. However, despite the fact that the
PIMS project has been discussed extensively in the literature [6, 10, 11] and that the BCG developments have similarly reached a wide audience,[4, 5, 8] a critical examination and comparison does not appear to have been made. [2]
One difficulty encountered by these authors in presenting
such an examination is that of availability of information,
for the complete results of the PIMS project have never
been published, nor have all the relevant developments of
BCG. Nevertheless, the purpose of this paper is to provide
a critical examination and comparison. A detailed discussion of the two approaches is not presented but rather each
is highlighted in order to provide a basis for examination.

## DESCRIPTION OF PIMS AND BCG

### PIMS

Now located at the autonomous, non-profit Strategic Planning Institute, Cambridge, Massachusetts, the PIMS project,
originally designed to obtain better measures of managerial
performance, has previously passed through introductory
stages at General Electric and the Harvard Business School.
Its one hundred and fifty, or more, participating corporations comprising consumer product manufacturers (20%),
capital equipment manufacturers (15%), new materials producers (12%), components manufacturers (24%), industrial
supplies manufacturers (10%), service industries businesses
(8%), and distribution businesses (5%), submit annual data,
securely maintained at the University of Massachusetts, on
over one thousand individual business units.

The heart of the PIMS project is the extensive data base,
and the key tool is a regression model which attempts to
determine critical variables, both those controllable by

by the firm and others within its environment, which impact Return on Investment (ROI). [3] Thus far, thirty-
seven such variables, falling into the seven major categories of Industry/Market environment, competitive position,
capital structure, production process, budget allocation,
company characteristics and change action factors have been
identified as impacting ROI.

The major findings from the PIMS Project are presented as
four main effects of variables on ROI and fifty-eight two-
way effects [13b]. [4] The four major elements are market
share, relative market share (the subject company's market
share divided by the combined share of the three largest
competitors), and relative product quality, which are
positively related to ROI and investment intensity (investment divided by value added), which is negatively related.
The two-way effects are typically presented as three by
three matrices in which the cell entry is ROI as shown
by the example in Table 1 [13b, p. 32]. The interpretation
of this example is that high R & D spending hurts profitability, especially when market share is weak.

Member companies receive reports on these general findings,
"what if" and "par"[5] reports on individual businesses and
access both to the models and the data base, subject to
security procedures.

### Table 1

#### R & D as a Percent of Sales

| | | Low 1.3% | 3.7% High | |
|---|---|---|---|---|
| Relative Market Share | Low | 17 | 12 | 4 |
| | 26% | | | |
| | 63% | 14 | 20 | 10 |
| | High | 27 | 30 | 30 |

---

[3] Latest developments of the PIMS project include the
introduction of cash flow models in addition to the major
focus on ROI.

[4] According to PIMS, the selected findings are not a
complete inventory of all significant effects, for instance
twelve main effects are claimed. However, the selected
findings are presumably the most important results.

[5] A "what if" report is a sensitivity analysis of possible specific strategic actions for a particular business,
while a "par" report rates the performance of a business
with respect to other businesses in the model that exhibit
similar characteristics.

---

[1] The authors wish to acknowledge the helpful comments
of Richard P. Rumelt, and Allan D. Shocker, Assistant
Professor and Visiting Associate Professor, Graduate School
of Management, UCLA.

[2] A brief discussion of the two approaches has been
presented by Blackwell [2] following a presentation of
each approach separately by Gale (PIMS) [10] and Cox (BCG)
[5] at this conference in 1974.

Although the Boston Consulting Group's work does contain empirical foundations, it is more conceptual than empirical in its four major dimensions. First, analysis of industry price data and subsequent individual firm cost analyses led to the concept of the experience curve [5], related to, but more encompassing than the learning curve [1]. This experience curve theory predicts that unit product costs reduce by twenty to thirty percent in constant currency units every time the total output of the product ever produced is doubled.[6] Second, the relationship of experience, and therefore costs, to market share and the treatment of market growth rate and market share as two key dimensions affecting business performance led to the development of the product portfolio concept. In this framework, products are designated either as "cash cows" (high market share/low market growth), "dogs" (low market share/low market growth), "stars" (high market share/high market growth) and "problem children" (low market share/high market growth) [7]. The prescription for the firm is to develop a product portfolio consisting of a sufficient number of "cash cows" to finance "stars" and a suitable number of high risk "problem children." "Dogs" are, in general, condemned to liquidation or sale. As the product life cycle matures and market growth slows, well managed stars and problem children ultimately become cash cows and in turn are used to finance replacement stars and problem children.

Third, this portfolio framework is employed not only as an analytic framework to examine the firm, but also to examine its competitors, so that feasible strategic actions can be assessed and plans made to respond to possible competitive threats. Finally, the relationship between financial strategy and market strategy is made explicit and the costs and benefits, respectively, of conservative and aggressive financial strategies are determined in some detail [14].

## COMPARISON OF PIMS AND BCG SIMILARITIES

### Unit of Analysis

The key similarities between PIMS and BCG relate to the unit of analysis employed and to the importance of market share as a crucial strategic variable. For both approaches, the traditional concepts of profit centers and divisions are eschewed in favor of the Strategic Business Unit. Such a unit is defined in terms of a product or product line and a well-defined customer group and set of competitors. The correct identification of these three items is critical for both approaches. For PIMS, if an incorrect diagnosis is made of the customer group and, therefore, of the market size and growth, incorrect data is entered into the data base, thus affecting the totality of the findings. Further, strategic implications for a particular product line are incorrectly diagnosed since the firm has an erroneous view of its market position. For BCG, the problem is equally critical, for the portfolio analysis rests on the twin concepts of market share and market growth rate. Incorrect diagnosis of the market leads to erroneous views of market share and market growth and, consequently, invalid strategic prescriptions.

### Market Share Findings

The second similarity relates to the major finding from both approaches, that of the critical nature of market share. While industry has, in general, perceived high market share as a desirable characteristic, both PIMS and BCG emphasize its overriding importance. For BCG market

share is inexorably linked with experience and experience linked with costs. At the mature stage of the product life cycle the firm with the highest market share has the most experience, the lowest costs and is, hence, the most profitable and, assuming no major reinvestment, is highly cash generating. Since market share is easiest to obtain when market growth is high (when competitors may be lulled by sales increases into an unintentional loss of market share), the BCG approach argues for setting market share objectives early in the product life cycle, gaining and maintaining market share through the growth phases and only in maturity sacrificing market share objectives for cash. The PIMS data also lead to high market share prescriptions on the basis of the empirical findings. The most recent data highlight the percent of businesses with pre-tax ROI greater than 25% and are indicated in Table 2 [13b, p.24]. At less than twenty-five percent market share the percent of businesses with a pre-tax ROI greater than 25% is less than thirty, but this rises sharply to sixty-four percent,[7] as market share is increased to over thirty-seven percent.

Table 2
Percent of Businesses with Pre-Tax ROI Greater Than 25%

| Market Share (%) | Percent of Businesses |
|---|---|
| 9 | 23 |
| 9-15 | 27 |
| 16-23 | 29 |
| 24-36 | 37 |
| 37 | 64 |

Read: Of those firms which have a market share of 9% or less, 23% have a pre-tax ROI greater than 25%.

Interpretation of the PIMS data does not, however, lead to the prescription of seeking high market share under all conditions. Rather, three market share strategies – building, holding and harvesting – are highlighted, each to be employed under the appropriate conditions [6]. While there is some resemblance here to the BCG conceptualization, PIMS does not tie the timing of such strategies into the product life cycle concept in the explicit manner of BCG.[8] Although the PIMS data prescribes seeking market share early in the product life cycle, its rationale is based largely on findings that, for high market share businesses, ROI is highest early in the product life cycle. BCG's rationale for high market share early in the life cycle is completely different. Indeed, they argue that to focus on high ROI early in the product life cycle will result in a damaging loss of market share. The crucial difference here is one of objectives. Following PIMS, the firm sets ROI objectives and market share is a means to reach these objectives; whereas for BCG, in the early stages of the product life cycle, market share functions as an objective in and of itself. The BCG approach of tying market share objectives explicitly to the stage of the product life cycle appears to ignore the effect of industry concentration on growth potential for the business. Thus, if in the mature stage of the product life cycle competition is relatively atomistic, growth objectives for a business (A) might be perfectly sensible even if the business has lower market share

---

[6] The costs include all costs involved in producing and distributing the product: capital, research, administrative, production and promotional, and are best viewed as a smoothed rate of cash outflow [5, p.3].

[7] Market shares of over thirty-seven percent are not, however, disaggregated and interesting findings may, therefore, be masked.

[8] None of the businesses in the main PIMS data base have been in existence less than five years, a limiting factor given an increasing tendency for product categories to reach maturity sooner. However, a subsidiary start up business project has been designed to give more explicit attention to strategy early in the product life cycle.

than its competitors (Market Shares A = 2%, B = 3%, C=4%). A strict interpretation of the BCG portfolio concept would argue for non-growth objectives since market growth rate is low and since the business is competitively weak.

## Relative Market Share

In addition to treating market share as an important concept, both approaches also employ the concept of relative market share and attest to the importance of high relative market share. However, the operationalization of this concept is different for each approach. BCG typically defines relative market share as the business unit sales divided by those of the major competitor. It functions, therefore, as a proxy for relative market power, and is closely tied to the concepts of relative experience and costs. PIMS, by contrast, is more concerned with competitive concentration and defines relative market share as the business unit sales divided by the sum of the three major competitors. The use of either method exclusively may result in the incorrect interpretation of certain situations. For instance, if in two quite different hypothetical markets the actual market shares of the four leaders were: Market 1, A=20%, B=23%, C=4%, D=3%; Market 2, A=20%, B=10%, C=10%, D=10%; PIMS relative market share index for company A would be identical, in either case (RMS=0.67). However, the BCG measure would suggest that in Market 1 Company A's position (RMS=0.87) is more tenuous than in Market 2 (RMS=2.0). The BCG measure thus appears to capture the competitive essence more clearly. However, the BCG measure is unable to distinguish between the competitive positions in markets 3 and 4 where the market shares are: Market 3, A=10%, B=10%, C=10%, D–10% and Market 4: A=10%, B=10%, C=1%, D=1%. While the competitive position of business A would appear to be different in the two markets, for BCG the relative market share of A is 1.0 in each market. By contrast the PIMS measure gives 0.33 and 0.83 respectively, and seems to better capture A's competitive positions. The argument in favor of the BCG measure is that relative cost positions with respect to individual competitors is the critical issue and whether there are one or three equi-cost competitors is irrelevant. The PIMS measure argues that having three equi-size competitors is more dangerous than having one.

Neither approach, however, explicitly considers the dangers of high market share. Their findings implicitly suggest that monopoly is the most desirable market structure for any business. Such a view is not, however, held by government and other interested parties [9] and for this reason Bloom & Kotler [3] have developed the concept of an optimal market share, somewhat less than one hundred percent, which is sufficiently high to gain the benefits forecast by PIMS and BCG, yet low enough to avoid damaging non-market activity.

## COMPARISON OF PIMS AND BCG - DIFFERENCES

### Objectives

Counterposed to the similarities between PIMS and BCG are, however, a number of major differences. First, and related to the market share findings, is the question of business unit objectives. For PIMS a principal objective of ROI is set equal to net pre-tax income (after deduction of corporate expenses but prior to interest charges), divided by investment (working capital plus book value of fixed capital). Variables are examined primarily for the effect that they have on ROI. BCG, by contrast, has no place for ROI in its schema. Product lines are managed for one of two objectives, growth (market share) in the early stages of the product life cycle and cash in the later stages. The firm is viewed as an entity which consumes cash to grow and grows to produce cash [14]. At the appropriate stage in its life cycle a product's market share is viewed as an end in itself rather than as a means to reach an end, that of ROI, as in the PIMS framework.

Not only has BCG moved away from traditional measurement criteria for product lines, it has avoided the problem of perturbations caused by accounting conventions. Not so PIMS, whose choice of ROI as a measuring device is predicated on its widespread employment and whose use gives rise to a number of accounting problems. Thus, in the numerator, income is affected by corporate conventions on allocation of corporate overhead while the denominator is highly dependent on depreciation schedules employed. Further, ROI results are affected by patents, trade secrets and other proprietary elements. Although PIMS researchers recognize many of these problems [6], nevertheless, in using data from many different companies the ROI figures are derived on many different bases, with attendant problems in analysis and interpretation.

### Data

In addition to the market data problems mentioned earlier, PIMS has a variety of other related data problems, while BCG suffers from a data problem of a different nature. For its empirical base, PIMS requires annual data on about one hundred variables from over one thousand businesses. In general, these data are prepared by line management working off data sheets and definitions provided by PIMS. Despite both considerable effort by PIMS to train and work with managers and the advantages to management of inputting good data, line management may be neither sufficiently sophisticated nor have sufficient time to ensure that accurate data is delivered to the project. Further, a number of data inputs such as relative product quality are extremely subjective. Thus, despite training and consistency checks, to the extent that poor data is entered into the system, poor results will be obtained.[9] The data problem for BCG is of a somewhat different nature. Their conceptual framework is heavily dependent on the experience curve phenomenon. While the existence of downward-sloping price experience curves is well documented [5], since individual firm cost data are less available, there is little published data to support a generalized, across-firm cost experience curve. BCG is forced to rely on proprietary cost data from their own client companies and the existence of downward-sloping price curves to argue for such a generalized cost experience curve. However, obtaining suitable data for construction of an experience curve can be very difficult, since it may be unavailable in the form required, having been gathered on a time or departmental basis, rather than on a units of production basis, and may be subject to arbitrary allocations for joint costs and overhead. They do, however, present underlying reasons to expect the presence of cost experience curves. In particular, the factors of economies of scale in R&D, purchasing, production, promotion, and distribution, the learning curve, product standardization, product redesign to meet better identified performance criteria, the substitution of lower cost components, and the introduction of new production technology, all argue for finding the cost experience curve and indicate that the data problems for BCG may be less acute than for PIMS.

### Methodology

Methodologically there are critical differences between the BCG approach and that of PIMS. Although starting from observed phenomena, that is, the relationship between price and competitive behavior in the electronics and chemicals industries, the major thrust of the BCG work has been to develop a conceptual framework of behavior.

---

[9] Since PIMS seeks robust general patterns, data outliers are eliminated from the analysis [12]; however, this procedure may result in the loss of interesting insights.

This framework, though containing few constructs, affords powerful insight to the manager in suggesting strategic courses of action. However, no statistical tests appear to have been performed by BCG on the price/cost and cumulative volume relationships, nor have any data been presented on the explanatory power of market share and market growth rates in determining business performance.

By contrast to the conceptual thrust of the BCG work, the developments of PIMS may be viewed as at a more elemental stage of theory development. There appears to have been relatively little systematic development of constructs and their interrelationships; rather an extensive number of variables have been constructed and probed for their correspondence with the dependent variable, ROI. Such a procedure leaves open major questions with respect to the validity of the many relationships presented. Thus, in the selected PIMS findings, four main variable effects and fifty-eight two-way effects are highlighted.[10] However, in the absence of information on how many variables were searched to obtain these relationships, or the extent to which cross validation studies were carried out, it is impossible to say whether or not these are real relationships or whether a large number of them are due to chance. Such reasons could account for non-intuitive and seemingly contradictory results. For instance, the PIMS data suggests that if, on the one hand, market position is weak, R & D and marketing efforts should be avoided but, on the other hand, states that new products are helpful,[11] a seeming contradiction, since a "follower" strategy is likely to require significant marketing expenditures.

A further problem with the methodology is possible multicollinearity of the large number of predictor variables involved. This multicollinearity can effect the estimates of the regression coefficient.[12] Finally, cross sectional analysis does not appear appropriate for all the relationships presented, for instance the effect of R & D expenditures on ROI and a time series anaylsis may be more meaningful.

Despite these problems, the relationships which have been found can be used to develop better theory and hypotheses, which can be tested subsequently on new data from the data base, leading to greater understanding of business phenomena.

Competition

A further difference between PIMS and BCG is the manner in which they treat competition. Thus, the BCG approach leads to use of the portfolio framework to assess the capabilities and likely objectives to be set by individual competitors, but does not deal in detail with the elements of their strategy. The basic PIMS model does not deal with competitors at all at the individual level, but they have developed a limited information model (LIM) which can be employed to gain insights on individual competitors. Both approaches rely on indices of relative market share but, as mentioned earlier, the two approaches give a somewhat different competitive insight from the differing definitions of relative market share that are employed.

Level of analysis

A final difference between the approaches is the level of analysis employed and the corresponding amount of detail involved. In the PIMS project the level of analysis is identical to the unit of analysis, that of the strategic business unit. The major focus is on the identification of variables which are related to ROI and as a consequence the analysis is highly detailed with many variables being examined. Very specific recommendations regarding such decisions as the degree of product quality, the level of R & D spending, and the volume of marketing effort are presented. Further, strategic business units within a company are essentially treated as independent entities, each striving to maximize ROI. By contrast, the level of analysis for BCG is that of the firm. Strategic Business Units are seen as elements in an interacting product portfolio.[13] Market share and cash generation objectives are only set in regard to all items in the portfolio. It makes no sense to pursue market share objectives for some items in the portfolio unless other items can perform the cash generation function. Further, financial policy is closely tied to the two operating objectives to provide an integrated financial and operational conceptual framework. However, the framework does not always function as it should. Thus, when a specific company is analyzed, low share, low growth businesses might be relatively highly cash generating (golden dogs) while high share, low growth businesses might throw off relatively little cash (sick cows).[14] The framework offers little suggestion on what action to take in such cases. In any event, working at a higher level of analysis, the BCG approach offers much less in the way of direction to guide the manipulation of specific variables in order to obtain the required objectives.

In a sense, then, rather than being contradictory, the approaches are complementary. Working at the level of the firm, the major impact of BCG is to develop strategic objectives for the Strategic Business Unit. PIMS, on the other hand, is far more concerned with isolating the specific variables which can lead to achievement of objective for the Business Units, albeit with no clear correspondenc between objectives for different business units.

CONCLUSION

While the PIMS and BCG approaches to strategy have some similarities, there appear to be more differences. The PIMS approach focuses on identification of profit determinants of the individual business unit by searching for stable relationships in a large data base. While a variet of interesting findings have been presented, their interpretation is difficult because of the lack of a conceptual development to guide the testing of relationships. Thus, from the academic's viewpoint, the results are perhaps best viewed as theory generating, to be tested later on new data sets. In any event, contributing companies appear to value participation in the project, if for no other reason than as a useful educational device to alert line management to possible critical variables and likely interrelationships.[15] By contrast, the work of BCG is focused primarily at the level of the total enterprise. The firm is viewed as a total cash system and individual

---

[10]Data has not been presented on the total number of significant effects isolated.

[11]See [13a], Exhibits 30, 32 and 41 respectively.

[12]PIMS claim to have solved this problem by the development of "multicollinear clusters" of variables, but in the absence of published details of the methodology little comment can be made.

---

[13] While companies belonging to PIMS can enter many businesses into the system and thus examine the firm from the perspective of a business portfolio, this has not, hitherto, been a major focus of the project.

[14]Personal communication from Richard P. Rumelt.

[15]Personal communication from Roger Cope, Vice President of Corporate Planning, Dart Industries, Inc., Los Angeles.

businesses are examined for their potential to provide either cash today, or growth today and cash tomorrow. Further, the impact of financial policy on operations is considered crucial. In contrast to the empirical focus of PIMS, the BCG approach is largely conceptual. BCG offers little in the way of insight into the variables which determine performance but rather focuses more on the objectives of businesses than on their strategy. To this extent, then, the approaches may be seen as complementary rather than competitive.

From the perspective of the academic it is unfortunate that both of these developments include proprietary material, for complete understanding of both BCG and PIMS is obscured and critical comparison can only be partially complete.

## REFERENCES

1. Abernathy, William J. and Kenneth Wayne. "Limits of the Learning Curve", Harvard Business Review,52 (September-October, 1974), 109-119.

2. Blackwell, Roger D., "Strategic Planning in Marketing: Discussion", in Ronald C. Curhan, ed., Combined Proceedings, Chicago: American Marketing Association (1974), 476-477.

3. Bloom, Paul N. and Philip Kotler, "Strategies for High Market-Share Companies", Harvard Business Review, 53 (November-December, 1975), 63-72.

4. Perspectives, Boston: Boston Consulting Group, Inc., A Pamphlet Series, 1968-1977.

5. Perspectives on Experience, Boston: Boston Consulting Group, Inc., 1972.

6. Buzzell, Robert D., Bradley T. Gale and Ralph G. M. Sultan, "Market Share A Key to Profitability", Harvard Business Review, 53 (January-February, 1975), 97-106.

7. Conley, Patrick, "Experience Curves as a Planning Tool: A Special Commentary", Boston: Boston Consulting Group, Inc., 1970.

8. Cox, William E., "Product Portfolio Strategy: A Review of the Boston Consulting Group Approach to Marketing Strategy" in Ronald C. Curhan, ed., Combined Proceedings. Chicago: American Marketing Association (1974), 471-475.

9. Dholakia, Ruby Roy and Louis W. Stern, "Market Power and the PIMS Data", in Kenneth L. Bernhardt, ed., Combined Proceedings. American Marketing Association (1976), 451-455.

10. Gale, Bradley, T., "Selected Findings from the PIMS Project: Market Strategy Impacts on Profitability", in Ronald C. Curhan, ed., Combined Proceedings, Chicago: American Marketing Association (1974), 471-475.

11. Schoeffler, Sidney, Robert Buzzell, and Donald Heany, "Impact of Strategic Planning on Profit Performance", Harvard Business Review, 52 (March-April, 1974), 137-145.

12. Schoeffler, Sidney, "Cross Sectional Study of Strategy Structure and Performance: Aspects of the PIMS Program," SSP Conference, Indiana University, November 1975.

13. The PIMS Program, Selected Findings, Cambridge, Mass.: The Strategic Planning Institute, 1976(a), 1977(b).

14. Zakon, Alan J., "Strategy and the Growth Business", Boston: Boston Consulting Group.

# TEST MARKETING AND COMPETITIVE REACTION: WHEN DOES IT MATTER?

Johny K. Johansson, University of Washington
John J. Wheatley, University of Washington

## ABSTRACT

The value of test marketing information is evaluated in light of the possibility of competitive reaction. A previously published model is used as a vehicle to demonstrate the sensitivity of test market information to different dimensions of potential competitive reaction. In general, the sensitivity tends to be relatively high, making test marketing of dubious value in strongly competitive markets.

## INTRODUCTION

The usefulness of Bayesian statistics in dealing with the question of whether or not to conduct a test marketing effort has been demonstrated by Bass [1]. This work was recently extended by Johansson et al. to take into account the impact of competitive reaction to the test marketing programs of firms initiating such activities [4]. The present paper explains in managerial terms the mechanics of the model and explores the sensitivity of the model to changes in certain key competitive parameters. It discusses the significance of the results obtained and suggests some future research opportunities in this area that should prove to be of value to those marketing managers who must make test marketing decisions.

## MODEL OVERVIEW: A MANAGERIAL ILLUSTRATION

### Uncertainty of Future Sales

Since the underlying rationale for test marketing lies in the uncertainty a new product faces in the market, the decision maker's first task is the assessment of how uncertain future sales really are. In the present case, this assessment of possible future sales levels is conceptualized as "prior" probabilities denoting the chance, subjectively assessed where no objective information is available, for each of the alternative sales outcomes. Although in principle an infinite number of sales levels are possible, the decision maker can and need usually specify only a limited number of them.

Suppose there is an option to test market a new product for two periods and that the decision maker considers 3 possible sales levels in the national market. Sales could be about \$3,000,000 with probability .2, \$5,000,000 with probability .3, and \$7,000,000 with probability .5. Without testing, this would generate an expected sales level of (\$3,000,000 · .2 + \$5,000,000 · .3 + \$7,000,000 · .5) = \$5,600,000. Let the payoff to dropping the product equal a payoff of \$3,500,000. Thus, if there were no test option, to maximize expected revenue, a "Go" decision would be indicated.

### Precision of Test Market Information

Given an assessment of the chances for various sales levels, the benefit from test marketing comes largely from improved knowledge about future sales provided by the test results. The degree to which test marketing is useful, then, depends upon two factors: (1) Exactly how uncertain is the decision maker about future sales? and (2) How precise is the test market information? The answer to (1) is given directly by the assessment of the prior; and to (2) by the assessment of the precision of the test marketing results.

The degree to which the test will correctly "mirror" the state of the national market is evaluated in the "likelihood function" or simply the "likelihoods." To assess the likelihoods several approaches have been proposed in the literature [7, pp. 14-21; 8, Ch. 8; 9]. Basically, the decision maker will have to answer the following "hypothetical" question: If the sales are really above average, what are the chances that the test will indicate this? And what are the chances that the test will indicate "below average"? This procedure will then have to be followed for all possible sales levels, considering each possible test outcome--a computationally tedious task. The basic idea to keep in mind when doing the assessment is that one is really appraising the reliability of the new information, and one can therefore rely on past records to guide such judgments.

The likelihoods are thus assessed as probabilities for various test outcomes, conditional upon some given "true" state of the world, and iterated for all possible "true" states. Suppose the following likelihoods are specified by our decision maker on the basis of previous experience (assume there are only two possible test outcomes):

Sales = \$3,000,000

Probability of test "high" = .3
Probability of test "low" = .7

Sales = \$5,000,000

Probability of test "high" = .5
Probability of test "low" = .5

Sales = \$7,000,000

Probability of test "high" = .8
Probability of test "low" = .2

Using the well known relationship between a marginal and joint probability distribution (see, for example, [3]) we can derive the unconditional distribution of test results in the following manner:

Probability of test "high" = .3·.2 + .5·.3 + .8·.5 = .61
Probability of test "low" = .7·.2 + .5·.3 + .2·.5 = .39.

### Probability of Competitive Entry

Now assume that our decision maker faces one strong competitor who would be able to enter the market with a product of his own on short notice. If the chances are very small that he will do so before we begin our test program, the probability of competitive entry can be set equal to, say, .05 in the first period. The question arises, what will this probability be after our test market results indicate a "high" sales potential or conversely, a "low" sales potential? To answer this directly will sometimes be possible and if the decision maker feels comfortable doing so, such a new value can be directly introduced into the model. Alternatively, the model provides the option of calculating a reasonable estimate of what the market promises to the competitor using the following approach.

Suppose the test shows a "high" sales potential. What then should the decision maker take as his new or "posterior" distribution of sales? Using Bayes' formula [7, p. 18] we can compute the new figures:

FIGURE 1

DECISION TREE FOR THE NUMERICAL EXAMPLE (Sales in $000)

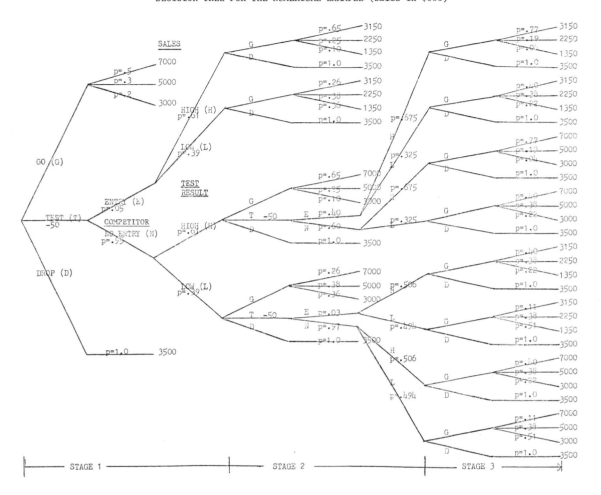

is possible to use the model to identify the competitive characteristics which do make a difference and those aspects of competitive actions which seem of less importance. This can be done by first solving the model for a set of reasonably normal parameter values, and then conducting a sensitivity analysis of the competitive factor of interest. The effect of varying the probability of at least one competitor entering, the cost of testing, the effect of varying the number of potential entrants, the timing of their possible entry, the size of the challengers, the portion of the market staying loyal to the first entrant and the dependence of the solution on the difficult-to-assess likelihoods are all significant issues. A few of these results are presented below in so-called "crossover" graphs commonly employed in this type of research [6]. The name derives from the fact that most of the effects of interest here are unidirectional—if, for example, the originally optimal decision is to "Test," a gradual increase in the test costs will sooner or later change the optimum solution to a "Go" or "Drop" decision. Where this happens constitutes the "crossover" point.

Parameter Settings

The "standard" parameter settings for the sensitivity analyses were selected on the basis of empirical assessments and experience [2, 6]. Since all possible decisions are treated directly in the model—"Go," "Test," and "Drop"

basically exhaust the options available. What matters are relative, not absolute, parameter levels. Even so, the parameter settings chosen here are based upon realistic magnitudes.

The first parameter setting involves the sales levels and their priors, and the "Drop" payoff. These figures will decide whether the "Test" option will have to compete with a "Go" or "Drop" decision. In the present model sales were approximated by 10 discrete equally likely levels as suggested by Schlaifer [8, p. 510].

The "Drop" payoff, which occurs with probability 1.0, was set at a level just below the expected payoff from a "Go" decision. Thus, the "Test" option is compared directly only to "Go" since "Drop" is a dominated choice. The expected net sales based on the prior distribution was set at $617,790 with a high sales level of $2,750,000 and a low sales level of $1,800,000.

The Test outcomes were set at three levels ("high," "medium," "low"). Although test market results tend to be more exact than this, the pooling of several markets and the adjustment for specific situational characteristics usually leads to rather crude overall assessments, often given as intervals rather than point estimates. With ten sales levels and three test outcomes, there are 30 values necessary to specify the likelihoods. In the

Probability of sales $7,000,000 = (.5·.8)/.61 = .65
Probability of sales $5,000,000 = (.3·.5)/.61 = .25
Probability of sales $3,000,000 = (.2·.3)/.61 = .10.

Similarly, if the test shows "low" sales potential the posterior distribution becomes:

Probability of sales $7,000,000 = (.5·.2)/.39 = .26
Probability of sales $5,000,000 = (.3·.5)/.39 = .38
Probability of sales $3,000,000 = (.2·.7)/.39 = .36.

As one would expect a "high" test raises the probability of large sales, whereas a "low" test increases the chances of a small total market.

We can now use these posterior probabilities and compute the expected sales, conditional upon the test outcomes. If the test shows "high," the expected sales are (.65·$7,000,000 + .25·$5,000,000 + .10·$3,000,000) = $6,100,000. If the test result is "low," the expected sales are (.26·$7,000,000 + .38·$5,000,000 + .36·$3,000,000) = $4,800,000. If no competitor has entered we can treat these figures as our new payoff.

One can often reasonably assume that the competitor's estimate of the market will be similar to ours after observing the test results. If so, our decision maker can assign the required subjective probabilities for the competitor's entry given the posterior distributions. The proper question to ask is: "Given that our test indicates "high" sales potential in the first period, leading to expected national sales of $6,100,000, what is the chance that the competitor will challenge us by an introduction of his own product?" (and similarly for "low" test results).

If the probability of competitive entry is still too difficult to assess, there is need for further analysis. The impact of an early competitive entry can often be conceptualized as arising from two related sources. One is that the first entrant in many markets will enjoy and hold a captive (loyal) portion of the market in subsequent periods. Another is the "harvesting" of the pioneer buyers for a new product, some of whom switch to another brand when competitive brands become available but who, in the meantime, buy our brand. The size of these two market portions will have to be assessed by our decision maker before testing begins. Neither of these figures are easy to come by since existing market knowledge for the new product is limited a fortiori. On the other hand, the decision maker can usually draw upon his knowledge and experience from existing, related markets to identify reasonable "guesstimates".

Suppose the portion of the market that stays with the first entrant is set at 10%. Furthermore, there is a portion of the market, say 50% which will accept the early brand(s) but which will switch to new brands as they enter. The rest of the market will be distributed in a stable manner among all introduced brands. Thus, if a competitor enters before us, we will lose 10% of the projected sales of our brand. Furthermore, switchers, who constitute 50% of the market, will not be limited to our brand but may purchase a competitor's brand. Now this market segment (and the remaining 40%) will divide themselves between us and our competitor depending upon our relative differential advantage. Suppose, however, that our product offering is about on a par with that of our competitor. It then becomes reasonable to assume that we will divide both of the segments equally between us. Our total sales become:

Sales after entry = Sales without entry - 10% of Sales
                    - .5·90% of Sales.

This is the estimate of payoffs after a competitive entry.[1]

It is possible to treat the competitor's decision situation in an analogous manner, and attempt to "second-guess" his sales and profit picture. On the basis of these figures one should be able to derive a quite reasonable assessment of his entry probability. This analysis provides the third level at which the probability of competitive entry after the first test period can be assessed. If the decision maker even at this level of detailed analysis feels uncomfortable with his probability assignment, the solution lies in a sensitivity analysis of the entry probability.

Let the entry probabilities after the first period test results are known be as follows:

| Test "high" | Test "low" |
|---|---|
| Probability of entry = .40 | Probability of entry = .03 |

The sales figures in the second period after competitive entry can be computed now. They are as follows:

Sales with entry = $7,000,000 - .1·$7,000,000
                   - .5·.9·$7,000,000
                 = $3,150,000 for the $7,000,000 level

Sales with entry = $5,000,000 = .1·$3,000,000
                   - .5·.9·$5,000,000
                 = $2,250,000 for the $5,000,000 level

Sales with entry = $3,000,000 = .1·$3,000,000
                   - .5·.9·$3,000,000
                 = $1,350,000 for the $3,000,000 level.

The probability of occurrence of these various sales levels stays the same as for the no-competitive-entry case discussed above.

Incorporating a test cost of, say, $50,000 per period, we have all the assessments necessary to solve the model. The complete decision tree is laid out in Figure 1. As can be seen there, the two test periods give rise to a three stage tree, where the third stage decision options are "Go" or "Drop" only. In the tree the "Test" option is also eliminated for the branches after a competitor has entered since in most cases the value of a test market would be considerably diminished (future sales might be assessed fairly accurately from sales of the competitive product, for example).

In the tree the probabilities and payoffs corresponding to the third stage are also displayed. The computations needed to arrive at these values are equivalent to the ones already displayed for the second stage and there is no need to go through them here. For the tree in Figure 1 the standard "backward induction" approach [7, pp. 21-26] can be used to arrive at an expected value for the "Test" option in the first period. The answer is $5,438,000. Since the first-stage payoff to "Go" is $5,600,000 the payoff to "Drop" is only $3,500,000 the optimal first-period decision is to "Go."

### SELECTED SENSITIVITY ANALYSES

The primary use of the model presented here is test marketing situations where competitive reactions are likely. It

---

[1]With more than one potential competitor entering the market, the "switcher" segment cannot be treated as the stable segment—the model accounts for the timing of entry by additional competitors to further reduce the "switcher" segment sales.

present context we simply assigned a reasonably strong
chance of a low market being uncovered if that was the
true state of the world. The probability of the test
"low" given that the true market was at -$1,800,000 was
set at 80% and similarly for the upper end of the scale
the chance a "high" test would occur when the market was
at $2,750,000 was set at 85%. Then the likelihoods were
basically gradated in equal steps between these two
extremes--the full set are shown in the Appendix.

The utility function employed was linear throughout. A
quadratic function or a logarithmic function can also be
incorporated into the model, but was not tested here. Similarly, a discount rate of 4% per period (about 16% per year)
was used throughout the simulation runs presented here.

## Probability of One Competitive Entrant

To introduce the basic mode of analysis, the sensitivity
of the solution to variations in the probability that at
least one competitor will enter in the first period is
displayed in Figure 2. The probability of competitive

FIGURE 2

CROSSOVER GRAPH FOR PROBABILITY OF AT LEAST
ONE ENTRANT IN PERIOD ONE

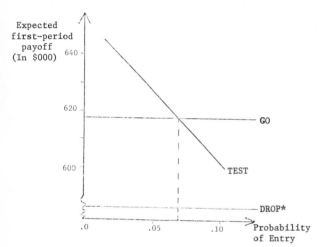

*The payoff to DROP was set at a constant "scrap" value of
$10,000. Since the crossover points of interest occur
between GO and TEST, the constant DROP payoff is not
graphed in the succeeding figures.

entry affects the optimal decision very dramatically. The
important thing to note is that the "Test" option very
quickly turns into a "Go" decision when competitive entry
chances go up, with a crossover point at about 7%. The
relationship in linear. The linearity exists despite the
multiple effects of competitive entry which threaten the
"captive" first-entrant portion of the market, forces a
sharing of the switchers, and does not allow "our" brand
to take its customers initially.

## Timing of Competitive Entry

In Figure 3 the sensitivity of the model is analyzed with
respect to the timing of entry--can competitor(s) enter
right away, or are there delays in their coming into the
market? The crossover graph reveals testing is a viable
option unless competition is capable of immediate entry.
The non-linearity shows, however, that the value of testing
does not increase much if competitor(s) are unable to enter
the market until the second or third period.

FIGURE 3

CROSSOVER GRAPH FOR TIMING OF
POSSIBLE COMPETITIVE ENTRY

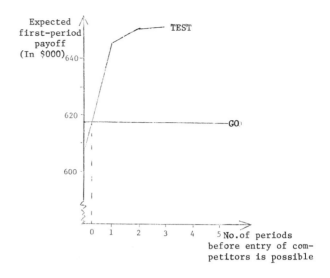

### Likelihoods

The likelihoods also need to be analyzed to identify the
sensitivity of the indicated decision to competitive interference. Although a simple crossover chart is not really
sufficient to display the many possible variations in the
assessed likelihoods, we have carried out two simple
analyses. One consisted of changing the precision of the
indication of extremely low net sales (-$1,800,000) and
the other the precision of extremely high sales
($2,750,000). The manipulation consisted of decreasing
both from a probability of .8 for a correct indication
down to .7, .6, and .5. The two incorrect indications
were allotted equal probabilities to make the sum equal
to 1.0. The results are shown in Figure 4.

The slope of the line representing changes in the lower end
of the likelihoods is steeper, indicating that the sensitivity of the optimal choice is higher for impreciseness
in the indication of losses. This happens even though the
objective function is linear, and would presumably be even
more accentuated for a risk-averse decision maker. The
result points out that if there is a possibility of great
losses, test precision becomes especially critical in
assessing the true state of the market. In other words,
it seems particularly desirable to evaluate the precision
of the test procedure when it comes to the discovery of a
low-selling product.

### Test Costs, Number and Size of Potential
Competitors, Captive Market Share[2]

An increase in test costs affects the expected "Test" payoff in a negative manner. The relationship is linear since
the increased costs will have to be paid with a constant
probability of 1.0. If the test cost is greater than
$95,000 per period, the optimal first period decision
changes from "Test" to "Go."

---

[2]Space limitations prevent the inclusion of the crossover graphs of these simulations. Copies of them may be
obtained however by writing to either of the authors.

## FIGURE 4

### CROSSOVER GRAPH FOR CHANGES IN LIKELIHOODS*

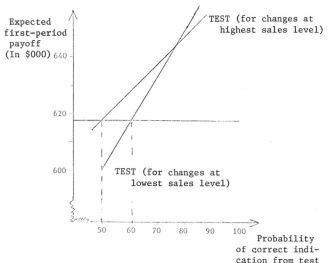

One conclusion from the preceding sensitivity analyses is that in general competitive reactions can have a strongly negative effect upon the value of test marketing. At the same time there are some factors whose impact is lower than one would generally have expected. Also, it should be pointed out that the analysis has been concerned throughout with the case where it is reasonable to assume that competitors do monitor the test markets. If, for some reason, this assumption is invalidated even large and capable competitors might be disregarded. In most cases such an approach would seem far from realistic, however.

The sensitivity analyses presented only represent a partial picture of the possible effects from competitive reactions. Not only are some competitive dimensions omitted--the most important one might well be a more complete treatment of various promotional "interference" strategies--but no interactions between the various dimensions are explicitly accounted for. These additional complications will have to be dealt with in a paper less restricted in scope than the present one. The results presented here serve to underline the need and feasibility of such a larger scale effort.

### APPENDIX

#### BASIC PARAMETER SETTINGS FOR THE SENSITIVITY ANALYSES

| | |
|---|---|
| Number of Decision Options: | 3 (GO, TEST, DROP) |
| Number of Sales Outcomes: | 10 (Equally likely) |
| Number of Test Outcomes: | 3 ("High," (Medium," "Low") |
| Number of Competitive Actions: | 2 ("Entry," "No entry") |

Values of Payoffs (in $000):

| Net Sales | Scrap Value |
|---|---|
| -1800 | 10 |
| - 700 | |
| - 200 | |
| 325 | |
| 500 | |
| 750 | |
| 1100 | |
| 1550 | |
| 2150 | |
| 2750 | |

Likelihoods: The probability of the test outcome given the actual sales level

| | | Test Outcome | | |
|---|---|---|---|---|
| | | High | Medium | Low |
| | -1800 | .10 | .10 | .80 |
| | - 700 | .20 | .20 | .60 |
| | - 200 | .30 | .40 | .30 |
| Net Sales | 325 | .50 | .30 | .20 |
| Level | 500 | .50 | .40 | .10 |
| | 750 | .60 | .35 | .05 |
| | 1100 | .70 | .25 | .05 |
| | 1550 | .80 | .17 | .03 |
| | 2150 | .82 | .15 | .03 |
| | 2750 | .85 | .10 | .05 |

Test cost per period (in $000): 40
Discount rate: 4% per period

---

*A value of 80%, for example, indicates a .8 probability that the test shows "low" sales when actual sales are net -1800. The probabilities for an incorrect indication are spread equally between a "medium" test indication (with probability of .1) and a "high" test indication (with probability of .1). The same formula was applied to the other levels shown in the graph, and also to the sensitivity testing for the highest sales (at 2750) shown above.

Although the "Test" option is still viable with one potential entrant, the possibility that two or more competitors are capable of entering indicates the avoidance of a test.

If the first entrant can be expected to capture no more than about 10% of the market, testing is still a viable option. If the potential entrant provides more of a threat than that, testing should be foregone in favor of a "Go" decision. (It should be pointed out here that "our" firms competitiveness matters. Its likely market share in the mature market was set at 25% for these runs.[3]

Increasing captive market share levels from 0% to 30% shifts expected payoffs only about $25,000 with a crossover point at 27%. The relative insensitivity of the model to such a wide range of values for this variable is comforting, since the assessment of the level of the captive market share will generally be difficult. It should be emphasized however, that where the expected payoffs between the "Test" and "Go" options are close, the captive portion might still provide the decisive influence.

---

[3] The non-linearity here is an example of a result which is not immediately obvious. The explanation for the decreasing slope of the function at either end is the self-limiting nature of the payoffs: At some expected market shares one option (TEST or GO depending on what part of the function is analyzed) will be completely dominated by the other so that further variations in the size of a competitor make very little difference.

REFERENCES

1. Bass, F. M., "Marketing Research Expenditures: A Decision Model," The Journal of Business, January, 1963.

2. Davis, L., "Market Forecasting Ultimately May Obviate All Test Marketing," Marketing News, November 19, 1976, X, No. 10.

3. Hirshlaifer, J., "The Bayesian Approach to Statistical Decision: An Exposition," The Journal of Business, October, 1961.

4. Johansson, J. K., D. M. Roberts, & J. J. Wheatley, "Competitive Reaction in Test Marketing: A Bayesian Solution," Proceedings, K. L. Bernhardt, ed., American Marketing Association, Chicago, 1976.

5. Moskowitz, H. & W. L. Berry, "A Bayesian Algorithm for Determining Optimal Single Sample Acceptance Plans for Product Attributes," Management Science, July, 1976.

6. Newman, J. W., Management Applications of Decision Theory, New York, Harper & Row, 1971.

7. Raiffa, H., Decision Analysis: Introductory Lectures on Choices Under Uncertainty, Reading, Mass.: Addison-Wesley, 1968.

8. Schlaifer, R., Analysis of Decisions Under Uncertainty, New York: McGraw Hill, 1969.

9. Spetzler, C. S. & C. A. S. Stael von Holstein, "Probability Encoding in Decision Analysis," Management Science, November, 1975.

# A STRATEGIC APPROACH TO INTERNATIONAL MARKET SELECTION

Peter Doyle, Bradford University, U.K.
Zeki B. Gidengil, Concordia University

## ABSTRACT

This paper introduces the notion of a portfolio approach to international market planning and suggests the number and type of markets chosen should be related to overall portfolio balance and performance. A technique for operationalizing this approach is outlined.

## INTRODUCTION

Most companies have moved into exporting and international marketing over the years in a piecemeal and unplanned manner. Consequently, many now find they do business in a large number of ill-considered markets many of which provide little or no contribution to the company's overall performance. This paper suggests management should adopt a portfolio approach to international marketing and select opportunities only when they contribute to the aggregate performance or balance of this portfolio. The first section describes the principles which apply in such strategy formulation. In the following section the means of operationalizing it are illustrated.

## INTERNATIONAL MARKETING STRATEGY

In international marketing the firm faces a sequence of decisions (Figure 1). Logically international planning does not begin with the selection of international markets but with the dimensionalizing of the market portfolio - determining the number of markets in which to operate and the desired characteristics of these markets. Individual markets are then chosen which are consistent with the market portfolio strategy of the company. The alternative strategies can be distinguished along two dimensions: the number and type of markets.

### Number of markets: concentration vs. multiplication

One of the most common phenomena in business is the "80:20 rule" - 80 per cent of the results are generated by 20 per cent of the activities [1]. Nowhere is this more apparent than in exporting. One British study found two-thirds of exporters selling to over 30 countries, with a third selling to between 60 and 180 countries.[8]. Yet this and other studies found that almost all firms had four or five key markets and usually their best ten markets accounted for almost 90 per cent of exports. Clearly there is rarely justification for establishing an export organization to deal with 100 or more countries when 90 of them make an insignificant contribution. For most companies, concentration on a limited number of key markets increases profits. Such companies can invest adequate resources in markets offering the greatest expected returns, they can establish an effective market presence and level of customer service, and they can develop the detailed knowledge of markets and competition necessary to retain a long-term differential advantage. In general, the smaller the firm, the more restricted its export experience and the more diverse and complex its products the greater are the gains from market concentration.

A company can calculate its degree of export concentration and compare it over time or with other firms using the Herfindahl index [12], defined as the sum of the squares of the percentage of sales in each foreign country,

$$C = \Sigma s_i^2 \tag{1}$$

Where
$C$ = the export concentration index for the firm
$s_i$ = exports to country i as a percentage of the firm's total exports ($\Sigma s_i = 1$)

Thus maximum concentration $C = 1$ occurs when all the exports of the firm are made to one country only; minimum concentration $C = 1/n$ exists when exports are equally distributed over a large number of countries.

FIGURE 1

INTERNATIONAL MARKETING DECISIONS

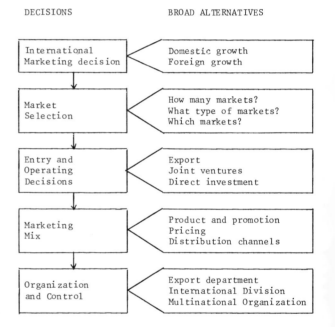

| DECISIONS | BROAD ALTERNATIVES |
|---|---|
| International Marketing decision | Domestic growth / Foreign growth |
| Market Selection | How many markets? / What type of markets? / Which markets? |
| Entry and Operating Decisions | Export / Joint ventures / Direct investment |
| Marketing Mix | Product and promotion / Pricing / Distribution channels |
| Organization and Control | Export department / International Division / Multinational Organization |

### Market Characteristics: Similarity vs. Diversity

The second dimension of the market portfolio is market type. Should the firm seek to add markets which are similar to one another and to the home market, or should it seek markets which are diverse or complementary? Most companies do not have a strategy and their markets are based upon chance orders or uncoordinated ventures 10 . This is unfortunate because different portfolio strategies produce different results.

The arguments for selecting new overseas markets which are similar to the company's existing markets are usually persuasive. Similar markets permit broadly consistent marketing approaches to be used, reducing the problems of coordination and control, this in turn facilitates the development of a common international image for a company's products [11]. Similar markets too, often produce economies in production and marketing costs.

Ther are two possible reasons for choosing diverse markets. First, market diversity is an inevitable consequence of a company deciding to penetrate a very large number of markets. Second, dissimilar markets may be chosen to balance cyclical fluctuations across markets or to reduce risks. The latter portfolio strategy, however, is only rational if the markets have individual profit variances which are negatively correlated. Thus in choosing diverse markets to reduce risks, the manager must establish that the added complexity does not have a deleterious effect on the overall expected return and that these markets are not likely to be positively correlated to their reactions to environmental changes.

FIGURE 2

EXPORT MARKET STRATEGY MATRIX

Type of Market

|  | SIMILAR | DIVERSE |
|---|---|---|
| FEW | Concentrated Similarity | Concentrated Diversity |
| MANY | Multiple Similarity | Multiple Diversity |

Number of Markets

The International Market Strategy Matrix

The choices among market concentration strategies can now be defined in an international market strategy matrix (Figure 2). The four alternatives are:

Concentrated similarity. Under this strategy the company concentrates on exploiting a small number of similar markets. The advantages of concentration and the synergy from operating in similar markets make this strategy optimal for most companies. It is especially advantageous for smaller, less experienced firms and those marketing products requiring high customer contact and sales control.

Concentrated diversity. Here the company chooses a small number of markets which are dissimilar in character. For e. ple, a machine tool manufacturer might be selling to Canada, Nigeria and Italy. Each market is different in terms of level of development and market structure but their small number makes control possible. The strategy is viable as long as the number of markets do not expand beyond the firm's capability to effectively service them.

Multiple similarity. Here the company exports to a large number of countries but all these countries have important market characteristics in common. For example, a tractor manufacturer may have developed a basic unit suitable for most developing countries. Market similarities mean that considerable standardization may be attainable in product and market planning. Nevertheless, the company should regularly monitor whether marginal markets represent an effective use of resources.

Multiple diversity. This strategy involves selling to a large number of markets which have little in common. Only the largest and most experienced exporters selling simple product lines can make this policy effective. Effectiveness is threatened by both the large number of markets which stretch resources thinly and by a lack of any compensating similarity among markets permitting standardization in efforts.

ANALYSIS OF MARKET TYPOLOGIES

Once the firm has determined its market concentration strategy, it operationalizes this strategy by choosing a portfolio of markets consistent with it. Managers can perform this task judgmentally. But multidimensional techniques may be used to support and give precision to these judgments. The most obvious way of grouping countries analytically is by clustering techniques. Indeed several writers have used this approach, [5, 6, 9]. The main drawback of these earlier studies is that they have failed to supply any clear theoretical rationale for the methodology. Without a concept of a portfolio of markets, the empirical results have no obvious managerial utility. Additionally they exhibit various technical shortcomings notably in choice of similarity measures and clustering methodology. In this section we employ Wishart's mode analysis as the clustering scheme for inter-country comparisons.

Choice of Variables

In choosing indices of market response the exporter must use product specific measures. To illustrate the approach here, however, a more general example is used. Twenty six variables were chosen to measure the essential market characteristics of 85 of the world's major economies (Table 1). A number of important variables, notably political and cultural indicators, had to be omitted from lack of reliable data. The data base refers to 1974.

Use of Factor Scores

To obtain reliable measures of complex concepts, several variables were collected on each concept. For example, level of economic development is measured by such variables as per capita income, energy consumption, education etc. This results in a problem of collinearity. To deal with this, factor analysis was used to reduce the dimensionality of the original 85 x 26 data matrix. Table 1 shows the principle components and varimax solutions for the major factors.

The main aim of the factor analysis was data reduction but it is possible to interpret the varimax factors. The high loadings (indicated in parentheses) suggest that the first factor may be labelled "economic development"- the second "industrialization"; the third "distribution potential"; the fourth "urbanization" and the firth a "trade" factor.

Next a set of unique factor scores for each country was obtained using the formula:

$$x_i = \sum_k a_{ki} b_k \tag{2}$$

Where  $x_i$ = the country's score on factor i.

  $a_{ki}$ = factor score coefficient for variable k and factor i.

  $b_k$ = the country's standardized value on variable k.

The advantage of using such scores to compare countries is that, unlike the 26 original variables, they are uncorrelated and thus provide independent information on the 85

TABLE 1

THE FACTOR MATRICES FOR THE 26 MARKET CHARACTERISTIC VARIABLES

| VARIABLES | FACTORS | | | | | | | | | |
|---|---|---|---|---|---|---|---|---|---|---|
| | UNROTATED | | | | | VARIMAX | | | | |
| | 1 | 2 | 3 | 4 | 5 | 1 | 2 | 3 | 4 | 5 |
| 1) Population/million | -0.156 | -0.813 | -0.035 | -0.277 | -0.118 | 0.118 | 0.012 | (0.738) | -0.245 | -0.397 |
| 2) Past 5-year % increase in population | 0.655 | 0.017 | 0.422 | -0.021 | -0.375 | -0.441 | 0.008 | -0.019 | 0.075 | |
| 3) Population Density | -0.355 | 0.017 | -0.432 | -0.681 | 0.165 | 0.066 | (0.631) | 0.491 | -0.019 | 0.398 |
| 4) Cement production, Kg/per Capita | -0.813 | 0.057 | -0.307 | 0.036 | 0.121 | 0.584 | (0.597) | 0.053 | 0.269 | -0.044 |
| 5) Electric energy, production Mil.Kwh/per capita | -0.924 | -0.002 | 0.162 | 0.106 | 0.145 | (0.909) | 0.253 | 0.008 | 0.143 | -0.029 |
| 6) Energy consumption, Kg/per capita | -0.868 | 0.034 | 0.199 | 0.160 | 0.093 | (0.873) | 0.176 | -0.041 | 0.182 | -0.038 |
| 7) Steel consumption, Kg/per capita | -0.939 | -0.076 | -0.026 | 0.063 | 0.129 | (0.834) | 0.405 | 0.106 | 0.173 | -0.094 |
| 8) No. of passenger cars/per 1000 population | -0.905 | -0.022 | 0.307 | 0.080 | -0.183 | (0.930) | 0.106 | 0.137 | 0.132 | 0.074 |
| 9) No. of commercial vehicles/per 1000 population | -0.811 | -0.073 | 0.348 | 0.152 | 0.075 | (0.842) | -0.083 | 0.161 | 0.280 | -0.062 |
| 10) Mfg. as % of domestic product | -0.592 | 0.040 | -0.688 | -0.248 | -0.156 | 0.225 | (0.732) | -0.005 | 0.356 | -0.222 |
| 11) Civil aviation passengers/Km. thousands | -0.713 | -0.483 | 0.193 | -0.420 | -0.200 | (0.674) | 0.010 | 0.630 | 0.072 | -0.157 |
| 12) Civil aviation freight/Ton Km. | -0.690 | -0.420 | 0.122 | -0.214 | 0.303 | 0.607 | 0.104 | (0.698) | 0.045 | -0.005 |
| 13) No. of population/per hospital bed | 0.598 | -0.462 | 0.053 | -0.172 | 0.450 | -0.436 | -0.133 | 0.198 | (-0.670) | -0.114 |
| 14) No. of population/per physician | 0.555 | -0.284 | 0.248 | -0.042 | 0.107 | -0.292 | -0.206 | 0.002 | (-0.744) | 0.042 |
| 15) No. of telephones/per 100 population | -0.918 | -0.012 | 0.160 | -0.013 | -0.252 | (0.882) | 0.253 | 0.131 | 0.141 | 0.059 |
| 16) No. of radio sets/per 1000 population | -0.777 | -0.106 | 0.009 | 0.026 | 0.069 | (0.638) | 0.159 | 0.294 | 0.386 | -0.105 |
| 17) No. of television sets/per 1000 population | -0.964 | -0.006 | -0.036 | -0.028 | 0.134 | (0.832) | 0.405 | 0.119 | 0.253 | -0.031 |
| 18) Daily newspaper copies sold/per 1000 pop. | -0.888 | 0.078 | -0.157 | 0.057 | 0.115 | (0.711) | 0.515 | 0.080 | 0.238 | 0.047 |
| 19) GDP per capita | -0.906 | 0.070 | 0.261 | | | (0.924) | 0.163 | 0.002 | 0.156 | 0.071 |
| 20) Consumption of printing and writing paper Kg./per capita | -0.899 | -0.032 | 0.090 | -0.130 | 0.158 | (0.834) | 0.334 | 0.187 | 0.090 | 0.097 |
| 21) Total export as % of GDP | 0.051 | 0.615 | 0.064 | -0.412 | 0.160 | 0.115 | -0.239 | -0.179 | -0.083 | (0.826) |
| 22) Total imports as % of GDP | -0.025 | 0.689 | 0.057 | -0.572 | 0.044 | -0.046 | 0.092 | -0.022 | 0.145 | (0.881) |
| 23) Agriculture as % of GDP | 0.736 | -0.351 | -0.057 | -0.058 | 0.356 | -0.587 | -0.081 | -0.008 | (-0.649) | -0.159 |
| 24) Wholesale and retail trade as % of GDP | 0.122 | 0.106 | -0.326 | -0.427 | -0.462 | -0.384 | 0.077 | (0.419) | 0.382 | 0.231 |
| 25) % of school enrolment of 14 year olds | -0.858 | 0.242 | -0.145 | 0.035 | -0.015 | (0.663) | 0.434 | -0.008 | 0.424 | 0.100 |
| 26) University enrolment/per 1000 population | -0.847 | -0.069 | -0.059 | 0.057 | -0.113 | (0.697) | 0.295 | 0.186 | 0.346 | -0.124 |
| PERCENTAGE OF TOTAL VARIANCE | 53.9 | 9.5 | 7.0 | 6.3 | 4.5 | 42.0 | 12.5 | 8.2 | 10.2 | 8.3 |

SOURCES: U. N. Statistical Yearbook, U. N. Demographic Yearbook, U. N. Yearbook of Accounts Statistics, Business International, U.N.E.S.C.O. Statistical Yearbook.

countries.

## Similarity Indices

All clustering methods begin with a similarity matrix. Unfortunately, there are a variety of similarity indices and each gives different results. The Euclidean distant coefficient, for example, may overemphasise certain variables in the process of squaring. Here, this index would place Sweden closer to Afghanistan than to the USA simply because its score on the "distribution potential" factor differs greatly from the US score.

Another common similarity index is the product-moment correlation. But again this creates distortions because it measures only pattern and not magnitude similarity. To illustrate this distorting effect, the patterns for the Netherlands and Malawi are plotted in Figure 3. Despite very large differences in levels, the similarity of patterns leads to a correlation of + 0.97.

To avoid these problems a similarity coefficient was chosen which reflects both magnitude and pattern similarities. This is the cosine coefficient which like the correlation coefficient ranges from +1 to -1 but unlike that statistic does not standardize countries to a common mean and variance. The cosine between countries j and k is

$$\cos \theta_{jk} = \frac{\sum_i x_{ij} x_{ik}}{(\sum_i x_{ij}^2)^{\frac{1}{2}} (\sum_i x_{ik}^2)^{\frac{1}{2}}} \qquad (3)$$

where $x_{ij}$ is the value of factor i for country j.

## Mode Analysis

In classifying countries to define market concentration

FIGURE 3

THE PATTERN SIMILARITY OF THE NETHERLANDS AND MALAWI

strategy, the researcher is trying to determine whether countries fall into natural groups. A problem with the earlier approaches which utilized hierarchical clustering is that they are not generally suitable for detecting such groups, unless they are clearly separated (7, 14). Such procedures are termed "minimum variance" methods since they partition a population into clusters by minimising total within-group variation. Unfortunately, by imposing such variance constraints they easily yield partitions that actually cut across natural groups in the data.

The present study, by contrast, uses a procedure - Wishart'

mode analysis – which allows some internal variation within clusters (14). Natural clusters can be described as regions containing a relatively high density of points separated from other clusters by low density regions (3). Mode analysis conforms to this concept of natural clusters since it isolates only as many clusters as there are modes, unlike other hierarchical methods which yield all groupings from n-1 clusters down to two clusters, even if no natural groupings are in fact present. Table 2 shows the 11 clusters yielded from the data on the 85 countries.

### TABLE 2

#### GROUPING OF 85 COUNTRIES BY MODE ANALYSIS

CLUSTER 1

Afghanistan
Central African Rep.
Ethiopia
Ghana
Haiti
Kenya
Malawi
Nigeria
Uganda
Korea
Saudi Arabia

CLUSTER 2

Algeria
Bolivia
Ecuador
Iraq
Panama
South Africa
Venezuela

CLUSTER 3

Bulgaria
Czechoslovakia
German Dem. Rep.
Greece
Hungary
Poland
Roumania
Portugal
Yugoslavia

CLUSTER 4

Burma
Chile
Columbia
Paraguay
Peru
Argentina
Brazil
Mexico
Thailand
Uruguay

CLUSTER 5

Costa Rica
Dominican Republic
Guatemala
Jordan
Nicaragua
Syria
El Salvador
Lebanon

CLUSTER 6

Austria
Denmark
Finland
Norway
Sweden
Switzerland
Australia
Belgium
Israel
New Zealand

CLUSTER 7

Egypt
Iran
Turkey

CLUSTER 8

France
German Fed. Rep.
Italy
Japan
U.K.
U.S.A.
Canada
Netherlands
Spain

CLUSTER 9

Gabon
Honduras
Tunisia
Zaire
Tanzania
Kuwait
Libya
Morocco

CLUSTER 10

Guyana
Malaysia
Zambia
Hong Kong
Ireland
Jamaica

CLUSTER 11

India
Indonesia
Pakistan
Phillippines

FIGURE 4

THE MEAN PROFILES OF THE 11 COUNTRY CLUSTERS

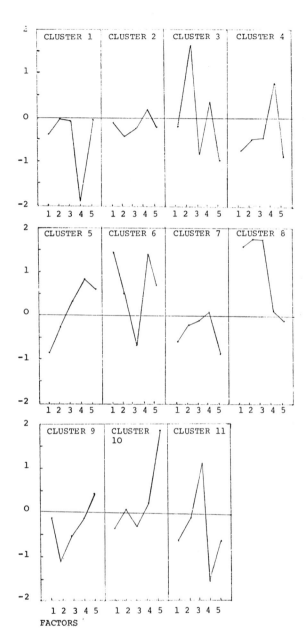

### Results

The mean profiles of each of the 11 clusters on the five factors are plotted in Figure 4. All five factors are important in differentiating clusters of countries. The first factor, it will be recalled, was labelled "economic development", having its highest loadings on such variables as GDP per capita, electric energy production per capita, passenger cars per 1,000 inhabitants, and energy consumption per capita. Two clusters – clusters 6 and 8 – had means on this factor that were considerably higher than the overall mean for all countries. Not surprisingly, these clusters included such countries as the U.S.A., West Germany, Japan, France and the Scandinavian countries. Examination of the mean profiles for these two clusters indicates, however, that is could be misleading to consider these countries on just this one dimension for their patterns on the other four factors show marked differences. Thus, these two clusters of countries were far apart on their mean values for the third factor, which had been labelled "distribution potential" from its loadings on the population size, civil aviation freight and wholesale and retail trade variables.

The situation was similar for the clusters which had low mean values on the "economic development" factor. Clusters 1 and 4, for example, differed considerably on their mean scores for the fourth factor, identified as an "urbanization" factor because of its negative loadings on the agriculture and health service variables. Clusters 9 and 10, on the other hand, were differentiated most clearly by their mean values on the fifth factor, the "trade" factor, and on the second factor, labelled an "industrialization" factor for its positive loadings on the manufacturing, cement production and population density variables and negative loading on the population increase variable.

Implications for Strategy

The analysis illustrates the formulation of a market concentration strategy. The company basing its strategy on exporting to similar markets would initially evaluate countries in the same or similar clusters. Companies wanting complementary countries would examine dissimilar mean profiles to identify candidate clusters.

The results also demonstrate the ability of multidimensional techniques for identifying these complex relationships. For example, the analysis suggests it is not enough to use level of economic development as an index of market similarity. Two countries at a comparable level of development may differ greatly on other important dimensions. The degree of industrialization, for instance, is an important consideration for industrial goods producers. Another relevant dimension is degree of urbanization since the marketing strategies for urban and rural populations can differ significantly.

Equally inadequate are purely regional or geographic forms of classification. For example, the results show that the Israel market has much more in common with European countries than its neighbours Egypt, Iraq or Syria. Similarly lessons learned in such Latin American countries as Chile or Peru might assist the company venturing into Burma or Thailand. Conversely, experiences gained in Korea may have limited value if used in the formulation of a strategy for penetrating the Japanese market.

CONCLUSIONS

Export market planning should begin with a statement of market concentration strategy. Without such a strategy most companies fail to concentrate their resources on countries offering the best potential, instead they allow resources and efforts to be dissipated across an increasing range of marginal markets. Drucker observed, "concentration is the key to economic results ...... no other principle of effectiveness is violated as constantly today as the basic principle of concentration". (2).

To identify countries which are consistent with one of the four strategy choices, the company must group candidate markets in terms of their similarity to one another. Essentially this implies three steps: choosing data which is relevant to that company's export products and overseas markets, rating countries along these dimensions, and

finally finding meaningful groupings of countries in terms of these dimensions. Wishart's mode analysis was used to illustrate, on general country measures, an analytical solution to this problem.

Nevertheless, the export market strategy matrix does not necessarily have to be based upon a multidimensional technique. Management judgment and insight will often be sufficient to dimensionalize the alternatives. The concept of market concentration strategy is not a technique but a fundamental building bloc in international marketing planning.

REFERENCES

1.  Drucker, Peter F. "Managing for Business Effectiveness", Harvard Business Review, 40 (May - June 1963), 59.

2.  Drucker, Peter F. Management: Tasks, Responsibilities and Practices, London: Heinemann, 1974

3.  Forgey, E. W. "Cluster Analysis of Multivariate Data: Efficiency Versus Interpretability of Classification", Biometrics, 21 (September 1965), 768 - 9.

4.  Hall, A. V. "Group Forming and Discrimination with Homogeneity Functions", in A. J. Cole, ed., Numerical Taxonomy: Proceedings of the Colloquium in Numerical Taxonomy. London: Academic Press, 1969.

5.  Hansz, James E. and James D. Goodnow. "A Multivariate Classification of Overseas Country Market Environments" in Marketing Education and the Real World, Combined Proceedings of the Spring and Fall Conferences of the American Marketing Association, V. W. Becker and H. Becker, eds. Chicago: AMA, 1972, 191 - 98.

6.  Liander, Bertil, Vern Terpstra, Michael Y. Yoshiao and A. A. Sherbini. Comparative Analysis for International Marketing: Boston: Allyn and Bacon, 1967.

7.  Marriott, F. H. C. "Practical Problems in a Method of Cluster Analysis", Biometrics, 27 (September 1971), 501 - 14.

8.  Royal Society of Arts. Concentration on Key Markets: A Development Plan for Exports. London: Royal Society of Arts, 1975.

9.  Sethi, Prakash S. "Comparative Cluster Analysis for World Markets", Journal of Marketing Research, 8 (August 1971), 348-54.

10. Simmonds, Kenneth and Helen Smith. "The First Export Order: A Marketing Innovation", British Journal of Marketing, 2 (Summer 1969), 3 - 13.

11. Sorenson, Ralph Z. and Ulrich E. Wiechmann. "How Multinationals View Marketing Standardization", Harvard Business Review, 53 (May - June 1975), 38 - 56.

12. Stigler G. J. The Organization of Industry. Homewood, Ill.: Irwin, 1968. Chapter 4.

13. Tookey, D. Export Marketing Decisions. London: Penguin Books, 1975.

14. Wishart, David. "Mode Analysis: A Generalization of the Nearest Neighbour Method Which Reduces Chaining Effects", in A. J. Cole, ed., op. cit.

SOCIOLOGY: THE MISSING CHUNK OR HOW WE'VE MISSED THE BOAT

Gerald Zaltman, University of Pittsburgh
Melanie Wallendorf, University of Pittsburgh

## ABSTRACT

Consumer behavior is not a solely psychological phenomenon, yet this could be the conclusion reached by examining
published literature in the area. The contention of this
paper is that a sociological perspective must also be used
to develop a comprehensive understanding of consumer
behavior. The value added by using a sociological perspective is demonstrated by discussing a sample of neglected topics.

## INTRODUCTION

The study of consumer behavior has, for the most part,
missed the boat by omitting from consideration a large
chunk of phenomena which are sociological in nature. As
consumer behavior researchers, we have consistently found
low predictive capabilities for many of the explanatory
variables we have used. Yet we have frequently assumed
that this was due to poor measurement or poor statistical
techniques. In response to this definition of the problem,
we have then tried to construct better measurement scales
and use more sophisticated statistical techniques. And,
sadly, the effort has missed the boat.

In this paper we offer an alternative definition of the
problem. It is our contention that the study of consumer
behavior is woefully incomplete if sociological phenomena
are not included. In this paper we shall identify a small
sample of areas in sociology which we feel are important
for understanding consumer behavior. We must make clear
the fact that our position is not that less attention
should be paid to psychological issues. These, too, are
important. However, they leave unexplained substantial
amounts of variance in consumer behavior. Adding sociological perspectives, we contend, would at least equal in
explanatory power what psychological perspectives provide.
The consistent exclusion of sociological concepts soundly
applied to consumer behavior phenomena has left a large
gap in our inventory of knowledge about consumer behavior.
An argument can be made to the effect that sociological
explanations are increasing in importance as society
becomes increasingly complex, and rapid social change
becomes a permanent fixture of social life. It is as if
we are standing on a dock loaded with psychological merchandise, while the boat we're concerned with is chugging
off to the horizon.

## A SAMPLE OF NEGLECTED TOPICS

### Social Roles

First, a basic characteristic of sociology is that it is
concerned with social relationships. For too long now we
have focused on the individual as the unit of analysis.
What is needed is a focus on social relationships as the
unit of analysis. A detailed development of this position
may be found in Bonoma, Bagozzi, and Zaltman [3]. Studying relationships highlights the importance of social
roles in defining relationships. To be sure, marketers
have been concerned with social roles in the past, and
some very fine studies of social roles exist in the marketing literature. But only the surface has been touched.

An issue which has not been addressed yet is the study of
role acquisition. Consumer behavior studies, and many in
sociology, construe a social role as static. In the portrayal used by these studies, a person either occupies a
social role or he does not, and the dynamics of role enactment are unchanging. A fruitful recent approach to
this problem suggests role behavior to be an evolutionary
process [9]. For example, there is, first of all, an
anticipatory stage prior to the formal occupancy of a role.
At this stage consumers are exposed to the expected behavior associated with a role relationship. At the formal
stage the individual assumes the role and begins to view
it as an incumbent rather than as an outsider. An informal stage is begun when the consumer encounters informal
and unofficial role expectations. Finally, a personalization stage may be entered during which the consumer
attempts to impose on others his or her own ideas about
appropriate behavior in the role. Each stage may differ
from the others in the sources of information used, the
content of information sought, and the types of expectation
about one's own behavior and the behavior of others. Thus,
in promoting goods and services it may be desirable to
segment ultimate consumers according to role acquisition
stages. A salesperson calling upon a purchasing agent for
the first time might want to differentiate the approach,
depending on the agent's role stage. An important caveat
is in order. This progression from anticipatory through
personalization stage is not inevitable. For various
reasons consumers may remain in an earlier stage or proceed
through different stages with differential speed.

Another important dimension of role study involves the
notion of role strain. Different social roles, such as
employee and parent, may conflict. A salesperson with a
large territory requiring frequent and lengthy travel may
experience strain when his or her parental obligations
require spending more time at home or officiating in local
athletic events. The mechanisms whereby role strain
develops and is responded to have important marketing
implications. For example, some products and services
might be presented in terms of how they release resources,
e.g., time, which are demanded by the various roles the
consumer must perform. Role strain reduction activities
might also explain why in some firms senior management
with obligations to many roles may delegate considerable
authority to purchasing agents in making major product
purchase decisions. The delegation of authority and
responsibility attendant upon a particular role is one way
in which strain involving that role is resolved.

Perhaps the most intriguing concept to develop in current
research on social roles is the notion of role accumulation. People may deliberately acquire roles even when
role strain may arise if there are additional net rewards
from the additional roles [8]. Space does not permit here
the development this idea warrants. However, we would like
to identify some of the implications of this idea. There
is substantial evidence in the literature to believe that
people who accumulate many social roles, i.e., people who
are role accumulators, are early learners of the availability of new products, early adopters of those products,
and active in word-of-mouth communication about new products. Moreover, and most importantly, it appears that
there is only modest overlap between people who are role
accumulators and people who are opinion leaders, innovators, and gatekeepers. That there may be a previously
unacknowledged group of people more influential in new
product diffusion than those people we customarily study
is of profound importance. This means that we have been
studying opinion leaders and innovators when they are not
the most important market segment for new product diffusion.
Considering the enormous resources expended on new product

marketing, this oversight is not inconsequential.

It might be added at this point that very little is known about the causal impact of particular social roles on consumption behavior. The effects of occupation on consumption behavior are little studied. Studies of broad occupational groups, such as blue collar/white collar or unskilled/semi-skilled/skilled, have reported differences in associated consumption patterns. However, these gross classifications are increasingly weak for descriptive, explanatory, or predictive purposes. A much more refined classification scheme is necessary, taking into account job culture variables such as (1) formal training required; (2) certification procedures; (3) whether travel is involved; (4) degrees of contact with specific types of co-workers and the clients of the firm; and (5) night shift versus day shift. This list could be extended considerably. There is substantial variation on all these factors within each of the categories of occupation currently used in consumer studies. These are some of the important factors to look at in the sociology of occupation literature.

## Societal Level Analysis

Cross-cultural studies of consumer behavior are coming into vogue (again). This is to be encouraged. From a marketing management standpoint, we have much to learn about current and potential foreign markets or for identifying what consumer characteristics should be considered in actual marketing practice in other countries. However, cross-cultural studies which compare the psychological traits of individuals in the cultures studied miss the boat by omitting the interesting sociological comparisons which could be made. This can be accomplished by shifting the unit of analysis from the individual to the social system. Important social system characteristics studied by sociologists and others include: (1) perceived need for change; (2) openness to change; (3) potential for change; (4) perceived control over the social change process; and (5) commitment to change. It is important to add that a social system's rating on these dimensions is not the average of where individual members of that system or society fall or rank. There is something added which Blau [1] refers to as an emergent phenomenon, which has an impact on individuals beyond what a paper and pencil test of individuals might show. Social norms are examples of emergent phenomena.

Social imitation processes, general socialization processes, cosmopolitanism, migration patterns, status mobility, communication infrastructure, influence systems and elitism, innovativeness, literacy/education, and political system variables are a few of the important variables which may change as one shifts from one culture to another. Yet we know little about the impact of these variables on consumers in any culture despite their demonstrated importance for human behavior.

Consumer behavior studies have also largely ignored the unique culture of particular social sectors in which consumption occurs. There is, for example, a health culture, an educational culture, a legal culture, and an entertainment culture. Each culture consists of the network of agencies and individuals who shape the choices consumers make in those cultures, as well as consumers themselves. The health culture consists of the U.S. Public Health Service, medical personnel in individual and group practice, health insurance agencies, the American Public Health Association, the American Medical Association, and hospitals. The overall pattern of interactions in this culture, including consumer actions, help shape the health purchase opportunities and constraints faced by consumers. Importantly, what consumers face in the health culture will differ significantly from the purchase process opportunities and constraints they face in the educational culture or the entertainment culture. If we want to understand consumer behavior, we must also understand the cultures of the

different social sectors within whose sphere consumption occurs. The literature on the occupational sociology, industrial sociology, and the sociology of the professions can be of help here. The idea of sector analysis is not new. Economists often choose social sectors as their unit of analysis. And, of course, each social sector has its own participant observers analyzing its social dynamics. In studying various sectors consumer behavior researchers will discover that there are very substantial variations among social sectors. For example, the health area is very different from the educational sector (compare descriptions in Blum [2] and Zaltman, et al [14]). Even subcultures within these sectors may differ from one another considerably. Thus, failing to take into consideration the impact of various sectors on consumer behavior will result in a source of unexplained variance.

## Collective Decision Making

Once we acknowledge that people do not purchase and consume goods in isolation of other people, we step into the arena of collective decision making. Nobody seriously disputes that nearly all consumption involves "significant others." At the same time few studies of consumer behavior take this into account. The few exceptions include studies of family decision making, children's consumer socialization processes, and word-of-mouth communication. Curiously, even these studies are often silent in citing the rich sociological literature on these issues.

Perhaps the largest deficiency stemming from the lack of attention to collective decision-making processes is the ignoring of collectivities other than families and friendship groups as units of consumption. A substantial portion of all goods and services consumed are consumed by formal organizations. If our focus is on consumption processes and their antecedents and consequences, or if we are concerned with consumers in the generic sense, then we must admit formal organizations into the set of entities covered by consumer research. Interestingly, the literature on formal organizations has not dwelled heavily on purchase decision processes.

The literature on organizational behavior is rich with studies describing how organizational structure impacts decision making. For example, organizational complexity, formalization, and centralization have important implications for understanding purchase decisions. So, too, do formal and information communication structures influence purchase behavior. The degree to which organizations monitor their environment and the way this is done is correlated with organizational innovativeness.

## Demography

Traditionally, demographic variables, such as age, income, family size, and geographic location, are used as control variables or as general descriptions of a sample being studied. Exactly how these variables influence consumer behavior is seldom discussed. Nor is their impact always as obvious as their neglected discussion implies. The effect of family income on food and transportation expenditures may vary, depending on whether that income is derived from two working spouses or from one. Cohabitation without the benefit (detriment?) of a legally certified marriage is increasing in frequency among both younger people and people at or around retirement age. Savings and investment patterns and the way consumer durables are purchased may vary, depending upon whether the male and female adult members of the family are legally married. Thus, if we want to understand changing patterns in the purchase of, say, kitchen appliances, it is necessary to go beyond mere household formation counts or trends and look at the social dynamics present in the formation of those households. Sex roles in families impact consumption and those sex roles are changing [7]. Social demography can help us understand

236

the marketing implications of these changes.

It might be added in this section about demography that current life-cycle concepts are rapidly being outdated. First, there are, in effect, new family life-cycle stages, that is, stages which are being entered into by many more people but which were previously ignored because they applied to too few persons. Divorce is a case in point. Cohabitation prior to marriage is now a significant stage, as it is much later after the so-called "empty nest" stage when the children have left the home and a marriage partner is deceased. Also, childless marriage is a more frequent, deliberately selected family state which warrants special attention by marketers. There are still other stages after the "solitary survivor" stage in which older persons may move into their children's home or into retirement homes or communities. All of these phenomena have important implications for the study of consumer behavior.

Furthermore, there is evidence that the single person living alone does behave differently from persons living with others. For example, males over 65 years of age living alone differ in their consumer behavior from the same aged males living with others. Moreover, this pattern of differences is not always the same when comparing women over 65 years of age living alone and women in this same age range but living with others. This evidence is found in a panel survey of both older and younger consumers being conducted at the University of Pittsburgh.

Our thinking about age has been almost entirely in terms of chronological age when we should be thinking in terms of social definitions of age status and the normative divisions of the life course [4]. A more sociocultural perspective on age would highlight not just different life cycles or life course stages, but, importantly, the transition processes from one point in the cycle to another. With the addition of more stages, e.g., cohabitation among unmarrieds, divorce, entry into children's "nests" or those of various institutions and communities, employment/re-employment, and so forth, the need to study the effects of transition from one social state to another increases in importance.

Life-Style

The sociological literature is rich with life-style studies (for a good review, see Zablocki and Kanter [13]). Sociologists view life-style in terms of shared values and tastes among a group whose members are similar to one another and dissimilar from others in terms of their consumption patterns and the motivations underlying these patterns. This is not the same as a culture or social class and social status, although these phenomena affect life-style. A sociological approach to life-style study goes beyond property-dominated life-styles, occupation-dominated life-styles, and poverty-dominated life-styles. Sociologists have addressed the interactions of life-style with life-cycle stage and particularly with life-cycle transitions. For example, the transition from adolescence to adulthood and the transition from work to retirement tend to be characterized with life-style experimentation. Life-style experimentation also characterizes transition from married life to being divorced. The sociological phenomena associated with these transitions need to be understood if we are to explain consumption patterns and their motivation during these transition periods.

Nearly all studies of consumer behavior are concerned with describing and, to a lesser extent, explaining the present life-style of one or more groups. By and large, these descriptions and expectations are developed in terms of economic and social status. But this, too, misses the boat, although the approach does make it to the gangplank. New life-styles develop when consensus is lost about the appropriateness of values, or at the very least, a loss in value coherence or consensus concerning the appropriate ways to express values. In fact, the proliferation of life-styles in the U.S. may be attributed to the breakdown of preexisting cultural values prior to the establishment of new values. We shall not address here the issue of how new life-styles emerge and their relationship to changing value systems. We simply point out that if students of consumer behavior want to understand life-style behavior, they need to review the literature on value (in)coherence in sociology [13].

Social Class

A discussion of sociology and consumer behavior cannot be concluded without a discussion of social class. Conventional treatments of social class rely on an approach put forth by W. Lloyd Warner [12]. A major difficulty with the customary approach is that the kind of society it is most relevant to does not generally exist today.

The study of social class and consumer behavior would be more fruitful if more overtly sociological approaches were followed. Consumer behavior researchers should be concerned with the processes whereby a stratification system develops. That is, how and why do certain positions become associated with certain levels of prestige? We should also consider status inconsistencies and not simply use as a social class measure the average position of a consumer on several prestige hierarchies. Perhaps the concept of social class is differentially relevant to consumer behavior as the degree of status inconsistency changes. There is a need to examine the effects of intergenerational mobility, career mobility, and status persistence, that is, the persistence of characteristics of an earlier social class once a consumer moves into another social class. For some reason, the literature on social class and consumer behavior has assumed social class to be a stable trait. This is evidenced not only by the ignoring of post-social classes, but also ignoring the effects on consumption of aspirations to a higher social class.

There is also occasional confusion of the variables which are indices of social class with the concept of social class itself. Education, income, occupation, and possessions are not social class -- they are merely proxy variables used to make estimations of a person's social class. One sociologist suggests that social class is essentially a phenomenon of opportunity availability [5]. Another error in measurement is often made when the social status of an entire family is determined by the characteristics of the adult male wage earner. This ignores such effects on consumption as family size and the employment and education of the adult female in the family. This is especially important when introducing the notion of opportunity availability as the basic phenomenon of social class.

Illegal Exchanges

Students of consumer behavior have frequently over-identified with the corporate marketing manager and thus have narrowly defined their scope of interest. Consistent with broadened marketing [6], this limitation must be overcome. Almost all studies of marketing behavior have focused on how consumers or firms go about purchasing and using products and services which are legally produced, sold, and used. However, sociological studies of deviance and crime have focused on another aspect of consumer behavior -- marketing exchanges which violate a societal norm which is enforced by laws. A few examples include:

Selling stolen goods (fencing)
Selling illegal drugs
Shoplifting
Prostitution
Gambling (i.e., illegal numbers games)
Hiring someone to kill someone else (hit men)

Illegal abortions (prior to 1973 Supreme Court ruling)
Selling liquor during Prohibition
Sales of certain goods (cigarettes, liquor) to minors
Political bribery (the selling of "favors")

Why should the study of illegal exchanges be a part of the study of consumer behavior? Why not leave it to sociologists interested in deviance?

The first reason is that illegal exchanges constitute a large sector of the economy. It has been estimated that in 1973 the resale of stolen goods amounted to $16 billion [10]. Legal gambling at race tracks amounts to about $5 billion annually. Compare with this the estimates of annual illegal gambling which range from $7 billion to $50 billion. Most law enforcement officials agree that the figure totals at least $20 billion a year -- four times the amount spent on legal gambling. Not only do the illegal exchanges themselves constitute a large segment of the economy, but large expenditures are also made on efforts to enforce the laws associated with these practices.

Secondly, the perhaps most importantly for those interested in consumer behavior, the study of illegal exchanges can provide a way to study the isolated effects of interpersonal communication as promotion. Since media promotion is not used to advertise illegal drugs, prostitution, or hit men, consumers must rely on information they receive from other people. Thus, this is an area for studying interpersonal communication about products without the confounding effects of media advertising. This is an excellent area for researching the effects of role accumulation mentioned earlier. What is learned here about the communication process can be used for drawing up propositions about behavior related to legal products which rely heavily on interpersonal communication or which are prohibited from using media advertising.

A third reason for studying illegal exchanges is that it provides a mechanism for studying the isolated effects of extended search for information and for the product by the potential consumer. In illegal exchanges consumers must actively search for the product as well as information about it. For instance, how does one go about finding a hit man? Although one knows that in our society hiring a hit man violates a norm and a law, how does one go about finding out the norms of the subculture in which this type of exchange exists? How does one find out how to buy heroin, let alone where to buy it?

A fourth reason for examining illegal exchanges is that it gives clues about what needs or preferences are not met within the legal marketing system. For instance, the fact that some consumers will buy stolen television sets is evidence that they are sensitive enough to price deals to take the risk (price is usually lower on knowledgeable purchases of stolen goods).

Finally, studying illegal exchanges and comparing them with legal marketing exchanges can help identify the effects of norms which are strong enough to be enforced by laws. For instance, comparing the sale of legal goods with that of fencing stolen goods, or the sale of legal prescription drugs with illegal drugs, provides insights into the effect of legality.

Thus, taking a sociological perspective generates several research questions which remain to be answered. What structures organize illegal exchanges and how are these structures similar to or different from the structures organizing legal exchanges? What are the role expectations for an illegal seller and an illegal buyer? What are the patterns underlying their interactions? How do word-of-mouth communication processes occur when there are legal risks in mentioning the product or service? Preliminary work on these questions has begun [11], but the study of illegal exchange remains an open area for contributions

and insights by researchers in the consumer behavior area.

## CONCLUSION

Seven areas of interest to consumer researchers have been briefly discussed. These are: (1) social roles, (2) societal level analysis, (3) collective decision making, (4) demography, (5) life-style, (6) social class, and (7) illegal exchange. These areas are only a small sample of those which a sociological perspective adds to the study of consumer behavior. Our purpose has been to discuss these areas in the hope of getting us back on the boat toward a comprehensive understanding of consumer behavior.

## REFERENCES

1. Blau, Peter. Exchange and Power in Social Life. New York: Harcourt, Brace & Jovanovich, 1964.

2. Blum, Henrik. Planning for Health. New York: Human Services Press, 1973.

3. Bonoma, Thomas V., Richard Bagozzi, and Gerald Zaltman. "The Dyadic Paradigm with Specific Application Toward Industrial Marketing," Proceedings, AMA Workshop, 1977.

4. Elder, Glen H., Jr. "Age Differentiation and the Life Course," in Alex Inkeles, et al (eds.), The Annual Review of Sociology. Palo Alto, CA: Annual Reviews, Inc., 1975, 165-190.

5. Felson, Marcus. "A Modern Sociological Approach to the Stratification of Material Lifestyles," in Advances in Consumer Research, Vol. 2. Chicago, 1975.

6. Kotler, Philip and Sidney Levy. "Broadening the Concept of Marketing," Journal of Marketing, 33 (January 1969), 10-15.

7. Lipman-Blumen, Jean and Ann R. Tickamyer. "Sex Roles in Transition: A Ten-Year Perspective," in Alex Inkeles, et al (eds.), The Annual Review of Sociology. Palo Alto, CA: Annual Reviews, Inc., 1975.

8. Sieber, Sam. "Toward a Theory of Role Accumulation," American Sociological Review, 39 (August 1974), 567-578.

9. Thornton, Russell and Peter M. Nardi. "The Dynamics of Role Acquisition," American Journal of Sociology, 80 (January 1975), 870-885.

10. U.S. Congress, Senate Hearings Before the Selected Committee on Small Business. Criminal Redistribution (Fencing) Systems, 93rd Congress, 1st Session, Part 1, 1.

11. Wallendorf, Melanie. "A Comparative Analysis of the Structure of Illegal Exchanges: Abortion, Drugs, Fencing, Gambling, and Prostitution," M.A. thesis, Department of Sociology, University of Pittsburgh, May 1977.

12. Warner, W. Lloyd. American Life, Dream and Reality. Chicago: The University of Chicago Press, 1953.

13. Zablocki, Benjamin D. and Rosabeth M. Kanter. "The Differentiation of Life-Styles," in Alex Inkeles, et al (eds.), The Annual Review of Sociology. Palo Alto, CA: Annual Reviews, Inc., 1975, 269-298.

14. Zaltman, Gerald, David Florio, and Linda Sikorski. Dynamic Educational Change. New York: Free Press, 19

# NEW CONTRIBUTIONS OF SOCIOLOGY TO CONSUMER RESEARCH

Robert Nathan Mayer, University of Utah
Francesco M. Nicosia, University of California, Berkeley

## ABSTRACT

The main use of sociology in consumer research has been in studying the influence of group memberships on individual awareness, preferences, and decisions. The sociology of consumption is an extension of current consumer research in at least two ways. First, it emphasizes the study of consumption as a property of groups rather than just of individuals. Second, it examines consumption in relation to other group properties. Among these correlates of consumption are group properties that are not based on information about individual members--for example, institutional arrangements, technology, and cultural values. This paper provides several examples of how the sociology of consumption can be helpful in addressing problems of marketing management.

## INTRODUCTION

Marketers have always been sensitive to the fact that consumer behavior takes place in a social environment. Over time, though, consumer researchers have increasingly focused their efforts on social psychological variables and, especially in recent years, on a few psychological constructs (see, for example, the review article by Hansen [7].

A more balanced approach seems appropriate. There are certainly many avenues to explore in the area of the "sociology of consumer behavior," that is, the influence of group memberships on the individual consumer. The family, in particular, is receiving renewed attention as a source of social influences on individual consumer behavior [3].

We are most intrigued, however, by the possibilities of a "sociology of consumption." This emerging area of research should bear on the applied problems of private managers and public officials. In addition, it should help update the images of society used by basic researchers. For although we increasingly characterize modern industrial societies with phrases which imply consumption--"affluent," "service-oriented," or "post-industrial"--we have very little systematic knowledge about a society's consumption.

## THE FOCUS ON GROUP CHARACTERISTICS

The distinctive feature of the sociology of consumption is that it studies groups rather than individuals; hence, consumption rather than consumer behavior. It takes consumption as one characteristic of a group and relates consumption to other group properties.

Group properties can be either "aggregate" or "global" [9]. Aggregate properties are derivable from the attributes of individuals. Global properties are not; they are inherent to a group. A society's crime rate would be an aggregate property, but its criminal laws would be global properties, inherent to a specific society. Similarly, the average age of a firm's employees is an aggregate property, but its degree of centralization or specialization is not. For our purposes, global properties refer to a group's institutional arrangements, its culture, and its technology. Aggregate properties refer to the activities of group members.

Consumption per se is an activity, so it is an aggregate characteristic of groups. However, institutions in which consumption occurs (for example, supermarkets, laundromats, bars, restaurants), consumption rituals (for instance, gift giving), and cultural values pertaining to consumption (for example, freedom of choice or standards of cleanliness) may also characterize and differentiate groups, and these would be global properties. They could be used as correlates of consumption.

Thinking, then, of consumption as an aggregate property, some examples are:

1 the rates of purchase of particular goods (whether potatoes or antibiotics);

2 the social distribution in the ownership of particular goods;

3 the degree of differentiation in the content of the typical "baskets" of goods which consumers buy; and

4 the allocation of time to buying, use, and disposal activities in total and relative to each other.

It is also possible to characterize a collectivity on the basis of the individual attributes of a subgroup. Societies could be compared, for instance, according to the consumption of jet travel by their political leaders, mass transit by their urban residents, alcohol by their adults, baby food by their infants (or elderly), dresses by their women, or suits by their men.

In summary, the sociology of consumption relates consumption (an aggregate property of a group) to either aggregate or global properties of a social group. The aggregate correlates can refer, by definition, to any types of human activity other than consumption. They might include, for instance, a group's average years of schooling, its income distribution, or its rates of family formation and dissolution. The global correlates of consumption may refer to both consumption and nonconsumption, however. One may speak of the influence of marketing institutions as well as work institutions, consumption rituals as well as religious ones.

## RELEVANCE TO MARKETING PROBLEMS

Many marketers already consider the implications of demographic changes in a group or society. They note the importance of changes, for example, in the rate of female participation in the work force or in the age distribution of a society. Why, then, do we need a sociology of consumption?

We would suggest that the sociology of consumption can (1) illuminate the meanings and motivations behind some types of consumer behavior, (2) help identify more precise market segments, (3) improve the content of promotional material, (4) aid new product introduction, and (5) improve the public perception of firms as well as business in general.

Some of the illustrations that follow are impressionistic; others can be backed up with data. The examples also range from marketing management narrowly conceived to the new social roles marketers and firms are being asked to assume. Our final example refers to a research project in which we are currently engaged--it addresses the problem of how firms may interpret and respond to consumer problems with technologically complex goods (for other examples, see Nicosia and Mayer [14]).

## The Meaning of Products

We know from consumer research that, given certain physical properties, consumers can attribute a variety of meanings or definitions to a particular good. For example, a car may mean transportation to and from work, but it can also mean recreation or procreation. Toothpaste can be defined in terms of sex appeal, not just oral hygiene.

Generally, we analyze differences in the meaning of goods at the level of the individual consumer. If we ask why a person employs a certain definition rather than another, we look at other personal characteristics--say, age, gender, or income. This hopefully becomes the basis of market segmentation.

The sociology of consumption helps identify group properties which promote definitions that are shared by all or some of its members. We have suggested elsewhere [10], for instance, that ecologically conscious consumption is defined more as political than as consumer behavior. Furthermore, our interpretation holds that ecologically conscious consumption by a society's upper strata occurs when there are (a) cultural values of humanitarianism (that is, helping those less privileged than oneself), and (b) an absence of institutions which facilitate the expression of this cultural value (say, political and religious institutions). This interpretation clearly differs from one that tries to correlate ecologically conscious consumption with either individual beliefs about nature or a cultural value concerning ecology.

Our interpretation of ecologically conscious consumption contains many implications for marketing ecologically oriented products. For one, it suggests new bases of market segmentation. It also suggests that the content of advertising should reflect the political rather than the environmental motivations underlying ecology conscious consumer behavior. Rather than show the prospective customer running through a field of daisies, the more effective ad might picture the consumer returning from a community fund-raising event.

## The Group Function vs. the Contrast Function

The classic sociological insight into consumption is that people strive for status through consumption [5, 6, 16, 17]. Sometimes consumption style merely expresses and reinforces membership in a group that is defined on the basis of how people make their money. In other cases, consumption itself defines a group on the basis of how people spend their money.

In a study of the consumption patterns of Swedish girls, Ann-Mari Sellerberg [15] notes that goods can be used not only to express belongingness to a certain group (the group function), but also to mark the contrast between situations (the contrast function). Furthermore, she found that the group function characterizes middle-class Swedish girls, while the contrast function characterizes the working-class girls. For example, middle-class girls are concerned with having a personal style of dress, whereas working-class girls "used" clothes to mark the distinction between past and present, leisure and work, festive occasions and everyday.

Most marketers would take this finding as an indication that social class is an important basis for market segmentation. These research findings raise a more fundamental question, however, one which may ultimately tell us much more about what social characteristics promote either the group or the contrast function.

Fred Hirsch, in a recent book, The Social Limits to Growth [8], states that the group function of consumption becomes increasingly problematic as a society grows more affluent. "If everyone stands on tiptoe, no one sees better." A study of automobile workers by Eli Chinoy [2] suggests that the group function occurs when cultural values emphasizing individual success exist alongside work institutions that do not distribute rewards on the basis of individual effort.

Therefore, social class may be both too specific and too general as a basis for market segmentation. Hirsch indicates that a society's level of industrialization is the relevant variable for discussing the use of the group function. Hence, market segmentation on the basis of class may be effective in some societies but not in others. Chinoy, on the other hand, implies that not all members of a particular social class will employ consumer goods to express their status aspirations (that is, aspirations for membership in a status group). Rather, it is only those people who adhere to the success ethic and are blocked by institutional arrangements from pursuing individual advancement. Again, more precise market segmentation as well as more effective promotional content follows from attention to group characteristics such as cultural values and institutional arrangement rather than just the characteristics of individual consumers.

## Introducing New Products

In a sense, marketers are sociologists of consumption when they analyze the "readiness" of a particular group or market area for the introduction of a new product. Marketers will typically assess the existence of competing products, marketing channels, and the number of potential consumers, as well as the income level and age distribution of an area before trying to market a new product. In other words, they study the characteristics of an area and its consumers in order to increase the probability of success.

The sociology of consumption simply suggests a more systematic and thorough assessment of the community characteristics relevant to the introduction of a new product or the location of a new store. These characteristics are most obvious when expanding into a new country. Differences in cultural values concerning time and cleanliness or differences in institutional arrangements concerning the length of the lunch hour and the distance between home and work will partially determine, for instance, the prospects of a new fast-food outlet.

Characteristics relevant to consumption need not pertain to differences among nations. They may refer to differences within them as well. A somewhat laughable but suggestive example is provided by Conrad Kottak, an anthropologist at the University of Michigan. Kottak feels that visiting a McDonald's restaurant has virtually become a religious experience for millions of Americans. He observes that repeated pilgrimages to the Golden Arches assure customers of uniformity in an otherwise chaotic world. "The menu is located in the same place, contains the same items and has the same prices," he says. "We know what we're going to see, say and hear from that first request for a Big Mac to the final 'Have a nice day.' Every move is ritualized like a religious service" [11].

Kottak's interpretation may seem a bit far-fetched, but it does raise interesting marketing questions. For instance, will the success of a new McDonald's be related to the number and kind of religious institutions in a community? Are alienated, uprooted residents of urban communities more likely to welcome the security provided by the Golden Arches? Should promotion stress the ritualized aspects of the McDonald's experience?

McDonald's not only imbues consumption with a religious character, according to Kottak. His findings also raise relevant questions at the societal or group level: Is consumption replacing religion as a source of personal security and social cohesion? What societal characteristics promote the ritualization of consumption? Finding the answers to these questions should greatly aid marketing of a wide range of products.

## Consumer Coping

A final example of how consumption can be related to both the aggregate and global properties of groups comes from a research project now in progress [13]. The project is studying how different types of consumers deal or "cope" with breakdowns and malfunctions of technologically complex products. In the process, issues that fall within the sociology of consumption are being raised.

Several studies have found a striking disparity between the occurrence of problems involving consumer products and the active pursuit of redress for these problems by consumers [1, 4, 12]. Andreasen, for instance, speaks of the 20-40-60 relationship. Using a broad definition of product problems, his national study of 2,400 households found that 20 percent of products and services spell problems for consumers. Forty percent of these problems are reported to business and, of these, about 60 percent are resolved by business to the consumer's satisfaction.

Findings such as these raise two interrelated questions: (1) What societal (or group) characteristics help to explain why so many consumers cope by accepting product malfunctions? and (2) What can explain the difference between those consumers who actively pursue the solution of their problems and those who do not?

The first question calls for analysis of the rate of kinds of consumer coping in different societies or in one society at more than one point in time. It seeks to explain differences in consumption by reference to the characteristics of societies. The second question speaks to differences among the consumers of one country. It analyzes individual differences according to other attributes of individuals. These individual attributes can be aggregated and then used to generate market segments. These market segments may not, however, correspond to a previously existing social group.

The Nicosia project entails a cross-sectional survey. Therefore, it is best suited to addressing the second of these two questions. Regardless of which of these questions one addresses, however, the alternative hypotheses are quite similar. In both cases we seek to explain variation in the rates of "active" coping vs. acceptance of product problems and/or replacement with a new product. In one case, these rates refer to a clearly defined and previously existing group. In the second case, analysis of individual differences may generate groups within society which are homogeneous in terms of their coping.

The hypothesis is that the rate of active coping depends on the existence of certain cultural values. For example, a society which emphasizes achievement, frugality, and individual rights should be conducive to active coping. When studying individual differences, research would assess the extent to which these cultural values have been internalized.

A second hypothesis is that the rate of active coping depends on the existence of facilitating institutions. These institutions could include consumer affairs depart-

ments within firms, consumer affairs offices within government, and private consumer action groups. The objective availability of these facilitating institutions may be analyzed at the societal level or in terms of subgroups within it. For instance, if there are more private consumer groups in middle-class communities than in working-class communities, one can anticipate differences in coping.

Third, even when actual coping opportunities are constant across groups or nations, important differences may exist in perceived coping opportunities. Perceptions imply an aggregate property of the collectivity, but one could then seek the reasons for these differences in perceptions by examining other global characteristics of the collectivity. For example, if opportunity does not exist with respect to occupational mobility or political participation (a statement about institutions), then people may generalize their experiences and fail to perceive actual coping opportunities. Again, differences in the perception of coping opportunities may be analyzed across or within societies. Within societies, market segments would be defined according to their perception of coping opportunities.

A fourth hypothesis is that coping is a function of the personal resources of consumers. Hence, collectivities would be described by the aggregate properties of individuals rather than by global properties. Some of these individual resources can clearly be expected to vary across and within societies--for example, leisure time, knowledge of coping alternatives and rights, knowledge of product technology, mechanical skills, and social contacts. Other individual resources are more subtly related to membership in particular market segments or countries. These might include self-confidence, feelings of personal efficacy, cognitive complexity, verbal ability, and tolerance of ambiguity.

In either case, differences in these aggregate properties may be related to global properties. For instance, the educational institutions that characterize a nation may affect the amount and distribution of knowledge and verbal ability. Similarly, the degree of industrialization and the occupational structure may influence the amount and distribution of mechanical skills.

Finally, a fifth hypothesis is that those societies and market segments in which coping is least active (remember that active coping does not include buying a replacement, according to our definition) are those in which consumers place a high value on discretionary time relative to discretionary income. In other words, consumers may not have sufficient incentive or motivation to cope actively with product malfunction if they do not highly value the income required to ignore the malfunction by buying a replacement, but they do highly value the time they spend in more rewarding and enjoyable leisure-time pursuits [12]. We are speaking of the utilities that a person assigns to their time and income. These utilities are related to, but are conceptually distinct from, the actual amount of discretionary time and income a person possesses. Utilities concerning time and money may be taken as an aggregate property of a predefined group, but, again, market segments may also be defined on differences in these utilities. In either case, these utilities become an aggregate property of a group.

Of course, more than one of these hypotheses can be involved in explaining differences in the coping of societies or groups. For example, consumers in affluent societies may lack the incentive and motivation to cope actively and therefore rationalize their behavior by perceiving that there is no coping opportunity (a combination of hypothesis two and four). One would therefore expect that the relationship between perceived coping opportunity and active coping would depend on how much a person values his/her leisure time and money.

Each of these hypotheses and combinations of hypotheses have important implications for the marketer's task of building and maintaining consumer satisfaction with a brand and consumer loyalty to the firm. Specifically, it bears on the allocation of resources to aid consumers in using, maintaining, and repairing goods.

Suppose consumers are too busy to care about product malfunctions and that they have the income to buy replacements. This has different implications for the firm and the private sector in general than the finding that consumers perceive firms as unresponsive to consumer problems--that is, as providing little coping opportunity.

It may be that firms have little influence over the correlates of consumer coping. The individual firm has, for instance, very little control over cultural values and the distribution of personal resources. These depend more on educational, familial, and occupational institutions than they do on business institutions. Nevertheless, attention to the changing correlates of consumer coping, even when they are beyond the control of the marketing manager, can help in determining and evaluating the demands raised by consumers and by their elected and appointed representatives.

## CONCLUSION

The sociology of consumption is an extension of current consumer research in at least two ways. First, it emphasizes the study of consumption as a property of groups rather than just of individuals. Second, it examines consumption in relation to other group properties. Among these correlates of consumption are group properties that are not based on information about individual members-- for example, institutional arrangements, technology, and cultural values.

This distinctive focus allows the sociology of consumption to help in addressing the problems of managers in both the private and public sectors. For marketers, it is useful in market segmentation, new product introduction, and the maintenance of brand and firm loyalty. The sociology of consumption should aid government officials in dealing with those national problems in which consumers are implicated, especially the management of natural resources and environmental quality.

## REFERENCES

1. Best, Arthur and Alan R. Andreasen. "Talking Back to Business: Voiced and Unvoiced Consumer Complaints," Working Paper, Center for Study of Responsive Law, Washington, D.C., 1976.

2. Chinoy, Eli. "The Tradition of Opportunity and the Aspirations of Automobile Workers," American Journal of Sociology, 57 (March 1952): 453-459.

3. Davis, Harry L. "Decision Making within the Household," in Robert Ferber, ed., A Synthesis of Selected Aspects of Consumer Behavior. Washington: National Science Foundation, 1976.

4. Day, Ralph L. and E. Laird Landon, Jr. "Collecting Comprehensive Consumer Complaint Data by Survey Research," in Beverlee B. Anderson, ed., Advances in Consumer Research, 3, Cincinnati Association for Consumer Research, 1976.

5. deTocqueville, Alexis. Democracy in America. New York: Schocken, 1961).

6. Fallers, Lloyd A. "A Note on the Trickle Effect," Public Opinion Quarterly, 5 (1954): 314-321.

7. Hansen, Flemming. "Psychological Theories of Consumer Choice," Journal of Consumer Research, 3 (December 1976): 117-142.

8. Hirsch, Fred. Social Limits to Growth. New York: Twentieth Century Fund, 1976.

9. Lazarsfeld, Paul F. and Herbert Menzel. "On the Relation between Individual and Collective Properties," in Paul F. Lazarsfeld, Ann K. Pasanella, and Morris Rosenberg, eds., Continuities in the Language of Social Research. New York: Free Press, 1972.

10. Mayer, Robert N. "The Socially Conscious Consumer: Another Look at the Data," Journal of Consumer Research, 3 (September 1976): 113-115.

11. Moneysworth, March 14, 1977, p. 2.

12. Nicosia, Francesco M. "Technology and Consumers: Individual and Social Choices," Vol. 1, in Francesco M. Nicosia, ed., Technological Change, Product Proliferation, and Consumer Decision Processes. Berkeley: Institute of Business and Economic Research, University of California, 1974.

13. _____. "Coping Behavior: An Empirical Study of the Consumer-Technology Interface," Research Proposal, Institute of Business and Economic Research, University of California, Berkeley, 1976.

14. Nicosia, Francesco M. and Robert N. Mayer. "Toward a Sociology of Consumption," Journal of Consumer Research, 3 (September 1976): 65-75.

15. Sellerberg, Ann-Mari. "On Differing Social Meanings of Consumption," Journal of the Market Research Society, 18, no. 4 (1976).

16. Veblen, Thorstein. The Theory of the Leisure Class. New York: Macmillan Company, 1899.

17. Weber, Max. Economy and Society. Edited by Guenther Roth and Claus Wittich. New York: Bedminster Press, 1968.

# ANALYZING THE RELATIVE POWER OF PARTICIPANTS
## IN INDUSTRIAL BUYING DECISIONS

James R. Cooley, California State University, Chico
Donald W. Jackson, Jr., Arizona State University
Lonnie L. Ostrom, Arizona State University

## ABSTRACT

The relative power of various functional groups in the modified rebuy purchasing decision for industrial components were analyzed. Power differed significantly between the supplier selection decision and the product selection decision. Size of firm, type of product, and type of manufacture each affected the perceived power of the various participants. Traditional product characteristics were shown to have mixed results in affecting the power of the various functions.

## INTRODUCTION

Industrial purchasing decisions typically involve a complex set of smaller decisions which are made or influenced by several participants. While several studies support the existence of multiple buying influences in the industrial buying process, little is known about the factors that affect the number of participants or the extent of these influences [1, 9, 11, 13]. The need for additional research in this area is supported by the fact that one study found that 64 percent of all industrial sales calls were made on the wrong person [10]. The complex set of decisions in the buying process makes knowledge about the participants and how power is distributed among them crucial to the marketer. This knowledge is critical in developing the content and timing of the industrial marketing program, in directing promotional efforts to appropriate people, and in giving direction to the sales force for developing selling strategies. Webster and Wind conclude that:

> . . . it is useful to understand (the) relative power (of the participants in the purchasing decision) . . . A key question in virtually every buying organization is the extent to which the purchasing agent actually influences the decision process at each of the buying stages . . . There is no more important task in the planning of marketing strategy than identifying those individuals . . . [12, p. 67]

A major concept useful in identifying the relationships among participants in the buying process is power; power refers to the amount of say, or influence, an individual has in a decision. In a group situation, such as the industrial buying decision, power and influence are synonymous. A major shortcoming of prior research was that responsibility and authority were used as implicit indicators of power [5, 7]. These measures, however, do not consider the informal relationships in the firm.

The purpose of this study is to investigate the relative power of participants in the purchase of industrial components; and to determine if the power structure varies in relation to types of decisions, types of manufacture, types of products, product characteristics, and other corporate specific factors. The study examines three major hypotheses. Stated in null form for ease of testing, the hypotheses are as follows:

H1 There is no difference in the relative power of the decision making functions in the product selection decision or the supplier selection decision.

H2 There is no difference in the power perceptions of the various functions based on type of manufacture, type of product, or company size.

H3 There is no difference in the power perceptions of the various functions based on the product characteristics: technical complexity, product modification, product installation, product similarity, rate of product improvement, or supplier similarity.

## THE STUDY

Focus of the research centered on a study of modified rebuys of component items [3]. According to Haas, the modified rebuy is much more difficult to understand than the new buy or straight rebuy and as such, confuses many marketing managers [6, p. 58]. In addition, the modified rebuy requires the evaluation of new alternatives based upon past experience with the product. Component items were selected since they were widely used and would minimize the number of firms in the study that did not purchase the products. Fasteners, electronic components and castings were selected to represent components based on a pretest of nine component products. The use of three products, rather than one, was believed to permit stronger generalizations to be made concerning component items as a class of products.

Fifteen industrial manufacturing firms were identified in Phoenix, Arizona, and twenty-three firms were identified in Orange County, California, as being likely buyers of the products specified in this research. A total of twenty-six of the thirty-eight firms were included in the study, generating 122 responses. All companies were from Standard Industrial Classifications 3400 to 3800. The median size of the participating firms was 1,000 employees; the smallest had 400 employees and the largest had over 15,000. A majority of the respondents had more than five years of experience with the company and products under investigation.

Initial contact with each firm was made with the top purchasing executive who identified the buyers responsible for purchasing the specified products. The buyers, in turn, identified those in production, engineering or other functions who were involved in the procurement process for these items. The questionnaire was administered through personal interviews with each of the participants in the purchasing decision.

For purposes of the study, the industrial purchasing process was divided into two decision stages: the product selection decision, and the supplier selection decision. The dependent variable power was measured by adapting Marsh's "measure of attributed influence" [8]. This method required each participant in the study to allocate a fixed sum, in this case 100 percent of the total power in a decision, between the decision makers (purchasing, production, engineering or other functions) based upon their perceptions of how power was distributed. Type of manufacture, type of product, and the corporate specific variables were used to classify the power responses. The product related factors were measured on a five point Likert type scale.

Since the dependent variable, power, was a vector variable having three elements (purchasing, production, and engineering) for each measure of the dependent variable, the basic analytical technique used to test the hypotheses concerning power was a one-way multivariate analysis of variance (Manova). Manova was used to determine if there were overall differences in the power distributions. If the overall relationship was significant, then univariate F tests were explored to note the source of variation. Univariate F tests should only be interpreted if the Manova null hypothesis has been rejected [2]. Thus, where the Manova F was not significant univariate F statistics are not reported.

## FINDINGS

The hypothesis of no difference in relative power between functions was rejected. As can be seen in Table 1, in both the product selection decision and supplier selection decision, there were significant differences in the power of purchasing, production and engineering. Engineering had the dominant power in selecting products; while purchasing had the dominant power in selecting suppliers.

The second hypothesis tested was that there would be no difference in the perceptions of the various functions based on the corporate specific variables: type of manufacture, type of product, or size of firm. Results here were mixed. Table 2 indicates significant differences in the relative power distributions between firms which produced to customer order and those which produced for stock. The differences were significant for the product selection decision but not for the supplier selection decision. As can be seen from the table, purchasing had significantly more power in the product selection decision in those cases where production was for stock than in those cases where production was for specific customers orders. In contrast, engineering had more power when production was for customer order than when it was for stock. There were no significant differences in the power of production in either case.

The next factor investigated was the type of product being selected. Three different categories of industrial components were investigated: fasteners, castings and electronics. Table 3 indicates that there were no significant differences in power for the product selection decision between the three different product categories. There were, however, differences in relative power in the supplier selection decision. Purchasing had the greatest power in selecting the supplier of castings, while engineering had the greatest relative power in selecting suppliers of electronic components. Again, there were no significant differences in the power of production based upon the type of product.

The last factor examined was company size. Companies were divided into those with 1,000 or less employees and those with more than 1,000 employees. Table 4 indicates that power perceptions differed significantly based on size of the company for both the product selection decision and the supplier selection decision.

In the product selection decision, purchasing was perceived as having relatively more power in small companies than in larger companies. Neither of the other functions showed significant differences between different sized companies in the product selection decision. In the supplier selection decision, each of the functions showed relative differences in power between different sized firms. Purchasing had more relative power in smaller companies, while production and engineering had more relative power in large companies.

TABLE 1

ANALYSIS OF DIFFERENCES IN POWER
BASED ON TYPE OF DECISION

| Function | Product Selection Decision | | | Supplier Selection Decision | | |
|---|---|---|---|---|---|---|
| | Mean | $F^a$ | P Less Than | Mean | $F^a$ | P Less Than |
| Purchasing | 19.5 | | | 67.5 | | |
| Production | 16.6 | | | 4.9 | | |
| Engineering | 61.1 | | | 24.5 | | |
| Other | 2.8 | | | 3.1 | | |
| | | 405.1 | .001 | | 497.2 | .001 |

[a] $F_{(2,363)}$

TABLE 2

POWER PERCEPTIONS
BASED ON TYPE OF MANUFACTURE

| Function and Decision | Mean Power Score by Type of Manufacture | | $F^a$ | P Less Than |
|---|---|---|---|---|
| | Customer Order | For Stock | | |
| Product Selection | | | 7.9 | .001 |
| Purchasing | 14.3 | 23.4 | 20.5 | .001 |
| Production | 14.1 | 15.6 | .5 | .499 |
| Engineering | 60.4 | 52.0 | 8.9 | .003 |
| Supplier Selection | | | 2.0 | .117[b] |
| Purchasing | 61.3 | 68.0 | – | NS |
| Production | 5.1 | 2.6 | – | NS |
| Engineering | 20.3 | 18.3 | – | NS |

[a] Value for product selection and supplier selection decisions based on $F_{(3,118)}$. Values for functional power are based on $F_{(1,120)}$.

[b] Unvariate F scores are only meaningful when overall Monova results are significant, thus, they are not reported.

TABLE 3

POWER PERCEPTIONS
BASED ON TYPE OF PRODUCT

| Function and Decision | Mean Power for Decisions Involving | | | $F^a$ | P Less Than |
|---|---|---|---|---|---|
| | Fasteners | Castings | Electronics | | |
| Product Selection | | | | 1.17[b] | .104 |
| Purchasing | 21.2 | 15.5 | 16.0 | – | NS |
| Production | 12.5 | 19.6 | 14.4 | – | NS |
| Engineering | 56.0 | 54.7 | 59.2 | – | NS |
| Supplier Selection | | | | 3.8 | .001 |
| Purchasing | 64.1 | 75.8 | 58.6 | 7.4 | .001 |
| Production | 5.0 | 3.0 | 3.9 | .6 | .560 |
| Engineering | 17.7 | 8.9 | 25.5 | 11.0 | .001 |

[a] Values for the product selection decision and the supplier selection decision are based upon $F_{(6,234)}$. Values for functional power are based upon $F_{(2,119)}$.

[b] Unvariate F scores are only meaningful when overall Manova results are significant, thus, they are not reported.

244

TABLE 4

POWER PERCEPTIONS
BASED ON SIZE OF COMPANY

| Function and Decision | Mean Power for Size of Firm | | F[a] | P Less Than |
| | 1,000 or Less Employees | More than 1,000 Employees | | |
|---|---|---|---|---|
| Product Selection | | | 5.7 | .001 |
| Purchasing | 22.1 | 13.8 | 17.0 | .001 |
| Production | 13.3 | 15.9 | 1.4 | .232 |
| Engineering | 54.7 | 59.5 | 2.9 | .095 |
| Supplier Selection | | | 4.7 | .004 |
| Purchasing | 70.0 | 58.2 | 13.3 | .001 |
| Production | 2.8 | 5.4 | 4.0 | .049 |
| Engineering | 15.3 | 23.4 | 8.6 | .004 |

[a]Values for the product selection decision and the supplier selection decision are based upon F (3,118). Values for functional power are based upon F (1,120).

The third hypothesis tested was that there would be no difference in the perceptions of the various functions based on the product characteristics of technical complexity, product modification, product installation, product similarity, rate of product improvement, or supplier similarity. These six product factors were developed from Fisher [4]. The factors are defined in the appendix.

Results of this hypothesis, as indicated in Table 5, were mixed. Analysis of the power distribution showed that purchasing had significantly more power in the product selection decision when products were technically simple than when they were technically complex. There were, however, no overall differences in the power distributions of the functions in the supplier selection decision based upon the technical complexity of the products. No overall differences in the power distributions of the functions were observed in the product selection decision based upon the amount of product modification need. There were, however, differences in the power distributions in the supplier selection decision based upon the amount of product modification needed. Purchasing power was significantly greater for products requiring much modification while engineering had more relative power at lower levels of modification. Purchasing had significantly more power in the selection of products that did not require significant amounts of complicated installation. Power of the other functions did not vary significantly. Product installation did not cause any significant variation in the power distribution in the supplier selection decision. There were no significant differences in the relative power of the functions based upon the amount of product similarity or upon the rate of product improvement. Finally, no significant differences in the product selection decision were observed based upon similarity of suppliers. In the supplier selection decision, the power of engineering and purchasing varied significantly based upon supplier similarity, however, inspection of the actual power means did not reveal any pattern in the changes.

TABLE 5

ANALYSIS OF VARIANCE FOR PRODUCT FACTORS

| Source of Variation | F[a] | P Less Than |
|---|---|---|
| Technical Complexity | | |
| Product Selection | 2.0 | .022 |
| Purchasing | 4.4 | .002 |
| Production | .4 | .816 |
| Engineering | 1.4 | .224 |
| Supplier Selection | 1.1 | .358[b] |
| Product Modification | | |
| Product Selection | 1.0 | .487[b] |
| Supplier Selection | 2.1 | .019 |
| Purchasing | 5.7 | .001 |
| Production | .4 | .780 |
| Engineering | 3.7 | .007 |
| Product Installation | | |
| Product Selection | 2.0 | .026 |
| Purchasing | 3.3 | .014 |
| Production | 2.1 | .086 |
| Engineering | 1.5 | .218 |
| Supplier Selection | .8 | .236[b] |
| Product Similarity | | |
| Product Selection | .4 | .946[b] |
| Supplier Selection | .6 | .846[b] |
| Rate of Product Improvement | | |
| Product Selection | 1.7 | .056[b] |
| Supplier Selection | 1.1 | .385[b] |
| Supplier Similarity | | |
| Product Selection | 1.6 | .098[b] |
| Supplier Selection | 2.3 | .007 |
| Purchasing | 5.8 | .001 |
| Production | 1.0 | .395 |
| Engineering | 5.6 | .001 |

[a]Values for the product selection and supplier selection decisions are based upon F (12,305). Values for individual functions in each case are based upon F (4,117).

[b]Univariate F's are only meaningful when overall Manova results are significant, thus, they are not reported when the Manova is not significant.

CONCLUSIONS AND IMPLICATIONS

Industrial buying was shown to be a complex process. Many factors determined the relative power of the participants. While the present study cannot be generalized to all industrial purchasing decisions, several factors were found to affect the relative power of the various participants. The power of the participants, purchasing, production, and engineering was found to differ significantly between the selection of suppliers and the selection of products. Purchasing was found to have more relative power in the selection of suppliers, the selection of products which are produced for stock, the selection of suppliers of castings, and the selection of products and suppliers in smaller companies. Relative to product characteristics, purchasing was found to have more relative power in the selection of products which were technically simple, or required minimal installation, while it had more relative power in the selection of suppliers when there was supplier similarity or extensive product modification.

On the other hand, engineering had more relative power in the product selection decision. Engineering had more power in the selection of products which were produced for customer order, the selection of suppliers of electronic components, and the selection of suppliers in larger companies. Engineering was found to have more relative power in the selection of suppliers when there was supplier similarity and when minimal product modification was required. The only area where production had more relative power was in the selection of suppliers in larger companies.

The results of this study reinforce previous findings that several groups of participants play an influential role in the industrial buying decision. In addition, the study supports previous findings that engineering dominates the selection of products while purchasing dominates the selection of suppliers. Size of firm and the type of manufacture have a significant impact on the distributions of power within the buying firm. These two factors may provide important insights for developing marketing strategies aimed at industrial firms.

Traditional product factors which are often cited as important in identifying the extent of participant involvement in the industrial buying decision were not shown to be good predictors of relative power. It appears that these factors have limited value in uncovering insights about the power relationships in modified rebuys of industrial components. Care should be exercised when using product factors as a basis for developing marketing strategy. Further research should be undertaken to extend the results to other types of purchase decisions and products.

## APPENDIX

### PRODUCT FACTOR DEFINITIONS

1. Technical Complexity - the amount of technical capabilities required to develop and manufacture the product.

2. Product Modification - the amount of physical change made to the product between the time it was received by the firm until the firm product was completed.

3. Product Installation - the amount of special skilled installation required.

4. Product Similarity - the amount of product similarity between manufacturers of the same product class.

5. Rate of Product Improvement - the rate of product improvement changes within the product class.

6. Supplier Similarity - the amount of similarity between the various firms supplying the product class. Similarity was based upon factors such as ability to meet delivery schedules, quality control, and ability to perform in accordance with the terms of contract.

### REFERENCES

1. Buckner, Hugh, How British Industry Buys, (London: Hutchinson & Co., 1967).

2. Cooley, William W., and Paul R. Lohnes, Multivariate Data Analyses, (New York: John Wiley and Sons, Inc., 1971).

3. Faris, Charles W., and Patrick J. Robinson, Industrial Buying and Creative Marketing, (Boston: Allyn & Bacon, Inc., 1967).

4. Fisher, Lawrence, Industrial Marketing, (London: Business Books Limited, 1969).

5. Gorman, Ronald H., "Role Conception and Purchasing Behavior," Journal of Purchasing, 7 (February, 1971), 57-61.

6. Haas, Robert W., Industrial Marketing Management, (New York: Petrocelli/Charter, 1976).

7. Hall, Ogden H., "An Analyses of Power and Its Role in the Decision-Making Process of the Formal Organization," unpublished Ph.D. dissertation, Louisiana State University (Baton Rouge, Louisiana: Louisiana State University, 1964).

8. March, James G., "An Introduction to the Theory and Measurement of Influence," American Political Review, 69 (June, 1955), 445-451.

9. Meier, Robert E., "A Factor Analytic Investigation of the Industrial Purchasing Manager Position," unpublished Ph.D. dissertation, University of Illinois, (Urbana, Illinois: University of Illinois, 1972).

10. "64 Per Cent of Industrial Calls are on the Wrong Man," Sales Management, 82 (February 6, 1959), 53-56.

11. Scientific American, Inc., How Industry Buys, (New York: Scientific American, Inc., 1969).

12. Webster, Frederick E., Jr., and Yoram Wind, Organizational Buying Behavior, (Englewood Cliffs, New Jersey: Prentice-Hall, Inc., 1972).

13. Wilson, Aubrey, The Assessment of Industrial Markets, (London: Hutchinson & Co., 1968).

RECONCEPTUALIZING INDUSTRIAL BUYING BEHAVIOR:
TOWARD IMPROVED RESEARCH APPROACHES

Wesley J. Johnston, University of Pittsburgh
Thomas V. Bonoma, University of Pittsburgh

## ABSTRACT

The authors begin by discussing two anomalies characterizing the study of industrial buying behavior: they refer
to (1) the amount of utilizable research knowledge available, and (2) the perceived importance of this area to
marketing thought. To explore these anomalies they move
to a consideration of the traditional assumptions made by
researchers in their attempts to understand the industrial
buyer. These assumptions are viewed as unrealistic and
not parsimonious with the nature of the industrial buying
transaction; they are cited as perhaps the cause of a lack
of cumulative progress in industrial buying behavior research. A new conceptual paradigm for studying buyer behavior is then presented with an examination of what it
could mean to this area of study. A model of exchanges in
industrial buying behavior is also presented as a fallout
of the "dyadic" approach or paradigm offered here.

## INTRODUCTION

The importance of understanding industrial buying behavior
to an integrated marketing science is undebatable by any
criteria. Yet, the general topic of industrial buying is
a study in contradictory beliefs. In a recent exhaustive
review of the literature [15] over 1,000 references were
cited. As the author of this review pointed out, however,
the popular belief is that there is not a substantial
amount of research or knowledge about organizational-in-
dustrial buying behavior. It is apparently the case, then,
that a very vast amount of industrial buying literature
has made little impact either in terms of its summary value
or explanatory power within marketing. When all excuses
about the obscure industrial publication outlets or the
"boring" subject matter are put aside, the critical question is "why?".

Secondly, industrial buying behavior has traditionally
been conceptualized as a special sub-area of industrial
marketing [9, 13, 21]. Industrial marketing, as a field
of study, has itself been frequently defined by default or
by what type of marketing it is not: It is not consumer
marketing, it is not (necessarily) international marketing,
and it is not at all "direct marketing" [11]. Industrial
marketing may be said to consist of those residual categories of "other markets," including producer (industrial),
reseller and government markets, which although not of
"prime importance" or a "major rationale for the existence
of the other markets," nonetheless are "large ones and
challenging to the marketer" [11, p. 98].

As these summary phrases tend to indicate, industrial marketing has apparently been considered a less immediate,
exciting, or clearly delineated subject than others among
the marketing subdisciplines. It is what marketing academicians study when they are not addressing consumer issues of "prime importance,"[1] even if the dollar compari-

sons indicating that these attributions of importance may
be very displaced [7, 9, 11, 19]. For instance, the dollar volume involved in industrial purchases far exceeds
those of the consumer market in the United States. By
1980, it is estimated that the dollar volume of the industrial, reseller and government markets combined will exceed the gross national product.[2]

Leaving out the government and reseller markets, over 9
million different industrial production units currently
exist in the country, employing over 52 million workers
and generating an annual national income of 705 billions
of dollars. It was estimated that even the smallest of
these firms spend over $70,000 each on industrial purchases
in their manufacturing process [9]. Since this estimate is
almost 10 years old, let us update it with a conservative
estimate allowing only for the general wholesale price index increment. This would put the total industrial purchasing costs closer to $150,000 for small business expen-
ditures today.

The two anomalies we believe exist for industrial buying
behavior in summary read as follows:

(1) A significant amount of the industrial buying behavior
literature seems to have failed to impact on marketing
thought or practice.

(2) The tendency for marketers to overlook the importance
of studying the industrial buyer is unfortunate as well as
unfounded when the relative importance of the consumer and
industrial areas are compared.

We believe the reasons for these puzzling inconsistencies
can perhaps be partially found in current methods of conceptualization and what in our opinion are inappropriate
research approaches. We initially examine the traditional
assumptions found in the study of industrial buying behavior before offering a reconceptualization designed to help
remove these inconsistencies and increase the payback from
industrial buying researchers.

## TRADITIONAL ASSUMPTIONS OF INDUSTRIAL BUYING BEHAVIOR

1. Industrial buying behavior may be studied separately
from selling behavior as actions taken by a separate individual or individuals in the firm.

With the possible exceptions of Swallow's [17] introductory
remarks and the recurrent "problem" of reciprocity in the
industrial buying process [1, 12, 20], we found no cita-
tion in over 200 articles reviewed [4] counter to this
"separation" assumption. One of the major consequences of
this separation assumption has been a primary focus in the
study of industrial buying behavior on "individualistic"
variables as these affect the industrial buying process.
Thus, such constructs as (individual) choice processes,

---

[1]A review of both the Journal of Marketing Research
and the Journal of Marketing for 1976 revealed that articles oriented toward consumer behavior issues out numbered
those concerned with industrial buying behavior by almost
to 1.

---

[2]The reader may ask how this is possible, for certainly the GNP includes all $ sums of products and services
produced. The reason is that the GNP figure operates on a
value added basis not calculating all of the myriad transfer payments that occur in any market.

personality and intrapersonal dynamics, economic notions of individual expected utility and rationality are seen as appropriate theoretical variables for investigation of the industrial buyer.

Clearly, the theoretical coherence of these variables depends totally on acceptance of the "separation" assumption. Nonacceptance, construing industrial buying behavior in some other manner, would generate a different set of constructs.

For example, there are several other ways to view industrial buying behavior --- two major competing alternatives can be called the "dyadic" model and the "system" model [3]. The former asserts that buying is an interactive process which cannot be studied in isolation from selling, and that buyer seller dyads (two person groups) are the basic units of analysis for studying transactions of the firm. The systems assumption goes one step further than the dyadic paradigm and asserts that buying behavior can only be understood as some systemic component affected by all inputs, throughputs and outputs affecting the corporation generally.

2. The appropriate way in which to approach understanding of industrial buying behavior is through Stimulus (S)-Response (R) models.

Closely related to the "separation" assumption is the Stimulus-Response view of causal inference. The industrial buying process is viewed as a "response" generated by an (individual) buyer as a result of his or her subjection to various stimuli by industrial salesmen, promotions, and so on. "A model of organizational buying behavior can take one of two forms: (1) a stimulus-response type model which relates inputs (marketing stimuli) to output (buyers' response); or (2) a stimulus-respondent-response model which consists of a set of propositions about how the buyer responds to marketing stimuli, and may provide some generalizable answers about how inputs lead to outputs [19, p. 8]." There are other options for use besides these S-R or S-O (organism)-R models. For instance, a base assumption more oriented to the transactional nature of industrial buying would not select an SOR viewpoint, but rather one which made interactive constructs (say, interdependence) the critical mediators between parties to a purchase transaction.

3. Choice processes, and intraindividual notions of decision "rationality" or "optimality", as well as information processes are the heart of the industrial purchase.

The assumption that choice processes and prescriptive decision optimality indices should be the major explanatory construct in the industrial buying area is not surprising in light of the two previous assumptions. The emphases on cost factors and personal selling processes in industrial marketing are viewed as the major distinguishing variables between this market and the consumer market. There is nothing inherent in the industrial purchasing transaction which demands that this assumption be made -- if minor or cost trivial decisions were accorded equal focus with unique purchases of expensive items -- we would venture to suggest the descriptive bulk of the literature would indicate that such concerns are not central to explaining the ongoing process [4].

4. The phenomena studied in industrial buying area are significantly different in nature from those occurring in the consumer behavior area.

This assumption has several subparts: it is said that more individuals, with more widely disparate utility schedules, are involved in the industrial buying process; the type and importance of goods bought and sold is said to differ; the type of advertising approach (personal

selling vs. mass media) to be widely divergent between the two areas of marketing; the reciprocity phenomenon is said to be absent from the consumer behavior area; as well as other differences. In reality, the differences between the markets can be widely disparate or highly similar depending upon the type of transactions examined [6, 10]. The amount of generalizability between industrial buying behavior and consumer behavior depends on whether one compares like or different-type interaction settings.

## MOVING AWAY FROM THE TRADITIONAL ASSUMPTIONS

Because we do not see the current assumptions and variable focus of research on industrial buying behavior as ones that have led to a coherent attack on the phenomenon, we felt the need to attempt a reconceptualization of the subject. We desired that this re-thinking of industrial buying behavior be more conducive toward the development of explanatory attempts, and more directive for a concerted empirical effort. The essential seed for this reconceptualization requires a shift in the paradigm used to structure research approaches to industrial buying behavior. The shift we recommend moves from a noninteractive, primarily individually based paradigm that takes the purchasing agent or the firm as its central focus toward a transactional, interactive, mutual interdependency paradigm taking interactions between the purchasing agent and relevant others both internal and external to buying firm as the basic units of analysis.

Just as it is impossible to understand or even successfully examine "leadership" as some innate characteristic of the leader, so it is impossible to come to terms with industrial marketing when one sees buying as a function or characteristic of only the buyer. Marketing has perhaps been best categorized as exchange [2, 11]. This in itself makes studying only the buyer in a transaction a meaningless exercise, since the essential phenomena observed are interactional and relational, not individualistic. One needs to ask not only what happens to the buyer in industrial marketing but also what is happening to the seller: how is he influenced by the transaction(s). For instance, isn't it important to know what effects reciprocal sales tactics have on the seller using them as well as on the buyer? Does it require the seller to reorganize his managerial hierarchy by adding a trade relations department? Does it weaken the seller's marketing department by making the sales representatives fat, lazy, and dependent upon the trade relations contacts? Such research hypotheses become not only evident but essential from a dyadic perspective on industrial buying.

The unit paradigm is limited in scope and explanatory power. It poses a number of obstacles for the growth of marketing theory, and is quite possibly the cause of the two anomalies cited in the introduction.

## NEW LAMPS FOR OLD, NEW PARADIGMS FOR OLD

Comparing the suggested new dyadic paradigm with the current unit paradigm is perhaps the best way to highlight both the benefits and consequences of each.

The unit paradigm is primarily limited in its subject matter to investigations of the behavior or actions of single buyers (or groups of buyers acting in a concerted way) or to the properties or characteristics of these actors. Typically, under unit examination are individual purchasing agents, suppliers, salesmen, or advertisers. Occasionally, the unit of analysis will be a channel of distribution, an industry, or a market or bazaar. Thus, under the current paradigm such behaviors as the preferences of industrial consumers, the response of middlemen to various deals, the risk of taking bribes by purchasing agents, and the closing activities of salesmen are the "meat" of research investigations.

In order to explain the variations in the concept being examined under the unit paradigm of analysis, marketers have primarily relied on the classical S-R model or variants of it. The focus is thus limited to the "functional relationship" between observed changes in behavior and changes in the environment. The individualist S-R approach, with its focus on choice processes and rationality within the purchasing agent, has been applied extensively in industrial marketing. Even at the macro level, the industrial organization is viewed as "pushed" or "pulled" by environmental forces (stimuli) [5]. Problems that can be identified as a result of the use of the unit paradigm for analysis of industrial buying behavior are:

1. The unit paradigm takes a naive and unidirectional view of social causation in the industrial buying behavior area as "moving" from stimulus to response; it is not acknowledged that responses also influence their stimuli, as in classical operant conditioning.

2. The well known problem of reductionism is prevalent in the unit paradigm. Forcing what is in reality a transactional phenomenon into an individualistic framework, and then attempting to paste or tape it back together is essentially futile.

3. The most basic, and most serious, problem is the neglect of unit paradigm views of the social character of industrial buying behavior. Purchases are better viewed as negotiated settlements between all those individuals involved internally in the buying firm and those external to it (i.e., intermediate marketers, competing sales representatives, the government, and the general public). These interactions lead to a purchase decision that is truly some social resultant of these interactive forces rather than any individual response.

In contrast, our proposed view of reconceptualization can be called a dyadic paradigm [3, 4]. It has as its basic tenent the required assumption that the smallest analyzable and meaningful unit of marketing behavior is the resultant of the _interaction_ of two individuals or groups, i.e., the _exchange_ itself and not the _change_ in either party. Thus the dyadic approach begins with the smallest irreducible socially meaningful unit, and marketing _is_ social science. Theory building with the dyadic paradigm, in contrast to the unit paradigm, is a matter of degree, not a difference in kind. Complex _social_ behavior is explained with simpler _social_ concepts. These relationships are inferred from events, actions, or other observable phenomena and often depend on the shared meaning's mediating the interaction. The characteristics of a dyadic interaction can be classified as the following:

The parties in the sales/purchasing relation share some values or have mutual interests. They may want something the other has or in some way be dependent on each other. The mutuality of interests will sometimes take the form of cooperation, alliances, coalitions, or other relationships. Sometimes the interaction will involve conflict of interest of disagreement over certain issues.

The dyadic relationship will invariably contain instances of social influence attempts by one or both parties. These social influence attempts may involve promises, threats, warnings, recommendations, or the attempt to control information or other cues [18]. Deception, flattery, ingratiation, or similar strategies may involved in the purchasing agent-sales representative interaction as well as between the purchasing agent and relevant others within the buying firm [16].

3. The nature of the buyer-seller relationship and its outcome may be constrained or shaped by forces in the purchasing situation. Alternative sources of supply outside the relationship, the influence of a powerful third party within the buying center lobbying for a different vendor, or socio-economic restrictions in the immediate environment such as a budget cut may affect the outcome of a buyer-seller interaction.

4. The characteristics of the parties involved may affect the course of an exchange. Bargaining and negotiation have been shown to be affected by such variables as the historical pattern of offers made, personality characteristics, individual or organizational needs, channels of distribution, and the availability of resources [14].

5. Norms concerning how one ought to behave may play a structuring role in dyadic relations. They can invoke compelling behavioral expectations and demands upon either or both sides in the buyer-seller interaction. Caveat emptor is not really an acceptable position for an industrial seller to take. Norms of bargaining require that "within acceptable limits" each party tries to improve his position. Once either party is too disadvantaged in the negotiations a "walkout" or deadlock is the likely resultant with no transaction taking place. In most sales representative-purchasing agent exchanges norms of etiquette, reciprocity, deference, demeanor and often times respect and sometimes close friendship can be seen to exist. As a matter of fact the number of high value sales that are accomplished through high level friendships would probably totally swamp any rationalistic, stimulus-response, unit analysis model. Of course purchases are often subject to competitive bidding, but even this does not eliminate friendship bonds from being influential, for industrial buyers can certainly "work with their friends" to help make them competitive. These norms often generate behaviors of a ritual-like character. Take the courtesy call the industrial salesman makes on his small buyers or those he "knows" will not buy at this time, these fulfill expectations and demands of the members of the dyad. The "business lunch" is another example of an almost ritualistic interaction [8].

6. Dyadic relations ebb and flow with the individual actions and purposive behavior of the parties involved. The sales representative and the buyer both have plans, goals, set ways of behaving, and intentions they hope to satisfy. Sometimes, these are the object of negotiation. Invariably, they set restrictions on what is acceptable or not in an exchange and serve as the starting point for the give and take of the interaction. Hence, while a dyadic view of industrial buying allows incorporation of the S-R perspective, the reverse is definitely not true.

7. A common element in most dyads is the uncertainty of the outcome. The course of the relation depends upon the offers, counteroffers, and mutual adjustments made by the parties in the on-going involvement. Interpretation, evaluation, decision making, and exchange are all processes occurring in this dyadic process. Table 1 contrasts the traditional unit paradigm with the new dyadic paradigm.

We are not evil magicians as in the story of Alladin; will the reader make the trade? If one is willing to accept the dyadic view of industrial buying behavior the process can then be modeled as in Figure 1.

THE INDUSTRIAL BUYING PROCESS AS EXCHANGE

As mentioned before marketing has been typologized as exchange [2, 11]. This is perhaps the best of the general conceptualizations of marketing and certainly the most flexible. It is built, as well, upon dyadic interactions. As our model depicts there are at least 5 different types

*TABLE 1
TWO FUNDAMENTAL PARADIGMS IN INDUSTRIAL BUYING BEHAVIOR

| | PERSPECTIVE | |
| FEATURE | UNIT PARADIGM | DYADIC PARADIGM |
| --- | --- | --- |
| Structure | Learning Model | Social Model |
| | S $\longrightarrow$ O $\longrightarrow$ R | A $\longleftrightarrow$ B |
| Major Process | Exogenous Influence | Reciprocal influence, mutual problem solving |
| Explanatory Mechanisms | Stimulus-Response | Interdependence |
| Typical Models or Pre-Models | Sheth's organization Buying Model  Attitude and Multi-Attribute Information Processing Models | Ammer's "Realistic Reciprocity" Bagozzi's exchange model |
| Typical Foci | Reactivity Closed Systems Prediction Control | Social exchange. Power/influence relations. Bargaining & negotiations. Conflict, cooperation, competition. Other social relationships. Explanation and understanding. |
| Typical Shortcomings | Reductionistic/Mechanistic Violates social character of marketing Neglect of the meaning of products, actions, etc., in mediating behavior (e.g., through symbols) Failure to account for purposeful behavior. | Most approaches have been applied to only customer-salesmen situation. A majority of models have represented only a limited set of social processes. |

*Adapted from reference 3.

of dyadic relations in the process of industrial buying behavior which recommend themselves for study:

1. The sales representative-purchasing agent relationship is obviously an exchange of information and help in problem solving on the part of the seller for credit for the specific "sale" given by the buyer. Other exchanges can take place as well. In a deteriorated situation, fraud and chicanery can be exchanged for distrust.

2. The sales representative exchanges his sales efforts with his own company for money in the form of his commission. Sometimes there are side payments such as a trip to the Bahamas for meeting a special sales quota. Recognition and praise are often exchanged for loyalty.

3. The purchasing agent exchanges his talents and abilities of buying and problem solving efforts with his company for money usually in the form of a salary. However, sometimes buyers are rewarded in the form of a percentage of the volume of purchases. If this reward is insufficient in the eyes of the purchasing agent or if his own interests come before those of the company, he may look elsewhere for more rewarding exchanges, i.e., bribery.

4. The most clear cut exchange occurs between the buying and selling firm where the product/service is exchanged for money or credit. Reciprocal trade relations may often develop between the two companies. An interesting type of reciprocity has arisen recently in critical shortage periods of essential production materials. This reciprocity has not been of the type "I'll buy from you if you'll

FIGURE 1
EXCHANGES IN INDUSTRIAL MARKETING

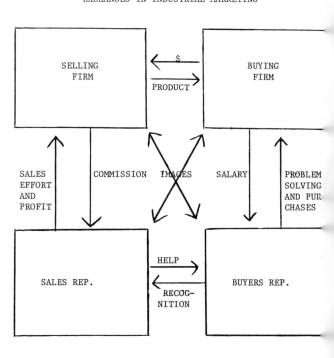

buy from me" but "I'll sell to you if you'll sell to me" a critical difference.

5. Images of the buying firm are held by the sales representative while the purchasing agent harbors feelings about the selling firm these are also exchanges generated in the industrial buying process.

An exchange which we will not list but need to mention is the exchange that becomes obvious if we move our industrial buying process model into a system perspective. This exchange is the one that occurs between the model and the environment for the industrial buying process is clearly an open system, one that takes inputs from the environment, processes the throughput and returns output back in the environment.

## CONCLUSION

It is always easy to offer to barter new lamps for old, for there is a natural human desire for novelty which makes "tradeup marketing" easy with academicians or with queens. Yet, in this case there is a purpose to model replacement. We feel that by the adoption of a "dyadic" view of industrial marketing coherence, understandability and parsimony will be added to the industrial buying process. The transactional nature of industrial purchasing we have depicted requires a research approach that has at its core relational constructs. So that we will not be accused of performing "merely another exercise in theory construction sin validation in the area of industrial marketing," we feel compelled at this point to offer some specific suggestions for further operationalization and empirical research:

1. View the causal relationships in industrial marketing as bidirectional. Not only is the buyer affected by actions the seller takes, but the seller is also affected by the buyer. The buyer may even initiate the interaction.

2. Concentrate on the exchanges, power and influence relations that take place.

3. Examine the bargaining and negotiation processes that are typically present in industrial marketing.

4. Finally, understand that the result of any buyer-seller interaction is more than just the actions taken by the buyer. The selling firm, its representative, the buyer and the firm he or she represents are all changed by any and every interaction.

## REFERENCES

. Ammer, D.S. "Realistic Reciprocity," Harvard Business Review, 40 (January-February, 1962), 116-24.

. Bagozzi, R.P. "Marketing as Exchange," Journal of Marketing, 39 (October 1975), 32-9.

. Bonoma, T.V., R.P. Bagozzi and G. Zaltman. "The Dyadic Paradigm with Specific Application Towards Industrial Marketing," University of Pittsburgh Working Paper #138, University of Pittsburgh, 1975.

. Bonoma, T.V., G. Zaltman and W.J. Johnston. Organizational Buying Behavior: Review, Reanalysis and Reconceptualization. Marketing Science Institute Monograph, in press.

. Cyert, R.M. and J.G. March. A Behavioral Theory of the Firm. Englewood Cliffs, N.J.: Prentice-Hall, Inc., 1963.

6. Cyert, R.M., H.A. Simon and D.B. Trow. "Observation of a Business Decision," Journal of Business, 29 (October 1956), 237-48.

7. Dening, J. Marketing Industrial Goods. London: Business Publications Ltd., 1968.

8. Halvorson, P.J. and W. Rudelius. "Is There a Free Lunch?" Journal of Marketing, 41 (January 1977), 44-9.

9. Hill, R.M., R.S. Alexander and J.S. Cross. Industrial Marketing, 4th Ed. Homewood, Ill.: Richard D. Irwin, Inc., 1975.

10. Hill, R.W. and A. Meidan. "The Use of Quantitative Techniques in Industrial Marketing," Industrial Marketing Management, 4 (June 1975), 59-68.

11. Kotler, P. Marketing Management: Analysis, Planning and Control, 3rd Ed. Englewood Cliffs, N.J.: Prentice-Hall, Inc., 1975.

12. Moyer, R. "Reciprocity: Retrospect and Prospect," Journal of Marketing, 34 (October 1970), 47-54.

13. Risley, G. Modern Industrial Marketing: A Decision Making Approach. New York: McGraw Hill Book Company, 1972.

14. Rubin, J.Z. and B.R. Brown. Social Psychology of Bargaining and Negotiations. New York: Academic Press, 1975.

15. Sheth, J. "Recent Developments in Organizational Buying Behavior," University of Illinois Faculty Working Paper #317, University of Illinois, 1976.

16. Strauss, G. "Tactics of Lateral Relationship: The Purchasing Agent," Administration Science Quarterly, 7 (September 1962), 161-86.

17. Swallow, S. "Industrial Marketing: The Buyer's Viewpoint," in New Ideas in Industrial Marketing. P. Coram and R. Hall (Eds.) London: Staple Press, 1970.

18. Tedeschi, J.T., B.R. Schlenker and T.V. Bonoma. Conflict, Power, & Games: The Experimental Study of Interpersonal Relations. Chicago: Alding Publishing Company, 1973.

19. Webster, F.E., Jr. and Y. Wind. Organizational Buying Behavior. Englewood Cliffs, N.J.: Prentice-Hall, Inc., 1972.

20. Weigand, R.E. "The Problems of Managing Reciprocity," California Management Review, University of California reprint, 1973.

21. Wilson, A. The Assessment of Industrial Markets. London: Hutchinson of London, 1968.

# AN EXPLORATORY STUDY OF COMPLIANCE GAINING
## TECHNIQUES IN BUYER BEHAVIOR

Noel Capon, University of California, Los Angeles
John Swasy, University of California, Los Angeles

## ABSTRACT

A role playing methodology was employed to examine the effectiveness of a variety of compliance gaining techniques in achieving a purchase response in buyer-seller interation. The compliance gaining techniques were differentially effective overall, suggesting that the assumptions underlying the methodology were met. Further, situational dimensions of the interaction were found to have an impact on the perceived effectivenss of a number of the techniques. A factor analysis was employed to develop a structure of the compliance gaining techniques. The structure differed from general typologies of power and influence, suggesting that for the study of buyer-seller interaction, more specific typologies are required.

## INTRODUCTION

Many consumer and organizational buyer situations involve active attempts by one party to gain compliance from another. Such compliance gaining techniques are fundamtal to the study of social influence and power, a broad field of research which spans many disciplines. However, despite an extensive research tradition, the impact of the social influence and power literature on the study of buyer-seller interaction has been relatively minor. Only Busch and Wilson [2] and Spiro and Perreault [20] appear to have used concepts drawn directly from the field for the development of their research studies.[1]

The focus of this paper is on the effectivenss and structure of various compliance gaining techniques within the framework of the buyer-seller interaction. Specifically, (1) several theoretical frameworks of social influence are reviewed, (2) a role-playing methodology for the study of compliance gaining techniques is presented and (3) the results of an exploratory study aimed at assessing the structure underlying various compliance gaining techniques and the relationship between several situational factors and the perceived effectiveness of various compliance gaining techniques are presented.

Theoretical Background

A rich source of ideas for application to the study of buyer behavior in salesmen-influenced situations is the extensive number of power and influence typologies that have been developed in organizational theory, sociology, and social psychology. In organizational theory Etzioni [9] has described three mechanisms of influence: the mediating of physical sanctions (coercive power), material resources (remunerative power) and symbolic rewards and deprivations (normative power).

From sociology Parsons [17] has suggested four broad types of influence. Two influence types (inducement and deterrence) occur when the influencer emphasises the situational advantages and disadvantages of compliance or non-compliance. In persuasion, the reasons why compliance would result in positive outcomes for the influencee, independent of the situation, are emphasized. Finally, activation of committments occurs when the influencer emphasises why non-compliance would be "wrong", based on the influencee's own beliefs.

In the social psychology literature, Kelman [14] and French and Raven [11] offer additional perspectives on methods of interpersonal influence. Kelman suggests the three different concepts of compliance, identification, and internalization to explain attitude change. The first process, compliance, describes those changes which stem from influencer's ability to reward or punish the influence. Changes described by the identification process result from the influencee's desire to be similar to the influencer. Finally internalization, describes changes which are due to the influencee's acceptance of the influencer's reasoning, beliefs or values.

The French and Raven typology describes influence processes in terms of the "bases" for the influencer's (A) power over the influencee (B). These power bases include expert, coercion, reward, referent, legitimate and information. The expert power basis stems from the influencee's attribution of superior skills or knowledge to the influencer. Coercion power rests on B's belief that A will punish him for not complying. The reward power of an influencer (A) over an influencee (B) is based on A's ability to mediate positive outcomes and to remove or decrease negative outcomes received by B. Referent power results largely from the influencee's feelings of identification with the influencer and desire to maintain similarity with the influencer. Legitimate power stems from internalized values of the influencee (cultural values and norms, group norms, or role prescriptions) which dictate that the influencee is obligated to comply with the influencer. Finally, information power differs from the previous bases in that it is "independent" of the influencing agent, per se, and rather stems from the logic or reasoning of the communication provided by the influencing agent.[2]

While these theoretical perspectives clearly overlap, there has been little empirical work aimed at integrating these approaches. Only Marwell and Schmidt [15] who assessed the relationships among the perceived effectiveness of many of these influence techniques across a wide variety of interpersonl influence situations have attempted such integration. Using an oblique factor analysis they claimed support for general factors similar to French and Raven's reward, coercion and expert based power.

Many of these influence concepts have direct relevance to the study of buyer-seller interactions, and have been studied in this context [2]. However, there has been no empirical attempt to specify and formulate a general taxonomy of influence techniques for the buyer-seller situation Such a taxonomy might provide a valuable structure for guiding research on the buyer-seller situation.

Methodology for the Study of Compliance Gaining Techniques

An ideal method for investigating the structure and effectiveness of a variety of compliance gaining techniques migh involve collecting behavioral and other measures on a larg sample of buyers who were subjected to a variety of techni ques, from a large number of salesmen, in many different buying situations. Effectiveness in such a study might be measured by sales or changes in a buyer's intentions to

---

[1]Busch, Bush and Hair [3] have recently reviewed the use of social power theory in marketing.

[2]Information power does not appear in French & Raven' original conception of power. It was introduced by Deutsc and Gerhard [7]. For a discussion of this typology see Raven and Kruglanski [18].

purchase, attitude towards, or knowledge of the product.

One step in making such a study more manageable, albeit with some loss in external validity, would be to have subjects respond with "perceptions of effectiveness", rather than using actual effectiveness, in a series of simulated buying environments using scenarios. While such perceptions could be measured from either side of the exchange process, the buyer or the seller, it is likely that each actor would have different perceptions of the effectivenss of specific compliance gaining techniques [13]. A focus on buyer behavior suggests that measuring effectiveness as perceived by the buyer is the appropriate route to follow, but the likelihood of socially desirable responses seems high.

One approach to this problem of response bias is to employ a role playing methodology. By placing buyers in selling roles, buyer's perceptions of compliance gaining techniques might be tapped indirectly. Thus, when asked how effective a compliance gaining technique would be if they used it, the subjects' belief of their own experiences and personal responses to the technique would perhaps be obtained.

In summary, the employment of this methodology for the study of buyers' models of compliance gaining techniques requires the following assumptions which are made for this exploratory study:

1) The responses of "perceived effectiveness" represent meaningful surrogates for changes either in behavioral, attitudinal or cognitive states towards the compliant act; and

2) Subjects are aware of and will utilize their own personal reactions towards a compliance gaining technique when assessing perceived effectiveness.

METHOD

Scenarios

Scenarios which depicted a cross section of buyer-seller situations were developed. Two levels on three dimensions thought likely to influence the perceived effectivenss of compliance gaining techniques were chosen, the resulting combinations producing eight different scenarios. The three dimensions were type of buyer, level of perceived risk of decision, and type of relationship. Type of buyer, whether a consumer or acting on behalf of an organization, is a dichotomy much employed within marketing. Theoretical frameworks of buyer behavior have tended to be developed for consumers [8,12,16] and organizations [19,21] separately. Second, the extensive research on perceived risk has highlighted different behavior patterns at different levels of perceived risk [1,6], and high and low perceived risk were selected.[3] Third, the type of relationship in which the influence attempt takes place, whether continuing or a one-time relationship, was thought likely to be important [20], and was therefore selected.

Since one portion of the study sought to assess the impact of these dimensions on the perceived effectiveness of the compliance gaining techniques an attempt was made to match each scenario in terms of other factors thought to be important, such as product, level of seller competition and buyer knowledge of the product. Thus, in each situation the product was a camera, other competing sellers were available to the buyer and the buyer appeared to have average knowledge of the product. Each scenario ended

with a statement emphasizing the three manipulated situation factors.[4] The operationalizations of the manipulated situation factors are noted in Table 1 and an example of a scenario is presented in Figure 1.

TABLE 1

OPERATIONALIZATIONS OF MANIPULATED DIMENSIONS

| Buyer Type | 1. Consumer | Buyer is shopping for a camera for personal use. |
| | 2. Organizational | Buyer is purchasing agent for company planning camera purchase |
| Perceived Risk | 1. High a. Consumer | An expensive camera (app. $300) is required for taking pictures on vacation and in future for photography as a hobby |
| | b. Organizational | Several very expensive cameras are sought for a critical aspect of the production monitoring system |
| | 2. Low a. Consumer | An inexpensive camera (less than $30) is sought to use for snapshots on vacation |
| | b. Organizational | Several inexpensive cameras are sought for a non-critical aspect of the production monitoring system |
| Relationship | 1. Continuing a. Consumer | Buyer is a regular customer at the camera and photography store |
| | b. Organizational | Buyer is meeting with regular salesman from established supplier |
| | 2. One Time a. Consumer | Buyer from out of state, passing through town en route to a vacation resort |
| | b. Organizational | Buyer is meeting with an unfamiliar salesman who does not anticipate any repeat business |

Compliance Gaining Techniques

Twenty three compliance gaining techniques were selected for the study. Sixteen were identical to those used by Marwell and Schmidt. These techniques and their operationalizations, which were matched with complete accuracy by three judges, are noted in Table 2. Seven additional techniques which were added as being particularly appropriate in a buyer behavior context are also noted in Table 2.

Procedure

Each scenario was typed on a separate page, followed by twenty-three statements, each statement representing a

_____

[3]Perceived risk was conceptualized in a general sense for this study. Cost and the importance of the product to the buyer were manipulated to operationalize the perceived risk factor.

[4]This procedure was employed to direct the subject's attention to these situational factors. While manipulation checks might have been used to verify the treatments, it was the authors' opinion that the manipulations were obvious to the subject.

253

particular compliance gaining technique.[5] Subjects were
asked to rate the effectiveness of each technique in producing a purchase response in the situation described in
each scenario, given that the subject actually used the
technique. A seven point semantic differential response
scale was employed, with end points of "very effective" and
"very ineffective." The subjects, who were sixty-two second year MBA students, rated both an organizational and a
consumer scenario.[6]

## FIGURE 1

### SCENARIO EXAMPLE

You are a sales representative for an industrial photography
equipment and supply company. There are several other competing sales representatives also working in your area.

You have heard via the grapevine, that the DEMCO Corporation,
a company which you have not sold to before, plans to purchase several relatively inexpensive cameras.

You have met with the DEMCO purchasing agent, Mr. Burns,
and you have confirmed that he plans to purchase the cameras.
He indicates that the needed cameras are for a non-critical
aspect of their production monitoring system. He also
states that it is highly unlikely that there will be any
repeat business. Mr. Burns appears to have average knowledge about photography and photographic supplies.

Given the above situation (i.e., you are a sales representative attempting to sell several inexpensive cameras to a
company with whom you do not expect to deal in the future),
please consider each of the following techniques you might
use to convince Mr. Burns to purchase your product.

## TABLE 2

### COMPLIANCE GAINING TECHNIQUES
### EXAMPLE FROM CONSUMER SCENARIOS

Promise*
(If you comply, I will reward you) "You offer
to throw in a free roll of film if Mr. Smith
buys this camera."

Threat*
(If you do not comply, I will punish you)
"You threaten that if Mr. Smith doesn't buy,
you will use him as an example of someone who
doesn't care about quality photography and
equipment when you talk with other customers."

Expertise*
(Positive)
(If you comply you will be rewarded because of
"the nature of things") "You show Mr. Smith
information indicating that people who buy this
camera will not have to buy an expensive adapter
later when a new type of film is sold."

Expertise*
(Negative)
(If you do not comply you will be punished because of the nature of things") "You show Mr.
Smith information indicating that people who do
not buy this camera may have to buy an expensive adapter later when a new type of film is
sold."

---

[5] A typing error resulted in Self Feeling (Negative)
not being rated. The analysis therefore proceeded on the
remaining twenty-two compliance gaining techniques.

[6] The small number of subjects made it necessary for
each subject to rate two scenarios, one consumer and one
organizational. While single scenario rating would have
been preferred, the treatment of each scenario rating as
independent was not believed to be a critical matter in
this exploratory study.

Table 2 Continued

Liking*
(Salesman is friendly and helpful to get customer in "good frame of mind.") "You attempt
to be as pleasant as possible, trying to get
Mr. Smith to like you by projecting a favorable 'personal image.'"

Pre-Giving*
(Salesman rewards customer before requesting
compliance) "You give Mr. Smith a free roll of
film before asking him to buy the camera."

Aversive*
Stimulation
(Salesman continuously punishes customer, making compliance an effortless way of producing
cessation) "You persist in your sales pitch in
an outspoken and aggressive manner and try to
wear down his resistance."

Debt*
(You owe me compliance because of past favors)
"You tell Mr. Smith that since you have spend
so much time waiting on him and answering his
questions he owes it to you to buy this camera."

Moral*
Appeal*
(You are immoral if you do not comply)
"You point out that by not buying this camera
he would be depriving his family of the advan-
tages of high quality photographs."

Self*
Feeling
(Positive)
(You will feel better about yourself if you
comply) "You tell Mr. Smith that he will feel
proud of himself for having obtained the advantages of this new camera."

Self*
Feeling
(Negative)
(You will feel worse about yourself if you do
not comply) "You tell Mr. Smith that he will
feel bad if he does not take this opportunity
to purchase this new camera."

Altercast-*
ing
(Positive)
(A person with good qualities would comply)
"You tell Mr. Smith that since he is a perceptive critic of good photography, he will
naturally want to purchase this new camera."

Alter-*
casting
(Negative)
(Only a person with bad qualities would not
comply) "You tell Mr. Smith that only someone
who had very little knowledge of cameras would
not purchase this camera."

Altruism*
(I need your compliance very badly so do it
for me) "You tell Mr. Smith that your sales
have been poor and that you will be unable to
meet your sales quota if he does not purchase
this camera."

Esteem*
(Positive)
(People you value will think better of you if
you comply) "You tell Mr. Smith that his
family will appreciate him very much if he
purchases this camera."

Esteem*
(Negative)
(People you value will think worse of you if
you do not comply) "You tell Mr. Smith that
his family will be very disappointed in him if
he does not purchase this new camera.

Market
Standing
(Many others have already made the choice I'm
asking you to make) "You show Mr. Smith statistics indicating that many more people purchase from your store than from other stores
in the city."

Social
Standing
(Others will ascribe high status to you if you
comply) "You tell Mr. Smith that his friends
will be very impressed when they hear that he
has purchased this new camera."

Table 2 Continued

| | |
|---|---|
| Competitive Comparison | (Salesman points out superiority to competition) "You emphasize the quality of this camera compared to those available from your chief competitor in the city." |
| Personal Experience | (Salesman expresses personal experience and satisfaction with the product) "You tell Mr. Smith you have an identical camera at home and that you are completely satisfied with it." |
| Personal Similarity | (You and I have similarities and therefore you should accept what I say) "You tell Mr. Smith that from talking with him you can tell that you have similar tastes in photography and that buying this camera would be a good decision for him." |
| Company's Experience | (The supplier has a good reputation) "You tell Mr. Smith that the camera manufacturer has been in business for many years and has an excellent reputation." |
| Product Information | (Salesman supplies data on product attributes) "You describe in detail the construction and features of the camera." |

*Techniques derived from Marwell and Schmidt.

## Analysis

A preliminary analysis phase involved testing whether the compliance gaing techniques differed in perceived effectiveness. This was achieved by means of a one way ANOVA over all situations.

The analysis then proceeded in two stages. First, a 2 x 2 x 2 (type of buyer x level of perceived risk x type of relationship) multivariate analysis of variance was performed for all main and interaction effects, using the perceived effectiveness ratings for the twenty-two compliance gaining techniques as the dependent measures [10]. When significant main and interaction effects were obtained, the univariate effects significant at p < 10 were also investigated to aid in the interpretation.

The item ratings were obtained under eight different treatment conditions which may have affected the correlation between the items. Therefore, the structure of compliance gaining techniques was obtained by performing an orthogonal factor analysis of the pooled within cell variance - covariance matrix derived from the multivariate analysis, resulting in a factor structure independent of treatment effects.

The factor extraction and rotation procedure for this study was performed as suggested by Comrey [5, pg. 188]. The basic components of this method are: (1) extraction of factors by the minimum residual method until convergence on vectors of opposite sign is obtained; (2) rotation of substantial factors (those with several loadings of at least 0.2) by the criterion that two variables which are correlated should appear on the same factor; (3) dropping of residual factors (those with no loadings greater than 0.3) and rotation of the remaining factors by the criterion that uncorrelated variables should not appear on the same factor.

## RESULTS

The overall perceived effectiveness ratings for the twenty two compliance gaining techniques are presented in Table 3. One way ANOVA produced a highly significant result $p<.001$, $F(21,2706)=158.9$). The factor structure underlying these techniques and the situational dimensions impact on the perceived effectiveness of the techniques will now be reviewed.

TABLE 3

PERCEIVED EFFECTIVENESS OF COMPLIANCE GAINING TECHNIQUES

| Technique | Overall Mean[1] Perceived Effectiveness | Standard Deviation |
|---|---|---|
| Company Experience | 1.84 | 1.03 |
| Competitive Comparison | 2.08 | 1.33 |
| Product Information | 2.30 | 1.47 |
| Expertise (Positive) | 2.32 | 1.41 |
| Liking | 2.39 | 1.36 |
| Personal Experience | 2.50 | 1.44 |
| Expertise (Negative) | 2.69 | 1.65 |
| Altercasting (Positive) | 3.30 | 1.69 |
| Personal Similarity | 3.30 | 1.53 |
| Esteem (Positive) | 3.72 | 1.51 |
| Self-Feeling (Positive) | 3.82 | 1.66 |
| Promise | 3.92 | 2.01 |
| Social Standing | 3.92 | 1.62 |
| Moral Appeal | 3.97 | 1.76 |
| Market Standing | 4.24 | 1.94 |
| Pre-Giving | 4.77 | 1.78 |
| Esteem (Negative) | 4.98 | 1.69 |
| Altercasting (Negative) | 5.66 | 1.50 |
| Aversive Stimulation | 5.82 | 1.38 |
| Altruism | 6.31 | 1.02 |
| Debt | 6.70 | 0.71 |
| Threat | 6.78 | 0.61 |

[1] Based on Unweighted Means of the eight cells (1 = very effective, 7 = very ineffective)

## Factor Structure

The item loadings for the seven derived factors and the estimated communalities for each item are presented in Table 4. The items used in inferring the factor meaning (items with loadings greater than 0.40) are underlined. Factor 1, Social Esteem is composed of items emphasizing the buyer's personal values based upon his relationship to important others. Sanctions, factor II, is defined by the three least effective items, altruism, threat and debt. These items suggest personal coercive types of appeal. Factor III, Expertise, consists of positive and negative expertise items. Promise and pre-giving form factor IV, Reward. Factor V, Comparison Information is composed of the marked standing and competitive comparison items. Self Perception, factor VI, is defined by items reflecting aspects of the buyer's self image. The last factor, VII, Experience, is composed of items reflecting the product's merits based on the manufacturer's reputation and the salesman's stated experience with the product.

## Impact of Situational Dimensions on Technique Effectiveness

The results of the MANOVA indicated no significant three way interaction, and only one significant two-way interaction - the Buyer x Risk interaction (F(22,95)=2.03; $p<0.0097$). Esteem (negative) and social standing compliance techniques evidenced this interaction with univariate F (1,116) ratios of 5.62 ($p<0.019$) and 5.92 ($p<.016$) respectively. The effectiveness of esteem (negative) was perceived as highest for low price-consumer, followed by high price-organizational, low price-organizational, and least effective for the high price-consumer situation. The effectiveness of social standing was in completely the opposite sequence with the high-price consumer situation being perceived as most effective. In absolute terms, however, neither technique was viewed as being very effective.

Significant main effects were obtained for Price (F(22,95)= 2.47, $p<0.0014$) and Buyer (F(22,95)=3.44, $p<0.0001$) but not for type of relationship (F(22,95)=0.77, $p<0.74$).

The Price main effect was caused primarily by the univariate effects of price upon promise (p<0.0001), market standing (p<0.045), pre-giving (p<0.053), and altruism (p<0.089). These five techniques were all perceived as being more effective in the lower priced situations.

The main effect of buyer type indication that market standing (p<0.001), moral appeal (p<0.021), expertise-negative (p<0.033), and competitive-comparison (p<0.089) were viewed as more effective in organizational situation, while personal experience (p<0.0006), personal similarity p<0.0031), liking (p<0.031), and debt (p<0.062) were perceived as more effective in consumer situations.

## TABLE 4

FACTOR LOADINGS     FACTORS

| Techniques | I | II | III | IV | V | VI | VII | h |
|---|---|---|---|---|---|---|---|---|
| Promise | -03* | 06 | 00 | 60 | 14 | -05 | 10 | .41 |
| Threat | 07 | -59 | -04 | 05 | 14 | -07 | -18 | 42 |
| Market Standing | 22 | -07 | -17 | 26 | 42 | 19 | 07 | 38 |
| Expert-Neg | 07 | -01 | 81 | -02 | 05 | 03 | 00 | 67 |
| Liking | 00 | -15 | 16 | 24 | 27 | -07 | 09 | 20 |
| Pre-giving | 04 | -15 | -01 | 52 | 06 | -01 | 07 | 31 |
| Aversive Stimulation | 13 | -28 | 02 | -24 | 04 | 00 | 23 | 21 |
| Debt | 07 | -48 | 16 | -01 | -13 | 00 | 20 | 32 |
| Moral Appeal | 44 | -17 | 06 | 16 | 11 | -39 | 09 | 43 |
| Self-feeling-Pos | 24 | -13 | 12 | 23 | 05 | -54 | 37 | 58 |
| Altercasting-Pos | 10 | -03 | -08 | 11 | 20 | -64 | 22 | 54 |
| Altercasting-Neg | 27 | -25 | -06 | 14 | 17 | -27 | 14 | 29 |
| Altruism | 03 | -60 | -02 | 09 | -01 | 02 | -04 | 38 |
| Esteem-Pos | 64 | -06 | 06 | 18 | 14 | -24 | 21 | 58 |
| Esteem-Neg | 69 | -23 | 06 | 11 | 07 | -14 | 05 | 58 |
| Social Standing | 42 | -18 | 02 | 21 | 20 | -38 | 31 | 55 |
| Competitive Comparison | -04 | 07 | 16 | 00 | 65 | 00 | -01 | 46 |
| Personal Experience | 00 | 08 | 05 | 33 | 04 | 05 | 63 | 52 |
| Personal Similarity | 21 | 07 | -05 | 23 | 08 | -57 | 25 | 51 |
| Company Experience | -01 | 09 | -07 | 00 | 29 | -08 | 56 | 42 |
| Product Information | -18 | -02 | 05 | -08 | 35 | -05 | 00 | 17 |
| Expert-Pos | -01 | 08 | 63 | 07 | 06 | -01 | 09 | 42 |
| SSQS | 1.59 | 1.33 | 1.23 | 1.23 | 1.14 | 1.56 | 1.32 | 9.42 |

*Cell entry equals factor loading x 100

## DISCUSSION

The results of this exploratory study suggest that it may be possible to construct a model of buyer's perceptions of compliance gaining techniques. Overall, the techniques illustrated a wide range of perceived effectiveness, and, in a general sense, are as might be expected intuitively. The more rational problem solving techniques of company experience, competitive-comparison and expertise received high ratings of effectiveness while the negative techniques of threat, debt, altruism, aversive stimulation and negative altercasting received low ratings.

The results of the factor analysis indicate a moderate resemblance with more general influence typologies. The factors of Expertise, Reward and Sanctions are clearly analogous to influence methods developed elsewhere in the social sciences, while the Comparison Information and Experience factors appear to reflect informational types of appeal. Two other factors seem less related to the general influence typologies and suggest more personal approaches of influence. Social Esteem represents using relevant others' attributions toward the influence target,

while Self Perception employs the influencee's self attributions.

To the extent that the items composing each factor are uncorrelated with other factors and also have a high degree of common variance, one would expect that the situation dimensions would affect each item of a particular factor in a consistent manner. A review of the situation dimensions impact upon factor items indicates that the Reward and Comparison Information factor items were uniformly affected by price and buyer-type respectively but that the other factors' items were not uniformly affected by situation dimensions.

These findings suggest that further refinement of the factors is necessary before detailed interpretations of the impact of situational dimensions can be made. Nevertheless, it does appear that buyers perceive Reward type appeals as more affective in lower priced situations, possibly because of their greater relative salience and that Comparison Information type appeals are more affective for organizational buying situations where more objective problem solving procedures are followed.

Refinement and extension of the methodology employed in the study to develop deeper insight into buyer-seller interaction could take a number of forms. First, the set of compliance gaining techniques employed to develop the factor structure could be expanded by tapping salemen's experience, and adding to the techniques used in the study which were largely developed from theoretical perspectives In addition to the external validity derived from the procedure, the increase in the number and the refinement of the compliance gaining techniques should lead to a better factor structure.

Second, the use, of actual buyers and actual sellers, rather than students would also add external validity to the results obtained. Further, by having buyers take both salesman and buyer roles, the question of social desirability of responses in the buyer role, assumed for this study, could be probed. Finally, comparisons of the perceptions of both buyers and sellers could provide interesting insights into the different ways in which both sets of actors view the buyer-seller interaction.

## REFERENCES

1. Bauer, Raymond A. "Consumer Behavior as Risk Taking," in R.S. Hancock, ed., Dynamic Marketing for a Changing World. Chicago: American Marketing Association, 1970 389-398.

2. Busch, Paul, and David T. Wilson. "An Experimental Analysis of a Salesman's Expert and Referent Bases of Social Power in the Buyer-Seller Dyad," Journal of Marketing Research 13 (February 1976), 3-11.

3. Busch, Paul, Ronald F. Bush, and Joseph F. Hair. "Social Power Theory in Marketing," in A.G. Woodside, P.D. Bennett and J.N. Sheth, eds., Foundations of Consumer and Industrial Buying Behavior, forthcoming, 197

4. Capon, Noel, Morris B. Holbrook and James Hulbert. "Selling Processes and Buyer Behavior: Theoretical Implications of Recent Research," in A.G. Woodside, P.D. Bennett, and J.N. Sheth, eds., Foundations of Consumer and Industrial Buying Behavior, forthcoming, 1977.

5. Comrey, Andrew L. A First Course in Factor Analysis, New York: Academic Press, 1973.

6. Cox, Donald F., ed., Risk Taking and Information Handling in Consumer Behavior. Boston: Harvard University Press, 1967.

7. Deutsch, Morton and K. B. Gerhard. "A Study of Normative and Social Influence Upon Individual Judgment," Journal of Abnormal and Social Psychology, 51 (1955), 629-36.

8. Engel, James, Kollatt, David T., and Roger D. Blackwell. Consumer Behavior, New York: Holt, Rinehart and Winston, 1968.

9. Etzioni, Amitai. A Comparative Analysis of Complex Organizations, New York: The Free Press of Glencoe, 1961.

10. Finn, Jeremy D. A General Model for Multivariate Analysis, New York: Holt, Rinehart and Winston, 1974.

11. French, John R.P. and Bertram Raven. "The Bases of Social Power," in D. Cartright, ed., Studies in Social Power, Ann Arbor: University of Michigan, Institute for Social Research, 1959, 150-67.

12. Howard, John A. and Jagdish N. Sheth. The Theory of Buyer Behavior, Englewood Cliffs, New Jersey: Prentice Hall, 1969.

13. Jones, Edward E. and Richard E. Nisbett. "The Actor and the Observer: Divergent Perceptions of the Causes of Behavior," in E.E. Jones et. al. eds., Attribution: Perceiving the Causes of Behavior, Morristown, N.J. General Learning Press, 1972.

14. Kelman, Herbert C. "Processes of Opinion Change," Public Opinion Quarterly, 25 (Spring, 1961), 57-78.

15. Marwell, Gerald and David R. Schmitt. "Dimensions of Compliance-Gaining Behavior: An Empirical Analysis," Sociometry, 30 (December, 1967), 350-364.

16. Nicosia, Francesco M. Consumer Decision Processes, Englewood Cliffs, New Jersey: Prentice-Hall, 1966.

17. Parsons, Talcott, "On the Concept of Influence," Public Opinion Quarterly, 27 (1963), 37-62.

18. Raven, Bertram, M. and Arie W. Kruglanski. "Conflict and Power" in The Structure of Conflict, New York: Academic Press, 1970, 69-109.

19. Robinson, Patrick J., Charles W. Faris and Yoram Wind. Industrial Buying and Creative Marketing, Boston: Allyn and Bacon, 1967.

20. Spiro, Rosann L. and William D. Perreault, Jr. "Influence Strategy Mixes and Situational Determinants," Working Paper, Graduate School of Business Administration, University of North Carolina, Chapel Hill, September, 1976.

21. Webster, Frederick E., Jr. and Yoram Wind. "A General Model for Understanding Organizational Buying Behavior," Journal of Marketing, 36 (April 1972), 12-19.

# INFORMATION SOURCE PREFERENCE IN THE INDUSTRIAL ADOPTION DECISION

Michael J. Baker, Strathclyde University
Stephen T. Parkinson, Strathclyde University

## ABSTRACT

This paper reports the results of a study of the adoption of a new type of earth moving machine in the UK building and construction industry which provides some insight into information acquisition and use in the industrial adoption decision.

## INTRODUCTION

While there are many different models of the buying decision process all are agreed upon the crucial importance of information. In light of this agreement it is surprising that relatively little research has been undertaken which improves our understanding of the way in which organizational buyers find out about new products or processes. It is clear that this topic is of central interest to the innovator in developing a communications strategy which will maximize the probability of early market acceptance.

The Role of Information in Adoption Decisions

Research into the use of information in the industrial adoption decision is firmly founded upon that undertaken in other research traditions. A central concept is that of stages in the adoption decision process as developed by rural sociologists, extended by medical sociologists and, more generally, by students of consumer behavior [11]. Studies of the industrial adoption decision undertaken by Ozanne & Churchill [10], Webster [14], Martilla [8], Hayward [6], and Monoky, Mathews & Wilson [9] all support the general concept. They also confirm the findings of earlier research that as the buyer moves from an awareness of an innovation through evaluation of it to a decision to accept or reject it so the preference for information sources changes from formal to informal. It also appears that at each stage of this process different types of information may be required leading to preference for different sources of information.

Clearly the industrial buyers' preference for different sources of information at different stages is a phenomenon which should be useful in devising a company's communications strategy. However, this is of little direct use to the industrial marketing manager unless he understands the reasons which underlie the phenomenon. Without an understanding of why the potential buyer prefers one information source to another, the innovating organization is still not in a strong position to provide the most useful information (from a buyer's point of view) at the appropriate time.

In the consumer behavior literature there is already evidence that the differential preference for alternative sources of information at various stages in the adoption process can be explained by the uncertainties of the adoption decision, see for example Bauer [3], Cox [5], and Arndt [1]. However, there is little reported research evidence of the relationship between information search and perceived risk in the organizational buying decision, despite the fact that this relationship has been suggested by several researchers in models of organizational buying behavior. (See for example Cardozo [4], Sheth [12], and Webster [13].)

Exceptions are two experimental studies by Levitt [7] and Wilson [15] which support the view that perceived risk influences the industrial buyers' pattern of information acquisition and use.

These issues were central to broadly based study of the diffusion of two industrial innovations conducted in the UK between 1973 and 1976. Specifically, the study examined the following two hypotheses:

(a) The early adopter of an industrial innovation will prefer different sources of information from later adopters;

(b) The early adopter of an industrial innovation will perceive less risk in adopting than later adopters.

## METHODOLOGY

In selecting innovations for study approaches were made to firms which had received the Queen's Award for Technological Innovation. Where willingness to co-operate in the study was forthcoming, a survey of merit was made to check whether the innovation was perceived as significant in terms of a set of criteria established in an earlier survey conducted by the authors [2]. As a result of this procedure a new type of earth moving machine was selected for detailed investigation.

The field research comprised two stages - semi - structured interviews in a cross section of 22 adopter organizations and a postal census of the remaining adopters. The qualitative interviews were used in the preparation of nine case histories of the adoption decision, reflecting the behavior of early, middle and late adopters, and provided the basis for the test instrument used in the postal census.

From the semi-structured interviews with the 22 adopting organizations it emerged that the actual purchase decision was usually made by the plant manager, or his equivalent, assisted or influenced by other managers at different stages in the decision process. The plant manager tended to be the manager most involved in the purchasing decision, with the greatest responsibility for collecting and using information on alternative machines (i.e. he was the 'gate keeper' in many instances).

A single questionnaire was piloted, reworked, and mailed to each of the companies which had adopted the machine, addressed to the Plant Manager. The response to the survey was relatively poor, in that it elicited a usable response from plant managers in only 49 companies from a total population of 219 adopters. However, analysis of the response revealed no significant differences between the type of respondents and the population from which they were drawn. The profile of respondents and of population were similar on both the dispersion of the dependent variable, time to adoption, and size of organization.

## RESULTS

Usefulness of Different Sources of Information

Table 1 compares the ratings of usefulness given to each source of information by three arbitrarily defined categories of adopters.

In Table 1 some differences are evident in the usefulness ratings given by each of the three categories of adopters, to the different sources of information. These differences, although fairly consistent are only statistically significant for one source of information. Generalizing from relatively weak evidence it would appear that the early adopter tends to find each commercial source of information less useful than do the later adopters. However, the early adopter appears to find the only non-commercial source of information, i.e. members of his own company, to be significantly more useful than do later categories of adopters.

In overall terms the most useful source of information appears to be demonstrations (highly appropriate for judging earth moving equipment) followed by the local distributor. Since most demonstrations tended to be organized by the local distributor the local distributor clearly played an important role in providing information used by adopters to evaluate this machine. This finding clearly illustrates the value of the manufacturer establishing a sound dealer network before trying to launch a new product of this type.

Overall the table underlines the importance of personal selling. If this responsibility is delegated to a distributor or dealer then it is critical that they should be seen as a credible source by potential users. The corollary of this is that a poor dealership is likely to prove a positive deterrent to early adoption which first class promotion, trade shows, etc., would have great difficulty in overcoming.

Opinion Leadership

The respondents to this survey were asked to indicate whether they asked anyone else in the industry for advice before buying the new machine, or if anyone asked them. 36% of the sample indicated that they had approached someone else in the industry for advice or opinion on the machine, and 55% of this same sample indicated that someone had asked them for advice.

The average number of weeks to adoption of the respondents who said they were approached by someone for advice was 84.48 weeks. The average number of weeks to adoption of respondents who said they were not approached by someone for advice was 110.10 weeks. This difference was significant at the 90% level of confidence. Those respondents who were asked for advice tended to be earlier on average to adopt, than those who were not asked for advice. The result supports the view that opinion leaders tended to be those companies which had already bought the machine, and shown some commercial commitment to their views.

There was also support for the view that membership of trade associations may provide a source of information and perhaps support for adoption decisions. The average number of weeks to adoption of respondents who were members of trade associations was 84.33 weeks, the corresponding figure for non-members was 110.47 weeks. (A difference which was not statistically significant.)

Rate of Adoption and Perceived Risk

Table 2 illustrates the degree to which each of the three categories of adopters were confident about certain aspects of the new machine.

There appears to be a relationship between category of adopter and perceived risk in adopting, albeit one which is not statistically significant. Moreover this relationship appears to be one which goes contrary to the direction which the work of previous authors in the area would have predicted. From Table 2 early adopters of this innovation appear to have been considerably less confident rather than more confident than later adopters, about certain aspects of its performance when they were evaluating the machine.

Caution in accepting this conclusion is merited due to the lack of statistical significance of this finding, but we feel it is a theoretically significant result.

The results of the qualitative interviewing stage suggest that the early adopter may have seen greater risks in adopting the new machine before it was proven, but was prepared to take them relying in doing so on the innovator's reputation for looking after its customers. (i.e., the credibility of the manufacturer counter-balanced the risk perceived in adopting.)

TABLE 1

COMPARISON OF RATINGS OF USEFULNESS OF DIFFERENT SOURCES OF INFORMATION BETWEEN ADOPTER CATEGORIES

| Source of Information | Category of Adopter | | | |
| --- | --- | --- | --- | --- |
| | Bought before 1st Jan. 1973 | Bought during 1973 | Bought since 1st Jan. 1974 | |
| | 'Early Adopters' | 'Middle Adopters' | 'Late Adopters' | |
| | (n = 16) | (n = 22) | (n = 11) | |
| | | | | (F) |
| Leaflets & Brochures | 4.2* | 3.1 | 3.5 | 0.81 |
| Trade Shows | 4.6 | 3.8 | 3.6 | 0.42 |
| Trade Journals | 5.5 | 4.2 | 6.0 | 0.75 |
| Demonstrations | 1.9 | 1.6 | 1.6 | 0.12 |
| Local Distributor | 2.9 | 2.5 | 1.7 | 0.67 |
| Members of own firm | 1.8 | 2.6 | 5.2 | 4.67** |

    * To be read: The average rating of usefulness of leaflets and brochures given by firms which adopted before 1st January 1973 was 4.2 on a scale running from 1 (very useful) to 9 (not useful at all).

    ** Significant at 95% level of confidence.

TABLE 2

RATE OF ADOPTION AND PERCEIVED RISK

| Attribute of Machine | Category of Adopter/Degree of Confidence | | |
|---|---|---|---|
| | Early Adopter (n = 16) | Middle Adopter (n = 22) | Late Adopter (n = 11) |
| That it would have a good resale price | 5.3* | 4.3 | 4.7 |
| That it would match up to manufacturers' claims on output and performance | 3.0 | 2.8 | 1.8 |
| That it would be reliable | 3.7 | 4.1 | 2.7 |
| That its tracks would have an acceptable life | 4.3 | 3.8 | 3.5 |
| That it would be easy to service | 3.7 | 3.7 | 2.1 |

* To be read: The average rating of confidence in the machine having a
good resale price given by firms which adopted before
1st January 1973 was 5.3 on a scale running from 1 (very
confident) to 9 (not at all confident)

---

In addition it is possible that the early adopter may have been prepared to discount the risks perceived in adopting against the potential advantages to be gained by being the first to adopt. (See Table 3)

A review of Table 3 readily indicates that the early adopter tended to see the new machine as being comparatively less well matched to his requirements than did later adopters, on resale price, reliability, track life and ease of servicing. However, the early adopter did see the comparative advantages of the new machine in terms of output and performance, and appeared prepared to discount disadvantages and uncertainty against potential benefits. Again it should be stressed that these differences were not statistically significant.

Discussion

Data presented above suggests that the patterns of information source preference exhibited by the early adopter differ significantly and consistently from the pattern of information source preference of later adopters. The early adopter tended to find sources of information within his own firm more useful than did later adopters.

This preference may be partially explained by the finding that the early adopter perceives more risk in adopting than do later adopters. He attempts therefore to involve other members of his own company in the decision to share the risk with him by asking them for information and opinion (i.e., risk sharing by involvement). In doing so he raises the level of risk which he is prepared to take as an individual, and can involve other managers in the decision by pointing out the comparative advantages of the new machine over the machines which it competed with. (See Table 3). Such a conclusion would be consistent with the findings of the 'risky-shift' tradition of research which suggests that a group consensus on the level of risk which should be tolerated, is frequently greater than the level of risk which each of the individual members of the group would tolerate on his or her own without consultation.

TABLE 3

COMPARATIVE ADVANTAGE PERCEIVED BY DIFFERENT CATEGORIES OF ADOPTERS

Question: At the time of purchase of your company's first machine how well did it
compare with competitive machines in meeting your company's requirements
on the following features?

| Attribute of Machine | A Good Match 1+3* | A Bad Match 5+7+9 | F. ratio |
|---|---|---|---|
| Resale Price | 100.79(14)** | 98.93(15) | 0.22 |
| Output & Performance | 91.27(22) | 111.00(11) | 1.4 |
| Reliability | 102.87(21) | 97.50(18) | 0.12 |
| Track Life | 98.41(17) | 95.84(19) | 0.02 |
| Ease of Servicing | 113.00(23) | 85.81(16) | 3.56 |

* The original scale went from 1 (a good match) to 9 (a bad match). It has been
collapsed for purposes of comparison into two classifications on an arbitrary
basis.

** To Be Read: The average time to adoption in the 14 companies where the manager
responding said that the machine was a good match to their requirements on resale price was 100.70 weeks.

260

Later adopters on the other hand appear to show a greater preference for essentially commercial sources of information and the opinions of existing owners which by definition, the early adopter cannot use. As the risks from adopting appear to diminish for the later adopters so there appears to be less need for support by members of the adopter's own organization. It also seems reasonable to suppose that the innovator's promotional mix develops over time, as salesmen for example learn about the machine, leaflets and brochures become more widely available and more machines become available for demonstrations in commercial situations etc. Such factors would naturally make the 'commercial' sources of information more useful to later adopters than early adopters. Validation of this finding is clearly desirable and has obvious practical implications.

## REFERENCES

1. Arndt, J. "Perceived Risk, Sociometric Integration and Word of Mouth Advertising in the Adoption of a New Food Product," in R.M. Haas, ed. "Science Technology and Marketing," Proceedings of A.M.A. Conference, Chicago, 1966.

2. Baker, Michael J., and Stephen T. Parkinson. "Predicting the Adoption and Diffusion of Industrial Innovation." Report to the Social Science Research Council, University of Strathclyde, Glasgow, 1976.

3. Bauer, R. "Consumer Behavior as Risk Taking." Proceedings of the 43rd National Conference A.M.A., Chicago, 1960.

4. Cardozo, R.N. "Segmenting the Industrial Market," Proceedings of the A.M.A., Fall Conference, 1968.

5. Cox, D.F. "Information and Uncertainty: Their Effects on the Consumer's Product Evaluation," D.B.A. Thesis, Harvard Business School, 1963.

6. Hayward, G. "Diffusion of Innovation in the Flour Milling Industry," European Journal of Marketing, Vol. 6, No. 3, (1972).

7. Levitt, T. Industrial Purchasing Behavior: A Study of Communications Effects, Harvard University, Graduate School of Business Administration, (1965).

8. Martilla, J.A. "Word of Mouth Communication in the Industrial Adoption Process," Journal of Marketing Research, (May 1971) pgs. 173-178.

9. Monoky, J.F., H.L. Mathews and D.R. Wilson, "Information Source Preference by Industrial Buyers as a Function of the Buying Situation," Working Series in Marketing Research, No. 27, College of Business Administration, Pennsylvania State University, February 1975.

0. Ozanne, U.B., and G.A. Churchill, "Adoption Research: Information Sources in the Industrial Purchasing Decision," Proceedings, A.M.A. Fall Conference, 1968, pgs. 352-359.

1. Rogers, E.M., and F.F. Shoemaker. Communications of Innovations, 2nd ed. New York: Free Press, 1971.

2. Sheth, J.N. "Model of Industrial Buyer Behavior," Journal of Marketing, Vol. 37, (October 1973) pgs. 50-53.

13. Webster, F.E., Jr., "Modelling the Industrial Buying Process," Journal of Marketing Research, Vol. 11 (November 1965).

14. Webster, F.E. "Informal Communication in Industrial Markets," Journal of Marketing Research (May 1970) pgs. 186-189.

15. Wilson, D.T. "Industrial Buyers' Decision Making Styles," Journal of Marketing Research, Vol. VIII, (November) pgs. 433-436.

# THE PERSONAL SELLING COURSE:
## AN OPPORTUNITY FOR EXPERIENTIAL LEARNING

Anthony J. Alessandra, University of San Diego
John S. Wright, Georgia State University

## ABSTRACT

Business courses undergo constant change and revitalization in the search for better methods of preparing people for suitable careers. Currently experiential learning is in vogue. By happy coincidence a revival in the personal selling course is also underway. This paper reports on an innovative response to these two important trends in business education.

## INTRODUCTION

Many schools and departments of business administration moved away during the 1960s from the offering of such "practical" marketing courses as advertising, retailing, and personal selling. In their place were substituted newer, more abstract courses including consumer behavior, marketing communications, and marketing information systems. This action was taken largely in response to the foundation-sponsored studies of business education which appeared at the beginning of the decade. After its abandonment by many schools of business, the advertising course found a home in schools of journalism where it prospered. Retailing and personal selling courses did not fare so well. These courses lost favor with marketing academicians and were dropped because the subjects were felt to be lacking in sophistication [4], emphasized description and vocational training [3], and/or were of little teaching interest to professors [2].

The academic pendulum moved back to a certain degree of pragmatism in the 1970s [3]. Students started to demand better preparation for entry-level jobs; recruiters preferred students who had taken more practical college courses; and, marketing department chairpersons desired more majors in their discipline. Pent-up student demand for meaningful, "real-world" courses that impart usable job skills led to frequent overcrowded conditions in retailing and selling classes at many colleges and universities. The regenerated demand for these course offerings seems to agree with Lazer's prediction of the mid-1960s that the 1970s would bring more specialized courses in marketing [5].

The increased interest in more pragmatic, experiential learning in marketing courses is best demonstrated by the quantity of papers devoted to this topic at the 1976 American Marketing Association Educators Conference [1]. The Marketing Department at Georgia State University has long believed in the need for experiential student learning exercises due to the type of student who normally attends an urban university with a large evening program. One example of this orientation, the Principles of Selling course as offered at GSU, is presented in this paper. The approach can, of course, be adapted to institutions located in the non-urban setting although there will be some problems locating suitable persons to participate in the role playing described below.

## NEW APPROACH

### Course Objectives

The course is geared primarily toward the industrial selling situation. Although some students enter insurance, real estate, and various direct selling fields, the majority of marketing graduates at GSU and most institutions around the country enter the selling profession at the industrial level. Therefore, one of the course objectives is to provide these students with in-depth awareness and appreciation of the professional buying process in industry. It is felt the principles and techniques learned will serve the needs of other students in a satisfactory manner.

Another objective is to familiarize students with the professional opportunities in selling. In addition, the students are exposed to the complexities of the selling process with its ups-and-downs, hopes and fears, and feasts and famines.

A further objective of this course is to teach the students how to relate to buyers in an open, honest manner. It is hoped that students will acquire a sensitivity to the needs and feelings of others, learn how to build trust relationships and how to help others discover solutions to their problems.

### Teaching Materials

Conceptual material for the course is provided by a combination of a traditional textbook and a series of mini-lectures. The latter are usually provided during the first half of the course with each lecturette dealing with a separate topic which is not included in the textbook or which needs amplification. A sampling of lecturette topics is shown in Exhibit 1.

### Micro-Training

Micro-training is a process of learning individual skills one at a time and then in combination with each other. This process allows students to understand and learn a complex interactive series of skills, such as those needed for success in personal selling.

Early courses in personal selling usually required that students make a full sales presentation before the class without any previous role playing. This procedure necessitated that each student internalize and perform all the selling skills covered in the course at one time. Personal trauma, mass confusion, and fear often resulted. On the other hand, if students are allowed to practice (role play) each individual skill (such as questioning, listening, probing, approaching, presenting, objection-handling, and closing) separately and then employ combinations of these skills, they should assimilate and understand the complex materials much better. Micro-training, as the technique is utilized in our selling class, has this as its objective.

Students first practice questioning skills, feedback skills, listening skills, nonverbal awareness skills, creative presentation skills, negotiating skills, and commitment skills separately, then in combination with each of the other skills. Essentially these skill-developing exercises are performed in the classroom in a fashion somewhat akin to the in-basket simulation approach. A student is given a short problem which he or she is to solve before the class with either the instructor or another student acting as the obverse side of the role play. This allows students to become comfortable and competent with one skill before attempting to build another skill on top of it. A more meaningful and successful experiential learning experience results.

Video Tape Role Plays

Once the textbook has been studied, the lecturettes given, and micro-training completed, each student makes a full-length sales presentation on video tape. The tape is played back before the entire class for purposes of critiquing. The learning value is enhanced because the tape can be replayed and stopped at selected points, both of which are not feasible in before-class presentations. Another advantage of video taping, of course, is that the presentation is made in the quiet of the studio absent from the embarrassment of performing before one's peers. If an error is made, the presentation continues without a breakdown due to the laughter of classmates.

A fellow classmate simulates the buyer in the video tape role play. In order to lend more realism to this exercise, each student buyer is fully acquainted with the product, company, and competition of the student salesperson. The briefing form (Exhibit 2) must be completed by each student salesperson and given to the buyer at least one week before the actual taping session. This gives the student buyer enough time to review the briefing form, do additional research on the product, or ask the student salesperson to clarify any points on the form before the role play exercise takes place. A considerable amount of realism is added to the video tape role play as a result of the increased buyer competence gained through the use of the buyer's briefing form. Furthermore, the student knows that his or her performance in the buyer role will be evaluated by the instructor and members of the class.

In order to increase the learning potential of this exercise several rules are followed. First, sales presentations are video taped outside of class. Student sellers and buyers make an appointment with the college's audio-visual (educational media) center to tape their presentations. The presentations are taped outside of regular class periods on students' own time. In addition, playback of the tapes is delayed for at least 24 hours, thereby giving each student salesperson a chance to "cool off" so that he can view the tape of his sales presentation in a more objective manner. Secondly, the class is instructed to be aware of both the good and bad selling skills utilized by the student salespeople in the video tape sales presentations. Lastly, each video tape sales presentation is played back twice before the class. After the initial viewing, the student salesperson's overall reaction is first obtained before the those of the rest of the class. The initial showing is played through from the beginning to end without stopping. However, the second playback may be stopped at particular points to emphasize particularly good or bad selling skills. The usual length of presentations is from twenty to thirty minutes.

Effective utilization of the video tape technique in the personal selling course generates involvement and holds student interest at high levels throughout the entire course.

Real-Life Sales Presentations

A new dimension has been added to role playing in the sales course offering at Georgia State University. In addition to the video tape role play, each student is required to make an actual in-office sales presentation before a professional purchasing agent. This teaching innovation has been made possible through the cooperation of the Purchasing Management Association of Georgia (PMAG).

The PMAG, a non-profit professional association of men and women engaged in the field of purchasing, supplies a professional buyer before whom each student makes a formal sales presentation. Approximately two dozen buyers, each from a group of Atlanta's leading business firms, participate in this program. Represented are manufacturing firms, financial institutions, airlines, retailers, recreational parks, and universities.

At the beginning of each quarter, a list of purchasing agents who are willing to cooperate is developed. The products or services which the purchasing agents buy are isolated on a separate sheet of paper. During the first week of class, students select the available products or services which they wish to "sell." The instructor then assigns each student to a specific purchasing agent who buys that particular product or service.

From here on, students play the role of an actual salesperson in the real business world. They must thoroughly research product strengths and weaknesses, company history, competition, as well as the customer's company, and its customers.

After a student has viewed the video tape sales presentation (selling the same product or service which he is going to sell to the purchasing agent) in class, he is free to contact the purchasing agent for an appointment. The student then actually goes to the firm for the sales interview with the buyer just as any professional salesperson would in the pursuit of an actual sale. Each purchasing agent agrees to set aside time for the student to make the presentation without interruption and to make a thorough evaluation of the student's presentation. An evaluation form (see Exhibit 3) is filled out by the buyer immediately after the student sales interview and returned by mail and in confidence to the instructor.

The evaluation by the purchasing agent is a factor to be considered when the student's final grade in the personal selling course is determined. Admittedly, this facet of the course is difficult for the instructor, as he has no real control over rating standards. Before a purchasing agent becomes a participant in the program, however, the instructor does schedule an orientation meeting to explain the importance of the evaluation process, both to the student and to the university and its standards. Furthermore, over a period of time, the performance of participating purchasing agents can be traced and "soft touches" and "hard noses" are isolated. Moreover, students are given an opportunity to provide feedback, in writing, on their opinion of how the interview was conducted by the buyer-- the P.A. is rated, as it were, by the student salesperson. All in all, the rating by the purchasing agent carries a weight of approximately twenty percent of the total grade.

The student who makes the best sales presentation is invited to a regular monthly dinner meeting of the PMAG where a plaque recognizing his or her accomplishment is presented. The choice of the student to be honored is based on the rating received from the purchasing agents, class evaluation of the video taped presentations, and the instructor's opinion.

This unique experiential learning exercise is enthusiastically acclaimed by both students and purchasing agents. Students are permitted to engage in a role playing exercise which closely simulates real life conditions. It enables students to experience first hand the role of a professional salesperson and provide the kind of pragmatic business experience that many students are seeking. In addition, the purchasing agents find the program rewarding to themselves. They feel that their cooperation helps to put better qualified salespeople into the companies from whom they buy. The student sales presentations are, in the stated opinions of the purchasing agents, often better than ones given by the majority of the salespeople who call on them in the day-to-day conduct of their buying efforts.

CONCLUSION

The preparation and implementation of this learning exercise requires inordinate amounts of the instructor's time. The administrative detail is considerable. Nevertheless, we believe that the results are worth the bother. Under this plan, the selling course moves ahead on a goal-directed path throughout the quarter; there is no letdown. Study of the textbook and absorbing lecturettes lead into micro-training, which passes into video tapes sales presentations, culminating in real-life purchasing agent sales presentations. This progression allows students not only to learn and talk about selling, but to actually "experience" selling.

Marketing education is entering a new era of experiential learning wherein new and unique "involvement" approaches will be increasingly employed and well received by today's students, businesspeople, and educators. This pragmatic swing of the pendulum is likely to last for a number of years. We hope that the example presented in this paper will prompt other marketing educators to develop more and better methods of experiential learning in their classes.

### EXHIBIT 1
### SELECTED LIST OF PERSONAL SELLING LECTURETTES

The Role of Selling in the Economic, Business and Marketing
    Environments
Opportunities in Selling
Overview of the Buying Process
Overview of the Selling Process
Understanding the Human Interaction Process
Non-Manipulative Selling
Transactional Analysis (TA) in Selling
Questioning Skills
Listening Skills
Nonverbal Communication Skills
Creative Presentation Skills
Commitment Skills
Follow-Through Skills

### EXHIBIT 2
### BUYER'S BRIEFING FORM

Student_____ Date_____
Product Name_____
What is this product/service?_____
Who makes it?_____
How is it used?_____
Who uses it?_____
What additional services are provided?_____
    Type of Product/

| Competitor | Service | Advantages | Disadvantages |
|---|---|---|---|
| 1. | | | |
| 2. | | | |

| Features* | Related Benefits | Proofs/Supports |
|---|---|---|
| 1. | | |
| 2. | | |
| 3. | | |
| 4. | | |

*Describe each distinctive feature.

| Common Objections* | Benefits Used in Answer |
|---|---|
| 1. | |
| 2. | |
| 3. | |
| 4. | |

*Fill.in both the type of objection and how it might be verbalized.

### EXHIBIT 3
### SALES PRESENTATION EVALUATION

Student_____ Purchasing Agent_____
Company_____ Date _____
Directions: Please circle the number on the scale which ranks closest to describing the performance of the student in each category. Your personal evaluation is very impor-

tant, so I urge you to make careful and thoughtful choices. Your cooperation is greatly appreciated.

Example: If the student had good knowledge of your needs, but did not exactly give an impression of exceptional knowledge, you may give him/her a 4. If the student had reasonable knowledge of your needs, but failed to impress you that he/she had a good grasp of your needs, you may circle a 3 or a 2.

1. Knowledge of Agent's Needs and Wants
  5      4      3      2      1      0
  Very thorough                 Ignorant of
  knowledge of                 my needs
  my needs

2. Knowledge of Business Operation
  5      4      3      2      1      0
  Thorough knowl-             Ignorant of
  edge of operation           operation

3. Opening Remarks
  5      4      3      2      1      0
  Excellent;                 Stiff and
  gained and held            boring
  my interest

4. Probing Techniques
  5      4      3      2      1      0
  Excellent                 Very poor

5. Questioning
  5      4      3      2      1      0
  Chose perti-               Undirected,
  nent questions            unnecessary
                           questions

6. Attentiveness
  5      4      3      2      1      0
  Listened care-           Too interested in
  fully to my re-         talking rather
  sponses and questions    than listening

7. Exploration of Needs and Wants
  5      4      3      2      1      0
  Thoroughly and           Oblivious to my
  effectively ex-          needs; sold what
  plored my needs         he/she wanted to
                           sell

8. Focus on Benefits of Product
  5      4      3      2      1      0
  Emphasized and           Only sold
  concentrated on          features of
  benefits of the          the product
  product

9. Product Knowledge
  5      4      3      2      1      0
  Had thorough            Superficial
  knowledge of            knowledge
  product

10. Presentation
  5      4      3      2      1      0
  Very logical            Illogical
  and lucid            and vague
  presentation          presentation

11. Promotion
  5      4      3      2      1      0
  Built my confidence       Caused serious
  in his/her product,       doubts about
  price, service,         product, price,
  future support, etc.     service, etc.

12. Self-Confidence

| 5 | 4 | 3 | 2 | 1 | 0 |
|---|---|---|---|---|---|

Convinced I would buy the product

Convinced that he/she could not <u>give</u> me the product

13. Closing

| 5 | 4 | 3 | 2 | 1 | 0 |
|---|---|---|---|---|---|

Recognized when to close

Missed several buying cues from me

14. Actual Sale

| 5 | 4 | 3 | 2 | 1 | 0 |
|---|---|---|---|---|---|

Made a tactful request for the order

Untactful when asking for the order

15. Anticipation of Objections

| 5 | 4 | 3 | 2 | 1 | 0 |
|---|---|---|---|---|---|

Anticipated and/or uncovered any objections not mentioned

Never tried to probe for hidden objections

16. Meeting Objections

| 5 | 4 | 3 | 2 | 1 | 0 |
|---|---|---|---|---|---|

Handled objections logically and smoothly

Lacked poise when meeting objections; illogical and tactless

17. Punctuality

| 5 | 4 | 3 | 2 | 1 | 0 |
|---|---|---|---|---|---|

Was on time

Late

18. Appearance

| 5 | 4 | 3 | 2 | 1 | 0 |
|---|---|---|---|---|---|

Well groomed

Dressed in an unbusinesslike fashion

19. Attitude

| 5 | 4 | 3 | 2 | 1 | 0 |
|---|---|---|---|---|---|

Very enthusiastic, persistent, and creative

Couldn't care less

20. Personal Impression

| 5 | 4 | 3 | 2 | 1 | 0 |
|---|---|---|---|---|---|

Very favorable

Unfavorable

You are encouraged to suggest improvements in the student's overall performance. Feel free to make any additional comments you may have. Thank you very much!

## REFERENCES

1. Bernhardt, Kenneth L., ed. Marketing: 1776-1976 and Beyond. Chicago: American Marketing Association, 1976. See: T.E. Barry, M.G. Harvey, and R.A. Kerin, "Marketing Practicum: Career Exposure for Students." J.S. Armstrong, "The Panolba Role Playing Case." R.A. Mittelstaedt, "Word-of-Mouth Advertising in Action." A.G. Woodside, J.T. Sims, and J.R. Foster, "Manufacturing and Wholesaler Channel Exercise in Seller and Buyer Interactions." L.J. Rosenberg, "A Mock Problem Exercise: Vocational Schools Regulation." G.A. Smith, "Student Oriented - Multi Media Approach to Teaching Principles of Advertising Course."

2. Dyer, Robert F. and Shrimp, T. A. "An Attitudinal Analysis of Marketing Educators and Executives: Suggestions for Curriculum Design," in Edward M. Mazze, ed., 1975 Combined Proceedings. Chicago: American Marketing Association, 1975.

3. Enis, Ben M. and Smith, Sam V. "The Marketing Curriculum of the Seventies: Period of the Pendulum or New Plane of Performance," in Kenneth L. Bernhardt, ed., Marketing: 1776-1976 and Beyond. Chicago: American Marketing Association, 1976.

4. Hardin, David K. "Can Marketing and Marketing Education Survive?" in Boris W. Becker and Helmut Becker, eds., 1972 Combined Proceedings. Chicago: American Marketing Association, 1973.

5. Lazer, William. "Education for Marketing in the 1970s." Journal of Marketing (July 1966), 36.

MARKETING RESEARCH FOR PUBLIC TELEVISION:
A PROMISING CLASS PROJECT OPPORTUNITY

Richard K. Robinson, Marquette University

## ABSTRACT

As a result of a recent FCC directive, public television stations are now required to ascertain significant community needs and to maintain a list of those programs broadcast which address those needs. This paper discusses the joint effort of a university marketing research class and a public television station to conduct a survey as the basis for a special program concerning a previously ascertained community problem. The survey provided the students with a realistic and beneficial class project and enabled the station to develop a program relevant to its service area. Marketing educators are encouraged to pursue similar efforts in helping students experience marketing research in action and in assisting public television to provide programming in the public interest.

## INTRODUCTION

The growing interest of managers of nonprofit organizations in marketing principles can be seen in the increased use of marketing research to study their markets. In the public services, in particular, there has been a research emphasis on (1) measuring the needs of the target market, and (2) determining whether the needs are being met or how they might be better satisfied. The impetus to put the marketing concept into action through researching the public's needs has come in part from management but also, to a greater degree, from government regulatory commissions. A relevant example is public television.

Within the past year, the FCC has issued a new directive for license renewal that requires all public television stations to ascertain ten significant needs within the service area of each station and to keep a list of programs broadcast during the preceding twelve months to help meet these needs [2] . Faced with this new marketing research task, public television stations can pay for the services of a research firm or can turn to a community resource, such as a local university, for assistance. This paper reports the recent combined effort of a university marketing research class and a public television station to develop a special program designed to address a significant community problem.

## ONE STATION'S COMMUNITY ASCERTAINMENT EXPERIENCE

WMVS, public television serving Milwaukee and Southeastern Wisconsin, began its community ascertainment program in 1971. At that time, non-commercial broadcast stations were not required by the FCC to participate in the survey effort to be performed by commercial broadcasters for license renewal. WMVS believed, however, that its ascertainment efforts should be no less exhaustive than those of the commercial stations in the market [4] . From two formal surveys, one a random telephone survey of the community and the other a survey of community leaders, WMVS developed a list of ascertained community needs, against which its programming performance during the license period could be judged.

The FCC issued a revised directive regarding rules and regulations for the ascertainment of community needs in early 1976 [2] , which was the license renewal year for broadcast stations in Wisconsin. It required that all

stations, both commercial and non-commercial, perform a general public survey at any time during the license period and conduct community leader interviews continuously throughout the license term. Since WMVS was the only station in the Milwaukee market with first-hand survey experience (all other stations had contracted the service to outside research firms), it undertook the leadership role. Public television station WMVS contracted with area radio and television broadcasters to administer a total market cooperative ascertainment package consisting of the public survey and interviews between area broadcast managers and recognized community leaders.

The results of the general public survey of 959 persons in the Milwaukee area and the interviews with 220 community leaders indicated that crime was mentioned most frequently as the most important problem in the community. To develop a local program relevant to the community, WMVS decided to follow up on its ascertainment effort with an in-depth analysis of the crime issue. The station reasoned that marketing research techniques similar to those used in the ascertainment study could be applied in a telephone survey as a basis for a special program on crime. As a further indication of its desire to work with other area institutions in addressing community needs, WMVS pooled its resources with those of Marquette University to conduct the survey and develop the program.

## A COMBINED UNIVERSITY-PUBLIC TELEVISION STATION EFFORT

A requirement of the undergraduate marketing research course at Marquette University is the completion of a semester research project, often in the form of an overall class project. Recent projects have involved surveys for a variety of non-profit organizations, including the Better Business Bureau and Goodwill Industries.

### Course and Survey Objectives

The crime survey for public television represented a challenging semester project that fit one of the writer's goals for the course -- to bring marketing research reality into the classroom. It was presented to the students as a survey project that would give them an opportunity to apply research tools to an actual problem and would yield results that would be used and seen on public television. Their enthusiastic acceptance of the survey as a class project enabled the professor to meet another course objective: to help students learn from their own efforts that doing good marketing research is a rewarding experience.

The objective of the survey was to provide a general assessment of Milwaukee area residents' attitudes toward and perceptions of (1) crime, (2) the police, and (3) the courts. WMVS wanted to know what relationships exist among variables such as the area in which a person lives, standard demographics, feelings about personal safety, and attitudes and perceptions about crime, criminals, the police and the court system. The station desired a random sample of 500 respondents for the telephone survey.

### A Committee Approach

To accomplish the research objectives, the class of 38 students was divided into six committees: executive, questionnaire design, sampling, pretest, data editing and analysis, and report writing. Committee sizes ranged from four on the executive committee to eight on the data analysis committee. Each committee was required to report to the class on its procedures as the project evolved. All students participated in the final telephone interviewing in addition to their committee work.

Questionnaire Design. The Executive Committee, in addition to its job of overseeing the project and coordinating the other committees, further developed the set of research objectives and prepared a list of guidelines for the questionnaire design. Both the objectives and the guidelines were reviewed and approved by WMVS. The Questionnaire Committee faced the challenge of formulating a questionnaire that would not only cover all the objectives but would also be concise. A trial run of their initial questionnaire, conducted by the Pretest Committee, demonstrated the importance of a proper sequence of questions and brief, comprehensible response formats. Pretest problems and suggestions for improvement were discussed with WMVS.

The result of the consultation between the Pretest and Questionnaire Committees and WMVS was a highly structured telephone survey form consisting of brief questions with dichotomous, multiple-choice, or rating-scale response formats. Emphasis was placed on a smooth flow of questions so as to maximize the likelihood of interview completion. The telephone questionnaire required about five minutes to complete.

Sampling. The Sample Committee supplied the addresses and telephone numbers of households to be contacted in the pretest and in the final survey. A street address/telephone directory was used because it offered the most consolidated and convenient coverage of the survey area. The sample selection process involved the use of a random number generator and computer program devised so that every entry in the directory had an equal chance of being chosen.

With a survey objective of 500 respondents, the committee followed the "ten percent rule" for the pretest by supplying enough telephone numbers to the pretest callers so that at least 50 responses would be achieved. Although 70 phone interviews were completed, the pretest indicated the need to compile a list of well over 1000 telephone numbers to allow for losses due to not-at-homes and refusals and still yield at least 500 completed interviews for the survey. Using the random number combinations provided by the computer, the committee prepared a list of phone numbers for each student to call.

Data Editing and Analysis. The survey responses were transcribed onto optical scanner sheets to facilitate computer processing. The Data Analysis Committee double-checked the process to insure the accuracy of the data. A final sample of 574 usable responses was obtained. The data were then processed by the Statistical Package for the Social Sciences (SPSS) to provide response frequency totals for each survey question and crosstabulations between variables. WMVS provided some guidelines for organizing the results. The committee spent considerable time going over the computer output to determine which findings were relevant and should be presented in the final report.

Report Writing. The initial task of the Report Writing Committee was one of organizing the materials provided by the other committees for the report. Committee members then divided the writing responsibility as equally as possible and prepared a first draft for the professor. A problem of differing writing styles was resolved with the help of two members who prepared the final draft according to the professor's guidelines.

## REPORT OF AN EVALUATION OF THE COMBINED EFFORT

After reading the report and further developing plans for the special program to be based on the survey, WMVS representatives, including the special programs manager and the producer of the program, met with the class to thank them for their work and to report on the program plans. They told the students that the program would be aired in February during National Crime Prevention Week. They also entertained ideas from the students as to possible program content and points of emphasis.

Student Response

At the end of the semester, the students were asked to evaluate the project as an educational experience. Their anonymous critiques indicated an overwhelming support for the combined university - public TV effort as a valuable supplement to the formal materials covered in class. Among specific benefits mentioned were the following:

- the project made the course more relevant

- able to see theory put into practice

- gave practical experience with some case concepts

- excellent way to see how people must work as a team to do research

- gave me greater confidence for any future projects

- that the findings were to be used later made it more meaningful

- able to see the results of our work on TV.

The benefit most frequently mentioned was the experience of putting into practice the marketing research concepts and techniques which were presented in the classroom. Several students reported a much better grasp of sampling theory and questionnaire construction because of their project work. The project also enabled students to experience the reality of working cooperatively in fulfilling committee responsibilities. The team efforts involved a beneficial exchange of ideas with the rewarding byproduct of greater confidence for some students in their abilities to contribute to research efforts. Finally, the significance of meeting "business-like" deadlines, the reality of having committee efforts monitored and evaluated by a "client," and the meaningfulness of seeing the results used by the station, all combined to reinforce the rewards of the project.

Although most of the comments addressed the benefits of the experience, some also offered insights into problems encountered in such a project. The following were specific problems recognized by the students:

- one problem was getting a large group to generate useful ideas

- it is difficult coordinating a group to accomplish a task

- after I did my part, I got lost on what was happening -- maybe if the whole class were involved in bringing it together, it would be better

- the amount of work done by some individuals far surpassed that of the average person in the class

- it will be difficult to judge the contribution of each student.

Among the limitations associated with the committee approach, the inherent problems of coordination and motivation within groups were evident in a few instances. But these, too, are part of the realism of team research efforts. It was apparent from the student evaluations that the quality of the learning experience varied with the amount of involvement and effort of the individual members of the committees. A number of the students were highly involved, devoting considerable time to the project. Some of these individuals, after completing their own committee task, worked on the final stages of data analysis and report writing because they wanted to see the project through to completion.

Unfortunately, a few students regarded the committee approach as an opportunity to sit back and let their classmates do the work. The involved students inevitably experienced the aggravation which arose when some committee members delayed progress by a lack of cooperation and concern for the committee's work. As a means of evaluating the students, committee leaders were asked to rate the contributions of individual members to the overall committee efforts. While the professor was able to work more closely with the leaders and some other committee members, and thus could assess the quality of their efforts, he inevitably had to rely on the leaders' ratings for grading most of the class. A word of caution is therefore offered with respect to the problem of grading inherent in such a project. It should be made clear to the students at the outset that their contributions, or lack thereof, will be recognized in the project grades.

Station Reactions

WMVS personnel involved with the project were asked whether the class' efforts had fulfilled their objectives for the combined university-station survey and whether they would work with marketing research classes on similar survey projects in the future. Station personnel were unanimous in their praise of the work done by the class and the quality of the final report. They felt that the project demonstrated the advantages of a public television station working with a university marketing research class to address community problems, and that this was a logical approach for future in-depth research into significant community issues.

Interestingly, the special programs manager and the producer felt this was as much of a learning experience for them as it was for the students. For example, they had developed a new appreciation of the need for clear, comprehensive research objectives to guide the project. These are essential not only in gaining student understanding and commitment but also in guiding question formulation. In addition, they learned the value of pretesting the questionnaire. At this point in the liaison relationship the professor's guidance is especially important in helping the station representatives see which questions should be clarified and which should be dropped. For example, it was concluded that a question on the reasons people commit crimes was not only troublesome to the respondents but also inappropriate to the survey. The station representatives also gained a better understanding of the limitations of telephone interviewing, such as the required brevity of the questionnaire and the respondent's unwillingness to divulge some information (i.e., precautionary measures taken to prevent crime) over the telephone. Finally, they had come to realize the caution required in interpreting survey results. The special programs manager indicated, in summary, that the station, because of its experiences with this project, was better prepared to guide and support future university-public television research.

SUMMARY

In the report which prompted the passage of the Public Broadcasting Act of 1967, the Carnegie Commission noted that "cities are suddenly confronted with an unending series of new problems ... that demand the engagement of each individual citizen, who must be both informed and moved to act " [3, p. 17] . Public television can best fulfill its promise and responsibility to serve in the public interest by addressing the problems of America's communities and by providing an open forum for the discussion of solutions to these problems. Indeed, the FCC has directed that public television stations be held accountable for ascertaining community programming needs and providing programs that deal with the issues involved.

This paper has reported the combined effort of a public television station and a university marketing research class to conduct a survey as the basis for a special program on a community problem. The survey represented a class project in which student committees were responsible for the various research stages, from the setting of research objectives to the actual report writing. The benefits of this educational experience for the students included the opportunity to put research concepts and techniques into practice, the realism of working on a research project as a team, and the meaningfulness of contributing to research results that would actually be used and could be seen on television. The chief benefit to public television station WMVS was the opportunity to pool its resources with those of the university to provide programming which matches "the high standards that the community deserves" [4] .

This combined public television station-marketing research class approach to more relevant local programming can and should be repeated in other cities. Table 1 lists forty cities in which there is a public television station with a university as licensee. This list is by no means exhaustive, for there are many more cities with colleges and public television stations with boards of education or other organizations as licensees.

In assessing the prospects for similar joint program research efforts in these and other cities, both marketing educators and public television management should realize that such efforts are totally consistent with public television programming goals to report and interpret public issues and to provide means for community participation in the making of public decisions and the solution of problems [1] . Public television stations would surely welcome marketing educators' ideas for program research and students' help in conducting community surveys. Besides furnishing students with new insight into the role of marketing research in dealing with public issues, projects similar to that reported in this paper would help students experience the marketing concept in action through public television stations' efforts to meet community programming needs. Marketing educators should pursue this excellent opportunity to provide students with a beneficial class project.

TABLE 1

CITIES WITH UNIVERSITY-LICENSED PUBLIC TELEVISION STATIONS

| City | Public Television Station | University Licensee |
|------|---------------------------|---------------------|
| Albuquerque, NM | KNME | Univ. of New Mexico |
| Athens, GA | WGTV | Univ. of Georgia |
| Athens, OH | WOUB | Ohio Univ. |
| Bloomington, IN | WTIU | Indiana Univ. |
| Boise, ID | KAID | Boise State Univ. |
| Bowling Green, OH | WBGU | Bowling Green St. Univ. |
| Brookings, SD | KESD | South Dakota St. Univ. |
| Burlington, VT | WETK | Univ. of Vermont |
| Carbondale, IL | WSIU | Southern Illinois Univ. |
| Chapel Hill, NC | WUNC | Univ. of North Carolina |
| University Park, PA | WPSX | Pennsylvania St. Univ. |

TABLE 1 (continued)

| City | Public Television Station | University Licensee |
|------|---------------------------|---------------------|
| College Station, TX | KAMU | Texas A & M Univ. |
| Columbus, OH | WOSU | Ohio State Univ. |
| Durham, NH | WENH | Univ. of New Hampshire |
| East Lansing, MI | WKAR | Michigan State Univ. |
| Fairbanks, AK | KUAC | Univ. of Alaska |
| Gainesville, FL | WUFT | Univ. of Florida |
| Houston, TX | KUHT | Univ. of Houston |
| Las Cruces, NM | KRWG | New Mexico State Univ. |
| Lubbock, TX | KTXT | Texas Tech Univ. |
| Lincoln, NE | KUON | Univ. of Nebraska |
| Madison, WI | WHA | Univ. of Wisconsin |
| Marquette, MI | WNMU | Northern Michigan Univ. |
| Morgantown, WV | WMVU | West Virginia Univ. |
| Moscow, ID | KUID | Univ. of Idaho |
| Muncie, IN | WIPB | Ball State Univ. |
| Orono, ME | WMEB | Univ. of Maine |
| Phoenix, AZ | KAET | Arizona State Univ. |
| Pocatello, ID | KBGL | Idaho State Univ. |
| Provo, UT | KBYU | Bringham Young Univ. |
| Pullman, WA | KWSU | Washington State Univ. |
| Salt Lake City, UT | KUED | Univ. of Utah |
| San Diego, CA | KPBS | San Diego State Univ. |
| Seattle, WA | KCTS | Univ. of Washington |
| Tallahassee, FL | WFSU | Florida State Univ. |
| Tampa, FL | WUSF | Univ. of South Florida |
| Topeka, KS | KYWU | Washburn Univ. |
| Tucson, AZ | KUAT | Univ. of Arizona |
| Urbana, IL | WILL | Univ. of Illinois |
| Vermillion, SD | KUSD | Univ. of South Dakota |

REFERENCES

1.  Blakely, Robert J.  The People's Instrument:  A
    Philosophy of Programming for Public Television.
    Washington: Public Affairs Press, 1971.

2.  Primer on Ascertainment of Community Problems by
    Broadcast Applicants.  41 FCC 75-1361, Dkt. 19715
    (1976).

3.  Public Television: A Program for Action, The Report of
    the Carnegie Commission on Educational Television.
    New York: Bantam, 1967.

4.  Turner, Tom.  "Conducting a Cooperative, Market-Wide
    Community  Ascertainment Effort...and Making It Pay,"
    report prepared under a grant from The Corporation for
    Public Broadcasting, WMVS, Milwaukee, 1976.

# NEGOTIATION IN MULTINATIONAL MARKETING: THE RUM GAME

James H. Sood, American University
Arch G. Woodside, University of South Carolina

## ABSTRACT

An educational classroom case and exercise in multinational marketing is presented. The experiential exercise involves seven student teams role-playing six countries and the EEC in negotiating U.S. tariff changes on rum. Results in testing the exercise indicated heightened student interest and understanding of the role of negotiations in multinational marketing.

## INTRODUCTION

Kotler [3] has proposed that the essence of marketing is the transaction, that is, the exchange of values between two parties. "Marketing is specifically concerned with how transactions are created, stimulated, facilitated, and valued" [3, p. 49]. The Willett and Pennington study [5, 6, 9] of consumer buyer-seller transactions within retail stores using a wireless recording system is one of the best and most well-known exchange studies in marketing. Capon, Holbrook, and Hulbert [2] have provided an extensive review of the available transaction literature in marketing. While Sheth [8] has formally incorporated exchanges between members of the buying center in his model of industrial buying, limited theory or research is available on buyer-seller transactions for classroom use in marketing education. Outside of sales presentations in the undergraduate personal selling course, marketing students are asked infrequently to study or participate in transactions.

The purpose of this article is to provide a classroom experiential learning exercise in marketing negotiations within a multinational setting. Participating students are requested to study background materials on marketing rum, prepare a brief position paper as representatives of an assigned country, and negotiate the question of United States rum tariff reductions with students representing other countries.

## GOALS OF THE RUM GAME

The Rum Game is designed for students to learn (1) the role of multiple government intervention in multinational marketing, (2) pricing and distribution strategy effects on market shares and sales volumes, (3) the experience of negotiating and bargaining in a marketing setting, and (4) the role of the multinational corporation in affecting government regulations. Thus, the aim of the game is to achieve multiple educational objectives and to increase student active participation in the classroom. The Rum Game may be a useful complement to lectures on transactions in multinational marketing between governments', buyers, and sellers.

Negotiation and other transaction exercises in marketing education were presented in a workshop session of the 1976 American Marketing Association's Educators' Conference [1, 4, 7, 10]. Similar to this previous workshop program, an additional purpose of the Rum Game is to promote greater interest and use of experiential approaches by marketing educators in the classroom.

## METHOD

### Group Size

Seven to thirty students may be included as participants in the Rum Game, one to four students to represent the governments of the United States, Barbados, Jamaica, Brazil, Puerto Rico, Trinidad and Tobago, and the European Economic Community (EEC). The balance of the students in the class may be assigned as judges in the game. Brazil, Trinidad and Tobago, and the EEC may be eliminated if class size is small.

### Time Required

The Rum Game requires fifty to seventy minutes for the negotiations and thirty to fifty minutes for class discussion following the exercise. Some outside classroom assigned reading time of the exercise is necessary (fifty minutes). The class discussion following the exercise is necessary for many students to understand the complexities in multinational negotiations.

### Materials and Instructions

Students should be instructed at least one week before the exercise that they are to represent one of seven multinational entities. Students should form into teams of up to four members and they should be assigned to represent one of the six countries, EEC, or to act as judges. The case for the Rum Game (appended) should be given to each student for reading. Each student group should be requested to prepare a brief (three to five page) position paper on recommended changes to U.S. tariff regulations on rum. The students should be informed that a representative of their group is to present their position paper during class in the following week and they should be prepared to negotiate with representatives of the other countries on the U.S. rum tariff.

A classroom with moveable chairs should be used during the actual exercise. The students should sit with their respective team members, and the teams organized in a large circle. The use of a tape recorder is particularly helpful in analyzing the critical points in the negotiations during the class discussion following the exercise.

### Process

The class may be instructed that each team is to present a five minute opening statement on their country's position on the U.S. rum tariff regulations. Students representing Puerto Rico should present the first opening statement of their country's position. Students representing the U.S. should present the last statement. All students should be encouraged to offer comments and ask questions during these opening statements. Also, students should be instructed to insure that their country's statement is presented at the meeting.

The teams should be permitted to present counterarguments, plead, offer concessions, and make threats following the opening statements. Then, the U.S. student team should be requested to leave the room for five minutes and reach a decision on changes, if any, to be made on the U.S. rum tariff. The U.S. team should return, announce their decision and provide reasons for their action.

Students acting as judges should offer oral evaluations of each team's performance and suggest actions they believe should be taken by U.S. tariff authorities on rum.

The instructor should provide instructions for this process in writing to the participants before the negotiation meeting. The instructor should keep a low profile in the class during the negotiations by sitting to the rear of the class and not interrupting the discussions. (The discussions are likely to slowly develop into international alliances and conflicts.)

The Rum Game case material may be used as the only source of data. However, students might be encouraged to research secondary data using the United Nations Yearbook, World Bank Atlas, and The Liquor Handbook. Managers of liquor retail stores and liquor distributors may be contacted by students for primary information.

## RESULTS

Both authors have had similar results in playing the Rum Game with their classes. Graduate students grasped the concept of role playing much quicker than undergraduates. A substantial amount of explanation was not required for graduate students to understand the instructions and to proceed with the negotiations.

Both graduate and undergraduate students made use of secondary and primary research ranging from two to twelve and zero to five sources for 21 graduate and 21 undergraduate teams, respectively.

Written reactions to the Rum Game was over 80% favorable among both undergraduates and graduates. Both authors had to stop the discussions on two occasions because class time was over. "I liked this exercise because I felt that I could get my hands into the problem" was the most typical open-ended student reaction to the Rum Game.

Instructors using the Rum Game should expect 25% to 50% of their students not to negotiate across countries, i.e., with students representing other countries. Most teams appoint one spokesperson for the opening statement and the negotiation. However, nearly all students do contribute to the discussions, at least, within their own teams by providing suggestions, comments, and arguing with their own spokespersons during the negotiations.

Heightened student interest and understanding of negotiation in multinational marketing were observed in class meetings following the exercise. Student comments in later classes included more remarks on likely reactions to decisions made unilaterally in multinational marketing than prior to playing the game. While these findings are limited to the authors' experiences, the results support the recommendation to classroom test the Rum Game.

The instructor (facilitator) may want to list the advantages and disadvantages of three decisions for the United States: (1) an increase, (2) decrease, (3) and no change in the rum tariff. Students may be requested to offer profit or loss estimates resulting for the multiple parties (including U.S. consumers) for each of the three decisions. Then, total profit or loss for each decision may be calculated. This procedure should produce greater student awareness and benefit of free trade.

## APPENDIX: THE RUM GAME

The Federal Alcohol Administration Act is the principal legislation that regulates the production and marketing of alcoholic beverages in the United States. This Act defines rum as "an alcoholic distillate from the fermented juice of sugar cane, sugar cane syrup, sugar molasses, or other sugar cane by-products, produced at less than 190 proof and in such manner that the distillate possesses the taste, aroma, and characteristics generally attributed to rum, and bottled at not less than 80 proof; and also includes mixtures solely of such distillates."

## The Market

The growth of the whiskey market in the United States has been decreasing in recent years. Whiskey blends, straights, and bonds have actually decreased while Scotch and Canadian whiskeys are increasing at a decreasing rate. The consumption of non-whiskeys such as vodka, gin, and rum, however, has been increasing markedly.

Industry analysts have observed that the predominant trend is away from the traditional whiskeys and toward the lighter (in color), more bland (in taste), lower proof ( around 80°) distilled spirits. In addition, there has been a significant movement of trading down or switching to lower priced brands, which were lightly advertised or not advertised at all. A large youth market (20's and early 30's) has also emerged rather suddenly, together with a diversification or broader buying of different types of distilled spirits by consumers. The consensus of the industry is that the U.S. rum market will continue to grow at an annual rate of 4-6% until 1985. The relative growth of the rum market is shown in Table 1.

TABLE 1

RUM SALES IN U.S. AS PERCENTAGE OF ALL
DISTILLED SPIRITS SALES

| 1970 | 1971 | 1972 | 1973 | 1974 | 1975 |
|------|------|------|------|------|------|
| 3.1% | 3.3% | 3.4% | 3.8% | 3.7% | 3.9% |

Source: Time, Marketing Report #1940, 1976.

The sources of supply of rum in the U.S. market are shown in Tables 2 and 3.

The rum industry in the United States and most other countries is dominated by Bacardi which has between 65-70% of the market. Bacardi has established this position by the development of an effective distribution system of over 200 wholesalers; by an extensive advertising program; and by a considerable marketing research effort. The success of Bacardi's marketing program is illustrated by the fact that Bacardi is almost synonymous with rum. Bacardi produces all of its rum for the U.S. market in Puerto Rico. Most of the rum is shipped in bulk containers to Jacksonville, Florida where it is aged, blended, and bottled. Bacardi rum for the West Coast is bottled in Puerto Rico and shipped directly to that area.

## Marketing Mix

The dominance of Bacardi and the difficulty of increasing market share is demonstrated by a project undertaken by a Jamaica rum producer in 1974. This producer and its import agent lowered the bottle price of their rum from 90¢ higher to within 25¢ (per fifth) of Bacardi throughout the State of Texas. At the same time, they heavily increased the display promotion in the retail stores. This effort was continued for an entire year, at a loss of about $200,000, without increasing their market share. While the result was disappointing to the producer, the demand curve for this brand of rum was shown to be inelastic in this price range.

The vast majority of bottled rum products on the market today are "light" rums. The heavy, dark rums are essentially products of the past. About the only difference be-

TABLE 2

ESTIMATED RUM ENTERING TRADE CHANNELS IN U.S. MARKET
(1,000's of wine gallons)

| | 1970 | 1971 | 1972 | 1973 | 1974 | 1975 |
|---|---|---|---|---|---|---|
| Puerto Rico | 9,049 (73.2%) | 10,591 (76.8) | 9,623 (70.4) | 11,931 (79.0) | 11,895 (76.7) | 13,601 (77.6) |
| Virgin Islands | 249 (2.0) | 199 (1.4) | 401 (2.9) | 872 (6.5) | 1,012 (6.5) | 1,309 (7.5) |
| Other Domestic | 2,909 (23.6) | 2,448 (17.8) | 3,083 (22.5) | 1,662 (11.0) | 1,905 (12.3) | 1,902 (10.9) |
| Total Domestic | 12,207 (98.6) | 13,238 (96.0) | 13,107 (95.9) | 14,465 (95.8) | 14,812 (95.5) | 16,812 (95.9) |
| Imported | 141 (1.1) | 546 (4.0) | 566 (4.1) | 638 (4.2) | 694 (4.5) | 714 (4.1) |
| Total | 12,348 | 13,784 | 13,673 | 15,103 | 15,506 | 17,526 |

Percentages of total for each year are in parentheses.
Source: Distilled Spirits Council of U.S. Washington, D.C. 1975 Annual Statistical Review.

TABLE 3

U.S. RUM IMPORTS FROM SELECTED COUNTRIES
(1,000's of proof gallons)

| | | | | | | |
|---|---|---|---|---|---|---|
| Barbados | 35.9 | 16.9 | 16.7 | 34.8 | 35.9 | 37.9 |
| Brazil | 0.2 | 0.2 | - | 0.2 | 0.2 | 98.0 |
| Guyana | 48.5 | 53.4 | 98.5 | 60.6 | 63.3 | 63.7 |
| Jamaica | 322.9 | 255.4 | 446.6 | 515.2 | 579.4 | 504.9 |
| Trinidad | 2.2 | 1.2 | 2.4 | 7.3 | 3.0 | 10.1 |

Source: U.S. Department of Commerce, Bureau of the Census, Schedule A: U.S. Imports by Country of Origin.
OTHER SOURCES OF U.S. RUM IMPORTS: Antigua, Bahamas, British Virgin Islands, Canada, Cayman Islands, Columbia, Dominican Republic, French West Indies, Haiti, México, Netherlands Antilles, Turks & Caicos Islands.

tween the white rums and the golden rums is that the latter are colored with caramel and the former usually filtered through charcoal. The ratio of white to golden rum sold in the U.S. is about three to one. Thus, the product has been designed to meet the present needs of the market which are light, bland, 80° rums.

All imported rum, including Puerto Rican and Virgin Island rum, pass through the same type of distribution channel. The one exception is Bacardi which does its own importing and bottling. Because of the many economies in handling, shipping, bottling, taxes, etc., there is a decided trend toward shipping rum in bulk (usually at about 150° and in 4,500 gallon steel containers) from the producing countries to the importers in the U.S. The importers age, blend, bottle, label, and distribute the rum to wholesalers and the control states.

Government regulations prohibit advertising of distilled spirits on radio or television. Most of the national advertising is in magazines and is sponsored by the producers and importers, usually on a joint basis. Local advertising primarily uses the newspaper medium, and private retailers use this form of promotion to announce specific sales. The major national advertiser in the rum industry is "Rums of Puerto Rico." This organization is supported by the Puerto Rican Government and it currently spends about $3 million annually to advertise Puerto Rican rum in an institutional manner. The Bacardi Company spends approximately $2.5 million per year on advertising. The other companies in the industry allocate relatively much smaller amounts to this form of promotion. Personal selling, or pushing the product through the channel, is still a major form of promotion in the rum business.

Taxes and Regulations

The federal excise tax is $10.50 per proof gallon if the alcohol content is 100 proof or more and $10.50 per wine gallon if the proof is less than 100. The proof gallon is calculated by dividing the proof of the distilled spirits by 100, when the proof is 100 or more. When the proof is less than 100, it is considered to be the same as 100 proof and equals one proof gallon. The wine gallon is simply the same as the liquid volume of measure, that is, one gallon equals 231 cubic inches. For example, one gallon at 150 proof equals one proof gallon. Both of these examples equal one wine gallon.

The federal excise tax is on all alcoholic beverages produced or imported in the United States. The amount of the excise tax has not been changed since 1951. Senators Jacob Javits and Charles Percy sponsored a bill in the 1975 Congress which would raise the federal excise tax by 50%. This bill did not clear the Senate Finance Committee, but there is a chance that this bill in some form might be passed in the coming session of Congress.

The distribution and sale of alcoholic beverages are controlled by the state governments in 18 states. The approval of that state's alcoholic beverage control board is required to sell a particular brand of alcoholic beverage in one of these states. The requirements to obtain this approval vary by state, but essentially the seller must convince the board that the brand will satisfy a need that is not being satisfied by the brands that the state is presently offering its customers. The state taxes in the states other than control states range from $1.50 to $4.30 per gallon, with an average of $2.60 per gallon.

The special situation of Puerto Rico and the Virgin Islands stems from the fact that these countries are political territories of the United States. It was established by legislative act in 1954 that the federal excise tax on applicable products produced in these territories and exported to the U.S. will be rebated to the producing territory. In approximate terms, this amounts annually to over $100 million for Puerto Rico and $20 million for the Virgin Islands as a result of rum shipments to the U.S. These revenues are about 10% and 15% respectively of the total government budgets of these territories. The rebate of the federal excise tax is the singular aspect of the industry that makes it a unique situation for negotiation.

Table 6 shows that the tariffs on all other alcoholic beverages have been reduced substantially, particularly since the Kennedy Round, while the tariff on rum has been held constant at $1.75 per proof gallon. The present position of the United States on this question is that it is highly sensitive to the interests of all parties concerned with the tariff on rum imports in the United States. On one hand is a strong desire to work with the countries in the Western Hemisphere, and on the other hand is the special consideration of Puerto Rico and the Virgin Islands.

TABLE 6

IMPORT DUTIES ON DISTILLED SPIRITS
(per proof gallon if 100 proof or more,
wine gallon if less than 100 proof)

| Class and type | 1970 | 1971 | 1972-1973 | 1974-1975 |
|---|---|---|---|---|
| WHISKEY--(Scotch and Irish)............... | $.71 | $.61 | $.51 | $.51 |
| OTHER WHISKEY--(Canadian, etc.) ............. | .87 | .75 | .62 | .62 |
| RUM ...................... | 1.75 | 1.75 | 1.75 | 1.75 |
| GIN ...................... | .70 | .60 | .50 | .50 |
| BRANDY in containers each holding: | | | | |
| One gallon or less valued not over $9.00.... | .87 | .75 | .62 | .62 |
| Valued $9.00 to $17.00... | 5.00 | 5.00 | 5.00 | 1.25 |
| More than one gal. valued not over $9.00........... | .70 | .60 | .50 | .50 |
| Valued $9.00 to $17.00... | 5.00 | 5.00 | 5.00 | 1.00 |
| Valued over $17.00....... | -- | -- | -- | 5.00 |
| CORDIALS................... | .70 | .60 | .50 | .50 |
| BITTERS fit for beverage purposes............ | .70 | .60 | .50 | .50 |
| Other................... | 1.31 | 1.12 | .94 | .94 |
| ETHYL ALCOHOL for beverages................. | 1.57 | 1.35 | 1.12 | 1.12 |
| BEVERAGE SPIRITS other than above: | | | | |
| Arrack.................... | 1.40 | 1.20 | 1.00 | 1.00 |
| Aquavit.................. | .59 | .51 | .42 | .42 |
| OTHER spirits and preparations: | | | | |
| Chief value of distilled spirits: | | | | |
| Spirits................. | 1.25 | 1.25 | 1.25 | 1.25 |
| Other·................. | 1.75 | 1.50 | 1.25 | 1.25 |

SOURCE: U.S. Tariff Commission, 1976.

All potential negotiations concerning the tariff on rum imports would be held within the framework of the Multilateral Trade Negotiations in Geneva, Switzerland. Under the authority of the Trade Act of 1974, the President can negotiate tariff reductions up to 60% of the tariff without specific approval of Congress if the tariff is greater than 5% ad valorem, and he can eliminate the tariff completely if the tariff is 5% ad valorem or less. The U.S. tariff on rum would fall into the former category. All concessions on non-tariff barriers must be approved by Congress.

One other possibility is the Generalized System of Preference (GSP). By executive order, the U.S. could eliminate the tariff on rum for five years to all Most Favored Nations, except a country which supplies more than 50% of the imports of that product.

Perhaps the only non-tariff barrier to the U.S. rum market is the method of assessing the federal excise tax and the duty on imported bottle spirits. Both of these levies are calculated on a proof gallon basis if the product imported for consumption is 100 proof or more and on a wine gallon if less than 100 proof. Since most bottled rum is imported at 80 proof (40% alcohol) rather than 100 proof (50% alcohol), this means that 10% water is subjected to the federal excise tax and the tariff. If this assessment were applied to the domestic producers, there would not be a non-tariff barrier. However, U.S. producers (and bulk importers) pay the tax on withdrawal from bonded warehouses at a time when the spirits are usually about 100 proof. This method of assessment provides the domestic producers and bulk importers with a relative 10% advantage in the excise tax, and also a 10% advantage in the tariff in the case of the bulk importers, vis-a-vis the bottled rum importers. This has been one of the motivating factors behind the increased importation of alcoholic beverages in bulk in the U.S.

Another regulation that has probably had some effect on the rum market in the U.S. is that American tourists can bring back only one quart of spirits duty free, while before 1965 they could bring back one gallon duty free. One effect of this is shown by an example that occurred in Barbados a few years ago. One of the Bajan (Barbadian) rum producers heavily promoted its rum to a large group of tourists from Winnipeg. Without any additional advertising or sales promotion, sales to the Province of Manitoba have increased substantially since the initial promotion effort.

While Puerto Rico and the Virgin Islands can ship goods to the U.S. without tariff, other countries have similar opportunities with other regional or national markets. For example, the former British Commonwealth countries can export rum to the European Economic Community (EEC) countries duty free, within prescribed import quotas, under the Lome Convention of 1975. The French Caribbean countries of Martinique and Guadalupe also have this advantage since they are French Departments. The multinational operational approach of the Bacardi Company illustrates the importance of the tariff and non-tariff barriers. In order to avoid these difficulties, Bacardi supplies the French market from its facility in Martinique; the English market from its operations in the Bahamas and Bermuda; the U.S. market from Puerto Rico; and so on. Of course there are many other factors that influence the trend and level of exports.

The barriers to the U.S. market are considerably less than the barriers to the rum markets of other countries. Nevertheless, rum has not received equal treatment with the other alcoholic beverages in past multilateral negotiations.

The cause of this unequal treatment in the case of rum is

TABLE 7

RUM INDUSTRIES IN SELECTED COUNTRIES, 1975
(millions of proof gallons)

| | Production | Domestic Market | Exports | Distilling Capacity | Domestic Sugar Capacity[b] | Sugar Cane Production |
|---|---|---|---|---|---|---|
| Barbados | 1.5 | 0.6 | 0.9 | 5.0 | 2.7 | 90,000 tons |
| Jamaica | 6.5 | 2.0 | 4.5 | 11.5 | 11.4 | 380,000 " |
| Trinidad and Tobago | 3.8 | 1.8 | 2.0 | 6.0 | 7.5 | 250,000 " |
| Puerto Rico | 13.8 | 4.0 | 9.8[a] | N/A | 9.0 | 300,000 " |

[a]Exports include shipments to U.S.

[b]One ton of sugar cane = 50 gallons of molasses = 30 gallons of rum (approximate).

that the U.S. cannot negotiate concessions that would undermine the Puerto Rican economy. Most probably, any U.S. gain in negotiations would tend to help the overall U.S. economy, while any U.S. concession would tend to hurt the Puerto Rican economy. It is not a quid pro quo negotiating situation. No possible concessions to Puerto Rico exist that would compensate them for a reduction of Puerto Rican rum sales in the U.S. market, since this would mean, in effect, a reduction in government revenue because of the decreased rebate of the excise tax. Since no other likely source for this amount of revenue exists, the U.S. reluctance to jeopardize the situation is understandable.

Bacardi, which represents about 75-80% of the Puerto Rican rum industry, was initially a Cuban company that moved its primary operations to Puerto Rico after the revolution. The company is now a multinational operation with production facilities in nine countries and bottling plants in six countries. Bacardi cannot be considered a Puerto Rican company, either in ownership or management, and thus would appear to have little allegiance to Puerto Rico.

REFERENCES

1. Armstrong, J. Scott. "The Panalba Role Playing Case," in Combined Proceedings, Kenneth L. Bernhardt, ed. Chicago: American Marketing Association, 1976, 213-217.

2. Capon, Noel, Morris B. Holbrook, and James H. Hulbert. "Selling Processing and Buyer Behavior: Theoretical Implications of Recent Research," in Consumer and Industrial Buying Behavior, Arch G. Woodside, Jagdish N. Sheth, and Peter D. Bennett, eds. New York: Elsevier North-Holland, 1977, forthcoming.

3. Kotler, Philip. Marketing Management. Englewood Cliffs, NJ: Prentice-Hall, 1976.

4. Mittelstaedt, Robert A. "Word-of-Mouth Advertising in Action," in Combined Proceedings, Kenneth L. Bernhardt, ed. Chicago: American Marketing Association, 1976, 217-218.

5. Olshavsky, Richard W. "Customer-Salesman Interaction in Appliance Retailing," Journal of Marketing Research, 10 (May 1973), 208-12.

6. Pennington, Allen L. "Customer-Salesman Bargaining Behavior in Retail Transaction," Journal of Marketing Research, 5 (August 1968), 255-62.

7. Rosenberg, Larry J. "A Mock Problem Exercise: Vocational Schools Regulation," Combined Proceedings, Kenneth L. Bernhardt, ed. Chicago: American Marketing Association, 1976, 222-23.

8. Sheth, Jagdish N. "A Model of Industrial Buyer Behavior," Journal of Marketing, 37 (October 1972), 50-6.

9. Willett, Ronald P. and Allen Pennington. "Customer and Salesman: The Anatomy of Choice in a Retail Setting," in Proceedings, Peter D. Bennett, ed. Chicago: American Marketing Association, 1966, 598-616.

10. Woodside, Arch G. "Manufacturer and Wholesaler Exercise in Seller and Buyer Interactions," in Combined Proceedings, Kenneth L. Bernhardt, ed. Chicago: American Marketing Association, 1976, 219-21.

MARKSTRAT: A NEW APPROACH FOR TEACHING MARKETING STRATEGY

Jean-Claude Larreche, INSEAD, Fontainebleau, France

## ABSTRACT

Markstrat is a new game specifically designed to teach marketing strategy. The basic guidelines developed from pedagogical objectives to direct the design of the game are presented, and the main features of Markstrat are described. Markstrat generates a very large number of competitive market situations, from which a diversity of alternate product/market strategies can be formulated, evaluated and implemented. A high degree of transfer from experience gained in participating in Markstrat, to real world situations has been observed.

## INTRODUCTION

Marketing strategy usually refers to the selection of product/market positions in a dynamic and competitive environment. It represents the marketing component of a corporate strategy, and guides the design of marketing plans and programs. Although marketing strategy issues have received increasing attention in the literature, most marketing management courses are organized around, and concentrate on, the marketing mix. There is a lack of integration of some components of the strategic process, such as market opportunities analysis [13], and of the complete marketing curriculum, despite an increasing need in this direction [7]. Moreover, the traditional pedagogical approaches, such as readings, lectures, and cases, are of limited value to teach marketing strategy beyond the basic concepts. Students tend to feel that they understand these concepts easily, but get frustrated with the lack of tangible feedback on their ability to implement them in a realistic situation.

Some more innovative approaches such as course projects or "New Venture Analysis" [12] create a high level of involvement among students, and give them an opportunity to apply previously acquired marketing knowledge to a real situation. They however cover only the analysis stage of the strategic process and do not adequately illustrate the actual problems involved in the selection, implementation and adaptation of a marketing strategy. It is only through practice in a competitive and dynamic environment, over a number of planning periods, that students can assimilate and see the implications of marketing strategy concepts over the entire strategic process. It is for this purpose that a marketing strategy game, Markstrat, was developed.

## GUIDELINES FOR THE DESIGN OF A
## MARKETING STRATEGY GAME

Over the last 20 years, much experience has been gathered in the development and use of business games [11]. In marketing, the trend has been to move from the earlier more complex games [2,4] to much simpler ones [6,8]. These games allow the students to investigate market reactions to changes in the elements of the marketing mix, and to formulate marketing programs in a competitive environment. They tend, however, to deal with the management of existing products rather than with strategic marketing issues.

By giving the students the opportunity to manage the marketing department of a simulated company, a marketing strategy game should take them through the complete process of: (a) analyzing market opportunities; (b) selecting product/market strategies; (c) implementing these strategies with marketing programs, including product management,

and interaction with other departments of the firm; (d) controlling and updating the marketing strategy. While most marketing games concentrate on stage (c), and the determination of market response to specific marketing instruments, a marketing strategy game should emphasize stages (a), (b), and (d).

It is obvious that some basic choices in the design of a game will have a major influence on its ability to illustrate alternative pedagogical concepts. It should be expected, for instance, that a small and fixed number of products and markets will limit the importance of the marketing strategy and will instead direct the attention of students towards marketing instruments. For this reason, the following guidelines were set prior to the design of Markstrat:

### A Long-term Perspective

The simulated time horizon should be of the order of 5 to 10 years to be able to evaluate the long-term effects of marketing strategies, and to cover a wide variety of market situations (for instance, in terms of the product life cycle.) Moreover, short-term marketing activities, such as promotions, are relatively unimportant given the pedagogical objectives of the game and should not be considered.

### A Multiplicity of Markets

Several markets of different sizes, with different needs, and at different stages of their development should be present to stress the importance of the analysis of market opportunities and of strategic choices. It was also felt that interdependent markets, such as consumer segments which can buy the same products, shop in the same distribution channels or be exposed to the same advertising messages, would provide a richer pedagogical environment than independent markets, defined geographically for instance. This orientation allows in particular the consideration of synergy effects and company/product/distribution/market fit in the design of a marketing strategy.

### Product Line Management

Companies should not be able to introduce new brands as well as improving or suppressing others. Product development should be made possible along a number of product dimensions. Market information should be available to guide the adaptation of products to market needs, while at the same time stressing the difference between product perception, and product physical characteristics.

### A Graphical Representation of Product/Market Positions

It was felt that a graphical representation of product/market positions would help the students to think in terms of marketing strategy. The perceptual maps of brands similarities and preferences obtained through multivariate analyses, such as non-metric multidimensional scaling, offer a convenient representation of these product/market positions.

### An Indirect Effect of Marketing Instruments on Brand Sales

A direct effect of a marketing instrument on brand sales, through the use of an aggregate response function. If, on the opposite, the effect of a marketing instrument on the market is represented in a more indirect and complex fashion, students will concentrate more on understanding market phenomena, and will rely more on marketing research data.

In addition, students will realize that, while some patterns may be generalizable, the aggregate impact of an instrument on sales is very often situation specific. For instance, the game may be modeled to include disaggregated effects of advertising on consumer awareness, brand positioning, purchase intents and distribution acceptance. Although an aggregate response of sales to advertising may still be estimated, this response will automatically evolve over time and situations, according to the relative importance of the intermediate relationships. In particular, in a maturing market, with increased awareness levels, stronger brand positions, and higher distribution coverages, the aggregate effect of advertising on sales is expected to decrease. It is certainly pedagogically more satisfactory for students to try to understand the market behavior in this fashion, and draw inferences for marketing strategies, rather than trying to "beat the game."

## Environmental Changes

In addition to the obviously high level of competition, the game environment should be dynamic to force the students to permanently consider uncertainty in the design of their marketing strategy, and to encourage contingency planning.

## A Comprehensive Set of Marketing Research Studies

Companies should be able to buy a number of marketing research studies which should give, within the limits set by the accuracy of measuring instruments, a good grasp of the market behavior.

## Additional Features Enhancing Strategic Marketing Issues

The game should obviously illustrate marketing strategy concepts such as experience effects or product portfolio analyses [3]. In addition, to relieve students from some operational problems, it should include automatic short-term adjustments such as a partial adaptation of production planning to sales evolution within a simulated year.

These guidelines do not make a game. A great number of other decisions have to be taken in the design of the game, before it is "finalized." Moreover, modifications are inevitably made when testing the game and as new experience is acquired. But these guidelines ensure that the original pedagogical objectives are preserved when, in the midst of developing the game, design choices are made in the light of new ideas, and of software as well as hardware problems. In the end, these guidelines also summarize the distinctive qualities of the Markstrat structure for the teaching of marketing strategy.

## DESCRIPTION OF MARKSTRAT[1]

Five firms are competing in Markstrat, each under the management of a group of students. These firms start with different characteristics, and have global market shares from 10 to 30%, so that marketing strategies should be adopted by each firm according to its particular competitive situation. Each firm makes a set of decisions for yearly simulated periods, and the game should be run for a minimum of six simulated years to have a meaningful pedagogical impact.

[1]Markstrat has been developed at the Center Europeen d'Education Permanente (CEDEP) and at the European Institute of Business Administration (INSEAD), Fontainebleu, France. The authors wish to acknowledge the financial support of these institutions in the development of the game. The Markstrat programs have been written in Basic for the Hewlett Packard Series of computers, but can obviously be adapted for other systems. A more complete description of Markstrat is given in [10].

In Markstrat, only the operations of the marketing department are detailed. The students do not thus have to consider Balance Sheets and other "external" financial reports. Instead, they are allocated a Budget which should cover all marketing expenses. Revenues and expenses are detailed in the Marketing Department Contribution Statement which indicates the gross marketing contribution for each brand, and the total net contribution for the department. Obviously, this contribution does not represent disposable cash for the marketing department, and it is primarily a measure of performance, among others. In addition, it will generally have an impact on the budget made available to the marketing department for the next period.

The marketing department has thus all freedom in designing and implementing its marketing strategy. It can use its budget freely to introduce new brands, to modify others, to advertise, to buy marketing research studies, to request specific projects from the R & D department, or to increase its sales force. In addition it specifies required production levels for each brand to the production department. In the end, the marketing department is also fully responsible for its actions: for example, it does have to pay for R & D projects which were requested but then not used, and the cost of excess inventories will be included in its contribution statement in case of too optimistic forecasts.

The Markstrat industry manufactures and markets a consumer durable good, the Sonite. At the start of the game each firm carries two brands, which enjoy different positions in the market. The physical characteristics of these brands are known by all firms. The overall market is growing but industry experts have isolated over the years five main consumer segments which present different needs and behaviors, and which are at different stages of their development. The Sonites are sold through three distribution channels, and the Markstrat firms organize their sales force by channel type. Naturally, the five consumer segments present different shopping habits in these three distribution channels.

New Sonite brands are expected to be introduced in this growing market, as the existing brands do not fully satisfy the needs of the various segments, and the competitive structure is far from being stable. However, experience effects have been observed in this industry, and a proliferation of brands could be detrimental to the profitabilit of the firms.

The Markstrat environment has experienced relatively high GNP growth and inflation rates. It is likely that the government will impose price controls if the inflation rat increases beyond some undefined level. Finally, a recent technological breakthrough in the space industry makes feasible the development of a new product, the Vodite. Although there may be a market for this product, its devel opment would require relatively high R & D investments by the Markstrat firms. The Vodite would fulfill a different need than the Sonite, and there would be no substitution or complementarity effects between the two products, although they would be distributed through the same channels by a common sales force.

At the start of the game, each Markstrat firm possesses a detailed account of its situation, as well as information on a number of trends. They can gather additional information by purchasing, within the limit of their budget, up to 15 marketing research studies which include consumer surveys, consumer and distributor panels, semantic scales, perceptual mapping, market forecasts, estimates of competi tive advertising and sales forces, as well as advertising and sales force tests.

For each annual simulated period, the firms have to make a number of deicisions which are represented in Table 1. These decisions concern product management, sales force management, R & D, and marketing research. In addition other decisions can be negotiated with the game administrator who can incorporate them by modifying the firm's marketing budget or specifying exceptional profits or losses.

## TABLE 1

### Decisions in Markstrat

PRODUCT MANAGEMENT (for each brand)

- brand name, in case of introduction
- new product characteristics, if any
- price
- advertising budget
- advertising research budget
- advertising positioning objectives
- production planning

SALES FORCE MANAGEMENT

- Number of salesmen
- Allocation among three distribution channels

R & D (for each R & D project)

- Project name
- Budget
- Physical characteristics of researched product

MARKETING RESEARCH

- List of marketing research studies purchased

OTHER DECISIONS

- Other decisions may be made by the firms after negotiation with the game administrator. As a result of the negotiations, the administrator can modify the firm's marketing budget or specify exceptional profits or losses.

In fact, the decisions made by the firms represent only the implementation of their marketing strategy, while most of the students' time will be spent elaborating their marketing strategy. The comprehensive set of marketing research studies, as well as environmental and competitive information routinely provided with the annual reports, allow the students to make an in-depth analysis of opportunities. The formulation of a product/market strategy is then the major task of the groups. The multiplicity of markets (five segments in the Sonite market, plus a new Vodite market), and the possibility to introduce new brands or to reposition existing ones create a very large number of alternatives. A major aid in the visualization of these alternatives is provided by the perceptual maps, an example of which is represented in Figure I.

## FIGURE 1

### EXAMPLE OF A MARKSTRAT PERCEPTUAL MAP

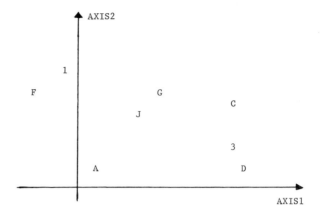

| IDEAL POINTS | SEGMENT | COORD.AXIS1 | COORD.AXIS2 |
|---|---|---|---|
| 1 | 1 | -1.5 | 8.1 |
| 2 | 2 | -5.7 | -4.0 |
| 3 | 3 | 15.8 | 2.9 |
| 4 | 4 | 12.9 | -8.0 |
| 5 | 5 | -12.4 | -7.8 |

| POSITIONING | BRAND | COORD.AXIS1 | COORD.AXIS2 |
|---|---|---|---|
| A | SAMA | 2.0 | 2.0 |
| B | SALT | 12.0 | -14.4 |
| C | SEMI | 15.5 | 5.3 |
| D | SELF | 17.0 | 1.8 |
| E | SIRO | -7.1 | -11.9 |
| F | SIBI | -6.0 | 7.2 |
| G | SOLD | 8.4 | 6.9 |
| H | SONO | -13.5 | 18.0 |
| I | SUSI | -7.8 | -10.3 |
| J | SULI | 5.7 | 5.0 |

This example represents only part of a fictitious Markstrat Perceptual Map. The letters and the numbers in the graph correspond to the positions of brands and ideal points of segments, respectively. The correspondence between the letters and the brands, as well as the coordinates on the two axes, are given in the table accompanying the perceptual map. Students are also told that an adequate stress level was obtained for two dimensions, and that no significant difference was found in brand similarities between segments, which makes a two-dimensional joint representation reasonable. Finally, when purchasing the appropriate marketing research studies, an interpretation of the two axes is given, based on semantic scales projections.

In this example, the brands SEMI and SELF are marketed by the same firm while each other brand belongs to a different competitor. The perceptual map indicates that SEMI and SELF are adequately positioned for segment 3, and SIBI for segment 1, while the three other brands may draw partly from both segments, illustrating single and multi-segments strategies. The most direct competitors of a given brand appear clearly, as well as potential cannibalization, as it is the case for SEMI and SELF.

Comparison of this perceptual map with those gathered in previous planning periods shows the dynamics of the market in terms of evolution of ideal points and brand positions. The evaluation of alternate positions on this map requires the consideration of a number of factors such as: market potential, growth and evolution of needs for each segment; market power of existing brands in terms of awareness, preferences, distribution coverage; intensity of competition; cannibalization; and synergy effects.

After an analysis of the opportunities present in each of the segments, of potential competitive undertakings, and of its own situation, a firm will select a given product/market strategy. In implementing its product/market strategy, it may position new brands or reposition existing ones. Repositioning may be achieved through advertising. In this case, repositioning objectives may be given as coordinates on the perceptual map, to guide the advertising agency in the development of advertising platform and themes, and for media selection. Repositioning through advertising will be easier to achieve for low awareness brands than for high awareness ones. The capacity of advertising to change perceptions is however limited, and effective repositioning may sometimes require product modifications through R & D.

### CONCLUSIONS: A NEW APPROACH FOR TEACHING MARKETING STRATEGY

Although the above description of Markstrat is obviously incomplete, it has hopefully illustrated how this game has been specifically designed for the teaching of marketing strategy concepts. It should also be clear that Markstrat is not only a new pedagogical tool, but that it represents also a new approach for teaching marketing strategy. This approach is based on an exposure to a large number of competitive market situations, the assimilation of a diversity of marketing strategies, and the formulation of strategic propositions.[2]

1. An exposure to a large number of competitive market situations. In the course of the game, a very large number of situations are generated, which are different across the various product/market domains, over time, and between the competing firms. Students have to recognize these situations, and to learn how to react to each of them. In the process, the judgements they could have previously acquired on the relative merits of alternative marketing instruments tend to become less absolute, to the benefit of a greater sensitivity to the specificities of market situations.

2. The assimilation of a diversity of marketing strategies. Various authors [1, 5, 9] have proposed mappings of alternate marketing strategies. In Markstrat, the students are given the opportunity to evaluate these marketing strategies in a number of situations, and to assimilate their implications for a firm in a competitive environment.

3. The formulation of strategic propositions. After having evaluated a number of strategies over a wide range of situations, students will attempt to develop some generalizations. These generalizations can be expressed as rules of thumb, or strategic propositions, which have been observed to be valid in a certain class of situations. These strategic propositions allow students to readily integrate their past experience in the elaboration of a marketing strategy, when faced with a similar situation

---

[2]I am indebted to Professor Harper W. Boyd, Jr. who proposed the concept of formulating strategic propositions and who first applied it in the administration of the Markstrat game.

This approach is in contrast with more traditional ones which rely on readings, lectures and case studies. These latter approaches provide on one hand very general concpets, and on the other one experience on selected cases. The transferability of the knowledge thus acquired to the multitude of situations that a student may encounter in his professional life is certainly limited.

The experience gathered in the dozen MBA or executive programs in which Markstrat has been used to date supports the validity of this new approach. Each of these applications has been highly successful, especially in terms of: (a) motivation and immediate satisfaction of students, (b) acquisition of a deeper sensitivity to marketing strategy issues, (c) recognition by students of the transferability of the knowledge acquired to practical marketing situations. The more satisfactory elements in the pedagogical evaluation of Markstrat have certainly been the assertions made by several executives, of the value of their Markstrat experience in better understanding the strategic choices which they face in their job, as well as their implications. It is hoped indeed that Markstrat will contribute to bridge the gap between academia and business in a critical area of the marketing curriculum.

### REFERENCES

1. Adler, L. "A New Orientation for Plotting Marketing Strategy," in R. C. Shirley, M. H. Peters, and A. I. El-Ansary, ed., Strategy and Policy Formulation: A Multifunctional Orientation. New York: John Wiley, 1976, 116-133.

2. Amstutz, A. E. and H. J. Claycamp. "The Total Market Environment Simulation. An Approach to Management Education," Industrial Management Review, 5, No. 2 (Spring 1964) 47-60.

3. The Boston Consulting Group. Perspectives on Experience. Boston: The Boston Consulting Group, 1972.

4. Cohen, K. J. and R. M. Cyert, W. R. Dill, A. A. Kuehn, M. H. Miller, T. A. Van Wormer and P. R. Winters. "The Carnegie Tech Management Game," Journal of Business, 33, No. 4 (1960), 309-316.

5. Cravens, D. W. "Marketing Strategy Positioning," Business Horizons, 18, (December 1975), 53-61.

6. Day, R. L. and T. E. Ness. Marketing in Action: A Decision Game. Homewood, Ill.: Richard D. Irwin, 1973.

7. Enis, B. M. and S. V. Smith. "The Marketing Curriculum of the Seventies: Period of the Pendulum or New Plane of Performance?" in K. L. Bernhardt, ed., Marketing: 1776-1976 and Beyond. Chicago: American Marketing Association, 1976, 25-28.

8. Faria, A. J., D. G. Johnstone, and R. O. Nulsen. Compete: A Dynamic Marketing Simulation. Dallas: Business Publications, Inc., 1974.

9. Johnson, S. C. and C. Jones. "How to Organize for New Products," Harvard Business Review, 35 (May-June 1957), 49-62.

10. Larreche, J. C. and H. Gatignon. Markstrat: Design and Implementation of Marketing Strategy in a Competitive Environment. Palo Alto, California: The Scientific Press, in press.

11. Meurs, F. and J. M. Choffray. "Business Games: Their Role in Training and Development," Journal of European Training, 4, No. 2, (1975), 81-112.

12.  Reizenstein, R. C. and D. J. Sweeney. "New Venture Analysis - A Pragmatic Approach to Learning Transfer in the Marketing Strategy Curriculum," in T. W. Greer, ed., <u>Combined Proceedings</u>. Chicago: American Marketing Association, 1973, 31-36.

13.  Woodruff, R.B., "Analyzing Market Opportunities: A Neglected Area of Learning in Marketing Curricula?" in K.L. Bernhardt, Ed. <u>Marketing: 1776-1976 and Beyond</u>. Chicago: American Marketing Association, 1976, 299 - 304.

AN EMPIRICAL TEST OF A PUBLIC POLICY DECISION MODEL:
THE EVALUATION OF PRESCRIPTION DRUG PRICE ADVERTISING

Robert L. Anderson, The University of South Florida
R. Eugene Klippel, The University of South Florida

ABSTRACT

Consumer research in public policy is becoming increasingly
important. Currently the thrust of much of the research
is aimed at providing information for decision making prior
to implementation rather than after. This paper presents
a general model for assessing information requirements. In
addition, it presents empirical research findings related
to a key public policy decision . . . the advertising of
prescription drug prices. The research deals with both the
consumer sector and the retail sector of the prescription
drug industry and relates these data to the overall decision model.

INTRODUCTION

The usefulness of consumer research in the formulation of
public policy is now being realized (1,3,9). Unfortunately, much of the consumer research conducted in the past
has been ex-post-facto and the findings of the research
could not be incorporated into the laws since they had already been enacted. Most of the consumer research has
focused upon the "full disclosure" laws and the results
have not been encouraging (4,5). Many of the problems with
previous public policy decisions could have been alleviated
had consumer research been conducted prior to the enactment
of the decision. Recognizing this need, the authors in a
previous effort have proposed a generalized model to evaluate proposed public policy decisions prior to their enactment. (See Figure 1.) This model focuses on a series of
cost/benefit decision stages that may ultimately suggest
the "test marketing" of proposed public policy decisions
before they are enacted.

A major criticism of this model and other models of similar
format is that while they represent a logical guide for
decision making purposes they lack realism in terms of
implementation. Taking issue with the above position the
purpose of this paper is to utilize the general model presented in Figure 1 to investigate a specific public policy
decision and evaluate its impact on a designated "target"
group. The specific issue under consideration is the en-
couragement by the federal government of price advertising
of prescription drugs by the retail members of industry
and its potential impact on the elderly consumer (target
group) of such products.

FIGURE 1

A GENERAL MODEL FOR PUBLIC POLICY RESEARCH AND DEVELOPMENT

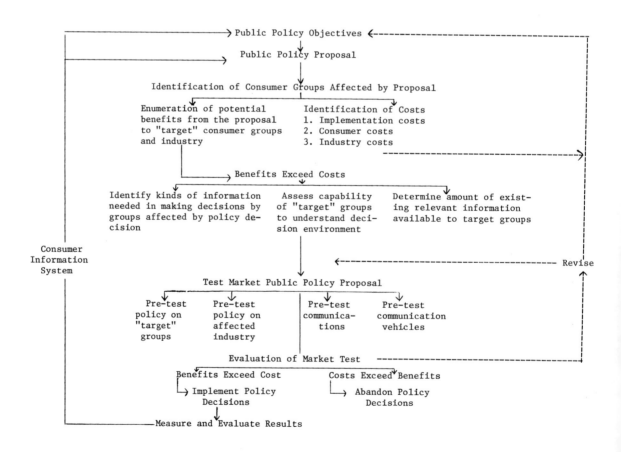

## Rx PRICE ADVERTISING

In January of 1976 the staff of the Federal Trade Commission recommended that the commission should issue a ruling prohibiting all states from enforcing laws against the advertising of prescription drugs. In June of 1976 the U.S. Supreme Court ruled that restrictions against the advertising of Rx prices was unconstitutional and thus accomplished what the FTC had begun to do. This ruling was very significant for a number of reasons. The decision gave the individual retailer the right to advertise Rx prices if he chose to do so. Further, it offers insight as to the direction of future FTC efforts. For example, the FTC is now encouraging price advertising of dentist and physician services. Given the FTC's efforts in these areas, the presentation of these research findings is believed to be both timely and relevant.

The elderly were selected as the "target group" in the research study because there are more elderly in the lower income groups. In addition, the elderly segment of our population also consumes a higher proportion of all prescription drugs than any other age group.

Focusing on the first phase of the model presented in Figure 1, the primary thrust of this research is to develop inputs for a cost/benefit analysis relative to the specific issue allowing Rx advertising in the State of Florida, and to recommend if additional decision phases of the model should be pursued.

The potential benefits of allowing Rx price advertising have been identified to be:

### Potential Benefits to Consumers

1. Lower drug prices

2. Allow the dissemination of more information about drugs in general

3. Allow more consumers to afford proper medication levels

4. Increase overall health level among special interest groups

### Potential Costs to Consumers

1. Higher prescription drug prices

2. Higher prices of over-the-counter drugs

3. Higher prices of non-drug merchandise sold by drugstores

4. Force small drugstores out of business

5. Increase shopping time

### SAMPLE PROCEDURE

In an effort to provide inputs to the above cost/benefit analysis in Phase I of the model, survey research was conducted utilizing both consumer and retail industry representatives as subjects. A convenience sample of 131 senior citizens was taken from a community association consisting of primarily retired people. One member of each household completed the questionnaire. The respondent from each household was the member who purchased most of the prescription drugs for the household. The respondents in groups of approximately thirty were provided with a three-part self-administered questionnaire. The first section dealt with their prescription drug usage, amount of income spent for prescription drugs and the distance from place of residence to the drug outlet used. The second section dealt with factors the elderly consider when choosing drug outlets, factors that might cause people to change drug outlets and general statements about different aspects of purchasing prescription drugs. The third section of the questionnaire requested demographic information.

The industry sample consisted of a random sample of 300 independent pharmacists located in the State of Florida. A survey questionnaire was mailed to each of the pharmacists in the sample, and 115 questionnaires were completed and returned. The purpose of the survey was to gather information on the following questions:

1. Do the independent pharmacists currently advertise and if not, why not?

2. Will the independent pharmacist advertise in the future now that the restrictions have been removed?

3. Do they post prices of prescription drugs in their pharmacies?

4. Do they quote prices of prescription drugs over the phone to consumers?

### FINDINGS

Consumer Survey

The respondents rated on a four point scale the importance of nine factors that they might consider when choosing an outlet to purchase prescriptions. These factors are shown in Table 1. The respondents rated the factors of "A pharmacist who knows your doctor" and "professional service" as being most important when they select a drug outlet. These two factors were followed by "low prices" and "a ready source of drug information." The factor of "advertised drug prices" was rated low but this could be the result of the consumers not being accustomed to seeing prescription drug prices readily available.

The second set of statements shown in Table 2 dealt with reasons why consumers might change their usual source of prescription drugs. As with the first set of factors, the senior citizens' relationship to their physician seems to be very important when they consider a retail drug source. The factor of another store advertising lower prescription drug prices was also rated high. This may be an indication that senior citizens would use price information if it were readily available and would change their shopping patterns if the information were available.

The results summarized in Table 3 indicate that their shopping behavior would change if price information were more available. A very high percentage of the respondents indicated that they would shop for the "best buy" if stores advertised their prescription prices and disagreed with the statement that they would never shop for prescriptions on the basis of price. Almost all of the respondents believe that drug prices should be advertised.

The results indicate that the senior citizens want and would use price information if it were made more available to them. What is unknown from the results of the survey is how having the price information made more available would affect the importance they place on their physician's personal advice.

TABLE 1

IMPORTANCE RATINGS OF FACTORS IN CHOOSING A
PRESCRIPTION DRUG OUTLET
(in percentages)

| Factors | Factor Designation | Ratings Very Important | Quite Important | Somewhat Important | Not al all Important | Median |
|---|---|---|---|---|---|---|
| A pharmacist who knows your doctor | P | 41.2 | 39.7 | 15.3 | 3.8 | 1.260 |
| Professional service | P | 64.9 | 22.9 | 10.7 | 1.5 | 1.488 |
| Low prices | E | 35.9 | 42.7 | 19.1 | 2.3 | 1.813 |
| A ready source of drug information | E | 34.4 | 32.8 | 27.5 | 5.3 | 1.977 |
| Outlet is close to consumer's residence | E | 26.0 | 38.9 | 33.6 | 1.5 | 2.118 |
| Personal attention given by pharmacist | P | 19.8 | 35.1 | 32.1 | 13.0 | 2.359 |
| Advertised drug prices | E | 22.9 | 24.4 | 35.9 | 16.8 | 2.574 |
| A large variety of non-drug merchandise | P | 2.3 | 18.3 | 33.6 | 45.8 | 3.375 |
| Outlet is close to physician's office | E | 1.5 | 8.4 | 41.2 | 48.9 | 3.472 |

Very important = 1  Somewhat important = 3
Quite important = 2  Not at all important = 4

TABLE 2

REASONS TO CHANGE SOURCE OF PRESCRIPTION DRUGS
(in percentages)

| Factors | Factor Designation | Ratings Very Important | Quite Important | Somewhat Important | Not at all Important | Median |
|---|---|---|---|---|---|---|
| The consumer's doctor recommends another drug outlet | P | 35.9 | 38.9 | 16.0 | 9.2 | 1.863 |
| The consumer changes place of residence and now lives closer to a different drug outlet | E | 28.2 | 43.5 | 24.4 | 3.8 | 2.000 |
| Another store advertises lower prices | E | 29.8 | 35.9 | 29.0 | 5.3 | 2.064 |
| A new store opens that is closer to the consumer's residence | E | 26.0 | 32.8 | 36.6 | 4.6 | 2.233 |
| Store will not fill prescriptions under Medicaid or Medicare plans | E | 29.8 | 20.6 | 8.4 | 41.2 | 2.481 |
| Pharmacist is very impersonal in the store used | P | 17.6 | 24.4 | 45.0 | 13.0 | 2.678 |
| Store now used does not advertise prices of prescription drugs | E | 12.2 | 21.4 | 35.9 | 30.5 | 2.936 |

Very important = 1  Somewhat important = 3
Quite important = 2  Not at all important = 4

TABLE 3

ATTITUDES TOWARDS DRUG PRICES AND SHOPPING FOR PRESCRIPTION DRUGS

| Statements | Definitely Agree | Agree Somewhat | Disagree Somewhat | Definitely Disagree | Median |
|---|---|---|---|---|---|
| | Ratings | | | | |
| Drug prices should be advertised in the store | 49.6 | 40.5 | 7.6 | 2.3 | 1.509 |
| I think I would shop for the "best buy" in drugs if the stores advertised their prices | 43.5 | 43.5 | 11.5 | 1.5 | 1.895 |
| If I could find out the prices the various outlets charged for prescription drugs, I would shop around before I filled my prescription. | 29.7 | 40.5 | 23.7 | 6.1 | 2.000 |
| Prescription drug prices are reasonable | 3.9 | 29.0 | 42.0 | 25.2 | 2.909 |
| The larger the store, the cheaper the prescription price will be | 3.5 | 24.4 | 46.6 | 26.0 | 2.984 |
| There is no difference between drug stores and discount stores that have drug departments | 9.2 | 22.1 | 34.4 | 34.4 | 3.044 |
| All prescription drug outlets charge about the same for prescription drugs | 4.5 | 27.5 | 31.3 | 36.6 | 3.073 |
| I would never shop for prescription drugs on the basis of price | 5.3 | 18.3 | 38.9 | 37.4 | 3.176 |

Definitely agree = 1    Agree somewhat = 2    Disagree somewhat = 3    Definitely disagree = 5

## Pharmacy Survey

Of the 115 pharmacists who replied to the question, "Do you currently advertise Rx prices (advertising other than in-store advertising)"? only two responded yes. The major reasons why there are very few independent pharmacists advertising are personal ones. The pharmacists indicated that it is against their personal code of ethics and comparatively don't believe they need to.

The pharmacists presently do not post prices (91% said no) and 83% said that they do not intend to do so in the future. The majority of the pharmacists said they do not quote prices over the phone. What promotion there is (quoting of prices over the phone) is primarily involuntary and only done if the consumer calls and requests the information. Two open-ended replies to the questions concerning price-posting, and quoting prices over the phone tend to set the flavor of the pharmacists' feelings:

--The customer doesn't know how to read the prescription correctly; how can they look up the price?

--I prefer that the patient present such prescription for pricing or dispensing. Many patients do not read the prescription correctly and once the price is quoted based on the Rx, I am held to it.

There seems to be a perceived lack of need to provide price information to the consumer. This perception is based on the cost (in time) to the pharmacist and the consumers' perceived inability to use the information correctly.

Table 4 gives the answers to two questions in the survey that dealt directly with the cost of advertising. Taking the information obtained from the consumer and retail surveys and utilizing it as the basis for the previously identified cost/benefit analysis, it can be stated that a clear decision is not discernable. Thus, the model would suggest that the "test market" phase be conducted before a final policy decision is rendered. Had the costs clearly outweighed the benefits, the decision process could have stopped at Phase I; however, this was not the situation. While Phase I information did not provide sufficient inputs for a final decision regarding the policy issue of Rx drug advertising, it did isolate several key issues that should form the major thrust of the "test marketing" phase. For example, from the replies to the questions it appears that prescription drugs and other items purchased at a pharmacy would increase in cost if Rx advertising became mandatory. The replies also indicate that the present level of services now provided by the pharmacies would decrease.

As with most public policy decisions in the past, the advertising of prescription drug prices is not without its problems. Problems have been identified in both the consumer sector and the retail sector of the drug industry. From the consumer's viewpoint the problem is wanting price information about prescription drugs and the inability to obtain it. The survey research indicates that if price information were made available that the senior citizens would use it in making their prescription purchases. However, a secondary problem arises in the consumer sector and that is the heavy reliance placed upon the consumer's physician as a source of drug information. Whether price information being made more available at the point of purchase would diminish the physician's

TABLE 4

PHARMACISTS' ATTITUDES TOWARDS THE COST OF ADVERTISING Rx PRICES

Question 1  If the advertising of prescription drug prices was made mandatory in the near future, could you cover the cost from your present profit margin?

Yes: 27% (n = 31)   No: 73% (n = 84)

Question 2  If you could not cover the cost of the advertising from your present profit margins, how would you attempt to cover the cost?

| | |
|---|---|
| Raise the price of all prescription drugs | 73% (n = 62) |
| Raise only the prices of non-advertised drugs | 29% (n = 24) |
| Increase prices of over-the-counter drugs | 55% (n = 46) |
| Reduce services now offered | 65% (n = 52) |
| Increase prices of non-drug merchandise | 13% (n = 11) |
| Reduce help in the store | 8% (n = 7) |
| Reduce hours that the store is open | 4% (n = 4) |

Base was 84 and the respondents could check more than one category.

influence is unknown at this time. One can only hypothesize that the physician's influence is due to the lack of price information in the past. As more information becomes available from the retailers, the consumer's reliance on the physician could diminish.

From the industry data the problems appear to be the pharmacists not really believing that the consumer needs the information and a personal ethical problem with providing it. The pharmacists consider themselves as professionals and price is only one attribute of the product/service that they provide to the consumer. Of the many problems with this public policy decision that have arisen from the research, the central issue is very simplistic: The senior citizens desire the price information and they are not likely to receive it from the pharmacist. Price advertising is very minimal at the present time and the indications are that it will not increase in the future.

Rx price advertising should remain at a minimum level for two reasons. First, the pharmacists perceive no real benefits to advertising but do see costs associated with it. Second, price advertising of prescription drugs is voluntary, not mandatory as with "truth-in-lending." Since the pharmacists perceive no benefits from advertising and given that it is voluntary, one should not expect the consumer to receive the information he wants. Is making Rx price advertising mandatory the solution? Not necessarily. From the answers given to the questions posed to the pharmacists concerning mandatory prescription price advertising, it appears that the costs of advertising would be passed along to the consumer. The question that remains to be answered is: Would the price level be higher due to advertising than it would be if there was no advertising?

Hopefully, the findings of this research effort demonstrate the importance of the role of consumer research in public policy formulation and the material use of the model presented in this paper.

REFERENCES

1. Day, G. S. and W. K. Brandt. "Consumer Research Contributions to the Evaluation of Public Policy: The Case of Truth-in-Lending." Journal of Consumer Research 1 (June 1974), 21-32.

2. Federal Trade Commission. "Prescription Drugs: Retail Price Disclosures." Washington, D.C. (January 28, 1975).

3. Jones, M. G. "The FTC's Need for Social Science Research," in David M. Gardner, ed. Proceedings: Second Annual Conference of the Association for Consumer Research. College Park, Maryland: Association for Consumer Research, 1971, pp. 1-9.

4. Kripke, Homer. "Gesture and Reality in Consumer Credit Reform." New York University Law Review (March 1969), pp. 1-12 and 51-52.

5. Mandell, Lewis. "Consumer Knowledge and Understanding of Consumer Credit." Journal of Consumer Affairs (Summer 1973), 35-44.

6. Monroe, Kent B. and Peter J. LaPlaca. "What are the Benefits of Unit Pricing?" Journal of Marketing 36 (July 1972), 16-22.

7.  Shoaf, F. Robert and Edward J. Melnick.  "Fair Packaging and Labeling Act."  Journal of Retailing 50 (Summer 1974), 3-10, 102.

8.  Wilkes, Robert E.  "Consumer Usage of Base Price Information."  Journal of Retailing 48 (Winter 1972), 72-85.

9.  Wilkie, W. L. and D. M. Gardner.  "The Role of Marketing Research in Public Policy Decision-Making."  Journal of Marketing 38 (January 1974), 38-47.

COMPARATIVE ADVERTISING: CONSUMER ISSUES AND ATTITUDES

Gordon H. G. McDougall, Wilfrid Laurier University*

## ABSTRACT

A significant issue in the comparative advertising controversy is the information value of direct comparisons for
consumer brand decisions. The Federal Trade Commission
has encouraged advertisements that "name names" rather
than indirect comparisons in the belief that more complete
information is provided. However, critics have argued
that the new guidelines have resulted in consumer confusion and reduced credibility for advertising.

A survey was undertaken to assess consumer attitudes
towards comparative advertising and comparative claims.
The results revealed that a majority of consumers held
negative attitudes towards various aspects of comparative
advertising. Further, direct claims (competing brands
named) were not seen as more reliable or helpful than
indirect claims (competing brands not named). Considering
the findings, it may be appropriate to revise the guidelines to allow either type of advertisement provided that
acceptable comparison standards can be established.

## INTRODUCTION

In late 1971, The Federal Trade Commission altered its
position on comparative advertising and encouraged advertisers to "name names" rather than use the more conservative "Brand X" approach. The rationale was that consumers
would be provided with better information upon which to
base their purchase decisions. Since that time the use of
direct comparative advertisements has increased, accompanied by numerous arguments for and against this advertising
form.

One of the controversial aspects of direct comparative
advertising is its effectiveness as an information source
for the consumer. Direct comparisons provide the consumer
with a standard against which the advertised brand is compared whereas indirect comparisons, where no competing
brands are named, omit that critical piece of information.
This paper outlines the major consumer issues involved
with comparative advertising and provides empirical evidence concerning consumer attitudes towards comparative
advertising and reaction to specific comparative claims.
The objective is to determine the perceived usefulness of
comparative advertising from the consumer's viewpoint.
The results suggest that unexpected consequences can occur
when well intended plans are put into practice.

## BACKGROUND

### History

Prior to 1972, most comparative ads took a disguised form
using "Brand X" or "Beeps" or "Other leading brands" as
the basis for comparison. [8] This approach allowed advertisers to attack phantom brands with impunity and the
consumer was given incomplete information because the
standard for comparison was not stated. To rectify this
situation, the FTC issued a series of guidelines encouraging the use of comparative ads which named the competing
brands. It was felt that these ads would provide information similar to Consumer Reports.

*The support of the Associates' Workshop, School of
Business Administration, University of Western Ontario is
gratefully acknowledged.

Since the FTC guidelines were introduced the use of direct
comparative advertising has increased. Depending on the
definition employed, comparative advertising constitutes
somewhere between 7 and 25 percent of all advertising in
the major media and the increase has been calculated at
between 20 to 80 percent from 1972 and 1976. [5,6,7]
While precise data on the amount or increase of comparative
advertising may not be available, it is clear that the FTC
rulings have had a significant impact on advertising. It
is appropriate to determine if consumers perceive the benefits that the FTC and other proponents have suggested for
comparative advertising.

### Definition

An aspect of the comparative advertising controversy has
been one of definition. Comparative advertising has been
narrowly defined as advertising that compares two or more
specifically named brands and makes the comparison in terms
of one or more specific product attributes. [9] The rationale for this definition is that explicit comparisons
will evoke consumer responses which are different than
those evoked by more traditional advertising appeals. Subsequent discussion and research has shown that this definition is too restrictive because it omits comparisons which
do not name other brands or specific attributes. In fact,
only a small percentage of "comparative" advertising falls
within the narrow definition. [5,7] Comparative advertising should be defined more broadly to incorporate advertising forms which imply a competitive superiority on any
dimension. It is proposed that comparison advertising be
defined as:

> Any advertisement that compares, implicitly or
> explicitly, two or more products and states or
> implies that information has been obtained or a
> test has been conducted on a comparative basis,
> or that states or implies a particular market
> standing in relation to other similar products,
> whether the other products are named or not,
> shall be deemed comparative. [5]

The argument favoring this definition is that if an implicit or explicit comparison is made consumers could assume
a factual basis for the claim. The unique aspect of comparative ads is the implication that factual information,
often in the form of scientific tests or independent
research, has been gathered as a basis for the claim. This
factual information can provide a legitimizing function for
the ad and may be an influence on a consumer's decision to
purchase a particular brand. From both the strategic
(marketing) and policy (government) viewpoint, it is important to recognize that when an advertiser states that a
product is "better", a comparison has been made, regardless
of what else is said.

Using the definitional framework, a typology was developed
(Table 1) which incorporates the three main characteristics
of comparative ads; claim, substantiation, and comparison.
These different forms of comparative ads need to be recognized because the information value, in a theoretical
sense, can vary depending on the form. In addition, consumer's perceptions of the information value of various forms
may differ. In the latter case, it is necessary to determine how consumers perceive the different forms, particularly direct versus indirect comparisons, in order to
assess the predicted benefits of the FTC guidelines.

# TABLE 1

## TYPOLOGY OF COMPARATIVE ADVERTISEMENTS

### Substantiated

| | Product Attribute | Market Standing |
|---|---|---|
| Direct | Tests show Brand A lasts longer than Brand B | Surveys prove consumers prefer Brand A over Brand B |
| Indirect | Tests show Brand A lasts longer than other brands | Surveys prove consumers prefer Brand A over other brands |
| Generic | Tests show Brand A lasts longer than (generic product) | Surveys prove consumers prefer Brand A over (generic product) |

### Unsubstantiated

| | Product Attribute | Market Standing |
|---|---|---|
| Direct | Brand A lasts longer than Brand B | Consumers prefer Brand A over Brand B |
| Indirect | Brand A lasts longer than other brands | Consumers prefer Brand A over other brands |
| Generic | Brand A lasts longer than (generic product) | Consumers prefer Brand A over (generic product) |

## Consumer Issues

The main arguments for comparative advertising, particularly direct comparisons, are; the consumer is provided with better information, the brand choice decision is made easier, rational decisions are encouraged, competition is increased, and product quality is improved. [1,2] The major thrust of these arguments is that the consumer will benefit in two ways. First, the consumer can make brand decisions more efficiently and effectively because direct comparisons provide relatively complete information on brands and the dimensions of superiority. Second, the market system will improve because more direct competition is encouraged and companies offering inferior brands will be forced to upgrade their products to avoid continuous unfavorable comparisons.

The arguments against comparative advertising are; it increases consumer confusion, it causes a decline in advertising credibility, consumers are not obtaining better information, it leads to unhealthy competition, and comparative claims are often misleading. [2,4] Probably the most serious of these criticisms is that the information in comparative ads is not "better" because it is selective. Unlike Consumer Reports which provides complete information, comparative ads provide data only in areas where the brand excels. Further, some comparative claims are clearly designed to confuse the consumer, as exemplified by the "Coca Cola-Pepsi" comparative war which has been unanimously criticized by the advertising industry. [3]

In attempting to reconcile these arguments it is apparent that the idea of theory and practice can be utilized to understand if not completely explain the differences. The arguments for comparative advertising are primarily theoretical. By allowing advertisers to name competing brands and claim superiority on product characteristics the consumer is given useful information. However, firms employing comparative advertising frequently use minor product differences for comparative purposes. They use selective rather than complete information and the standards for

comparisons are often questionable. This is not unexpected because advertisers are not going to provide comparison information which is detrimental to their brand. Firms see the role of advertising primarily as persuasive in nature, not informative. Advertisers have at times employed the new guidelines to benefit themselves, not necessarily the consumer.

To gain a better perspective, it is necessary to determine consumers perceptions of comparative advertising. Do consumers view comparative advertising as being useful and helpful in making buying decisions, as suggested by the FTC, or do they regard it as just another form of advertising? Are direct comparisons perceived as more helpful than indirect comparisons? A consumer survey was undertaken to answer these and related questions.

## METHODOLOGY

The two primary objectives of the research were to determine consumer attitudes towards comparative advertising and their reaction to the certain types of comparative ads. To accomplish these objectives a consumer survey was undertaken which measured attitudes towards various aspects of comparative advertisements. In addition, three different tests were conducted to determine respondents reactions to the four types of comparative claims (Table 2). The tests, involving scenerios which ranged from actual comparative claims that had been made by advertisers to a hypothetical situation, all measured the reliability and helpfulness to other consumers of the comparative claims. Table 3 lists the claims made for the three tests.

# TABLE 2

## TYPES OF COMPARATIVE ADS

| | Direct | Indirect |
|---|---|---|
| Substantiated | Tests show Brand A lasts longer than Brand B | Tests show Brand A lasts longer than other brands |
| Unsubstantiated | Brand A lasts longer than Brand B | Brand A lasts longer than other brands |

Data was collected from 225 females, 18 years of age or over, by means of a personal interview. The pretested questionnaire took approximately 15 minutes to complete. Sampling was done on an area basis, using voter polls to generate random starting points for the interviewers. The interviewers completed between four and ten interviews in a polling area depending on the size of the poll and the contacts-to-completion ratio. No call-backs were conducted if a dwelling did not contain a qualified respondent. The sampling was restricted to females because of the product categories used in the questionnaire, the fact that a substantial proportion of comparative advertising is aimed at this segment, and because of time and cost constraints.

In comparison to larger populations the sample was slightly younger, better educated, and higher in annual income. The sample closely resembled larger populations in terms of marital and employment status.

## RESULTS

Attitudes Towards Comparative Advertising

Analysis of the statements concerning comparative adverti-

TABLE 3

COMPARATIVE CLAIMS TESTED

Test 1 - Product Category - Deodorants

| Type of Claim | Claim |
| --- | --- |
| Indirect-Unsubstantiated | Arrid Extra Dry keeps you 50% drier than the other leading brands. |
| Indirect-Substantiated | Most anti-perspirant sprays go on wet and oily, compared to Sure which goes on dry. And Sure keeps you drier. |
| Direct-Unsubstantiated | Right Guard calls itself anti-stain. Sure promises to keep you drier. Arrid says it isn't sticky. New Dial Very Dry Anti-Perspirant does it all. |
| Direct-Substantiated | Tests have shown Ban Roll-on will help stop wetness better than Arrid Extra Dry, Right Guard, Soft and Dry and Dial. |

Test 2 - Product Category - Laundry Detergents

| Indirect-Unsubstantiated | Brand L detergent gets your clothes cleaner. |
| --- | --- |
| Indirect-Substantiated | Laboratory studies have shown that Brand L detergent gets your clothes cleaner. |
| Direct-Unsubstantiated | Brand L detergent gets your clothes cleaner than Brand M or Brand N. |
| Direct-Substantiated | Laboratory studies have shown that Brand L detergent gets your clothes cleaner than either Brand M or Brand N. |

Test 3 - Product Category - Bleach

| Indirect-Unsubstantiated | Javex Bleach removes stains better than other bleaches. |
| --- | --- |
| Indirect-Substantiated | Laboratory tests show that Javex Bleach removes stains better than other bleaches. |
| Direct-Unsubstantiated | Javex Bleach removes stains better than either Clorox Bleach or Purex Bleach. |
| Direct-Substantiated | Laboratory tests show that Javex Bleach removes stains better than either Clorox Bleach or Purex Bleach. |

sing produced two interesting results. As shown in Table 4, the average response to most of the statements was negative and few positive attitudes were held concerning comparative advertising. On average, the respondents felt that; advertisers should not be allowed to name other brands in their ads, comparative ads did not provide the consumer with more useful information, comparative ads were not more believable than other types of advertising, and comparative ads which name other brands did not help consumers in their buying decision. In light of these results it was somewhat surprising to find the respondents felt that if an advertiser has a better product than other firms, he should say so in his ads. This apparent conflict may be reconciled by suggesting that respondents feel the advertiser should make superiority claims but not by directly naming the competing brands.

Respondents were skeptical of the test claims made in comparative ads. They felt, on average, that tests were not fairly and reliably conducted and that advertisers may not have the facts to "back-up" their claims. Further evidence of respondent skepticism is their strong agreement that the government should control advertising more closely and that most advertisers were not considered honest.

While these results present a fairly negative picture of respondents attitudes towards advertising in general and comparative advertising in particular, the responses for most statements revealed a bimodal distribution. With two exceptions, the majority of respondents either agreed or disagreed with the statement, rather than remaining neutral. The significance of the bimodal distribution is that a substantial minority of respondents held positive attitudes towards comparative advertising.

Further analysis was conducted to determine if attitudes towards comparative advertising were related to respondent demographics. One way analysis of variance was performed between each of the fourteen attitude statements and six demographic variables (marital status, education of respondent, education of spouse, age, employment status, and income).

It was found that most of the fourteen statements were not related to any of the six demographic variables. Only one statement "Advertising often provides the consumer with useful information," provided differences across more than one demographic variables. Where differences were found in some instances a clear relationship was not present (e.g. - more education, more skepticism). Since few significant differences occurred, it is apparent that attitudes towards comparative advertising are formed mainly by factors other than demographic characteristics. This is consistent with other research that has attempted to use demographics for segmentation. Based on these results policies or strategics concerning comparative advertising should consider segmentation methods other than demographics. These results also suggest that the findings can be extrapolated to larger populations because respondent demographics did not influence attitudes.

In conclusion, the majority of respondents did not regard comparative advertising as a surrogate for Consumer Reports. These respondents exhibited skepticism towards comparative advertising which lowers its potential information value. It is likely that most consumers perceive comparative claims in the same manner as other advertising forms. That is, advertising is advertising, regardless of the package in which it is delivered.

Reactions to Comparative Claims

Three tests were conducted for respondent reaction to comparative claims to test the effects of indirect versus direct comparisons and substantiated versus unsubstantiate claims. The effects were analyzed using paired "t" tests in the first two cases and "t" tests for independent samples for the third case. The mean ratings for all the claims are reported in Table 5 and the complete results of the significance tests are reported in Table 6.

The first test measured respondent reaction to four comparative claims for deodorants. In terms of reliability, all the average scores were on the negative side of the scale. The Arrid claim received the highest reliability rating which was less than slightly reliable. The results for helpfulness to other consumers were more positive and all four claims were seen in the "slightly helpful" range. Again, the Arrid claim received the highest rating while the Dial claim was the least favorably received. Based on these results, it can be concluded that respondents did no completely reject the claims and they saw some value, albeit slight, in the information.

Additional analysis, not reported here, revealed the brand

## TABLE 4

### ATTITUDES TOWARDS COMPARATIVE ADVERTISING (PERCENTAGES)

| | Strongly Agree | Agree | Neither Agree nor Disagree | Disagree | Strongly Disagree | Total | Average |
|---|---|---|---|---|---|---|---|
| Advertisers who use test results in their ads should be required to have the ads approved by the government | 29.3 | 61.4 | 4.4 | 4.9 | .0 | 100.0 | 1.85 |
| The government should introduce more laws to control advertising. | 26.2 | 44.0 | 12.9 | 16.5 | .4 | 100.0 | 2.21 |
| Advertising often provides the consumer with useful information. | 6.7 | 67.6 | 11.6 | 13.2 | .9 | 100.0 | 2.34 |
| If an advertiser has a better product than other firms, he should say so in his ads. | 2.2 | 58.7 | 16.0 | 23.0 | .0 | 100.0 | 2.60 |
| Advertisers should not be allowed to name other brands in their ads. | 11.1 | 42.7 | 15.6 | 30.2 | .4 | 100.0 | 2.66 |
| The consumer buying decision is made easier when test results are provided in ads. | 2.2 | 52.9 | 7.6 | 36.9 | .4 | 100.0 | 2.80 |
| Comparative ads provide the consumer with more useful information than other types of ads. | .9 | 39.5 | 12.0 | 45.8 | 1.8 | 100.0 | 3.08 |
| Ads which name other brands are confusing to the consumer. | 1.3 | 39.6 | 5.8 | 52.0 | 1.3 | 100.0 | 3.12 |
| Advertisers should use more comparative advertising in the future. | 1.3 | 31.2 | 17.3 | 48.4 | 1.8 | 100.0 | 3.18 |
| When ads state that "test results show the product is better", the tests were fairly and reliably conducted. | .9 | 24.9 | 31.5 | 39.6 | 3.1 | 100.0 | 3.19 |
| Comparative ads are more believable than other types of advertising. | 1.3 | 32.9 | 11.6 | 52.0 | 2.2 | 100.0 | 3.21 |
| Comparative ads which name other brands help consumers in their buying decision. | 1.3 | 32.4 | 11.6 | 51.1 | 3.6 | 100.0 | 3.23 |
| When advertisers state their brand is better than other brands, they have the facts to "back them up". | 1.3 | 24.4 | 18.2 | 51.6 | 4.4 | 100.0 | 3.33 |
| Most advertisers are honest. | .4 | 25.8 | 17.3 | 46.7 | 9.8 | 100.0 | 3.40 |

N = 225

## TABLE 5

### COMPARATIVE CLAIMS - MEAN RATINGS

Test 1 - Product Category - Deodorants

| Type of Claim | Reliable | Helpfulness | N |
|---|---|---|---|
| Indirect-Unsubstantiated (Arrid) | 3.64* | 3.07 | 225 |
| Indirect-Substantiated (Sure) | 3.77 | 3.22 | 225 |
| Direct-Unsubstantiated (Dial) | 4.09 | 3.47 | 225 |
| Direct-Substantiated (Ban) | 3.74 | 3.28 | 225 |

Test 2 - Product Category - Laundry Detergents

| | | | |
|---|---|---|---|
| Indirect-Unsubstantiated | 4.15 | 4.13 | 225 |
| Indirect-Substantiated | 2.90 | 2.79 | 225 |
| Direct-Unsubstantiated | 4.09 | 3.73 | 225 |
| Direct-Substantiated | 3.12 | 2.67 | 225 |

Test 3 - Product Category - Bleach

| | | | |
|---|---|---|---|
| Indirect-Unsubstantiated | 3.57 | 3.50 | 56 |
| Indirect-Substantiated | 2.95 | 2.81 | 57 |
| Direct-Unsubstantiated | 3.50 | 3.10 | 56 |
| Direct-Substantiated | 3.25 | 2.98 | 56 |

*Read: The indirect-unsubstantiated claim for Arrid received a reliability rating of 3.64 by the 225 respondents, with a value of 1.00 representing extremely reliable and a value of 7.00 representing extremely unreliable.

loyalty affected responses to the comparative claims. Users of the advertised brand rated the claims significantly more favorably than did users of competing brands or nonloyal users (i.e. - purchase any brand). In order to remove the effects of brand loyalty, the sample for the "t" tests excluded all respondents who were loyal to one of the advertised brands. The "t" tests (Table 6) found that the direct, unsubstantiated claim for Dial was perceived as significantly less reliable than the other three claims. The indirect, unsubstantiated claim for Arrid was seen as significantly more helpful than either the Dial claim or the direct, substantiated claim for Ban. These findings must be considered with some caution because respondent reaction was probably influenced by the brand as well as the type of claim. At best, a tentative conclusion might be drawn suggesting that direct claims naming competing brands are rated more negatively than indirect claims, particularly if they are not substantiated.

The second test asked respondents to rate the four types of claims for a theoretical laundry detergent, Brand L. This test was conducted to eliminate the possible bias that could have been caused by using existing brand names. The results clearly show that the substantiated claims were perceived as significantly more reliable and helpful than the unsubstantiated claims. The indirect claims were rated slightly higher on the reliability dimension but the situation was reversed on the helpfulness dimension. This reversal may be attributed to the overwhelming effect of the substantiated dimension. That is, respondents may have differentiated the claims primarily on the basis of whether the statements were substantiated or not and the

TABLE 6

EFFECTS OF COMPARATIVE CLAIMS - SUMMARY STATISTICS

Test 1 - Product Category - Deodorants

| Comparison | Distribution of Statistic | Statistic Reliable | Helpfulness |
|---|---|---|---|
| I-U (Arrid) vs. I-U (Sure) | $t^a$ | .79 | -1.28 |
| I-U (Arrid) vs. D-U (Dial) | t | -1.73** | -2.71* |
| I-U (Arrid) vs. D-S (Ban) | t | .09 | -1.86** |
| I-U (Sure) vs. D-U (Dial) | t | -2.56* | -1.28 |
| I-U (Sure) vs. D-S (Ban) | t | - .79 | - .51 |
| D-U (Dial) vs. D-S (Ban) | t | 1.93** | .82 |

N = 138 (Excludes all loyal to advertised brands)

Test 2 - Product Category - Laundry Detergents

| | | | |
|---|---|---|---|
| D-S vs. I-U | $t^a$ | - 6.18* | - 9.25* |
| D-S vs. I-S | t | 2.10* | - 1.18 |
| D-S vs. D-U | t | - 9.54* | -11.17* |
| I-U vs. I-S | t | 10.20* | 12.59* |
| I-U vs. D-U | t | .43 | 3.38* |
| I-S vs. D-U | t | -10.78* | 9.08* |
| Direct vs. Indirect | t | .80 | - 2.60* |
| Substantiated vs. Unsubstantiated | t | -11.17* | -13.40* |

N = 225

Test 3 - Product Category - Bleach

| | | | |
|---|---|---|---|
| I-U vs. I-S | $t^b$ | 1.85** | 2.41* |
| I-U vs. D-U | t | .20 | 1.27 |
| I-U vs. D-S | t | 1.00 | 1.78** |
| I-S vs. D-U | t | -1.57 | -1.06 |
| I-S vs. D-S | t | - .93 | - .64 |
| D-U vs. D-S | t | .74 | .45 |
| Indirect vs. Direct | t | - .56 | .49 |
| Substantiated vs. Unsubstantiated | t | -1.85* | -2.01* |

N = 56

[a] t calculated for paired samples

[b] t calculated for independent samples

*p  .05 (two tailed)
**p  .10 (two tailed)

"direct" characteristic was of little importance.

The effect of different comparative claims was also tested by means of a quasi-experimental design in the survey. It was recognized that the previous test, where no real brands were mentioned, was somewhat artificial. Consequently four dummy ads were constructed for an existing brand of bleach, the ads differing only in the type of comparative claim. A respondent was shown one of the four ads and was asked to rate the ad in terms of reliability and helpfulness.

The substantiated claims were perceived as significantly more reliable and helpful than the unsubstantiated claims. Again, the results for the indirect-direct dimension were mixed and the difference between the types of claims was not significant. The most important claim characteristic was substantiation and whether or not a competing brand was named did not significantly affect respondents' actions. However, the statement receiving the greatest acceptance was the indirect-substantiated claim. Respondents considered this claim to be the most reliable and most helpful of the four claims.

In summary, the results of the three tests were relatively consistent in spite of the different scenerios constructed to measure the effects of the different types of comparative claims. In most cases, substantiated claims were perceived as significantly more reliable and offering more helpful information to other consumers than unsubstantiated claims. Respondents did not see direct claims being more reliable or helpful than indirect claims although there was a slight preference for indirect claims when actual deodorant claims were tested.

## CONCLUSIONS

When the new FTC guidelines were introduced it was expected that direct comparisons, with the "names named", would provide better consumer information than indirect comparisons. Theoretically this is a reasonable position because the consumer knows the standard of comparison when direct claims are made whereas with indirect or "Brand X" comparisons, the standard is unknown. However, when direct claims began to appear with increasing frequency, certain negative aspects of this practice became apparent. Advertisers used secondary product attributes for comparison, conflicting comparative claims were made, claims and counter-claims have been made to either confuse the consumer or cloud the issue.

This study has provided a view of the consumers perception of comparative advertising in general and reaction to specific comparative claims. Overall, consumers held more negative than positive attitudes towards comparative advertising. These negative attitudes reduce the potential information value of comparative ads and indicate that this advertising form is not perceived as more beneficial than other advertising forms. The evidence showed that comparative advertising, which is presumably based on factual information, is treated with skepticism by a majority of respondents. For these individuals the idea that comparative advertising could act as a kind of Consumer Reports is not valid. They perceive comparative advertising as lacking in reliability, usefulness, and helpfulness. Consequently, it would be unlikely that comparative ads would contain very much useful information for these people.

On the other hand, a substantial minority of respondents held favorable attitudes towards comparative advertising as a useful information form. For example, one-third or more of the respondents felt that comparative ads were useful, reliable and helpful. The overall negative attitudes must be tempered by the fact that a sizeable minority favored comparative advertising. This minority saw positive benefits in this advertising form. Unfortunately, the respondents who held favorable views were not different on a demographic basis from those who held unfavorable views which precludes identification for strategy or regulation purposes.

The expectations of the FTC concerning the usefulness of direct claims over indirect claims was not matched by the survey results. Consumers did not see direct claims as being more reliable or helpful than indirect claims. In fact, most consumers felt that advertisers should not be allowed to name other brands in their ads. While the information contained in a direct claim may be superior in a theoretical sense, consumers, in practice, view direct and

indirect claims similarly in terms of reliability and helpfulness. In some cases, the consumer may feel a direct
claim is not fair play because one advertiser is promoting
his product at the expense of another.

Given these results, one problem is to provide the consumer
with information that is reliable and helpful and perceived
as reliable and helpful. The solution may be to allow advertisers to make either direct or indirect comparisons
provided an adequate standard for comparison is established.

This could be accomplished by a number of mechanisms including; developing standards for products similar to the
E.P.A. ratings, allowing advertisers to make comparisons
against a limited number of leading brands (precluding
comparisons against clearly inferior brands with marginal
market shares), or screening all comparative claims through
an independent agency. It would be appropriate for each
industry to establish these guidelines because of the
specific knowledge required to establish controls. In
addition, all data upon which comparisons were based should
be available to the public. This would, at a minimum,
allow consumer advocates to examine and comment on the
basis for the claims. Regardless of the approach taken,
the objective is to improve the perceived and actual reliability of the claims.

Finally, a comment is appropriate concerning the idea that
direct comparisons could act as a kind of Consumer Reports.
Advertisers are going to use direct comparisons only if
they think the ad will be effective in persuading consumers
to purchase their brand. The information contained in
these ads is designed primarily to persuade and it will be
selective and unbalanced. It will not be a comprehensive
comparison as is Consumer Reports. Regulatory officials
need to recognize this and adopt a more practical view of
the basic role of advertising in society.


FOOTNOTES

1. Barry, T. E., and Tremblay, R. L., "Comparative Advertising: Perspectives and Issues," Journal of Advertising,
   No. 4, 1975, pp. 15-20.

2. "For and Against Comparative Advertising", Advertising
   Age, July 5, 1976, pp. 25, 26, 28.

3. Giges, N., "Coca-Cola-Reluctant Entrant Into Comparative
   Ad Warfare," Advertising Age, January 3, 1977, pp. 2,
   35.

4. Kershaw, A., "The Mischief of Comparative Advertising,"
   Talk delivered to The American Association of Advertising Agencies, 1976 Annual Meeting.

5. McDougall, G. H. G., "Comparative Advertising in
   Canada," Consumer Research Council, Ottawa, 1976.

6. Rockey, E. A., "Comparative Advertising, Fair or Unfair,
   Effective or Ineffective?", ANA Television Workshop,
   New York, February 24, 1976.

7. Shimp, T. A., "Comparison Advertising in National
   Television Commercials: A Content Analysis," paper
   presented to the Fall Conference of the American Marketing Association, Rochester, N.Y., August 1975.

8. Ulanoff, S. M., "Comparison Advertising: A Historical
   Perspective," working paper, Marketing Science Institute, Cambridge, Mass., February 1975.

9. Wilkie, W. L. and Farris, P. W., "Comparison Advertising: Problems and Potential," Journal of Marketing,
   Volume 39, (October 1975), pp. 7-15.

# THE EFFECTS OF ATTACKS AND INOCULATIONS IN A PUBLIC
# POLICY CONTEXT: A COGNITIVE STRUCTURE APPROACH

Meryl Gardner, Carnegie-Mellon University
Andrew Mitchell, Carnegie-Mellon University
Richard Staelin, Carnegie-Mellon University

## ABSTRACT

Alternative approaches for measuring the effects of corrective advertising are evaluated and a typology of beliefs is presented for use with a cognitive structure approach. The results of an experiment which investigates both the effect of attacking different types of beliefs and whether a firm can inoculate consumers against an attack are discussed.

## INTRODUCTION

A critical public policy problem today is the regulation of information in the market place. One aspect of this problem concerns the identification and correction of deceptive advertising. This paper is concerned only the latter issue, the correction of deceptive advertising.

Although the impact of the Federal Trade Commission as a consumer protection agency is greatly influenced by the method selected to correct deceptive advertising and the effects of corrections on consumer behavior, surprisingly little research has been conducted in the area. In a review of the literature, Mazis and Adkinson [9] found only four papers containing empirical research on the topic and most of these lacked a strong theoretic base which makes their results difficult to generalize.

In this paper, we used a "cognitive structure" approach [8] to examine a) the effects of an FTC attack on different types of beliefs and b) whether a firm may successfully inoculate consumers against an FTC attack.

### Research Approach

Lutz [8] has identified the use of three different approaches in previous research to examine communication effects. The first, or "black box" approach[1] measures the effect of a communication on either an attitude toward an object or another measure farther down the response hierarchy. The second approach, or "cognitive structure" approach[2] measures the effect of a communication on those factors thought to mediate attitude change (i.e., beliefs). The final approach, or "cognitive response" approach[3] examines the cognitive processes that an individual goes through when exposed to a communication (e.g., counterarguing).

The distinction between these different approaches can be made clearer by using an information-belief basis of attitude formation and change [5, 13] and are presented in Figure 1. We see that upon being exposed to a communication, the "cognitive response" approach examines factors which may mediate a belief or evaluation change while the "cognitive structure" approach monitors belief and evalua-

tion changes which in turn mediate attitude change. Finally the "black box" approach is concerned only with the output measure, in this case the attitude change.

### FIGURE 1

Domains of the Different Approaches
to Communication Research

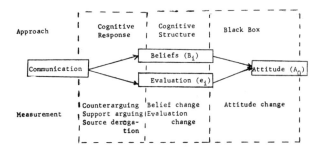

As pointed out by Wilkie and Gardner [18], the "black box" approach is clearly inadequate for examining the effects of corrective advertising even though most of the previous research in the area has used this approach. The FTC is concerned only with correcting what is thought to be a false belief and, as will be pointed out later, a change in a particular belief may or may not lead to an attitude change. Consequently, the fact that exposure to a corrective advertisement did not result in an attitude change does not necessarily indicate that the false belief was not corrected.

The above implies that it is necessary to go to at least a "cognitive structure" approach to examine the effects of a corrective advertising program. This is the approach we take. However, if procedures to correct deceptive beliefs are found to be unsuccessful, it may then be necessary to examine the factors which mediate belief changes.

### Theorectial Framework

In using a cognitive structure approach, we follow most other researchers by using the framework developed by Fishbein [5] where an attitude toward an object is a function of both the strength of beliefs about the object ($B_i$) and the evaluation of each belief ($e_i$).

In examining the effects of an attempt to change a false belief, it is useful to define the following types of beliefs.[4] First, a <u>primary</u> <u>belief</u> is a belief that is a direct determinant of an attitude. In his research, Fishbein has found that generally there are only a relatively small number of beliefs in this category for a specific object. In order to achieve a change in attitude, generally, one of these primary beliefs has to be changed.[5] A second type of

---

[1]The Yale research program on communication effects (Hovland, Janis and Kelley [6]) used this approach. Most mass communication research in marketing has followed this approach until recently.

[2]See Mitchell and Olson [12] and Mazis and Adkinson [9] for examples of this approach.

[3]See Wright [19] for an example of this approach.

---

[4]Except for secondary beliefs, the terms and definitions use here are from Fishbein and Ajzen [5].

[5]Attitude change may also be induced by a change in the evaluations of the attributes ($e_i$), however, since these evaluations are connected to the value system of the individual it is generally believed that these are more difficult to change.

belief is a <u>supportive belief</u>. A supportive belief is a nonprimary belief that is related to a primary belief. Consequently, a change in a supportive belief will lead to a change in a primary belief which, in turn, will lead to an attitude change. A third type of belief is what we shall call a <u>secondary belief</u>. This is a nonprimary belief that is uncorrelated with any of the primary beliefs. Therefore, a change in a secondary belief should not lead to an attitude change. Finally, we define a <u>target belief</u> as the belief that the sender of the communication wants to change.

In our context, then, the false belief that the FTC wants to change becomes the target belief and the differential effect of a change in this belief on an attitude depends on whether the target belief is a primary, supportive or secondary belief.

## RESEARCH PURPOSE

There are two main goals of this research. The first is to examine the effects of an attempt to change different types of beliefs, in this case, primary and supportive beliefs. The use of supportive beliefs is quite common in advertising. A "reason why" copy strategy basically uses supportive beliefs. For instance, the old Shell advertising campaign mentioning "Platformate" was a "reason why" approach. Shell wanted to create the primary belief that "Shell gives better gas milage" and used "Shell contains platformate" and "platformate gives better gas milage" as supportive beliefs.[6]

If the FTC determines that one of the supportive beliefs is false (e.g., platformate does not necessarily yield better gas milage) the inference that "Shell gives better gas milage" is false. What should the FTC do? Should it attempt to change the supportive belief or should it attempt to change the primary belief? Will changing the supportive belief have the same effect as changing the primary belief?

The second goal of this research is to determine whether a firm can successfully inoculate consumers against an FTC attack. Inoculation Theory as developed by McGuire [10] provides a procedure for making beliefs resistant to persuasion. The procedure is analogous to a biological inoculation. The individual is presented with refuted arguments[7] against a particular belief. These arguments motivate him or her to generate counterarguments against an attack on that belief, thereby making that belief more resistent to an attack.[8]

_____

[6]Conceptually, we might think of this example in terms of the primary belief being formed from two levels of supportive beliefs. In other words, an individual has a supportive belief connecting Shell and platformate ($B_1$) and the individual's evaluation of platformate ($e_1$) is determined by his belief that platformate gives better gas milage ($B_k$) and his evaluation of "better gas milage" ($e_k$). Consequently, this individual's primary belief that "Shell gives better gas milage" ($B_i$) might be $B_i = B_1 B_k e_k$. Consequently, a change in either of the support beliefs would lead to a change in the primary belief.

[7]Two types of refutations have been used in inoculation theory, refutation-same and refutation-different. In the former case, the refuted arguments are the same arguments used in the attack while in the latter case they are different. Most of the research in inoculation theory has indicated that refutation-same is the more effective inoculation when attacks occur shortly after the inoculation [11].

[8]Notice that counterarguing is one of the factors from the "cognitive response" approach that is hypothesized to mediate a belief change.

Although it has been suggested that inoculation theory might be an approach that a marketing manager could use to make consumer's beliefs about his product resistant to attack ([1]), there are two elements in the original experiments on inoculation theory which differ from the typical marketing situation. The first of these is the use of "cultural truisms" as the target beliefs in the original experiments. These were defined as "...beliefs so widely shared within the person's social mulieu that he would not have heard them attacked and indeed would doubt an attack possible" (McGuire [10]). Obviously, most beliefs about products or brands would not fall into this category. Second, the inoculations were always presented in a forced exposure situation, e.g., subjects read statements containing the inoculation and underlined key passages in the statements. In a marketing situation an individual is not forced to perceive a given advertisement and cognitive consistency theory suggests that an individual would probably ignore an inoculation message since it would present information which is discrepent with his or her beliefs [2].

There is some indication that the basic tenents of inoculation theory will hold when the target beliefs are less strongly held than "cultural truisms", however, in these experiments forced exposure to the inoculation was used (Bither, Dolich and Nell [4], Szybillo and Heslin [17], Hunt [7]). In our research, we relax both conditions to determine if inoculation theory will hold in a more typical marketing situation.

## METHOD

### Subjects

The 52 subjects were almost equally divided between both sexes and were recruited from a university subject pool. Although our sample consisted mostly of high school students, it was drawn from a fairly representative sample of the general population. Participants were paid $3.00 upon completion of the experiment which lasted approximately 1 hour.

### Experimental Design

To minimize demand characteristics [14, 15] measurements were taken after the treatment and the association between the treatment and the measurements was disguised so they appeared as two different experiments to the subjects. In the treatment part of the experiment, subjects were told that the purpose of the study was to get their opinions of a new radio show format. They then listened to a tape recording of a music and interview program conducted by a professional disk jockey which lasted approximately 15 minutes. Interspersed in the music portion of the program were the control and treatment advertisements. The interview portion of the program contained an interview with an "FTC official" who talked about deceptive advertising. After listening to the tape of the radio show, subjects were asked to fill out a questionnaire which asked for their opinions about the radio show. Included in the questionnaire were questions about the content of all the advertisements in the show.

After filling out this questionnaire, the subjects were taken to another room where another individual asked them to fill out a consumer survey questionnaire about three brands in each of four different product categories. Two of these twelve different brands were the same as the brands used in the treatment advertisements. After completing the questionaire, the subjects were debriefed and then dismissed.

In the experiment, the subjects were randomly placed in three different groups which contained 17, 18 and 17 subjects. The radio programs for the three groups differed only in the treatment advertisements and the content of the interview with the FTC official. The treatment advertisements were for Listerine (a mouthwash) and a hypothetical suntan lotion called Burnfree. The specific treatments for each group are given in Table 1.

TABLE 1

TREATMENTS

| | Listerine | | Burnfree |
| | Advertisement | Attack | Attack |
|---|---|---|---|
| Group 1 | Inoculation | FTC Attack | No Attack (Control) |
| Group 2 | Control | FTC Attack | Attack on the supportive belief |
| Group 3 | Control | FTC Attack | Attack on the primary belief |

Products and Advertisements

Listerine was chosen for the inoculation study because it was representative of a well established brand which is now subject to the FTC's corrective advertising program. The basic message used in our experiment was Listerine's claim to "aid in the prevention and treatment of colds and sore throats", a theme long emphasized by the company.

The control advertisement for Listerine omitted any mention of the claim but instead emphasized its ability to stop bad breath. The inoculation advertisement stated that a "group" has wrongly challenged Listerine's claim that it aids in the prevention and treatment of colds and sore throats and gave evidence to support the company's position. The attack message on Listerine said that the brand's claim was false and attacked precisely those points on which Listerine had already defended its position. In the no attack condition, the interview contained no mention of Listerine.

It should be noted that our design does not control for the fact that the subjects may have heard prior to the experiment about the FTC's actions against Listerine. Consequently our subjects may have received "attacks" via media accounts whether or not they received an attack from us. We will have more to say about this in a latter section.

To simplify our investigation of supportive and primary beliefs, a non-existant product was used so that the subjects' responses would not be confounded by previously formed beliefs and attitudes about the product. All the subjects received an identical message for Burnfree emphasizing the primary belief that Burnfree "prevents burns" as well as the supportive belief that Burnfree "contains a specific sun screening ingredient, BCI, that screens out the sun's rays".

Like the Listerine attack, the Burnfree attack was a reply by the "FTC official" to the interviewer's inquiry about corrective advertising. The attack on the primary belief denied the brand's ability to prevent sunburns, but made no mention of BCI, while the attack on the supportive belief said that BCI was ineffective in screening out the sun's rays, but made no mention of the brand's ability to prevent sunburn. Both attacks included evidence supporting their positions. Again, the no attack condition contained no FTC mention of Burnfree.

Dependent Variables

The dependent variables used in the study measured different elements of the cognitive structure suggested by Fishbein [5] including the belief strength ($B_i$) for the salient brand attributes, evaluations of each attribute ($e_i$), attitude toward each brand ($A_0$) and attitude toward the act of purchasing and using a brand ($A_B$). The measurements of belief strength and attribute evaluations followed Mitchell and Olson's [12] modification of Ahtola's [3] vector model.

Belief strengths were measured on seven point scales anchored by how likely or unlikely it was that each attribute level was associated with a particular brand. The evaluations of each attribute level were taken on bipolar scales labeled good-bad ($+3$ to $-3$). See Tables 2 and 3 for the attributes used for the two brands of interest.

In order to increase reliability and reduce measurement error, the mean score of three bipolar evaluative scales (good-bad, dislike very much-like very much, pleasant-unpleasant) for each brand was used as our measure of attitude toward specific brand (A). Similarly the mean score of three other evaluative scales (good-bad, foolish-wise, beneficial-harmful) was used as a measure of attitude toward purchasing and using each brand ($A_B$).

RESULTS

Demand Characteristics

To check for demand characteristics, the subjects were asked, after completing the consumer questionnaire, to write a brief paragraph discussing why they thought the data were being collected. Their comments indicated that no one recognized the connection between the content of the radio show and the consumer questionnaire.

Effects of Attack on Burnfree

The data from this manipulation were analyzed by a one way ANOVA. Two of the three belief strength measures for the target belief "prevents sunburn" were significant ($p < .05$). Only one of the belief strength measures on the 6 levels of the other two attributes was significant ($p < .10$) indicating that halo effects were minimal. The same analysis run on all the belief strength scores for the other two brands of suntan lotion indicated no significant effects ($p > .10$) so that the significant effects on the target beliefs were not due to group effects.

The attitude toward Burnfree and the attitude toward purchase were analyzed with the same type of ANOVA model. The results indicated that the attack effects were significant ($p < .05$).

The content levels for the belief strength and attitude measures for the different treatments are given in Table 2. These results indicate that the no attack group had higher belief strength scores for the "prevents sunburn better" attribute and a more favorable attitude toward the brand and its purchase than did the group receiving the attack on the supportive belief who, in turn, had higher belief strength scores for the "prevents sunburn better" attribute and a more favorable attitude toward the brand and its purchase than the group receiving the attack on the primary belief.

TABLE 2

SUMMARY OF RESULTS FOR BURNFREE

| Dependent Measure | Group Means | | | F Value |
|---|---|---|---|---|
| | No Attack Group | Attack on Supportive Belief Group | Attack on Primary Belief Group | |
| Beliefs: | | | | |
| Easier to Apply | 3.333 | 2.824 | 3.688 | 1.414 |
| As Easy to Apply | 5.333 | 4.824 | 5.500 | 0.662 |
| Less Easy to Apply | 2.800 | 2.824 | 2.250 | 0.810 |
| Tans Deeper | 3.133 | 3.353 | 2.313 | 1.844 |
| Tans as Deeply | 5.000 | 4.647 | 3.688 | $2.483^a$ |
| Tans Less Deeply | 3.857 | 3.882 | 3.813 | 0.005 |
| Prevents Burns Better | 4.467 | 3.471 | 2.438 | $3.591^b$ |
| 1 Prevents Burns As Well | 4.857 | 5.235 | 3.000 | $8.257^c$ |
| Prevents Burns Worse | 3.600 | 2.882 | 4.313 | 2.146 |
| Attitude: | | | | |
| Toward Brand | 3.063 | 2.825 | 2.125 | $8.503^c$ |
| Toward Use | 3.111 | 2.561 | 2.166 | $3.735^b$ |

1 - 7 scales of belief strength where 7 = very likely and 1 = very unlikely.

1 - 5 scales of attitude where larger numbers reflect more positive feelings.
    a: $p < .1$    b: $p < .05$    c: $p < .001$

TABLE 3

SUMMARY OF RESULTS FOR LISTERINE

| Dependent Measure | Group Means | | | F Value | |
|---|---|---|---|---|---|
| | Inoculation Ad Attack Group | Control Ad Attack Group | Control Ad No Attack Group | Attack Effect | Ad Effect |
| Beliefs: | | | | | |
| Stops bad breath more effectively | 4.647 | 3.944 | 4.000 | 1.163 | 0.860 |
| Stops bad breath as effectively | 5.235 | 5.111 | 5.429 | 0.187 | 0.038 |
| Stops bad breath less effectively | 2.588 | 2.667 | 1.786 | 2.467 | 0.019 |
| Kills germs better | 5.176 | 4.000 | 4.143 | 0.338 | 2.225 |
| Kills germs as well | 5.059 | 5.000 | 5.071 | 0.006 | 0.010 |
| Kills germs worse | 2.353 | 2.667 | 2.000 | 1.087 | 0.354 |
| Prevents and helps colds and sore throats better | 3.529 | 3.778 | 3.429 | 0.085 | 0.888 |
| Prevents and helps colds and sore throats as well | 5.059 | 4.944 | 4.857 | 0.046 | 0.026 |
| Prevents and helps colds and sore throats worse | 2.882 | 2.722 | 1.857 | $3.218^a$ | 0.081 |
| More pleasing taste | 2.294 | 3.000 | 2.286 | 0.479 | 1.514 |
| As pleasing taste | 3.118 | 3.833 | 2.286 | $4.012^a$ | 1.248 |
| Less pleasing taste | 6.235 | 4.333 | 5.500 | 0.188 | $10.064^b$ |
| Attitude: | | | | | |
| Toward Brand | 2.759 | 2.842 | 3.466 | $5.713^b$ | 0.076 |
| Toward Use | 3.407 | 3.209 | 3.755 | 1.875 | 0.315 |

1 - 7 scales of belief strength where 7 - very likely and 1 = very unlikely.

1 - 5 scales of attitude where larger numbers reflect more positive feelings.

a: $p < .1$    b: $p < .05$    c: $p < .001$

Listerine Manipulation

A two way ANOVA was run for the 3 target and 9 other primary belief strength measures. The two factors were whether an individual received an inoculation or a control advertisement and whether an individual was exposed to an "FTC" attack on the brand or not. Since only three groups were used, one cell of the ANOVA was missing.

The attack effect was significant (p < .10) for one of the three target beliefs (see Table 3). The inoculation effect was insignificant for all three target beliefs. Of the 18 possible significant results for the 9 non-target primary belief measures, two were found significant (p < .10), an occurrence which is minimally above chance. The same ANOVA was also run for attitude, toward a) the brand and b) its purchase. Only in the former case were the results significant (p < .10) and then only for the attack effect.

To control for usage effects on attitude scores [9], the sample was split between respondents who said that Listerine was their favorite brand and all others. Unfortunately, only eleven respondents fell into the former category. Since the size of this category was so small, we did not treat it as a seperate factor in the ANOVA. Instead, we repeated our previous analysis on the 41 subjects who did not consider Listerine to be their favorite brand. The results of this analysis was similar in all respects to the analysis using the entire sample.

We also compared the three groups on what they remembered about the advertisements. The control advertisement was correctly perceived by 17 of the 18 subjects in the no attack condition, but only 5 of the 17 subjects in the attack condition. In the latter condition, many of the subjects mistakenly thought that the advertisement mentioned the brand's ability to prevent sore throats and colds or to kill germs. Finally, the inoculation advertisement was correctly perceived by all subjects in that condition. Thus, when the advertisement and the attack contained similar information (inoculation advertisement-attack) or when the advertisement was not followed by an attack (control advertisement-no attack), there was no opportunity for confusion and the advertisement was correctly perceived. However, when the advertisement and the attack contained different information (control advertisement-attack) most subjects confused the source and the direction of the message and attributed the distorted information to the advertisement.

IMPLICATIONS

The results of the Burnfree phase of the experiment indicated that a greater change in a primary belief can be obtained by attacking the primary belief directly instead of attacking a supportive belief. This would seem to indicate that the FTC should concentrate corrective advertising on primary beliefs even though the primary belief may have been infered from a supportive belief. A greater change was noted in both attitude measures and primary belief measures when the attack dealt with a primary belief as opposed to a supportive belief.

The manipulated beliefs for Listerine were found to be bimodal for the control-no attack group indicating that the respondents had thought about and had decided to either accept or reject the Listerine message concerning the prevention of sore throats and colds prior to any inoculation treatment. Since the respondents had apparently already applied counterarguing and support arguing to their beliefs, the value of the inoculation in motivating these processes was minimal. This suggests that the use of inoculation theory to make beliefs about brands resistant to persuasion probably will not be effective in most marketing situations.

The recall data are consistent with the hypothesis that consumers who are paying only partial attention to an announcement may, when they later think about the message, be triggered into recalling previously heard "deceptive" concepts (even if these concepts were heard a long time ago) as well as the "correct" concepts. In other words, the attack served the purpose of getting the consumers to also think about the company's message, i.e., the consumers were "inoculated." This would explain the confusion in recall of the messages as well as the fact that the control-attack group and the inoculation-attack groups were very similar in attitudes and target belief measures, and consequently why the inoculation effect was insignificant.

A comparison of the two phases of the experiment indicates that the attack on the primary belief in the Burnfree situation was more successful than the attack on the primary belief in the Listerine situation. One possible reason for these differences is that the Burnfree beliefs were newly formed whereas the Listerine beliefs had been formed and reinforces through advertising for many years. This is consistent with the hypothesis that it is easier to change newly formed beliefs than well formed ones and also points out that the FTC may have difficulty "correcting" well-established deceptive beliefs.

REFERENCES

1. Aaker, David A. and John G. Myers. Advertising Management. Englewood Cliffs, N.J.: Prentice-Hall, Inc., 1975.

2. Abelson, Robert P., et. al. Theories of Cognitive Consistency: A Sourcebook. Chicago: Rand McNally, 1968.

3. Ahtola, Olli T. "The Vector Model of Preferences: An Alternative to the Fishbein Model," Journal of Marketing Research, 12 (February 1975), 52-59.

4. Bither, Stewart S., Ira J. Dolich and Elaine B. Nell. "The Application of Attitude Immunization Techniques in Marketing," Journal of Marketing Research, 8 (February 1971), 56-61.

5. Fishbein, Martin and Icek Ajzen. Belief, Attitude, Intention and Behavior: An Introduction to Theory and Research. Reading, Mass.: Addison-Wesley Publishing Company, 1975.

6. Hovland, Carl, Irving L. Janis and Harold H. Kelley. Communication and Persuasion. New Haven, Conn.: Yale University Press, 1953.

7. Hunt, Keith H. "Effects of Corrective Advertising," Journal of Advertising Research, 13 (October 1973), 15-24.

8. Lutz, Richard J. and John L. Swasy. "Integrating Cognitive Structure and Cognitive Response Approaches to Monitoring Communications Effects," in William D. Perreault, Jr., ed., Advances in Consumer Research, Vol. 4. Association for Consumer Research, 1977.

9. Mazis, Michael B. and Janice E. Adkinson. "An Experimental Evaluation of a Proposed Corrective Advertising Remedy," Journal of Marketing Research, 13 (May 1976), 178-83.

10. McGuire, William J. "Inducing Resistance to Persuasions," in L. Berkowitz, ed., Advances in Experimental Social Psychology, Vol. 1. New York: Wiley, 1964.

11. McGuire, William J. "Persistence of the Resistance to Persuasion Induced by Various Types of Prior Belief Defenses," Journal of Abnormal and Social Psychology, 64 (1962), 241-248.

12. Mitchell, Andrew A. and Jerry C. Olson. "Cognitive Effects of Advertising Repetition," in William D. Perreault, Jr., ed., Advances in Consumer Research, Vol. 4. Association for Consumer Research, 1977.

13. Olson, Jerry C. and Andrew A. Mitchell. "The Process of Attitude Acquisition: The Value of a Developmental Approach to Consumer Attitude Research," in M. J. Schlinger (ed.), Advances in Consumer Research, Vol. 3. Association for Consumer Research, 1976, 168-175.

14. Orne, M. T. "On the Social Psychology of the Psychological Experiment: With Particular Reference to Demand Characteristics and Their Implication," American Psychologist, 17 (November 1962), 776-783.

15. Sawyer, Alan G. "Demand Artifacts in Laboratory Experiments in Consumer Research," Journal of Consumer Research, 1 (March 1975), 20-30.

16. Sawyer, Alan G. "The Need to Measure Attitudes and Beliefs Over Time: The Case of Deceptive and Corrective Advertising," in Kenneth Bernhardt, ed., Marketing: 1776-1976 and Beyond, Series 39. American Marketing Association, 1976, 380-385.

17. Szybillo, George J. and Richard Heslin. "Resistance to Persuasion: Inoculation Theory in a Marketing Context," Journal of Marketing Research, 10 (November 1973), 396-403.

18. Wilkie, William L. and David M. Gardner. "The Role of Marketing Research in Public Policy Decision Making," Journal of Marketing, 4 (January 1974), 38-47.

19. Wright, Peter L. "The Cognitive Processes Mediating Acceptance of Advertising," Journal of Marketing Research, 10 (February 1973), 53-62.

# ARE COMPARATIVE ADVERTISEMENTS MORE INFORMATIVE FOR OWNERS OF THE MENTIONED COMPETING BRAND THAN FOR NONOWNERS?

William M. Pride, Texas A&M University
Charles W. Lamb, Texas A&M University
Barbara A. Pletcher, California State University, Sacramento

## ABSTRACT

The use of comparative messages in both print and broadcast advertisements is increasing. Yet, there is very little empirical research regarding the effectiveness of comparative advertisements. The laboratory experiment discussed in this paper focused upon the questions of (1) whether noncomparative and comparative messages are perceived differently, with respect to their informativeness, by owners and nonowners of the competing brand mentioned in the advertisements and (2) whether variations in the direction and intensity of comparison in comparative advertisements create differential effects on owners and nonowners with respect to informativeness. A factorial design, using seven mock print advertisements, was employed in this study.

## INTRODUCTION

In the October 1975 issue of the Journal of Marketing, Wilkie and Farris presented an overview of the practice of comparison advertising [3, p.7]. They defined comparison advertising as advertising that:

1. Compares two or more specifically named or recognizably presented brands of the same generic product or service class, and

2. Makes such a comparison in terms of one or more specific product or service attributes.

Wilkie and Farris also described the evolution of comparison advertising; discussed a number of issues that concern regulatory groups, industry leaders, media representatives, and brand strategists; and suggested several research hypotheses regarding the differential effects of comparative and noncomparative advertisements.

The utilization of direct comparisons in both print and television advertisements is increasing. Currently, about one out of every twelve commercials in prime time television is a comparison advertisement [2]. Although the use of direct comparisons is rapidly becoming a pervasive advertising practice, only a few studies have been aimed at evaluating the effectiveness of comparative messages. Research findings by Ogilvy and Mather [5], Mazis [3], Wilson [7], Golden [1] and Prasad [4] regarding the effects of comparative advertising are somewhat inconsistent. The Ogilvy and Mather [5] findings revealed that the comparative format leads to lower sponsor identification greater sponsor misidentification, and is less believeable and more confusing than the noncomparative format. Mazis' [3] results did not support any of the conclusions, but Wilson found comparative advertisements less believeable and more confusing than noncomparative advertisements. Golden [1], on the other hand, found no significant differences in the effectiveness of comparative versus noncomparative advertisements. Ogilvy and Mather [5] also found that there were no differences in the unaided brand identification of subjects exposed to comparative, noncomparative, or Brand X formats. This finding was supported by Mazis [3] and Prasad [4]. Prasad [4] also found that message and claim recall was greater for subjects exposed to comparative advertisements than those exposed to the Brand X format. Mazis'

[3] findings regarding these measures were mixed and inconclusive.

The need for empirical, comparative advertising has been emphasized and justified by Wilkie and Farris. They indicate that the use of comparison advertising is increasing, that comparative advertising copy is becoming more explicit and specific, and that the competitive atmosphere is becoming more obviously heated posing important questions for industry leaders, brand strategists, and advertising regulators [6]. In suggesting possible research dimensions regarding comparative advertising effectiveness, Wilkie and Farris raised the issue of whether comparative advertisements are more informative than are noncomparative advertisements [6].

## BACKGROUND AND PERSPECTIVE

One major reason for using comparative advertising is to inform owners or users of the mentioned competing brand or brands that the sponsored brand is equal to or superior to the competing brand in order to convince those individuals to switch to the sponsored brand. One of the major issues raised in the research reported in this paper was whether owners of the competing brand found comparative advertisements to be more informative than did nonowners of the competing brand. Informativeness was measured in two ways. First, subjects' perceptions of the level of informativeness of comparative or noncomparative advertisements were measured. Second, the relative informativeness of comparative and noncomparative messages were analyzed by measuring respondents' awareness of product features discussed in the advertisements. Perceived informativeness and product feature awareness were the two dependent variables of the study.

It appears reasonable that not all comparative advertisements are equally informative. From among the multitude of factors that may affect the informativeness of comparative messages, this study focused upon two -- directionality and intensity. Directionality refers to whether the sponsored brand is associated with or differentiated from the competing brand [6, p. 12]. An associative comparative advertisement is one in which most of the references to a competing brand or brands point out the similarities between the sponsored brand and the competing brand or brands. A differentiative comparative advertisement is one in which most of the references to a competing brand or brands point out the differences between the sponsored brand and the competing brand or brands. One question that arises is whether an associative or a differentiative comparative message is more informative than the other? There are no empirical findings that answer this question of directionality.

Intensity refers to the degree of specificity of comparison that is made in a comparative advertisement. Intensity can range from a very casual mention of the existence of a competitive brand to a very high level, point-by-point comparison of the sponsored and competitive brands. The level of intensity is a function of (1) whether the competing brand (or brands) is identified by brand name or whether it is identified in another way in the copy, (2) whether it is illustrated, and (3) the frequency at which it is compared to the sponsored brand. A low-intensity comparative message neither identifies the competing brand (or brands) by name nor illustrates the brand, but it does refer to the competitor in other ways such as "the leading brand" or "the major competitor." References to the competing brand are infrequent. A moderate-intensity comparative message is one in which the competing brand (or brands) is identified by name but is not shown, and there is not a high-frequency, point-by-point comparison of the sponsored and competing brands. In a high-intensity comparative advertisement the competing brand is identified by name and is illustrated if the sponsored brand is illustrated. Additionally, the sponsored brand is illustrated. Additionally, the sponsored brand and the competing brand are compared in a high-frequency, point-by-point manner.

Directionality and intensity were the two independent variables of this research effort. These dimensions and their various levels are shown in the framework in Figure 1.

FIGURE 1

CONCEPTUAL FRAMEWORK FOR COMPARATIVE ADVERTISING

PURPOSE OF THE STUDY

The purpose of the empirical study reported in this paper was to focus on the following questions.

1. Do comparative and noncomparative advertisements have differing effects, with respect to informativeness, on owners of the competing brand as compared to the effects on nonowners of the competing brand?

2. Do variations in directionality have differing effects, with respect to informativeness, on owners of the competing brand compared to the effects on nonowners of the competing brand?

3. Do variations in the intensity of comparison have differing effects, with respect to informativeness, on owners of the competing brand compared to the effects on nonowners of the competing brand?

RESEARCH DESIGN

A factorial design was utilized in this research. Seven mock magazine advertisements were developed including one noncomparative advertisement in which no reference was made to the competing brand, and six comparative advertisements, one for each form identified in Figure 1. The product used in all seven advertisements was a calculator; it was selected because it is both familiar and important to college students. A ficticious brand, Acco X410, was employed to avoid confounding effects that might have arisen due to predispositions toward an existing brand. The competing brand identified or referred to in each comparative advertisement was the Texas Instrument SR-11.

Data were obtained from 210 undergraduate students enrolled in business administration courses. Each subject was exposed to one advertisement and was given one minute to read it. At the end of the reading time the advertisements were collected, and the subjects were asked to complete a questionnaire. Each subject was requested to rate the advertisement on a seven point scale (ranging from extremely informative to extremely uninformative) in terms of its informativeness. Additionally, each was instructed to list as many product features as possible that appeared in the advertisement. Subjects were also asked whether or not they owned a calculator, and if so, what brand. Finally, they were asked to identify the leading national brand of calculator.

Of the 210 respondents, 126 reported that they owned a Texas Instruments calculator, and 84 reported that they owned another brand or did not own a calculator. Over 80 per cent of the subjects identified Texas Instruments as the leading national brand.

ANALYSIS AND FINDINGS

Analysis of the data occurred in three steps. First, the questionnaires were divided into 14 groups based upon the treatment given, and whether or not the subjects indicated that they owned Texas Instruments calculators. There were twelve respondents in each cell in the nonowner groups and eighteen per cell in the owner groups. Second, analysis of variance (ANOVA) was performed to analyze the main effects of the independent variables and possible interactions. Third, the means were computed for each of the respondent groups for the two dependent variables and orthogonal contrasts were used to determine if the differences in the treatment means were statistically significant.

The general models of analysis of variance for the dependent variables are shown in Tables 1 and 2. With respect to the two independent variables, none of the P-values were significant at the .10 level. No statistically significant interactions were found at the .10 level either.

TABLE 1

THE GENERAL MODEL OF ANALYSIS OF VARIANCE FOR OWNERS AND NON-OWNERS OF THE COMPETING BRAND FOR THE DEPENDENT VARIABLE, PERCEIVED INFORMATIVENESS

| Source | d.f. | Sum of Squares | F-Value | P-Value |
|---|---|---|---|---|
| Non-Owners: | | | | |
| Intensity (I) | 2 | 4.3611 | 1.6370 | .2007 |
| Directionality (D) | 1 | 0.0139 | 0.0104 | .9156 |
| I X D | 2 | 3.6944 | 1.3867 | .2560 |
| Owners: | | | | |
| Intensity (I) | 2 | 4.0185 | 1.9973 | .1389 |
| Directionality (D) | 1 | 1.5648 | 1.5555 | .2127 |
| I X D | 2 | 4.5740 | 2.2734 | .1061 |

Table 3 contains the treatment means and the P-values for the dependent variables for both owners and nonowners of the competing brand (Texas Instruments). In regard to the question of whether comparative and noncomparative advertisements generally produce different levels of informativeness for owners of the competing brand compared to nonowners, the data in Table 3 indicate that there were no differential effects. None of the P-values for perceived informativeness and product feature awareness for either owners or nonowners were significant at the .10 level of significance.

## TABLE 2

THE GENERAL MODEL OF ANALYSIS OF VARIANCE FOR OWNERS AND NON-OWNERS OF THE COMPETING BRAND FOR THE DEPENDENT VARIBLE, FEATURE AWARENESS

| Source | d.f. | Sum of Squares | F-Value | P-Value |
|---|---|---|---|---|
| Non-Owners: | | | | |
| Intensity (I) | 2 | 11.0833 | 0.7453 | .5172 |
| Directionality (D) | 1 | 13.3472 | 1.7950 | .1817 |
| I X D | 2 | 2.6944 | .1812 | .8359 |
| Owners: | | | | |
| Intensity (I) | 2 | 32.2963 | 2.2109 | .1127 |
| Directionality (D) | 1 | 10.7037 | 1.4655 | .2267 |
| I X D | 2 | 36.7407 | 2.5151 | .1139 |

Do variations in directionality have differing effects, with respect to informativeness, on owners of the competing brand compared to the effects on nonowners of the competing brand. The data in Table 3 suggest a negative answer to this question. The P-values for both owners and nonowners were not significant at the .10 level for either one of the dependent variables. Irrespective of whether a reader is an owner or a nonowner of the competing brand, differentiative comparative advertisements appear to be no more or no less effective for producing product feature awareness or perceived informativeness.

Do variations in the intensity of comparison have differing effects, with respect to informativeness, on owners of the competing brand compared to the effects on nonowners of the competing brand? Variations in intensity seem to have very limited effects on nonowners of the competing brand. The only contrast that was statistically significant at the .10 level was low intensity versus moderate intensity for the dependent variable, perceived informativeness. The P-value for this contrast was .0685. The same contrast for owners of the competing brand was also significant with a P-value of .0985. The direction of the differences between the contrasted means indicates that moderate intensity comparative advertisements create higher levels of perceived informativeness in both owners and nonowners of the competing brand than do low intensity comparisons. The remaining contrasts for nonowners, regarding variations in intensity for both dependent variables, were not statistically significant at the .10 level.

For owners of the competing brand all contrasts regarding intensity for both dependent variables were significant at the .10 level. The contrasts that were statistically significant for the dependent variable, perceived informativeness, are also the ones that were significant for the dependent variable, product feature awareness. Looking at the direction of the differences in the means for the statistically significant contrasts one can ascertain that, among owners, low intensity comparisons produced higher levels of perceived informativeness and product feature awareness than did high intensity comparative messages. Also moderate intensity comparisons created greater levels of perceived informativeness and product feature awareness than did either low or high intensity comparison advertisements.

## IMPLICATIONS OF THE FINDINGS

Relative to noncomparative messages, comparative advertisements are, in general, no more or no less informative for either owners or nonowners of the competing brand mentioned in the advertisement. Even though comparative ad-

## TABLE 3
## ORTHOGONALLY CONTRASTED MEANS AND RESULTING P-VALUES

### NON-OWNERS

| Contrasts | Perceived Informativeness | | Feature Awareness | | Perceived Informativeness | | Feature Awareness | |
|---|---|---|---|---|---|---|---|---|
| | Means* | P-Values | Means | P-Values | Means* | P-Values | Means | P-Values |
| Noncomparative versus Comparative | 2.4167 2.5139 | .7830 | 5.4167 5.1251 | .7225 | 2.2222 2.4537 | .3752 | 6.0556 5.7408 | .6433 |
| Associative versus Differentiative | 2.4999 2.5277 | .9171 | 5.5556 4.6945 | .1679 | 2.5741 3.5000 | .2232 | 5.4259 6.0556 | .2218 |
| Noncomparative versus Associative | 2.4167 2.4999 | .8270 | 5.4167 5.5556 | .2417 | 2.2222 2.5741 | .1466 | 6.0556 5.4259 | .1926 |
| Noncomparative versus Differentiative | 2.4167 2.5277 | .8472 | 5.4167 4.6945 | .1560 | 2.2222 3.5000 | .4075 | 6.0556 6.0556 | .3278 |
| Low Intensity versus High Intensity | 2.7083 2.6667 | .4189 | 5.6250 4.6667 | .2980 | 2.4444 2.6945 | .0859 | 5.6667 5.1111 | .0850 |
| Low Intensity versus Moderate Intensity | 2.7083 2.1667 | .0685 | 5.6250 5.0833 | .9244 | 2.4444 2.2222 | .0985 | 5.6667 6.4445 | .0546 |
| Moderate Intensity versus High Intensity | 2.1667 2.6667 | .1241 | 5.0833 4.6667 | .5841 | 2.2222 2.6945 | .0524 | 6.4445 5.1111 | .0355 |

*The lower values represent higher levels of perceived informativeness and the higher values represent lower levels of perceived informativeness.

vertisements are not more informative than noncomparative
ones, the fact that they appear to be no less informative
may be important for advertisers because by knowing that
comparative messages are no less informative, advertisers
have a broader range of approaches to use when developing
advertisements.

Directionality does not appear to influence the informativeness of comparative messages for either owners or
nonowners of the competing brand. This finding suggests
that an advertiser has the freedom to use either associative or differentiative messages since neither format is
more informative than the other.

With respect to variations in intensity, owners of the competing brand respond differently from nonowners. For nonowners, variations in the intensity of comparison have
very little impact on the informativeness of comparative
messages. One exception to this general finding is that
low intensity advertisements were perceived to be less
informative than moderate intensity ones. However, for
owners of the competing brand shown in the advertisement
variations in intensity seem to have significant effects
on informativeness of the advertisements. The objective
of many comparative advertisements is to attract and
appeal to the owners of the competing brand mentioned in
the advertisement because often that brand is the market
leader. If this is a primary goal, the findings suggest
that the advertiser should avoid the use of high intensity
comparisons and should attempt to achieve a moderate intensity of comparison in order to maximize the informativeness of the advertisement.

This study represents one attempt to evaluate the impact
of variations in intensity and directionality on the informativeness of comparative advertising for owners and
nonowners. A considerable amount of research is needed
to provide relevant data to the advertisers. Future research dealing with the dimensions of intensity and directionality could focus on the effectiveness of advertisements in which both the sponsored brand and the competing brand are known brands, on advertisements for different types of products, and on advertisements trans-
mitted through different media.

## REFERENCES

1. Golden, Linda L., "Consumer Reactions to Comparative
   Advertising," in B.B. Anderson, ed., Advances in Con-
   sumer Research, Volume III, Association for Consumer
   Research, 1976, 63-67.

2. Hickey, Neil, "It's Goodbye 'Brand X,'" TV Guide
   (October 2, 1976), 44-46.

3. Mazis, Michael B., "A Theoretical and Empirical Examination of Comparative Advertising," Working Paper,
   Gainesville, Florida, University of Florida, 1976.

4. Prasad, V. Kanti, "Communications-Effectiveness of
   Comparative Advertising: A Laboratory Analysis,"
   Journal of Marketing Research, 13, (May 1976), 128-137.

5. "The Effects of Comparative Advertising When You Name
   The Competition," Research Department, Ogilvy and
   Mather, Inc., 1975.

6. Wilkie, William L. and Paul Farris, "Comparison Advertising: Problems and Potential," Journal of Marketing,
   39 (October 1975), 7-15.

7. Wilson, R.D., "An Empirical Evaluation of Comparative
   Advertising Messages: Subjects' Responses on Perceptual Dimensions," in B.B. Anderson, ed., Advances
   in Consumer Research, Volume III, Association for
   Consumer Research, 1976, 53-57.

RETAIL CONSUMER TYPOLOGIES AND MARKET SEGMENTATION:
STRATEGIC IMPLICATIONS

W. Thomas Anderson, Jr., The University of Texas at Austin
William H. Cunningham, The University of Texas at Austin
John H. Murphy, The University of Texas at Austin

## ABSTRACT

The paper reports the results of an empirical study designed to evaluate the relative usefulness of alternative segmentation criteria in differentiating consumer typologies
based on store patronage. The findings provide the basis
for designing improved marketing strategies for both hard
and soft goods retailers.

## INTRODUCTION

There have been a number of studies reported in the literature dealing with the characteristics of consumers that
shop at particular forms of retail institutions. These
studies have, for the most part, attempted to assess the
usefulness of demographic and behavioral variables in identifying shopper typologies [2,3] and such segmentation criteria as psychographics, imagery, personality, and life
style [1,6,7,8,9,10,15,16]. The present study examined the
ability of a broad spectrum of potential segmentation variables to delineate retail store shoppers categorized on the
basis of generic store type patronization.

Specifically, the objective of the study was to evaluate
the relative usefulness of alternative segmentation criteria in differentiating shopper typologies based on store
patronage. Purchasers of a variety of hard and soft goods,
categorized as to store patronage, were contrasted on the
basis of selected (1) demographic variables, (2) behavioral
variables related to retail purchases, (3) sources utilized
in obtaining information about products, and (4) decision
factors influencing product selection. The study was conducted across a mix of both hard and soft goods in order to
provide a foundation for merchandising strategy in a number of retail environments.

## METHODOLOGY

### Data Collection

A self-administered questionnaire was developed to collect
the desired information and was mailed to a random sample
of 1,200 female residents of Austin, Texas. Subjects were
selected from the most recent metropolitan area telephone
directory and asked to participate in a study sponsored by
the marketing department of The University of Texas. Subjects were assured of the anonymity and confidentiality of
their responses.

Three hundred seventy-eight women returned the survey instrument properly completed, for a response rate of 32%. A
comparison of the demographic profile of the households in
the sample with the most recent U.S. census data indicated
that in terms of the age of the household head and the
presence of children the sample was representative of the
population. However, with respect to annual family income
and education of the household head, the sample had a sign-
nificantly higher income and educational level than the
population. Thus, as with most mail surveys, individuals
of lower socioeconomic status were underrepresented among
the respondents.

### Product Categories Examined

A total of six generic product categories were studied.
The three hard goods categories examined were: (1) major
appliances; (2) furniture; and (3) television and/or stereo
equipment. The three soft goods categories examined were:
(1) women's accessories, including shoes and handbags;
(2) women's lingerie, hosiery, and sleepwear; and, (3)
women's sports and casual wear.

Subjects were asked to identify the store in Austin where
they or a member of their family purchase each of these
items most frequently. Subjects were instructed to omit
the individual question if they or a member of their family had not purchased such an item in Austin.

### Shopper Typologies

Each subject was classified as being either a department
store shopper or a specialty store shopper for the product
categories. An insufficient number of subjects purchased
the products surveyed from discount stores or mail/catalog
stores to permit separate analysis of these shoppers.

### Segmentation Variables

Four sets of variables were examined in the research. The
first two sets consisted of demographic and behavioral variables. The demographic variables surveyed were: (1) occupation and (2) education of the chief wage earner, (3)
annual family income, (4) socioeconomic status [14], (5)
age of the chief wage earner, (6) marital status, (7) stage
in the family life cycle [12], (8) employment status of
the spouse, and (9) present dollar value of residence.
The behavioral variables analyzed were: (1) frequency of
downtown shopping, (2) mode of payment for merchandise
(cash, credit card, or charge account), (3) dollar volume
of charge account purchases, (4) dollar volume of credit
card purchases. The demographic and behavioral variables
were selected because they have previously been used in
consumer research and segmentation studies [4,5,11] and
were felt to be of potential value in delineating shopper
typologies.

The third set of variables consisted of sources utilized in
acquiring information concerning each of the product categories studied. Subjects were asked to indicate the most
important source in acquiring information about each of
the product classes from the following information sources:
going shopping, talking with friends, reading magazines,
reading newspapers, reading store circulars, observing
what others own, watching television, and, listening to
the radio.

The fourth set of variables consisted of decision factors
influencing the choice of products within each product
category. Subjects were asked to designate the most important factor influencing the selection of the hard and
soft goods studied from the following alternatives: store
location and parking, price, brand name, sales personnel,
service and warranty, availability of credit, selection of
products, store reputation, recommendation by a respected
person, delivery and installation. Both information source
categories and decision criteria alternatives were derived
from a review of relevant literature and extensive open-
ended pretesting among local residents.

Analysis

Chi square analyses were used to test for differences that might exist between department and specialty store customers on each of the variables examined. In several cases response categories had to be eliminated from consideration because the expected frequencies of responses were not sufficient for inclusion in the contingency table analyzed by chi square [13]. The chi square values were corrected for continuity, thus yielding conservative measures of statistical significance.

## FINDINGS [1]

Demographic and Behavioral Variables

Hard goods purchases. Of the demographic variables analyzed, marital status, education, and occupation of the chief wage earner, annual family income, and socioeconomic status significantly differentiated department from specialty store furniture purchases at the <.05 level. A higher proportion of specialty store furniture purchasers were married or widowed than department store furniture purchasers. Moreover, specialty store furniture purchasers were of relatively higher socioeconomic status, educational and occupational attainment, and annual family income, in contrast with department store furniture purchasers. Marital status marginally differentiated department from specialty store major appliance purchasers, with a slightly higher percentage of specialty store major appliance purchasers married. All other demographic variables examined failed to significantly differentiate department from specialty store purchasers of major appliances and television and/or stereo equipment. (See Table 1)

Of the behavioral variables analyzed, only mode of payment for merchandise significantly differentiated department from specialty store major appliance purchasers at the <.05 level. Frequency of downtown shopping and dollar volume of charge account purchases yielded differences between department and specialty store major appliance purchasers at the <.10 level. In general, specialty store major appliance purchasers shopped downtown with relatively greater frequency and charged a higher dollar volume of merchandise than department store major appliance purchasers. Alternatively, department store major appliance purchasers were more reliant on retailer credit.

Mode of merchandise payment and dollar volume of charge account purchases also significantly differentiated department from specialty store purchasers of television and /or stereo equipment. Department store television and/or stereo equipment purchasers were substantially more active charge account clients and charged a significantly higher dollar volume of merchandise, while specialty store television and/or stereo equipment purchasers were more exclusively reliant on cash purchases. Only frequency of downtown shopping significantly differentiated department from specialty store furniture purchasers, with specialty furniture purchasers shopping downtown with relatively greater frequency than department store furniture purchasers. (See Table 2)

Soft goods purchases. With respect to soft goods purchases, only education of the chief wage earner significantly differentiated department from specialty store sports and casual wear purchasers, while marital status yielded differences at the <.10 level. Specialty store sports and casual wear purchasers were of relatively higher educational attainment than department store sports and casual wear purchasers. Conversely, a relatively higher proportion of department store sports and casual wear purchasers were married than specialty store purchasers. None of the demographic variables surveyed yielded significant differences between department and specialty store purchasers of either of the other two soft goods categories--accessories and lingerie.

Of the behavioral variables tested, only mode of payment for merchandise significantly differentiated department from specialty store purchasers of accessories. Department store accessories purchasers made greater use of charge accounts, while specialty store accessories purchasers were more reliant on cash purchases. Dollar volume of charge account purchases provided marginal differences between department and specialty store sports and casual wear purchasers, with department store customers charging a proportionately higher dollar volume of merchandise.

Information Sources

An overall $x^2$ test of differences between department and specialty store customers in information sources used in the selection of commonly purchased hard and soft goods tested for significant relationships. Respondents were asked to indicate the most important of alternative information sources concerning each of the six categories of goods.

Hard goods purchases. It is noteworthy that while the same information source (going shopping) was found to be most important for the highest number of both department and specialty store purchasers of hard goods, the relative importance attached to secondary information sources was found to differ across product categories. Only with respect to television and/or stereo equipment purchases were department and specialty store customers found to differ significantly in the relative importance associated with alternative sources of product information. Both types of customers relegated major importance to shopping and secondary significance to conversations with friends. Specialty store television and/or stereo equipment purchasers interpreted comparative shopping as relatively more important than did department store customers. Important third and fourth-ranking sources of information concerning television and/or stereo equipment purchases among specialty store customers were magazines and observations of others, respectively. Alternatively, newspapers ranked as the third most important source of product information among department store television and/or stereo equipment purchasers. (See Table 3)

Both department and specialty store purchasers of major appliances and furniture placed major reliance on shopping. However, major appliance purchasers placed secondary importance on conversations with friends, while furniture purchasers placed secondary importance on newspaper reading.

Soft goods purchases. As in the case of hard goods purchases, the same information source (going shopping) was found to be most important to both department and specialty store purchasers of soft goods. However, the relative importance associated with other information sources was found to differ across product categories. For all three soft goods categories surveyed, both department and specialty store customers placed principal reliance on comparative shopping and secondary importance on reading newspapers. Specialty store customers were relatively more reliant on comparative shopping as the principal source of product information concerning accessories and sports and casual wear, while department store lingerie purchasers indicated newspapers as a relatively more important secondary source of product information.

Only in the case of accessories purchases were department

---

[1]Due to length limitations, the four tables which present the findings of the study have been abbreviated. Complete copies of the tables are available from the authors.

TABLE 1

SELECTED DEMOGRAPHIC VARIABLES AND STORE PATRONAGE

| Demographic Variables | Hard Goods – Furniture | | | Soft Goods – Sport & Casual Wear | | |
| --- | --- | --- | --- | --- | --- | --- |
| | Specialty Store | Department Store | P | Specialty Store | Department Store | P |
| Martial Status | 94% married 1% single 5% other | 81% married 3% single 16% other | .01 | 80% married 6% single 14% other | 88% married 1% single 11% other | .07 |
| Education of chief wage earner | 51% college graduates or advanced deg. | 66% less than completed college education | .03 | 46% college graduates or advanced deg. | 60% less than completed college education | .05 |
| Annual family income | 50% above $14,000 | 64% below $14,000 | .01 | – | – | n.s. |
| Occupation of chief wage earner | Professional & white collar | Light blue and blue collar | .002 | – | – | n.s. |
| Socioeconomic status | High & high average | Average & lower | .001 | – | – | n.s. |

TABLE 2

SELECTED BEHAVIORAL VARIABLES, PRODUCTS AND STORE PATRONAGE

| Behavioral Variable | Major Appliances | | | Hard Goods – Furniture | | |
| --- | --- | --- | --- | --- | --- | --- |
| | Specialty Store | Department Store | P | Specialty Store | Department Store | P |
| $-value of annual charge account purchases | 41% spend ≥ $150 22% spend $50-150 37% spend < $50 | 31% spend ≥ $150 21% spend $50-150 48% spend < $50 | .06 | – | – | n.s. |
| Mode of payment for merchandise | 56% cash 2% credit card 43% charge acct. | 36% cash 5% credit card 59% charge acct. | .02 | – | – | n.s. |
| Frequency of downtown shopping | 10% ≥ once/week 29% 1-3 times / month 46% 2-6 times/ year 15% < twice/year | 6% ≥ once/week 32% 1-3 times/ month 34% 2-6 times/ year 28% < twice/year | .06 | 11% ≥ once/week 31% 1-3 times/ month 34% 2-6 times/ year 24% < twice/yr | 5% ≥ once/week 27% 1-3 times/ month 46% 2-6 times/ year 22% < twice/year | .02 |

| Behavioral Variable | Soft Goods – Accessories | | | Soft Goods – Sports & Casual Wear | | |
| --- | --- | --- | --- | --- | --- | --- |
| | Specialty Store | Department Store | P | Specialty Store | Department Store | P |
| $-value of annual charge account purchases | – | – | n.s. | 28% spend ≥ $150 26% spend $50-150 46% spend < $50 | 33% spend ≥ $150 24% spend $50-150 43% spend < $50 | .06 |
| Mode of payment for merchandise | 64% cash 6% credit card 30% charge acct. | 43% cash 11% credit card 46% charge acct. | .001 | – | – | n.s. |

TABLE 3

DISTRIBUTION OF SUBJECTS BY SOURCES OF PRODUCT INFORMATION

| Purchase/Product Category | Maga-zines % | News-papers % | Store Cir-culars % | Shop-ping % | Talking with friends % | Observing others % | Tele-vision % | Total n | Total % | $x^2$ |
|---|---|---|---|---|---|---|---|---|---|---|
| **Hard goods purchases** | | | | | | | | | | |
| Major appliances | | | | | | | | | | |
| Specialty store | 12.9 | 9.7 | 4.8 | 38.7 | 24.2 | 8.1 | 1.6 | 62 | 100.0 | n.s |
| Department store | 8.6 | 12.3 | 6.2 | 43.8 | 17.3 | 11.1 | 0.6 | 162 | 100.0 | |
| Furniture | | | | | | | | | | |
| Specialty store | 5.1 | 16.5 | 1.3 | 63.3 | 10.1 | 3.8 | – | 79 | 100.0 | n.s |
| Department store | 3.2 | 20.2 | 4.8 | 62.1 | 4.8 | 3.2 | 1.6 | 124 | 100.0 | |
| Television/stereo | | | | | | | | | | |
| Specialty store | 12.0 | 5.0 | 3.0 | 51.0 | 19.0 | 10.0 | – | 100 | 100.0 | 9.70[a] |
| Department store | 4.5 | 10.2 | 9.1 | 48.9 | 20.5 | 4.5 | 2.3 | 88 | 100.0 | |
| **Soft goods purchases** | | | | | | | | | | |
| Accessories | | | | | | | | | | |
| Specialty store | 1.0 | 21.6 | – | 73.4 | 1.0 | 2.5 | 0.5 | 199 | 100.0 | 17.33[b] |
| Department store | 1.6 | 21.3 | 8.2 | 63.9 | 0.8 | 2.5 | 1.6 | 122 | 100.0 | |
| Lingerie | | | | | | | | | | |
| Specialty store | 5.4 | 16.3 | 2.2 | 68.5 | 2.2 | 2.2 | 3.3 | 92 | 100.0 | n.s |
| Department store | 1.0 | 19.5 | 7.1 | 68.6 | 2.4 | 1.4 | – | 210 | 100.0 | |
| Sports & Casual Wear | | | | | | | | | | |
| Specialty store | 3.2 | 16.8 | 1.6 | 73.6 | 1.6 | 3.2 | – | 125 | 100.0 | n.s |
| Department store | 3.2 | 17.4 | 5.2 | 65.2 | 3.9 | 3.9 | 1.3 | 155 | 100.0 | |

[a] $p < .10$; [b] $p < .001$

TABLE 4

DISTRIBUTION OF SUBJECTS BY SELECTED DECISION CRITERIA INFLUENCING PRODUCT SELECTION

| Purchase/Product Category | Store Location & parking % | Price % | Brand Name % | Service & warranty % | Selection of Products % | Store repu-tation % | Other % | Total n | Total % | $x^2$ |
|---|---|---|---|---|---|---|---|---|---|---|
| **Hard goods purchases** | | | | | | | | | | |
| Major appliances | | | | | | | | | | |
| Specialty store | – | 30.9 | 38.2 | 17.6 | 2.9 | 2.9 | 7.3 | 68 | 100.0 | 8.42[a] |
| Department store | 3.3 | 26.1 | 31.5 | 16.8 | 2.7 | 10.9 | 8.6 | 184 | 100.0 | |
| Furniture | | | | | | | | | | |
| Specialty store | 40.4 | 37.1 | 11.2 | – | 5.6 | 4.5 | 1.1 | 89 | 100.0 | 7.70[a] |
| Department store | 36.2 | 29.7 | 9.4 | 0.7 | 18.1 | 2.9 | 2.8 | 138 | 100.0 | |
| **Soft goods purchases** | | | | | | | | | | |
| Accessories | | | | | | | | | | |
| Specialty store | 10.1 | 30.3 | 19.7 | 0.5 | 31.3 | 4.8 | 3.3 | 208 | 100.0 | 9.29[a] |
| Department store | 10.5 | 43.5 | 20.2 | – | 17.7 | 4.8 | 3.2 | 124 | 100.0 | |

[a] $p < .10$; [b] $p < .05$

and specialty store customers found to significantly differ in the relative importance attached to alternative sources of product information. Department store accessories purchasers apparently considered store circulars or leaflets as an important third source of product information.

Hard versus soft goods purchases. It is noteworthy that the findings appear to suggest that there are greater differences in the relative importance associated with alternative sources of product information between hard and soft goods purchase decisions, irrespective of store patronage, than within hard or soft goods purchase categories. In both soft and hard goods purchase decisions customers appear to be highly reliant on point-of-purchase promotion and retailer contact as sources of product information. However, both department and specialty store customers appear to ascribe relatively greater importance to comparative shopping in soft goods purchase decisions.

More profound differences emerge with respect to major secondary sources of product information. In general, customers regard newspapers as the principal secondary source of product information concerning soft goods purchases, while in hard goods purchase decisions customers seem to balance media sources against interpersonal channels of communication concerning product information.

Decision Criteria

An overall $x^2$ test of differences between department and specialty store customers in the decision criteria utilized in the selection of commonly purchased hard and soft goods was used to test for significant relationships. The respondents were asked to designate the most important criteria influencing the selection in each of the product categories. (See Table 4)

Hard goods purchases. Significant differences were observed in all hard goods classes. Brand names carried was the most important decision criteria for both department and specialty store customers in the purchase of both major appliances and television and/or stereo equipment. Specialty store customers placed significantly greater importance on brand names carried for both major appliance and television and/or stereo equipment purchases than department store customers. Both department and specialty store major appliance purchasers were in agreement, however, on the secondary importance of price and service/warranty. Department store television and/or stereo equipment purchasers regarded price as a major secondary consideration and service/warranty an important third-ranking decision factor, while the reverse was true for specialty store television and/or stereo equipment purchasers.

In furniture purchase decisions both department and specialty store customers displayed a substantially different pattern of priorities in product selection criteria from that which characterized major appliance and television and/or stereo equipment purchases. Both department and specialty store customers regarded store location and parking and price as the principal and secondary decision criteria influencing product selection. However, specialty store furniture purchasers regarded brand names carried as an important third-ranking criteria, while department store customers viewed product selection as the third-ranking criteria influencing furniture purchases.

Soft goods purchases. In soft goods purchases, department and specialty store customers displayed a mixed pattern of priorities in decision criteria influencing product selection. Only in the case of accessories purchases were department and specialty store customers found to differ significantly in the relative importance associated with alternative purchase decision criteria. While specialty store accessories purchases regarded product selection and price as essentially equivalent primary purchase criteria,

department store customers relegated major importance to price by a wide margin over brand names carried and product selection as the principal decision criterion influencing the purchase of accessories. Both, however, interpreted store location and parking to be an important fourth-ranking decision factor.

In lingerie purchase decisions, specialty store customers apparently regarded brand names carried and product selection as equally, but not significantly more important selection criteria than price. Store location and parking was viewed as another important denominator of store patronage.

A parallel pattern of priorities in purchase decision criteria was found for sports and casual wear. Department store customers again apparently regarded price as the most significant decision factor in the purchase of sports and casual wear by a wide margin, followed by product selection, brand names carried and store location and parking. Specialty store customers apparently considered product selection and price to be essentially equally important purchase criteria, while store location and parking and brand names carried important third and fourth-ranking factors.

Hard versus soft goods purchases. As was the case with alternative sources of product information, the findings suggest that there are greater differences in the relative importance attached to alternative decision criteria influencing product selection between hard and soft goods purchase decisions, irrespective of store patronage, than within hard or soft goods purchase categories. Although both department and specialty store customers interpret price as a significant denominator of store patronage for both hard and soft goods, product selection and store location apparently receive relatively greater emphasis in soft goods purchase decisions, while brand names carried and service and warranty seem to be relatively more important in hard goods purchases. An exception to this generalization is furniture purchase decisions, where store location and parking and price constitute the principal decision criteria influencing product selection and store patronage.

These findings suggest that convenience, as reflected in product selection and store location, assumes relatively greater significance as a determinate of store patronage in soft goods purchase decisions. Conversely, security, reflected in brand names carried and service and warranty, appears to be a significant determinant of store patronage in hard goods purchase decisions.

## CONCLUSIONS AND STRATEGIC IMPLICATIONS FOR RETAIL MARKETERS

The results of the research indicate that the selected demographic and behavioral variables examined appear useful as disciminators of retailer preference for hard and soft goods on a product specific basis. Overall, the variables analyzed were found to be more appropriate for use as segmentation criteria for hard goods than soft goods.

More importantly, the research revealed differences both between and within hard and soft goods shopper categories with respect to information sources and decision criteria used in the selection of hard and soft goods. Moreover, there appear to be greater differences in the relative importance associated with alternative sources of product information and decision criteria influencing product selection between hard and soft goods purchase decisions, irrespective of store patronage, than among shopper typologies for either hard or soft goods.

Comparative shopping provides the principal source of product information for both hard and soft goods purchases, suggesting the importance of retailer contact and point-of-purchase promotion as sources of product information and store preference formation. The greater reliance on conventional media information sources in soft goods purchase decisions suggests the importance of advertising and sales promotion in the formation of both product and retailer preferences for soft goods. Alternatively, the importance of interpersonal channels of communication in hard goods purchase decisions underscores the significance of personal selling in shaping consumer patronage and product preferences for hard goods retailers.

With respect to purchase decision criteria, product selection and store location are high priority considerations for soft goods purchase decisions, while brand names carried and service and warranty are major determinants of store patronage for hard goods purchases. Thus, in soft goods purchases customers appear to be significantly more convenience oriented than in hard goods purchases, while in hard goods purchase decisions customers appear to be highly security conscious. By implication hard and soft goods retailers should appropriately incorporate security and convenience dimensions of consumer patronage in locational and product, promotional, and pricing decisions.

A further finding which has direct strategic implications revolves around the differences in secondary sources of product information. These differences suggest alternative marketing communications strategies to most effectively merchandise to specialty and department store soft and hard goods purchasers. Likewise, major contrasts in decison criteria influencing product and retailer selection between specialty and department store hard and soft goods purchasers suggest differences in the allocation of marketing resources to distribution and promotion, in contrast to the product component of the marketing mix.

An important thread of continuity running through these findings is the conclusion that consumers of a spectrum of commonly purchased hard and soft goods, irrespective of store patronage, are perhaps more appropriately distinguished on the basis of product information sources and decision criteria which would appear to be directly linked to the formation of product and dealer preferences than on the basis of conventional, although generally accessible, demographic and behavioral segmentation criteria. Thus, while such demographic and behavioral variables as socio-economic status, income, occupation, education, and mode of merchandise payment may provide a basis for segmenting shopper typologies for selected goods, and a partial focus for marketing strategy, it appears that improved strategies could perhaps emanate from consumer informational and decision-making styles which are more directly related to the formation of product and retailer preferences.

## REFERENCES

1. Arnold, S. J. and D. J. Tigert. "Market Monitoring Through Attitude Research," Journal of Retailing, 49 (Winter 1973-1974), 3-22.

2. Dardis, R. and M. Sandler. "Shopping Behavior of Discount Store Customers in a Small City," Journal of Retailing, 47 (Summer 1971), 60-72.

3. Dodge, H. R. and H. H. Summer. "Choosing Between Retail Stores," Journal of Retailing, 45 (Fall 1969), 21.

4. Frank, R. E. "Market Segmentation Research: Findings and Implications," in Applications of the Sciences in Marketing Management, F. Bass, C. King and E. Pessemier, eds., New York: Wiley, 1968.

5. Hisrich, R. E. and M. P. Peters. "Selecting the Superior Segmentation Correlate," Journal of Marketing, 38 (July 1974), 60-63.

6. Kassarjian, H. H. "Personality and Consumer Behavior: A Review," Journal of Marketing Research, 8 (November 1971), 409-419.

7. Lazer, W. and R. G. Wyckham. "Perceptual Segmentation of Department Store Markets," Journal of Retailing, 45 (Summer 1969), 3-14.

8. Pernica, J. "Psychographics: What Can Go Wrong? Proceedings, American Marketing Association, 1976, pp. 45-50.

9. Plummer, J. T. "The Concept and Uses of Life Style Segmentation," Journal of Marketing, 38 (January 1974), 33-37.

10. _____. "Psychographics: What Can Go Right?" Proceedings, American Marketing Association, 1975, pp. 41-44.

11. Rich, W. U. and S. C. Jain. "Social Class and Life Cycle as Predictors of Shopping Behavior," Journal of Marketing Research, 5 (February 1968), 41-49.

12. Rodgers, R. H. Improvements in the Construction and Analysis of Family Life Cycle Categories. Unpublished Ph.D. Dissertation, Western Michigan University, 1962.

13. Siegel, S. Nonparametric Statistics for the Behavioral Sciences. New York: McGraw-Hill, 1967.

14. U.S Bureau of the Census. U.S. Census of Population: 1960. Subject Reports. Socioeconomic Status. Final Report PC (2)-5C. Washington, D.C.: U.S. Government Printing Office, 1967.

15. Wells, W. D. and D. J. Tigert. "Activities, Interests and Opinions," Journal of Advertising Research, 11 (August 1971), 27-35.

16. Ziff, R. "Psychographics for Market Segmentation," Journal of Advertising Research, 11 (April 1971), 3-10.

TRADE AREA ATTRIBUTES, CONSUMER PATRONAGE BEHAVIOR,
AND RETAIL SALES -- A RECURSIVE MODEL

Dale M. Lewison, University of South Carolina
John F. Willenborg, University of South Carolina
Robert E. Pitts, University of South Carolina

## ABSTRACT

In this paper, a recursive model is developed to explain sales performance of retail outlets. The model includes two sets of explanatory variables: (1) trade area attributes of residential and non-residential units; and (2) consumer store choice (patronage) behavior based on origin and destination, and proximity of the origin/destination to the retail outlet. A test of the model was carried out utilizing data from a chain of convenience steakhouse restaurants. Consumer patronage behavior explained a significant amount of variation in average daily sales among restaurants as well as sales variation in noon hour, coffee hour, and dinner hour periods.

## INTRODUCTION

Sales performance of a retail outlet is often explained in terms of attributes of the trading area in which the outlet is located. In cases where product/service mixes remain fairly constant from one outlet to another, as is often the case with most chain operations, trade area locational attributes are often assigned the dominant role in explaining outlet to outlet sales variations. The inclusion of trade area attributes in numerous studies dealing with sales forecasting is indicative of their perceived importance [3, 4, 7, 9].

While macro-level trade area attributes such as accessibility [5], cumulative attraction [11], interception [6], compatibility [11], store association [1], and saturation [2, 8] are generally conceded to be important to retail sales success, the nature, degree, and direction of their relationship to sales sometimes have been established in an intuitive manner. Moreover, use of micro-level variables such as traffic count, front footage, and competitor count as surrogates of trade area attributes has met with mixed success in explaining sales both conceptually and statistically. The usual approach has been to measure the degree to which each of a large number of variables helps to explain sales variation. Those variables which add significant statistical explanation are included in the model. While this approach sometimes provides a respectable statistical explanation of sales variation between site alternatives, the conceptual interrelationships among sales, micro-level variables, and macro-level trade area attributes are often poorly developed.

A conceptual limitation of sales performance models which have used measures of trade area attributes is that the attributes serve as surrogates for actual consumer behavior. Clearly, consumers--not trade area attributes--generate retail sales. Trade area attributes, however, often directly influence choice of a retail outlet. Therefore, a logical approach to the prediction and explanation of retail sales is to view consumer store choice behavior in relation to trade area attributes and then to use behavior to explain the sales performance of retailers. In this way, a recursive model for forecasting retail sales would be developed.

The major purpose of this study is to demonstrate the applicability of a recursive model for estimating sales performances of retail outlets. The specific recursive model developed is a sequential series of linkages between the attributes of trade areas, store choice behavior of consumers, and retail sales.

## THE MODEL

The recursive model for explaining retail sales is illustrated in Figure 1. The general model describes the rela-

FIGURE 1

A RECURSIVE MODEL FOR EXPLAINING SALES

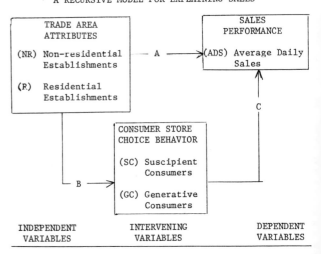

| INDEPENDENT VARIABLES | INTERVENING VARIABLES | DEPENDENT VARIABLES |

tionships between "trade area attributes," "store choice behavior," and several dimensions of retail sales. Common practice of using trade area attributes as independent variables to explain and/or predict the sales of a given retailer is illustrated by Flow A in Figure 1. In this study, a set of intervening consumer variables is interjected (Flows B and C, Figure 1) in an attempt to improve both statistical and conceptual explanation of the relationship between locational attributes of trading areas and sales.

Trade Area Attributes

As used in this study, trade area attributes are described in terms of the number and type of establishments found within the retail trading area. Assuming that the trading area serves as an important source of consumers for retailers, characteristics of the trading area also help to define both the consumer and his store choice behavior. While any number of typologies could be constructed in an attempt to isolate the consumer attraction capabilities of various outlets, "real world" operational considerations require that the simplest and most aggregate typology be constructed. Therefore, a two-class typology of trade area attributes is used in this study, residential establishments (R) and non-residential establishments (NR). A residential establishment is a housing unit occupied or intended for occupancy as separate living quarters. A non-residential establishment is a single physical location at which business (profit and/or non-profit) is conducted.

Conceptually, the number of trade area residential establishments is used as a proxy for the patronage potential of consumers who actually reside in the retailer's immediate vicinity. The number of non-residential establishments is a proxy for the patronage potential of consumers who reside outside the retailer's immediate vicinity, but who are attracted to the area for various purposes such as working or shopping. Trade areas vary greatly with regard to the mix of residential and non-residential establishments and to their absolute numbers. Consumer store choice (patronage) behavior is linked to the number of such trade area units in this model. The relative capabilities of residential and non-residential establishments to serve as sources of consumers for retailers during various daily sales periods are key factors in explaining sales variations.

## Consumer Store Choice Behavior

There are two general types of store choice (patronage) behavior. "Generative" behavior describes the case in which the consumer patronizes the store under consideration because it is conveniently located within the general vicinity of his place of residence. "Suscipient" behavior describes the case in which a consumer patronizes the store under consideration because it is conveniently located within the general vicinity of another non-residential establishment at which the consumer is/was engaged in an activity at any given time. Nelson [11] has provided further explanation of the terminology.

Consumers are classified on the basis of two spatial considerations relative to store choice: (1) the classification of trip origins and destinations as residential or non-residential; and (2) the proximity of origin/destination to the retail store. A consumer who patronizes a store is described as generative (GC) when (1) both his immediate origin and destination, relative to the store being patronized, was the consumer's place of residence; or (2) either his immediate origin or destination is the consumer's place of residence and it is closer to the store than the trip's counterpart (origin or destination). A consumer is described as suscipient (SC) when (1) both his origin and destination, relative to the store being patronized, is a non-residential establishment; or (2) either the immediate origin or destination is a non-residential establishment which is closer to the store than the trip counterpart (origin or destination). In this study, it is the trip behavior of suscipient and generative consumers that is the linkage between the attributes of a trading area and the sales performance of the retailer within that area.

## Daily Retail Sales

The third component of the model is a measure of retail sales. According to the model, average daily sales are a function of the nature of trip behavior undertaken by store patrons. Variations in sales by retailer will occur based on the number of generative and suscipient consumers who patronize a store.

The relationship between consumer store choice behavior and sales is even more meaningful when sales are differentiated in terms of daily peak periods. Many retailers depend on one or more relatively short time periods each day to generate satisfactory sales levels. For example, food outlets which are open throughout the day may experience wide sales variations from breakfast to lunch to coffee hour to dinner periods. Store choice behavior based both on type of trip origin/destination and proximity to the retail outlet is logically related to sales occurring during different periods of the day.

## RESEARCH DESIGN

### Methodology

A midwestern regional chain of company-owned and operated convenience steakhouse restaurants was used to test the model. The firm can be described as a rapid preparation, self-service, family-priced operation designed to handle a high volume of customers. The chain possessed three operating characteristics which were important to the test of the model: (1) a high degree of site-to-site standardization of the retailing mix variables, that is, the product-service offering, price structure, store atmosphere, and promotional strategy were consistent; (2) a high level of management control through a centralized management structure; and (3) location of stores in locales with diverse trade area characteristics.

Ten restaurants were selected to represent a variety of locational environments. The sample included seven sites from major metropolitan areas with both inner city and suburban locations represented. The remaining sample sites were from a range of smaller urban areas, the smallest city with a population of less than 20,000.

Sales data were obtained from the firm's management. They consisted of monthly sales volume for each of the ten sites over a 2-year period. The proportion of sales generated during each of three daily periods--noon hour (11:00 a.m. - 2:00 p.m.), coffee hour (2:00 p.m. - 5:00 p.m.), and dinner your (5:00 p.m. - 9:00 p.m.)--was also provided.

Data on the number of residential and non-residential establishments were obtained via field observation. Each primary trade area from which the data were obtained was defined as the area within an adjusted one mile radius of each restaurant. Justification for the somewhat arbitrary definition was a previous survey which determined that 52% of the firm's consumers had, either as their immediate origin or destination, a location which was within one mile of the restaurant. The 52% value is consistent with the range of values reported in other studies [1, 10].

The number of suscipient and generative consumers was generated through a survey of randomly selected consumers, carried out at the 10 restaurant sites. Each consumer interviewed was asked to identify: (1) his immediate origin and its distance (miles) from the restaurant and (2) his immediate destination and its distance (miles) from the restaurant. A total of 2,485 interviews were completed.

### Analysis Procedures

The principal analysis technique employed was multiple linear regression. The relationships depicted in the recursive model which were explored included: (1) the direct relationship between trade area attributes and sales (Figure 1, Flow A); (2) trade area attributes and consumer store choice behavior (Flow B); and (3) consumer store choice behavior and sales (Flow C).

The regression model resulting from the analysis was utilized in several specific ways: (1) to describe the direction of the posited relationships; (2) to identify the specific variables which contribute to explanation of both consumer store choice behavior and sales; and (3) to express the degree to which variations in sales among restaurants and by daily peak periods can be explained by consumer store choice behavior.

## RESULTS

The expectation that inclusion of the store choice behavior variable in the regression model would improve the explanation of sales behavior was borne out. Results of these regression analyses are summarized in Table 1. The trade

## TABLE 1

### THE DEGREE OF EXPLANATION OF VARIATIONS IN RESTAURANT SALES [a]

| Explanatory Factors | Dimensions of Sales | Coefficient of Determination ($R^2$) | F | Level of Significance |
|---|---|---|---|---|
| Trade Area Attributes | | | | |
| R + NR[b] | Average Daily Sales | .07 | 0.26 | N.S. |
| R + NR | Noon Hour Sales | .32 | 2.54 | N.S. |
| R + NR | Coffee Hour Sales | .11 | 0.44 | N.S. |
| R + NR | Dinner Hour Sales | .22 | 1.04 | N.S. |
| Consumer Store Choice Behavior | | | | |
| SC + GC[c] | Average Daily Sales | .84 | 18.74 | .01 |
| SC + GC | Noon Hour Sales | .65 | 6.50 | .05 |
| SC + GC | Coffee Hour Sales | .61 | 5.56 | .05 |
| SC + GC | Dinner Hour Sales | .74 | 10.03 | .01 |

[a]Based on multiple linear regression analysis.

[b]Number of trade-area residential units plus non-residential units.

[c]Number of suscipient consumers plus generative consumers.

area attributes of residential (R) and non-residential (NR) establishments directly explained only 7% of the variation in average daily sales. The sales performance of fast food steakhouses clearly is not a linear function of the number of residential and non-residential establishments in each trading area.

When sales were differentiated on the basis of peak periods, the result was the same. The regression equations explained from 11 to 32% of sales variation, but none were statistically significant.

The number of suscipient and generative consumers explained 84% of the variance in average daily sales among restaurants. This finding lends support to the contention that daily restaurant sales are a function of the consumer's immediate origin and destination and their proximity to the restaurant. Further, average daily sales are a function of two consumer types: (1) those who actually reside in the store's vicinity and choose to patronize the store due to its locational convenience to their residence; and (2) consumers who reside outside of the store's vicinity but are attracted to it because of its proximity to another place at which activity is car-

ried on.

The explanatory power of generative and suscipient patronage behavior is almost as great relative to peak period sales as it was regarding average daily sales (Table 1). The regressions explained 74% of the total variance in dinner hour sales, 65% of noon hour sales, and 61% of coffee hour sales. All were significant at the .05 level or above.

Results relative to the relationship of suscipient versus generative consumers based on the number of residential and non-residential units in the store trading area were encouraging. The $R^2$ of .73 for suscipient consumers was significant at the .01 level (Table 2). Somewhat less signif-

## TABLE 2

### THE INFLUENCE OF TRADE AREA ATTRIBUTES ON CONSUMER STORE CHOICE BEHAVIOR

| Explanatory Factors | Dependent Variables | Coefficient of Determination ($r^2$) | F | Level of Signification cance |
|---|---|---|---|---|
| Trade Area Attributes | Consumer Store Choice Behavior | | | |
| (R + NR)[a] | Generative | .43 | 2.62 | .10 |
| (R + NR) | Suscipient | .73 | 9.38 | .01 |

[a]Number of trade area residential units plus non-residential units

icant (.1) was the $R^2$ of .43 for generative consumers. Yet, the results provide evidence that R and NR are respectable proxies for patronage potential of consumers who reside either inside or outside the restaurant's vicinity.

In Table 3, standardized regression coefficients (betas) are presented. Both the degree of importance of each variable in the regression equation and the direction of each relationship can be ascertained.

The coefficients associated with Path B, that is, the relationship of trade area attributes to store choice behavior, were all statistically significant. The impact of the attributes on suscipient consumers was particularly strong. An inverse relationship was discovered between non-residential units and generative consumer behavior and between residential units and generative behavior. As a restaurant trading area becomes more residential, the potential patronage from suscipient consumers decreases.

Coefficients of residential and non-residential units relative to sales were not significant; however, the directions of their impact were of interest. The number of residential units in a trade area was inversely related to noon hour sales, but the positive impact of non-residential units on noon sales was far greater in magnitude. Also, non-residential units were inversely related to both coffee and dinner hour sales.

Five of the eight standardized regression coefficients of the store choice behavior variables relative to sales were significant at the .01 level (Table 3). Generative consumers have nearly twice the impact on average daily sales as suscipient consumers. The differential impact is even more pronounced regarding coffee hour and dinner hour sales, emphasizing the importance of restaurant location relatively near a consumer's place of residence where the objective is to maximize sales during those hours.

TABLE 3

THE RELATIVE IMPACT OF THE EXPLANATORY VARIABLES AS
INDICATED BY STANDARDIZED REGRESSION COEFFICIENTS

| Explanatory Variables | Store Choice Behavior | | Sales | | | |
|---|---|---|---|---|---|---|
| | Susci-pient | Gener-ative | Noon-Hour Sales | Cof-fee Hour Sales | Din-ner Hour Sales | Aver-age Daily Sales |
| **Trade Area Attributes** | | | | | | |
| Residential Units | -.82[a] | .76[b] | -.19 | .38 | .48 | .30 |
| Non-Residential Units | .96[a] | -.59[c] | .73 | -.13 | -.53 | .08 |
| **Store Choice Behavior** | | | | | | |
| Suscipient | | | .79[a] | .34 | .10 | .46[a] |
| Generative | | | .36 | .77[a] | .87[a] | .89[a] |

[a]Significant at p < .01

[b]Significant at p < .05

[c]Significant at p < .10

Finally, noon-hour sales seem to be more dependent on suscipient rather than generative patronage behavior. Suscipient behavioral influence was far greater than generative impact for noon-hour restaurant sales.

CONCLUSIONS AND IMPLICATIONS

The recursive retail sales model presented in this study provides the convenience retailer with a simple, but effective measure of the relative worth of alternative sites. The usefulness of the model lies in its ability to help explain variations in daily sales as well as variations in sales of the noon, coffee, and dinner peak demand hours. The significant relationships established in the model lend support to the notion that daily sales maximization requires maximization of sales in each of the peak demand periods. This effort, in turn, requires that fast-food restaurants attract both suscipient consumers (necessary to noon hour sales maximization) and generative consumers (necessary to coffee and dinner hour sales maximization).

A site's potential to attract both suscipient and generative consumers is, in part, a function of the number of residential and non-residential units within the restaurant's trading area. The implication is that a trade area combination of residential and non-residential establishments is required to develop the needed mixture of suscipient and generative consumers.

In summary, the model implies that certain trade area attributes may be necessary to initiate both generative and suscipient store choice behavior. The number of consumers exhibiting this behavior then helps to explain daily, noon, coffee, and dinner hour sales. The model does not suggest, however, that these trade area attributes and consumer types are sufficient conditions for total explanation of shopping behavior and sales variation. Future

application and development of the model requires that it be tested with regard to new store sites to measure its predictive power. While there is some risk in generalization, the model did provide considerable explanation of sales for the steakhouse restaurants. Thus, there is some likelihood that the model can be applied successfully to other retail outlets characterized by peak period daily sales.

REFERENCES

1. Applebaum, William and Saul B. Cohen. "Store Trading Areas in a Changing Market," Journal of Retailing, 37, (Fall, 1961); 14-35.

2. Applebaum, William and Saul B. Cohen. "Trading Area Networks and Problems of Store Saturation," Journal of Retailing 38 (Winter, 1961-1962), 32-43,55.

3. Applebaum, William. "Methods for Determining Store Trade Area Market Penetration and Potential Sales," Journal of Marketing Research, 3 (May 1966), 127-141.

4. Applebaum, William. "The Analog Method for Estimating Potential Store Sales." in Curt Kronblau (ed.), Guide to Store Location Research with Emphasis on Supermarkets. Reading, Mass.: Addison Wesley,1968.

5. Cohen, Saul B. and William Applebaum. "Evaluating Store Sites and Determining Store Rents," Economic Geography, 36 (January, 1960), 1-35.

6. Gist, Ronald E., Retailing: Concepts and Decisions. New York: John Wiley and Sons, Inc., 1968.

7. Heald, G.I. "Application of the Automatic Interaction Detector (ID) Programme and Multiple Regression Technique to the Assessment of Store Performance and Site Selection," Operations Research Quarterly, 23 (December, 1972) 445-457.

8. LaLonde, Bernard J. "The Logistics of Retail Location." Proceedings, Winter Conference, American Marketing Association (December, 1961), 567-575.

9. MacKay, David B. "A Microanalytic Approach to Store Location Analysis." Journal of Marketing Research, 9 (May 1972), 134-40.

10. Mertes, John A. "A Retail Structure Theory for Site Analysis." Journal of Retailing, 40, (Summer, 1964) pp. 19-30,56.

11. Nelson, Richard L. The Selection of Retail Locations. New York: F.W. Dodge Corporation, 1958.

# THE MARKETING OF SERVICES:
## A CATEGORIZATION WITH IMPLICATIONS FOR STRATEGY

Adrian B. Ryans, Stanford University
Dick R. Wittink, Stanford University

## ABSTRACT

Much of the literature on the marketing of services has tended to be descriptive rather than normative. In this paper we propose a simple conceptual framework for categorizing services that does have normative implications for developing marketing strategies for services. The framework is based on two dimensions: degree of differentiation of the service offering and the ability of the customer to switch between competing offerings or to discontinue use of the service entirely. Implications for marketing strategy are discussed.

## INTRODUCTION

Services of all kinds are taking an increasing share of American consumer spending [8]. However, successful application of marketing concepts and strategies appears to be lagging behind the profitable use of marketing in the product sector of the company [3,4]. Levitt has suggested that there are no service industries, only industries that involve services to a greater or lesser degree [7,8]. However, his observations about the successful "automization" of services by, for example, McDonald's emphasize the "production" aspects of service activities. While Levitt notes and suggests an increasing industrialization of services, it appears that many firms operating in the so-called service sector have lacked a marketing orientation as well [1,4].

To a large extent the debate about marketing services has centered around the extent to which it differs from marketing products. Stanton devotes a separate chapter to the marketing of services [10, Chapter 24] and the Handbook of Marketing includes several chapters on services [2, Chapters 4-2, 4-4, 4-6, 5-1, 10-12]. It is not clear, however, whether this treatment is the result of a belief that the marketing aspects are fundamentally different or that increasing interest in the marketing of services warrants separate coverage. Some authors have suggested that services are different from products on various grounds, including intangibility, inseparability, perishability and heterogeneity [12]. However, Wyckham et.al. have suggested that the development of taxonomies based on such characteristics is not useful [12].

We feel that much of the debate dealing with the similarities and differences between products and services and with the transferability of marketing knowledge from products to services has not been particularly productive. Instead of comparing the generic class of all products with the generic class of all services, we will limit our focus to services. We suggest a simple framework (amenable to further refinement) for categorizing services on the basis of market offerings and market characteristics. Using two specific dimensions we obtain a basis for discussing marketing activities of companies operating in selected service industries. Finally, implications of the framework for marketing strategy are explored. While the proposed framework may also be useful for categorizing products, our focus is on services in an attempt to structure marketing thinking in this area.

## A TAXONOMY OF SERVICES

Three approaches to the discussion of service marketing were identified by Blois [1]. One approach consists of a listing of differences between products and services. A second approach is the listing of services, which by itself has no implications for marketing strategy, and, as mentioned by Blois, listings tend to be outdated quickly due to new service developments [1]. The third approach is a taxonomy of services based on identifiable characteristics of services. Usually such taxonomies are based on offering characteristics which may or may not have direct implications for marketing strategy.

In developing marketing strategies for firms operating in the service sector, we believe that two dimensions are particularly important: the degree of differentiation of competing service offerings and the ability of the consumer to switch between alternative offerings or to stop using the service entirely. Degree of differentiation represents the extent to which the individual service has been differentiated from competing services in an attempt to provide a unique offering to the consumer. By appealing to a particular segment of the market, the firm may be sheltered somewhat from competing firms in the industry, possibly resulting in higher profitability. This dimension, therefore, does not focus on inherent differences between groups of services, but rather on the distinctions between competing services within a certain group. The opportunity to differentiate competing offerings is often a direct result of government regulation. In fact, many of the major service industries in our society are regulated in ways that have a major impact on their ability to develop differentiated marketing strategies. For example, both the banking and airline industries have only limited opportunities to use price as a competitive weapon. This results in firms in these industries attempting to differentiate their service offerings on what are probably less useful (but unregulated) dimensions.

The second dimension, the ability of the consumer to switch between competing offerings, results more directly from the characteristics of the offering. It is also closely related to what Wilson [11] has termed commitment; that is the time period of obligation a purchase of the service involves for the consumer. In several service (and also product) categories where brand switching is relatively easy, an S-shaped relationship between outlet- or capacity share and market share has been observed [5,9]. Such "additional" benefits that accrue to the firms with the larger outlet - or capacity shares were not observed in one study involving a service (banks) with infrequent switching [6]. Thus the degree of switching may have implications for marketing strategy.

Using differentiation and switching as the dimensions we suggest the following framework (Figure 1) for analyzing services by dichotomizing each continuum into low and high "regions." While there may be a considerable amount of variation along each of these dimensions, within a particular service industry, each service industry tends to be confined by its inherent nature or the environment in which it operates to only a part of the space defined by the two dimensions. We have placed some selected service industries in this framework to illustrate our perception of the degree of switching and differentiation that characterizes each of these industries (see Figure 1). To clarify our judgment we now discuss each of the four cells in this matrix.

FIGURE 1

A CLASSIFICATION OF SELECTED SERVICES IN
TERMS OF THE DEGREE OF DIFFERENTIATION
AND AMOUNT OF SWITCHING

DIFFERENTIATION

| | LOW | HIGH |
|---|---|---|
| SWITCHING | | |
| LOW | Banks<br>Life Insurance<br>Legal and Medical Services | Brokerage Institutions<br>Consulting Companies<br>Educational Institutions |
| HIGH | Airlines<br>Car Rentals<br>Taxi Cabs | Restaurants<br>Entertainment<br>Courier Services |

Low switching - low differentiation. In this cell we have classified professional services such as those provided by doctors, lawyers, dentists and public accountants as well as retail banks and life insurance companies. Most service industries in this category tend to be regulated or self-regulated with respect to marketing activities. Banks are constrained in their pricing strategies due to ceilings on the interest rates they can offer. The professional groups are restricted in the extent to which they can advertise (although these restrictions are being challenged), and such restrictions may have the effect of minimizing switching between alternative offerings. The quality of alternative offerings is difficult to evaluate (testability in Wilson's [11] terms), and the personal nature of the service, involving, for example, medical records, undoubtedly contributes to the relatively infrequent switching. The very nature of most life insurance contracts leaves little flexibility for changing companies, although lapsed policies can be a significant problem.

Low switching - high differentiation. Advertising agencies, management consulting and marketing research firms tend to fall in this category. Because of the recent abandonment of fixed commission rates, stock brokerage firms are becoming more differentiated. Many of the leading firms in these industries tend to stake out specialized "positions" in an attempt to appeal particularly to selected segments of the population. If the firms on the one hand, and the segments on the other are well matched, switching will be minimal. Professional service firms such as management consultants often stay abreast of a client's business even if there is no current project involving the client. By doing this the consultant believes that the client will be less likely to switch to a new consultant for a future project since the client realizes the present consultant is familiar with his operations and personnel and will only need a very short period to start making a positive contribution. Given the characteristics of these services, heavy reliance is placed on personal selling and word-of-mouth, while advertising is often designed to create awareness or interest and to support personal selling efforts.

High switching - low differentiation. The airline and car rental industries tend to be characterized by a lack of differentiation although there are clear differences between, say, international, national and regional airlines. The lack of differentiation is partly a result of government regulation (airlines) or it is due to an inability to develop truly differentiating features (taxicabs). The lack of differentiation between offerings in combination with the recurring need to choose between offerings on the part of consumers leads to a high degree of switching. For rental cars, the convenience of having a rental car counter at airports clearly differentiates the larger companies from many of the rest of the industry. Yet, within such a

subcategory, switching is quite frequent unless preferences are strong for the car manufacturer selected by a particular car rental company or the convenience offered by the reservations systems of some of the largest firms. In general, the firms in this category tend to rely more heavily on mass communication than firms in the group categorized by low switching and low differentiation. The frequency of customer choice and the low level of commitment dictates higher levels of advertising spending.

High switching - high differentiation. Many consumer services, especially in the restaurant and entertainment industries tend to fall in this category. By the very nature of these services, variety is important, and the choice of a particular offering depends crucially on the occasion. In the restaurant business, for example, the restaurant chosen is unlikely to be the same for an anniversary dinner and a quick meal for a family with young children. Thus, a restaurant may aim to establish a differentiated position within one or more occasion segments. For these types of businesses there is considerable potential for achieving a differentiated position. Advertising is often used extensively to help create and communicate the position.

IMPLICATIONS FOR MARKETING STRATEGY

For any service the most desirable position in the matrix is generally to be as close to the upper right hand corner as possible, that is, to be highly differentiated from its competitors (on dimensions that provide a meaningful customer value to the target segment) and to have low customer switching. We have indicated that the degree to which this position can be attained in a particular service industry depends critically on that industry's external environment, particularly on the regulatory environment and the basic customer needs with respect to the service. Nevertheless, the likely success and profitability of the service firm will be enhanced as the firm moves closer to the "ideal" combination of high differentiation and low switching.

Developing an appropriate differentiated service strategy (as is the development of any marketing strategy) is dependent on a meaningful segmentation of the market and the creation of a marketing mix to meet the needs of the target segment(s). The differentiation of the offering should be along dimensions that are important to the target segments and that cannot easily be imitated by competitors. For example, Emery Air Freight positioned its offering against the air freight operations of the major airlines by indicating that since it used all the major airlines, it could provide more frequent service to more destinations than any individual airline. The customer therefore, received two major benefits from using Emery: it only had to deal with one company for air freight service and there was the implied promise of faster delivery. By choosing to "position" itself and differentiate its offering in this manner, it was difficult for the major airlines to respond to or imitate this strategy. However, a recent entrant to this industry has avoided the regulatory and other constraints of the major airlines and has been able to turn Emery's apparent differential advantage into somewhat of a liability. Federal Express has pointed out that it uses its own fleet of planes and trucks and thus has complete control over parcels from the start of the journey to the destination, thereby reducing the chances of loss or delay. While it is a fairly common strategy now for service firms to try to differentiate their offerings, many appear to pay little attention to whether or not their differential advantage can be readily imitated. "Champagne and steak" promotional campaigns by airlines on selected routes are of this kind.

In developing their marketing strategies and in particular in differentiating their service offering many service firms appear to pay inadequate attention to the switching dimension. For example, in recent years many banks and savings and loan institutions have made extensive use of premiums as a differentiating tactic to encourage customers to switch to them. Unfortunately the premiums merely attract the customers, and the rest of the banks' services are generally not sufficiently differentiated from the competition to retain the newly acquired customer when a competitor also offers an attractive premium. Other service firms have been able to develop service features that differentiate their service and also contribute to reduced customer switching. The Hertz No. 1 Club and the Avis Wizard reservation systems are examples of this. The expense of such a system is probably only justifiable for very large car rental firms with many rental locations. Such a system does serve to differentiate these firms from most of their smaller competitors and the systems do provide a customer value to frequent renters in the form of shorter waiting times at the car rental counter. A strategy that encourages customer loyalty may in the long run reduce the firm's marketing communication costs since with a larger loyal customer base, the firm may have to spend less resources attracting new customers to replace those that would have switched away from the firm, ceteris paribus.

Ideally, therefore, the marketing manager in a service firm should search for strategies that both differentiate his service offering from those of his competitors on dimensions that are meaningful to customers in the target segment(s), difficult for competitors to imitate and inhibit customer switching.

## SUMMARY

Much of the literature on the marketing of services has tended to be descriptive rather than normative. In this paper we propose a simple conceptual framework for categorizing services that does have normative implications for developing marketing strategies for services. The framework is based on two dimensions: degree of differentiation of the service offering and the ability of the customer to switch between competing offerings or to discontinue use of the service entirely. Most service industries are restricted to a portion of the total space defined by these two dimensions due to the constraints placed on these firms by the external environment in which they operate. The regulatory environment and the inherent characteristics of the particular service are often particularly important in this regard. Nevertheless, within these general industry constraints individual firms do have an opportunity to position themselves favorably on these dimensions relative to their competitors. Generally a strategy that results in the firm's offering being

strongly differentiated from its competition (in a manner that makes it difficult for the competitors to imitate) and that inhibits customer switching is likely to place the firm in a favorable market position.

## REFERENCES

1. Blois, K.J. "The Marketing of Services: An Approach," European Journal of Marketing, 8 (Summer, 1974), 137-45.

2. Buell, Victor P. Handbook of Modern Marketing. New York: McGraw Hill, 1970.

3. Davies, D.G. "Marketing Financial Services: A Review Note," European Journal of Marketing, 8 (Spring, 1974), 83-88.

4. George, William R. and Hiram C. Barksdale. "Marketing Activities in the Service Industries," Journal of Marketing, 38 (October 1974), 65-70.

5. Hartung, Philip H. and James L. Fisher. "Brand Switching and Mathematical Programming in Market Expansion," Management Science, 2 (August 1965), 231-43.

6. Kinberg, Yoram and Ambar G. Rao. "A Model for Planning Bank Branching Strategy," paper presented at joint ORSA/TIMS Meeting, Las Vegas, Nevada, November 1975.

7. Levitt, Theodore. "Production-Line Approach to Service," Harvard Business Review, 54 (September-October 1972), 41-52.

8. Levitt, Theodore, "The Industrialization of Service," Harvard Business Review, 54 (September-October 1976), 63-74.

9. Lilien, Gary L. and Ambar G. Rao. "A Model for Allocating Retail Outlet Building Resources Across Market Areas," Working Paper 739-74, Alfred P. Sloan School of Management, Massachusetts Institute of Technology, September 1974.

10. Stanton, William J. Fundamentals of Marketing. Fourth edition. New York: McGraw Hill, 1975.

11. Wilson, Aubrey. The Marketing of Professional Services. New York: McGraw Hill, 1972.

12. Wyckham, R.G., P.T. Fitzroy and G.D. Mandry. "Marketing of Services: An Evaluation of the Theory," European Journal of Marketing, 9 (Spring 1975), 59-67.

# EXTENDING THE MCI MODEL TOWARD A THEORY OF INDIVIDUAL CHOICE BEHAVIOR[1]

Lee G. Cooper, University of California, Los Angeles
Masao Nakanishi, Kwansei Gakuin University, Japan

## ABSTRACT

In this paper we present a theory of individual choice which has evolved from our collaboration on the multiplicative competitive interaction (MCI) model. The development of the MCI model as an extension of the work of Huff (1962) [2] and the development of the theoretical side have run a course roughly together. While the general form of the model has broad applicability across domains and units of analysis, the theoretical developments only came clearly into focus by considering the processes occurring at the individual level. The propositions of the theory are presented at the individual level. The mathematical model which represents the theoretical elements is presented. A study of political choice is briefly described and evidence supporting the theory is presented.

## AN INDIVIDUAL IN THE PROCESS OF CHOOSING

### The Evoked Consideration Set

Consider a person who is presented a menu of alternatives, from which one is to be selected. It is well known that the menu does not necessarily correspond to the list (i.e. evoked set) of alternatives which the person really considers choosing. If you want to know what a person's evoked set contains, you could simply ask him/her to list the alternatives "you would really consider choosing." A researcher who decides that the consideration set is "such and such" without asking, has introduced a potential source of error.

### Meaningful Choice

Since the case of meaningless choice can easily be arrived at by reduction, we are free to assert that choosing is a meaningful process to a person. One way, and a good one, to find out the role of meaning in the process is to ask the person what he/she values knowing about each alternative in the evoked consideration set. There are qualitative questions, (e.g. "What qualities [things or attributes] would you like to know about these alternatives?") This would result in another kind of list which we could call a frame of reference. For each item in the list we could ask quantitative questions (e.g. the unipolar questions "How important is this attribute?" or "How important is it to know about this attribute?", or the bipolar question "How much do you value [positively or negatively] this quality?"). A very good list of qualities consists of all attributes for which value diverges from neutrality.

Since alternatives may be seen as differentially possessing qualities, we may also ask such questions as "To what extent does this alternative possess this attribute?"

### Distinctiveness of Possession

We assert that it is the distinctiveness of possession to which importance or value is attached. "Distinctiveness" is similar to the concept of "determinant" attributes in Myers and Alpert (1968) [4], but they do not develop this concept in a way which is useful to our theory.

If all alternatives possess an important attribute, the importance is not diminished, just the distinctiveness. Distinctiveness is a calculable aspect. It is not a parameter to be estimated. We have recently come to see distinctiveness as a representation in a choice context of the Jungian principle of the "regulating tensions of opposites" (Jung, 1966)[3]. Possession is valued in opposition to non-possession. It is the distinctiveness of possession that forms a basis for comparison. The particular way we choose to represent this transformation (from possession to distinctiveness of possession) may be improved upon, but the assertion that distinctiveness forms the basis of comparison is central to our theory at the individual level.

### An Attitude Toward Choosing

An attitude toward choosing from an evoked set of alternatives is formed in response to a total gestalt. A person forms an attitude toward selecting an alternative considering the total profile of all comparisons on all attributes. This is another central assertion, though it may be less controversial. "Value" or "importance" serves to shrink or stretch the impact of the distinctiveness. An attitude toward choosing is the result of all the value-distinctiveness pairs interacting fully with one another.

### From Attitude to Choice

This theory asserts that the transformation of attitudes into choice probabilities is a simple normative judgement. The probability of choosing a single alternative is just the ratio of the attitude toward that alternative referenced to the totality of attitudes for all alternatives in the evoked consideration sets. (N.B. It is only this sense of choice probabilities being a share of the total evaluative pie that makes the model derived from this theory a "special case" of the Luce Choice Axiom.)

## THE MODEL

The model has an element or relation for every assertion of the theory. This must be so if there is to be the possibility of gaining evidence for all deductions from the theory.

Let the evoked set of alternatives be represented as the objects $j = 1, 2, 3....m$. Let the frame of reference be established in terms of the set of attributes $k = 1, 2, 3, ....q$. Let the degree of possession of attribute $k$ for alternative $j$ be $Z_{jk}$. Let the distinctiveness transform of $Z_{jk}$ be represented as $X_{jk}$. And let $B_k$ be the "value" of possession of an attribute reported by a person. Then the attitude toward choosing alternative $j$ is:

$$A_j = \prod_{k=1}^{q} X_{jk}^{B_k} \tag{1}$$

and the probability of choosing alternative $j$ is:

$$\pi_j = \frac{A_j}{\sum_{j*} A_{j*}} \tag{2}$$

The first equation represents algebraically the notions that a) attitudes are formed toward a fully interacting

[1] This research was supported by a grant from the Division of Social Sciences of the National Science Foundation.

gestalt, as represented by the multiplication of distinctivenesses over attributes; and b) valuing is identifiably attached to the distinctiveness of each attribute, as represented by using value as an exponent. It is because we represent interaction algebraically as multiplication that value is represented as exponentiation, not vice versa. Distinctiveness is calculated with respect to a consideration set. This means the attitude toward a single alternative evolves in comparison to all other alternatives. Changes in the evoked set of alternatives may lead to changes in attitudes even if the frame of reference is unchanged.

The probability of choosing as shown in equation 2 is just a norming of the attitudes toward $j$ in relation to the aggregation of attitudes toward the whole evoked set.

## The Distinctiveness Transformation

There are three cases of the distinctiveness transform which we will consider. It originally evolved from attempts to deal more adequately with binary data on the possession or non-possession of attributes (c.f. Nakanishi, Cooper and Kassarjian, 1974) [5].

For binary data of this sort it seemed appropriate to develop an index which relied only on counting of candidates who possessed or did not possess an attribute. If we let $c_k$ be the number of candidates (choice-objects) who possess attribute k; then $X_{kj} = m/c_k$ if $j$ possesses the attribute and $(m-c_k)/m$ if $j$ does not possess the attribute.

The more general form for the binary (0,1) variable $Z_{kj}$ indicating non-possession or possession is given by:

$$X_{kj} = \frac{mZ_{kj} + (m-c_k)(1-Z_{kj})}{c_k \cdot Z_{kj} + m(1-Z_{kj})} \quad (3)$$

This index is symmetric in that it equals one if either all or none of the choice objects possess attribute k. It has its maximum value of m for the choice object j which is the sole possessor of an attribute. There is a natural symmetry to the binary cases which makes it unnecessary to consider whether possession or nonpossession of an attribute is the more ideal condition. When we move to the more general case of collecting data about possession on multistep discrete scales (e.g. semantic differential scales) we must consider two cases. The first is a straight generalization which is appropriate when the most ideal amount of possession of an attribute is perceived to be at or beyond the maximum (or minimum) scale value. In this case we can let Mn & Mx represent the minimum and maximum values of the measure on the scale incorporated into a particular study. And let $Z_{k\cdot}$ represent the arithmetic mean of the measure for the $k^{th}$ attribute summed over choice objects.

Then:

$$X_{kj} = \frac{(Z_{kj}-Mn)(Mx-Mn) + (Mx-Z_{kj})(Mx-\bar{Z}_{k\cdot})}{(Z_{kj}-Mn)(\bar{Z}_{k\cdot}-Mn) + (Mx-Z_{kj})(Mn-Mn)} \quad (4)$$

For convenience in seeing the relation of (4) to (3) we report the special case of data for which $0 \leq Z_{kj} \leq 1$

$$X_{kj} = \frac{Z_{kj} + (1-\bar{Z}_{k\cdot})(1-Z_{kj})}{Z_{kj}(\bar{Z}_{k\cdot}) + (1-Z_{kj})} = \frac{1-\bar{Z}_{k\cdot}(1-Z_{kj})}{1-Z_{kj}(1-\bar{Z}_{k\cdot})} \quad (5)$$

The development of a distinctiveness transform when the ideal amount of possession of an attribute is neither the maximum or minimum available presents certain problems. Most fundamentally, we need to address the possibility that departure from the ideal in different directions has different impact. Does possessing more than the ideal amount

of an attribute have a different impact than having less? A partially overlapping issue stems from the natural symmetry of the distinctiveness transform in the prior cases. It most likely is not naturally present in the ideal point case. Consider a seven-point scale measuring the (1) liberalness---conservativeness (7) of a candidate running for some office. If a person feels the ideal candidate would be rated as "3" on this scale, the largest departure available for real candidates on the more liberal side is smaller than the largest departure available on the more conservative side. Expanding the scale has no beneficial impact on the general issue since the process of psychological measurement converts <u>all</u> scales to multistep discrete scales for which other examples of this problem could be constructed. Does being as far away as is possible in one direction have the same meaning as being as far away as possible from the ideal in the other direction? Is absolute distance all that matters?*

One option we have discarded is splitting the attribute at the ideal point and treating all alternatives with less than an ideal amount as another group. This, however, would belie the tenet that information on the possession of attribute is transformed into a basis for comparison over the entire evoked consideration set of alternatives.

This issue is not fully resolved. We have decided to pursue, for this time, the formulation which uses absolute distances from the ideal regardless of direction of departure.

As we chose in the original generalization of the distinctiveness from the binary to the multistep case we will represent the maximum distance as the maximum available on the measurement scale as opposed to using the range of the measure present for any given set of alternatives.

With these restrictions, we may proceed to specify the ideal point version of the distinctiveness transform. Let $R_{Ik}$ be the available range (i.e. the distance from the ideal point to the most distant endpoint on the $k^{th}$ attribute). Let $d_{Ikj}$ be the absolute distance of alternative j from the ideal on the $k^{th}$ attribute. Let $\bar{d}_{Ik}$ be the average distance of the alternatives from the ideal rating on the $k^{th}$ attribute. Then the ideal point distinctiveness transform is given by:

$$X_{kj} = \frac{(R_{Ik} - d_{Ikj})*R_{Ik} + (d_{Ikj} * \bar{d}_{Ik\cdot})}{(R_{Ik} - d_{Ikj})*(R_{Ikh} - \bar{d}_{Ikj}) + (d_{Ikj} *R_{Ik})}$$

Of course, this reduces to the original formula if the data are binary.

It must be remembered that this is not an inferential statistic. We do not have to investigate properties such as bias, consistency or relative efficiency. Rather, it is a calculable descriptive index. It is valued in accord with its ability to describe the distinctiveness of an attribute in a given set of alternatives.

---

*We could also also consider whether distance or some function of distance (e.g. squared distance) is more appropriate. We have already adopted a partial stand on this in the formulas for the distinctiveness transform. In those equations we treat absolute distance rather than squared distance or some other function. We will do the same here. This is an aspect of the distinctiveness transform that we would be very willing to modify if strong evidence were developed that some other distance function were more appropriate.

## SOME EVIDENCE

One of the nice things about articulating a theory at the individual level is that it highlights the assumptions that are being made if the researchers choose to aggregate over individuals. Reflecting back on the analysis performed in Nakanishi, Cooper and Kassarjian (1974) [6] all the voters in Los Angeles were considered as a unit, the same evoked set of candidates, the same frame of reference, an analytic procedure was used to estimate the value of each attribute in a completely aggregate sense. Even with all these assumptions very favorable evidence was found for the superiority of this kind of theory over a linear, additive, nondistinctive representation. An average of 87% of the variance was explained in cross validation by our representation compared to 53% of the variance explained in cross validation by a more standard representation. This is, however, only a small step toward confirmation of the central propositions of our theory.

It will be necessary to gather evidence at the individual level. While the measurement models have been developed for the individual level analysis (Cooper and Nakanishi, 1975) [1], at this writing the data collection is some months off.

Some valuable evidence can be gained from the results from data originally collected for other purposes. Approximately 500 registered Democrats and Republicans in 40 precincts in Los Angeles County were interviewed in the weeks preceeding the 1974 statewide elections. The 90 to 120 minute in-person interview included a sample ballot for the Democratic and Republican candidates for Governor, U.S. Senator, Lt. Governor, and Attorney General; seven-point rating of each candidate on nine attributes (1. wants government to do more for people/wants people to do more for themselves, 2. favors integration/favors segregation, 3. favors capital punishment/favors rehabilitation of criminals, 4. pro-management/pro-labor, 5. conservative/liberal, 6. honest/dishonest, 7. active/passive, 8. doesn't have experience and ability/has both experience and ability, and 9. weak/powerful); ratings of a single ideal candidate's position on each of the nine attributes; and unipolar ratings of the importance of each of these attributes to the interviewee.

Because of extreme proportions (0 and 1) in the raw dependent variable (vote) at the individual level the results were aggregated to the precinct level. For each individual the distinctiveness transformation was calculated for an attribute and exponentiated by the reported importance for that attribute; the log of this was taken and averaged for all individuals in the precinct. This procedure summarizes the individual process as much as possible before aggregation while still allowing the analytical procedure to be used to estimate the proper sign for the unipolar importance of each attribute. Ordinary least square procedures estimate coefficients of which the sign indicates the direction of the reported importance and the magnitude of the raw coefficients indicates a combination of inconsequential scale effects and the relative extent of over or under reporting of the "actual" impact of importance.

Table 1 displays the distinctiveness model, the linear, additive, belief times importance model where

$$A_j = \sum_{k=1}^{q} B_k Z_{kj} \qquad (7)$$

and $\pi_j$ is defined as in equation (2) and a belief only model where

$$A_j = \sum_{k=1}^{q} Z_{kj} \qquad (8)$$

and $\pi_j$ is defined as in equation (2) in terms of the portion of explained variance. All models do very well in fitting the gubenatorial race with the distinctiveness model fitting minimally better. The senate race was best fitted by the distinctiveness model, but the overall fit of all models was not highly impressive. In the race for lieutenant governor the fits were not highly impressive and both the belief times importance and the belief only model fit slightly better than the distinctiveness model. In the attorney general race the distinctiveness model fit well and substantially outperformed the other models.

TABLE 1

PROPORTION OF VARIANCE EXPLAINED FOR EACH OFFICE

| MODELS | OFFICE | | | |
|---|---|---|---|---|
| | Governor | U.S. Senator | Lt. Governor | Attorney General |
| 1. Distinctiveness | .83 | .56 | .54 | .72 |
| 2. Belief x Importance | .79 | .38 | .59 | .42 |
| 3. Belief Only | .79 | .34 | .60 | .42 |

We also evaluated the ideal distinctiveness form of the model and compared it to an ideal distance multiplicative model where, letter $d_{Ikj}$ be the distance between a candidate's rating on an attribute and the ideal candidate's rating on an attribute,

$$A_j = \pi_{k=1}^{q} (d_{Ikj} + 1)^{B_k} ; \qquad (9)$$

a linear ideal distance model where

$$A_j = \sum_{k=1}^{q} (d_{Ikj} + 1)^{B_k} ; \qquad (10)$$

and a linear ideal distance, without importance model where

$$A_j = \sum_{k=1}^{q} (d_{Ikj} + 1) \qquad (11)$$

In all these models $\pi_j$ is defined in equation 2.

The aggregation was performed analogous to the method already described. Table 2 displays the results of each office in terms of the proportion of variance explained by each model. The essential difference between the ideal distinctiveness model and the multiplicative ideal distance is in the distinctiveness transformation versus a straight distance from ideal point. In three of the four offices the distinctiveness transformation fit better. The differences between the ideal distinctivenss model and the linear ideal distance model are in terms of the distinctiveness transform and the multiplicative versus linear formulation. In the same three of four offices the ideal distinctiveness model fit better. The linear ideal distance, without importance, model fits better than the ideal distinctiveness model in two offices and worse in two offices.

All of these results should be viewed with caution. Only one ideal candidate was used to apply to all four offices. The ideal point data to be most useful should be collected for each actual choice context. The ideal profile for governor and attorney general might well differ substantially. Further, a detailed analysis of the OLS coefficients

317

TABLE 2

PROPORTION OF VARIANCE EXPLAINED
FOR EACH OFFICE -- IDEAL POINT MODELS

| | OFFICE | | | |
|---|---|---|---|---|
| MODELS | Governor | U.S. Senator | Lt. Governor | Attorney General |
| 5. Ideal Distinctiveness | .72 | .53 | .76 | .79 |
| 6. Ideal Distance (Multiplicative) | .76 | .44 | .70 | .42 |
| 7. Ideal Distance (Linear) | .75 | .39 | .70 | .50 |
| 8. Ideal Distance (Linear without importance) | .79 | .44 | .78 | .30 |

currently being prepared reveals anti-ideal points on certain attributes in several models. This points toward a capitalization on chance. It is clear that the ideal point data were collected in a less than ideal manner considering our current purposes.

The next steps have to take us even closer to being able to validate the model on a purely individual level. Certain improvements are clearly called for: broader consideration sets, individuals having more choice over which alternatives they are to consider, individuals having more influence on the attribute used in evaluating the alternatives, doing more to minimize the impact of social desirability on personal report, and getting a richer collection of data regarding the dependent variable--choice. To consider choice to be perfectly represented by a binary vector of what was chosen and what was not, impoverishes the phenomena to a certain extent. All of the unchosen alternatives are not the same to the person choosing. Being able to deal with choice and go beyond choice to an understanding of the process of choosing is our real goal.

### REFERENCES

1. Cooper, Lee G. and Nakanishi, Masao. "On integrating attitudes with choice." 5th Management Science Summer Colloquim, Osaka, Japan, August, 1975.

2. Huff, David L. Determination of Intraurban Retail Trade Areas. Los Angeles: Real Estate Research Program, University of California, Los Angeles, 1962.

3. Jung, Carl G. Two Essays on Analytical Psychology. The Collected Works of C.G. Jung, Volume 7. Second Edition. Princeton University Press, 1966.

4. Myers, James H. and Alpert, Mark I. "Determinant buying attitudes: meaning and measurement." Journal of Marketing, 32, October, 1968, 13-20.

5. Nakanishi, Masao and Cooper, Lee G. "Parameter estimation for a multiplicative competitive interaction model--least squares approach." Journal of Marketing Research, XI, August, 1974, 303-311.

6. Nakanishi, Masao, Cooper, Lee G. and Kassarjian, Harold H. "Voting for a political candidate under conditions of minimal information." Journal of Consumer Research, 1, September, 1974, 36-43.

# AN EXAMINATION OF OPERATIONAL PROBLEMS WITH MULTIPLICATIVE COMPETITIVE INTERACTIVE MODELS

Vijay Mahajan, State University of New York at Buffalo
Arun K. Jain, State University of New York at Buffalo

## ABSTRACT

The paper is directed towards two operational problems encountered in the calibration of MCI models, namely, the problem of zero criterion variable and that of the transformation performed on binary explanatory variables. Alternative strategies to deal with these problems are discussed with examples.

## INTRODUCTION

Several approaches have been proposed in the marketing literature to evaluate the store location decisions. These approaches include checklist methods, Analog methods, Multiplicative Competitive Interactive (MCI) models, Entropy models, Environmental models, additive models, Sectogram techniques and Micro analytic models [9, 17, 19]. Attempts have also been made to combine the various approaches [16, 17]. Of the various approaches, Analog and MCI models seem to be the most popular ones. A review of the application of the Analog models can be found in the works of Applebaum and his associates [1, 2]. The MCI model, which is an extension of the Gravitational market share model of consumer spatial behavior originally suggested by Huff [5], has found its application in such areas as site selection [5, 10], estimation of sales potential [4], identification of trading area [3], and market share estimation [9]. The initial application of the MCI model was limited because of the problem in parameter estimation. However, it has been demonstrated by Teekens [20] and Nakanishi and Cooper [14] that the MCI model can be calibrated by using least squares procedures. Recently, the MCI model has been extended to include store image variables [12, 18] and to analyze the competitive environment on location decisions [7]. The superiority of the MCI model over additive model has also been demonstrated in nonmarketing application of predicting outcome of election results [15]. In the coming years we would expect a much wider use of this model due to the ease of estimation and sophistication of the model.

Some of the conceptual problems associated with the model were presented by Huff and Batsell at the 1974 ACR Conference in Chicago [6]. The purpose of this paper is to point out some of the data analysis problems associated with the model. Towards this, we first briefly discuss the model. Next, we identify operational problems and evaluate various approaches to handle them.

## THE MODEL

Huff's model [5] states that the probability ($P_{ij}$) of consumers in region $i$ ($i$, $i = 1, 2, ..., n$) choosing a particular retail facility $j$ ($j$, $j = 1, 2, ..., m$) is in proportion to the ratio of their utility to disutility derived from the facility. More formally, the model states:

$$P_{ij} = (\text{Utility})(\text{Disutility})^{-1} \tag{1}$$

The utility and disutility of retail facilities emanate from two sets of characteristics:

. The characteristics which are independent of the consumer such as sales area in the store, quality of product and service, in-store convenience level, etc.

. The characteristics which are dependent on the consumer such as the distance (or travel time) involved in

getting from a consumer's travel base $i$ to a given retail facility $j$.

The relevant characteristics may include categorical -- presence or absence of certain characteristics (e.g., location in a shopping plaza, type of the store -- independent or chain store) and interval scaled information (e.g., number of aisles in the store, size of the parking lot). Assuming a multiplicative function the consumer's choice from among m alternative stores may be described as follows:

$$P_{ij} = ( \prod_{k=1}^{q} A_{kj}^{\beta_k} ) \cdot ( \prod_{e=1}^{r} B_{eij}^{\beta_e} ) / \sum_{j=1}^{m} [ ( \prod_{k=1}^{q} A_{kj}^{\beta_k} ) \cdot ( \prod_{e=1}^{r} B_{eij}^{\beta_e} ) ] \tag{2}$$

where, $i = 1, 2, ..., n$ and $j = 1, 2, ..., m$.

$P_{ij}$ = The probability that a customer at location $i$ will shop at retail facility $j$

$A_{kj}$ = The $k$-th attribute of the retail facility $j$ which is independent of the consumer's point of origin; $k = 1, ..., q$

$\beta_k$, $\beta_e$ = Empirically determined parameters which reflect the sensitivity of the retail outlet characteristics of the probability to shop at a particular store

The MCI model can be calibrated by least squares methods using the following log transformed-centered form of (2):

$$\log (P_{ij}/\hat{P}_i) = \sum_{k=1}^{q} \beta_k \log (A_{kj}/\hat{A}_k) + \sum_{e=1}^{r} \beta_e \log (B_{eij}/\hat{B}_{ei})$$
$$= \sum_{k=1}^{q} \beta_k Z_{kj} + \sum_{e=1}^{r} \beta_e Z_{eij} \tag{3}$$

where,

$\hat{P}_i = ( \prod_{j=1}^{m} P_{ij} )^{1/m}$ = Geometric mean of the probabilities of consumer in point of origin $i$ shopping at m retail facilities

$\hat{A}_k = ( \prod_{j=1}^{m} A_{kj} )^{1/m}$ = Geometric mean of $k$-th attribute of m retail facilities which is independent of the consumer's point of origin

$\hat{B}_{ei} = ( \prod_{j=1}^{m} B_{eij} )^{1/m}$ = Geometric mean of $e$-th attribute of m retail facilities which is dependent on the consumer's point of origin

## SOME OPERATIONAL PROBLEMS

The calibration of (2) by means of (3), although intuitively appealing and operationally simple, possess two serious computational problems for the analyst:

1. Criterion Variable. If consumers from any region $i$ ($i$, $i = 1, 2, ..., n$) do not shop at a retail facility $j$ ($j$, $j = 1, 2, ..., m$), the resulting $P_{ij}$ and the geometric mean -- $P_{ij}$ -- for the region will be equal to zero. In such an event, the transformation of the ratio $P_{ij}/\hat{P}_{ij}$ will not be possible for parameter estimation in the model.

319

2. Explanatory Variable. The multiplicative character of the model requires that all the explanatory variables be coded either as interval or ratio-scaled. This excludes the use of variables in the model which can only be assigned values of zero or one to reflect their absence or presence in the environment being analyzed. The use of such variables in the model will make their geometric mean -- $\hat{A}_k$ or $\hat{B}_{ei}$ -- zero and log transformation of their ratio -- $A_{kj}/\hat{A}_k$ or $B_{eij}/\hat{B}_{ei}$ -- undefined and parameter estimation impossible.

## TRADITIONAL APPROACHES TO HANDLE THESE PROBLEMS

A literature search indicates the popularity of the following strategies to handle the problems outlined above:

1. Criterion Variable. In order to overcome the problem of zero criterion variable, two approaches are popular: (a) arbitrarily set the criterion variable to be equal to one so that log-value is zero; i.e., Log $P_{ij}/\hat{P}_i =$ log 1 = 0, or to (b) discard the corresponding observation.

2. Explanatory Variable. Nakanishi, Cooper and Kassarjian [15] have proposed the following transformation to handle the binary variables in the model (3):

   A. $B_{eij}$ = m/$C_{ei}$ if the retail facility $j$ patronized by consumers at region $i$ possess the characteristic e.

      = $(1 - C_{ei}/m)$, otherwise.

      Where, $C_{ei}$ is the number of retail facilities among the m facilities patronized by consumers at region $i$ which possess the characteristic $e$.

   B. $A_{kj}$ = m/$C_k$ if the retail facility $j$ possesses the characteristic k

      = $(1 - C_k/m)$, otherwise

      Where, $C_k$ is the total number of retail facilities among the m facilities which possess the characteristic $k$.

The various approaches to handle the data problems seem intuitively appealing and computationally expedient. However, little effort has been made to examine their potential impact on the parameters being estimated. The objective of this paper is to illustrate the effect of alternative research strategies to cope with these problems on parameter estimates. Towards this, data provided in Tables 1, 2, and 3 on four retailing facilities patronized by the residents from four regions is used. These tables provide information about the proportion of reported frequency of store selection by members of different regions, distance of stores from each region and two store characteristics. It should be noted that in Table 1 cells (1,3), (1,4), (2,1), (2,4), (3,1), (3,2), (4,2), and (4,4) are visited by only 1% of the total population from the respective regions. Such distributions are likely to occur in a typical application of this model.

### TABLE 1

FREQUENCY OF STORE SELECTION

| Region | Stores | | | |
|---|---|---|---|---|
| | A | B | C | D |
| I | 60 | 38 | 1 | 1 |
| II | 1 | 70 | 28 | 1 |
| III | 1 | 1 | 18 | 80 |
| IV | 20 | 1 | 78 | 1 |

Criterion Variable

It has been demonstrated by Young and Young [21] that arbitrarily setting the log-value of the criterion variable to zero totally changes the estimation equation, and for parameter estimation it is better to discard such observations. This approach -- discarding the observation with zero value

-- has statistical appeal. However, from an empirical model building point-of-view, such an approach might be risky. In particular, discarding of observations will result in reduction in the total number of observations which may effect the magnitude and sign of the estimated parameters [8]. To examine this, two regressions were performed using the data presented in Tables 1 - 3. In both regressions the variable location in a plaza was ignored. In the first case using (3), the $P_{ij}$'s are regressed against sales area and distance from the store. In the second case, we assumed that residents from region I visit only stores A and B, residents in region II visit only stores B and C, residents in region III visit only stores C and D, and residents in region IV visit only stores A and C. The $P_{ij}$'s for the remainder of the data were adjusted so that the total across stores within each region equals to 1. Columns 1 to 4 (Regressions I and II) of Table 4 present results of the analysis.

### TABLE 2

DISTANCE OF STORES FROM DIFFERENT REGIONS
(CONSUMER DEPENDENT CHARACTERISTICS)

| Region | Stores | | | |
|---|---|---|---|---|
| | A | B | C | D |
| I | 1 | 2 | 3 | 3 |
| II | 3 | 1 | 1 | 3 |
| III | 3 | 3 | 2 | 1 |
| IV | 2 | 3 | 1 | 3 |

### TABLE 3

STORE CHARACTERISTICS
(CONSUMER INDEPENDENT CHARACTERISTICS)

| Characteristic | Store | | | |
|---|---|---|---|---|
| | A | B | C | D |
| Sales area (Square yards) | 2000 | 3000 | 3000 | 4000 |
| Location in a shopping plaza[a] | 1 | 1 | 0 | 0 |

[a]Value 1 indicates the store is located in a shopping plaza while a 0 states that the store is not located in a plaza.

### TABLE 4

RESULTS OF THE MULTIPLE REGRESSION ANALYSIS
USING STORE DATA

| Variable | Regression I Total Sample | | Regression II Partial Sample | |
|---|---|---|---|---|
| | β | Significance | β | Significance |
| Size of the store | -0.05 | 0.60 | 0.36 | 0.10 |
| Distance from the store | -0.94 | 0.00 | -0.75 | 0.10 |
| R-square | 0.88 | | 0.84 | |

*Standardized parameter values.

We observe that parameters estimated from the two data sets differ sharply. First, the sign of the coefficient representing size of the store changes from negative to positive in the second data set. Second, the absolute value of the estimated parameters for the second data set decreases by close to 25% in the case of distance from the store and increases more than seven times for the size of the store. Finally, in the second data set, the parameters representing size of the store becomes statistically significant ($\alpha$ = 0.1) while it was insignificant ($\alpha$ = 0.6) when the total data set was used. The results highlight the problem an empirical model builder is likely to face if certain observations from the data sets are ignored. It suggests need for extreme care in sample selection and study design to ensure that the data closely approximates the market conditions. For example, the probability of observing zero $P_{ij}$'s may be reduced by increasing the sample size per origin or by using data collection techniques at individual respondent level which guarantee that there is no zero $P_{ij}$ in the data. Furthermore, the reduction in the degrees of freedom caused by discarding of observations can be compensated by increasing the number of origins (n) in the study.

## Explanatory Variables

In order to examine the effect of transformations used to convert binary explanatory variables to interval-scaled variables on the original data structure and values of regression coefficients in (3) consider the store dependent variables ($A_{kj}$). Let,

$$X_{kj} = a, \text{ if retail facility } \underline{j} \text{ possesses the characteristic } \underline{k}, (A_{kj} = 1)$$

$$= w\,a, \text{ otherwise } (A_{kj} = 0)$$

where a is an arbitrary value and w is the discriminant ratio between non-possession and possession of the $\underline{k}$-th attribute. For example, on an interval scale of 1 to 7, if possession of the attribute is assigned a value of 7, non-possession of the attribute a value of 1, the value of w is 1/7. The value of w reflects the relative importance of non-possession of the attribute to the possession of the attribute.

Next, let us derive the log transformed-centered value for binary explanatory variables in (3). If $c_k$ out of m facilities possess attribute $\underline{k}$, the geometric mean is:

$$\hat{X}_k = (\prod_{j=1}^{m} X_{kj})^{1/m} = [(a)^{c_k}(w\,a)^{(m-c_k)}]^{1/m} = a(w)^{(1-c_k/m)}$$

Therefore, in (3), the log transformed-centered term for attribute $\underline{k}$, i.e., $Z_{kj}$ is:

$$Z_{kj} = \text{Log } [X_{kj}/\hat{X}_k] = \text{Log } X_{kj} - \text{Log } a - (1 - c_k/m) \text{ Log } w, \text{ or}$$

$$Z_{kj} = - (1 - c_k/m) \log w, \text{ if retail facility } \underline{j} \text{ possesses attribute } \underline{k} \tag{4}$$

$$= (c_k/m) \log w, \text{ otherwise}$$

However, if the choice set m varies across the n originating regions, the log transformed-centered term in (3) is:

$$Z_{ikj} = - (1 - c_{ik}/m_i) \log w, \text{ if retail facility } \underline{j} \text{ in choice set } m_i \text{ possesses attribute } \underline{k} \tag{4a}$$

$$= (c_{ik}/m_i) \log w, \text{ otherwise}$$

In other words, the log transformed-centered value, $Z_{kj}$ (or $Z_{ijk}$) in (3) depends upon the ratio $c_k/m$ (or $c_{ik}/m_i$) and on the discriminant ratio. However, since for a particular problem $c_k/m$ (or $c_{ik}/m_i$) is determined by the choice set, the only factor influencing the value of $Z_{kj}$ (or $Z_{ikj}$), and hence the regression coefficient $\beta_k$ in (3) is the discriminant ratio w.

Now let us consider the alternative strategies available to a model builder in selection of the value for the discriminant ratio w:

i.   Consumers from all the originating regions ($\underline{i}$, i = 1, 2, ..., n) are assigned the same value of w for all the binary explanatory variables ($\underline{k}$, k = 1, 2, ..., q) (discriminatory ratio = w for all $\underline{k}$ and $\underline{i}$).

ii.  Consumers from all the originating regions are as-

signed the same values of w but different values may be assigned to different binary explanatory variables (discriminant ratio = $w_k$ for all $\underline{i}$).

iii. Consumers from each originating region are assigned the same value of w for all the binary explanatory variables. However, the value of w may vary across the region (discriminant ratio = $w_i$ for all $\underline{k}$).

iv.  Consumers from each originating region may be assigned different values of w for different binary explanatory variables and these values may vary across the regions (discriminant ratio = $w_{ik}$).

It will be observed from above that, first, in strategy (i) all the observations are being scaled by a constant term. Second, in strategy (ii) observations for the same attribute are being scaled by the same constant term. However, different attributes are being scaled by different constant terms. Third, in strategies (iii) and (iv) observations for the same attribute are being scaled by different constant terms. Finally, the set of standardized regression coefficients $\beta_k$ in (3) may vary across the strategies except for strategies (i) and (ii) where they will be the same.

We will now consider three possible transformations to convert binary variables into interval scaled variables (to extimate w) -- exponential, semantic differential, and the one proposed by Nakanishi, Cooper and Kassarjian [15] -- which can be used in the above four strategies. It will be demonstrated that the choice of transformations will not effect the values of the regression coefficients estimated in (3) for strategies (i) and (ii). However, the choice of a particular transformation used to convert binary variables may effect the set of regression coefficients obtained in strategies (iii) and (iv).

## EXAMPLES OF POSSIBLE TRANSFORMATIONS

### A. Exponential Transformation

For the first strategy (i) outlined above, let,

$$X_{kj} = \exp(A_{kj}) \tag{5}$$

$$X_{kj} = \exp(1) = e, \text{ if facility } \underline{j} \text{ possesses attribute } \underline{k} \ (A_{kj} = 1)$$

$$= 1, \text{ otherwise } (A_{kj} = 0)$$

Therefore, w = 1/e and the log transformed-centered term in (3) from (4) is (log e - 1):

$$Z_{kj} = (1 - c_k/m), \text{ if facility } \underline{j} \text{ possesses attribute } \underline{k}$$

$$= - (c_k/m), \text{ otherwise} \tag{6}$$

If the choice set m varies across the region, substitution of log w = - 1 in (4a) yields the required log transformed-centered term.

Similarly, the log transformed-centered term in (3) for the remaining three strategies can be obtained by introducing a scalar in the exponential term in (5). For example, in strategy (iv), $X_{ikj} = \exp(d_{ik}A_{ikj})$. Therefore, $w_{ik} = 1/\exp(d_{ik})$ and,

$$Z_{ikj} = (1 - c_{ik}/m_i)d_{ik}, \text{ if facility } \underline{j} \text{ in choice set } m_i \text{ posses attribute } \underline{k} \tag{7}$$

$$= - (c_{ik}/m_i)d_{ik}, \text{ otherwise}$$

Note in (7) that the log transformed-centered term varies across the originating regions and the attributes.

## B. Semantic Differential Scale Transformation

In strategy (i) the model builder may use a semantic differential scale of say, 1 to 7 to reflect the non-possession and possession of the attribute $k$. In such a case, the discriminant ratio $w = 1/7$ and the log transformed-centered term in (3) from (4) is:

$$Z_{kj} = (1 - c_k/m) \log 7, \text{ if facility } j \text{ possesses attribute } k$$
$$= -(c_k/m) \log 7, \text{ otherwise} \qquad (8)$$

It should be noted that the only difference between the transformations (6) and (8) is an additional scalar term, i.e., log 7. Therefore, in the parameter estimation in (3) use of (6) or (8) will yield the same value of the standardized regression coefficient $\beta_k$ for the $k$-th attribute. In other strategies, the log transformed-centered term in (3) may be obtained by varying the range of the semantic differential scale $(s_{ik})$. For example in strategy (iv):

$$Z_{ikj} = (1 - c_{ik}/m_i) \log s_{ik}, \text{ if facilty } j \text{ in choice} \atop \text{set } m_i \text{ possesses attribute } k \qquad (9)$$

$$= -(c_{ik}/m_i) \log s_{ik}, \text{ otherwise}$$

Again, it may be noted that the log transformed-centered term in (9) varies across the originating regions and the attributes. If $\log s_{ik}$ in (9) equals $d_{ik}$ in (7), for all $i$ and $k$, the set of regression coefficients $\beta_k$ in (3) obtained after using (7) and (9) will be the same. However, if this condition is violated, use of (7) and (9) will yield different sets of regression coefficients.

## C. Nakanishi, Cooper and Kassarjian (NCK) Transformation

Nakanishi, Cooper and Kassarjian [15] have proposed the following transformation:

$$X_{kj} = m/c_k, \text{ if the facility } j \text{ possesses attribute } k$$

$$= 1 - (c_k/m), \text{ otherwise}$$

or the discriminant ratio, $w = (1 - c_k/m)/(m/c_k)$. Therefore,

$$Z_{kj} = (1 - c_k/m) \{-\log [(c_k/m)(1 - c_k/m)]\}, \text{ if facility} \atop j \text{ possesses attribute } k \qquad (10)$$

$$= -(c_k/m) \{-\log [(c_k/m)(1 - c_k/m)]\}, \text{ otherwise}$$

It will be noted that the only difference between equation (6), (8) and (10) is in the value of $w$ used in the log transformed-centered term. The values of $w$ in these equations are, respectively, $1/e$, $1/7$ and $[(c_k/m)(1 - c_k/m)]$. It will be observed that whereas in transformation (A) and (B) the value of $w$ is prespecified by the analyst, in the NCK transformation, it is determined by the ratio $c_k/m$. If the ratio $c_k/m$ is the same for all $k$, $w$ will be the same for all the attributes and this will represent strategy (i). On the other hand if the ratio $c_k/m$ varies across the attributes $w$ will differ for all the attributes and this will represent strategy (ii). Since for a particular problem $c_k/m$ is pre-determined by the data, $(c_k/m)(1 - c_k/m)$ is constant. Therefore, the value of the standardized regression coefficients $\beta_k$, after using (6), (8) or (10) will be the same. If the ratio $c_{ik}/m_i$ is the same for all $k$ in each $i$, this will represent strategy (iii). For strategy (iv) log transformed-centered term m in (3) is:

$$Z_{ikj} = (1 - c_{ik}/m_i) \{-\log [(c_{ik}/m_i)(1 - c_{ik}/m_i)]\}, \text{ if} \atop \text{facility } j \text{ possesses attribute } k \qquad (11)$$

$$= -(c_{ik}/m_i) \{-\log [(c_{ik}/m_i)(1 - c_{ik}/m_i)]\}, \atop \text{otherwise}$$

Again, it may be noted that the log transformed-centered term in (11) varies across the originating regions and attributes. If in (7), (9), and (11), then $d_{ik} = \log s_{ik} = \{-\log [(c_{ik}/m_i)(1 - c_{ik}/m_i)]\}$, the set of regression coefficients $\beta_k$ in (3) obtained after using (7), (9), and (11) will be the same. However, violation of this condition will yield different sets of regression coefficients.

### Example

The parameters in (3) were estimated for the data presented in Tables 1, 2 and 3 by using the three transformations [equations (6), (8), and (10)]. The results for the total and partial sample are presented in Table 5. As expected from the above discussion, the beta coefficients under the three transformations within each sample are identical. However, the values of the standardized regression coefficients, $\beta_k$, vary across the samples due to the exclusion of observations with very small $P_{ij}$'s.

### TABLE 5

RESULTS OF MULTIPLE REGRESSION ANALYSIS
FOR DIFFERENT TRANSFORMATIONS*

| | Exponential Transformation | | | |
| | Regression III Total Sample | | Regression IV Partial Sample | |
| Variable | $\beta$ | Significance | $\beta$ | Significance |
|---|---|---|---|---|
| Size of the store | 0.03 | 0.85 | 0.52 | 0.00 |
| Distance from the store | -0.95 | 0.00 | -0.90 | 0.00 |
| Location in a shopping plaza | 0.10 | 0.44 | 0.46 | 0.00 |
| R-square | 0.89 | 0.00 | 0.98 | 0.00 |

*Standardized parameter values.

### TABLE 5 (Continued)

| | Semantic Differential | | | |
| | Regression V Total Sample | | Regression VI Partial Sample | |
| Variable | $\beta$ | Significance | $\beta$ | Significance |
|---|---|---|---|---|
| Size of the store | 0.03 | 0.85 | 0.52 | 0.00 |
| Distance from the store | -0.95 | 0.00 | -0.90 | 0.00 |
| Location in a shopping plaza | 0.10 | 0.44 | 0.46 | 0.00 |
| R-square | 0.89 | 0.00 | 0.98 | 0.00 |

### TABLE 5 (Continued)

| | NCK Transformation | | | |
| | Regression VII Total Sample | | Regression VIII Partial Sample | |
| Variable | $\beta$ | Significance | $\beta$ | Significance |
|---|---|---|---|---|
| Size of the store | 0.03 | 0.85 | 0.52 | 0.00 |
| Distance from the store | -0.95 | 0.00 | -0.90 | 0.00 |
| Location in a shopping plaza | 0.10 | 0.44 | 0.46 | 0.00 |
| R-square | 0.89 | 0.00 | 0.98 | 0.00 |

### SUMMARY AND DISCUSSION

In a typical application of the MCI model, the analyst will encounter data with certain very small or zero $P_{ij}$'s. Discarding of such observations is shown to effect the sign and magnitude of the sensitivity parameters of the MCI model. This may lead to misinterpretation of the results.

The log transformation used in the estimation of sensitivity parameters in the MCI model requires that binary explanatory variables be expressed as interval scaled variables. We identified four strategies and discussed three different transformations to convert binary explanatory variables. The basis for the identification of the four strategies was a discriminant ratio, w, used to express the relative importance of non-possession from possession of a given attribute. In a particular data structure it was suggested that value of w could be held constant (i) across all the attributes and originating regions, (ii) across all the regions but varied across attributes, (iii) across attributes but varied across regions, and (iv) varied across all regions and all attributes. It was shown that the choice of a transformation from the three discussed does not influence the values of the sensitivity parameters in MCI model under strategies (i) and (ii). However, since in strategies (iii) and (iv) observations are being differentially scaled across attributes and originating regions, the sets of sensitivity parameters estimated using the three different transformations may be different. It is debatable whether the strategies (iii) and (iv) should be used. Whereas in strategies (i) and (ii) the data is scaled across attributes, in strategies (iii) and (iv) it is also scaled across the originating regions, resulting in a completely different data structure within each originating region. It is questionable whether in the latter case, data across the regions can be combined to estimate the sensitivity parameters in the MCI model. This problem is further examined in [11].

## REFERENCES

1. Applebaum, William. Guide to Store Location Research with Emphasis on Super Markets. Reading: Addison-Wesley, 1968.

2. Green, Howard L. and William Applebaum. "The Status of Computer Applications to Store Location Research," AIDC Journal, 11 (April 1976), 33-52.

3. Haines, George H., Leonard S. Simon and Marcus A. Alexis. "Maximum Likelihood Estimation of Central City Food Trading Areas," Journal of Marketing Research, 9 (May 1972), 154-159.

4. Hlavac, T. E., Jr., and J. D. C. Little. "A Geographic Model of An Automobile Market," Working Paper 180-66, Alfred P. Sloan School of Management, Massachusetts Institute of Technology, Cambridge, 1966.

5. Huff, David L. "A Probabilistic Analysis of Consumer Spatial Behavior," in William S. Decker, ed., Emerging Concepts in Marketing. Chicago: American Marketing Association, 1963, 443-461.

6. _____ and Richard L. Batsell. "Conceptual Operational Problems with Market Share Models of Consumer Spatial Behavior," in Mary J. Schlinger, ed., Advances in Consumer Research, Vol. 2. Chicago: Association for Consumer Research, 1975, 165-172.

7. Jain, Arun K. and Vijay Mahajan. "Evaluating the Competitive Environment in Location Decisions," in Jagdish N. Sheth, ed., Research in Marketing, Vol. 2. Connecticut: JAI Press, Forthcoming in 1977.

8. Johnston, J. Econometric Methods. New York: McGraw-Hill, 1963.

9. Kotler, Philip. Marketing Decision Making: A Model Building Approach. New York: Holt, Rinehart and Winston, 1971.

10. Lalond, Bernard J. "Differentials in Supermarket Drawing Power," Marketing and Transportation Paper 11, Bureau of Business and Economic Research, Michigan State University, East Lansing, 1962.

11. Mahajan, Vijay and Arun K. Jain. "Voting for a Political Candidate Under Conditions of Minimal Information: A Re-examination of Data," Working Paper, School of Management, State University of New York at Buffalo, 1977.

12. _____, _____ and Michel Bergier. "Parameter Estimation in Marketing Models in The Presence of Multi-collinearity: An Application of Ridge Regression," Journal of Marketing Research, (Forthcoming).

13. Muller, John E. "Choosing Among 133 Candidates," Public Opinion Quarterly, 34 (Fall 1970), 395-402.

14. Nakanishi, M. and L. G. Cooper. "Parameter Estimate for Multiplicative Competitive Interactive Model -- Least Squares Approach," Journal of Marketing Research, 11 (August 1974a), 303-311.

15. _____, _____, and H. H. Kassarjian. "Voting for A Political Candidate Under Conditions of Minimal Information," Journal of Consumer Research, 1 (September 1974b), 36-43.

16. _____. "A New Technique for Forecasting New Store Sales," Proceedings. Fall Conference, American Marketing Association, 1976, 224-229.

17. Openshaw, S. Some Theoretical and Applied Aspects of Spatial Interaction Shopping Models. London: The Institute of British Geographers, 1975.

18. Stanley, Thomas J. and Murphy A. Sewall. "Image Inputs to A Probabilistic Model: Predicting Retail Potential," Journal of Marketing, 40 (July 1976), 48-53.

19. Stern, Louis W. and Adel I. El-Ansary. Marketing Channels. Englewood Cliffs: Prentice-Hall, 1977.

20. Teekens, R. Prediction Methods in Multiplicative Models. Netherlands: Rotterdam University Press, 1972.

21. Young, Kan H. and Lin Y. Young. "Estimation of Regressions Involving Logarithmic Transformation of Zero Values in The Dependent Variables," The American Statistician, 29 (August 1975), 118-120.

# A NOTE ON THE INFORMATION CONTENT OF RATING SCALES

Robert A. Peterson, The University of Texas
Subhash Sharma, The University of Texas

## ABSTRACT

This paper provides insights on the "How many rating scale categories to use" question. An experiment was conducted wherein the number of rating scale categories was systematically increased from 2 to 15. The major finding was that, as the number of scale categories increased, the gap between potential and actual scale information increased.

## INTRODUCTION

How many categories, positions or intervals should be used in a rating scale? Debate over this question has raged for at least a half century, with most discussions centering on the criterion of reliability. Much of the controversy started with Symonds [12], who theorized that reliability increased monotonically as the number of scale positions increased. However, he concluded that above nine scale categories the increase in reliability was negligible and, for most purposes, the optimal number of scale categories was seven. Several researchers [e.g., 2, 8] have taken issue with these conclusions, and recently there has been relatively wide agreement that scale reliability is independent of the number of scale positions.

Apart from reliability, there are several other criteria which have been put forward as bases for determining the appropriate number of scale categories to employ. Illustrative of these are the purpose of the research [e.g., 7, 9], and capabilities of the scaler [e.g., 6].

### Purpose

The purpose of the present research was not to provide a definitive answer to the "How many..." question. Even a cursory review of the relevant research literature will reveal that the only possible appropriate answer is "it depends". Often some sort of pretest may even be required in making the precise decision. Indeed, Guilford [5] has suggested an extreme procedure: the number of scale categories is a matter for empirical determination in each individual research situation.

Hence, rather than attempting a "once and for all" answer, the purpose of the present study is to merely provide some insights into the information content of rating scales. Specifically, this research addresses the question of how much information, both actual and potential, is provided by rating scales with differing numbers of categories. As such, information content is measured using the concept of entropy, where entropy is an information-related concept derived primarily from work in engineering [e.g., 1] and communication theory [e.g., 11].

Certain researchers, notably Green and Rao [4], have indirectly touched upon the information content issue (with some disagreement from Benson [3]). However, the present research possesses a different focus from their work, one that has not been previously addressed.

## THE CONCEPT OF ENTROPY

In general terms, entropy is a measure of the average amount of information available in a communication. As such, it is typically measured in bits per symbol...word message...or scale. Mathematically, entropy is given by the following formulation:

$$\text{Entropy} = -\sum_{i=1}^{n} p_i \log_2 p_i \tag{1}$$

where $n$ = number of symbols (e.g., scale positions)
$p_i$ = probability of $i^{th}$ response

As information increases, entropy increases. If entropy is standardized on a 0.0 - 1.0 continuum (a common procedure facilitating interstudy comparisons), a value of .0 would indicate complete redundancy of information. In such a situation researchers would only need a sample size of $n = 1$ since all information provided would be identical for every respondent. A value of 1.0 would mean respondents (communicators) possessed complete freedom of choice in responding (communicating).

Put another way, in a rating scale context, redundancy implies all respondents select exactly the same scale category alternative; hence the variance of that scale would be zero. At the other extreme, an entropy value of 1.0 implies all category alternatives are responded to equally; this is equivalent to a uniform response distribution.

To illustrate the concept of entropy, consider the data in Table 1.

TABLE 1

HYPOTHETICAL RESPONSE DISTRIBUTIONS
FOR A FOUR-CATEGORY RATING SCALE

| Response Distribution | | | | Entropy |
|---|---|---|---|---|
| 1 | 2 | 3 | 4 | |
| 0.00 | 0.00 | 0.00 | 1.00 | .00 |
| .01 | .01 | .01 | .97 | .24 |
| .05 | .05 | .05 | .85 | .85 |
| .05 | .10 | .20 | .65 | 1.42 |
| .10 | .40 | .40 | .10 | 1.72 |
| .10 | .20 | .30 | .40 | 1.85 |
| .25 | .25 | .25 | .25 | 2.00 |

This table contains seven hypothetical proportion response distributions for a four-category rating scale. For the sixth distribution, entropy was calculated in the following manner:

Entropy = - (.1x-3.3219 + .2x-2.3219 + .3x-1.7369 + .4x-1.3219)

= - (- .33219 - .46438 - .52107 - .52876)

= 1.85

In these example distributions, entropy varies from 0.0 to 2.0. The latter value is the maximum entropy for a four-category rating scale. As such, it represents the theoretical or potential information available from a four-category scale.

Briefly, then, the concept of entropy is similar to that of variance and can be interpreted in an analogous manner.

An eloquent statement of this is given by Miller [10]:

> The "amount of information" is exactly the same concept...(as that of) "variance". The equations are different, but if we hold tight to the idea that anything that increases the variance also increases the amount of information we cannot go far astray.

Miller goes on to discuss the merits of entropy, citing its dimensionless nature (freedom from measurement unit) as facilitating easy interpretation and cross study comparisons.

## METHODOLOGY

### Procedure

To collect requisite data for investigating the information content of rating scales an experimental design was employed. This was carried out in the following manner.

A product evaluation questionnaire containing ten bi-polar rating scales was constructed. At the top of the questionnaire was given the name of the product and a short instruction set. Subjects were requested to evaluate the product on the ten rating scales as they perceived it, regardless of their experience with the product.

The product used was (unbranded) yogurt. Yogurt was selected as broadly representative of the type of food product commonly rated, and one likely to be tested using the procedure followed here.

The rating scales used were typical of those used in product evaluation work. Each scale was anchored, but no internal category descriptions were given. Anchors included

> nutritional...not nutritional
> bad taste...good taste.

Both scale and anchor ordering were randomly determined. With few exceptions [e.g., 2], this particular approach (i.e., using individual rating scales) has seldom been employed in studying rating scales.[1]

The number of scale categories being studied varied from 2 to 15. Thus there were fourteen different questionnaire sets and treatment levels. The only difference among treatment levels was the number of scale categories.

Subjects were undergraduate advertising and marketing students. Each of the 14 questionnaire sets was randomly distributed to an independent sample of 75 subjects. Because there was no questionnaire-subject overlap, this resulted in 1050 different subjects being used. While there may be some question concerning the use of students or the product-subject fit, given that the experiment was strictly comparative, absolute individual entropy values were inconsequential.

### Analysis

Following data collection the entropy of each treatment level was computed for each respondent across the ten scales and an average calculated across respondents. This resulted in a mean scale entropy for each number of scale categories from 2 to 15.

For comparison purposes two additional measures of entropy

were computed. The first was the theoretical (upper limit) entropy for each number of scale categories. The second was the simulated (expected) entropy for each number of scale categories. The former was computed by simple application of the entropy formula.[2] The latter was carried out by drawing a sample of 100 observations from a normal probability distribution and calculating entropy based upon these observations.[3]

## RESULTS

The results of this study are relatively straightforward and are presented in summary form in Figure 1. Several observations are apparent from the figure.

FIGURE 1

A= Empirically-Derived Entropy
B= Theoretical Entropy
C= Simulated Entropy

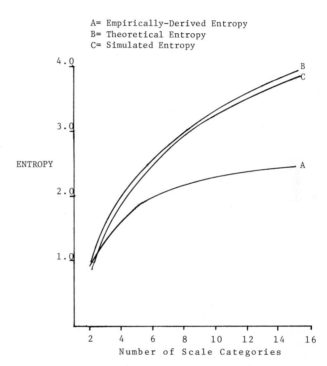

First, except for sampling error, the theoretical and simulated entropy curves exhibit little difference in their shapes. On the average, their levels differ a little more than 4 percent.

On the other hand, the empirically-derived entropy curve is significantly different from the theoretical and simulated entropy curves. This is so both with regard to shape and level. The level of the empirically-derived curve

---

[1]Most research in the area has focused upon pre-selected, multi-item, homogeneous psychological scales rather than individual scale items as are employed in most market research.

[2]A short formula for theoretical entropy is $E = -\log_2 \frac{1}{m}$, where m equals the number of scale positions.

[3]An alternative distribution was the uniform distribution. However, this was not used for two reasons. First, the simulation results from a uniform distribution would have been equivalent to the theoretical results, given the procedure for calculating (maximum) entropy. Second, it is widely assumed in behavioral research that perceptual phenomena occur in a normally distributed fashion. Hence a normal distribution was employed in the simulation to emulate typical response patterns.

is constantly and significantly (p < .005) lower than that of the other two with one exception. The simulated entropy curve is slightly below the empirically-derived curve at the 2-position treatment level. However, this is more than likely a statistical artifact due to sampling error, rather than a substantive difference. Moreover, the empirically-derived curve appears to be slightly flatter and more linear than the two others. Indeed, a straight line fits the empirically-derived points with $R^2$ = .82. Interestingly enough, though, an additional quadratic term increased $R^2$ to .97, and was statistically significant. This may suggest an "inverted bathtub" curve sometimes found in engineering-related applications of entropy.

Of perhaps most importance is the trend in relative entropy. Relative entropy (empirically-derived entropy divided by corresponding theoretical entropy for each number of scale categories) consistently declined as the number of scale categories increased. This can be seen visually by the widening gap between the two curves in the figure.

With two scale positions relative entropy equals 92% while at 15 scale positions it has declined to 63%. Theoretical entropy keeps increasing as a logarithmic progression as the number of scale positions increases. Likewise, empirically-derived entropy increases as the number of scale positions is increased, but at a decreasing (relatively slower) rate.

Hence, relative to the potential information available in a rating scale, actual information obtained in this particular situation declined as the number of scale categories increased. This discrepancy appeared to be relatively more rapid at first; the largest difference occurs in moving from two to three scale categories (a relative percentage decline of nearly 10%).

DISCUSSION AND CONCLUSIONS

As previously noted, it was not the purpose of this study to once and for all answer the "How many categories" question. Rather, the purpose was to provide some insights into the information content of rating scales. Hopefully this has been accomplished, and a new perspective added to the number-of-categories-to-use decision.

Certainly there were limitations associated with the study. For example, the stability of the empirically-derived entropy measures at higher category numbers is questionable given the number of categories-to-subjects ratios. Still, it is clear that, in this situation, as the number of scale positions increased, a gap emerged between the potential information available from the scale and the actual information provided by the scale. This implies there are diminishing returns in the amount of information obtainable in rating scales as the number of scale categories is increased.

Obviously more research needs to be conducted on this subject. The present work is only the beginning. It needs to be validated against and replicated with other samples, scale configurations, stimulus objects, category numbers, and the like. Moreover, attempts should be made to assess the usefulness of the information content concept in selecting the number of scale categories to use. For instance, it may be possible to treat the relative entropy curve as analogous to a "stress" curve in factor analysis or multidimensional scaling, and determine the "best" number of categories in this manner.

Perhaps more importantly, however, it is necessary to determine why this phenomenon occurs. Each of the four classes of influencing factors needs to be examined in a research setting to understand the potential--actual information gap.

Finally, from a decision-theoretic perspective, information content is an exceedingly important consideration. Hence, an additional research direction might be to study, say, trade-offs between the amount of information from a particular rating scale, its associated costs, and its decision usefulness.

REFERENCES

1. Abramson, Norman. Information Theory and Coding. New York: McGraw-Hill, 1963.

2. Bendig, A.W. "Reliability and the Number of Rating Scale Categories," Journal of Applied Psychology, 38 (February 1954), 38-40.

3. Benson, Purnell H. "How Many Scales and How Many Categories Shall We Use in Consumer Research--A Comment," Journal of Marketing, 35 (October 1971), 59-61.

4. Green, Paul E. and Vithala R. Rao. "Rating Scales and Information Recovery--How Many Scales and Response Categories to Use?" Journal of Marketing, 34 (July 1970), 33-9.

5. Guilford, J.P. Psychometric Methods. New York: McGraw-Hill, 1954.

6. Hulbert, James. "Information Processing Capacity and Attitude Measurement," Journal of Marketing Research, 12 (February 1975), 104-6.

7. Jacoby, Jacob and Michael S. Matell. "Three-Point Likert Scales are Good Enough," Journal of Marketing Research, 7 (November 1970), 495-500.

8. Komorita, S.S. and William K. Graham. "Number of Scale Points and the Reliability of Scales," Educational and Psychological Measurement, 25 (November 1965), 987-95.

9. Lehmann, Donald R. and James Hulbert. "Are Three-Point Scales Good Enough?" Journal of Marketing Research, 9 (November 1972), 444-6.

10. Miller, George A. "The Magical Number Seven, Plus or Minus Two: Some Limits on Our Capacity for Processing Information," Psychological Review, 63 (March 1956), 81-97.

11. Shannon, Claude and Warren Weaver. The Mathematical Theory of Communication. Urbana, Ill: The University of Illinois Press, 1949.

12. Symonds, P.M. "On the Loss of Reliability in Ratings Due to Coarseness of the Scale," Journal of Experital Psychology, 7 (December 1924), 456-61.

SOME METHODOLOGICAL CONSIDERATIONS AND EMPIRICAL FINDINGS CONCERNING
THE USE OF THE DUAL QUESTIONING METHOD TO IDENTIFY DETERMINANT ATTRIBUTES

Terence A. Shimp, Kent State University
John H. Lindgren, Jr., Kent State University

ABSTRACT

Dual questioning is a useful methodology for identifying which product attributes determine brand preference and choice. Associated with its use, however, are some potentially serious problems. The results from this study reveal that the empirical identification of determinant attributes is dependent upon: (1) the number of brands compared; (2) whether one of the brands is fundamentally different from the others; and (3) whether the brands chosen for comparison conform with respondents' evoked sets. Circumspection when using dual questioning in marketing research is indicated.

## INTRODUCTION

Myers and Alpert [7] introduced the attribute determinance concept in 1968. In various writings they have explained how it is distinct from the related concepts of attribute importance and salience [8], and methodological procedures for operationalizing it have been offered and tested [1, 7]. The most significant feature of the concept is that an attribute may be important but not determinant. Myers and Alpert have illustrated this point with automobile safety [1, 7, 8]. Although most consumers regard safety as an important product feature, they do not perceive alternative models as varying in the degree to which they provide it; consequently, safety is an important but not determinant attribute. Brand preference and purchase behavior are logically linked more closely to attribute determinance than to attribute importance.

Various methodological procedures can be used to empirically identify determinant attributes. The technique which constitutes the focus of this paper is dual questioning. It has been found to be superior to alternative methods for predicting brand preference [1].

The dual questioning procedure requires two measurements. Respondents rate the importance of various product attributes, and they rate a set of comparison alternatives (brands, stores, etc.) for degree of similarity/dissimilarity on each attribute. The product of the two measures yields a single "determinant attribute score" for each respondent on each attribute. Symbolically,

$$DAS_{ij} = I_{ij} \cdot D_{ijk} \qquad (1)$$

where:

$DAS_{ij}$ = individual i's determinant attribute score for attribute j.

$I_{ij}$ = individual i's rating of the importance of attribute j.

$D_{ijk}$ = individual i's perceived dissimilarity of the k alternatives on attribute j.

A determinant attribute score vector of size j is generated for each respondent. Across the total sample, attributes identified as determinant are those which, depending on scaling convention, have the highest or lowest average $DAS_j$.[1]

---

[1]Alpert [1] has offered one method for testing statistically which attributes are determinant.

Although the dual questioning method is straightforward and intuitively attractive, some potentially serious pitfalls are associated with its use in marketing research. The procedure per se will not be disputed in this paper. Instead, the intent is to indicate some methodological considerations and potential biases which should be taken into account when applying dual questioning.

## METHODOLOGICAL CONSIDERATIONS

The dual questioning procedure shares with other measurement methods (e.g., multidimensional scaling) the problem of determining which objects or consumption alternatives to compare. Since determinant attribute scores are composed of similarity ratings, and since similarity ratings are a function of the particular alternatives compared, it follows logically that the determinant attributes identified will depend upon the specific alternatives chosen. For illustration, consider the following two Comparison Alternative Sets (CAS hereafter). One CAS consists of brands A, B, C, D and the other contains brands A, B, C, E. No matter how similar brands A through C are, if D and E are decidedly different, it is probable that major differences in determinant attribute scores will result.

This, in short, is the potential pitfall of the dual questioning procedure: results are idiosyncratic to the particular CAS selected. Indeed, for most product/market situations, the researcher must display some degree of selectivity in determining which brands are to be compared. A particular product category may consist of as many as ten or more major competitors. It would be unreasonable, however, for respondents to be required to evaluate simultaneously the similarity of 10 or more brands. Clearly, there is an upper limit on individuals' discriminatory ability [6]. Consumers also are limited to a relatively small number of brands of which they possess brand comprehension [4] and are thus capable of evaluating for similarity. The marketing researcher must therefore selectively choose a CAS which is a subset of the available brands.

Three specific methodological considerations that are associated with selecting the CAS and which may potentially bias results are addressed: (1) The effect which CAS size (i.e., the number of alternatives evaluated simultaneously for similarity) has on the empirical assessment of determinant attributes; (2) Effect of including an alternative in the CAS which, though competitive with other CAS members, is fundamentally different in at least one important respect; (3) The effect of selecting a CAS which conforms with respondents' evoked sets [4].

### The Effect of CAS Size

A recent study [2] which used the dual questioning method provides an excellent example of the potential bias associated with CAS size. Respondents rated the importance of various bank features and evaluated five banks simultaneously for similarity on each feature. Determinant attributes were designated as those features which had the highest average determinant attribute scores.

The study received varied criticism [3, 5, 9], with one critic claiming: "This forced aggregate evaluation (i.e., all five banks evaluated simultaneously for degree of similarity on each bank feature) may have concealed or distorted individual bank characterizations" [9]. Although the critic failed to offer theoretical arguments or empirical data to support the statement, one can only wonder how different the results may have been had fewer than five banks been compared. Or, instead of having respondents evaluate all five banks simultaneously, would the same results have been obtained had the researchers disaggregated the similarity measures by having respondents rate various subsets of the five banks (e.g., all combinations of two, or three, or four banks)?

Effect of Including a Dissimilar Alternative in CAS

Many product categories are characterized by marked differences among competitive offerings; the automobile market is illustrative. Models within each sub-category reflect major distinguishing characteristics. Suppose, for example, a researcher is interested in analyzing determinant attributes associated with choice in the sub-compact market and a CAS is selected composed of four domestic models and one foreign model. Assuming origin of make is an important attribute, the dual questioning procedure would also assess it to be determinant as it is likely that respondents would rate the five models as dissimilar in this regard. If another domestic automobile were used in place of the foreign car, it is probable that a different set of determinant attributes would result.

Conformity of CAS with Respondents' Evoked Sets

A careful inspection of the dual questioning method suggests that determinant attribute scores will depend on whether the CAS conforms to respondents' evoked sets. This will be illustrated with two different CASs--one which closely conforms with respondents' evoked sets and one which does not. We suspect that determinant attribute scores will differ sharply between the two CASs.

In the case of the "evoked set confirming" CAS, it is expected that respondents will rate the alternatives as highly similar on attributes which receive high importance ratings, otherwise the alternatives would not be evoked set candidates. It is unlikely, therefore, that important attributes will be assessed as determinant since high importance scores will be offset with low dissimilarity scores.

In effect, if the CAS conforms closely with respondents' evoked sets, then results will be systematically biased against important attributes. If the selected CAS does not conform with respondents' evoked sets, the results will not be biased since there is no reason to suspect that dissimilarity ratings will be influenced by importance ratings.

RESEARCH METHODS

A study was designed to empirically assess the above methodological considerations. Over 500 college students were selected on a convenience basis and used at various phases in the research project. The product category chosen for investigation was fast food (FF) chains. This is an appropriate product for college students, and it is also amenable to determinant attribute analysis since distinct competitive features prevail. Five FF chains surrounding the campus provided the CAS. Hamburgers represent the major type of food for four of the chains (McDonald's, Burger King, Burger Chef, and Red Barn), and the fifth chain (Arby's) is most noted for its roast beef sandwiches.

Initial data collection was performed to identify the important features of FF chains. Sixty students responded to the question: "What features of fast food chains are important to you when deciding where to eat?" Responses were grouped into related categories with seven facets of FF chain operations accounting for the vast majority:

quality of food, type of food, speed of service, atmosphere, prices, cleanliness of store, and location. These seven attributes were used throughout the remaining data collection activities with the intent of identifying which were determinant.

Dual Questioning with CAS Size Varied

This research phase was performed to assess the effect of CAS size on the empirical identification of determinant attributes. Two hundred and sixty students were chosen on a convenience basis and randomly divided into four equal-sized groups of 65. The dual questioning methodology was then administered. Each group responded to the identical importance rating procedure. The seven attributes were each rated on a seven-point scale anchored with "not important" and "very important".

The similarity rating procedure differed for each group by adjusting the CAS size. One group evaluated all five FF chains simultaneously for degree of similarity on each attribute. A six-point scale ranging from "very similar" to "very different" was used. A single set of seven determinant attribute scores (the product of the importance and similarity ratings) was obtained from each respondent in this group.

A second group responded to a CAS of four FF chains. All combinations of four chains from the full set of five chains were isolated. Five combinations resulted (5!/4! (1!)), and respondents rated the four chains in each combination for attribute similarity. This procedure yielded five sets of determinant attribute scores, one set for each combination of four chains.

In a similar manner, a third group responded to all ten combinations of three FF chains from the full set of five chains. Ten sets of determinant attribute scores were generated by this group.

The final group received all ten combinations of paired-chain comparisons, and ten sets of determinant attribute scores were obtained. A total of 26 sets of determinant attribute scores were yielded by the four groups.

Dual Questioning with CAS Self Selected by Respondents

This research phase was performed to assess whether the same attributes identified as determinant in the previous phase would remain determinant provided each respondent self-selected and compared for similarity his/her own evoked set of FF chains. A total of 222 additional students were selected. After rating the seven attributes for importance, the five FF chains were presented, and respondents were requested to list "those chains you would consider eating at if you were to go to a fast food chain in the next two weeks". Respondents were permitted to select only one chain, all five chains, or any combination of the five chains.[2] They then rated these self-selected chains for similarity on each of the seven attributes. One set of determinant attribute scores was thereby obtained from each respondent.

RESULTS

The Effect of CAS Size

The typical dual questioning research project [1, 2] obtains similarity measures by having respondents evaluate simultaneously all alternatives composing the CAS. Important differences between brands are potentially lost or

_____
[2]Eleven of the 222 students selected only one FF chain. They had to be deleted from further analysis since the similarity measurement aspect of the dual questioning procedure was not applicable.

distorted by this approach. Empirical evidence is provided in Table 1. Results from the simultaneous evaluation group (group 1) are compared against results from the three disaggregated evaluation groups. Explanation of the method used to prepare Table 1 is needed initially.

findings.

Effect of Including a Dissimilar Alternative in CAS

The five FF chains consisted of four predominantly hamburg-

TABLE 1

DETERMINANT ATTRIBUTE SCORES AND ATTRIBUTE RANKS AT VARYING CAS SIZES

| | CAS SIZE | | | |
| Attributes | Group 1:[a] All five FF chains | Group 2: All combinations of four chains | Group 3: All combinations of three chains | Group 4: All combinations of two chains |
|---|---|---|---|---|
| Quality of Food | 20.48(1)[b] | 19.54(1)[c] | 22.04(1) | 20.96(1) |
| Type of Food | 16.57(4) | 18.68(2) | 20.11(2) | 18.28(2) |
| Speed of Service | 15.02(6) | 14.60(5) | 16.33(5) | 15.96(4) |
| Atmosphere | 10.75(7) | 8.55(7) | 12.20(7) | 11.39(7) |
| Prices | 16.60(3) | 16.88(3) | 18.25(3) | 16.90(3) |
| Cleanliness | 15.63(5) | 14.08(6) | 15.74(6) | 14.69(6) |
| Location | 19.65(2) | 14.83(4) | 16.68(4) | 15.91(5) |

[a] $n_1 = n_2 = n_3 = n_4 = 65$.

[b] Cell entries in group 1 represent mean determinant attribute scores, with accompanying rankings, averaged across respondents. The range of possible scores was from 0 (least determinant) to 42 (most determinant).

[c] Cell entries in groups 2, 3, 4 represent mean determinant attribute scores averaged both across all respondents and all combinations of 4, 3, and 2 chains respectively. Possible scores ranged from 0 to 42.

First, scores presented in Table 1 represent the product of importance ratings and similarity ratings. Separate MANOVAs were performed on the four groups' attribute importance ratings, similarity ratings, and determinant attribute scores. The MANOVA on the determinant attribute scores was statistically significant at .10 (F transformation of Wilks Lambda = 1.36 with 21; 718 d.f.). The MANOVA on the importance ratings was not significant (F = 1.16 with 21;718 d.f.), but the similarity rating's MANOVA was significant at .01 (F = 1.98 with 21;718 d.f.). Thus, there are significant differences in determinant attribute scores in Table 1 which are attributable to differences in the four groups' similarity ratings.

A second matter concerns the method used to aggregate determinant attribute scores in the three disaggregated groups (groups 2, 3, 4) which had yielded, respectively, 5, 10, and 10 sets of determinant attribute scores. Two methods were used: (1) the mean determinant attribute score for each attribute was computed across all respondents and all combinations of comparisons in each group; (2) determinant attribute scores for each combination of FF chains in a particular group were ranked and then the average rank position across all combinations was calculated for each attribute. The two methods yielded identical results; the rank ordering of mean attribute scores in Method 1 was reproduced by the average rank position of attributes in Method 2. All tabular results are based on Method 1.

Table 1 reveals that all four groups identified quality of food as the most determinant attribute; atmosphere was always least determinant; and price was consistently third. Results obtained from groups 2, 3, and 4 were identical (with one reversal in group 4), but group 1 differed in two major respects. In particular, location was identified as the second most determinant attribute in group 1, but it only achieved fourth and fifth place in the three disaggregated groups. Quality of food was second in determinance in all three disaggregated groups but fourth in group 1.

This one major flip flop in attribute rank position suggests that the dual questioning procedure may fail to detect significant differences among brands when respondents are required to evaluate simultaneously a relatively large number of brands (five in the present effort). A plausible reason for this is revealed in the following set of

er outlets and a roast beef chain (Arby's). It was expected that the one major difference (type of food) between Arby's and the other chains would have a significant impact on determinant attribute scores, particularly at lower levels of aggregation when Arby's was compared with only 1, 2, or 3 chains. This is a reasonable supposition since at lower levels of aggregation differences between/among alternatives are perceived more readily by respondents.

Table 2 displays the differences in determinant attribute scores based on whether Arby's was contained in the CAS. (Group 1 is presented for reference purposes only.) One-way ANOVAs corrected for replicated measures were performed on each attribute in each group. Fifteen of the 21 tests were statistically significant at the .05 level or below, indicating that the exclusion of Arby's from the CAS had a major impact on determinant attribute scores.

The same statistical testing was performed to determine whether "with" and "without" differences would also result for any other FF chains. Space limitations preclude detailed reporting, but results did reveal some significant differences for other chains--although the differences were not as extensive as they were in the with and without Arby's case. This detection of statistical significance for some of the non-Arby's chains may appear to undermine the above research premise. However, at the sake of engaging in post hoc interpretation, these significant differences in fact provide additional support for the premise, i.e., failure to include any chain in the CAS may result in decidedly different determinant attribute scores. Although the argument has been discussed from the perspective of Arby's (the most dissimilar chain), every chain is in fact dissimilar in certain regards; therefore, the same potential bias exists regardless of which chain is excluded from the CAS.

Two further facets of the findings in Table 2 are perhaps more significant. First, it will be noted that average determinant attribute scores are consistently higher when Arby's is in the CAS. This suggests the operation of something akin to a halo effect. The fact that Arby's differed in one important respect evidently carried over to respondents' evaluations of Arby's dissimilarity on the remaining attributes. (An alternative explanation is that Arby's is different from the other chains on all attributes.) Regardless of the correct explanation, it is obvious that Arby's had a major impact. The implication for

TABLE 2

DETERMINANT ATTRIBUTE SCORES AND ATTRIBUTE RANKS WHEN DISSIMILAR ALTERNATIVE IS CONTAINED IN CAS

| | CAS SIZE | | | | | | |
| --- | --- | --- | --- | --- | --- | --- | --- |
| Attributes | Group 1: All five FF chains | Group 2: All combinations of four chains[a] | | Group 3: All combinations of three chains[b] | | Group 4: All combinations of two chains[c] | |
| | | with Arby's | without Arby's | with Arby's | without Arby's | with Arby's | without Arby's |
| Quality of Food | 20.48(1)[d] | 20.34(1) | 16.34(1)[e] | 23.58(2) | 19.73(1) | 23.36(2) | 19.36(1) |
| Type of Food | 16.57(4) | 19.98(2) | 13.48(6) | 23.94(1) | 14.38(6) | 27.79(1) | 11.95(6) |
| Speed of Service | 15.02(6) | 14.87(5) | 13.51(5) | 17.19(4) | 15.04(5) | 16.91(4) | 15.33(3) |
| Atmosphere | 10.75(7) | 8.74(7) | 7.79(7) | 12.95(7) | 11.08(7) | 13.29(7) | 10.13(7) |
| Prices | 16.60(3) | 17.63(3) | 13.86(3) | 20.31(3) | 15.15(4) | 21.30(3) | 13.96(5) |
| Cleanliness | 15.63(5) | 14.15(6) | 13.80(4) | 15.95(6) | 15.42(3) | 15.65(6) | 14.05(4) |
| Location | 19.65(2) | 14.93(4) | 14.40(2) | 16.59(5) | 16.82(2) | 15.70(5) | 16.06(2) |

[a]Arby's was included in 4 of the 5 combinations.

[b]Arby's was included in 6 of the 10 combinations.

[c]Arby's was included in 4 of the 10 combinations.

[d]Cell entries represent mean determinant attribute scores. In group 1 they were averaged across all respondents, and in groups 2, 3, 4 they were averaged both across all respondents and all combinations of comparisons.

[e]One way ANOVA for replicated measures was performed to test for significant differences between the "with Arby's" and "without Arby's" means. Significant differences at the .05 level are indicated with a dashed line, while a solid line indicates significance at the .01 level.

other marketing researchers is that if one of the alternatives is different in at least one important regard, then determinant attribute analysis should be done separately, both with and without the divergent alternative.

A second significant aspect of the Table 2 findings is that the average determinant attribute scores in groups 1 and 2 are consistently lower than group 3 and 4 scores (with the single exception of the location score in group 1). Since, as previously indicated, the four groups did not significantly differ on attribute importance ratings, the lower scores are due to differences in similarity ratings.[3] This suggests that as more brands are aggregated for similarity ratings, the effect of including a divergent brand in the CAS is masked--a possibility which is explored further in Table 3.

TABLE 3

ABSOLUTE RELATIVE CHANGE (ARC)
IN DETERMINANT ATTRIBUTE SCORES

| | Effect of Including Chain in CAS | | |
| --- | --- | --- | --- |
| FF Chain | From CAS = 2 to CAS = 3 | From CAS = 3 to CAS = 4 | From CAS = 4 to CAS = 5 |
| Red Barn | 1.9%[*] | 4.5% | 10.9% |
| McDonald's | 4.2 | 4.5 | 13.6 |
| Burger King | 2.5 | 5.5 | 12.2 |
| Burger Chef | 3.0 | 4.8 | 11.7 |
| Arby's | 16.4 | 13.2 | 6.0 |

[*]Cell entries reflect the absolute change in determinant attribute scores. See Figure 1 for illustration of how computed.

Table 3 reflects the "absolute relative change" (ARC) in determinant attribute scores attributable to a particular FF chain. In order to compute ARC for a particular chain, X, it was necessary to compare the determinant attribute scores for all chain comparisons at a given CAS level from which X was absent with the determinant attribute scores for all chain comparisons at the next larger CAS level in

[3]There is no reason to suspect that students in the four groups differed with regard to factors influencing the perceptual process, but this is a feasible alternative explanation.

which X was present.[4] The mean determinant attribute score for each attribute was obtained at both CAS levels. Each attribute's percentage of the total determinant attribute score was computed at each CAS level, and the differences between these relative scores were summated to yield ARC.

Figure 1 illustrates this method by indicating how the first cell entry in Table 3 was obtained. It shows that Red Barn had a minimal, 1.9% effect on determinant attribute scores as CAS size increased from two to three chains. The same procedure was repeated for every FF chain when moving from CAS = 2 to CAS = 3, from CAS = 3 to CAS = 4, and from CAS = 4 to CAS = 5. In all instances, ARC is a summary statistic indicating the effect which a particular chain had on determinant attribute scores.[5]

Table 3 vividly indicates that a dissimilar alternative (viz., Arby's) had a major effect on determinant attribute scores when the CAS contained only three or four chains but only a slight effect when all five chains were evaluated simultaneously for similarity. The ARC was 16.4% and 13.2%, respectively, when Arby's was compared with two or three other chains, but only 6% when compared with all four chains. In effect, Arby's impact on determinant attribute scores decreased as CAS size increased. The four hamburger chains, on the other hand, had relatively little impact when included with two and three other chains, but all of them had greater impact than Arby's when compared with all four chains. The effect of each hamburger chain increased as CAS size increased.

[4]Each chain was contained in four of the ten total comparisons with CAS = 2 and absent from six comparisons; with CAS = 3, each chain was present in six comparisons and absent from four; with CAS = 4, each chain was present in four comparisons and absent from one; for CAS = 5 there was only one comparison which contained all the chains.

[5]The calculation of ARC required that the data be treated as if it had been generated by a single sample of respondents. This is a strong assumption since in actuality four groups were involved. Although it cannot be known for sure how comparable the data would have been had one group responded to all 26 comparisons, the four groups were fundamentally equivalent in terms of attitudes and purchase behavior toward the five FF chains which suggests that results would not have been substantially different.

330

FIGURE 1

AN ILLUSTRATION OF THE COMPUTATION OF ABSOLUTE RELATIVE CHANGE (ARC) IN DETERMINANT ATTRIBUTE SCORES

| Attributes | Average Determinant Attribute Scores of All CAS = 2 Comparisons Not Containing Red Barn (1) | Each Attribute's Relative % of Total Score (2) | Average Determinant Attribute Scores of All CAS = 3 Comparisons Containing Red Barn (3) | Each Attribute's Relative % of Total Score (4) | Absolute Relative Change in Determinant Attribute Scores (5) $\lvert(2)-(4)\rvert$ |
|---|---|---|---|---|---|
| Quality of Food | 20.93[a] | .184[b] | 22.77[c] | .185 | .001 |
| Type of Food | 18.68 | .165 | 20.16 | .164 | .001 |
| Speed of Service | 15.30 | .135 | 16.77 | .137 | .002 |
| Atmosphere | 11.23 | .099 | 12.52 | .102 | .003 |
| Prices | 17.08 | .150 | 18.07 | .147 | .003 |
| Cleanliness | 14.34 | .126 | 16.02 | .130 | .004 |
| Location | 15.93 | .140 | 16.57 | .135 | .005 |
| Totals | 113.49 | 1.000 | 122.88 | 1.000 | .019 = 1.9% |

[a]Cell entries represent the mean determinant attribute score obtained by taking the average for each attribute across all six CAS = 2 comparisons which did not include Red Barn.

[b]Cell entries represent the proportion of the total determinant attribute score which each attribute accounted for. For example, .184 = 20.93/113.49.

[c]Cell entries represent the mean determinant attribute score obtained by taking the average for each attribute across all six CAS = 3 comparisons which did include Red Barn.

The implication of this finding is clear. A dissimilar brand will have a major impact on determinant attribute scores when the CAS contains relatively few brands. As the CAS size increases, however, the impact will be masked. Similarity ratings, in effect, appear to regress toward the common denominator of brands when a relatively large number of brands are compared (five in the present research), but they tend to regress toward the least common denominator when fewer brands are in the CAS.

Conformity of CAS with Respondents' Evoked Sets

It was argued previously that dual questioning results are systematically biased against important attributes if the CAS conforms with respondents' evoked sets. This possibility was tested by administering the dual questioning method to 211 students who self-selected their evoked sets of FF chains to serve as the CAS. Results from this group were then compared (see Table 4) against results from the four other groups for whom the CAS was fixed by the researchers.

evoked set and non-evoked set groups. It was also the most determinant attribute in all four non-evoked set groups. Never was it most determinant, however, for the evoked set respondents.

The implication of this finding is that researchers using the dual questioning method should measure respondents evoked sets and perform separate analyses on the evoked set conforming and non-conforming respondents. Otherwise, results will be confounded since the two groups likely make similarity judgments from different perceptual bases.

CONCLUSION AND DISCUSSION

Dual questioning is a useful measurement method for discerning which attributes determine brand preference and choice. Associated with its use in marketing research, however, are some potentially serious problems. It has been argued that results will depend in large part on: (1) the number of brands (i.e., CAS size) respondents are

TABLE 4

COMPARISON OF ATTRIBUTE RANK ORDERINGS BETWEEN EVOKED SET CONFORMING AND NON-CONFORMING GROUPS

| | CAS SIZE | | | | | | | |
|---|---|---|---|---|---|---|---|---|
| | All five FF chains | | All combinations of four FF chains | | All combinations of three FF chains | | All combinations of two FF chains | |
| Attributes | Evoked Set | Non-Evoked Set | Evoked Set | Non-Evoked Set | Evoked Set | Non-Evoked Set | Evoked Set | Non-Evoked Set |
| Quality of Food | 22.71(2)[a] | (1)[b] | 18.05(3) | (1) | 15.90(4) | (1) | 15.32(4) | (1) |
| Type of Food | 23.08(1) | (4) | 17.97(4) | (2) | 19.98(1) | (2) | 20.91(1) | (2) |
| Speed of Service | 17.71(5) | (6) | 13.82(6) | (5) | 13.95(5) | (5) | 13.46(5) | (4) |
| Atmosphere | 9.92(7) | (7) | 10.76(7) | (7) | 10.65(7) | (7) | 12.52(6) | (7) |
| Prices | 20.96(3) | (3) | 18.69(2) | (3) | 18.51(2) | (3) | 17.78(3) | (3) |
| Cleanliness | 16.54(6) | (5) | 15.05(5) | (6) | 12.79(6) | (6) | 12.50(7) | (6) |
| Location | 19.79(4) | (2) | 19.26(1) | (4) | 18.32(3) | (4) | 17.89(2) | (5) |
| Sample Size | 24 | 65 | 38 | 65 | 95 | 65 | 54 | 65 |

[a]Evoked set cell entries represent mean determinant attribute scores, with accompanying rankings, averaged across all respondents who selected the same CAS size.

[b]Because of space limitations, only the rank orderings of the non-evoked set attributes are presented. See Table 1 for the mean determinant attribute scores.

Table 4 provides support for the research premise, particularly for the quality of food attribute. Quality of food received the highest average importance rating in both the

required to evaluate simultaneously for attribute similarity; (2) whether one of the brands is fundamentally different from the other CAS alternatives in one or more important respects; (3) whether the CAS conforms with respondents' evoked sets.

The present study has provided empirical evidence concerning all of these issues. Although the methodological procedures do not permit definitive conclusions, the results do support the research premises. The need for circumspection when using the dual questioning procedure is indicated. Several factors should be taken into account by marketing researchers when administering dual questioning:

1) The typical procedure for measuring attribute similarity requires respondents to evaluate simultaneously all CAS alternatives. This imposes a heavy burden on respondents' discriminatory abilities when the CAS is relatively large.[6] As a result, actual attribute differences between or among some brands may be lost or distorted. It appears that the larger the CAS, the greater the probability that error will enter into the similarity measures. To prevent this, we recommend that researchers keep CAS size to an absolute minimum by including only those brands of primary competitive concern.

2) A related matter concerns the effect of including a brand in the CAS which is competitive with the other brands but fundamentally different with respect to one or more product features. When this brand is simultaneously evaluated with all other brands, its distinguishing characteristic (a characteristic which may actually determine brand preference and choice) will be masked. To prevent this, the researcher should disaggregate the CAS by having respondents perform similarity ratings on subsets of the full CAS. The advantage of this is that it enables the researcher to compute determinant attribute scores for each subset, free of the masking effect of the simultaneous evaluation procedure.

3) Which attributes are identified as determinant by the dual questioning method will depend on whether the CAS conforms with respondents' evoked sets of brands. When the CAS is specified by the researcher, it is probable that the CAS corresponds with the evoked sets of some respondents but not others. Individual differences are lost, however, when data is aggregated across all respondents. To avoid this problem, two phases of data collection are recommended. Phase 1, following the suggestions in points 1 and 2 above, should employ dual questioning based on a researcher-specified CAS. Phase 2, performed on the same respondents or another sample of matched or randomly selected ones, would then perform dual questioning based on respondents' self-selected brands comprising their evoked sets.

---

[6]How large is "large" is an empirical question which depends both on product complexity and on respondents' product knowledge and discriminatory ability. A CAS consisting of five FF chains appeared to be "too large" in the present study.

## REFERENCES

1. Alpert, Mark I. "Identification of Determinant Attributes: A Comparison of Methods," Journal of Marketing Research, VIII (May 1971), 184-91.

2. Anderson, W. Thomas, Jr., Eli P. Cox III, and David G. Fulcher. "Bank Selection Decision and Market Segmentation," Journal of Marketing, 40 (January 1976), 40-45.

3. Dupuy, George M. and William J. Kehoe. "Comments on Bank Selection Decision and Market Segmentation," Journal of Marketing, 40 (October 1976), 89-90.

4. Howard, John A. and Jagdish N. Sheth. The Theory of Buyer Behavior (New York: John Wiley & Sons, Inc., 1969).

5. Linneman, Robert F. and Raymond N. Davis. "Comments on Bank Selection Decision and Market Segmentation," Journal of Marketing, 40 (October 1976), 90.

6. Miller, George A. "The Magical Number Seven, Plus or Minus Two: Some Limits on Our Capacity for Processing Information," Psychological Review, 63 (1956), 81-97.

7. Myers, James H. and Mark I. Alpert. "Determinant Buying Attitudes: Meaning and Measurement," Journal of Marketing, 32 (October 1968), 13-20.

8. _____. "Semantic Confusion in Attitude Research: Salience Vs. Importance Vs. Determinance," Proceedings of the Association for Consumer Research, IV (November 1976).

9. Reed, Jim D. "Comments on Bank Selection and Market Segmentation," Journal of Marketing, 40 (October 1976), 90.

# DETERMINING AN APPROPRIATE MEASURE OF RELIABILITY
## FOR PSYCHOGRAPHIC MEASURES

Donald R. Lehmann, Columbia University
Kathryn E. A. Britney, Columbia University

## ABSTRACT

This paper examines the appropriateness of the correlation coefficient to determine the test-retest reliability of psychographic test items. It shows that with discrete scale measures, if there is little variation in the responses across respondents, the correlation coefficient provides a meaningless indicator of the relative or absolute stability of test items.

## INTRODUCTION

Among the many issues concerning psychographic research in marketing is the need to assess the reliability of psychographic measures. Wells points out that although reliability is not the sole determinant of whether or not marketers will have confidence in psychographic research results, it plays an important role in determining their usefulness for predictive and decision-making purposes [11, p. 203].

A few studies have been published which examine the reliability of several psychographic items and scales developed specifically for marketing research purposes [1, 3,6,10,11]. In all cases, the test-retest reliability coefficients [1,7,11] and the split-half reliabilities [4] for individual items have been determined using correlation analysis.

In this study we will show, however, that correlations can be misleading as indicators of the reliability of psychographic items. Not only do they suffer from usually being biased downward in absolute value due to the discrete nature of the rating scales [5,8], but also under certain circumstances they are invalid measures of the rank order of the reliability of the numerous test items.

## METHOD

The study was based on psychographic data collected in 1971 and 1973 from 504 adult female heads of households from a sample of 1500 Home Testing Institute (HTI) panel members. Each respondent completed identical, self-administered, mailed, psychographic questionnaires in the Fall of both years. The psychographic questionnaire contained 152 life style questions to which the respondent was asked to indicate her degree of agreement with each statement using a 5-point scale [9].

For this study the data were collapsed from the 5-point scale (strongly agree, agree, neither agree nor disagree, disagree, strongly disagree) to a 3-point scale by combining the strongly agree/agree responses and the strongly disagree/disagree responses. This collapsing was done for practical reasons, in particular to simplify the analysis of the cross-tabulations of the 1971 and 1973 responses by reducing the pattern of response changes from 25 cells to 9 cells. The results using the collapsed scales were essentially identical to the 5-point scale results.

## RELIABILITY MEASURES

Three measures which seemed related to the test-retest reliability of the respondents' 1971 and 1973 scores for the 152 psychographic items were used. These were based on two different calculations:
(1) simple correlations between the 1971 and 1973 responses across all respondents;
(2) cross-tabulations of the 1971 and 1973 responses for all sample members.
Thus, the following measures should indicate the reliability of the 152 psychographic items:
(1) The simple correlations--the higher the correlation coefficient, the greater the test-retest reliability of the item.
(2) The percent of the respondents who show no change in response between 1971 and 1973--the larger the percentage of total respondents in cells on the diagonal, the greater the reliability of the item.
(3) The percentage of the respondents who made "extreme" changes in responses between 1971 and 1973--the smaller the percentage of total respondents who made extreme changes in the responses (i.e., went from agree to disagree or vice versa), the greater the reliability of the items.

## ANALYSIS AND RESULTS

To test whether the above three methods of reliability measurement were similar, three simple correlations were computed between all possible pair-wise combinations of the three different reliability measures across the 152 psychographic questions. The results are shown in Table 1. All the correlations between the different measures of reliability are very low, indicating that at least in absolute value, the different measures of reliability do not provide a very similar list of which of the 152 items are "reliable" and which are not. Examples of the disparity between the correlation and % diagonal measures are shown in Table 2.

### TABLE 1

PAIRWISE CORRELATIONS BETWEEN DIFFERENT RELIABILITY MEASURES FOR 152 PSYCHOGRAPHIC ITEMS

| Reliability Measures Correlated | R |
| --- | --- |
| Correlation Coefficients, Percent of Respondents on Diagonal | 0.15 |
| Correlation Coefficients, Percent of Respondents with Extreme Changes | -0.19 |
| Percent of Respondents on Diagonal, Percent with Extreme Changes | -0.28 |

To directly examine the issue of whether or not similar rank orders of reliability for the 152 items are indicated by the reliability measures of correlation coefficients and percent responses on the diagonal, Spearman's rank order correlation coefficient was calculated. As one might expect from the above correlation results, it was found to be a low 0.24. That is, the rank order of the reliability of the 152 items indicated by the correlation coefficients showed little resemblance to the rank order of the reliability of the same items

TABLE 2

TEST-RETEST CORRELATIONS FOR SIX PSYCHOGRAPHIC ITEMS
WITH THE "% NO CHANGE" IN RESPONSES RANGING BETWEEN
75 AND 79

|  | Correlations Between 1971 and 1973 Responses (r) |
|---|---|
| 1. Our family is a close knit group (% on Diagonal - 79) | 0.62 |
| 2. I use one or more household disinfectants (% on Diagonal - 77) | 0.27 |
| 3. I try to wash the dishes promptly after each meal (% on Diagonal - 76) | 0.58 |
| 4. Our family is too heavily in debt (% on Diagonal - 76) | 0.58 |
| 5. Once I find a brand I like, I stick with it (% on Diagonal - 75) | 0.25 |
| 6. Legal penalties for false advertising should be increased (% on Diagonal - 75) | 0.20 |

as determined by the percent of the total sample responses
that were the same in both time periods (i.e., on the
cross-tabulation diagonal).

## EXPLANATION OF LACK OF CORRESPONDENCE BETWEEN STABILITY MEASURES

The apparent disparity between the stability measures
leads one to wonder which is "right". The remainder of
this paper will examine this question and show that the
following four processes influence the stability measures
(and usually in different ways in terms of direction and
magnitude):
(1) the number of discrete scale points
(2) skewness of the mean
(3) heterogenity of the mean
(4) heterogenity of the variance

Before describing these 4 influences on the 3 reliability
measures, it is useful to recall how a correlation coefficient is calculated. As shown in Table 3, if the responses are distributed "reasonably" across the possible
scales, the correlation of the line for which 80% of the
respondents give the same answer both times (i.e., are on
the diagonal) and 20% make "extreme" changes is .46.
However, in the same case (i.e., where 80% of the respondents give the same response in both time periods and 20%
change) and the question is not discriminating (i.e., most
of the respondents give the same scale point answer), the
correlation coefficient is determined mainly by the out-
lying variables which are not close to the mean. The result, as we see in Table 4, is a relatively low
correlation coefficient (.31).

TABLE 3

CORRELATION COEFFICIENT FOR A "DISCRIMINATING" QUESTION

|  | 1 | 2 | 3 |
|---|---|---|---|
| 1 | 40 |  | 15 |
| 2 |  | 40 |  |
| 3 | 15 |  | 40 |

r = .455    $\overline{X} = \overline{Y} = 2$
% on diagonal = 80%
% extreme change = 20%
N = 150

Obviously, in the latter case of a greatly skewed distribution of responses, the correlation coefficient is a
relatively unstable and unrepresentative measure of the
degree to which respondents are consistent in their responses. Unfortunately this type of distribution is

common for many life style and personality measures. Such
psychographic items as "I am satisfied with life," and so
on, tend to elicit the same answer from a great majority
of the respondents. One might question the usefulness of
such an item that has so little discriminating power that
most people give the same answer to it; however, that
issue is beyond the scope of this paper. What is important here is that for those psychographic items that
are relatively undiscriminating across respondents, the
correlation coefficient is often a misleading measure of
reliability of such items in typical test-retest situations.

TABLE 4

CORRELATION COEFFICIENT FOR A "NON-DISCRIMINATING QUESTION"

|  | 1 | 2 | 3 |
|---|---|---|---|
| 1 | 10 |  | 15 |
| 2 |  | 10 |  |
| 3 | 15 |  | 100 |

r = .309    $\overline{X} = \overline{Y} = 2.73$
% on diagonal = 80%
% extreme change = 20%
N = 150

## THE NUMBER OF SCALE POINTS

If we assume that the individual's responses to a life
style question lie on a continuum, it has been shown that
measurement using discrete scales will lower the expected
correlation even if we have a "perfect" model [4]. Also,
the number of scale points used will affect the correlation coefficient such that, in general, the fewer the number of scale points the greater the downward bias on the
correlation coefficient [7]. In contrast, fewer scale
points will tend to increase the percent of respondents
who exhibit no change in their responses in a test-retest
situation.

## SKEWNESS OF THE MEAN

The observed frequency distributions for the responses to
many of the life style questions in this study were
skewed. As one might expect, many of the questions, such
as "I like convenience in cooking," generate a disproportionately high number of positive responses. If the
observed skewed distribution is reflective of the individuals' true underlying distribution, what effect would
this have on the stability measures?

Assume individuals' responses to a life style question are
measurable on a scale from 1 to 3, are homogeneous, and
are drawn from a normal distribution with a standard
deviation of 0.5. The following examples will show that
in such a situation the percent of respondents who exhibit
no or great changes in the life style responses at two
points in time depends on the mean life-style response.

Consider first the case where the mean is located at 2
(the center of the scale). In this case, the probabilities of the life style response falling into the three
scale categories are given by .1587, .6827, and .1587
respectively. If we assume the responses are independent between the two time periods (i.e., the mean remains the same but the "error"/random component changes
randomly), then the expected "joint" probabilities are
given in the following matrix.

|  |  | Response at Time 1 | | |
|---|---|---|---|---|
|  |  | 1 | 2 | 3 |
| Response | 1 | .0252 | .1083 | .0252 |
| at | 2 | .1083 | .4661 | .1083 |
| Time 2 | 3 | .0252 | .1083 | .0252 |

Based on these probabilities, the expected values for: the correlation (r) between the responses given in time 1 and time 2; the percent of responses that do not change in the two time periods (% on diagonal); and the percent of responses that change from one extreme on the scale to the other, are:

E(r) = 0
E(% on diagonal) = .52
E(% extreme change) = .0504

Now assume the mean response on the underlying scale is 2.75 instead of 2. The expected probabilities of the three responses are .0062, .3023, and .6915 respectively. The expected joint probability matrix thus becomes:

|  |  | Response at Time 1 | | |
|---|---|---|---|---|
|  |  | 1 | 2 | 3 |
| Response | 1 | .0000 | .0019 | .0043 |
| at | 2 | .0019 | .0914 | .2090 |
| Time 2 | 3 | .0043 | .2090 | .4782 |

Based on these probabilities, the expected values are as follows:

E(r) = 0
E(% on diagonal) = .57
E(% extreme change) = .0086

In comparing the expected values in these two cases we find that even though the correlation remained constant, movement of the mean toward an extreme end of the scale increases the percent of respondents who exhibit no change. That is, even in the unlikely case of a homogeneous population, if the distribution of probable responses to a life style question is skewed, this will tend to have a positive effect on the percent of no change responses expected, a negative effect on the percent of the respondents exhibiting extreme changes, and no effect on the correlation expected between the responses given in the two time periods.

## HETEROGENEITY OF THE MEAN

The previous assumption of homogeneity of responses is obviously inappropriate if one hopes to use life style measures for any type of segmentation purpose [3,6,8,10]. In the following example we will show that a direct result of the heterogeneity of the respondents is a positive effect on the correlation (r) found between the responses in the two time periods.

To show how this works, consider the simplest form of mixing distribution with 50% of the respondents having a mean of 2 and 50% having a mean of 2.75. The expected probabilities for the three responses (1, 2 and 3) become .0825, .4925, and .4251, respectively and the expected joint probability matrix is shown below.

|  |  | Response at Time 1 | | |
|---|---|---|---|---|
|  |  | 1 | 2 | 3 |
| Response | 1 | .0126 | .0551 | .0148 |
| at | 2 | .0551 | .2788 | .1586 |
| Time 2 | 3 | .0148 | .0586 | .2517 |

Thus, the expected values for the three different stability measures are as follows.

E(r) = .30
E(% on diagonal) = .5411
E(% extreme change) = .0295

We see therefore, that the heterogeneity produces a large shift in the correlation measure with relatively little change in the % on the diagonal measure from those found in the homogeneous cases. Thus, if the aggregate distribution of responses is the result of combining subsets of respondents with different mean responses, it appears that this heterogeneity will have a positive effect on the correlation between the life style measures at two points in time while having little or no effect on the percent no change or extreme change measures.

## HETEROGENEITY OF VARIANCE

If a group of respondents exists with very large variances in their responses, the overall correlation between the responses in the two time periods will decrease and the percent of respondents who exhibit extreme shifts will increase in comparison with the situation where all the respondents have "average" variances.

TABLE 5

SUMMARY OF EFFECTS OF DIFFERENT RPOCESS AND MEASUREMENT

FACTORS ON STABILITY MEASURES

Influencing Factor

| Stability Measure | Number of Scale Points | Skewness of True Mean | Heterogeneity of Mean | Heterogeneity of Variance |
|---|---|---|---|---|
| r | Fewer the scale points the lower the r | No effect on r | If heterogeneity, tends to increase r | If heterogeneity, tends to decrease r |
| % on diagonal | Fewer the scale points the higher the % diagonal | If skewed, tends to increase the % diagonal | Little effect | Little effect |
| % extreme change | Fewer the scale points the higher the % extreme shifts | If skewed, tends to decrease % extreme shifts | Little effect | If heterogeneity, tends to increase % extreme shifts |

## CONCLUSION

We have shown that the absolute levels of the three stability measures (r, % on the diagonal, % extreme changes) are influenced not only by true stability but also by a variety of process and measurement factors listed in Table 5. Specifically we have shown that the distribution of the responses can have an overwhelming effect on the correlation coefficient, to the point that in those cases where the responses are highly skewed, the correlation coefficient can be an unstable and unrepresentative measure of reliability. Also, the number of scale points used to measure the responses will affect the different reliability measures but in different directions. Finally, the skewness of the true mean of the distribution and the heterogeneity of the mean will also have varying influences on the reliability measures.

The main implication of this study is that researchers must look more closely at what is an "appropriate" measure of reliability of psychographic items. From a measurement standpoint, the researcher should first examine the frequency of responses across the scale values for each test item. Only when the psychographic items tend to be "discriminating" is the use of the correlation coefficient and the distribution of the coefficients a meaningful reflection of the relative reliability of the items. Also, regardless of the reliability measure used, some recognition of the influence of the number of scale points should be incorporated in the interpretation of the results. Finally, some consideration should be given to the underlying situation and processes from which the data are drawn and their impact on different reliability measures.

These findings also have wider application to any reliability/validity testing technique of psychological testing instruments which rely on correlation as the basic measure. For example, the multitrait-multimethod matrix technique for testing validity [2] interprets high correlations on the diagonal and low correlations on the off-diagonal as support that two independent tests are valid and measuring the same trait. However, if the two tests measure individuals' responses in terms of discrete scales (which is typical in most psychological testing) and if there is little variation in the responses across individuals, the diagonal correlations might be relatively low because of the factors mentioned in this paper and not because the tests are not measuring the same trait.

Due to the generally skewed nature of the responses to psychographic questions, it would appear that the past attempts at examining the reliability of the test items through correlation of test-retest scores [1,3,6,10] have provided information of limited value about the absolute or relative reliability of these items. Any future research in the area of examining the reliability of psychographics should begin therefore, with research that helps determine appropriate and meaningful measures of reliability.

## REFERENCES

1. Bruno, Albert V. and Edgar A. Pessemier. "An Empirical Investigation of the Validity of Selected Attitude and Activity Measures," Proceedings. Third Annual Conference, Association for Consumer Research (1972), 456-74.

2. Campbell, Donald T. and Donald W. Fiske. "Convergant and Discriminant Validation by the Multitrait-Multimethod Matrix," Psychological Bulletin, 56 (February 1970), 67-76.

3. Darden, William R. and Fred D. Reynolds. "Backward Profiling of Male Innovators," Journal of Marketing Research, 11 (February 1974), 79-84.

4. Hustad, Thomas P. and Edgar A. Pessemier. "Industry's Use of Life Style Analysis: Segmenting Consumer Market with Activity and Attitude Measures," Combined Conference Proceedings. American Marketing Association, Spring & Fall 1971, 296-301.

5. Morrison, Donald G. "Regression with Discrete Random Variables: The Effect on $R^2$," Journal of Marketing Research, 9 (August 1972), 338-340.

6. Pessemier, Edgar A. and Albert V. Bruno. "An Empirical Investigation of the Reliability and Stability of Selected Activity and Attitude Measures," Proceedings. Second Annual Conference, Association for Consumer Research, 1971, 389-403.

7. Plummer, Joseph T. "The Theory & Uses of Life Style Segmentation," Journal of Marketing, 38 (January 1974), 33-7.

8. Toy, Norman E. "Correlation Analysis with Discrete Mappings of Continuous Variables," Working paper, Columbia University.

9. Villani, Kathryn E.A. "Personality/Life Style and Television Viewing Behavior," Journal of Marketing Research (November 1975)

10. Villani, Kathryn E.A. and Donald R. Lehmann. "An Examination of the Stability of A10 Measures," Proceedings. American Marketing Association Conference (August 1975), 484-8.

11. Wells, William D. "Segmentation by Attitude Types," in Robert L. King, ed., Marketing and the New Science of Planning, Chicago: American Marketing Association.

12. Wells, William D. "Psychographics: A Critical Review," Journal of Marketing Research, 12 (May 1975), 196-213.

# STATEMENT POLARITY IN ATTITUDE STUDIES: ADDITIONAL EVIDENCE

John R. Nevin, University of Wisconsin-Madison[1]

## ABSTRACT

Several research efforts have focused on the "polarity of attitude statement" issue. A recent study by Falthzik and Jolson found that the polarity of the attitude statements used influenced the answers respondents provided researchers. This research re-examines the differences in response, if any, between favorably versus unfavorably or positively versus negatively worded versions of the same attitude-eliciting statements. In addition, the agreement phenomenon (yeasayers) and disagreement phenomenon (naysayers) is examined as possible explanations of any significant statement wording effects.

## INTRODUCTION

Although seemingly much progress has been made, the wording of questions is still very much an art and not a science. Most of the important ideas on the wording of questions are more rules of thumb or admonitions that have been learned from experience than underlying concepts learned through research. Most researchers in marketing recognize the important role played by question wording in gathering accurate and reliable information. As one author claimed, "There has been widespread agreement among those who engage in research in marketing that 'how you ask the question' is often as important as 'what you ask'" [4, pg. 102].

Recently, there seems to be an increase in research efforts investigating the impact of question wording on responses [1, 2, 4, 5, 6]. Several research efforts have specifically focused on the "polarity of attitude statement" issue [1, 4, 5]. Greyser investigated the differences in response to favorable and unfavorable attitude-eliciting statements on the same issues [5]. Falthzik and Jolson suggest that researchers have been arbitrarily choosing positive statements without serious concern as to whether a reversal to negative phrasing would produce significantly different results [4]. The results from these pioneering research studies strongly suggest that the polarity of the statements used may influence the answers respondents provide researchers.

The purpose of this research is to re-examine the differences in response, if any, between favorably versus unfavorably or positively versus negatively worded versions of the same attitude-eliciting statements. In addition, the agreement phenomenon (yeasayers) and disagreement phenomenon (naysayers) will be examined as possible explanations of any significant statement wording effects. This rejoinder type of research enhances the validity and maturity of the marketing discipline by insuring that initial empirical research results are not uncritically absorbed into the body of marketing thought [3].

## METHOD AND PROCEDURE

Data for this study were derived from questionnaires mailed to 1,040 names systematically selected from a list of residents provided by University of Wisconsin Residence Halls. The initial mailing plus one follow-up generated a response rate of 71.1% or 739 completed questionnaires.

The focus of the research was in the area of student attitudes toward University of Wisconsin Residence Halls. Residents were asked to score each of 21 statements about University Residence Halls along a 5-point scale ranging from "strongly agree" to "strongly disagree."

Favorably versus unfavorably or positively versus negatively phrased versions of the 21 statements are presented in Illustration 1. Statements 1 through 8 are the favorably and unfavorably worded versions, whereas statements 9 through 21 are the positively and negatively ("not" has been added) worded versions being investigated.

Two different questionnaires were developed, one using approximately half of the favorable and positive statements and half of the unfavorable and negative statements in an interspersed way; the second using the other half of the statements. Residents were randomly assigned to receive one of the two questionnaires. Each resident also was requested to indicate his or her age, sex, year in school, and grade point average.

## RESULTS

To assess the homogeneity of the sample groups completing the two questionnaire forms, chi-square tests were performed for all demographic characteristics. There were no significant differences using the 10 percent level of significance between the two groups in terms of age, sex, year in school, or grade point average.

The data in Table 1 compare responses to favorable versus unfavorable and positive versus negative versions of attitude statements. If statement polarity were not an influencing variable, the aggregate sample response distribution for a favorable or positive statement would be the mirror image of the response distribution for an unfavorable or negative statement. According to the results in Table 1, statement polarity is a significant factor in only 2 of the 8 favorable versus unfavorable statements (statements 1 through 8). In contrast, however, statement polarity is a significant factor in 10 of the 12 positive versus negative statements (statements 9 through 21). The simple act of inserting the word "not" in an attitude statement definitely affected the responses of residents.

An analysis of the quartile deviations in Table 1 indicates no systematic dispersion pattern between favorable versus unfavorable or positive versus negative statements. An analysis of the medians, however, indicates that for all but two of the 12 statements with significant differences (statements 6 and 21), the intensity of disagreement with a positively posed version is significantly higher than the intensity of agreement with a negatively posed version. Thus, these results suggest that the double disagreement ("naysaying") phenomenon prevails, but not sufficiently to reverse the direction of attitudes drawn from any of the statements.

Residents of University Residence Halls are obviously only moderately satisfied at best and this might help explain their general tendency to disagree. Given this disagreement (naysaying) tendency, the use of negative statements would tend to portray University Residence Halls in a more

---
[1]John R. Nevin is an Assistant Professor, Graduate School of Business, University of Wisconsin-Madison. He wishes to gratefully acknowledge the constructive criticisms of an earlier draft of this manuscript by Professor Michael J. Houston, University of Wisconsin-Madison.

ILLUSTRATION 1

FAVORABLE VS. UNFAVORABLE AND POSITIVE VS. NEGATIVE VERSIONS OF ATTITUDE STATEMENTS

<table>
<tr><td colspan="2" align="center">FAVORABLE</td><td colspan="2" align="center">UNFAVORABLE</td></tr>
<tr><td>1.</td><td>The food served in the University Residence Halls is of good quality.</td><td>1.</td><td>The food served in University Residence Halls is of poor quality.</td></tr>
<tr><td>2.</td><td>The serving hours are convenient.</td><td>2.</td><td>The serving hours are inconvenient.</td></tr>
<tr><td>3.</td><td>The cost of food service is reasonable.</td><td>3.</td><td>The cost of food service is unreasonable.</td></tr>
<tr><td>4.</td><td>I am satisfied with the furnishings in my dorm room.</td><td>4.</td><td>I am unsatisfied with the furnishings in my dorm room.</td></tr>
<tr><td>5.</td><td>The dorm rooms have adequate space.</td><td>5.</td><td>The dorm rooms have inadequate space.</td></tr>
<tr><td>6.</td><td>The dorm rooms have adequate lighting for study purposes.</td><td>6.</td><td>The dorm rooms have inadequate lighting for study purposes.</td></tr>
<tr><td>7.</td><td>I do a lot of studying in my dorm room.</td><td>7.</td><td>I do very little studying in my dorm room.</td></tr>
<tr><td>8.</td><td>I think it is a good idea to require freshmen to live in University Residence Halls.</td><td>8.</td><td>I think it is a poor idea to require freshmen to live in University Residence Halls.</td></tr>
</table>

<table>
<tr><td colspan="2" align="center">POSITIVE</td><td colspan="2" align="center">NEGATIVE</td></tr>
<tr><td>9.</td><td>There is usually enough food served at meal times.</td><td>9.</td><td>There is usually not enough food served at meal times.</td></tr>
<tr><td>10.</td><td>The lines are very short at meal time.</td><td>10.</td><td>The lines are not very short at meal times.</td></tr>
<tr><td>11.</td><td>The housefellow is a worthwhile part of the Residence Hall System.</td><td>11.</td><td>The housefellow is not a worthwhile part of the Residence Hall System.</td></tr>
<tr><td>12.</td><td>I would be willing to pay $120 to $150 premium for a single room.</td><td>12.</td><td>I would not be willing to pay $120 to $150 premium for a single room.</td></tr>
<tr><td>13.</td><td>My room and floor are quiet enough for studying.</td><td>13.</td><td>My room and floor are not quiet enough for studying.</td></tr>
<tr><td>14.</td><td>"Night owls" should be separated from students who are "early risers" for roommate and house assignments.</td><td>14.</td><td>University Residence Halls should not attempt to separate "night owls" from students who are "early risers" for roommate and house assignments.</td></tr>
<tr><td>15.</td><td>Most of my activities are focused around the dorm.</td><td>15.</td><td>Most of my activities are not focused around the dorm.</td></tr>
<tr><td>16.</td><td>I think the Residence Halls provide ample opportunities for cultural and intellectual exchange.</td><td>16.</td><td>I think the Residence Halls do not provide ample opportunities for cultural and intellectual exchange.</td></tr>
<tr><td>17.</td><td>Sponsoring social activities is an important function of the dorm.</td><td>17.</td><td>Sponsoring social activities is not an important function of the dorm.</td></tr>
<tr><td>18.</td><td>Living in my house gives me a sense of community feeling.</td><td>18.</td><td>Living in my house does not give me a sense of community feeling.</td></tr>
<tr><td>19.</td><td>If my building is closed, it would definitely have an effect on my decision about returning to University Residence Halls.</td><td>19.</td><td>If my building is closed, it would definitely not have an effect on my decision about returning to University Residence Halls.</td></tr>
<tr><td>20.</td><td>I feel there should be houses in which visitation is only permitted on weekends.</td><td>20.</td><td>I feel there should not be houses in which visitation is only permitted on weekends.</td></tr>
<tr><td>21.</td><td>The University should move toward unlimited visitation for all residents who want it.</td><td>21.</td><td>The University should not move toward unlimited visitation for all residents who want it.</td></tr>
</table>

TABLE 1

COMPARISON OF RESPONSES TO FAVORABLE VS. UNFAVORABLE AND POSITIVE VS. NEGATIVE VERSIONS OF ATTITUDE STATEMENTS

| Statement Number & Polarity | Scale score[a] | | % of Respondents | | | Chi-square Value | N | Median | Quartile Deviation |
|---|---|---|---|---|---|---|---|---|---|
| | 1 | 2 | 3 | 4 | 5 | | | | |
| 1 Favorable | 11 | 26 | 23 | 35 | 5 | .5 | 348 | 3.6 | 1.1 |
| 1 Unfavorable | 11 | 27 | 22 | 34 | 6 | | 386 | 3.5 | 1.1 |
| 2 Favorable | 7 | 18 | 13 | 49 | 13 | 4.0 | 348 | 4.2 | .5 |
| 2 Unfavorable | 6 | 19 | 17 | 43 | 15 | | 388 | 4.2 | .6 |
| 3 Favorable | 14 | 29 | 30 | 26 | 1 | 4.5 | 348 | 3.2 | .8 |
| 3 Unfavorable | 13 | 25 | 37 | 23 | 2 | | 390 | 3.3 | .7 |
| 4 Favorable | 15 | 24 | 24 | 32 | 5 | 1.6 | 349 | 3.4 | 1.0 |
| 4 Unfavorable | 15 | 25 | 26 | 28 | 6 | | 388 | 3.4 | 1.0 |
| 5 Favorable | 32 | 24 | 14 | 25 | 5 | 6.1 | 348 | 2.8 | 1.0 |
| 5 Unfavorable | 28 | 30 | 17 | 21 | 4 | | 389 | 2.7 | .8 |
| 6 Favorable | 13 | 18 | 10 | 49 | 10 | 8.5* | 349 | 4.0 | 2.6 |
| 6 Unfavorable | 11 | 20 | 16 | 43 | 10 | | 390 | 3.2 | 1.5 |
| 7 Favorable | 15 | 18 | 13 | 32 | 22 | 2.5 | 349 | 3.4 | 2.0 |
| 7 Unfavorable | 18 | 20 | 13 | 28 | 21 | | 390 | 4.0 | 2.0 |
| 8 Favorable | 37 | 21 | 15 | 16 | 11 | 11.2** | 349 | 2.6 | 1.2 |
| 8 Unfavorable | 30 | 17 | 18 | 25 | 11 | | 389 | 3.2 | 1.4 |
| 9 Favorable | 7 | 14 | 12 | 46 | 21 | 2.6 | 349 | 4.4 | .5 |
| 9 Unfavorable | 7 | 16 | 13 | 47 | 17 | | 388 | 4.3 | .5 |
| 10 Positive | 38 | 32 | 20 | 9 | 2 | 58.2** | 349 | 2.4 | .8 |
| 10 Negative | 25 | 29 | 15 | 20 | 11 | | 389 | 2.9 | .9 |
| 11 Positive | 20 | 21 | 26 | 25 | 8 | 16.3*** | 349 | 3.3 | 1.0 |
| 11 Negative | 13 | 19 | 22 | 31 | 15 | | 389 | 3.8 | 1.1 |
| 12 Positive | 31 | 28 | 19 | 14 | 8 | 6.98 | 345 | 2.7 | .9 |
| 12 Negative | 25 | 32 | 16 | 15 | 12 | | 389 | 2.8 | .8 |
| 13 Positive | 22 | 27 | 20 | 27 | 4 | 1.20 | 348 | 3.1 | 1.2 |
| 13 Negative | 23 | 24 | 22 | 26 | 5 | | 389 | 3.1 | 1.2 |
| 14 Positive | 11 | 15 | 31 | 24 | 19 | 12.6** | 349 | 3.8 | .8 |
| 14 Negative | 5 | 17 | 30 | 30 | 18 | | 389 | 3.9 | .8 |
| 15 Positive | 28 | 33 | 19 | 17 | 3 | 12.9** | 349 | 2.7 | .8 |
| 15 Negative | 18 | 34 | 22 | 21 | 5 | | 390 | 2.9 | .7 |
| 16 Positive | 12 | 26 | 37 | 22 | 3 | 9.8** | 349 | 3.3 | .7 |
| 16 Negative | 6 | 30 | 35 | 24 | 5 | | 386 | 3.4 | .7 |
| 17 Positive | 9 | 24 | 28 | 31 | 8 | 33.1*** | 349 | 3.6 | .9 |
| 17 Negative | 4 | 17 | 21 | 39 | 19 | | 388 | 4.2 | .6 |
| 18 Positive | 19 | 24 | 27 | 26 | 4 | 25.1*** | 348 | 3.3 | .9 |
| 18 Negative | 10 | 31 | 20 | 30 | 9 | | 389 | 3.4 | 1.2 |
| 19 Positive | 19 | 20 | 25 | 19 | 17 | 13.82*** | 346 | 3.5 | 1.0 |
| 19 Negative | 15 | 26 | 16 | 22 | 21 | | 388 | 3.6 | 1.5 |
| 20 Positive | 42 | 18 | 24 | 12 | 4 | 33.2*** | 348 | 2.4 | 1.4 |
| 20 Negative | 28 | 18 | 22 | 19 | 13 | | 388 | 3.2 | 1.1 |
| 21 Positive | 6 | 5 | 6 | 18 | 65 | 11.0** | 349 | 5.2 | .4 |
| 21 Negative | 8 | 8 | 11 | 19 | 54 | | 389 | 5.1 | .5 |

e positive statements are scored "strongly disagree" (1), "disagree" (2), "neither agree nor disagree" (3), "agree"
), and "strongly disagree" (5). The negative statements are oppositely scored, "strongly agree" (1), "agree" (2),
either agree nor disagree" (3), "disagree" (4), and "strongly disagree" (5).
gnificant at the .10 level; **significant at the .05 level; ***significant at the .01 level.

favorable light, while the use of positive statements would provide a more unfavorable perspective.

## DISCUSSION

The evidence indicates that the intensity of residents' expressed attitudes depends to some degree on whether the researcher's statements are phrased positively or negatively but not on whether they are phrased favorably or unfavorably. Further, the evidence indicates that the double disagreement ("naysaying") phenomenon exists. This tendency for residents to disagree with any statement might be attributed to the existence of some strong negative attitudes toward University Residence Halls. In this case, the researcher can somewhat manipulate the expressed attitudes by the choice of positive versus negative statements of an issue.

These results conflict with studies conducted by Payne that indicate that when people have strong convictions, the wording of the statement should not greatly change the stand they take [6]. In this case, the residents have very strong convictions and yet the positive versus negative wording of statements affects their responses.

The evidence in this study provides additional support for the conclusion by Falthzik and Jolson [3, pg. 104] that:

> ... A substantial number of the Likert-type or dichotomous statements currently used in marketing research are loaded, that is, they may lead some respondents to give different answers than they would give to another wording of what was intended to be the same issue.

Loading by statement polarity choice, whether it is done consciously or unconsciously by the researcher, may have undesirable consequences. For instance, a researcher may, by choosing positive statements, unconsciously distort research results that management relies upon for decision-making. Another possibility that emerges is the conscious distortion of attitudes and opinions to support particular hypotheses or managerial decisions.

Marketing researchers need to become aware of this problem area in attitude studies. Falthzik and Jolson suggested that researchers conduct a pre-test of positive versus negative statements to determine whether the results differ significantly [3]. Significant differences in results would suggest employing a split ballot where one phrasing is used on one-half of the questionnaires, and the alternative phrasing is employed on the other half.

In light of the findings in this study, positive and negative statements could be restructured into favorable and unfavorable statements of the same issues to minimize the potential distortion of respondents' attitudes. Other less desirable alternatives would be to restructure the statements to include both polarities (alternative phrasings). This could be accomplished by including both polarities in a question (i.e., Are the serving hours convenient or inconvenient?), or asking respondents to rate an issue on a scale between the polarities (i.e., convenient hours |_|_|_|_|_|_|_| inconvenient hours). Restructuring the statements to include both polarities eliminates the bipolarity problem, but somewhat complicates the task of getting attitudinal data from respondents.

Marketing researchers need to use greater caution in designing and interpreting the results from studies that rely on responses to attitude-eliciting statements. The results from this study may not be generalizable to all situations since the sample had a relatively high education level and the issue was moderately involving. To the extent that the results from this study and Falthzik and Jolson's study are generalizable, however, researchers should either avoid the use of positive and negative attitude statements altogether, employ a split ballot technique, or at a minimum, consider the potential effects of the polarity problem in interpreting the results from attitude studies.

## REFERENCES

1. Arndt, Johan and Edgar Crane. "Response Bias, Yea-Saying, and the Double Negative," Journal of Marketing Research, 12 (May 1975), 218-20.

2. Belkin, Marvin and Seymour Liberman. "Effect of Question Wording on Response Distribution," Journal of Marketing Research, 4 (August 1967), 312-13.

3. Brown, Stephen W. and Kenneth A. Coney. "Building a Replication Tradition in Marketing," in Kenneth L. Beanhardt, ed., Educator's Proceedings of the American Marketing Association, 1976, 622-625.

4. Falthzik, Alfred M. and Marvin A. Jolson. "Statement Polarity in Attitude Studies," Journal of Marketing Research, 11 (February 1974), 102-5.

5. Greyser, Stephen A. "Businessmen Re Advertising: 'Yea, but ...'," Harvard Business Review, 40 (May-June 1962), 26-8.

6. Hubbard, Alfred W. "Phrasing Questions," Journal of Marketing, 15 (July 1950), 48-56.

7. Payne, Stanley L. The Art of Asking Questions. Princeton: Princeton University Press, 1963.

# IDENTIFYING OPINION LEADERS BY SELF-REPORT

Danny N. Bellenger, Georgia State University
Elizabeth C. Hirschman, Georgia State University

## ABSTRACT

The study reported here replicates a portion of a study done by Corey on the validity of self-report as a measure of opinion leadership, using a different product category -- clothing. It also adds analytical cross-validation to this previous work. The results support the validity of the self-report measure of opinion leadership. This approach appears to offer a simple yet valid alternative in this particular consumer research task.

## INTRODUCTION

Opinion leaders are people who are well informed and who hold the trust of others. The influential individuals exist in almost all primary groups. Given their impact on group behavior, they are vitally important to many marketing efforts. Their impact is derived from word-of-mouth communications with other group members. As described in several earlier works [3, 4, 5], the opinion leader acts as a group mediator for passing mass communications to other group members. They have been described as both channels of information and as a source of social pressure to behave in a specific way [3]. Thus, communicating with, persuading, and perhaps creating [5] opinion leaders is critical to the success of such marketing activities as new product introduction.

In order to effectively deal with the opinion leader, the marketing manager must know who he is, or at least what general characteristics the opinion leader possesses. Numerous studies have been directed toward this identification task [2, 6, 8]. One interesting possibility is to simply ask the group members to self-report whether they are an opinion leader or not. If the consumers who are opinion leaders can successfully identify themselves, the measurement task in this type of consumer research can be greatly simplified.

How valid is the self-reported identification of opinion leaders? Corey has reported that in two studies he conducted on automotive topics and food preparation and in research by Stewart on grocery product topics the self-report measure of opinion leadership had criterion-related validity [1]. That is, the opinion leaders identified by self-report had characteristics that are ascribed to them in the literature. Other works have also indicated success with the self-report measurement [7, 9].

The research reported by Corey consisted of an examination of three different consumer product studies, each of which utilized a single item, self-report technique for measuring opinion leadership. The three topics under investigation in Corey's research included ideas on food preparation, automobiles, and grocery products. The data on which his analyses were based were gathered in 1964 and 1969.

Each study used a self-report technique for classifying respondents into one of two opinion leadership groups:

1) Individuals who claim that associates come to them for advice and information about specific consumer topics (i.e. opinion leaders).

2) Individuals who claim that they go to associates for such advice and information (i.e. nonleaders).

The study reported in this paper is aimed at replicating the Corey study [1] with a different product category (clothing) and extending the analysis by cross-validation to provide additional insights into the validity of the self-report measurement of opinion leadership.

This research effort in some ways adds to the previous work done on opinion leaders, but it relates much more directly to the methodology issue; is the self-report measure of opinion leadership valid? Thus it builds on the work of Corey [1] and on earlier work by Rogers and Cartano [7] and Tittle and Hill [9]. The trend of findings in all this work suggests that self-report is a relatively valid measurement device.

## METHODOLOGY

### Sample

Data for the study were gathered in a series of 495 telephone interviews conducted in Birmingham, Alabama, during the second and third weeks of August, 1976. The interviews were conducted by trained, professional interviewers. A random digit dialing technique was utilized to insure adequate representation of newcomers and unlisted numbers. All interviews were conducted during the hours of 6:00 p.m. to 9:30 p.m. to gather a representative sample of working as well as non-working persons.

The sample was apportioned according to population density in each telephone exchange area. A 15 percent subset of all interviews were validated by call backs; completion rate for the interview, once initiated, was 87 percent.

### Opinion Leadership Measurement

As in the Corey study [1], respondents were categorized as opinion leaders or non-opinion leaders by their response to the following question:

> Which answer most nearly characterizes you?
> For ideas of fashion and clothing,
>
> 1. People come to me.
> 2. I go to other people.

Respondents who gave response number 1 were categorized as opinion leaders; those who gave response number 2 were classified as non-opinion leaders.

### Criterion Variables

The criterion variables consisted of demographics, social activities, self-descriptive statements, and the importance ratings for store features which are shown in Table 1. The first three sets of variables were selected because the literature provides a basis for validating the opinion leader profile they provide [2, 6, 8]; the final set was included to provide direction for retailers in attracting opinion leaders if in fact the self-reporting measure could be validated.

### Analysis

The data collected in the study were analyzed through the use of discriminant analysis. First, the sample was divided into male and female. This was done because previous studies of opinion leadership for clothing provide separate male and female profiles [2, 8]. The sample contained 198 males and 297 females.[1] Next, the male and female sub-samples were split in half and discriminant functions developed for each half. The functions were then applied to the other halves of the sample to cross-validate the analysis. This allowed an internal validity check on the self-report measure. After the discriminant functions and the resulting opinion leader profiles were cross-validated, the profiles were compared to those expected from the literature. This provides a test of criterion-related validity for the measure.

## FINDINGS

### Male Sub-Sample

The results of the discriminant analysis for the male sub-sample are shown in Table 2. The three most powerful discriminating variables are shown in the table. Two key elements in the profile for the male clothing opinion leader are that it involves people who want to "look different than others" and a disproportionate number of non-whites. The profile for the two male subgroups is similar and the aggregate relationship of the independent variables to

TABLE 1

CRITERION VARIABLES

| Demographic | Social Activity[1] | Self Descriptors[2] | Store Features[3] |
|---|---|---|---|
| Possession of national department store credit cards | Hunting/fishing | I am very active. | Sales clerk service |
| Possession or regional department store credit cards | Camping/backpacking | I usually act on the spur of the moment. | Store location |
| Possession of discount store credit cards | Tennis | I am willing to try new ideas. | Merchandise pricing |
| Possession of Bank Americard | Entertaining in your home | Appearance is more important than comfort in the way I dress. | Credit or billing policies |
| Possession of Master Charge | Photography | I want to look different than others. | Store layout or atmosphere |
| Marital status | Concerts/ballet | | Merchandise quality |
| Number of children living at home | Plays | | Merchandise variety and assortment |
| Children in various age groups | Bridge clubs | | Merchandise display |
| Spouse's age | Spectator sporting events | | Store's guarantee, exchange or adjustment policies |
| Respondent's age | Social organizations | | Store sales represent real savings |
| House as a residence (yes/no) | Religious organizations | | |
| Length of time lived in metropolitan area | Business organizations | | |
| Respondent's education | Community organizations | | |
| Spouse's education | | | |
| Income | | | |
| Sex | | | |
| Race | | | |
| Life cycle[4] | | | |
| Social class[5] | | | |

[1]Dichotomous response based on question, "Do you participate (or attend) regularly in _____?"

[2]Respondents were asked to indicate how well each statement described them -- very true, mostly true, mostly false, or very false.

[3]Respondents were asked to indicate whether each characteristic was Very Important, Moderately Important, or Not Important at All to them in deciding where to shop. Responses were scored 3, 2, and 1, respectively.

[4]Life cycle was broken into six categories:
  (1) Single, under age 34, with no children.
  (2) Married, under age 34, with no children.
  (3) Married, with children under age 10.
  (4) Married, with children over age 10.
  (5) Married, over age 34, with no children.
  (6) Single/widowed, over age 34.

[5]Social class was operationalized as a weighted composite of:
  (1) number of years education.
  (2) total family income.
  (3) status of occupation.

---

[1]Approximately 27% (134) of the total sample consisted of non-white respondents. Of these, 60% were female and 40% were male, which was proportional to the overall sample composition.

opinion leadership is highly significant in both cases.

The male sub-sample cross-validation is shown in Table 3. It indicates that the discriminant functions developed for each subgroup are reasonably successful in predicting both opinion leaders and non-opinion leaders in the other subgroup. The predictions were significant to the .05 level in both cases. This internal consistency lends support to the validity of the self-report opinion leader measure.

Turning to the criterion-related validity of Corey, Darden and Reynolds found that men's apparel fashions opinion leaders tended to have a high level of "fashion venturesomeness." [2] This is consistent with the finding in this study, that male clothing opinion leaders "want to look different than others." This supports Corey's contention that the self-reported opinion leader measure has criterion-related validity.

Female Sub-Sample

The results of the discriminant analysis for the female sub-sample are shown in Table 4. The three most powerful discriminating variables are shown in the table. The profile for the female clothing opinion leaders, as with the case with males, involves people who "want to look different than others." It also suggests an active woman who attends spectator sporting events and movies. As with the males, the profiles for the two subgroups are similar and the aggregate relationship of the independent variables to opinion leadership is highly significant for both groups.

The female sub-sample cross-validation is shown in Table 5. The cross predictions by the discriminant functions are significant to the .001 level. The validity of the self-report measurement is again supported by this internal consistency.

Research reported by Summers provides a basis for evaluating the criterion-related validity of the measure [8]. Summers' work indicated that women's clothing fashion opinion leaders tend to show more venturesomeness in clothing and to be more active than non-opinion leaders. This is consistent with the findings reported here, lending additional support to the validity of the self-report measure of opinion leadership.

### TABLE 2

### DISCRIMINANT ANALYSIS RESULTS: MALES

Subgroup 1 Discriminant Function Coefficients*

   -.35 Possession of a discount store credit card
   .30 Race (non-white)
   .18 I want to look different than others

Subgroup 2 Discriminant Function Coefficients*

   .29 Race (non-white)
   .20 I want to look different than others
   .15 Attend movies regularly

*The statistical significance of the discriminant functions was p < .0001 in both cases using the Wilks Lambda criterion.

### TABLE 3

### CROSS-VALIDATED DISCRIMINANT ANALYSIS RESULTS: MALES

Subgroup 1 Discriminant Function Applied to Subgroup 2

|  | Prior Probability | Correctly Classified* |
|---|---|---|
| Opinion Leader | .42 | 70.4% |
| Non-opinion Leader | .58 | 63.2% |

Subgroup 2 Discriminant Function Applied to Subgroup 1

|  | Prior Probability | Correctly Classified* |
|---|---|---|
| Opinion Leader | .49 | 72.7% |
| Non-opinion Leader | .51 | 67.6% |

*The Chi-squared statistic values associated with both cross-validated classifications had probabilities of p < .05.

### TABLE 4

### DISCRIMINANT ANALYSIS RESULTS: FEMALES

Subgroup 1 Discriminant Function Coefficients*

   .33 Attend spectator sporting events
   .28 I want to look different than others
   .25 I am very active

Subgroup 2 Discriminant Function Coefficients*

   .30 I want to look different than others
   .18 Attend spectator sporting events
   .18 Attend movies regularly

*The statistical significance of the discriminant functions was p < .0001 in both cases using the Wilks Lambda criterion.

### TABLE 5

### CROSS-VALIDATED DISCRIMINANT ANALYSIS RESULTS: FEMALES

Subgroup 1 Discriminant Function Applied to Subgroup 2

|  | Prior Probability | Correctly Classified* |
|---|---|---|
| Opinion Leader | .43 | 68.5% |
| Non-opinion Leader | .57 | 60.5% |

Subgroup 2 Discriminant Function Applied to Subgroup 1

|  | Prior Probability | Correctly Classified* |
|---|---|---|
| Opinion Leader | .48 | 73.4% |
| Non-opinion | .52 | 72.9% |

*The Chi-squared statistic values associated with both classifications had probabilities of p < .001.

### IMPLICATION

This study supports the validity of self-report as a measure of opinion leadership among consumers. There are several complex methods for identifying this group which can be used in consumer research. They are, however, relatively difficult to apply. The self-report technique appears to offer a simple and yet valid alternative. No doubt, some accuracy is sacrificed for economy and expediency but the measure does seem to have considerable validity.

REFERENCES

1.  Corey, Lawrence G. "People Who Claim to Be Opinion
    Leaders: Identifying Their Characteristics by Self-
    Report," *Journal of Marketing*, 35 (October 1971),
    48-53.

2.  Darden, William R. and Fred D. Reynolds. "Predicting
    Opinion Leadership for Men's Apparel Fashions," *Jour-
    nal of Marketing Research*, 9 (August 1972), 324-7.

3.  Glock, Charles Y. and Francesco M. Nicosia. "Sociol-
    ogy and the Study of Consumers," *Journal of Advertis-
    ing Research*, 3 (September 1963), 21-7.

4.  Katz, Elihu and Paul F. Lazarsfeld. *Personal Influ-
    ence*. New York: Free Press of Glencoe, 1955.

5.  Mancuso, Joseph R. "Why Not Create Opinion Leaders
    for New Product Introductions?" *Journal of Marketing*,
    33 (July 1969), 20-25.

6.  Robertson, Thomas S. and James H. Myers. "Personality
    Correlates of Opinion Leadership and Innovative Buy-
    ing Behavior," *Journal of Marketing Research*, 6
    (May 1969), 164-68.

7.  Rogers, Everett M. and David G. Cartano. "Methods of
    Measuring Opinion Leadership," *Public Opinion Quarter-
    ly*, 26 (Fall 1962), 435-41.

8.  Summers, John O. "The Identity of Women's Clothing
    Fashion Opinion Leaders," *Journal of Marketing Re-
    search*, 7 (May 1970), 178-85.

9.  Tittle, Charles R. and Richard J. Hill. "The Accuracy
    of Self-Reported Data and Prediction of Political Ac-
    tivity," *Public Opinion Quarterly*, 31 (Spring 1967),
    103-6.

SOCIOECONOMIC RISK AND PERSONAL INFLUENCE
IN PURCHASE DECISIONS:   REPLICATION AND EXTENSION

James H. Barnes, Jr., University of Oregon

ABSTRACT

This article reports a study that explores the relationship between the importance of personal influence as an
information source and degree of risk in 24 purchase decisions.  The findings suggest that the higher the degree of
perceived risk, the greater the importance of personal
influence in making a purchase decision.

INTRODUCTION

The potential usefulness of socioeconomic risk and personal
influence variables in the formulation of segmentation policies has frequently been discussed in the literature of
consumer behavior.  (See for example [3, 4, 5, 6, 7].  The
concept of perceived risk in purchase decisions was first
introduced by Bauer [2].  He argued that purchase decisions
involve risk in the sense that any action of the consumer
will produce consequences which cannot be anticipated with
anything approximating certainty, and some of which at
least are likely to be unpleasant.  Bauer further argued
that consumers develop decision strategies or ways of reducing risk that enable them to act with a relative degree
of confidence and to proceed with ease in situations in
which their information is inadequate and the consequences
of their actions are in some meaningful sense incalculable.
Among these strategies, according to Bauer, are cues the
consumer receives from his reference group as to the type
of consumption that is valued by people whose esteem he or
she in turn values.

A number of authors have presented empirical results which
elucidate the relationships between interpersonal influence -- the dependent variable -- and perceived socioeconomic risk -- the independent variable.  Arndt, for example, studied the relations between perceived risk and
word-of-mouth and found that "the high risk perceivers
tended to make more effort to seek word-of-mouth information" [1].

This paper is concerned with one study which has attempted
to quantify the effects of risk and personal influence on
purchase decisions.  More specifically, it reports a replication of some aspects of a survey research project
which related respondents perceived risk toward a purchase
decision with their evaluation of the importance of interpersonal influence on that purchase decision.

Perry and Hamm took socioeconomic risk as their independent variable [12].  Their data were derived from a sample
of 101 male Oklahoma State University undergraduates. They
conclude that "the higher the risk involved in a particular purchase decision, the greater the importance of personal influence."  In those cases where canonical correlation was significant at the (p < .05) level, "the social
risk contributed more than the economic risk."

RESEARCH DESIGN AND METHOD

The purpose of the research reported here is to investigate the relationship between the importance of personal
influence and the degree of risk in 24 purchase decisions
by replicating the work of Perry and Hamm and extending it
to both male and female consumers.  The study utilizing
students at the University of Oregon replicated the Oklahoma State study in that it employed the same dependent

variable (socioeconomic risk) and derived its independent
variables from the same information sources as the Oklahoma State study.  The purchase decisions were altered somewhat so that they would apply to both male and female respondents.  The purchase decisions for the present study
were, however, also chosen on the following basis:

1.  Each must be the kind of a purchase decision that the
respondent might face as a college student.

2.  Each must be the kind of purchase decision that would
be suitable for advertising promotion.

3.  The list must include purchase decisions on both goods
and services.

4.  The list of decisions must cover a significant range of
potential socioeconomic risks.

Using these requirements, the 24 purchase decisions listed
in Table 1 were chosen and presented randomly to a sample
of 34 graduate and 65 undergraduate students.

The questionnaire was divided into two primary sections.
In the first part, the respondents were asked to rate, on a
seven-point scale, with the score of 1 indicating very
little or no significance and the score of 7 indicating
high significance, the significance of social risk and that
of economic risk, separately, for each decision.  The two
kinds of risk were explained as follows:

Social significance refers to how the purchase decision
will affect the opinion other people hold of the individual.
Thus, social significance varies with such factors as a
product's social importance and its social conspicuousness.

Economic significance refers to how the purchase will affect
the individual's ability to make other purchases.  Thus,
economic significance varies with the financial considerations or price in relation to factors such as the individual's income, ability to pay, and alternate uses for the
money.

In the second part of the questionnaire, respondents were
given the following situation.

A good friend and fellow student has been impressed by an
advertisement for Product L.  He or she is now in the process of deciding whether or not to purchase it.  Listed below are seven possible sources of information from which
the student might draw to assist him or her in making the
decision.  With the same seven-point rating scale used in
Part I, estimate the significance of each source as an influence upon your friend's purchase decision....

A friend, rather than the respondent, was placed in the
hypothetical risk situation to produce a more objective
evaluation of the decision process since there is a closer
congruence between ones ideal self and the concept of a
close friend than there is between that of ideal self and
one's own self concept [11].

The seven information sources given for the purchase decisions were:

1.  Information contained in the ad.

2.  Information contained in a different ad (either for the

product or a competitor).

3. Unbiased information sources (such as Consumer's Report).

4. Observed attitude of others toward the product (such as the product's ownership and use by others).

5. Verbal opinion of others toward the product (such as a friend's personal recommendation).

6. Past personal experience.

7. Information from some source other than (1-6).

As with the Perry and Hamm study, sources (4) and (5) only are included in the final analysis since they were selected to represent the interpersonal influence on the purchase decision.

## SCALE CONSTRUCTION

The final data used in the present analysis consisted of four scores for each respondent and each purchase decision. Canonical analysis can be used to determine the weights for each score and the degree of correlation such that the indices of total risk and personal influence may be thus computed:

$$X_j = A_s X'_s + A_e X'_e \qquad (1)$$

where

$X_j$ is the index of total purchase risk

$X'_s$ is the mean value for the degree of social risk

$X'_e$ is the mean value for the degree of economic risk

$A_s$ and $A_e$ are the canonical weights for the purchase risk set.

$$Y_j = B_a Y'_a + B_y Y'_y \qquad (2)$$

where

$Y_j$ is the index of personal influence for that purchase decision

$Y'_a$ is the mean value for the significance of observed attitude

$Y'_y$ is the mean value of the significance of verbal opinion

$B_a$ and $B_y$ are the canonical weights for the personal influence set.

The use of canonical weights as opposed to the mean values for each set insures that the indices are optimal in terms of the maximum linear correlations between the two sets of variables. Canonical correlation is a subclass of multivariate analysis which may be defined as that "branch of statistical analysis which is concerned with relationships of sets of dependent variates" [10]. "In canonical correlation we desire to find linear combinations of both the criterion and predictor sets whose correlation is maximized when the linear combinations are treated as two derived variates in a two-variable correlation" [9].

## FINDINGS

Table 1 reports the mean score for each of the risk and influence variables separately for each of the 24 purchase decisions. It is significant to note that in every case, verbal opinion of others toward the product was greater than observed attitude. This tends to support the finding of Burnkrant and Cousineau in that people "use the evaluations of others as a basis for inferring that the product is indeed, a better product" [4].

All decisions were subsequently ranked - first according to their weighted risk index ($X_j$) and then according to their weighted risk index ($Y_j$). These scores and ranks are given in Table 2. Kendall's rank-order correlation coefficient (tau$_a$) [13] is .902. This correlation shows a significant relationship between influence and risk and supports the findings of Perry and Hamm and the hypothesis that the higher the perceived socioeconomic risk in a purchase decision, the greater the personal influence on that decision.

TABLE 1

PURCHASE DECISION MEAN SCORES

| Purchase Decision | Social Risk | Economic Risk | Observed Influence | Verbal Influence |
|---|---|---|---|---|
| Automobile | 5.18 | 6.03 | 5.06 | 5.33 |
| Stereo Hi-Fi | 4.66 | 5.49 | 4.95 | 5.59 |
| Apartment | 4.27 | 4.88 | 4.48 | 5.15 |
| Magazine | 4.20 | 2.60 | 3.68 | 4.56 |
| Bicycle | 4.06 | 4.04 | 5.18 | 5.37 |
| Color TV | 3.96 | 5.11 | 4.67 | 5.24 |
| Haircut | 3.66 | 2.43 | 4.19 | 4.63 |
| Checking Account | 3.57 | 3.33 | 3.31 | 4.23 |
| Life Insurance | 3.39 | 4.42 | 3.91 | 4.54 |
| Blue Jeans | 3.34 | 2.79 | 4.14 | 4.58 |
| Beer | 3.33 | 2.39 | 3.73 | 4.25 |
| Automobile Tires | 3.30 | 4.22 | 4.35 | 5.14 |
| Watch | 3.22 | 3.95 | 4.16 | 4.75 |
| Tennis Shoes | 3.01 | 2.72 | 4.66 | 5.16 |
| Cologne | 3.01 | 2.19 | 3.83 | 4.18 |
| Sun Glasses | 2.68 | 2.19 | 3.60 | 3.82 |
| Soap | 2.67 | 2.05 | 2.97 | 3.54 |
| Class Ring | 2.46 | 2.35 | 3.16 | 3.35 |
| Undergarments | 2.39 | 1.98 | 2.79 | 3.07 |
| Hamburger | 2.30 | 1.90 | 3.34 | 4.09 |
| Cigarettes | 2.30 | 1.41 | 2.86 | 3.14 |
| Ballpoint Pen | 1.85 | 1.70 | 2.94 | 3.11 |
| Hair Spray | 1.79 | 1.27 | 2.91 | 3.24 |
| Sleepware | 1.67 | 1.61 | 2.66 | 2.97 |

346

## TABLE 2

### RANK AND CORRELATION OF PURCHASE DECISIONS

| Purchase Decision | Socioeconomic Risk | | Interpersonal influence | | Canonical Correlation Coefficient |
|---|---|---|---|---|---|
| | Weighted Index | Rank | Weighted Index | Rank | |
| Automobile | 6.17 | 1 | 3.78 | 14 | .295 |
| Stereo Hi-Fi | 5.35 | 2 | 5.38 | 3 | .372[b] |
| Color TV | 4.97 | 3 | 4.73 | 5 | .211 |
| Auto Tires | 4.50 | 4 | 3.40 | 16 | .382[b] |
| Watch | 4.44 | 5 | 4.03 | 11 | .329[a] |
| Bicycle | 4.14 | 6 | 6.03 | 1 | .330[a] |
| Checking Account | 3.94 | 7 | 4.31 | 7 | .369[b] |
| Apartment | 3.82 | 8 | 4.24 | 9 | .316[a] |
| Life Insurance | 3.78 | 9 | 4.44 | 6 | .339[a] |
| Haircut | 3.76 | 10 | 4.75 | 4 | .417[b] |
| Blue Jeans | 3.66 | 11 | 4.05 | 10 | .253 |
| Beer | 3.32 | 12 | 3.94 | 12 | .280 |
| Magazine | 3.25 | 13 | 5.47 | 2 | .234 |
| Cologne | 3.11 | 14 | 4.29 | 8 | .406[b] |
| Tennis Shoes | 2.92 | 15 | 2.08 | 23 | .253[a] |
| Sun Glasses | 2.86 | 16 | 3.92 | 13 | .479[b] |
| Soap | 2.71 | 17 | 3.54 | 15 | .220 |
| Hamburger | 2.69 | 18 | 1.26 | 24 | .195 |
| Undergarments | 2.36 | 19 | 2.67 | 22 | .267 |
| Class Ring | 2.31 | 20 | 2.81 | 21 | .323[b] |
| Ballpoint Pen | 1.93 | 21 | 3.09 | 19 | .324[b] |
| Sleepware | 1.92 | 22 | 2.87 | 20 | .210 |
| Hair Spray | 1.90 | 23 | 3.10 | 18 | .300[a] |
| Cigarettes | 1.82 | 24 | 3.13 | 17 | .229 |

[a]Significant at .05 level.

[b]Significant at .01 level.

Canonical analysis also provides an opportunity to examine the relationship between risk and influence for each product individually. The canonical correlation coefficient was computed for each product and is also reported in Table 2. Fourteen of these coefficients were significant at or below the .05 level.

Table 3 presents the cannonical coefficients for the purchase decisions with significant correlation (p < .05). It reveals that in all but three decisions (Sun Glasses, Ballpoint Pen, and Tennis Shoes), social risk played a more important role in forming the risk index than did economic risk. In the Perry and Hamm study only one such exception was found. This variation could result from the difference

in the economic climate between the two studies. That is, consumers are perhaps more economically aware of risk in their purchase decisions as a result of reduced purchasing power.

## TABLE 3

### CANONICAL RESULTS ON STATISTICALLY SIGNIFICANT PURCHASE DECISIONS

| Purchase Decision | Correlation Coefficient | Canonical Weight | | | |
|---|---|---|---|---|---|
| | | Risk | | Influence | |
| | | Social | Economic | Observed | Verbal |
| Sun Glasses | .479 | 0.56 | 0.62 | 0.34 | 0.71 |
| Haircut | .417 | 0.63 | 0.60 | 0.37 | 0.69 |
| Cologne | .406 | 0.71 | 0.45 | 0.69 | 0.39 |
| Auto Tires | .382 | 0.70 | 0.52 | 1.18 | -0.34 |
| Stereo Hi-Fi | .372 | 0.81 | 0.29 | 0.88 | 0.19 |
| Checking Account | .369 | 0.63 | 0.51 | 0.53 | 0.61 |
| Life Insurance | .339 | 0.95 | 0.13 | 0.48 | 0.57 |
| Bicycle | .330 | 0.97 | 0.05 | 0.60 | 0.55 |
| Watch | .329 | 0.68 | 0.57 | 1.04 | -0.60 |
| Ballpoint Pen | .324 | 0.31 | 0.80 | -0.04 | 1.03 |
| Class Ring | .323 | 1.04 | -0.10 | 1.31 | -0.40 |
| Apartment | .316 | 1.08 | 0.16 | 1.05 | -0.08 |
| Hair Spray | .300 | 0.95 | 0.15 | 0.76 | 0.27 |
| Tennis Shoes | .253 | 0.13 | 0.92 | -1.03 | 1.33 |

The present study employed an additional step in the investigation of the data. In addition to the canonical coefficients derived from the risk and personal influence indexes, respondents demographic characteristics were combined with the influence index in order to examine their effects on the predictive ability of the model. The results for the ten product decisions not found to be statistically significant (p < .05) are reported in Table 4. The coefficients of the canonical functions (A and B weights), indicate a variables contribution to the canonical correlations. These weights are generally interpreted as the importance of each variable in forming the general index. However, caution must be used in interpreting the results when dummy variables (coded 0 or 1) are used to deal with nominal classifications, i.e., male-female, married-single, and U.S. citizen-non U.S. citizen. The group coded 1 indicates that that variable is part of the model and the group coded 0 indicates that the variable does not affect the predictive model.

The inclusion of demographic data produced significant correlations (p < .05) on four of the ten product decisions -- Sleepware, Cigarettes, Automobiles, and Beer. Age does not appear to be an important variable in the model. A constant negative value for the citizenship variable indicates that native respondents perceive less risk than do non-native respondents for each of the purchase decisions. This result is expected since most people probably tend to proceed with less confidence in another

TABLE 4

CANONICAL RESULTS ON SELECTED PURCHASE DECISIONS

| Purchase Decision | Corre-lation Coeffi-cient | Risk | | Influence | | Demographic | | | | | | |
|---|---|---|---|---|---|---|---|---|---|---|---|---|
| | | Social | Economic | Observed | Verbal | Age | Citizen | Sex | Class | Income | Marital | Major |
| Sleepware | .548[b] | 0.82 | 0.31 | -0.01 | 0.30 | 0.33 | -0.79 | 0.14 | -0.33 | -0.32 | 0.02 | 0.1 |
| Cigarettes | .529[a] | 0.60 | 0.61 | 0.24 | 0.16 | 0.28 | -0.55 | 0.46 | 0.47 | 0.35 | 0.11 | -0.2 |
| Automobile | .515[a] | 0.95 | 0.07 | 0.36 | -0.13 | 0.02 | -0.13 | 0.17 | -0.62 | 0.17 | 0.23 | -0.1 |
| Beer | .499[a] | 0.95 | 0.11 | 0.44 | 0.01 | 0.06 | -0.15 | 0.35 | 0.45 | 0.24 | 0.14 | -0.0 |
| Soap | .474 | 1.15 | -0.31 | -0.02 | 0.25 | -0.11 | -0.11 | 0.27 | 0.45 | -0.32 | 0.25 | -0.2 |
| Color TV | .471 | 0.79 | 0.37 | 0.38 | -0.06 | -0.11 | -0.31 | 0.04 | -0.58 | -0.03 | 0.35 | -0.1 |
| Magazine | .450 | 0.28 | 0.83 | 0.29 | 0.54 | -0.35 | -0.15 | 0.49 | -0.27 | -0.10 | 0.16 | -0.3 |
| Undergarments | .443 | 0.14 | 0.95 | 0.19 | 0.49 | -0.23 | -0.23 | 0.55 | 0.01 | -0.44 | 0.22 | 0.2 |
| Hamburger | .438 | 0.19 | 0.94 | -0.35 | 0.61 | -0.06 | -0.11 | 0.76 | 0.11 | -0.57 | 0.01 | 0.3 |
| Blue Jeans | .373 | 0.79 | 0.37 | 0.45 | 0.13 | -0.67 | -0.19 | 0.21 | -0.42 | -0.54 | 0.08 | -0.1 |

[a]Significant at .05 level.

[b]Significant at .01 level.

cultural environment. This result deserves further study, however, since the non-U.S. citizen respondents were represented on only 10% of the sample and were not selected as representative of that group.

Marital status and college major fail to contribute to the results in any significant pattern. Males and females both hold similar views on risk for most of the 24 purchase decisions. Class and income when viewed together tend to indicate that the more educated, higher income individual perceives less risk in purchase decisions. This result is expected, based on other studies which have had similar findings [8].

Four products in Table 4 (Cigarettes, Magazine, Undergarments, and Hamburger) highlight an interesting aspect of economic risk. For each of those product decisions, economic risk is perceived to be greater than social risk although the amount of money at stake in each case is relatively small. Such factors as newness, variability in performance along with price, to name only a few, combine to form the concept of economic risk as perceived by the consumer.

SUMMARY AND IMPLICATIONS

The work of Perry and Hamm was replicated in this study. The higher the perceived risk in a particular purchase decision, the greater the importance of personal influence on that decision. Using canonical analysis it was found that social risk contributed more than economic risk in those cases where correlation was significant. It was found that the results were the same for males and females. Additionally, the study found that respondents valued the verbal opinion of others toward the product more than they valued their own ability to deduce others opinion through observation of product use and ownership.

The present study also reveals several areas for additional study. First is the different degree of risk as perceived

by native citizens and others in their evaluation of various products. Second is the delineation of the parameters of economic risk. It was shown in this report that monetary value is not sufficient within itself as a measure of economic risk.

Several important implications may be derived from the present study. In those purchase decisions where the consumer perceives a high degree of socioeconomic risk, promotional strategies which try to reach the buyer through personal channels (opinion leaders, word-of-mouth) as opposed to the general media will be more successful. The amount of perceived risk varies with the social visability of the product, the amount of money at stake, and the amount of consumer self-confidence. The marketer must understand these risk provoking factors and develop aids that will help to reduce this risk.

REFERENCES

1. Arndt, Johan. "Role of Product-Related Conversations in the Diffusion of a New Product," Journal of Marketting Research, 4 (August 1967), 294.

2. Bauer, Raymond A. "Consumer Behavior as Risk Taking," in R. S. Hancock, ed., Dynamic Marketing for a Changing World, Proceedings of the 43rd National Conference, American Marketing Association, (1960), 389-98.

3. Bettman, James R. "Perceived Risk and its Components: A Model and Empirical Test," Journal of Marketing Research, 10 (May 1973), 184-90.

4. Burnkrant, Robert E. and Alain Cousineau. "Informational and Normative Social Influence in Buyer Behavior," Journal of Consumer Research 2 (December 1975), 206-15.

5. Cohen, J. B. and E. Golden. "Informational Social In-

fluence and Product Evaluation," Journal of Applied Psychology, 56 (1972), 54-9.

6. Cox, Donald F., ed. Risk Taking and Information Handling in Consumer Behavior. Boston: Graduate School of Business Administration, Harvard University, 1967.

7. Dash, J. F., L. G. Schiffman, and C. Berenson. "Risk- and Personality-Related Dimensions of Store Choice," Journal of Marketing, 40 (January 1976), 32-9.

8. Engel, James F., David L. Kollat, and Roger D. Blackwell." Consumer Behavior, 2nd ed. New York: Holt, Rinehart and Winston, 1973.

9. Green, Paul E. and Donald S. Tull. Research For Marketing Decisions, 3rd ed. Englewood Cliffs, New Jersey: Prentice Hall, Inc., 1975.

10. Kendall, Maurice G. A Course in Multivariate Analysis. New York: Hafner, 1957.

11. McKenna, Helen V., Peter R. Hofstaetter, and James P. O'Connor. "The Concept of Ideal Self and of a Friend," Journal of Personality, 24 (April 1956), 262-71.

12. Perry, Michael and B. Curtis Hamm. "Canonical Analysis of Relations Between Socioeconomic Risk and Personal Influence in Purchase Decisions," Journal of Marketing Research, 6 (August 1969), 351-4.

13. Siegel, Sidney. Nonparametric Statistics. New York: McGraw Hill Book Company, 1956.

CONSUMER PURCHASE ORIENTATION AND RACE:
REPLICATION AND EXTENSION

Phillip B. Niffenegger, Murray State University
Patrick D. McElya, Murray State University

## ABSTRACT

This research replicates a previous application of Stone's shopper typology to white and black urban shoppers. The relationship of shopper orientation to ecological concern is also examined. The findings suggest that shopper orientation is dependent on city size and retail structure, and is related to ecological concern, as measured by a multi-item index.

## INTRODUCTION

Based on in-depth interviews with 150 white middle-class housewives in the early 1950's, sociologist Gregory P. Stone developed a typology of shoppers which has been widely reproduced in consumer behavior texts [7,10,13]. Stone suggested that urban shoppers tend to establish certain relationships with stores and their personnel as a means of forming identifications which bind them to the larger urban community [15]. Although Stone's data was gathered in Chicago, a later replication carried out in the Southwest by Boone and Johnson [2] suggests that differences exist both between the purchase orientations of modern white shoppers and those of Stone's era, and between non-white and white shoppers.

The Stone study classified four distinct types of shopping orientation. These were the basis for the present study, and consist of economic, personalizing, ethical, and apathetic shoppers.

Economic shoppers emphasized the importance of the price, quality and variety of stores' merchandise. Store personnel were seen primarily as instruments to facilitate the efficiency of shopping and acquiring of goods.

Personalizing shoppers saw shopping as a fundamentally positive interpersonal experience. Store patronage was based on the strong personal attachments that were formed with store personnel. A good clerk was one who treated the shopper in a personal, relatively intimate manner.

Ethical shoppers sought to "help the little guy out" by selecting a small business, if possible, to shop. Identification was primarily with the store as a whole rather than its clerks.

Apathetic shoppers were not interested in shopping and sought to minimize the expenditure of effort in shopping for goods. Convenience of location was the crucial factor in store selection.

One purpose of the present study was to attempt to replicate the results of the recent Boone and Johnson study of shopper orientations [4], and its findings on the relative difference between the orientations of black shoppers as compared to white shoppers. In the Boone and Johnson study the largest proportion of black shoppers (41%) were found to be of the ethical orientation, while white shoppers were about evenly divided between the economic (35%) and the personalizing orientation (37%), only 6% having the ethical orientation.

A second and related purpose was to explore the relationship between shopper orientation and ecological concern.

A recent study by Kinnear and Taylor [9] found that the level of ecological concern among a group of 500 Canadian consumers had a definite effect on their brand perceptions in the laundry product category. Although the Kinnear and Taylor study did not report specifically on the relationship between ecological concern and intended brand purchase, it might reasonably be expected that consumers with a high level of ecological concern would express the intention to purchase ecologically "safe" products at a higher rate than consumers having a low level of ecological concern.

A study of household residents in Austin, Texas by Anderson and Cunningham [1] found that degree of Social Responsibility, (as measured by the Berkowitz-Daniels scale) was inversely correlated with alienation and directly correlated with cosmopolitanism. Alienation was defined as "a feeling of isolation from one's community, society, and/or culture" while cosmopolitanism was "a global, nonparochial perspective and orientation". Overall, a group of six sociopsychological variables were more sensitive discriminators of social consciousness than a group of six demographic measures. A later study by Anderson, Henion, and Cox [2] attempted to develop a profile of ecologically responsible consumers. Both alienation and cosmopolitanism were found to be highly sensitive discriminators of ecologically responsible consumers; ecological responsibility was found to be positively correlated with both alienation and cosmopolitanism. However, a study by Nelson [11] found that housewives having a high degree of ecological concern had a lower degree of alienation, which was inconsistent with the findings of Anderson, Henion, and Cox on alienation. Thus, there is some empirical basis for the view that ecologically concerned shoppers would have above average interest and involvement with the welfare of their community and its institutions.

In the Stone shopper typology, the two categories of ethical and personalizing consumers have an orientation that indicates a high degree of involvement with community retailing institutions. Ethical shoppers expressed a desire to keep a balance in the mix of community stores, by "helping the little guy out" in his competition with the larger chain stores. Personalizing shoppers formed a strong relationship with the stores they shopped, based on the clerks in the stores. Both types demonstrated a greater involvement with their respective business communities than the economic shoppers (who sought to maximize product value) and apathetic shoppers (who sought to minimize expenditure of effort in purchasing goods). Thus ethical and personalizing shoppers would be expected to be more concerned about ecological problems such as pollution and litter that would lower the living quality of their communities than would economic or apathetic shoppers, who might put lower price ahead of environmental welfare or simply not have strong feelings about the effect of their own consumption on the environment.

The final objective of the present study was to determine if a significant relationship existed between shoppers' race and their ecological concern. A previous study reported by Henion [8] found that the ecologically concerned consumer is more likely to be of above average education and socioeconomic status, but little research on the effect of shopper race on ecological concern or intention to purchase ecologically "safe" products has been reported.

The consensus of a number of published studies on black consumers [3,6,13] is that blacks in America are increasingly developing values similar to those of middle class white consumers. Thus, it was postulated that there would be no significant difference in the level of ecological concern between black shoppers and white shoppers.

## HYPOTHESIS

In accordance with the previous cited research on shopper orientation, attitudes of ecological concern, and race, three research hypotheses were developed.

$H_1$: Black shoppers will be of a predominantly ethical orientation, while the majority of white shoppers will be of an economic or personalizing orientation.

$H_2$: Shoppers of an ethical or personalizing orientation will express a significantly higher degree of ecological concern than shoppers of an economic or apathetic orientation.

$H_3$: There will be no significant difference in the degree of ecological concern expressed by black shoppers and white shoppers.

## METHOD

A structured questionnaire was developed containing items for the measurement of ecological concern and shopper orientation. Attitudes concerning ecology and the purchase of ecologically desirable products were collected on five-point Likert-type scales. Items were coded one through five respectively for the responses strongly agree, agree, undecided, disagree, and strongly disagree. Three attitude measures covered in the six ecological items included concern about pollution, placement of government controls on polluting products, and use of peer influence against polluting products. Also included were questions on the purchase intentions for each of three ecologically desirable products. The three product purchase questions were based on an exploratory study of 20 middle-class housewives. Each of the house wives was asked to write a description of a housewife whom she felt "had a high level of concern about ecology and the environment," stating what products the concerned housewife would buy or avoid buying. The resulting descriptions were then content analyzed, and the three most frequently mentioned products were included in the present study. The three items dealing with general pollution were selected from an instrument developed by Kinnear and Taylor for measurement of ecological concern [9].

In order to develop an overall index of ecological concern, each item was scored in a Likert manner, and hence the sum of the numbers associated with an individual's response on the items comprising the scale constituted the respondent's final score. Items were coded such that a low total score represented a high degree of ecological concern.

The item for classification of respondents' shopping orientation was developed from the descriptions contained in the original Stone study [15] and the shopper orientation scales of Darden and Reynolds [5]. Each respondent was asked to pick one of four shopper descriptions which best fit the way she shopped, see Appendix.

A total sample of 115 female shoppers were interviewed in the central business district and major suburban shopping center in Paducah, a city of 50,000 population located in western Kentucky. The city is of a racially segregated type, having a black population of 23 percent and similar to many cities of like size in the United States. The social demography of the city has produced a forced form of integration at the retail level, in that the city lacks a clearly defined ghetto area where black stores service black customers. Interviews were approximately equally divided between the central business district area and the suburban shopping center, and among black and white shoppers. Two interviewers, one black and the other white, were instructed to divide their interviews equally between the two retail sites, and between black and white shoppers. A variety of store locations at each site were sampled, and prior to each interview a coin was flipped to randomize selection of individual shoppers exiting from the stores. Subsequent sample tabulations indicate that the incomes of white and black respondents were fairly closely matched.

In order to remove as much measurement error as possible from the index of ecological concern, the six ecology items were subjected to an analysis for internal consistency using the data secured from the 115 respondent sample. Cronbach's alpha coefficient, a measure of reliability based on the internal consistency of the test items, was calculated for various combinations of scale items in the manner suggested by Nunnally [12]. Individual items were added or subtracted until the level of .62 was reached for Cronbach's alpha. Nunnally recommends an alpha coefficient in the range of .50 to .80 as sufficient for basic research. The resultant four item index was then computed for each of the sample respondents.

## RESULTS

Table 1 shows the consumer type distribution for respondents in Chicago, Paducah, and Tulsa with shopper race also shown for the latter two cities. Comparison of the consumer types in the Paducah study indicate a greater similarity in shopper orientation across race than was hypothesized, with the differences not statistically significant. The largest proportion of black shoppers in the present study were of an economic orientation (37.9%) in contrast to the Tulsa study, where the black consumers were predominately of an ethical orientation (41.2%). A much larger proportion of the Paducah black shoppers were of the personalizing type (19.0%) than was true of the Tulsa black consumers (6.1%). A possible explanation for these differences lies in the high degree of shopper integration of the Paducah area, and the absence of a concentration of black owned neighborhood retail stores characteristic of the Tulsa area. Boone and Johnson reported that the moral

TABLE 1

COMPARATIVE DISTRIBUTION OF SHOPPER TYPES IN THREE CITIES

| Consumer Type | Chicago Stone Study (n=124) | Paducah[a] Black Shoppers (n=58) | Paducah[a] White Shoppers (n=57) | Tulsa[b] Black Shoppers (n=136) | Tulsa[b] White Shoppers (n=147) |
|---|---|---|---|---|---|
| Economic | 33.1% | 37.9% | 22.8% | 29.4% | 35.4% |
| Personalizing | 28.2% | 19.0% | 24.6% | 5.1% | 36.7% |
| Ethical | 17.8% | 24.1% | 28.1% | 41.2% | 6.1% |
| Apathetic | 16.9% | 19.0% | 24.6% | 24.3% | 21.8% |
| Indeterminate | 4.0% | --- | --- | --- | --- |
| Total | 100.0% | 100.0% | 100.0% | 100.0% | 100.0% |

351

TABLE 1 (Continued)

$$a_{\chi2} = 3.59, \text{ d.f.} = 3, p = .31.$$
b Boone and Johnson Study

obligations among black shoppers to shop black owned neighborhood stores were "apparently extremely strong" [4]. Lacking an identifiable group of black owned and operated stores, Paducah blacks apparently failed to develop the strong ethical orientation characteristic of the Tulsa blacks, but a relatively large proportion did develop a personalizing orientation to the white owned Paducah stores, which do employ a visible percentage of black clerks. A smaller proportion (22.8%) of Paducah shoppers were classified as economic than in either the Stone study (33.1%) or the Tulsa study (35.3%). The largest proportions of Paducah white shoppers (28.1%) were classified as ethical, a greater proportion than was found in the Stone (17.8%) or Tulsa (6.1%) studies. White shoppers in a smaller city like Paducah may be less "chain-oriented" than white shoppers of large urban areas, where the number and range of large chain outlets is greater.

Shopper Orientation and Ecological Concern

The mean scores on the index of ecological concern are shown for the combined ethical and personalizing shoppers in comparison to the combined economic and apathetic shopper group in Table 2. It was expected from Hypothesis 2 that the ethical/personalizing group would have a significantly lower score on the index than shoppers in the economic/apathetic group, and the results support this hypothesis.

TABLE 2

COMPARISON OF ECOLOGICAL CONCERN
SCORES OF ETHICAL/PERSONALIZING SHOPPERS
VERSUS ECONOMIC/APATHETIC SHOPPERS

| | Ethical and Personalizing Shoppers (n=52) | Economic and Apathetic Shoppers (n=63) | T Value |
|---|---|---|---|
| Ecological Concern Index Score[b] | 9.17 | 10.87 | -3.02[a] |

a p = .002, one tail test
b Actual Score range = 4 (high concern) to 15 (low concern).

In order to better understand the underlying reasons for the difference in ecological concern between the two aggregated shopper groups, mean scores were computed for each of the individual test items, which are shown in Table 3.

Both groups of aggregated shoppers agreed with the statement that pollution was a problem in America, indicating a fairly general awareness of the problem among all the shopper groups. However the aggregated groups differed in their attitudes towards the use of government regulation and peer pressure to help reduce pollution. The ethical/personalizing group was more strongly in favor of both government and individual action (urging friends not to use polluting products) than the economic and apathetic shopper group. And the ethical/personalizing shoppers also

expressed stronger intentions to purchase low phosphate detergent.

TABLE 3

MEAN ITEM SCORES OF ETHICAL/PERSONALIZING
SHOPPERS VERSUS ECONOMIC/APATHETIC SHOPPERS

| Item | Ethical and Personalizing Shoppers (n=52) | Economic and Apathetic Shoppers (n=63) |
|---|---|---|
| 1. Pollution is a problem in America today. | 1.98 | 2.02 |
| 2. The Government should force all products that pollute off the market | 2.29 | 2.74 |
| 3. I think that a person should urge her friends not to use products that pollute. | 2.29 | 2.73 |
| 4. I would buy a low phosphate detergent that doesn't pollute, even if it made my laundry less white or bright. | 2.62 | 3.38 |

Scale ratings: 1 = strongly agree, 2 = agree, 3 = undecide 4 = disagree, 5 = strongly disagree.

Shopper Race and Ecological Concern

The mean scores on the ecological concern index for white shoppers in comparison to black shoppers is shown in Table 4. Based on Hypothesis 3, no significant difference would be expected, however the findings show that white shoppers expressed a significantly higher ecological concern on the average than did black shoppers.

TABLE 4

COMPARISON OF INDEX OF ECOLOGICAL CONCERN
SCORES OF BLACK SHOPPERS TO WHITE SHOPPERS

| | Black Shoppers (n=58) | White Shoppers (n=57) | T Value |
|---|---|---|---|
| Ecological Concern Index Score[b] | 9.24 | 10.95 | -3.09[a] |

a p = .003, two tail test
b Actual score range = 4 (high concern) to 15 (low concern

A comparison of score differences by race on each of the four test items is shown in Table 5.

## TABLE 5

### MEAN ITEM CONCERN SCORES OF BLACK SHOPPERS IN COMPARISON TO WHITE SHOPPERS

| Item | Black Shoppers (n=58) | White Shoppers (n=57) |
|------|------|------|
| 1. Pollution is a problem in America today. | 2.35 | 1.65 |
| 2. The Government should force all products that pollute off the market. | 2.53 | 2.54 |
| 3. I think that a person should urge her friends not to use products that pollute. | 2.62 | 2.44 |
| 4. I would buy a low phosphate detergent that doesn't pollute, even if it made my laundry less white or bright. | 3.45 | 2.61 |

Scale ratings:  1 = strongly agree, 2 = agree,
3 = undecided, 4 = disagree,
5 = strongly disagree.

White shoppers expressed stronger agreement than did black shoppers with the statement that pollution is a problem in America. Both shopper groups agreed about equally that the government should take action against polluting products, and that individuals should urge friends to avoid use of polluting products. White shoppers did express greater agreement with the use of low phosphate detergents than black shoppers. Perhaps black housewives in the sample were not convinced that the gains in pollution abatement are worth the potential loss in laundry whiteness.

## DISCUSSION

This study attempted to replicate and extend the findings of two earlier studies on shopper orientation by Stone [15] and Boone and Johnson [4]. The Boone and Johnson study findings suggested that some shifts had occurred in the relative proportions of shoppers belonging to each of the four categories in the two decades since the original Stone study was performed. The Boone and Johnson study also suggested that in urban areas of multi-racial composition, black shoppers will most frequently develop an ethical orientation, while the majority of white shoppers adopt either an economic or a personalizing orientation. The present study findings suggest that in small size cities of multi-racial composition, white and black shoppers will tend to have less pronounced differences in their shopping orientations. The urban area of the present study has a population of approximately 50,000 and has not developed clusters of black owned and operated neighborhood stores, with result that blacks and whites alike shop the central business district stores and the suburban stores. These conditions have been less condusive to a development of the strong ethical orientation which characterized the largest portion of black shoppers in the Tulsa study. Additionally, the present study included a wider socio-economic range of shoppers than the Tulsa study, which was restricted to middleclass neighborhoods. The present findings suggest that inclusion of a balanced but broader range of shoppers tends to diminish the differences in white versus black orientations that characterize the middle class segment. The variances in all three studies suggest that the relative proportions of shopper membership in the Stone typology vary from city to city, dependent on such factors as city size and retail structure. This would be a productive area for further research.

The findings with respect to shopper orientation and ecological concern indicate that while all shoppers in the Stone typology share a degree of concern about pollution, their willingness to purchase ecologically desirable products varies according to their orientation. Shoppers having a high degree of identification with the stores in their community (ethical and personalizing orientations) were more willing to purchase low phosphate detergents and urge their friends to avoid products that pollute. This suggests that manufacturers of ecologically safe products should not overlook the importance of smaller retailers and retailers who emphasize the maintenance of personal customer service, in their channel strategy. Such products may gain faster acceptance through these types of outlets.

The findings on the relationship between shopper race and ecological concern suggest that white shoppers felt a greater concern for ecology although both races agreed with the desirability of both government and individual actions to reduce pollution. Additional research is needed to determine if this finding holds true for other geographic areas. The lower purchase intention for low phosphate detergent among black shoppers suggests that manufacturers of low phosphate detergents may encounter greater buyer resistance from the black shopper segment. Extra promotional effort explaining the merits of low phosphate detergent and directed through black oriented media may be necessary to fully develop the sales potential of this segment.

## APPENDIX

### Definition of the Shopper Orientation Measures

On the questionnaire respondents were asked to pick one of the following statements which best fit their shopping philosophy.

1. I make it a point to shop with local merchants because it is good for the community. (This response denoted the Ethical category.)

2. All stores are about the same, it makes very little difference where you shop. (This response denoted the Apathetic category.)

3. I always shop the stores where prices are lowest. (This response denoted the Economic category.)

4. I always shop the stores where the clerks are friendly and try to get to know you. (This response denoted the Personalizing category.)

REFERENCES

1.  Anderson, W. Thomas, Jr. and Cunningham, William H.,
    "The Socially Conscious Consumer", Journal of
    Marketing (July, 1972), 23-31.

2.  Anderson, W. Thomas, Jr. Henion, Karl E., and Cox,
    Eli P., "Socially vs. Ecologically Responsible
    Consumers", Curhan, Ronald C. (ed.) American
    Marketing Association Combined Conference
    Proceedings (Spring & Fall 1974), 304-311.

3.  Bauer, Raymond A., Cunningham, Scott M., and Wortzel,
    Lawrence H., "The Marketing Dilemma of Negros",
    Journal of Marketing (July, 1965), 1-6.

4.  Boone, Louis E. and Johnson, James C., "Purchase
    Orientations of the Black Shopper," E. M. Mazze
    (ed.), Marketing in Turbulent Times and Marketing:
    The Challenges and the Opportunities, Combined
    Proceedings of the American Marketing Association
    (1975), 250-252.

5.  Darden, William R. and Reynolds, Fred D., "Shopping
    Orientations and Product Usage Rates," Journal of
    Marketing Research (November, 1971), 505-508.

6.  Duker, Jacob M., "Value Orientations of Middle-Class
    Blacks," American Marketing Association Combined
    Conference Proceedings (1972), 429-433.

7.  Engel, James F., Kollat, David T., and Blackwell,
    Roger D., Consumer Behavior (New York:  Holt,
    Rinehart & Winston, 1973), 458-461.

8.  Henion, Karl E., Ecological Marketing (Columbus:
    Grid, 1976), 35.

9.  Kinnear, Thomas C. and Taylor, James R., "The Effect
    of Ecological Concern on Brand Perceptions,"
    Journal of Marketing Research (May, 1973), 191-197.

10. McNeal, James U., An Introduction to Consumer Behavior
    (New York:  John Wiley & Sons, 1973), 57-58.

11. Nelson, James E., "An Empirical Investigation of the
    Nature and Incidence of Ecologically Responsible
    Consumption of Housewives," (Unpublished Doctoral
    Dissertation, University of Minnesota, 1974).

12. Nunnally, Jum C., Psychometric Theory (New York:
    McGraw Hill, 1967), 192-235.

13. Pettigrew, Thomas F., A Profile of the American Negro
    (Princeton:  D. Van Nostrand Co., 1964), Chapters
    1 and 2.

14. Robertson, Thomas S., Consumer Behavior (Glenview,
    Ill.:  Scott Foresman & Co., 1970), 106.

15. Stone, Gregory P., "Sociological Aspects of Consumer
    Purchasing in Northwest Side Chicago Community,"
    (Master's Thesis, University of Chicago, 1952).

INFORMATION IN THE MARKET PLACE:  A BEHAVIORAL
VIEW OF CAVEAT VENDITOR VERSUS CAVEAT EMPTOR

M. D. Bernacchi, University of Detroit
Ken Kono, University of Detroit

## ABSTRACT

Marketplace protection has long been a focus of attention
between business and industry interests on the one hand
and consuming interests on the other hand.  The normative
balance of power has dramatically shifted from caveat
emptor to caveat venditor in recent years.  This paper considers the goal of equilibrium between these interests as
a product of positive marketplace interactions.

## INTRODUCTION

This paper focuses on some of the many aspects of information theory and their marketplace application to the
consumer.  It stresses that marketplace liabilities be
based upon a realistic balancing of caveat emptor with
caveat venditor using behavioral data as opposed to accepting the legal perception which assumes a power struggle
between these two public policies.  These data should consider the information search process, and quantity and
quality, on usage of marketplace information.  The pivotal
position of information in this balancing process has
never been better captured than by Tibor Scitovsky when he
offered that:
> ...the buyer's information as cause and the market's
> organization as effect...the market's perfection
> depends on the buyer's expertness.  For it is only
> the expert buyer who insists on comparing rival
> products before every purchase (the economic man
> standard); and it is only his insistence on making
> comparisons that forces the seller-or rather makes
> it profitable for him-to make this product easily
> comparable to competing products. [16]

In essence there should be an equilibrium between the marketers' efforts to provide market information and the consumers' use of the information.  The sweeping cross-current
of the recent consumerism movement, however, has focused
our attention on seller-product liability based upon tenets
of protecting the consumers from seller error, while all
but totally neglecting the protection of the seller from
consumer error.  More specifically, recent product liability case law has held the manufacture and/or seller liable
either based on his marketplace pronunciations or the lack
of them.  On the other hand, the law has all but ignored
how and to what extent consumers should volitionally seek
and use such market information.

## MARKET INFORMATION IN ECONOMICS AND LAW

Any inquiry into information must confront both traditional economic theory and legal analysis at the outset.
Traditional economic theory has generally stated that information in the marketplace is sought, accessible, cost-
less, complete, usable and used. [1, 11, 14, 19, 21]  In
that competitive ideal, the consumer is assumed to be
"economic man" seeking information for a "rational" selection between purchase alternatives. [11, 19]

Behavioral research indicates that the extensive problem
solving behavior supposedly exhibited by the economic man
is not the typical consumer response with the actual range
of behavior varying greatly among potential consumers.
There are substantial data that consumers respond

differently to differing products, some which are more
amenable to problem solving behavior and some which are
not. [20]

Traditional legal analysis has generally ignored the economists' unrealistic assumption and adopted its own.  That
is, legal analysis has assumed that it is able to weigh
the quality and quantity of information by its own infinite
conventional wisdom, parceling out liability where it has
assumed an inequality of bargaining power. [17]  This, of
course, implicitly recognizes the unequal information
status of the various marketplace participants accepting
the buyer's informational disadvantage and the sellers
relatively superior possession of marketplace information.
This same conventional wisdom posits that a consumer's
defective purchase is a direct consequence of inadequate
information.

The law has committed errors of commission and omission in
its treatment of information.  It has neither omissively
ignored the issue of information completely or commissive-
ly made some very determinative assumptions concerning the
existence of information or the lack of it rarely ever
seeking behavioral substantiation. [10]

A very good example of the law's omissive treatment of information occurs every time a legislative and/or judicial
decision is founded on the "unequal" "bargaining power" or
"basis of the bargain" rationale [17] rather than pursuing
a determination of ordinary marketplace expectations,
product performances, and frustrations.  Despite the
seriousness of the law's errors of omission, it must be
admitted that commissive errors are potentially more
dangerous because they may well become generally accepted
tenets.  This danger is very well exemplified by Karl
Llewellyn's empathetic belief that the consumer "takes
what he gets, because he does not know enough technically
to test even what it is before his eyes." [12]  Llewellyn's
statement is the type of generalization which has encar-
cerated the legal profession's active pursuit of behavioral
reality.  Where not ignored, the consumer's assumed information disadvantage is a theme which has been adopted by
various legal scholars.

This assumed information disadvantage must increasingly be
viewed as suspect where there are 1) a variety of purchase
stimulants or information available to the consumer ranging from implied to express warranties and 2) a well known
variety of likely negative consumer effects ranging from
mild consumer dissatisfaction to serious consumer injury
induced by purchase misinformation being anticipated.  The
point is that consumers have an information base at the
time of mild dissatisfaction or serious injury which demands investigation and determination rather than the law's
authoritarian assumptions.

## BEHAVIORAL EMPIRICISM ON MARKET INFORMATION

It is quite clear that market information as reflected in
either economics or law does not reflect marketplace
reality.  A number of empirical studies has consistently
documented this point.  For consumers are neither really
"rational" decision-makers in the "economic man" sense nor

possess perfect knowledge of the marketplace. At the same time, consumers are not always disadvantaged in their access to and use of market information as the law seems to maintain. For example, consumers may freely exercise their rights 1) to screen out the information, no matter how informative it may be from either buyers' or sellers' view points, and 2) may either fail to use or even misuse information, in some cases. In effect, it can truly be stated that these consumers have assumed the risk of their ill-informed purchase.

It must, therefore, be realized that the disturbingly low use of market information on the part of consumers should not unilaterally be interpreted as further evidence of their "unequal bargaining" position. Many consumers even opt for under-utilizing available information because of their lethargy or perceived marginal cost/benefit relationship of the additional market information to them. [12a, p. 510; 25, p. 50-52] Furthermore, it has even been suggested that there may be finite limits to the availability of consumers to assimilate and process information during any given unit of time, and that once these limits are surpassed, behavior tends to become confused and dysfunctional. [9] While this latter point has been rebutted [22, 26] it nonetheless sheds further light on information processing by consumers. Human information processing appears to be neither infinite nor automatic.

## IRRESPONSIBLE CONSUMPTION

Implicit in much of the discussion concerning information and the consumer is the concept of responsible consumption. The nexus between consumer information and responsible consumption is, of course, the duty (both legal and moral) which the consumer has on the one hand to discover information and on the other hand to use that information reasonably and responsibly in his/her consumption.

There are two basic types of irresponsible consumption, ignorant and dishonest. The data concerning information seeking behavior and usage suggests that the majority of consumers are not only ignorant but almost blissfully accept their ignorance. [2, 3, 4, 5, 6, 23, 25] The evidence to this time, however, is incomplete for there has been, for example, virtually no attempt to discover what percentage of consumers are either ignorant by their choice or by the choice of the message sender having made the message unpalatable. This information is critical for all those concerned with consumer protection since the very basic foundation of consumer protection could well change if the data indicated a definitely recognized (if not totally patent) volitional desire on the part of the consumer to be a "risk consumer."

For products' liability more specifically, the consequence could well be a rebalancing of liability and risks between the producer and/or seller, and the consumer. That is, liability and risks would be reallocated between the producer and consumer to better display marketplace realities. This reallocation process would result in a behaviorally based relationship between caveat emptor and caveat venditor shifting liability and risks away from the presently highly revered caveat venditor position more towards a caveat emptor philosophy.

In essence, the kind of question being asked, for example, is whether a consumer perceiving the likely need for external search would zealously guard his ignorance by either: 1) steadfastly refusing to leave his home in quest of useful consumption information without even so much as a pretense of making a "cost-benefit" analysis (to determine the worth of information seeking) or, 2) perhaps, just refusing to seek useful purchase-consumption information from a retail establishment when they should be held blameless as a matter of policy in a wide variety

of circumstances. [25] Needless to say the above is inapplicable if the information stored is both perfect as well as perfectly applicable.

Beyond the general issue whether a consumer who actively pursues ignorance should either be held to have assumed the risk or be held blameless there is the status of the consumer who misuses, or uses a product in an abnormal or unintended manner. [13, 24] While case law has generally shrouded these types of abhorrent consumption practices with a cloak of "foreseeability" [8] one must, nevertheless, recognize the patent opportunity for such abusive consumptive practices as well as their likely marketplace impact.

Irresponsible consumption may also take the form of dishonest consumption. According to Prof. Sabriskie [15] dishonest consumption is a continuum ranging from unrealistic expectations to provable fraud. From his study which analyzed consumer complaints, it was determined that slightly less than 23% of all consumer complaints had virtually no honest basis for recovery. That is, the consumers either made honest complaints based on a less than realistically honest assessment of the product's performance in view of their expectations or were guilty of dishonesty in a premeditated sense in that they lodged their complaints through a variety of fraudulent practices.

The dishonest consumer is of particular importance to any parsimonious treatment of products liability because he measurably affects the remedies available to honest consumers. That is:
1. He directly raises the costs of products to other consumers by forcing greater insurance coverage by the producer and/or the seller. Also, one must consider the costs the consumer incurs as a direct consequence of "consumerism" departments in most major firms and with the addition of the "hot line" [7] and similar programs;
2. He indirectly raises the costs of products with the continued proliferation and growth of consumer protection agencies at all government levels which are of course supported by taxpayer dollars with the consequence of fewer available personal disposable income or consumable dollars; and
3. He raises questions of legitimacy for all products liability claims by his very existence.

## MARKETING VIEW OF INFORMATION IN THE MARKETPLACE

Considering the behavioral reality discussed above with regard to consumers' perceptual use of market information, we must realistically measure the distance between the two extreme polar viewpoints of caveat venditor and caveat emptor. In other words, marketplace liability should encounter marketplace realities, rather than blindly accepting the age old tenet that sellers and legislators should produce (either by their own volition or by legislative fiat) an infinite quantity of marketplace information. Some of these marketplace realities are:
1. The existance of predictable and possibly alterable information seeking behavior and usage by the consumer;
2. The marketplace freedom of the consumer to "choose" to remain ignorant in the face of accessible information opportunities, and consumer products according to his own whims, an albeit unwise and/or nonrational choice, but nonetheless a free choice; and
3. That the seller, perhaps, rather than the buyer deserves "protection against incompetent or fraudulent buyers." [18]

Needless to say, further hard empirical and behavioral data are necessary on the consumers' use, misuse, and neglect of market information. It is believed, however, that it is due time to take a closer and more careful look at seller-product culpability in the light of consumer risk taking. This scrutiny will result in behaviorally based products liability relationships. That is, liability will no longer be determined by the highly revered public policy of caveat venditor, but it will be determined by a balancing of the polar policies of caveat venditor and caveat emptor based on behavioral realities rather than speculative assumptions.

In conclusion, it should be noted that the purpose of this paper has been a positive rather than a negative one. That is, the purpose of this paper has been one of forcing the recognition, acceptance and usage of positive marketplace considerations in conjunction with the normative ones of marketplace information, when determining the seller-buyer liability-protection relationship rather than one of upsetting the present liability-protection balance of the marketplace.

## REFERENCES

1. Boulding, K., The Image (1957).

2. Brandt, W. and Day, G., "Information Disclosure and Consumer Behavior: An Empirical Evaluation of Truth-in-Lending," 7 U. of Mich. J.L. Reform, 297, 1974.

3. _____, "Consumer Research and the Evaluation of Public Policy: The Case of Truth in Lending," J. of Consumer Research, June 1974, at 21-32.

4. Cunningham and Cunningham, "More Information or More Regulation?", J. of Marketing, Apr. 1976 at 63.

5. Day, G., "Assessing the Effects of Information Disclosurer Requirements," J. of Marketing, Apr. 1976 at 42-52.

6. _____, "Full Disclosure of Comparative Performance Information to Consumers: Problems and Prospects," J. of Contemporary Business, Jan. 1975 at 53-68.

7. Diamond and Ward, "Consumer Problems and Consumerism: Hot Line Analysis," J. of Marketing, Jan. 1976, at 58.

8. Green, "Foreseeability in Negligence Law," 61 Colum L. Rev. 1401 (1961).

9. Jacoby, J., Speller and Kohn, C., "Brand Choice Behavior as a Function of Information Load," Journal of Marketing Research (February 1974).

10. Jonescue v. Jewel Home Shopping Service, 16 Ill. App. 3d. 339, 306 N.F. 2d. 312 (1973).

11. Katona, G., "Rational Behavior and Economic Behavior," 60 Psychological Review 307 (1953).

12. Llewellyn, K. "On Warranty of Quality and Society: II," 37 Colum. L. Rev. 341 404 (1937).

12a. Markin, R., Consumer Behavior, Ronald Press, New York, New York (1974).

13. Noel, "Defective Products: Abnormal Use, Contributory Negligence and Acceptance of Risk, 25 Vanderbilt Law Review 93 (1972).

14. Posner, R., Economic Analysis of Law (1973).

15. Sabriskie, "Fraud by Consumers," J. of Retailing (Witer 1972, 1973) at 22.

16. Scitovsky, T., "Ignornace as a Source of Oligopoly Power," 40 American Economic Review 49 (1950).

17. Seely v. White Motor Company, 63 Cal. 2d. 403P 2d 145, 45 Cal Rptr. 17 (1965).

18. Shapo, "A Representative Theory of Consumer Protection," 60 Va. L. Rev. 1109, 1304 (1975).

19. Simon, H. and Sterdy, A., "Psychology of Economics," The Handbook of Social Psychology 269-283 (G. Lindzey & E. Aronson eds. 1969).

20. Stanton, W., Fundamentals of Marketing 1971.

21. Stigler, G., "The Economics of Information," The Journal of Political Economy (June 1961).

22. Summers, John O., "Less Information is Better?" Journal of Marketing Research Vol. 11 (November 1974) 467-68.

23. Thorelli, Hans, H. Becker and J. Engledow, The Information Seekers, (1975).

24. Trombette, W. and T. Wilson, "Forecastability of Misuse and Abnormal Use of Products by the Consumer," Journal of Marketing Vol. 39 (July 1975) 48-55.

25. Udell, J., "Prepurchase Behavior of Buyers of Small Appliances," Journal of Marketing, October 1966.

26. Wilke, William L., "Analysis of Effects of Information Load", Journal of Marketing Research, Vol. 11 (November 1974) 462-466.

INFORMATION CONTENT IN TELEVISION ADVERTISING:
A FURTHER ANALYSIS

Bruce L. Stern, Portland State University
Alan J. Resnik, Portland State University
Edward L. Grubb, Portland State University

## ABSTRACT

The content of 378 randomly-chosen network television advertisements was analyzed to determine if they communicated
useful informational cues. Less than one-half of the sampled advertisements were judged as informative. Statistical
analysis of the data indicated that the informativeness of
ads varied significantly by broadcast times, classifications
of products, and stage in their product and brand life
cycles.

## INTRODUCTION

Fifteen years ago in a speech before the House of Representatives, John F. Kennedy outlined what has come to be known
as the Consumer Bill of Rights, the second article of which
is: The right to be informed - to be protected against
fraudulent, deceitful, or grossly misleading information,
advertising, labeling, or other practices, and to be given
the facts he needs to make an informed choice [4].

Advertising, with 30 billion dollars in expenditures, is
obviously a major force in providing consumer information.
However, many social critics and advertising practitioners
differ in their views of the extent to which advertising
provides useful information for consumer decision making
[1]. It is interesting to note that despite the controversy
about whether advertising is informative, 87% of U.S. businessmen surveyed believed that advertising should provide
sufficient information for making logical buying decisions
[2, pg. 52]. Howard and Hulbert state: "Despite the dia-
tribes of social critics, advertising is a key means of
providing information to the consumer and helps in making
many shopping decisions. However, to the extent that advertising deviates from this role, its burden of criticism is
likely to grow." [3, pg. 33]. The controversy does continue
and remains almost totally unresolved.

Television advertising because of its vast integration into
our lives and its intrusive nature has become the center of
the dispute. The information content of television advertising or the lack of it, may have major public policy
implications. Robert Pitofsky, former FTC chairman believes
that non-informative advertising contradicts the economic
justifications for advertising and questions its "fundamental fairness" [6, pg. 39]. Thus, the role of information in advertising is an issue related to the very foundations of the free enterprise system.

Despite the profound implications of questions concerning
the information content of advertising, there is a dearth
of research evidence in the area. Howard and Hulbert
established six criteria of advertising's informational
adequacy: timeliness, intelligibility, relevance, truth-
fullness, completeness and proper segmentation. The authors
through reasoning only concluded that advertising was in
fact informative [3]. A recent study investigated the
question empirically through random selection of television
advertising. The results indicated that less than half of
the commercials communicated any useful information. Useful information was conceptualized as that which allows
the viewer to make a more intelligent choice between alternatives after viewing the commercial. This concept was
operationalized into fourteen specific criteria. Applying

these criteria the study also reported that advertising for
certain classes of products tended to be more informative [5].

Correlates of Information Content

The present study using these same criteria investigates
relationships between the information content of advertisements and the characteristics of the advertised product,
where the commercials were shown, and when they were shown.
The study attempts to determine whether the time block
during which a commercial is aired affects the likelihood
of its being informative or non-informative or if there are
any differences between the major networks. The advertised
products were classified by stage in their life cycle to
determine whether information content varied by these
stages.

## METHODOLOGY

An operational definition of useful information was constructed in order to investigate the aforementioned relationships. Fourteen criteria which a buyer might use in
his decision process were the basis for classifying each
commercial as informative or non-informative. Only one of
the informational cues presented in Table 1 needed to be
present for the commercial to be deemed informative.

### TABLE 1

CRITERIA FOR CLASSIFICATION
AS INFORMATIVE OR NON-INFORMATIVE

1. Price-Value

   -What does the product cost?
   -What is the need satisfaction capability/dollars?
   -What is its value retention capability?

2. Quality

   -Product characteristics which distinguish a particular
   product from competing products based upon an objective
   evaluation of workmanship, engineering, durability, excellence of materials, structural superiority, superiority of personnel, attention to detail, or special
   services?

3. Performance

   -What does the product do and how well does it do what
   it is designed to do in comparison to alternative
   purchases?

4. Components or Contents

   -What is the product composed of?
   -What ingredients does it contain?
   -What ancillary items are included with the product?

5. Availability

   -Where can the product be purchased?
   -When will the product be available for purchase?

## TABLE 1
### (continued)

6. Special Offers

   -What limited-time non-price deals are available with a
   particular purchase?

7. Taste

   -Is evidence presented that the taste of a particular
   product is perceived as superior in taste by a sample
   of potential customers?  (The opinion of the advertiser
   is inadequate.)

8. Nutrition

   -Are specific data given concerning the nutritional content of a particular product or is a direct specific
   comparison made with other products?

9. Packaging or Shape

   -What package is the product available in which makes it
   more desirable than alternatives?
   -What special shapes is the product available in?

10. Guarantees and Warranties

    -What post-purchase assurances accompany the product?

11. Safety

    -What safety features are available on a particular
    product compared to alternative choices?

12. Independent Research

    -Are results of research gathered by an "independent"
    research firm presented?

.13. Company Research

    -Are data gathered by a company to compare their product
    with a competitor's presented?

14. New Ideas

    -Is a totally new concept introduced during the commer-
    cial?
    -Are its advantages presented?

The contents of each advertisement, to which the criteria
was to be applied, was taken at "face value" with no attempt
made to evaluate the veracity of the commercial.

A multi-stage sampling procedure was used to randomly select
a good representation of commercials by time blocks for
weekdays and weekends and by the major networks. No advertisement was used more than once.

Two researchers reviewed each advertisement for information
content based upon the fourteen criteria that were established.  Each advertisement which was selected was color
video-taped and later played back in order to avoid rushed
evaluations.  The video-taping also allowed researchers to
replay advertisements where disagreements concerning classification occurred.  The following information was noted
about each commercial:  the network, time, day, brand name
and which, if any, of the information criteria were communicated.[1]

---

[1]For a more detailed explanation of the methodology
see [5, pg. 51].

## RESULTS

The previous study indicated that only 49.2% of the sampled
commercials were informative [5].  While this information
is of value, it is essential to determine where this informative advertising is more likely to be found.

Time of Day

Chi-square analysis of the information content of commercials by time of day (see Table 2), shows that statistically significant differences do occur beyond the .01 level.
Specifically, the proportion of advertisements broadcasted
in the evening are far more informative than those broadcasted during the morning or afternoon -- with the latter
showing a much higher proportion of non-informative advertisements.

### TABLE 2

#### NUMBER OF INFORMATIVE AND NON-INFORMATIVE
#### ADVERTISEMENTS BY TIME OF DAY

|  | Morning | Afternoon | Evening |
|---|---|---|---|
| Informative Advertisements | 58 | 52 | 76 |
| Non-informative Advertisements | 68 | 74 | 50 |

Chi-square equals 9.91, $p < .01$

Time of Week

When the previous time-of-day analysis is stratified by
weekday and weekend periods, more conclusive results
emerge (see Table 3).

### TABLE 3

#### NUMBER OF INFORMATIVE AND NON-INFORMATIVE
#### ADVERTISEMENTS OCCURRING BY WEEKDAY TIME PERIODS

| | WEEKDAY | | |
|---|---|---|---|
|  | Morning | Afternoon | Evening |
| Informative Advertisements | 36 | 21 | 38 |
| Non-informative Advertisements | 27 | 42 | 25 |

Chi-square equals 10.96, $p < .005$

Both weekday morning and evening viewing includes a higher
incidence of informative than non-informative commercials;
while during weekday afternoons the proportion of non-
informative advertisements is double that of informative
advertisements.

Analysis by weekend time stratifications, indicates a different pattern from that of the weekday (see Table 4).
The advertisements appearing during the weekend evenings
are as informative as weekday evening advertisements.
Weekend afternoon commercials are about equally split between the frequency of informative and non-informative
commercials compared to the heavy incidence of non-
informative commercials occurring during the same time
period during the weekday.  Weekend morning times contain
a higher proportion of non-informative commercial messages

compared to either the weekday morning time period or the weekend afternoon and evening viewing times.

TABLE 4

NUMBER OF INFORMATIVE AND NON-INFORMATIVE ADVERTISEMENTS OCCURRING BY WEEKEND TIME PERIODS

| | WEEKEND | | |
| | Morning | Afternoon | Evening |
|---|---|---|---|
| Informative Advertisements | 22 | 31 | 38 |
| Non-informative Advertisements | 41 | 32 | 25 |

Chi-square equals 8.18, p < .02

In visually comparing the differences in the informativeness of advertisements between weekday and weekend time periods, it appears that differences in audience composition influence the type of product and/or advertising content aired. For instance, in predominantly mixed adult viewing times (evenings) the advertisements are more informative; while during the weekend morning the audience shifts to predominantly children and the information value of commercials diminishes. During the weekday afternoon the audience composition is largely adult female and the numbers of commercials with positive information value is lowest for all time periods analyzed.

In addition to time placement, the category of product accounted for significant differences in the informativeness of commercials. The sampled commercials were grouped into six relatively homogeneous product classifications.

TABLE 5

NUMBER OF INFORMATIVE AND NON-INFORMATIVE ADVERTISEMENTS BY PRODUCT CLASSIFICATION

| | Food | Institutional | Personal Care Products |
|---|---|---|---|
| Informative Advertisements | 66 | 18 | 37 |
| Non-Informative Advertisements | 78 | 6 | 56 |

| | Laundry & Household Products | Hobbies, Toys, and Transportation | Other |
|---|---|---|---|
| Informative Advertisements | 24 | 20 | 21 |
| Non-Informative Advertisements | 28 | 9 | 15 |

Chi-square equals 16.27, p < .01

The results (reported in Table 5) indicate that advertisements for food, personal care, and laundry and household products were informative in fewer than 50% of the cases; while institutional, toys, hobbies and transportation, and "other" advertisements were informative in greater than 50% of the cases. These findings should be tempered by the

fact that the product categories which contained a higher proportion of informative commercials represented only 23.5% of the 378 sampled commercials.

Network Transmission

The number of informative advertisements communicated by the three major television networks (as presented in Table 6) was not statistically different. This occurrence not only supports the similarity between the networks' review board tolerances, but lends credibility to the true randomness of the study's sampling design and the reliability of the classification system.

TABLE 6

NUMBER OF INFORMATIVE AND NON-INFORMATIVE ADVERTISEMENTS APPEARING ON THE MAJOR TELEVISION NETWORKS

| | ABC | CBS | NBC |
|---|---|---|---|
| Informative Advertisements | 63 | 62 | 61 |
| Non-Informative Advertisements | 63 | 64 | 65 |

Chi-square equals .06, p < .97

Life Cycle

The authors classified the products and the brands of the commercials by the stages in their life cycle: introduction, growth, and maturity. Each product and brand was rated by the criteria of length of time on market, number of competing items, and uniqueness of brands or product attributes. It is recognized that, while these criteria and their application only allow for a limited approximation of the life cycle stage, they do provide a means for beginning analysis. Other commercials were not classified because of lack of data or because what is advertised in institutional or government commercials is difficult to fit into the life cycle concept.

The data in Table 7 represent the relationship between a product's life cycle stage and the informativeness of its television advertising. Commercials for products in the introductory stage tend to be more informative, while the opposite is true for products in the maturity stage.

TABLE 7

NUMBER OF INFORMATIVE AND NON-INFORMATIVE ADVERTISEMENTS BY STAGE IN THE PRODUCT LIFE CYCLE

| | LIFE CYCLE STAGES | | |
| | Introduction | Growth | Maturity |
|---|---|---|---|
| Informative Advertisements | 7 | 7 | 88 |
| Non-Informative Advertisements | 2 | 7 | 123 |

Chi-square equals 4.82, p < .10

These results imply that for newer products, informative advertising may be essential in order to educate the audience to the value of the unique offering; while for more mature products, information is of less importance.

The relationship between a brand's life cycle stage and the informativeness of its television advertising is very similar to the previously mentioned product life cycle results. As presented in Table 8, brands in the introductory stage of their life cycle are more likely to use informative advertising, while brands in the maturity stage are less likely to use informative advertising.

TABLE 8

NUMBER OF INFORMATIVE AND NON-INFORMATIVE ADVERTISEMENTS
BY STAGE IN THE BRAND LIFE CYCLE

LIFE CYCLE STAGES

| | Introduction | Growth | Maturity |
|---|---|---|---|
| Informative Advertisements | 15 | 11 | 75 |
| Non-Informative Advertisements | 8 | 13 | 106 |

Chi-square equals 4.70, p < .10

## SUMMARY AND CONCLUSIONS

It is apparent that significant differences do exist in the number of advertisements which contain factors that meet operational criteria of informativeness. During the evening there was more likely to be advertisements which contained information leading to a more informed choice. The opposite was true for weekday afternoons and weekend mornings. The advertisements for food, personal care, and laundry and household products were more likely to not contain information or use informational appeals. The brands and/or products in their development stages were more likely to be advertised in an informational manner, while for mature products advertising had a greater probability of not containing information. These results certainly will not quiet the critics of advertising and on the surface do provide further support for at least questioning the legitimacy of advertising as for seeking corrective action.

The results indicate that television commercials have room for improvement in providing useful information to consumers. It is possible that non-informative advertising might be an implicit admission that the product fails to fulfill any unique or relevant needs of the customer. It is also possible that the copywriter has overlooked potential advertising effectiveness by ignoring features and competitive advantages which the consumer can use in making an intelligent decision in the marketplace.

**If** a significant portion of advertising continues to be non-informative, a provocative question for advertisers is whether it will be effective in persuading an increasingly better educated, more aware, and sophisticated consumer. This problem may be more acute in inflationary times, as customers seek relevant product information that will allow them to purchase products that optimize economic returns.

From a more empirical view, this study raises a number of interesting and important questions which should be answered before more generalized conclusions are drawn.

A basic assumption is made that all decisions involve a process that must incorporate additional information and therefore each advertisement should provide this additional information. Yet from the standpoint of many consumers, this may not be true. They may not want or need new information. The time and risk factor may be such that the benefits of additional information may be less than the costs of getting new information; even if the cost is only watching

and absorbing the message of a 30 second commercial.

In many cases the consumer may only want to be made aware of something; which might only be the brand, the product, or the company. If this is so, then a major function of advertising is to revitalize awareness, which may require creativity but not additional information. Of course it may be equally interesting to investigate whether advertising as an institution has fostered a lack of reliance on information.

Therefore, research should be undertaken which questions the total importance of information from the standpoint of the consumer rather than totally accepting the normative view of the total importance of information in advertising.

Closely related is the question of what is relevant information to consumers. This study developed fourteen criteria, which from a marketing standpoint, should be most important. Yet from the standpoint of the consumer there may be other factors. The consumer may be more interested in what might be called "soft" criteria that more relate to enhanced self images. It may be useful to analyze non-informative advertisements with regard to these soft criteria in an attempt to learn their function.

If volume of sales, market share, and profit data were available for particular products, it would be important to compare the information content of their advertisements with these data. What relationships exist between information and these business measures of success? Theoretically the more informative advertisements should be associated with success, but if not, why are non-informative ads successful? Is the consumer wrong in his choice or do we marketing experts have some wrong views about the role and place of information in advertising. Or perhaps advertising is indeed the powerful manipulative force that critics claim. Additional research into the information content of advertising and the role of information in advertising may lead to important insights into these basic issues.

REFERENCES

1. Backman, Jules. "Is Advertising Wasteful?" Journal of Marketing, 32 (January 1968), 2-8.

2. Greyser, Stephan A. and Steven L. Diamond. "Business in Adapting to Consumerism," Harvard Business Review, 74 (September-October 1974), 38-58.

3. Howard, John A. and James Hulbert. "Advertising and the Public Interest," Journal of Advertising Research, 14 (December 1974), 33-39.

4. Kennedy, John F. Message to Congress, Document No. 364, House of Representatives 187th Congress, 2nd Session, March 15, 1962.

5. Resnik, Alan J. and Bruce L. Stern. "An Analysis of Information Content in Television Advertising," Journal of Marketing, 41 (January 1977), 50-53.

6. Wight, Robin. The Day the Pigs Refused to be Driven to Market. New York: Random House, 1972.

BANNING UNSAFE PRODUCTS:
A FRAMEWORK FOR POLICY ANALYSIS

Brian T. Ratchford, State University of New York at Buffalo

## ABSTRACT

Using an extension of Lancaster's economic model of consumer choice, this paper explores the desirability of an outright ban on relatively unsafe products vs. providing better information on safety hazards. A methodology for applying the model presented in this paper in simulating policy alternatives is also developed.

## INTRODUCTION

Under what circumstances should unsafe products be banned from the market? Perhaps no other public policy issue in marketing is more in need of a rational framework for analysis. Consumerists would argue that any product which poses a substantial safety hazard ought to be banned from the market no matter what its redeeming features. On the other hand, consumers themselves often appear to be indifferent to safety hazards, and to continue to buy products with known safety risks. An excellent current example of this conflict is the controversy over safety standards for power lawnmowers. Concerned over the high cost of injuries from mowers, influential consumerist groups such as Consumers' Union support rigorous safety standards even though these would probably double the minimum cost of a mower. Judging from their reaction, many individual consumers would prefer to pay the lower price and take their chances.

What should the policy maker do? Inspired by some recent work in economics by Colantoni, et al., [1] this paper presents a framework for analyzing the consumer's choice problem for a risky product under conditions of imperfect information. This framework is used to explore the feasibility of public policy alternatives, and to develop a market research approach to obtaining the information needed to make a wise policy decision. While the approach used in this paper is essentially that of [1], the numerical example and policy implications presented in this paper differ considerably from [1], and the suggested framework for empirical analysis presented here is, to my knowledge, new.

## A MODEL OF CONSUMER CHOICE
## WITH IMPERFECT INFORMATION

Suppose that consumers derive utility or satisfaction from the properties or characteristics which goods possess, rather than goods themselves. Given the view that consumers derive utility from characteristics, an economic model of consumer choice may be stated in Lancaster's [5] terminology as follows: A consumer maximizes an ordinal preference function for characteristics $U(Z)$, where $Z$ is a vector of characteristics $1, \ldots, r$, subject to the usual budget constraint $PX \leq K$, where $P$ is a vector of prices for each of these goods and $K$ is income. Goods, $X$, are transformed into characteristics, $Z$, through the relationship $Z = BX$, where $B$ is an $r \times n$ matrix which transforms the $n$ goods into $r$ characteristics. The model may therefore be written succinctly as:

$$\text{Maximize } U(Z) \quad (1)$$
$$\text{Subject to } PX \leq K$$
$$\text{With } Z = BX$$

In this model, goods, $X$, would refer to each brand available to the consumer: for example, each brand of lawnmower would constitute a separate good. While the original Lan-

caster model assumes that each good is available in a continuous range of units (for example, one could buy 1 1/2 lawnmowers), the model can easily be modified so that $X$ is restricted to feasible values, e.g., integer amounts of each brand [6]. The consumption technology $B$ describes how $X$ is transformed into the characteristics $Z$ which are the object of utility. While this technology is known objectively and the same for all consumers in Lancaster's original model, the model can be modified to allow each consumer to have a unique consumption technology, i.e., a unique way of defining the characteristics he purchases [1,4].

Given perfect information about the characteristics yielded by each good, as defined by the matrix $B$, the consumer would choose the quantities of $X$ that maximize $U(Z)$. But there are at least two reasons why consumers will ordinarily not have perfect information. First, consumers will rarely have access to all information about a product's salient characteristics. Second, there are limits on a consumer's ability to process information without error. Because of this the perceived consumption technology, $B^*$, will ordinarily differ from the actual consumption technology $B$. Instead of solving the problem in (1), the consumer actually solves:

$$\text{Maximize } U(Z^*) \quad (2)$$
$$\text{Subject to } PX \leq K$$
$$\text{With } Z = B^*X$$

Because of the imperfect information, a welfare loss $U(Z) - U(Z^*)$ occurs. A monetary measure of this loss could be obtained as the increment in income $\Delta K$, needed to purchase enough additional goods $\Delta X$ to make $U(Z^*) = U(Z)$. Given that people's perceptions were seriously distorted so that the monetary loss due to misinformation were large, public policy action might be required. This might either take the form of providing better information, or banning certain products which the policy maker knew to be a poor choice. Using the above framework, a numerical example illustrating the welfare implications of various options open to product safety regulation is presented in the following section.

## WELFARE CONSEQUENCES OF SAFETY REGULATION

Suppose that the product class being analyzed is lawnmowers, and that lawnmowers have two salient characteristics, safety ($z_1$), defined as the probability of noninjury, and grass cutting power ($z_2$). The consumer has three lawnmowers to choose from, all of which have equivalent grass cutting power. Mower 1 costs $50, and has a probability of noninjury of .8; Mower 2 costs $110 and has a probability of noninjury of .9; Mower 3 costs $100 and has a probability of noninjury of .95. To focus on lawnmowers, define all other goods as $y$ where units of $y$ are measured so that price per unit of $y$ is $1.[1]. Also, assume that only integer amounts of lawnmowers can be consumed, and that no consumer would buy more than one mower. Then any consumer's maximization problem could be stated as:

---

[1] This convention is commonly used by economists. For example, see [3,6].

Maximize: $U(z_1, z_2, z_3)$  (3)

Subject to: $\begin{bmatrix} z_1 \\ z_2 \\ z_3 \end{bmatrix} = \begin{bmatrix} .8 & .9 & .95 & 0 \\ 1 & 1 & 1 & 0 \\ 0 & 0 & 0 & 1 \end{bmatrix} \begin{bmatrix} x_1 \\ x_2 \\ x_3 \\ y \end{bmatrix}$

$50 x_1 + 110 x_2 + 100 x_3 + y \leq K$

$x_1 + x_2 + x_3 \leq 1$

$x_1, x_2, x_3 = 0$ or $1$

where each mower is assumed to generate one unit of grass-cutting power, and each y is assumed to generate one unit of characteristic $z_3$.

Since each mower performs equally well in grass cutting, that attribute is irrelevant for determining the choice between mowers, and the analysis can be limited to the trade-off between $z_1$ and $z_3$.[2] For consumers having incomes of $10,000, attainable amounts of the two attributes are plotted in Figure 1 as points $M_1$, $M_2$, $M_3$. Mower 2 (point $M_2$) is dominated by Mower 3 (point $M_3$), and no fully informed consumer would choose it regardless of his income. However, whether consumers would choose the risky mower ($M_1$) over the unsafe mower ($M_3$) is a matter of preference: consumers in group G1 with indifference curves $I_1$-$I_1$, $I_2$-$I_2$, etc., would choose the risky Mower 1; consumers in group G2 with indifference curves $J_1$-$J_1$, $J_2$-$J_2$, etc., would choose the safe Mower 2.[3] The decision is purely a personal one: if a consumer valued a .15 reduction in the probability of an injury more than an extra $50 expenditure on other goods, he would choose Mower 3 in the above example, otherwise he would choose Mower 1.

FIGURE 1

Tradeoff Between Safety
and Other Goods
Given Perfect Information

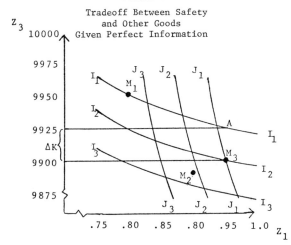

This leads to one important, but often overlooked, policy implication: because a ban on a risky product would inflict a welfare loss on those who would otherwise prefer it, bans on risky products are unwarranted if consumers

are fully informed **about** the risks.[4] In the above example for instance, because of a ban on Mower 1 would force consumers in group G1 to buy the less preferred Mower 3, the ban would force them from indifference curve $I_1$-$I_1$ to the less preferred $I_2$-$I_2$. Under the ban consumers could achieve their initial position only if they had an additional A-$M_3$ = $\Delta K$ dollars to spend on other goods; $\Delta K$ is therefore a measure of the welfare loss accruing to each member of group G1 resulting from the ban.

With respect to imperfect information, it is useful to distinguish between three cases, each of which have somewhat different implications for consumer welfare and public policy:

1. Consumers underestimate the safety risk of a brand which is actually dominated.
2. Consumers overestimate the relative safety of the most risky brand(s).
3. Consumers underestimate the relative safety of the most risky brand(s).

Each of these three cases is considered below using the numerical example outlined above.

Riskiness of a Dominated Brand is Underestimated

This section considers the case of a brand which perfectly informed consumers would consider to be dominated in all salient attributes. However, because they underestimate the safety risk associated with the brand, some consumers continue to buy it. In terms of the above example, suppose that the probability of noninjury arising from Mower 2 is perceived by all consumers to be 1.0, when it is actually .9.[5] Then the elements in the first row of the consumption technology matrix in equations 3 would be changed to: .8, 1, .95, 0. Consumers would then perceive the amounts of $Z_1$ and $Z_3$ attainable from the three mowers as points $M_1$, $\overline{M}_2$, $M_3$ in Figure 2, while the amounts really obtainable are given by points $M_1$, $M_2$, $M_3$. Because of this misperception, consumers in Group G2 would buy Mower 2 rather than Mower 3 since they would believe that Mower 2 would put them on indifference curve $J^*$-$J^*$. Their error in judgment, however,

FIGURE 2

Safety of Dominated
Brand Overestimated

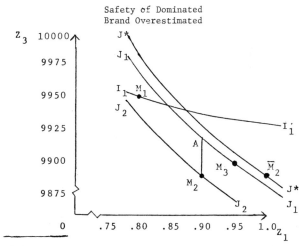

---

[2]The only reason for not allowing $z_2$ to vary between brands in the example is to allow a graphical analysis of the problem in two dimensions. Obviously, the analysis could proceed with any number of brands and attributes.

[3]Indifference curves represent alternative combinations of attributes which yield the same amount of utility. In this example, more of both attributes are preferred to less, and therefore indifference curve $I_1$-$I_1$ implies higher utility than $I_2$-$I_2$, etc.

[4]With the qualification that only safety hazards which accrue to individual consumers are being considered, and not harm to third parties.

[5]In the following examples it is assumed, for simplicity, that all consumers share the same distorted information B*. However, the essential conclusions drawn here extend to the more likely case in which the distorted perceptions are idiosyncratic.

would actually put them on indifference curve $J_2$-$J_2$ rather than $J_1$-$J_1$; by reasoning analogous to that presented above, they would each suffer a welfare loss of A-$M_2$.

One way to eliminate this distortion and to lead consumers to the correct choice, would be to ban the dominated brand. However, a ban would not be the only way to achieve the desired effect: disseminating information about the safety hazards of the brand, for example, could lead the manufacturer to lower its price in the face of the unfavorable publicity, thereby making it the best buy for some consumers. Moreover, if a ban could only be achieved by promulgating safety standards, certain desirable but less safe brands (such as Mower 1) would have to be eliminated as well.

### Relative Safety of the Most Risky Brand is Overestimated

The case in which unwary consumers unwittingly purchase a dangerous product because it appears to be a good buy seems to be the one which consumer advocates fear the most. This case is considered in this section. To illustrate, suppose that the perceived probability of noninjury arising from Mower 1 is .95, Mower 2 is .97, and Mower 3 is .98. Then the elements in the first row of the consumption technology matrix in Equations 3 would become: .95, .97, .98, 0, and the perceived amounts of $Z_1$ and $Z_3$ attainable from the three mowers would be given as points $\bar{M}_1$, $\bar{M}_2$, $\bar{M}_3$ in Figure 3. Because they underestimate its safety risk, consumers of type G2 would now perceive that Mower 1 would lead them to indifference curve J*-J*, and would therefore choose this cheaper brand. However, since Mower 1 would actually lead them to indifference $J_2$-$J_2$ rather than $J_1$-$J_1$, the misinformed choice would cause each of them to suffer a welfare loss of A-$M_1$.

FIGURE 3

Relative Safety of Risky Brand Overestimated

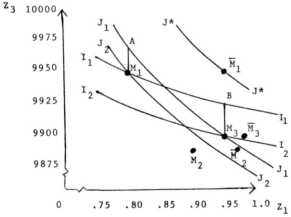

At the same time, however, consumers of type G1 would not suffer any welfare loss due to the misinformation since they would choose Mower 1 even if fully informed. On the other hand, if Mower 1 were banned in order to correct for the faulty decision of group G2 described in the preceeding paragraph, type G1 consumers would each suffer a welfare loss equal to B-$M_3$ in Figure 3 because they could no longer buy their most preferred brand. Thus a ban (or, equivalently, a safety standard which would remove Mower 1 from the market) would help one group, but harm the other. If there are $N_1$ consumers in group G1 and $N_2$ consumers in group G2, and if welfare levels of consumers could be compared, the ban would be socially beneficial if $N_2$(A-$M_1$) > $N_1$(B-$M_3$), where A-$M_1$ estimates the gain in Figure 3 to each consumer in G2 resulting from the ban, and B-$M_3$ measures the loss to each consumer in G1. On the other hand, policy makers could disseminate information to correct consumer

misperceptions sufficiently that they would make the same choice as under full information. If the cost of the information were less than the loss that would result to consumers of the banned product, this would be the best course.

### Relative Safety of the Most Risky Brand is Underestimated

In their goal to protect the unwary, consumerists often seem to overlook an important point: potential buyers may be just as likely to overestimate the safety hazard of a product as to underestimate it. A case in point is the common fear of flying among people who think nothing of car travel, even though commercial air travel is demonstrably safer than auto travel. As illustrated in Figure 4, underestimating the relative safety of the most risky brand can also lead to welfare losses. Suppose that the probability of noninjury from Mower 1 is estimated to be .7 rather than the actual .8, so that the first row of the consumption technology matrix in Equations 3 becomes: .7, .9, .95, 0. Then the perceived amounts of $Z_1$ and $Z_3$ attainable from the mowers is given in Figure 4 by the points $\bar{M}_1$, $M_2$, $M_3$. Consumers in group G1 would now shift to Mower 3 on perceived indifference curve $I_2$-$I_2$. A welfare loss of A-$M_3$ would result (the same loss that would result if Mower 1 were banned). The point is that misinformation can cause a consumer to purchase a less risky as well as a more risky product, with a consequent welfare loss.

FIGURE 4

Relative Safety of Risky Brand Underestimated

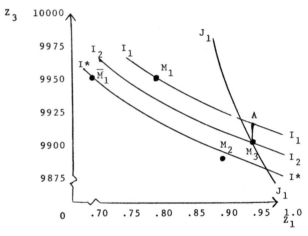

To summarize, banning risky products by promulgating safety standards, or by other means, is clearly a desirable course only if the unsafe brands are dominated in all of their attributes, including price. In other cases, a ban will result in a welfare loss to some consumers, and the questions to be asked are whether this loss exceeds the gain to other consumers who benefit from the ban, or whether this loss exceeds the gain to other consumers who benefit from the ban or whether better results could be obtained through the dissemination of safety information about the product.

### AN EMPIRICAL FRAMEWORK FOR PUBLIC POLICY RESEARCH ON PRODUCT SAFETY

The model presented in this paper not only provides a theoretical guide to policy decisions, but it also suggests how to apply rather standard market research techniques in providing input information for policy makers. Basically three things must be known in order to apply the model in practice: (1) each consumer's utility function, i.e., how he trades off between safety and other salient attributes; (2) an objective matrix B by which goods are transformed into characteristics; (3) the consumer's perceived matrix B* which provides his estimates of how goods are transformed into characteristics. In studying any product, these paramaters might be estimated on a representative sample and used to simulate alternative product safety policies.

As in the numerical illustration, parameters in the utility function are comprised of three types of attributes: safety of the product being studied, $Z_1$, possibly a vector of several safety attributes; a vector of non-safety attributes of the product, $Z_2$; a composite attribute representing all other goods. However, given an individual consumer's income, expenditures on other goods are directly proportional to $-m$ or $-1/m$, where $m$ is the expenditure on the product, under study. Therefore, in empirical work it is sufficient to estimate utility functions of the form $U(Z_1, Z_2, -m)$ or $U(Z_1, Z_2, 1/m)$ [6].

One approach to estimating either of these utility functions on a representative sample of individual consumers would be conjoint measurement [2], in which each consumer was given different scenarios of safety attributes, $Z_1$, other attributes, $Z_2$, and expenditure, $m$. Safety attributes might be defined in terms of "probability of an accident" for one or more accident categories, i.e., "probability of an accident leading to a minor injury," etc.

Another approach to estimating the utility function would be to use PREFMAP, [2] or some alternative algorithm, to establish the functional relation between preference rankings of actual brands of the product in question and values of $Z_1$, $Z_2$, $m$ for each of the brands. The latter values could be obtained from data on individual perceptions of the levels of $Z_1$, $Z_2$, $m$ for each brand. In estimating the transformation matrices B and B* for each subject, it would probably be reasonable to adopt a partial view and worry only about misperceptions of safety. Scores for each brand $i$ on non-safety attributes, $B_{2i}$, and on price, $p_i$, could therefore be the same for both matrices, and across all consumers. These scores could either be obtained from attribute ratings, objective data, or some combination. The safety component of the matrix B would be the actual safety record of each brand; the safety component of B* for each subject would be on his own perceptions of each brand's safety.

Given estimates of the utility function, and the matrices B and B*, the maximization problems described in Equations 1 and 2 would be solved for each consumer. If the problem were one in which the consumer makes one choice between several alternative brands as in Equations 3 (this formulation would be appropriate for most durable goods), solutions to the maximization problems could be found by simply computing U and U* for each successive brand. As in the numerical example, the welfare cost of a non-optimal choice could be estimated by comparing utility for the optimal choice, U*. This could be converted to monetary terms by computing the increment to income $\Delta K$, or alternatively the change in expenditure $\Delta M$ needed to make $U^* = U$.[6] This procedure would be followed for each subject (or each segment if subjects had been grouped into segments), and the welfare costs added across consumers to get an estimate of the aggregate welfare cost due to misinformation. While the numerical example presented above assumed a monotonically increasing utility function for expositional purposes, there is nothing in this computational procedure to preclude use of the more general utility functions employed in conjoint measurement or the ideal point version of PREFMAP.

Employing the same data on utility functions, B and B*, the welfare cost (gain) of alternative safety standard policies could then be estimated by removing brands affected by the policy, simulating choice, and estimating utility and welfare costs or gains as above. Similarly, if the impact of different information dissemination policies on the perceived consumption technology B could be determined, the same procedure could be used to compute the welfare cost (gain) from each policy. In this way, the theoretical framework outlined in this paper could be used to develop a method for simulating various policy alternatives.

## CONCLUSIONS

Using a version of Lancaster's demand model [5] modified to handle the problem of misinformation about safety by Colantoni, et al., [1] this study has explored the theoretical implications of misinformation about product safety for consumer welfare, and has developed a framework for the analysis of alternative policies toward product safety. The theoretical discussion suggested that bans on unsafe products promulgated through safety standards may be beneficial in relatively few instances. While such bans may have the beneficial effect of saving unwary consumers from safety hazards, they tend to create welfare losses at the same time by restricting the range of consumer choices. On the other hand, providing information does not have the disadvantage of restricting the range of consumer choice. This suggests that, in many cases, a policy of information dissemination will be superior to outright bans. Which policy is best, however, will depend on a complex set of circumstances. That is why attempts to apply the empirical approach outlined in the final section would appear to have great potential for improving public policy decisions in this area.

## REFERENCES

1. Colantoni, Claude S., Otto A. Davis and Malati Swaminuthan. "Imperfect Consumers and Welfare Comparisons of Policies Concerning Information and Regulation," Bell Journal of Economics, 7 (Autumn 1976), 602-15.

2. Green, Paul E. and Yoram Wind. Multiattribute Decisions in Marketing: A Measurement Approach. Hinsdale, Illinois: The Dryden Press, 1973.

3. Hicks, J.R. A Revision of Demand Theory. London: Oxford University Press, 1956.

4. Ironmonger, Duncan. New Commodities and Consumer Behavior. Cambridge, Massachusetts: University Press, 1972.

5. Lancaster, Kelvin. "A New Approach to Consumer Theory," Journal of Political Economy, 74 (April 1976), 132-57.

6. Rosen, Sherwin. "Hedonic Prices and Implicit Markets: Product Differentiation in Pure Competition," Journal of Political Economy, 82 (January/February 1974), 34-55.

---

[6] That is, a consumer could be brought to a utility level U* which is the same as U either by increasing his income $\Delta K$, or cutting the price of the product by an equivalent amount $\Delta M$.

STUDENT EVALUATIONS--A MEASURE OF
VALIDITY IN THE INTRODUCTORY MARKETING COURSE

Ronald B. Marks, University of Wisconsin-Oshkosh
J. Dale Molander, University of Wisconsin-Oshkosh

## ABSTRACT

In academe increasing attention is being given to the assessment of teaching effectiveness. Student evaluations are the most common method of measurement because of their assumed objectivity. Most evaluation instruments, however, have been developed with little effort at validation.

In this study, a measure of the extent of student learning was obtained in the introductory marketing course, and then related to student evaluations of the instructor and course. Using multiple regression, evaluation items were able to explain only 14% of the variance in amount learned. In contrast, the evaluation items were able to explain 54% of the variance in perceived teacher rank. This result raises questions about the ability of student evaluations to assess teaching effectiveness in marketing courses.

## INTRODUCTION

Teaching, research and service--these three words strike a common cord among university faculty, for they are the criteria for nearly all performance evaluations in higher education. While the criteria have remained constant over the years, the relative importance of each criterion and the manner in which they are measured have been in a state of ferment. This has been particularly true of teacher performance.

Traditionally, evaluation of classroom performance has been subjective. Colleagues and department chairpersons would make judgments from occasional student comments and the ability of a faculty member to attract students into his or her section. These judgments would be further "refined" by assumed relationships between teaching and such variables as research, committee performance, and the willingness of faculty to interact with students outside of the classroom.

In the late 1960's, formal student evaluations became a major input into the evaluation of teacher performance on many campuses [6, p. 59]. This influence has continued to expand through the 1970's [2, 5]. From an administrative point of view, student evaluations offer the advantage of specificity. A standard set of questions are used with responses tabulated on a rating scale thereby permitting direct quantitative comparisons across faculty. What is being measured by these scores, however, remains open to question.

### Problems Associated with Rating Forms

Over the years, considerable research has been undertaken to identify criteria associated with instructor ratings by students [5]. These studies in turn have led to the development of student rating forms that have received widespread attention. Among the better known forms are the Student Instructional Report (SIR) developed by the Educational Testing Service in conjunction with Northwestern University, the Student Instructional Rating System (SIRS) developed at Michigan State University and the Purdue rating scale for instructors [3, 8, 10]. While the factors isolated in existing forms vary, most would fit within the following framework.
1) Student-Instructor Interaction
2) Instructor Teaching Methods
3) Student Interest in Course
4) Challenge or Difficulty of Course
5) Enthusiasm or Expressiveness of the Instructor

These five factors were developed by factor analyzing a large number of questions posed to students regarding their assessment of instructors. A question of validity arises with this methodology. Do these rating criteria necessarily reflect the ability of the instructor to convey knowledge of his discipline to the student? Without relating these criteria to a concrete measure of the extent of student learning, there must remain a measure of doubt about what student evaluation forms are really assessing.

Moreover, some studies seem to indicate the importance of considerations not directly associated with instructor teaching ability. Some of these, in fact, are exclusively student characteristics and not at all associated with instructor effectiveness. Two issues are involved, then, in using student evaluations: 1) To what extent are student responses affected by variables unrelated to the instructors ability; and, 2) To what extent are student responses independent of student learning?

Factors unrelated to instructor ability. In recent years, considerable attention has been given to the question of the impact of grades, both actual and expected on evaluations. The results have consistently shown that a positive relationship does exist [1, 12]. This relationship is strongest where a disparity exists between the grade a student had initially expected and the grade actually received. Other factors that have been considered include a student's year in school, curriculum, sex, and grade-point average [7, 13].

Evaluations and student learning. The ultimate measure of a good teacher is his or her ability to enhance learning. An instructor who receives favorable student evaluations may or may not be effective as measured by student achievement.

The evidence to date on this relationship is mixed. In a well publicized study involving students in an undergraduate calculus class, comparisons were made between the amount learned by students based on solutions to problems and the performance of instructors as measured by student evaluations. Differences in initial ability were controlled. The correlation between these two variables was -.754 [11]. Other studies, however, show a positive correlation between test scores and student evaluation of teachers [4, 9].

The problem with many of the research studies into the validity of student evaluation of teachers is that student achievement has been measured on the basis of grades or on the basis of an examination at the end of the course. A more useful approach would be a pretest and posttest of all students in the course so that change data would be available for measuring student achievement.

## PURPOSE OF THIS STUDY

As with other academic departments, the assessment of teaching effectiveness is of critical concern to marketing faculty. Not only is assessment necessary for promotion and salary decisions, but it is important to measure student satisfaction with marketing faculty to maintain an adequate number of marketing majors. As student evaluations are commonly employed by marketing departments for these purposes, it appears critical to determine what these instruments are, in fact, measuring. Specifically, the research questions to be addressed in this study are:

1) Which student evaluation criteria are most predictive of the amount learned in the introductory marketing course? Are these criteria associated with instructor teaching ability, or with strictly student characteristics?

2) Which evaluation criteria are most predictive of student satisfaction with the instructor (i.e. overall teacher rank)?

3) Are these two sets of predictor criteria comparable?

## METHODOLOGY

Students enrolled in the introductory marketing course constituted the subjects for the study. The students were administered a test both at the beginning and end of the course. The test was composed of one hundred forty multiple choice and true-false questions that the researchers thought adequately reflected material covered in the introductory course. Primary emphasis was given to the behavioral objectives of knowledge and comprehension. To minimize differences in emphasis by individual instructors, the questions were restricted to material appearing in the text. Much of this material, of course, was also covered in class lectures, but no attempt was made to standardize lecture material among instructors. Differences in the score between the pre and posttest constituted the measure of the amount learned in the course.

The pre-post test approach is not without fault. The extent to which the course material is retained over time remains unknown. In addition, recall of knowledge is but one objective of learning. Changes in the way students think, feel and act toward marketing issues is of equal importance. Still, the pre-post test approach is preferable to the limited conclusiveness of grades or a solitary achievement test administered at the end of the course.

At the end of the course, students were asked to answer twenty-five questions concerning their evaluations of their instructor and course. These twenty-five items were selected as representative of the five factors enumerated earlier that appear in some of the more common rating forms [8, 10]. In addition, several factors unrelated to instructor effectiveness, such as student grade point average and expected course grade were included in the instrument. The items were administered in the form of a bipolar five point scale. Because of the research requirements, students were asked to provide their student identification numbers, but not their names on the forms. They were assured that the evaluations would not be used by the instructor in a punitive manner. Comparison with past evaluations where no identification was required appeared to indicate no bias. Useable forms from one hundred ninety-six students for three instructors of the introductory course made up the data for analysis.

## RESULTS

The initial analyses entailed stepwise regressions of two criterion variables--amount learned and overall perceived instructor rank--with the remaining items of the student evaluation as the predictor variables. Results of the regressions are shown in Tables 1 and 2. Iteration for the stepwise procedure continued until no further entering variables possessed coefficients significantly different from zero by the F-test at the .10 level of significance. In Tables 1 and 2, predictor variables are listed in order of contribution to $R^2$.

The regression of student evaluation criteria on the amount learned explained approximately 14% of variance. Of the five entering variables of Table 1, grade point average contributed most to variance explained, roughly half of the total. In order of contribution, the other four variables were: instructor friendliness to students, grade expectation, discussion of recent developments by the instructor, and preparation by the instructor.

TABLE 1
VARIANCE EXPLAINED AND COEFFICIENTS
FOR AMOUNT LEARNED

| PREDICTOR VARIABLES | CUMULATIVE $R^2$ | CHANGE IN $R^2$ | BETA COEFFICIENT |
|---|---|---|---|
| Grade Point Average | .074 | .074 | 0.260 |
| Instructor Friendliness Towards Students | .099 | .025 | 0.110 |
| Grade Received In Comparison With Expected Grade | .119 | .019 | 0.146 |
| Instructor Discussion Of Recent Developments | .131 | .012 | 0.102 |
| Instructor Was Well Prepared | .140 | .009 | 0.103 |

With teacher rank as the criterion variable (lower 25% to upper 10%), eight entering evaluation criteria explained approximately 54% of total variance. As indicated in Table 2, instructor enthusiasm, intellectual challenge of the course, how the instructor was liked as an individual, and possession of an interesting style of presentation contributed 46% towards $R^2$. Other significant but lesser contributing variables were course organization, instructor knowledge of student understanding, instructor preparation, and discussion of recent developments.

TABLE 2
VARIANCE EXPLAINED AND COEFFICIENTS
FOR TEACHER RANK

| PREDICTOR VARIABLES | CUMULATIVE $R^2$ | CHANGE IN $R^2$ | BETA COEFFICIENT |
|---|---|---|---|
| Instructor Enthusiasm | .226 | .226 | 0.105 |
| Intellectual Challenge Of Course | .341 | .115 | 0.262 |
| How Well The Instructor Was Liked As An Individual | .435 | .094 | 0.297 |
| Instructor Has An Interesting Style Of Presentation | .476 | .041 | 0.149 |
| Course Was Well Organized | .504 | .029 | 0.142 |
| Instructor Knowledge Of Student Understanding | .521 | .016 | 0.138 |
| Instructor Was Well Prepared | .535 | .013 | 0.151 |
| Instructor Discussion Of Recent Developments | .544 | .009 | -0.099 |

A question of comparability arises with these two sets of predictor variables. That is, to what extent will the best predictor set for amount learned (i.e. items of Table 1) explain teacher rank? Correspondingly, to what extent will the best predictor set for teacher rank (i.e. items of Table 2) explain amount learned? The results are shown respectively in Table 3. Making use of the forcing option of the computational routine (SPSS), Table 3 shows that the predictor variables for learning explain approximately 26% of variance if teacher rank is the dependent variable. Correspondingly, those variables that are most predictive of teacher rank explain only 5% of variance in the amount learned.

### TABLE 3
### VARIANCE EXPLAINED USING ALTERNATIVE PREDICTOR SETS

| PREDICTOR VARIABLES | TEACHER RANK USING SET FOR AMOUNT LEARNED | |
|---|---|---|
| | CUMULATIVE $R^2$ | CHANGE IN $R^2$ |
| Grade Point Average | .0004 | .0004 |
| Instructor Friendliness Towards Students | .0735 | .0726 |
| Grade Received In Comparison With Expected Grade | .1059 | .0329 |
| Instructor Discussion Of Recent Developments | .1064 | .0004 |
| Instructor Was Well Prepared | .2685 | .1621 |

| PREDICTOR VARIABLES | AMOUNT LEARNED USING SET FOR TEACHER RANK | |
|---|---|---|
| | CUMULATIVE $R^2$ | CHANGE IN $R^2$ |
| Instructor Enthusiasm | .0175 | .0175 |
| Intellectual Challenge Of Course | .0193 | .0018 |
| How Well The Instructor Was Liked As An Individual | .0206 | .0013 |
| Instructor Has An Interesting Style Of Presentation | .0226 | .0019 |
| Course Was Well Organized | .0342 | .0116 |
| Instructor Knowledge Of Student Understanding | .0362 | .0020 |
| Instructor Was Well Prepared | .0476 | .0114 |
| Instructor Discussion Of Recent Developments | .0502 | .0026 |

### DISCUSSION

While predictor variables explain much of the variance in instructor ratings, little or no success is experienced in predicting the amount learned. Of the five predictor variables that resulted in at least a 1% change in $R^2$, two of the variables could not be strictly associated with instructor effectiveness. These two variables, grade point average and grade received in comparison with expected grade accounted for 9.3% of $R^2$. The remaining 4.7% variance explained related to student-instructor interaction and instructor teaching methods.

The inability of the student rating scale to measure student learning is reinforced by the findings shown in

Table 3. When the best predictor set for teacher rank is applied to learning, only 5% of the variance is explained. None of the eight predictor variables used was able to explain even 2% of the variance.

With overall teacher rank as the dependent variable, a much greater proportion of variance is explained (54%). Three variables, instructor enthusiasm, how well the instructor is liked as an individual, and an interesting style of presentation account for approximately 36% of the variance. The personality of the instructor and his enthusiasm and expressiveness appear critical to student satisfaction with the instructor. By contrast, variables more closely associated with teaching ability--course organization, knowledge of student understanding, preparation, and discussion of recent developments--account for a little over 6% of explained variance. If one construes the intellectual challenge of the course as primarily a function of the instructor, then this total might be inflated to approximately 18%. In either instance, it would appear that satisfaction with the instructor in the introductory marketing course is primarily associated with "expressive" rather than substantive factors. This result would not be of great concern if these best predictors of teacher rank also predicted a large proportion of variance in the amount learned. However, as the lower portion of Table 3 indicates, such is not the case. If the best predictors of teacher rank are employed as predictors of amount learned, then only 5% of variance is explained.

### CONCLUSION

The findings of this study support the contention that teacher evaluations provide useful information about the level of student satisfaction with their instruction. As members of the marketing profession, we cannot discount the importance of "customer satisfaction." However, it is equally apparent that the measurement of instructor effectiveness, as most members of the profession would choose to define it, is not adequately handled by student evaluation forms.

A possible cause of this difficulty is that the success of a course from the students point of view may involve many variables in addition to or even instead of learning. The entertainment value of a course, the effort required to earn a desired grade, the relationship between effort required and preceived value of the course material are examples of variables whose impact on student evaluations require further study. The complexity of this area is increased if one assumes that each student has a different set of needs which he or she is trying to satisfy.

While such studies may give us new insights as to how to satisfy students, the decisions regarding promotion, tenure and salary must continue to be made. If instructor effectiveness is to be a part of these decisions, perhaps direct measures of student achievement are required. If course objectives can be specifically spelled out, then student achievement can be measured with regard to these objectives. This approach raises a number of questions including the issue of academic freedom. Nevertheless, it may be the best approach to obtaining meaningful results.

### REFERENCES

1. Anderson, Ralph E., Kwang S. Choi, and Gerald V. Boyles. "Disconfirmed Student Expectations and Instructional Evaluations: An Empirical Study," in Proceedings: Southern Marketing Association, ed. by Robert L. King (1973), 511-516.

2. Centra, John A.  "The Student as Godfather; The Impact of Student Ratings on Academia," Educational Researcher, 2 (1973), 4-8.

3. Centra, John A.  The Student Instructional Report: Its Development and Uses.  Princeton, New Jersey: Educational Testing Service, 1972.

4. Cohen, S. A., and W. G. Berger.  "Dimensions of Students' Ratings of College Instructors Underlying Subsequent Achievement on Course Examinations," in Proceedings of the 178th Annual Convention of the America Psychological Association, (1970), 605-606.

5. Costin, Frank, W. T. Greenough, and R. J. Menges.  "Student Ratings of College Teaching: Reliability, Validity and Usefulness," Review of Educational Research 41 (1973), 511-535.

6. Eble, Kenneth E.  Professors as Teachers. San Francisco, California: Jossey-Bass, Inc., 1972.

7. Guthrie, D. R.  The Evaluation of Teaching.  Seattle, Washington: University of Washington, 1954.

8. Hildebrand, Milton, Robert C. Wilson, and Evelyn R. Dienst.  Evaluating University Teaching.  Berkeley, California: A Handbook published by the Center for Research and Development in Higher Education, University of California, 1971.

9. McKeachie, W. J.  Teaching Tips:  A Guidebook for the Beginning College Teacher (6th ed.) Lexington, Massachusetts: D. C. Heath, 1969.

10. Michigan State University.  Student Instructional Rating System (SIRS).  Ann Arbor, Michigan: Office of Evaluation Service, January, 1974.

11. Rodin, Miriam, and Burton Rodin.  "Student Evaluations of Teachers," Science, 177 (1972) 1164-1166.

12. Snyder, C. R., and Mark Clair.  "Effects of Expected and Obtained Grades on Teacher Evaluation and Attribution of Performance," Journal of Educational Psychology, 68 (1976), 75-82.

13. Spencer, R. E.  The Course Evaluation Questionnaire: Manual of Interpretation.  Urbana, Illinois: Office of Institutional Research, University of Illinois, 1965.

AN EXPERIMENTAL INVESTIGATION OF STUDENT
PREFERENCES FOR MARKETING INSTRUCTORS

Bruce Seaton, Florida International University
Ronald H. Vogel, Florida International University

## ABSTRACT

Enrollment in marketing courses, and the effectiveness of
the instructor in these courses, may be increased if the
student preferences for marketing instructors are measured.
This paper outlines an institution-specific method of determining the preferred characteristics of an instructor of
marketing. These preferred characteristics include factors
which could be considered in the course design such as the
work load, grading, classroom format and style, and teacher
style.

## INTRODUCTION

As the value of higher education appears to be increasingly
questioned the traditional hallowed sanctity of the professor's classroom is being challenged. Enis [5] provides
evidence that teachers of marketing have shown resistance
to such incursions as mandatory faculty ratings by students.
He presents a comprehensive outline of the issues involved
in the evaluation of marketing faculty teaching effectiveness and concludes that the formal evaluating of teachers
of marketing is consistent with the consumer ("student")
perspective we adopt in our classes. French and Jones [6]
develop the argument that students should play the primary
role in the teaching evaluation process. Cox [4] suggests
that teaching is the primary focus of a university and that
the changing environment in which universities operate makes
change inevitable. One of the changes he predicts is an
increasing emphasis on formal evaluation procedures for
teaching faculty. His recommendations are basically to accept the trend and actively participate to ensure maximum
faculty input into the process, and to incorporate teaching
effectiveness into the faculty reward system.

There is evidence of the increasing importance of teaching
effectiveness in business faculty evaluations. For example,
Jolson's [11] nationwide survey of business faculty indicated that faculty members themselves regard teaching competence as the most important criterion for promotion and
tenure decisions. Seldin [17] reports a survey of 147 Business Deans inquiring into factors used to evaluate faculty
performance. His findings indicate that the sources of information for evaluating faculty have moved substantially
in the direction of formal student evaluations and away from
colleague opinion as a major input. Enis [5] also reports
on the relative importance of teaching performance in assessing faculty members. Fifty-eight percent of responding
marketing chairmen of A.A.C.S.B. schools indicated that
they assigned a weight of 1/3 to 2/3 to teaching performance
in evaluating marketing faculty for salary increments. There
is evidence of differing perceptions of the weight assigned
to teaching performance. Miller [15] found that business
professors themselves perceived that research was the most
important criterion for promotion.

The apparent trend toward an increased role for formal
teacher evaluation and the increasing acceptance of formal
student input as the primary ingredient in this evaluation
raises the question of what factors students are using, or
should be using, in the evaluation process. There have
been a number of attempts to determine which attributes
possessed by a teacher of marketing are evaluated by students and how they are assessed. Some of the findings are
summarized below.

Tauber [18] attempted to determine those criteria which
were a necessary condition for an effective teacher. His
research indicated that the prerequisites for effective
teaching were that an instructor be "knowledgable in the
field," "communicate well," "give fair tests" and "grade
fairly." It should be noted that the meaing of "fair" and
"fairly" is probably highly subjective. Painter and Granzin [16] studied the relationship between business student
course ratings and an extensive set of independent variables. They suggested that those teachers interested in
high student ratings should (i) attempt to convince the
students of the relevance of the course, (ii) make the
course as entertaining as possible, (iii) avoid making the
course too easy, and (iv) not be too concerned about giving
high grades as their findings suggested grades were of minor
importance. McGann, Marquardt and Jakubauskus [14] found a
positive relationship between type of examination (essay-
type favored over multiple choice) and the awarding of
higher grades and the overall evaluation received by an instructor. In contrast to McGann, et.al., Barry [2] determined that there was no relationship between instructor
evaluation and testing method (essay-type contrasted with a
term paper). Barry and Lundstrom [3] found that a "parti-
cipative" teaching style was evaluated more highly than an
"authoritarian" style of teaching. Each of the above
studies was performed at a single university. Kerin, Peterson and Martin [12] conducted a study encompassing 32 different business schools for a total of 101 instructors.
They found that instructor enthusiasm, preparedness, knowledge of the subject, teaching enjoyment, and oral presentation were the principal correlates with the overall instructor
rating. Such uncontrollable factors as the "halo effect"
of the school and all other instructors, enrollment size of
the school, class size, and the number of courses taught by
the instructor also affected overall teacher ratings. The
above studies differ sufficiently to suggest either that
there is no specific model of the effective teacher or that
the model has not yet been formulated and that perhaps we
are dealing with a segmented market.

Generally, studies attempting to correlate teaching effectiveness with more specific teacher attributes have been
performed "ex post facto." However, if a true marketing
orientation is to be adopted in the marketing classroom and
a legitimate goal is to serve the students' perceived needs
then more specific research into student preferences (in
addition to assessment of the "product" that they have been
provided) would seem to be of value. The value of such research should be particularly true in cases of stable or
declining enrollment, as is apparently the situation in
marketing [19]. The purpose of this paper is thus to:

(a) Outline an institution-specific method of determining the preferred characteristics of a
teacher of marketing.
(b) Provide the results of the process on a commuter
university with a diverse student body.

More specifically the research was undertaken primarily to
provide the answers to the following questions:

(a) What are the realtive utilities of the factors
related to student preferences for marketing
instructors?
(b) Are the utility values and related preferences of
administrators and the faculty review group

congruent with that of the students?

## METHODOLOGY

The investigative technique used was additive conjoint measurement, a specific method of exploring the area of trade-off analysis. Trade-off analysis is based on the premise that individuals' preference behavior is based on the simultaneous consideration of a number of object attributes and the derived judgements represent a compromise or "trade-off" in that, in general, no object will be optimal with respect to all attributes. An important special case is the additive model of conjoint measurement which is analogous, in the absence of interactions, to the analysis of variance of a factorial design. The procedure requires ordinal input but generates interval-scaled output. The appropriateness of the assumption of lack of interaction effects has been discussed by Green [7]. Experimental designs are extremely parsimonious using this approach, as has been noted by Addelman [1] in his review of the subject area. For example, using the procedures described in his paper, the main effects for a full factorial design for six factors at five levels could be investigated with a 25-cell experiment. In contrast, a full factorial design (all interactions estimated) would require 15,625 cells.

In the research reported in this paper an asymmetrical factorial design was utilized and the data was collected in accordance with an orthogonal main effects plan. The approach is being used to an increasing extent in marketing research [9].

## RESEARCH DESIGN

The research design employed may be essetnially considered as a five-step process. The steps are outlined below:

1. The identification of the salient dimensions of student preferences for marketing instructors.
2. The development of the required number of hypothetical teacher profiles - in this research, sixteen.
3. The collection of preference data from a sample of students and faculty.
4. The analysis of the preference data as a main effects experimental design.
5. The comparison of faculty and student results.

The Identification of the Salient Dimensions of Student Preferences

Hughes [10] has discussed the various techniques of determining the salient attributes of an object evaluation. As outlined below, the technique used was primarily the unstructured techniques of depth questioning.

The delineation of the salient dimensions of student preferences was primarily based on a series of assignments for students of a marketing research class. The students were required to interview a number of their fellow marketing students to determine what qualities they (the interviewed students) looked for in a teacher. The interviewing process also probed the array of levels that students perceived for each dimension. Those dimensions that were beyond the control of an instructor (such as class size and schedule) were eliminated. This was not intended to imply that these factors are unimportant in students' preferences for marketing instructors but merely to focus on factors that might vary between teachers in the specific university environment. The second phase of this process consisted of a class discussion of the findings. The appropriateness and value of this procedure was greatly enhanced by the fact that the class members themselves were part of the population of interest. Based on class evaluation of the dimensions identified, a preliminary set of profiles

(nine in all) was developed for the purposes of pretesting the research instrument. The pretest established the viability of the data collection technique.

The ease that subject students experienced in **ranking the** nine teacher profiles facilitated the expansion of the scope of each profile to five **dimensions** and the 16 treatments necessary to investigate these more substantial profiles. It should be noted that one of the dimensions (classroom format and style) represents the collapsing of two separate dimensions, some of whose combinations of levels is directly contradictory. The five dimensions and the levels associated with each have been reproduced in Table 1.

### TABLE 1

#### SALIENT DIMENSIONS OF STUDENT PREFERENCES AND THE ASSOCIATED LEVELS

| | |
|---|---|
| 1. Education and Experience: | 1. Instructor has doctorate in Marketing with several years of practical experience. |
| | 2. Instructor has minimum educational requirements but has several years of practical experience. |
| | 3. Instructor has doctorate in Marketing and little practical experience. |
| 2. Work load: | 1. Little work required. |
| | 2. Busy work only required. |
| | 3. Much work but student **learns** a lot. |
| 3. Grading: | 1. Instructor has a reputation as an easy grader. |
| | 2. Instructor has a reputation as a hard grader. |
| | 3. Instructor grades on a normal curve ("C" average). |
| | 4. Instructor grades on a normal curve ("B" average). |
| 4. Classroom Format and Style: | 1. (a) Primarily lecture. |
| | (b) Instructor seems to discourage students from asking questions. |
| | 2. (a) Primarily lecture. |
| | (b) Instructor welcomes student questions. |
| | 3. (a) Primarily a participation and discussion format. |
| | (b) Instructor welcomes student questions. |
| 5. Teacher style: | 1. Instructor has a reputation as a very humorous person. |
| | 2. Instructor occasionally shows a sense of humor. |
| | 3. Instructor has a reputation as a very serious-minded person. |

Development of a Hypothetical Set of Alternatives

As previously noted the number of treatments for a full factorial design was inordinately large and thus the ease of an incomplete design was necessary. As there was no reason to suspect that any of the variables would interact, the most parsimonious of experimental designes, the "main effects" only, was chosen. The specific set of 16 profiles was based on the array of designed developed by Addelman [1]. The design has been reproduced in Table 2. On the assumption that there are no interaction effects, such a design allows an independent estimate of the impact of each variable on respondents' preferences.

### TABLE 2

#### THE EXPERIMENTAL DESIGN
#### Variable

| Cell | Education and Experience | Work Load | Gra-ing | Classroom Format and Style | Teacher Style |
|------|------|------|------|------|------|
| 1 | 1 | 1 | 1 | 1 | 1 |
| 2 | 1 | 1 | 1 | 3 | 2 |
| 3 | 1 | 1 | 4 | 2 | 2 |
| 4 | 1 | 1 | 4 | 2 | 3 |
| 5 | 1 | 2 | 2 | 3 | 2 |
| 6 | 1 | 2 | 3 | 2 | 1 |
| 7 | 1 | 3 | 2 | 1 | 3 |
| 8 | 1 | 3 | 3 | 2 | 2 |
| 9 | 2 | 1 | 2 | 2 | 2 |
| 10 | 2 | 1 | 3 | 1 | 2 |
| 11 | 2 | 2 | 1 | 2 | 3 |
| 12 | 2 | 3 | 4 | 3 | 1 |
| 13 | 3 | 1 | 2 | 2 | 1 |
| 14 | 3 | 1 | 3 | 3 | 3 |
| 15 | 3 | 2 | 4 | 1 | 2 |
| 16 | 3 | 3 | 1 | 2 | 2 |

### Data Collection

The primary population of interest consisted of students attending advanced undergraduate marketing classes in the Fall Quarter of 1976. The secondary population of importance was comprised of those faculty members who had a role in evaluating the teaching effectiveness of the marketing faculty members. These consisted of the Dean of the Business School, the Departmental Chairman and members of the school-wide Faculty Development Committee.

Approximately 50 percent of the students in the advanced marketing classes were included in the sample. The sampling was accomplished by cluster sampling with clusters being defined as specific classes in advanced marketing. The choice of classes was made to reflect a balance of both required and elective and day and night classes. Precautions were taken to ensure that no student responded more than once.

Student responses were obtained in the regular sessions of the sampled classes. Students were reminded that each quarter the University administered teacher evaluations but that a major problem in making use of these evaluations was the lack of knowledge of what students looked for in a teacher of marketing. They were told the purpose of the research was to explore this problem and that their cooperation was essential. Each of the sixteen profiles was reproduced on a 3 x 5 index card and the written instructions accompanying the cards included "...examine carefully the 16 cards and arrange them in order of preference, placing the most preferred profile on top (face up), the second most preferred next through to the least preferred on the bottom. To simplify this procedure, we suggest that you first sort the cards into 3 piles corresponding to a favorable pile, a neutral pile and a less favorable pile. This will allow you to rank the smaller number of cards in each

pile and then, after checking that the transition cards are correctly ordered, combine the 3 piles to complete the ranking."

At the completion of the ranking the students were asked to provide basic demographic information and also the numbers of hours worked per week, the hours carried, and also their current grade point average.

Faculty responses were elicited on an individual basis. The written instructions were similar to those given the students as reproduced above.

### Data Analysis

Profile rankings were obtained from 89 students and a total of 7 faculty members. Each of these 96 sets of ordinal data was analyzed by MONANOVA (Monotone Analysis of Variance). MONANOVA is a procedure for transforming data from a factorial experiment by searching over all monotone transformations of the data and selecting the "best" one [8, 13]. The "best" transformation results in the greatest percentage being accounted for by the main effects.[1] The algorithm seeks to minimize the "stress" (which is effectively the residual variance divided by the total variance). Thus a utility value is computed for each level of each dimension (16 levels in this research) subject to the requirement that the sum of utilities for the levels of each variable equals zero. A comparison of the moduli of the differences between the most and least preferred levels within each variable can be used to estimate the importance of a dimension in determining profile rankings (indicates the proportion of variation due to a specific attribute of the profile).

MONANOVA has a replication feature but the size of the data matrix for this research (a total of 1424 observations) precluded its use. Thus a summary of results was achieved by averaging the results for the students and faculty. These results have been summarized in Table 3. The major differences in emphasis between these two different groups is seen by examining the proportion of variation due to each dimension. The faculty emphasized "Education and Experience" and "Work Load" whereas the students placed more importance on "Classroom Format and Style" and "Teacher Style." "Grading" showed a minimal difference. Within each dimension the evaluation of the various levels showed a similar pattern with the strong exception of "Grading." Students showed a preference for the "easy" and "B" levels and a strong antipathy toward "hard" grading. In contrast, the faculty showed a strong preference for "hard" grading and were extremely negative on "easy" grading. The most favored profile for each group is outlined in Table 4.

### IMPLICATIONS

The institution at which this research was performed conducts an extensive instructor evaluation program based on student input. The form of this evaluation is extremely simple requiring the student to provide an overall evaluation of the instructor on a four-point scale with extreme values of "excellent" and "poor." In addition, the evaluation form invites and provides opportunity for open-ended student comments. Thus the mode of collecting this feedback on teacher performance effectively leaves the criteria to the individual student. In a situation such as this the student evaluation could be expected to vary depending on how well the students' expectations are met with these

---

[1] As previously noted, the design used in this research was restricted to the measurement of main effects and so the use of MONANOVA did not imply the rejection of information contained in the data. Conventional ANOVA requires interval level data.

TABLE 3

SUMMARY OF FACULTY AND STUDENT RESULTS:  RELATIVE
IMPORTANCE OF EACH DIMENSION AND UTILITY
VALUES OF EXPERIMENTAL TREATMENTS

| Dimension | Level Level | FACULTY Proportion of Variation* | Mean Utility Value | STUDENTS Proportion of Variation | Mean Utility Value |
|---|---|---|---|---|---|
| Education and Experience | 1 | 27.9% | 1.113 | 14.6% | 0.456 |
| | 2 | | -1.134 | | -0.200 |
| | 3 | | 0.021 | | -0.256 |
| Work Load | 1 | 35.0% | -0.585 | 10.8% | -0.113 |
| | 2 | | -1.119 | | -0.207 |
| | 3 | | 1.704 | | 0.320 |
| Grading | 1 | 21.5% | -0.918 | 23.5% | 0.210 |
| | 2 | | 0.813 | | -0.714 |
| | 3 | | 0.333 | | 0.072 |
| | 4 | | -0.228 | | 0.431 |
| Classroom Format and Style | 1 | 13.5% | -0.661 | 38.9% | -1.095 |
| | 2 | | 0.428 | | 0.301 |
| | 3 | | 0.234 | | 0.795 |
| Teacher Style | 1 | 2.0% | 0.096 | 12.1% | 0.181 |
| | 2 | | -0.027 | | 0.204 |
| | 3 | | -0.069 | | -0.385 |

*The proportion of variation is found by dividing the difference between the high and low values for each dimension by the sum of those differences for all dimensions.  It indicates the relative importance of the particular dimension.

TABLE 4

MOST AND LEAST FAVORED PROFILES OF
THE FACULTY AND STUDENTS

| Dimension | FACULTY Most Favored | Least Favored | STUDENTS Most Favored | Least Favored |
|---|---|---|---|---|
| Education and Experience | Doctorate and Experience | Practical Experience Only | Doctorate and Experience | Doctorate, no Experience |
| Work Load | Much Work | Busy Work | Much Work | Busy Work |
| Grading | Hard | Easy | Normal,"B" | Hard |
| Classroom Format and Style | Lecture plus Questions | Lecture, no Questions | Discussion plus Questions | Lecture, no Questions |
| Teacher Style | Very Humorous | Serious | Somewhat Humorous | Serious |

...pectations reflecting the students' preferences as indi-
...ted by the measured utility values.

...ile the resulting evaluations may, or may not, reflect
...e effectiveness of the instructor, the interesting point
...this research is that the Dean of the School and the
...mbers of the Faculty Development Committee differed from
...e students in the relative importance of the dimensions
...asured.  Since the criteria for evaluation are not ex-
...icitly given in the evaluation form the faculty percep-
...on of favorable student evaluations may ascribe qualities
...an instructor rather different from those the students
...ve used.

In addition, the instructor could initially use the measured utility values in making course decisions related to the
measured dimensions.  Thus the product, the consumers'
(students') perceptions of the product, or the dimensions
on which the product is judged could be changed.

This could result in increased enrollment, increased satisfaction, and possibly more effective teaching and better
instructor evaluations.

REFERENCES

1. Addelman, Sidney.  "Orthogonal Main-Effect Plans for
   Asymmetrical Factorial Experiments," Technometrics,
   4 (February, 1962), 21-46.

2. Barry, Thomas E.  "Tests vs. Term Papers: Some Empirical
   Results and Implications," Combined Proceedings, Chicago:
   American Marketing Association, 1975.

3. Barry, Thomas E. and William J. Lundstrom.  "The Effect
   of Classroom Teaching Styles on Student Performance and
   Evaluation," Proceedings, State College, Missippi:
   Southern Marketing Association, 1975.

4. Cox, Keith K.  "Changes in the Reward System for Marketing Professors," Combined Proceedings, Chicago: American
   Marketing Association, 1972.

5. Enis, Ben M.  "Some Thoughts and a Little Data on a
   Formal Evaluation of Teaching Effectiveness in Market-
   ing," Combined Proceedings, Chicago: American Marketing
   Association, 1971.

6. French, Warren A. and J. Richard Jones.  "The Case for
   Teacher Evaluation: A Position Paper," Combined Proceed-

ings, Chicago: American Marketing Association, 1972.

7. Green, Paul E. "On the Analysis of Interactions in Marketing Research Data," Journal of Marketing Research, 10 (November, 1973), 410-20.

8. Green, Paul E. and Vithala R. Rao. "Conjoint Measurement for Quantifying Judgement Data," Journal of Marketing Research, 8 (August, 1971), 355-63.

9. Green, Paul E. and Donald S. Tull. "New Way to Measure Consumer Judgements," Harvard Business Review, 53 (July-August, 1975), 107-17.

10. Hughes, G. David. Attitude Measurement for Marketing Strategies. Glenview, Illinois: Scott, Foreman and Company, 1971.

11. Jolson, Marvin. "Criteria for Promotion and Tenure: A Faculty View," Academy of Management Journal, 17 (March, 1974), 149-54.

12. Kerin, Rober, Robert Peterson and Warren Martin. "Teaching Effectiveness: How Do We Rate?" Combined Proceedings, Chicago: American Marketing Association, 1975.

13. Kruskal, Joseph B. "Analysis of Factorial Experiments by Estimating Monotone Transformations of the Data," Journal of the Royal Statistical Society, Series B, 27 (March, 1965), 251-63.

14. McGann, Anthony F., Raymond Marquardt and E. B. Jakubauskas, "Student Evaluations, Professional Responsibility, and Career Advancement," Combined Proceedings, Chicago: American Marketing Association, 1975.

15. Miller, Thomas R. "Factors of Faculty Promotion in Collegiate Schools of Business," AACSB Bulletin, 12 (January, 1976), 13-9.

16. Painter, John J. and Kent L. Granzin. "An Investigation of Determinants of Student Course Rating," Combined Proceedings, eds. Chicago: American Marketing Association, 1972.

17. Seldin, Peter. "Current Practices in Evaluating the Business Faculty," AACSB Bulletin, 12 (April, 1976), 1-6.

18. Tauber, Edward M. "Student Criteria for Judging Instructor Performance," Combined Proceedings, Chicago: American Marketing Association, 1973.

19. Twedt, Dik. "Business Degrees Show Steady Increase, but Marketing Education's Share Shrinks," Marketing News, 10 (July 30, 1976), 1, 15.

# FACULTY ATTITUDES TOWARD MONITORING
## OF MARKETING CLASSES

Marvin A. Jolson, University of Maryland
Thomas E. Barry, Southern Methodist University

## ABSTRACT

Despite the widespread dominance of formal student evaluations of teaching effectiveness, there is limited agreement
that such methods are valid and reliable for improving and
appraising teaching. This paper investigates the current
potential of the traditionally forbidden technique of
classroom visitations by decentral administrators or their
appointees.

## INTRODUCTION

In consuming most products, one has the assurance that a
rigorous inspection process will reduce the likelihood of
receiving faulty products. In this age of consumerism,
quality control systems abound. Yet, such protection is
rarely offered to the purchaser of higher education.
Information concerning teaching quality that makes its way
to those in administrative positions is necessarily second
or third hand. To the extent that peer and administrative
surveillance exists, it is primarily focused on the faculty
member's qualifications as a scholar, not as a teacher. [3]

Almost all colleges or universities recognize teaching as
one of three major criteria for evaluating faculty members;
moreover, faculty members in all business school disciplines
have unanimously agreed that teaching effectiveness should
be the major criterion for promotion and tenure [4]. However, as indicated by one survey of A.A.C.S.B. accredited
schools, the difficulties involved in developing objective
evaluations of teaching have influenced central and decentral administrators and faculty members to attach more
weight to research achievements [5].

### Student Evaluations

Few graduate schools of business offer doctoral level
courses on "how to teach." Yet, the awarding of the terminal degree carries with it the stamp of approval as a
teacher.

Past research has shown and this study confirms the fact
that student evaluations serve as the major source of influence for administrators who evaluate teaching effectiveness. Such input makes a major contribution to the student
grapevine system and is welcomed by some instructors and
ignored by others. There are many objections to the use of
student opinions, particularly by those who relate teaching
ability to student achievement. First, some academicians
say that students are not in a good position to judge and
that they do not know when they are getting a worthwhile
experience; that they judge in terms of pain and pleasure
rather than in terms of merit. Second, instructors knowing that opinions are being collected may teach to enter-
tain students rather than to help them to learn. Similarly,
some professors may become presenters of subject matter and
organizers and spoon-feeders of information that will enable students to do well on examinations. Finally, the
argument is offered that instructors who are teaching
basic, dreary, or theoretical materials are penalized
whereas those who deal in practical and exciting visionary
type courses are overly rewarded [2].

Conversely, students are somewhat qualified to respond to
the mood or the warmth of the classroom setting, to the
interest and style of the instructor, to the format of the
instructional program, to the worthiness of the readings
and assignments, and to the appropriateness of the exams.
When accepted by the instructor, these findings serve as
guides for self-improvement and eventual student benefits.

Most schools have their own faculty and course evaluation
instruments and many attempts have been made to develop
elaborate student rating instruments that provide a valid
and reliable measure of teaching effectiveness. For example, one of the more sophisticated instruments is the
Temple University FACE program that employs 160 rating
dimensions [6].

### Other Sources of Teaching Evaluation

Business school educators are far from agreed that teaching evaluations by students are valid and reliable indicators of an instructor's proficiency. The typical reaction is that the student evaluation is the best of an
imperfect lot of approaches.

Yet, in this day of dynamic change on campuses and elsewhere, the classroom visitation method may offer more hope
than any other method. As far back as 1961, one group of
educators indicated that the only tangible evidence of
quality in teaching requires at least a minimum program of
classroom monitoring by the department chairman or persons
designated by him [2].

But, is the academic community ready for widespread classroom monitoring? The mores of academe define the visitation to a college class by someone in authority as an
impermissible intrusion [3]. Balyeat's studies conclude
that academic freedom is the most important influence upon
a professor's propensity to continue his current position
or to seek an employment change [1].

### Objectives of the Study

This study examines the current state of readiness for
classroom monitoring, at least among marketing faculty
members. After investigating present methods of improving
and evaluating marketing instructors, the research focuses
on the following major issues:
1. Would classroom monitoring contribute to the improvement and evaluation of teaching effectiveness?
2. Who should be monitored?
3. What is the ideal monitoring format?
4. What should the monitoring group look for?
5. How should the findings be dispersed?
6. Would monitoring threaten "academic freedom"?
7. Do attitudes toward monitoring vary among selected
   faculty segments?
8. Would faculty members accept monitoring in their own
   classes?

### Sample and Instrument

Data were collected by mailing questionnaires to a random
sample of 195 marketing educators taken from the 1975
American Marketing Association Directory. One hundred
twenty-one responses were usable for a response rate of
62 percent.

In addition to the use of Likert scales and other forced
choice sections, a number of questions solicited open-
ended responses. A final section generated information

about the respondents' terminal degree, rank, tenure status, level of courses taught, time spent in teaching, and self-reported teaching proficiency.

It was recognized that self-ratings of teaching effectiveness would be biased in an upward direction and that few faculty members would rate themselves as poor or fair teachers. However, the authors reasoned that poor or fair teachers who sought to elevate their status would rate themselves as good rather than superior. Accordingly, for the purpose of partitioning the independent variable, teaching effectiveness, the results placed 40 percent of the respondents in the superior category and 60 percent in the fair/good category. No respondents rated themselves as poor teachers.

## FINDINGS

Current Evaluation Methods

Much of the introductory material was based on the supposition that decentral administrators do not have information at their disposal to qualify them to either appraise or improve the teaching competence of faculty members. The first statement in Table 4 specifically addresses this issue and discloses that only 63 percent of the sample felt that such information was available to deans and/or department chairmen.

By asking respondents to rank various teaching information sources in the order in which they think administrators at their own schools are influenced, the researchers were able to compile the data in Table 1. The student evaluation system is overwhelmingly predominant. As shown in Table 2, in about two-thirds of the schools, such evaluations are required for each course and the results are published and/or placed in the hands of department administrators at a majority of the schools. Formal student evaluations are omitted at less than 3 percent of the schools. Yet statement 2 of Table 4 indicates that 56.4 percent of the respondents are not convinced of the validity and reliability of such instruments.

### TABLE 1

PERCEIVED IMPORTANCE OF INFORMATION SOURCES
FOR EVALUATING TEACHING EFFECTIVENESS

| Source | Number of Respondents Ranking | | | | |
|---|---|---|---|---|---|
| | 1st | 2nd | 3rd | 4th | 5th |
| Written student evaluations | 71 | 19 | 9 | 8 | 3 |
| Informal comments by colleagues | 16 | 21 | 35 | 22 | 6 |
| Casual comments by students | 10 | 39 | 32 | 12 | 11 |
| Casual self-reports by faculty (e.g., conversations at lunch, etc.) | 6 | 12 | 16 | 22 | 19 |
| Formal self-reports by faculty | 8 | 12 | 10 | 17 | 18 |
| Formal classroom monitoring | 6 | 8 | 2 | 2 | 8 |
| Informal class visits | 4 | 4 | 5 | 2 | 6 |

Table 1 discloses that the only other mildly popular sources are informal or casual comments by students and faculty peers. As shown in Table 3, more than 80 percent of the respondents' schools avoid the use of formal classroom monitoring and the method is mandatory at less than 10 percent of the schools.

### TABLE 2

DEPARTMENTAL POLICIES REGARDING FORMAL WRITTEN TEACHING
EVALUATIONS BY STUDENTS (n = 121)

| | % of Respondents Indicating Applicability to Own Institution |
|---|---|
| Required and prepared each semester/quarter for each course | 66.1 |
| Results automatically published and/or submitted to departmental administrator | 58.7 |
| Subject to option of individual instructor | 28.9 |
| Results available to instructor only | 18.2 |
| Not used | 2.5 |

### TABLE 3

EXTENT OF CLASSROOM MONITORING BY FORMALIZED
VISITS (n = 121)

| Does it occur? | % of Respondents Indicating Applicability to Own Institution |
|---|---|
| No | 80.2 |
| Yes, but only when authorized by instructor | 7.4 |
| Yes, mandatory for some courses of all instructors | 4.1 |
| Yes, mandatory for all courses of some instructors | 3.3 |
| Yes, mandatory for all courses of all instructors | 1.7 |

Attitudes toward Classroom Monitoring

Data from Tables 4, 5, and 6 lead toward one surprising conclusion--that is, a majority of faculty members support a more widespread use of classroom monitoring and feel that implementation of the method would be helpful in the evaluation and teaching improvement process. Even more surprising is the finding in Table 5 that nearly half of the respondents feel that all teachers should be subjected to monitoring. Table 6 discloses that a majority of the respondents condone a visit by the administrator or his appointee(s) following prenotification and nearly half are willing to permit unannounced visitations.

About 70 percent of the faculty members feel that the monitoring person or group should be from the monitoree's own discipline (Table 4). Untabulated findings indicate that about two-thirds of the respondents would require the visitors to be either administrators or those who are confirmed as excellent teachers. Several respondents recommended students, business people, former students, members of promotion and tenure committees, experts in measuring effectiveness, and others as acceptable visitors.

The list shown in Table 7 offers some clues as to a few of the major items that should be included on the checklist of the monitoring person or committee. The major dimensions of teaching seem to center on the instructor's preparedness, his quality of lecture content, his ability to explain new or difficult concepts, and his capability of encouraging students to think.

TABLE 4

FACULTY ATTITUDES TOWARD TEACHING EVALUATION
AND CLASSROOM MONITORING

| | SA 5 | A 4 | U 3 | D 2 | SD 1 | n |
|---|---|---|---|---|---|---|
| 1. My department chairman and/or dean has information at their (his) disposal which qualifies them (him) to make valid statements about the teaching competence of individual faculty members. | 10.1 | 52.9 | 12.6 | 19.3 | 5.1 | 119 |
| 2. In general, teaching evaluations by students are valid and reliable indicators of an instructor's proficiency. | 3.4 | 40.2 | 21.4 | 26.5 | 8.5 | 117 |
| 3. Under certain conditions, classroom monitoring by the departmental chairman, dean, or appointed committees would be helpful in improving teaching effectiveness. | 11.0 | 45.8 | 16.9 | 12.7 | 13.6 | 118 |
| 4. Under certain conditions, classroom monitoring by the departmental chairman, dean, or appointed committees would be helpful as a teaching evaluation tool. | 8.6 | 47.4 | 12.9 | 16.4 | 14.7 | 116 |
| 5. Classroom monitoring should be unannounced. | 19.0 | 13.7 | 25.9 | 15.5 | 25.9 | 116 |
| 6. A professor should have the option to reject monitoring of his classes. | 31.6 | 21.4 | 19.7 | 17.0 | 10.3 | 117 |
| 7. The findings of the monitoring group should be confidential and given only to the instructor. | 27.4 | 17.7 | 22.1 | 20.4 | 12.4 | 113 |
| 8. The findings of the monitoring group should be submitted to departmental administrators. | 12.6 | 26.1 | 24.3 | 18.9 | 18.1 | 111 |
| 9. The person or group that does the classroom monitoring should be from the monitoree's discipline. | 39.2 | 29.5 | 17.9 | 8.0 | 5.4 | 110 |

% of Respondents

SA = Strongly Agree,  A = Agree,  U = Undecided,  D = Disagree,  SD = Strongly Disagree

TABLE 5

WHO SHOULD BE MONITORED?
(n = 121)

| | % of Respondents |
|---|---|
| All teachers | 47.1 |
| Teachers being considered for promotion/tenure | 24.0 |
| Teachers receiving poor or marginal student ratings | 22.3 |
| Only those who are perceived by administrators to be poor or marginal teachers | 14.9 |
| Only new teachers | 13.2 |
| Administrators should decide | 4.1 |
| Other responses | 17.4 |

The reader should not overestimate the level of support for a monitoring system in marketing classrooms. About 52 percent of the respondents felt that the technique would limit "academic freedom" which was defined in the questionnaire as "the provision of autonomy in the classroom environment with any limitations understood and acceptable by the teacher" [6]. Moreover, despite the expressed level of support for monitoring, the findings of Table 6 reveal that more than 30 percent of the professors would not permit an announced classroom visit and more than 40 percent would object to an unannounced approach. In addition, Table 4 shows that a substantial number of marketing educators would give the professor the option to reject monitoring and would restrict the findings of the monitoring group to the confidential use of the monitoree.

TABLE 6

WILLINGNESS TO PERMIT MONITORING
OF PERSONAL CLASSES

| Type of Monitoring | % of Respondents | | |
|---|---|---|---|
| | Willing | Undecided | Not Willing |
| Announced | 54.9 | 15.0 | 30.1 |
| Unannounced | 46.5 | 13.2 | 40.4 |

Respondent Subgroups

Logically, one may assume that response functions such as "support of the monitoring process" and "willingness to direct monitoring information to department administrators" would be directly related to the teacher's self-reported effectiveness. Table 8 presents these data. In comparing the attitudes of superior (S) versus fair or good (F/G) teachers, it was found that:

1. A significantly larger proportion of S teachers were supportive of unannounced monitoring of their own classes.
2. A significantly larger proportion of S teachers were supportive of announced monitoring of their own classes.
3. A significantly larger proportion of S teachers supported the transmission of monitoring findings to decentral administrators.

TABLE 7

## WHAT SHOULD THE MONITOR(S) LOOK FOR IN THE CLASSROOM?

| Factors | Very Important 3 | Somewhat Important 2 | Not Important 1 | n |
|---|---|---|---|---|
| Are lectures delivered effectively? | 70.6 | 28.4 | 1.0 | 102 |
| Are materials presented at a proper speed? | 35.6 | 53.5 | 10.9 | 101 |
| What is the quality of lecture content? | 80.8 | 18.2 | 1.0 | 99 |
| Does the instructor synthesize, integrate, and summarize effectively? | 64.0 | 35.0 | 1.0 | 103 |
| Can the instructor explain new or difficult concepts? | 80.6 | 18.4 | 1.0 | 103 |
| Does the instructor maintain organization with meaningful sequence of material? | 54.4 | 43.7 | 1.9 | 103 |
| Is the instructor prepared? | 84.5 | 12.6 | 2.9 | 103 |
| Does the instructor coordinate lectures with other components such as reading and labs? | 28.7 | 64.4 | 6.9 | 101 |
| Does the instructor hold the students' interests? | 48.0 | 50.0 | 2.0 | 102 |
| Are students encouraged to think? | 79.6 | 18.5 | 1.9 | 103 |
| Does the instructor encourage verbal expression of opinion and questions in class? | 59.2 | 36.9 | 3.9 | 103 |
| Are students stimulated and motivated? | 64.1 | 32.0 | 3.9 | 103 |
| Does the instructor tolerate disagreement? | 58.8 | 39.2 | 2.0 | 102 |
| Does the instructor emphasize learning rather than teaching for the "test" or "good grade"? | 64.4 | 28.7 | 6.9 | 101 |
| Does the instructor adjust to the class level of comprehension? | 36.9 | 56.3 | 6.8 | 103 |
| What is the superficial appearance of the teacher? | 13.7 | 39.2 | 47.1 | 102 |

Approximately equal proportions (37 percent vs. 40 percent) of the tenured and non-tenured faculty groups condone the use of monitoring information by departmental administrators. However, a larger proportion of the latter segment seems to "straddle the fence" on this proposition in that less than 3 percent strongly agreed while more than 37 percent were undecided. The corresponding figure for the tenured group is 19.2 percent for both scale ratings. Although these findings are not tabulated for this report, the results are significant at the .01 level. These observations may reflect the doubts and anxieties of newer faculty members relative to the weighting of teaching as a criterion for promotion and tenure. However, variables such as academic rank, degree held, level of courses taught, and time spent in teaching were found to be tenuous predictors of faculty response.

TABLE 8

## RESPONSES TO CLASSROOM MONITORING AS FUNCTION OF SELF-REPORTED TEACHING PROFICIENCY

| Self-Rating | SD | D | U | A | SA |
|---|---|---|---|---|---|
| **1. Unannounced monitoring of respondent's classes** | | | | | |
| Superior | 30.6 | 8.3 | 8.3 | 19.4 | 33.4 |
| Fair/good | 20.0 | 20.0 | 10.9 | 40.0 | 9.1 |

$$\chi^2 = 13.05, \; df = 4, \; p < .02$$

| Self-Rating | SD | D | U | A | SA |
|---|---|---|---|---|---|
| **2. Announced monitoring of respondent's classes** | | | | | |
| Superior | 19.4 | 8.3 | 8.3 | 22.3 | 41.7 |
| Fair/good | 14.5 | 16.4 | 20.0 | 38.2 | 10.9 |

$$\chi^2 = 13.93, \; df = 4, \; p < .01$$

| Self-Rating | SD | D | U | A | SA |
|---|---|---|---|---|---|
| **3. Submission of monitor's findings to administrators** | | | | | |
| Superior | 21.2 | 9.1 | 21.2 | 27.3 | 21.2 |
| Fair/good | 11.5 | 25.0 | 30.8 | 25.0 | 7.7 |

$$\chi^2 = 7.72, \; df = 4, \; p < .10$$

SD = Strongly Disagree, D = Disagree, U = Undecided, A = Agree, SA = Strongly Agree

## SUMMARY AND CONCLUSIONS

A review of currently-employed methods of evaluating and improving teaching proficiency reveals the dominance of the student evaluation instrument. Because of continuing imperfections in the latter method, this exploratory study has attempted to elicit the attitudes of marketing faculty members toward classroom monitoring.

The findings offer evidence that the approach is no longer academically taboo and that approximately half of the faculty members would be receptive to monitoring of their own classes. Yet, there is substantial support for the propositions that a professor should have the option to reject monitoring of his classes and that the findings of monitors should be confidential and given only to the instructor.

The authors conclude that the monitoring program would be fruitful even if implemented under the latter conditions. If the primary purpose is improved teaching, the confidential findings should serve to supply observations, hints, and friendly suggestions which will allow the teacher the freedom to structure his pedagogical approach with few intrusions, demands, and threats. Surely it will benefit those who are willing and able to improve. In addition, this approach may be sufficient to persuade a number of the devoted but skeptical teachers to convert to "monitorism."

Continued student feedback, both formalized and casual, will soon communicate the remedial impact of the plan and identify those who are unwilling or unable to improve. At the same time, recalcitrants will be uniquely conspicuous to their leaders and peers. Once accepted as a useful mode for teaching improvement, the subsequent stage of "monitoring for appraisal purposes" may reach a new level of acceptance.

REFERENCES

1. Balyeat, Ralph E. "Factors Affecting the Acquisition
   and Retention of College Faculty," Cooperative Research
   Project No. 7D-033, College of Business Administration,
   University of Georgia, 1972.

2. Clark, Kenneth E. Studies of College Faculty.
   Boulder, Colorado: Western Interstate Commission on
   Higher Education, 1961.

3. Dykstra, John W. "America's Forgotten Consumer," The
   Educational Forum, 36 (January 1972), 209-13.

4. Jolson, Marvin A. "Criteria for Promotion and Tenure:
   A Faculty View," Academy of Management Journal, 17
   (March 1974), 149-54.

5. Luthans, Fred. "Faculty Promotions: An Analysis of
   Central Administrative Control," Academy of Management
   Journal, 10 (December 1967), 385-93.

6. Sockloff, Alan L., and Vincent T. Deabler, The Con-
   struction of the Faculty and Course Evaluation
   Instrument. Philadelphia: Temple University Testing
   Bureau, March 1971.

J. Steven Kelly, DePaul University
J. Irwin Peters, DePaul University

## ABSTRACT

A review of the empirical research into vertical channel conflict shows a lack of concern, on the part of past researchers, for the differences in types of channel systems being studied. The goal of the investigation discussed here was to ascertain whether the nature and incidence of vertical conflict is the same within and across different types of channel systems. Using a measure of conflict developed earlier by other researchers, i.e., frequency of disagreements, the perceptions franchisees and distributors held toward their franchisors and suppliers were examined.

## INTRODUCTION

Vertical channel conflict, as opposed to horizontal conflict, takes place between two members of the same channel, but at two different levels [19, p. 416]. A review of the literature on vertical conflict reveals analysis of the causes of conflict [17], the potential constructive/destructive nature of conflict [1,6,7], how to measure its intensity [13], and the impact of conflict on efficiency and performance [1,5,14]. However, little concern has been shown regarding the unit of analysis, the type of channel being studied. Little research has studied conflict outside one type of channel organization. Past empirical studies of vertical conflict have focused within a grocery operation [12], franchised automobile dealerships [1,5,13], and an experimental setting [20]. There appears to be an assumption made, on the part of these researchers, that conflict is conflict and whether it has a positive, negative or curvilinear influence on performance has little to do with the type of channel relationship under review. Without research to ascertain the validity of that assumption, conclusions drawn from research based on that assumption may be premature.

The franchise business is a contractual channel system where the buyer of the franchise, the franchisee, agrees to sell a product or service under the guidance and supervision of the franchisor [19, p. 124]. There are many advantages and disadvantages to both the franchisee and franchisor in entering into such an agreement [3], yet one might suggest that this arrangement involves a great deal of cooperation, and therefore little conflict. On the other hand, certain pressure tactics to increase the number of franchisees in the system as well as policies on buying back franchises may lead to more conflict than other channel relationships. Some have suggested that unless steps are taken to carefully outline the nature of the contract between franchisee and franchisor, the attempts to integrate the work-flow and activities in the channel may yield vertical conflict [16, p. 40]. Recent press coverage regarding federal legislation on franchising [2, 15] as well as efforts to organize franchisees within separate systems [8] and national associations [9] may indicate that countervailing forces are being brought together to resolve apparent conflicts between sellers and buyers of franchisees.

Therefore, one may wonder whether the dependency relationship implicit in the franchised type of channel system generates more or less vertical conflict than independent systems of distribution. Further, questions may arise regarding whether conflicts prevalent in one type of franchise system are consistent with those found in other types.

It is the purpose of this paper to shed some light on the above questions. What follows is a discussion of a research project on the comparative conflict between franchisors and franchisees as well as between manufacturers and their distributors.

## METHODOLOGY

The elements of the study set forth here are part of a larger project carried on by the authors at a private, midwestern university. The purpose of the main project, in addition to examining the nature of vertical channel conflict, was to study the incidence and range of promotional support, technical assistance, and communication patterns between franchisors and franchisees as well as between suppliers and distributors. Findings in these areas will be presented at a later date when they become available. The following discussion relates specifically to seeking answers to the questions raised in the introductory section.

### The Sample

The study was based on interviews with franchisees and distributors located basically in the midwest, relatively close to the Chicago area. The types of franchisees and distributors interviewed were determined by (1) geographic constraints, the economic feasibility of interviewing respondents; (2) the desire to have a diverse sample; and (3) the ability of the interviewers to question the owner of the operation or a responsible, knowledgeable manager.

A total of 145 interviews were completed successfully and form the data base for this study. The breakdown is as follows:

Fast Food Franchisees:
16 different chains, 44 interviews.

Automotive Service (mufflers, transmissions, rustproofing) Franchisees:
4 different chains, 24 interviews.

Hotel/Motel Franchisees:
7 different chains, 26 interviews.

Independent Distributors of Industrial Goods:
7 different manufacturers, 26 interviews.

Independent Distributors of Consumer Goods:
5 different manufacturers, 25 interviews.

The inclusion of both franchisees and distributors in the sample was based on the following considerations. Both are middlemen in the channel of distribution. They provide a product or service to consumers of different types. In order to do so successfully, they must be supported in many ways by channel members at prior stages. This support includes, of course, training, promotion, offering the "right" product, etc. The middlemen must be "sold," i.e., the franchisor and the manufacturer must market his product or service to them. If the franchisor or manufacturer does not satisfy his customer (the franchisee or distributor) by managing him properly or offering him proper support, the middlemen may perceive conflict.

Examination of the sample according to size showed the following distribution. Those units reporting less than $2 million annual sales included: fast-food franchisees, 93%; hotel/motel franchisees, 57%; auto-service franchisees, 79%; industrial goods distributors, 38%; consumer goods distributors, 88%. The rest of the sample had greater than $2 million annual sales with 39% of the industrial distributors having greater than $3 million annual sales.

The Interview

The 145 interviews were conducted by graduate students from an Industrial Marketing class and several undergraduate students selected from a class in Promotion Management. The students were involved in the creation of the survey instrument and they were trained in the method of obtaining and conducting the interviews. The interviewers were instructed to talk with the owner rather than the manager whenever possible. It was felt that, in most instances, the perspective and knowledge of the manager was not likely to be as complete as that of the owner.

The interview form was divided into four distinct sections. Section I identified the interviewee, his location and whether he was the owner or manager.

Section II dealt with the general size of the channel system, the ratio of privately to company-owned dealerships and whether there was evidence that the supplier organization was trying to buy out this particular distributorship.

Section III dealt with the issues of conflict between the interviewee and the franchisor or supplier. The definition of conflict was made in terms of the frequency of disagreement between the two levels in the channel. This definition as well as most of the issues of conflict conform with research carried out by Lusch [5]. The interviewee was asked to indicate whether, in reference to each of 21 possible conflict issues, he was very frequently, frequently, infrequently, or very infrequently in disagreement with his franchisor or supplier. These specific issues will be discussed later. Lusch found the issues he used to have a high degree of validity and reliability. Although an attempt was made to duplicate these issues, some changes in the statements had to be made to conform with the situations studied. Time and economics did not allow for similar testing.

The other sections of the questionnaire dealt with the amount and type of communications transacted between the dealer and his supplier, the amount and effectiveness of various types of promotional support made available, and the interviewee's own performance.

RESULTS

Table 1 shows the comparative results to the questions regarding the franchisees' and distributors' frequency of disagreement with their franchisors or suppliers. The average scores were derived from the four-interval disagreement scales. A score of 1 represents high disagreement and a score of 4 indicates low or "very infrequent" disagreement. A one-way analysis of the variance was employed on each disagreement issue across the five groups: fast food, hotel/motel, and auto service franchisees and distributors of industrial goods and of consumer goods. The purpose of this was to determine whether there was a significant difference in level of disagreement among each of the groups studied, for each particular conflict issue.

The first point to be made is that for two-thirds of the issues there was not a significant difference between any of the franchisee or distributor groups in terms of the frequency of disagreement. Only seven showed a difference near or below the .05 level of significance. Those issues were:

3. Handling dissatisfied customers.
7. Location of other franchisees/distributors too near you.
8. Remodeling and/or expansion.
11. Local advertising you may do.
14. Availability of supplies.
19. Sales contests sponsored by franchisor/suppliers.
20. Cooperative advertising offered to you.

They will be analyzed more closely later.

The second point to be made is that the group means on each issue are generally 3.0 or better, indicating infrequent disagreement. This seems to say that the respondents had a tendency more toward agreement than disagreement with higher levels in the channel. In fact, the only time the average level of agreement falls below 3.0 is on the issues noted above. In addition, except for the one case of auto service franchisors regarding the location of other dealers, these lower scores were generated by the distributors of industrial goods. These operations are independent and, it will be recalled, represent the highest yearly sales of the five groups. Low levels of conflict among the groups studied raise some questions which will be addressed in the conclusions.

Tables 2a and 2b represent a closer analysis of the seven issues which showed a significant level of difference in frequency of disagreement. Table 2a shows a pair-wise comparison within the franchisee groups. Fast-food franchisees are compared to hotel/motel franchisees and auto service franchisees. Then hotel/motel franchisees are compared to auto service franchisees. These comparisons were done to examine the points of difference among franchisees. The comparisons were made using t-tests, so a negative t-value indicates that the second group had a higher mean score and thus was more often in agreement with the franchisor than was the first group, on that particular issue.

There is only one issue on which all of the franchisees differ at a significant level in frequency of disagreement: location of other franchisees near their places of business. It appears that hotel/motel franchisees are least often in disagreement and auto service are most often in disagreement regarding the location of other dealers in the chain.

TABLE 1

AVERAGE FREQUENCY OF DISAGREEMENT AMONG
FRANCHISEES AND INDEPENDENT
DISTRIBUTORS

| DISAGREEMENT TYPE[a] | FAST FOOD $X_1$ n=44 | HOTEL/ MOTEL $X_2$ n=26 | AUTO SERVICE $X_3$ n=24 | INDUST. DIST. $X_4$ n=26 | CONSUM. DIST. $X_5$ n=25 | F RATIO | F PROB.[b] |
|---|---|---|---|---|---|---|---|
| 1. Minimum sales you are expected to make. | 3.75 | 3.58 | 3.67 | 3.42 | 3.80 | 1.46 | NS |
| 2. Size of inventory you should carry. | 3.84 | 3.60 | 3.67 | 3.42 | 3.58 | 1.94 | NS |
| 3. Handling dissatisfied customers. | 3.77 | 3.15 | 3.46 | 3.19 | 3.70 | 4.10 | .00 |
| 4. Quality of products required to carry. | 3.66 | 3.42 | 3.61 | 3.58 | 3.71 | .63 | NS |
| 5. Assortment of goods you offer. | 3.34 | 3.53 | 3.57 | 3.57 | 3.40 | .51 | NS |
| 6. Your store location. | 3.61 | 3.70 | 3.38 | 3.60 | 3.63 | .47 | NS |
| 7. Location of other franchisees/ distributors too near you. | 3.09 | 3.63 | 2.32 | 3.00 | 3.05 | 4.52 | .00 |
| 8. Remodeling and/or expansion. | 3.61 | 3.46 | 3.46 | 3.91 | 3.89 | 2.37 | .06 |
| 9. Number of employees you have. | 3.89 | 3.76 | 3.78 | 3.50 | 3.79 | 1.34 | NS |
| 10. Hours you stay open. | 3.67 | 3.72 | 3.58 | 3.92 | 3.74 | .49 | NS |
| 11. Local advertising you may do. | 3.77 | 3.50 | 3.17 | 3.69 | 3.80 | 3.72 | .01 |
| 12. Local advertising parent may do. | 3.46 | 3.23 | 3.13 | 3.50 | 3.35 | .85 | NS |
| 13. Your purchases of supplies. | 3.75 | 3.52 | 3.50 | 3.65 | 3.61 | .81 | NS |
| 14. Availability of supplies. | 3.59 | 3.23 | 3.21 | 2.88 | 3.08 | 2.84 | .03 |
| 15. Your relations with your community. | 3.82 | 3.73 | 3.70 | 3.63 | 3.76 | .23 | NS |
| 16. Prices of your products. | 3.45 | 3.46 | 3.13 | 3.08 | 3.23 | 1.06 | NS |
| 17. Promotional allowances. | 3.48 | 3.40 | 3.18 | 3.04 | 3.54 | 1.35 | NS |
| 18. Sales promotion displays. | 3.24 | 3.42 | 3.22 | 3.38 | 3.55 | .58 | NS |
| 19. Sales contests sponsored by franchisor/supplier. | 3.28 | 3.42 | 3.00 | 2.83 | 3.59 | 2.58 | .04 |
| 20. Cooperative advertising offered to you. | 3.38 | 3.12 | 3.27 | 2.92 | 3.85 | 3.17 | .02 |
| 21. Timing and frequency of promotional campaigns. | 4.00 | 3.16 | 3.24 | 3.04 | 3.57 | 2.13 | NS |

Source: One way analysis of variance from SPSS computer package: ONEWAY subroutine.

[a]Comparison made on 21 scales of agreement. Respondent was asked to indicate how frequently he was in disagreement with his franchisor/supplier. Each scale had four intervals ranging from Very Frequently (1) to Very Infrequently (4). A lower score indicates less frequent disagreement on the situation in question.

[b]F-Probability indicating NS fell well below the .05 level of significance.

382

TABLE 2

| | Table 2a — COMPARISON OF AVERAGE FREQUENCY OF DISAGREEMENT AMONG FAST FOOD, HOTEL/MOTEL, AND AUTO SERVICE, FRANCHISEES | | | | | | Table 2b — COMPARISON OF AVERAGE FREQUENCY OF DISAGREEMENT BETWEEN EACH FRANCHISEE GROUP AND DISTRIBUTORS OF INDUSTRIAL GOODS | | | | | |
|---|---|---|---|---|---|---|---|---|---|---|---|---|
| Group 1 = / Group 2 = | Fast Food: Hotel/Motel | | Fast Food: Auto Service | | Hotel/Motel: Auto Service | | Fast Food: Distributors | | Hotel/Motel: Distributor | | Auto Service: Distributor | |
| DISAGREEMENT TYPE[a] | $T^{b}$ Value | 2 Tail Prob. | T Value | 2 Tail Prob. | T Value | 2 Tail Prob. | $T^{b}$ Value | 2 Tail Prob. | T Value | 2 Tail Prob. | T Value | 2 Tail Prob. |
| 3. Handling of dissatisfied customers. | 2.68 | .01 | 1.82 | NS | -1.18 | NS | 3.06 | .00 | -.14 | NS | 1.20 | NS |
| 7. Location of other franchisees/distributors too near you. | -2.43 | .02 | 2.59 | .01 | 4.33 | .00 | .30 | NS | 1.99 | .06 | -1.82 | NS |
| 8. Remodeling and/or expansion. | .91 | NS | .84 | NS | .02 | NS | -2.27 | .03 | -2.70 | .01 | -2.46 | .02 |
| 11. Local advertising you may do. | 1.78 | NS | 2.63 | .01 | 1.34 | NS | .54 | NS | -1.10 | NS | -2.14 | .04 |
| 14. Availability of supplies. | 1.79 | NS | 1.58 | NS | .08 | NS | 3.50 | .00 | 1.45 | NS | 1.18 | NS |
| 19. Sales contests sponsored by franchisor/supplier. | -.61 | NS | 1.03 | NS | 1.50 | NS | 1.69 | NS | 2.16 | .04 | .54 | NS |
| 20. Cooperative advertising offered to you. | 1.04 | NS | .42 | NS | -.52 | NS | 1.69 | NS | .67 | NS | 1.20 | NS |

SOURCE: SPSS package: T-Test subroutine.

[a] Only shows scales from Table 1 which fell close to .05 level of significance.

[b] The t-test used is for independent samples, unequal variances. It compares the average disagreement scores of one group to another. Mean values may be found on Table 1 for each group. The sign of the t-value indicates relative value of group means. On the scales a high score indicates agreement, thus a (-) t-value sign shows group #2 is more in agreement with its suppliers than group #1.

There are two other areas where there appears to be significant difference. One is between fast food and hotel franchisees regarding the handling of dissatisfied customers. Hotel franchisees have significantly more frequent disagreements about this than fast food operators. The other area of difference is between fast food and auto service dealers regarding the local advertising they are allowed to do. Auto service franchisees are more frequently in disagreement on this issue.

Table 2b reviews the relation of frequency of disagreement between franchisees and independent distributors. This comparison was made with only one of the independent distributors due to space limitations. Industrial distributors were chosen for purposes of example because it was felt they would make a greater conrast due to their lower levels of agreement noted earlier. Overall, out of 21 pair-wise comparisons only 8 were found to differ at the .05 level.

Distributors disagree more often than fast food operators on the matter of handling dissatisfied customers and on the availability of supplies.

Each franchisee differed with the industrial distributor regarding remodeling and/or expansion. The industrial distributor had a higher level of agreement than any of the franchisees.

Distributors differ at a significant level with hotel/motel franchisees both on location of other operators near-by as well as on sales contests issued by the franchisor or supplier. In both instances the distributor is more frequently in disagreement.

The only significant difference between distributors and auto service franchisees, aside from the remodeling issue noted earlier, relates to local advertising they are allowed to do. It appears that auto service dealers are in less agreement than distributors on this issue.

## CONCLUSIONS

The objective of this study was to examine whether or not there are differences among channel system types in terms of the nature and incidence of conflict. Two questions were investigated. Does the level of conflict between franchisor and franchisee vary among franchise types? Does the level of conflict vary between contractual systems, such as franchises and independent distributor systems?

A relatively low number of differences was uncovered when pair-wise comparisons were made among the franchisee groups and between each of these groups and the independent distributors. Therefore, one should not generalize, at this point, that there is more or less conflict in a contractual as opposed to an independent channel system. In addition, it would be unwise to generalize that there is much variance in conflict among franchise types. The following points may offer some explanation for the low number of differences in vertical conflict.

Earlier research [1,5] found that the performance of the channel member was usually negatively correlated with conflict. That is to say, those operators with higher levels of conflict often performed at lower levels. Preliminary investigation of this data set could suggest support for this relationship. When asked to rank the profitability of their operations with respect to other similar operations, the franchisees and distributors of consumer goods ranked themselves well above average. The distributors of industrial goods often ranked themselves at or below average. It will be recalled that the industrial distributors most often showed the most disagreement with their suppliers. One might suggest that it was this relatively high level of profitability, perceived by most of the interviewees, that yielded a sample composed of low levels of conflict. That is to say, there may have been a rather limited range in levels of conflict because there was a limited range in relative profitability. It might also be suggested that, if further research is to be done into various levels of conflict, the study should represent fairly diverse levels of performance.

## REFERENCES

1.  Assael, Henry. "Constructive Role of Interorganizational Conflict," Administrative Science Quarterly, 14 (December, 1969), 573-82.

2.  Barnhart, Bill. "Franchise Power Struggle Heats Up," Chicago Daily News, (January 14, 1977), p. 30.

3.  Franchised Distribution. New York: The Conference Board, Inc., 1971.

4.  Levi, Robert. "So You Want to Run a Franchise?," Dun's Review, (January, 1969), pp. 36-38.

5.  Lusch, Robert F. "Channel Conflict: Its Impact on Retailer Operating Performance," Journal of Retailing, 52 (Summer, 1976), pp. 3-12.

6.  Mallen, Bruce. "A Theory of Retailer-Supplier Conflict, Control, and Cooperation," Journal of Retailing, 39 (Summer, 1963), 24-31.

7.  Mallen, Bruce. "Conflict and Cooperation in Marketing Channels," in The Marketing Channel: A Conceptual Viewpoint, Bruce E. Mallen, ed., New York: John Wiley and Sons, Inc., 1967, pp. 124-134.

8.  McDonald's Operators' Association Newsletter, (December, 1976).

9.  National Franchise Association Coalition News, (September, 1976).

10. Nie, Norman H., et. al. SPSS: Statistical Package for the Social Sciences. New York: McGraw-Hill, 1975.

11. Oxenfeldt, Alfred R. and Anthony O. Kelly. "Will Successful Franchise Systems Ultimately Become Wholly-Owned Chains?," Journal of Retailing, 44 (Winter, 1968-69), pp. 69-83.

12. Pearson, Michael M. "An Empirical Study of the Operational Results Associated With Conflict and Cooperation In Channels of Distribution," Unpublished Ph.D. thesis, University of Colorado, 1972.

13. Rosenberg, Larry J. and Louis W. Stern. "Conflict Measurement in the Distribution Channel," Journal of Marketing Research, 8 (November, 1971), 437-42.

14. Rosenbloom, Bert. "Conflict and Channel Efficiency: Some Conceptual Models for the Decision Maker," Journal of Marketing, 37 (July, 1973), 26-30.

15. S. Bill 2335, 94th Congress, 1st Session, 1975.

16. Stephenson, P. Ronald and Robert G. House. "A Perspective on Franchising: The Design of an Effective Relationship," Business Horizons, 14 (August, 1971), 35-42.

17. Stern, Louis W. and Ronald H. Gorman. "Conflict in Distribution Channels: An Exploration," in Distribution Channels: Behavioral Dimensions, Louis W. Stern, ed. Boston: Houghton Mifflin, 1969, pp. 156-75.

18. Thompson, Donald N. "The Literature on Franchising: A Selected, Classified Bibliography," Journal of Retailing, 44 (Winter, 1968-69), pp. 84-88.

19. Walters, C. Glenn. Marketing Channels. New York: The Ronald Press, 1974.

20. Walker, Orville C. "An Experimental Investigation of Conflict and Power In Marketing Channels," Unpublished Ph.D. thesis, University of Wisconsin, 1970.

TOWARD IMPROVED MEASURES OF DISTRIBUTION CHANNEL CONFLICT

James R. Brown, Indiana University

## ABSTRACT

The seriousness of conflict within distribution channels
depends upon the importance of certain issues and the
frequency with which disagreements over these issues
occur.  Previous researchers in this area have not
attempted to directly measure the relative importance of
these issues.  The results of a pilot study indicate that
conjoint measurement may be a feasible technique for
directly measuring the relative importance of conflict
issues.

## INTRODUCTION

The behavioral construct of conflict within channels of
distribution is one which has received a growing amount of
attention by marketing scholars [1, 2, 4, 5, 8, 10, 11,
13, 14, 15, 16, 18, 19].  Much of the previous research
in this area has been conceptual in nature but there appears to be some interest in empirically examining this
concept [1, 2, 8, 11, 15].  One area of particular interest is that of developing better measures of conflict
within distribution channels with the hope of gaining a
deeper understanding of this construct.

The purpose of this paper, then, is to suggest a method
of improving present measures of channel conflict.
Specifically, this paper will present the results of a
pilot study undertaken to examine the feasibility of
utilizing conjoint measurement in operationalizing conflict and to evaluate the contribution of various
factors to perceived conflict.

## CONCEPTUAL FRAMEWORK

### Toward a Definition of Conflict

Exactly what is meant by conflict?  "Researchers for
decades have sought an adequate definition of conflict..."
[17, p. 359].  For example, Rosenberg and Stern have defined conflict as an adversary relationship [14] as well
as "...the distance between reciprocal channel members'
perceptions of issues, which are symptomatic of conflict"
[15, p. 437].  Stern and Gorman view conflict "...as a
process of changes--changes in the task environment, within
individual firms in a channel system, and/or in the relationships between elements of the environment and
channel members--which induce realignment in the relationships between the channel system members" [18, p. 157].
Boulding, on the other hand, defines conflict "...as a
situation of competition in which the parties are aware
of the incompatibility of potential future positions and
in which each party wishes to occupy a position that is
incompatible with the wishes of the other" [3, p. 5].

One view in these various definitions is the process aspect of conflict.  One approach to this aspect considers
conflict as a "dynamic process" composed of a series of
"conflict episodes."  Each episode is posited to be comprised of five states--the latent state, the cognitive
state, the affective state, conflictful behavior, and
conflict aftermath [12].

Another aspect of conflict implied in these definitions
is the incompatibility of the goals held by the parties
of the conflict situation.  The incompatibility of "po-

tential future positions" is a necessary condition for
conflict to exist.  If there is no incompatibility,
there will be no conflict.  This notion, along with that
of the process aspect of conflict, should be included in
a general definition of conflict.

One such useful definition of conflict as it applies to
distribution channels is as follows:  <u>conflict</u> is the
evolution of the incompatibility of the channel members'
goals from its latent state through its aftermath.  A
schematic diagram of channel conflict as it is defined
here is shown in Figure 1.

FIGURE 1

A MODEL OF CHANNEL CONFLICT

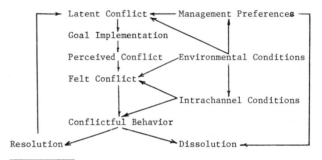

Source:  Adapted from Pondy [12, p. 306] and Rosenberg
[13, p. 69].

Management preferences and environmental conditions may
cause a channel member to change one or more of its goals
and objectives such that they become incongruent with
those of other members in the channel.  This goal incompatibility remains in its <u>latent state</u> until at least
one member of the distribution channel perceives the
members' goals as now being incompatible with each other.
The <u>perceived state</u> of channel conflict results as the
channel members attempt to implement their incompatible
goals.  Incompatible goals within a channel may cause
inconsistent demands to be made upon channel members.
These inconsistent demands as well as environmental conditions may create tension and anxiety within those
channel members.[1]  This tension or anxiety is known as
the <u>felt</u> or <u>affective state</u> of conflict.  Conditions
either within the channel, within the environment, or
both may again serve to further exacerbate the situation
by triggering apathetic, noncooperative, or aggressive
behavior by one or more channel members.  These forms of
behavior comprise the <u>conflictful behavior state</u> of the
conflict process.  The final state of this evolution of
goal incompatibility is that of <u>conflict aftermath</u>.  In

---

[1]Since much of the conflict literature is in terms of individuals in conflict within themselves or with other individuals or organizations, felt conflict is a perfectly
reasonable element within the evolutionary states of conflict.  The emphasis here, however, is on institutions
and instituions are not usually thought of as having
affective states.  An argument can be made for this
though, since their affective states may be considered
to be reflections of the institution's top decision
makers.

this state the goal incompatibility may be either partially or completely resolved or may lead to the dissolution of the channel relationship if it cannot be resolved. The degree to which the goal incompatibility has been resolved determines, in part, the latent state for the next evolutionary process. Thus conflict may be viewed as the evolution of the incompatibility of channel members' goals from its latent state through its aftermath.

Since the construct of conflict within distribution channels is a broad one, any one research attempt must be restricted to a portion of such a construct. This study represents a preliminary investigation into a refinement of the measurement of the perceived state of conflict.

Perceived Conflict

If the underlying goals of a firm are incompatible with other channel members' goals, the strategies used by the various channel members to implement them are likely to be incompatible. For conflict to be in the perceived state, these incompatible strategies must be recognized as such by at least one member of the channel.

A schematic representation of the construct of perceived conflict is presented in Figure 2. Through strategies, incompatible goals are implemented. The number and importance of these goals determine the number and importance of the incompatible strategies. The number of incompatible strategies and their relative contribution to overall perceived conflict determine the existence and extent of that conflict state. The relative contribution, then, may be thought of as a measure of the relative importance of a particular strategy to the channel member.

FIGURE 2

PERCEIVED STATE OF CONFLICT

Any instrument attempting to measure an overall level of perceived conflict should, therefore, include an assessment of the importance of incompatible strategies to each channel member. A good indicant of that importance is the relative contribution of that strategy to an overall level of perceived conflict.

PREVIOUS MEASURES

Rosenberg and Stern [15], Pearson [11], and Lusch [8] have all attempted to measure conflict. Although the former two studies were measuring perceived conflict while the latter was measuring manifest conflict, all three employed a similar method of measuring the conflict state of interest. Essentially, the procedure is to first identify items over which firms within a distribution channel might disagree (e.g., promotional allowances, pricing, delivery time). Respondents are then asked to provide direct subjective estimates as to the degree of conflict contained in an item (or conflict issue) [15, 11] or to provide some subjective estimate as to the frequency of

disagreement over each issue [8]. These estimates are then summed or averaged, over the conflict issues considered, to arrive at some index of conflict within the distribution channel under study. None of these three studies deals directly with the relative importance of the conflict issues. It would seem, as indicated in the previous section of this paper, that the level of the conflict state under study depends upon the number (or frequency) of disagreements and the importance of the conflict issues involved. An improved measure of conflict should, therefore, include the relative contribution of incompatible issues to the overall level of the conflict state being studied.

PRESENT STUDY

Objectives and Scope

To test the feasibility of utilizing conjoint-measurement to assess the relative contribution of certain issues to an overall level of conflict, a pilot study was developed. Conflict in this study was restricted to the perceived state and was operationally defined to be the overall level (i.e., seriousness) of disagreement between a manufacturer and a retailer pertaining to the goals, policies, and activities of their relationship. Implicit in this operational definition was the assumption that conflict is perceived by at least one of the parties in the channel. In addition, the channel membership was restricted to a manufacturer and a retailer to reduce the confounding effects of the presence of other intermediaries.

The conflict issues selected for measurement were (1) disagreement over the functions performed; (2) disagreement over the target market served; (3) disagreement over the assortment of products carried by the retailer; and (4) differences in the interpretation of information pertaining to the channel relationship. Since these four issues (or some form of them) have been defined as "causes" of channel conflict [1, 4, 18, 19], their use in this pilot study seemed justified.

The primary objective of this study was to determine if an additive conjoint-measurement model could be used to represent the composition rule (or evaluation function) for an individual or group of individuals. This composition rule, then, may be used to predict the seriousness or overall level of perceived conflict. A second objective was to test for convergent validity in the model by comparing the part-worth contributions derived by the additive conjoint-measurement model with those derived by direct estimates. These objectives may be expressed in the form of the following research hypotheses:

1. The additive conjoint-measurement model adequately represents both each individual's and the group's composition rule used to predict some overall level of conflict.

2. The direct-estimates of the relative contribution of the four issues to an overall level of perceived conflict are significantly correlated to those derived from the conjoint-measurement model. This relationship is hypothesized to be true for both individual and group data.

Methodology

A convenience sample of forty-seven undergraduate business students enrolled in an introductory marketing course was used in this exploratory study. The subjects were first given a brief introduction to the concept of channel conflict after which they were presented a scenario describing a contrived relationship between a manufacturer and a retailer. The purpose of this scenario was to provide the subjects with a common frame of reference. Following a procedure described by Green and Wind [6], the subjects were then given sixteen cards each containing a different conflict circumstance. In each of these circumstances, the four issues were assigned one of two levels, that of either being present or absent in the circumstance. The subjects were asked to rank and then mark the cards from the highest degree of perceived conflict present to the lowest degree present.

The second task asked of the subjects consisted of their weighting the four conflict issues--disagreement over the markets served, disagreement over the functions performed, disagreement over the assortment of products carried by the retailer, and differences in the interpretation of information relevant to the channel relationship--on the basis of their relative contribution to the overall level of perceived conflict. Again following Green and Wind [6], each subject was asked to assign "11" to the issue believed to contribute the most to perceived conflict and then to assign numbers from 1 to 10 to the remaining issues based on their degree of contribution to perceived conflict relative to that of the highest contributor.

Analysis and Findings

The first task required of the subjects resulted in ordinal ratings of sixteen different conflict circumstances. These nonmetric data were then submitted to the MONANOVA program [7] to derive the part-worth contribution for each issue for each subject. To determine the applicability of the additive conjoint-measurement model, two criteria were applied to each individual's results. First, a low stress level (0.05 to 0.125) indicated that the program was reasonably able "... to find a monotone transformation of the input data whose values ... [were] represented as an additive combination of main effects" [6, p. 118]. A second criterion used was whether or not the a priori assumption of monotonicity held true. Since the four issues were expected to contribute to the overall level of perceived conflict in a positive manner, the signs of each of the part-worth contributions were expected to be positive.

Eight subjects had evaluation functions that could not minimize stress below the cutoff level of 0.125 and one individual's part-worth contributions did not conform to the assumption of monotonicity. Since the remaining 38 subjects (81%) had low stress values and monotonic composition rules, the additive conjoint-measurement model can be said to accurately represent their evaluation functions of overall perceived conflict.

To determine how well the additive conjoint-measurement model represented the group's[2] composition rule, the mean rankings for each of the sixteen conflict circumstances were computed. These mean rankings were then submitted to the MONANOVA program to determine the group's part-worth contributions for each of the four conflict issues. The resulting composition rule was found to be monotonic and to have a stress value of much less than 0.125. As an additional check of the adequacy of this model, a metric ANOVA program was used to determine the total interaction sums of squares as a percentage of total sums of squares [6]. This percentage, found to be 2.09%, can only be used as a rough guage of the absence of interaction effects since nonmetric data were submitted to a metric program. Thus the absence of large interaction effects confirm that the additive conjoint-measurement model adequately represents the group composition rule. The part-worth contribution of each conflict issues as a percentage of the sum of the part-worths for the group appear in Table 1.

---

[2]Since the additive conjoint-measurement model seems to adequately describe the composition rules for 38 of the subjects, subsequent analysis will be based upon this group of 38 individuals.

TABLE 1

Percentage Contribution of the Issues to Overall Perceived Conflict for MONANOVA and Direct-Estimates for the Sample Evaluation Function

| Issue[a] | MONANOVA | Direct-Estimate |
|---|---|---|
| A | 27.0% | 28.2% |
| B | 20.1% | 20.6% |
| C | 25.9% | 24.9% |
| D | 26.9% | 26.3% |

---

[a] Issue A represents disagreement over the functions performed.
Issue B represents differences in the interpretation of relevant information.
Issue C represents disagreement over the assortment of products carried by the retailer.
Issue D represents disagreement over the target market served.

Also presented in Table 1 are the group mean percentage contributions for each issue to the overall level of perceived conflict derived from the direct-estimate method. As can be seen, the two methods appear to produce quite similar results. If the additive conjoint-measurement model produces part-worth contributions that reasonably represent the subject's beliefs, the part-worths derived from this model should be significantly correlated with those derived by the direct-estimate method. To test this hypothesis, correlation analysis was performed on the part-worths derived by the two methods for each individual as well as for the group. The correlation coefficient was significantly different from zero for 24 individuals (63% of the group) at $\alpha = 0.05$ and for 31 individuals (82%) at $\alpha = 0.10$. In addition, the mean correlation coefficient ($r = .9547$) was also found to be significantly different from zero ($\alpha = 0.05$).

As a matter of curiosity, an analysis of variance was performed on the percentage part-worth contributions derived by MONANOVA for the 38 subjects to test the null hypothesis that the four conflict issues contributed equally to the overall level of perceived conflict. As can be seen from Table 2, the null hypothesis could not be rejected at a significance level of 0.05. Thus for this sample differences between the part-worth contributions of these four issues could not be found.

TABLE 2

Analysis of Variance Table to Test Differences Among the Mean MONANOVA Part-Worth Contributions

| Source of Variation | SS | df | MS | F[a] |
|---|---|---|---|---|
| Among Groups | 0.098 | 3 | 0.033 | 0.764 |
| Within Groups | 1.469 | 34 | 0.043 | |
| Total | 1.567 | 37 | | |

---

[a]$F_{3,34} = 2.88$ at $\alpha = .05$

Discussion

For 38 of the 47 original subjects (i.e., 81%), the additive conjoint-measurement model adequately represented their composition rules used to predict an overall level of perceived conflict. Had the task required of the subjects been more difficult or had the additive model not been applicable, a much smaller percentage of subjects would have been expected to have low stress values and to adhere to the criterion of monotonicity. Thus uncovering the relative contribution of conflict issues to an overall level of perceived conflict appears to be feasible using the additive conjoint-measurement model.

An additional check on this model was to compare its resulting part-worth contribution percentages with those derived from direct-estimates. For nearly two-thirds of individuals and for the group, the correlation coefficient between the two methods is significant at the 0.05 level. This result indicates that the additive conjoint-measurement model produces relative contributions similar to those derived by direct-estimates and, thus, provides evidence for convergent validity.

The results of this pilot study indicate that the additive conjoint-measurement model provides a method to uncover the relative contribution of conflict issues to an overall level of perceived conflict. These part-worth contributions may then be used to weight the frequencies of the conflict issues. The sum, over all issues, of these weighted frequencies, thus, represents the overall level of the particular conflict state under study. Such a measure of conflict would seem to better portray the construct than do present measures.

Limitations of the Study

A very obvious limitation is the sample that was selected. Most of the subjects were college juniors with little or no experience with the management or the operation of distribution channels. The intent of this study was to determine if the tasks associated with uncovering the relative contributions of certain conflict issues could be performed. Regardless of the sample chosen, these tasks would be similar; thus the use of undergraduates as subjects seems justified.

Another limitation of this pilot study is the failure to provide the respondents with a precise specification of the degree of the issue present or absent. This may partially explain why no significant differences were found among the mean MONANOVA part-worth contributions for the four conflict issues. A more precise specification of the levels of these issues plus the use of businessmen who are involved in channel relationships as subjects might have led to significant differences among these issues of conflict.

This lack of significant differences may also be attributed to experimenter-induced bias. Since the course instructor served as the experimenter, the subjects may have tailored their responses to be consistent with what they had been taught rather than what they actually perceived.

Summers and MacKay [21] have shown that multidimensional scaling results may shift over time; the same may be true for conjoint-measurement results. A test-retest should have been performed in this pilot study to determine the reliability of these results. Although some evidence for convergent validity was found, no tests for discriminant validity were undertaken. Future studies of this sort should correct these deficiencies.

Implications

The use of a valid measure of channel conflict would enable marketing scholars to test the relationships underlying this construct. Combining the relative contribution of various issues with the frequencies of disagreement over those issues is one step toward an improved measure of channel conflict. Use of this measure will, hopefully, lead to a better understanding of the construct.

Since channel conflict may have either functional or dysfunctional consequences [16, 19], managers involved with channel relationships should attempt to monitor and control it. A valid measure of channel conflict would enable a manager to investigate the current level of conflict within the channel; it would also point out how various issues contribute to conflict. The relative part-worth contributions derived from conjoint-measurement indicate how much various issues affect overall conflict. Knowledge of these part-worths would enable a manager to know which issues are less tolerant to disagreements. By controlling the frequency of disagreement over these sensitive issues, the manager may be able to control conflict within the distribution channel.

CONCLUSION

This paper has examined the feasibility of using conjoint-measurement to operationalize conflict and to evaluate the contribution of various factors to perceived conflict. The pilot study reported on here indicates that this may be a useful technique in determining the relative contribution of conflict issues to the seriousness or overall level of perceived conflict.

Future research in the area of conflict measurement should be aimed at determining the stability of the MONANOVA part-worth contributions over time. In addition, the validity of such a measure should be examined to insure that the relative contributions of conflict issues to the overall level of the conflict state being studied is actually what is being measured. A third area for future research is to compare the relative contributions of the conflict issues across conflict states to determine the change in contribution (if any) that these issues undergo during the process of conflict.

Including a measure of the relative contribution as well as the frequency of conflict issues in an overall measure of conflict provides a more realistic approach to the measurement of that construct. The pilot study reported on here indicates that conjoint-measurement may be a feasible technique for uncovering the relative contribution of conflict issues to an overall level of perceived conflict. Although the study does have limitations, hopefully, it will stimulate further research and thinking into the measurement of channel conflict.

REFERENCES

1. Assael, Henry. "The Political Role of Trade Associations in Distributive Conflict Resolutions," Journal of Marketing, 32 (April 1968), 21-8.

2. _____. "Constructive Role of Interorganizational Conflict," Administrative Science Quarterly, 14 (December 1969), 573-82.

3. Boulding, Kenneth E. Conflict and Defense: A General Theory. New York: Harper & Row, Publishers, 1962.

4. Carlson, Bjorn and Bertil Kusoffsky. "Distributor Brands and Conflicts in Distributive Organizations," in Louis W. Stern (ed.), Distribution Channels: Behavioral Dimensions, Boston: Houghton Mifflin Company, 1969.

5. Dommermuth, William P. "Profiting from Distribution Conflicts," Business Horizons, 19 (December 1976), 4-13.

6. Green, Paul E. and Yoram Wind. Multiattribute Decisions in Marketing: A Measurement Approach. Hinsdale, Illinois: The Dryden Press, 1973.

7. Kruskal, J. B. and Frank Carmone. "Use and Theory of MONANOVA, A Program to Analyze Factorial Experiments by Estimating Monotone Transformations of the Data," unpublished paper, Bell Laboratories, 1968.

8. Lusch, Robert F. "Sources of Power: Their Impact on Interchannel Conflict," Journal of Marketing Research, 13 (November 1976), 382-90.

9. Mallen, Bruce. "A Theory of Retailer-Supplier Conflict, Control, and Cooperation," Journal of Retailing, 39 (Summer 1963), 24-32, 51.

10. Palamountain, Joseph C. The Politics of Distribution. Cambridge, Mass.: Harvard University Press, 1955.

11. Pearson, Michael M. "The Conflict-Performance Assumption," Journal of Purchasing, 9 (February 1973), 57-69.

12. Pondy, Louis R. "Organizational Conflict: Concepts and Models," Administrative Science Quarterly, 12 (September 1967), 296-320.

13. Rosenberg, Larry J. "A New Approach to Distribution Conflict Management," Business Horizons, 17 (October 1974), 67-74.

14. _____ and Louis W. Stern. "Toward the Analysis of Conflict in Distribution Channels," Journal of Marketing, 34 (October 1970), 40-6.

15. _____ and _____. "Conflict Measurement in the Distribution Channel," Journal of Marketing, 8 (November 1971), 437-42.

16. Rosenbloom, Bert. "Conflict and Channel Efficiency: Some Conceptual Models for the Decision Maker," Journal of Marketing, 37 (July 1973), 26-30.

17. Schmidt, Stuart M. and Thomas A. Kochan. "Conflict: Toward Conceptual Clarity," Administrative Science Quarterly, 17 (September 1972), 359-70.

18. Stern, Louis W. and Ronald H. Gorman. "Conflict in Distribution Channels: An Exploration," in Louis W. Stern (ed.), Distribution Channels: Behavioral Dimensions, Boston: Houghton Mifflin Company, 1969.

19. _____ and J. L. Heskett. "Conflict Management in Interorganization Relations: A Conceptual Framework," in Louis W. Stern (ed.), Distribution Channels: Behavioral Dimensions, Boston: Houghton Mifflin Company, 1969.

20. Summers, John O. and Dvaid B. MacKay. "On the Validity and Reliability of Direct Similarity Judgements," Journal of Marketing Research, 13 (August 1976), 289-95.

# THE OPERATING PERFORMANCE OF RETAIL ORGANIZATIONS DURING DOWNTURN ECONOMIC PERIODS[1]

Albert D. Bates, University of Colorado
Wesley E. Patton, III, University of Colorado

## ABSTRACT

Large scale retailers seem poorly equipped to cope with major economic recessions. During the downturn of 1974 retailers did not cut prices, reduce their work force, cut expenses or reduce inventories. Their major response was to reduce long-term capital expenditures, but this was done only after the recession had bottomed out.

## INTRODUCTION

Marketing as a discipline has never been overly concerned with the subject of economic recession and recovery. Instead, the study of cyclical economic activity has been considered almost exclusively the domain of classical economic analysis. From a marketing viewpoint, though, the discussion of recession by economists is rather hollow. Most of the economist's attention is focused on understanding the macro-impact of recessions and forecasting future downturns or recoveries, with only limited attention devoted to developing prescriptive programs for overcoming the vagaries of recessionary periods [2, 3, 5, 10].

Even though marketing has somewhat ignored the business cycle as a concept, marketing remains an ideal subject area in which to analyze the firm's performance during recession. For one thing, the economic climate is a major environmental variable that influences market potential and buying patterns, much in the same way as demographic factors or consumer attitudes. Thus its impact should be more clearly understood. In addition, many of the most commonly suggested actions for the firm to take during recession--such as price reductions or counter-cyclical advertising--are marketing actions. When it is considered that a number of analysts argue that the economy in the future is likely to be characterized by a series of cyclical fluctuations [12] then the value of understanding recession and recovery should be apparent.

This paper attempts to provide an insight into the relationship between managerial actions during recession and recovery and the operating performance of the firm, by using large scale retailers as an analysis group. Retailers are a particularly good economic segment to study since they are in direct contact with the consumer, which causes economic changes to be felt immediately and without the amplification effects frequently experienced by wholesalers and manufacturers.

## RESEARCH METHODOLOGY

The research focuses on the base year of 1973, the economic downturn of 1974 and the recovery of 1975. From an analytical viewpoint the 1974 recession had both good and bad characteristics. On the negative side the 1974 recession was markedly atypical (assuming that a typical recession exists). In particular, the downturn of 1974 not only had the normal decline in real growth and high levels of unemployment, but it also had rapid rates of inflation. Such a mixed bag economy could possibly have caused firms not to take actions that they might normally follow during a more precisely defined recession. For example, while a reduction in aggregate retail sales might normally cause firms to take actions to reduce inventory levels, the inflationary pressures that existed in 1974 would augur for increased inventory investments to generate possible inventory profits.

Offsetting this negative aspect of the recession are two very positive analytical attributes. First, the recession was quite severe, popularly characterized as the worst economic downturn since 1929. Given its severity, most retail executives felt compelled to take some sort of corrective action. In previous, less severe, recessions, such as in 1958 or 1970, it was possible to simply wait patiently for the economic recovery. Such a waiting game did not seem to be a viable strategy in 1974. Second, the recession coincided very closely with the 1974 calendar year, starting down early in the first quarter of 1974 and bottoming out in the first quarter of 1975. This unusual characteristic made it possible to study the recession using annual rather than quarterly data, thus greatly increasing both the quantity and accuracy of available financial information.

The financial and operating results of 90 firms were reviewed. For analytical purposes the companies were divided into three categories which probably should be affected by economic conditions in different ways.

-Necessities Retailers--These firms, primarily supermarkets and drug stores, concentrate on products that must be purchased in both good times and bad. As a result such firms should be only minimally impacted by economic conditions.

-General Merchandise Retailers--These firms sell a wide spectrum of goods from near necessities to almost totally discretionary items. Thus they should be moderately impacted by recession and recovery. For purposes of this study the general merchandise category includes department stores, discount stores and variety stores.

-Discretionary Goods Retailers--The final category includes firms selling goods whose purchase can be easily postponed. Companies in this category--including apparel and accessory stores, home furnishing stores and appliances stores--should be especially hard hit by recession.

Data for the firms were obtained from the Compustat Financial Tapes which summarize information derived from SEC 10-K reports and company annual reports. Since the Compustat Tapes cover only large national and regional firms, the results of the study are applicable only to relatively large retail organizations. This factor is rather important in that the sample retailers were less severely impacted by the recession than their smaller counterparts. Specifically, the firms sampled felt less than a one percent decline in real dollar sales in 1974, compared to 3.7 percent for total retail sales.

The analysis was conducted using a variety of non-parametric tests, particularly the Kruskal-Wallis one-way analysis of variance and the Wilcoxon matched-pairs signed-ranks test. The non-parametric approach was employed because the research involved convenience sampling and because some of

[1]The authors express their appreciation to the Business Research Division, University of Colorado for providing the funding to support this research project.

the assumptions underlying most parametric tests (such as variance homogeneity) were violated.

As a final point, it should be noted that the study looks only at operating results. It makes no attempt to determine the extent to which management tried to produce certain results and simply failed.

## MAJOR RESEARCH FINDINGS

This paper focuses only on the most interesting findings of the research project and those with the most compelling managerial implications. For discussion purposes the findings are divided into four categories: the overall impact of the recession and the recovery on sales and profits, the extent to which gross margin and expense controls were used to counter recessionary pressures, attempts by retailers to minimize their investment levels, and the degree to which supplier financing was employed as a counter-recessionary device.

### Sales and Profits

To probably nobody's surprise, retailers faced major economic challenges during 1974. The seriousness of the downturn is shown in Table 1 which traces the aggregate performance of the 90 retailers from 1970 to 1975. As can be seen, economic results were virtually constant during that time period, except for 1974. During the recovery of 1975 retailers rebounded to almost the exact same financial position they had in 1973.

Interestingly, current dollar sales actually increased rather substantially for retailers during 1974, thanks to inflation. The sales increase was not experienced uniformly, though, with necessity merchants, as expected, having the largest sales increase during 1974 (p = .0001). When inflation is removed the results are not altered in any meaningful way. In addition, the sales growth pattern during recovery was almost the same as that during the recession.

Profits demonstrated a markedly different pattern than sales. During the downturn profits fell sharply with no appreciable differences between groups (p = .345). During recovery, however, there were sharply differential rates of profit growth--90.9% for necessity retailers, 35.8% for general merchandise retailers and only 12.7% for discretionary goods retailers (p = .039). Both the sales and profit information suggests that necessity retailers perform considerably better than the other groups, particularly during recovery while discretionary goods retailers are especially vulnerable to economic fluctuations.

There are two other factors worth noting before leaving Table 1. First, the widely discussed liquidity crisis of 1974 was largely illusory, at least for retailers. Liquidity ratios demonstrated only the most minimal downward movement. Second, the combination of poor economic performance and high interest rates was staggering to most firms. In 1974 the rate of earnings before interest and taxes actually fell below the effective interest rate on borrowed funds for the firms sampled.

In summary, the economic recession of 1974 was a damaging, but transitory, occurrence. Most retailers experienced very large profit declines in 1974 and a few even faced temporary problems with survival. However, almost all firms were able to return to more normal levels during the recovery of 1975.

### Gross Margin and Expense Control

Two of the most frequently discussed responses to an economic downturn are a series of more aggressive price actions and a greater emphasis on internal cost control. Available evidence suggests that price competition was probably not actively employed during the recession and that expense controls may have been attempted, but if so they met with very little success.

During the recession of 1974, there was no noticeable movement in gross margin percentages for the total group sampled (p = .346). In addition, none of the individual categories demonstrated a movement in gross margin. This is somewhat surprising since the trade press of the day was full of articles regarding aggressive markdown actions being taken by many retailers [6, 8, 9, 11]. It may well be that retailers took earlier markdowns than usual to stimulate sales, but not larger than normal markdowns, or that the markdown activity was aggressive in particular product categories, but was not substantial in total. In addition, a sizeable amount of price reduction activity was engaged in by manufacturers, thus reducing prices to the consumer without affecting retailers' markup percentages.

TABLE 1

COMPOSITE FINANCIAL RATIOS FOR NINETY LEADING RETAIL ORGANIZATIONS
1970 - 1975

| Ratio | 1970 | 1971 | 1972 | 1973 | 1974 | 1975 |
|---|---|---|---|---|---|---|
| **Profitability Ratios** | | | | | | |
| Net Profits (after-tax) to Net Sales | 2.3% | 2.4% | 2.3% | 2.3% | 1.6% | 2.1% |
| Net Sales to Total Assets | 2.3 | 2.3 | 2.3 | 2.4 | 2.4 | 2.5 |
| Net Profits (after-tax) to Total Assets | 5.3% | 5.7% | 5.5% | 5.5% | 3.9% | 5.2% |
| **Liquidity Ratios** | | | | | | |
| Current Assets to Current Liabilities | 1.9 | 1.9 | 1.9 | 1.8 | 1.7 | 1.8 |
| Current Assets (less Inventory) to Current Liabilities | .9 | .9 | .8 | .8 | .8 | .8 |
| **Growth Potential Ratios** | | | | | | |
| Times Interest Earned | 5.7 | 6.8 | 6.5 | 5.3 | 3.5 | 5.3 |
| Earnings before Interest and Taxes to Total Assets | 12.3% | 12.3% | 11.5% | 12.2% | 10.4% | 12.0% |
| Effective Interest Rate | 7.8% | 7.1% | 7.0% | 8.7% | 10.5% | 8.9% |

## TABLE 2

### OPERATING EXPENSES AS A PERCENT OF SALES FOR
### NECESSITIES, GENERAL MERCHANDISE AND DISCRETIONARY GOODS RETAILERS
### 1973 – 1975

| Retail Categories/Year | Total Expenses | Illustrative Expense Categories | | |
| --- | --- | --- | --- | --- |
| | | Interest Expenses | Advertising Expenses | Rental Expenses |
| Necessities Retailers | | | | |
| 1973 | 19.79 | .33 | 1.07 | 1.69 |
| 1974 | 20.42 | .37 | 1.09 | 1.69 |
| 1975 | 20.27 | .33 | 1.24 | 1.57 |
| General Merchandise Retailers | | | | |
| 1973 | 27.75 | 1.52 | 2.42 | 2.32 |
| 1974 | 28.13 | 1.97 | 2.57 | 2.37 |
| 1975 | 28.14 | 1.42 | 2.36 | 2.41 |
| Discretionary Goods Retailers | | | | |
| 1973 | 30.22 | .61 | 3.29 | 6.35 |
| 1974 | 30.54 | .90 | 3.30 | 6.67 |
| 1975 | 30.92 | .48 | 3.21 | 6.94 |
| Total Sample | | | | |
| 1973 | 25.70 | 1.17 | 2.47 | 2.28 |
| 1974 | 26.22 | 1.50 | 2.80 | 2.32 |
| 1975 | 26.19 | 1.10 | 2.42 | 2.33 |

During the recovery of 1975 gross margins increased (p = .006) with no one group lagging behind (p = .170). This upward movement represents a resumption of a long-term upward trend in gross margin percentages that has been noted in many lines of retail trade. Taken in aggregate the results suggest an ability on the part of retailers to control gross margin levels, but a reluctance to use gross margins aggressively in recessionary periods.

Operating expenses by their very nature are quite difficult to control during down economic periods. Most studies of retail cost structures indicate a high level of fixed expenses [1, 4]. This is because retailers must have the air conditioning and lights on and retail clerks covering all sales positions regardless of the level of sales generated. This expense structure has the pleasant characteristic of producing high levels of expense leveraging and rapid increases in profits as sales rise. It also has the disquieting characteristic that as the sales base declines expense leveraging works against the firm and many expenses automatically rise as a percent of sales.

The major expense changes during the 1973 to 1975 time period are outlined in Table 2. While the table reflects the negative aspects of expense leveraging during recession, it fails to suggest the positive impact of expense leveraging during recovery. Specifically, during recession expenses increased as a percent of sales (p = .001), but during recovery they did not decline (p = .741).

When the expense information is viewed in total it suggests that retailers probably have relatively little control over operating expense percentages during a downturn environment. Thus, there appear to be limited payouts from attempting additional expense control activities unless they are accomplished through some dramatic changes in operating methods.

The combination of the expense and gross margin data points up one very interesting observation--expense deterioration creates the profit problem while gross margin improvement leads to recovery. This ratchet effect is a very important point that should be closely reviewed by retail management.

Investment and Productivity Control

It is difficult to appraise the exact value of productivity and investment control activities in influencing profitability. Some studies have suggested that inter-firm variations in capital utilization and productivity ratios have only a slight relationship to profitability [1]. However, simulation studies have suggested that for individual firms productivity improvements can have major profitability payouts [7].

Four major categories of investment control are reviewed in this paper. Three of the categories are short-term in character. These areas include inventory, accounts receivable and employee productivity, which are reviewed in Table 3. The final decision category, capital expenditures, involves a more delayed payout.

The sales-to-inventory ratio rose during both the recessionary period (p = .0001) and recovery (p = .0002). All three groups performed in the same fashion during the downturn, but general merchandise retailers experienced smaller increases in the sales-to-inventory ratio during recovery than did the other groups (p = .039).

The sales-to-accounts receivable ratio remained relatively constant during 1974 (p = .402), but climbed significantly in the 1975 recovery (p = .0006). No major inter-group variations were prevalent in either period (p = .350, p = .786).

The ratio of current dollar sales per employee rose during both recession and recovery (p = .0001 for both periods) as sales increased while the number of employees remained stable in both periods. There was no significant difference in the rate of increase among the three categories of retailers (p = .285, p = .438).

Such a decidedly mixed pattern of results is somewhat difficult to interpret with any precision. On the one hand the results suggest some decided management actions to improve results. However, the ratios are also consistent with what might be expected to happen as a matter of course during a

TABLE 3

PRODUCTIVITY RATIOS FOR NECESSITIES,
GENERAL MERCHANDISE AND DISCRETIONARY GOODS RETAILERS
1973 - 1975

| Retail Category/Year | Sales to Inventory | Sales to Accounts Receivable | Sales per Employee ($000) |
|---|---|---|---|
| Necessities Retailers | | | |
| 1973 | 10.98 | 96.71 | 59.17 |
| 1974 | 11.46 | 110.50 | 65.43 |
| 1975 | 12.46 | 114.95 | 72.47 |
| General Merchandise Retailers | | | |
| 1973 | 5.67 | 6.29 | 31.42 |
| 1974 | 5.98 | 6.35 | 33.92 |
| 1975 | 6.17 | 6.60 | 37.31 |
| Discretionary Goods Retailers | | | |
| 1973 | 4.88 | 13.92 | 35.27 |
| 1974 | 5.39 | 13.52 | 37.98 |
| 1975 | 5.72 | 15.63 | 39.52 |
| Total Sample | | | |
| 1973 | 7.06 | 10.67 | 39.24 |
| 1974 | 7.50 | 11.03 | 42.99 |
| 1975 | 7.87 | 11.53 | 47.36 |

highly inflationary time period as the improvements came
from sales increases, not investment reductions.

One area of investment control that apparently did show a
clear sign of management action is the area of capital expenditures. In aggregate, capital expenditures as a percent of sales fell slightly in 1974 to 2.66% from 2.69%
($p = .036$), and then plummeted sharply to 2.15% in 1975
($p = .0001$). The expenditure levels fell soundly across
all retailing categories ($p = .567$).

The drop in capital expenditures is disquieting in light
of the fact that such actions have such a long-term impact
on corporate performance. However, such actions are understandable given the environment that existed during 1974.
Executives were simply hesitant to make low payout commitments during high interest rate periods. The failure to
resume capital expenditure patterns during the recovery of
1975 does not fit such a logical pattern, though.

The long-term impact of capital spending decisions poses
a serious problem for retailers when decisions are made in
periods of economic turbulence. It appears that the retailers may be forced to forego the full fruits of recovery
because of the limitation in growth potential fostered by
prior investment decisions. The lack of return to a systematic capital investment program calls into question the
ability of retail firms to gauge the timing of future expansion needs.

Supplier Financing

Since the 1974 time period was one of high interest rates
as well as an economic downturn, most retailers had difficulty financing growth. One way to continue growth in
such an environment is by employing interest-free sources
of money, particularly supplier credit. In the present
study the use of supplier financing was measured through
the accounts payable to inventory ratio which indicates
the proportion of the total inventory investment that is
supplier financed.

In total, such outside financing fell in 1974 and then rose
substantially in 1975. Specifically, the ratio of accounts
payable as a percent of inventory fell from 74% in 1973 to
71% in 1974 and then rose to 81% in 1975.

During 1974 there was a marked difference in the ability of
different types of retailers to utilize supplier financing
($p = .0009$). Only necessity retailers--which were least
impacted by recession and least in need of such support--
experienced an increase, with the ratio rising from 70% to
77%. Both general merchandise retailers and discretionary
goods retailers actually experienced declines in the ratio.

During the recovery of 1975 the accounts payable to inventory ratio rose ($p = .0001$), with no apparent differences
between retail categories. While supplier financing is
important at any time and the increase in 1975 was certainly welcome, such improvements are not retroactive and the
lack of success in raising the ratio in 1974 aggravated the
recessionary pressures.

Summary of Findings

To summarize, the pattern of change shown in the data is
suggestive of a somewhat imprecise and ill-defined response
to economic challenges as opposed to a programmed and systematic response. In particular, the failure to use price
competition more aggressively, the failure to control expenses, the lack of control over assets and the inability
to use supplier financing more aggressively are particularly discouraging.

MANAGERIAL ACTIONS FOR COMBATING RECESSIONARY CYCLES

Traditional managerial thinking argues that during recessions retailers should employ counter-cyclical advertising,
reduce prices, and emphasize the sale of counter-cyclical
product categories such as home repair products, sewing
items and auto parts. In addition the present research
suggests some other tactics, some of which run counter to
prevailing management thought.

- Inventory control procedures should probably be loosened somewhat. This is clearly counter to conventional thinking and requires some elaboration. During
  low sales periods normally slow moving items tend to
  drop to very low sales levels, while fast movers tend
  to continue to enjoy relatively brisk sales. By
  reducing inventory levels during down periods, most of
  the reduction is forced to come from the fast selling
  items, precipitating excessive out-of-stock conditions
  and placing further constraints on sales. This difficulty must be overcome.

- Retailers should negotiate more aggressively for extended datings from manufacturers during recessions.
  During the down period most manufacturers are offering
  substantial price incentives, but the retailers' problem is really not one of adequate discounts. In addition to seeking extra discounts retailers should seek
  extended terms on merchandise to compensate for the
  possible increase in inventory levels.

- Retailers should review more carefully the types of
  investment decisions they face and consider the timing
  of investments more precisely. In particular, long-
  term expansion decisions should not be deferred based
  on short-run operating problems. During the recovery
  phase of the business cycle retailers have a distinct
  opportunity to gain ground on competitors through a
  more aggressive growth policy.

In summary, retail executives should try to respond to recessionary periods in a meaningful way. Where possible
they should try to counter the impact of recession with
counter-cyclical programs. Where that is not possible they
must work with the flow of the economy and use it to their
advantage.

## SUMMARY AND CONCLUSIONS

It appears that the retailers sampled in this study resort-
ed to few of the traditional defenses against recession.
Despite the fact that the recession of 1974 was the most
severe since the Great Depression, these retailers did not
cut prices, did not reduce the size of the work force, did
not drastically cut expenses, and did not make large cuts
in inventories. However, there is no way of knowing
whether retailers attempted some of these strategies and
failed or whether, for reasons of their own, made little
attempt at defense.

The retailers studied here are among the largest and
strongest, and despite apparent lack of active counter-
cyclical defense activity, they outperformed retailers as
a whole. The 1974 recession does seem to have had a
sobering effect, however, as noted in the drop in capital
spending during the recovery of 1975. It is quite possible
that retailers are now assessing their performance through
the past economic turbulence and are formulating strategies
for the next one.

## REFERENCES

1.  Bates, Albert D. "The Correlates of Profitability for
    Large-Scale Retail Organizations" (unpublished manu-
    script).

2.  Colberg, Marshall, W. C. Bradford and Richard M. Alt.
    Business Economics. Homewood, Ill.: Richard D.
    Irwin, Inc., 1957.

3.  Dunckel, E. B., W. K. Reed, and I. H. Wilson. The
    Business Environment of the Seventies. New York:
    McGraw-Hill Book Co., 1970.

4.  The Economics of Food Distributors: McKinsey-General
    Foods Study. White Plains, New York: General Foods
    Corporation, 1963.

5.  Galbraith, J. K. The New Industrial State, 2nd ed.
    Boston: Houghton-Mifflin, 1971.

6.  Gordon, Ben. "Is Cream-Skimming the Wave of the
    Future?" Chain Store Age, (December 1974), 7.

7.  Lusch, Robert F. "The Oklahoma Retailer: Doing Time
    in a Turbulent Economy," Oklahoma Business Bulletin,
    (March 1976), 1-3.

8.  "President Cheers Rebate Marketing," Advertising Age,
    (February 10, 1975), 1.

9.  "Price Cutting Seen as Paradox," Merchandising Week,
    (March 31, 1975), 1.

10. Rautenstrauch, Walter. The Economics of Business
    Enterprise. New York: John Wiley and Sons, Inc.,
    1939.

11. Robertson, W. "Merchants Fight It Out in a Less
    Affluent Society," Fortune, (December 1974), 128-33.

12. Sommers, Albert T. "Inflation, Unemployment, and
    Stabilization Policy," Conference Board Record,
    (September 1976), 52-64.

# EFFECTS OF DEBRIEFINGS THAT IDENTIFY A RESEARCH DECEPTION[1]

Daniel Toy, The Pennsylvania State University
Jerry Olson, The Pennsylvania State University
Robert Dipboye, University of Tennessee[2]

## ABSTRACT

Issues involved with the use of deception in applied research are discussed. An experiment is described in which the effects on consumer subjects of a relatively minor marketing research deception were examined. In addition, the effectiveness of a post-experimental debriefing in alleviating any aversive consequences of the deception was examined. Explanations are offered for the generally weak effects of deception and debriefing, as are suggestions for further research.

## INTRODUCTION

As Tybout and Zaltman [18] have embarrassingly noted, little attention has been devoted by marketing researchers to ethical issues involving consumers who serve as research subjects. Of the various research procedures which may have ethically questionable effects on research subjects, perhaps the most frequently criticized is deception. Much of this criticism has originated in psychology [8]. In contrast, the American Marketing Association and the Association for Consumer Research have essentially ignored issues involving the use and impact of deception in consumer research [12, 18]. It is the purpose of this paper to briefly discuss several issues involved with deception use in applied research and, furthermore, to describe the results of an experiment which examined (a) the effects on consumer subjects of a deception sometimes used in marketing research, and (b) the efficacy of debriefing in alleviating the potentially harmful or aversive consequences of the deception experience.

### What is Deception?

Basically, there are two types of deception of research participants. Deception by omission involves telling subjects less than the whole truth. Such deceptions are very common in applied research. They are often employed to avoid sensitizing subjects by not divulging the sponsor of the research. Deceptions involving incomplete information are also used to reduce demand characteristics which could result if subjects knew all the research details prior to their participation.

In contrast, deception by commission involves giving false information (i.e., deliberately lying) to research subjects. Such deceptions may be used to create a credible cover story or guise for a particular investigation. Other reasons for providing research participants with false information include reduction of demand characteristics by creating a false justification for a particular research

procedure (e.g., collecting certain data under the false guise that it is for another, unrelated purpose), manipulation of an independent variable (e.g., falsely telling subjects that a message comes from a certain source), or measurement of a dependent variable (e.g., use of behavioroid measures [2] such as obtaining a commitment from subjects to engage in an activity which is never intended to occur).

### What are the Consequences of Deception?

Although no research in the consumer behavior literature was found which measured the effects of deception, the social psychology literature contains several such studies. In general, the negative effects of deception experiences on research subjects depend upon the absolute severity of the deception and whether or not the subjects were aware of being deceived.

Certain types of deception may have severe negative consequences which occur as a direct result of the deception manipulation. That is, the false or incomplete information provided in the study may itself have harmful effects on the research participants. The psychology literature contains numerous examples of such deceptions, including telling male subjects that they evidence tendencies toward homosexuality [4], telling subjects in a war-stress experiment that they were responsible for the deaths of several fellow soldiers [3], or allowing subjects to believe that they have subjected another person to very strong electric shocks which seemingly had severe physical consequences [14]. In such studies, the deception manipulation may have direct negative impact on research subjects ranging from a state of mild anxiety to a major trauma. A debriefing may or may not substantially reduce these effects.

In contrast, for relatively "mild" deceptions, negative consequences are likely to occur only if subjects become aware that they have been deceived. In well-designed studies, awareness of deception is usually generated by debriefing the subjects, i.e., providing a truthful description of the study upon its completion. There seem to be several potential negative consequences of informing research subjects that they have been deceived. One problem is that the deception may sensitize the subjects and increase their suspiciousness, making them more prone to demand characteristic biases in future research participation [1, 16]. A potential long-run effect of the wide-spread use of deception which is of greater concern to applied psychologists is the apparently growing number of persons in our society who may have a distrust of behavioral research and researchers, or even of science in general [13]. A third and more immediate impact of deception awareness involves the negative effects on subjects who may feel foolish, gullible, or stupid at having "fallen" for the deception.

### Alleviating the Negative Consequences of Deception

Some investigators might recommend that the most effective way to eliminate the harmful outcomes of deception is simply never to use deception in one's research. Substitute research methods available to the researcher who follows this advice include role playing and simulation; unfortunately, most research has found these procedures to be

---

[1]This study was funded by a grant from the Krannert Graduate School of Industrial Administration, Purdue University to Howard Fromkin whose advice and useful criticisms we gratefully acknowledge along with those of Jacob Jacoby. Preparation of this paper was partially supported by a grant to the second author from the Center for Research, College of Business Administration, Pennsylvania State University.

[2]Doctoral candidate in Marketing, Associate Professor of Marketing, and Assistant Professor of Organizational Behavior, respectively.

unsatisfactory [11] and excessively costly and difficult [10], respectively.

Alternatively, a researcher may decide to use deception but attempt to alleviate its harmful consequences by using one or both of two procedures--informed consent and debriefing. Informed consent involves forewarning the subject about the experimental procedures, or perhaps telling him that the study will involve a deception without providing many of the details, and receiving his voluntary consent to participate. However, many applied researchers may be unwilling to tell their subjects "all", prior to data collection.

In contrast, debriefing is a relatively direct method of handling the negative effects of a deception experience, after the data are collected. A debriefing may be considered to have two purposes: (a) to completely inform subjects of the procedures and purpose of the research and their contribution to it (this may bring the deception to the subjects' attention), and (b) to alleviate any harmful consequences of the experimental procedures, including the effects of any deceptions used.

Prevalence of Deception and Debriefing

Few, if any, investigations in marketing involve deceptions with directly harmful effects on subjects of the type and magnitude described earlier. However, it is likely that many studies conducted by marketing researchers involve (perhaps less directly aversive) deceit and falsehoods. To obtain a rough estimate of the prevalence of deception in one type of marketing research, the authors reviewed all 32 experimental studies published in the Journal of Marketing Research from 1972 to 1975[3]. The analysis revealed that all 32 investigations involved some type of deception (78% deception by omission and 22% deception by both commission and omission).[4] However, none of the deceptions involving false information seemed severe enough to have directly harmful consequences on subjects.

Although the APA "Ethical Principles" [8] require that research subjects be debriefed about their participation, only five of these 32 studies (6%) reported having conducted a postexperimental debriefing. Perhaps a major reason for omitting the debriefing is the researcher's concern that telling subjects about a relatively "mild," innocuous deception may cause more negativity, greater upset, etc., than not conducting a debriefing. The general purpose of the present research was to probe this issue by examining the effects of debriefings which identified a relatively "mild" deception.

METHODS

Research Purpose and Overview

The two-fold purpose of this research was (a) to examine the impact on selected attitudes, values, suspicions, and behavioral intentions of informing consumer subjects through a debriefing, of a consumer research deception involving false information, and (b) to assess the effects of a good, high quality debriefing on alleviating these possibly negative reactions. To more meaningfully assess the impact of the deception, two situations were created that were intended to differ in the extent to which the deception personally affected each subject. In the more involving condition, subjects were falsely led to believe that they would soon possess a desirable product (which did not, in fact, exist), while in the less involving condition subjects were told they would not be possessors. The deception was identified during a post-experimental debriefing. To more clearly determine the efficacy of the debriefing in alleviating the possible negative consequences of deception, two levels of debriefing quality were created. In the "poor" debriefing condition, the experimenter made a minimal effort, bluntly identifying the deception and providing only a cursory description of the study. In contrast, the "good" debriefing treatment was much more extensive and included a general discussion of the experiment in which the experimenter gradually allowed the subjects to recognize for themselves the possibility of a deception and then presented a logical rationale for its use, as well as a thorough description of the study and its purposes.

Experimental Design and Procedures

The experimental procedures which created the necessary deception were part of a nearly exact replication of an earlier study [9] which tested, in a consumer product evaluation context, hypothesis "a" from Brock's [6] commodity theory. Specifically, this hypothesis states that a product perceived to be scarce or unavailable is valued more highly than if it is perceived to be plentiful and widely available. The replication involved two between-subjects manipulations of consumer perceptions of a new product: (a) an availability factor with two levels--scarce and plentiful, and (b) a possession factor with two levels--possessor and nonpossessor. Only the possession manipulation is relevant to this paper.

Deception. The basic deception involved in this study was that the "new product" did not in fact exist. Additional deceptions described below were used in order to increase the impact and experimental realism of the basic deception. All of these deceptions were considered to be relatively "mild" in the sense that subjects would have to be made aware of the deceptions through a debriefing in order that negative reactions be evidenced.

Following a 15-minute "warm-up" discussion about nylon hose and pantyhose led by the female experimenter, 41 women undergraduate subjects were told that their participation was part of a nationwide marketing research study to determine the potential demand for a new brand of nylon pantyhose manufactured in Europe. To convince subjects of the product's authenticity and its outstanding attributes, they were shown a 5-minute film supposedly made by an independent U.S. testing institute.[5] The film deceptively depicted the fictitious brand out-performing "leading American hosiery brands" on five machines which scientifically measure a fabric's abrasion and tear resistance, stretchability, etc. In reality, all of the filmed comparisons were rigged so that it appeared the "new brand" had somewhat better performance characteristics than the comparison hose.

Manipulation of Perceived Possession. Then, the two levels of the possession factor (possessor or not) were manipulated by telling the approximately 20 subjects in each group that, due to a delayed shipment, not everyone in the group could receive a free pair of these hose. However, subjects were told that the experimenter did have enough hose so that about half of the group could receive a free pair. Forthcoming receipt of the complimentary pair of hose (i.e., perceived possession or nonpossession) was randomly determined by whether or not the face-down questionnaire before each subject had a large "X" stamped on the first page. If an "X" was present when a subject turned over her questionnaire, she would receive a free pair of

---

[3]A complete description of this review can be found in [15].

[4]Certainly, some survey research employs deception involving false information. Moreover, some proprietary and/or unpublished research may also use deceptive procedures.

---

[5]In reality, the film was created by the second author using the facilities of the Home Economics Department's temperature- and humidity-controlled textile lab at Purdue University.

of hose following the study; no "X", no free pair.

The subjects then completed a nine-page questionnaire containing several measures of their evaluation of the "new brand" (none of these data are relevant to this article), plus several measures of potential experimental artifacts such as suspiciousness, evaluation apprehension, demand characteristics, etc.

Manipulation of Debriefing Quality. The debriefing (poor or good) was conducted following completion and collection of the questionnaire. To reduce subjects' inhibitions about responding frankly and possibly negatively to the experiment, a different (male) experimenter administered the quality-of-debriefing manipulation.

In the minimal or poor debriefing condition, the experimenter simply and bluntly told the subjects that there was no "new, European hose," no one would receive a pair, the film was a hoax, etc. He said he had to lie in order to conduct the study of how scarce products were evaluated. A more thorough description of the study's purposes, a justification for the subjects' behavior, and the rationale for the procedures were not provided. Thus, this four-minute "debriefing" merely served to identify the deception for the subjects, but did nothing to alleviate the possibly negative consequences of knowing one was deceived. Then, the experimenter said he was interested in the effects of deception and had a short questionnaire for subjects to report their feelings about the study and deception. After finishing the questionnaire, the subjects received a thorough (i.e., good) debriefing in which all procedures were completely explained, were promised a free pair of American hose (actually delivered about 2 months later), and left the room.

In the extensive or good debriefing condition, the experimenter first led the subjects through a general discussion of the experiment. During this conversation, he gradually focused on subjects' suspicions, following the procedures advocated by Aronson and Carlsmith [2]. After the subjects became aware that the study was not quite as it seemed, the experimenter described the deceptions and provided a detailed rationale for the necessity of using deception in order to achieve the purposes of the study. Subjects were further told that alternative methods were considered but were not feasible and the experimenter had reluctantly decided to use deception. In order to insure the success of the basic deception, the experimenter described how he had developed, through extensive pretests, an elaborate set of experimental "props" or "scenery" which made the "new hose" seem very real and desirable (e.g., a sign on the laboratory door, a sound film, etc.). Thus, the experimenter said no subjects should feel foolish or gullible for believing the experimental procedures, since they were designed to be successful. After the 15-minute debriefing, subjects responded to the questionnaire, were promised a free pair of American hose and were dismissed.

Dependent Variables--Deception Questionnaire. The effects of the deception and debriefing were measured by 16 dependent variables administered in a "Deception Evaluation Questionnaire." This instrument was designed specifically to measure the negative effects identified in the literature [e.g., 5] as potential and important outcomes of deception.[6] Table 1 presents the 16 questions in skeleton form.

_____
[6]The questionnaire construction and its pilot testing were primarily the work of Michael Flanagan to whom we are grateful for permission to use his instrument. Copies are available from the second author.

Check for Experimental Artifacts

A content analysis of subjects' written responses to several questions at the end of the pre-debriefing questionnaire provided no evidence that (a) major suspicions had been aroused by the study, (b) any subjects had accurate insights into the experimental hypothesis (i.e., no evidence of demand characteristics), or (c) previous experimental experiences had a sensitizing effect on subjects or otherwise affected the obtained results. Thus, no measurable biases due to experimental artifacts were found.

Manipulation Checks--Possession/Deception Impact

An ANOVA of responses to the question "how likely are you to receive a free pair of hose?" yielded only a significant main effect of Possession ($F = 86.60$, $df = 1/37$, $p < .0001$). Perceived possession mean scores were 4.22 for possessors and 1.98 for nonpossessors, on a 1-5 point scale from extremely unlikely to extremely likely, respectively. Clearly, the two manipulations of perceived possession (yes and no) had strong and successful effects on subjects' belief expectations. The perceived possession manipulation was also expected to have a differential impact on subjects' experimental involvement and thus affect the impact of the deception. To check on this effect, seven measures of how subjects felt were included in the pre-debriefing questionnaire. ANOVAs of these "feeling state" measures (5-point scales) revealed that subjects who expected possession of the product felt (a) more lucky than nonpossessors (2.08 vs. 2.96 $p < .02$) and (b) more rewarded than nonpossessors (1.76 vs. 2.77 $p < .005$). Possessors felt slightly less jealous than nonpossessors, although this difference was marginally significant (3.47 vs. 3.02 $p < .06$). No significant differences were found between possessors and nonpossessors in terms of boredom, sadness, feelings of uniqueness, or anger, and no other main or interaction effects were significant for any of these seven variables. In sum, the possession manipulations had a measurable differential impact on the consumer subjects of this research and thus may be legitimately interpreted as having created two different conditions of deception impact, one more and the other less involving for the research subjects.

Effects of Deception Impact and Debriefing Quality

Table 1 presents the grand mean and treatment condition cell means responses to the 16 questions that measured the effects of deception impact and debriefing quality. Perhaps the most surprising result in Table 1 is the overall lack of differential reaction due either to Debriefing Quality or Deception Impact (Possession). Only one of the 16 measures yielded a clearly significant difference between treatment conditions. In an ANOVA of responses to Question #2 ("Now that I have heard the debriefing and all things considered, I am glad to have been in the experiment."), the interaction between Possession and Debriefing Quality was significant ($F = 7.89$, $df$, $p < .008$, $\omega^2 = .15$). The disordinal interaction was such that if a subject was a possessor (higher impact), the extensive debriefing resulted in lower ratings of "gladness" than did the minimal debriefing, while under the nonpossessor (lower impact) conditions, the extensive debriefing caused significantly higher ratings of "gladness." No other effects were found involving the possession (deception impact) treatment.

Three measures yielded marginally significant main effects of Debriefing Quality (Questions 4, 13, and 14). Subjects in the good debriefing condition agreed slightly more with the statement that "debriefing helps alleviate negative feelings brought about by deception research" ($M = 4.18$) than did subjects in the poor debriefing condition ($M = 3.91$; $F = 3.11$, $df = 1/37$, $p < .083$, $\omega^2 = .05$). Second, subjects receiving the good debriefing indicated that they understood the experiment somewhat better ($M = 1.76$) than

TABLE 1
MEAN RESPONSES TO QUESTIONS MEASURING SUBJECTS' REACTIONS TO DECEPTION

| Measure of Deception Effect | Grand Mean (n=41) | Good Debriefing | | Poor Debriefing | |
|---|---|---|---|---|---|
| | | Non-Possess (Low Impact) (n=8) | Possess (High Impact) (n=9) | Non-Possess (Low Impact) (n=12) | Possess (High Impact) (n=12) |
| 1. Ss should follow instructions exactly | 3.17 | 3.30 | 3.22 | 2.83 | 3.25 |
| 2. I am glad to have been in experiment | 3.61 | 4.13 | 3.22 | 3.42 | 3.75 |
| 3. Ss look foolish if "duped" in experiment | 2.29 | 2.62 | 2.44 | 1.67 | 2.58 |
| 4. Debriefing alleviates negative feelings | 4.03 | 4.25 | 4.11 | 3.92 | 3.92 |
| 5. Deception is necessary in research | 3.56 | 3.63 | 3.78 | 3.67 | 3.25 |
| 6. I will expect deception in next experiment | 3.10 | 3.25 | 3.44 | 2.92 | 2.91 |
| 7. Deception may upset Ss in this study | 2.12 | 2.00 | 2.22 | 2.08 | 2.17 |
| 8. Ss should anticipate purpose of experiment | 2.61 | 2.00 | 2.67 | 2.67 | 2.92 |
| 9. This exp. could be done w/out deception | 1.86 | 1.63 | 1.89 | 2.17 | 1.67 |
| 10. I will disbelieve instruc. in next exper. | 2.64 | 2.75 | 3.00 | 2.67 | 2.25 |
| 11. How interesting was the experiment? | 2.78 | 2.25 | 2.89 | 3.00 | 2.83 |
| 12. Willing to be in another experiment? | 2.85 | 2.50 | 3.33 | 3.08 | 2.50 |
| 13. How well do you understand experiment? | 2.17 | 1.75 | 1.78 | 2.58 | 2.33 |
| 14. How necessary was deception? | 1.93 | 1.25 | 1.78 | 2.25 | 2.17 |
| 15. How justified was deception? | 1.73 | 1.63 | 1.78 | 1.83 | 1.67 |
| 16. How much did you learn about the research? | 3.00 | 2.88 | 2.89 | 3.17 | 3.00 |

Note: Responses to questions 1-10 were taken on a 5-point scale, where 1 = strongly disagree and 5 = strongly agree. Responses to questions 11-16 were taken on a 7-point scale, where 1 = most positive end (e.g., Q. 11, 1 = extremely interesting, 7 = extremely uninteresting).

those receiving a poor debriefing ($\underline{M}$ = 2.46; $\underline{F}$ = 3.80, df = 1/37, p < .056, $\omega^2$ = .067). Finally, subjects in the good debriefing condition felt that the deception was somewhat more necessary ($\underline{M}$ = 1.51) than did the subjects receiving the poor debriefing ($\underline{M}$ = 2.21; $\underline{F}$ = 3.48, $\underline{df}$ = 1/37, $\underline{p}$ < .067, $\omega^2$ = .158).

Yet another perspective on the results is provided by the grand means for the 16 questions (see Table 1). The consistent pattern of reactions evidenced by the absolute magnitude of these overall mean responses, indicates that, in general, subjects reacted rather positively, or at least neutrally, to the study.

### DISCUSSION AND CONCLUSION

The few significant effects that were obtained warrant brief discussion. The significant interaction effect of Debriefing Quality and Possession on subject's gladness in having participated in the study has interesting implications for future research on debriefing effects. This finding suggests that a debriefing in which subjects are led to a self-discovery of deceptions may be less useful in alleviating certain negative reactions when subjects have some reason to regret the deception (i.e., as the result of high involvement and personal impact) than when subjects have little reason to regret a deception. In the latter situation, such as when subjects anticipating nonpossession of a product learn that the product does not exist, a thorough debriefing may induce more positive feelings regarding the study than a more limited debriefing. One explanation for this interaction is that it is but one of 16 possible effects and thus could be due to chance variation. Although this is a possibility, the data for this inter-

action are somewhat unique in that they are derived from the only question (#2) which directly tapped subjects' affective, personal reactions to their experimental participation. This was in contrast to the other questions which primarily measured subjects' beliefs and behavioral intentions. Therefore, this interaction effect suggests a need for special attention to subjects' affective feelings in future research.

No other main or interaction effects due to the deception impact/possession factor were found. One potential explanation might be that the supposedly enhanced level of involvement which the deception created by the possession treatment does not approach the impact levels achieved in other deception experiments, particularly those in psychology [e.g., 14]. Rather, it may be more accurate to consider the perceived possession condition in the present study as only slightly more impactful than the nonpossession treatment. A manipulation that successfully creates a truly high level of deception impact may significantly affect subjects' reactions to their deception experiences. However, it may be that extremely high levels of impact cannot be obtained with the relatively "mild" types of deceptions commonly used in consumer and other types of applied research.

The only other effects were three marginally significant main effects of Debriefing Quality. Two of these (questions 13 and 14, Table 1) seem due primarily to the differences in the amount of information contained in the good and poor debriefings, rather than to their qualitative differences (i.e., the experimenter's demeanor, his overt concern for the subjects, etc.). The third (question 4) is more affective in nature and this main effect is more easily traceable to the qualitative differences in the debriefing quality manipulations.

Clearly, three weak main effects and one interaction (out of 48 possible effects) do not provide strong evidence of substantial impact due to the debriefing quality treatments. In fact, examination of the small magnitude of the obtained differences as well as the generally positive absolute scale values of the cell and grand means indicates that most subjects reacted favorably to the experiment regardless of the quality of debriefing. The apparent lack of a negative reaction to this deception was somewhat surprising. The experiment consisted of an elaborate system of interrelated lies that seemed to be accepted by virtually all the subjects. As a consequence of these deceptions, subjects believed that the product did exist and was valuable. Analysis of questionnaire data revealed a desire to possess the product. Further, it appeared obvious during the debriefing that many subjects were quite disappointed when they learned that the product did not exist--i.e., faces "fell," frowns appeared, spontaneous verbalizations were evidenced (e.g., nervous laughter, "groans," etc.). Yet, upon learning of these deceptions, even when bluntly told in the poorest debriefing we could develop, most subjects expressed generally favorable attitudes toward this particular experiment and experimentation in general. There are several possible explanations for the absence of differences between the debriefing conditions, each of which could be examined in future research. It may have been that many subjects in this study were accustomed to rather poor debriefings as a result of their previous experimental participation. Thus, though they reacted favorably to the good debriefing, the poor debriefing treatment did not create any particular frustration or violate expectations derived from earlier experience and, therefore, subjects reacted relatively favorably to it as well. Also, one should not neglect the possibility that the lack of deception and debriefing quality effects may be because substantial negative feelings about the deception were not aroused by participation in this particular experiment. That is, there may have been no major negative reactions for a good debriefing to alleviate. Much more severe deceptions may be necessary for overt hostility or the effects of debriefing quality to emerge. Another explanation is related to the fact that nearly all of the 16 dependent measures tapped the cognitive reactions of the subjects in terms of their beliefs about research and deception in general. Variations in debriefing quality may have weaker effects on beliefs about experimentation than on affective responses to one's personal participation. Also, it may be that differential reactions to deception and debriefing quality are likely with certain subject populations, for example, with males rather than females. Cook et al. [7] found female subjects to like an experiment more and to perceive the deception as more legitimate and to be less annoyed than were the male subjects, whereas Stricker, Messick, and Jackson [17] found girls to be less suspicious than boys. Moreover, it may be that other populations more commonly studied in marketing research (such as housewives, workers, professional managers), under other types of incentives than used here, are more sensitive to deception experiences than are women college students. Finally, it may be that more negative reactions to deception are found in more natural research settings, away from the role demands of the academic research lab. Therefore, nonliteral replications of this study using different research subject populations and differing deceptions would be useful in determining the magnitude of negative reactions to deception experiences as well as in identifying the mediators and boundary conditions of these effects.

In conclusion, it is our opinion that a post-experimental debriefing of research subjects in a deception study has three major goals or purposes. First, a debriefing should identify any deceptions and reduce, to a pre-experimental level, any possible anger, hostility, and other negative reactions directly caused by experimental participation or indirectly caused by awareness of having been deceived. The present findings suggest that at least for relatively "mild" deceptions, researchers should not omit the debriefing for fear of creating negative effects. Second, a debriefing should educate subjects about the meaning of their participation and about scientific research in general. The present results suggest that a debriefing can do this fairly well, with a thorough debriefing performing somewhat better than a cursory debriefing. Finally, a debriefing should provide insights for the experimenter into how the subjects reacted to the procedures and measures.

In most research a well-designed debriefing seems able to accomplish all three goals, while elimination of the debriefing accomplishes none of them. For these three reasons, and because adherence to a professional standard of research ethics requires it, we believe that a complete, extensive, and honest debriefing is the right of each participant in experimental consumer/marketing research.

REFERENCES

1. Altemeyer, R. A. "Subject Pool Pollution and the Postexperimental Interview." Journal of Experimental Research in Personality, 5 (1971), 79-84.

2. Aronson, E., and J. M. Carlsmith. "Experimentation in Social Psychology," in G. Lindzey and E. Aronson, eds., The Handbook of Social Psychology: Volume Two. Reading, Mass.: Addison-Wesley, 1968.

3. Berkum, M. M. "Performance Decrement Under Psychological Stress." Human Factors, 6 (1964), 21-30.

4. Bramel, D. "A Dissonance Theory Approach to Defensive Projection," Journal of Abnormal and Social Psychology, 64 (1962), 121-129.

5. Baumrind, D. "Some Thoughts on the Ethics of Research: After Reading Milgram's Behavioral Study of Obedience," American Psychologist, 19 (1964), 421-423.

6. Brock, Timothy C. "Implications of Commodity Theory for Value Change," in A. Greenwald, T. Brock, and T. Ostrom, eds., Psychological Foundations of Attitudes. New York: Academic Press, 1968.

7. Cook, Thomas D., J. R. Bean, B. J. Calder, R. Frey, M. L. Krovetz, and S. R. Reisman. "Demand Characteristics and Three Conceptions of the Frequently Deceived Subjects," Journal of Personality and Social Psychology, 14 (1970), 185-194.

8. Ethical Principles in the Conduct of Research with Human Participants. American Psychological Association, Washington, D.C., 1973.

9. Fromkin, H. L., J. C. Olson, R. L. Dipboye, and D. Barnaby. "A Commodity Theory Analysis of Consumer Preferences for Scarce Products," Proceedings of the 79th Annual Convention of the American Psychological Association, 6 (1971), 653-654.

10. Fromkin, H. L., and S. Streufert. "Laboratory Experimentation," in M. Dunnette, ed., The Handbook of Organizational and Industrial Psychology. Chicago: Rand McNally, 1976.

11. Holmes, D. S., and D. H. Bennett. "Experiments to Answer Questions Raised by the Use of Deception in Psychological Research: I, II, III," Journal of Personality and Social Psychology, 29 (1974), 358-367.

12. Jacoby, J. "History and Objectives Underlying the Formation of ACR's Professional Affairs Committee," in W. Perreault, ed., Advances in Consumer Research: Vol. IV. Atlanta: Association for Consumer Research, 1977.

13. Kelman, H. C. "Human Use of Human Subjects: The Problem of Deception in Social Psychological Experiments," Psychological Bulletin, 67 (1967), 1-11.

14. Milgram, S. "Behavioral Study of Obedience," Journal of Abnormal and Social Psychology, 67 (1963), 371-378.

15. Olson, J. C., R. Dipboye, and D. Toy. "Effects of Deception Impact and Debriefing Quality In Consumer Subjects," Paper No. 35, Working Series in Marketing Research, College of Business Administration, Pennsylvania State University, 1975.

16. Rubin, Z., and J. C. Moore, Jr. "Assessment of Subjects' Suspicions," Journal of Personality and Social Psychology, 17 (1971), 163-170.

17. Stricker, L. J., S. Messick, and D. N. Jackson. "Suspicion of Deception: Implications for Conformity Research," Journal of Personality and Social Psychology, 5 (1967), 379-389.

18. Tybout, A. M., and G. Zaltman. "Ethics in Marketing Research: Their Practical Relevance," Journal of Marketing Research, 11 (1974), 357-368.

# IMPROVING THE REPRESENTATIVENESS OF SURVEY RESEARCH:  SOME ISSUES AND UNANSWERED QUESTIONS

Robert A. Hansen, The Ohio State University
Carol A. Scott, The Ohio State University

## ABSTRACT

Implementation of the marketing concept implies a direct line of communication between the company and the consuming public.  This paper presents a definition of an adequate line of communication using the concepts of a sampling frames and representativeness of results.  This is followed by a discussion of some of the major threats to the operational success of such a line of communication.

## INTRODUCTION

The past decade has been characterized by a tremendous growth in the pressure placed on business institutions to be more responsive to consumer and societal needs.  And increasingly, there are signs to indicate that at least some corporate leaders agree that they must make greater efforts to identify and service customer needs and wants. Operationalizing this concern, however, is problematic.

Traditionally, the establishment of communication links between marketers and consumers has been suggested as one means of achieving that adjustment of marketing activities that will result in greater consumer satisfaction.  That is, marketers should listen better through traditional channels of marketing research and through alternative communication mechanisms such as customer complaint monitoring. This implies that while the marketing concept may be basically sound [2], it is difficult for even the well-intentioned company to collect the information necessary to completely and consistently implement the concept.

A primary issue often overlooked in these calls for more communication between company and its public is that of defining the relevant group of consumers or sampling frame. From a managerial point of view, the answer to this question is generally that group of consumers who represent the company's current and potential target markets.  From a broader perspective, however, it is clear that communication lines should be open between marketers and government officials and all segments of consumers.  As businesses are called upon to be more responsive to the needs and expectations of women, minority groups, and other relatively disadvantaged members of society, marketing research methods and practices must be scrutinized to determine whether they are capable of eliciting information such as suggested product improvements or satisfaction with current product alternatives from these groups.  If present or current research methods do not afford minority populations an adequate means of communication, more marketing research will merely result in improved conditions and greater satisfaction among those consumers already relatively well served by the marketplace and already well equipped to deal with its intricacies.

This paper attempts to examine current marketing research methods and practices (both commercial and academic) in order to identify those activities which directly or indirectly effect the ability of minorities (the disadvantaged, minorities, elderly, etc.) to receive adequate representation in the data upon which decisions are made.  It is argued that merely increasing the number of these individuals in the sample will not necessarily result in better representation.  Rather, preliminary examination of several recent studies suggests that other methodological improvements must be made to insure that survey sample results reflect the feelings of the entire population including the disadvantaged.

## BACKGROUND OF THE PROBLEM

The goal of developing lines of communication between business and the consuming public should be complete representativeness.  That is, any market monitoring program or broad-based research for consumer input should be designed, implemented, and evaluated with the goal of obtaining input from all segments of the consuming population.  For a variety of reasons, however, large segments have been ignored in the past as sources of feedback for marketing strategists.  These individuals have had little or no voice in the marketing process (see [20] for a survey of the problems and consequences).  Blacks and the elderly are perhaps the most obvious examples of special interest groups frequently overlooked by marketing researchers.  Households headed by women, rural Americans, low-income consumers, and the poorly educated are only infrequently considered in the data collection process [21].  These special groups are important for reasons of social concern as well as economic viability, as they are relatively large segments of consumers with a substantial amount of aggregate purchasing power.  As such, they represent a potentially significant opportunity for those marketers who understand their special needs.

Whether the motivation for reaching these segments is social or economic, the immediate concern is for mapping an operational strategy for building the necessary lines of communication with these minority consumers.  One method of increasing the representativeness of a sample drawn from a heterogeneous population, of course, is statistical in nature and relates to the choice of a sampling plan [22].  A stratified sampling plan can be employed in which the strata are formed on the basis of the relevant variable (e.g., race, education, income).  These strata are then oversampled.  By increasing the potential contacts, the researcher fills his quota of subjects of special interest.  The obvious question here is whether this method actually achieves representative results.  A consideration of the unique characteristics of some special interest groups suggests that a number of other problems of a non-statistical nature remain which may adversely affect the ability of the researcher to obtain information from a representative sample even when using such a disproportional stratified sampling plan.

These non-statistical problems can be broadly classified as being related to data collection and data content.  The discussion of the problems associated with data collection and data content focuses on the use of mail surveys, since this is perhaps the most widely used method of information gathering.  However, many of the problems identified also affect telephone and personal interviewing procedures.

## DATA COLLECTION

The major concerns in data collection involve:  (1) identifying potential respondents, (2) motivating them to participate in the study, and (3) generating useable returns. The impact of these processes on the representativeness of marketing data is examined in this section.

Identifying Potential Respondents

Identification of potential special interest group respondents can often be accomplished by purchasing mailing lists or by using selected census tract information (e.g., [3]). Unique characteristics of these groups must be considered, however, to determine the utility of this approach and to assess the need for additional precautions to insure delivery of the questionnaire. For example, low-income areas are often characterized by less home ownership and greater renting. Individuals in these areas are more likely to move frequently, making city directories and mailing lists less accurate.

A potential solution for this problem is the use of an occupant mailing format. Questionnaires addressed to a particular street number rather than to an individual will at least be deliverable. This may be a reasonable compromise if the overall demographic profile of the area remains stable even though the renter turnover is high. And, some evidence suggests that the response rate to an occupant mailing is not necessarily lower than that to a personalized mailing [14]. Unfortunately, no evidence is available which addresses the possibility of differential effects of occupant mailings across types of consumers (e.g., low income or non-white).

Clearly, the problems associated with identifying members of some minority groups pose a threat to the implementation of a representative sample of subjects for a marketing study. Merely increasing the total sample size and hence the absolute number of responses will not suffice. More work is needed on the development and evaluation of alternative methods of identifying potential respondents from minority populations.

Motivating Participation

As is evident from the discussion of identifying respondents, attention must also be given to motivating individuals to participate once they have received the survey. While many empirical studies on methods of inducing people to respond to and return questionnaires have been conducted (see [13, 15, 17,] for reviews of these studies), few have dealt specifically with motivating minority respondents or members of other special interest groups. Most discussions of the response problems associated with low-income, poor, or less-educated individuals are generalizations [5, 18], but at least one study suggests that the effects of strategies to increase response rates vary across social classes [7]. Although this study was plagued by several methodological problems, it is indicative of the kind of research questions which must be addressed. As more emphasis is placed on eliciting responses from the special segments of the population, more must be learned about how to do it.

Generating Useable Returns

The final issue of concern in the data collection process is that of generating complete and useful responses. The efforts to identify and motivate respondents will not result in greater representation of special segments if the returned questionnaires are incomplete and contain errors. These problems are not unique to minority groups, but little has been done to determine effective methods of insuring data quality in surveys in general, let alone in surveys of minority respondents. Unfortunately, item nonresponse and errors in completing questionnaires seem in many cases to be problems more closely associated with traditionally under-represented consumer groups. If even modest literacy skills are required to fill out a questionnaire properly, lower completion rates will be evidenced by low income, less well-educated respondents [5, 18, 23].

A survey recently conducted by the authors, in which housewives were asked to evaluate and indicate usage rates of types of food products, illustrates the bias that can occur from item non-response. As shown in Tables 1-4, the

average number of missing items per questionnaire is greater for black, low education, elderly, and low income respondents.

TABLE 1

RESPONSE RATE AND AVERAGE NUMBER OF MISSING ITEMS BY RACE OF RESPONDENT

| Race | Total Sent | Total Returned | Avg. Missing Items |
|------|-----------|----------------|--------------------|
| White | 1915 | 1386 (72.3%) | 7.5 |
| Black | 77 | 41 (53.2%) | 10.9 |
| Other | 4 | 2 (50.0%) | 0.0 |

TABLE 2

RESPONSE RATE AND AVERAGE NUMBER OF MISSING ITEMS BY EDUCATION OF HOMEAKER

| Education | Total Sent | Total Returned | Avg. Missing Items |
|-----------|-----------|----------------|--------------------|
| Some grade school | 45 | 32 (71.2%) | 21.5 |
| Grade School graduate | 72 | 50 (69.4%) | 17.7 |
| Some high school | 229 | 162 (70.7%) | 13.2 |
| High school graduate | 871 | 601 (69.0%) | 6.9 |
| Some college | 423 | 316 (74.7%) | 5.8 |
| College graduate | 283 | 216 (76.3%) | 4.5 |
| Graduate degree | 76 | 55 (72.4%) | 4.8 |

TABLE 3

RESPONSE RATE AND AVERAGE NUMBER OF MISSING ITEMS BY AGE OF HOMEAKER

| Age | Total Sent | Total Returned | Avg. Missing Items |
|-----|-----------|----------------|--------------------|
| Under 30 | 476 | 314 (65.9%) | 2.4 |
| 30-39 years | 414 | 285 (68.8%) | 4.9 |
| 40-49 years | 414 | 286 (69.0%) | 6.0 |
| 50-59 years | 364 | 281 (77.1%) | 8.7 |
| 60 years and older | 332 | 266 (80.1%) | 17.3 |

TABLE 4

RESPONSE RATE AND AVERAGE NUMBER OF MISSING
ITEMS BY FAMILY INCOME

| Income | Total Sent | Total Returned | Avg. Missing Items |
|--------|-----------|----------------|--------------------|
| Less than $6,000 | 386 | 274 (70.9%) | 13.7 |
| $6,000 - $9,999 | 398 | 291 (73.1%) | 9.3 |
| $10,000 - $14,999 | 510 | 360 (70.5%) | 4.9 |
| $15,000 - $19,999 | 334 | 245 (73.3%) | 5.6 |
| $20,000 and over | 372 | 262 (70.4%) | 5.1 |

Although in this case the demographic profile was not sub-stantially altered by failure of some respondents groups to return the instrument, less useable information was re-ceived from the relatively disadvantaged consumers. These findings are even more distressing when one considers that these survey participants were members of a National Fam-ily Opinion, Inc. (NFO) consumer panel. These problems occurred despite the advantages that are typically associ-ated with panels [6, 9] and the fact that these individuals have had a substantial amount of experience in completing forms of this type. Thus, it is our conclusion that these are conservative estimates of item non-response bias. In-deed, in a general population survey conducted by the se-nior author, 89% of the errors in a constant-sum task were from questionnaires returned by low income (< $5,000), low education (not a high school graduate), or more senior (50 years or older) persons.

The problems related to data collection are not insurmount-able. They are at present simply questions which have not received much attention. It should be noted, however, that simple solutions such as sending out more questionnaires, making instructions clearer, and the like will not be suf-ficient remedies. Specific studies are needed which have as their primary goal the investigation of one or more of these problems.

DATA CONTENT

Putting the data collection process aside for the moment, and assuming that the researcher is able to generate use-able responses from a representative population, the focus of concern must shift to assessing the quality of the data collected. More specifically, the researcher must assess the appropriateness of the questions used in the survey. Two specific problem areas can be identified here, errors of omission and errors in phrasing. Both of these problems result from potential differences between members of the special target groups and the rest of the population.

Unlike the problems associated with the data collection process, the solution to these data quality issues is not found in simply increasing the sample size. Increasing sample size, and in particular increasing the number of re-spondents from minority groups, helps solve problems asso-ciated with statistical error in measurement. The issue of data quality as discussed here is more appropriately con-sidered a problem of bias, and bias issues can only be handled by insuring that all relevant questions are includ-ed and are properly worded [4].

Errors of Omission

Biased information can result from a failure to include items that reflect all dimensions of the topic of interest. Most surveys, of course, undergo a substantial amount of

pretesting. A researcher may schedule focus group inter-views or arrange for discussions of drafts of questionnaires to elicit any dimensions that he may have originally over-looked. Unfortunately, these pretesting sessions seldom include sufficient numbers of minority groups members whose perspectives may be qualitatively different from those of the dominant population group [1]. Some examples taken from several recent research projects illustrates the po-tential seriousness of this omission.

In store image studies, for example, the researcher assumes that the store receiving the highest score on the total set of measurement scales will be the most preferred. Semenik and Hansen [19] conducted such a study using a store image measurement instrument developed after an extensive review and consolidation of previously used dimensions [10], and found significant differences in the preference profiles of low income and non-low income consumers. These findings, however, may be conservative estimates of differences be-tween the two populations since there is a strong possibil-ity that low income consumers use entirely different di-mensions, not included in the instrument, to evaluate stores. For example, Gensch and Staelin [8] observed that race of store owner was of some importance in the store evaluation and selection process of black shoppers. This variable has not been included in past attempts to measure store images, and thus was not included in the instrument used by Semenik and Hansen [19]. This error of omission suggests that researchers must examine source literature carefully to determine for which populations the instru-ments have been validated.

The same type of problem could occur with the use of a new-ly developed measure of consumer discontent [16]. This scale was constructed using the judgements of faculty and doctoral students of a university, and "validated" on mem-bers of the Arizona Consumers Council and the Denver Better Business Bureau. If this scale were to be used to assess consumer discontent of selected minority groups, the results would be extremely difficult to interpret. As reported thus far, there is no reason to believe that this scale is not population specific.

Errors in Phrasing

A second data content problem area is the wording of items used in scale construction. This issue again centers a-round the possibility that some groups of interest are in-herently different from those individuals represented in most scale construction processes. In this case, the dif-ferences relate to cultural issues, and may or may not in-clude the specific issue under investigation. Differences in interpretation of the questions across various respond-ent groups have been observed in other areas (e.g., "cul-turally fair" intelligence tests), and there is reason to believe that marketing research instruments are subject to the same types of biases. Hilger [12], for example, found that a questionnaire developed, pre-tested and administered to white, middle class subjects was inappropriate when used to assess the attitudes and opinions of Mexican Americans. Clearly this is an area in which research must be conducted to determine which specific question formats are most sus-ceptible to this source of bias.

CONCLUSIONS

As one marketing scholar has noted, the consumption prob-lems of relatively disadvantaged consumers are qualitative-ly as well as quantitatively different from those of the white middle-class consumers who fill the ranks of consum-erist organizations [1]. While we agree with this author that it will be difficult to grasp these differences, we do not feel that it is impossible or even undesirable to make the effort. Rather, we feel that it is imperative for academic and commercial researchers to identify potential difficulties in communication and to devise methods to overcome them.

A particularly troubling conclusion which results from even a cursory review of the marketing literature is that much published research is conducted on an extremely narrow population base. Some years ago, social psychologists began to worry that they were creating a psychology of college sophomores. Marketers are to be congratulated on their attempts to include members of the general public in their samples and the decreasing frequency with which researchers turn to a convenience sample of their students. It is clear, however, that marketing researchers must expand their concern for relevant samples to include more diverse segments of the general population. As we have noted, representativeness is difficult to achieve and requires great sensitivity to the indirect as well as direct impact of traditional research methods. To ignore these problems, however, is to consign much marketing research to social irrelevance.

## REFERENCES

1. Andreasen, Alan R. "The Differing Nature of Consumerism in the Ghetto," The Journal of Consumer Affairs, 10 (Winter 1976), 179-90.

2. Bell, Martin L. and William Emory. "The Faltering Marketing Concept," Journal of Marketing, 35 (October 1971), 37-42.

3. Churchill, Gilbert A. Jr. Marketing Research: Methodological Foundations. Hinsdale, IL.: Dryden Press, 1976.

4. Cook, Thomas and Donald T. Campbell. "The Design and Conduct of Quasi-Experiments and True Experiments in Field Settings," in Martin D. Dunnette ed., Handbook of Industrial and Organizational Psychology. Chicago: Rand McNally, 1976, 273-326.

5. Erdos, Paul L. Professional Mail Surveys. New York: McGraw-Hill, 1970.

6. Ferber, Robert. Collecting Financial Data by Consumer Panel Techniques. Champaign, IL.: Bureau of Economic and Business Research, University of Illinois, 1959.

7. Gelb, Betsy D. "Incentives to Increase Survey Returns: Social Class Considerations," Journal of Marketing Research, 12 (February 1975), 107-9.

8. Gensch, Donald H. and Richard Staelin. "The Appeal of Buying Black," Journal of Marketing Research, 9 (May 1972), 141-8.

9. Granbois, Donald H. and James F. Engel. "The Longitudinal Approach to Studying Market Behavior," in Peter D. Bennet, ed., Marketing and Economic Development. Chicago: American Marketing Association, 1965, 205-21.

10. Hansen, Robert A. and Terry Deutscher: "An Empirical Investigation of Attribute Importance in Retail Store Selection," Journal of Retailing (forthcoming).

11. Hansen, Robert A., Terry Deutscher and Eric Berkowitz. "Retail Image Research: A Case of Significant Unrealized Potential," Unpublished Working Paper, The Ohio State University, 1976.

12. Hilger, Marye Tharp. Personal Communication, August 1976.

13. Kanuk, Leslie and Conrad Berenson. "Mail Surveys and Response Rates: A Literature Review," Journal of Marketing Research, 12 (November 1975), 440-53.

14. Kernan, Jerome B. "Are Bulk-Rate Occupants Really Unresponsive?" Public Opinion Quarterly, 35 (Fall 1971), 420-2.

15. Linsky, Arnold S. "Stimulating Responses to Mailed Questionnaires: A review," Public Opinion Quarterly 39 (Spring 1975), 82-101.

16. Lundstrom, William J. and Lawrence M. Lamont. "The Development of a Scale to Measure Consumer Discontent," Journal of Marketing Research, 13 (November 1976), 373-81.

17. Pressley, Milton M. Mail Response: A Critically Annotated Bibliography. Greensboro, N.C.: Faber and Company, 1976.

18. Selltiz, Claire, Marie Jahoda, Morton Deutsch, and Stuart W. Cook. Research Methods in Social Relations. Revised edition, New York: Holt, Rinehart and Winston, 1959.

19. Semenik, Richard J. and Robert A. Hansen. "Low Income vs. Non-Low Income Consumer Preference Data as Input to Socially Responsive and Economically Profitable Decision-Making," Proceedings. American Marketing Association Educators' Conference, 1976, 205-8.

20. Sturdivant, Frederick D. "Better Deal for Ghetto Shoppers" in F. D. Sturdivant (ed.). The Ghetto Marketplace. New York: The Free Press, 1969, 142-7.

21. Sturdivant, Frederick D. and Terry Deutscher. "Disadvantaged Consumers: Research Dimensions," paper presented at the American Marketing Association Marketing and Minorities Workship, Columbus, Ohio, May, 1976.

22. Sudman, Seymour. Applied Sampling. New York: Academic Press, 1976.

23. Zeisel, Hans. Say it With Figures. 5th ed., New York: Harper and Row, 1968.

# ON CLASSIFICATION IN THE PRESENCE OF SPARSENESS
## AND/OR DISPROPORTIONATE SAMPLE SIZES

William R. Dillon, University of Massachusetts
Matthew Goldstein, Baruch College, C.U.N.Y.

## ABSTRACT

This article presents and discusses two new multinomial
classification methods which have advantages over other
available discrimination procedures in situations of
sparseness and/or disproportionate sample sizes. The two
methods are illustrated with examples and their superiority
over such standards procedures as Fisher's LDF and the full
multinomial procedure is clearly evident.

## BACKGROUND

Although much of the informative data collected in marketing research studies do not possess those good properties
of interval or ratio scaled data, the treatment of such
data has, in general, received scant attention in the
marketing literature. Consequently, a tendency in applied
research has been to ignore the nominal or ordinal nature
of the data and to proceed with continuous variable techniques. In the case of classification or discrimination
this leads to the use of a linear discriminant function
(LDF), which was originally proposed by Fisher [3].

The use of Fisher's LDF in marketing research has been, by
any standards, extensive, and detailed summaries of its
uses can be found elsewhere (see [4,8,16,18]). However, a
natural question which arises when discussing applied
research concerns the notion of performance or, in more
general terms, the compatibility of the data with underlying assumptions. As is the case with many of the multivariate techniques, herein lies the problem for the situation covered by Fisher's LDF is in reality rare. In particular, use of Fisher's LDF cannot be justified, in the
sense of minimizing the Bayes risk, unless multivariate
normality and equal covariance matrices are assumed present.

Problems of this nature have led as a start to research in
classification procedures whereby the underlying distributions are discrete, and in particular multinomial. In
multinomial classification, the data are qualitative with
each measurement assuming a finite number of distinct
values. In general, if there are v measurements with
measurement j taking on $s_j$ values, then the number of
states s is equal to $\Pi_j s_j$. If the predictor variables are
binary, for example, $v$ measurements yield $2^v$ states. Papers, appearing in the statistical literature, of fundamental importance and interest dealing with issues in
multinomial classification include: Cochran and Hopkins
[1], Hills [9], Gilbert [5], Glick [6], Moore [15], Goldstein and Rabinowitz [7], Krzanowski [10], and Dillon and
Goldstein [2]. In particular, several of these studies
[1,2,10,15] have shown that the uncritical use of Fisher's
LDF is to be avoided.

In practice, however, the use of multinomial classification
procedures is likely to entail several problems. Perhaps
the most serious of these problems is state sparseness.
For example, if the number of respondents is small relative
to the number of possible states, then it is likely that
many of the states will be empty and, therefore, no observations are available for computing the state frequency
estimates. In addition, in the case where the sample from
one group is small relative to the other, there is a

tendency for most classification methods (including the
LDF) to misclassify most of the members of the smaller
group into the larger group.

Problems such as these have prompted research into different methods of allocating less sensitive to sparse data
sets. Toward this end, the present study discusses two
procedures which the authors feel can be potentially
useful to marketing researchers as multinomial classification rules, particularly in the case of sparseness and/or
disproportionate sample sizes.

## MULTINOMIAL CLASSIFICATION --
## PROBLEMS IN PRACTICE

To motivate the procedures to be discussed assume, for
simplicity, v binary predicator variables. To be more
specific, suppose a multivariate vector $\underline{X}=(X_1,x_2,...,X_v)$
is characterized by each of its components, $X_i$,
$i = 1, 2, ..., v$, assuming only two possible values 0 or 1
(all of the following can be extended to the case where $X_i$
can assume any finite number of values). A v-dimensional
binary vector generates $s = 2^v$ possible patterns of zeros
and ones. Each unique pattern we call a state, and associated with each state is a probability or parameter.
Since the sum of the state probabilities (parameters) is
unity, it follows that $2^v-1$ independent parameters are
needed in order to completely characterize a multinomial
density generated in this fashion.

In the two-group classification problem , the underlying
populations, say $G_1$ and $G_2$, are characterized by the
parameter vectors $(p_1, p_2, ..., p_v)$ and $(q_1, q_2, ..., q_v)$,
respectively. An optimal rule for classifying an observation from state j is given by: classify into $G_1$ if
$p_j/q_j > c$ and into $G_2$ if $p_j/q_j < c$, where c is the ratio of
the prior odds of $G_2$ to $G_1$. If $p_j/q_j = c$, then the observation is usually assigned randomly.

In any practical problem, the vectors of parameters
$(p_1, p_2, ..., p_v)$ and $(q_1, q_2, ..., q_v)$ are unknown, and
some sample-based procedure needs to be utilized. There
are two basic sampling situations which generally are
employed: (1) independent samples of size n and m are
available from $G_1$ and $G_2$ respectively, and (2) one sample
is generated from the mixed population and then observations are identified as to which population they belong.
We will assume throughout that independent samples are
available, however, all that we discuss is completely
applicable to the other sampling scheme. Continuing,
suppose on the basis of samples of size n and m the relative frequencies of each state are used as estimates of
state probabilities, viz., $n_j/n$ for $p_j$ and $m_j/m$ for $q_j$,
where $n_j(m_j)$ is the number of sample observations out of
n(m) from state j. A rule for assigning a future observation x belonging to state j is then simply given by:
classify x into $G_1$ if $n_j/n > m_j/m$, into $G_2$ if $n_j/n < m_j/m$,
and randomly assign if otherwise. Note that for simplicity we have assumed c=1, i.e., equal prior probabilities.

The appeal of this rule, sometimes called the full multinomial rule, is the ease in which it can be applied and
its intuitiveness. Further, the rule is consistent since
as n and m increase without bound, it and the optimal rule
behave the same in that the probability they assign any

given pattern to different groups tends to zero.

However, this sample-based procedure is fraught with problems. In many studies the number of responses is small relative to the number of possible states or patterns. As an example, if seven binary predictor variables are used in a study, then 128 possible patterns can be realized. In order that reasonable state estimates for all state probabilities be obtained, at least five observations in each state will be required or a total sample of 640, at a minimum. Generally, however, many of the states remain empty, and hence no observations are available for computing frequency estimates. In addition, further difficulties can arise in that if a given state is empty in both populations no classification outside randomization is possible.

Another difficulty, which is particularly common to diffusion of innovation studies, arises when the samples taken from $G_1$ and $G_2$ are disproportionate in size. As in contingency table analysis, zero frequencies in certain cells may mean something entirely different from zeros in other cells. Translating this to the multinomial classification problem, a zero in state j from $G_1$ may really represent a greater theoretical frequency than a nonzero in state j from $G_2$, especially if the total sample size from $G_1$ is disproportionately small with respect to the total sample size from $G_2$. The usually sample-based multinomial rule is: if x belongs to state j then allocate x to $G_1$ if $n_j/n > m_j/m$ is insensitive to this problem since, all other things remaining equal, as soon as state j is zero in $G_1$ and nonzero in $G_2$, then x is allocated to $G_2$. It should be noted that Morrison [16] discusses this problem in the context of the LDF, and demonstrates a similar result. To summarize, when the sample size for one group is very much larger than the other, almost all the observations will be classified into the larger group.

In the following two sections we present two procedures potentially useful in overcoming these problems.

THE PROBLEM OF DISPROPORTIONATE SAMPLE SIZES:
A PROCEDURE BASED ON A DISTRIBUTIONAL DISTANCE

The crux of the problem concerning grossly unequal sample sizes is that although in situations where one group is very much larger than the other, the total misclassification probability is likely to be good, almost all of the members of the smaller group will be misclassified into the larger group. This is particularly troublesome since in many applications we are often more interested in the smaller group. To provide a remedy for this problem, we develop a new sample-based multinominal rule, which is completely general, based upon the notion of distance (or affinity) between two distributions.

In a series of papers Matusita [12,13,14] proposed a measure of distance between two distributions as a means of analyzing a large number of statistical problems. To show how one may utilize his measure of distributional distance in defining a multinomial classification rule, suppose $(n_1, n_2, ..., n_v)$ and $(m_1, m_2, ..., m_v)$ are the respective state frequencies based upon samples of size n and m. Then the distance between the empirical distributions $S_n$ and $S_m$ generated by these frequencies is given by

$$||S_n - S_m||^2 = \sum_{i=1}^{v} (\sqrt{n_1/n} - \sqrt{m_j/m})^2 \qquad (1)$$

The rule for assigning a future observation x which we propose assumes the following form:

Classify x into $G_1$ if $||S_{n+1} - S_m|| > ||S_n - S_{m+1}||$,

Classify x into $G_2$ if $||S_{n+1} - S_m|| < ||S_n - S_{m+1}||$, $\qquad (2)$

Randomly allocate if $||S_{n+1} - S_m|| = ||S_n - S_{m+1}||$,

where $S_{n+1}$ is the empirical distribution function based upon n+1 observations; similarly for $S_{m+1}$. The rationale for the rule, which we refer to as the distance rule, is simply that if assigning x to $G_1$ results in greater sample distributional distance than if x is assigned to $G_2$, then x should be classified into $G_1$.

After some algebra it is easy to see that the rule given in (2) has an equivalent representation with the first inequality in (2) replaced by

$$\sqrt{m_j(n_j+1)/m(n+1)} + \sum_{i \neq j}\sqrt{m_i n_i/m(n+1)}$$
$$< \sqrt{n_j(m_j+1)/n(m+1)} + \sum_{i \neq j}\sqrt{n_i m_i/n(m+1)}. \qquad (3)$$

Note that when m=n, the rule given in (3) is equivalent to the full multinomial procedure. However, when n≠m, the case of real interest, the rules are different.

In discussing some of the deficiencies of the full multinomial procedure, we indicated that as soon as state j has no observation under $G_1$ but at least one observation in $G_2$, any future observation from that state will automatically be assigned to $G_2$. However, suppose n<m, so that $m(n+1)/n(m+1)>1$, and $n_j = 0$ but $m_j>0$. Then, (3) allows us to classify x into $G_1$ provided

$$\sqrt{m_j} < \sum_{i \neq j} \sqrt{n_i m_i} \{[m(n+1)/n(m+1)]^{1/2} - 1\}. \qquad (4)$$

It is not difficult to construct examples where the inequality given in (4) is satisfied provided that samples are disproportionate in size, and $m_j$ is small relative to the other $m_i$'s. This is a most desirable property in that it will assist in an area where the full multinomial rule has no value. Also, as is demonstrated in the example to follow, the distance procedure, in general, will yield better performance (lower misclassification probability) in the smaller of the two groups since it permits us to allocate x into $G_1$ even in situations where n(x)/n<m(x)/m.

An Example

The data used to demonstrate the relative efficiency of the distance procedure were collected in a 1975 study designed to examine the consumption behavior for a major household service. The grouping (dependent) variable was the extent of customer usage, where usage was in terms of actual dollar expenditures for a fixed period. Of a total of 464 respondents, 54 were identified as heavy users, while the remaining 410 were identified as light users. Assume throughout the following that we are more interested in the smaller of the two groups, the heavy users.

Nine socio-economic and demographic variables were selected to form the basis for classification. A description of these variables can be found in Table 1. Note that each predictor variable is binary. With each variable assuming a value of zero or one, there are in total $2^9$=512 states. While we illustrate the distance procedure on binary predictor variables, it is completely applicable to the

---

[1] In their original form, each variable was not uniformly binary; however, all variables were of a nominal or ordinal nature. Therefore, we chose to standardize the coding by determining a critical category (value) for each polytomous (three or more categories) variable such that the distributions above and below that category across the two groups have maximum separation.

general case where each variable can assume any finite number of distinct values.

Table 2 presents summary results, in the form of a classification matrix, for the full multinomial, LDF, and distance procedures. As Morrison has indicated, when the groups are of grossly unequal size, there is some difficulty in interpreting the classification table [16, pp. 159-160]. For example, according to the table the LDF misclassifies only 54 observations, but all of these come from $G_1$, the smaller of the two groups. Therefore, while its total efficiency $(410/464 = .884)$ is satisfactory as compared to either the distance method $(390/464 = .841)$, the maximum chance model $(c_{max} = .884)$, or the proportional chance model $(c_{prop} = .794)$,[2] it is of no value to us in identifying heavy users. Similarly, use of the full multinomial procedure yields better total performance $(419/464 = .903)$ than the other methods, and compares favorably to the maximum and chance models, but compared to the distance method it does poorly in the smaller group.

TABLE 1

VARIABLE CODINGS AND DESCRIPTIONS

| Variable | Descriptions | |
| --- | --- | --- |
| | Coding 1 | Coding 0 |
| Home ownership $(x_1)$ | Own | Rent |
| Number of rooms in home $(x_2)$ | At least 5 rooms | Less than 5 rooms |
| Length of residence $(x_3)$ | At least 5 years | Less than 5 years |
| Location of previous home $(x_4)$ | Outside of county, state, or U.S.A. | Within the same town or county |
| Marital status $(x_5)$ | Married | Single, widowed, or divorced |
| Head of household's occupation $(x_6)$ | Professional or Manager | Sales, Craftsman, Clerical worker (or below) |
| Head of households' education $(x_7)$ | Some college or above | No college |
| Family income $(x_8)$ | At least $11,000 a yr. | Less than $11,000 a yr. |
| Stage in family life cycle $(x_9)$ | 55 years or older, employed or unemployed | Less than 55 years old |

TABLE 2

CLASSIFICATION RESULTS FOR THE FULL, LDF AND
DISTANCE PROCEDURES

| | | PREDICTED | | | | | |
| --- | --- | --- | --- | --- | --- | --- | --- |
| | | FULL | | LDF | | DISTANCE | |
| | | $G_1$ | $G_2$ | $G_1$ | $G_2$ | $G_1$ | $G_2$ | Total |
| Actual | $G_1$ | 10 | 44 | 0 | 54 | 35 | 19 | 54 |
| | $G_2$ | 1 | 409 | 0 | 410 | 55 | 355 | 410 |
| | | 11 | 453 | 0 | 464 | 90 | 374 | |

Clearly, what we are arguing is that in situations of disproportionate sample sizes total efficiency may not be the best estimte of discriminatory efficiency. Further, in cases such as this, analysis of the individual group classification is warranted, with particular emphasis on the accuracy of classification obtained in the smaller group. This translates into examining the conditional efficiency. For example, it seems most important to ask what the probability of correctly identifying an observation given its group membership? That is: given that an individual is a heavy (light) user, what is the probability of classifying the individual as a heavy (light) user? These probabilities are estimated from the classification matrix by the proportion of heavy user correctly classified out of the total number of heavy users, and the proportion of light users correctly classified out of the total number of light users, respectively. In our case the values are: .185(10/54) and .997(409/410) for the full multinomial; .000(0/54) and 1.00(410/410) for the LDF; and .648 (35/54) and .866(355/410) for the distance method. Using the proportional chance model, the conditional chance probabilities are .116(54/410) and .884(410/464). Hence, we see that the distance method correctly classifies 64.8% of the heavy users, which is far superior to the full multinominal and LDF procedures. Also, its conditional efficiency in the ligher user group is only slightly different from the conditional proportional chance model.

THE CASE OF SPARSENESS: A RULE RESULTING FROM
REPARAMETIZATION OF STATE PROBABILITIES

Unlike the distance procedure, the allocation rule to be discussed is restricted to the case of multivariate binary predictor variables. The procedure developed is an extension of a method originally proposed by Ott and Kronmal [17], and entails a reparametization of state probabilities. In particular, we extend their procedure to the case of independent samples and more importantly, we indicate through a process of achieving parismony in modeling how sparse data may potentially be dealt with.

For a given $x$ Ott and Kronmal show that the corresponding state probabilities denoted by $f(x)$ takes the form

$$f(x) = \frac{1}{2^v} \sum_r d_r \Psi_r (x), \tag{5}$$

where $r$ is an indexing vector which assumes the same values as the predictor variables $x$, $d_r$ is an unknown parameter, and $\Psi_r(x) = (1)^{x'r}$ where $x'r = \sum_{i=1}^v x_i r_i$. To simplify notation, we will from now on drop the symbol $\sim$ under x and r, but remember that both are vectors.

Based on a sample of size n, the $d_r$ are estimated by

$$\hat{d}_r = \sum_x \Psi_r(x) \, n(x)/n, \tag{6}$$

[2]The maximum change $(c_{max})$ and proportional chance $(c_{prop})$ models were seemingly first discussed in the marketing literature by Morrison [16]. Letting $\alpha$ be the proportion of individuals in $G_1$, and $1-\alpha$ the proportion of individuals in $G_2$, then

$$c_{max} = \max(\alpha, \ 1-\alpha),$$

and

$$c_{prop} = \alpha^2 + (1-\alpha)^2.$$

407

and the state probability $f(x)$ is estimated by

$$\hat{f}(x) = \frac{1}{2^v} \sum_r \Psi_r(x)\hat{d}_r. \tag{7}$$

The representation given in (7) is in disguised form just the usual frequency estimates for the state probability at x. A fundamental contribution in the Ott and Kronmal paper is that certain of the estimates in (6) may be set equal to zero because their inclusion in (7) will not lead to a decrease in

$$E\Sigma(\hat{f}(x)-f(x))^2, \tag{8}$$
$$\phantom{E\Sigma}_x$$

and the mean summed squared error. The condition on whether to maintain a given estimate $d_j$ in (7) is shown by the authors to be

$$\hat{d}_j^2 > 2/(n+1). \tag{9}$$

Based upon independent random samples of size n and m from $G_1$ and $G_2$ respectively, a condition analogous to (8) for the classification problem is maintaining only those estimates which lead to a decrease in

$$E\Sigma[(\hat{f}_1(x)-\hat{f}_2(x)) - (f_1(x)-f_2(x))]^2, \tag{10}$$

where $f_i(x)$ is the state probability for pattern x for $G_i$, $i=1,2$, and $\hat{f}_i(x)$, $i=1,2$, are the corresponding two estimates. It is not hard to show that this will be satsified provided

$$\hat{d}_{1,r}^2 > \frac{2}{n+1}, \quad \hat{d}_{2,r}^2 > \frac{2}{m+1}, \tag{11}$$

where $\hat{d}_{i,r}$ is the estimate of parameter $d_r$ under $G_i$, $i=1,2$.

If all the estimates $\hat{d}_r$ are used in (7) under both groups, then the sample-based classification procedure assuming equal priors is equivalent to the full multinomial rule. However, we consider the following rule:

Classify x into $G_1$ if $\sum\limits_{S_{1,r}} \Psi_r(x)\hat{d}_{1,r} > \sum\limits_{S_{2,r}} \Psi_r(x)\hat{d}_{2,r}$,

Classify x into $G_2$ if $\sum\limits_{S_{1,r}} \Psi_r(x)\hat{d}_{1,r} < \sum\limits_{S_{2,r}} \Psi_r(x)\hat{d}_{2,r}$, (12)

Randomly allocate if $\sum\limits_{S_{1,r}} \Psi_r(x)\hat{d}_{1,r} = \sum\limits_{S_{2,r}} \Psi_r(x)\hat{d}_{2,4}$,

where $S_{1,r}$ is the set of indices where $\hat{d}_{1,r}>2/(n+1)$, and $S_{2,r}$ is the set of indices where $\hat{d}_{2,r}>2/(n+1)$.

The potential use of the rule (12) in dealing with sparse data sets rests in its ability to reduce the number of $d_r$ parameters in each group. Not only do we achieve a degree of parsimony in modeling, that is, reducing the number of parameters to estimate, but it also becomes possible to generate nonzero estimates for probabilities corresponding to states for which no data are available. Especially in the case where under both groups a given state is sparse can the potential for a rule other than randomization be realized, and yet still maintain a property of optimality given by (10). We illustrate this by way of an example in the next section.

## An Example

Table 3 presents summary information for two data sets generated by three dichotomous variables. The data was first presented by Martin and Bradley [11], and consists of a subset of data collected in a preliminary study of the behavioral consequences following hypoxic trauma (damage caused by oxygen deficiency). The groups are $G_1$: Infants whose physiological functioning was suggestive of damage and $G_2$: Infants physiological functioning was normal. The three variables used are: (i) race; (ii) suggestive or non-suggestive previous medical history of mother; and (iii) infant first breath before or after 5 seconds.

As can be seen from the table, certain of the states are relatively sparse and for states (0,0,1) and (1,0,1) no data are available in either group. However, straightforward calculation of the $d_r$ parameters shows

TABLE 3

FREQUENCIES ON $G_1$ AND $G_2$ INFANTS

| | $G_1$ (Suggestive of Damage) | | $G_2$ (Normal) | |
|---|---|---|---|---|
| State | Frequency | Relative Frequency | Frequency | Relative Frequency |
| 000 | 24 | .226 | 31 | .274 |
| 001 | 0 | .000 | 0 | .000 |
| 010 | 48 | .453 | 36 | .319 |
| 011 | 3 | .028 | 0 | .000 |
| 100 | 8 | .075 | 22 | .195 |
| 101 | 0 | .000 | 0 | .000 |
| 110 | 21 | .198 | 24 | .212 |
| 111 | 2 | .019 | 0 | .000 |
| | 106 | | 113 | |

$\hat{d}_{1,1}=.999$, $\hat{d}_{1,2}=.905$, $\hat{d}_{1,3}=-.397$, $\hat{d}_{1,4}=-.303$, $\hat{d}_{1,5}=.415$, $\hat{d}_{1,6}=.397$, $\hat{d}_{1,7}=-.113$, $\hat{d}_{1,8}=-.095$

$\hat{d}_{2,1}=1.000$, $\hat{d}_{2,2}=1.000$, $\hat{d}_{2,3}=-.062$, $\hat{d}_{2,4}=-.062$, $\hat{d}_{2,5}=.186$, $\hat{d}_{2,6}=.186$, $\hat{d}_{2,7}=-.028$, $\hat{d}_{2,8}=-.028$

Now, using condition (10) and (11), the following estimates are set equal to zero

$\hat{d}_{1,7}$, $\hat{d}_{1,8}$, $\hat{d}_{2,3}$, $\hat{d}_{2,4}$, $\hat{d}_{2,7}$, and $\hat{d}_{2,8}$.

The state probabilities using the above deleted parameters are under $G_1$ and $G_2$ given by

$\hat{f}_1(0,0,0) = .253$, $\hat{f}_1(0,0,1) = .002$, $\hat{f}_1(0,1,0) = .427$, $\hat{f}_1(0,1,1) = .026$

$\hat{f}_1(1,0,0) = .049$, $\hat{f}_1(1,0,1) = .000$, $\hat{f}_1(1,1,0) = .224$, $\hat{f}_1(1,1,1) = .021$

$\hat{f}_2(0,0,0) = .297$, $\hat{f}_2(0,0,1) = .000$, $\hat{f}_2(0,1,0) = .297$, $\hat{f}_2(0,1,1) = .000$

$\hat{f}_2(1,0,0) = .204$, $\hat{f}_2(1,0,1) = .000$, $\hat{f}_2(1,1,0) = .204$, $\hat{f}_2(1,1,1) = .000$

Note that for this data set the full multinomial rule required that sixteen parameters be estimated while in the above only ten need be used. Also, for state (0,0,1) which has no observations in both groups, we were able to generate a nonzero estimate under $G_1$, and hence effect a classification. Note further that the rule given in (12) correctly classified 60% of the observations, and is slightly better than the full multinomial rule which correctly classifies 59% of the observations.

## CONCLUDING REMARKS

Given the discrete nature of the data commonly collected in marketing research studies, the authors believe that discrete and, in particular, multinomial classification procedures can be potentially useful. However, in general, one finds little mention or use of discrete discrimination techniques in the marketing literature, where there is almost exclusive use of Fisher's LDF. As discrete classification procedures gain wider acceptance, those practical problems that are likely to arise in most reasonable applications demand serious attention.

Toward this end, we have considered the classification problem in situations of sparseness and/or disproportionate sample sizes. Two new multinomial classification models have been discussed and illustrated with examples. While some care must be exercised when drawing conclusions from both examples, since a bias is introduced when the same data are used to estimate a procedure and evaluate its performance, the results obtained clearly demonstrate the superiority of the distance and reparametization methods over other available techniques. In particular, when the sample from one group is small relative to the other, the distance method leads to an increase in the accuracy of classification in the smaller group and, in this sense, was clearly superior to either the LDF or full multinomial procedures. On the other hand, in the case where no observations are available for computing the state frequency estimates, the reparametization method allowed us to generate a nonzero estimate, and hence effect a classification.

## REFERENCES

1. Cochran, William G. and Carl E. Hopkins, "Some Classification Problems with Multivariate Qualitative Data," Biometrics, 17 (March 1961), 10-32.

2. Dillon, William R. and Matthew Goldstein. "On the Performance of Some Multinomial Classification Rules," unpublished paper, University of Massachusetts, 1976.

3. Fisher, R.A., "The Use of Measurements in Taxonmonic Problems," Annuals of Eugenics, 7 (1936), 176-84.

4. Frank, Ronald E., William F. Massy and Donald G. Morrison. "Bias in Multiple Discriminant Analysis," Journal of Marketing Research, 2 (August 1965), 250-58.

5. Gilbert, Ethel S. "On Discrimination Using Qualitative Variables," Journal of the American Statistical Association, 63 (December 1968), 116-27.

6. Glick, Ned. "Sample-Based Multinomial Classification," Biometrics, 29 (June 1973), 241-56.

7. Goldstein, Matthew and M. Rabinowitz. "Selection of Variates for the Two Group Multinomial Classification Problem," Journal of the American Statistical Association, 70, No. 352 (December 1975), 776-81.

8. Green, Paul and Donald Tull. Research for Marketing Decisions, 3rd edition, New Jersey: Prentice-Hall, Inc., 1975.

9. Hills, M. "Discrimination and Allocation with Discrete Data," Journal of the Royal Statistical Society, Series C, 16, No. 3 (1967), 237-50.

10. Krzanowski, W.J. "Discrimination and Classification Using Both Binary and Continuous Variables," Journal of the American Statistical Association, 70 (December 1975), 782-90.

11. Martin, D.C. and R.A. Bradley. "Probability Models, Estimation and Classification for Multivariate Dichotomous Population," Biometrics, 28 (March 1972), 203-22.

12. Matusita, Kameo. "Decision Rules, Based on the Distance for Problems of Fit, Two Samples and Estimation," Annuals of Mathematical Statistics, 26, No. 2 (December 1955), 131-40.

13. _____. "Decision Rules, Based on the Distance for the Classification Problem," Annuals of the Institutes of Statistical Mathematics, 7 (1957), 67-77.

14. _____. "Classification Based on Distance in Multivariate Gaussian Cases," Proc. 5th Berkeley Symp. Math. Statistic. Prob. 1, (1967), 249-304.

15. Moore, D.H., II. "Evaluation of Five Discrimination Procedures for Binary Variables," Journal of the American Statistical Association, 68 (June 1973), 399-404.

16. Morrison, Donald G. "On the Interpretation of Discriminant Analysis," Journal of Marketing Research, 6 (May 1969), 159-163.

17. Ott, J. and R.A. Kronmal. "Some Classification Procedures for Multivariate Binary Data Using Orthogonal Functions," Journal of the American Statistical Association, 68 (June 1976), 366-72.

18. Sheth, J.N. "Multivariate Analysis in Marketing," Journal of Advertising Research, 10 (February 1970), 29-37.

ON THE NONRESPONSE PROBLEM IN LONGITUDINAL MAIL SURVEYS

Leendert de Jonge, N.V. Philips' Gloeilampenfabrieken

## ABSTRACT

In literature on mail-survey research almost no attention
is paid to the problem of cumulating nonresponse that occurs in repeated measurements of the same sample population.
This paper suggests that the nature and the seriousness of
nonresponse in longitudinal mail surveys provide the impetus for the adoption of some specific variables to control
that nonresponse through time. The usefulness of these
variables is illustrated by some empirical findings.

## INTRODUCTION

Longitudinal analysis may be described as "the analysis of
measurement data from observations taken at more than one
point in time of a fixed set of objects, whose purpose is
to describe or explain change in those objects over the
specific period of observation" [1]. Hence the longitudinal method is in part a method of generating data and in
part a method of analyzing given data. Its implementation
involves problems that are partly common to all survey methods and partly unique. The main problems of longitudinal
measurement are reviewed by Nicosia [16], Granbois and
Engel [6], and Nestel [15]. Literature on analytical methods for detecting relationships among panel data is mainly
contributed by sociologists and psychologists [for example
2, 7, 20].

With a few exceptions [3, 18] techniques of longitudinal
analysis received almost no attention in published marketing research studies. This might, at least partly, explain
why longitudinal analysis, despite its important potential
contributions, has still not been widely used in marketing.
Literature on the problems of mail surveying are reviewed
by Scott [19], Kanuk and Berenson [11], and Linsky [14].
In contrast to the extensive body of literature devoted to
the more specific problem of nonresponse in single mail-
interviews, the problem of cumulating nonresponse in repeated mail-interviews receives almost no attention.

The purpose of the present paper is to focus on some typical aspects of controlling the level of nonresponse in longitudinal mail surveys.[1] It reports on some empirical experience gained from the so-called "Longitudinal Anticipations Research" project that is presently being performed
in the Netherlands. This project is aimed at the development and testing of a micro-model of household purchasing
behavior concerning specific durable goods like private
cars, television sets, and vacuum-cleaners. According to
this model [8] the household's purchase is conceived as a
function of the household's situation (economic, demographic,
sociological, psychological), the household's anticipations
and changes in both these. For the model's descriptive and
predictive validity and for gaining an understanding of the
dynamics of change that takes place through time, measurement and analysis are to be performed at the level of the
individual consumption unit, vix. the household. To this
end, it was planned to have a fixed group of households in-

terviewed five times within a period of two years. The
final number of households having cooperated each time will
form the critical mass to which longitudinal analysis is to
be applied. The size of this critical mass is, given the
initial sample, determined by the magnitude of nonresponse
in successive interviews. The structure of the paper is as
follows. Firstly, the nature and the seriousness of the
nonresponse problem in longitudinal mail surveys are explored. Next, some variables suggested for monitoring nonresponse are briefly reviewed. Then, the survey design employed in the "Longitudinal Anticipations Research" project
is described. Finally, the nonresponse found in the first
and the second measurement is described in terms of the
suggested variables to illustrate their usefulness.[2]

## DISCUSSION OF THE NONRESPONSE PROBLEM

In survey research nonresponse is usually defined as the
failure to obtain observations from elements which are eligible for interview. Consequently, the nature of nonresponse is dependent on the sample design, the sampling procedure and the particular method of data collection. The
seriousness of nonresponse relates to the cost of data-
gathering and the seriousness of nonresponse bias.

The Nature of Nonresponse

The sample design. One can distinguish between four types
of sample design which each yield nonresponse of a specific
nature, namely:

A. one measurement of one single sample
B. repeated measurement of independent samples
C. repeated measurement of one sample maintained over
   time with periodic additions of new sample units to
   replace drop-outs or to maintain representativeness
D. repeated measurement of one sample maintained over
   time without any additions

These designs typically fulfill the data-requirements of
cross-section studies, trend studies (or repeated cross-
section studies), cohort studies, and longitudinal studies
respectively. Only with design D do nonrespondents in cons
utive measurements all belong to the group of respondents i
earlier measurements. The unique character of nonresponse
in longitudinal surveys is that it is cumulative in nature.
Nonrespondents in subsequent measurements form disjunct
subgroups of one and the same initial sample.

The sampling procedure. If the composition of the ultimat
sample is influenced by an interviewer through the employment of a particular selection procedure, then, in fact,
also the non-coverage component of nonresponse might be influenced. Non-coverage denotes failure to include element
of the defined survey population in the sample frame. In
mail surveys, where the ultimate sample is pre-determined
in terms of a fixed list of sample members, the particular
sources of non-coverage due to the interviewer's performance will be absent.

---

[1]Other aspects of the nonresponse problem, such as treatment of nonresponse in estimation (procedures to cope with
the problem of nonresponse bias), and assessing the effectiveness of particular devices to control (increase) the
response rates to reduce nonresponse bias, to improve response quality, or to increase the completeness of returns
(less missing data) are beyond the scope of this paper.

[2]This is a preliminary paper. Because of the permitted
length of the paper the findings are only briefly describe
Nevertheless, these findings are thought to be of interest
to support the suggestions made. A more thorough analysis
of these findings will be possible in the further stages o
the research project.

The data-collection method. The nature of the non-interview component of nonresponse is dependent on the interview technique. Non-interview refers to the failure to obtain responses from elements included in the sample. Some of the possible sources of non-interview bias relate only to interviewer's performance in the area of gaining respondent cooperation and do not occur in mail surveys. Unfortunately, however, the real causes of non-interview in mail surveys often remain unknown. Only "non-contacts" due to "vacant households" (i.e. questionnarie returned by the post in case of non-delivery), "overt refusal" (i.e., empty questionnaires returned by the households or other negative reactions), and "interview not possible" (due to failure to understand the questionnaire, respondent too old, incompleteness of returns, etc.) can be established explicitly.

The Seriousness of Nonresponse

The cost of data-gathering. The average cost per interview is inversely proportional to the number of respondents. Obviously, this is only true if the survey is aimed at the collection of data on a pre-determined number of sample units within a specified period for completing interviews. Therefore, nonresponse seriously affects the cost of data collection as it requires larger samples to obtain a fixed quantity of respondents. In longitudinal mail surveys this problem is particularly serious since mail surveys are generally believed to produce relatively high nonresponse rates [11, 14, 19] and moreover, because of the "compounding" nature of nonresponse in longitudinal measurement [7, 8, 15].

Nonresponse bias. As the purpose of most survey research is to arrive at valid and reliable inferences about the population, nonresponse bias is quite serious. Nonresponse bias is denoted as the phenomenon that the average value of an estimator determined over all respondents is not equal to the true value of the complete sample. In longitudinal research however, the nonresponse bias problem can be considered differently. Unrepresentativeness of the interviewed population at repeated measurements is inherent in the longitudinal design. Just the passage of time will make the sample atypical.

For this reason the primary purpose of longitudinal analysis should not be to obtain findings that are representative of the population. Rather, it will be concerned with detecting basic relationships between variables, their causal structure and interaction patterns. The assumption behind longitudinal analysis is that these basic relationships generally remain relatively unbiased [13, 16].

In conclusion, nonresponse in longitudinal mail surveys is rather serious because of the cost involved in obtaining a sufficient number of respondents in the final measurement. Implications of nonresponse bias are less serious than they are for most other types of survey.

VARIABLES SUGGESTED FOR MONITORING NONRESPONSE

The nature and the seriousness of nonresponse provide the impetus for the adoption of some other criteria besides response rate to evaluate the overall effectiveness of the survey design in obtaining respondent cooperation.

1. The response pattern through time. The level of nonresponse is usually indicated indirectly by the response rate. The evaluative character of this measure is based on the empirical experience that response rates can be effectively influenced by a great number of devices. These devices have been extensively investigated and reviewed [11, 14, 19] and will therefore not be discussed in this paper. In studies not aimed at the testing of particular devices like the one described in this paper, the response rate just reflects the overall effect of the complete set of devices used. This implies that response rates, as

such, are not comparable from one survey to another. Whether a response rate is considered high, moderate or low should reasonably depend on the efforts (and its associated cost) made to obtain sample units' cooperation. In longitudinal research, however, comparison of response rates relating to subsequent measurements makes sense since the devices used do not differ, or differ only slightly, between measurements. The response pattern through time then reveals each measurement's contribution to the total nonresponse, both in absolute and relative figures.

2. The sources of nonresponse through time. In single mail surveys the distribution of nonresponse according to its sources ("vacant households," "overt refusal," "interview not possible," and "other") can be used only for an ex-post evaluation. In longitudinal surveys, however, insights into the changes in this distribution over time could be helpful in identifying additional devices for reducing the level of nonresponse in later measurements. To experimental studies these cahnges may imply an extra criterion to assess the effectiveness of these devices.

3. Nonresponse bias through time. Longitudinal studies offer the opportunity to study the variability of nonresponse bias between subsequent measurements. This might contribute to an evaluation of the procedures which are presently used in many panel studies for making allowance or corrections for nonresponse bias.

4. Speed of response. This variable measures the length of the period elapsing between the first mailing date and the date of return. Estimating nonresponse bias on the basis of differences between early and late respondents has its origine in the so-called "extrapolation hypothesis," advanced by Ferber [4]. This hypothesis says that late respondents are more like nonrespondents than early respondents. For a long time this hypothesis has been a controversial subject [5, 10, 19]. Longitudinal studies provide the opportunity to test it more thoroughly than is usually possible. In later measurements, respondents and nonrespondents can be compared on the basis of the variables recorded in earlier measurements.

Other opportunities regard an examination of: how the distribution of speed of response varies over time, to what degree the individual's speed of response shows stability over time, and last but not least, to what extent speed of response in one measurement is indicative of nonresponse in later measurements. Prediction of future nonresponse is of special importance from a cost point of view. The efficiency of follow-up efforts to obtain more (late) respondents will clearly depend on the extent to which these late respondents will become nonrespondent in future measurements.

5. Other variables that may be indicative of nonresponse in later measurements are item omission and completion time. In this paper, no further attention can be paid to these response characteristics of potential nonrespondents.

THE METHOD OF DATA COLLECTION

In the "Longitudinal Anticipations Research" project, essentially the same method of data collection will be employed in each of the five measurements scheduled in the period from January 1976 to January 1978. The unit under observation is the private household.

The sample. The sample population (N = 2600) was defined as all individual households which either were members of the "Attwood Household Panel" in the Netherlands at Jauuary 1st, 1976, or were removed from this panel during the latest five months prior to this date. The first group included 2.290 so-called "Life Panel" members. The second group consisted of 310 so-called "Removal-1" households.

"Life Panel" members report each week their purchases of a

large variety of consumer goods by means of a diary, most often completed by the housewife. In incomplete households and one-person households, the head of the household completes the diary. The "Life Panel" was representative of the Dutch population of households with respect to: district, degree of urbanization, age of the housewife, size of the household, social class, age of the youngest person and occupation of the head [12].

In operating with such a panel the organizer has to tackle the problems of panel mortality and attrition. Replacement of drop-outs is necessary to maintain representativeness. However, for the purpose of the "Longitudinal Anticipation Research" project the sample must remain the same. Therefore, "Life Panel" members which have been removed since January 1st were kept in the sample, as "Removals-2", while newly added "Life Panel" members were left out.

The respondent. The designated respondent is the housewife [9]. Should there be no housewife, the head of the household is the designated respondent. If neither of these is available another member of the household is asked to do the job.

The questionnaire. The 48-page mimeographed mail-questionnaire covers 272 questions dealing with variables relating to the household's situation, anticipations, and changes in both [8]. Personalization of the questionnaire is achieved by asking respondents to provide their name and address at the end.

The covering letter. The purpose of the survey and the procedures are briefly explained in a separate covering letter. The properties of this letter are: non-personal salutation, a named sender, and facsimiled personal signature. The content further comprises the request to respond promptly without reference to any deadline data and the promise of strict confidentiality of answers. No reference is made to sponsorship.

In later measurements the covering letter also draws the respondent's attention to the household's earlier cooperation in the survey for which thanks is expressed. It is requested to let the same respondent complete the questionnaire as the one who did before.

The cover envelope. The questionnaire with the covering letter and a paid-return envelope are sent by mail under normal delivery conditions. The white cover envelope clearly reveals the name and address of the sender.

Incentives. The respondent is offered the choice between Dgld. 5.- and a gramophone record. A record can be selected out of a list of our "singles" for each of which the retail price is about Dgld. 7.-.

Mailing data and reminders. The first mailing is on Thursday to ensure that the questionnaire is received by the household just before the weekend. In each measurement three written reminders are sent out at subsequent Thursdays to all households which have not yet responded. The first reminder (one week after the first mailing) is a postcard follow-up which just mentions the respondent that he might still not have returned the questionnaire and which asks him to do so promptly because of the importance of his answers. The second reminder (two weeks after the first mailing) is a follow-up letter enclosing a new copy of the questionnaire. The third reminder (three weeks after the original mailing) is a postcard follow-up like the first one.

All these follow-ups are personalized in a way similar to the covering letter of the original mailing. Cover envelopes are identical to those used in the original mailing in all cases except one: cover envelopes sent to removals in the third follow-up of the second measurement did not reveal name and address of the sender. The reason behind this is, as was found from the first measurement, that households who voluntarily removed from the "Life Panel" might be more inclined to drop signed envelopes unopened in the waste-paper basket.

In the first measurement, "Life Panel" members who did not respond in spite of three follow-up letters, were telephoned if they had one. In the second measurement no fourth reminder was used.

SOME ILLUSTRATIVE FINDINGS

To show how nonresponse develops through time, the total sample is decomposed into the following components:

LP1 = "Life Panel" members at the date of measurement I.
LP2 = "Life Panel" members at the date of measurement II.
R1  = "Removal 1" households, removed from the Life Panel in the latest five months prior to the date of measurement I.
R2  = "Removal 2" households, removed from the Life Panel in the period between measurements I and II.

The response pattern through time. The overall effectiveness of the data collection method is indicated by the relatively high overall response rates shown in Table 1. It appears that response rates for the Life Panel are substantially higher than for removals. Because of these high response rates in the Life Panel and the increasing number of removals through time, nonresponse is to an increasing extent determined by the incidence of becoming removal. Fortunately, response rates appear to increase for both the Life Panel and removals: this results in an absolute decrease of the number of nonrespondents over time (from 269 at measurement I to 195 at measurement II).

It can also be observed that removals account for an increasing part of total response (from 178 out of 2.331 at measurement I to 443 out of 2.133 at measurement II). Therefore, the decision to keep removals in the sample can be considered of critical importance to the feasibility of longitudinal research in an existing panel.

The sources of nonresponse through time. Table 2 shows that the importance of the different sources of nonresponse changed over time. In particular, the category "interview not possible" decreased sharply, while "vacant households" became more serious, as could be expected [7, 15].

Nonresponse bias through time. From the panel registration file information regarding six reference variables was available on nonrespondents in measurement I (see Table 3, first column). Only the year of birth of the housewife and the household size appeared to be significantly different between respondents and nonrespondents. At measurement II, nonresponse bias is tested on the same variables as they were recorded during measurement I (see Table 3, second column). Besides the year of birth of the housewife and the household size also the age of the youngest person appeared to be biased. This, however, does not prove that nonresponse bias changed over time since these three variables are highly interdependent.

An additional test on nonresponse bias at measurement II is performed on some other variables observed at measurement I (lower part of the second column of Table 3). This test revealed that the answers to questions on ownership of cars, recent purchase of vacuum cleaners, year of marriage, and sex of the respondent show a significant nonresponse bias. These findings underline how dangerous it is to draw conclusions about the existence of nonresponse bias, solely on the basis of general reference variables [5]. Moreover, they suggest the desirability of investigating nonresponse bias over time with respect to the variables that are most critical to the survey.

412

TABLE 1

The Response Pattern Through Time

| Sample components | | LP1 | R1 | R2 | Total sample |
|---|---|---|---|---|---|
| Measurement I (January '76) | Mailed | 2.290(100.0) | 310(100.0) | - | 2.600(100.0) |
| | Nonresponse | 137( 6.0) | 132( 42.6) | - | 269( 10.3) |
| | Response | 2.153( 94.0) | 178( 57.4) | - | 2.331( 89.7) |
| Respondents removed from LP2 to R2 | | - 422 | | + 422 | |
| | | LP2 | R1 | R2 | Total sample |
| Measurement II (Sept. 1976) | Mailed | 1.731(100.0) | 178(100.0) | 422(100.0) | 2.331(100.0) |
| | Nonresponse | 38( 2.2) | 41( 23.0) | 116( 27.5) | 195( 8.5) |
| | Response | 1.693( 97.8) | 137( 77.0) | 306( 72.5) | 2.136( 91.5) |

TABLE 2

The Sources of Nonresponse Through Time

| Sources of Nonresponse | Measurement I | Measurement II |
|---|---|---|
| Vacant households | 7 ( 2.6) | 12 ( 6.2) |
| Overt refusals | 72 (26.8) | 49 (25.1) |
| Interview not possible | 36 (13.4) | 6 ( 3.1) |
| Unknown | 154 (57.2) | 128 (65.6) |
| Total | 269 (100%) | 195 (100%) |

Nonresponse bias may vary between the different components of the total sample. The third column of Table 3 shows that removals might have an influence on nonresponse bias which differs from that of "Life Panel" members.

Finally, the changes in nonresponse bias can be tested more directly by comparing nonrespondents in measurement I with nonrespondents in measurement II. The fourth column of Table 3 shows that this test might produce results that differ from comparisons between respondents and nonrespondents for each measurement separately.

The speed of response (SOR). Table 4 shows that Life Panel members responded more promptly than removals. Further, SOR increased through time for those respondents who stayed in the Life Panel during both measurements (LP2). In contrast, SOR decreased for those who left the Life Panel (R2). Table 5 shows that the stability of SOR over time is much greater in the Life Panel than for removals. SOR I and SOR II are equal for 72.7 percent of the LP2-group, while 15.4 percent is speeding up and 11.9% is speeding down. For the R2-group these percentages are 48.7, 21.7 and 29.7 respectively.

The finding (from Table 4) that those respondents who became removals between the two measurements (R2) already had a lower SOR in measurement I, at least suggests that SOR might be indicative of becoming removal in the next measurement. Table 6 shows that the probability of becoming a removal decreases as SOR I increases. As removals have higher nonresponse rates, this finding might imply that SOR is also indicative of becoming nonrespondent in the next measurement. Table 7 shows that SOR I is negatively correlated with the probability of becoming nonrespondent in measurement II insofar as the Life Panel is concerned. This relationship does not apply to the removals. It must be noticed, however, that even for the LP2-group, nonresponse in measurement II is mainly composed of early respondents to measurement I (24 out of the 38).

CONCLUSIONS

The purpose of this paper was just to illustrate the usefulness of some particular variables for monitoring nonresponse in longitudinal mail surveys.

It is shown that response rates do change over time while essentially the same set of devices to control nonresponse is used. The importance of the different sources of nonresponse appears to vary over time. It is indicated that the study of nonresponse bias and changes through time in it, is facilitated by the availability of data on nonrespondents from earlier measurements. The hypothesis that speed of response is indicative of future nonresponse is enforced in two respects. Firstly, the speed of response appeared to be a direct, but weak, indicator of nonrespondents in the Life Panel. Secondly, the speed of response is found to be indicative of becoming removal in the near future. Since removals do have lower response rates, the speed of response may be considered an indirect predictor of nonresponse due to removals.

Of course, a more definite assessment of the usefulness of the suggested variables requires further research. In particular, the availability of more longitudinal data would enable the testing of the hypothesis that go beyond the findings presented before. The possible implications of insights gained from such studies would not be limited to only longitudinal surveys: they might also be useful to help improve the efficiency of other types of survey research in gaining sample members' cooperation.

FINAL NOTE

The preliminary findings of this report need further verification and explanation. The author and his colleagues intend to extend the study of nonresponse bias to other behavioral variables than the ones included in this report. Also, a further elaboration of speed of response as an indicator of future nonresponse -- one of the main findings -- is considered particularly challenging. Hopefully, some new findings from the third measurement can be presented verbally at the congress.

REFERENCES

1. Andreason, A.R. "Potential Marketing Applications of Longitudinal Methods." In P.D. Bennet (ed.), "Economic Growth, Competition, and World Markets," AMA Proceedings, September 1965, 261-75.

2. Blalock, H.M. Jr., (ed). Casual Models in the Social

TABLE 3

Nonresponse Bias Through Time

| Variables recorded at measurement I | CHI-square statistics relating to differences between: *) | | | |
|---|---|---|---|---|
| | 2.153 respondents and 137 nonrespondents from LP1 | 1.999 respondents and 154 nonrespondents from (LP2+R2) | 306 respondents and 116 nonrespondents from R2 | 137 respondents from LP1 and 154 nonrespondents from (LP2+R2) |
| Social class | 3.20(4) | 7.28(4) | 9.84(4) | 9.29(4) |
| Household size | 9.59(5) | 10.69(5) | 2.42(5) | 12.53(5) |
| Year of birth of housewife | 15.29(5) | 10.94(5) | 2.74(5) | 4.96(5) |
| Age of youngest person | 1.34(3) | 9.35(3) | 2.36(3) | 7.58(3) |
| Urbanization degree | 4.63(4) | 3.74(4) | 2.94(4) | 4.63(4) |
| District | 5.29(4) | 6.11(6) | 9.12(6) | 1.92(4) |
| Ownership of: | | | | |
| - car | | 5.48(2) | 5.68(2) | |
| - TV-set | | 0.27(1) | 2.20(1) | |
| - Vacuum cleaner | | 0.03(1) | 0.32(1) | |
| Recent acquisition of: | | | | |
| - Car | | 1.42(1) | 3.05(1) | |
| - TV-set | | 1.28(1) | 1.75(1) | |
| - Vacuum cleaner | | 3.61(1) | 2.33(1) | |
| Education housewife | | 0.74(2) | 0.02(2) | |
| Year of marriage | | 8.10(4) | 2.17(4) | |
| Sex of respondent | | 3.13(1) | 0.02(1) | |
| Annual income | | 7.28(7) | 4.60(7) | |
| Completion time | | 2.88(5) | 4.67(5) | |

* Numbers between brackets refer to the number of degree of freedom; CHI-square statistics in boxes are significant at the .10-level.


TABLE 4

Speed of Response (SOR) Through Time

| SOR \ Sample-components | Measurement I | | | Measurement II | | |
|---|---|---|---|---|---|---|
| | LP2 | R2 | (LP2+R2) | LP2 | R2 | (LP2+R2) |
| 1. (First week) | 78.6 | 65.4 | 75.3 | 82.4 | 59.5 | 78.9 |
| 2. (Second week) | 18.9 | 22.9 | 20.1 | 14.1 | 22.2 | 15.4 |
| 3. (Third week or later) | 2.5 | 11.8 | 4.6 | 3.5 | 18.3 | 5.7 |
| Total response | 1.693 | 306 | 1.999 | 1.693 | 306 | 1.999 |

TABLE 5

Turnover Table of Speed of Response

| SOR II \ SOR I | LP2 | | | | R2 | | | |
|---|---|---|---|---|---|---|---|---|
| | 1 | 2 | 3 | Total | 1 | 2 | 3 | Total |
| 1 | 1.148 | 226 | 21 up | 1.395 | 124 | 38 | 20 up | 182 |
| 2 | 149 down | 76 | 14 | 239 | 43 down | 17 | 8 | 68 |
| 3 | 34 | 18 | 7 | 59 | 33 | 15 | 8 | 56 |
| Total | 1.331 | 320 | 42 | 1.693 | 200 | 70 | 36 | 306 |

TABLE 6

Speed of Response as Indicator of Becoming Removal

| SOR I | 1 | 2 | 3 | Total |
|---|---|---|---|---|
| Became Removal 2 | 267( 16.5) | 106( 24.5) | 49( 50.0) | 422( 19.6) |
| Stayed in Life Panel | 1.355( 83.5) | 327( 75.5) | 49( 50.0) | 1.731( 80.4) |
| Totals | 1.622(100.0) | 433(100.0) | 98(100.0) | 2.153(100.0) |

TABLE 7

Speed of Response as Indicator of Becoming Nonrespondent

| | SOR I: | 1 | 2 | 3 | Total |
|---|---|---|---|---|---|
| R2 | Nonrespondents | 67( 25.1) | 36( 34.0) | 13( 26.5) | 116( 27.5) |
| | Respondents | 200 | 70 | 36 | 306 |
| | Total | 267(100.0) | 106(100.0) | 49(100.0) | 422(100.0) |
| LP2 | Nonrespondents | 24( 1.8) | 7( 2.1) | 7( 14.3) | 38( 2.2) |
| | Respondents | 1.331 | 320 | 42 | 1.693 |
| | Total | 1.355(100.0) | 327(100.0) | 49(100.0) | 1.731(100.0) |

Sciences. The Macmillan Press Ltd., London, 1974.

3. Christopher, M.G. and C.K. Elliot. "Causal Path Analysis in Market Research." Journal of the Market Research Society. 12, No. 2 (April 1970), 112-24.

4. Ferber, R. "The Problem of Bias in Mail Returns: A Solution." Public Opinion Quarterly, 12 (Winter 1948), 669-76.

5. Ford, R.N. and H. Zeisel. "Bias in Mail Surveys Cannot be Controlled by One Mailing." Public Opinion Quarterly, 13 (Fall 1949), 495-501.

Granbois, D.H. and J.F. Engel. "The Longitudinal Approach to Studying Marketing Behavior." In P.D. Bennet (ed.),"Economic Growth, Competition and World Markets," AMA Proceedings, September 1965, 205-221.

Hall, G.E. "Recent Census Bureau Experiences with Longitudinal Surveys." Proceedings American Statistical Association, Social Statistics in Section, 1968, 160-62.

Jonge, L. de, and W.M. Oppedijk van Veen. "A Micro Model of Purchasing Behaviour for Consumer Durable Goods: I and II." European Research, 3 (July 1975), 151-161; 4 (May 1976), 129-41.

Jonge, L. de, and W.M. Oppedijk van Veen. "Some Problems of Collecting Data on Households' Purhcasing Behaviour Concerning Durable Goods." Internal Philips

Report (publ. nr. M.M:R./11/1977).

10. Jonge, L. de, W.M. Oppedijk van Veen and C. Pooters. "The Speed of Response in Mail-Panel Surveys." Internal Philips Report (publ. nr. M.M.R./12/1977).

11. Kanuk, L. and C. Berenson. "Mail Surveys and Response Rates: A Literature Review." Journal of Marketing Research, 12 (November 1975), 440-53.

12. Koning, C.C.J. de. "Technical Aspects of Running Panels." ESOMAR, Seminar on "Panels," Amsterdam (1972), 23-38.

13. Kosobud, R.F. and J.N. Morgan (eds.). Consumer Behavior of Individual Families Over Two and Three Years. The University of Michigan, Monograph No. 36, 1964.

14. Linsky, A.S. "Stimulating Responses to Mailed Questionnaires: A Review." Public Opinion Quarterly, 39 (Spring 1975), 82-101

15. Nestel, G. "A Longitudinal Study of Labour Market Behavior -- Advantages and Some Methodological Problems in Analysis." Proceedings A.S.A., Social Statistics Section, 1970, 26-31.

16. Nicosia, F.M. "Panel Designs and Analyses in Marketing." In P.D. Bennet (ed), "Economic Growth, Competition and World Markets," AMA Proceedings, September 1965, 244-60.

17. Pelz, D.C. and F.M. Andrews. "Detecting Casual

Priorities in Panel Study Data." <u>American Sociological Review</u>, 29 (December 1964), 836-48.

18. Pratt, R.W., Jr. "Understanding the Decision Process for Consumer Durable Goods: An Example of the Application of Longitudinal Analysis." In P.D. Bennett (ed.), "Economic Growth, Competition and World Markets," <u>AMA Proceedings</u>, September 1965, 244-60

19. Scott, C. "Research on Mail Surveys." <u>Journal of the Royal Statistical Society</u>, 124, Series A, Part 2 (1961), 143-91.

20. Yee, A.H. and N.L. Gage. "Techniques for Estimating the Source and Direction of Causal Influence in Panel Data." <u>Psychological Bulletin</u>, No. 2 (1968), 115-26.

# CHANGING ROLES OF WOMEN -- SOME EMPIRICAL FINDINGS
## WITH MARKETING IMPLICATIONS

Alladi Venkatesh, State University of New York at Binghamton

## ABSTRACT

The paper examines the impact of the women's movement on marketing. Three groups of women, Feminists, Moderates and Traditionalists, were included in the study, and differences and similarities between the groups were observed in some selected life style and demographic characteristics. The study throws light on some sociological aspects of consumer behavior with serious implications for product and communication strategies.

## INTRODUCTION

Traditionally a marketer's interest in women as consumers has centered around the roles of wife, mother, homemaker, and hostess, or single girl preparatory to these roles [7]. Roles outside the family such as career woman, professional worker which may be called 'social roles' were given little or no attention. These social roles are assuming considerable importance with the impact of women's movement on the American scene. In one of the earlier studies, Koponen [16] reported that "men were higher in their expression of needs for achievement, autonomy, dominance and sex and aggression. Women received higher scores on association, assistance, dependence, order compliance and self-depreciation." Demby [9] reacts to this by saying, "one might warn that as the role of women changes in society, the latter type of response may change over time -- very directly as a result of the effects of the women's liberation movement."

The significance of women's movement to marketing may be summarized as follows:

- The women's movement is a forerunner of significant changes in the social values and in the social system.

- The life styles of women will be significantly affected with some bearing on economic behavior of the consumers at large.

- The traditional household decision making will undergo significant changes.

- The economics of the household especially in the allocation of women's time in acquiring and processing commodities will change considerably.

- As a result of anticipated changes in the life styles of women, we can expect changes in life styles of men.

Only recently have marketers begun to address themselves to some of the social and economic issues arising out of the changing feminine environment. However, empirical research has been limited to the issue of role portrayals of women in advertisements [6, 26, 28] and some tangential issues [11, 12, 18].

The purpose of this exploration study is to investigate the significance of the women's movement to marketing. For this study the aims of the movement are defined as the attempts to bring about a change in the role and status of women in the direction of equality with men. The term feminism embodies these aims. The focus of this study is on three groups of women, designated as Traditionalists, Moderates and Feminists. The specific objectives of the

study are three fold:

1. To examine the life style characteristics of the members of the three groups and focus attention on those dimensions which reveal some differences.
2. To examine the extent to which demographic variables contribute to the differences between the groups.
3. To evaluate the implications of the study for marketing.

## BACKGROUND

The traditional family structure in the U. S. includes the bread-winning and status-giving father-husband, the domesticated wife-mother-homemaker. It is well known that the extended family in the U. S. is on the way to extinction and only the nuclear family is most common. Factors affecting nuclear family include changing saliency of marriage and parenthood, rising divorce rates, increasing proportion of families headed by a single parent [24]. There is also evidence that more families are becoming 'egalitarian' where the couples share 'husband-father' and 'wife-mother' roles [30].

The reason for changing views on marriage can be attributed to the transition from an 'institutional' to 'companionship' approach to marriage. While the institutional approach represents a normative framework embedded in duty bound tradition and religion, the companionship approach stresses such values as mutual gratification of needs, equal sharing of emotional needs and other secular aspirations [19]. Liberal views on abortion and contraception are also contributing toward the changing attitudes toward family and marriage.

Women's choice and commitment to careers are also having an impact on the social structure. The shift is occurring from the traditional two-person career (where husband's career[1] is the focus of attention for both) to dual careers. The dual career (or two career) family system strikes at the very heart of sex-linked division of labor and is creating new stresses and strains as well as challenges not found in the conventional framework [14].

The feminist movement can be considered a revolt against psychological oppression, social and economic discrimination and an effort to establish a female ideology separate from and not subservient to male ideology [10, 31]. Its basic aims include redefinition of concepts of marriage, motherhood and housewifery; realization of equitable sharing of responsibilities between men and women in almost all walks of life; and removal of the false and stereotype image of women now prevalent in the mass media, texts, ceremonies, laws and practices of our major social institutions. Major topics of current interest found to be of concern to women in general and feminists in particular include, Career Commitment, Child Care and Orienta-

---

[1]'Career' as opposed to 'Job' refers to a conceptualization of work that extends beyond fulfilling a financial need or avoiding boredom through domestic existence. It incorporates societal values such as self-expression, achievement, etc., which have been traditionally limited to male aspirations.

tion, Homemaking, Problems of Employment, Attitude Toward Marriage, Contemporary Issues, Social and Economic Injustice, Sex Equality in all Spheres of Life, Abortion, Occupational and Social Status, Sexual Stereotyping, and Political and Civil Rights. These issues are, of course, interrelated.

## METHODOLOGY

For the purpose of the study, three groups of women, Traditionalists, Moderates and Feminists were identified by administering Arnott's Feminism Scale. The specific hypotheses to be verified were:

H1: Life style dimensions are stable across the three groups.

H2: Hypothesized life style dimensions and the extracted dimensions (factors) will be the same.

H3: Life style dimensions do not discriminate significantly between the groups.

H4: There are no significant differences between the groups on the basis of demographics variables.

### Survey Design

The population included in the study consisted of all women between the ages of 18-45 living in the urbanized area of Syracuse, New York, as defined by the U. S. Census Bureau [25]. The study was restricted to these age categories primarily because the feminist movement being of more recent origin, one could evaluate more meaningfully the similarities and differences between comparable groups of women. The sampling method used was a three stage stratified cluster sampling of the designated area, to the household level. The total sample size of respondents was determined to be 748 which was arrived at by methods suggested by Hansen et al. [13]. All the respondents were contacted by mail and various measures were taken to increase the response rate and remove possible biases. The initial response rate was 41%. Non-respondents were sampled and were compared to the respondent sample on some demographic characteristics. The differences were negligible and consequently both respondents and non-respondents were merged into one consolidated sample. The final sample size was 333 after discarding 26 unusable questionnaires.

### Questionnaire Design

The questionnaire was made up of three parts (a) Feminism Scale (b) Life Style Statements and (c) Demographic Variables.

The Feminism Scale consisted of ten items and was originally developed by Arnott [3] as Autonomy Inventory Scores which was, in turn, based on the original scale of Kirkpatrick [15]. The scale has been used in marketing by Green and Cunningham [12]. The scale incorporates Feminism construct with an equal number of positive and negative statements[2] measured on a five point scale. The response categories are "Strongly Agree', "Agree', "Neither Agree nor Disagree', "Disagree', "Strongly Disagree". The range of scores on the Feminism scale is from a minimum of 10 to a maximum of 50.

Life style dimensions were selected on the basis of three criteria, (a) relevance to feminism (b) relevance to marketing and (c) their measurability. Selected dimensions include Innovative Behavior [22], Opinion Leadership [23],

Role Portrayal of Women in Ads [6], Toys and Sex Symbolism [21], Social Responsibility [5], Attitude Toward Television [8], Life Simplification Products [1], Fashion and Personal Appearance [29], Frozen Foods [1], Leisure Activities [44]. Included under each dimension were a set of statements [Table 1] against which the respondent was asked to indicate her agreement or disagreement on a five point scale similar to the Feminism Scale described earlier. The questionnaire also sought information on some demographic variables such as Age, Education, Family Income, Race, Marital Status, Work Status, Household Status, and Religion. The questionnaire was pretested by administering it to 50 women and was modified in length, phrasing and appeal as found necessary.

Feminism Scores: In order to classify an individual respondent into one of the three groups the range of feminism scores for each group was established. Both methods of Arnott [3] and Green and Cunningham [12] were considered arbitrary raising some questions relative to validity of their classification procedure. Green and Cunningham do not mention the classification method used in their study, but one gets the impression from reading their article that they simply followed Arnott's procedure. Arnott used a seven point scale for the ten items with the potential scores ranging from 10 to 70. Keeping the midpoint as 40, she arbitrarily assigned the scores of 10 thru 25 to conservatives, 33-47 to moderates and 55-70 to liberals. She does not explain what group assignment was made for individuals who scored either 26 thru 32 or 48 thru 54. If they were not included in the study, one doesn't know why.

In the present study, this was avoided by first administering the Feminism scale to groups of women with known views on feminism, ranging from extreme pro to con. A total of 150 women were selected (these are different from the sample selected for the study) who also received a self-designating questionnaire in which they were asked about their knowledge and support of certain feminist issues, their readership interest in magazines devoted exclusively to women's political and social issues and finally, how they would identify themselves on two self-designating constructs, Traditional-Feminist and Conservative-Liberal. The scores on the two constructs were then correlated with the scores on the Feminism Scale and this yielded a highly significant .58 correlation. The idea was to check whether a person who designated herself Feminist/Liberal (or Conservative/Traditional or Middle of the Road) would accordingly score high (or low or middle) on the Feminism Scale. Taking the mean value for each group, the cut-off points established were (a) Traditionalists 10 thru 36, (b) Moderates 37 to 42 and (c) Feminists 43 to 50. These scores were obviously different from the equal ranges established by Arnott and by implication followed by Green and Cunningham.

## DISCUSSION OF RESULTS

Demographic Variables: In the first state of the analysis the groups were compared on demographic characteristics.

In the Feminists category, 74% of the respondents were between the ages of 18-30 whereas 46% of the Traditionalists and 64% of the Moderates were in this age group. The remaining were in 31-45 age group. The age characteristics showed significant differences between the groups. In an earlier study on changing "female ideology", Lipman-Blumen [17] found no significant difference in the age characteristics of two groups of women whom she labeled "Traditional" and "Contemporary".

Feminists were generally more educated than members of other groups, with 61% of them in the college graduate and post-graduate categories compared to Moderates and Traditionalists (43% and 34% respectively). The Feminist

---

[2]An example of a positive statement is "The word obey should be removed from the marriage ceremony." A negative statement would be "Motherhood is the 'ideal' career for most women."

movement has been viewed by some as basically an elitist-intellectual affair [10] and it is not surprising that the Feminists appear to enjoy higher educational qualifications.

In all the three groups, the largest proportion of women were full-time employed; Traditionalists - 34%, Moderates - 48%, Feminists - 42%, and for the total sample the figure was 41% which compared well with national average. However, more Feminists (20%) reported being still in school compared to Moderates (12%) and Traditionalists (10%) presumably because they are also younger. Similarly more Traditionalists (36%) were "keeping house" than Moderates (16%) and Feminists (14%).

More Traditionalists reported (25%) themselves as 'housewives' compared to Moderates (15%) and Feminists (7%). A large proportion in all categories addressed themselves as 'Cohead of Household'; with Feminists (74%) leading and followed by Moderates (56%) and Traditionalists (46%). Roughly equal proportion of women in each category used the term 'Head of Household' (16%-18%).

While there were about equal proportion of Protestants in each group (36%-40%), there were more Catholics among Traditionalists (50%) compared to Moderates (36%) and Feminists (26%). More Feminists (16%) classified themselves as Jewish than Moderates (4%) and Traditionalists (2%) did.

No significant differences were found between the groups on the basis of Income and Marital Status.

Factor Analysis of Life Style Statements

Factor Analysis was performed in two stages, (a) separate factor analysis for each group, the purpose of which was to check the stability of the dimensions across the groups and, (b) combined group factor analysis, where the objective was to extract life style dimensions, compare them with the hypothesized dimensions and use the factor scores in further analysis.

The factor analysis technique used in the study was the principal component technique. Only those factors (a) whose eigen values were at least equal to 1 and, (b) offered some conceptual meaning, were included in the study. Factors were rotated orthogonally and only those life style statements with a minimum loading of 0.30 or more were further considered.

Separate analyses were performed on individual groups. Of the 11 hypothesized dimensions only one dimension "Social Responsibility" was not accounted for by the extracted factors. The purpose of the analysis was to check visually for the stability of factors across different samples. The stability appears to hold true with a variation. Factors were not extracted in the same order in all groups and this is to be expected, if not desirable, to show that while the groups think in terms of same dimensions, these dimensions do not mean the same to them. In the second stage of the actor nalysis group data were combined and factors were extracted. Except for one factor "Social Responsibility" all others were extracted. However, two dimensions "Women's Role Portrayals in Ads" and "Toys and Sex Symbolism" emerged as a single dimension because of a common underlying construct, which has been designated as "Sex Stereotyping". Similarly, a single hypothesized dimension, Leisure Activities, emerged as two distinct factors labeled as "Leisure-Work Attitude" and "Active-Leisure Behavior". Each of these dimensions are discussed individually.

Sex Stereotyping: This dimension emerged as a result of the merger of two related constructs, Toys and Sex Symbolism and Women's Role Portrayal in Ads. The individual items under this dimension indicate significant differences between the groups. In fact, this dimension may be viewed

as the most important in the analysis. Feminists strongly believe that toys should be non-sexist and that TV ads still portray women in stereotype roles and do not reflect the reality of the situation. Traditionalists hold opposite views on both these issues with Moderates taking a middle stand. The implications of this to the marketers are that as Feminists' views become popular and widespread, changes in product and communication strategies have to reflect new thinking.

Self-Confidence: Bardwick [4] theorized that in traditional sex stereotyping of values, self-confidence was associated with men more than women. If Feminists are trying to eliminate this distinction, one would expect them to demonstrate greater self-confidence than other groups. The individual statements under this dimension do not give any conclusive evidence as to which group appears more self-confident, although there are some minor differences between the groups. In persuasive communication, self-confidence has been discussed as an important personality variable [32]. In the present study, no significant result was obtained.

Attitude Toward Television Viewing: This dimension revealed some significant differences with Feminists appearing to be less sympathetic to television viewing than other groups.

Leisure-Work Attitude,

Active Leisure Behavior: These two factors have resulted from one hypothesized factor "Leisure Activities". Both extracted factors have been subject to much theoretical discussions in sociological literature [20]. Regarding Leisure-Work Attitude, the Traditionalists seem to favor self-definition through leisure while Moderates and Feminists appear less inclined to think that way. This may be because of the emerging career patterns of the two groups which make work appear less as a drudgery. On the other factor, Active Leisure Behavior, all groups indicated (with more feminists, however) positive approval of physically demanding leisure activities for women on par with men.

Innovative Behavior: This dimension has figured in marketing literature rather prominently in the context of diffusion of innovations. Some significant differences were found between the groups, and one can infer in general terms that, Feminists' attitude toward risk taking is more positive and so is their willingness to try new ideas.

Opinion Leadership: There is no reason to infer that any one group has significantly more opinion leaders than the other. In general, about half the members in each group appear to have been in opinion leadership situations.

Life Simplification Products: This dimension was included (as was Frozen Foods) for making the life style analysis more product specific. Life simplification products can be considered either an end in themselves (a cultural artifact, a manifestation of modern living and a status symbol) or merely an instrument which frees up time. Out of the four products included, three of them, Automatic Coffee Maker, Dishwasher, and Food Dispoal Unit were considered less essential to American families than Washer and Dryer, by the three groups. However, among those who agreed that these products were essential, Traditionalists showed greater appreciation of the need for them.

Frozen Foods: This is another marketing specific dimension which showed no real differences between the groups in terms of their dependence on frozen foods. In general, all the groups felt less dependent on frozen foods in their meal preparations.

Social Responsibility: This dimension was introduced into marketing literature by Anderson and Cunningham [2] who found major differences between high social conscious and low social conscious consumers. In the present study, the factor failed to emerge at all and even the individual statements did not reveal any specific differences between the groups.

In the following stage, a multiple-discriminanat analysis was performed with all the life style dimensions and demographic variables included in the model.

## Multiple Discriminant Analysis (Table 2)

A step-wise discriminant analysis technique was used to evaluate the discriminating ability of the life style and demographic characteristics. The input to discriminant analysis were the factor scores from the combined group factor analysis and the measures on demographic variables. Since each group membership in the sample was almost equal, the prior probability of group membership was made equal to 0.33. Half the sample in each group was used to generate the discriminant function and the other half as the validating sample for prediction of new group membership.

The uni-variate F-ratios indicate highly significant differences on one construct, Sex Stereotyping and moderate to low differences on Age, Education, Religion, Life Simplification Products and Household Status.

Table 2 presents the order in which the discriminating variables entered in the step-wise procedure. It is interesting to note that some variables which were found significant in the uni-variate F-test did not appear in the list, while variables not found significant were included. Although two discriminant functions were generated, the first function dominated the second completely with the second function showing a very low level of significance. Out of a possible 19 variables, only 8 were retained in the discriminant model. In order of entry, these are Sex Stereotyping, Life Simplification Products, Age, Education, Self-Confidence, Marital Status, Fashion and Personal Appearance and Active Leisure Behavior. The inclusion of Marital Status is surprising because of its low significance in earlier crosstab analysis. It is possible that some demographic characteristics which earlier appeared to differentiate the groups were dropped in the discriminant analysis because of collinearities.

A more important result than the order of entry of variables is the magnitude of standardized coefficients. In the order of their relative strength they are Sex Stereotyping, Age, Education, Self-Confidence, Marital Status, Active-Leisure Behavior, Fashion and Personal Appearance and Life Simplification Products. The results confirm earlier findings that Sex Stereotyping, Age, and Education are the most important variables that differentiate between the groups.

The discriminant function is also evaluated for its predictive ability. Table 2 presents the hits and misses. Using the validating sample the discriminant function correctly classified 61% of the Traditionalists, 72% of the Feminists but only 35% of the Moderates. More Moderates were classified as Feminists than Traditionalists. The difficulty with Moderates, as the name suggests, is that they are a middle group and straddle both the other groups. The overall prediction is impressive, especially in the two extreme groups.

## SOME CONCLUSIONS AND MARKETING IMPLICATIONS

In this study an attempt was made to evaluate the perceptions of three groups of women who were identified as Traditionalists, Moderates and Feminists on the basis of the scores they received on a Feminism Scale. Significant differences were found between the groups on some life style and demographic characteristics. In particular, the three variables that differentiated them most were Sex Stereotyping, Age and Education. Other variables that accounted for some differences were Life-Simplification Products, Active-Leisure Behavior, Self-Confidence, and Fashion and Personal Appearance.

Feminists appear to be generally younger, better educated,

have a greater sense of independence, sympathetic to risk behavior, willing to try new ideas and are very vehemently opposed to Sex Stereotyping. Traditionalists are on the other extreme, while Moderates are somewhat in between though leaning toward Feminists on various life style and demographic characteristics. These differences may appear to be stressing the obvious but that is only one aspect of it. The most important or critical dimension to emerge from this study is Sex Stereotyping which symbolizes a whole range of issues for marketers. The implications for communication strategies, product appeals, segmentation and new products and services are obvious. Although the study did not address itself to any specific products which are conventionally sold to female markets, one can develop a scenario of changes in consumption patterns.

In family purchasing decisions, the focus of attention has to shift from women as purchasing agents to both men and women as purchasing agents of home products. Careers and professional goals are becoming important to women thus introducing new value systems for men and women. Women are engaging in physically demanding activities and participating in leisure activities that have been traditionally associated with men. These create a new set of demands for products and services. Women engaging in such activities are not doing so merely to satisfy recreational needs, but realize higher needs of self-definition and self-expression. There is also a growing emphasis from sexist to non-sexist image of some products. The research amply demonstrated relevant perceptions in this direction. Much has already been written on image of women in current advertising. The attitudes toward role portrayal of women in ads are unfavorable as confirmed in the present study. While marketers develop appropriate strategies in response to the changing world of women, they should try to understand the deep currents so that their responses are made with serious intentions and are not merely cosmetic.

### TABLE I

#### FREQUENCY ANALYSIS OF LIFE STYLE STATEMENTS INCLUDED UNDER EACH HYPOTHESIZED DIMENSION
(With Chi-Square Test Results)

#### Life Style Dimension

#### Innovative Behavior

-I often try new ideas before my friends do. (49, 48, 59) .02[1]
-When I see a new brand of product on the shelf, I often buy it just to see what it is like. (32, 24, 28) NS[2]
-I feel I am a member of more organizations than most women are. (20, 14, 18) NS
-Sometimes I buy things impulsively and do not feel sorry about it later. (44, 52, 52) NS
-I feel I can talk to most people in the neighborhood any time I feel like it. (48, 46, 41) NS
-I like people who take risks in life without fear of what may happen. (34, 44, 51) 0.08

#### Opinion Leadership
-My friends or neighbors often come to me for advice. (57, 55, 58) NS
-I sometimes influence what my friends say. (33, 41, 50) NS
-People come to me more often than I go to them for information about brands. (23, 25, 18) NS

#### Self-Confidence
-I feel capable of handling myself in most social situations. (78, 75, 86) 0.08

---

[1] Read 49% of Traditionalists, 48% of Moderates, 59% of Feminists agreed with the Statement. Level of significance .02.

[2] Not significant

(Table I cont'd)

420

-I seldom fear my actions will cause others to have a low opinion of me.(43, 56, 39) 0.01
-It doesn't bother me to have to enter a room where other people have gathered already and are talking. (66, 63, 68) NS
-In group discussions, I usually feel my opinions are inferior. (23, 13, 14) 0.00
-I don't make favorable first impressions on people. (17, 18, 10) NS
-I would feel extremely uncomfortable if I accidentally went to a formal party in ordinary clothes. (55, 44, 51) NS
-When confronted by a group of strangers, my first reaction is one of shyness and inferiority. (24, 24, 23) NS
-I don't spend much time worrying about what people think of me. (55, 55, 55) NS
-I am rarely at a loss for words when I am introduced to someone. (42, 50, 57) NS

### Frozen Food Consumption
-I couldn't get along without frozen foods. (18, 18, 20) NS
-I depend on frozen food for at least one meal a day.(17, 12, 11) NS

### Women's Role in Advertising
-American advertisements picture a woman's place to be in the home. (38, 64, 89) 0.00
-American advertisements seem to have recognized the changes in women's roles. (48, 33, 22) 0.00
-American advertisements depict women as sexual objects. (44, 56, 81) 0.00
-American advertisements depict women as independent without needing the protection of men. (14, 8, 4) 0.00

### Toys and Sex Symbolism
-I would like to see more and more young girls play with mechanical toys. (18, 42, 75) 0.00
-I would like to see boys playing with dolls just the way girls do. (10, 30, 66) 0.00
-Boys and girls should play with the same kind of toys. (30, 64, 80) 0.00

### Life Simplification
-I consider it essential for most American families to own an automatic coffee maker. (12, 1, 4) 0.00
-I consider it essential for most American families to own a dishwasher. (17, 6, 11) NS
-I consider it essential for most American families to own a food disposal unit. (13, 4, 4) 0.02

-I consider it essential for most American families to own a washer and dryer. (68, 53, 47) 0.04

### Leisure Mindedness
-Leisure activities express one's talents better than does a person's job. (48, 41, 38) NS
-Leisure activities are more satisfying than a job. (32, 30, 28) NS
-Ambitions are more realized on the job than in one's free time. (33, 39, 30) NS
-I indulge in sports activities in my free time. (53, 52, 62) 0.08
-It is encouraging to see women participate in outdoor sports as men do. (78, 92, 96) 0.00
-During leisure time I like to relax by reading a book or listening to music. (72, 82, 94) 0.02
-If I am not working I feel bored. (52, 43, 50) NA

### Fashion and Personal Appearance
-An important part of my life and activities is dressing smartly. (39, 38, 38) 0.06
-I love to shop for clothes. (49, 46, 47) 0.00
-I like to feel attractive. (86, 92, 90) 0.04
-I would like to go to beauty parlor as often as I can. (17, 12, 5) 0.00
-I enjoy looking through fashion magazines to see what is new in fashions. (60, 63, 57) NS
-I like to do lot of partying. (26, 39, 38) NS

### Television Viewing
-Television has added a great deal of enjoyment to my life. (38, 27, 26) NS
-I don't like watching television and so I rarely do. (24, 37, 39) 0.01
-I watch television to be entertained. (50, 47, 52) 0.00
-I watch television more than I should. (29, 18, 37) 0.01
-I don't pay much attention to television commercials. (59, 72, 71) 0.00

### Social Responsibility
-It is no use worrying about current events or public affairs; I can't do anything about them anyway. (26, 17, 16) 0.00
-Every person should give some of their time for the good of the country. (62, 58, 52) NS
-Our country would be better off if we didn't have so many elections and people didn't have to vote so often. (9, 4, 7) 0.04
-At school I volunteered for special projects. (58, 62, 70) NS

TABLE 2- DISCRIMINANT ANALYSIS RESULTS

| Variable | Uni-variate F-Ratio (2 and 161 df) | Order of Entry (Relative Importance) | Discriminant Function 1 Standardized Coefficients | Unstandardized Coefficients |
|---|---|---|---|---|
| Constant | | | | -0.336 |
| Sex Stereotyping | 36.9441 (Sig 0.00) | 1 (1) | -0.834 | -0.851 |
| Self-Confidence | 0.6633 NS | 5 (4) | 0.204 | 0.209 |
| Fashion Behavior | 0.7709 NS | 7 (7) | -0.595 | -0.065 |
| Television Viewing | 0.7099 NS | | | |
| Life Simplification Products | 4.1307 (Sig 0.05) | 2 (8) | -0.035 | -0.036 |
| Leisure-Work Attitude | 0.0184 NS | | | |
| Innovative Behavior | 0.5847 NS | | | |
| Active-Leisure Behavior | 2.3693 NS | 8 (6) | 0.150 | 0.149 |
| Opinion Leadership | 0.0558 NS | | | |
| Frozen Foods | 0.0585 NS | | | |
| Marital Status | 1.3946 NS | 6 (5) | -0.175 | -0.105 |
| Work Status | 2.0152 NS | | | |
| Household Status | 3.8624 (Sig 0.05) | | | |
| Religion | 3.4980 (Sig 0.05) | | | |
| Race | 0.0292 NS | | | |
| Age | 3.6781 (Sig 0.05) | 3 (2) | -0.248 | -0.170 |
| Education | 6.4899 (Sig 0.01) | 4 (3) | 0.235 | 0.215 |
| Income | 0.5171 NS | | | (cont'd) |

421

| Actual Group | No. of Cases | Predicted Group Membership | | | Eigen Value | 0.659 |
|---|---|---|---|---|---|---|
| | | Group 1 | Group 2 | Group 3 | Relative Percentage | 88.96 |
| Traditionalists | 56 | 34 | 20 | 2 | Canonical Correlation | 0.630 |
| | | 60.7% | 35.7% | 3.6% | Wilks' Lambda | 0.5573 |
| | | | | | Chi-Square | 92.074 |
| Moderates | 54 | 20 | 19 | 15 | Degrees of Freedom | 16 |
| | | 37% | 35.2% | 27.8% | Significance | 0.000 |
| Feminists | 58 | 4 | 12 | 42 | Group Centroids: | |
| | | 6.9% | 20.7% | 72.4% | Traditionalists | -0.688 |
| | | | | | Moderates | -0.154 |
| | | | | | Feminists | 0.830 |

# REFERENCES

1. Anderson, W. T., Jr., "Identifying the Convenience-Oriented Consumer," Journal of Marketing Research, Vol.8, May 1971, pp. 179-183

2. _____and W. H. Cunningham, "The Socially Conscious Consumer," Journal of Marketing, Vol. 36, July, 1972, pp. 23-31.

3. Arnott, C. C., "Husbands Attitudes and Wives' Commitment to Employment," Journal of Marriage and Family, Vol. 34, 1972, pp. 673-681.

4. Bardwick, J. J. and E. Douvan, "Ambivalence: the Socialization of Women," Women in Sexist Society, Gornick, Vivian and B. K. Moran, New York: Basic Books, 1971, pp. 147-1459.

5. Berkowitz, L.and L. R. Daniels, "Affecting the Salience of Social Responsibility Norm," Journal of Abnormal and Social Psychology, Vol. 68, Mar., 1964, pp. 274-281.

6. Courtney, A. E. and S. W. Lockeretz, "A Woman's Place: An Analysis of the Roles Portrayed by Women in Magazine Advertisements," Journal of Marketing Research, Vol. 8, February, 1971, pp. 92-95.

7. Davis, H. L., "Decision Making within the Household," Journal of Consumer Research, Vol. 2, No. 4, March, 1976, pp. 241-260.

8. Day, R. C. and R. L. Hamblin, "Some Effects of Close and Primitive Styles of Supervision," The American Journal of Sociology, Vol. 69, Mar. 1964, pp. 499-511.

9. Demby, Emanuel, "Psychographics and from Whence it Came," W. Wells, ed., Life Style and Psychographics, Chicago, American Marketing Assoc., 1974, pp. 9-30.

10. Dixon, M., "Public Ideology and the Class Composition of Women's Liberation (1966-1969)" Berkley Journal of Sociology, Vol. 16, 1971-2, pp. 149-179.

11. Douglas, S. P., "Cross-National Comparisons and Consumer Stereotypes: A Case Study of Working and Non-Working Wives in the U.S. and France," Journal of Consumer Research, Vol. 3, No. 1, June, 1976, pp. 12-20.

12. Green, R. T., and I. Cunningham, "Feminine Role Perceptions and Family Purchase Decisions," Journal of Marketing Research, August, 1975, pp. 325-332.

13. Hansen, M. H., W. N. Hurwitz, and W. G. Madow, Sampling Survey Methods and Theory, Vol. 1, New York, John Wiley and Sons, 1953.

14. Holmstrom, L. L., The Two-Career Family, Cambridge, Mass., Schenkman Pub., 1972.

15. Kirkpatrick, C., "The Construction of a Belief-Pattern Scale for Measuring Attitudes Toward Feminism," Journal of Social Psychology, Vol. 7, 1936, pp. 421-437.

16. Kopenen, A., "Personality Characteristics of Purchasers," Journal of Advertising Research, Vol. 1, No. 1, September, 1960.

17. Lipman-Blumen, Jean, "How Ideology Shapes Women's Lives," Scientific American, Vol. 226, No. 1, 1972, pp. 34-42.

18. McCall, S., "Analytical Projections of Life Style Identification in Consumer Behavior," American Marketing Association Proceedings, 1976, pp. 354-359.

19. Mulligan, L. W., "Wives, Women and Wife Role Behavior: An Alternative Cross-Cultural Perspective." International Journal of Comparative Sociology, Vol. 13, March, 1972, pp. 36-47.

20. Neulinger, J. and M. Breit, "Attitude Dimensions of Leisure," Journal of Leisure Research, Vol. 3, No. 2, Spring, 1971.

21. Pogrebin, L. C, "Toys for Free Children," Ms., Vol. 2, No. 6, December, 1973, pp. 48-53.

22. Robertson, T. S., "Determinants of Innovative Behavior," American Marketing Association Proceedings, Reed Moyer, ed., 1967 Winter Conference.

23. Rogers, E. M. and D. G. Gartano, "Methods of Measuring Opinion Leadership," Public Opinion Quarterly, Vol. 26, Fall, 1962, pp. 435-441.

24. Ross, H. L. and A. MacIntosh, "The Emergence of Households Headed by Women", Washington, D.C., The Urban Institute, Working Paper, 1973.

25. U.S. Bureau of Census, Census of Housing: 1970, Block Statistics, Syracuse, N.Y., Urbanized Area

26. Venkatesan, M. and J. Losco, "Women in Magazine Ads: 1959-71", Journal of Advertising Research, Vol. 15, October, 1975, p. 51.

27. Villani, K. E. A. and D. R. Lehmann, "An Examination of the Stability of AIO Measures," American Marketing Association Fall Conference at Rochester, New York, August, 1975.

28. Wagner, L. C. and J. B. Banos, "A Woman's Place: Follow-up Analysis of the Roles Portrayed by Women in Magazine Advertisements," Journal of Marketing Research, Vol. 10, May, 1973, pp. 213-214.

29. Wells, W. D., and D. J. Tigert, "Activities, Interests, and Opinions," Journal of Advertising Research, Vol.2, No. 4, August, 1971, p. 31.

30. Poloma, M. M. and T. N. Garland, "The Married Professional Woman: Study in the Tolerance of Domestication," Journal of Marriage and the Family, August, 1971, pp. 522-531.

31. Rossi, Alice S., "Equality Between the Sexes: An Immodest Appeal," Daedalus, Vol. 93, 1964, pp. 607-652.

# MASCULINITY-FEMININITY RELATED TO CONSUMER CHOICE

James W. Gentry, Kansas State University
Mildred Doering, Kansas State University

## ABSTRACT

Sex roles are undergoing major change in the United States today, and it has been hypothesized that the changing sex roles will be evidenced in changed consumer behavior. This study looks at a demographic variable (sex) and two measures of masculinity-femininity (the California Psychological Inventory's Fe-scale and the Personal Attributes Questionnaire) and their relationships with marketing stimuli. Sex was found to be a better explanatory variable than the personality variable, and the traditional single-continuum CPI measure was found to explain more than the newer PAQ with its concept of androgyny. Possibly, however, the most interesting finding was the lack of significance in the male or female usage rates of some traditionally sex-stereotyped products. Also, those respondents categorized as being androgynous were more likely to take part in leisure activities, watch documentaries and news programs on television, and prefer R-rated movies.

## INTRODUCTION

Tucker [12, p. 353] strongly emphasizes the impact of changing sex roles on marketing, "During most of the rest of the century marketers will increasingly miss the center of their markets because they will not understand them. And the change in the relations of the sexes will be the primary cause." The emergence of women into the top echelon of business and government symbolizes the growth of decision-making power at the household level. The trend toward less stereotypic sex roles is evidenced by women smoking cigars, hunting, and playing professional football and by men sewing, cooking, and wearing cologne. One might speculate that, someday, there will be a large female segment for lava soap and a large male segment for Virginia Slims.

That sex roles are changing in our society may be sufficient impetus for the marketer to become less interested in the male-female dichotomy and more interested in the level of masculinity or femininity. As Sechrest [10, p. 6] states, "That a respondent is male is in itself of little psychological impact. What is of consequence are the patterns of attitudes or abilities or problems or interests that are presumed to go along with being male." Aiken [1] was one of the first to relate masculinity-femininity to purchasing behavior. He found that more feminine women were more likely to belong to the "Decoration," "Interest," and "Conformity" clusters of female dress buyers. Masculinity-femininity was not related to membership in the "Comfort" and "Economy" clusters. Vitz and Johnson [13] found that, within each sex, a person's masculinity (femininity) is positively related to the masculine (feminine) image of the cigarette smoked. Fry [5] found that more feminine men were more likely to smoke cigarettes that were identified as being less masculine. Morris and Cundiff [9] found that masculinity-femininity was not related to the rating of hair spray by males. However, a strong interaction between manifest anxiety and masculinity-femininity was found.

[1] The authors wish to thank Rene Klaassen for his help in the data collection and the data coding, Gail Holtman for her help in the analysis, Terry O'Brien for his comments on an earlier draft, and the Bureau of General Research at Kansas State University for financial assistance.

This study was designed to explore male and female perceptions of a wide variety of products, activities, and brands, and also to explore whether masculinity-femininity within each sex is related to the individual's perception.

## RESEARCH DESIGN

The population chosen for study consists of college students. One reason was convenience, but more important is the belief that if there is a strong tendency toward changing sex roles in our society (and also a corresponding change in purchasing behavior), it will be more evident currently in college-aged individuals than in their elders. On the other hand, it may well be that blue-collar, non-college young adults are fiercely adherent to traditional sex-roles. The group studied in this study (college students) certainly limits generalization of the results.

The selection of the leisure activities, products, and brands to be evaluated was done through a three-stage process. First of all, the individuals involved in the research listed all activities and products that they felt would be related to the lifestyles of the subjects. An informal survey of local retail outlets yielded a list of the available brands of the listed products. Second, one pretest was run concerning attitudes toward the stimuli and frequency of usage of them. A second pretest was run to investigate the perceived masculinity-femininity of the stimuli. Stimuli were deleted if they were used very infrequently by most of the respondents. Also, the brands included in the study were chosen if they were among the most masculine, the most feminine, or those near the middle. For some products, all brands were deleted because there was a very strong delineation between male- and female-oriented brands (for instance, boots) or because there was a general lack of awareness of most of the brand names. The third stage consisted of a final pretest of the instrument after the deletions mentioned above were made. Then additional stimuli were deleted because of their perceived similarity to some of the other stimuli and because of the felt need to shorten the instrument. The specific leisure activities, products, and brands used in the study are listed in Tables 1 and 2.

TABLE 1

### LIST OF LEISURE ACTIVITIES INVESTIGATED

Watching Ballet

Going to Basketball Games

Bicycle Riding

Watching Car Races

Going Fishing

Going Hunting

Ice Skating

Knitting

Swimming

Going to the Movies
    Rated G
    Rated GP
    Rated R
    Rated X

TABLE 2

LIST OF PRODUCTS AND BRANDS INVESTIGATED

| Products | Brands |
|----------|--------|
| Beer | Black Label, Buckhorn, Budweiser, Coors, Falstaff, Hamms, Lite, Millers, Old Milwaukee, Pabst, Schlitz |
| Boots | None |
| Cigarettes | Alpine, Benson & Hedges, Camel, Chesterfield King, Eve, Lark, Marlboro, Vantage, Virginia Slims, Winchester |
| Cologne | None |
| Deodorant | Arrid, Ban, Brut, Dial, Hour After Hour, Manpower, Mitchum, Secret, Soft and Dry, Sure |
| Hair Spray | Brut, Clairol, Final Net, Command, Dry Look, Helene Curtis Spray Net, Miss Breck, Protein 21, Style, Suave |
| Jeans | Big Mac, Gotch Ya Covered, Levi, Loving Stuff, Statler, Strut, Wrangler, Wright |
| Mouthwash | Cepacol, Lavoris, Listerine, Micrin, Scope |
| Razor Blades | None |
| Sandals | None |
| Shampoo | Breck, Brut, Clairol, Head & Shoulders, Herbal Essence, Johnson's Baby Shampoo, Prell, Selsun Blue, Tegrin, White Rain |
| Soap (Bar Soap) | Brut, Camay, Caress, Castile, Dial, Dove, Irish Spring, Ivory, Lava, Palmolive, Phase III |
| Tennis Shoes | None |

After the data were collected, but before they were coded, another survey was made in order to help classify the magazines read regularly (at least every other issue) by the respondents. Some general classifications of magazines were available in Wolseley [14] and in Koester and Adkins [8], as well as the grouping of magazines by factor analysis by Bass, Pessemeier, and Tigert [2]. However, there was considerable question as to which category best fit certain magazines. A survey was made that required respondents to classify magazines in pre-designated categories. The final magazine categories and example magazines in each category are listed in Table 3.

Two-hundred college students at Kansas State University were recruited through an advertisement in the student newspaper, 100 males and 100 females. While there was no attempt to randomly select subjects, the procedure did result in a representative mix of curricula. Further, the subjects' scores on a standardized personality instrument (the California Psychological Inventory Fe-scale) were nearly identical with the results published for college students in Gough [7]. The mean and standard deviation for the females (23.22 and 2.85, respectively) and the males (16.35 and 3.82, respectively) in our study closely approximate the CPI norms (23.16, 3.27; and 16.65, 3.73;

respectively). Consequently, there is some evidence that the sample of students was a representative one.

TABLE 3

MAGAZINE CATEGORIES AND EXAMPLES

| Category | Examples |
|----------|----------|
| Sports & Outdoor Activity | "Sports Illustrated," "Car & Driver," "Field & Stream" |
| News | "Time," "National Observer," "Life" |
| Hobby (other than home) | "Dog World," "Popular Photography," "Scale Models" |
| Women's | "Cosmopolitan," "Ms," "Redbook," "Seventeen" |
| Home | "Ladies Home Journal," "Workbasket," "Better Homes & Gardens" |
| Sex | "Playboy," "Playgirl" |
| Curriculum-Related, Professional | "Business Week," Journal of Animal Science |
| Fans, Humor, & Entertainment | "Mad," "True Story," "TV Guide" |
| General | "National Geographic," "Reader's Digest," "People" |

Each subject was paid four dollars for completing the series of questionnaires dealing with their ratings of different consumer products and leisure-time activities. Also, the subjects completed two masculinity-femininity scales, the CPI Fe-scale [7] and the Personal Attributes Scale (PAQ) [11]. The last section included a set of demographic questions, usage measures of various media, and ratings of the products, brands, and activities as to their perceived masculinity or femininity. Each subject was told to complete all forms, and each of the 56 sheets of information for each subject was checked by a monitor before the subject was paid.

## DISCUSSION OF SCALES

Gough's [7] CPI Fe-scale consists of 38 true-false items. This procedure views "masculinity-femininity" as a continuum, and a low score indicates masculinity while a high score indicates femininity. This scale was chosen because of its long tradition, being published first in 1952 [6], and because it has been commonly used in marketing studies [1, 5, 9, 13].

The PAQ views masculinity and femininity as two distinct dimensions, which permits individuals to be identified as being "androgynous," or masculine and feminine. The androgynous classification is applied to those who are both independent and tender, assertive and yielding, tough but sweet. The first androgyny scale was developed by Bem [3], but we preferred the PAQ because of the way "androgyny" is defined operationally. The Bem Sex Role Inventory (BSRI) identifies someone as "androgynous" if his/her score on the masculine and feminine scales are comparable. Thus the BSRI identifies respondents as masculine, feminine, or androgynous. The PAQ is more restrictive in the identification of androgynous individuals; only those who score high on both the masculine and feminine dimensions are identified as being androgynous. Those ranking low on both dimensions are grouped in a fourth category, labeled low-masculine, low-feminine. The only marketing study that we have seen that used the concept of androgyny was that by Tucker [12], and he used the PAQ rather than the BSRI.

The attitude measures consisted, in part, of the four seven-point, bipolar scales used in the Morris and Cundiff study [9]: valuable-worthless, sociable-unsociable, nice-awful, and useless-useful. In addition, an overall brand, product, or activity attitude was obtained using a seven-point, bipolar scale with very unfavorable attitude and very favorable attitude as the end points. Numerical frequencies were required where applicable, usually with the leisure activities. Most of the product usage questions required the subject to select a response such as "once a month," "once a day," etc. Brand usage was obtained using always use-never use semantic differentials, and media usage was obtained using very frequently-very infrequently semantic differentials.

After the respondents provided some standard demographic information, they were asked to rate the products, brands, and leisure activities as to their masculinity-femininity. The inclusion of these measures at the end of the session was to hide the intent of the study as much as we could. The purpose of these questions was to investigate whether various sex types consciously choose marketing stimuli because of their correspondence to an ideal or an actual self typology. Due to the complex variety of results found and to space limitations, these relationships will not be discussed here.

One measure that might be included in future research of this nature, but unfortunately was not included in this study, is a social desirability scale such as the Crowne-Marlowe instrument [4]. Such a measure would act as a control for social desirability if respondents perceive or misperceive the intent of the study.

## ANALYSIS

The respondents were grouped in different masculinity-femininity categories based upon their scores on the two scales. For the CPI Fe-scale, boundaries were established at approximately the 33rd and 66th percentiles. The groups are labeled Masculine (60 males, 2 females), Neither (33 males, 39 females) and Feminine (7 males, 59 females). For the PAQ, the subject population was split at the median on both the male-valued and female-valued scales (59 and 50, respectively). The resulting four groups are low masculine and low feminine (32 females, 25 males), low masculine and high feminine (32 females, 13 males), high masculine and low feminine (10 females, 34 males), and high masculine, high feminine (26 females, 28 males).

The respondents' attitudes toward and usage of the stimuli were related to their sex and their masculinity-femininity through one-way analysis of variance.

## RESULTS

Table 4 provides an overview of the analysis of variance results for Stage 1. A general conclusion is that the demographic variable (sex) is a far better predictor variable for differences in attitudes or usage than the personality variables (CPI Fe-scale and PAQ masculinity-femininity measures). Overall, 48% of the possible relationships with sex were significant at the .05 level, while 36% and 21% of the relationships with the CPI Fe-scale and the PAQ, respectively, were significant. It is most likely to find significant relationships with the leisure activities and least likely with the specific brands.

TABLE 4

SUMMARY OF RELATIONSHIPS BETWEEN THE STIMULI
AND SEX AND MASCULINITY-FEMININITY

| General Category or Stimuli | Number of Possible Relationships | Number of Significant[a] Relationships with Sex | Number of Significant Relationships with Masculinity-Femininity CPI Fe-Scale | PAQ |
|---|---|---|---|---|
| Leisure Activities | 60 | 37 | 29 | 24 |
| Products | 78 | 39 | 26 | 12 |
| Brands | 156 | 67 | 50 | 26 |
| Media | 43 | 19 | 16 | 10 |

[a]All relationships are significant at the .05 level.

Leisure Activities

Overall, sex (male-female) related with the attitudes toward and usage of leisure activities more frequently than did the masculinity-femininity measures. Sex predicted relationships with watching ballet (females more likely), going to car races (males), going fishing (males), going hunting (males), ice skating (females), knitting (females), and swimming (females). These relationships, with the possible exception of the more favorable attitude toward swimming held by females, are obvious. Most of the relationships between the masculinity-femininity measures and the leisure activities were consistent with the sex-stereotype; for example, those categorized as feminine or low masculine, high feminine were more likely to give favorable responses if it had been found that females were more favorable.

However, there were some activities which related more strongly with the masculinity-femininity measures than with sex. For example, the low masculine, high feminine group held more positive attitudes toward going to basketball games, finding that activity to have more value, nicer, more sociable, and generally more favorable than did their counterparts. These findings were somewhat surprising, as sports are generally stereotyped as more masculine activities. It may well be that basketball games are associated with dating by college coeds, and that these findings can not be generalized to other groups of subjects.

Another interesting finding is that androgynous (high masculine and high feminine) respondents are more likely to watch ballet, ride bicycles, go to car races, go to movies, and to go swimming. In fact, when there were significant differences in the participation in leisure activities, the androgynous group was the most likely to participate in each case. The activities in which differences in participation were found are wide-ranging, from ballet with its feminine stereotype to car racing with its masculine stereotype, with relatively non-sexist activities like movie watching, swimming, and riding bicycles in between. A possible conjecture is that androgynous individuals tend to be more active recreationally.

425

### Products

Overall, sex (male-female) related with the attitudes toward and usage of the selected products more frequently than did the masculinity-femininity measures. Furthermore, the traditional CPI Fe-scale related more frequently than did the newer PAQ. Males were found to drink more beer and wear boots more frequently, while females were more likely to use and/or had more favorable attitudes toward cologne, deodorant, hair spray, jeans, razor blades, sandals, shampoo, and bar soap. Males wore tennis shoes more, but females had more favorable attitudes toward them. Most of the relationships between the masculinity-femininity measures and the leisure activities were consistent with the sex-stereotype; for example, those categorized as feminine or low masculine, high feminine were more likely to give favorable responses if it had been found that females were more favorable.

When significant differences in usage patterns existed, androgynous individuals (high feminine and high masculine) were either the most likely to use the product (razor blades and tennis shoes) or the second most likely (sandals).

### Brands

There were relatively fewer significant relationships between the brands selected and sex and the masculinity-femininity measures than with leisure activities, products or media. Sex more frequently explained differences in brand attitudes or brand usage than did the masculinity-femininity measures. Similarly, the traditional CPI Fe-scale was a better predictor variable than the PAQ. Most of the relationships are not surprising; females use more and have a more favorable attitude toward Camay while males use and are more likely to prefer Lava. Males were more likely to prefer X-rated movies while females were more likely to prefer G and GP movies.

Some non-intuitive relationships were found. Where significant differences toward cigarettes were found, the low masculine, low feminine group held more favorable attitudes while the androgynous group held the most negative views. Androgynous individuals held more favorable views toward R-rated movies, which comprised the most frequented category of movie. Neither sex nor the CPI Fe-scale measures related with R-rated movie attitudes or attendance.

One interesting result dealt with the Mitchum brand of deodorant. A relatively new brand, Mitchum's advertisements have shown a shirt-less man and emphasized its "staying power." Those individuals categorized as feminine or masculine used Mitchum much more than those categorized as neither. No other brand had such a noticeable tendency to attract the ends of the continuum and have an unfavorable impact on those in between.

### Media

Overall, sex (male-female) related with the respondents' media usage more frequently than did the masculinity-femininity measures. Furthermore, the traditional CPI Fe-scale related more frequently than did the newer PAQ. Many of the relationships were intuitive: females were more likely to watch daytime dramas on television while males were more likely to watch sports. In most cases, when one of the masculinity-femininity variables was significantly related to usage of a medium, the corresponding sex was also more likely to use the medium. For instance, if feminine individuals used a medium more than masculine or "neither" individuals, females were also found to use the medium more. Non-obvious relationships were that males and masculine individuals were more likely to watch talk shows on television and listen to them on the radio. Males, masculine individuals, and androgynous individuals (high masculine and high feminine) were more likely to watch news programs on television and to read magazines categorized as "news."

## DISCUSSION

Tucker's contention [12] that marketers should concentrate on the changing sex-roles of consumers has not been strongly supported in this study. Sex (male-female) explained much more variance in the respondents' attitudes towards and usage of the stimuli than did the masculinity-femininity measures. At this point it should be pointed out that the sample under study (college students) is likely to be somewhat more progressive in their views on sex-roles than the general populace, although this is modified somewhat since most of them come from a conservative state (Kansas).

Most of the significant differences should not have been unexpected. That males are more likely to go to car races; go fishing; go hunting; drink beer; wear tennis shoes; use Brut bar soap, deodorant, and shampoo; use Lava soap and Manpower deodorant; go to X-rated movies; watch sports shows on television, listen to them on the radio, and read sports-oriented magazines; watch more television during the day on weekends; and read sex-oriented magazines is consistent with most individuals' stereotypes. Similarly, we are not surprised to find that females are more likely to watch ballet; have positive attitudes toward ice skating; knit; use cologne; use bar soap and deodorant; use Camay, Caress, Dove, and Ivory bar soaps; drink Lite beer; smoke Eve and Virginia Slims cigarettes; use Arid, Secret, Soft and Dry, and Sure deodorants; go to G- and GP-rated movies; use Clairol and White Rain Shampoo; watch daytime dramas; read the society page in newspapers; and read women's- and home-oriented magazines. These relationships would argue, contrary to Tucker's hypothesis, that stereotypic sex roles are still very important in the consumer purchase decision.

On the other hand, the lack of significant differences for some stimuli may be construed as support for Tucker's hypothesis. Smoking was once considered to be restricted to the male domain (if we are to believe the Virginia Slims advertisements). However, there were no significant differences found between the sexes as to their frequency of smoking. Furthermore, there were no significant differences between the sexes in the attitudes or usage of cigarette brands such as Camel, Marlboro, and Winchester, which have consistently emphasized a masculine image in their advertisements. Also, no significant differences were found in the usage of hair spray (stereotypically considered a feminine product) or razor blades (stereotypically considered a masculine product). In addition, no significant differences were observed in the attitudes toward or attendance of R-rated movies; the sex, violence, and language commonly associated with R-rated movies might have led us to expect males to be more favorable.

Many of the significant relationships between one's masculinity-femininity and the attitudes toward or usage of the stimuli were consistent with the findings with the male-female dichotomy. However, the androgyny concept does provide some basis for future research since androgynous individuals were more likely to participate in several of the leisure activities and to use some of the products. Androgynous individuals were also more likely to have a favorable attitude toward R-rated movies, to watch documentaries on television and to read news-oriented magazines. Thus the androgyny concept seems to have some "psychographic" implications. Care needs to be taken, though, in the development of these implications since there is overlap between the type of question included in instruments used to obtain psychographic profiles and those instruments used to measure masculinity-femininity.

In summary, we do not feel that one's sex-role orientation, as measured by his/her masculinity-femininity, is terribly crucial now in determining his/her consumer behavior. However, the results do provide some support for Tucker's contention [11] that changing sex roles will greatly affect consumer behavior in the future.

## REFERENCES

[1] Aiken, Lewis R., Jr. "The Relationships of Dress to Selected Measures of Personality in Undergraduate Women," Journal of Social Psychology, 59 (1963), 119-128.

[2] Bass, Frank M., Edgar A. Pessemier, and Douglas J. Tigert. "A Taxonomy of Magazine Readership Applied to Problems in Marketing Strategy and Media Selection," Journal of Business, 42 (July 1969), 357-363.

[3] Bem, Sarah L. "The Measurement of Psychological Androgyny, "Journal of Consulting and Clinical Psychology, 42 (1974), 155-162.

[4] Crowne, D. P. and D. Marlowe. "A New Scale of Social Desirability Independent of Psychopathology," Journal of Consulting Psychology, 24 (1960), 349-354.

[5] Fry, Joseph N. "Personality Variables and Cigarette Brand Choice," Journal of Marketing Research, 8 (August 1971), 298-304.

[6] Gough, Harrison G. "Identifying Psychological Femininity," Educational and Psychological Measurement 12 (1952), 427-439.

[7] Gough, Harrison G. Manual for the California Psychological Inventory, Palo Alto, Cal.: Consulting Psychologists Press, Inc., 1975.

[8] Koester, Jane and Rose Adkins. Writer's Market '75, Cincinnati: Writer's Digest, 1974.

[9] Morris, George P. and Edward W. Cundiff. "Acceptance by Males of Feminine Products," Journal of Marketing Research, 8 (August 1971), 372-4.

[10] Sechrest, Lee. "Personality," In M. R. Rosenzweis and L. W. Porter (Eds.), Annual Review of Psychology, Palo Alto: Annual Reviews Inc., Vol. 27 (1976), 1-27.

[11] Spence, Janet T., Robert Helmuich, and Joy Stapp. "The Personality Attributes Questionnaire: A Measure of Sex Role Stereotypes and Masculinity-Femininity," Journal Supplement Abstract Service Catalog of Selected Documents in Psychology (Ms. No. 617), 4 (1974), 43.

[12] Tucker, W. T. "A Long Day of Discrepant Behavior," Proceedings, Fall Conference, American Marketing Association, 1976, 351-353.

[13] Vitz, Paul C. and Donald Johnston. "Masculinity of Smokers and the Masculinity of Cigarette Images," Journal of Applied Psychology, 49 (No. 3, 1965), 155-159.

[14] Wolseley, Roland E. Understand Magazines, Ames, Iowa: Iowa State University Press, 1965.

# FAMILY DECISION MAKING: EMERGING ISSUES AND FUTURE OPPORTUNITIES

Donald J. Hempel, University of Connecticut

## ABSTRACT

The roles of family members in buying decisions has become a major area of consumer research. Existing studies provide the basis for some generalizations about intrafamily buying influences and role structure. Several critical issues need further research to develop the strategy implications of changing role patterns.

## INTRODUCTION

The study of family roles in buying decisions is a rapidly growing area of consumer research interest. This trend has been stimulated by speculations concerning the impact of changing life styles and role expectations upon consumer behavior. Pervasive social changes, such as the promotion of sexual equality and the fuller integration of women into the economic fabric of society, have generated increasing uncertainty about the relative influence of different family members. The existing information gap is a significant problem for anyone concerned with the development of effective marketing programs or relevant theories of consumer behavior. Without additional research, they must contend with the predicament of either working with findings that ignore these intrafamily relationships or accepting the limited evidence available as a reliable basis of generalization and speculation. Given the rate and scope of the apparent changes, these are not likely to be regarded as an acceptable set of alternatives!

The purpose of this paper is threefold: (1) to present a brief summary of some major research findings and explanations concerning family decision-making; (2) to identify some important issues in need of further study; and (3) to discuss some practical implications of this research in terms of marketing opportunities. It attempts a response to the fundamental research questions of what has been done, what should be done, and why?

## RELEVANT FINDINGS AND EXPLANATIONS

Much of the empirical research concerning family buying decisions has been summarized in a series of review articles published during the past five years [2,3,5,9]. Those who are interested in household decision-making regarding other aspects of family life should examine the review of family power structure and the theoretically-oriented work by Burr [1] or by Safilios-Rothschild [8] and Goode, Hopkins, and McClure [4]. These studies provide a basis for the following generalizations about husband-wife involvement in consumer decisions. Since the available findings are not always supported by interpretations, the explanations presented are more speculative in nature.

### Variance Among Families

The variability in buying decision roles associated with family characteristics tend to support three general hypotheses: (1) the greater the resources, contribution, and status of the individual relative to his or her spouse, the greater the influence; (2) more extensive experience as a decision-making unit is associated with a reduction in joint decisions; and (3) greater "connectedness" of the family's social network is inversely related to the degree of joint decision-making.

Relative resources are usually measured in terms of education, occupational prestige, income contribution, and employment status. These socioeconomic characteristics probably reflect a set of culturally determined expectations concerning the appropriate bases for legitimate use of power. Since the relative position of women on many of these variables is shifting toward a more egalitarian relationship, they may serve to predict and explain the trend toward syncratic role structures (i.e., joint decision-making). The significance of these variables is likely to depend upon intrafamily perceptions of each member's relative competence, personal attractiveness, and ability to reward or punish.

The family's experience as a decision-making unit has been measured in terms of life cycle stages, ages of each spouse, and the number of years they have been married. All of these variables are associated with the accumulation of knowledge concerning both the purchase and use of products and the preferences and expectations of other family members. This knowledge facilitates the shift away from joint decisions by increasing confidence in one's ability to execute buyer roles. It also provides more accurate perceptions of family role expectations, thereby improving performance and gaining reinforcement for more individual action. The experience variables may reflect greater recognition of the economies achieved through specialization. A somewhat different explanation of this relationship is that product use patterns become more personalized with experience, and the decision roles that emerge depend upon who is likely to be the main user of the product (e.g., multiple automobiles or checking accounts).

The social "connectedness" of family members can be measured in terms of the similarity of friends and interests. This factor probably reflects the propensity of the family to engage in joint activity and the extent of agreement in their preference structures. High levels of agreement on important social decisions, such as the choice of friends, may create conditions of mutual trust and confidence that facilitate greater separation of roles in less salient product decisions. Joint social activity and commonality of interests enhance communications among family members, and may make it more feasible for one spouse to fulfill the expectations of others in buying situations. Joint involvement in buying decisions may serve as a means of gaining tacit acceptance and agreement from the less interested spouse in families with low social connectedness.

### Variance Among Products

There is considerable evidence that husband-wife involvement varies with the product category, but the product-role relationships have not been determined. The most consistent findings indicate that joint participation in decision making is more likely as the importance of the purchase increases. This important factor is usually expressed as some combination of the level of expenditure involved, the consumption cycle, the newness of the product, and the expected usage of the product by various family members. In general joint decision-making tends to be most frequent for durable goods that are collectively consumed (e.g., house or automobile), and least frequent for non-durables individually consumed (e.g., cosmetics).

Joint decision-making is more likely for durable goods because their purchase often involves an extensive problem-solving process. As the time required for the progression of interrelated decisions and activities increases, there are more opportunities for the participation of other family members. The number of decision points at which additional information and judgments are required also increases with the social, economic, and technical complexity of the product. New products, multiple users, and extended use periods may increase the perceived risk of not meeting the expectations of others. Thus, some combination of participation opportunities, need for functional assistance in buying tasks, and risk avoidance strategies probably account for the tendency toward shared decisions on major products.

Variance Among Decisions

It would be inappropriate to simply classify any product category as dominated by one spouse or syncratic because family-member participation varies with the type of decision and decision stage. One of the more consistent findings is that husbands perform the instrumental role and wives play the expressive role in family buying decisions. There is considerable evidence that the family member who initiates the buying decision process may not be equally involved in other stages. The extent of joint participation tends to be lowest for the search phase and highest for the purchase phase.

The instrumental-expressive split of husband-wife involvement is probably due to cultural norms concerning role performance. Role perceptions and expectations determine the kinds of decisions one attends to, and the type of information acquired. As these experiences are accumulated over product buying situations, they also determine the type of role specializations which the household is likely to find most efficient, and the role structures which are considered appropriate and therefore reported to others. The variations in role allocations across decision stages may reflect family efforts to share the work involved and to realize the benefits gained from specialization in areas of relative advantage. Joint participation at the purchase stage may represent a form of risk-reduction behavior in which one spouse seeks the tacit approval of other family members through their participation. Such strategies are not uncommon in industrial buying situations or in other organizational decision processes such as planning.

ISSUES AND RESEARCH PRIORITIES

Although the empirical basis for understanding family buying decisions is rapidly expanding, there are several recurring problems which need further research. Perhaps the most significant obstacle to the development of more practical theories is the conceptual ambiguity in the determination of family member involvement. The need for conceptual refinement is most evident in the definition of "relevant others" and the measurement of their influence.

Unit of Analysis

The choice of the appropriate unit of analysis is a major issue in consumer research. There is growing acceptance of the belief that a multi-person unit rather than the individual should be the unit of analysis for many product categories. Who are the relevant others? Should the definition include the broader kinship system to recognize the advice of relatives and intergenerational influences? Most studies of family decision making treat husbands and wives as the appropriate unit, and the influence of other family members is relatively unexplored. Studies of the influence of children on family buying decisions for products such as toys and cereals have not been adequately integrated into this research [11].

More information is needed on the dynamics of family interaction in purchase and consumption decision processes before this issue can be resolved. The determination of who are the relevant others and the extent of their influence is fundamental to the evaluation of cost-effectiveness in collecting data from more than one household member. This information is also necessary before their responses can be weighted and combined into valid summary measures. Several recent articles have suggested new methodologies for dealing with this problem [e.g., 12].

Measurement

Should family member involvement in buying decisions be measured in terms of influence, decision-making responsibility, or in the performance of a particular task (e.g., purchase or information gathering)? The power or dominance of one spouse may be reflected throughout the buying process, but their apparent relative importance in determining the final outcome is likely to depend upon the particular measurement used. Many of the earlier studies used measures of "who decided" whereas the more recent investigations have shifted towards measures of relative influence. Perhaps the reported trends toward shared or syncratic decisions is partially attributable to insufficient differentiation of concepts and measurements. The research by Turk and Bell (1972) indicates that the type of influence measures used affects the apparent decision-making power of different family members.

The concept of influence needs further exploration in the context of consumer decision processes. This research should include methodological questions such as the ability of respondents to recall with accuracy the effects of others upon their actions. For example, the assumption that felt influences can be recalled for purchases of durables and services made up 12 months earlier may add a significant source of variance into the measures of husband-wife differences. Analysis of the relationship between reported influence and elapsed time since the purchase would help to clarify this issue.

The related question of how to measure influence is certainly not unimportant, but the conceptual refinements should take precedence. Several relevant scales (e.g., Likert and constant sum) have been used with apparent success for specific buying decisions. The problem of aggregating these separate measures into an overall measure of relative influence needs further study. A basic issue is the use of structural vs. process measures of influence and involvement. Granbois [6] suggests that a single summary measure may be sufficient when there is (e.g., a conflict resolution model) intrafamily agreement on role allocations, but a more complex measure of the interaction process is more appropriate when disagreement occurs.

The Effects of Role Allocations

Does it make any difference how family roles are allocated? The growing concern for the practical implications of research has increased sensitivity to the fact that relatively little is known about the impact of family roles on buyer behavior. This issue is critical to management decisions concerning the choice of target markets, the design of marketing programs, and investments in consumer research. Investigation of the effects of family roles on behavioral variables such as search expenditures, brand choice and satisfaction should be considered a major research priority. A preliminary study of these relationships was recently reported [7].

The effects of family member involvement on buying efficiency and consumer satisfaction are likely to be of particular importance. Exploration of these consequences may help to supplement descriptive studies of _how_ families make decisions with insights into the reasons _why_ they adopt different buying strategies. They may also indicate instructive patterns of family role allocations for consumer education programs. In either case, these effects are relevant feedback for performance evaluation and will probably contribute to the evolution of family role patterns over time.

## IMPLICATIONS AND OPPORTUNITIES

How might the available research findings on family decision making-be used to develop marketing strategy? What are some of the more promising research opportunities in this area?

### Growth Constraints

The need for information concerning family member influences on consumer behavior is expanding so rapidly that there is considerable risk of hasty generalizations and redundant research efforts. Although the roots of concern are well established in both theoretical and practical foundations, a well-defined conceptual framework is needed to provide a basis for effective synthesis. This framework should distinguish the product categories and buying situations in which different patterns of family member influence are likely to emerge.

Perhaps the greatest obstacles to this integration are the validity and reliability problems resulting from the rapidly changing role perceptions in our society. One implication is that relevant research findings may be rejected by managers because the results are inconsistent with their own beliefs and life styles (i.e., they lack face validity). For example, it has been difficult to convince insurance executives that women (or some market segments) are a significant influence in the family's long-range financial planning decisions. Of course, the rather sparce and somewhat inconsistent evidence available does not provide a very strong challenge to well-established beliefs.

The reliability implications are equally troublesome because of the rate at which some of the role transitions are developing. For instance, the reallocation of roles stimulated by the women's liberation movement and the entry of wife-mothers into the labor force may have contributed to the trend toward syncratic role allocations. As these new roles become more comfortable and definite role expectations are developed, the efficiencies of role specialization may result in a reversal of this trend (i.e., toward autonomic and spouse dominated role structures). Thus, there may be some very reasonable but frustrating resistance to the acceptance of research findings until a critical mass of consistent evidence is accumulated.

### Emerging Market Segments

The changing roles and expectations of women outside the home are likely to significantly influence intrafamily role allocations. For example, the instrumental vs. expressive role splits may occur less frequently as the working wife acquires more instrumental role experiences in her job outside the home. The movement of women into professional occupations with career orientations could bring about new buying styles and greater planfulness in consumer decision processes. This occupational trend is likely to impact not only the households directly involved, but many others who stay at home and use the career woman as a role model. Greater participation of husbands in household chores and child care may increase their concern for the expressive aspects of purchase and consumption. Consequently, male-oriented hobbies and crafts may move away from the work bench into the living room and kitchen.

The husbands of working women may emerge as an important market segment, particularly for some food and home-care products that have been traditionally purchased by women. Greater involvement of children is also likely in working-wife families, especially teenagers who assume part of the family purchasing agent role. The possible interaction among family life cycle, life style, and the wife's employment status has important implications for both strategy and research. In the short run, an increase in the total amount of time husbands and wives spend outside the home in occupations may be reflected in greater expenditures for convenience foods and appliances, meals away from home, and concentrated family-type vacation experiences. Over a decade, entirely new life styles with much greater emphasis upon individual self-sufficiency and personal priorities may develop. One implication would be greater independence among family members who purchase more of their own products for their own consumption--perhaps an extension of the multi-automobile family patterns to include many other goods and services.

### Research Opportunities

The comparison of families as problem solving groups with buying committees and other groups in formal organizations may provide some useful insights. There is considerable research in-process concerning organizational buying behavior in industrial settings. These studies may help to articulate and operationally define some of the more subtle and less observable processes in household decision-making. For example, the intracompany interactions involved in buying decisions involving negotiation and compromise should provide relevant perspectives of conflict resolution within households. Such efforts may contribute to the merger of information on consumer and industrial buyer behavior that is beginning to occur.

Group level analysis has been largely ignored in studies of the diffusion of innovation [12]. There is some evidence that husbands and teenagers are frequently involved in new or different purchase incidents, although the extent of their involvement varies significantly by product category. The interaction among family members in the course of evaluating new products and services should be a productive area for research. If this can be linked to life style variations, a useful framework for selecting target markets and directing promotional efforts over stages of the adoption process might be developed.

Studies are needed of how families accumulate information through search behavior and feedback from past experiences. The storage and pooling of the information obtained by various family members should be of particular interest to those involved in selecting communication targets. Roles of children and relatives in this knowledge development process should be included.

Some useful insights into the evolutionary path of family buying decisions may be derived from research on role accumulation and role transition. The concept of role accumulation may provide a relevant explanation for some of the experience effects associated with life cycle and years married. The concept of role transition may account for the variability in the patterns of husband and wife involvement associated with a single product. It might be interpreted as a threshold phenomena where intrafamily attitudes toward role performance undergo change without emerging as an overt restructuring of expectations until the stress factors build up beyond some critical level. The time required to learn how to perform different roles and the need to make effective use of total family resources may result in the development of family decision-making across the following states:

Stage I--Conformity to Perceived Role Norms: During the early years of marriage a great deal of the decision-making is syncratic because both partners are lacking confidence in many areas of product evaluation. The exceptions may be for products such as automobiles or meal planning where one partner perceives the other's knowledge to be significantly superior. These perceptions and the actual acquisition of skills is influenced by cultural patterns of child rearing and formal education (e.g., until recently, home economics classes were "for girls" and auto repair classes were "for boys").

Stage II--Role Specialization: As the time pressures on the family increase (because of growing children, larger housing unit, and more diverse activities), there is greater need to depend upon the role specializations that have developed and the separations become more imbedded. This may also happen because the partners recognize certain preferences and differential abilities in performance of the tasks.

Stage III--Role Personalization and Experimentation: The search for variety and experimentation increases as many aspects of family management become more routine. This may result in role switching or partial occupancy of the other's role on a trial basis to explore new activities. The patterns are reflected in more syncratic decisions, particularly on the large-ticket items and on the products purchased for special occasions.

## CONCLUSIONS

Most of the available evidence on family buying decisions is based upon simple measures of general influence derived from the perceptions of wives. Considerable work has been done on the determinants of family role patterns and the role variations associated with different product categories. Perhaps the most critical area for future research is the impact of family member influences on various stages of the buying process.

## REFERENCES

1. Burr, W.R. Theory Construction and the Sociology of the Family. New York: John Wiley and Sons, 1973.

2. Davis, H.L. "Decision Making Within the Household," Journal of Consumer Research, 2 (March 1976), 241-260.

3. Ferber, R. "Family Decision Making and Economic Behavior," in E.B. Sheldon, ed., Family Economic Behavior: Problems and Prospects. Philadelphia: J.B. Lippincott Company, 1973.

4. Goode, W.J., E. Hopkins, and H. McClure. Social Systems and Family Patterns: A Propositional Inventory. New York: Bobbs-Merrill, 1971.

5. Granbois, H. "Decision Processes for Major Durable Goods," in G. Fish, ed., New Essays in Marketing Theory. Boston: Allyn and Bacon, 1972.

6. Granbois, D.H. "A Multi-Level Approach to Family Role Structure Research," David M. Gardner, ed., Proceedings. Association for Consumer Research, 1971, 99-107.

7. Hempel, D.J. "Family Role Structure and Housing Decisions," in M. Schlinger, ed., Proceedings. Association for Consumer Research, 1975, 71-80.

8. Safilios-Rothschild, C. "A Study of Family Power Structure: A Review of 1960-1969," Journal of Marriage and the Family, 32 (November 1970), 539-552.

9. Sheth, J.N. "A Theory of Family Buying Decisions," in P. Pellemans, ed., Insights in Consumer and Market Behavior. Belgium: Namus University, 1971.

10. Turk, James L. and Norman W. Bell. "Measuring Power in Families," Journal of Marriage and the Family, 34 (May 1972), 215-222.

11. Ward, S. and D.B. Wackman. "Children's Purchase Influence Attempts and Parent Yielding," Journal of Marketing Research, 9 (1972), 316-319.

12. Wind, Y. "Preferences of Relevant Others and Individual Choice Models," Journal of Consumer Research, 3 (June 1976) 50-57.

COMMUNICATING ENERGY CONSERVATION INFORMATION
TO CONSUMERS:  A FIELD EXPERIMENT[1]

C. Samuel Craig, Cornell University
John M. McCann, Cornell University

### ABSTRACT

This paper reports the results of a field experiment aimed
at reducing the amount of electricity used for air conditioning.  Subjects were 2,000 residential consumers of
electricity.  Three factors were experimentally manipulated:  the source of the communication, the channel used to
convey it, and the nature of the appeal.  Measurements were
taken on consumer's interest in and intention to conserve
electricity.  Additionally, actual consumption of electricity was monitored.  Results were mixed, with the treatments having an effect on the interest and intention
measures, but not on actual consumption.

### INTRODUCTION

Energy problems, whether in the form of brownouts, or
shortages of gasoline, heating oil, and natural gas are
going to be a continuing reality.  The fact that there has
been a fundamental shift from a seemingly limitless supply
of cheap energy to a quite finite supply of increasingly
expensive energy is inescapable.  What is less clear is the
best way to deal with the energy problem both in terms of
what will be most effective and at the same time somewhat
palatable to consumers of energy.

Ultimately, the success or failure of any comprehensive
energy program is determined by how well the intent of the
strategy is communicated to consumers, whether they are
able to grasp its implications, and whether they are able
to respond to it.  In this paper the impact of an experimental energy conservation program aimed at one particular
energy problem, summer brownouts, is assessed.  Electric
utilities face both seasonal and daily fluctuation in the
demand for electricity.  Occasionally, utilities do not
have sufficient capacity available to meet peak demand.
For urban utilities this is most apt to occur during the
hottest part of the summer when air conditioning use is at
its highest.  While there are many types of consumers that
account for the total demand for electricity, only one type,
individually metered residential consumers are examined.
The intent of the experimental program was to see whether
communications could influence the amount of electricity
consumed for air conditioning.  Intermediate measures of
interest and intention were also taken to provide additional measures of communication effectiveness.

Consumer Information Processing Perspective

There has been considerable interest recently in the application of consumer information processing (CIP) to assist
in making more enlightened public policy decisions.  Much
of the initial work has been aimed at identifying and

[1] We would like to gratefully acknowledge the funding
support of the Federal Energy Administration and the
New York Public Service Commission.  We would also
like to thank the many people at Con Edison who helped make this research project possible through their
cooperation.  Finally, we would like to acknowledge
the assistance of Jerry Spencer, Wilson Chung, and
Diane Stewart.

articulating a framework to guide future CIP research in
the area [10,11].  While there are alternative views of
exactly what consumer information processing is [see 4] the
view taken here is consistent with that advanced by McGuire
[5,6].  The following example may help ·clarify the approach
and relate it to the particular problem setting.

One potential source of information about energy conservation is a bill enclosure.  The effect of the bill enclosure
would depend on a number of factors which are linked hier-
archically with one factor being necessary but not sufficient for a subsequent factor.  For example, if the bill
enclosure about energy conservation is included with a
consumer's monthly bill there is some probability that the
consumer will be exposed to it.  Exposure, in turn, is
necessary but not sufficient for communication reception.
Reception entails whether the consumer actively begins to
process and pay attention to the information contained in
the bill enclosure.  Given that reception occurs and the
consumer begins to process the information, there is some
probability that he will respond to the bill enclosure.
The consumer must understand (comprehend) the contents of
the bill enclosure in order to be able to take subsequent
action on it.  Then, the consumer either accepts or rejects
the contents as being valid.  Finally, the information is
retained and may form the basis for energy conserving
action.  The key aspect of the above sequence is that each
proceeding step must occur before a subsequent step may.
Also given that a step does occur there is only some probability that the one immediately following it will.

An attitude toward energy conservation is formed or modified on the basis of the communication, but only if information processing has taken place.  The attitude in turn
influences a consumer's behavior.  As a result of the
energy conservation communication the consumer may begin to
run his air conditioner at a higher setting or wait longer
before turning it on.  It should also be noted that while
attitudes are linked to behavior, behavior may influence
attitudes.  For example, a consumer may run the air conditioner at a higher setting because of an attitude change
induced earlier.  However, after engaging in this behavior
for a while the consumer may find that he is hot and uncomfortable.  This changes his attitude toward the behavior
and alters his subsequent behavior.

In addition to information processing per se, there are
factors which moderate the process.  There are uncontrollable moderators such as an individual's education or age,
which moderate information processing, but cannot be influenced or altered.  There are also controllable moderators
which moderate information processing and that the policy
maker has some element of control over.  Communication
effectiveness can be enhanced by manipulating factors
known to influence the various components of information
processing.  For this study three controllable moderators
were selected.  These were the channel used to communicate
the message, the source, and the message content.

Communication Channel.  Utilities presently employ a variety of channels to communicate energy conservation information to their customers.  These include:  television,
radio, newspapers, transit media, and bill enclosures.  One
of the present channels, bill enclosures was compared to
an alternative communication channel, separate direct mail
pieces.  These were the only two channels that could be
looked at in a rigorous controlled fashion.  With any of

the mass media approaches, it is impossible to reach only certain groups to the exclusion of others.

Communication Source. The source of the communication is another controllable moderator. By using a source that is perceived as being trustworthy, expert or attractive by the intended audience, the persuasiveness of the communication can be enhanced. The value of credible sources has been well documented [see 9]. It only remains for the effectiveness of this approach to be assessed in the context of energy conservation information. The impact of two different sources was examined. The first source was the cooperating utility, Con Edison of New York. The second source was the New York Public Service Commission.

Communication Content. Various appeals have been used to try and persuade consumers to conserve energy. A Federal Energy Administration document [3] provided some insights into the goals that consumers consider good reasons to conserve energy. The main goal consumers indicated was that of personal monetary savings followed by having enough energy for oneself in the future. A third goal was to achieve independence from the influence of others. Goals one and three were selected for the study. Goal one, saving money, was selected since it seemed to be most important to consumers. Goal three, independence from others, was selected because Con Edison is highly dependent on imported oil. Thus, the appeal could be made very concrete. Closely related to the communication's appeal is the recommendation that the communication makes. The appeal captures a consumer's attention and the recommendation tells him explicitly what to do. The recommendation is an important part of the overall communication as research suggest that people do not always know what they can do to achieve energy conservation goals [3]. The recommendation employed eleven energy saving tips that consumers could follow to reduce their use of electricity for air conditioning.

## METHOD

### Sample Selection

The subjects were single metered residential consumers of electricity in the Con Edison service territory. Selection of subjects was further limited to those who consumed more than 5,000 kilowatt hours per year and whose July-August consumption was at least 20 percent greater than their December-January consumption. This allowed selection of those who were likely to have air conditioning units. From earlier research it was determined that over 90 percent of the consumers with this characteristic had air conditioners [1]. A final selection criterion was that all subjects had to be billed on the same day. Temperature varies from day to day and temperature fluctuations affect air conditioning usage. Therefore, it was important that all subjects received their communications on the same day. Further, the meter readings for both the experimental and control groups had to be for the identical 30 day period so that the same conditions prevailed for all.

### Communication Design

The main elements of the experiment were the communications and the manner in which they were presented to consumers. Two different appeals were used: (1) save dollars, "Air conditioning will cost more this summer" and (2) independence, "Help reduce our dependence on foreign oil." All communications contained the same recommendation, a summary of 11 different ways people can reduce their consumption of electricity for air conditioning. The actual communications were prepared in conjunction with Con Edison personnel with the final art work and printing being handled by Con Edison.

Since the two communications had no source identification on them, a letter was used to identify the originator of the communication. Letterhead stationery was used along with matching envelopes (when appropriate). To heighten the source manipulation, an individual within each organization was used: The Manager of Consumer Affairs at Con Edison and the Chairman of the N. Y. Public Service Commission. All communication materials may be found in [2].

The channel used to deliver the communication was either the monthly bill or a separate direct mail piece. In the case of the monthly bill, all other bill enclosures were removed and the customer received his bill along with one of two communications and one of two cover letters. The material sent for the direct mail was the same and an envelope with the organization's logo on it was used. Those customers who received the direct mail piece received their bill as they normally did. The direct mail communications were mailed out at the same time the bills were mailed so that they should have been received on the same day. In addition to the communications each mailing had a postage paid return card that the consumer could send in to receive more information about ways to control their electric bill.

### Experimental Design

Experimental variables manipulated were: source of the communication (Con Ed or PSC), type of appeal (save dollars or independence), and the channel used to communicate the message (bill or direct mail). An after-only design (with control group) was employed. In addition to monitoring electricity consumption a questionnaire was sent to all experimental and control groups in early August. The above independent variables were combined to form a 2x2x2 full factorial experimental design with 200 subjects in a cell and a control group of 400.

The first dependent variable was the number of subjects who returned the postage paid card included with each mailing. The return card requested additional information on ways to save electricity. A second dependent variable was behavioral intention measure taken using a questionnaire. A questionnaire was mailed out to all 2,000 experimental and control consumers one week after they had received the communication. Questionnaires were returned by 432 individuals for an overall response rate of 23 percent. Earlier it had been determined that there was no difference between those who returned questionnaires and those who did not with respect to the number of kilowatt hours consumed [1]. Thus, the 23 percent who did respond were felt to be representative, on the dimension of electricity consumption. A third dependent variable was the amount of electricity consumed for one month after receipt of the communication.

### Research Hypotheses

$H_1$ There are significant differences between experimental treatments with respect to post card return rates.

$H_2$ There are significant differences between experimental treatments and between experimental treatments and the control with respect to behavioral intention.

$H_3$ There are significant differences between experimental treatments with respect to kilowatt hours consumed during the 30 day test period.

## RESULTS

### Immediate Impact of Communication

Post card returns by treatment provided an indication of how effective each experimental variation was in generating requests for energy conservation material. While it cannot be determined unequivocally, the return rate was considered as a surrogate for two underlying factors.

First, return rate provided an indication of the attention getting characteristics of the communication. Obviously, customers other than those who returned the cards read the communication, but ceteris paribus more would have read those with a higher return rate. Second, return rate provided an indication of the immediate persuasive impact of the communication in generating requests for energy conservation material. The treatment with higher return rates were more successful in convincing customers that it would be beneficial to get more information on ways to control their electric bill.

Overall ten percent of the subjects requested energy conservation information. The only treatment that was significant was the channel manipulation (Table 1). Over 12 percent of those who received their communication as a bill enclosure requested energy conservation information versus only seven percent of those who received the same communications as a direct mail piece. The source and appeal conditions obtained return rates very similar to the overall rate. The channel main effect may be explained by the increased saliency of the communication when it accompanied the bill. Receiving a large electric bill along with a card offering free information on ways to reduce the bill has considerable impact. Opening a separate letter on the same day with the same offer appears to have less impact.

Intention to Conserve Electricity

Consumers may request energy conservation information and not intend to conserve electricity. Alternatively, consumers may be influenced to conserve electricity through reduced use of their air conditioner(s) but not feel the need for additional information. Therefore, the next dependent measure to be examined is intention to conserve electricity. This intention was measured by asking subjects to indicate at what outside temperature they would turn on their air conditioner. Those who indicate they would wait until it got hotter would ceteris paribus use less electricity.

None of the main effects were significant; however, a number of the interactions were (see Table 2). The source by appeal interaction and the source by appeal by channel interaction were significant. An inspection of Table 3 suggests what is behind this. The PSC source was most effective when used in conjunction with direct mail and the independence appeal. Con Edison as a source was most effective with direct mail and the save dollars appeal.

In order to assess what the effect of the experimental manipulations were with respect to no manipulation, the experimental groups were compared to the control group (see Table 3). For 5 of the 8 message conditions the experimental groups indicated they would wait until it got hotter outside than the control group. The control group, on the average, indicated that they would turn their air conditioner on when the outside temperature got to be 81.5°F. When the PSC was the source, the appeal independence from foreign oil, and the communication came with their monthly bill, subjects indicated they would wait 1.5 degrees more than the control (this was the smallest significant difference). When the PSC was the source, the appeal save dollars, and the communication came as a separate direct mail piece, subjects indicated they would wait 3.2 degrees more than the control (this was the largest observed difference).

Thus, the communications appear to have a positive effect in terms of getting people to say they will wait until it gets hotter to turn their air conditioner on. If this stated behavior carries through to their actual behavior than there should be a corresponding reduction in the amount of electricity used.

Actual Consumption of Electricity

All subjects had their electric meter read on the same day (August 3) just prior to their receipt of the communications. Thirty days later their meters were read again. Any differences in kilowatt hours between groups would be attributable to the experimental treatments. It should be stressed that many household devices account for the number of kilowatt hours used during any 30 day period. This posed a problem in analysis which was somewhat mitigated by the use of two covariates in the analysis of variance. The two covariates used were the July kilowatt hour consumption and urban density (number of people per square mile in the service district). If the variation attributable to these factors can be accounted for then the precision of the experiment can be increased.

Both of the covariates were highly significant, but none of the treatments effects were significant (See Tables 4, 5). There was a large unadjusted difference between bill enclosures and direct mail but when the effect of the other variables were taken into account this difference was not significant (in fact the direction of the effect was reversed).

TABLE 1

POST CARD RETURN RATES:  REQUESTS
FOR ENERGY CONSERVATION INFORMATION[a]

| Source | Channel | | | | Row Totals |
| | Bill Enclosure | | Direct Mail | | |
| | Appeal | | Appeal | | |
| | Dollars Percent Returned | Independence Percent Returned | Dollars Percent Returned | Independence Percent Returned | |
| --- | --- | --- | --- | --- | --- |
| Public Service Commission | 17.2 | 11.7 | 5.6 | 7.2 | 10.4 |
| Con Edison | 11.1 | 10.6 | 10.6 | 5.6 | 9.4 |

| Column Totals | | Column Totals | |
| --- | --- | --- | --- |
| Bill Enclosures | 12.6 | Dollars | 11.1 |
| Direct Mail | 7.2 | Independence | 8.8 |

[a]Channel effect was significant with the communications sent out as bill enclosures resulting in higher requests for more information. Actual significance testing was done using the log linear model. See: [7,8] for a discussion of the procedure used and [2] for the complete analysis.

TABLE 2

ANALYSIS OF VARIANCE SUMMARY TABLE[a]

| Source of Variation | Sum of Squares | DF | Mean Square | F |
|---|---|---|---|---|
| **Main Effects** | | | | |
| Source | 30.12 | 1 | 30.12 | 0.85 |
| Channel | 2.93 | 1 | 2.93 | 0.08 |
| Appeal | 23.50 | 1 | 23.50 | 0.67 |
| **Interactions** | | | | |
| Source x Channel | 6.20 | 1 | 6.20 | 0.18 |
| Source x Appeal | 252.20 | 1 | 252.20 | 7.15[b] |
| Channel x Appeal | 38.68 | 1 | 38.68 | 1.10 |
| Source x Channel x Appeal | 150.61 | 1 | 150.61 | 4.27[c] |
| **Error** | 9943.28 | 282 | 35.26 | |

[a]Independent Variables: Source -- Public Service Commission and Con Edison; Channel -- Bill enclosure and direct mail; Appeal -- Save dollars and independence. Dependent Variable: Stated temperature at which air conditioner would be turned on.

[b]$p < .01$

[c]$p < .05$

TABLE 3

EXPERIMENTAL VERSUS CONTROL GROUPS

| | Message Conditions | | Variable |
|---|---|---|---|
| Source | Channel | Appeal | Temperature[a] |
| PSC | Bill | Dollars | 83.4[c] |
| PSC | Bill | Independence | 83.0[b] |
| CON ED | Bill | Dollars | 83.7[c] |
| CON ED | Bill | Independence | 81.2 |
| PSC | Mail | Dollars | 81.3 |
| PSC | Mail | Independence | 84.7[c] |
| CON ED | Mail | Dollars | 84.3[c] |
| CON ED | Mail | Independence | 81.5 |

[a]Mean of control group is 81.5, significance tests indicate whether mean of experimental group is greater than mean of control group. Dunnett's t statistic was used for the test, see [12] for the procedure.

[b]$p < .05$

[c]$p < .01$

The lack of significant differences can be attributed to either a failure of the communications to induce differential consumption or to the lack of precision in measurement of the dependent variable. The general purpose of the experiment is to reduce the consumption of electricity. More specifically, it attempts to accomplish this through persuasive communications aimed at reducing air conditioning usage. However, the dependent measure is the total number of kilowatt hours consumed during the month of August, not just the kilowatts used to run air conditioners. The relationship is as follows:

$$TK_{ij} = AK_{ij} + BK_{ij} \tag{1}$$

where,

$TK_{ij}$ = Total kilowatt hours consumed for household i during month j.

$AK_{ij}$ = Kilowatt hours consumed by air conditioning for household i during month j.

$BK_{ij}$ = All other electricity consumed by household i during month j.

For the month of August 1976 BK is approximately 60 percent of TK. The communications are aimed at influencing the remaining 40 percent, AK. However, in determining whether the differences in AK between experimental groups is significant the variance of TK must be used. Also a large change in AK is a much smaller change in TK. For example, if a particular communication were successful in persuading consumers to reduce their air conditioning by 10 percent this would only be a 4 percent reduction in their overall consumption for the month. In testing for differences the variance of total consumption is used, making it more difficult to pick up small but important changes in the amount of air conditioning usage. The only real solution is to monitor $AK_{ij}$ directly through the use of a separate meter.

TABLE 4

ANALYSIS OF COVARIANCE SUMMARY TABLE[a,c]

| Source of Variation | Sum of Squares | DF | Mean Square | F |
|---|---|---|---|---|
| **Covariates** | | | | |
| July | 156418240. | 1 | 156418240. | 2070.27[b] |
| Density | 702535.69 | 1 | 702535.69 | 9.30[b] |
| **Main Effects** | | | | |
| Source | 533.97 | 1 | 533.97 | 0.01 |
| Channel | 47332.70 | 1 | 47332.70 | 0.63 |
| Appeal | 25004.65 | 1 | 25004.65 | 0.33 |
| **Interactions** | | | | |
| Source x Channel | 46117.73 | 1 | 46117.73 | 0.61 |
| Source x Appeal | 129412.38 | 1 | 12 412.38 | 1.71 |
| Channel x Appeal | 3.56 | 1 | 3.56 | 0.00 |
| Source x Channel x Appeal | 45406.76 | 1 | 45406.76 | 0.60 |
| **Error** | 113633968. | 1504 | 75554.50 | |

[a]Independent Variables: Source -- Public Service Commission and Con Edison; Channel -- Bill enclosure and direct mail; Appeal -- Save dollars and independence. Dependent Variable: August -- kilowatt hours consumed during August; Covariates: July -- kilowatt hours consumed during July, Density -- population per square mile for service district.

[b]$p < .01$

[c]Explained variance overall, significant $p < .001$, $R^2 = .59$.

SUMMARY AND CONCLUSION

Two types of conclusions can be drawn from the present study. The first involves the substantive recommendations that can be made to those concerned with implementing energy policies. The second concerns the usefulness of a CIP approach to energy conservation programs.

In the first area the findings suggest approaches and courses of action which are appropriate for any large urban utility faced with summer peaking. If the utility or other organization is interested in getting consumers to request information about energy conservation it appears that the response rate can be enhanced if the offer is included with the bill rather than being sent as a separate direct mail piece. The reason for this effect may be explained by the increased saliency of the communication

TABLE 5

DEVIATION OF TREATMENT MEANS FROM GRAND MEAN
FOR AUGUST KILOWATT HOUR CONSUMPTION

| Treatment | Unadjusted Mean Deviation | Adjusted Mean Deviation |
|---|---|---|
| Source | | |
| Public Service Commission | 1.7 | - .6 |
| Con Edison | - 1.7 | .6 |
| Channel | | |
| Bill Enclosure | 17.4 | -5.6[a,b] |
| Direct Mail | -17.3 | 5.6 |
| Appeal | | |
| Save Dollars | -12.2 | 4.1 |
| Independence | 12.2 | -4.1 |

[a]Read, communication sent as separate direct mail piece resulted in an average decrease of 5.6 kilowatt hours during the month of August, net difference between treatments 11.2 kilowatt hours.

[b]None of the differences between treatments were significant, see Table 4 for analysis of covariance summary table.

when it accompanies the bill. At that moment consumers are made aware (possibly painfully) of exactly how much energy they are consuming. Thus, they are more likely to be receptive to offers concerning ways to reduce their bill. This finding suggests that there is little to be gained by experimenting further with the more expensive direct mail approach.

The implications of the intention and actual consumption results are less clear. None of the main effects for the intention to conserve electricity were significant. However, the combined communication factors frequently resulted in a significantly greater conservation intention than the control group which received no communication. None of the experimental manipulations were successful in getting consumers to reduce their actual consumption of electricity. While this is disappointing it is not surprising. The impact of any one communication is small and given the measurement problem it is not likely that small, but important, changes in the amount of electricity used for air conditioning could be detected.

Using a CIP approach seems very fruitful. It can not only guide selection of message content, structure, channel and so on, but it suggests the importance of taking intermediate measures. If only the ultimate dependent variable, kilowatt hour consumption, had been measured the experiment would have been considered a failure. Utilization of intermediate measures, interest and intention, afforded a better understanding of what the communications' impact was and the limits of their impact. As additional communication approaches are tested, the validity of the present findings can be ascertained and more effective ways of communication energy conservation information to consumers can be developed.

REFERENCES

1. Craig, C.S. and J.M. McCann. "Marketing Energy Conservation to Residential Consumers of Electricity," A report prepared for the Federal Energy Administration, 1977.

2. _____ and _____. "Communicating Energy Conservation to Consumers: A Field Experiment on Alternative Ways of Communicating Energy Conservation to Residential Consumers of Electricity," A report prepared for the Federal Energy Administration, 1977.

3. Federal Energy Administration, "Summary of Energy Research on Consumers," Mimeo, 1976.

4. Hughes, G.D. and M.L. Ray (eds.). Buyer/Consumer Information Processing, Chapel Hill, N.C.: University of North Carolina Press, 1974.

5. McGuire, W.J. "An Information - Processing Model of Advertising Effectiveness," paper presented to Symposium on Behavioral and Management Science in Marketing, University of Chicago, June 1969.

6. _____. "Some Internal Psychological Factors Influencing Consumer Choice," Journal of Consumer Research, 2(March 1976) 302-319.

7. Ne er, J.A. "Log Linear Models for Contingency Tables: A Generalization of Classical Least Squares," Applied Statistics, Vol. 23, No. 3, 1974, 323-329.

8. _____, and R.W.M. Wedderburn, "Generalized Linear Model," Journal of the Royal Statistical Society, Series A, Vol. 135, Part 3, 1972, 370-384.

9. Sternthal, B. and R.R. Dholakia. "Processes Underlying the Persuasive Effect of Source Credibility: A Review," Working paper, Northwestern University, 1975.

10. Wilkie, W.L. How Consumers Use Product Information, Washington: U.S. Government Printing Office, 1975.

11. _____ and P.W. Farris. Consumer Information Processing: Perspectives and Implications for Advertising. Cambridge, Ma.: Marketing Science Institute, 1976.

12. Winer, B.J. Statistical Principles in Experimental Design, second edition, New York: McGraw-Hill, 1971.

# A PROPOSAL TO INCREASE ENERGY CONSERVATION THROUGH PROVISION OF CONSUMPTION AND COST INFORMATION TO CONSUMERS

J. Edward Russo,[1] Carnegie-Mellon University[2]

## ABSTRACT

It is proposed that monthly residential utility bills provide better feedback about energy consumption and cost. Without such information, it is difficult for consumers to determine whether their energy conservation actions have been successful, and how much money they are saving (or not saving) as a result. A simple version of this proposed feedback was printed on the monthly bills of all residential customers of Atlantic City Electric Company for 15 months during 1974-75. By comparing the resulting energy usage patterns with those of four neighboring electric companies, it is possible to estimate that the energy consumption feedback caused a 2-3% decrease in consumption.

## INTRODUCTION

Everyone is aware of the national energy crisis: a continually increasing demand in the face of dwindling, more expensive supplies. A consensus is forming that conservation must form a major part of any solution to this problem. Essential to any conservation effort is a reduction in residential energy use, which currently accounts for 29% of total consumption [3]. Whereas industrial users have made important gains in energy conservation since the Oil Embargo of November, 1973, residential energy use decreased only temporarily. Furthermore, a comparison of energy use between the U.S. and several Western European countries with similar standards of living strongly supports the conclusion that major reductions are possible (e.g., [6]). The evidence indicates that we ought to be able to find ways to reduce significantly our residential energy consumption.

The purpose of this paper is to propose one method for improving residential conservation. The problem is analyzed from the viewpoint of consumer decision making. Energy, in this case electricity and natural gas, is subject to the same principles of decision making as more conventional consumer goods. The proposal that follows is based on the fundamental need of all good decision making: relevant information in a timely, usable format. Specifically, householders need more precise feedback on their energy consumption and, especially, on the cost of this consumption.

## THE CONSUMPTION DECISION: LOCUS OF THE PROBLEM

All consumption decisions consist of a trade-off between goods and price. A vendor offers to sell certain goods at a specified price; or when several brands are available, differences in quality or performance can usually be compensated by differences in price. Consider the purchase of a typical product like dish detergent. The price (posted by law) is known with certainty. The same, however, is rarely true of our perception of quality/performance. How confident is the average shopper that the chosen brand will really wash more dishes per penny than some other brand?

Our uncertainty about the value of a good has important implications for the quality of consumer decisions. A characteristic of human decision processes is that an attribute tends to be discounted if its values are not clear and easy to "process" [8,9, and 5]. Applying this finding to product purchases implies that the quality/performance attribute is typically underweighted relative to the price attribute.

The situation for energy purchases is exactly the opposite: the cost is known only imprecisely while the value is relatively clear. Consider householders who decided to save money by lowering their thermostats from 68° to 65° during this past winter. The difference in value, namely the discomfort, was easily perceived. In contrast, how could these householders determine the money they saved? There is no price tag on individual energy consumption actions. All the purchaser receives is a monthly bill for the total energy consumed (see Figure 1). Something as

### FIGURE 1

A SIMPLIFIED UTILITY BILL OMITTING INESSENTIAL INFORMATION

| Billing Period: Nov 30 to Dec 29 | Amount Due |
|---|---|
| Consumption (Kwhr) 2275 | $118.30 |
| | Date Due Jan 15 |

major as lowering the thermostat by 3° might be detected on this bill, but only imprecisely.

For energy consumption decisions of less magnitude, price information is even more obscure. For example, how many people know how much money is saved by hanging out a load of wash to dry in the sun rather than using a clothes drier? Or the cost of a frost-free relative to a regular refrigerator? Or whether baths or showers use less energy?[3] All of these energy costs are aggregated into the monthly bill, and it is impossible for the ordinary householder to estimate them separately.

---

[1] The author gratefully acknowledges the cooperation of the five utility companies whose residential usage rates comprise the data for the main empirical results reported in this paper. I would like to acknowledge several early discussions with my former colleague, Vladimir Konecni of the University of California, San Diego.

[2] Current address: Graduate School of Business, University of Chicago, Chicago, IL 60637.

---

[3] It costs about 20¢ to dry a load of clothes. Frost-free refrigerators use two-thirds more energy than manual defrost models. Showers are cheaper than baths.

In summary, a decision analysis of residential energy purchases suggests that householders lack the price information needed to make a sound trade-off between value and price. The relatively clear perception of the discomfort or inconvenience resulting from energy conservation leads to an imbalance favoring consumption over conservation. Although there are many other causes of excess residential energy consumption, like poorly insulated homes, the problem described above is particularly unfortunate. It results neither from inadequate technology nor from pro-consumption attitudes [7], but simply from uncertainty about the money saved by specific conservation actions.

## PROVISION OF INFORMATION AS THE SOLUTION

The preceding analysis suggests a straightforward solution. Informing householders of energy costs should lead to a better balance between cost and value in the energy consumption decision. This, in turn, should lead to a reduction in energy use.

Let us return to the householders who lowered their thermostats from 68° to 65° during this past winter. The energy (and money) that they saved cannot be determined from the information provided on a typical monthly utility bill (Figure 1). Energy saved can be determined, however, if the householders know their energy consumption for a comparison period when the thermostat was set at 68° and all other conditions were identical.

The same billing period during the previous year approximates such a comparison. Of course, this comparison is not perfect because all conditions cannot be held equal between the two years. However, the major hindrances to comparability can be removed if we adjust for weather variation and for differences in the billing period, especially the total number of days. Weather normalization capability is now possessed by many utility companies, with many others in the process of developing it. (The ability to normalize consumption levels for differences in weather is important to companies for predicting future system loads). Some utility companies are experimenting with average daily consumption rates as a means of eliminating fluctuations in total monthly bills caused by different numbers of days per month.

The essential point is that both adjustments, for weather and for billing period, can be efficiently performed by the utility company. This suggests that utility companies could provide an adjusted version of last year's energy consumption on this year's bill. This proposed version of the monthly utility bill is shown in Figure 2. The house-

### FIGURE 2

THE BASIC PROPOSAL: INCLUSION ON THE UTILITY BILL OF LAST YEAR'S CONSUMPTION AND THE PERCENT CHANGE IN CONSUMPTION

| Billing Period: Nov 30 to Dec 29 | | | Amount Due |
|---|---|---|---|
| Consumption (Kwhr) | | | $118.30 |
| Current Billing Period | Same Period Last Year Adjusted for Weather Changes | Change in Energy Consumption | |
| 2275 | 2472 | 8% drop | Date Due Jan 15 |

holders who lowered their thermostats can now see that they succeeded in reducing energy consumption by 8%.

This calculation assumes that the energy consumption behavior of the household is constant over the two periods, except for the lowered thermostat. Changes like upgrading insulation or purchasing a major appliance will violate this constancy. When such changes occur the individual householder will have to factor them into the change in energy consumption.

One might ask why consumers can't determine the change in energy consumption for themselves. It is possible to maintain a file of past utility bills and to compute the percent change in consumption for each month. The effort involved in such record keeping and calculation is considerable and poses a major obstacle. Few householders have a professional accountant's discipline, or skills. Moreover, even if householders kept the records and performed the calculations, the resulting comparison would be inaccurate because of changes in billing periods and in weather. With some effort, the former might be overcome; but it is unreasonable to expect even the most determined consumer to attain weather normalization capability. Most important of all, the fact is that few, if any, consumers actually generate even an approximate version of the information shown in Figure 2. If this information is to be available to them, it will have to be provided by utility companies.

The proposed solution, the use of a comparison period, works only for major energy purchases. These are of sufficient magnitude to stand above the normal variation in monthly consumption. The energy cost of minor purchases has to be communicated more directly. However, we can still take advantage of the monthly bill to deliver this information. An energy cost message can be added to each billing statement, as shown in Figure 3.

### FIGURE 3

THE BASIC PROPOSAL AUGMENTED BY ENERGY COSTS OF INDIVIDUAL CONSUMPTION BEHAVIORS

| Billing Period: Nov 30 to Dec 29 | | | Amount Due |
|---|---|---|---|
| Consumption (Kwhr) | | | $118.30 |
| Current Billing Period | Same Period Last Year | Change in Energy Consumption | |
| 2275 | 2472 | 8% drop | Date Due Jan 15 |
| Energy Saving Reminder | A clothes dryer uses ten times the energy of a washer. Let the sun dry your clothes for free. | | |

## INFORMATION FORMAT

It is easy to underestimate the value of information format. If consumers are to be encouraged to use the consumption feedback provided in the preceding proposals, this information must be provided in the most meaningful, usable form [1]. Consider unit pricing in supermarkets. (A unit price is a cost per measure, i.e., the price of an item divided by its quantity.) When unit prices are posted beside the total price, a significant purchasing shift toward the less expensive items occurs [4]. This shift is due solely to computational convenience because the price and quantity values are already posted, although separately. In a similar way, it is important to calculate the percent change in consumption shown in Figure 2. The more clearly price information is communicated, the more it will be used.

Carrying this reasoning further, the change in energy consumption can be translated into a change in energy cost.

That is, consumers can be informed not only of how much energy they saved (or failed to save) but also how much money they saved (or failed to save). This direct reporting of the dollar savings produced by energy conservation behaviors is pictured in Figure 4.

FIGURE 4

THE BASIC PROPOSAL WITH THE CHANGE IN ENERGY CONSUMPTION
TRANSLATED INTO DOLLARS

| Billing Period: Nov 30 to Dec 29 | | | | Amount Due |
|---|---|---|---|---|
| Consumption (Kwhr) | | Change from Last Year | | |
| Current Billing Period | Same Period Last Year | Energy Consumed | Cost at Current Rate | $118.30 |
| 2275 | 2472 | 8% drop | $10.29 less | Date Due Jan 15 |

Besides providing the most relevant form of the price attribute the dollar format should motivate consumers to reduce energy use. To those who have successfully conserved energy, the dollar savings is a tangible reward. To those who increased their energy consumption, the increased dollar cost is brought home to them in the clearest terms. They cannot avoid the unpleasant recognition of exactly how much they are paying for their increased use of energy.

A final aspect of the optimal presentation of information is timing. The best time to influence any decision is while the decision is being made. Unfortunately, there are very many individual energy consumption decisions. We cannot hope to intervene with the relevant cost information during each one. However, all these energy purchase decisions have one thing in common: their cost is communicated through the monthly bill. Every household receives it, reads it, pays it, and wishes it were lower. The ideal time to deliver an energy conservation message based on the cost of energy is when the bill is read.

PROPOSED EXPERIMENT

The only good way to decide whether the consumption information provided in Figures 2, 3 and 4 will help people save energy is to test these proposals in a complete field study. A test could be performed along the following lines. From a cooperating utility company's total set of residential customers, several groups of approximately 1000 should be selected. These groups should be similar on characteristics related to consumption, such as past consumption, location (for weather comparability), income, and education level (which may be related to the tendency to utilize the consumption/cost feedback). Each group is mailed a different type of monthly billing statement. The three proposed improvements (Figures 2, 3 and 4) would require three groups. In addition, there should probably be two control groups that receive an unaugmented bill (see Figure 1). One control group would know that it was in an energy conservation study, the other would not. (The problem of the knowledgeable control group's feeling cheated because they know that they are not receiving a benefit available to others can be avoided by using a procedure suggested by Wortman, Hendricks and Hillis [10].)

The measure of interest is actual energy consumption. The five groups should be compared on the amount of energy saved. Differences among the three experimental groups will identify the most effective information and format. The study should run for a full year, although preliminary

results will be available each month. At the conclusion of the study, a questionnaire should be administered to all participants. It should be designed to determine the behavioral details of how the consumption/cost information was used to conserve energy.

Finally, confidence in the results of such an experiment will be enhanced by its being performed by several different utility companies. Especially important are different geographic locations (and climates) and different numbers and types of customers. The proposals are equally applicable to electricity and natural gas. And although only residential use is discussed in this paper, a test involving commercial customers should be performed. In general, the widest set of conditions will provide the best test of the conservation proposals.

EXISTING EVIDENCE: ATLANTIC CITY ELECTRIC
COMPANY'S "ENERGY MESSAGE"

The study just proposed has not been performed. However, similar energy consumption feedback was provided to consumers for a limited time by one electric utility company. In response to the energy crisis of November, 1973, the management of Atlantic City Electric decided to add the following statement to the monthly bill of every residential customer: "You used __% less (more) energy than the same period in 1973 (1974)." [4] This energy message, as it was called, was implemented in the belief that making consumers aware of consumption changes would increase their conservation efforts. This was a belief of top management; it was not treated as a proposition to be experimentally tested. Thus, there was no control group of customers who continued to receive the traditional billing statement. [5] All residential customers received the new information.

The "energy message" is similar to the proposal described in Figure 2. It differs from that proposal mainly in not adjusting the previous year's consumption for changes in weather or in billing period. Nonetheless, this "energy message" contains the essence of our proposal, providing the percent change in consumption between two (approximately) comparable billing periods. Thus, it is important to know whether this message was actually successful at reducing energy consumption.

Comparison Groups

The determination of the effect of the energy message requires separating this effect from the decrease in residential consumption that resulted from the energy crisis of November, 1973. What is needed is a control group that did not receive the energy message. Because Atlantic City printed the energy message on all residential utility bills, the necessary control group must be obtained from other companies. There are four electric companies whose

---

[4] In some instances, households more than doubled their use of electricity. When this occurred, the energy message read: "You used over 100% more energy than same period in 1973 (1974)." All other cases received the actual percentage change in consumption.

[5] The message was not printed on utility bills if: (1) the change in consumption was less than 0.5%; (2) no comparison period was available because the account was new; (3) it was a closing bill; (4) consumption was zero; (5) merchandise was included in the bill; (6) the meter had been replaced during the month; or (7) if the bill was based on estimated rather than metered consumption. In addition a few consumers (fewer than ten) found the message offensive and requested that they not receive it. In all, about 25% of Atlantic City's residential customers did not receive the energy message during any given month.

service territories abut Atlantic City's[6]. The consumption
pattern of Atlantic City's customers can be compared to the
patterns of each of these four companies. If the energy
message was effective, Atlantic City's customers should
show a reduced use of electricity relative to the customers
of the four comparison companies.

## Test Period

The energy message first appeared on utility bills mailed
between early March and early April of 1974. Thus, its
effects should be reflected in all utility bills beginning
with May, 1974. It was discontinued in mid-July, 1975 (for
reasons that will be discussed later). Thus, the effect of
the message should terminate after mid-August, 1975. Therefore, the months where a decrease in energy consumption
might have been caused by the energy message are May, 1974
through July, 1975.

Any decrease during this period must be measured against
some prior period. November, 1970 through October, 1973
was chosen because it safely precedes the oil embargo of
November, 1973, and it is long enough to provide a stable
estimate of consumption. A twelve month period was chosen
because energy consumption varies markedly with month, and
a full year cycle is needed to reflect average consumption
accurately. The fifteen months of the energy message were
converted into a twelve month cycle by counting all overlapping months one-half, as described in Table 1.

### TABLE 1

MEAN CONSUMPTION (Kwhr/Month) OVER A TWELVE MONTH PERIOD
Period

| Company | Pretest Nov 70 Oct 73 | Test May 74 July 75[a] | Posttest Jan 76 Dec 76 | Nov 70 Oct 71 | Nov 71 Oct 72 | Nov 72 Oct 73 |
|---|---|---|---|---|---|---|
| Atlantic City | 591.8 | 587.3 | 610.8 | 565.6 | 596.5 | 613.3 |
| Delmarva | 626.2 | 635.4 | 662.7 | 598.3 | 611.0 | 669.3 |
| Jersey Central | 614.2 | 651.1 | 676.2 | 575.0 | 604.6 | 663.1 |
| Philadelphia | 534.8 | 543.7 | 559.3 | 513.7 | 523.0 | 567.7 |
| Public Service | 451.4 | 447.2 | 449.3 | 431.9 | 440.4 | 482.0 |

a   The months of May, June and July for both years were
each given a weight of one-half in estimating the average monthly consumption over a full year cycle. This
adjustment permitted all 15 months of the test period
to be included in the twelve month average.

In a similar way, a period after the end of the energy
message should be examined for an increase in Atlantic
City's consumption relative to the comparison companies.
The period January, 1976 through December 1976 was chosen.
This period could have begun as early as September, 1975
(the first month with no effect of the message), but one
of the comparison companies changed its billing system during this time. This change was fully effective prior to
January, 1976. Thus, there are three time periods whose
consumption data are to be compared: Pretest, November,
1970 through October, 1973; Test, May, 1974 through July,
1975; and Posttest, January, 1976 through December, 1976.

[6]The four companies, followed by their size (number of
residential customers in December, 1976 given in
thousands) and distance from Atlantic City Electric
(based on the distance between customer-weighted geographic centers) are: Delmarva Power and Light,198,
32 mi southwest; Jersey Central Power and Light, 586,
58 mi north; Philadelphia Electric, 1138, 46 mi north-
west; and Public Service Electric and Gas, 1424, 70
mi north. Atlantic City Electric served 283,000 residential customers during December, 1976.

## Consumption Data

The consumption data for these three time periods is shown
in Table 1. For each of the five companies the mean monthly consumption (in kwhr) for all residential customers is
shown. For Atlantic City, the consumption value during
the Test period includes those customers who did not receive the energy message (about 25%, see Footnote 5) as
well as those who did. The three years of the Pretest
period are shown separately in the right of the table in
order to expose trends over time.

The primary consumption data are plotted in Figure 5.

### FIGURE 5

AVERAGE CONSUMPTION FOR THE PRETEST, TEST
AND POSTTEST PERIODS

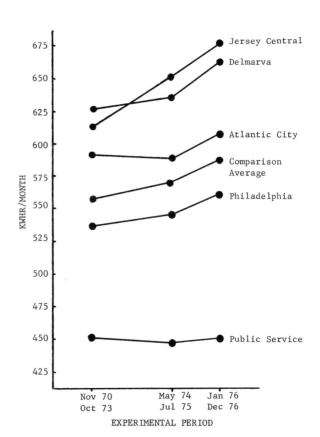

Notice that Atlantic City is one of only two companies
whose consumption decreased between the Pretest and Test
periods. To facilitate identifying trends, the average
consumption over the four comparison companies is also
plotted. Relative to this average, Atlantic City's customers clearly reduced consumption during the Test period.
Also, they show a slight tendency to increase their consumption faster between the Test and Posttest periods.
Both of these relations suggest that the energy message
had a positive effect on conservation.

### Estimation of Energy Message Effect

To estimate the effect of the energy message, the percent
change in energy consumption was computed between the Pre-
test and Test periods and between the Test and Posttest
periods for each of the five utility companies. These values are shown in Table 2. In order to normalize over
differences in consumption levels among the five companies

TABLE 2

EFFECT OF THE ENERGY MESSAGE

| Company | Percent Change from prior period | | Effect of the Energy Message | |
|---|---|---|---|---|
| | Test | Posttest | Test | Posttest |
| Atlantic City | -0.76 | 4.00 | - | - |
| Delmarva | 1.47 | 4.30 | 2.23 | -0.30 |
| Jersey Central | 6.01 | 3.86 | 6.77 | 0.14 |
| Philadelphia | 1.66 | 2.87 | 2.42 | 1.13 |
| Public Service | -0.93 | 0.47 | -0.17 | 3.53 |
| Mean | | | 2.81 | 1.12 |

the change is reported as a percentage rather than as a difference in kwhr. The effect of the energy message is estimated by subtracting Atlantic City's change (in percent) from that of each of the four comparison companies for the Pretest and Test periods and reversing this for the Test and Posttest periods. The mean of the four Pretest-Test values is 2.8%. This average can be interpreted as a 2.8% reduction in energy use caused by the energy message. However, the four individual estimates cover a large range, and one (for Public Service) is slightly less than zero. A t-test (df = 3, one-tailed) only marginally rejects the hypothesis of a zero effect (p = .07). The corresponding 95% confidence interval is (-1.8%, 7.4%). Although the mean estimate of 2.8% is very encouraging, variation among the four comparison companies prevents the attainment of the traditional level of statistical confidence (.05). The differences among the four estimates are explored further in the next section. The estimate of 2.8% should be treated with caution for one further reason. The period just after November, 1973 was unique with respect to consumer response to energy conservation. In spite of the use of comparison companies, the estimate of energy message may depend on conditions unique to the Test Period.

The Test-Posttest comparison suggests that when the energy message was terminated some of its beneficial effects were lost fairly quickly. The "rebound" effect averages 1.1% although again the four individual estimates are highly variable. The 95% confidence interval is (-1.6%, 3.8%); and the corresponding t-test (df = 3, one-tailed) is again not significant at the .05 level (p = .12). Nonetheless, the best estimate is that after about a year 40% of the conservation value of the energy message was lost. It will be interesting to examine the 1977 consumption rates to see if more than 40% of the value of the energy message has now been lost.

Differences among the Five Companies

The consumption data in Tables 1 and 2 indicate important differences among the five utility companies. It will not be possible to explore all differences for their effect on our estimates, but one issue deserves attention.

In addition to large differences in numbers of customers (see Footnote 6), there is wide variation in the proportions of customers who use electricity for home heating. In December, 1976 these proportions were: Atlantic City, .13; Delmarva, .16; Jersey Central, .10; Philadelphia, .03; and Public Service .02. Any increase in average consumption per customer could be caused solely by adding new customers with electric home heating. The larger (smaller) the increase in the proportion of these such customers, the larger (smaller) the increase in mean kwhr per household. Since it is these increases (or decreases) that are used to compute the effect of the energy message, our estimates could be confounded with the proportion of electrically heated households. An examination of the data shows that this is not the case, not for the absolute proportions

given above nor the rate of change of these proportions (not shown). For example, consider the companies most similar to Atlantic City in the proportion of electrically heated households, Delmarva and Jersey Central. (These two are also most similar in the rate of change of the proportions.) By holding the proportions constant or nearly so across companies we remove any effect due to this factor. Since the estimates of message effect (2.2% and 6.8%) are not lowered, we can conclude that this factor is not responsible for the observed effect of 2.8%. This analysis illustrates the complexities of comparing total energy consumption across different samples of customers. The limitations of such comparisons strongly argue for controlled experimental studies like the one proposed earlier.

COST/BENEFIT ANALYSIS

Any change like the one proposed here deserves a full cost/benefit analysis. Such an analysis is advisable if for no other reason than the inequity of asking utility companies to absorb the costs while consumers derive the benefits.

Costs

There are two classes of costs, implementation and maintenance. Implementation of any one of the proposals shown in Figures 2, 3 and 4 entails expanding customer records, calculating necessary values, and printing additional information on the monthly bill. All of these activities are currently performed by utility companies, usually with the aid of large computers. The expansion of these capabilities to include our proposals should not be difficult, although staff time and other costs will be incurred. Only if a company does not have weather normalization capability will a new activity have to be added. Here, however, there is considerable value to the company apart from implementing the preceding proposals. Once such a system is established, maintenance costs should be small. Indeed, the largest maintenance cost may result from special problems like those described in Footnote 5. Although specific dollar values cannot be assigned to these costs at the present moment, it seems safe to assume that most of the costs will be incurred to implement rather than to maintain the system. And the implementation costs should not be high relative to the current accounting expenses of major utility companies.

Benefits

The benefits of the proposed energy consumption information are considerable. First, it has just been estimated that an early version of our proposal produced a 2-3% decrease in residential energy consumption. Although this value is not as reliable as desired, it strongly suggests a major conservation benefit. Since only 75% of households received the message, this effect can be increased by improving the accounting and other systems to reach more customers. In addition, the proposals made here are more sophisticated than Atlantic City's energy message and should only further increase the conservation effect.

There are other important benefits of these proposals. They require no new technology (such as a "smart" thermostat) that requires extended development time and capital expenditure. These proposals involve no major economic or social changes, such as new energy-based taxes or massive consumer education programs. There should be little or no delay in implementation. The main obstacle is creating a software system to retrieve, calculate, and print the new information on the regular monthly bill. This process is practically instantaneous compared to solutions to the energy crisis that involve the development of new technology or new sources of energy. Also, the present proposals can be implemented at almost no risk to the cooperating utility companies. If a few companies will respond to the call to implement a field test of these proposals, all others will have solid estimates of energy conservation and costs. Finally, note that the proposed systems are very likely to be upward compatible with future systems. Future systems might include monthly comparisons to detect more quickly the effects of changes in energy consumption, or energy use predictions tailored to individual households as a function of the household's appliance package. These changes involve augmenting the original system, not replacing it.

All in all, the benefits both to individual consumers and to the country as a whole seem considerable. The cost to the utility companies appears to be relatively small, and one which customers would be willing to have passed on to them. Of course, precise estimates of cost and benefits still await a full field test. However, the analysis presented above indicates that the field test itself has a high benefit/cost ratio.

CONCLUSION

An analysis of consumer decision making has indicated that the provision of better consumption information will aid in energy conservation. In the only study testing the presentation of such information,[7] a 2-3% reduction in energy use was obtained. Given this evidence, and the cost/benefit analysis just presented, why did Atlantic City stop printing its energy message in July, 1975?

When consumers received their monthly electric bills, many realized that they had used less energy than a year earlier, but that their bill had still increased. Angered by the increase in rates that was made so clear by the new billing format, many complained to the company's customer service department. Eventually, the negative effects of customer complaints became so great, that in spite of the energy message's (unknown) ability to reduce energy consumption, the program was cancelled.

Atlantic City Electric's decision to terminate the energy message was based on a clearly perceived "discomfort" versus a presumed (but unknown) energy saving. This problem brings us back to where we started. It is the same one that faces householders who lower their thermostats in winter. The discomfort of a colder house is directly and continually perceived, but the amount of energy saved is unknown. This imbalance favoring the value of an energy purchase over its price leads to discounting the price attribute and to the failure to conserve energy. The problem is not confined to individual consumers, but extends even to the management of utility companies. It is hoped that this paper will make clear to management that the energy message did have an important conservation effect. Then, maybe they will provide the same information to their customers.

---

[7]For related examples of providing energy conservation information to consumers, see [2] and [7].

REFERENCES

1. Bettman, James R. "Issues in Designing Consumer Information Environments", Journal of Consumer Research, 2 (December 1975), 169-177.

2. Craig, C. Samuel and John M. McCann. "Communicating Energy Conservation to Consumers: A Field Experiment on Alternative Ways of Communicating Energy Conservation Information to Residential Consumers of Electricity," Cornell Energy Research Group, Graduate School of Business and Public Administration, Cornell University, 1977.

3. Hirst, Eric. "Residential Energy Use Alternatives: 1976 to 2000," Science, 194 (17 December, 1976), 1247-1252.

4. Russo, J. Edward. "The Value of Unit Price Information," Journal of Marketing Research, 14 (May 1977), in press.

5. Russo, J. Edward and Barbara A. Dosher. "An Information Processing Analysis of Binary Choice," unpublished manuscript, Graduate School of Industrial Administration, Carnegie-Mellon University, 1976.

6. Schipper, Lee and Allan J. Lichtenberg. "Efficient Energy Use and Well-Being: The Swedish Example," Science, 194 (3 December 1976), 1001-1013.

7. Seligman, Clive, John M. Darley and Lawrence J. Becker. "Psychological Strategies to Reduce Energy Consumption: First Annual Progress Report," Report No. 41, Center for Environmental Studies, Princeton University, 1976.

8. Slovic, Paul and Douglas MacPhillamy. "Dimensional Commensurability and Cue Utilization in Comparative Judgment," Organizational Behavior and Human Performance, 11 (1974), 172-194.

9. Tversky, Amos. "Intransitivity of Preferences," Psychological Review, 76 (1969), 31-48.

10. Wortman, Camille B., Michael Hendricks and Jay W. Willis. "Factors Affecting Participant Reactions to Random Assignment in Ameliorative Social Programs," Journal of Personality and Social Psychology, 33 (1976), 256-266.

# A COMPETENCY-BASED METHOD OF GRADING FOR THE MARKETING PRINCIPLES COURSE

Jerome B. Reed, California State College, San Bernardino

## ABSTRACT

This paper presents a method of providing a differentiated product to the heterogeneous group of students in the marketing principles course. It is the use of competency-based grading. This grading system requires that a student understand marketing principles and how each is applied to attain a "C"; be able to integrate these principles to attain a "B"; and that an "A" requires the above plus the application of the integrated principles in the solution of a major marketing case. A theoretical rationale for this approach based on learning hierarchies is provided. The method of application is then presented as are initial student reactions to it. Student reactions are generally positive.

## INTRODUCTION

The basic marketing course is a multi-purpose course and is taken by a variety of students. These students come from many different areas of the university and for different purposes. As a result the total enrollment in marketing principles is large and consists of a heterogeneous mix of students. Because of various constraints, the marketing department in the large southwestern university at which I taught could not provide specialized courses or sections for each of the segments. Thus each section had this diverse mix of students. They had different motivations, abilities, backgrounds and expectations. How could the course offerings and requirements--the product--be differentiated within each section of about fifty students to serve the goals of the student segments?

An undifferentiated approach did not work. A standard mix of requirements was originally applied to all students. They were expected to learn the material from the book and lectures and then, on exams, show that they understood it. They were also expected to analyze several short cases and one long one during the semester. These analyses had to be written and submitted for grading. There were also short written reports of field studies.

Because of the diversity of the students, some were able to complete all of the requirements and get a high grade. Others, for various reasons, were unable or unwilling to put forth the effort required. Still others, as much as they wanted to do a better job in the course, were just unable to meet the requirements, especially the analyses of the cases.

The problem became how to provide a differentiated product to this diverse mix of students which would let them make their own choices and at the same time allow me to "certify" them as having attained a specific level of competency in marketing.

## SEGMENTATION

An undifferentiated approach did not work and a differentiated approach was required. Taking the marketing concept into account, consumers--the students--had to be considered and segments developed. The problem became to identify the dimensions to use for segmentation.

First, consider the sources of student heterogeneity. As mentioned, there were four key variables; motivations, abilities, backgrounds and expectations. Because of prior constraints, little could be done with the latter pair and it was decided to focus on motivation and ability, and their interaction, as the primary segmenting variables.

### Motivation

The first element to be considered is the intrinsic motivation that each student brought to the course. Based on experience, all students within a state university are not highly motivated. Further, an individual's motivation varies between courses. Some students do not want the highest grade obtainable in a course and will not work to their maximum potential. Marketing majors and/or others who are grade conscious want to get as much of the course as possible. However, for many students the marketing principles course is another of the many hurdles on their way to their terminal degree. These latter students come in with a low level of intrinsic motivation.

Some potential heresy. The majority of professors cannot provide the positive extrinsic motivation required to get students with low levels of intrinsic motivation to achieve their highest potential. Some, yes; but not all. Adding this extrinsic motivation to existing intrinsic motivation leads to a higher level of performance. However, the form of these extrinsic motivators is extremely critical in developing student attitudes towards the course. Deci [3] has shown that the application of positive motivators in the form of work oriented rewards can oftentimes lead to a decrease in the intrinsic motivation of the student. Further, the use of negative motivators, such as fear, does lead to a lessening of intrinsic motivation.

### Ability

The next segmenting variable is ability. Not all students who take the introductory marketing course have the ability to obtain an "A". Within a large state university, some students will be of high ability and are the equivalent of the best students at an outstanding school. But the majority, albeit of above average ability, cannot, on ability alone, achieve an "A" in every course.

### Interaction

However, the most important aspect of these variables is their interaction. Studies in psychology show that quality of performance is not a function of either variable alone [5]. Rather, Anderson and Butzin [1] following Heider [5] have empirically shown that performance is a multiplicative function of motivation and ability. These findings show that a high level of motivation can overcome a low level of ability and a high level of ability can overcome low level motivation. Conversely, a low level of motivation coupled to a high level of ability can lead to only average performance.

Other attempts have been made to solve this problem of lack of motivation and/or ability in developing other approaches to courses. These include such things as self-paced instruction and contract grading. Experiences of mine and others who have used these approaches have been somewhat equivocal. They do work in many situations but not all and not with all students. However, the specific problem being considered is how to develop an approach which will solve this problem, yet be suitable for the standard classroom approach. How can we provide a differentiated product to the students.

## COMPETENCY-BASED GRADING

A solution has been found that meets this goal of differentiation. It is a competency-based grading approach which allows each student to set their own grade given their unique combination of abilities and motivations. It is based in theory and preliminary data show that students like it. At the same time it allows the instructor to certify that a grade of "A" denotes clearly superior performance and not just a larger quantity of work.

Let us consider what this grading system must do. The first goal is that the grade be based on quality and not just quantity. However, additional effort must be required of the student to achieve a higher grade. As mentioned, performance is primarily a function of motivation and ability along with background and expectations. The grading system must be such that if a person has high ability but low motivation, then a "C" can be obtained. At the same time it must be possible for a student who has a modest level of ability but high motivation to attain an "A" through increased quality of performance. The grading criteria must reflect performance only.

The second objective is that the grade be based on previously established criteria that are well known to both students and instructor. Each student knows in advance exactly what is required for each grade and can estimate the amount of effort required, given their ability, to attain the desired grade. This follows Mager's philosophy [6].

Finally, the grading system must be well grounded in theory. This requirement of being theoretically sound will now be considered.

## THEORETICAL BACKGROUND

Within the general area of learning theory the objectives and requirements for learning have been extensively discussed. The specific area which this paper considers is that of the domains of learning and the different hierarchies within these domains. The specific cognitive domain hierarchies considered are Bloom's Taxonomy of Educational Objectives [2] and Gagne's The Conditions of Learning [4]. Both of these authors posit a series of levels of mental learning abilities and performance. Bloom's hierarchy consists of six steps, from simplest to most complex: knowledge (recall), comprehension (relating and association), application (use in concrete situations), analysis (breaking down into elements), synthesis (putting together of elements to form a structure or system), and evaluation (judgements and standards). Gagne's conditions are similar but they start at a more elemental level. They are signal learning (involuntary reflex response), stimulus-response learning (voluntary response to a signal), chaining (linking a series of stimulus-response), verbal association (verbal chaining), multiple-discrimination (choosing among a class of possibilities), concept learning (memorizing names and properties), principle learning (chaining of two or more concepts and relationships), and problem solving (combining old principles into new ones). A consideration was made of the specific activities of the two parallel hierarchies which the authors intended and defined in their original works.

Based on this consideration, the minimum acceptable performance level for a university course, especially an introductory course, should be the understanding of the specific ideas and concepts and how these are used. On the other hand, the optimum level would be problem solving--

the ability to make an integrated whole of the material learned and then apply this to solve new and unique problems. An intermediate level would be the ability to integrate the ideas, to chain them, to synthesize them, to make principles, to see the course content in an holistic manner. But application to new and unique problems would not be required.

These three levels of achievement thus become the basis for a competency-based grading system. The ability to solve new and unique problems using all course materials results in an "A" while understanding the various ideas and concepts and their applications leads to a "C".

How does this help to differentiate the course? If students are aware at the beginning of the course of the exact requirements to achieve the different grades they can set their own goals relative to a grade. A highly motivated student with average ability knows that with extra effort he can achieve an "A". On the other hand, the lesser motivated student, whether of high or low ability, knows exactly what is required to achieve a "C". At the same time the instructor can certify that the student who achieves a particular grade has a stated level of competency. This latter is very important to me.

## APPLICATION

The application is handled in the following manner. At the beginning of the semester students are given a list of marketing concepts which they must understand. Examples of these are shown in Appendix I. Students are told that to achieve a "C" in the course that on an essay exam they must be able to accurately define and show the usage of 80% of the concepts chosen at random. In practice the exams have consisted of a five-question essay type. Typical questions are shown in Appendix II.

In order to achieve a "B" in the course they must pass the "C" level satisfactorily and also be able to relate ideas and concepts to each other and develop and apply these principles. This was done by adding "B" questions to each exam. An example question which would get at these abilities would be one such as "Given a heterogeneous shopping good in the maturity stage of the product life cycle which is purchased primarily by families in the full nest one and two stage of the family life cycle, develop an appropriate advertising strategy." Again students are given an 80% level of competency requirement in order to achieve a "B".

The "A" level is obtained by doing a satisfactory level of performance on a case utilizing the previously learned principles. Thus the "A" student can integrate course material and can apply this in the analysis of a specific marketing problem. The problem can either be a case or a live marketing situation.

For each level of competency students are given several chances to show their ability. The "B" and "C" exams on each area of the course are given twice, once as a midterm and once as a part of the final. For the "A" level students are given at least two opportunities to analyze a specific major marketing problem.

The major question remaining is how the students respond to this approach. Preliminary data show that they respond favorably. A survey was taken of two sections of the beginning marketing course on the first day of class after the approach had been presented to them and the students showed they understood it. They were asked to provide free-form, anonymous responses to two questions: "Advantages to you of this approach?" and "Disadvantages to you of this approach?" These types of questions have been used before and have been validated through both group and individual discussions. The results of this survey are shown in Table 1. Since there were multiple responses to the first question, the responses totaled more than 100%.

## TABLE 1

### INITIAL SURVEY RESPONSES

Advantages to you of this approach?

| | |
|---|---|
| Set your own grade; set your own goals; get as much or as little as you want from the course. | 73% |
| Fairer; several chances to show your ability. | 44% |
| Make classes more interesting and enjoyable. | 8% |
| Able to work at own pace. | 7% |
| Other | 7% |

Disadvantages to you of this approach?

| | |
|---|---|
| Too much time involved, can't catch up if you fall behind. | 34% |
| Requirements for grade of "C" too high. | 8% |
| Not motivating enough. | 7% |
| Other | 12% |
| No response | 39% |

(n = 59)

The major advantages seen by the students were oriented toward their knowledge of their motivation and ability. They liked the idea of being able to set their own grade, to set their own standards, to get as much or as little out of the course as they wanted. One of the interesting aspects to the list of advantages is that it did not include the aspect of non-competitive grading. It was felt that this would be important to them. But none mentioned it. The major disadvantage seen to the approach was that it could take more time than they were willing to spend. Later discussions uncovered two facets to this problem: The first was that the exams were so laid out that if they did not achieve the required performance level on the first one covering a particular part of the course they had to take a second exam. The students perceived this as being a requirement to cover the material twice. The other was the amount of time required on their part to learn more than just the basic material. Apparently this was new to many of them. They had not previously been required to do some thinking, to integrate material, to make a whole of it and then apply it.

A limited survey of a random subset of students later in the semester showed that students felt that the approach gave them more motivation than the standard approach to grading. They saw that the grade they earned was entirely up to them. They could blame no one else. They were becoming aware that the competency-based grading system relied heavily on intrinsic motivation.

A separate, unforeseen, advantage to both the students and instructor was that students of lower ability soon became aware of their level of competency. Once aware they saw what they could realistically achieve and stopped at that level. They did not continue beating their heads against the wall, trying to reach a level of competency that their ability kept them from reaching. This was an advantage to them. It was also an advantage to the instructor in that

the students made the decision for themselves. It was not the instructor providing negative feedback in the terms of continuous low grades on items such as cases.

## SUMMARY

The technique is applicable in almost any basic, introductory course in any field. It is possible to develop a set of concepts, principles, and application requirements for any course. Using these levels of performance and the students can be told in advance exactly what is expected of them to achieve different grades. It is a method that is theoretically sound, it has met with student approval, and I feel it has wide application.

## APPENDIX I

### SAMPLE MARKETING CONCEPTS

| | |
|---|---|
| General | Marketing Concept<br>Marketing Mix<br>The External, Uncontrollable Environment<br>Internal Corporate Constraints |
| Consumers | Market Segmentation: People are Different<br>Demographics<br>Family Life Cycle<br>Social Class/Income<br>Psychographics<br>Self-Concept Theory<br>Life Style<br>Reference Group Influence<br>Usage Rates<br>Usage Situations<br>Consumer Decision Process |
| Research | The Search for the Dissatisfied Consumer<br>Problem Definition<br>Primary Data<br>Secondary Data<br>Marketing Information Systems<br>Sales Forecasting |

## APPENDIX II

### SAMPLE EXAMINATION QUESTIONS

Define the concept, "The Search for the Dissatisfied Consumer." Show why this is one of the major aspects of market research.

In your own words restate the Self-Concept Theory and give an example of how a marketer might use it.

Define the first three steps in the consumer decision process. Use a recent purchase of yours as an example and show how the steps applied to it.

What is the Marketing Mix and where does it fit in the overall approach used in this course?

## REFERENCES

1. Anderson, Normal H. and Clifford A. Butzin. "Performance = Motivation X Ability: An Integration-Theoretical Analysis." Journal of Personality and Social Psychology, (November 1974), 598-604.

2. Bloom, Benjamin S. Taxonomy of Educational Objectives, The Classification of Educational Goals, Handbook I: Cognitive Domain. New York: David McKay Company, 1965.

3. Deci, Edward L. _Intrinsic Motivation_. New York:
   Plenum Press, 1975.

4. Gagne, R. M. _The Conditions of Learning_. New York:
   Holt, Rinehart and Winston, 1970.

5. Heider, F. _The Psychology of Interpersonal Relations_.
   New York: Wiley, 1958.

6. Mager, Robert F. _Preparing Instructional Objectives_.
   Palo Alto: Fearon Publishers, 1962.

# SIMULATIONS DO INCREASE LEARNING

Ernest F. Cooke, University of Baltimore
Thomas J. Maronick, University of Baltimore

## ABSTRACT

Although marketing simulations are frequently used in a variety of marketing classes there is some question as to how effective they are in increasing learning. The authors have tested with positive results the proposition that simulations do increase learning. Special efforts were made to hold all variables constant so as not to cloud the results with extraneous issues.

## INTRODUCTION

The wide use of simulation as an aid to learning is well documented: texts and manuals of simulations published by several publishers, two organizations devoted to simulations (ABSEL and NASAGA)-each with an annual meeting and proceedings, a bi-monthly journal (Simulation/Gaming), and several regional and national intercollegiate simulation competitions. In addition, the fact that each proceeding of the AMA educators conference for the past several years has had at least one article on simulation testifies to the fact that marketing faculty are using simulations to aid in teaching marketing courses.

Up to now it seems to have been universally accepted that simulations do aid in the learning process, but now Neuhouser (3) has questioned the whole process in a paper which was accepted for publication by The Academy of Management Review after extensive review and revision. Neuhouser (3) claims, without documentation (2), that business games have failed.

It is not the purpose of this paper to refute Neuhouser's thesis but rather to answer his call and Frazer's (2) call for validation of the learning that does take place when simulations are used in the classroom. In answering his call, the authors have designed a simple test of the hypothesis that the use of a simulation in the classroom will increase learning. As Neuhouser notes (3) this is a complicated subject requiring careful experimental design starting with clear-cut learning objectives.

## EXPERIMENTAL DESIGN

Four introductory marketing classes taught by two different instructors (two classes each) were used for the experiment. Each instructor offered exactly the same material in each of his classes with the one exception that each used a simulation in one class and not in the other. Table I describes the four classes used in this study. Every attempt was made to hold all factors constant between the two classes taught by one instructor except for the simulation.

The experimental design used in the study was a before-after with control group design (1) where students in each class were tested (see Appendix A) at the beginning of the semester and then again at the end of the semester, using the same instrument. Students were not told the purpose of the test but were left with the impression that it was important.

The hypothesis tested in the study was that: If learning is increased by a simulation, then the classes where the simulation was used should show more of an improvement between the pre-test and post-test than the classes where simulation was not used.

## LEARNING OBJECTIVE

The objective of the experiment was to determine how the students were able to handle basic marketing concepts with a high but easy quantitative content. Three concepts were used: Breakeven analysis, mark-up and sales analysis. The simulation used required a considerable amount of numerical manipulation. Although the three concepts were not directly treated in the simulation, the student could use all three to advantage. Thus, the goal of the simulation was to increase the student's experience in working with numbers in a context similar to that found on the pre- and post-test. The simulation used is briefly described in Appendix B.

### TABLE 1

DESCRIPTION OF MARKETING CLASSES USED IN EXPERIMENT

| INSTRUCTOR/ SECTION | TIME | STUDENTS | SIMULATION |
|---|---|---|---|
| X-1 | M-W-F 8:00-8:50 | 34 | Yes |
| X-2 | M-W-F 1:00-1:50 | 39 | No |
| Y-3 | Tu-Th 8:00-9:15 | 29 | No |
| Y-4 | Tu-Th 9:30-10:45 | 38 | Yes |

## IMPLEMENTATION

To hold as many factors as possible constant and to keep the experiment as simple as possible, the only difference between each class as taught by one instructor was the use of the simulation. Students competed as individuals not teams and the students knew that they would earn a grade based on individual results in the simulation.

The instructors limited the amount of class time devoted to the simulation. They did not discuss the simulation or the results unless specifically requested. The classes that did not have the simulation did not have a specific substitute for the simulation. In those classes, the instructors just lectured more than in the classes with the simulations.

This was a rather severe test of the simulation since the instructor was not using the simulation in the traditional sense of incorporating it directly into his class plan. Rather, it was extra work which one class had but the other class did not. This was done so that any difference between results of the pre- and post-test could be attributed to the simulation and not to how the instructor used it.

Each instructor gave the pre-test and post-test to his two classes in the same general way, but there were some minor variations between instructors. No connection was made by the students between the tests and the simulation.

The experiment was conducted at an upper-division school (third and fourth year plus graduate) with an open admission policy. The course was an introductory level course and most of the students in the course were in their first semester in the school. The mean test scores (pre- and post-test) for all students was 46.8%.

Finally, there did not seem to be any important differences between the two instructors. They both used the same method in teaching the courses (lecture plus tests), both were trained at the same graduate school, and both were approximately the same age. However, even if other minor differences did exist, the experimental design should have controlled for them since each instructor taught one experimental and one control group.

## RESULTS

The results are shown in Tables II and III. In the case of both instructors, there was a greater change in learning in the classes that used the simulation, but in the case of instructor Y, the change was not statistically significant. Using a t-test, the differences were statistically significant at 0.05 for instructor X.

Instructor X inadvertently put both of his classes under time pressure for the post-test which resulted in lower post-test scores in both classes. In the class using the simulation, there was an insignificant 0.5% drop in test average scores (from 51.9% to 51.4%) for the 34 students. In the class which did not use the simulation, there was a substantial drop in average test scores of 12.8% (from 49.7% to 43.4%) for the 39 students. This suggests that more learning of the type measured by the test occurred in the class with the simulation.

The results for instructor Y are not as obvious. In the class with the simulation, the average test scores increased 24.6% while the class without the simulation showed a lower 19.1% increase. The difference in post-test scores is not statistically significant.

Two factors may have contributed to the inconclusive results for instructor Y. First, the differences in class size were greater than the two classes taught by instructor X. One of instructor Y's classes had 29 students and the other 38 students. The smaller class did not use the simulation. Instructor X had classes of 34 and 39 with the smaller class using the simulation.

Second, there was a sizable difference in the pre-test scores for Y's two classes as compared to X's classes As noted on Table II, Y's class that would be using the simulation had a mean pretest score of 36.9 compared to 46.0 for Y's class that would not be using the simulation and compared to a score of 51.9 for X's class that would have the simulation.

While no explanation could be determined for these differences since the pretest instrument was the same for both groups, it is possible that both factors (class size and pre-test scores) could have biased the results in favor of the class which did not use the simulation. The smaller class may have had more of the instructor's attention and since the smaller class was the brighter class as far as the pre-test was concerned, it did not have as far to go. It should be noted, however, that despite these differences, the class using the simulation did have a slightly larger, though not statistically significant, percentage increase in learning as measured by the pre- and post-test (24.6% with the simulation versus 19.1% without).

As noted in Table 2, there was no difference in the final grades given by each instructor to his two classes, although instructor X did grade higher (grade point 2.47 and 2.49) than instructor Y (grade point 2.24 and 2.28). Each of the four classes had students who earned all grades and each class had at least 4A's and 2F's. The only surprise is that instructor Y did not have a greater difference between his two classes since the pre-test scores were so different. Of course, the pre-test and post-test measured only a very small part of the total course content so it might be too much to expect a high correlation between the final grades and these tests.

## STUDENT INTEREST

Another claim made for simulations is that they result in increased interst on the part of students. Independently of the experiment, the faculty and the courses were evaluated by the students at the end of the semester. These evaluations are also shown in Table 2 and in every case, the students rated the courses or instructors with the simulation higher than the courses or instructors without the simulation. In the case of instructor Y, the results are very close. In these student evaluations, 4.0 means every student in the class rated the factor in the top 10% in his experience at the school and 0.0 means every student in the class rated the factor in the lowest 10%.

## FURTHER ANALYSIS

Neuhouser (3) suggests that only "competitive" students will benefit from simulations. Since the only measure of competitiveness is the final grade, the suggestion is that the more competitive students will likely earn the higher grades. Although this suggestion is by no means known to be correct, it was decided to examine the changes in learning as measured by the pre- and post-test by final grades. The results are shown in Table 3.

The most interesting result of this analysis has nothing to do with the idea that prompted it. This unexpected result is that analysis of the data in Table III further supports the validity of the results for instructor X's two classes and it helps explain the weakness in the results for instructor Y's two classes.

Specifically, there seems to be a strong positive relationship between final grade and the post-test scores in both of instructor X's classes: A & B+ students scored higher than B students who scored higher than C+ & C students who scored higher than D & F students. This relationship does not hold up in Y's classes. However, it is noteworthy that among A & B+ students in Y's classes, several students who did not use the simulation, did much better than those who did use it. If these students were taken out of the analysis of both of Y's classes (9 and 8 students respectively) then the balance (29 and 21 students) would show significantly higher learning with the simulation.

Going back to the original thought that prompted this part of the analysis, the B students seem to have benefited the most from the simulation in X's class while the D & F students seem to have benefited the most in Y's class.

## CONCLUSION

The key to an experiment of the type described in this paper is to hold all factors constant except for the variable under study, in this case the simulation. Since the student registration process is not controllable, and the class schedule pre-determined, it was necessary to conduct the experiment in classes of unequal size and unequal ability.

In the experiment with instructor X, the two classes were close in size (34 and 39 students) and as far as this factor might be measured by the pre-test, close in ability (51.9% and 49.7%). In this experiment, the class with the simulation did significantly better on the post-test and in both classes the scores are consistent with the final grades, with A & B+ students getting higher post-test scores than B students, etc.

The results of the experiment conducted in X's classes indicate that, given a clearly defined learning objective, and an appropriate simulation, greater learning occurs when a simulation is used to aid the process. This was a severe test of the simulation since it was not an intergral part of the class plan as noted above in the section on implementation.

The experiment conducted in instructor Y's classes does not confirm the conclusion stated in the last paragraph, but at the same time it does not lead to rejection of this conclusion. Taken as a percentage increase in post-test over pre-test, more learning did occur in the class with the simulation (24.6%) than in the class without the simulation (19.1%) but the results are not statistically significant.

In this latter experiment there were factors which were not as constant as in the first experiment. A minor factor was class sizes (29 and 38 students) with the larger class using the simulation. A more important factor was the relative ability of the two classes as measured by the pre-test.

In Y's class with the simulation, the pre-test mean score was 36.9%, while Y's class without the simulation had a pre-test mean score of 46.0% which was almost 25% better. Both classes had lower pre-test scores than did the classes taught by instructor X. Breaking down both of Y's classes by grade groups showed an inconsistency between final grades and the post-test in both classes. An inconsistency not present in the experiment using X's classes.

Given that there is some indication of more learning in Y's class with the simulation, given that class sizes were different in a direction to favor the class without the simulation, given that the classes did not start out (or end up) showing equal ability as measured by the tests and this was in a direction to favor the class without the simulation, it may be safe to conclude that had all factors been equal in the second experiment (Y), the results might have been more in line with the first (X).

## REFERENCES

1. H.W. Boyd, Jr. and R. Westfall, Marketing Research: Text and Cases, (Homewood, Ill., Richard D. Irwin, 1972), p. 88.

2. J. Ronald Frazer, ABSEL News, Simulation/Gaming, January/February, 1977, p. 17.

3. John J. Neuhouser, "Business Games Have Failed", The Academy of Management Review, October, 1976, pp. 124-29.

## APPENDIX A

The test used for both the pre-test and the post-test consisted of three questions of different degrees of difficulty. One objective in writing the test was to design one that would not put a large number of students at either extreme. In that regard, the test was very successful. Only one student (out of 140 total) received zero's on both the pre-test and the post-test and the highest grade was 93.3%. This was done by using one fairly easy question and one difficult question. Overall, the test was difficult for the students who took it since the mean test score for the 280 tests was 46.8%. The three questions were:

1. An important concept in business and marketing is the breakeven point. Breakeven is the quantity of a product which must be sold to cover all expenses. At breakeven, profit is zero. The most common equation for breakeven says that the breakeven point in units is equal to the fixed cost (or overhead) divided by the difference between the unit selling price and the unit variable cost.

   You are a small business reselling a single product. Your salary is $5,600.00 per year, your rent is $200.00 per month. You buy the product for 60¢ each and you sell it for a dollar. How many do you have to sell every year to breakeven? Show your calculations.

2. Retailers talk about markup. They buy something, mark it up and then sell it at the marked-up price. The mark-up is expressed as a percentage and this percentage is based on the retailer's selling price or cost. In the previous question, what is the mark-up percentage? Show your calculations.

3. You have three retail locations in three different cities. Your product has about the same appeal to all the people in each city. You are studying last year's results for all three of your stores:

| STORE | STORE LOCATION | YOUR SALES | TOTAL SALES | LOCAL POPULATION | STORE PROFIT |
|---|---|---|---|---|---|
| A | New York City | 200,000 | 800,000 | 10 Mil | $30,000 |
| B | Baltimore, Md. | 100,000 | 200,000 | 2 Mil | 20,000 |
| C | Wilmington, Del. | 20,000 | 50,000 | .5 Mil | 1,000 |

Your sales and total sales are in units. Total sales means your sales plus the sales of all your competitors. Calculate the market share (that is, the share of total sales) of each of your three stores. How would you compare the performance of each of your three stores to each other? That is, which store is doing the best job and which store the worst job? Why?

## APPENDIX B

The simulation used was, The Quaker Oats Company Supermarket Management Decision Game, published in 1969 by Quaker Oats in cooperation with Purdue University, IBM and the National Association of Retail Grocers of the United States. Each student made two practice decisions and then made eight consecutive decisions in a competition which lead to a grade based on final simulation results.

Decisions were highly interactive within the firm and competition between firms was intensive with one firm's decisions affecting all other firms. Twenty separate decisions were required each period in the area of inventory, price, promotion, staffing and financing for four separate departments: Grocery, Meat, Produce and Dairy.

As an example of the interaction between firms, one firm's market share is a function of ten pricing and promotional decisions (two for each department and two for the entire operation) in relation to all the same decisions made by all other supermarkets in the area.

Although not specifically called for, a student could make use of breakeven analysis, mark-up and sales analysis in this simulation.

TABLE 2

RESULTS OF AN EXPERIMENT TO TEST
LEARNING THROUGH THE USE OF A
SIMULATION

| CLASS | X-1 | X-2 | Y-4 | Y-3 |
|---|---|---|---|---|
| Simulation | Yes | No | Yes | No |
| Students | 34 | 39 | 38 | 29 |
| Pre-Test Mean Score | 51.9 % | 49.7 % | 36.9% | 46.0% |
| Post-Test Mean Score | 51.4 % | 43.4 % | 46.0% | 54.8% |
| Mean Change (Pre-test minus Post-test) | -0.5 % | -6.4 %[1] | +9.1% | +8.8%[2] |
| Standard Deviation of Change | 15.9 % | 20.3 % | 23.6% | 23.4% |
| % Change (Mean Change ÷ by Mean Pre-Test) | -0.9 % | -12.8 % | 24.6% | 19.1% |
| Average Final Grade (A=4 points) | 2.47 | 2.49 | 2.24 | 2.28 |
| Student Evaluation of Subject Matter (0 to 4) | 2.58 | 2.38 | 2.19 | 2.10 |
| | (X-1 is 8.4% higher than X-2) | | (Y-4 is 4.3% higher than Y-3) | |
| Student Evaluation of Instructor (0 to 4) | 3.32 | 2.88 | 2.52 | 2.43 |
| | (X-1 is 15.3% higher than X-2) | | (Y-4 is 3.7% higher than Y-3) | |

(1) Significant at $\alpha = .05$; (2) N.S.

TABLE 3

COMPARISON OF PRE- AND POST-TEST[2]

BASED ON FINAL COURSE GRADES

| FINAL GRADE | PRE-TEST | POST-TEST | % CHANGE | NUMBER OF STUDENTS | PRE-TEST | POST-TEST | % CHANGE | NO. OF STUDENT |
|---|---|---|---|---|---|---|---|---|
| X-1 (with simulation) | | | | | X-2 (without simulation) | | | |
| A&B+ | 69.2% | 66.0% | -4.5% | 8 | 64.6% | 57.8% | -10.6% | 9 |
| B | 54.2% | 61.3% | +13.1% | 8 | 57.5% | 53.8% | -6.5% | 12 |
| C&C+ | 55.5% | 51.7% | +6.8% | 11 | 50.0% | 43.7% | -12.6% | 9 |
| D&F | 23.8% | 22.9% | -4.0% | 7 | 24.3% | 14.8% | -38.9% | 9 |
| Y-4 (with simulation) | | | | | Y-3 (without simulation) | | | |
| A&B+ | 48.7% | 55.4% | +13.7% | 9 | 48.5% | 66.3% | +36.5% | 8 |
| B | 47.5% | 56.9% | +19.9% | 6 | 54.3% | 52.7% | -3.1% | 5 |
| C&C+ | 33.8% | 42.9% | +27.2% | 12 | 49.2% | 61.9% | +26.0% | 6 |
| D&F | 24.8% | 35.6% | +43.3% | 11 | 38.0% | 42.5% | +11.8% | 10 |

(2) Grade ranges were selected to maximize sample
size (number of students) while still breaking
the class down into several catagories.

# PROGRAMMABLE CALCULATOR ASSISTED CASES

Ronald Stiff, University of Baltimore

## ABSTRACT

Card programmable calculators can provide greater portability and accessibility than computers and substantially more power than non-programmable calculators. Their use to supplement case analysis through developing programs allowing the user to ask many "what-if" questions is described in general and through four case study examples. An increase in managerial ability in the use of quantitative models is likely to follow the diffusion of programmable calculators.

## INTRODUCTION

Calculators and computers have had significant impact on both marketing management and marketing education. The recent introduction of key and card programmable calculators provides a middle ground to the convenience of calculators and the power and logic of computers. The programmable calculator offers significant benefits in teaching and management development applications.

## BENEFITS OF PROGRAMMABLE CALCULATOR USE

Business Week reported a number of management uses of programmable calculators including financial ratio calculation, interest schedule calculations, evaluation of stock options, experience curve analysis, and a variety of statistical routines [6]. Managers find programmable calculators to be more accessible and economical than time-shared computers, to be a stimulus to learning quantitative and statistical analysis and to be a great convenience in portability on business trips and at home where time-shared computers frequently are difficult to access.

All of these benefits are present for marketing faculty. The portability benefit is especially valuable to faculty involved in management development programs where distance and/or economics discourage the use of computers. The programmable calculator encourages working at home which some faculty may view as a benefit.

Students benefit from an introduction to a tool which will have an increasing impact on management analysis. The programmable calculator also minimizes the frustration of students who are exposed to a well developed university computer center only to find the lack of such resources on their first job.

A natural and realistic use of the programmable calculator is through programmable calculator assisted cases. Computer and model assisted cases are becoming increasingly used and documented [1, 2, 3, 5]. Programmable calculator assisted cases offer a useful supplement and alternative to computer assisted cases. When used for in class demonstrations the programmable calculator requires less set-up time and is more reliable than many time sharing computer systems.

## A GENERAL MODEL OF PROGRAMMABLE CALCULATOR USE

Programmable calculators are available in key and card programmable models. The card programmable models are by far the most flexible allowing programs to be written on and read from chewing gum stick size cards. Manufacturers also provide statistical and business program libraries which extend the usefulness of the card programmable models. Library programs permit flexible use of time value of money, forecasting, and curve fitting routines as a supplement to case analysis.

Card programmable calculators provide virtually all the function keys of non-programmable calculators plus the additional power of programming. Programming capabilities generally include read/write on magnetic cards, editing, subroutines, conditional and unconditional branching, memories, and user defined keys. These capabilities allow rather flexible analysis of cases.

One possible model for programmable calculator use in case analysis is shown in Figure 1.[1] The program written specifically for a case is entered with Initial Conditions for most or all of the relevant case variables read directly into calculator memory. These initial conditions are specified by the program writer using case facts. The user then keys in any specified Input Variables using one or more of the user defined keys.

FIGURE 1

GENERAL MODEL FOR PROGRAMMABLE CALCULATOR USE

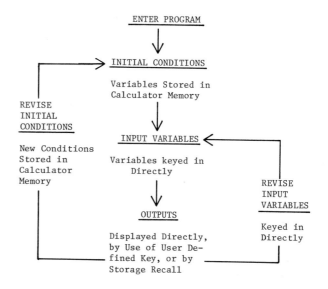

---

[1] Programming techniques are not described in this paper since they are readily available in the manufacturers documentation. Card programmable calculators were available in retail outlets and by mail order in April 1977 for under $200 with libraries selling from $20 to $30 for 10 to 15 programs.

Output is displayed directly and additional outputs may be requested, if programmed, by pressing a specified user defined key. The user may repeat this procedure by keying in any desired revised Input Variables. The user may also revise the Initial Conditions by storing new values for these variables. At any point during this procedure the user can make use of the calculator's abilities and calculate per-cent increases, linear or compound growth, present values, etc. to create new input variables. For example, if a program calculated profits expected from a specific price the user could easily calculate the effect on profits of a ten per-cent price change.

The power of the calculator is best demonstrated through the following examples.

### EXAMPLES OF PROGRAMMABLE CALCULATOR USES

The following four examples of programmable calculator uses have been field tested in management development seminars with very positive results.[2] Each case is readily available in published form or through the Intercollegiate Case Clearing House.[3]

Gillette Safety Razor Division (Figure 2)

Gillette is faced with a new product decision, whether or not to enter the blank recording tape market. The costs are well defined in the case and the analyst must decide if any combination of price, market size, and market share is reasonable in obtaining Gillette's profit goal. The user quickly realizes that the initial conditions require over 40 per-cent market share to reach the profit goal. This encourages the user to revise either the cost structure or the first year profit goal to develop a reasonable new product introduction market plan. The calculator model is essentially a pro-form income statement that allows the user to skip performing the actual calculations and concentrate on relationships such as the effects of suggested retail price changes on the sales target required to achieve the profit goal. The user is encouraged to ask many "what if" questions which quickly demonstrate that Gillete cannot profitably enter either low or high price tape markets.

The calculator eliminates the rather boring computations required if the user wishes to change underlying assumptions such as the price, cost structure, or market potential. Since the user can rapidly produce a variety of answers he has a strong tendency to focus on the marketing issues in the case rather than becoming overly enchanted with "the single answer." For example, in the Gillette case students are generally reluctant to calculate by hand a variety of market size-market share-profit relationships. With the calculator they focus on key issues of can Gillette obtain their objectives under any one of a variety of marketing programs.

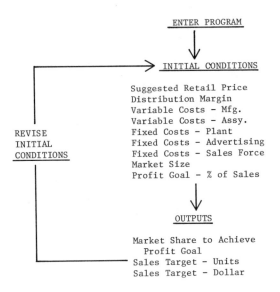

FIGURE 2

GILLETTE SAFETY RAZOR DIVISION
THE BLANK CASSETTE PROJECT

ENTER PROGRAM

INITIAL CONDITIONS

Suggested Retail Price
Distribution Margin
Variable Costs - Mfg.
Variable Costs - Assy.
Fixed Costs - Plant
Fixed Costs - Advertising
Fixed Costs - Sales Force
Market Size
Profit Goal - % of Sales

REVISE
INITIAL
CONDITIONS

OUTPUTS

Market Share to Achieve
Profit Goal
Sales Target - Units
Sales Target - Dollar

In this, as in other cases described, any single analysis can be accomplished or checked without great difficulty by hand. The advantage provided by the calculator is that it encourages recalculations under a variety of assumptions freeing the user to deal with issues.

Gould, Inc. - Graphics Division (Figure 3)

Gould must decide if a new electrostatic printer should be sold directly to computer users or to original equipment manufacturers to integrate and sell with their computer systems. The program calculates break-even points under the initial conditions given in the case. The user may then enter a profit goal which generally leads to greatly increased sales targets due to the cost structure facing Gould. On the other hand, the student also learns that a fairly low sales target will net a fairly small short run loss and that the downside risks of market entry are not large. Students and managers often fail to do the quantity of calculations required to understand these relationships. The calculator encourages more sensitivity testing.

---

[2] Texas Instruments SR-52 programs are available from the author.

[3] Cases, except for Fanta Chemicals [2] are available from: Intercollegiate Case Clearing House, Soldiers Field, Boston, Massachusetts.

FIGURE 3

GOULD, INC. - GRAPHICS DIVISION

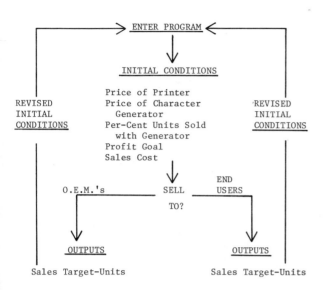

Poly Fiber Plastics Group (Figure 4)

Poly Fibers must make a pricing decision for a plastic material which is a potential replacement for metals and other plastics. The program library can be used to fit a demand curve for case data. A power curve results in an excellent fit.[4] This curve is used in the Poly Fiber program.

FIGURE 4

POLY FIBER PLASTICS GROUP

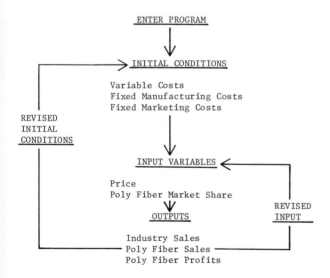

---

[4]Academic users have reported some problems with manu-facturer's program libraries [6].

The program user inputs price and Poly Fiber's expected market share and obtains industry sales, Poly Fiber sales, and Poly Fiber profits. The calculator's conditional branching logic allows a step function for fixed manufacturing and marketing costs and the user can calculate a profit maximizing price under different marketing programs. It would not be difficult to program the calculator to solve directly, rather than through successive price inputs, for the optimum price, but this would likely reduce the quality of the learning experience by producing a single answer under somewhat doubtful assumptions regarding competitive response.

Fanta Chemical Company (Figure 5)

Fanta must plan ethyl glycol production expansion based on knowledge of past trends and expert opinion of the future growth rates of motor vehicle sales, radiator size, ethyl glycol share of the anti-freeze market, and their own market share. The program uses an exponential growth model based on expert opinion of the growth rates. The user can request the total ethyl glycol demand and Fanta's market share and demand for any future year. The user may then question and revise any of the expert opinions and calculate a new forecast. If the user prefers to use past data to project trends, library programs can be used to fit linear or other relationships.

FIGURE 5

FANTA CHEMICAL COMPANY

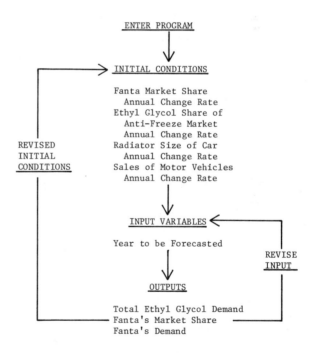

FUTURE OPPORTUNITIES

Computer programs often require substantial investments of development time. Most faculty are reluctant to make this investment and seek packaged programs, if they even use the computer. Packaged programs often do not fit one's teaching style.[5] The programmable calculator permits easy creation and "personalization" of programs to an individual's teaching style. As a result programming concepts and approaches to case analysis are more valuable than the actual programs.

Anyone with modest programming ability would quickly be tempted to revise an existing program to meet his specific needs.[6] Program exchange, therefore, is much more flexible than with computer programs since each user is likely to make personalized revisions. Several channels for program exchange currently exist. Programmable calculator manufacturers offer user's exchanges. A more useful means of exchange for calculator assisted cases is the Intercollegiate Case Clearing House where Teaching Notes can be written supplementing cases.

Due to their current moderate cost the initial use of programmable calculators is likely to be achieved by teachers performing in-class demonstration analysis of cases which students have analyzed. Variables can be revised rapidly allowing many "what if" questions to be answered. The calculator display can be picked up in low light by a television camera with a zoom lens allowing calculator demonstrations to be viewed remotely or video-taped.

Expanded use of programmable calculators can be accomplished through the use of slave printers which permit the calculator to be locked down. Calculator and printer can be purchased far more cheaply than any terminal device for either laboratory or home check-out use.

Considering the calculator power-price history relationship it is quite possible that widespread student use of programmable calculators will occur before or shortly after this paper is published. Student use of programmable calculators could substantially reduce the "number crunching" aspects of case analysis, leave the more substantive issues, and make modelling a commonplace activity. When faculty are more concerned with the student learning relationships than programming, program listings and directions may be distributed with the case. The student can then rapidly key in the program, test it and use it in his analysis.

## CONCLUSIONS

A rapid diffusion of programmable calculators into management as a result of a dynamic power-price relationship will place substantial logic and computing power literally in the hands of most managers. As educators and professional developers we are challenged to educate future and present managers in the effective use of this power. Pro-

grammable calculator assisted cases provide a natural setting for use of this innovation. If the student becomes involved with the case material the use of calculators and reasonable models are likely to be viewed as a natural part of analysis.

## REFERENCES

1. Aaker, David A. and Charles B. Weinberg. "Interactive Marketing Models." Journal of Marketing, (October 1975), 16 - 23.

2. Bursk, Edward C. and Steven A. Greyser. Advanced Cases in Marketing Management. Englewood Cliffs, N.J., Prentice-Hall, Inc., 1968.

3. Day, George S., Gerald T. Eskin, David B. Montgomery, and Charles B. Weinberg. Cases in Computer and Model Assisted Marketing: Planning. Cupertino, California, Hewlett-Packard, 1975.

4. Day, George S., David B. Montgomery, and Charles B. Weinberg. "New Tools For Teaching Marketing: Computer and Model Assisted Cases." Stanford University Graduate School of Business Research Paper Number 253, 1975.

5. Eskin, Gerald J. and David B. Montgomery. Cases in Computer and Model Assisted Marketing: Data Analysis. Cupertino, California, Hewlett-Packard, 1975.

6. "Tiny Computers that Speed Business Decisions." Business Week, (January 10, 1977), 40 - 44.

---

[5]S.P.S.S. is one of the most widely used and most flexible of computer program packages. Even so the programmable calculator is a useful alternative for rapid statistical analysis, such as T-Tests, with small amounts of data.

[6]Programming these calculators, while a good deal easier than many computers from conceptualization to testing, is still a highly personal matter. As a result time estimates of program creation or revision are generally quite unreliable.

DYNAMIC CHANGES IN AN EXPECTANCY-VALUE ATTITUDE MODEL
AS A FUNCTION OF MULTIPLE EXPOSURES TO PRODUCT INFORMATION[1]

Philip A. Dover, The Pennsylvania State University
Jerry C. Olson, The Pennsylvania State University[2]

## ABSTRACT

This study examined the cognitive effects of information
derived from advertising and product trial measured in
terms of a multi-attribute, expectancy-value, attitude model. Of particular interest were the changes in the relationships between model components that occurred over time
as a function of information exposure. Substantial increases in the predictive power of the model over time were
obtained, as were changes in other cognitive relationships.
Implications and future research directions are discussed.

## INTRODUCTION

Innumerable attempts have been made to test the basic expectancy-value (E-V), multi-attribute attitude model in
marketing contexts [21]. Unfortunately, much of this
research contains serious flaws, including misspecifica-
tions and improper operationalization of the E-V model components and disregard of the theory underlying the model
[see 4, and especially 14]. In addition to these common
problems, this research evidences other similarities.
Very few of these multi-attribute model studies were experimental in the sense that the effects of manipulating
components of the model were investigated (see [12, 13]
for an exception). Virtually all of these studies were
static in that the cognitive states comprising the model
were measured only once for each subject. Few studies
have examined how the components of a multi-attribute model form within each subject and/or change over time as a
function of informational input [17]. Thus, consumer
researchers have not considered the possible dynamic
changes which may occur within the expectancy-value attitude model,[3] as a function of informational exposure or
simply with the passage of time [19].

The present research represents an initial examination of
the possible dynamic changes in the multi-attribute E-V
model. Specifically, this study investigates the formation
of and changes in a cognitive (belief) structure for an
initially unfamiliar brand, over a series of exposures to
product information. This longitudinal approach allowed
multiple tests of the E-V model, one at each informational
exposure. The study also involved two different sources
of product information, marketer dominated advertising and
a consumer's own personal experience with the product,
thus allowing an evaluation of the relative impacts of
these sources on cognitive structure and the attitude model itself. The direct impact of these informational manipulations on specific cognitive elements has been reported
elsewhere [18]. The present paper is more concerned with
the impact of multiple information exposures on the rela-

tionships between the cognitive elements specified in the
E-V model.

## METHODS

### Research Design

Two experimental conditions were created. In group A, the
major experimental manipulation involved five "stages" in
which consumer subjects were exposed to product information.
These five stages provided product information that could
be acquired by the consumers and integrated into their cognitive structures. In stages 1, 2, and 3, consumers were
presented with three different, ad-like communications,
each of which stressed that the product had a specific,
highly salient product characteristic. These messages
were specifically designed to create beliefs that the product possessed this particular attribute. Stage 4 involved
a single product trial or usage experience, while stage 5
involved an extended trial period in which the product was
used in the consumer's home. Members of a second experimental group B received none of the three advertisements,
but did try the product in the same two usage experience
settings. For subjects in both groups, extensive measures
of attitude structure were taken following each informational exposure.

### Subjects

The respondents were 38 married women homemakers recruited
from two social groups in return for a cash payment. Vol-
unteering members of each social group were randomly assigned to either the five- or two-stage experimental conditions (n = 20 and 18, respectively).

### Product Selection

An unfamiliar brand of ground coffee was selected as the
attitude object for several reasons. For the adult housewives used as subjects, coffee has a well-developed but
relatively limited attitude structure in terms of the number of salient belief attributes, thus simplifying the
measurement of each consumer's belief/attitude structure.
Also, because the product was unknown to the research participants, no brand-specific attitudes or beliefs existed
prior to the experiment. Although the actual brand name of
this product was used throughout the experiment to increase
mundane realism, the product is referred to as "coffee" in
this paper.

### Dependent Variables

Because this research required precise and sensitive
measurement of the belief elements in the multi-attribute
model, Ahtola's [1] vector model adaptation of the Fishbein
E-V attitude model was used for this research. Ahtola's
model maintains the theoretical properties of the attitude
model as specified by Fishbein [9], while separating the
strength and content components of the belief construct
[1]. Implementation of Ahtola's procedure requires
detailed knowledge about the major belief dimensions in a
cognitive structure (i.e., the salient product attributes),
plus the discriminable attribute levels or amounts along
each dimension [15]. Once these cognitive aspects are
identified, product beliefs are measured not for a specific
attribute dimension such as sweetness, but for each

---

[1]This study is based upon research conducted for the senior
author's M.S. thesis. Funding was provided by a Research
Initiation Grant to the junior author from the Pennsylvania
State University. We are grateful for the critical comments received from many of our Penn State colleagues and
an anonymous ACR reviewer.

[2]Doctoral candidate and Associate Professor, Marketing
Department, Pennsylvania State University.

[3]This dynamic aspect of attitude or belief structures has
received attention in the social psychology literature
[e.g., 16, 23].

discriminable level or category along that dimension (e.g., not sweet at all, somewhat sweet, very sweet; see [1]). To identify the modally salient dimensions of cognitive structure for ground coffee, extensive interviews were conducted with 20 housewives using a modified Kelly Repertory Grid Procedure [22]. This procedure identified five attributes of ground coffee (bitterness, caffeine content, expense, strength of flavor, and quality consistency) and their respective four or five discriminable levels as the most frequently appearing elements of consumers' cognitive structures [see Table 2 in 17 or 18].

It should be noted that adoption of Ahtola's modification of the Fishbein attitude model requires a minor change in the familiar E-V (or belief-evaluation, $b_i$-$e_i$) model:

$$A_o = \sum_{i=1}^{n} b_i e_i. \tag{1}$$

In using the vector model one must combine the "n" $b_{ij}e_{ij}$ products (corresponding to "n" levels or amounts of the attribute) within each attribute vector "j,"

$$\sum_{i=1}^{n} b_{ij}e_{ij}, \tag{2}$$

and then combine the "m" vector scores (corresponding to the "m" salient attributes),

$$\sum_{j=1}^{m} \sum_{i=1}^{n} b_{ij}e_{ij}. \tag{3}$$

For convenience, the double subscripting is dropped in the remainder of this paper. Models (2) or (3) are obviously indicated by the number of summation signs used.

Ahtola's [1] operational procedures were used to measure the strength of each consumer's belief that the "coffee" possessed each amount or level of each attribute. Consumers assigned 10 points among the 4 or 5 belief levels, $b_{ij}$, of each attribute dimension, j, such that the number of points allocated to each attribute level represented the strength of their belief about the likelihood that the product possessed that particular level of the attribute dimension. In addition to the belief strengths ($b_{ij}$), measures of several other cognitive elements were taken at each experimental stage. These included the evaluative aspect ($e_{ij}$) for each of the 22 belief levels, confidence ($C_j$) in the belief strength ratings for each attribute vector j, the overall evaluation of the "coffee" ($A_o$), and the behavioral intention (BI) to purchase the "coffee."[4]

## Experimental Procedures

To maximize the potential impact on cognitive structure and attitude toward the "coffee," the belief chosen for manipulation was the most salient coffee attribute. The repertory grid analysis identified "bitterness" as the most important characteristic of ground coffee, with the most desirable level sought being "not bitter." Based on this knowledge, three ad-like messages were created, each typed on official-appearing stationery made up with the corporate logo as letterhead and written in nonformal language to simulate advertising copy. Each of the three messages emphasized that the "coffee" had no bitterness. Because no other product attributes were explicitly mentioned in the messages, only beliefs about coffee bitterness were directly manipulated. Although the basic message was the same, each ad was slightly different to provide support for the experimental guise and to minimize suspicions.

Care was taken to devise a credible guise for the study. All respondents were told that the overall aim of the research was to examine how companies introduce new products, with the specific goal of more accurately predicting product success or failure. Subjects in the five-stage condition were told that their reactions to three promotional communications and to the "coffee" itself were desired. Control group respondents were told only that their reactions to tasting the "coffee" were desired. It was stressed to both groups that the experimenter had no specific involvement with, or prior predictions about this particular product and only desired each subject's frank and honest reactions.

The three communications were personally delivered to each experimental group respondent at her home along with a questionnaire containing the dependent variables. Approximately four days intervened between each exposure. Subjects were told to read the communication at their convenience and then immediately complete the questionnaire and mail it back to the researcher in an enclosed envelope. Then, approximately four days after the third exposure, the two social groups met for a regular meeting. At this and the following stage, subjects in conditions A and B were treated identically. During each group's meeting, subjects were taken singly to another room for the tasting of the "coffee."[5] Although all subjects were informed that the coffee had been prepared exactly as specified on the container, in fact, the "coffee" had been prepared using 50% more product than specified by the package directions.[6] In earlier pilot tests this composition had been judged to have substantial bitterness. Thus, the trial experience was intended to cause changes in product beliefs which might, in turn, be evidenced by changes in the E-V attitude model.

For the tasting, each consumer was seated at a table and given one-half cup of black "coffee" (i.e., no cream or sugar was allowed so that the product trial experience was consistent for all respondents). Each consumer was allowed to sip and sample the taste and aroma of the "coffee" for two minutes, following which she responded to a questionnaire containing the same cognitive structure measures described above.

At the conclusion of the initial trial, all participants were given a free one-pound can of "coffee" to take home and use in their own homes. Approximately 10 days later, each subject received by mail another questionnaire containing the same cognitive structure measures as before. When the experimenter arrived about two days later to pick up this questionnaire, subjects were debriefed, paid, and thanked for their participation.

## RESULTS AND DISCUSSION

### Check for Demand Characteristics

Subjects were asked, upon completion of stage 5, to state

---

[4]Belief strength ($b_{ij}$) was measured on a 0-10 scale, $e_{ij}$ was measured on a 7-point scale (-3 to +3), labeled bad-good, $C_j$ was measured on a 5-point scale with bipolar labels "not at all confident" and "very confident," $A_o$ was measured by the average of three, bipolar evaluative scales (good-bad, high quality-low quality, and like very much-dislike very much), and BI was measured on a 5-point scale with bipolar labels "not at all likely to buy" and "very likely to buy." In all cases these variables were coded such that larger numbers indicated stronger or more favorable reactions.

[5]Since subjects from both experimental conditions were present in each social group, the experimenter was blind as to the treatment condition of any given subject.

[6]This manipulation was necessary to accomplish the original purpose of the research—namely, to determine the effects of a negative disconfirmation of pretrial expectations.

their opinions of the research purpose. All essentially repeated the original explanation for the study given them at the time of recruitment. No subjects mentioned that the research might deal with the effects of disconfirming trial experience, with the development of product beliefs, or with changes in cognitions over time or as a function of product trial. Thus, it seems unlikely that the present results are due to direct insight into the true purpose of this research.

## Effects on Specific Cognitive Elements

The direct effects of the informational stages on individual cognitive variables are not of major importance for this paper and have been reported in detail elsewhere [17, 18]. However, for background, they are briefly summarized here.

Beliefs ($b_i$). The information provided in the five stages for experimental group A should most directly affect product beliefs [10], especially the "not-at-all-bitter" belief. One-way ANOVA's were run on the strength ratings for each of the 22 belief levels. Only the "not-at-all-bitter" belief strength varied over the five stages ($F$ = 2.50; $df$ = 4,19; $p <$ .05; see Figure 1). Probing this effect revealed a marginally significant decrease in "not bitter" belief strength after the initial product trial (6.70 to 4.35, $p <$ .10).

Evaluative Aspects of Beliefs ($e_i$). The evaluations associated with each of the 22 product beliefs were stable over the five experimental stages and evidenced no changes (all $p$'s > .10).

Attitudes ($A_O$) and Intentions (BI). Although the pattern of changes in $A_O$ and BI followed that of the not-at-all-bitter belief (see Figure 1), neither $A_O$ nor BI evidenced statistically significant changes over the five stages ($p$'s > .10).

In sum, the multiple exposures to product information produced significant changes in brand beliefs about product bitterness. Similar, but not statistically significant changes were obtained for the other major cognitive variables. Attention is now directed toward the major issue in this paper--the dynamic effect of these cognitive changes and perhaps other time-correlated influences on the relationships described by the multi-attribute, E-V model.

## Effects on E-V Model

Column 1 of Table 1 presents the correlation coefficients for Ahtola's multi-attribute attitude model at each of the experimental stages for the two treatment groups. For group A, the predictive validity of the E-V model increased steadily over successive stages from a not-unusual correlation of .37 to a respectable .78 at the conclusion of the study.[7] That is, the predictive power of the model increased from an $r^2$ of .14 after a single ad exposure (stage 1) to an $r^2$ of .61 after about 3 weeks of varying experiences with the product (stage 5). Group B, with about 10 days of direct product experience, yielded a model $r^2$ of .46 at study's end. Differences between the two conditions at stages 4 or 5, however, were not statistically significant ($Z$ = .610, N.S.; $Z$ = .664, N.S.), due in part to the small sample sizes. Also of immediate interest in Table 1 (column 2) is the steadily increasing relationship between $A_O$ and purchase intentions (BI) over the five stages for Group A. At the end of the five experimental stages, $A_O$ accounted for 90% of the variance in BI compared with an initial 29%. Moreover, the relationship between attitudes and intentions was significantly higher group A than for group B at stage 4 (.93 vs. .49, $Z$ = 3.17, $p <$ .01) and at stage 5 (.95 vs. .63, $Z$ = 2.81, $p <$ .01).

TABLE 1
CORRELATIONS RELEVANT TO MAJOR THEORETICAL
RELATIONSHIPS BETWEEN COGNITIVE VARIABLES

| Experimental Stages | Selected Relationships | | |
|---|---|---|---|
| Group A (n = 20) | $\Sigma\Sigma b_i e_i = A_O$ (1) | $A_O \simeq BI$ (2) | $\Sigma\Sigma (b_i e_i) C_j = A_O$ (3) |
| 1. Ad A | .37 | .54 | .43 |
| 2. Ad B | .39 | .70 | .48 |
| 3. Ad C | .59 | .76 | .66 |
| 4. Initial trial | .64 | .93 | .72 |
| 5. Extended trial | .78 | .95 | .69 |
| Group B (n = 18) | | | |
| 4. Initial Trial | .48 | .49 | .57 |
| 5. Extended Trial | .68 | .63 | .70 |

Note: All correlations in this table are significantly greater than zero ($p <$ .05, one-tailed test).

[7]The authors were unable to find a computational procedure for testing differences among correlations between the same variables measured at different points in time for the same subjects.

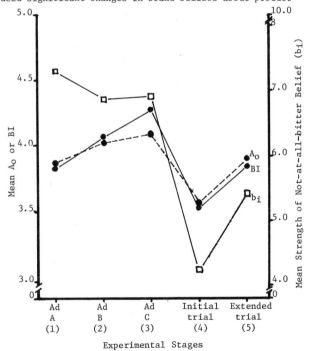

FIGURE 1. CHANGES IN SELECTED COGNITIVE ELEMENTS OVER FIVE EXPERIMENTAL STAGES

If reliable (i.e., replicable in other studies), these dramatic increases over time in the strength of relationships between cognitive structure ($\Sigma\Sigma b_i e_i$) and $A_o$, and $A_o$ and BI, raise several theoretical issues as well as questions about measurement methodology in attitude research. Several possible explanations for the increase in strength of these theoretical relationships are addressed below.

## Measurement Effect

Perhaps the first explanation that a critical reader might propose is that the observed predictable increases are a function of the repeated measures procedures. This possibility is appealing in its simplicity but somewhat lacking in explanatory clarity. That is, it is not readily apparent how the repeated measurements caused the observed increases in $r^2$. For instance, it seems unlikely that the increase was caused by subjects remembering their answers to individual questions from previous measurements and thus becoming (intentionally or unintentionally) more consistent over time. Both the complexity of the questionnaire (many responses) and the rather long time between the measurements (at least four days) argue against such an explanation. Moreover, if this explanation were true, Group A whose members were measured five times should yield a much stronger E-V model correlation than the twice-measured Group B. In fact, however, these correlations were quite similar in magnitude (.78 vs. .68, see Table 1) and not significantly different statistically. Additionally, if a measurement explanation is valid, the intercorrelations between successive time periods for each cognitive element should increase dramatically over the five stages. Table 2 presents these correlations for selected cognitive elements. A consistent pattern of increasing correlations was not obtained. In sum, the basis for "pure measurement" explanation to the present results is not clear. This is not to say, of course, that multiple measurement has no effect. The relative influence of multiple information vs. multiple measurement could be more carefully examined in future longitudinal studies by using control groups whose members are exposed to multiple information, but are not measured until the final stage. This might be supplemented by another control condition whose members are repeatedly measured but who receive no product information.

## Change in Cognitive Structure

A more theoretically interesting, and perhaps more compelling explanation involves the possibility that some dynamic change occurs within the cognitive structure itself as a partial function of processing information derived either from advertisements or from actual product experience. This change would not necessarily be evidenced in the absolute magnitudes or levels of measured cognitive variables but rather might be more subtly represented by the changing interrelationships between cognitions.[8] In fact, in the present study, the cognitive variables increased and decreased over the five stages (see Figure 1), whereas the E-V model validity estimates increased consistently. Perhaps over time, as additional information (either positive or negative) is acquired and integrated with previously stored information about a product, and as the consumer consciously considers her beliefs, attitudes, and intentions (as required in conscientiously completing a questionnaire), there is a tendency for the developing cognitive structure to "mature"--that is, to become more stable and reliable, more "clearly defined," and more internally consistent among its components. This increase in the internal stability of cognitive states and consistency among cognitive cognitive elements would be reflected in an increasing strength of empirical relationships between those cognitive elements, rather than the magnitude or evaluative direction of the cognitive states. Although the present data cannot, of course, be used to rigorously test this post-hoc notion, additional data was collected which is somewhat relevant to this issue.

The present study included measures of confidence in the belief strength allocations among the attribute levels along each vector, yielding five confidence measures at each measurement stage.[9] Table 3 presents these mean confidence ratings for the entire study. One-way ANOVA's of these scores indicated significant increases in confidence for each of the belief vectors over the five experimental stages for Group A (all p's < .10). For all vectors, self-reported confidence was stronger at stage 5 than at stage 1. Moreover, the confidence scores for the five-stage group (after 3 weeks of product "experiences") were stronger than for the two-stage group (after less than 2 weeks experience and no written information about the product) for all vectors except "bitterness" (p's < .10). These changes and differences in confidence are consistent with the proposition that an increasingly "well-defined," more internally consistent cognitive structure develops over time as one becomes more knowledgeable and familiar with the attitude object.

Consistent with previous findings [2], inclusion of confidence as a component in the multi-attribute, E-V model had no significant effects on the predictive power of the model (compare columns 1 and 3, Table 1). Rather, it is suggested that self-reported confidence is best considered as an indication of the clarity with which a consumer holds certain beliefs. Thus, confidence should indirectly reflect the reliability and validity of the belief strength measures. And, to complete the logic, an E-V

---

TABLE 2

CORRELATIONS BETWEEN SUCCESSIVE EXPERIMENTAL STAGES
FOR SELECTED COGNITIVE ELEMENTS

| Cognitive Elements | Experimental Stages--Group A | | | |
| --- | --- | --- | --- | --- |
| | 1-2 | 2-3 | 3-4 | 4-5 |
| $b_i$ | | | | |
| not at all bitter | .54 | .80 | .26 | .60 |
| $e_i$ | | | | |
| not at all bitter | .23 | .33 | .77 | .31 |
| $\Sigma b_i e_i$ | | | | |
| bitterness | .26 | .56 | .10 | .80 |
| caffeine | .56 | .40 | .15 | .60 |
| expense | .39 | .40 | .24 | .21 |
| strength of flavor | .56 | .45 | .46 | .57 |
| consistency | .18 | .30 | .14 | .42 |
| $\Sigma\Sigma b_i e_i$ | .44 | .53 | .48 | .66 |
| $A_o$ | .67 | .74 | .50 | .48 |
| BI | .58 | .88 | .52 | .53 |

Note: Correlations greater than .369 are statistically significant (p < .05).

---

[8]For example, McGuire [16] has discussed dynamic changes over time in the logical consistency among syllogistic beliefs. More recently, Wyer and his colleagues have examined this so-called Socratic effect in some detail [11, 24]. Although the present study does not involve syllogistic beliefs or Socratic effects, a conceptually similar explanation can be advanced for the present results.

[9]The construct of self-reported confidence or certainty in one's belief strength judgments has received research attention in the social psychology literature on belief formation and consistency among beliefs [7, 23]. However, confidence has been only infrequently examined in the consumer behavior area [2].

model should predict $A_O$ more accurately when based on reliable, valid cognitive elements than when not. The pattern of results obtained here is consistent with this interpretation.

TABLE 3

MEAN CONFIDENCE[a] IN BELIEF STRENGTH JUDGMENTS
FOR EACH ATTRIBUTE VECTOR

| Experimental Stages | Belief Vectors | | | | |
|---|---|---|---|---|---|
| Group A (n = 20) | Bitter-ness (1) | Caffeine (2) | Expense (3) | Strength of Flavor (4) | Consistency (5) |
| 1. Ad A | 3.70 | 3.35 | 3.65 | 3.70 | 3.45 |
| 2. Ad B | 3.95 | 3.70 | 4.25 | 4.05 | 3.50 |
| 3. Ad C | 4.15 | 3.75 | 4.10 | 4.05 | 3.80 |
| 4. Initial trial | 4.40 | 3.40 | 3.95 | 4.35 | 4.05 |
| 5. Extended trial | 4.55 | 3.95 | 4.10 | 4.60 | 4.20 |
| Group B (n = 18) | | | | | |
| 4. Initial trial | 4.44 | 2.50 | 2.55 | 3.88 | 2.72 |
| 5. Extended trial | 4.05 | 3.05 | 3.22 | 3.89 | 3.55 |

[a]Confidence scores vary from 1 = not at all confident to 5 = very confident.

## CONCLUSIONS AND IMPLICATIONS

A fitting summary of the results presented above might be to note that more questions have been raised for future research than have been answered. These data identify a number of interesting and heuristic issues about multi-attribute model research specifically, and cognitive structure research in general.

For one, the present results raise the possibility that the typical cross-sectional marketing study using E-V or other multi-attribute attitude models, especially for relatively unfamiliar products or brands, may have tapped into fairly unstable, "vaguely defined" sets of consumer cognitions about the product/brand. If so, the weak model correlations found in many studies (.20 - .40) should not be surprising, even for carefully constructed models. In fact, such weak validity estimates are consistent with those obtained in the early stages of this study when relatively little information was available and when consumers had thought relatively little about the product to be rated.

If the dynamic phenomena observed here are reliable, questions regarding the cause of changes in cognitive structure become salient. From a cognitive theory point of view, the issues raised are fascinating. For example, the present results may reflect that a brand-specific cognitive structure--made up of beliefs, attitudes and intentions--develops or is acquired rather slowly, only as a result of rather substantial processing of information and conscious effort in reviewing and considering the stored information. This notion is not consistent with most attitude acquisition and change literature that seems to assume rather immediate changes in the entire structure upon receiving some information [12].

However, such a view is essentially consistent with a currently popular conceptual perspective in cognitive psychology which proposes that a variety of memory processes can be explained in terms of the "depth" of processing at which the to-be-remembered stimulus was initially processed [5, 6]. The present results may be somewhat clarified by a depth of processing explanation. In this view, the process of receiving and considering product information from either ads or trial and the act of completing the questionnaire about the product literally forces the consumer to process the information at a rather "deep" (i.e., semantic or meaningful) level. That is, a substantial degree of conscious processing effort is demanded of the subject in encoding this product information and integrating it with other information or with one's value system. Several such experiences over time would be expected to create an increasingly well-defined, meaningful, internally consistent cognitive structure which, in turn, should yield increasing model correlations over time.

A related issue involves the impact that actual product trial has on cognitive structure relative to that of other sources of product information. For instance, are attitude and intentions more likely to be closely related after product trial than before?

Space limitations preclude a deeper analysis of these, and other unmentioned issues (e.g., halo effect explanations). Our major purpose in this paper was to identify and briefly discuss an interesting set of data relevant to the E-V model that result from taking a longitudinal approach to the development and modification of cognitive elements. We agree with several others who have suggested that experimental studies [12, 14], and especially longitudinal experiments [20], are the best way to increase our knowledge about multi-attribute attitude models. We further suggest that such an approach may yield interesting and useful findings about broader issues of information processing and cognitive structure.

## REFERENCES

1. Ahtola, Olli T. "The Vector Model of Preferences: An Alternative to the Fishbein Model," Journal of Marketing Research, 12 (February 1975), 52-59.

2. Bennett, Peter D. and Gilbert D. Harrell. "The Role of Confidence in Understanding and Predicting Buyers' Attitudes and Purchase Intentions," The Journal of Consumer Research, 2 (September 1975), 110-117.

3. Campbell, Donald T. and Julian C. Stanley. Experimental and Quasi-Experimental Designs for Research. Chicago: Rand McNally, 1963.

4. Cohen, Joel B., Martin Fishbein, and Olli T. Ahtola. "The Nature of Uses of Expectancy-Value Models in Consumer Attitude Research," Journal of Marketing Research, 9 (November 1972), 456-460.

5. Craik, Fergus I. M., and Robert S. Lockhart. "Levels of Processing: A Framework for Memory Research," Journal of Verbal Learning and Verbal Behavior, 11 (1972), 671-684.

6. Craik, Fergus I. M. and Endel Tulving. "Depth of Processing and the Retention of Words in Episodic Memory," Journal of Experimental Psychology: General, 104 (3, 1974), 268-294.

7. Feldman, Jack M. "Note on the Utility of Certainty Weights in Expectancy Theory," Journal of Applied Psychology, 59 (December 1974), 727-730.

8. Fishbein, Martin. "A Consideration of Beliefs and Their Role in Attitude Measurement," in M. Fishbein ed., Readings in Attitude Theory and Measurement, New York: John Wiley, 1967.

9. Fishbein, Martin. "A Behavior Theory Approach to the Relations Between Beliefs about an Object and the Attitude Towards the Object," in M. Fishbein ed., Readings in Attitude Theory and Measurement, New York: Wiley, 1967, 389-400.

10. Fishbein, Martin and Icek Ajzen. Belief, Attitude, Intention and Behavior, Reading, Mass.: Addison-Wesley, 1975.

11. Henninger, Marilyn and Robert S. Wyer, Jr. "The Recognition and Elimination of Inconsistencies Among Syllogistically Related Beliefs: Some New Light on the 'Socratic Effect,'" Journal of Personality and Social Psychology, 34 (October 1976), 680-693.

12. Lutz, Ricahrd J. "Changing Brand Attitudes Through Modification of Cognitive Structure," The Journal of Consumer Research, 1 (March 1975), 49-59.

13. Lutz, Richard J. "An Experimental Investigation of Causal Relations Among Cognitions, Affect and Behavioral Intention," Journal of Consumer Research, 3 (March 1977), 197-208.

14. Lutz, Richard J., and James R. Bettman. "Multiattribute Models in Marketing: A Bicentennial Review," in A. Woodside, J. N. Sheth, and P. D. Bennett, eds., Foundations of Consumer and Industrial Buying Behavior, New York: American Elsevier, 1977, in press.

15. Mazis, Michael B., Olli T. Ahtola, and Eugene R. Klippel. "A Comparison of Four Multi-Attribute Models in the Prediction of Consumer Attitudes," Journal of Consumer Research, 2 (June 1975), 38-52.

16. McGuire, William J. "A Syllogistic Analysis of Cognitive Relationships," in Milton J. Rosenberg et al., eds., Attitude Organization and Change, New Haven, Conn.: Yale University Press, 1960.

17. Olson, Jerry C. and Philip Dover. "Effects of Expectation Creation and Disconfirmation on Belief Elements of Cognitive Structure," in B. Anderson, ed., Advances in Consumer Research: Vol. III, Cincinnati: Association for Consumer Research, 1976, 168-175.

18. Olson, Jerry C. and Philip A. Dover. "Disconfirmation of Consumer Expectations Trhough Product Trial," Paper No. 53, Working Series in Marketing Research, College of Business Administration, Pennsylvania State University, 1976.

19. Olson, Jerry C. and Andrew A. Mitchell, "The Process of Attitude Acquisition: The Value of a Developmental Approach to Consumer Attitude Research," in M. J. Schlinger ed., Advances in Consumer Research, Vol. II, Chicago: Association for Consumer Research, 1975, 249-264.

20. Sawyer, Alan G. "The Need to Measure Attitudes and Beliefs Over Time: The Case of Deceptive and Corrective Advertising," in K. L. Bernhardt, ed., Marketing: 1776-1976 and Beyond, Chicago: American Marketing Association, 1976, 380-385.

21. Wilkie, William L. and Edgar A. Pessemier. "Issues in Marketing's Use of Multi-Attribute Attitude Models," Journal of Marketing Research, 10 (November 1973), 428-441.

22. Wilson, David T. and Philip Dover. "A Test of the Repertory Grid Technique as a Means of Developing Attributes for Use in Choice Models," Paper No. 34, Working Series in Marketing Research, College of Business Administration, Pennsylvania State University, 1975.

23. Wyer, Robert S., Jr. Cognitive Organization and Change: An Information-Processing Approach. Potomac, Md.: Erlbaum, 1974.

24. Wyer, Robert S., Jr. "Some Implications of the 'Socratic Effect' for Alternative Models of Cognitive Consistency," Journal of Personality, 42 (1974), 399-419.

# LONGITUDINAL DECISION STUDIES USING A PROCESS APPROACH: SOME RESULTS FROM A PRELIMINARY EXPERIMENT

Richard Green, Carnegie-Mellon University
Andrew Mitchell, Carnegie-Mellon University
Richard Staelin, Carnegie-Mellon University

## ABSTRACT

The value of longitudinal decision studies using a process approach is discussed and a simplified choice model with feedback is presented. The results of a preliminary experiment using a longitudinal design indicate that learning and feedback have an effect on the amount of information sought by individuals and that if an individual knows that he will be making more than one decision on the same set of alternatives, it may have an effect on the processing strategy used.

## INTRODUCTION

A major area of research in marketing and consumer behavior has been directed at understanding and predicting the choice behavior of individuals when confronted with a number of alternative stimuli. In the early 1960's, most of the research on the topic centered on predicting choice behavior from either past choice behavior (Massy, Montgomery and Morrison [5]) or individual characteristics such as personality or demographic variables (Frank [3]). Since then most researchers have directed their attention to how individuals select and integrate information about alternative stimuli to reach a choice decision.

We also address these latter questions. Since we are primarily interested in understanding the process that individuals use in making a choice as opposed to simply predicting the choice, we use a process approach as opposed to a static approach (Bettman [1]). However, our research focus differs from previous process studies in that rather than examining the effect of the task environment on the choice strategies used by individuals, we hold this constant and instead look at the effect of learning and feedback.

The next section briefly summarizes the findings of previous research that has used a process approach. Then we discuss the value of a longitudinal design in studying choice behavior and present a simplified model of sequential decision making which provides a foundation for our research. Finally, we present some tentative findings from a pilot experiment.

### Single Decision Studies

A number of studies have examined the case of a single decision--one which is not repeated or, in the case of consumer non-durables, examines only a single decision from a sequence of decisions [2,4,10,12,13,14]. Although space limitations prevent a thorough review of these studies here, we will briefly summarize what we consider to be the important findings of these studies. Later we compare the results of our preliminary study, where relevant, with the results of these studies.

Since the above referenced studies use different methodologies, different types of purchase situations and different methods of analysis, the comparison of results between studies tends to be somewhat difficult. Even so, a number of findings pertaining to the effects of the environment on the choice process seem to be generalizable across studies. Among these are:

(1) As the number of alternatives and attributes increase, individuals use proportionately less of the available information.
(2) When the number of alternatives is large, individuals use a phased strategy--first eliminating some alternatives and then comparing the remaining alternatives.
(3) There are substantial individual differences in the way subjects process information in situations with a large number of alternatives and attributes.
(4) When the acquisition costs associated with a processing-by-attributes strategy and a processing-by-brand strategy are the same, the former seems to be favored by individuals in single decision situations.

Despite these generalizations, many of the specific results, for instance, in the amount of information sought, vary considerably across studies. We believe that some of these differences in results can be explained by using a longitudinal design to examine the learning effects that occur with multiple decisions.[1]

### Longitudinal Decision Studies

In any consumer choice situation where the individual is concerned with satisfying a new need or goal, the individual must go through a number of cognitive operations before making a purchase decision. These include the development of information search, encoding, storage and processing strategies. In other words, the individual must determine what information to acquire, how and where to acquire it, how to interpret this information, how to store it and how to process it in order to reach a decision.

We believe that these steps may change significantly depending on the purchase situation. For instance, we might differentiate between a situation where the individual knows that he or she will be frequently making the same decision on approximately the same set of alternatives and one where an individual makes a choice knowing it will not be repeated on the same set of alternatives.

In the former case, the consumer may concentrate on acquiring and storing information in long term memory for retrieval a number of times in the future as opposed to the latter situation where the consumer may concentrate on developing information search and processing strategies. Also, in the former case, it would seem useful for the individual to develop some overall evaluations of the brands that may be used in future decisions. In situations where the "cost" of information is high and/or the information is considered unreliable (e.g., advertising) individuals may

---

[1] Learning effects can be thought of in two different ways. The first concerns learning to make decisions with the same alternative stimuli. Here much of the learning is based on obtaining information about the alternatives. The second type of learning concerns making a series of decisions on similar, but different alternatives in each decision situation. Here much of the learning is based on learning to process information to make a choice as opposed to obtaining information about the alternatives. In this paper, we are primarily concerned with the first type of learning. See Russo and Dosher [12] for an example of experiments that might be used to examine the second type of learning.

use a simple heuristic to narrow the number of alternatives to an acceptable set ("eliminate nonadvertised brands") and then randomly sample the remaining alternatives (Nelson [6]). In other words, product purchase and use also represents a method of obtaining information; one which, in some respects, provides "perfect" information.

Since these differences between one-shot decisions and repeat decisions may occur, it is important to design studies under both conditions. More specifically, longitudinal studies which concentrate on how consumers make repeated decisions can address a number of interesting issues. Among these are:

(1) The effect of feedback on information processing strategies.
(2) The effect of feedback on the stability and size of the acceptable or evoked set.
(3) The content and form of information stored in memory.
(4) The development of evaluations of alternatives.
(5) How strategies will change under conditions of "risky" and "perfect" information.
(6) Strategies used when the first choice is unavailable.
(7) The effect of minor changes in the available information.
(8) Reaction to new alternatives with respect to the acceptable set and information processing strategies.

In this study, we will direct our attention to the first two issues.

Model of the Multiple Decision Process

In Figure 1, we present a simplified model of the multiple decision process. The model is not meant to be testable, as proposed by Popper [11], or to be a literal representation. Rather, it serves as a guide in developing and presenting our experimental work. The model is a simplified representation of the process in that we expect continued looping backward and forward between the different stages.

At the start of the process (Step 1), an individual is confronted with a situation that requires a choice to be made from a set of alternatives. In Step 2, the individual establishes a cognitive framework for the task. This framework might include determining the importance of the different attributes, what range or combination of values for the attributes might be feasible and how the information should be integrated. At this point, some individuals may use a constructive processing approach (Bettman [1]) by developing a strategy for the first few moves while others may develop a strategy for the entire decision.

After a cognitive framework has been developed, the individual begins to search for information. With a new purchase situation, most of this search will probably be for external information as opposed to information stored in memory.

Previous research suggests that if the set of alternatives is large, then individuals initially eliminate some of the alternatives, thereby forming a reduced set of alternatives (Step 3). At Step 4 the alternatives in the reduced set are more completely evaluated. In the final step (Step 5), one is selected and, in some cases, other acceptable alternatives may be determined, forming an acceptable set. This is where almost all of the previous research has stopped.

However, in most choice situations, certainly in most consumer choice situations, some type of feedback is obtained. The information obtained from feedback (Step 6) may cause individuals to make adjustments in their cognitive framework (Step 7). These adjustments may involve the subsequent use of new attributes, changing the perceived importance of the attributes, or eliminating the previous chosen alternative from the acceptable set.

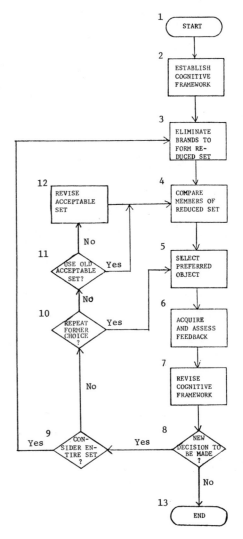

In this preliminary model, feedback will be classified as positive, neutral, or negative. If positive feedback is received, it seems likely that individuals will simply repeat their previous choice, following Steps 9, 10 and then back to Step 5. If an individual receives neutral feedback, he may either select the same alternative again, as with positive feedback, or he may select another alternative from the acceptable set, following Steps 9, 10, 11 and then back to Step 4. It seems rather unlikely that, after receiving neutral feedback, the individual would reconsider the entire set of alternatives. If the individual receives negative feedback, he may either select another alternative from the acceptable set, as with neutral feedback, or he may choose to reconsider the entire choice set, following stage 9 to stage 3.

RESEARCH DESIGN

The purpose of our preliminary experiment was to test our experimental design and measurement devices while getting an initial understanding of how subjects would react to feedback.

In this longitudinal design subjects first acquired information about the alternatives from an information board and then selected an alternative. Up to this point, the basic design is similar to the work of Jacoby et. al. [4], Payne

[10], Bettman and Jacoby [2] and Staelin and Payne [14]. However, after this choice subjects received feedback[2] about their decision, and then were told to seek as much information as they desired to come to another decision.[3]

Since one of the major goals of the study was to examine learning effects, an unfamiliar choice situation was used in order to maximize learning and minimize the use of information already stored in memory. Because we wanted to encourage substantial information acquisition during the second choice process, subjects were given negative feedback concerning their first choice.

A potential problem with information board procedures is that subjects may store some or all of the acquired information in long term memory and then access this internally stored information during the decision making process. In such cases, the information tracing procedure will not capture the actual processing strategy used by the subjects to reach a decision. It is possible, however, to examine to what extent internal memory was used and how the information was encoded by asking subjects to recall information about the alternatives after making a decision. This recall measure should be taken only after the final decision since earlier questioning or forewarning might suggest to subjects that they are being tested on how much information they can memorize.

The subjects were a convenience sample of non-academic staff and graduate students at Carnegie-Mellon University. The results of 14 subjects were analyzed in this preliminary study.

Description of Task

Subjects were asked to imagine that they had been assigned to a special project group that has been designing a new electronic product and will soon be building prototypes for testing.

Subjects were then presented with an information board describing ten resistors that "met basic engineering specifications". Each resistor differed along four attributes (life, stability, delivery time and supplier reputation) described in simple, non-technical terms to insure that they would be comprehensible to the subjects despite the technical nature of the product. The resistor descriptions were designed so that no single resistor dominated all other resistors and in fact all resistors would receive an equal total score if all attributes were weighted equally. Our procedures are similar to those of Jacoby et. al. [4] and Payne [10] in that the information describing each alternative on each attribute was on a card mounted face

down on the board. To examine a specific piece of information, a subject took a card from the information board, looked at it and then placed it face down on a spindle, thereby recording the sequence in which he acquired information. Each cell of the information board contained a number of identical cards, enabling subjects to obtain the same information several times.

After seeking as much information as they desired, the subjects placed an order for one brand of resistors and then were asked to name any other resistors that they considered acceptable. After providing this information, subjects received negative, attribute-specific feedback on their choice, the attribute being the one on which the chosen resistor rated most poorly. (Each resistor had an attribute on which it had the poorest possible rating.) The feedback was purposely neither critical of the subject nor threatening to him.[4]

After receiving the feedback, the subjects were asked to place a new order for a second batch of resistors needed for additional test models. They were again allowed to seek additional information which was recorded as described above. After obtaining as much information as they desired, subjects again selected a single resistor and recorded all acceptable alternatives. Finally, they were given a questionnaire which attempted to obtain additional information about the strategies used, the amount of information remembered about the chosen resistors, the respondent's shopping habits, and some demographics.

RESULTS

The analysis of the choice decisions followed the general framework suggested by Jacoby et. al. [4] in that the depth and sequence of the information acquired was examined. However, since the experiment was longitudinal we were also able to explore such issues as the reaction to feedback and the effect of the acceptable set on the processing strategy for the second decision.

Depth of Information Acquisition

Four measures were taken of each subject's depth of information acquisition: (a) number of pieces of information sought, (b) percent of available information examined, (c) repeat information as a percent of total information acquired and (d) cells examined more than once as a percent of available information. These variables are shown in Tables 1 and 2 for the first and second decisions respectively. These data show that considerably less external information acquisition took place during the second decision (the mean number of cards sought was 69 for the first choice and only 11 for the second choice), suggesting that the extent of external search is strongly influenced by the subject's prior experience with the choice situation.

Care must be taken in comparing our results with previous experiments since the choice situation and/or the process tracing methodology is not constant across experiments. However, some comparison is possible. Bettman and Jacoby

---

[2]If the feedback is verbal or written (as it was in this experiment) it might be thought of as varying along two dimensions. The first of these would be defined by a continuum from very positive to very negative. The zero point might be thought of as the absence of feedback. The second dimension would be whether the feedback was specific to a particular attribute or general in nature. For instance, if the product category was soft drinks and the attributes were sweetness, carbonation and flavor, feedback that was attribute-specific might say that one alternative was too sweet, while general feedback might simply state that an alternative had a poor taste. In the latter case, the subject must try to interpret the general information in terms of specific attributes.

[3]This basic design can, of course, be generalized to make the situation more realistic. For instance, the information might be in the form of a realistic message from neighbors or advertisements, the pause between decisions may be as long as two weeks and the feedback may involve actually having individuals use the selected product (see Olson and Dover [9] for an example of a more realistic longitudinal experiment of this type).

[4]An example of feedback for a subject that had selected a resistor with poor supplier reputation would be as follows: First, the subject would be informed that the initial tests "were quite successful", that the project was going well and that it was time to order another batch of resistors "to build a few assembly prototypes". Next, the feedback specific to the attribute supplier reputation was given. "As far as these resistors go, the test was OK, but we had some trouble with the supplier. They sent us 2,000 resistors and even though we returned the extra 1,000 resistors, they billed us for 2,000. They corrected that, of course, and promised not to let it happen again."

[2], using an identical methodology reported a mean search length of 11 for consumers selecting among cereals which were identified by brand name. One might hypothesize that the second purchase decision in our experiment closely paralleled the cereal experiment since in both situations the subjects were familiar with the available alternatives. In fact, the average depth of search is almost identical in both situations.

## TABLE 1

### DEPTH OF INFORMATION ACQUISITION

#### First Decision

| Sub-ject | Number of Cards Sought | Cells Examined (% of all Cells | Repetition Measure 1 | Repetition Measure 2 |
|------|------|------|------|------|
| 1 | 55 | 82.5 | 40.0 | 42.5 |
| 2 | 49 | 75.0 | 38.8 | 37.5 |
| 3 | 27 | 52.5 | 22.2 | 15.0 |
| 4 | 30 | 67.5 | 11.1 | 7.5 |
| 5 | 89 | 100.0 | 55.1 | 77.5 |
| 6 | 41 | 65.0 | 36.6 | 30.0 |
| 7 | 32 | 57.5 | 28.1 | 20.0 |
| 8 | 101 | 87.5 | 65.3 | 52.5 |
| 9 | 191 | 100.0 | 79.1 | 97.5 |
| 10 | 37 | 62.5 | 32.4 | 22.5 |
| 11 | 111 | 100.0 | 64.0 | 82.5 |
| 12 | 75 | 100.0 | 46.7 | 57.5 |
| 13 | 61 | 92.5 | 39.3 | 47.5 |
| 14 | 68 | 85.0 | 50.0 | 60.0 |
| Mean | 69 | 80.4 | 43.5 | 46.6 |

Legend: Repetition Measure 1: Repeat cards (% of all cards acquired).
Repetition Measure 2: Cells examined more than once (% of all cells).

## TABLE 2

### DEPTH OF INFORMATION ACQUISITION

#### Second Decision

| Sub-ject | Number of Cards Sought | Cells Examined (% of all Cells) | Repetition Measure 1 | Repetition Measure 2 |
|------|------|------|------|------|
| 1 | 6 | 15.0 | 0.0 | 0.0 |
| 2 | 2 | 5.0 | 0.0 | 0.0 |
| 3 | 18 | 42.5 | 5.0 | 2.5 |
| 4 | 0 | --- | --- | --- |
| 5 | 13 | 32.5 | 0.0 | 0.0 |
| 6 | 0 | --- | --- | --- |
| 7 | 0 | --- | --- | --- |
| 8 | 21 | 30.0 | 42.9 | 15.0 |
| 9 | 3 | 5.0 | 33.3 | 2.5 |
| 10 | 12 | 25.0 | 16.7 | 5.0 |
| 11 | 4 | 7.5 | 25.0 | 2.5 |
| 12 | 28 | 55.0 | 21.4 | 15.0 |
| 13 | 34 | 75.0 | 11.8 | 10.0 |
| 14 | 13 | 32.5 | 0.0 | 0.0 |
| Mean | 11.3 | 23.9 | 11.1 | 3.8 |

Legend: Repetition Measure 1: Repeat cards (% of all cards acquired).
Repetition Measure 2: Cells examined more than once (% of all cells).

Staelin and Payne [14] conducted an experiment concerning the selection of hypothetical apartments. However, after turning up a card, their subjects were allowed to see it for the rest of the experiment. Thus, comparing the number of cards sought is not possible, since Staelin and Payne did not record instances where the subject's "resought" information from a turned-up card. However, it is possible to compare percentage of available information sought. They ran 4 by 8 (attributes by brands) and 4 by 12 conditions and reported percentages of 67 and 63 percent respectively. This compares rather closely to our figure of 80 percent if contrasted to the 24 percent observed in the second decision. This suggests that the extent of information search may descrease as task familiarity increases.

Finally, it should be noted from Table 1 that during the first decision all of our subjects re-acquired information already sought. In fact, 44 percent of all cards acquired were repeat cards, which is substantially higher than the 8 percent reported by Bettman and Jacoby [2]. Interestingly, our repeat percentage for the second choice was 11. The high repeat percentage in the first choice situation may be due to our specific instructions not to view the experiment as a test of memory or the relative unfamiliarity of the subjects with resistors as opposed to breakfast cereals. The lower percentage of repeat information on the second decision may indicate that as the subjects became more familiar with the task they were more easily able to store and recall information from long term memory and therefore avoid the "cost" of reacquiring the information from the information board.

### Acceptable Set

The acceptable set of each subject was operationally defined as the set of resistors that the subject reported as being almost as good as the chosen resistor. The size and content of the acceptable set for each decision is given in Table 3. For the first decision four subjects reported a minimal acceptable set (i.e., consisting of the chosen resistor only), six reported an acceptable set of size two, and four reported an acceptable set for size three.

## TABLE 3

### SIZE AND CONTENT OF THE ACCEPTABLE SET

| Sub-ject | First Decision Size of Acceptable Set | Content[a] | Second Decision Size of Acceptable Set | Content[a] |
|------|------|------|------|------|
| 1 | 3 | E(A,F) | 2 | F(E) |
| 2 | 2 | E(G) | 2 | E(G) |
| 3 | 1 | E | 1 | D |
| 4 | 1 | E | 1 | E |
| 5 | 1 | A | 2 | B(E) |
| 6 | 2 | H(F) | 1 | F |
| 7 | 3 | H(B,C) | 1 | H |
| 8 | 2 | D(H) | 2 | F(C) |
| 9 | 2 | F(E) | 1 | E |
| 10 | 1 | B | 2 | I(B) |
| 11 | 3 | C(F,G) | 2 | C(G) |
| 12 | 3 | B(E,G) | 1 | A |
| 13 | 2 | F(E) | 1 | G |
| 14 | 2 | C(G) | 1 | G |

[a]Selected resistor and, in parentheses, resistors reported as being equally or almost as good as the selected resistor.

Of the <u>four subjects naming the minimal acceptable set</u>, only Subject 4 did not revise his cognitive framework on receipt of the negative, attribute-specific feedback ("I discounted that information"). Instead, he simply chose the same resistor in his second decision. The three remaining subjects (Subjects 3, 5 and 10) conducted moderately long second searches (18, 13 and 12 pieces of information, respectively) examining most (8, 10 and 6) of the brands on at least one attribute. All three picked a different resistor than they had previously, although Subject 10 left her original first choice in the acceptable set. These subjects thus exhibited substantial revision of their cognitive framework.

Of the <u>ten subjects who chose a non-minimal acceptable set</u>, seven made their second selection from that set, while three chose resistors from outside their original acceptable sets. These two sub-groups differed markedly in the extent of their second searches. The first seven had a mean search length of 4.0 cards (range zero to 13), while the remaining three had a mean search length of 27.7 cards (range 21 to 34). Furthermore, six of the first seven only examined information about resistors in the original acceptable set (the seventh, Subject 14, examined six brands) while the other three looked very similar to the minimal set group, examining 6, 10 and 8 brands respectively.

A further analysis of three subjects who did not stay within their acceptable set during the second decision indicated that for two of the three subjects, all of their acceptable alternatives happened to have a value on the feedback attribute which was equally bad as the one selected. It appears that negative feedback forced them to revise their cognitive framework sufficiently to start their decision process over. This hypothesis is supported by Newman and Staelin [7, 8] who reported that major durable purchasers who said they were dissatisfied with their previous brand on the average behaved much more like first time purchasers than satisfied previous users.

The above can be summarized as follows. About half of the subjects sought little or no information on their second search and confined that search and choice to their original acceptable set. The other half conducted quite extensive searches over the whole set of objects. The strategy of conducting a limited search on the second decision is strongly associated with the naming of a non-minimal acceptable set of the first decision.

These findings suggest that future research on information processing should recognize that in purchase situations that are familiar, subjects may have already formed acceptable sets and that the existence of these sets can influence significantly the information sought on subsequent decisions. Also, marketing decision makers should recognize that many consumers will limit their search activity to an acceptable set of alternatives unless they receive feedback which causes them to revise their cognitive framework.

Structure of Search

There does not currently seem to be any generally accepted method for measuring a search strategy from the data generated in our type of experiment. In our analysis we first followed an approach suggested by Bettman and Jacoby [2] by calculating a Same Brand Index (SBI) and Same Attribute Index (SAI) for each subject[5] for the first decision situation and found that one subject was classified as processing information by attribute, five by brand and the rest were following a mixed strategy. Not finding these re-

sults particularly insightful, we used an alternative measure suggested by Van Raaij [15]. Under this approach a subject's search pattern is compared against a random search pattern.[6]

The results for the first decision are shown in Table 4. First of all, the hypothesis that the process is random is clearly rejected.[7] Moreover, all but one subject (S4) had significantly more brand pairs than would be expected by chance, indicating that subjects tended to look at more than one attribute of a brand before switching their attention to another brand. Finally, only five of these subjects also showed a tendency to group their acquisition of data by attribute at greater than random levels, as did S4. We thus infer that our subjects' acquisition strategy was in general to seek enough information on a particular brand to form an overall impression of the brand before seeking information pertaining to another alternative. However, if the brand pairs are removed from the analysis, 13 of the 14 subjects had significantly more attribute pairs than expected under a random process. This leads us to believe that subjects tended to use attribute comparisons whenever they were not acquiring overall brand impressions.

TABLE 4

OBSERVED VERSUS EXPECTED PAIR TYPES

First Decision

Observed(Expected) Number of Pairs

| Subject | Attribute Pairs | Brand Pairs | Other Pairs | Total[a] Pairs |
|---|---|---|---|---|
| 1 | 11(11)[b] | 30(4)[c] | 6(33) | 47 |
| 2 | 13(10) | 24(3) | 9(32) | 46 |
| 3 | 13(5) | 10(2) | 1(17) | 24 |
| 4 | 22(6) | 1(2) | 5(20) | 28 |
| 5 | 10(17) | 51(6) | 16(54) | 77 |
| 6 | 11(8) | 22(3) | 4(26) | 37 |
| 7 | 11(7) | 13(2) | 7(22) | 31 |
| 8 | 51(21) | 24(7) | 19(66) | 94 |
| 9 | 37(35) | 111(12) | 11(111) | 159 |
| 10 | 13(8) | 11(3) | 10(24) | 34 |
| 11 | 31(22) | 56(7) | 10(68) | 97 |
| 12 | 16(16) | 42(5) | 11(48) | 69 |
| 13 | 3(11) | 43(4) | 1(33) | 47 |
| 14 | 15(14) | 32(5) | 16(44) | 63 |

[a]Excludes forced switches.   [c]$47 \times .075 = 4$

[b]$47 \times .225 = 11$

We conducted the same analysis for the seven subjects who examined at least 12 cells in the second choice situation (Table 5). It should be noted that prior to this second task, subjects had received feedback specific to a particular attribute, so one might suspect that they would be more sensitive to attribute information.[8] However, all

---

[5]The problem with this approach is that it does not capture the dynamics of the strategy being used. Unfortunately, the other measurement approaches used in the literature (Jacoby, et. al. [4], Russo and Dosher [12]) do not capture this either.

[6]For example, in a 4 x 10 display the probability of a subject picking the same attribute twice in a row (without replacement) is 9/39 or .225. Similarly for a same brand pair the probability is 3/39 or .075.

[7]The chi-squared value was significant at the .01 level for every subject.

[8]It should be noted, however, that all seven of these subjects either had minimal acceptable sets or broadened their search outside of their non-minimal acceptable sets. Consequently, these subjects may, in effect, be starting the decision process again.

seven still sought significantly more brand pairs than one would predict if the process were random. In contrast, three of the four subjects who sought just a few (6 or less) pieces of information for the second decision processed the information almost entirely be attribute.

These results suggest that subjects may favor a processing-by-brand strategy over a processing-by-attribute strategy. The previous single decision studies obtained the opposite findings. We hypothesize that these differing results may be due to the decision situation, a new product, and the fact that respondents knew they would be making the same decision again. When respondents know that they will be repeating a decision they may find it useful to determine brand evaluations for a number of brands. This would be best accomplished by using a processing-by-brand strategy. When respondents are making only a single decision they need only select one brand and with large number of alternatives a processing-by-attribute strategy is easier to execute.

TABLE 5

Second Decision

Observed (Expected) Number of Pairs

| Sub-ject | Attribute Pairs | Brand Pairs | Other Pairs | Total[a] Pairs |
|---|---|---|---|---|
| 3 | 3(3) | 9(1) | 3(11) | 15 |
| 5 | 7(2) | 3(1) | 1(8) | 11 |
| 8 | 7(5) | 7(2) | 6(14) | 20 |
| 10 | 3(2) | 5(1) | 2(7) | 10 |
| 12 | 8(6) | 14(2) | 3(17) | 25 |
| 13 | 0(6) | 25(2) | 1(18) | 26 |
| 14 | 6(3) | 5(1) | 1(8) | 12 |

[a]Excludes forced switches.

SUMMARY

In this paper we have discussed the value of using longitudinal decision studies to understand the effects of learning and feedback on decision strategies, to examine how individuals may encode and store information and to obtain an understanding of the evaluation process. Problems in designing these types of studies were discussed and a simplified model of sequential decision making was presented.

A preliminary experiment was conducted where subjects were placed in an unfamiliar purchase situation and asked to make two decisions on the same set of alternatives and received negative feedback on the first decision. The results indicated that subjects sought substantially less information during the second decision and substantially less repeat information. The amount of information sought prior to the second decision was largely determined by whether an individual formed an acceptable set of more than one brand and if some of the members of the acceptable set were better than the chosen brand on the attribute on which they received negative feedback.

The results also indicated that in this type of choice situation, individuals seem to favor a processing-by-brand strategy as opposed to a processing-by-attribute strategy. These results are the opposite of those found in single decision studies.

In summary, these results indicate that learning and feedback have an important effect on the amount of information sought by respondents. Also whether a single decision or

a sequence of decisions on a set of alternatives is to be made may have an effect on the type of processing strategies used by respondents.

REFERENCES

1. Bettman, James R. A Theory of Consumer Information Processing and Choice. Reading, Massachusetts: Addison-Wesley, forthcoming.

2. Bettman, James R. and Jacob Jacoby. "Patterns of Processing in Consumer Information Acquisition," in B. B. Anderson, ed., Advances in Consumer Research, Vol. III. Chicago: Association for Consumer Research, 1976, 315-320.

3. Frank, Ronald E. "Market Segmentation Research: Findings and Implications," in Frank Bass, et. al., eds., Applications of the Sciences in Marketing Management. New York: John Wiley & Sons, Inc., 1968.

4. Jacoby, Jacob, Robert W. Chestnut, Karl C. Weigl and William Fisher. "Pre-Purchase Information Acquisition: Description of a Process Methodology Research Paradigm, and Pilot Investigation," in B. B. Anderson, ed., Advances in Consumer Research, Vol. III. Chicago: Association for Consumer Research, 1976, 306-314.

5. Massy, William F., David B. Montgomery and Donald G. Morrison. Stochastic Models of Buying Behavior. Cambridge, Mass.: The M.I.T. Press, 1970.

6. Nelson, Phillip. "Information and Consumer Behavior," Journal of Political Economy, 78 (1970), 311-329.

7. Newman, Joseph W. and Richard Staelin. "Why Differences in Buyer Decision Time--A Multivariate Approach," Journal of Marketing Research, 8 (May 1971), 192-198.

8. Newman, Joseph W. and Richard Staelin. "Prepurchase Information Seeking for New Cars and Major Household Appliances," Journal of Marketing Research, 9 (August 1972), 249-257.

9. Olson, Jerry C. and Philip Dover. "Effects of Expectation Creation and Disconfirmation on Belief Elements of Cognitive Structure," in B. B. Anderson, ed., Advances in Consumer Research, Vol. III. Chicago: Association for Consumer Research, 1976, 168-175.

10. Payne, John W. "Task Complexity and Contingent Processing in Decision Making: An Information Search and Protocol Analysis," Organizational Behavior and Human Performance, 11 (1976).

11. Popper, Karl. The Logic of Scientific Discovery. New York: Harper & Row, 2nd Torchbook ed., 1968.

12. Russo, J. Edward and Barbara Anne Dosher. "An Information Processing Analysis of Binary Choice," Pittsburgh: Carnegie-Mellon University, 1976.

13. Russo, Edward J. and Larry D. Rosen. "An Eye Fixation Analysis of Multialternative Choice," Memory & Cognition, 3 (1975), 267-76.

14. Staelin, Richard and John W. Payne. "Studies of the Information Seeking Behavior of Consumers," in John Carroll and John Payne, eds., Cognition and Social Behavior. New York: Erlbaum Assoc., 1976, 185-202.

15. Van Raaij, Fred W. "Consumer Information Processing for Different Information Structures and Formats," in W. D. Perreault, Jr., ed., Advances in Consumer Res., Vol. IV. Chicago: Association for Consumer Res., 1977, 176-184.

# CONSUMER JUDGMENT ANALYSIS

Robert B. Settle, San Diego State University
James R. Beatty, San Diego State University
John V. Kaiser, Jr., San Diego State University

## ABSTRACT

A judgment analysis model for capturing consumer buying
policies is presented and evaluated. The project example
uses eleven fictitious brands of pocket calculators with
five characteristics used as regression predictor
variables and ratings from 54 respondents of likelihood to
purchase used as dependent variables. Consumer buying
policy consistency is measured, and the consumers are
segmented by a hierarchical clustering process into four
homogeneous and distinct segments. Self-reported policies
are compared with those revealed by the model; the capabilities and limitations of the model for segmentation are
cited; and future applications are suggested.

## INTRODUCTION

Market segmentation has become increasingly important to
marketing managers in recent years. Some firms still provide their public with a single "universal product" for
the "average customer" because they consciously reject the
concept of segmentation. Many other firms recognize the
wisdom of segmentation, but the success of its application
depends on the ability of the marketer to partition
product markets into segments characterized by consumers
with homogeneous buying policies. This paper presents
and evaluates a relatively new policy capturing technique,
Judgment Analysis [1], with emphasis on its application as
a method of identifying market segments.

### The Judgment Analysis Model

Judgment models are usually derived by having a group of $J$
judges evaluate a set of $N$ objects based on a previously
quantified set of $K$ profile characteristic values. The $K$
profile values are then used as independent (predictor)
variables and the $N$ ratings or judgments as dependent
variables in a standard multiple regression analysis. For
each $J$, a set of $K$ regression weights plus a constant term
are obtained. The weights associated with the independent
variables or characteristics represent estimates of the
judge's "model" or "policy," while the square of the
multiple correlation coefficient (RSQ) provides a measure
of variance explained in the judge's policy by a knowledge
of each characteristic variable.

The use of the scientific method of studying human judgmental processes began in clinical psychology and
philosophy, with earliest efforts focusing on accuracy of
estimates and the degree to which linear regression models
could represent judgments [4,5,6,9,11,12,13,15,16,17].
Slovic and Lichtenstein [18] provide a summary of applications of the linear regression model, including judgment
topics such as personality characteristics [6,9], performance in college [2,3,14,16], performance on the job
[11,13], attractiveness of common stocks [17], other types
of risky decisions or gambles [18], quality of patient
care in hospitals [8], physical and mental pathology
[4,7,15,21], and legal decisions [10,20].

In the studies cited above, some judgment tasks were
familiar to the judges while others were not, some were
artificial situations while others were real; yet typical
RSQ values ranged from the .70's to the .90's. Thus the
linear regression model appears to provide satisfactory
representation of more complex real-world situations for
a wide variety of circumstances and topics.

### Judgment Analysis (JAN)

JAN was developed by Bottenberg and Christal [1], and the
method incorporates both regression analysis and one form
of hierarchical grouping. The technique first evaluates
the judges' policies by determining regression weights for
each of the various characteristics of the object which
serve as independent variables. It then clusters the
judges into groups beginning with J-1 groups in the first
iteration and continuing through a series of steps until
all are grouped into a single cluster. At each step in
the clustering procedure, JAN considers all the $J(J-1)/2$
possible pairs of judges, where J represents the number of
judges. For each possible pairing, the RSQ value is
obtained, and these values are sequentially compared. The
pairing resulting in the least loss of predictive value is
identified and consummated by calculation of a new regression equation for the combination. At any step, one individual judge may be combined with another, one judge may
be combined with a group, or one group may be combined
with another group.

### Product Judgments

Judgment Analysis appears to be particularly applicable
for studying buying decisions. The regression would furnish a measure of the value each individual places on each
product characteristic and the clustering would congregate
buyers into relatively homogeneous segments on the basis
of their decision policies. Within this context, J consumers would judge $N$ products (or brands) on the basis of
$K$ characteristics or attributes. The decision policies
of each segment and their relative consistency and homogeneity could be studied in this way.

## METHODOLOGY

To present and evaluate the JAN technique for studying
consumer judgment policies and segmenting markets, a self-
administered questionnaire was prepared to present the
product alternatives. Responses were obtained from 54
undergraduate business students, and these were submitted
to the JAN program and other statistical analyses.

### Product and Attributes

The products selected for this project were "pocket" calculators. Eleven fictitious "brands" of electronic calculators were described in terms of five attributes: the
price in dollars, the number of digits shown on the display, the presence or absence of a power function, the
number of special functions or single-stroke buttons to
calculate special numeric values, and the number of
addressable storage registers. These are shown in
Table 1, with the values of the predictor variables for
regression. The yes-no values are expressed as one-zero
dummy variables.

Table 1

FICTITIOUS CALCULATOR PRODUCT CHARACTERISTICS

| Characteristics | Calculators | | | | | | | | | | |
|---|---|---|---|---|---|---|---|---|---|---|---|
| | 1 | 2 | 3 | 4 | 5 | 6 | 7 | 8 | 9 | 10 | 11 |
| Price | 39 | 49 | 49 | 59 | 59 | 99 | 159 | 159 | 159 | 169 | 179 |
| Number of Digits | 6 | 8 | 6 | 8 | 8 | 8 | 6 | 10 | 8 | 10 | 10 |
| Power Function | No | No | Yes | Yes | No | Yes | Yes | Yes | No | Yes | Yes |
| Special Function | 0 | 0 | 0 | 0 | 0 | 1 | 8 | 4 | 8 | 8 | 8 |
| Registers | 1 | 1 | 1 | 1 | 2 | 2 | 4 | 4 | 2 | 2 | 4 |

Table 2

CORRELATIONS AMONG PREDICTOR VARIABLES

| | Price | Digits | Power | Special | Storage |
|---|---|---|---|---|---|
| Price | 1.00 | 0.58 | 0.42 | 0.94 | 0.81 |
| Number of Digits | | 1.00 | 0.26 | 0.40 | 0.41 |
| Power Functions | | | 1.00 | 0.28 | 0.43 |
| Special Functions | | | | 1.00 | 0.69 |
| Storage Registers | | | | | 1.00 |

In the "real world" there is ordinarily a high degree of covariance between price and several attributes of any given product. Since the attribute value profiles become the predictor variables for regression, this multi-colinearity can seriously jeopardize the stability of the beta weights obtained from the regression. The fictitious brands used in this study were patterned after actual brand alternatives, but attributes were modified to some extent to lower the intercorrelations of predictor variables within the constraints of acceptable face validity for the respondents. The correlation matrix is shown in Table 2. Further, the ratio of five characteristics to eleven calculators will tend to take considerable advantage of chance. Such a ratio is not of concern here, as the example is only used as an illustration of the technique; however, in actual practice a more appropriate ratio would be required, as with any regression model.

Questionnaire and Administration

A three-part questionnaire was used to obtain the data. Part one contained questions about the respondents' academic background and characteristics. Part two contained the listing of fictitious calculators and their characteristics. To avoid order bias, the computer-generated questionnaire listed both the brands and the characteristics in random order for each respondent. Judges recorded their probability of purchase for each brand by using a ten point scale, ranging from zero to nine. Part three of the questionnaire again listed the descriptions of the various characteristics of the product. Respondents were asked to apportion a total of 100 points to each of the five characteristics according to their importance to him or her. In this way, the self-rated importance of characteristics was obtained so that these ratings could be compared with the regression weights calculated by JAN.

The questionnaires were group administered to 56 undergraduate business students at this university. Two failed to comprehend the instructions or complete the instrument properly; thus, they were excluded from the respondent group. The remaining 54 responses were substantially complete, and they constitute the sample used for analysis.

Statistical Analysis

The pre-coded data were edited, keypunched, verified, and submitted to the JAN program and other appropriate statistical analyses. Within JAN, each respondent was treated as a "judge," each characteristic profile value as an independent or predictor variable for regression, and each fictitious brand of calculator rated was treated as a "case." Thus, there were 54 judges rating 11 cases on 5 predictor variable characteristics.

The JAN program first calculated individual regression coefficients for each respondent for each characteristic, plus individual RSQ values and a composite RSQ value for all respondents taken separately. Next, the hierarchical procedure was employed, combining the two respondents who were most similar in their policies, so as to minimize the decrement in explained variance. The procedure continued to combine individual and group "systems" from the full model of 54 individual systems to the final step of one system containing all 54 in a single group.

At each step in the grouping process, the composite RSQ value, the decrement from the previous step, the decrement from the full model RSQ, the RSQ for each group system, and the group memberships were reported, together with other details. Such information permitted identification of steps with radical decrements in the composite RSQ value, indicating combinations of respondents with widely differing evaluation policies, identification of segments containing homogeneous policies, and calculation of the regression coefficients for individual segments that differed from one another. Identification of market segments is, then, a subjective judgment on the part of the analyst, but it is based on quantified assessment of the similarity or dissimilarity of buying policies.

In addition to the segmentation derived from the JAN procedure, the self-rated importance of various product characteristics were rank correlated with the regression coefficients for each respondent obtained from regression analysis. This procedure was performed to assess the degree to which the individual was cognizant of his or her own buying policies and the degree to which he or she could or would report them accurately.

## RESULTS

The results of the analysis are oriented around four fundamental questions: Can JAN adequately capture the buying policies of consumers? Can JAN cluster consumers into segments, with similar buying policies within groups and distinct policies among groups? Which product characteristics are important to each segment? Can consumers adequately identify and report their own buying policies? Each set of results will be presented in turn.

Individual Buying Policies

A summary of the distribution of RSQ values obtained from regression for individual buyers is presented in Table 3. Based on the criteria suggested by Slovic and Lichtenstein [18], only 13% of the sample provided inadequate consistency. With over two thirds of the sample in the clearly acceptable range, it appears that the individual regressions within JAN can adequately capture the buying policies of this set of individual consumers. The results provide an adequate basis for clustering consumers into segments.

If the investigator so desires, tests of significance could be computed for individual RSQ values. However, since the present data were generated for the expressed purpose of illustrating the JAN technique, such tests are irrelevant, and the approach suggested by Slovic and Lichenstein seems useful for discussion purposes. Of course, it should again be noted that the eleven to five ratio of cases to variables tends to provide an overfit of the data; actual applications would hopefully use a more appropriate ratio.

Table 3

INDIVIDUAL RSQ VALUES

| Degree | Range | Number | Percent |
|---|---|---|---|
| Acceptable | $.70 \leq RSQ \leq 1.00$ | 36 | 67 |
| Marginal | $.50 \leq RSQ \leq .70$ | 11 | 20 |
| Inadequate | $.00 \leq RSQ \leq .50$ | 7 | 13 |

Clustering Consumers into Segments

A summary of the RSQ values and losses during the last ten steps of the clustering sequence is shown in Table 4. The first row of the table contains the information for the full model of 54 individuals; the remaining rows summarize only the last ten steps, since more segments than ten would be completely impractical. Inspection of the incremental drop in RSQ at each step reveals a very sharp decrement from four to three groups. Such a marked change in the trend of incremental drops from one stage to another would tend to indicate that a point has been reached when two rather heterogeneous groups have been clustered together. Consequently, the preceding set of clusters should be used, since the objective is to identify groups with similar buying policies.

Buying Policies by Segment

The four segments identified for further study are described in Table 5. Inspection of the percentage distribution of the sample into the segments indicates the largest segment contains over one third of the market and the smallest contains fifteen percent. The largest segment contains over one third of the market and the smallest contains fifteen percent. The largest segment also contains the highest percent of explained variance, with 74% explained. The values of the standardized regression coefficients and the unique contributions of the variables in the full models provide a sketch of the policies of the four segments. Uniqueness of product characteristics can be evaluated by examining the contribution of each individual variable to each full regression model. Such contributions are determined by subtracting the RSQ obtained from the restricted model (based upon all variables except the one of interest) from the RSQ obtained from the full model. Since the predictor variables are not orthogonal, standardized regression weights need to be compared to their appropriate standard error terms. However, an examination of the uniqueness of variables allows for the same interpretation. The unique RSQ losses and the standardized regression weights are presented in Table 5.

Table 4

SUMMARY OF RSQ LOSS IN GROUPING

| Groups Remaining | Cumulative RSQ | Incremental Drop in RSQ | Cumulative Drop in RSQ |
|---|---|---|---|
| 54 | .7971 | .0000 | .0000 |
| . | . | . | . |
| . | . | . | . |
| . | . | . | . |
| 10 | .6534 | .0144 | .1437 |
| 9 | .6387 | .0147 | .1584 |
| 8 | .6257 | .0150 | .1743 |
| 7 | .6072 | .0165 | .1900 |
| 6 | .5868 | .0240 | .2343 |
| 5 | .5628 | .0240 | .2343 |
| 4 | .5368 | .0260 | .2343 |
| 3 | .4839 | .0538 | .3141 |
| 2 | .4231 | .0598 | .3739 |
| 1 | .0920 | .3313 | .7057 |

Table 5

MARKET SEGMENTATION STATISTICS

| Group | J | % | Z Weights | | | | |
|---|---|---|---|---|---|---|---|
| | | | Price | Digits | Power | Spec. Func. | Storage |
| I | 19 | 35 | 0.4273 | 0.1879 | 0.2847 | 0.0347 | 0.1379 |
| II | 8 | 15 | 2.4657 | -0.4944 | 0.3490 | -1.8646 | -0.4007 |
| III | 13 | 24 | 0.3591 | 0.0849 | 0.1782 | -0.7374 | -0.2497 |
| IV | 14 | 26 | -0.7914 | 0.1552 | 0.1482 | -0.0602 | 0.1147 |

| Group | Full RSA | Unique RSQ Loss | | | | |
|---|---|---|---|---|---|---|
| | | Price | Digits | Power | Spec. Func. | Storage |
| I | .7398 | .0025 | .0133 | .0521 | .0002 | .0053 |
| II | .4611 | .1274 | .0802 | .0760 | .1381 | .0377 |
| III | .2998 | .0038 | .0014 | .0183 | .0245 | .0156 |
| IV | .4088 | .0134 | .0082 | .0134 | .0001 | .0032 |

The decision policy of Segment I hinges around the existence of power functions on the calculator, while the number of digits and storage registers are also important. Segment II tends to evaluate price and the number of digits and storage registers are also important. Segment II tends to evaluate price and the number of digits somewhat more than other characteristics, but considers everything. Segment III looks most to the special functions, although the overall RSQ for this segment is rather low. Segment IV appears to consider only price and the availability of power functions.

The RSQ values for each segment indicate fairly homogeneous individuals within segments. The configuration of unique contributions of predictors indicates heterogeneity of decision policies among groups. The differences among segments are also revealed in the drop in cumulative RSQ value when the sample is clustered into less than four segments. These results seem to indicate that JAN is able to capture buying policies for individuals, cluster consumers into segments with similar buying policies, and reveal which characteristics are important to each segment.

Self-reported Policies

Respondents were asked to indicate the rating of importance of each of the five characteristics of calculators. These ratings were rank ordered for each individual, as were the standardized regression coefficients for characteristics. Table 6 summarizes the results, showing that 80% of the RSQ values were below .50. If the regression coefficients are regarded as the criteria, this indicates that the vast majority of respondents were unaware of their policies or would not report them accurately. On the other hand, the multicolinearity among characteristic variables mentioned earlier may have distorted the true rank order values of the regression weights, making further analysis difficult for this example.

Table 6

REGRESSION COEFFICIENTS VS. SELF-REPORTS

| Percent | Range[a] | Number | Percent |
|---|---|---|---|
| Acceptable | $.70 \leq RSQ \leq 1.00$ | 6 | 11 |
| Marginal | $.50 \leq RSQ \leq .70$ | 5 | 9 |
| Inadequate | $.00 \leq RSQ \leq .50$ | 43 | 80 |

[a]Spearman Rank Order RSQ ranges for individuals.

CONCLUSIONS

The results of this project indicate there is some promise of future success in the use of Judgment Analysis to capture the buying policies of consumers. The process is summarized very briefly below, and a capsule evaluation is presented. Several of the most identifiable limitations are cited, and a few suggestions for future application of the technique are offered.

Summary of JAN

The procedural outline used in this study was:

1. Identify a _few_ of the most salient attributes of the product being considered.

2. Invent a sufficient number of fictitious brands with varying amounts of each attribute.

3. Control the intercorrelations of the values of the attributes within the limitations of face validity.

4. Obtain probabilities of purchase of each brand from a sample of typical consumers, based on descriptions of brands in terms of attributes.

5. Perform individual regressions, noting degree of linear consistency for respondents.

6. Perform hierarchical grouping from J groups to one group, noting losses in consistency at each step.

7. Select feasible number of market segments, based on (a) incremental drop in consistency and (b) size and number of identifiable segments.

8. Obtain group regression coefficients to indicate group policy, note group consistency, and examine uniquely contributing attributes.

9. Compare self-rated attribute importance with regression coefficients to estimate accuracy of self-reporting.

Evaluation of JAN Segmentation

Evaluation is oriented around the four basic issues:

1. JAN can adequately capture the buying policies of consumers, given that they do use policies.

2. JAN can provide information with which adequately homogeneous and distinct segments can be identified.

3. JAN can assist in the identification of the relative importance of product characteristics for individual segments.

4. JAN can assist in determining whether respondents are capable of reporting accurately their own buying policies.

Limitations to this JAN example

Among the major limitations to this study are these:

1. The study used product descriptions rather than real products.

2. Product attributes used were "functional" rather than comprehensive, so that the effects of factors such as brand loyalty or appearance were eliminated.

3. The respondent sample consisted of college students, rather than the general buying public.

4. The reliability and validity of the data collection remain unproven.

471

5. Only linear, first order effects were comprehended, while interactions and configural effects were ignored.

6. The ratio of cases to predictor variables was eleven to five, resulting in the possibility of an overfit of the data.

## Future Applications

Despite the existence of the limitations cited above, and possibly several other limitations of a serious nature, this method of segment identification offers some very real advantages and opportunities to the marketing manager. Extending the process, analysis of competitive product offerings might lead to improved selection of product attributes to meet consumer needs. It also seems advisable to measure individual consumer characteristics of respondents, which can then be related to segment membership. If membership corresponds closely to some of the variables on which segmentation is conventionally based, the conditions for deliberate segmentation may be met. If not, there still remains the possibility of "self-segmentation" based on the attribute evaluations and buying policies of individual segments, with product offerings tailored to target segments.

With additional applications and exploration of JAN for segmentation, additional knowledge of consumer buying policies might also result. In short, the technique is more than just predictive. By providing insight into individual and group evaluations of attributes and decision policies, and with the exploration of the relationship between policies and consumer characteristics, the method may become another link between consumer variables and product or brand choice. If so, JAN studies could enhance our understanding of consumer behavior in general.

## REFERENCES

1. Bottenberg, R.A. and R.E. Christal. "Grouping Criteria - A Method Which Retains Maximum Predictive Efficiency," Journal of Experimental Education, 36(1968), 28-32.

2. Dawes, R.M. "Graduate Admissions: A Case Study," American Psychologist 26(1971), 180-88.

3. Einhorn, H.J. "Use of Nonlinear, Noncompensatory Models in Decision Making," Psychological Bulletin, 73(1970), 221-30.

4. Goldberg, L.R. "Man versus Model of Man: A Rationale, Plus Some Evidence, for a Method of Improving on Clinical Inferences," Psychological Bulletin, 73(1970), 422-32.

5. Gough, H.G. "Clinical versus Statistical Prediction in Psychology," in L. Postman, ed., Psychology in the Making: Histories of Selected Research Problems. New York: Knopf, 1962.

6. Hammond, K.R., C.J. Hursh, and F.J. Todd. "Analyzing the Components of Clinical Inference," Psychological Review, 71(1964), 438-56.

7. Hoffman, P.J., P. Slovic, and L.G. Rorer. "An Analysis-of-Variance Model for the Assessment of Configural Cue Utilization in Clinical Judgment," Psychological Bulletin, 69(1968), 338-49.

8. Huber, G.P., V.K. Sahney, and D.L. Ford. "A Study of Subjective Evaluation Models," Behavioral Science, 14(1969), 483-89.

9. Knox, R.E., and P.J. Hoffman. "Effects of Variations on Profile Format on Intelligence and Sociability Judgments," Journal of Applied Psychology, 46(1962), 14-20.

10. Kort, F. "A Nonlinear Model for Analysis of Judicial Decisions," The American Political Science Review, 62(1968), 546-55.

11. Madden, J.M. "Policy-Capturing Model for Analyzing Individual and Group Judgments in Job-Evaluation," Journal of Industrial Psychology, 2(1964), 36-42.

12. Meehl, R.E. Clinical versus Statistical Prediction. Minneapolis: University of Minnesota Press, 1954.

13. Naylor, J.C., and R.J. Wherry, Sr. "The Use of Simulated Stimuli and the 'JAN' Technique to Capture and Cluster the Policies of Raters," Educational and Psychological Measurements, 36(1965), 28-35.

14. Newton, J.R. "Judgment and Feedback in a Quasi-Clinical Situation," Journal of Personality and Social Psychology, 1(1965), 336-42.

15. Oskamp, S. "Overconfidence in Case Study Judgments," Journal of Consulting Psychology, 29(1965), 261-65.

16. Sarbin, T.R. "A Contribution to the Study of Actuarial and Individual Methods of Prediction," American Journal of Sociology, 48(1942), 593-602.

17. Slovic, P. "Analyzing the Expert Judge: A Descriptive Study of a Stock-broker's Decision Processes," Journal of Applied Psychology, 53(1969), 255-63.

18. Slovic, P., and S.C. Lichenstein. "Comparison of Bayesian and Regression Approaches to the Study of Information Processing Judgments," in L. Rappoport and D. Summers, eds., Human Judgments and Social Interactions. New York: Holt, Rinehart & Winston, 1971.

19. Summers, D.A. and T.R. Stewart. "Regression Models of Foreign Policy Judgments," Proceedings of the 76th Annual Convention of American Psychological Association, 3(1968), 195-96.

20. Ulmer, S.S. "The Discriminant Function and a Theoretical Context for Its Use in Estimating the Votes of Judges," in J. Grossman and J. Tanenhaus, eds., Frontiers of Judicial Research. New York: John Wiley & Sons, 1969.

21. Wiggins, N., and P.J. Hoffman. "Dimensions of Profile Judgments as a Function of Instructions, Cue-Consistency, and Individual Differences." Multivariate Behavioral Research, 3(1968), 3-20.

# THE QUESTIONABLE FOREIGN PAYMENTS CONTROVERSY: DIMENSIONS OF THE PROBLEM

Barbara J. Coe, New York University

## ABSTRACT

Americans were shocked in 1976 by revelations of question-able foreign payments by over 200 U.S. corporations, yet such payments are viewed in many developed and underdeveloped countries as "business as usual." The dimensions of the problem are examined in terms of the nature and types of payments, the interdependence of U.S. foreign policy and trade policy with corporate policy, corporate social responsibility, varying host country cultures and societies, and suggested solutions.

## INTRODUCTION

The Germans call it "schmiergelder" or literally "greasing money." Though they don't talk about international bribes, bribes are deductible items for income tax purposes. [16]

Though Americans were shocked in 1976 by revelations of questionable foreign payments by over 200 U.S. corporations such payments are viewed in many developed and underdeveloped countries as "business as usual."

Some Europeans consider the stir about the foreign payoffs silly and even immature. "It's an Americanism" says one German businessman. "Journalism masochism," adds another. [16] These views are shared by many businessmen around the world. Given this, it is not surprising that Americans experienced in international trade are concerned that the U.S. reaction to these questions of business ethics is out of perspective. Disagreement over what has been done, its legality, what should be done and by whom is widespread. The key problem around which the foreign payment question swirls is that such areas are not all black and white. Many are complex questions involving not only difficult ethical and cultural questions but consideration of corporate public policy and national policy and assessment of the honesty and integrity of third parties with whom the corporation is dealing. [11, 17]

The major aspects of the foreign payment question as it relates to U.S. marketing firms, the interdependence of these aspects, and the marketing as well as the corporate public policy implications of some of the proposed solutions to foreign payments are considered in the paper.

## PAYMENTS AND PRACTICES

Concealment of **questionable** foreign payments (payoffs) on the books of a corporation violates the reporting requirements of the Security and Exchange Commission. Penalties levied usually are no more than public disclosure of what payments have been made.[3] No other legal restrictions exist under current U.S. law regarding foreign payments including bribes.

The questionable payments at the center of the current controversy take four basic forms. The first and by far the most common class are small amounts paid to low-salaried public employees to facilitate clearance of shipments, documents or other routine transactions. Foreign governments frequently take such amounts into account when setting wage and salary levels for employees. These types of payments can normally be made in compliance with the law and in conformance with the custom of the host country. [8, 12] Payoffs in about the 5-10 percent of total sales range appear to be standard in many areas.[3]

A second class of payments involve distributing or selling products or services through agents to whom a commission is normally paid. What is an acceptable commission rate and what is excessive are not precisely defined. In this situation, typical current corporate policy is "fees paid will be at competitive rates and commensurate with services performed" which allows for excessive payments.[8] There have been charges that many companies prefer to pay their agents and then do not want to know what the agents do to sell the product.

Political contributions comprise a third class. Strictly political contributions which constitute outright bribes are usually crimes in whatever country they take place. But contributions are viewed as socially and culturally acceptable in many developed and underdeveloped areas.[5, 7,8] The fourth class constitutes payments which are clearly in violation of both law and custom in the host country.[1] Countries like England, Holland and Belgium have legal and cultural histories opposing bribes.

The current controversy has focused primarily on financial and political conduct relating to activities in categories three and four.

Some industries appear more likely to be involved in questionable foreign payments than others. A majority of bribes and kickbacks appear to have occurred among natural resource companies, those heavily regulated by government, or capital-intensive firms, such as aerospace, and where the government is often the sole customer.[6] Heaviest users of revealed payoffs have been oil companies, aircraft and weapons makers.[3] Such payments were found to be less common among consumer products companies, high technology product companies, and those with strong market position. The oil companies are especially vulnerable to unfavorable government action-expropriation, revocation of drilling concessions, tax increases, price control. The aircraft makers do not have a steady flow of sales for standard products; their prosperity for years to come may depend on a single big contract for new planes.

Competition alone does not explain the pervasiveness of payoffs abroad. Another factor is that many officials at almost every level appear to be on the take.[10] Part of the reason is that in many parts of the world, notably the Middle East, Asia and Africa, a true market system based on the price and quality of goods has never existed.[2] Instead, commerce is carried on through intricate webs of associations and social connections that are lubricated by many forms of payment including money. Even in a nation as developed as Japan there is a bewildering and deeply rooted system of extramarket arrangements that shape and guide the way that business is done. One of these is the custom of "on," which requires that all favors be repaid, often in the form of cash. Another reason U.S. firms face problems is that in many developing countries all Western companies are regarded as neo-imperialist, extracting from the host all they can from its land and labor. It is almost patriotic to take foreign **companies** for as much as possible.[3, 7] Sometimes the demands for payoffs are presented directly and bluntly but in most cases the demands are much more subtle; bribegiver and receiver may never meet, but deal through middlemen or agents.

## INTERDEPENDENT NATURE OF THE PROBLEM

If the problem of foreign payments was a simple question of what we in the U.S. would deem to be acceptable from a legal, ethical, and social perspective, then suggestions regarding the passage of strict laws and the jailing of corporate **executives** would seem to be deterents to such payments. But the problem is complicated by the interdependence of the corporate perspective, U.S. government policy, including foreign policy, balance of payments, and the legal, ethical and cultural environment of host countries.

### Corporate Perspective

While international commercial transactions go back well over a thousand years, it has been the recent rise of the multinational enterprise that has made international business a major commercial phenomenon. Moreover, this trend can continue since executives around the world stress the importance of their firms' becoming more multinational.[9] A recent Wharton School survey of executives in forty-five top American multinational enterprises revealed that about 85 percent felt that pulling out of foreign operations would be catastrophic or cause permanent damage; about 70 percent expected that by 1980 over one quarter of their firms' after-tax income would come from foreign operations. [14] Currently, foreign sales by exporting or overseas manufacturing account for 20 percent of U.S. corporate profits and support roughly 8 million jobs.[3]

While most business executives were shocked by the size and clumsiness of the Lockheed bribery, the prominence of the receivers and the potential damage to friendly governments, they were not surprised that bribery did take place.[13] This lack of surprise may be a matter of "cosmopolitanism", of losing one's innocence through dealing with other cultures. On one hand, companies can be viewed as cynical, but businessmen prefer to see it as sensitivity to other people's cultures. As one prominent business leader expressed it: "Why should the U.S. have the right to impose its values on other cultures. There are gray areas in which American companies must accept the moral standards of the countries where they operate, like it or not."[3] Another president, in defending his company's activities overseas, argued that the "payments were a defense strategy to defend ourselves in the game of international trade... **they were worthwhile since they amounted to less than 3 per**cent of the expected sum of about $430 million that would be received for the sale of the aircraft...Bribes are the admission to a ball game. If you didn't pay the admission you were not even qualified to participate in the game... your product would not even be considered."[7] Of course, some executives, such as W. Michael Blumenthal, now Secretary of the Treasury, indicated the payment of bribes was not acceptable and that it was management's responsibility to set the moral tone in the corporation and to make sure that all understand that foreign markets will not be bought with bribes or other types of questionable payments.[4]

While there is a wide range of opinions in the business world concerning such payments, the results of independent studies by the Conference Board and by Opinion Research Corporation [8] both indicated that 48 percent of the upper and middle level executives polled answered yes when asked if bribes should be paid to foreign officials.

### Interdependence of Corporate and Government Policy

Payoffs probably involve many basic issues of corporate structure and American foreign policy and the relation between the two. During the decades after World War II, American government, American business and American labor were happily united in the belief that our overseas invesments -- like overseas defense and aid programs -- were clearly in the national interest.

The question must be posed as to whether foreign payments and bribes were essentially in harmony with American foreign policy, with its goals of maximizing American sales abroad and of supporting anti-Communist regimes around the world. In recent years the Pentagon has pushed to increase exports of U.S. made weapons. U.S. military assistance groups are constantly touting the benefits of American arms in almost every non-Communist country where the U.S. has an embassy. There is no evidence that the Pentagon has actually encouraged payment of bribes to expand exports of arms, but it has been tolerant of agents' fees.[3,6]

Aside from the arms sale question, the bribes appear to have been consistent with a second aspect of American foreign polity -- most of the money has gone to support such anti-Communist parties and powers as the ruling Christain Democratic Party in Italy and the Park regime in South Korea. The sensitivity of the relationship between some international payment activities of U.S. corporations and our foreign policy was highlighted when former Secretary of State Henry Kissinger asked that details of foreign payoffs **be kept secret, citing foreign policy interests as the reason. He cited such revelations could jeopardize relations with allies and weaken friendly governments. [6]**

In addition to foreign policy, government policy regarding balance of trade also appears to be involved in the foreign payment question. Several business executives estimated that refusing to make payments viewed as customary in host countries would cut U.S. international sales by a minimum of 12-18 percent a year.[5] At a time when the U.S. government is stressing the need to increase the strength of our balance of payment system, this would seem to present a conflict of interest. Satisfying the demands for more ethical behavior, as defined by U.S. standards, could result in a weakening of our trade position in the critial period nicknamed the "aging Eighties" by some analysts.[1] A consideration of the projected trade balance in 1985 for selected products as shown in Figure 1, reveals that the areas of projected strength include many of the industries earlier identified as being the most flagrant users of bribes. If, as these companies maintain, they cannot sell to governments and major manufacturing combines without meeting the demands for payments perceived as suitable in the host country, then failure to pay bribes could have a strong negative impact on the balance of trade.

FIGURE 1

Projected Trade Balance in 1985
(in billions of 1972 $)

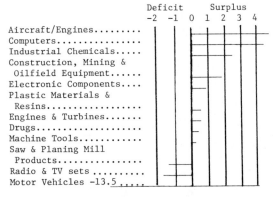

Source: Interindustry Forecasting Project: University of Maryland: The Conference Board

Business and government have developed their interdependence to a degree **where** a great many business people find it difficult to accept or even understand. But the fact remains that decisions regarding U.S corporations and their behavior overseas involves serious aspects of public policy and the responsibility of U.S. firms to aid the government in activities perceived to be good for the country as a whole.

## Interdependence of Corporations and Hosts

"The most important element by far in setting payment patterns is the attitude of the host country."[15] The host country's attitude was identified as the number one determinent of questionable payment patterns in a Business International study of 55 multinational companies in the U.S., Canada and Western Europe.[5] In many developed and developing host countries, it is both customary and legal to permit or overlook gratuities of various forms to lower-placed government officials designed to expedite or advance the process of business.[15] The U.S. is a government by statute, where what is legal and what is illegal are relatively well defined. Many other countries are ruled by administrative decision and as ministers and administrations change so do the rulings. Things are not as black and white in other countries as they are in the U.S. The acceptable cultural norms in a host country may be more revealing of what type of business process exist than the laws of that country.[18] Laws which may be ignored, winked at, or evoked only selectively.[16] In Mexico, for example, payoffs in amounts of more than $100,000 occur with distressing and unsettling frequency in spite of laws against bribery. In the Business International study, Saudi Arabia and **Kuwait** emerged as the two countries most tolerant of bribes. In Kuwait payoffs have been institutionalized by requiring that companies wanting to do business there hire local agents who often perform no services. In parts of Europe attitudes can be equally cynical. One company took a case to court when a tax agent demanded $5,000 on top of the company's tax bill of $30,000. The judge told the company's lawyer that the case was ridiculous, saying: "I am a busy man. This is a busy court with no time for such idiocies. Go take care of your tax man." [5]

In all countries, with the possible exception of China, there have been documented cases of companies being pressured for questionable payments in legal, social, and cultural environments which take no real action to stop the practices unless there was a major scandal causing possible embarrassment to the host country. Unlike American competitors, foreign firms are rarely exposed by their governments for making payoffs. For example, in the 1960s a West German arms maker, Heckler & Koch, managed to elbow out a Belgian rival for an army-rifle contract in Colombia by paying a tribute of $200,000 to the committee of officers who approved the weapon. The rifles proved extremely unpopular with the troops. But not a whisper of criticism has been raised in Germany.[3]

If foreign operations are to be successful there must be a concentration on culture. Culture is a key to understanding the real attitude of host countries toward "business as usual."

## DOES A SOLUTION EXIST?

At the heart of the question concerning foreign payments is the unanswered question relating to what is the corporate social responsibility to its consumers, employees, government and the governments of host countries. Further if the responsibility toward one group represents a violation of the responsibility to one or more other groups, who decides which takes precedence?

The case of questionable foreign payments presents this type of quandary. If the company cooperates with their own government in helping certain friendly countries and groups or shields them in domestic U.S. investigations,

these may be, from government perspective, viewed as socially responsible acts. On the other hand, the same acts may be viewed as socially irresponsible acts by customers, shareholders and the mass of society. Which groups, in such a case, should be the arbitrator of what is socially responsible? The maze of possible solutions for the questionable foreign payments situation do not deal with possible conflicting views of the social desirability of corporate acts. Suggested solutions ranged from doing nothing to enactment and enforcement of strict laws with criminal penalties. From the range of suggestions, three emerge as being among the most likely in terms of eventual adoption.

### Strict Laws

Federal Reserve Board Chairman Arthur Burns has supported a law making the payment of bribes a crime.[6, 13] This solution has possibly the greatest potential impact on an international marketing firm. The impact could be:

| (1) domestic markets | (2) international markets |
|---|---|
| -if violated, public disclosure leading to loss of goodwill | -possible loss of access to host countries where bribes are acceptable |
| -fines and imprisonment of executives | -where bribes not acceptable, host countries may break off business contact |
| -possible loss of domestic market share | -loss of revenues |
| | -shrinking of potential overseas markets |

Besides not defining exactly what is a bribe, this solution completely ignores the possibility that "bribes," in some circumstances, may be desirable from a foreign policy or trade balance point of view. The prevailing views of consumers and the mass of society that such payments are socially undesirable are upheld by this solution. No attention is paid to the prevailing business or cultural environment of the host country.

### Required Public Reporting of Foreign Payments and Receivers

This approach represents a modification of current S.E.C. reporting rules. Supporters of the modification feel required public disclosure by the company will make firms question the advisability of making such payments and perhaps, will make receivers less likely to request them. Opponents of this approach claim that the use of fines rather than harsh penalties is an impediment to its adoption. If adopted, this approach could affect a marketing firm in both markets:

| (1) domestic markets | (2) international markets |
|---|---|
| .could create hostile public image | .pressure for payments from current non-receivers |
| .pressure for better local terms of sale | .loss of business due to exposure of receiver |
| .loss of market share | .closed out of countries where payments viewed as unethical |
| .legal problems | |
| | .pressure to pay but not reveal receiver |

As in the first solution, this approach is best suited to the domestic U.S. perception of what is socially correct behavior in the international market. It goes one step further though and also names receivers regardless of whether the act is illegal or unacceptable in the host country. This solution more directly presents a situation in which enforcement could lead to a direct confrontation between what is socially desirable for the U.S. government and what is socially desirable for the general public. This could lead to avoidance of the law and/or companies refusing to name recipients under U.S. as well as host government pressure.

## Reporting in Financial Statements for S.E.C. and Stockholders

This is the current requirement which has not been successful given that the S.E.C. has had to cite 200 firms for non-reporting. If this remains as the means for overseeing foreign payments, and more companies feel pressure to adhere to it, the expected impact could be:

(1) domestic markets
   -knowledge among own people may adversely affect morale
   -could damage stockholder relations

(2) international markets
   -no real change except for continued pressure for questionable payments in some host countries

This solution hasn't worked historically. Of the three solutions it is the weakest in terms of dealing with the dual social responsibility standards.

## SUMMARY

The first two solutions accept the perceived social view of U.S. culture and society while ignoring how to handle situations in which these views conflict with accepted views and interests of the U.S. and host governments. The third solution hasn't been effective in the past and there is no reason to believe it will be in the future.

All the solutions are surface bandaids. None deals with the real problem: when there is a conflict between the social responsibilities of a U.S. firm dealing in the international market, which responsibility should dictate its actions. Until there is some agreement as to what is socially "acceptable behavior" the international marketing firm will be operating in a "no-man's land" of conflicting norms. The business firm cannot serve several masters when some of all will have different bases for evaluating socially responsible behavior in the international market.

Before developing solutions it is critical to establish the philosophical basis on which the question of foreign payments can be evaluated. We have not as yet developed a national philosophy as to the role of the U.S. corporation in relation to our own society and culture and its responsibility to other societies and cultures. Until we come to grips with the philosophical question, no solution will be successful.

## REFERENCES

1. Bauer, David. "The Disappearnace of the U.S. Trade Surplus." The Conference Board Record (June 1976), 14-17.

2. Behrman, Jack N. U.S. International Business and Governments. McGraw-Hill Series in International Business, 1971.

3. "The Big Payoff." Time (February 23, 1976) 28-34.

4. Blumenthal, W. Michael. "Top Management's Role in Preventing Illegal Payments." The Conference Board Record (August 1976), 14-16.

5. Crittenden, Ann. "Business Bribery Abroad: A Deeply Etched Pattern." The New York Times (December 20, 1976), D1-D3.

7. Halloran, Richard. "Lockheed Ex-Official Says Initiative in Bribe Cases Came From Japanese," The New York Times (December 20, 1976), 23.

8. Hamilton, Walter A. "Corporate Behavior -- A Status Report." The Conference Board Record (August 1976), 6-8.

9. Heenan, David. Multinational Management of Human Resources: A Systems Approach. Austin, Texas: Bureau of Business Research, University of Texas, 1975.

10. "Italian Panel Urges 2 Ex-Aides Be Tried in Lockheed Scandal," The New York Times (January 30, 1977), 1.

11. Jensen, Michael C. "Bribery Dilemma Grows," The New York Times (January 25, 1976) 44.

12. McCloy, John J. "Improper Payments and the Responsibility of the Board of Directors." The Conference Board Record (August 1976), 9-13.

13. "Payoffs: The Growing Scandal." Newsweek (February 23, 1976), 26-33.

14. Perlmutter, Howard V., Franklin R. Root and Leo V. Plante. "Responses of U.S.-Based MNCs to Alternative Public Policy Futures." Columbia Journal of World Business (Fall 1973) 78-86.

15. Simmons, R. P. "The Thumbs on the Trade Scales." Business Week (February 9, 1976), 11-12.

16. Spiers, Joseph N. and Kenneth A. Kovaly. "An International Perspective on Business Ethics." Industry Week (October 27, 1975), 30-34

17. Taylor, John C., 3rd. "Preventing Improper Payments Through Internal Control." The Conference Board Record (August 1976), 17-19.

18. Wallin, Theodore O. "The International Executive's Baggage: Cultural Values of the American Frontier." MSU Business Topics (Spring 1976), 49-58.

# THE IMPACT OF CORPORATE POLICY ON REPORTED
## ETHICAL BELIEFS AND BEHAVIOR OF MARKETING PRACTITIONERS

K. Mark Weaver, University of Alabama
O. C. Ferrell, Illinois State University

## ABSTRACT

Findings of a survey of marketing practitioners (all members of the American Marketing Association) indicate that the existence and enforcement of corporate policy may improve some ethical beliefs and behavior. Therefore, corporate policy makers must assume at least part of the responsibility for the ethical conduct of marketing practitioners in their organization.

## INTRODUCTION

The exposure or bribery, illegal campaign donations, dishonest communication, and potentially dangerous products has led to questions about the ethics of marketing practitioners. The public is concerned there is pressure to compromise personal ethics to attain corporate goals. Carroll [5] found that young managers in business said they would go along with their superiors to show their loyalty in matters that related to judgments on morality. "Almost 60 percent of the respondents (N=236) agreed that young managers in business would have done just what junior members of Nixon's reelection committee had done" [5]. A follow-up study by Bowman supports these results [3].

A survey by Pitney-Bowes Inc., a manufacturer of business equipment, (N=236) revealed that 59% of its managers feel pressure to compromise personal ethics to achieve corporate goals [8]. A similar study of Uniroyal managers found 70% (N=252) feel pressure to compromise ethics. Most managers at Pitney-Bowes and Uniroyal believe most of their peers would not refuse orders to market off-standard and possibly dangerous products. "In general, managers want leadership to show them what to do. They want to believe their job can be done with a high degree of ethics. It is up to corporate management to confirm this belief" [8].

A survey of Harvard Business Review readers by Brenner and Molander was compared to a similar survey conducted by Baumhart fifteen years ago [4,2]. There was substantial disagreement among respondents [4,2] in the latest study as to whether ethical standards in business have changed over the past fifteen years, but respondents were more cynical today about the ethical conduct of their peers. Honesty in communication (advertising, providing information to top management, clients, and government agencies) was a significantly greater problem in 1976 than it was in 1961. Also there was a feeling that ethical codes alone would not substantially improve ethics, although most respondents favor ethical codes.

While marketers have developed creeds, codes and models of ethics [1,7,11] the impact of these actions is debatable. Normative models of ethics do not always consider the "pressure for results" environment that many marketing practitioners face. For many firms, success is measured in dollars and not by the welfare of society or the means used to obtain results.

A recent public opinion survey sponsored by U.S. News and World Report, states that "dissatisfaction with business runs wider and deeper than many experts suspected" [10]. The findings show marketing is weakest in communication with its publics openly and honestly. These failures have led to attitudes toward marketing which are marked by "lack of enthusiasm, uncertainty, suspicion or downright

opposition" [10]. Since ethics deals with <u>all</u> forms of managerial behavior and its purpose, it cuts through many of the dimensions of the crisis of confidence today" [3].

Traditionally, personal values and the behavior of one's superiors (top management) have been considered important determinants of a manager's ethical behavior. According to Brenner and Molander [4] managers believe formal company policy is a somewhat distant secondary influence on ethical beliefs and behavior. The current rationale for ethical or non-ethical behavior is that the immediate organizational environment provides guidance when the manager faces conflict in making ethical judgments. The behavior of superiors is considered more important in guiding behavior than the behavior of peers or the existence of policies within the organizational environment.

The purpose of this study is to examine the perceived relationships between corporate policy, ethical beliefs and ethical behavior within organizations. While previous studies have focused on direct measures of the impact of policy on ethics, this study takes a more indirect approach by first measuring beliefs toward behavioral situations, then determining if relationships exist between beliefs and the existence and enforcement of corporate policy.

## METHODOLOGY

The problem is to determine if the existence and enforcement of corporate policy is related to the following constructs designed to measure ethical beliefs toward internal organizational relationships.

1. Individual Beliefs (What I believe)
2. Individual Behavior (What I do)
3. Reported Peer Beliefs (What I think my peers believe)
4. Reported Peer Behavior (What I think my peers do)
5. Reported Top Management Beliefs (What I believe top management believes)

These constructs are used to test the hypothesis that the existence and enforcement of corporate policy will not be associated with reported ethical beliefs and behavior.

### Sample

The data for the study were collected through a systematic random sample of 280 marketing managers selected from the 1975 American Marketing Association (AMA) roster. Academic members were excluded from the frame. Questionnaires were mailed to the cross-sample of marketing practitioners who represent a variety of firms. These practitioners (primarily middle managers) who have joined the AMA would be expected to have a strong professional orientation and may have higher ethical standards than non-AMA members. A usable mail survey response rate of 47.5% (133/280) was an encouraging result.

### Instrument

The data collection phase utilized a self-administered questionnaire with six response areas. Each response scale contained the same seventeen individual behaviors. (See Table 1) The questionnaire is a modification of the instrument developed by Newstrom and Ruch in a previous study of ethical beliefs and conduct of managers enrolled in a

TABLE 1
IMPACT OF THE EXISTENCE AND ENFORCEMENT OF CORPORATE POLICY
ON REPORTED INDIVIDUAL BELIEFS

| | Existence of Policy | | Enforcement of Policy | |
|---|---|---|---|---|
| | No Policy | Policy Exists | Not Enforced | Enforced |
| 1. Using company services for personal use. | 2.65 | 3.18* | 3.20 | 3.90*** |
| 2. Padding an expense account up to 10%. | 4.00 | 4.35 | 4.09 | 4.68*** |
| 3. Giving gifts/favors for preferential treatment | 3.46 | 3.93 | 3.89 | 4.18 |
| 4. Taking longer than necessary to do a job | 3.62 | 3.68 | 4.04 | 3.67 |
| 5. Divulging confidential information | 4.64 | 4.68 | 4.37 | 4.81*** |
| 6. Doing personal business on company time. | 2.59 | 2.95 | 3.16 | 3.52 |
| 7. Concealing one's errors. | 3.43 | 3.73 | 3.71 | 4.25* |
| 8. Passing blame for errors to an innocent co-worker. | 4.85 | 4.88 | 4.84 | 4.92 |
| 9. Claiming credit for someone else's work. | 4.71 | 4.80 | 4.83 | 4.78 |
| 10. Falsifying time/quality/quantity reports | 4.76 | 4.73 | 4.62 | 4.80 |
| 11. Padding an expense account more than 10% | 4.68 | 4.75 | 4.73 | 4.78 |
| 12. Calling in sick to take a day off. | 3.63 | 3.71 | 3.87 | 3.97 |
| 13. Authorizing a subordinate to violate company rules | 4.27 | 4.23 | 3.84 | 4.52** |
| 14. Pilfering company materials and supplies | 3.95 | 4.59*** | 4.59 | 4.70 |
| 15. Accepting gifts/favors in exchange for preferential treatment. | 3.86 | 4.43*** | 4.30 | 4.58* |
| 16. Taking extra personal time (lunch hour, breaks, early departure, etc.). | 2.12 | 2.62** | 2.66 | 3.14 |
| 17. Not reporting others' violations of policies and rules | 2.51 | 2.85* | 3.06 | 3.67* |

*Sig. at .05 or >, **Sig. at .01 or >, ***Sig. at .00
Higher mean scores (scaled 1-5) indicate the behavioral situation is reported to be unethical.

TABLE 2
IMPACT OF THE EXISTENCE AND ENFORCEMENT OF CORPORATE POLICY
ON REPORTED INDIVIDUAL BEHAVIOR

| | Existence of Policy | | Enforcement of Policy | |
|---|---|---|---|---|
| | No Policy | Policy Exists | Not Enforced | Enforced |
| 1. Using company services for personal use. | 1.93 | 1.97 | 2.18 | 1.70*** |
| 2. Padding an expense account up to 10% | 1.90 | 1.44** | 1.82 | 1.21*** |
| 3. Giving gifts/favors for preferential treatment | 1.50 | 1.18*** | 1.25 | 1.17 |
| 4. Taking longer than necessary to do a job | 1.67 | 1.70 | 1.77 | 1.67 |
| 5. Divulging confidential information | 1.50 | 1.20 | 1.50 | 1.15*** |
| 6. Doing personal business on company time. | 2.27 | 2.05* | 3.05 | 3.43 |
| 7. Concealing one's errors. | 1.61 | 1.52 | 1.71 | 1.33 |
| 8. Passing blame for errors to an innocent co-worker. | 1.06 | 1.07 | 1.08 | 1.08 |
| 9. Claiming credit for someone else's work. | 1.17 | 1.06 | 1.17 | 1.00 |
| 10. Falsifying time/quality/quantity reports | 1.16 | 1.12 | 1.29 | 1.06*** |
| 11. Padding an expense account more than 10% | 1.23 | 1.11 | 1.13 | 1.10 |
| 12. Calling in sick to take a day off. | 1.47 | 1.30* | 1.31 | 1.28 |
| 13. Authorizing a subordinate to violate company rules | 1.40 | 1.36 | 1.65 | 1.21*** |
| 14. Pilfering company materials and supplies | 1.85 | 1.60* | 1.78 | 1.51** |
| 15. Accepting gifts/favors in exchange for preferential treatment. | 1.32 | 1.17 | 1.31 | 1.11** |
| 16. Taking extra personal time (lunch hour, breaks, early departure, etc.). | 2.32 | 2.17 | 2.44 | 1.91*** |
| 17. Not reporting others' violations of policies and rules | 2.57 | 2.34 | 2.61 | 1.91* |

*Sig. at .05 or >, **Sig. at .01 or >, ***Sig. at .00
Lower mean scores (scaled 1-5) indicate the behavior occurred less frequently.

professional development program [6]. The instrument was used by permission of Newstrom and Ruch and considers the following response areas: (1) "What I Believe," (2) "What I Think My Peers Believe," (3) "What I Think Top Management Believes," (4) "What I Do," (5) "What My Peers Do," (6) "The Existence and Enforcement of Corporate Policy."

The seventeen behaviors were repeated for each of the six constructs described above. A systematic rotation of these items was utilized to minimize response bias. The behavioral situations represent intra-organizational behaviors which confront nearly all individuals who participate in a corporate environment. The responses generated, as in the original Newstrom and Ruch study, were designed to elicit cross-perceptual data for comparison purposes. The belief and behavior responses were collected by use of a Likert-type scale consisting of five fixed standardized response categories. The responses for the belief section asked for

responses ranging from 1 "not at all unethical" to 5 "very unethical." The second set of responses related to how often individuals engaged in the behavior. The five response categories ranged from 1 "never" to 5 "very often." The policy question was used to place respondents into the categories of no policy exists, policy exists, and policy exists and is enforced, policy exists and is not enforced, for each behavioral situation. These choices then represented the ethical nature of the behavior, frequency of action, and perceptions of the existence and enforcement of policy.

Two-tailed t-tests were used to determine if there was a significant difference between policy exists, no policy exists categories and policy enforced, policy not enforced categories related to ethical beliefs and behavior (see Table 1). The t-test assumes two independent samples and it is a parametric test. Although the assumptions underlying the use of the t-test are subject to question in this example, it is believed that there is a close approximation. Although the Likert-type scales used possibly provide ordinal data they are analyzed by most social scientists as interval data. All subsamples used in t-tests are from the same sample but the categories are mutually exclusive. Therefore, some degree of independence may be assumed. Since all subsamples used in statistical tests are greater than 20, the Mann-Whitney U test (nonparametric) would yield approximately the same results as the t-test (parametric). The statistical tests used in this study indicate relationships and should not be construed as causal. The self-selected nature of the sample and small sample sizes compound the problems in developing causal implications.

Due to the sensitive nature of this research, the respondents were informed that no individual scores could be identified. This procedure was employed to help alleviate any undue reluctance to respond. The 47.5% response rate is an indication of the interest in this topic. Although no systematic attempt was made to determine why nonresponse occurred, personal contacts with respondents indicated a high level of concern with the area of internal behavior and ethics.

## FINDINGS

The findings report the results of the two-tailed t-tests for both the existence of policy and enforcement of policy for individual beliefs and behavior, peer beliefs and behavior and reported top management beliefs. All findings, including the existence and enforcement of policy, are based on the perceptions of marketing practitioner respondents.

### Impact of the Existence and Enforcement of Corporate Policy on Reported Individual Beliefs

Table 1 shows that the existence of policy is related to individual beliefs toward five ethical behaviors. Beliefs toward "using company services for personal use," "pilfering company materials and supplies," "accepting gifts and favors in exchange for preferential treatment," "taking extra personal time," and "not reporting others' violations of policies and rules" are improved (higher mean scores) when corporate policy exists. It can be observed from Table 1 that beliefs about seven of the behaviors are even "more ethical" when the policy is enforced. In the case of "using company services for personal use," "accepting gifts/favors in exchange for preferential treatment," and "not reporting others' violations of policies and rules" it is apparent that both existence and enforcement of policy are associated with more ethical beliefs. "Authorizing a subordinate to violate company rules," "concealing one's errors," "divulging confidential information," and "padding an expense account up to 10%" are only associated with the enforcement of policy.

For all other behaviors neither existence nor enforcement of policy is associated with individual beliefs. Of the behaviors not associated with the existence and enforcement of policy "passing blame for errors to an innocent co-worker," "claiming credit for someone else's work," "falsifying time/quality/quantity reports," and "padding an expense account more than 10%" represent strong positive ethical beliefs even though no policy exists.

### Impact of the Existence and Enforcement of Corporate Policy on Reported Individual Behavior

Table 2 shows that reported individual behavior was positively associated (lower mean scores) by the existence of policy in five cases while in nine cases individual behavior was positively associated with the enforcement of policy.

Note that for only two behaviors "padding an expense account up to 10%" and "pilfering company materials and supplies" did both existence and enforcement of policy relate to improved reported individual behavior. For "not reporting others' violations of policies and rules," "taking extra personal time," "accepting gifts/favors in exchange for preferential treatment," "authorizing a subordinate to violate company rules," "falsifying time/quality/quantity reports," "divulging confidential information," and "using company services for personal use" only the enforcement of behavior is associated with improved conduct.

In situations where improved behavior was associated with the existence of policy, it could be assumed that the existence of policy was effective in improving behavior and enforcement did not significantly change behavior, but in other situations the existence of policy apparently improved behavior and the enforcement of policy also possibly improved behavior.

### Impact of the Existence and the Enforcement of Corporate Policy on Reported Peer Beliefs

Table 3 indicates that the existence of corporate policy is associated with improved peer beliefs in seven behavioral situations. On the other hand, the enforcement of policy is associated with improved peer beliefs in twelve situations. As can be seen in all situations but "doing personal business on company time," the enforcement of policy is associated with improvements in reported ethical beliefs, even when the existence of policy also apparently improves reported peer beliefs.

These findings demonstrate the importance of enforcing policy. Even for behavior that was not statistically significant, it is obvious from Table 3 that mean scores are usually lowest when there is no policy. The increase of mean scores for some reported peer beliefs supports a hypothesis that enforced policy is associated with improved ethical beliefs of peers.

### Impact of Existence and Enforcement of Corporate Policy on Reported Peer Behavior

Table 4 illustrates that respondents perceive that the existence of policy has no impact on peer behavior. On the other hand, in eight of the seventeen behavioral situations the enforcement of corporate policy is associated with improved peer behavior (lower mean scores). For most behaviors, respondents believe that peers change behavior when policy is enforced. But a few exceptions to this generalization do exist. For example, "passing blame for errors to an innocent co-worker," "falsifying time/quality/quantity reports," and "accepting gifts/favors in exchange for preferential treatment" are not associated with improved ethical behavior when policy exists or when policy is enforced.

### Impact of the Existence and Enforcement of Corporate Policy on Reported Top Management Beliefs

Table 5 shows that many reported top management beliefs toward behaviors are improved by the existence and enforcement of policy. In eight behavioral situations the existence of policy is associated with improved reported top management ethical beliefs. In twelve behavioral situations the enforcement of policy improved reported top management ethical beliefs at a statistically significant level.

Only four situations "13," "12," "8," and "7" were not associated with improvements in either the existence of policy or the enforcement of policy. These findings suggest the importance of policy in structuring ethical beliefs even for top management. Also the enforcement of corporate policy may also contribute to improving reported top management beliefs toward ethical conduct.

TABLE 3
IMPACT OF THE EXISTENCE AND ENFORCEMENT OF CORPORATE POLICY
ON REPORTED PEER BELIEFS

| | Existence of Policy | | Enforcement of Policy | |
|---|---|---|---|---|
| | No Policy | Policy Exists | Not Enforced | Enforced |
| 1. Using company services for personal use. . . . . . . . . . . . . | 2.27 | 2.50 | 2.67 | 3.20** |
| 2. Padding an expense account up to 10% . . . . . . . . . . . . . . | 3.05 | 3.14 | 2.98 | 3.63*** |
| 3. Giving gifts/favors for preferential treatment . . . . . . . . . | 2.41 | 3.34*** | 3.23 | 3.77** |
| 4. Taking longer than necessary to do a job . . . . . . . . . . . . | 2.72 | 3.21** | 3.69 | 2.80** |
| 5. Divulging confidential information . . . . . . . . . . . . . . . | 4.09 | 4.33 | 3.74 | 4.56*** |
| 6. Doing personal business on company time. . . . . . . . . . . . . | 2.02 | 2.49** | 3.16 | 3.52 |
| 7. Concealing one's errors. . . . . . . . . . . . . . . . . . . . . | 2.94 | 3.30 | 3.43 | 3.75 |
| 8. Passing blame for errors to an innocent co-worker. . . . . . . . | 3.74 | 4.03 | 4.07 | 4.38 |
| 9. Claiming credit for someone else's work. . . . . . . . . . . . . | 3.21 | 3.67 | 3.83 | 3.56 |
| 10. Falsifying time/quality/quantity reports . . . . . . . . . . . . | 3.97 | 4.04 | 3.75 | 4.32** |
| 11. Padding an expense account more than 10% . . . . . . . . . . . . | 3.19 | 3.42 | 3.60 | 3.65 |
| 12. Calling in sick to take a day off. . . . . . . . . . . . . . . . | 2.56 | 2.78 | 2.94 | 3.50** |
| 13. Authorizing a subordinate to violate company rules . . . . . . . | 3.51 | 3.71 | 3.64 | 4.09** |
| 14. Pilfering company materials and supplies . . . . . . . . . . . . | 2.55 | 3.60*** | 3.28 | 4.14*** |
| 15. Accepting gifts/favors in exchange for preferential treatment. . | 2.75 | 3.40** | 3.24 | 3.85*** |
| 16. Taking extra personal time (lunch hour, breaks, early departure, etc.). . . . . . . . . . . . . . . . . . . . . . . . . . . . . . | 1.88 | 2.31** | 2.35 | 2.86* |
| 17. Not reporting others' violations of policies and rules . . . . . | 2.46 | 3.13*** | 3.14 | 4.17*** |

*Sig. at .05 or >, **Sig. at .01 or >, ***Sig. at .00
Higher mean scores (scaled 1-5) indicate the behavioral situation is reported to be unethical.

TABLE 4
IMPACT OF THE EXISTENCE AND ENFORCEMENT OF CORPORATE POLICY
ON REPORTED PEER BEHAVIOR

| | Existence of Policy | | Enforcement of Policy | |
|---|---|---|---|---|
| | No Policy | Policy Exists | Not Enforced | Enforced |
| 1. Using company services for personal use. . . . . . . . . . . . . | 3.13 | 2.78 | 3.12 | 2.97 |
| 2. Padding an expense account up to 10% . . . . . . . . . . . . . . | 3.00 | 2.63 | 3.29 | 2.68*** |
| 3. Giving gifts/favors for preferential treatment . . . . . . . . . | 2.31 | 2.17 | 2.61 | 2.21** |
| 4. Taking longer than necessary to do a job . . . . . . . . . . . . | 2.55 | 2.36 | 2.87 | 2.47 |
| 5. Divulging confidential information . . . . . . . . . . . . . . . | 2.18 | 1.86 | 2.44 | 1.86*** |
| 6. Doing personal business on company time. . . . . . . . . . . . . | 3.11 | 2.83 | 3.28 | 2.67** |
| 7. Concealing one's errors. . . . . . . . . . . . . . . . . . . . . | 2.45 | 2.34 | 2.78 | 2.73 |
| 8. Passing blame for errors to an innocent co-worker. . . . . . . . | 2.02 | 2.11 | 2.46 | 2.15 |
| 9. Claiming credit for someone else's work. . . . . . . . . . . . . | 2.44 | 2.33 | 2.30 | 2.33 |
| 10. Falsifying time/quality/quantity reports . . . . . . . . . . . . | 2.11 | 2.14 | 2.75 | 2.11*** |
| 11. Padding an expense account more than 10% . . . . . . . . . . . . | 2.45 | 2.22 | 2.50 | 2.32 |
| 12. Calling in sick to take a day off. . . . . . . . . . . . . . . . | 2.24 | 2.22 | 2.56 | 2.30 |
| 13. Authorizing a subordinate to violate company rules . . . . . . . | 2.02 | 1.96 | 2.24 | 1.89** |
| 14. Pilfering company materials and supplies . . . . . . . . . . . . | 2.44 | 2.42 | 3.07 | 2.32*** |
| 15. Accepting gifts/favors in exchange for preferential treatment. . | 2.48 | 2.17 | 2.66 | 2.92** |
| 16. Taking extra personal time (lunch hour, breaks, early departure, etc.). . . . . . . . . . . . . . . . . . . . . . . . . . . . . . | 3.26 | 2.94 | 3.38 | 2.77*** |
| 17. Not reporting others' violations of policies and rules . . . . . | 2.71 | 2.50 | 2.78 | 2.42 |

*Sig. at .05 or >, **Sig. at .01 or >, ***Sig. at .00
Lower mean scores (scaled 1-5) indicate the behavior occurred less frequently.

## CONCLUSIONS

The general hypothesis that the existence and enforcement of corporate policy will not be associated with reported ethical beliefs and behavior is rejected. The findings of Brenner and Molander that company policy is a somewhat secondary influence in ethical beliefs and behavior is challenged. While Brenner and Molander used a direct approach (asked respondents directly if policy influenced ethical beliefs and behavior) this study used an indirect approach in determining the impact of policy on ethical beliefs and behavior. Behavioral situations were evaluated; existence and enforcement of policy were determined independently. Also, the evaluation of reported peer beliefs and behavior may serve as surrogate indicators of respondent feelings. Tull and Albaum indicate that peer evaluations "may be interpreted, however, as a projection of the opinion of the respondent on the situation posed" [9].

A basic building block of the organizational environment is corporate policy. Formal policy is an explicit statement to encourage beliefs and behaviors either ethical or unethical. Based on these findings, policy appears to a viable consideration to influence ethical conduct. If the associations discovered in this limited study are typical, individuals that make policy decisions must assume some part of the responsibility for the ethical environment of the organization. Also, these findings question the impact of "codes of ethics" that are not enforced; top management should establish policy as well as express a commitment to ethical conduct.

This study reported beliefs and behavior related to selected internal organizational behaviors. Also, the social pressure for ethical conduct is always a source of bias in opinion research. Future research should analyze the relationship of ethical beliefs, behavior, and policy in

TABLE 5

IMPACT OF THE EXISTENCE AND ENFORCEMENT OF CORPORATE POLICY
ON REPORTED TOP MANAGEMENT BELIEFS

| | Existence of Policy | | Enforcement of Policy | |
|---|---|---|---|---|
| | No Policy | Policy Exists | Not Enforced | Enforced |
| 1. Using company services for personal use. | 2.50 | 3.34*** | 3.40 | 3.90** |
| 2. Padding an expense account up to 10% | 3.68 | 4.05 | 3.79 | 4.49*** |
| 3. Giving gifts/favors for preferential treatment | 3.00 | 3.81** | 3.51 | 4.28*** |
| 4. Taking longer than necessary to do a job | 3.41 | 3.67 | 3.95 | 3.67 |
| 5. Divulging confidential information | 4.64 | 4.77 | 4.42 | 4.89*** |
| 6. Doing personal business on company time. | 2.45 | 2.86* | 2.59 | 3.19** |
| 7. Concealing one's errors. | 3.52 | 3.86 | 4.00 | 4.07 |
| 8. Passing blame for errors to an innocent co-worker. | 4.15 | 4.48 | 4.46 | 4.67 |
| 9. Claiming credit for someone else's work. | 3.65 | 4.43*** | 4.67 | 4.38 |
| 10. Falsifying time/quality/quantity reports | 4.41 | 4.53 | 4.33 | 4.69*** |
| 11. Padding an expense account more than 10% | 4.19 | 4.64** | 4.33 | 4.79*** |
| 12. Calling in sick to take a day off. | 3.64 | 3.65 | 3.69 | 4.09* |
| 13. Authorizing a subordinate to violate company rules | 4.31 | 4.59 | 4.48 | 4.67 |
| 14. Pilfering company materials and supplies | 3.60 | 4.42*** | 4.32 | 4.63* |
| 15. Accepting gifts/favors in exchange for preferential treatment. | 3.43 | 4.15** | 3.97 | 4.42** |
| 16. Taking extra personal time (lunch hour, breaks, early departure, etc.). | 2.17 | 2.76** | 2.88 | 3.36* |
| 17. Not reporting others' violations of policies and rules | 3.33 | 3.60 | 3.75 | 4.18** |

*Sig. at .05 or >, **Sig. at .01 or >, ***Sig. at .00
Higher mean scores (scaled 1-5) indicate the behavioral situation is reported to be unethical.

behavioral situations dealing with the consuming public.
Increased awareness of the factors that influence ethical
conduct should improve the practice of marketing.

REFERENCES

1. Bartels, Robert. "Model for Ethics in Marketing."
   Journal of Marketing, 31 (January 1967), 20-26.

2. Baumhart. "How Ethical Are Businessmen?" Harvard
   Business Review, (July-August 1961), 6.

3. Bowman, James S. "Managerial Ethics in Business and
   Government." Business Horizons, 19 (October 1976),
   48.

4. Brenner, Steven N. and Earl A. Molander. "Is the
   Business of Ethics Changing?" Harvard Business Review
   (January-February 1977), 57-71.

5. Carroll, Archie B. "Managerial Ethics: A Post-
   Watergate View." Business Horizons, 18 (April 1975),
   79.

6. Newstrom, John W. and William A. Ruch. "The Ethics of
   Management and the Management of Ethics." MSU Business Topics, 23 (Winter 1975).

7. Patterson, J. M. "What Are the Social and Ethical
   Responsibilities of Marketing Executives?" Journal
   of Marketing, 30 (July 1966), 12-15.

8. "The Pressure to Compromise Personal Ethics." Business Week, (January 31, 1977), 107.

9. Tull, Donald S. and Gerald S. Albaum. Survey Research: A Decisional Approach. New York: Intext
   Educational Publishers, 1973, 153.

10. "Why Business Has a Black Eye." U.S. News and World
    Report, (September 6, 1976), 22.

11. "World Marketing Contact Group Proposes Creed for Mar-
    keters." Marketing News, (November 5, 1976), 1 and 9.

EXTENSION OF CRIMINAL LIABILITY TO CORPORATE
EXECUTIVES FOR SUBORDINATES' ACTIONS:
SOME IMPLICATIONS OF ACME MARKETS CASE

Robert N. Katz, University of California at Berkeley
S. Prakash Sethi, University of Texas at Dallas

ABSTRACT

Recent cases imposing criminal sanctions upon executives,
who have no knowledge of wrongdoing, set forth many implications for the firm and management decisions in marketing. The negative, as well as positive, effects of
increasing executive liability must be examined along
with evaluation of alternatives available to the firm.

## INTRODUCTION

Marketing activities by business firms, large and small,
have been historically subject to greater public scrutiny
and regulations than any other area of business activity.
This results principally from two factors. First, the
pricing function is one of the critical elements in the
maintenance of competitive markets and therefore is subject to governmental scrutiny. The second factor is the
nature of the marketing function itself; it is the closest
link between the manufacturer and the ultimate consumer.

This paper analyzes the impact of recent court decisions
imposing criminal liabilities upon corporate executives
for derelictions unknown to the executive. The decision
of the Supreme Court in U.S. v. John R. Park[1] has substantial implications for the marketing manager in areas
of marketing procedures, product innovation, and organizational structures. That decision provides a basis for
holding responsible supervisors criminally liable for
wrongful acts of subordinates. How will this decision
and orientation affect marketing decisions and behavior
of top executives?

Recent events have led to new regulatory approaches, creation of new government agencies and increased activism
by the courts. Thus, today there are significant uncertainties for marketing executives in otherwise normal
marketing decisions.[2] An example of changing orientation
by the courts is found in the broadened scope of product
liability.[3]

Commencing in the early 1960's, the courts began to eliminate the need for a direct contractual relationship in
product defect suits based on a theory of contract. More
importantly, in tort actions for product liability the
courts began a departure from the old common law doctrine
of requirement of a showing of negligence.[4] Today in
thirty-eight jurisdictions, even though there is no knowledge of negligence of no negligent act, a company can be
held liable without any fault.

The impact of the increased ease in obtaining redress
under the doctrine of strict liability has had major
implications for marketing. In the same manner in which
the courts and legislations have imposed tort liability,
in some areas without fault, courts and legislation are
imposing criminal liability and sanctions in the absence
of any direct, knowing or intentional wrongdoing. Thus
a new dimension has been added to the issue of public
intervention into a firm's discretion in planning its
marketing strategy. Not only are the marketing decisions
being extremely constrained by regulation, but more
ominously, recent court decisions have significantly
expanded the area of personal liability--civil and crim-
inal--of the corporate executive. Thus executives are
being held personally responsible for the activities of
subordinates where no direct complicity of negligence is
involved.

## ISSUES FOR ANALYSIS

This paper is an attempt to analyze the recent developments in the area of personal legal liability of corporate executives and its implications for corporate marketing management and public policy.

1.  What are the economic, social and political impli-
    cations of broad expansion in the personal liability
    of corporate officers for the activities of their
    subordinates? In particular, how would they affect
    the behavior of top executives and their responses
    to society's demand for more products, services, and
    employment?

2.  What are the reasonable and realistic limits on the
    extent on which a corporate officer can be held
    personally liable for the acts of his subordinates?
    How can these be ascertained, given the extreme
    complexity of modern large-scale organizations?

3.  In terms of corporate organizational behavior, how
    would increased liability affect product innovation,
    market development, organizational structures, deci-
    sion-making processes, and incentive and reward
    systems?

4.  Are there certain types of marketing activities that
    are particularly susceptible to exposing top execu-
    tives to personal liability? How should a firm
    develop procedures to minimize their impact?

5.  How should a corporate executive protect himself
    from exposure to personal liability?

The Supreme Court decision in U.S. v. John R. Park [421
U.S. 658 (1975)] has raised the spector of personal liability of corporate executives for the actions or in-
actions of their subordinates when they involve violation
of U.S. Food, Drug and Cosmetics Act of 1938. In that
case, John R. Park, president of Acme Markets, Inc., a
Philadelphia based national retail food chain, was held
personally liable for the presence of unsanitary conditions in one of the company's warehouses. The evidence
showed that Park was made aware of the unsanitary conditions by the FDA inspector, and had instructed the supervisor of the warehouse to correct those violations. When
a second inspection found that unsanitary conditions were
not removed, Park was nevertheless held criminally liable
along with the company because he "was the responsible
person in authority."

Acme Market, Inc. has approximately 36,000 employees, 874 retail stores, and 16 warehouses in various parts of the United States. The Federal Food and Drug Administration, after finding continuations of violations, brought suit against Acme Markets and John R. Park charging five counts of violations of the Food and Drug Administration Act. The company plead guilty to all five counts. Although Park plead not guilty, the jury found him guilty and that finding was upheld by the U.S. Supreme Court, although the Court of Appeals had reversed. Park admitted having ultimate responsibility within the company but urged that he had no direct involvement and that delegation of responsibility had been made. Several trade associations had filed **amicus curiae**, such as the National Association of Food Chains and the Grocery Manufacturers of America, briefs supporting Park's position.[5]

## Other Areas of Expanding Personal Liability of Corporate Executives

The demand for a greater degree of accountability and responsibility is not limited to the field of food, drugs and cosmetics. Indeed, recently enacted statutes, regulations and cases impose liability without fault. The increased adoption of the doctrine of strict liability in torts for defective products is an obvious example. As an aftermath of the Acme Markets decision against Park, the courts and the regulatory agencies have anticipated seeking criminal sanctions against individuals within the corporation with greater frequency. There is precedent for this outside the field of food and drugs.

**Antitrust.** Prior to Spring 1961, while there had been instances in which corporate employees had been fired, corporate individuals had not served sentences as a result of antitrust violations. The electrical industry conspiracy changed that, however, and may have heralded a new era of individual stringent sanctions.[6]

**Product Liability.** While not an example of imputing liability to "higher ups" for negligence, the concept of strict liability in tort does provide an example of imposing liability without fault. Thus, just as the old common law requirement for a showing of negligence in tort action has been eliminated, so appears a demise to be in the offing for the requirement of a showing of knowledge and intent in a criminal action.

**OSHA.** Pursuant to the provisions of the Occupational Safety and Health Act of 1970,[7] sanctions, including fines, are assessable against individuals who are "responsible" for, though unknowledgeable about, safety infractions. The constitutionality of administrative assessment of civil penalties that are tantamount to criminal sanctions is the issue in a case presently before the U.S. Supreme Court.[8] If the Supreme Court affirms the Court of Appeals and upholds administrative assessment of civil penalties, which are frequently assessed against individuals who have no knowledge of the specific wrongdoing, there may well be a rush by other regulatory agencies to expand their penalty assessment authority.

**IRS.** Additional precedent for liability without fault is found within the Internal Revenue Service.[9] If a person is a "responsible" officer or employee, that is, one who has check-signing authority, he may be liable to 100 percent penalty for federal taxes withheld but not remitted to the IRS even though he had no knowledge of or connection with the nonremission of taxes.

The consequences of the Acme Markets case and other Supreme Court decisions are far-reaching for the marketing manager in particular and corporate executives in general. If the pattern of expanding the scope of legal liability--civil and criminal--is sustained in future court decisions, which seems likely, it would cause significant changes in the development of the marketing mix and other operating strategies of the companies. It would also force some changes in the organizational structures and decision-making processes of corporations that deal in consumer products. Every corporate supervisor, whether or not that supervisor is an officer or a director, may under certain circumstances be held personally liable for the acts of his subordinates--regardless of whether that supervisor had any knowledge of or participation in the acts of the employees that have been determined to be wrongful or in violation of the law. This raises the difficult question of what are the reasonable limitations of the executive.

## Complexity of Products

The first consideration is the sheer impossibility of a corporate executive to monitor and supervise all corporate activities--corporate bylaws notwithstanding--even in a small area of a large corporation's product-related activities. Consider, for example, the problem of canning firms. In an **amicus curiae** brief filed before the Supreme Court in the Park case, the National Canners Association alludes to the increasingly complex technical requirements imposed by the Food and Drug Administration under the act since **Dotterweich**.[10] These now fill six volumes of the Code of Federal Regulations. In the case of the canning industry, regulations prescribing virtually every step of the canning process are so technical and complex that they are literally unintelligible to those who lack complete technological training in these areas. The current labelling requirements for certain medical diagnostic devices are an example.[11] Among the most detailedof the FDA's current labelling schemes, four pages of these regulations list required labelling information.

These and other similar detailed regulations require interpretation by different people with expertise in such diverse fields as medicine, engineering, and statistics. Since no company president can be expected to develop the requisite expertise in each of the fields needed to interpret and implement compliance with the bulk of the FDA's present regulations, he must rely on technically trained subordinates. Top management is equally dependent on these qualified persons for information as to any problems which might arise with respect to compliance.

## Product Innovation

Increased personal liability may make executives more cautious and reluctant to introduce new products and services in the marketplace. Not only would this be likely to have an adverse effect on the growth of the firm, but it may also restrict consumer choice. Furthermore, the uncertainty, risk, cost of testing, and quality assurance would increase the cost of doing business, which would fall disproportionately heavily on smaller firms thereby reducing market competition and social welfare.

There is indeed some evidence that increased regulatory requirements have adversely affected business investment in research on development and product innovation.[12] The increased regulatory requirements for disclosure, product safety, criteria for effectiveness, standards for substantiation of ad claims, coupled with liability suits for potential and indeterminable injury claims, have led many a marketer to withhold new products from the market, leading to greater homogeneity and standardization of products and thereby reducing consumer choice.

A contrary view which would assert that the increased regulatory requirements enhance product innovation may be found in other publications.[13]

In the area of prescription drugs, an econometric study conducted in 1972 by Professor Sam Peltzman of UCLA, concluded that consumers would have been better off if the 1962 amendments to the Food and Drug Administration Act had never been implemented because the benefits lost from drugs not developed were measured as several times greater than the savings that had accrued to the consumers as a result of being protected from unsafe and ineffective drugs.[14]

## Meeting Existing Legal Requirements is Not Enough

At present a company cannot escape liability by maintaining that it had fulfilled the existing legal requirements. For example, in the case of prescription drugs the courts have held that the mere compliance with regulations or directives as to warnings, such as those issued by the FDA in this case, may not be sufficient to immunize the manufacturer or supplier of the drug from liability. The warnings required by such agencies may be only minimal in nature, and when the manufacturer or supplier has reason to know of greater dangers not included in the warning, its duty to warn may not be fulfilled.[15] If one were to extend the notion of "person in a responsible position" to these situations, the implications for the marketing executive are indeed ominous.

## The Manner, Extent and Timing of An Executive's Awareness of a Legal Violation

In the Park case the government made a significant point in its briefs that the president of the company had been aware of the violation of the acts at another location some two years earlier. The implication was that if this had been the first violation by his company there would not have been the seeking of sanctions against him. From this it could be extrapolated that the supervisor gets one free bite of the apple. From the Acme Markets case it would further appear clear that a geographic separation of the responsible official from the wrongdoing employee would be no defense whatsoever.

Furthermore, in the Park case the government argued that Park was informed about the violation. Suppose now that the information regarding a violation came not from a FDA inspector but through an internal document informing the executive of a possible violation. Could this be used at a later date as evidence that he was aware of the situation and therefore personally responsible for noncompliance? Consider further whether the executive issued instructions to cure the possible violation. At issue would be whether such instructions were issued in a timely manner and whether, especially in light of the case, the executive checked to ensure that his instructions were followed. Thus, simply the issuance of a directive to correct would not be sufficient.

The above-mentioned situations illustrate the point that it is virtually impossible for a corporate executive to be kept personally informed of all the corporate activities with potential for public injury, and when well-thought out and executed control procedures fail, to be held personally responsible. The companies must therefore initiate new procedures and develop new safeguards to ensure their economic survival and well-being, as well as to protect their top executives from exposure to personal liability for good faith efforts made on a company's behalf during the normal course of business.

### Move Toward Centralization

Potential criminal liability or exposure to civil assessment is tantamount to criminal sanction and will, in all likelihood, lead executives to take steps to ensure that they have knowledge of and control over activities that could lead to their being the subject of imposition of sanctions. Thus, when faced with the option of decentralizing operations or delegating responsibility, the executive may reject those options. The lower-echelon manager will feel the close scrutiny of the "responsible" officer. This could limit initiative and stifle innovation. Because of a desire to maintain and exercise close supervision and control over company operations, growth may be sacrificed. This could lead to consumers being denied the fruits of the economics of size, availability of producers in closer proximity, and access to information. On the other hand, it could be argued that by compelling the executive to maintain closer supervision and control, the company will be more responsible to societal needs and demands and thus expansion and growth will only come with a clear and reasoned justification for such growth.

### Corporate Restructure

In an effort to limit the extent of activity for which an executive is the "responsible" individual, consideration may be given to creation of separate legal entities. This is already done to limit exposure to tort and other civil liabilities. We submit that it might also be done to limit executive exposure to criminal liability. Thus, there may be a growth in use of subsidiary corporations. This could lead to a result opposite to that sought by the advocates of imposition of stringent criminal sanctions. For example, a different result might have been obtained in Acme Markets if the offending warehouse in Baltimore were owned, say, by Acme Markets of Baltimore, Inc., John Doe, president, rather than by Acme Markets, Inc., John Park, president. The buck would have stopped with John Doe. Thus, the top level executives could be insulated from criminal liability. Would this detract from the public interest? It could be argued that it would since sanctions against higher-level officials gain more publicity, highlight demand for accountability, and serve as a deterrant to others. The countervailing argument is that the on-site responsible individual is the one who has immediate access to knowledge of a potential violation and the means to effect correction and he should not pass the buck on up. (Of course, both the on-site individual and the remote CEO could be deemed to be responsible.)

### Indemnification of the Officer for Financial Costs

A company may undertake to indemnify a corporate officer for any fines paid either through liability insurance or through the case of corporate funds. (Under the laws of some states this is limited or prohibited.) This cost would undoubtedly be borne by the shareholders or passed on to the consumer. However, there is no adequate way of compensating the executive for a possible jail term.

The question of restitution raises two issues of public policy: (1) whether negligence on the part of corporate executives should be compensated, thereby removing its deterrent effects; and (2) whether prison sentences and fines indeed act as deterrents. Fines have sometimes been referred to as cheap licenses to abuse the system. The evidence on both questions is inconclusive, and arguments can be advanced to support either the pro or con position. A detailed discussion of the indemnification by the corporation of employees who are not culpable, but nonetheless held liable and responsible for criminal sanctions, is beyond the scope of this paper; we must limit ourselves to simply raising the issue and its possible implications.

## CONCLUSION

It is contended that while there may be some element of deterrance in corporate wrongdoing if responsible executives are held personally liable, there are serious implications for the working of the firm and the national economy which must not be ignored. First, corporations would likely develop measures that would either insulate or indemnify executives against such risks, thereby minimizing this deterrant effect. Second, it would arguably have an adverse effect on product innovation, stifle creativity, reduce new offerings of products and services to consumers, thereby restricting consumer choice, and, overall, reduce competition and thereby consumer welfare. While the positive and negative effects of increasing executive liability are not easily measurable, they should be seriously considered before society undertakes any expansion of this measure as a social instrument for reform in corporate behavior.

## REFERENCES

1. United States v. John R. Park, 421 U.S. 658 (1975).

2. Werner, Ray O., "Marketing and the United States Supreme Court, 1968-1974," Journal of Marketing, January 1977, 32-43.

3. Gray, Irwin, "Product Liability: A Management Response," AMACOM, New York, 1975. Noel, Dix, and Jerry Phillips, "Products Liability in a Nut Shell" (St. Paul, Minn.: West Publishing Co., 1974). Prosser, William L., "The Fall of the Citadel," Minnesota Law Review, v. 50 (1966), 791.

4. Henningsen v. Bloomfield Motors, Inc., 32 N.J. 358, 161 App. 2d 69 (1960).

5. A detailed discussion of the case may be seen in "Acme Markets, Inc., Philadelphia." Case study by S.P. Sethi and R.N. Katz.

6. New York Times, February 7, 1961.

7. 84 Stat. 1590; 29 U.S.C. 651.

8. Frank C. Ivey, Jr., Inc. v. OSHRC, pending before the U.S. Supreme Court, argued November 1976.

9. Internal Revenue Code, Section 6672, etc.

10. United States v. John R. Park, No. 74-215, on writ of Certiorari to the United States Court of Appeals for the Fourth Circuit, Brief Amicus Curiae for the National Canners Association, Washington, D.C., 1974.

11. 21 C.F.R. 328.10 (1974).

12. See, for example, Knight, Kenneth, George Kozmetsky, and Helen R. Baka, Industry Views of the Role of the Federal Government in Industrial Innovation (Austin, Texas: Graduate School of Business, The University of Texas at. Austin, 1976); R&D in Industry, 1973 (Washington, D.C.: National Science Foundation, 1975); "The Silent Crises in R&D," Business Week, March 8, 1976, 90; "The Two Way Squeeze in New Products," Business Week, August 10, 1974, 130; "Where Private Industry Puts Its Research Money," Business Week, June 28, 1976, 62.

13. From Rubinstein, et al., "Factors Influencing Innovation Success," Research Management, 1976.

14. Statement by Sam Peltzman, Professor of Economics, University of California, Los Angeles. U.S. Congress, Senate, "Competitive Problems in the Drug Industry, Present Status of Competition in the Pharmaceutical Industry, Development and Marketing of Prescription Drugs," Part 23. Hearings Before the Subcommittee on Monopoly of the Select Committee on Small Business, 93rd Congress, March 14, 1973, 9802-9842. See also M. N. Baily, "Research Development Costs and Returns: The U.S. Pharmaceutical Industry," Journal of Political Economy, January-February 1972, 70-85.

15. See the case discussion of Stevens v. Parke, Davis & Company and A. J. Beland, M.D., in Sethi, S. Prakash, Up Against the Corporate Wall, 3rd ed. (Englewood Cliffs, N.J.: Prentice-Hall, 1977), 386. Also see Love v. Wolf (266 Cal. App. 2d 226, 395-96); Yarrows v. Sterling Drug Co. (263 F. Supp. 162-63); Incollingo v. Ewing [Pa. (1971), 282 A. 2d 206, 220].

# SEGMENTATION AS AN
# INDUSTRIAL MARKETING STRATEGY

J. S. Schiff, Pace University
Jose Fernandez, Pace University
Leon Winer, Pace University

## ABSTRACT

While consumer market segmentation has been one of the most widely discussed topics in the field of marketing, there has not been sufficient research on segmentation of industrial markets. To maximize their effectiveness, industrial marketers must realize that their markets consist of segments, which while internally homogeneous, differ from each other.

This paper reviews the segmentation literature, presents criteria for segmenting industrial markets, discusses implementation of an industrial segmentation strategy and suggests areas for further research.

## INTRODUCTION

Market segmentation is "the development and pursuit of different marketing programs by the same firm, for essentially the same product, but for different components of the overall market." [23].

While a great deal has been written about the segmentation of consumer markets, less research has been done on industrial market segmentation [24]. To begin to remedy this situation, the authors are conducting a two-part study. This paper, the result of the first phase of the project, briefly reviews the concepts of market segmentation and discusses the application of these concepts to industrial markets. It is not an exhaustive literature review, but rather is intended to serve as background for the second phase of the project, a field study of segmentation strategies employed by leading industrial marketers.

## CONCEPTS FROM CONSUMER MARKET SEGMENTATION

### Properties of Market Segments

To be used as the target of a segmentation strategy, a market segment must possess three properties. It must be of sufficient size to warrant the expenditure of marketing funds; it must be reachable through available promotional channels; and the segment must differ in market behavior from other segments with respect to marketing mix response [18, 44].

### Demographic Criteria for Segmentation

Several consumer attributes have been found to be related to buying behavior. For example, the differences in purchasing behavior between males and females is well documented [7, 31, 45, 50]. Age appears to influence both expenditure patterns [26] and attitudes towards products and promotion [46].

Similarly, life cycle stage, as defined by indices incorporating variables such as age, marital status, and number and age of children is related to both product and service expenditures [13, 20, 47] as well as to indebtedness [32].

Differences in buying behavior and communications responses between racial groups have also been observed [4, 25]. Additionally, nationality groups tend to exhibit various buying patterns that differ from other groups, but are fairly uniform within each group, even well into the assimilation process [3].

There are considerable variations in buying behavior among geographic regions, as well as among urban, suburban and rural areas [15, 46].

### Socioeconomic Criteria

Income is the most widely used basis for consumer segmentation [23]. Much research has pointed to relationships between income and buying behavior. For example, Banks observed that low income groups tend to patronize independent stores rather than chains for certain items [3]. while Udell found a relationship between low income and certain promotional efforts [45].

Social class, which in addition to income, considers education and various life style characteristics, has been found to be an important factor in explaining differences in consumption patterns, store patronage and media habits [35, 38, 42].

### Personality and Life Style Characteristics

There have been several efforts to measure the relationship between overall personality and buying behavior, but most systems used to assess general personality have had limited results [17, 19, 29, 46]. However, certain aspects of buying behavior have been linked to social personality traits. Cohen found that consumers who were classified as "aggressive" had different product preferences and media habits from "compliant" or "detatched" persons [12].

Life style, as measured by a person's activities, interests, opinions and values (AIOV) is another important factor in predicting promotion response and is related to usage of a wide range of products [48].

### Market Behavior Criteria

Another type of consumer segmentation, and one that has received considerable attention in recent years, uses differences in market behavior as criteria for segmentation. For example, it is often useful to segment markets by amount of usage. Different promotional approaches may be required to maintain present users, to induce light users to increase consumption, and to persuade non-users to try the product [18]. Promotion can also be designed to appeal to segments of the market defined by degree of brand loyalty [2, 34]. Blattberg and Sen studied segments of the aluminum foil market and found a relationship between various types of brand loyalty and certain demographic characteristics [6].

Yankelovich discussed segmentation based on consumer attitudes. He proposed independent variables such as susceptibility to change, purpose perceived needs and aesthetic concepts of products [51]. The ability to identify and reach the segment of the market who are opinion leaders can also be an effective aid in increasing the efficiency of the marketing effort. This is particularly true in the new product category. It appears, however, that opinion leadership varies from one product category to another, making identification difficult [9, 30, 33].

Developing a Segmentation Strategy

Once differences in buying behavior and promotional response have been observed, the remaining questions in determining the feasibility of incorporating these differences into a marketing strategy are:
1. Are the segments large enough to warrant the expense of tailoring the marketing effort to each group? and
2. Can the segments be reached through the available promotional media without excessive waste?

The question of reachability is particularly important in evaluating segments defined by market behavior criteria. These segments are often distributed throughout the whole of society. For example, several studies have been shown little relationship between brand loyalty and demographic or personality characteristics [2,34]. Thus it is unlikely that any media would have an extraordinarily high concentration of brand loyal consumers. If the segment is sufficiently large, however, a strategy that Frank, Massy and Wind call "self selection" may be in order [24]. This entails making the promotion available to the general market, with the intent of making segment members identify themselves, and respond to the marketing mix.

SEGMENTING INDUSTRIAL MARKETS

Among the ways that industrial markets may be segmented are by:
1. Characteristics of firms within the market.
2. The ways in which firms purchase goods and services.
3. Attributes and behavioral differences of the decision making units (DMU's) [24].

Organization Characteristic Criteria

Segmentation by industry is the most often mentioned basis for industrial segmentation [16, 21, 24]. The Standard Industrial Classification system (SIC) is a useful tool for categorizing sales prospects [41]. For firms involved in markets with a diversity of potential buyers, this type of segmentation is particularly valuable. Several large firms have found an advantage in dividing their markets by an SIC-like basis, and maintaining separate marketing forces for each segment. Each of these units is expert in the needs of the industry or industry group it services, and is well acquainted with ways that their products can be used to meet them [39]

Industrial markets can also be segmented by size of firm. Small firms will usually have different capital and cash requirements from that of larger firms and thus will respond to different marketing approaches. Moreover, the size of a firm will determine the degree of task specialization. A specialized purchasing agent in a large firm may have different priorities and perceptions than say, a plant manager in a smaller company who does his own purchasing. Geographic Location is another criterion that often will affect response to the marketing mix. For example, a firm located far from an emergency supply of a needed item will have greater concern for terms related to reliability of delivery than a firm that could pick up a needed supply in a hurry [21, 23].

The degree to which a firm makes use of technology may influence the effectiveness of alternative marketing mix variations. A firm that has an R & D capability sufficient to evaluate technical products will require a different marketing approach than a firm that relies on "faith" [51]. Profit situation may also affect the optimal marketing mix. A highly profitable firm will be more interested in long term benefits than a firm that is struggling to meet its current obligations.

Firms whose competitive marketing advantage consists of product quality and reliability of service will consider these aspects important in their own purchasing decisions. Firms whose market advantage lies in price will be more price conscious when they buy materials or components. The industrial marketer must then vary his strategy to meet the different needs of each of these segments. An evaluation of firms' supplier rating systems may lead to insights about what is considered important by each buyer [10, 49].

Industrial Buying Habit Criteria

The degree of centralization of the purchasing function has been shown to affect buying decisions [8, 24]. In a centralized buying office for a large firm, where a purchasing officer's day to day associations are mainly within the purchasing department, these associations will influence him in developing an economy point of view. In a decentralized structure, however, the purchaser will have more contact with people in other functions. In purchasing typewriters, for example, the buyer will look more receptively towards spending a few extra dollars for a superior typewriter if he has more contact with the typists who will use them.

Source loyal segments are evident in industrial as well as in consumer markets. Industrial source loyalty can be seen in terms of a necessary subjective analysis of risk and the buyer's perception of his ability to manage that risk. Cardozo identified two segments of industrial purchasers related to source loyalty [10]:

1. Sequential scanners. This method of supplier selection is employed by firms that are unwilling to assume the risk involved in buying from an unfamiliar source. Once the need for an item is established, this type of buyer will contact a familiar source who will be most likely in his opinion to fill the need. If the price quoted is reasonable, he will make the purchase; if not, he will contact the next most likely source. In this way, the buyer minimizes his risk but is not necessarily getting the best price. As a market segment, these types of firms are important to identify since they necessitate a distinct strategy from non-source loyal buyers. An "out" firm must offer sufficient guarantees of reliability to satisfy the buyer's reluctance. A supplier may even be willing to take a cut in price to get "in" in the belief that buyer satisfaction will lead to future business.
2. Simultaneous scanners. This segment generally consists of more confident buyers and firms whose competitive marketing advantages lies in price. This type of buyer will contact a large number of prospective suppliers, and make a decision based on the relative weights of price and reliability. Thus the purchaser is likely to get a better price, if he is willing to accept the risk of dealing with a less known supplier. Marketing directed at this segment will differ substantially from that used to reach source loyal buyers since taking a low or loss price to get "in" will not necessarily lead to future business. An effective marketing effort for this segment must consist of an accurate evaluation of the firm's perception of price and quality considerations.

Firms handle purchasing decisions at different levels of the organization [8]. While some firms have technically trained purchasing departments that are responsible for major buying decisions, others have purchasing functions whose sole task is to write orders, the decisions being made by general management, R & D, or production departments. Industrial marketers must pinpoint the level at which the effort can be most effectively directed. Robinson and Faris, in a study of several industries found that the organizational level at which purchasing decisions are made varies with the classifications of new purchase, modified rebuy and straight rebuy [41].
1. New Purchase. For the first time purchase of an industrial product, general management will generally have an active role in the buying process. R & D and production engineers will exert considerable influence through recommendations. The purchasing officer's role is usually at a minimum in this situation.
2. Modified Rebuy. In the situation where a product is being bought similar to one previously in use, general management tends to play a much less active role. The purchasing officer will have a greater say in the supplier selections.
3. Straight rebuy. Here the purchasing agent's authority is at a maximum.

Brand suggested that industrial markets can be segmented by categorizing firms by how far along in the decision making process they are. In purchasing plant equipment, it is general management that usually initiates the project [8]. So until the decision to expand or renovate is made, the marketing effort should concentrate on appealing to top-level executives. Once the project is initiated, and R & D is charged with developing specifications for the project, the marketer should attempt to have included characteristics that would give his firm a competitive marketing advantage. After the specs are formulated, the marketing effort should appeal to the point of view of the purchasing officer, or whomever is charged with the actual supplier selection.

Segmentation Based on DMU Characteristics

As noted, it has been argued by Frank, Massy and Wind that industrial markets can be segmented by attributes of the "decision making unit" within each organization [24]. This view is shared by Dichter, who found that certain engineers were found to identify with certain materials [14]. Some preferred glass bottles over metal cans and vice versa, and the reasons seemed to be less than rational. Preconceptions about aluminum were difficult to expel when large vats were manufactured that were proven to be as sturdy as steel.

In international marketing, it is particularly important to recognize how national and cultural differences affect the behavior of purchasing decision makers. Dichter notes that in marketing sophisticated machinery to engineers in Mexico, references to the excellence of German technology produced a negative effect, something that did not happen in the U. S. and other more industrialized countries.

Yankelovich suggested that the computer market can be segmented by differences in prospects' attitudes toward the inevitability of progress [51]. Roberts, in a study of the livestock chemical industry noted that veterinarians were quite 'touchy' about doing business with suppliers that also served the food industry [39].

The importance of decision maker characteristics can best be appreciated if the purchasing decision is understood in terms of a need satisfaction process [43]. Perceived needs differ from one individual to another. An effective marketing approach will appeal on different levels to different industrial purchasers. There are three categories of interacting needs that shape the buying decision.
1. Organizational Needs. Every industrial purchaser is affected by the large scale objectives of the firm, such as increasing sales, decreasing costs, etc.
2. Job Needs. Industrial buyers are influenced by their desire to perform their specific task in a professional manner.
3. Personal Needs. Needs for security, social interaction and esteem affect all human behavior, and buying decisions are no exception.

Industrial marketers should identify segments that are defined by the varying degrees of each one of these needs categories, and where appropriate, make available to their sales forces promotional tools to address properly selected needs. While it has been suggested that empirical research of DMU segments may be feasible, [24] preliminary results of our field research indicate that empirical DMU segmentation studies are virtually non-existent in industry.

Implementing an Industrial Segmentation Strategy

One of the circumstances that has contributed to the
need for sophisticated consumer segmentation research
has been the fact that in modern consumer markets,
there is little direct contact between manufacturer
and ultimate user.  Thus the marketing effort must be
fully contained in the formal promotional channels.
In industrial markets, which are generally characterized
by direct sales efforts, contact is more closely
maintained, and to an extent, segmentation can be
handled by informal variation of the sales approach.
On the other hand, in certain situations, industrial
segmentation seems to be better handled through formal
division of the marketing function.  Thus it seems
that industrial segmentation may have different implications for top level marketing management, middle
management and sales management. Our field research
will deal with the effectiveness of alternative methods
of structuring the marketing function to deal with
market segments.  In general, the options open to
industrial marketers in this regard are: [39]
   1.  Sales force diversification, which in its
       most extreme form is operation under quasi-
       independent subsidiaries in each market
       segment; or
   2.  Product line diversification, under one
       label and one marketing and sales management.
       The sales force is trained to be aware of
       different market segments, how to recognize
       them, and how to vary promotion and terms
       to more precisely meet the requirements of
       each segment.

It is safe to hypothesize that the first option is
better suited for segmentation based on stable characteristics such as organizational attributes, and the
second approach is more likely to be feasible for
dynamic or shifting segments such as groups defined by
DMU attributes.  However, there has been little
research to date devoted to developing a systematic
method for evaluating structural approaches in industrial segmentation.  The second phase of the present
study will attempt to remedy this lack by examining
segmentation strategies of a wide range of industrial
marketing firms.


CONCLUSION

Clearly, industrial markets are not homogeneous, but
consist of segments, which while internally homogeneous
with respect to a given variable, differ from each
other. To be more effective, industrial marketers
should learn to recognize these segments and tailor
product, pricing, promotion and distribution to more
precisely meet the needs of each segment.

The literature of industrial market segmentation
suggests that industrial markets may be segmented
according to:
   1.  Characteristics of organizations
   2.  Buying habits of organizations
   3.  Attitudes and preferences of firms

Additionally, the literature of consumer market segmentation suggests that markets can be segmented according
to:
   1.  Demographic and socioeconomic criteria
   2.  Market behavior criteria

It may be argued that since decision makers in the
industrial setting may be influenced by other than
rational considerations, these two sets of criteria
may also have some applicability to industrial
markets.  The field research we are presently conducting should help to determine which criteria are most
effective, to identify new criteria for industrial
market segmentation and to evaluate the effectiveness
of alternative methods of implementing an industrial
market segmentation strategy.

REFERENCES

1.  Adler, L., "A New Orientation for Plotting
    Marketing Strategy" Business Horizons, 4
    (Winter, 1960) 35-70 reprinted in Engel,
    et. al.  Market Segmentation N.Y.:  Holt
    Rinehart and Winston, 1972, 60-78.

2.  Advertising Research Foundation, Are there
    Consumer Types? N.Y.:  Advertising Research
    Foundation, 1964.

3.  Banks, S., "Some Correlates of Coffee and
    Cleanser Brand Shares" Journal of Advertising
    Research, 1 (June, 1961) 22-28.

4.  Bauer, R. A. and S. M. Cunningham, "The
    Negro Market" Journal of Advertising Research,
    10 (April, 1970) 3-13.

5.  Baumwoll, J. P., "Segmentation Research –
    the Baker vs. the Cookie Maker" Proceedings
    of the American Marketing Association
    Meeting, (1974) 14-21.

6.  Blattberg, R.C. and S. K. Sen, "Market
    Segmentation Using Models of Multidimen-
    sional Purchasing Behavior" Journal of
    Marketing, 38 (Oct., 1974) 17-28.

7.  Boomer, P., "Male Market:  Big, Rich and
    Tough" Printer's Ink, 280 (July 20, 1962)
    21-25.

8.  Brand, G. T. , The Industrial Buying Decision
    N.Y.:  Wiley, 1973.

9.  Bruno, A. V. , T. P. Hustard and E. A.
    Pesemier, "Media Approaches to Segementation"
    Journal of Advertising Research, (Apr., 1973)
    35-42.

10. Cardozo, R. N., "Segementing the Industrial
    Market" Proceedings of the American
    Marketing Association Conference, (Fall, 1968)
    433-40.

11. Claycamp, H. J. and W. F. Massy, "A Theory of Market Segmentation" _Journal of Marketing Research_, 35 (Nov., 1968) 388-94.

12. Cohen, J. B., "An Interpersonal Orientation to the Study of Consumer Behavior" _Journal of Marketing Research_, 4 (Aug., 1967) 270-78.

13. Crockett, J. and I. Friend, "A Complete Set of Consumer Demand Relationships" in I. Friend and R. Jones, eds. _Consumption and Savings_, Phil., PA: University of Pennsylvania Press, 1960.

14. Dichter, Erenst, "Industrial Buying is Based on the Same 'Only Human' Emotional Factors that Motivate Consumer Market Housewives," _Industrial Marketing_, 58 (Feb., 1973) 14-16.

15. Dobriner, W. M., _Class in Suburbia_, Englewood Cliffs. N.J.: Prentice Hall, 1963.

16. Dodge, H. R., _Industrial Marketing_, New York: McGraw Hill, 1970.

17. Edwards, A. L., _Edwards Personal Peference Schedule Manual_. N.Y.: Psychological, Corporations, 1959.

18. Engel, J.F., H. F. Fiorillo and M. A. Cayley, eds, _Market Segmentation_, New York: Holt, Rinehart and Winston, 1972.

19. Evans, F. B. , "Psychological and Objective Factors in the Prediction of Brand Choice," _Journal of Business_, 32 (Oct., 1959).

20. Ferber, R., "Factors Influencing Durable Goods Purchases" in L. H. Clark, ed., _The Life Cycle and Consumer Behavior_. N.Y.: New York University Press, 1955.

21. Fischer, L., _Industrial Marketing_, (N.Y., 1970).

22. Foote, N. L., "Market Segmentation as a Competitive Strategy" in Leo Bogard, ed., _Current Controversies in Marketing Research_, (Chicago, 1969).

23. Frank, R. E., "Market Segmentation Research: Findings and Implications" in Frank M. Bass, ed., _The Application of the Sciences to Marketing Management_, (N.Y., 1968) 39-68.

24. _____, W. M. Massy and Y. Wind, _Market Segmentation_. Englewood Cliffs, N.J.: Prentice Hall, 1972.

25. Gibson, D. P., _The $30 Billion Negro_. N.Y.: Macmillan, 1970.

26. Goldstein, S., "The Aged Segment of the Market" _Journal of Marketing_, 32 (Apr., 1968) 62-68.

27. Goluskin, N., "Every Man a Walter Mitty," _Sales Management_ 115 (July, 1975) 45-46.

28. Hustad, T. P., C. S. Mayer and T. W. Whipple, "Segmentation Research Works If" _Proceedings of the American Marketing Association Meeting_, (1974) 21-25.

29. Kassarjian, H. H., "Personality and Consumer Behavior: A Review" _Journal of Marketing Research_, 8 (Nov., 1971) 409-18.

30. Katz, E., and P. Larzfeld, _Personal Influence_. N.Y.: The Fall Press, 1955.

31. Kollat, D. R., and R. P. Willett, "Customer Impulse Purchasing Behavior" _Journal of Marketing Research_, 4 (Feb., 1967) 21-31.

32. Lansing, J. B., and L. Kish, "Family Life Cycles as an Independent Variable" _American Sociological Review_, 22 (Oct., 1967) 512-19.

33. Marcus, A. S. and R. A. Bauer, "Yes, There Are Generalized Opinion Leaders," _Public Opinion Quarterly_, 28 (Winter, 1964) 638-42.

34. Massy, W. and R. Frank, "Short-Term Price and Dealing Effects in Selected Market Segments" _Journal of Marketing Research_, 2 (May, 1965) 171-85.

35. Matthews, H. L. and J. W. Slocum, "Social Class and Commercial Bank Credit Card Usage," _Journal of Marketing_, 33 (Jan., 1969) 71-78.

36. Politz, A., _A 12 Month of Better Homes and Garden Readers_, (Des Moines, 1956).

37. "Researchers Categorize Beer Drinkers to Aid Anheuser-Bush Brand Efforts" _Advertising Age_, 46 (July, 1957) 17.

38. Rich, S. V. and S. C. Jaim, "Social Class and Life Cycle as Predictors of Shopping Behavior," _Journal of Marketing Research_, 5 (Feb., 1968) 41-49.

39. Roberts, A. A., "Applying the Strategy of Market Segmentation," _Business Horizons_, 4 (Fall, 1961) 65-72. reprinted in Engel, et al. _Market Segmentation_ (N.Y. 1972) 78-89.

40. Robinson, P. J. and C. L. Hinkle, _Standard Industrial Classification for Marketing Analysis_. Philadelphia: Marketing Science Institute, 1967.

41. _____ and C. W. Faris, _Industrial Buying and Creative Marketing_. Boston: Allyn and Bacon, 1967.

42. Rotzoll, K. B., "The Effect of Social Stratification on Market Behavior" _Journal of Advertising Research_, 7 (March, 1967) 22-27.

43. Schiff, J. S., "Why Pros Buy Like Amateurs," _Sales Management_ (Oct., 1970).

44. Smith, Wendell R., "Product Differentiation and Market Segmentation" _Journal of Marketing_, 21 (July, 1956) 3-8.

45.  Udell, J. G., "Can Attitude Measurement Predict
     Consumer Behavior" Journal of Marketing 29 (Oct.,
     1965) 46-50.

46.  Walters, C. G. and G. W. Paul, Consumer Behavior:
     an Intergrated Framework. Homewood, ILL: Irwin,
     1970.

47.  Wells, W. D. and G. Gubar, "Life Cycle Concept in
     Marketing Research" Journal of Marketing Research,
     3 Nov., 1966) 355-63.

48.  _____, Life Style and Psychographics,
     Chicago: American Marketing Association, 1974.

49.  Wieters, C. D., "The Design and Use of Supplier
     Performance Rating Systems in Selected Industries,"
     Unpublished doctoral dissertation, Arizona State
     University, (May, 1976).

50.  Wolff, J., What Makes Woman Buy?  New York:
     McGraw-Hill, 1958.

51.  Yankelovich, D., "New Criteria for Market Segmenta-
     tion," Harvard Business Review, 42 (March-April,
     1964) 83-90.

# A TYPOLOGY OF INDUSTRIAL NEW PRODUCT FAILURE

Roger J. Calantone, McGill University
Robert G. Cooper, McGill University

## ABSTRACT

This paper develops a typology of new product failures of industrial products. Each of the products was classified into groups based on the precipitating circumstances of market failure. Then scenarios are derived based on deficient activities, resources, and market factors of each type.

## INTRODUCTION

A definite pattern to industrial new product failure does exist. These are the conclusions of our research. Not only is there a pattern to new product failure, but most industrial failures fit into one of a set of typical scenarios or typologies.

Each year, the marketplace is witness to the introduction of thousands of new industrial products. And each year, the familiar story is repeated .... the majority of these products fail commercially. Indeed, reliable estimates place the failure rate at somewhere between 50% and 90%. As much as 80% of the thirty billion dollars spent annually on product innovation in the U.S. is spent on products which fail or are withdrawn from the market [1].

## PREVIOUS RESEARCH

The empirical evidence gathered to date points to marketing as the key problem area. Inadequate market analysis and a lack of effective marketing efforts were the main reasons for product failure cited by the Conference Board's Senior Marketing Executives Panel [8]. A lack of market orientation was the main cause of failures in industrial innovations found by Robertson in a study of 34 case histories [9].

Research into product failure is predicated on the belief that an understanding of one's past blunders will pave the way for more successful efforts in the future. Most such research has focussed on a simple listing and count of the reasons for failure, with little attention paid to the development of a framework for understanding what ails product innovation. Moreover this research has suffered from the fact that it usually involved a survey of management opinion without reference to specific product failures, or at best, a review of a very limited sample of failures [6, 8]. But in spite of the apparent methodological weaknesses, the results seem to point to a similar picture.

Our research focusses on the development of scenarios or typologies of industrial new product failures. The need for an empirical study of a large and representative sample of failures .... a valid post-mortem analysis .... is clear. Moreover, the prospect of moving beyond a simple listing of failure reasons and towards a framework for understanding these failures, is an appealing one. The development of groupings or clusters of product failures, each with its own typology, is not only of methodological interest, but also has managerial utility.

## A MODEL FOR THE STUDY

A conceptual model of new product failure was first developed. This generalized model was first proposed and

## FIGURE I: A CONCEPTUAL MODEL OF PRODUCT FAILURE

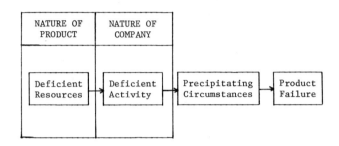

reported on by Cooper [2] in his original study of 114 new product failures. Later this model was used by Cooper [3] as a basis for studying the reason why certain new products were successful in their market introductions. This later paper presented several extended case studies of these new product introductions which avoided the pitfalls identified in the first paper. This paper extends the previous work in that methodological rigor is applied to the question of generalized types of failures and which specific causes tend to happen concurrently with each specific type of failure.

The new product development process can be viewed as a sequential, stagewise process, each step moving the product project closer to the ultimate goal of commercialization. These stages consist of activities, whose purpose in part is to provide additional information needed to proceed to the next stage or activity. At the final stage, the product is launched into the market, where its commercial viability is determined.

If the product fails commercially, the causes of failure can be directly attributed to decisions and/or events which occurred in and around the launch stage. These decisions/events immediately linked to the failure are the "precipitating circumstances" of failure. But often these precipitating circumstances have their roots earlier in the product development process; they can be traced back to one or more stages of the process which were poorly undertaken. Thus "deficient activities" are yet another set of reasons for failure.

Finally, the product development process takes place within a corporate environment. The extent to which the company possesses the vital resources needed to undertake the product project will certainly impact upon the eventual outcome of the product. In addition the nature of the company itself together with the type of new product are important considerations in the study of product failure.

Thus three sets of variables which are directly or indirectly related to product failure have been identified:

1. Precipitating circumstances: events and decisions:
   Example: "Our price was too high; customers opted for inferior competitive products at much lower prices"

2. Deficient activities:
   Example: "We failed to do a thorough market study"

3. Deficient Resources:
   Example: "We sadly lack marketing research skills and resources"

Two other sets of variables .... the nature of the product and the company .... are introduced as moderating variables.

## METHODOLOGY

### Data Collection

A sample of 150 industrial product firms were contacted to provide the product failure information. These firms were located in Ontario and Quebec, Canada, and were known to be active in product development [4][1]. The sample included the larger and more obvious product developers as well as a random selection of smaller firms. This bias towards larger firms was deliberate in order to reflect their greater importance in a study of product development.

In each firm, the manager most likely to be familiar with his company's new product activities was contacted.[2] A questionnaire was mailed to each manager, who was asked to answer general questions about his firm and the nature of its business. Next he was requested to select two typical product failures - products which had been commercialized but had fallen far short profitability expectations.[3] The criteria for selecting the two failures were:

- new products (new to the firm);
- recent failures (within last 5 years);
- products developed by the firm in Canada;
- products typical to the firm.

For each product the manager was asked to categorize the nature of the failure. In this study we were particularly interested in market failures .... those products where sales had failed far short of expectations. (Other failure categories such as "excessive investment", "excessive manufacturing costs and difficulties" were also offered). If the product was a market failure, the manager was then presented with a lengthy list of possible precipitating circumstances which might explain why sales failed to materialize. The response categories used for precipitating circumstances were: a main cause; contributing cause; or not a cause. An "other" category and space for comments was provided. Table I provides a listing of these causes of failure and their relative frequencies.

---

[1]Source of the sample was [4].

[2]All firms had been contacted in previous research.

[3]An exact operational definition of a "product failure" was not possible in this research. However, to the extent the research focussed only on product failures (rather than matched pairs of successes and failures), an exact and dichotomous operational definition was not essential. Managers were instructed to pick ventures which were clear and obvious financial failures from their firms' point of view.

TABLE I

SPECIFIC CAUSES FOR POOR SALES PERFORMANCE (N=89)

| Specific Cause | Percent of Product Failures | |
|---|---|---|
| | Main Cause | Contributing Cause |
| Competitors were more firmly entrenched in the market than expected | 36.4 | 13.6 |
| The number of potential users was overestimated | 20.5 | 30.7 |
| The price was set higher than customers would pay | 18.2 | 33.3 |
| The product had design, technical or manufacturing deficiencies/difficulties | 20.5 | 25.0 |
| Selling, distribution or promotional efforts were misdirect | 15.9 | 23.9 |
| The product was the same as competing products ... "a me too" product | 14.8 | 25.0 |
| Did not understand customer requirements; product did not meet his needs or specifications | 13.6 | 26.1 |
| Selling, distribution or promotional efforts were inadequate | 9.1 | 31.8 |
| A similar competitive product was introduced | 10.2 | 22.7 |
| Were unable to develop or produce product exactly as desired | 11.4 | 19.3 |
| Competitors lowered prices or took other defensive actions | 12.5 | 13.6 |
| Timing was too late | 8.0 | 13.6 |
| No market need existed for this type of product | 5.7 | 18.2 |
| Timing was premature | 6.8 | 13.6 |
| Government action/ legislation hindered the sale of the product | 2.3 | 3.4 |

Next the manager was presented with a list and brief description of a number of activities typically undertaken in a new product process. He was asked to rate how well each activity had been performed for each product failure. The response categories were: done more than adequately; done adequately; done inadequately; not done, but should have been; not applicable.

The manager was also shown a list of possible resource deficiencies, and asked to indicate how much each had contributed to the failure. The response categories were: very much, somewhat, or not at all. Finally, a number of questions were posed in order to characterize the company and the nature of the product.

The original sample of 150 firms was reduced to an effective sample of 101. A handful of firms were no longer in business. Another 46 firms actually had no recent product failures to discuss; in some cases, the firm was basically a one-or-two-product firm, and simply did not undertake enough innovative product development to encounter failures; in other cases, the firm undertook product development on a contract basis (for example, aerospace), and once the contract was awarded, was assured of a profitable product development. This was based on returned questionnaires and telephone follow-up discussions.

Of the sample of 101 firms which actually encountered product failures, 66 replied to the questionnaire for an effective response rate of 65%. Not all the firms were able to discuss two failures, and the eventual sample numbered 114 product failures. Thus, the sample of products is biased toward firms with more active product development programs. The sample of firms which responded represented a wide variety of industries, and ranged in size from very small companies to corporate giants.

Data Analysis

An examination of specific causes of low sales (Table I) suggested a considerable amount of interrelationship among the fifteen sales causes. Factor analysis was performed and a six factor solution explaining 66.8% of the variance was selected. Table II shows the important factor loadings - the loadings of specific causes on each factor, and provides an interpretation of each factor.

TABLE II

LOADINGS OF SPECIFIC CAUSES ON EACH FACTOR (N=89) AFTER VARIMAX ROTATION (Only the Main Loadings are Shown)

| Factor | Specific Causes Most Heavily Loaded on Factor | Loading* | Interpretation |
|---|---|---|---|
| 1 | Tech. difficulties with product | 0.918 | |
| | Could not produce product | 0.623 | Technical problems |
| | Inadequate selling effort (negative) | -0.305 | |
| 2 | "Me too" product | 0.722 | |
| | Timing too late | 0.688 | Timing too late |
| | Competitors firmly entrenched | 0.572 | |
| | Timing premature (negative) | -0.307 | |
| 3 | Lack of market need for product | 0.692 | Lack of understanding of customers' needs |
| | Did not understand customer requirements | 0.531 | |
| | Potential users overestimated | 0.439 | |

TABLE II (continued)

| Factor | Specific Causes Most Heavily Loaded on Factor | Loading* | Interpretation |
|---|---|---|---|
| 4 | Similar products were introduced | 0.967 | Defensive actions by competitors |
| | Competitive defensive actions | 0.491 | |
| 5 | Sales efforts misdirect | 0.441 | Lack of understanding of market environment |
| | Government action/ legislation | 0.466 | |
| | Inadequate selling effort | 0.268 | |
| 6 | Competitive defensive actions | 0.522 | Price competition |
| | Price too high | 0.534 | |

The next step in the analysis is a clustering of the product failures. In respect to the possibility of redundancy in the original measures, the factor scores of each case was used as the data input [7]. The factor scores of the 89 cases were input to the Howard-Harris [5] cluster routine, and the cases were successfully grouped into two thorough seven groups. Three cases were dropped at this point due to excessive missing data, thus reducing effective sample size to 86 failures. No systematic bias could be found in the three dropped cases.

In order to select a final cluster solution, the percent of the total sum of squares appearing as within group sum of squares was examined for each level of grouping. An evaluation of the results indicated a relatively drastic change in within group homogeneity between a clustering level of six and five groups.

A grouping level of six groups was chosen based on maximal heterogeneity between groups and managerial interpretability. Interpretation of each group was determined by simple ANOVAS with Duncan multiple range tests performed on the factor scores. At the six group level all the F's were significant at the $\alpha=.01$ level. The Duncan ($\alpha=.01$) multiple range tests showed which group(s) were significantly higher or lower on each factor.

To aid in further interpretation, the same analysis was performed on the original fifteen variables measuring sales specific causes of new product failure. In addition the same tests were performed on seven market situation descriptors, six company descriptors, seven resource deficiency measures, and twelve activity deficiency variables.

RESULTS

Six clusters of product failures were identified, each cluster representing a unique scenario or typology. The results are presented in Table III, and each cluster or scenario is described below:

TABLE III   RESULTS OF ANOVAS

SIGNIFICANT HIGH SCORE FROM DUNCAN ($\alpha = .01$)
MULTIPLE RANGE TEST INDICATED X

| Sales Causes | Grp 1 28% | Grp 2 24% | Grp 3 13% | Grp 4 7% | Grp 5 15% | Grp 6 13% |
|---|---|---|---|---|---|---|
| 1. Overestimated potential mkt. | X | | | | | |
| 2. No need for product | | | | | | |
| 3. A "me too" product | | X | X | | | |
| 4. Failed to match prod. to market | | | | X | X | |
| 5. Understood mkt. but failed to produce | | | | | X | |
| 6. Engineering Deficiencies | | | | | X | |
| 7. Price too high | | | | | | X |
| 8. Timing premature (ns) | | | | | | |
| 9. Timing too late | | | | | | |
| 10. Competitive prod. introduced | | | X | X | | X |
| 11. Competitors lowered price | | | | | | X |
| 12. Competitors firmly entrenched | | | X | X | | |
| 13. Inadequate promotion or selling | | | | X | | |
| 14. Misdirect promotion or selling | | | | X | | |
| 15. Govt. action interfered | | | | X | | |

| Deficient Activities | Grp 1 | Grp 2 | Grp 3 | Grp 4 | Grp 5 | Grp 6 |
|---|---|---|---|---|---|---|
| 1. Initial Screening | X | X | | | | |
| 2. Prelim. mkt. assessment | X | | | | | |
| 3. Prelim. tech. assessment | | | | | X | |
| 4. Mkt. potential study | | | X | X | | X |
| 5. Prod. Develop. | | | X | | X | |
| 6. Financial Anal. | | X | | X | | X |
| 7. Inhouse prototype test. | | | | | X | X |
| 8. Customer prototype test. | | | X | | X | X |
| 9. Pilot/test production | | | | | X | X |
| 10. Test Market/ Trial selling | | | | X | | |
| 11. Production start up | | | | X | | |
| 12. Product level | | | X | X | | X |

| Deficient Resources | Grp 1 28% | Grp 2 24% | Grp 3 13% | Grp 4 7% | Grp 5 15% | Grp 6 13% |
|---|---|---|---|---|---|---|
| 1. Financial | | | | | | |
| 2. Engineering Skills | | | | X | | |
| 3. R & D Skill | | | X | X | | |
| 4. Marketing Research | X | | X | | | |
| 5. Mgmt. Skills (ns) | | | | | | |
| 6. Production Resources (ns) | | | | | | |
| 7. Selling | | X | | X | | X |

| Nature of Market & Product | Grp 1 | Grp 2 | Grp 3 | Grp 4 | Grp 5 | Grp 6 |
|---|---|---|---|---|---|---|
| 1. New Market to Co. (ns) | | | | | | |
| 2. Product totally new to market | X | | | | | X |
| 3. Product new to Co. (ns) | | | | | | |
| 4. New type of R & D to Co. (ns) | | | | | | |
| 5. New selling & distribution for this prod. | | | | X | | |
| 6. Production newness (ns) | | | | | | |
| 7. Production is imp. to Co. (ns) | | | | | | |
| 8. Certainty | | | | X | | |
| 9. Risk | | | | X | | X |

### Company Attributes

1. Firm type (ns)
2. Annual Sales (ns)
3. % of sales due to new prod.
4. New prod. devel. success
5. % failures (ns)
6. Size of R & D budget (ns)

NOTE:  ns = not significant

Cluster I - "The Better Mousetrap No One Wanted" (28% of failures).

Product failures in this group were unique products that were rejected by the market. The number of potential customers who might buy and use the product was overestimated: there simply wasn't a widespread need for the product. But there were virtually no other obstacles to the product. Technical problems were absent in development, and no strong competitive market action was discerned. The selling effort was adequate and timing not a problem.

Several activities were mentioned as contributing to the failure, most notably a lack of initial screening and a failure to undertake preliminary market assessment. Executives indicated that a lack of market research skills and people certainly contributed to the failure. In summary, the development of a new and unique product without proper attention to customer and requirements doomed this type of product to be "the better mousetrap no one wanted".

Cluster II - "The Me-Too Product Meeting a Competitive Brick-Wall" (24% of failures)

These cases were products which were very similar to products already on the market, and also met customers' needs. But they were launched into a market in which competitors were firmly entrenched. The market potential was correctly estimated; market entry was not premature; and similar products were not launched concurrently by competitors. Moreover, competitors did not react with price cuts. It was simply more difficult to dislodge competitive products then anticipated. With a "me too" product and no differential advantage, the product never stood much of a chance.

These products tended to be product modifications of the company's existing product line. But typically they were targetted at new markets for the company. Little new technology was required by the company in their development. Of particular importance was the fact that a poor financial analysis and an inadequate selling effort were thought to be key activities contributing to the failure.

Cluster III - "Competitive One Upmanship" (13% of failures)

This group of failures consists of "me too" products which were hurt by the concurrent introduction of similar products by competitors. Premature timing was not a problem; nor was severe price competition. This was a case of being upstaged by competitive new products.

Products in this group tended to be regarded as relatively unimportant by the company. Thorough market studies, product development and market testing activities tended to be absent or poorly undertaken during the process. The product launch itself was also deficient. Managers believed that a lack of R & D skills contributed to the product's failure. To summarize, we are witness to products which went to market lacking adequate development, market studies and launch efforts. When competitive products were introduced, ours were easily displaced.

Cluster IV - "Environmental Ignorance" (7% of cases)

Products in this group typically were not well suited to customers' needs, and the product was deemed inappropriate for the market. Competitive products were introduced at about the same time, while competitors themselves were already firmly entrenched in the market. The selling and promotional effort was both inadequate and misdirected. Finally these projects tended to run a foul of government regulations. In the case of this small group of products, everything that could go wrong - did! This was due to a complete misreading of the environment: customers, competitors and government.

These products were characterized by a number of deficient activities: thorough market studies; financial analysis; test markets; production start-up; and product launch. A lack of marketing research resources and a lack of selling resources were thought to contribute to these failures. Usually, the company found itself in a new distribution method with such products. Management perceived the products as being important, fairly uncertain as to outcome, yet surprisingly, a low risk venture!

Cluster V - The Technical "Dog" Product (15% of cases)

These products were unique products, and certainly not "me too" designs. Their main drawback was that they did not perform in a technical sense as expected. The company was fully aware of what customers wanted, but were unable to turn these needs into the appropriate product design.

Engineering and production flaws and deficiencies plagued the product. The product was simply a "bad product".

These products typically represented a new addition to the company's product line, as opposed to a product modification. But these products were typically sold to familiar markets and through existing company channels.

Deficient activities centered around the preliminary technical assessment and product development efforts. Little prototype testing was done either in-house or with the customer. Pilot production was also inadequate. As might be expected, resource deficiencies cited were in the areas of R & D and Engineering skills.

Cluster VI - "The Price Crunch" (13% of cases)

These products were approximately designed and well suited to customers' needs. The fatal blow came when they were introduced at prices higher than customers were prepared to pay. Moreover competitors tended to react to their introduction by cutting prices. Finally, there was some evidence of competitive introductions of similar products. This scenario is a common one: "the company offered a Cadillac when the market wanted a Ford".

These products were typically modifications of existing company products, but were also somewhat unique in the marketplace. Market studies and market tests were judged to be inadequate, and product launch was poorly undertaken. Deficient marketing research skills and deficient selling resources were cited as contributing to the failure. Thus a failure to understand customer price sensitivities and likely competitive reactions together with a troubled launch were at the roots of the product failure.

## CONCLUSIONS

This post-mortem study of a large sample of industrial product failures permitted the development of six typologies of product failure. Besides having internal validity, the scenarios themselves appear to be intuitively plausible. Indeed, managers are quick to recognize some or all of these typologies as scenarios which beset their own new product failures.

The typology developed provides a convenient framework or classification system for analyzing past new product failures. To the extent that many firms do perform periodic reviews of failures, then this typology should assist him.

At the same time, the scenarios, which were based on precipitating circumstances of failure, tended to be related to groups of variables which preceded the failure: deficient activities; deficient resources; and characteristics of the product/market. Thus we gain a clearer understanding of the facilitating situations which lead to various types of product failure.

## REFERENCES

1. Booz, Allen & Hamilton (1965). Management of New Products, New York.

2. Cooper, R. (1975). "Why New Industrial Products Fail", Industrial Marketing Management, 4, pp. 315-326.

3. Cooper, R. (1976). "Introducing Successful New Products", European Journal of Marketing, Vol. 10, #6.

4.  Directory of Scientific Research and Development
    Establishments in Canada (1969).  Ottawa:  Department
    of Industry, Trade, and Commerce.

5.  Howard, N. and B. Harris (October 1966).  A
    Hierarchical Grouping Routine, IBM 360/65 Fortran
    in Program, University of Pennsylvania Computer
    Center.

6.  Konopa, L.J. (1968).  New Products:  Assessing
    Commercial Potential, Management Bulletin #88.
    New York:  American Management Association

7.  Morrison, D. (August 1967).  "On Measurement Problems
    in Cluster Analysis", Management Science, 13,
    pp. 775-780.

8.  National Industrial Conference Board (1964).  "Why
    New Products Fail", The Conference Board Record.

9.  Robertson, A. (1973).  "The Marketing Factor in
    Successful Industrial Innovation", Industrial
    Marketing Management, #2.

# THE DIFFUSION OF INNOVATION IN INDUSTRIAL MARKETS

Michael J. Baker, Strathclyde University
F. Abu-Ismail, Cairo University

## ABSTRACT

Most research into factors which distinguish between early
and late adopters in industrial markets has tended to emphasize economic variables (size and profitability).
This paper reports the results of a survey combining both
economic and behavioral variables and presents a multiple
regression equation which "explains" 63% of the variance
in the adoption sequence.

## INTRODUCTION

It is widely accepted that technological innovation embodied in new products constitutes a major source of
economic growth. However, while this contribution is
positive in the aggregate, there is much evidence to indicate that it is considerably reduced by the failure of
many new product introductions. Such failure is a waste
of scarce economic resources.

In that "failure" is usually measured in terms of elapsed
time to achieve some predetermined level of sales or profit,
it is clear that the speed of diffusion, or acceptance
of a new product is a vital determinant of success. If
this is the case, then a critical factor in determining
the speed of acceptance of a new product is the innovator's ability to pre-identify those potential users with
the greatest likelihood of early adoption and to focus
his marketing effort on them. (Adoption is defined here
as the decision to invest in and make full use of an innovation.)

An extensive review of the literature indicates that in a
marketing context most research into adoption/diffusion
has concentrated upon new consumer products while relatively little attention has been given to industrial innovation. In the particular, the collective influence
of economic, behavioral and managerial factors on "elapsed
time to adoption" have been explored by only a handful
of researchers including Mansfield [8], Peters and
Venkatesan [11], Webster [13], Ozanne and Churchill[10],
Czepiel [5], and Baker [2].

In this paper we report the findings of a survey designed
to test a refined version of the model proposed by Baker
(op. cit.) and described at length by Abu-Ismail [1].

The model distinguishes three major phases or stages in
the adoption decision. The first of these phases we
characterize as the "input" stage in which an innovation
is seeking to establish recognition by prospective adopters (i.e. awareness). Our findings confirm and extend
earlier work which suggests that product attributes and
especially their ability to fill an existing performance
gap coupled with the type and quality of product-related
communications (largely impersonal) are of crucial importance.

The second phase encompasses the decision making process
in which an extended and mainly formal analysis of the
innovation's advantages and disadvantages is undertaken.
Since most industrial adoption decisions are taken
jointly (e.g. see Wilson [14]) the identity of the decision making group, the flexibility of the organizational
system, the firm's ability to meet the capital investment
required by the innovation, and the ability to make the

innovation fit in with the manufacturing system are all
determinants during this phase.

Finally, the third stage represents the "output" whereby
the decision making unit commits the organization to
either adopt, reject or postpone judgement on the innovation.

Two assumptions are implicit in the model. First, if the
model is to have operational utility, one must regard the
firm as a single decision making unit (DMU) the future
behavior of which may be predicted under certain prescribed
conditions and, second, based on the hypothesis that firms
do exhibit a certain consistency in their response to
external stimuli, it is assumed that such consistency is
amenable to external observation and measurement.

## METHODOLOGY

An extensive survey of significant innovations launched
in the U.K. within the past ten years suggested that
needled fibrous backing materials for use in the manufacture
of tufted carpets would be a suitable subject for study.
(The criteria for determining "significance" and for
selecting this particular innovation are set out at length
in Baker and Parkinson [3].

Having secured the co-operation of the innovator, and
access to their sales records from which the precise
sequence of adoption was determined, a series of interviews
were conducted with firms in the industry. Of the 74 firms
in the population 41(55%) agreed to co-operate and were
found to constitute a representative sample of the population (see Abu-Ismail (op. cit.) for a full description.)

Data was collected on 39 independent variables. However,
a number of these variables reflected different approaches
to measuring a particular dimension of a firms characteristics and/or behavior so that 10 groups of variables may
be distinguished - Product attributes (9 vars.), Firm size/
performance (4 vars.), Organizational Structure (5 vars.),
Progressiveness of Personnel Policies (3 vars.), Marketing
Orientation (5 vars.), Scientific Orientation (8 vars.),
Creativity of DMU (1 var.), Cosmopoliteness (1 var.),
Opinion Leadership of Decision Makers (2 vars.), Professionalism of Decision Makers (1 var.). A full discussion
of all these variables is to be found in Abu-Ismail (op.
cit.) and a brief description of the general approach
must suffice here.

In the study reported in Marketing New Industrial Products,
Baker was concerned primarily with exploring the dimensions
of what Mansfield [8], Ray [12], and Carter and Williams
[4], had designated "managerial attitude". In essence
this factor embraced the unexplained variance in the
sequence in which firms adopted different innovations after
the economic variables such as size and profitability had
been accounted for. While the latter were excluded from
the earlier survey by Baker, in this case it was decided
to include them and also to incorporate other factors
which had been identified in subsequent studies by other
researchers. For example, Project Sappho (Science Policy
Research Unit, University of Sussex) had stressed the importance of a marketing orientation as a characteristic
of successful innovators and it was hypothesized in turn
that a marketing orientated firm would be more receptive to
innovations offered to it. Accordingly 5 measures of

marketing orientation were developed to test this basic hypothesis, e.g., use of market research, importance attached to the marketing function etc. A similar procedure was followed for the other major groups of variables, the titles of which are largely self explanatory.

## FINDINGS

Data yielded by the field survey were analyzed using multiple regression and factor analysis techniques - only the former is reported here.

From the correlation matrix of 39 independent variables for which data had been collected a set of 12 variables was selected for further investigation. The criteria for selection were that a variable should have a high correlation (relatively) with the dependent variable "elapsed time to adoption", low intercorrelation with other variables in the set and should not be a size or size related variable (i.e., total assets, sales volume, etc.). This latter constraint was applied as the main thrust of our analysis was to establish the contribution of non-"economic" variables, i.e., the nature of "managerial attitude".

The stepwise regression programme in the SPSS package (regression co-efficient not normalized) yielded Table 1 below.

The most powerful variable is one of the product attributes - specifically the compatibility of 'fit' of the innovation with the adopter's extant manufacturing system. Other product attributes such as the impact of the innovation upon raw material savings (a significant product plus) and on the quality of the finished product failed to distinguish early from late adoption. We hypothesize that these factors lack discriminatory power as the innovators' promotional campaign centered on the 'relative advantage' of the new material with the result that these benefits were obvious to all potential adopters and so were not determinant.

In fact, the appeal of product attributes depends not only upon their physical characteristics, but also upon the quantity and quality of their communicability (the correlation co-efficient between both resulted in 0.787). The quality of product-related communication was measured by its ability to reduce perceived risk, and to increase certainty of economic and technical advantages of the innovation. Among these variables, the rating of perceived risk did not conform to our hypothesis in that

early adopters perceive the innovation as <u>less</u> risky than do later adopters. (With hindsight, of course, it seems perfectly natural that early adopters should have lower perceived risk!)

The characteristics of the company were found also to be able to distinguish between earlier and later adoption of the innovation under investigation here. Among these characteristics, the type of organization, progressiveness of personnel policies, marketing orientation and size variables were the most significant predictors of why some firms use a new technique long before other firms. (It should be noted that there was intercorrelation between company size and the type of organization.)

One conclusion which comes from the analysis of multiple regression results is that by comparison with organic systems, mechanistic organization with their rigid rules and procedures, <u>centralization of authority</u>, greater number of hierarchical levels, etc., resulted in later adoption of the innovation.

Analysis of the degree of integration between major departments produced results which seem to contradict the view held by Lawrence and Lorsch [6, 7], in that integration is an important variable in the acceptance of innovation. We do not know yet if this was a result of the design of measures used in examining this dimension or if it was a result of the existence of a greater degree of differentiation between different parts of the organization in early adopter firms especially if we consider that they are larger than later adopters.

The dilemma in this case is that although the adoption of major innovations requires huge capital investments, and technological/marketing potentialities which are available mostly in large firms, the integration of departments becomes more difficult in the case of these firms than in the case of smaller firms. The qualitative data collected through interviews held in nine adopter firms indicated that some firms were able to overcome this dilemma and adopt earlier by having an influential and enthusiastic person behind the project (the "product champion").

As for marketing and scientific orientations, the results of the field study suggest that early adopter firms are marketing and scientific oriented to a greater extent than later adopters. Among variables relevant to <u>marketing orientation</u>, concern with trends in the overall market and product diversification, and the membership of the marketing manager on the company board proved to be linked to early adoption.

TABLE 1

THE EXPLANATORY POWER OF BEHAVIORAL AND PRODUCT RELATED VARIABLES

| Variable | Co-efficient | Standard Error | "t" value | Significance* | $R^2$ |
|---|---|---|---|---|---|
| Product Attributes | 5.141 | 1.385 | 3.712 | 0.0005 | 0.371 |
| Centralization of Authority | -2.273 | 1.158 | -1.964 | 0.02 | 0.161 |
| Marketing Orientation | -2.263** | 1.191 | -1.901 | 0.02 | 0.073 |
| Managers Creativity | 0.2665 | 0.2662 | 1.001 | 0.15 | 0.025 |

Multiple Correlation = 0.7936      $R^2$ = 0.6298

P under 0.001

\* Based upon one tail test

\*\* The negative sign is due to the phrasing of the question but not due to the inverse relationships with early adoption of needleweave.

As for scientific orientation, efficiency in knowing how to make the innovation fit in with the manufacturing system, the allocation of a greater number of persons full time on technical research and development work, and the membership of the R&D manager on the company board are associated positively with early adoption of the innovation.

The identity of the decision making group was also examined in its relation to the length of time the firm waits before accepting an innovation. Although this dimension (Managers creativity in the Table) resulted in a very low explanatory power of time lapse to adoption (it produced $R^2$ of 0.03) we believe that it is an important factor in differentiating between earlier and later adoption of innovation. We faced two difficulties when measuring decision group identity:

(a) We were unable to find established measure to capture the essence of decision group identity, especially creativity variables and so had to develop our own measures, the validity and reliability of which have not been established. Clearly, the failure to discriminate may well be due to deficiencies in our measures.

(b) We applied an arbitrary approach for summing the decision makers' scores in each firm to arrive at the group index concerning the variable in question. In other words, when more than one questionnaire was received from a firm, a total index concerning the variable in question was calculated for the firm based on the average index of all respondents from the firm. We realize that the decision making group identity might be more or less than the average index of its members. It should be mentioned also that among variables relevant to decision group identity, the membership of decision makers in scientific/technical societies failed to distinguish earlier from later adoption of the innovation under investigation here.

Although the foregoing analysis deliberately excluded "economic" variable some reference must be made to the explanatory power of what we term a 'performance gap'. March and Simon [9, pgs. 183-4] concluded that "the natural stimuli to innovation are the failure of the existing programme to attain satisfactory levels of its relevant criteria". We endeavored to measure this by comparing the individual firms rate of return on investment with that of the industry average and established an $R^2$ of 0.361 between the existence of a gap and early adoption. Clearly, a company seeking to innovate should seek to define the nature of existing performance gap(s) in prospective markets and plan its R&D, marketing and production policies accordingly - a somewhat self evident statement of the marketing concept!

## APPLICATIONS AND CONCLUSIONS

The findings presented in this paper have their application for companies producing innovations. In this respect, it appears that the decision to adopt earlier is a function of economic, behavioral and managerial variables. This in turn casts doubt on the view held by economists such as Mansfield and Ray [12] that adoption of industrial innovations is essentially an objective rational process controlled by economic factors alone. The profitability of innovation, for example, produced as low an $R^2$ as (0.02) in its relationship with earlier receptivity to the innovation.

However, perceived technological and economic attributes of innovation seems to be highly associated with earlier adoption. Compatibility of innovation to the manufacturing system proved to be the most significant attribute and hence it should be emphasized by the company introducing an innovation into the market place. Thus, the marketing information system in innovator firms should be

emphasized as a means for removing this gap.

Company size is an important factor in early adoption of innovation even in cases where such innovation does not need a huge amount of capital investment as, for example, the case of "needled fibrous materials". This is because the size variables do not only have their impact upon the financial capacity of firms, but also upon the technical and marketing resources needed to make the innovation fit in with manufacturing and marketing systems.

Finally, flexibility of organization and creativity of the decision-making group could be used as a source of planning the type and quantity of communication used in demonstrating the attributes of an innovation. It might be suggested here that the inflexibility of mechanistic organization and the conservatism and dogmatism of the decision-making group in certain segments of the market might require the use of personal rather than impersonal type of communication. Moreover, the innovator company should increase the quantity of communication directed to mechanistic organizations. This is because in mechanistic organization, the communication between departments tends to be very limited and hence innovator firms should be able to fill this gap through the use of their own communications strategy.

## REFERENCES

1. Abu-Ismail, F.A.F. "Predicting the Adoption and Diffusion of Industrial Product Innovations," unpublished Doctoral Dissertation, Strathclyde University, Glasgow, 1976.

2. Baker, Michael J., Marketing New Industrial Products. London: Macmillan, 1975.

3. Baker, Michael J., and Stephen T. Parkinson, Predicting the Adoption and Diffusion of Industrial Innovation. Report to the Social Science Research Council, April 1976.

4. Carter, C.F., and B.R. Williams. "The Characteristics of Technically Progressive Firms." Journal of Industrial Economics, Vol. VII, No.2, March 1959.

5. Czepiel, John A. "The Diffusion of Major Technological Innovation in a Complex Industrial Community: An Analysis of Social Process in the American Steel Industry," unpublished Doctoral Dissertation, Northwestern University, 1972.

6. Lawrence, P.R., and J.W. Lorsch. "Differentiation and Integration in Complex Organizations," Administrative Science Quarterly, Vol.12, No.1, June 1967.

7. Lawrence, P.R., and J.W. Lorsch. Organization and Environment, Harvard Business School, 1967.

8. Mansfield, Edwin. "The Speed of Response of Films to New Techniques," Quarterly Journal of Economics, Vol. LXXVII, No.2, May 1963.

9. March, James G., and Herbert A. Simon. Organizations Fifth Ed., New York: John Wiley and Sons, 1964.

10. Ozanne, Urban B., and Gilbert A. Churchill. "Five Dimensions of the Industrial Adoption Process", Journal of Marketing Research, Vol.VIII, No.3, August 1971.

11. Peters, M.P., and M. Venkatesan. "Exploration of Variables Inherent in Adopting an Industrial Product", Journal of Marketing Research, Vol.X, No.3, August 1973.

12. Ray, G.F.  "The Diffusion of New Technology: A Study
    of Ten Processes in Nine Industries", <u>National Insti-
    tute Economic Review</u>, Vol.48, May 1968.

13. Webster, Frederick E.  "New Product Adoption in Indus-
    trial Markets: A Framework for Analysis", <u>Journal of
    Marketing</u>, Vol.33, No.3, July 1969.

14. Wilson, David T.  "Industrial Buyers' Decision-Making
    Styles", <u>Journal of Marketing Research</u>, Vol.VIII,
    No.4, November 1971.

# THE PURCHASING MANAGER--FROM ORDER-TAKER TO DECISION-MAKER: SOME PRELIMINARY FINDINGS

Robert E. Spekman, University of Maryland

## INTRODUCTION

The purchasing manager has traditionally been viewed as a relatively low power organizational member, whose function was often described as little more than clerical in nature. More recently, and particularly since the severe materials shortages of 1973-74, there has been anecdotal evidence suggesting that the role of the purchasing manager has taken on new dimensions [3, 7]. After years of corporate obscurity, the purchasing manager is gradually gaining more corporate responsibility, accompanied by an increase in his corporate status. This paper presented description data suggesting that the purchasing manager is beginning to shed his "passive order-taker" image and is slowly becoming a more active participant in the purchasing decision-making process.

## METHODOLOGY

The sample consisted of 35 purchasing managers from 20 firms in the greater Chicago area. The term manager was used to denote purchasing personnel whose duties were administrative in nature. The open ended interviews focused on the materials shortages of 1973-74 and on the means by which the firm adapted to those turbulent economic conditions. During the course of the conversation each purchasing manager was asked to respond to the following question:

> In recent years the purchasing function has received a great deal of attention. Can you think of any events which have taken place in your company which would reflect the current status of the purchasing function?

The data consisted of a listing of the various responses elicited from each purchasing manager. Each statement was then categorized into response groupings.

## FINDINGS

These findings suggested that there has, for the most part, been an increase in the status afforded to the purchasing managers comprising this sample. While these results tended to concur with earlier research [2, 6], any inferences to enhanced status should be viewed in a relative sense. For instance, several respondents were quick to acknowledge that while "things" had improved, purchasing would probably not gain equal status with other departments. Despite this sense of inequality, there emerged from the data three major response categories. Among these, an increase in budgetary allocation (18%) and a heightened concern for professionalism within the purchasing function (13%) furnished insights into corporate events which presumably become manifest as a result of the greater status being given to the purchasing function.

A more interesting finding, however, showed that a large portion of those purchasing managers sampled felt that they had achieved greater participation in the purchasing decision-making process (60%) over the last few years. These results were quite compatible with research devoted to the examination of boundary role persons [1]. It was proposed that the characteristics of purchasing's boundary role position serve as the basis for a conceptual mechanism explaining the recent corporate recognition accorded to purchasing.

Specifically, it was posited that as an adaptive structural response to conditions of greater environmental uncertainty [4], those in boundary role positions (i.e., purchasing) presumably devote greater energy to gathering and processing relevant purchasing information. This "buffering" mechanism [5, 8], conceptually at least, places purchasing in a position in which it can monitor information entering the firm. Theoretically, the eventual recognition, by management, of the information gathering potential of purchasing was inevitable, the severe materials shortages of 1973-74 only accelerated the process. Although the environment within which a good portion of American industry presently operates has become relatively less uncertain, management has probably come to learn that it is better to anticipate environment change and has also come to acknowledge the potentially crucial role played by purchasing in this process. This would seemingly account for the purchasing manager's increased participation in the decision-making process and, concomitantly, his heightened organizational status.

## REFERENCES

1. Adams, J. Stacy. "The Structure and Dynamics of Behavior in Organizational Boundary Roles," in M. D. Dunnette, ed., Handbook of Industrial and Organizational Research. Chicago: Rand McNally, 1976.

2. Ammer, Dean S. "Top Management's View of the Purchasing Function." Journal of Purchasing and Materials Management, (August, 1974), 5-15.

3. "Buying Agents Find Suppliers Eager to Sell--But at Higher Prices," The Wall Street Journal, (February 26, 1976), 1.

4. Galbraith, Jay. Designing Complex Organizations. Reading, Ma.: Addison Wesley, 1973.

5. March, J. and H. Simon. Organizations. New York: John Wiley and Sons, 1956.

6. Rich, Stuart H. "The Impact of Materials Shortages on Purchasing Organizations." Journal of Purchasing and Materials Management, (Spring, 1975), 13-17.

7. "The Buyer Gains More Clout." Business Week, (January 13, 1975), 46-47.

8. Thompson, James. Organizations in Action. New York: McGraw Hill, 1967.

# EXPLORING THE IMPACT OF ORGANIZATIONAL VARIABLES IN A COMPLEX BUYING SITUATION

Kjell Grønhaug, The Norwegian School of Economics and Business Administration

## ABSTRACT

In a study conducted among 16 research and consulting organizations, variables like organizational type and size were found both to influence the need perception, the participation in, and the handling of a computer purchase.

## THE STUDY

The study explores the handling of a buying decision assumed to be of great perceived importance, the purchase of a computer. Of 25 research and consulting organizations randomly selected, 16 agreed to participate. In each of the organizations willing to cooperate, contacts were established with persons that had been heavily involved in the computer purchase. In using a "snowball"-approach, data about various internal and external conditions including organizational structure, buying influences, buying motives, use of information were gathered by means of semistructured personal interviews. In addition information from a variety of written sources such as letters, brochures, organizational charts were collected.

## FINDINGS

Seven of the organizations in the study can be classified as business organizations indicating strong market dependence, while the remaining nine organizations (research institutes related to universities, governmental and research organizations etc.) may be classified as "market-independent" depending on various regulatory groups (other than the buyer) [1].

### The buying process

Purchasing is often viewed as a decision process, where the final choice may be seen as the output of the process. And of course, a process has to start in order to go on. It is often assumed that instability under labels such as "felt need" or "problem recognition" represents the starting point of the process, where the underlying "mechanism" (in consumer buying the human need) is activated by internal or external stimuli. In making a distinction between "gradual" and "sudden" need perception related to type of organization "market" and "non-market" and organizational size, "sudden" need perception was found to occure more often in small compared to big organizations indicating that small compared to big organizations are confronted with more environmental disturbances.

In all the non-market organizations the purchase was related to budgets involving negotiations with regulatory groups as a necessary condition, which may be interpreted as political behavior [2], (i.e. behavior by individuals or groups which makes a claim against the resources sharing system). For market organizations, however, the necessary resources are obtained through exchange of output in the marketplace.

### The buying center

Three roles have been emphasized in the buying decision as it relates to the organizational levels of the various organizations. These are the initiative, the decider, and other influencers. Examination of the data reveals some striking differences:

In eight cases the initiative to the purchase came from the top level of the organization. Looking at type of organization, however, this is the case for all market-organizations, but only for one of the non-market organization. The initiative in non-market organizations primarily comes from "others" (i.e. users).

The deciders are in 12 of the 16 cases found at the top level of the organization. All the four non-top level decisions, however, were made in non-market organizations. Furthermore, three of these were team-decisions, of which two were made by appointed committees.

Different evaluation criteria were stressed by various members in nine of the purchase situations studied, and this was really demonstrated to be a source of conflict [3]. Seven of these nine situations were found in big organizations, which indicate that the conflict potential is positively related to number of participants.

## REFERENCES

1. Grønhaug, K. "Exploring Environmental Influences in Organizational Buying", Journal of Marketing Research, Vol. XIII (August 1976), 225-9.

2. Pettigrew, A.M. "The Industrial Purchasing as a Political Decision", European Journal of Marketing, Vol. 9 (No 1, 1975), 4-19.

3. Sheth, J.N. "A Model of Industrial Buyer Behavior", Journal of Marketing, Vol. 37 (Oct. 1973), 50-6.

# TRANSPORTATION MODE CHOICE FROM
## AN INDUSTRIAL BUYER BEHAVIOR PERSPECTIVE

Bernard J. LaLonde, The Ohio State University
James R. Stock, University of Notre Dame

## INTRODUCTION

There has been an increasing awareness of the necessity to understand and model the decision processes involved in the purchases of consumer and industrial goods. The literature abounds with models of consumer behavior, some of which have been operationalized to varying degrees. Several models of industrial buyer behavior have also been developed, although their development has not been as extensive. This development however, has not extended into the distribution area except in a few isolated instances. The processes underlying the transportation mode selection decision have been researched only infrequently. One can only infer that the transportation mode selection decision could be explained using theory and models developed from the industrial buyer behavior literature. This is intuitively appealing inasmuch as transportation mode choice is the purchase of "services" rather than the purchase of "goods." This paper: (1) examines the relationship between industrial buyer behavior and transportation mode selection; (2) presents the results of a study on the decision processes involved in mode choice; (3) develops a descriptive model of the process used to select a transportation mode; and, (4) compares the model of mode choice with the Robinson, Faris and Wind "Buygrid" model of industrial buyer behavior.

## METHODOLOGY

As a prerequisite to studying the transportation mode choice decision, it was necessary that those situations where a variety of mode choices were possible be identified. A review of secondary data sources indicated three industry groups suitable for examination: SIC 2033 (canned fruits and vegetables); SIC 2844 (perfumes, cosmetics, and other toilet preparations); and SIC 3662 (radio and television transmitting, signaling, and detection equipment and apparatus). A selected sample of 357 firms were sent mail questionnaires which asked a variety of questions on mode choice. In addition, 13 additional firms were interviewed. Distribution personnel interviewed were administered protocols, i.e., they were asked to verbalize the mode choice process in which they would engage if their firm had just recently introduced a new product (New Task Buy Class). A mode choice model was developed from the protocols. Seventy-four (74) firms responded to the mail questionnaire (20.7%). After including those firms which were interviewed, an effective sample size of 87 firms were used in the data analysis.

## FINDINGS

The model of mode choice developed from the protocols exhibited four (4) distinct stages or steps. These stages in order of occurrence, were: (1) problem recognition; (2) search; (3) choice, and, (4) post-choice evaluation. In the problem recognition stage the mode choice decision is initiated. Many factors can initiate mode choice including a desire to improve customer service, reduction of distribution costs, customer complaints, claims and/or loss experience, market expansion, and many others. At this stage of the mode choice process, established order routines are followed if available; otherwise, a search is undertaken for a feasible transportation alternative.

In the search process, a variety of information sources are reviewed by the decision-maker to be used as inputs into the mode choice decision. Past experience is the most important information source, but carrier's sales calls, directories, customers, users of the mode, marketing department, and others, are also examined. At the point where the decision-maker has examined a sufficient number of information sources to satisfy his or her information requirements, the decision becomes one of using the information obtained to select a particular mode alternative.

The choice process involves the decision-maker assimilating the information obtained and deciding upon a feasible mode alternative among the several modes available to him or her. Selection criteria vary considerably, but in general they are cost and/or service related. Respondents cited on-time pickup and delivery, freight charges, time-in-transit, routing and scheduling, loss and/or damage history, and others as being important in mode choice. The mode which best satisfies the decision-maker's selection criteria is selected and the shipment is routed via that mode.

On a regular or irregular basis, most firms re-examine their transportation mode choice decision. Some procedure of evaluation is employed to determine the performance level of each mode used. Many techniques are employed including cost studies or audits, analysis of customer complaints, shipment tracing, review of on-time pickup and delivery service, etc. During this final stage, order routines may be established.

A marked similarity existed between the model of transportation mode choice and the "Buygrid" model of industrial buyer behavior developed by Robinson, Faris and Wind. A comparison of the two models was made by several independent judges and all were in agreement that the models were at least 90 percent similar with respect to both containing the same steps or stages.

## CONCLUSIONS

The similarity between the mode choice model and the "Buygrid" model suggests that industrial buyer behavior theory is applicable to physical distribution problems such as transportation mode choice. Additionally, industrial buyer behavior can be applied to the purchase of services. This will allow expansion of existing theory into new areas of industrial purchasing.

With an era of shortages, uncertainty, inflation and the profit squeeze, it is vital that optimal decisions be made in all areas of the firm. A better understanding of the mode choice decision process should help to reduce some of the inefficiencies associated with freight distribution and provide a basic decision framework upon which the firm can develop its own transportation mode selection system.

# PERSONAL VALUES AS A DIMENSION OF CONSUMER DISCONTENT

Donald E. Vinson, University of Southern California

## INTRODUCTION

While the topic of consumerism has received a great deal of attention in marketing literature, its treatment has been extremely disappointing from a social scientific perspective. Rather than an attempt to identify or isolate those aspects of consumer behavior that contribute to the consumerism phenomenon, the vast majority of papers and articles have been entirely descriptive or "nose counting" exercises at best. The purpose of this paper is to report the results of a study investigating the underlying etiology of consumerism based upon personal values.

A review of existing value literature suggests that personal values exist at two mutually dependent and partially consistent levels of abstraction. The first is referred to as global or generalized personal values. Global values are highly salient in guiding an individual's actions and judgments and represent an important element in the determination of attitudes and opinion as well as overt behavior. The second level of values is referred to as domain-specific values and reflects the view that people acquire certain types of values in specific situations or domains of activity. These values are thought to intervene between the more abstract global values and the formation of evaluations and judgments in decision making situations.

## THE STUDY

In order to investigate the relationship between an individual's system of personal values and consumer discontent, a random sample of subjects were asked to respond to Likert-type scales designed to measure the importance of personal values as well as an inventory of items providing an overall index of consumer discontent. The level of consumer discontent for each subject was assessed by the individual's total score on the Lundstrom CDS inventory. As reported in JMR, the instrument has been shown to be a valid and reliable vehicle for assessing an individual's position on the content-discontent continuum.

## FINDINGS

To test the hypothesis that personal values are related to consumer discontent, the importance ratings of each of the value constructs were analyzed using multiple discriminant analysis. The investigation of the global values provide a profile of contented consumer suggesting a somewhat spiritual, humanistic, and perhaps introspective orientation. Values associated with discontented consumers imply more of a social, interpersonal or other directed orientation. These conclusions appear to be consistent with the analysis of the consumption-specific values as well. For those values related to consumer products, the discontented sample is characterized by the values Exciting, Stylish Products, Reasonable Prices, Health Promoting Products, and Products Easy to Repair. Contented subjects placed greater importance on the values Dependable, Trustworthy Products, a Wide Variety of Products, and Comfortable, Secure Products. The classification matrix for this analysis indicates that 70 percent of the respondents were correctly classified.

The final analysis was quite interesting. Only two values relating to "marketing behavior" effectively discriminate between the two groups and the discriminant function correctly classified 70 percent of the subjects. The "marketing behavior" related value important to discontented consumers in Work for Legislation to Protect Consumer. This finding is consistent with what one would expect from discontented consumers. Contented consumers on the other hand place greater importance on the value Compete for the Business of the Consumer. This finding suggests that while these people are presently satisfied with marketing and business practices, this attitude may be seriously jeopardized with the absence of aggressive marketing activities.

## CONCLUSION

The existence of consumerism is a behavioral phenomenon and should be examined as such. While historical and descriptive studies have helped provide a perspective of the problem, they have done very little to contribute to a sophisticated understanding of the underlying dimension of consumer discontent. Without this knowledge, the implementation of effective strategies and programs to mitigate consumer dissatisfaction will be exceedingly difficult.

Because personal values are regarded as antecedents of both attitudes as well as overt behavior, they appear to provide a fruitful approach to achieving a greater understanding of consumer discontent. The findings of this study reveal that certain values do appear to significantly differentiate contented from discontented consumers. People satisfied with current methods of marketing and the operation of the business system appear to possess a somewhat humanistic, introspective, and self deterministic value orientation. In contrast, discontented consumers were found to place greater importance on social or other directed values.

In terms of values relating specifically to consumption and economic exchange, the two groups were also quite different. Contented consumers tended to possess values consistent with a traditional view of the business system; that is, when the system is functioning effectively, there should be a wide variety of dependable and satisfactory products. Discontented consumers placed greater importance on values relating to the personal and social impact of products. This suggests that perhaps marketers should emphasize these values in product development and promotional activities in an attempt to mitigate the influence of consumerism.

The analysis of values relating to marketing behavior suggests that discontented consumers are more committed to external or government intervention as a protection of consumer welfare while contented consumers appear to prefer the competitive, business enterprise system to achieve this goal. This suggests the need for even greater adherence to the marketing concept on the part of marketing practitioners.

Finally, the results of this study demand replication and further research. Rather than the typical platitute stated in many academic papers, this request is based upon the need for greater insight into the role of values, attitudes and beliefs in this important area of consumer behavior.

# A SURVEY RESEARCH APPROACH TO MEASURING CONSUMER SATISFACTION WITH SERVICES

Ralph L. Day, Indiana University
Muzaffer Bodur, Indiana University

## INTRODUCTION

The effectiveness of government agencies and consumer organizations in protecting the interests of consumers depends largely on their ability to identify the particular products and services which are generating the greatest amounts of dissatisfaction among consumers. At least the following four kinds of information are needed to assess the level of dissatisfaction with any particular product or service: (1) the number of people in the population who use the item; (2) the fractions of users who express dissatisfaction with the item; (3) the degree of importance which consumers attach to the item; and (4) the extent of extreme levels of dissatisfaction. These factors can be combined into an "index of consumer satisfaction/dissatisfaction" and provide policy makers with a useful tool for assessing the "need for protection" by consumers of particular products and services and serve as basis for setting priorities and planning consumer protection programs.

Comprehensive data of these kinds have never been collected on a national basis over the entire range of consumer products. Consumer protection agencies have relied primarily on tabulations and summaries of the volunteered complaints of individual consumers or on isolated cases involving fraud or physical injury to consumers. The shortcomings of complaint letters and other volunteered information as the basis of diagnosing consumer protection needs has been recognized in recent years. The most fundamental difficulty with volunteered complaint data is that it is quite unrepresentative of either the kinds of problems being experienced throughout the population or of the kinds of people who are experiencing consumer problems. Complaint letters usually report unsatisfactory experiences with products that are very important to the consumer in some way, especially items which involve large expenditures of money. Volunteered complaints underrepresent dissatisfaction with items of lower cost or those which play a relatively modest role in the consumer's daily life. A more widely recognized problem of volunteered complaints is that complainers tend to be quite unrepresentative of the total consumer population.

In addition to biases caused by the self selection of complainers, bias results from a more mechanical factor. Using simple counts of the number of complaints related to particular product types as an index of consumer discontent implicitly assumes that all products are used by the same fraction of the population when there is an extremely wide range in the use rates of products. The apparent rate of dissatisfaction among users tends to be overstated for widely used products and understated for products used by a smaller segment of the population.

Although survey research offers a promising method for obtaining better data for consumer protection policy makers, surveys using national probability samples and asking respondents to recall the one most important or most upsetting recent unsatisfactory experience as a consumer are not flawless. Although these studies provide more information about the respondents themselves than is normally available with volunteered complaint data, they fail to provide incidence of use data or any other basis for systematically evaluating the relative severity of consumer problems other than counts of "single most important" complaints.

## A COMPREHENSIVE SURVEY DESIGN

A comprehensive study which overcomes many of the flaws of previous methods of estimating consumer dissatisfaction has been designed and pretested with a probability sample of 500 consumers in a single midwestern city. Plans are nearing completion for a large national study sponsored by a consortium of consumer protection agencies. This study will span the full range of consumer products and services in three major sections (durables, nondurables, and services) containing approximately 200 categories. The rather lengthy questionnaires obtain satisfaction/dissatisfaction data for each of the categories, probe for particularly unsatisfactory experiences, obtain data about the reasons for dissatisfaction, determine if any actions were taken after dissatisfaction, and obtain data on attitudes and demographics.

One of the three major sections of the survey instrument used in the present study contains 73 types of services and intangible products grouped into four major subsections as follows: (1) repairs and general services; (2) professional and personal services; (3) financial services and insurance; and (4) rentals, public transportation, and utilities. The results showed many variations in usage, importance, dissatisfaction and complaining behavior patterns both within and among the four subsections of services and intangible products.

## SOME RESULTS

The degree of dissatisfaction expressed by the users was highest for "appliance repairs," "services of home security agencies, private detectives," "services of stockbrokers, investment counselors, and security dealers," and "mobile home rentals," for the above mentioned subsections, respectively. The service items with lowest degrees of dissatisfaction were: "photographic services" and "furniture reupholstery and refinishing services" among the categories of repairs and general services; "computer dating and other matching services" in the case of professional and personal services; "liability insurance" in the case of financial services and insurances; and "furniture and appliance rentals" among the last subsection. On the average, the highest level of dissatisfaction was expressed for repairs and general services and lowest for financial services and insurance.

Respondents reported highly unsatisfactory experience within the last two years mainly with "auto repairs," services of "employment agencies," "banks and trust companies" and with "apartment rentals." The reasons for their dissatisfaction centered around quality and price aspects of the service item purchased or contracted for. Most of the dissatisfied consumers attempted to seek redress in order to resolve their complaints. When the unsatisfactory item was one from the categories of repairs and general services, financial services and insurance, or rentals, public transportation or utilities, respondents contacted the company to voice their complaint. Those who were dissatisfied with a professional and personal service item either decided to quit using the particular company or professional person and/or warned friends and family members about the service. The survey instrument was able to discriminate among categories of services and the data obtained has face validity as the basis of developing measures of relative satisfaction and dissatisfaction with consumer products and services.

# COMPARATIVE CONSUMERISM: AN ANALYTICAL APPROACH

Larry J. Rosenberg, New York University
Edward L. Melnick, New York University

## ABSTRACT

The purpose of this paper is to study comparative consumerism through development of an analytic framework. Tested with data from samples of business executives from the United States, Japan and France responding to a common research instrument, the framework received support.

## INTRODUCTION

Consumerism, a largely American experience of the 1960s, has been shifting to an international condition affecting marketing in countries with advanced economies. This area of inquiry is important for multinational corporations, because they confront consumerism in the several countries in which they are doing business. In addition, public policy makers, consumer spokespersons and marketing researchers need to understand the evolution of consumerism and its implications.

The examination of consumerism has consisted of descriptive case studies and observation of several countries and comparisons among them. More objective research is needed which defines measurable forces contributing to multinational consumerism, and is sensitive to the culturally-determined variance among national versions of consumerism. This paper presents a research approach for investigating the character and intensity of consumerism by measuring the opinions of executives from three advanced economies of different cultures: the United States, Japan and France.

From the international consumerism literature, certain "core variables" that cut across cultural contexts were identified to provide the basis for empirical comparisons. The set of seven core variables includes: consumer rights (choice, information, safety and grievance), economic goals (primary or balanced with social goals), corporate beliefs (values and pressures on corporate social performance), consumer organizations (their presence and power), government role (justification and thrust of consumer policy), mass media (extent in facilitating consumerism), and public attitudes (consumer awareness and the pursuit of life quality).

It should be possible to employ these core variables in a form that would discriminate among countries. Given an attitude study among executives from the selected nations, the first hypothesis is phrased: Core consumerism variables are capable of differentiating consumerism among business executives from the United States, Japan and France.

From the core consumerism variables, an "index" of consumerism in each country can be constructed, allowing observed qualitative differences to be measured in a composite form. Based upon reported differences in consumerism characteristics in the three countries, the second hypothesis is offered: Consumerism is perceived by American executives as further developed in the U.S. than consumerism by Japanese executives regarding Japan, which is more advanced than consumerism perceived by French executives regarding France.

## METHODOLOGY

For the sample, three countries were selected with mature economic systems and disparate cultures in which signs of consumerism were visible -- U.S., France and Japan. The respondents were designated as major business executives from these three countries, who were located in the United States. The sample was drawn from directories of American (300), Japanese (100) and French (100) firms. The questionnaires returned consisted of 100, 24, and 22, respectively. The research instrument consisted of a mailed, self-administered questionnaire, designed to obtain opinions of business executives regarding the state of consumerism in marketing. The questionnaire contained 39 statements regarding aspects of consumerism to which the respondent could express his or her degree of agreement on a Likert-type scale.

Limitations in the methodology include the selection of only three countries, a sample of executives who possess pro-business attitudes, modest return rates, the influence on the foreign respondents of living in the U. S., and the bias of their interpretations of the English-language questionnaire given their cultures.

## FINDINGS

The first hypothesis states that the consumerism core variables have a capacity to differentiate among the nationalities sampled. Computed linear discriminate functions were used to classify the pattern of responses of each individual into one of the three nationality groups. It was found that 60 percent of the overall sample are classified appropriately -- Americans (61 percent), Japanese (50 percent), French (64 percent) -- the differences being statistically significant. Next, the importance of the variables in the national consumerism profiles examined the multiplying coefficients of the seven core variables for the three groups. The signs of these variables indicated that the relationship to consumerism is either positive (public attitudes, mass media, consumer rights) or negative (economic goals, corporate beliefs, government role, consumer organizations). Furthermore, the seven core variables form a configuration of different contributions to consumerism, suggesting a profile for each of three countries. These profiles correspond to the descriptions found in the literature.

To verify the assumption of varying intensity levels of consumerism among countries, the mean responses to the core variables for the American, Japanese and French groups were computed; statistically significant differences were found. The second hypothesis, referring to the rank order of the three national groups, is explored with the index of consumerism -- a weighted average of the seven-category means for each nationality group. As hypothesized, the Americans have the highest index (3.66), the Japanese second (1.63), and the French third (0.49). Since the three groups are significantly different, this rank order of consumerism saliency seems a meaningful way to determine the relative scaling of differences among countries.

# EVOKED SETS AND CONSUMER MEMORY SYSTEMS

Frederick E. May, University of Missouri-St. Louis
Richard E. Homans, University of Missouri-St. Louis
R. Neil Maddox, University of Missouri-St. Louis

## INTRODUCTION

This study demonstrates how the evoked sets of new automobile buyers are related to their memory systems. Evoked sets are operationally defined by their size and by the familiarity of the brands considered before a purchase. Familiar brands are those reported to have been owned and used by the buyer or spouse.

We distinguish three types of evoked sets that are associated with different levels in the decision process typology. Evoked sets that include only familiar brands correspond to routinized response behavior. Extensive problem solving implies evoked sets whose brands are unfamiliar. Limited problem solving applies to sets some of whose brands are familiar and some unfamiliar.

We find that the size of evoked sets in automobile purchase is primarily a function of the decision process. To illustrate, completely familiar sets are typically the smallest (Average size = 1.23 in our sample of 132 new car purchasers). Completely unfamiliar sets are somewhat larger (1.39) than familiar sets; and mixed sets are significantly larger (2.61). By definition the minimum mixed set must include at least one familiar and one unfamiliar brand; whereas completely familiar and unfamiliar sets have a minimum of one brand.

Variations in the size of familiar and unfamiliar sets appear to be explained by the memory systems used by the consumer. That is, consumers who use a verbal system and abstract product concepts have larger evoked sets than those who use an imagery system and concrete product concepts and choice criteria.

## IMAGERY AND VERBAL MEMORY SYSTEMS

The imagery system specializes in processing information concerning concrete events and objects. It is closely tied to perception of sensory aspects of objects and the short-term memory for concrete experiences. For example, images of the shape of the Coca Cola bottle, the particular rounded configuration of Chevrolet cars, or the specific green color of Scope mouthwash are stored in the imagery system. The imagery system also includes memories of auditory and tactile perceptions.

The verbal system is specialized for dealing with abstracted information involving language. To illustrate, the words for salient functional or dimensional specifications of a product, and the attributes of brands are stored in the verbal system. For example, when asked to describe the type of car wanted at the problem recognition stage, verbal processors mention attributes and functions. "I wanted a heavy car for highway driving;" or, "I wanted a station wagon for a large family and hauling."

These quotes are typical descriptions that indicate a network or tree diagramatic product concept. That is, at the apex of the conceptual structure are the functions, or activities or performances that are desired. The attributes that are necessary to carry out the desired functions are then related, and positioned on salient dimensions.

In contrast, descriptions that are retrieved from the imagery system include the name of a brand, and unique attributes of the brand. For example, "I wanted a four-door, blue Chevrolet with an eight cylinder engine." Typical descriptions here refer to the phenotypic attributes of the product rather than the genotypic ones. Phenotypic attributes are readily-perceived --- colors, configurations, etc.

Because verbal processors have abstracted the dimensions of the product class and encoded and stored these, they are more likely to include unfamiliar brands under a general broad product concept. Imagers, by contrast appear to recall total, global, concrete images of brands. Imagers have a preference for the familiar brands in their memory. Thus, imagers tend to evoke significantly smaller sets for consideration than do verbalizers. Typically, imagers have to encounter inhibitors, such as unavailability, in order to evoke other familiar brands, or an unfamiliar brand.

There is now strong evidence from physiological studies that imagery and verbal systems are located in opposite cerebral hemispheres. In right-handed persons, the right hemisphere specializes in motor-sensory functioning, and the left hemisphere in abstraction and verbal processing. Furthermore, psychological research on imagery and verbal symbolic processes reveals individual differences in symbolic habits and skills. Thus, there appear to be cognitive styles of perception, learning, and memorizing that are related to habitual or preferred uses of imagery and verbal processes.

Discriminant analysis of automobile buyers indicates that imagers are more likely to be in occupations that are oriented toward "things" and verbalizers are more likely to be oriented toward "ideas" or "data" and "people". Education is a strong correlate of verbal processing and underlying verbal intelligence. Verbalizers are more likely to seek variety; that is, include unfamiliar brands in their evoked sets.

## IMPLICATIONS FOR MARKETING

The three types of decision processes imply entirely different marketing strategies, and different marketing research techniques in product concept and copy testing. More specifically, verbalizers are more likely to respond to print media and comparative, data based commercials. They are more likely to form attitudes before changing behavior.

# THE IMPACT OF BARGAINING ORIENTATION, EXPECTATION,
## AND PARTICIPATION ON CONSUMER SEARCH EFFORT

Bruce H. Allen, Kent State University
David R. Lambert, St. Louis University

## INTRODUCTION

Certain factors may influence the extent to which consumers are willing to expend effort bargaining with retailers in order to gain additional pre-purchase information. One factor could be the consumer's favorable or unfavorable orientation toward the bargaining process itself. Another factor could be consumer expectation as to whether bargaining is permitted by retailers. A third factor might be whether a consumer's actual participation in bargaining encourages, or discourages, additional search activity.

The cost-value explanation of consumer information search might be potentially useful in explaining the impact of bargaining expectation and participation in bargaining on consumer search effort. The cost-value explanation states that consumer perceptions of costs incurred, and value received, in gathering additional information will determine the extent of future search effort. If the additional perceived value of information outweighs the incremental costs of obtaining it, the consumer should continue to search for information. A consumer who expects to successfully bargain and receive concessions from retailers could perceive increased search effort as being very valuable in relation to cost. Conversely, participation in the bargaining process might be a factor which increases the cost of information search. A consumer could perceive negotiating with a retail salesman as being very costly, in terms of time invested and psychological exertion, leading to abbreviated search effort.

The purpose of this research is to determine whether consumer orientation toward retail bargaining, expectation concerning whether bargaining is appropriate, and participation in the bargaining process influence the amount of effort spent in pre-purchase information search. The relationship among these factors will be examined by testing the following null hypotheses:

$H_1$: An individual's orientation toward retail bargaining has no effect upon the amount of effort spent in pre-purchase information search.

$H_2$: An individual's expectation concerning whether retail bargaining is permitted has no effect upon the amount of effort spent in pre-purchase information search.

$H_3$: An individual's participation in bargaining has no effect upon the amount of effort spent in pre-purchase information search.

## METHOD

To test the study's hypotheses, a shopping simulation game was employed in an experiment. A 2x2x2 factorial design was used combining the following three variables: attitude toward bargaining, expectation as to whether or not bargaining was appropriate, and whether bargaining actually occurred. Sixty-three male college students, selected from introductory marketing classes participated as subjects in the experiment.

Subjects' expectations as to whether or not bargaining was appropriate were controlled via pre-experimental instructions. To permit bargaining for subjects assigned to certain treatments and prevent it for others, activities of persons acting as salesmen in the simulation were programmed and controlled. Based on their Attitude-Toward-Retail-Bargaining-Scale scores [1], subjects were divided into two groups, those more and less favorable toward bargaining, using the median attitude score.

The shopping simulation required the subject to act in the role of buyer. The subject was informed that his objective was to purchase a specified model of stereo system from one of three salesmen at the lowest possible price. It was also explained that the salesmen participating in the shopping simulation were doing so in order to win a prize based upon their sales and profit performance. Further, in an attempt to create involvement on the part of the subject, the instructions stated that he was also eligible for prizes based on his performance in the shopping simulation. Thus, a competitive market situation was described to the subject in which the salesmen attempt to maximize sales and profits and buyers seek to make a purchase at the lowest possible price.

The total number of visits a subject paid to the three salesmen in the shopping simulation was used as a measure of effort expended searching for information. Number of salesman visitations was employed as a measure of search effort because a subject had to: delay thirty seconds between visits, exert himself in walking back and forth between each salesman and the waiting area, and take the time to interact with a salesman.

## RESULTS AND DISCUSSION

The experiment took the form of a 2x2x2 fixed effects, fully crossed, factorial design, and the data were analyzed using analysis of variance. The dependent variable is effort spent in information search, operationalized as a subject's number of visits made to salespeople.

Two of the main effects are statistically significant, and one of the interaction effects approaches significance. Subjects' expectations concerning whether or not price bargaining was permissible produced increased search effort in the buying experiment ($F(1,55)=17.43$, $p < .001$). Subjects expecting to bargain made a significantly greater number of salesmen visitations than those not anticipating bargaining. Attitude toward bargaining also had a positive effect upon search effort ($F(1,55)=5.33$, $p < .023$). Those subjects with the most favorable attitudes toward bargaining became more involved in the shopping experiment. The bargaining participation x attitude interaction ($F(1,55)=3.67$, $p < .059$) does not reach the generally accepted .05 level, but it is too strong to dismiss without consideration. The mean scores suggest that a positive attitude toward bargaining produces a greater effort spent in information search when combined with a situation in which price bargaining is allowed.

## REFERENCES

1. Allen, Bruce H. "Post-Transactional Evaluation as a Consequence of Bargaining in an Experimental Setting." Unpublished Ph.D. Dissertation, University of Cincinnati, 1974.

# A CONTROL SYSTEM SPECIFICATION OF MULTIPLE ATTRIBUTE ATTITUDE MODELS

Beheruz N. Sethna, Clarkson College

## INTRODUCTION

A control system approach to buyer behavior is proposed, employing control system concepts such as those used in electrical engineering. The resulting attitude model is tested, with favorable results.

## BACKGROUND

The model is shown in Figure 1. The concepts of perception, attitude, confidence, intention, purchase and satisfaction are used and function in a manner similar to the constructs used by many researchers in Consumer Behavior (see Howard and Sheth [2]). The relatively "new" concepts of the reference signal and the error signal are defined and used below.

## EMPIRICAL WORK

The relationships postulated in this model have been tested by Sethna [3], with encouraging results. Those results are not reported here. The main purpose of the present work is to develop and test the attitude model that emerges from the control system approach and to compare it with another (the traditional) multiple attribute attitude model. The attitude model resulting out of the control system framework is:

$$A_j = \sum_{i=1}^{n} (R_i - P_i) \text{ for all } R_i > P_{ij}; \text{ and } A_j = 0 \text{ for all } R_i \leq P_{ij} \qquad (1)$$

where $A_j$ = attitude towards brand $j$
$R_i$ = the reference signal on attribute $i$
and $P_{ij}$ = the buyer's perception of brand $j$ on attribute $i$

FIGURE 1

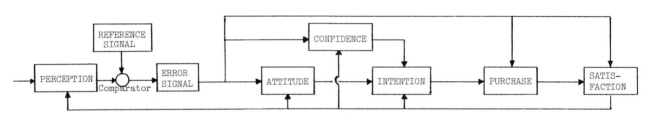

## THE CONTROL SYSTEM MODEL OF BUYER BEHAVIOR

The buyer has his perception[2] of a brand. This perception is compared with his reference signal[1] by which he evaluates the brand. The discrepancy between the two gives rise to an error signal[3]. Since this undesirable discrepancy between the reference signal and the perception of a brand is uncomfortable to live with, the buyer will tend to behave in a manner so as to reduce a large error signal to some acceptable minimum, if not to zero. The combined effect of the error signal and satisfaction (the feedback link) is to increase the probability of purchase of a brand that conforms to the buyer's reference signal, and to decrease the probability of purchase of a brand that does not match up to the buyer's reference signal.

Theoretical support for this model is found in the psychological literature. The substance of many of these theories in this context can be summarized in Cofer and Appley's [1] statement: "The concept of a stable equilibrium model is either stated or implied in all of the theories. A disequilibrium in the motivational system occurs, for example, when some need arises and elicits certain equilibrating responses such as some course of action expected to satisfy the need, and these responses cease when equilibrium is restored as a result of the need being met." (Heider, Festinger, Weiner and other researchers postulate a similar framework.)

This attitude model has been tested and compared with the traditional multiplicative multiple attribute model:

$$A_j = \sum_{i=1}^{n} W_i P_{ij} \qquad (2)$$

where $W_i$ is the weight assigned to attribute $i$, usually expressed as the importance rating ($I_i$) and the other symbols are defined as given above.

Both these models have been tested by pairwise correlations and by regression analysis along with other endogenous and exogenous variables. The results show that the control system model (equation 1) consistently performs better than the traditional model.

Perhaps the greatest contribution of this work is the effective integration of the concepts of the engineering control system into buyer behavior. Further, by noting the correspondence of the control system model with the work of Howard and Sheth on the one hand, and the "ideal point" of multidimensional scaling on the other, this work provides a common thread between these two widely differing schools of thought. In the opinion of the author, the literature will be the richer for such a link.

## REFERENCES

1. Cofer, C. and M. Appley. Motivation: Theory and Research, Wiley & Sons, 1964.

2. Howard, John A. and J. Sheth. The Theory of Buyer Behavior, Wiley & Sons, 1969.

3. Sethna, Beheruz N. "A Control System Approach to Consumer Behavior," unpublished doctoral dissertation, Columbia University, 1976.

---

[1]Reference signal: frame of reference by which a buyer evaluates a brand ($R_i$; $i = 1,...,n$).

[2]Perception: buyer's evaluation of Brand $j$ ($P_{ij}$).

[3]Error signal: a difference function of the Reference Signal and Perception.

IMPROVING FREQUENCY OF CHOICE PREDICTIONS: AN EMPIRICAL TEST

Kenneth E. Miller, University of Utah
James L. Ginter, The Ohio State University

## INTRODUCTION

Although most studies of consumer attitudes have used some
measure of preference as the criterion variable, substantial effort has been expended in trying to predict dichotomous brand choice. However consumers may not consistently
select the same brand from a product category but choose
differing brands in their evoked set or acceptance region.
In line with this argument several authors call for the
probability of choice to be used as the criterion for consumer decision model performance. Each individual's probability of purchase of brand j is defined as his normalized
frequency of purchase over a 12 week period. It is the
objective of this paper to investigate the relationship
between brand attitude and probability of choice and to
examine a method to improve the measured correlation
between these variables.

Nonlinear Transformation of Attitude

The nature of the attitude scores and the probability of
choice measure are dissimilar in that a consumer may only
choose a few of many brands in a product category. Ginter
and Pessimier [2] discussed a method which is equivalent to
stretching the attitude scale to account for the over
assignment of attitude scores to brands which have a near
zero chance of being chosen. The attitude scale is
stretched using the power function:

$$\hat{P}_{ij} = \frac{X_{ij}^B}{\sum_{i=j}^{m} X_{ij}^B} \qquad (1)$$

where B=parameter determining the degree to which the relative preference scale is differentially stretched.
$X_{ij}$=normalized attitude value of brand i for subject j.

In order to calculate the optimum value of the power parameter, the probability of choice must be available from
purchase history. Nakanishi [3] pointed out that

$$\ln (P_{ij}/P_j^\bullet) = \hat{B}_j \ln (X_{ij}/X_j^\bullet) \qquad (2)$$

where $^\bullet$ = geometric mean
$B_j$ = power parameter for individual j

OLS estimates could be derived for each subject. However
the derivation of $\hat{B}$ for each subject necessitates non zero
probability of choice for each brand as ln0 is defined. As
expected, respondents in this study did not choose all of
the available brands during the panel duration. Therefore
an aggregate $\hat{B}$ was computed using aggregate attitude and
aggregate choice (for all consumers) and the subsequent
improvement in the attitude-probability correlation was
ascertained.

## THE DATA

The data were collected from a mail panel in a midwestern
city of approximately one million population. The initial
panel of 744 was randomly generated from a list of names in
the telephone directory. The final panel size was 446.
Each respondent completed five questionnaires over a period
of three months concerning eight fast food hamburger restaurant chains. Responses were collected on belief and
importance components of the multi-attribute attitude model
along seven attributes. On each of the questionnaires

reported choice data were collected.

## THE ANALYSIS

An attitude score, using the form of the model found superior by Ginter [1], was calculated for each individual in
the panel using data provided at the beginning of the
study. The panel was then randomly split into two groups.
The aggregate normalized attitudes for all brands at
period one and subsequent aggregate purchase frequencies
during the panel study were calculated for the first group.
An aggregate B was derived by regressing ln $(X_i/X_i^0)$ on
ln $(P_i/P_i^0)$ on the first group data. The beta obtained from
this analysis was 6.78 and was applied to the normalized
attitude of each brand in the second split half at both the
individual and aggregate level of analysis. For the individual analysis this beta was applied to the vector of
brand attitudes for each individual while at the aggregate
level, beta was applied only once to the attitude vector
gained by averaging brand attitudes of all individuals.
The mean correlation coefficients for the individual analysis of normalized attitude and probability of choice for
both beta=1 (first group) and beta=6.78 (holdout group)
were .479 (.026) and .522 (.032) respectively. The correlation coefficients for the aggregate analysis with beta=
1 and beta=6.78 were .887 and .976 respectively. The null
hypothesis of no relationship between attitude and probability of choice must be rejected for both the individual
(p <.001) and the aggregate level (p <.01) of analysis. In
order to ascertain the efficacy of beta in improving the
measured attitude-behavior relationship, a test of differences was conducted between the mean correlation coefficients obtained from sample 1 and sample 2. The calculated
Z score was 3.38 which is significant at the .001 level.
The difference between the aggregate correlation coefficients was tested. The calculated t value of 2.85 is significant at the .05 level. The null hypothesis that application of the calculated beta does not improve the measured
attitude-behavior relationship must be rejected for both
the individual and aggregate analysis.

## DISCUSSION

The research found that attitude was significantly related
to probability of choice and the correlation was significantly improved when the attitude vector was differentially
stretched using a coefficient derived from an independent
sample. The possible variation of the power coefficient
across market segments and product categories should be
investigated. The use of this transformation may alter the
attitude measure, so further research on the issue appears
warrented.

## REFERENCES

1. Ginter, James L. "An Experimental Investigation of
   Attitude Change and Choice of a New Brand." Journal
   of Marketing Research, 11, 1974, 30-40.

2. Ginter, James L. and Edgar A. Pessemier "Profiles of
   Market Segments and Product Competitive Structures."
   Working Paper, The Ohio State University, 1974.

3. Nakanishi, Masao. "Measurement of Sales Promotion
   Effects at the Retail Level--A New Approach," Combined
   Proceedings of the American Marketing Association, 1972

# UTILIZING MULTIDIMENSIONAL SCALING TO PREDICT BRAND CHOICE

Phillip E. Downs, College of William and Mary

## ABSTRACT

Previous studies have attempted to compare the predictive capability of multidimensional scaling models with multiattribute models. Before a winner is announced, issues which may affect the outcome need to be discussed. This paper focuses on one such issue, and presents a new technique for determining model-derived preference estimates.

## INTRODUCTION

To date, only a few studies have used multidimensional scaling techniques to predict brand preference. Each of these studies compares the predictive capabilities of MDS models with those of multiattribute models [1-3]. Neither model has established a clear superiority. The purpose of this paper is to explore a modification of the manner in which MDS models are utilized to predict brand preference, and to determine if this modified technique will improve the predictive capability of MDS models.

## DETERMINING BRAND PREFERENCE

Each previous study examining the predictive capability of MDS models utilized a joint-space analysis, i.e., a multidimensional mapping of stimuli and subjects. The most popular technique for determining predicted brand preference is to select the stimulus closest to a given subject's ideal point as the preferred stimulus. An example will illustrate the limitations of this technique. Suppose there are 50 subjects, and 4 brands, and the intent is to predict (using MDS) brand preference for the fifty subjects. Further, suppose that from the joint-space analysis it is found that brand A is the closest brand to 26 subjects, brand B is the closest to 16 subjects, and brands C and D are the closest brands to 4 subjects each. The traditional approach for determining brand preference would hold that brand A is most preferred. However, by using the success/failure (closest/not closest) criterion, valuable information may be discarded. Let it be assumed that brands A through D are 9.5, 9.6, 10.4, and 20.5 units from subject 1. In applying the success/failure criterion, brand A is selected as the preferred brand, while all other information is lost. It may be informative to the researcher to know that 3 brands are nearly equally preferred. It is possible to retain this information by assigning fractions of a success to the 3 or 4 closest methods.[1] If these fractions of a success (brand preference weights) are calculated such that they are inversely proportional to the distance from each of 3 or 4 brands to the ideal point, then such fractions of success will reflect a subject's relative preference for several brands. The brand preference weights for each subject will sum to 1. An aggregate preference score for any given brand can be determined by summing individual preference weights across subjects. The "weighted technique" enables one to predict brand preference by utilizing valuable information that is discarded by the traditional approach.

---

[1]Allocating an individual's preference across 3 or 4 brands rather than across all brands or solely to one brand in a set is supported by Howard and Sheth's evoked set concept.

## EMPIRICAL SUPPORT FOR THE WEIGHTED TECHNIQUE

In a study designed to, among other things, examine perceptions of and preferences for contraceptives, similarity and preference data concerning a set of contraceptive methods were collected from 58 couples. An aggregate stimulus map was generated by ALSCAL and couples were positioned in the stimulus map by use of PREFMAP. Four sets of estimated preferences were generated from the joint-space analysis. The traditional success/failure approach was tested against 3 types of weighted techniques. Tested were 2-way, 3-way, and 4-way weighted techniques in which each couple's preference was proportionately allocated to the 2, 3, and 4 closest contraceptive methods. For each of the four techniques, preferences were summed across couples to yield an overall predicted preference score.

Couples were sent a follow-up letter roughly 9-12 months after childbirth and were requested to supply contraceptive use information. The predicted preference score was compared to actual contraceptive use via a chi-square analysis. The results are presented in Table 1. The traditional success/failure approach results in preference predictions which are significantly different from actual use (p<.001). The 4-way weighted technique results in preference estimates which are remarkably similar to actual use.

### TABLE 1

Chi-square Values Indicating the Differences Between Actual and Predicted Contraceptive Use as Predicted By 4 Alternative Techniques

|  | $x^2$ | p-value |
|---|---|---|
| Traditional (Success/Failure) Technique | 63.6 | <.001 |
| 2-Way Weighted Technique | 13.7 | <.03 |
| 3-Way Weighted Technique | 12.1 | <.04 |
| 4-Way Weighted Technique | 5.6 | <.36 |

## CONCLUSION

If the predictive capability of MDS models versus multiattribute (or any other) models is to be accurately tested, the appropriate technique for determining preferences from the results of an MDS joint-space analysis must be chosen. The traditional technique of choosing the brand which is closest to a subject's ideal point discards valuable information which thus affects the predictive capability of the model. The weighted technique utilizes all relevant information, and with the data presented, serves as a better predictor of actual brand choice.

## REFERENCES

[1]Dubois, Bernard. "Ideal Point Versus Attribute Models of Brand Preference; A Comparison of Predictive Validity" Advances in Consumer Research. Association for Consumer Research, Chicago, 1975, 321-33.

[2]Hanson, Flemming and Thomas Bolland. "The Relationship between Cognitive Models of Choice and Nonmetric Multidimensional Scaling," Proceedings. 2nd Annual Conference, Association for Consumer Research, 1971, 376-88.

[3]Miller, Kenneth E. "An Investigation of the Comparative Performance of the Multi-Attribute Attitude Model and Multidimensional Scaling in the Prediction of Reported Choice," Proceedings. Southern Marketing Association, 1975, 94-96.

# A STOCHASTIC ANALYSIS OF REPEAT PURCHASING
## BEHAVIOR AMONG AUTOMOBILE BUYERS

Wilke English, University of Georgia
W. H. Cunningham, University of Texas

## ABSTRACT

The objective of this research is to investigate the order of repeat purchasing behavior with respect to automobile purchases. Two stochastic models were used for this analysis which indicated that overall brand perception, as evidenced by the consumers' historical propensity to purchase, may be of more importance as a repeat purchase factor than even actual purchasing experience.

## INTRODUCTION

The use of stochastic models as a means of explaining consumer behavior is an established area of marketing thought. Although there has been much debate concerning the true nature of the process, evidence indicates that there exists a stochastic component in buyer behavior. [1] In addition, stochastic techniques possess a great deal of operational utility as a means of summarizing brand-switching data. These techniques also provide a means of examining such factors as the influence of past purchases upon present purchases, and in that manner, they give insight into the nature of buyer behavior.

To date, there has been very little research utilizing stochastic techniques in the analysis of the purchase process for consumer durables. Previous efforts have been concentrated in the areas of frequently purchased food and drug products. The emphasis upon consumer nondurables can be easily understood. If there is to be a model of brand-switching behavior there must be a record of several purchases which may not exist for many durable goods. Even when there is an adequate number of purchases, as for automobiles, differences in inter-purchase times may cast doubts upon the comparability of results.

## OBJECTIVES AND PROCEDURES

It is the objective of the present research to utilize two stochastic models of brand-switching for the analysis of automobile purchase data. The two models are the Bernoulli and the Markov, and the thrust of the investigation will be centered around the question of the order of the process. The order of a process relates to the number of previous purchases which have bearing upon a **present** purchase. Obviously, the concept of order has strong implications concerning the phenomena of repeat purchasing behavior.

In this investigation, a sample of consumers provided repeat purchasing data covering the purchase of four automobiles. These purchases will be modeled using both the Bernoulli and Markov model, and then each model will be tested with regard to the order of the underlying process.

## HYPOTHESIS

Although the tests used on the two models are somewhat different, the null hypothesis to be tested is the same for both models: that the process represented by the data is of zero-order. It is important to note that although both models involve chi-square tests of a zero-order null hypothesis, the mechanics of the tests are vastly different in that the Bernoulli model will be employing data which has been divided into sub-groups of homogeneous probability, while the Markov model uses the data in its aggregate form. An additional emphasis for this procedure is that it reproduces for durables the same type of analysis that has been performed for non-durables.

## FINDINGS

The results of this study with regard to consumer durables are similar to those studies of buyer behavior performed with regard to non-durables [2,3]. That is, the process appears to be of first-order when analyzed in the aggregate, but of zero-order when the analysis is performed on separate homogeneous classes. To the extent that this finding is valid, it is a rejection of the theory of the last purchase which states that what a person purchases last is most indicative of his current behavior. Rather the present research implies that the purchasing phenomena is very image dependent and may relate only secondarily to the actual purchasing experience.

## CONCLUSION

These results imply that the most important aspect relating to business success may well be the initial marketing decisions (along with their continued execution). Different market segments will have different propensities to purchase, and thus the crucial business decisions will revolve around such marketing factors as selection of the target market, brand placement, along with brand image and the builder and maintainer of brand image, advertising. This not only underscores the necessity of careful planning at the initial stages of target market selection and placement, but it also provides a warning to marketers of established products. Since these all-critical propensities to purchase are established over time, adjustments of the marketing mix, at least in the short run, may be of very limited effectiveness in changing these perceptions.

## REFERENCES

1. Frank M. Bass, "The Theory of Stochastic Preferences and Brand Switching," Journal of Marketing Research 11 (February 1974): 1-20.

2. William Massy, David Montgomery, and Donald Morrison, Stochastic Models of Buying Behavior (Cambridge, Massachusetts: The Massachusetts Institute of Technology, 1970): p. 90.

3. William Massy, "Order and Homogeneity of Family Specific Brand-Switching Processes," Journal of Marketing Research 3 (February, 1966): 48-54.

# AN INVESTIGATION INTO THE DIFFERENTIAL IN ATTRIBUTIONS OF HOUSEWIVES WHEN PROCESSING INFORMATION ABOUT GOODS VERSUS SERVICES

Richard W. Mizerski, University of Cincinnati
Marc G. Weinberger, University of Massachusetts

## INTRODUCTION

There have been many articles written about services but only Euguene Johnson's 1969 dissertation was designed to determine whether a difference between goods and services exists from a consumer's perspective. The findings of Johnson's study showed that while consumers perceived goods and services rather similarly, there were significant differences in the way consumers processed information about each type.

But what prompts these differences in processing information? The purpose of this paper is to develop and test several hypotheses based upon work in the area of psychological study known as attribution theory.

## ATTRIBUTION THEORY AND DIFFERENTIAL GOODS-SERVICE PERCEPTION

Attribution Theory studies the processes whereby people make causal explanations about the information they receive. This study employed a direct measure of attribution developed by Mizerski.

### Main Experiment

A study was executed in a field laboratory setting using 180 women from the Phoenix Metropolitan area as subjects. Each of the women was given standardized printed ratings about a product set of three items - one good, one service, and a dummy product. The final design consisted of a 3 (source levels) x 2 (information levels) x 4 (product sets) repeated measure (service and good) factorial. After receiving the treatments, the subjects responded to a measure of attributions that elicited: (1) their degree of stimulus attribution; and (2) the complexity of their causal array (a measure of causal complexity).

### Hypotheses

Based upon work by Mizerski and Johnson it was hypothesized that the greater subjectivity associated with services would result in more non-stimulus attribution than goods. Moreover, this difference in attributional allocation should be affected by principles of attribution which suggest that there be greater stimulus attribution when unfavorable information is presented and that more non-stimulus causes will occur when favorable information is received.

Hypothesis 1: Services, as compared to goods, will exhibit larger differences in causal complexity (a concept that measures a combination of the number of causes perceived and the causal allocation among those factors) mean scores between favorable and unfavorable information.

### Source Effects

Based upon Hovland et al. and Cox it was hypothesized that information from sources in different social locations (marketer-dominated, neutral, consumer-dominated) vary with regard to their credibility and their resulting value as influential information sources.

Hypothesis 2: When providing favorable market information, the marketer-dominated source should prompt the most complex causal array, followed by the consumer-dominated source and the neutral source.

Unfavorable information would tend to prompt an opposite attributional response.

Hypothesis 3: When providing unfavorable market information, the marketer-deominated source should prompt the simplest causal array, followed by the consumer-dominated source and the neutral source.

Finally, if the more subjective nature of evaluating services generally prompts a potentially larger (more complex) causal domain, the attribution differentials suggested with the information and source interaction (hypotheses 2 and 3) should be larger for services than for goods.

Hypothesis 4: Differences in attribution complexity, in response to the information x source interaction, should be larger for services than for goods.

## RESULTS

The first hypothesis was supported. Hypotheses 2 and 3 proposed an information x source interaction and these predictions were partially supported. Thus, the lack of complete support for Hypotheses 2 and 3 appears to be the result of the factors predicted in Hypothesis 4. Since direct comparisons of the complexity mean scores for services and goods was not possible, the failure to detect the same information x source interaction tends to support the fourth hypothesis.

## SUMMARY AND CONCLUSIONS

The results of this experiment give support to the suggestion that there are significant differences in consumer causal attributions when called upon to process information about goods versus services. These differences appear to be a product of the perceived complexity of each product type's causal array. Services tend to be seen as having more potential non-stimulus causes, causes other than the service's actual performance, for marketing information. This potentially more complex causal array provides a greater latitude for attributional changes to important information factors of source and information favorability.

# PREDICTIVE VALUE OF PRODUCT INFORMATION: AN APPLICATION OF THE BRUNSWIK LENS MODEL TO CONSUMER BEHAVIOR

Arch G. Woodside, University of South Carolina
James L. Taylor, Texas A&M University

## ABSTRACT

Brunswik's lens model was applied to consumer evaluations of peanut butter quality. Cue utilization, ecological validity and achievement of consumer's perceived quality and actual quality were measured for three brands of peanut butter. Actual quality was operationally defined in terms of Consumers Union ratings. Subjects (n=95) tasted and rated the peanut butters on the basis of quality and nine product attributes. Subjects had no knowledge of brand names or comparative qualities prior to the test. Stepwise multiple regression and correlation analysis were used to analyze the data. Non-significant correlation between actual quality of the brands and quality as perceived by the subjects was found. The major cues used by subjects in making their qualitative judgments (cue utilization) differed from the significant dimensions associated with quality (ecological validity). Results suggest a need for greater consumer education.

## INTRODUCTION

Cox [3] raised the question of why consumers do not always rely on information of high predictive value. He hypothesized a confidence value of information dimension to explain this behavior. Confidence value is a measure of how certain the consumer is that the cue is what the consumer thinks it is. A housewife may be unable to discriminate with confidence between good and bad internal components of a stereo amplifier. For her, this would be a low confidence value cue, even though it is high in predictive value.

Unfortunately, consumers' use of the predictive value of information has not been investigated well. The present study is focused on consumers' use of information of high and low predictive value. The analysis is based on the application of Brunswik's lens model [1, 2] on consumer evaluations of the quality of three brands of peanut butter.

The Brunswik's lens model requires that some "objective" criterion or "distal variable," such as some measure of a product's actual quality, be available. The correlation between a given cue dimension and this objective criterion ($Y_e$) is taken as an index of the cue's relevance with respect to the criterion; this correlation has been called the cue's ecological validity ($r_{e,i}$). In addition, computing the correlation between the individual's prediction and the actual criterion is possible. This correlation, called the achievement index ($r_a$), reflects the accuracy of the individual's judgment. The correlations of the subject's beliefs concerning cues and the subject's estimate of the criterion are the cue utilizations ($r_{s,i}$). The consumer's perception of product quality would be a measure of the "subject's estimate" ($Y_s$).

The cue utilization ($r_{e,i}$), ecological validity ($r_{s,i}$), and achievement ($r_a$) of consumers' perceived quality and actual quality are reported in this study for brands of peanut butter varying in actual quality. This type of analysis may be a useful research step for developing programs to improve consumer judgments of product quality.

## METHOD

The subjects were 95 female graduate students from the College of Education, University of South Carolina in August,

1976. Three different brands of peanut butter commonly found in local supermarkets were utilized. Consumers Union had tested the three brands prior to the study and rated them substantially different in quality. Actual quality was operationally defined for the purpose of this study in terms of these Consumer Reports ratings. No information concerning brand names or comparative qualities was given to the subjects.

A questionnaire was administered to each subject immediately after she had sampled the assigned brand of peanut butter. A seven point semantic differential with bipolar adjectives of very unlikely and very likely was used to measure perceptions of product quality and the extent to which the brand possessed eight attributes:(1) an aroma of freshly roasted peanuts, (2) a smooth texture, (3) a distinct peanut flavor, (4) tasted creamy, not gritty, (5) stuck to the roof of one's mouth, (6) was a nationally advertised brand, (7) would be liked by one's family and (8) was a high priced brand. A dichotomous response (yes or no) was required for a final question concerning whether the subject has eaten peanut butter within the last seven days.

## FINDINGS

Multiple regression and correlation analyses were used to analyze the data [4]. Actual quality ratings, consistent with the evaluations of Consumer's Union, were assigned to the three brands. Coding of actual quality for the purpose of analysis was as follows:(a) very good quality = 3, (b) good quality = 2 and (c) fair quality = 1.

The resulting achievement index of $r_a$ = .18 reflects the inaccuracy of the subjects' judgments of quality. Low correlation occurred between actual quality of the peanut butters and quality as perceived by the subjects. The major cues used by subjects in making their qualitative judgments (cue utilizations) differ from the significant dimensions associated with actual quality (ecological validities). Actual quality, for example, correlates highly with texture and creaminess whereas perceived quality correlates highly with family-liking, national advertising, aroma, and flavor. Two variables - texture and creamy taste - were found to be the major determinants of actual quality. Perceived quality was determined largely by (1) the extent to which the subject believed her family would like the brand and (2) the brand's aroma.

## REFERENCES

1. Brunswik, E. "Representative Design and Probability Theory in a Functional Psychology," Psychological Review, 62 (1955), 193-217.

2. Brunswik, E. Perception and the Representative Design of Experiments. Berkeley: Univ. of California Press, 1956.

3. Cox, D.F. "The Measurement of Information Value: A Study in Consumer Decision-Making," in J.A. Howard and L.E. Ostlund, eds., Buyer Behavior: Theoretical and Empirical Foundations. New York: Alfred A. Knopf, Inc., 1973, 210-16.

4. Hursch, C.J., K.R. Hammond, and J. Hursch. "Some Methodological Consideration in Multiple-Cue Probability Studies," Psychological Review, 71 (1964), 42-60.

RAIL PASSENGER SERVICE AND THE
HIERARCHY OF COMMUNICATIONS EFFECTS

Ronald E. Turner, Queen's University

## INTRODUCTION

Within the field of marketing communication, the hypothesis
of the hierarchy of effects provides a traditional view
of market behavior. The consumer proceeds through cognitive, affective, and conative responses to a market
stimulus such as advertising. A typical example would be
the viewer of an advertisement who first becomes aware of
a new product and acquires some knowledge about it. Subsequently, he develops positive attitudes toward the product and preferences for it. This leads to a decision to
buy the product and, ultimately, to actual purchase.

The hierarchy-of-effects hypothesis has not experienced
unqualified acceptance by marketing scholars in spite of
its apparent logic. Perhaps the most comprehensive critique was provided by Ray. He proposed that three different
orderings of the stages might occur, depending upon the
nature of the product and the market situation:

Learning hierarchy (cognitive→affective→conative)
Low-Involvement hierarchy (cognitive→conative→affective)
Dissonance-Attribution hierarchy (conative→affective→cogni-
tive)

This study represents an attempt to evaluate the applicability of these hierarchy-of-effects hypotheses to the marketing of passenger rail service. Data gathered before and
after a significant change in rail service are analyzed to
evaluate the relative suitability of the three orderings.

## CAUSAL INFERENCE

Several techniques have been used to explore the sequence
of relationships between variables, including the method
of path coefficients, single-equation regression, and
multiple-equation econometric analysis. This study employs
the method of partial cross-lagged correlations. The method has been used to infer the direction of causal influence
between variables, using repeated measures obtained from
the same respondents over time.

A rival explanation for an inference of causal influence
between variables x and y is spuriousness. If some exogenous effect represented by variable z causes both x and
y, and the magnitude of z changes over time, this could
provide the semblance of a causal relationship between x
and y. To test for spuriousness, one can test the null
hypothesis that the difference between the cross-lagged
correlations is zero. One interpretation of a non-zero
difference is that a causal effect exists between x and y.
This raises the question of whether an observed difference
can be considered non-zero. The traditional method for
testing the significance of observed deviations from zero
consists of relating them to a known probability distribution. Unfortunately, the distribution of the partial
cross-lagged correlation is not known.

The method used in this study consisted of constructing a
simulated distribution of partial cross-lagged differences
based upon randomly-generated data. Pairs of vectors of
random numbers were generated from an artificial data set
having "similar" characteristics to those of the real data
set. The differences between the partial correlations
computed from these artificial vectors were recorded, and
the cumulative frequencies of observing given differences
were computed. This permitted one to infer the magnitudes
of partial cross-lagged correlation differences which
would be statistically significant with specified α-risks.

## AN APPLICATION

The substantive issue addressed by this study was which of
Ray's three hierarchical orderings seemed most appropriate
to understand changes in awareness, preference, and intentions to use the train, among a survey sample of business
travellers. Canadian National Railways provides passenger
service through Kingston, Ontario, which is midway between
Toronto and Montreal. Matched samples of 100 business
travellers were contacted by telephone in Kingston, before
and after the train service was improved by CNR doubling
the number of trains which stopped each day.

Among the data collected on the two occasions were measures
of the following three concepts:

awareness of the number of trains per day between Kingston-
Toronto and between Kingston-Montreal;

preference for the train relative to the competing modes
(bus and automobile), based upon ten specified criteria;

intention to use the train on future trips to Toronto or
Montreal.

## RESULTS

Partial cross-lagged correlations were computed among the
measures of the above concepts. The non-significant
correlations were deleted, using the procedure for testing
the significance of a partial cross-lagged difference.
The remaining results were consistent with the following
sequence:

Intention→Preference→Awareness

This is similar to the ordering which Ray termed the
dissonance-attribution hierarchy.

The implied behavior of travellers is that attitudes toward the train are a result, rather than a cause, of
decisions to use the train. One scenario which is consistent with this interpretation is that travellers decide to
use the train because of circumstances which create the
need to travel. Having made a mental commitment to the
train, the travellers are predisposed to favourable attitudes toward it, and to assimilating factual knowledge
about the train.

If this interpretation is valid, it suggests that the marketing strategy for rail service should try to facilitate
the occasions for using the train. An obvious example is
to emphasize service frequency. In addition, rail service
is particularly well suited for sampling because trains
typically run with excess capacity. An aggressive marketing strategy based upon the results of this study would be
to offer attractive inducements, such as low-cost excursion
packages, to increase trial usage.

# A REPLICATION STUDY OF INNOVATION
## IN THE SERVICE SECTOR

Bruce Seaton, Florida International University
Ronald H. Vogel, Florida International University

## INTRODUCTION

This paper presents the results of a replication of the research conducted by Green, Langeard, and Farell [1]. The two primary objectives of the original research were to determine the characteristics of innovators in the retailing area of the service industry and to determine the overlap which exists between retail service innovators and product innovators.

## METHODOLOGY

With only slight variations the introduction, format, and wording of questions used in the original questionnaire were also used in the replication. However, since the original study was 4 years old, and since the cross-sectional method for identifying innovators requires a mix of items in various stages of the diffusion process, a different list of products and services was used.

Data for the replication were collected from a random sample of 118 persons in a major metropolitan area. Sixteen percent were classified as product innovators and 23% were classified as service innovators.

## FINDINGS

In both the original study and in the replication grocery product innovators are similar to the non-innovators on almost all of the measured characteristics. In the original study grocery product innovators tended to watch considerably more television than the non-innovators. This was considered an important finding. However, this difference was not found when the study was replicated. In the replication, age and number of children were found to vary between innovators and non-innovators. Non-innovators tended to be older than the innovators and to have more children. These differences were found to be significant in the original study.

Service innovators were found to be different from non-innovators on five dimensions in the original study. In the replication no significant differences were found on three of these five dimensions. Opinion leadership and TV viewership were the only variables in which a significant difference was found in the replication, as they were in the original study.

In the replication, as in the original study, an overlap between the product and service innovators was found. Also, in both studies people who had purchased more of the listed grocery products tended to have used more of the services. In the replication grocery product innovators had used more services than non-innovators. However, no significant difference was found in the number of grocery products used by service innovators and non-innovators. In the original study significant results were found in both cases. As in the original study, no significant differences were found when the dual innovators were excluded from the tests.

As in the original study, tests were performed to determine the differences between the product only innovators and the service only innovators.

While the original study found differences between the two single category innovator groups on six dimensions, the replication found a difference on only one -- the number of children. However, while service innovators were found to have more children in the original study, product innovators were found to have more children in the replication study.

## CONCLUSIONS

The conclusions reached in the original study were primarily that retail service innovators were a reasonably distinct group and that innovators do exist across product and service categories.

The replication results don't indicate that retail service innovators are a distinct group either when compared to service non-innovators or to product innovators.

The replication did support the finding that innovators do exist across product and service categories. Additional justification is thus given to extending this research to study further the characteristics of people who are general innovators across other product categories.

## REFERENCES

1. Green, Robert T., Eric Langeard and Alice C. Farell. "Innovation in the Service Sector: Some Empirical Findings," Journal of Marketing Research, 11 (August, 1974), 323-6.

# CONVERGENT AND DISCRIMINANT VALIDITY FOR METHODS OF MEASURING CONSUMER SATISFACTION:
## A REPLICATION AND EXTENSION OF A VALIDATION STRATEGY

R. Neil Maddox, University of Missouri-St. Louis

## INTRODUCTION

Marketers have recently evidenced a growing interest in direct assessments of the level of consumer satisfaction. Since satisfaction is commonly understood as a complex, internal and unobservable construct, particular care must be taken in selecting the measures to be employed.

Validity is the most important question to be raised with respect to any measure: "Does it measure what it purports to measure?" Marketers have frequently been chastised for failing to validate their instruments. Industrial psychologists have been similarly criticized. In the latter discipline the work of Smith and her various collaborators is notable exception.

Smith, Kendall and Hulin's monograph, The Measurement of Satisfaction in Work and Retirement, presents a detailed accounting of the validation of the Job Descriptive Index (JDI). A modest replication of their validation strategy in a different attitudinal domain is described here.

## MEASURE VALIDATION

There are a number of approaches for validating an instrument. Measure validation is particularly appropriate for psychological constructs, such as satisfaction, where the variable of interest has no obvious, observable behavioral correlates.

Measure validation requires that a scale exhibit both convergent and discriminant validity. Convergent validity is exhibited if a variable correlates highly with others supposedly measuring the same construct. Discriminant validity is demonstrated by low correlations with variables believed to measure other constructs.

Campbell and Fiske's multtrait-multimethod technique is frequently employed in the validation of psychological measurements. This approach requires that two or more maximally different methods be used to measure two or more constructs. The variables are intercorrelated and the matrix of correlations is examined for the following characteristics.

Convergent validity is demonstrated if the correlations among different measures of the same construct are statistically significant and large enough to encourage further validation.
The first criterion for discriminant validity is that two measures of a trait should correlate more highly with one another than with different traits measured by different methods.
The second criterion for discriminant validity specifies that two measures of a trait should correlate more highly than two different traits which happen to have been measured by the same method.

By convention, the preceeding discussion was couched in terms of trait validity. Assessing the relative performance of various forms of measurement is of primary interest here. Parallel tests may be applied.

## PROCEDURES

A self-administered questionnaire was used to gather ratings of satisfaction with a number of products. The re-
quirement for maximally dissimilar measures was met by including graphic scales, faces scales and batteries of verbal items in a single instrument. Appraisals of overall satisfaction and satisfaction with four distinct aspects of each product's marketing mix---its advertising, price, places where it is purchased and the product itself---were collected using all measures.

Direct and self-anchoring scorings were applied to the data. In direct scoring a response is given the same value for all respondents. Self-anchoring scorings individualize the scales; the individual's own most and least satisfying products serve as the anchors.

## FINDINGS

Space limitations preclude a detailed presentation of the results. In summary,

- --The faces, graphic direct and verbal direct scales had significant values for convergent validity.
- --These same scales, faces, graphic direct and verbal direct, satisfied the first criterion for discriminant validity.
- --The faces and graphic direct scales met the second, and most difficult criterion for discriminant validity. There were indications that the failure of the verbal direct scale could be attributed to some method variance common to the two nonverbal measures.
- --In no instance did the self-anchoring scorings perform satisfactorily.

## CONCLUSIONS

This replication of Smith, Kendall and Hulin's validation strategy seems to have been highly successful. The convergence of findings from substantive areas as diverse as jobs and consumer products lend support to the notion that the approach can be adapted to a wide range of attitudinal domains.

More specific conclusions may be drawn. The self-anchoring scorings did not perform well in either investigation. Given this convergence of findings, these scalings would not seem to warrant the extra respondent effort which they require.

The verbal scales performed quite satisfactorily. Further explorations of the properties of this item set definitely seem justified.

There were no clear-cut indications of the superiority of either nonverbal measure .... This is encouraging. Both performed well enough to justify their employment in future efforts requiring multiple measures. Were it necessary to select a single nonverbal measure of satisfaction, one could use either the graphic or the faces scale with considerable confidence in its validity.

# SOME FURTHER EVIDENCE CONCERNING CONFORMITY

David R. Gourley, Arizona State University
Donald W. Jackson, Jr., Arizona State University

## ABSTRACT

The experimental findings of Venkatesan's study of consumer conformity to group norms are replicated and extended. Findings indicate that consumers do tend to conform; that females as well as males are subject to group pressure; and that pressure to conform may be extended to consumer decisions besides men's suits.

## INTRODUCTION

The purpose of the present research was to replicate and extend Venkatesan's frequently quoted study of consumer conformity to group norms [2]. The study was replicated to the extent of using the same general laboratory procedures, research design, questionnaire, and methods of analysis. However, several changes were made in the form of the study (that would not affect its validity) to increase the generalizability of the results. First, the replication included both female and male participants. The second change was to use a food product, bologna, as the choice object. A food product was used in order to broaden the scope of products to which the findings might be applied and because it involved the additional sensual stimuli of taste to the findings. Bologna was chosen because of general uniformity of product taste, appearance, and aroma; ease of preparation and handling; and because it allowed the use of mixed groups, being assumed to be a product commonly bought and/or consumed by both sexes.

The sampling procedure was a judgemental quota sample composed of sophomore and junior level students taking business classes. The sampling frame for the study included 32 subjects in the control group, 16 males and 16 females. A total of 120 subjects were given the experimental treatment, 60 males and 60 females. The sample was further broken down so that half of each sex were exposed to all male confederates and half were exposed to all female confederates. The major hypothesis in the replication was the same one tested in the original study. That hypothesis stated in null form is that ($H_1$), in a consumer decision-making situation where no objective standards are present individuals who are exposed to a group norm will not tend to conform to that norm. Four additional sub-hypotheses were also tested: ($H_2$)...males exposed to a group norm will not tend to conform to that standard; ($H_3$)...females exposed to a group norm will not tend to conform to that standard; and ($H_4$) the sex of the confederates will not have any effect on conformity.

As in the original study, the control group, which was merely asked to choose among the three brands, showed no significant preference for any of the three brands ($X^2 = 2.72$). This supported the contention of no difference between the brands and showed that there was no order bias or foil bias in the experiment [1].

The experimental hypotheses were tested using a Z statistic and a one tailed test to see if the proportion of experimental subjects who chose brand B of bologna (the one chosen by the confederates) differed from what would be expected by chance. Table 1 presents the results of the experimental treatments. The first hypothesis, as in the original study, examines the overall group of 120, to see the effect of group pressure on the aggregate group. Analysis of the proportion of choices obtained for Bologna

B in the experimental condition indicate that it was significantly greater than one third ($Z = 3.487$). Therefore, as in the original study the null hypothesis of no conformity was rejected; and the individuals tended to conform to the group norm.

TABLE 1

Results of Experimental Group

| Experimental Group | Sample Size | Z | Significance |
|---|---|---|---|
| Aggregate Group | 120 | 3.49 | .001 |
| Males | 60 | 1.87 | .05 |
| Females | 60 | 3.11 | .01 |
| Males Exposed to Male Confederates | 30 | 1.11 | NS |
| Males Exposed to Female Confederates | 30 | 1.49 | NS |
| Females Exposed to Female Confederates | 30 | 1.83 | .05 |
| Females Exposed to Male Confederates | 30 | 2.59 | .05 |

Overall, the male group and the female group each chose bologna B significantly more than one third of the time ($Z$ males = 1.87; $Z$ females = 3.11). Therefore, null hypotheses number 2 and number 3 of no conformity for each of the sexes were rejected.

Next, the males in the experimental group were subdivided into those exposed to all male confederates and those exposed to all female confederates; neither differed significantly from what would be expected by chance ($Z$ males exposed to male confederates = 1.11; $Z$ males exposed to female confederates = 1.49). Interestingly, while the overall group of males reacted to group conformity in a significant manner, neither of the male subgroup null hypotheses could be rejected. This could be due to the smaller sample sizes in the subgroups.

Females, regardless of the sex of the confederates, chose bologna B more often than would be expected by chance ($Z$ females exposed to females = 1.83; $Z$ females exposed to males = 2.59). For females, the null hypothesis of no conformity was rejected. Thus, the overall results of hypothesis number 4 are mixed. Male subjects, whether exposed to all male or all female confederates, did not tend to conform to the group norm. On the other hand, females tended to conform to either the all male or the all female group of confederates.

## REFERENCES

1. Coney, Kenneth A. and James E. Van Dyke. "Order Bias: Fact or Artifact," Proceedings: Eighth Annual Meeting of the American Institute for Decision Sciences, Howard C. Schneider, Ed. (San Francisco, November, 1976) p. 275.

2. Venkatesan, M. "Experimental Study of Consumer Behavior Conformity and Independence," Journal of Marketing Research, 3 (November, 1966) pp. 384-87.

# TIME ORIENTATION AND CONSUMER ATTITUDES

Robert B. Settle, San Diego State University
Pamela L. Alreck, San Diego State University

## PURPOSE

This study is focused on a single set of personality characteristics, the *time orientation* of the consumer. Since marketing provides time utility, the individual's time orientation was expected to influence attitudes toward time related utility. A literature search revealed no *standardized* tests of time orientation. Thus, the project required the construction and standardization of the F-A-S-T Time Orientation Test. From an item pool of several hundred items, a test was built, administered, analyzed, and revised for standardization and use in this project. It included four dimensions: *Focus*, the location of consciousness on the time spectrum, past to present to future. *Activity*, the perceived time pressure and supply, relative to activity level. *Structure*, the tendency to see time in discrete blocks rather than a continuous flow. *Tenacity*, the willingness to delay gratification over substantial periods of time.

The test consisted of 64 items, 16 to a scale, randomly ordered and 8 inclined in each direction. Most were first person statements, such as *I hate following a schedule*, but other types were such as *Time drags*, or *My friends think I move too slowly*. Respondents indicated if each was *Exactly like me*, or *Not at all like me* on a seven-point scale. Hypotheses were: *Focus* would correlate with perceptions of current versus past product quality and the early adoption of innovation. *Activity* with acceptance of convenience stores and products and rejection of do-it-yourself products. *Structure* with planned versus impulse buying and with brand and store loyalty. *Tenacity* with saving versus personal credit and with large versus small purchases.

## METHOD

A survey of 930 adult respondents was conducted by field workers placing and collecting a self-administered questionnaire, using a convenience sample with quotas on demographics to insure representative distributions. The instrument contained five sections; The F-A-S-T test to measure time orientation, 12 items measuring consumer attitudes, 16 items for spouse ratings to test validity of the F-A-S-T scores in terms of overt, observable behavior, 24 items to measure occupational characteristics and job satisfaction concerning time, and the usual demographics. As an inducement, respondents were provided a six-page, computer-generated, individual report of their time test scores with interpretations.

The results of the internal consistency reliability and item analysis were well within acceptable ranges, and the distributions of scale scores were sufficiently near normal to permit use of parametric statistics. Some significant differences in scores by demographic status were revealed, but were not large enough to require separate norm reports. Comparisons of spouse observations with F-A-S-T scores for 240 couples supported external validity in that orientation did translate into observable behavior, particularly for *Structure* and *Tenacity*. Future oriented respondents often talked of their plans, low active people complained of being bored, structured individuals were the prompt schedule-makers, tenacious persons refused to stop until the job was finished, and so forth. Test results corresponded to spouse (and self) observations.

Comparison of test scores with occupational characteristics related to time revealed no systematic relationships, but *satisfaction* with the characteristics did differ according to time orientation. This result also supported the validity of the test.

## RESULTS

There were twelve statements of consumer attitudes, three for each test scale, for which respondents rated their agreement or disagreement. The first item relating to focus considered certainty concerning product quality at the present time, and the correlation was not significant. The second, suggesting a favorable attitude toward early adoption of innovation, also proved not to be systematically related to focus. The third, comparing product quality today with that a few years ago, was significantly related to focus, suggesting past oriented persons see past product quality as superior.

Two items associated with activity expressed favorable attitudes toward convenience stores and products, and neither provided a significant correlation with scale scores. The third, indicating a favorable attitude toward do-it-yourself products, was systematically related to activity, with highly active persons tending to disagree.

All three items devoted to structure of time were significantly related to the scale scores. Highly structured persons more often agreed that it was a good idea to plan large purchases and to budget, to have a shopping list and avoid impulse buying, and to be brand and store loyal.

The three items relating to tenacity were also significantly related to that scale. Low tenacious people more often liked to use credit cards, while highly tenacious respondents more often favored saving up and buying large items rather than several small things, and also favored setting aside money for large purchases.

In summary, the results indicate that *Focus* and *Activity* are only marginally related to consumer attitudes, while *Structure* and *Tenacity* scales provided somewhat more substantial evidence of a systematic relationship with consumer attitudes. It should also be noted that the number of consumer attitude items was relatively small, and the reliability of the individual items remains untested, so there is some suspicion that correlations with the F-A-S-T Time Orientation Test might be attenuated by this factor.

The results of the study were encouraging in regard to the time test, itself. The analyses of the test's performance consistently yielded results that were completely acceptable, relative to conventional norms for psychological tests of this nature. Because of these findings, the test has been employed in several studies subsequent to this initial effort, including measures of association between time orientation and: (1) several other standard tests of psychological constructs related to time, (2) lifestyles measured on the basis of over 400 activities, interests and opinions, (3) opinion leadership, innovativeness, brand and store loyalty, perceived risk reduction strategy and concern for types of consumer risk, (4) job satisfaction, performance and time use of field sales representatives, and (5) occupational values and financial opinions and behavior of consumers.

# WIVES' MASCULINE-FEMININE ORIENTATIONS AND THEIR PERCEPTIONS
# OF HUSBAND-WIFE PURCHASE DECISION MAKING

Alvin C. Burns, Louisiana State University

## INTRODUCTION

One possible explanation for the disappointing results to date lies in the failure of (our choice of) explanatory variables to embody factors which impinge on the husband-wife purchase decision making process. Researchers are subconsciously constrained by sex role stereotypes. A strong position against sex role stereotyping has been argued by Tucker (2) whose experiences with the instrument developed by Spence, Helmreich, and Stapp (1) has prompted him to urge marketers to revise the undimensional concept of masculinity and femininity. Androgyny, Tucker points out, is a prevalent condition in males and females. It follows that a wife's self-perceptions of her sex roles could provide greater understanding of husband-wife purchase decision making.

## METHOD, FINDINGS AND DISCUSSION

In an exploratory study wives were instructed to indicate on a five-point response scale ("husband alone","husband more than wife", "both equally", etc.) how they and their spouses would resolve each of thirty separate purchase decisions. Another section of the questionnaire contained two subtests of the PAQ (1). The masculinity subtest measures "reported pragmatic or instrumental character", while the femininity subtest measures "expressive and nurturant behavior". Each subtest consists of several five-point items anchored with polar opposite phrases. The questionnaire was administered to 81 wives chosen in a nonprobabilistic manner to include a demographically diverse set.

The two subtests for masculinity and femininity were scored using the group medians to split the sample and identify each wife's disposition as either high masculine or low masculine and high feminine or low feminine. Chi Square values were then computed on crosstabulations for each of the thirty decisions.

Three cases of association were found between femininity and stated decision making roles. All of the fourteen significant associations between (high) masculinity and decision making represented a shift away from husband influence toward wife influence.

### FIGURE 1
PATTERN OF RESULTS FOR ASSOCIATIONS BETWEEN
WIVES' MASCULINITY AND DECISION MAKING*

| Decision | Stereo | Auto | Television | Dinette | Sofa |
|----------|--------|------|------------|---------|------|
| When | | J | | W | W |
| How much | | | J | W | W |
| Brand/make | | | J | W | W |
| Style | | | | W | W |
| Color | | | W | | W |
| Where | | | | | W |

*Letters indicate the direction of association with high masculinity. J=Joint, W=Wife influence

The pattern in the matrix implies that the relationship is product-specific rather than decision-specific. No statistical test is appropriate; nevertheless, it is defensible to conclude that high masculine wives believe that they are more dominant across most or all of the purchase subdecisions for a sofa and a dinette set. Moreover, they are less willing to concede decision making power to the husband in the case of some television purchase decisions

than are wives who possess low masculinity.

Research with the PAQ has revealed that an individual may possess both high masculinity and high femininity, a condition of androgyny (2). From an exploratory standpoint, it seemed worthwhile to investigate the presence of androgny and its associations with these wives' descriptions of husband and wife purchase decision making.

A Chi Square test of the independence of masculinity and femininity in the respondents found a probability of significant association greater than .98. The association supported androgyny as high masculinity was paired with high femininity (33.3%) and low masculinity was paired with low femininity (30.9%). High femininity and low masculinity was the least frequent state (16.0%).

Successive Chi Square analyses were run between wives' masculinity-femininity dispositions and perceived husband-wife decision making. Each was compared to the other three groups combined. The condensed presentation of the results supports neither a product nor a decision-specific pattern. The associations met intuitive expectations generally.

### FIGURE 2
SIGNIFICANT ASSOCIATIONS BETWEEN WIVES' MASCULINITY-
FEMININITY DISPOSITIONS AND DECISION MAKING*

| Decision | Stereo | Auto | Television | Dinette | Sofa |
|----------|--------|------|------------|---------|------|
| When | | 1 | 3 | 2,3,4 | |
| How much | 2,4 | | 4 | 4 | |
| Brand/make | 1,2 | | 1 | 1,3 | 2,3 |
| Style | | | | | 1,4 |
| Color | | 3 | | | 2 |
| Where | 2 | | | 3 | 3 |

*Probability of significant association .90 or greater
1=Hi Masc, Hi Fem     2=Hi Masc, Lo Fem
3=Lo Masc, Hi Fem     4=Lo Masc, Lo Fem

In the case of this sample, femininity and masculinity are indeed separate dimensions within each wife, and their effects must be considered with this distinction in mind. Consequently, they hold promise of explaining individual differences. For the majority of wives, masculinity and femininity apparently work in concert or additively. Thus, wives high in femininity do not passively concede decision making authority nor do they automatically assume responsibility for decision areas such as color or style. Their masculine dispositions are determining factors. More research utilizing this approach seems advisable.

## REFERENCES

1. Spence, J. T., R. Helmreich, and J. Stapp. The Personal Attributes Questionnaire: A Measure of Sex Role Stereotypes and Masculinity-Femininity, mimeographed report, 1975.

2. Tucker, W. T. "A Long Day of Discrepant Behavior," Marketing: 1776-1976 and Beyond, Kenneth L. Bernhardt (ed.), AMA, 1976, 351-353.

# GAME PLAYING, CULTURE AND BUYER
## BEHAVIOR: AN EXPLORATORY INVESTIGATION

Wilbur W. Stanton, Oklahoma State University

## INTRODUCTION

Recently, in both micro and macro marketing research there has been found a common interest in individual responses to environmental attributes. Sheth, Brody and Cunningham, Fishbein, and Bellenger, Stanton and Steinberg, have suggested and/or demonstrated that individual characteristics influence the manner in which environmental attributes are perceived by individuals.

While many individual characteristics have come under analysis in this effort, the bulk of these have concerned psychologically oriented variables, such as personality dimensions, cognitive structure, etc. Few successful attempts have been made in recent years to explore sociologically derived variables to explain individual perceptions on environmental attributes. This study is an attempt to begin such an exploration.

This study is an attempt to add a viable new approach to the study of consumer behavior. This is attempted through an examination of autotelic folk-models. The expression, autotelic folk-model, names a concept found in the literature of sociology. Briefly, this concept can be defined as play-forms which are models or simulations of serious activities. It is believed that these play-forms are developed in a natural and unself-conscious way out of the life of the community. They are then placed into a separate domain containing social norms which define an activity as play and protect it from serious intrusions. Although this concept has been discussed on a societal or sub-cultural level in the literature of sociology since 1952, this study represents the first attempt to apply it to the micro level of the individual consumer.

## METHODOLOGY

Market segmentation, a concept based on the proposition that consumers are different, was selected as an appropriate decision area in order to test this concept. Specifically, an examination was made of data gathered from shoppers of four of the major department stores located in a regional shopping center in Atlanta, Georgia. The main thrust of the study was to isolate, analyze and interpret the contribution of autotelic folk-model orientations to the development of store loyalty of these stores for the purpose of market segmentation.

Data for this investigation was obtained by a convenience sample of 110 females. Each female was selected to participate based on her past shopping behavior at the selected regional center in Atlanta, Georgia. Once individuals were selected they were asked to complete three test instruments; (1) an instrument to measure loyalty toward each of the four test stores along the women's apparel lines; (2) an instrument to measure activities, interest and opinions; and (3); an instrument to measure folk-model orientations.

Sixteen major hypotheses were tested in this study. These were tested individually by means of the Kruskal-Wallis one way analysis of variance test in which the technique of fixed-effects analysis was utilized to assess the statistical significance of the influence exerted by the independent variable.

## FINDINGS

Of these sixteen hypotheses four were shown to be supported by the sample data. Consumers tended to have higher loyalty perception scores toward Store II and Store III as the level of their puzzle orientation increased. That is, consumers having a high puzzle orientation tended to have higher loyalty perception scores than did consumers having a medium or low puzzle orientation. Consumers tended to have higher loyalty perception scores toward Store I as the level of aesthetic orientation increased.

After conducting the tests on the sixteen hypotheses an attempt was made to show that individuals having different folk-model orientations also had different and identifiable life-styles. This was accomplished by first selecting 19 statements concerning activities, interest, and opinions and then using these to describe the respondents having various levels of folk-model orientations. It was concluded that there was a significant difference in the percentage of responses to several of the statements by individuals having differing folk-model orientations.

A MODEL FOR A STRATEGIC MARKETING PLAN

Robert J. Williams, Eastern Michigan University
Colin F. Neuhaus, Eastern Michigan University

## INTRODUCTION

The purpose of this paper is to develop a conceptual model of an annual marketing plan. The authors recognize that the precise make-up of the marketing plan will vary from industry to industry and from company to company.

## STRATEGIC MARKETING PLAN

Section 1. Existing Situation (What and Where You Are)
Description of the Planning Unit: (1) Mission: The mission statement should focus on the mission or purpose of the organization. This statement should be stated in terms of satisfying one or more customer needs. (2) Activity Definition: A brief statement providing an overview of the role of the planning unit and its contribution to the mission of the organization. (3) Brief Marketing History: An indepth analysis of the planning unit's past five years of marketing history. (4) Marketing Results/Accountabilities: One or more statistical tables showing sales, market share, etc. for the past five years. (5) Markets and Customer Groups: Target customer groups should be identified along with key buying influences. (6) Organization: An organization chart covering the marketing function is included.

Section 2. Environment/Competition (What and Where You Are)
The purpose of this section is to develop pertinent data regarding important environmental and competitive factors which have significant bearing on the planning unit.
A. External Environment: The external environment is concerned with those factors that are external to the firm and affect the unit's marketing plan. Basic categories that should be covered are: (1) Business/Economic Climate. (2) Government. (3) Social Aspects. (4) Resource Factors. (5) Customers.
B. Internal Environment: Major topics to be considered in this area are: organization, management style, personnel practices, motivation, etc.
C. Competition: Competitive strategies should be examined from the point-of-view of the competitor's marketing mix.

Section 3. Opportunity Analysis (Where Can You Go)
This section is more specific than sections 1 and 2 and is concerned with opportunity identification.
A. Business Outlook: A general statement covering the outlook for business over the next one to three years.
B. Assumptions: In developing an outlook statement, some assumptions are usually made. What are they?
C. Special Events: What special events will have an impact on market opportunities during the planning time frame?
D. Strengths-Opportunities-Action: Every company has certain strengths. What are they?
E. Weaknesses-Problems-Action: Weaknesses in a marketing organization should also be identified and corrective action planned.

Section 4. Objectives/Goals (Where You Want to Go)
Objectives should be continuing aims or targets for three years or longer. Goals, then are stated as "what by when" and support objectives.

A. Objectives: This section is designed to give the marketing manager a place to state long-range objectives in terms of where the unit wants to go.
B. Goals: A goal is a statement that clearly defines what is going to happen by when.

Section 5. Marketing Strategy (How Are You Going To Get There in the Long-Run)
The purpose of developing marketing strategy is to provide a blueprint of how one plans to accomplish long-range objectives. In a marketing plan, we are concerned with the elements under control of the marketing manager; namely, selection of market targets and development of a marketing mix.

Section 6. Marketing Tactics (How Are You Going To Get There in the Short-Run)
Marketing tactics is a series of a specific action designed to accomplish designated goals during the period covered by the plan. To describe marketing tactics, the organizational concept of programs and projects is used. Each goal is supported by a program that may consist of one or more projects.
A. Program Summary: The marketing manager develops a series of programs to accomplish stated goals established for the planning period.
B. Program Analysis: Each program listed in the program summary document should be supported by a program analysis which lists the key elements of the program.
C. Project Data: A project data form should be developed on each proposed project which supports a program.

Section 7. Programming (A Time Plan for Actions)
Marketing programs and projects are implemented throughout the planning period. It is useful to show these events using some type of calendar format.

Section 8. Organization (Manpower Support)
This section is concerned with organizational changes required to implement the Strategic Marketing Plan.

Section 9. Budget/Resources (Financial Support)
A marketing budget is developed covering the planning period.

Section 10. Control (Are We On Target)
This section is used to enable marketing managers to document actual results and planned benchmarks by comparing monthly and/or quarterly reports to plan during the planned year.

## CONCLUSION

It is hoped that this model will stimulate additional discussion from the marketing community on the development of marketing plans. By this, perhaps some pitfalls found in the marketing planning process can be avoided. Both the academic and the business community await contributions to a better understanding of the marketing planning process.

# DETERMINING THE ORGANIZATION'S GOAL STRUCTURE BY MEANS OF MULTIDIMENSIONAL SCALING: AN EMPIRICAL INVESTIGATION

Kenneth E. Miller, University of Utah
Kent L. Granzin, University of Utah

## INTRODUCTION AND BACKGROUND

Marketing organizations are increasingly turning to "management by objectives" as a means of coordinating decision-making. For many firms, management by objectives has become the standard mechanism for ensuring that marketing (and other) plans reflect the goals of the firm as a whole. And within the marketing department, setting objectives aids marketing employees to "pull together" toward a commonly-sought achievement.

As might be expected, the objectives held important in one part of the organization often clash with what is desired elsewhere: the production manager wants long production runs, the finance manager wants low inventory levels, and the marketing manager wants full, varied stocks kept in field distribution locations. Obviously, managers need a way to unify goal setting. That is, organizational efficiency will benefit if planners can give order to the many, often conflicting goals that appear salient to various decision-makers involved in the planning process.

Given the desirability of obtaining consensus among managers on the goals they are to pursue, there are several questions which, if answered, would provide them with useful information for resolving disagreement. What are the basic dimensions underlying the structure of relevant objectives? How are the candidate goals characterized by these dimensions? For example, do the maximizing objective "profit maximization" and the satisficing goal "satisfactory profit" lie at different points on the same continuum, or do they represent complex combinations of several attributes? What ideal point represents the best consensus goal as a blending of the set of proposed candidate objectives? Where do the goals preferred by the individual managers lie with respect to this consensus goal?

In short, a device for describing the structure of objectives as seen by disagreeing planners would be a useful aid to bringing about consensus among these managers. This exploratory study investigates the possibility of using a marketing research technique to define the objectives space. Multidimensional scaling holds promise for delineating this space, determining the relative positions of apparently competing goals, and positioning the planners' ideal objective(s).

## METHOD AND ANALYSIS

To test the efficacy of using the MDS technique to determine the underlying space of collective goal perceptions, 52 MBA students were asked to provide judgments on the similarity of eight corporate objectives. While the number and variety of objectives used as stimuli could be greatly expanded, these eight were selected as both applicable to decision-making at a single hierarchal level and typical of those espoused by authors in the relevant literature: (1) Profit maximization; (2) Growth in earnings per share; (3) Sales maximization; (4) Stable profit; (6) Maximize corporate size; (7) Maximize stock price; (8) Maximize market share.

The 28 possible pairwise combinations of the eight goals were presented to the respondents. They evaluated the similarity of each pair of objectives on a nine-point scale (1-almost identical to 9=completely different). The re-spondents were given no information on what attributes of objectives they should use in judging similarity of the pairs presented to them.

Ratings for each pairwise comparison were averaged over all respondents. These mean similarity judgments provided input to the KYST multidimensional scaling program. While different dimensionalities were possible outputs from this routine, a stress value of .0941 supported a two-dimensional portrayal of the perceptual space.

## RESULTS AND DISCUSSION

After an arbitrary rotation, the two resulting axes of the geometric space seem to represent financial achievement vs. sales achievement and monetary status quo vs. monetary advancement. Interpretation of MDS output spaces is subject to the same differences of opinion that accompany factor analysis. Nonetheless, the 2-space evolved here demonstrates the application of the technique to finding the perceptual structure of corporate objectives. The respondents for this study perceived two underlying attributes when judging similarities of the stimulus objectives. Here it appears that maximum profit and satisfactory profits do lie on the same continuum. But to maximize stock price includes consideration of more than just high profits; an element of financial management is interjected into the stock price objective. Growth in earnings per share represents a profit achievement that is higher than satisfactory but lower than maximum. This growth also includes an element of financial achievement perceived to be considerably removed from mere high sales volume.

For coordination purposes, the three sales achievement goals are perceived as relatively similar. Managers holding to these objectives would be in fairly high agreement. But they would be in opposition to a planner seeking growth in earnings per share. On the other hand, those seeking profit maximization would require a balance between sales achievement and financial achievement, and a sizable departure from either stable or satisfactory profit.

The MDS approach can provide a more powerful guide toward goal consensus than has been empirically demonstrated here. Given proper input data from planners, the next step is to provide the position of the ideal point and the extent to which individual planners' preferred goals differ from the aggregate ideal. Using one approach, an explicit ideal point can be specified by an outside source, perhaps by direction of the Board of Directors. Using preference judgments in addition to the similarity measures used here, the ideal goal for each planner can also be established in a joint perceptual-preference space. Managers can then see how far their preferences differ from the imposed ideal, and this information can guide subsequent compromises and shifts of orientation. Informing managers of the functional relationship between financial objectives may be in order. With another method, an implicit ideal point can be established in the joint space by working with some unweighted or weighted combination of the individual preferences. Again, the joint space can include aggregate goal perceptions, as well as the ideal point preferences for individual managers. With such portrayals of the joint perceptual/preference space, individual managers can visualize the trade-offs to be made within the objectives space. Better planning should be the result.

PLANNING AND THE PLANNING PROCESS:
OBSERVING AND VIOLATING THE RULES

James A. Constantin, The University of Oklahoma
Ronald D. Anderson, Indiana University
Roger E. Jerman, Indiana University

ABSTRACT

Having a strategic plan is the only way a company can control or influence its destiny.  Because marketing matters
are the basic focus of strategic planning it is important
that firms have planning programs.  It is almost as important that these programs adhere to certain basic "rules" of
planning.  The research underlying this paper was designed
to determine certain characteristics of planning programs
of the respondents' companies.

The specific points addressed were (1) whether written
plans and objectives exist in respondents' companies; (2)
the extent to which respondents participate in planning;
(3) whether objectives define responsibilities of the respondents and whether plans define respondents' work role;
and (4) attitudes of respondents toward objectives and detailed plans.  Four hypotheses were stated on relationships
among these domains, educational level attained, and satisfaction with career.  Statistical analyses of the hypotheses are followed by a discussion of some implications of
not following the "rules" of planning.

# INNOVATION LINKAGES BETWEEN
## MARKETING AND R & D

Dillard B. Tinsley, Stephen F. Austin State University

## INTRODUCTION

For a number of years, commercialization of R & D results has been one of the "most severe" problems faced by R & D managers. At present, new products involve increasingly higher risks, and more defensive approach to innovation may be developing.

Marketing's linkages to R & D have been extensively studied in terms of their general organizational characteristics. These linkages are seen as a key to successful innovation, for there is the expectation that a close integration between marketing and R & D increases the probability of successful innovation and commercialization. This paper reports on specific problems in the actual marketing - R & D linkages found in 25 large manufacturers of consumer products. Highly-placed marketers in these companies assert that linkage problems exist, although 84% of the respondents have marketing and R & D personnel working together in innovation teams. Joint project reviews are held in 92%.

## PROBLEMS STILL EXIST

Although the marketing concept influences product development in 84% and marketing participates in setting R & D goals in 52%, at least 64% feel that R & D has more influence in setting product characteristics, goals, or schedules. Marketing is not involved soon enough in innovation in 44%, and 32% feel that adequate company support is not provided to marketing personnel in innovation. (24% feel adequate rewards are not provided.)

The most common cause of disputes between marketing and R & D is time schedules--mentioned by 56%. Other common causes, each mentioned by 32%, are communication, personalities, and product characteristics. Disputes are usually resolved by time constraints or department heads, but 72% sometimes use joint committees.

Human behavioral problems are significantly involved in communications because the two most commonly mentioned communication problems (60% mentioning) are "communications from R & D not often enough" and "R & D does not understand marketing." The latter problem was mentioned most often (36%) as the worst problem. The second most-common problem (48%) is "R & D does not respond quickly enough to information or clarification requests." Tied with 40% are "not enough detail provided by R & D" and "R & D is closed minded."

## NEED FOR MARKETING UNDERSTANDING

Part of the communication problems are structured in that communications between the two are usually by personal conversation or telephone. Although all the companies have special forms for communicating between the two, these forms are seldom used. In general, however, communication problems seem to be due to a lack of R & D understanding of marketing. This shows up in the failure to communicate often enough, quickly enough, or in sufficient detail. Understanding of marketing would aid R & D in deciding when to respond and what details to include.

The lack of marketing understanding also shows up in other ways. In 32% marketing does not supply information to R & D on product characteristics; in 36% marketing does not supply information on middleman characteristics; and 48% do not have marketing supply R & D with information about which product characteristics are to be used in promotion. Only 24% have R & D suggest points to use in promotion.

If R & D better understood marketing, communication problems should decrease. An R & D understanding of marketing should also ameliorate the other significant causes of disputes. Closer agreement on product characteristics should result; and personality clashes should be reduced as a common, marketing frame of reference is developed. Even disputes concerning time schedules might be reduced if the underlying marketing needs are understood and appreciated.

## IMPROVING UNDERSTANDING

R & D must understand marketing because R & D must ultimately fulfill marketing objectives. Marketing needs condition R & D efforts, the subject matter addressed by R & D, and even the particular types of scientists hired. At present, there is some attempt to increase understanding through experience. In 32% interchanges of personnel take place between R & D and marketing--24% assign R & D personnel to marketing and 16% assign marketing personnel to R & D. In 24% there are marketing personnel with some formal technical training in their background. No respondents have R & D personnel with any formal marketing training.

Providing R & D personnel with a basic understanding of marketing should not be difficult. These people are highly intelligent. Introduction to the marketing concept, market segmentation, differential advantage, the AIDA model, and characterization of the firm's target markets might be sufficient. The problems of speed, detail, and frequency might be solved by a computerized MIS including R & D and marketing. However, only 8% presently have computerized communications between R & D and marketing. Although 72% use PERT, CPM, or some other mathematical scheduling of new product development, only 8% is computerized.

# ADVERTISING BUDGETING IN A MULTIPRODUCT FIRM

Michael Etgar, State University of New York at Buffalo
Meir Schneller, Hebrew University at Jerusalem

## INTRODUCTION

Advertising decisions in multiproduct firms often have to be made under conditions of uncertainty and when considerable interactions among advertising programs for the firm's different products take place. To arrive at optimal decisions, marketing and advertising managers in multiproduct firms have to acknowledge these aspects. While some models have dealt with the effects of uncertainty on advertising allocations [1], none have dealt with the issues of allocation of advertising outlays within a product line where advertising interactions take place. Such a model is developed here.

## ASSUMPTIONS OF THE MODEL

1. Consider a firm producing and selling i products. Each dollar spent on advertising of a product i ($i = 1, \ldots, n$) results in increased sales at the amount of $1 + R_i$. Where $R_i$ is called the return on advertising product i and its mean is denoted by $M_i$.

2. The returns on the various products are interrelated. This implies that at least some of the covariance $\sigma_{ij} \neq 0$ ($i,j = 1, \ldots, n$).

3. The firm makes its decisions on the basis of the expected return and the variances connected with the advertising budget in such a way, that for a given level of an overall expected return, it will prefer the advertising combination with the lower variance of return. This assumes implicitly that the variance is a good measure for the risk involved in advertising expenditures and that management holds a conservative position towards risk.

4. The cost of capital which is invested in advertising, $R_f$, is given to the firm. $R_f$ could be perceived as reflecting the alternative return which the firm can generate from investing its capital in other marketing strategies for example in product development.

## THE MODEL

The way in which the decision should be made by assumption 3 is by maximizing the objective function:

$$\text{Max } M - \lambda\sigma^2 \qquad (1)$$

where $M = \sum_{i=1}^{n} X_i M_i$

subject to: $\sigma^2 = \sum\sum_{ij} X_i X_j \sigma_{ij} \quad \sum_{i=1}^{n+1} X_i = 1 \qquad 1 \geq X_i \geq 0$

where $M$ and $\sigma^2$ stand for the mean and variance of the returns on the advertising budget. By denoting as $X_i$ the fraction of the advertising budget to be spent on product i and by using basic statistical relationships, the problem presented in equation (1) can be transformed into:

$$\text{Max } M = \sum_{i=1}^{n+1} X_i M_i - \lambda \sum_{i=1}^{n} \sum_{j=1}^{n} X_i X_j \sigma_{ij} \qquad (2)$$

subject to:

$$\sum_{i=1}^{n+1} X_i = 1 \qquad (3)$$

To solve this problem as a constrained optimization problem formulate the Langrangian:

$$L = \sum_{i=1}^{n} X_i M_i + X_{n+1} R_f - \lambda \sum_{i=1}^{n} \sum_{j=1}^{n} X_i X_j \sigma_{ij} - \delta(\sum_{i=1}^{n+1} X_i - 1) \qquad (4)$$

where $\delta$ is the Lagrange multiplier connected with the budget constraint and where $\lambda$ reflects management's trade-offs between risk and return.

The n+1 first order conditions will be:

$$M_i - \delta - \lambda \sum_{j=1}^{n} X_j \sigma_{ij} = 0 \qquad i,j = 1, \ldots, n \qquad (5)$$

$$R_f - \delta = 0 \qquad (6)$$

from which we can solve by means of Cramer rule [2]:

$$X_i = \frac{1}{\lambda} \sum_{j=1}^{n} V_{ij}(M_i - R_f) \qquad i,j = 1, \ldots, n \qquad (7)$$

where $(V_{ij}) i,j = 1, \ldots, n$ is the inverse of the variance-covariance matrix: $(\sigma_{ij}) \; i,j = 1, \ldots, n$

Equation (7) indicates that the size of $X_{n+1}$ cannot be determined unless we know $\lambda$, the management's coefficient of trade-off between risk and return. However, even if we do not know this coefficient we are able to determine the proportions to be allocated to each product i. Only the actual size of the budget will depend on $\lambda$.

The interesting result is that the decision as to how much to invest in advertising the various products depends only to a limited extent on the variability of the return on advertising of each product. Most important is the impact of the advertising of one product on the sales of other products, as expressed by the $(V_{ij})$ matrix in equation (7).

Notice that our model cannot solve for $X_{n+1}$. The meaning of this is that the firm once deciding about the distribution of the budget can now decide upon the size of the budget. Thus $X_{n+1} > 0$ will call for a reduction in the size of the budget whereas $X_{n+1} < 0$ will call for increasing the budget. The size of the budget depends on the level of risk or expected return that the manager wants to attain, but regardless of the budget size the distribution is dictated by equation (7).

## REFERENCES

1. Enis, Ben M. "Bayesian Approach to Advertising Budgets", Journal of Advertising Research, 12 (February 1972), 13-19.

2. Hadley, G. Linear Algebra. Reading: Addison-Wesley, 1961.

# CHOOSING THE BEST ADVERTISING APPROPRIATION WHEN
## APPROPRIATIONS INTERACT OVER TIME

Haim Levy, Hebrew University, Jerusalem, Israel
Julian L. Simon, University of Illinois, Urbana, Illinios

## INTRODUCTION

This paper provides operational methods of choosing the firm's optimum expenditure for advertising in some common situations in which the advertising expenditure in one period influences the results obtained from the expenditures in the following periods. A secondary aim is to analyze the size of the appropriations that will be spent if the firm acts rationally.

## THE CASES CONSIDERED

First we present a simplified explanation of an earlier method of choosing the advertising expenditure in situations where the budget in one period may be assumed not to affect the results of subsequent expenditures. This method is appropriate and easy to apply in most actual situations of advertising budget allocation. The only information needed are the advertising response function, the prior period's sales, the carryover rate, and the cost of capital.

Then we find the relationship of the response function to the carryover rate and money discount factor if the firm optimizes, still in the situation of no interaction among budgets in various periods. This relationship turns out to be a strong generalization of the well-known Dorfman-Steiner theorem.

Established products with bounded markets are discussed next. In such a situation, as the firm makes customers it reduces the number of potential customers that advertising may attract in following periods. We arrive at an easy-to-implement formula that tells what the optimizing appropriation should be in such a case. This calculation requires only an estimate of the total market in addition to the elements required for the simplest model.

New products are analyzed next. On a plausible assumption about how advertising works for new products, we show that the amount that should be spent in any period depends only upon the carryover rate and the money discount factor, just as in the no-interaction situation. But we also arrive at the rather surprising finding that after the first period the amount of advertising will be constant for the new product. And the amount of advertising in the first period will be greater than in subsequent periods by exactly the carryover rate multiplied by discount factor multiplied by the amount spent in the next period.

## CALCULATING FORMULAS

These are the methods we have arrived at:

1. When the brand's market share is relatively small, and the firm can assume that its advertising budget in period $t$ has no affect on the results of advertising in $t + k$, then the net present value (NPV) of any particular advertising budget $A_t$ can be calculated as follows:

$$NPV\ (A_t) = (S_t - bS_{t-1})\ \left(\frac{1}{1 - bd}\right) - A_t$$

where $S_t$ = sales

$b$ = the retention factor

$d$ = the discount factor.

The advertising budget that promises the highest NPV should be chosen. This result holds whether or not the firm's prior advertising budget was optimal. If the carryover is not regular and geometric, an extended form of this relationship may be used.

2. For a mature product that has an important share of the market, and for which it is reasonable to assume that the optimum budget will be the same in future periods, the firm may try various budgets with the formula.

$$NPV = \frac{1}{k}\ \{bS[1 - f(A)] + Mf(A) - A\}$$

where M is the total market in dollars, and $k$ is the cost of capital. Or it may solve, analytically or numerically, this equation,

$$\frac{\partial NPV}{\partial A} = \frac{1}{k}\ \{b\frac{\partial S}{\partial A}\ [1 - f(A)] - bSf'(A) + Mf'(A) - 1\} = 0.$$

3. For a new product the matter is even simpler. It is reasonable to assume that sales in any period for a new product are a function such as

$$S_t = f(A_t + bA_{t-1} + b^2A_{t-2} + \ldots .b^tA_0).$$

Then the firm should advertise at that point of the advertising response function at which the slope of the response is equal to 1 - bd. The advertising in the first period will be greater than in subsequent periods because no stock of advertising impressions is carried over into the first period. But the optimizing rule is nevertheless the same for the first and subsequent periods.

A second set of findings in the paper are the descriptions of the budgets that a profit-maximizing firm will reach.

# A GOAL PROGRAMMING "INDEX MODEL" FOR THE ALLOCATION OF ADVERTISING EFFORT

Paul F. Anderson, Virginia Polytechnic Institute
Bernard W. Taylor, III, Virginia Polytechnic Institute

## INTRODUCTION

This paper employs a goal programming (GP) algorithm to develop a market potential index for the geographic allocation of advertising effort. The model makes use of the preemptive priority capability of GP to "weight" a group of economic and demographic variables which are related to market potential. This somewhat nontraditional use of GP offers a practical, inexpensive, and flexible alternative to the use of optimization models for the allocation of advertising resources.

Regression and experimentation are the most frequently cited optimization models used for advertising allocation. Both approaches attempt to identify the marginal sales response to advertising relationship in different territories. Unfortunately, the implementation of these techniques can be costly and time-consuming. Moreover, the various statistical and design problems associated with their use may make them practical for only the most sophisticated users.

A widely used alternative to the application of optimization models involves the development of market potential indexes, such as Sales and Marketing Management's well-known Buying Power Index. With this approach, the firm allocates its promotional budget in accordance with the relative market potential of each area, as indicated by a group of economic and demographic variables.

## THE MODEL

The proposed GP model is a variant of the market potential index approach. The technique was demonstrated through the use of an example problem which considers the case of a furniture manufacturer which wishes to determine its promotional allocations for the seven SMSAs in the state of Virginia.

The general GP model may be expressed mathematically as:

$$\text{Minimize } Z = \sum_{i=1}^{m} \sum_{j=1}^{k} P_j (d_i^+ + d_i^-) \qquad (1)$$

$$\text{Subject to: } AX - Id^+ + Id^- = b \qquad (2)$$

$$X, d^+, d^- \geq 0 \qquad (3)$$

Where "b" is an "m" column vector, $(b_1, b_2, \ldots, b_m)$, corresponding to "m" goals. "A" is an "mxn" matrix expressing the relationship between goals and subgoals. "X" represents decision variables involved in the subgoals $(x_1, x_2, \ldots, x_n)$, "$d^+$" and "$d^-$" are "m" component vectors representing the deviation from goals, "I" is an "mxn" identity matrix, and the "$P_j$" represent priority coefficients.

The objective of the model is to allocate the firm's advertising efforts among the seven SMSAs in accordance with the market potential of each area. To this end, the first goal constraint becomes the exact achievement of a 100% allocation of effort across the seven markets:

$$X_1 + X_2 + X_3 + X_4 + X_5 + X_6 + X_7 + d_1^- - d_1^+ = 1.00 \qquad (4)$$

The remaining goal constraints are constructed from variables related to furniture market potential. A goal constraint for a given variable (e.g., furniture sales per household) represents the relative magnitude of the variable in the seven SMSAs. The coefficients (magnitudes) in a goal constraint equation (along with the specified goal levels and priority assignments) serve to direct resources toward those areas with the greatest potential. For example, equation (5) represents the goal constraint for total retail furniture sales:

$$9.1X_1 + 17.7X_2 + 49.4X_3 + 106.1X_4 + 14.1X_5 + 96.2X_6$$
$$+ 38.2X_7 + d_2^- - d_2^+ = 70.0 \qquad (5)$$

where the coefficients are furniture sales in millions of dollars for each of the seven markets. Six other goal constraints are employed in the model. These include variables related to furniture sales as well as variables on age, income, and growth patterns in the markets. Each goal constraint is assigned a priority coefficient reflecting its importance as an index of furniture market potential. An artificial priority must be established for equation (4) so that the top priority becomes the allocation of exactly 100% of the promotional budget.

In effect, the priority assignments serve to "weight" each of the variables included in the index. Promotional resources are assigned to the various markets in accordance with the priority of each variable. Allocations are made on a sequential basis starting with the highest priority variable and working downward through the lower priorities. The use of this preemptive priority capability avoids the problem of overallocating resources to low potential areas, as can occur with more traditional weighting schemes. On the other hand, experience with the model suggests a tendency to underallocate resources to low potential areas. This results because the priority weighting system will not sacrifice allocations made on the basis of top priority variables in order to satisfy low priority constraints. Thus, the procedure tends to force allocations toward the highest potential markets without regard for many of the lower priority variables.

## CONCLUSIONS

This experience suggests that the model is most appropriate to situations in which (1) only a few variables are necessary to identify the market potential of various areas, and (2) underallocation to high potential areas is deemed to be a more serious problem than underallocation to low potential areas. In these circumstances, the GP approach can provide a practical, flexible, and inexpensive alternative to regression or experimentation techniques for the allocation of promotional resources.

THE EVOLVING ROLE OF MARKETING TECHNOLOGY IN AN INNOVATIVE HEALTH
CARE DELIVERY SYSTEM:  A COMPARATIVE ANALYSIS

Richard C. Becherer, Wayne State University
Lawrence M. Richard, Wayne State University
William R. George, Virginia Commonwealth University

## INTRODUCTION

One traditionally non-business area of potential application for marketing technology, that of health care delivery,
has been conspicuously absent in the marketing literature
and has only recently been given serious attention by marketers.  The passage of the Health Maintenance Organization and Resources Act of 1973, however, requires that
Health Maintenance Organizations (HMO's) seeking federal
certification and funding submit detailed market feasibility and planning documents with their applications to HEW.
These documents must specify the organization's market
analysis, product offerings, promotional plans, distribution method, and pricing strategy.  Thus, this stipulation
effectively requires that all HMO's must either develop
or acquire expertise in the performance of traditional
marketing activities.

Health Maintenance Organizations as alternatives to the
existing health care delivery system are defined as legal
entities or organized systems of health care that provide
directly, or arrange for, comprehensive basic and supple-
mentary health care services to a voluntarily enrolled
population, in a defined geographical area, on a primarily
prepaid and fixed periodic basis.  The HMO Act's explicit
attention to marketing was based on the beliefs of HMO
experts in and out of government that marketing was one of
the major keys to success for any HMO.  The legislative
requirements for a market planning approach were an attempt
to ensure the success of HMO's.  It is the purpose of this
study to explore the status of marketing technology in
HMO's in the early stages of their evolution.

## METHODOLOGY

The data for this research were collected via a mail
questionnaire sent to a nationwide census of operative
HMO-type organizations.  Of the 179 questionnaires that
were mailed, 81 were returned for a response rate of 45
percent.  A total 69 of these were useable responses.

The items selected for inclusion in the study were designed to gather information on the performance of HMO
marketing activities across four specific areas: offerings, pricing, advertising and promotion, and marketing
research.  Comparative data from a previous study were
used as the basis for evaluating the scope and status of
HMO marketing activities [1].  Respondents were asked to
indicate if each marketing activity was performed primarily
internally (in the marketing department, some other department, jointly with another department), externally by a
consultant, or was not performed.  Chi-square analysis was
utilized to test for significant differences between the
responses of reporting HMO's and the previously collected
data for service firms.

## RESULTS

Findings from the data analysis revealed all Chi-square
values significant at p < .001, suggesting considerable
differences between HMO marketing and the marketing activities in other service firms.  In HMO's marketing departments tend to share responsibility for determination of
service offerings, demand analysis, and planning with
other departments.

Regarding pricing activities, joint responsibility was
reported quite frequently for the pretesting of prices and
pricing policy evaluation, and only in competitor pricing
analysis did the marketing department dominate.  The frequency of external responsibility for these three pricing
activities was very similar for HMO and other service firms,
but HMO's are more likely than other service firms to perform pricing policy evaluation.  This may reflect the newness of the HMO concept in the marketplace, and the importance placed on pricing for HMO's.

Differences between marketing technology in HMO's and other
service firms are perhaps most clearly evidenced in the
data relative to advertising and promotion activities.  A
considerable proportion of HMO's (33.3%) report that they
do not currently create and place any advertising, and
many are not currently developing any advertising programs
(33.3%) or sales training programs (42.9%) aimed at specific target groups.  These proportions for HMO's not performing promotion related activities are particularly high
relative to other service firms.

Two contrasts are evident between HMO's and other service
firms relative to marketing research activities.  First,
HMO's are much more likely than service firms to have a
joint approach to market analysis.  Second, HMO's are less
likely to perform their research activities externally,
except for evaluation of customer wants and needs.

Generally, the findings indicate that HMO organizations
are less likely than other service firms to employ external
consultants to perform designated marketing activities.
Since the internal marketing departments do not appear from
the data to be very highly developed, most HMO organizations are either not at a level of maturity which recognizes the value of more technical expertise or the technical expertise for marketing HMO services is not readily
available.

## CONCLUSIONS

In this research, the high proportion of HMO's reporting
that they currently perform marketing activities is an
indication of the universality of the marketing function in
non-profit areas.  Such performance is also an indication
that these organizations recognize the importance of marketing's role in their success.  However, the responding
HMO organizations represent a far less structured marketing
approach than other service firms.  Traditional marketing
activities in HMO's are often diffused and performed by the
marketing department in conjunction with other departments
in the organization.  In comparing these findings with
other service firms, one might expect that as HMO's continue to evolve, marketing responsibilities will become
more clearly defined and centralized in marketing departments.

## REFERENCES

1.  George, William R., and Hiram C. Barksdale, "Marketing
    Activities in the Services Industries," Journal of
    Marketing, 38 (October 1974) 65-70.

INTERFACING MARKETING AND MASS TRANSIT:
GUIDELINES FOR PLANNING AND CONTROLLING

Dennis R. McDermott, Syracuse University

## INTRODUCTION

The scope of this article is to identify the dimensions of the urban passenger transportation problem, i.e., its symptoms and causes, and to examine proposed solutions from the marketing perspectives of product management, promotional strategy, pricing decisions, and market research. A set of guidelines is then developed to enhance the marketing planning and controlling processes relative to mass transit decision-making.

## BACKGROUND

The energy crisis has forced a reassessment of social priorities and life styles in the U.S. Nowhere in our economy is this more true than in the transportation sector, which accounts for 25% of all energy usage, but over 52% of the consumption of petroleum products. The component of transportation consuming the largest proportion of energy is urban automobile passenger travel, which accounts for some 40% of the total. The dominance of the automobile as the major mode of urban travel has been increasing substantially since WW II. In 1950, mass transit, which is 3 to 4 times as energy efficient as automobiles, accounted for 15% of all urban passenger trips. By 1970, this had declined to only 3%. As urban passengers left mass transit for the automobile, not only did energy efficiency decrease, but other problems arose. Among the major problems of large cities are unsafe air pollution levels, rush-hour congestion, and the decline of the center-city area's economic viability. Perhaps the greatest cause of the demise of mass transit is the increased affluence and high standard of living enjoyed by most Americans. This has affected housing patterns and automobile usage in that suburbia and "urban sprawl" have proliferated in the last two decades. Other causes adding momentum to the demise of mass transit and the increased usage of automobiles include the historically low costs of gasoline in the U.S., the governmental policies regarding transportation, and the economics of the mass transit industry itself. Evidence that the problem will only increase in severity in the future includes projections of demographic trends in the U.S. and demand forecasts for automobiles. It is projected that by 1980, more than 80% of our population will reside in metropolitan areas. Automobile sales, which currently total some 10 million on an annual basis in the U.S., are projected to increase to 18 million annually by the end of this century.

## APPLICATION OF MARKETING VARIABLES

As a guide to mass transit operators and researchers, an integration of marketing application is required in the areas of product management, promotional strategy, pricing decisions, and market research. It is important to recognize the generic product or service concept, relative to urban transportation, in this case consisting of the combined set of attributes or factors affecting consumers' perceptions of the advantages and disadvantages of various transportation alternatives. The key to mass transit's future success is in redirecting its offering to those target market segments where it can effectively compete with the automobile along certain key attributes or service dimensions. Some bases for market segmentation in this industry include the trip purpose, the geographic base, and demographic characteristics of riders. For example, a segmentation strategy, focusing on demographic characteristics,

consists of park-and-ride services oriented to commuters travelling from suburban residences to downtown areas. These commuters typically assemble at one point in their residential area and then receive express service to the downtown area in a large capacity bus. These projects sometimes include bus-priority features such as the use of an exclusive, high-speed traffic lane or on-bus control of traffic signals. Park-and-ride services do have a constraint, however, in that they are generally oriented to downtown areas. As industries have relocated to the suburbs, the need exists to redirect mass transit routings. As a result, a version of park-and-ride service has evolved called subscription service, which also involves assembly at a central point, and then express service is offered to typically one destination, e.g. a large industrial employer away from the downtown area.

The impact of educating the automobile commuter of the actual costs of driving can be substantial. The public generally considers only the out-of-pocket or direct operating costs of using an automobile, without realizing the total costs. A recent study, which applied to an average 1976 model operating under average urban conditions, computed the per-mile cost of driving to be 18.7¢. Based on this cost, and assuming a subscription service rate of $5 per week which eliminates a 20 mile drive daily, the annual savings to an automobile commuter of using subscription service would approximate $700. In addition, promotional themes emphasizing the social impacts of mass transit usage, such as reduced energy usage and air pollution, have been popular campaigns for mass transit organizations.

The pricing variable does not seem to represent an elastic demand schedule for mass transit services as studies have shown the greatest effect on ridership was brought about by service improvements and not fare reductions. These results should not be interpreted as indicating pricing decisions are inconsequential. Pricing experiments have been shown to be effective in the case of either facilitating payment, e.g. through a payroll deduction plan for subscription service, adding complementary products to encourage high-volume consumption, or implementing off-peak-hour discounts to result in better capacity utilization.

Two emphases or focuses of market research applied to mass transit are: 1) market data serving as inputs for planning or setting strategy; and, 2) performance data serving as feedback measures for controlling marketing decisions. Strategic Data consists of assessing consumer profiles, competitive profiles, and market trends. Controlling data relates to evaluating the effectiveness of mass transit strategy by providing continued feedback as to whether or not operational objectives are being achieved in terms of ridership, growth, market share, or capacity utilization measures.

In the long run, the restoration of mass transit systems to their former demand levels of some 25 years ago will depend on changed life styles and land-use patterns in the U.S. Meanwhile, much can be done in the area of aggressively marketing mass transit services to specific consumer segments by recognizing the need for strategic planning and effective controlling of marketing decisions.

PLANNING AND CONTROL FOR PERFORMING ARTS' MARKETING: A SUMMARY

Gene R. Laczniak, Marquette University
Patrick E. Murphy, Marquette University

## INTRODUCTION

During the 1970's a prominent development within marketing has been a growing application of marketing techniques to nonprofit organizations. Recently, aspects of marketing have been utilized in Performing Arts' promotion. However, marketing the Arts represents a difficult task because it does not meet several assumptions that hold for economic goods. This paper's purpose is to outline these differences and to suggest a general planning and control model for marketing the Arts.

## HOW MARKETING THE ARTS IS DIFFERENT

Clearly, there are differences in the product development, pricing, promotion and distribution of the Arts which are encountered by the marketer familiar with selling economic goods. While modern marketers in the profit sector are guided by the "marketing concept," the Arts are dominated by a desire of artists (i.e., the product creators) to introduce more of an audience to new and progressive artistic expression. As a result, artists create or adapt the "Arts" product without consulting the audience; commonly, they rely solely on their artistic temperaments. Therefore, the Arts practice what marketing theorists label as the "product concept."

Contrary to economic goods, Arts are commonly priced below cost. If ticket prices reflected the actual cost of production, the Arts would be priced out of the reach of most patrons. The Arts survive because they depend on the contributions of business, government and wealthy benefactors to subsidize the gap between actual cost and ticket revenue. The primary justification for below cost pricing is that the Arts represent a form of cultural enrichment, important to society, that would otherwise be lost. Another reason for the high cost of the Arts stems from the commitment of performing artists to quality productions.

Convenience of location is a prime distribution criteria for profit marketers. Performing Arts companies cannot locate predominantly on the basis of selectivity. They need a large potential audience to survive; thus, they require a facility with expanded seating and exceptional support systems. Increasingly, Performing Arts companies are working out of Performing Arts Centers built and subsidized by government and usually located in the downtown metropolitan areas. Such facilities permit various Performing Arts companies to share overhead in an efficient economic manner. Therefore, these companies are not only saddled with a given location, but also have limited or fixed time slots for performances because of the sharing arrangement.

Admittedly, the strategies utilized in the promotion of the Performing Arts are not that dissimilar from those used to sell economic goods. However, major differences between traditional promotion and that utilized for Arts organizations exist. For example: (1) Most Arts companies have little or no advertising budget. Commonly, radio and TV commercials are subsidized by an outside source; (2) The Artistic Director of the Arts company will often demand a strong voice in shaping the promotional materials (e.g., direct mail brochures) utilized and his aesthetic standards may not be easily attainable by an ad agency; (3) Some artists feel that the Arts inherently possess their own attraction to the cultured and that any promotion degrades their nature.

## A PLANNING AND CONTROL MODEL FOR ARTS' MARKETING

### Objectives for Arts Organizations

Three possible objectives for Arts organizations are put forth. Of paramount importance is free artistic expression. The artist wants the freedom to develop new forms of expression and lead society in its quest for cultural appreciation. Since performing artists are as much "performers" as formulators of artistic expression, continuing and increasing patronage is a second desirable objective. Third, community financial support also appears to be important.

### Market Analysis for the Arts

For market analysis to be complete, audience identification and development are essential. Marketing research tools can be employed to identify demographic and psychographic features of current patrons as well as those who have never attended artistic performances. With audience profiles generated through research, it would be possible to develop "targeted" promotional strategies to reach greater numbers of an audience segment.

### Arts Programming and Implementation

Most essential to programming is the development of proper marketing strategy (i.e., target market selection and marketing-mix determination). The product element includes putting together the performances, coordinating management decisions with the companies' artistic directors and scheduling the number and times of performances. Competition among the other cultural institutions of public television, libraries and museums is becoming keener and the "product" offered by Performing Arts groups may not be as unique as previously believed. Although raising ticket prices for Arts performances to fully cover costs is not practical, some price increases to moderate projected expenses-earnings gaps appear necessary. Through market research, Arts organizations can establish the elasticity of their ticket prices so that maximum revenue can be obtained. While promotional budgets for the Arts are modest, determination of proper promotional mixes is essential. The use of television, magazines, radio and newspapers should be evaluated according to their impact upon potential audience segments. Since the location of most Performing Arts companies is fixed, the facilitation of convenient parking and possibly the provision of mass transit options are distribution decisions which affect program success.

### Evaluation of Arts Programs

The components of the Arts' evaluation effort involve effectiveness (i.e., degree to which objectives were attained), efficiency measures and feedback. An efficiency measure for an Arts organization would be to compare the cost of different advertising media with their contribution of new patrons. Feedback should be continuous and Arts organizations must periodically survey their audiences and local community for reactions concerning each type of event.

CONSUMER PARTICIPATION IN THE REGULATORY SYSTEM

Priscilla Ann La Barbera, New York University

ABSTRACT

This paper reports the results of an exploratory study concerning the attitudinal nature of consumers who are involved in Federal Trade Commission rule-making procedures. The data indicate that consumers who participate in shaping the regulations governing business have a consumer activist orientation and espouse increased government regulation to achieve consumer protection.

INTRODUCTION

General notices of all proposed federal agency rules necessary to implement a law are published in the Federal Register. Subsequent to notice, the federal agent must allow interested parties an opportunity to participate in the rule-making process through submission of written and/or oral data, views, or arguments. After consideration of all relevant material presented, the administrator then writes the final rule.

Historically, industry tended to be the major participant in the rule-making process. A comfortable relationship often existed between the regulators and the regulated industries [3,pp. 162-4]. Prior to the 1970's, files of proposed rules reflected extensive industry input while consumer input into federal agency decision making was essentially nonexistent [2].

Since 1970, however, projects focused on broadening the base of federal agency decision making have been initiated by the Office of the Federal Register, the Office of Consumer Affairs, and the federal agencies. Due to these efforts a proposed consumer protection rule which may have generated two or three public comments in the 1960's now results in two or three hundred [5, pg. 36]. The purpose of this exploratory study was to gain some insight into the attitudinal nature of consumers whose views are now competing with those of industry members for the attention of federal administrators.

ATTITUDINAL STUDY OF CONSUMER PARTICIPANTS IN
FEDERAL TRADE COMMISSION RULE MAKING

In the spring of 1976 a survey was undertaken to determine whether attitudes toward consumerism and government regulation differed significantly between consumers involved in Federal Trade Commission (FTC) rule making and members of the public at large. It was hypothesized that involved consumers would have more positive attitudes than the public at large toward the importance and effectiveness of consumerism. In addition, it was hypothesized that these consumers would have more positive attitudes than the general public toward increasing government activities to achieve consumer protection.

Methodology

Issues of the Federal Register were examined for the period November 1, 1974 to October 31, 1975 to cull FTC consumer protection rules which were proposed during that year. A systematic random sample of 420 consumer names and addresses was drawn from the files of individual consumer comments received for each rule proposal which are maintained by the FTC in Washington, D. C.

A research instrument comprising five point Likert-type items was designed to gather attitudinal data from subjects. To make a comparative analysis possible, the questions used were borrowed from a previous study undertaken by Barksdale et al. in 1975 to examine attitudes held by the general public [1]. A national random sample of consumers was surveyed by these researchers and after one follow up letter, 697 consumers or 45% of the sample responded to the survey.

Copies of the final research instrument were mailed to 400 members of the FTC sample in March 1976. Almost 85% of the sample, or 350, returned completed questionnaires within a one-month period.

Results and Discussion

Both major hypotheses were supported by the data. Responses to the Likert statements indicated more positive attitudes of the FTC than the national sample toward the importance and effectiveness of consumerism as well as increasing government activities to achieve consumer protection. All but one Likert statement also resulted in statistically significant more positive attitudes of the FTC than national sample respondents according to the Kolmogorov-Smirnov two-sample one-tailed test [4].

It was found, for example, that over 80% of consumers who present their views to the FTC believe that Ralph Nader and his work on behalf of consumers have been an important force in changing the practices of business. Nearly 75% of the respondents believed that the government should set minimum standards of quality for all products sold to consumers.

The attitudinal data, along with the activity of commenting on rule proposals, strongly suggest that the consumers studied have a greater consumer activist orientation than consumers at large. The data clearly indicated that these consumers will seek protection through increased government legislation and regulations. It appears that these individuals will present views on a proposed rule which are in conflict with views held by members of industry.

REFERENCES

1. Barksdale, Hiram C., William R. Darden, and William D. Perreault. "Changes in Consumer Attitudes Toward Marketing, Consumerism, and Government Regulation: 1971-1975," The Journal of Consumer Affairs, 10 (Winter 1976), 117-39.

2. La Barbera, Priscilla, Alvin Katzman, Richard Rose and Morris Shapero, "Decisions That Affect Your Future," Working paper. White House Office of Consumer Affairs, August 1971.

3. McCraw, Thomas K. "Regulation in America: A Review Article," Business History Review, 49 (Summer 1975), 162-68.

4. Siegel, Sidney. Nonparametric Statistics for the Behavioral Sciences. New York: McGraw-Hill Book Co., 1956, 127-36.

5. Shafer, Ronald G. "Federal Register, Written in 'Governmentese,' Tries to Make Itself Understood by the Public," Wall Street Journal, (October 23, 1975), 36.

STATUS REPORT ON CONSUMER
PROTECTION AT THE STATE LEVEL

Bernard A. Morin, University of Virginia
Thomas L. Wheelen, University of Virginia

## INTRODUCTION

This paper reports on two studies (1971 and 1975) undertaken by the authors to ascertain what activities were contemplated or implemented by states in response to the consumerism movement. The states were chosen because their
laws and regulations seem to have more direct impact on the
consumer in his normal dealings than those at the federal
level. The same questionnaire was submitted in 1971 and
1975 to the Attorney General of each of the 50 states, with
forty-six responses in 1971 and forty-two responses in 1975.

The authors wanted to determine whether changes had occurred
in the following: (1) states' budgetary commitments for
consumer protection; (2) attitudes toward the adequacy of
consumer legislation; (3) consumer awareness of legislation;
(4) staffs to administer programs; (5) the types and number
of media to inform the public; (6) attitudes toward the
role of the federal and state governments in the consumer
movement; and (7) offices or agencies responsible for the
consumer movement at the state level.

## FINDINGS

In 1971, less than 80 percent of the states responding to
the survey had a specific agency dealing with consumer protection. In 1975 all respondents had such an agency.
Also, for those states which replied to both surveys,
staffing and budgets increased. The average staff rose
from eight to 15.8 employees and the average yearly budget
increased from $342,461 to $539,927. The lower percentage
increase for budgets may be due to the possibility that
fixed costs of operating an agency may be constant over a
fairly wide range of activity.

Attorneys General felt that the affectiveness of state laws
changed considerably over the four year period. On a five
point scale, with a "5" response meaning 'highly effective,'
and a "1" response meaning 'poorly effective,' the mean
response increased from 2.83 to 3.94 between 1971 and 1975.
However, when questioned whether citizens of the state were
well informed concerning consumer legislation, and again
answering on a five point scale, the Attorneys General
responded that consumer knowledge did not increase significantly.

Since awareness is related to the ability of the state to
communicate with citizens, the authors requested data on
the use of toll-free phones and the media employed to inform citizens of important consumer legislation. In 1971,
only eight of forty-six respondents had toll-free numbers,
while twenty of forty-two respondents had the numbers in
1975. Also, although the same media were being used to
promulgate laws in 1971 and 1975, the percentage of states
using the media increased. The most popular means of communication involved state news releases to the media, and
heavy emphasis was placed on radio and television.

## CONCLUSION

In summary, the average Attorney General feels that his
state has effective laws and agencies to protect consumer
rights and that his state is making a greater effort to
insure that citizens are made aware of their rights.
However, a number noted that more consumer education is
needed, and the fact that the use of the media to promulgate the laws has increased considerably without a major
effect leads the authors to believe that continued use of
present media policies and messages may have only a marginal effect.

# THE IMPACT OF INFLATION:
## A COMPARATIVE STUDY OF THE BLACK POPULATION
## AND THE GENERAL POPULATION

Zoher E. Shipchandler, Indiana University-Purdue University at Fort Wayne
Marcia Wilson, Central Soya

## INTRODUCTION

The purpose of this paper is to determine the impact of inflation on families belonging to two groups - the overall American population and the black population which is a subset of the former. Past studies indicate that attitudinal, behavioral, and consumption differences exist between blacks and whites (2,3,4). However, research on a comparison of the impact of inflation between the general and black population is practically non-existent.

While the black population has made some economic gains, as a group it is more vulnerable to inflation. Barry and Harvey (1) state that due to the fact that blacks have not received the same quality of education as their nonblack counterparts, the black consumer's ability to rationally evaluate the alternative uses for his funds and thus maximize consumer utilities is drastically affected. In a period of shrinking purchasing power this would be even more accentuated.

## RESEARCH METHOD

The findings are based upon a research study that was undertaken in Fort Wayne, Indiana during the Summer of 1975. The exploratory phase of the study consisted of a focus group interview with eight housewives selected at random, and in-depth follow-up personal interviews. The second phase of the study consisted of a survey, using a structured questionnaire, of 183 adults representing the general population and 69 adults representing the black population. The two samples were selected using area sampling techniques.

## FINDINGS

The study revealed that both blacks and the general population are finding it necessary to make changes in lifestyle in order to cope with inflation. While the similarities are many, so are the differences. Some of the differences between the two groups may be just as much explained by income as by race as the black sample's median income was substantially lower than that of the overall population sample.

While a majority of both groups indicated that they were more careful than before in their use of household utilities and gasoline, the proportion of the general population is significantly greater than the corresponding proportion of blacks (Table 1). This is not surprising as the previous consumption level of blacks may be lower and hence it is more difficult for them to cut back.

### TABLE 1

#### CONSUMPTION PATTERN OF HOUSEHOLD UTILITIES AND GASOLINE[a]

| | Percent More Careful | |
| --- | --- | --- |
| | Black | General |
| Use of Household Utilities | 73.9 | 85.3 |
| Use of Gasoline | 68.1 | 80.0 |

[a]The difference between the proportions are all significant at p $\leq$ .05.

Both groups are doing comparison shopping and buying items on sale more than before. The general population, like the black population, has stepped up purchases from wholesale and discount outlets. Both groups are also consuming less of discretionary food items such as frozen prepared foods and ready-to-eat baked foods.

In connection with attitudes relating to inflation, blacks are more pessimistic than the general population (Table 2). These and other differences outlined above underscore the point that the true impact of inflation can only be appreciated by studying the impact on the various subgroups that make the total population.

### TABLE 2

#### ATTITUDES RELATING TO INFLATION

| | Percent Agreeing[a] | |
| --- | --- | --- |
| | Black | General |
| Has inflation cheated you out of the "good life"? | 65.2 | 27.3 |
| Each person should have one last happy fling. | 50.8 | 25.7 |
| It is difficult for a person to make any plans. | 60.9 | 40.5 |

[a]The difference between the proportions are all significant at p $\leq$ .05.

## REFERENCES

1. Barry, Thomas E. and Michael G. Harvey. "Marketing to Heterogeneous Black Consumers." California Management Review, 17 (February 1974), 50-7.

2. Bauer, Raymond A., Scott M. Cunningham and Lawrence H. Wortzel. "The Marketing Dilemma of Negroes." Journal of Marketing, 29 (July 1965), 1-6.

3. Cohen, Dorothy. "Advertising and the Black Community." Journal of Marketing, 34 (October 1970), 3-11.

4. Hills, Gerald E., Donald H. Granbois and James M. Patterson. "Black Consumer Perceptions of Food Store Attributes." Journal of Marketing, 37 (April 1973), 47-57.

# BLACK/WHITE EXPERIENCES WITH SUPERMARKET PRODUCT UNAVAILABILITY

J. B. Wilkinson, The University of Alabama
J. Barry Mason, The University of Alabama

## INTRODUCTION

As partial recognition of mispricing and unavailability problems in supermarkets, the Federal Trade Commission issued a trade regulation rule in 1971 designed to control these abuses. However, these practices continue to plague food shoppers and in the aggregate cause them both monetary loss and personal frustration. A recent shopper simulation based on actual information for one national supermarket chain estimated that, under varying assumptions, product unavailability could cost consumers as a group almost $18,000 per year in a single store (6). This and other research indicates that differences in promotion practices can be as important as market basket price differentials in their impact on consumer food costs (2,3,4,8).

However, the actual degree of economic loss is dependent upon shopper reliance on food specials. Recent research has shown that urban shoppers on the average now spend 14% of their food dollar on advertised food specials during a typical shopping trip (1,7) and that they are becoming increasingly price conscious in their behavior (5).

In summary, unavailability of advertised food specials is a frequent occurrence in the supermarket and advertised food specials are important to food shoppers. However, the food shopper's reaction to product unavailability and the store's management response to their behavior are still largely unknown.

## PURPOSES

Given the above information, the purposes of this research were to: (1) Profile the in-store price checking behavior of consumers and determine the extent of unavailability encounters for advertised food specials; (2) Analyze the behavior patterns of consumers when confronted with unavailability of advertised food products; (3) Determine the extent of consumer knowledge about the FTC trade regulation rule on unavailability of advertised food products.

Differences, if any, between the behavior patterns of and supermarket management responses to low-income black, low-income white and higher-income white customers were studied. Other differences in the socio-economic background of the shoppers were also related to behavior patterns. The research is based on responses from 219 persons who were selected through random sampling procedures in a Southeastern SMSA.

## FINDINGS

1. Black low-income shoppers bought supermarket specials less frequently than either white low-income or white higher-income shoppers.
2. Most shoppers were conscientious in their shopping behavior and few differences in behavior were noted. However, low-income blacks did less in-store checking of prices but were most likely to check cash register tapes upon returning home.
3. Seventy-two percent of the respondents had encountered an unavailable advertised special in the preceding six months. Sixty-four percent of these persons had asked someone about the unavailable item. Approximately 22% of the "askers" were offered a substitute, 34% a rain check, and 50% nothing.
4. Males were more likely to be offered a substitute than females, while rain checks were more likely to be issued

to white shoppers, shoppers with higher education and shoppers who do not use food stamps. Low-income blacks were more likely to be offered nothing than either of the white income groups. This overall pattern of store behavior suggests that substitutes and rainchecks are offered primarily to either "better" clientele or to more demanding shoppers.
5. Virtually all of the shoppers who reported an unavailability experience within the previous six months continued to shop at the store where the incident occurred. Further, all of the respondents who asked and received neither a raincheck nor a substitute reported continued store loyalty. Race/income was not a significant factor.
6. Most respondents, regardless of race/income characteristics, knew that unavailability of advertised products is illegal. However, specific knowledge of the FTC trade rule on this point was low. Few respondents knew that a Federal agency enforces it, that supermarkets can post a notice requesting shoppers to ask for unavailable items or that supermarkets can exclude certain stores in the advertisement from the promotion. Generally, both black and white low-income shoppers knew less than white higher-income shoppers about the law enforcement agency.

## DISCUSSION

Few significant race/income differences emerged in the analysis of shopping behavior for advertised specials and reactions to unavailability incidents. Low-income Blacks, however, purchase fewer supermarket specials, receive fewer raincheck offers and fewer substitutes than White shoppers and also have less knowledge of the FTC Trade Regulation Rule than Whites.

The similarities between the three race-income groups with respect to purchasing specials, price-checking, unavailability experiences, asking about unavailable items, and judging the legality of unavailability support the thesis that Blacks are careful shoppers. The subsequent differential treatment they receive in the supermarket after asking about an unavailable item is disappointing and offers further evidence of the continuing discriminatory marketing practices by many supermarkets.

## REFERENCES

1. Consumers in Crisis: They've Changed Their Ways of Shopping," Progressive Grocer, April 1974, p. 45.

2. Mason, Joseph Barry and Wilkinson, J.B., "An Intra-Chain Analysis of Supermarket Overpricing, Unavailability, and Advertisement Composition," Journal of Retailing, Winter 1975-76.

3. U.S. Department of Agriculture. Comparison of Prices Paid for Selected Foods in Chainstores in High and Low Income Areas of Six Cities. Washington,DC: Government Printing Office, 1968.

4. U.S. Federal Trade Commission. Economic Report on Food Chain Selling Practices in the District of Columbia and San Francisco. Washington, DC: Government Printing Office, 1969.

5. "Unit Pricing and Freshness Dates are Largely Ignored: True or False?" Progressive Grocer, October 1975, p. 48.

The remaining references can be obtained by writing the authors.

# ATTITUDES TOWARD BUSINESS:  SOME RACE AND SEX DIFFERENCES

James E. Stafford, University of Houston
Dan Rinks, University of Houston
Molly Friedman, University of Houston

## INTRODUCTION

Today, more than ever, decision-makers are aware that business in general, and marketing, specifically, operate within a political framework.  Much of the final output generated from components of this framework are legislation and regulation aimed at curbing the "excesses" of the private sector.  The political structure, in turn, is affected by the degree and intensity of citizen input and participation into the system.  In other words, the higher is the level of citizen participation in the political process, the greater the probability of change taking place regardless of whether or not the change is good or bad.  Most studies on participation show the importance of social and psychological conditions on shaping a citizen's involvement in the political area.  These theories of participation point to the conclusion that respondent characteristics often shape attitudes, and ultimately behavior, as much as conditions external to the individual.  Conditions such as education, income, occupation, race and sex, contribute to the ability and interest of the individual to engage actively in politics.

The purposes of this paper are (1) to determine whether or not two characteristics -- race and sex -- have any effect on attitudes toward business and marketing and (2) to delimit some of the possible implications of the findings toward citizen participation in social and political change.

## METHODOLOGY AND ANALYSIS

The data analyzed in this study was obtained from an area cluster probability sample of 1,000 male and female heads-of-households residing in Houston (Harris County), Texas.  The base study was sponsored by three large Houston based corporations for the purpose of generating citizen input useful to company management in making local social investment decisions.  Personal interviews were used to obtain the data with the average length of interview lasting ninety minutes.  A variety of question types and questioning techniques were utilized to stimulate citizen response.

One area of the survey was concerned with measuring the attitudes of citizens toward business and marketing.  The five specific variables were (1) business involvement, (2) advertising, (3) business profits, (4) big business, and (5) product quality.

Since we were dealing with multiple groups and multiple responses, multivariate tests of significance were first utilized to determine overall group differences.  Where significant differences were found, multiple discriminant analysis was applied to the data to ascertain the direction or dimensions along which the major differences occurred.  Hopefully, this analysis would allow us to reduce the multiple measurements to one or more weighted combinations which would have maximum potential for distinguishing among members of the different groups under study.

In comparing the responses of males and females, it was noted that on each of the five indices used, _males_ as a group displayed a more _positive_ orientation to business and marketing activities than females.  The percentage differences, however, tended to be small with the largest differences occurring on the Business Profits Index where 48.0% of the males had positive orientation scores versus only 39.2% of the females.  Overall, the data reflect the trend often reported by various national polls, i.e. the public's view of corporate activities is one of suspicion.

On a racial comparison bases, Blacks and Mexican-Americans both generally express more negative opinions of corporations than whites.  For example, on the Big Business and Product Quality indices, only 15% of the two minority groups had a positive orientation score as compared to 22% for whites.  Obviously, neither group responded very favorably to these indices.

For the two sex and three racial groups, multiple responses were obtained.  The first interest was in the determination of whether overall differences for the various groups existed on the multiple response measures.  Multivariate significance tests of group differences were applied here.  The derived discriminant function for groups based on sex was significant (.042 level); as a result, the null hypothesis that males and females do not differ in their overall orientation to business was rejected.  Turning to race, the first derived discriminant function was statistically significant (at the .0001 level).  At least one of the groups -- Whites, Blacks, Mexican-Americans -- differed, therefore, from the others in their overall orientation to business.  By doing test of hypothesis on the group centroids, it was determined that whites differed significantly from Blacks and Mexican-Americans, but that Blacks and Mexican-Americans did not differ significantly.

Once group differences were determined, the direction or dimensions along which the major differences occurred were analyzed.  The results provided further indication that the attitudes of both minority groups studied -- women, Blacks and Mexican-Americans -- were more negative toward business and marketing than men or whites.  A key question, therefore, is related to what potential impact do these findings have for business.

## CONCLUSION

Both groups (women and racial minorities) are growing as a proportion of the total population.  In addition, both groups are becoming more vocal and aggressive in their demands for equal rights, etc.  From a political perspective, it is likely that business will receive increasing attention from minority and women's activist groups.  As women, Blacks and Mexican-Americans expand their participation in the political process, business may be faced with the prospect of increased legislation and regulation aimed at curbing perceived excesses in (1) corporate size, (2) corporate profits, (3) product quality, and (4) advertising expenditures and content.

It is clear that business is fighting an up-hill battle.  No matter what they do, corporations are likely to be criticized.  Yet to do nothing may lead to the slow destruction of our free enterprise system as well meaning, but misguided, groups stimulate action against big business.  The findings of this study clearly indicate a problem exists and suggests that it is imperative for business to take the initiative in minimizing potential problems.

# MARKETING OPPORTUNITIES IN LESS-DEVELOPED COUNTRIES EXPERIENCING POLITICAL VIOLENCE

William R. Crawford, U.S. Army
Harry A. Lipson, University of Alabama

## ABSTRACT

The importance for an infrastructure to support the growth of each economic sector in every national economy has been universally accepted. Consistent with the importance given to this aspect of national development, one major objective of political activists has been to control or destroy the infrastructure.

Most of the studies which investigate the relationship between any elements of political instability and economic development do so on a cross-polity (nation) basis. In such studies it is difficult to focus on the long-term impact of political instability in any one particular polity.

The information which has been available about economic sector growth in less-developed countries experiencing internal political instability is limited. When researchers have attempted to investigate marketing opportunities in less-developed countries experiencing political violence, they turn to a body of knowledge which stems from studies of war economics and wartime experiences about the impact of conflicts among nations rather than internal political violence. What researchers need is an inventory of proven indicators and a tested method for evaluation to examine opportunities in less-developed countries experiencing political violence over an extended period of time.

This paper describes some of the findings from an empirical study made to measure the impact of political violence upon marketing and the marketing infrastructure in South Vietnam: 1955-1972.

South Vietnam was selected for this study for four reasons: (1) the wide spectrum of political violence extending over eighteen years and changing from a low-level of violence in the "pre-insurgency" period, 1955-1960, to a medium level of violence in the "insurgency" period, 1961-1964, and then to a high level of violence in the "limited war" period, 1965-1972; (2) the reported aggregate time series data available for the eighteen years of the development period; (3) the reported disaggregate time series data available concerning national marketing development and political violence, and (4) the extensive technical and economic assistance provided to South Vietnam over the eighteen-year period.

The case study answers the following questions:

How can a researcher measure the impact in less-developed countries of changing levels of political violence on: (1) primary, secondary, and tertiary economic sectors, (2) marketing infrastructure, (3) production of agricultural commodities, and (4) consumption patterns of basic foods, luxury foods, industrial commodities, and soft goods? The answers to each part of this question provide a sound basis for identifying potential marketing opportunities in less-developed countries experiencing political violence.

## Lessons Learned From The Study of South Vietnam: 1955-1972

Impact on Economic Sectors. The results clearly show that the major impacts were on the primary and tertiary sectors.

The wholesale and retail trade sub-sector of the tertiary sector grew rapidly during the limited war period.

Throughout the entire 18-year period the secondary sector was stagnant except during four years in the limited war period when there was extensive physical destruction.

Impact on Marketing Infrastructure. The entire marketing infrastructure grew despite the increasing level of violence, and it grew at even faster rate during the limited war period.

Impact on Agricultural Production. The rate of growth of rice production in the pre-insurgency period was very small, during the insurgency period it declined slightly, but during the limited war period it increased significantly.

The production of rubber, a plantation crop, declined throughout the entire period, but most dramatically during the limited war period when many were destroyed.

Impact on Consumption. Per capita consumption of rice, the dietary staple, remained at the same level throughout the entire study period.

Per capita fish consumption steadily tripled over the 18-year period.

The per capita consumption of sugar and beverages (soft drinks, beer, and rice wine), which are luxury foods in less-developed countries, increased during the pre-insurgency period, continued to increase at a more rapid rate in the insurgency period, and dramatically increased in the limited war period.

Per capita consumption of petroleum and cement, which are industrial goods, increased throughout the entire period.

Per capita consumption of paper products followed the same pattern as petroleum and cement and increased nearly 300 percent over the entire period. The per capita consumption of fabrics remained relatively constant until the limited war period when it declined dramatically. There was no significant relationship found between per capita consumption of pharmaceuticals and the increasing levels of violence.

## Implications of the Findings

The findings of this study have important implications for marketing researchers and public policy.

Marketing Researchers. This study demonstrates that marketing researchers should investigate the marketing opportunities in the less-developed countries. Contrary to the widespread belief, political violence does not have a devastating impact on marketing and related activities except during high-levels of violence.

There were many growth opportunities for marketing goods and services in South Vietnam despite the increasing levels of political violence.

Public Policy. The findings of this study need to be taken seriously by business executives and government officials interested in the economic and marketing development of their own less-developed countries, and by those business executives and government officials of advanced economies interested in providing technical and economic assistance to less developed nations.

# ECONOMIC DEVELOPMENT AND MARKETING

John V. Petrof, Université Laval

## INTRODUCTION

This paper suggests that marketing institutions in developing countries may be retarding economic development. The
marketing profession needs to cooperate with governments
in developing countries to serve the actual needs of
poorer nations rather than concentrating their efforts on
stimulating the consumption of non-utilitarian products.

## THE ROLE OF MARKETING IN ECONOMIC DEVELOPMENT

The profession of marketing has critized the literature
of economic development for its neglect of the improvement
of living standards by increasing the productivity of the
marketing function. However, most existing marketing
knowledge is not transferable to environments of scarcity.
An analysis of four vital areas indicates that marketing
institutions in developing societies may be retarding
rather than hastening economic development.

In general, we may say that marketing makes a positive
contribution to economic development when:
  a) the function of acquainting potential buyers and
     sellers as well as the transmittal of information
     concerning product quality is adequately performed,
  b) a minimum amount of resources is absorbed directly
     by institutions engaged in marketing activities,
  c) declines in import or domestic prices are rapidly
     transmitted throughout society and demand is
     stimulated for products with a high domestic and
     export growth potential or low import prices,
  d) in order to pass on the benefits of economic
     development and ameliorate the living standards of
     the population, institutions engaged in marketing
     activities are dispersed throughout the country.

These results require, in effect, a fully efficient
marketing system. The efficiency concept involved encompasses the availability of product and service
information, exchange, location, and quality as well as
quantity.

Modern marketing, as we know it, has been based on highly
developed technology oriented toward growth. Without
constantly rising production there is little use for
marketing. Even in developed countries economic growth
is based on the maximization of the growth rate in
manufacturing and the immediate diversion of this benefit
to the non-manufacturing sector of the economy. In an
environment of scarcity the excessive promotion of
imported products creates an unhealthy demand among the
population. Such a practice of demand stimulation,
advocated by some U.S. marketers, tends to retard the
transformation of trade capital into production capital
which is a crucial phase in the development process.

It has often been suggested that developing countries
should utilize the great deal of marketing experience
and knowledge accumulated over the past decades by the
developed countries. However, there exists in the
developing countries a psychological atmosphere which
results in an automatic negative reaction to any form of
change initiated by the powerful, technologically
advanced nations.

Existing marketing institutions are not likely to
willingly expedite the development process. Modernization
efforts are by definition in basic conflict with
established practices and interests. Even though per
capita incomes are low many strategic marketing institutions, usually controlled by minorities which are
disliked by the indigenous population, manage to earn
substantial profits. There is little incentive for
them to change the status quo.

Since most of the programs and policies to stimulate
marketing must be of a long-term nature, it follows
that in most instances they can be pursued only through
the involvement of the government. The influence of
government is of paramount importance to the establishment
of an efficient marketing system in three ways. First,
an essential feature of any development strategy is
the choice of forms of economic activity which will be
encouraged. Second, the channel in which creative
energies will flow depends in part on the degree to which
other possible channels are blocked. Third, in many
underdeveloped countries the programs of the government
are the only means for providing financial help, technical assistance, and other types of aid which private
enterprise needs to expand and ameliorate its marketing
activities.

The potential community value of applying marketing skills
to economic development is high. Kotler and Levy
pioneered the concept of marketing in many organizational
contexts. If marketing is to become a valuable technology
for serving humanity, marketers need to cooperate with
governments in developing countries to serve the actual
needs of poorer nations rather than concentrating their
efforts on stimulating the consumption of non-utilitarian
products.

CONSUMER ATTITUDE RESEARCH: HELP FOR THE PUBLIC MARKETER

Marye Tharp Hilger, The University of Texas at San Antonio
Edward W. Cundiff, Emory University
William H. Cunningham, The University of Texas at Austin

## INTRODUCTION AND BACKGROUND

Consumer research is a valuable and needed input into public policy decision-making, especially when a public enterprise is the agency for implementation of public policy goals. Several authors have alluded to the appropriateness of marketing concepts to public policy decision-making, but there continues to be resistance in the public sector to adoption of marketing techniques. The purpose of this paper is to illustrate how the management of a public marketing firm could better meet its goals through decision-making based on consumer research.

Several governments are currently experimenting with roles as marketing entrepreneurs for economic development purposes. Mexico, as an example is using its autonomous, public enterprise CONASUPO (Compania Nacional de Subsistencias Populares) for regulation of the market system and for protection of certain consumer segments. CONASUPO is a vertically-integrated distribution channel for staple goods and basic commodities. It is in direct competition with private wholesalers, retailers, and storage facilities in Mexico. There are over 4000 CONASUPO retail outlets in Mexico, and yet CONASUPO sales account for less than 1% of total food sales in the country. CONASUPO has an overall purpose of providing basic commodity goods at stable, and reasonable prices, to low income consumers. A second purpose of CONASUPO is to reduce speculative activities in staple products, and to reduce overall intermediary margins. CONASUPO stores are located in working class suburbs and are similar to the small 'tiendas' owned by private retailers. The 'tienda'-style stores allow CONASUPO to introduce modern merchandising methods, such as self-service, in an environment similar to that of traditionally patronized outlets. There has been on assessment of how well CONASUPO has met the above goals. However, consumer perceptions about the agency can be useful in determining how well they are serving the target population and in pinpointing CONASUPO efforts that need strengthening.

## RESEARCH DESIGN AND FINDINGS

A two-step, randomized survey of attitudes toward CONASUPO was made in low, medium, and high income neighborhoods in Monterrey, a large industrial center in northern Mexico. Sample size was about 200. Respondents were queried as to their overall shopping habits and attitudes about CONASUPO's activities in the marketplace.

Of primary interest to CONASUPO management should be feedback as to their success in appealing to the designated target market, low income consumers. Responses to the survey indicated that while the majority of the sample who shopped at CONASUPO stores were low income consumers, a significant minority of CONASUPO shoppers fell within middle income groups. Therefore, CONASUPO seems to have established itself as an appropriate outlet for low income consumers in Monterrey, and management should be pleased to know it is perceived to be meeting one of its foremost goals.

The image of persons who shop at CONASUPO stores could be helpful to management in directing future growth of the organization. It was predicted that the actual CONASUPO shopper would not see herself as distinct socio-economically. In the survey, mean scores of shoppers and non-shoppers were not found to be significantly different with respect to family size or income of the 'CONASUPO shopper'. In both cases, however, the absolute value of the means implied that the two groups believe that income and family size of the 'CONASUPO shopper' are different than those of other shoppers. CONASUPO's plans to begin serving middle income consumers may be stumped by its image as a poor person's store. Targeting retail stores to several socio-economic groups in Mexico poses many more problems than undifferentiated marketing in other cultures. Therefore, CONASUPO should reassess its future plans in light of the current image of its patrons.

A third topic of interest concerns shopping patterns in general for the low income consumer. In any urban market, a low income consumer can choose to shop at a supermarket, a public market, a 'despensa' (small dispensaries for employees of private firms), a 'tienda', or a CONASUPO store. In the analysis of low income shopping patterns in Monterrey, it was noted that the 'tienda' is most often patronized only for beverages, dairy products, and packaged breads; yet, for several other important product categories, the supermarket is the most preferred outlet. The popularity in Monterrey of supermarkets for low income consumers may necessitate an adaptation of CONASUPO retail operations to meet consumer preferences in northern Mexico.

Another question that management needs to ask at CONASUPO concerns whether it is providing a product mix that is desired by low income consumers in Monterrey. In an analysis of the difference in mean scores of low, middle, and high income respondents, several aspects of CONASUPO's responsiveness to low income consumers in Monterrey were measured. In general, it appeared that low and middle income respondents agreed that CONASUPO products are of a good quality for the price paid, while high income respondents believed the products were of inferior quality. Low, medium, and high income respondents seemed to agree, however, that CONASUPO offers stability of product quality. Management should take care in matching the desired store image with perceived product quality; consumer surveys would give CONASUPO an opportunity to have continual feedback on their merchandising policies.

Matching the stores' product mix to low income consumer product assortments is another CONASUPO goal. Again, findings suggest CONASUPO's product mix appears appropriate to low and middle income groups in Monterrey and not to high income respondents. This perception would ease CONASUPO's entry into merchandising for middle-class consumers in Mexico, but may be simultaneously confounding its image as a 'poor' person's store. Since product assortment in Mexico differs across socio-economic groups, merchandising needs more targeting precision. Lastly, CONASUPO has as an objective offering products at stable and reasonable prices. The study findings suggested CONASUPO may find it difficult to further penetrate low income markets in Mexico, if it cannot communicate its price advantages to the non-shoppers who indicated they did not believe its prices were lower than those of other stores.

The public marketer plays an important role in implementing public policy in many countries. Consumer research has not, however, been used to determine whether public policy goals are being met through the marketing strategies used by these public agencies.

# A NEW SOCIETAL MARKETING CONCEPT

William G. Nickels, University of Maryland
Earnestine Hargrove, Morgan State University

## ABSTRACT

This article describes a new marketing philosophy to replace the traditional marketing concept. It emphasizes
a societal, a systems, and a human orientation.

## INTRODUCTION

Many articles have described the problems and limitations
of the traditional marketing concept [1,2,4,7]. The
purpose of this paper is twofold: A. introduce a new
societal marketing concept that is applicable in all
organizations and to buyers as well as sellers, and B. show
how this new marketing concept can be implemented effectively and profitably.

## PROBLEMS WITH THE TRADITIONAL MARKETING.CONCEPT

The traditional marketing concept has three dimensions:
[1] a consumer orientation, [2] the coordination and integration of the firm, and [3] a profit orientation. Critics
of the marketing concept have cited its narrow focus on
consumers [2,7], its concentration on the firm rather
than the total marketing system, and its lack of implementation [1, 4].

The new societal marketing concept is a managerial philosophy that uses systems concepts to attempt to satisfy
the needs of individual consumers; of society as a whole;
and of employees, managers, and owners. The societal
marketing concept is not a philosophy for the marketing
department exclusively, but is an exchange philosophy for
the whole organization and for the buying public as well.
It consists of three main elements: 1. a new societal
orientation is replacing the more narrow consumer orientation [3], 2. a systems orientation is replacing the
traditional emphasis on coordination and integration of
individual firms, and 3. a human orientation is replacing
the traditional profit orientation [2].

## A SOCIETAL ORIENTATION

A societal orientation directs an organization's marketing activities toward generating consumer satisfaction
(as in the traditional marketing concept) plus creating a
healthy environment, using resources intelligently, and
generally responding to the broader needs of society.
Business and Society Review each year recognizes organizations that have done an outstanding job in societal
marketing. Many companies have found the new societal
orientation not only benefits society, but also benefits
their organizations as well. For example, the 3M Company
was able to structure pollution control methods so that
they saved $10 million.

## A SYSTEMS ORIENTATION

Today's organizations are also adopting a new systems
orientation. This means, for one thing, that marketing
management is expanding to mean management of the total
channel system, not just one firm. By employing other
systems concepts, including marketing information systems,
organizations can more effectively and efficiently serve
mass markets.

Nonprofit organizations are also adopting a new systems
orientation. For example, systems concepts have helped

make the health service program in Hartford, Connecticut
more efficient. Eight hospitals have formed a regional
consortium and are pooling their resources, sharing staffs
and purchasing jointly in bulk.

## A HUMAN ORIENTATION

The profit orientation of the past is being replaced with
a more responsive human orientation [2]. It is a managerial philosophy that focuses on the needs of people
within the organization including managers, employees, and
owners. One of those needs may be for profits [5]. There
is no inherent conflict between a human orientation and a
profit orientation. There is a direct link between a
human orientation and a societal orientation. Both are
concerned with human needs: a societal orientation seeks
to satisfy those outside the channel system and a human
orientation seeks to satisfy those within the system.

## SOCIETAL MARKETING CONCEPT APPLIES EVERYWHERE

The new societal marketing concept may be applied in non-
profit as well as business organizations. Furthermore, it
may be applied to buyers as well as sellers. Buyers can
learn to temper their demands by recognizing the possible
effects on the environment and on society as a whole (a
societal orientation) [6]. Buyers can also form coopera-
tives and generally apply systems concepts to their efforts. Finally, buyers can join with sellers in implementing a human orientation in all their marketing
relationships.

## REFERENCES

1. Bell, Martin and C. William Emory. "The Faltering
   Marketing Concept," Journal of Marketing, 35
   (October 1971), 37-42.

2. Dawson, Leslie M. "The Human Concept: New Philosophy
   for Business," Business Horizons, 12 (December 1969),
   29-38.

3. El-Ansary, Adel I. "Societal Marketing: A Strategic
   View of the Marketing Mix in the 1970 s," Journal of
   the Academy of Marketing Science, 2, (Fall 1974),
   553-66.

4. McNamara, Carlton P. "The Present Status of the Marketing Concept," Journal of Marketing, 36 (January
   1972), 50-7).

5. Phillips, Charles F. "What is Wrong with Profit
   Maximization?," Business Horizons, 6 (Winter 1963),
   73-80.

6. Rothe, James T. and Lissa Benson. "Intelligent Consumption: An Attractive Alternative to the Marketing
   Concept," MSU Business Topics (Winter 1974), 29-34.

7. Walters, C. Glenn, D. Wayne Norvell, and Sam J. Bruno.
   "Is There a Better Way than Consumer Orientation?," in
   Henry W. Nash and Donald P. Robins (eds.), Proceedings
   Southern Marketing Association, 1975 Conference, 1976
   79-81.

THE MANAGEMENT OF MARKETING-CONFLICT:  IMPLICATIONS
FOR PUBLIC POLICY

Rajendra K. Srivastava, University of Pittsburgh
Rohit Deshpande, University of Pittsburgh

## INTRODUCTION

Developments in the last decade indicate a process of
growing conflict between marketers and systems within
their environment.  Despite the continued emphasis on the
marketing concept, governmental regulatory agencies are
becoming increasingly involved in the ways in which marketing firms go about doing business.  Consumerist movements
have proliferated and larger percentages of the public
appear to be alienated in their participation in the mass
consumption society.  What must be realized is that
conflict is inevitable in the marketplace and that rather
than attempting to move toward a utopian state of complacent intrasocietal cooperation, marketers, consumers, and
regulatory bodies should attempt to enhance the management
of conflict.

## MARKETING CONFLICT AND CONFLICT-HANDLING MECHANISMS

The ubiquity of marketing-conflict is almost tautologically
obvious when one realizes that the marketplace serves to
further the simultaneous attempts of two or more persons
(or groups of persons) to maximize their gains and/or to
minimize their losses as they perceive them.  This
somewhat simplistic utility based viewpoint of marketing
transactions glosses over the myriad supra-economic considerations that become involved in the determination of
optimal marketing mixes for specific consumer market segments.  Yet the collaborative problem-solving processes
that we articulate later to better manage conflict do not
obviate the problems themselves--rather, the 'satisfactory'
resolution of marketing problems are but transient phenomena in the dynamics of marketing exchange.  The perpetua-
tion of cooperation would lead to the absence of motivation
to manufacture and market and to the cessation of transactional activity that characterizes a dead marketplace.

There exist five basic conflict-handling mechanisms -
competitive, avoidant, sharing, accommodative, and collaborative.  The competitive mechanism is illustrated by
cases such as that involving the "commercialization" of
religious holidays.  Marketers claim that consumers are
themselves demanding the products or services sold.  Here
marketers and the consumer public see each other as being
diametrically opposed to the maximization of their individual subjective expected utilities.

The avoidant mechanism is exemplified by complaint departments of large retail organizations which are alleged by
grievanced consumers to be simply "cooling off" junctions
rather than motivated by proactive remedial concern.

The sharing mechanism is an attempt at compromise in the
movement toward a collaborative marketing mode where
serious attempts are made to maximize the expected utilities of both consumers and marketers in both the short and
long run.

Finally, the accommodative mechanism is one of appeasement
where one party gives in entirely to the demands of the
the other.  Obviously this cannot be considered to be anything more than a transient process in its lasting effect.

Although marketers have been charged with causing a series
of diverse consumer ills, students of the consumerist
movement have frequently failed to realize that marketing
firms are often the convenient flogging horse for special
interest groups and their lobbyist representatives to the
regulatory agencies.  Indeed the misdemeanors of a few are
occasionally erroneously extrapolated onto the many when
catch-all labels such as "commercialism" and "big business
exploitation" are applied and the concomitant onus of proof
of innocence is generally placed on the firm with all its
consequential ramifications of extensive clarification and
litigation.

## THE MANAGEMENT OF MARKETING CONFLICT

Clearly it is possible to move from avoidant and competitive conflict-handling mechanisms to ones that involve more
sharing in the short run and eventually toward collaboration in the long run.

This movement is what we refer to as more effective management of marketing-conflict and involves the utilization of
one or more of a set of four management mechanisms.  The
first mechanism is mediation on the part of a third party.
For example, in the conflict situation between U.S. Steel
and environmentalists recently, the courts organized a
series of "pretrial conferences" between the parties that
ultimately led to a cooperative resolution.  Another mechanism is that of bargaining based on trust where primarily
confidence is generated between two parties (or their representatives) by bargaining over minor issues and then discussing the larger, more significant elements of disagreement.  A third mechanism is co-optation or "the process
of absorbing new elements into the leadership of an organization as a means of averting threats to its stability or
existence."  In our discussed scenarios this could be illustrated by the inclusion of an ex-regulator on the board of
directors of a marketing firm.  The final conflict-manage-
ment mechanism is self-encapsulation where "conflict situations may be modified or limited by rules or prior understanding which form 'capsules' or containment devices.
Through these rules, detrimental modes of conflict tend to
be excluded, and simultaneously, beneficial actions can be
legitimized.  This mechanism can be shown by a marketing
organization that invited a consumer interest group to discuss the pros and cons and the modifications necessary before the introduction of any potentially "sensitive" product.

Based on the above discussion, we suggest that governmental
regulatory agencies develop methodologies to mediate between conflicting interest groups before disruption occurs
and the parties end up in court.  Additionally, the system
should be geared to rewards rather than punishment to channel the energies of marketers away from trying to find loop-
holes in the often too-restrictive legislation.  Tripartite
representation of government, marketers, and consumer representatives on panels to chart new and modify extant legislation would also facilitate collaborative behavior among the
the groups concerned.  Finally, on the part of marketing
firms co-optation and self-encapsulation need to be legitimized so as to develop trust within the relationship between
marketers and their public interface.

# SOCIAL AND ECONOMIC DISCONTINUITY AND MARKETING

Leonard L. Berry, Georgia State University

## INTRODUCTION

Marketing, constantly buffeted by change and constantly producing it, is today functioning in the early aftermath of two, culture-shaking environmental discontinuities: the emergence in the late 1960's of a new set of value priorities placing people ahead of things and the emergence in the early 1970's of a new set of economic realities summing to instability and flux, conservation and caution, belt-tightening and lowered expectations.

## NEW VALUES, NEW ECONOMIC REALITIES

Characterizing the new values is a commonality of yearning--more quality and inner fulfillment in life--and a diversity of proponents--blacks and whites, young and old, men and women, factory workers and executives, consumers of goods and services and consumers of air and water.

Concerning the new economic realities, it can be expected that the period 1947-1973 will prove to be far more bountiful than the period 1973-1990 in terms of traditional economic criteria. That is, the post World War II economic era of abundance and ebullience has now ended, replaced by a new economic era that will include: higher inflation (particularly in necessity-consumption categories such as food, energy and shelter), lower real growth in GNP, growing entanglement of resource availabilities with international politics, uncertain capital availability, and a growing ethic of resource conservation and environmental protection.

## IMPLICATIONS FOR MARKETING

Among the marketing implications of the new values are (1) the need to build social criteria into the new product development process, (2) the opportunity to use corporate responsibility as a marketing tool, and (3) the growing market for products and services that restore more balance in life between permanence and impermanence, the old and the new, yesterday and tomorrow.

Among the marketing implications arising in part from the new economic realities are the likelihood of increasing numbers of consumers (1) moving towards scaled-down, waste-minimizing lifestyles and (2) becoming more interested in total use cost of goods and services in contrast to initial acquisition cost.

## CHALLENGES FOR THE PROFESSION

In addition to such direct and tangible implications to marketing as these, there are other more generalized, profession-oriented challenges that emerge. First, marketing practitioners and scholars must begin to think of strategic, long-range planning as part of the marketing discipline. Given that environmental change can and does dramatically affect the shape and nature of markets, marketing professionals have an important role to play in monitoring and assessing the future beyond the annual planning cycle and in developing long-term strategies in response to such assessments. Among other things, this means more attention within marketing to the "futures" movement in general and to the research techniques that futurists use in particular.

Second, the new values and the new economic realities present a rich opportunity for marketing to solidify its role beyond the traditional confines of commercial transactions between buyers and sellers. For example, in a period of changing values, when it is clear that a growing number of American workers require more from their jobs than income alone, the customer-oriented philosophy and tools of marketing have much to offer the managers of people.

In the same vein, the exigencies of the times require the marketing profession to move forward, despite the inevitable missteps and failures along the way, in marshalling its research, consumer behavior and communications knowledge base towards the marketing of socially significant ideas and skills, e.g., ways individuals can conserve energy.

Third, marketing educators can no longer afford to consider "marketing and society" types of issues the peripheral category of study they are so commonly considered to be. A momentous development, Watergate, seems to have spurred many law schools in America to seriously reappraise the adequacy of their curricula. Marketing educators, exposed in recent years to an unrelenting series of environmental developments that in a cumulative sense are no less significant in terms of societal change than Watergate, have much progress still to make towards sensitizing students to the new social, economic and other environmental realities impacting upon the profession.

In conclusion, tomorrow's marketing environment is going to be quite different from that which existed from the post World War II period to the late 1960's. What has been occurring since the mid-1960's is a steady stream of signals as to what lies ahead. In his book Future Without Shock, Louis Lundborg perhaps captures the spirit of what lies ahead as well as anyone when he rejects the dictum that "the business of America is business" and replaces it with his own: "the business of business and of America is man." [1, p. 127]

## REFERENCE

1. Lundborg, Louis B. Future Without Shock. New York: W. W. Norton and Co., 1974.

AN EXPERIENTIAL PROGRAM IN UNDERGRADUATE MARKETING EDUCATION

Julian Andorka, DePaul University

## INTRODUCTION

This paper describes a series of projects from an experiential program incorporated into several undergraduate
marketing courses. The program was designed to
substitute for the conventional textbook-case approach
and to focus upon contemporary unidentified marketing
opportunities available to several existing corporations.

The instructor selected probable marketing opportunities
for a brand or company. He informed the companies,
which are most likely to benefit from exploration of the
opportunities, about the project. He then requested
that the companies release information,which is not in
violation of confidentiality, to inquiring students.
In exchange he arranged to submit all final reports prepared by the students to the companies for executive
study.

By the second week of the quarter the instructor provided the students with a detailed description of the
product or service to be studied. A required minimum
outline for the final report is supplied to the students.
The final reports are to be submitted by the students
two weeks prior to the final examination.

After grading them himself the instructor submitted the
reports to the interested corporations for further
evaluation. The corporations may then choose to
acknowledge the best papers by means of a letter to the
individual students or with a monetary award for the
best paper(s).

## BRIEF SUMMARIES OF PROJECTS WITHIN THE PROGRAM

Summaries of some of the experiential projects, including
both those already completed and those currently underway, are provided below.

Project I: The program originated with a Marketing
Research class. The assignment to the class was to
determine the potential of the college student market for
car polishes and what is the best media for reaching
college students. Each student individually gathered
and analyzed data, reported on his/her findings and made
appropriate recommendations. The papers were sent to
the Simoniz Company. The best report was awarded with
$100. The second and third best received $50 and $25,
while six other students received gifts of the companies'
products.

Project II: The second project was conducted with a
class studying marketing strategies and tactics. The
instructor observed that the Bolens Company, a division
of the FMC Corporation, might better promote the unique
consumer benefits offered by the mulching lawnmower
within their product line. The assignment to the class
was to identify the critical problems which could be
turned into marketing opportunities and recommend solutions to Bolens. Bolens executives gave letters of
acknowledgement to the writers of the best papers.

Project III: The third project began in January 1977.
Participants were members of a Marketing Principles
class. The students were asked to advance new product

ideas. The most promising new idea centered around a
powertool. The assignment to the class was to evaluate
consumer buying interest regarding the new product. As
in the prior projects each student individually conducted
his/her concept test, analyzed and reported his or her
findings. In this instance the company requested
anonymity. The new product might be introduced.

Projects IV & V: At the time of this writing two other
projects are in process. The first project concerns the
optimal marketing area of foreign-car dealers and
whether competition among dealers of the same make of
imported car is detrimental or beneficial to the consumers and manufacturer.

The second study introduces the marketing approach to
the planning of continuing education. The assignment to
the class will be how best DePaul University can satisfy middle management's need for continuing education.

## ACHIEVEMENT OF PROGRAM OBJECTIVES

As previously stated, the program aims at involving
students directly with marketing problems and programs.
It further aims toward providing a contemporary view of
real and existing problems and opportunities.

The program requires much of the students. It requires
that they devote time and effort to independent exploration of data and to independent thought in coming to
grips with and making sense of the data they bring together. The program requires that students learn to conduct research which depends in many instances upon
secondary sources of data. This is a kind of research
which is too often pushed aside in favor of primary data
collection methods.

The program seems to succeed because it has a high component of reality. The students know that they are preparing, organizing and writing reports for corporate
executives to read and act upon. Further, they are preparing these reports in a competitive environment that
promises rewards only to three judged to be worthy.
Student evaluations of the program have thus far
focused upon the points outlined and the response has
been most gratifying.

Thus far the participating corporations have been most
responsive to the program. Experiential programs such
as that described in this report grow from the belief
that marketing is indeed a profession and marketing
students can profit from a professional "internship."

## CONCLUDING COMMENTS

The program exposes students to live problems and
opportunities in the marketplace. They are strongly
motivated by personal contacts with corporate officers
and plant visits initiated by the students themselves.
At the same time, a new business-student interaction is
created, where business becomes a contributor to marketing education.

THE EVALUATION OF A STUDENT LETTER PROJECT AS AN

INTRODUCTION TO MARKETING TOOL

Michael M. Pearson, Bowling Green State University
William R. Hoskins, Bowling Green State University
Gregory M. Gazda, San Diego State University

Over the past three years all beginning marketing students at Bowling Green State University have been introduced to marketing with an assignment requiring each to write a letter, of either praise or complaint, to a business firm about its product or service. An analysis of the 940 student responses to a series of questionnaires and rating forms administered before during and after the assignment is undertaken in this paper. The paper discusses whether the assignment is worthwhile from a student's point of view, and whether the students experienced an attitude change toward the firm, product, or service in completing this letter-writing experience.

## RESEARCH RESULTS

A total of 940 "student letter cases" were included in the study. A case consisted of the initial self report questionnaire, the rating form, and the self report questionnaire administered at the end of the quarter. These all needed to be present and in agreement for the "student letter case" to be included in the analysis.

Of the total letters written or sent, 51.9% were praise letters and 38.3% were complaint. (The remaining 9.8% were classified as requests for information, comment, or others. The firms written to consisted of 11% local firms, 12% regional firms, and 76% national firms. Fifty-eight percent of the firms were manufacturers and 30% retailers. Sixty-three percent concerned consumer durable goods, and fourteen percent services.

Overall, responses were received by 63.0% of the letters. Praise letters received a 58.6% response and complaint letters received 65.4% response. Letters dealing with consumer non-durable products received a higher rate of response (67.9%) than did those dealing with consumer durables (58.7%) or services (48.0%). Manufacturers responded more often than did retailers (53.0%). National firms responded at a higher rate (68.2%) than regional (58.5%) or local firms (33.3%).

### Did the Student View this as a Worthwhile Assignment?

Overall, 86% thought the assignment worthwhile. The key variable, and indeed the only variable that seemed to show any difference between the students rating the assignment worthwhile and those rating it as not worthwhile was response. For the group of students receiving responses to their letters, 92.6% rated the assignment as worthwhile. Seventy-five percent of the group receiving no response rated the assignment as worthwhile.

There was a significant difference as to whether the student perceived the response to be a form letter or a personal letter in determining whether the assignment was viewed as worthwhile. In addition, any extra response above and beyond a letter seemed to lead to the student rating the assignment as worthwhile. Tangible responses (money refunded, replacement products, and gift certificates) led to higher ratings of the assignment.

Despite the fact that the research results could not support a positive change in attitude as a result of the letter-writing experience, the assignment has several positive attributes. First, the assignment is a good way to introduce the marketing concept. Second, the assignment builds some degree of consumerism in an often complacent group of students. The fact that only 38.2% of the students wrote complaint letters in response to an assignment that was in many ways implying that the students should write letters of complaint partially defends this position. Third, the assignment brings out the importance of consumer feedback and how it can be often blocked and its workings slowed down. It should be emphasized that even the students not receiving a response still rated the assignment as being worthwhile.

### Did the Students' Attitudes Change as a Result of this Letter-Writing Experience?

To determine whether the students' feelings toward the firm, product, or service changed as a result of the letter-writing experience, two specific questions were asked: 1) What is your overall impression of the product/store/service that you wrote your letter about? 2) Would you purchase this product or service or shop at this store again?

The pre-ratings and post-ratings were compared to determine the number of students that showed higher or lower rankings on the post-rating questionnaire. A net rating was determined by subtracting the number of students showing a lower rating on the second questionnaire from the number of students showing a higher rating on the second questionnaire. The results are presented in Table 1.

TABLE 1

NET CHANGES IN STUDENT RATINGS OF FIRM, PRODUCT OR SERVICE

|  | Question Number | A Number Showing Higher Ratings | A Number Showing Lower Ratings | Net Rating (Differences between A & B) |
|---|---|---|---|---|
| Praise Letter - | (1) | +26 | -58 | -32 |
| Response | (2) | +27 | -59 | -12 |
| Praise Letter | (1) | + 5 | -76 | -71 |
| No Response | (2) | +11 | -76 | -64 |
| Complaint Letter- | (1) | +86 | -36 | +50 |
| Response | (2) | +74 | -42 | +32 |
| Complaint Letter- | (1) | +14 | -57 | -43 |
| No Response | (2) | +10 | -51 | -41 |

As can be seen in Table 1, only in the complaint letter--response classification did the attitude toward the firm, product, or service change positively during the letter-writing experience. For praise letters, students showed higher ratings in the pre-rating than in the post. As would be expected, students showed lower post-ratings for complaint letters with no response.

## CONCLUSIONS

Based upon the results, the students did consider this a worthwhile assignment. How worthwhile it was considered was largely dependent on whether students received a response and the nature of the response. However, it cannot be concluded that students attain a better attitude toward the firm, product, or service based upon this assignment. Only for complaint letters where a response was received did such a positive change take place.

USING CORPORATE SPONSORED MARKETING MANAGEMENT PROJECT

William G. Browne, Oregon State University

## INTRODUCTION

Six years ago the senior level Marketing Management course at Oregon State University was expanded from three to five hours of credit. The added credit was justified on the basis of expanding the content of the course to include a project to be run in conjunction with the text and required readings. The term-long project used in the course requires the student to work with marketing personnel in developing a marketing audit and a marketing plan for the next planning cycle.

The intent of this paper is to review, in detail, the preparation required, the content of, and the benefits realized by the student and corporate sponsor in a major real life marketing project. The expanded objectives of the course are outlined and discussed in the first section of the paper. An overview of the project and its relationship with the text and readings is explained in the second section. The third section contains information on the development and organization of the projects. The benefits observed from using the projects and conclusions are contained in the last section.

## COURSE OBJECTIVES

The five major objectives of the project are listed and then discussed below.

The project should provide an environment for constantly using and thus gaining confidence in using the marketing vocabulary;

It should provide an experience in gathering and analyzing both secondary and primary market data;

Verbal and written communication skills are developed and/or tailored for the real world professional climate;

The project work should furnish an appreciation of the complex relationship that exists between various marketing variables;

It should assist in developing career interests and simultaneously involve business marketing managers in classroom activities.

## OVERVIEW OF PROJECT

During the first half of the course, the marketing environment is studied and the marketing mix is explored in detail. On a weekly basis for the first five weeks, the variables, product, place (channels and physical distribution), price and promotion, (the 4 P's) are individually studied with the goal of identifying:

The alternatives available within the domain of each variable;

The environmental conditions that might surround each variable;

Simplistic models that may be used to analyze information associated with each variable;

The opportunities developed through a use of each variable.

Parallel with these assignments, the students are preparing descriptive papers concerning their corporate sponsor's marketing activities related to each individual variable. This is needed to familiarize the project group with their sponsor's marketing activities, set up channels of communication, and familiarize themselves with the sponsor's

markets. Later, using these and other data, the students attempt to appraise the success of the sponsor's marketing program, identify new opportunities, critique each feature in the program (both good and weak features), and then offer their suggestions in the form of an annual marketing plan.

There are numerous advantages in using such a project as part of the course. In many regards, it may be superior to the case method in that it requires the students to identify and fully articulate problems which appear as they study the sponsor's activities and markets. To support a problem's existence, the students have to gather data from many sources. This activity should serve to familiarize students with marketing data available through trade associations, government and industry statistics, trade magazines and journals, specialized marketing news magazines such as Advertising Age, and generalized news sources such as the Wall Street Journal or Business Week.

## RESULTS AND CONCLUSIONS

The outcome of the projects will first be viewed from the student's standpoint and then from the sponsor's standpoint. There are also both long and short run implications. An obvious short run outcome from the student's standpoint is that the project requires each individual to be current with respect to the text readings. The project re-enforces the text by requiring the students, in their groups, to verbalize the concepts and apply them to their project each week during the project audit. Test scores indicate that most of the students gain confidence and do well with the basic marketing concepts. Instructors of the specialty courses have also commented that a minimum review is needed, since the projects have served to provide a vehicle for remembering the basic concepts. This also appears to be true over a longer period.

Since, whenever possible, the students are assigned to projects that compliment their career interests (such as a marketing student with a forestry minor being assigned to a wood products firm) they have had an opportunity to learn about marketing in their chosen industry. In many cases this has given them leverage during job interviews.

In the short run, the sponsors have a very positive evaluation for the project. It provides them with an assortment of ideas, some of which have been tried, to improve and/or fine tune their marketing efforts. It has also provided them with a chance to review the total marketing mix and its applicability to their situation. Usually, a few of the recommendations offered in each project are implemented directly or indirectly by the firm. Some of the recommendations parallel the sponsor's current thoughts and the project has provided further evidence supporting possible implementation. A majority of the sponsors have complimented the resourcefulness of the students in gathering data for supporting their recommendations.

The sponsors have been generally impressed with the student's ability to conduct themselves during the interviews and have indicated that the students have a good grasp of the marketing world. In this sense, the sponsors have given it a positive evaluation. Most of the sponsors have either asked to or consented to sponsor another such project within two years. Also, a number of the sponsors have tried to hire our students as a direct consequence of the project.

# THE NATURE AND SCOPE OF MARKETING REVISITED:  THE THREE DICHOTOMIES MODEL

Shelby D. Hunt, University of Wisconsin-Madison

## INTRODUCTION

The "three dichotomies model" of marketing suggests that all of the activities, issues, theories, and research in marketing can be categorized by way of the following dimensions:  micro/macro, profit sector/nonprofit sector, and positive/normative.  Since its first publication in an article entitled "The Nature and Scope of Marketing" [1], the model has generated substantial controversy.  Although the positive/normative dichotomy has sparked the most spirited comments, it is fair to say that all aspects of the model have been questioned.  And this is as it should be, since no model is (or ought to be) inscribed in stone.

This paper will attempt to summarize in succinct fashion some comments of marketers concerning the model and then analyze and evaluate these comments.  The evaluation process will culminate in 1) a re-specification of the micro/macro dichotomy, and 2) some conclusions concerning the role of general paradigms in marketing.

Although numerous colleagues in marketing have volunteered their observations on the three dichotomies model, most of the observations discussed in this paper come from the participants at the Macro-Marketing Conference held at the University of Colorado in August of 1976 and also a written comment on the model by Robin [3].  The first two comments are the beliefs of Robin that the positive/normative dichotomy is 1) "meaningless," and 2) "unnecessary."  Comments 3 through 6 reflect some of the views of the Macro-Marketing Conference participants.

## ANALYSIS

The positive/normative dichotomy is "meaningless" because the information derived from a positive "study is of little interest unless it is given prescriptive overtones. ...That is, the positive issues are barren except where they have prescriptive implications" [3, p. 136].  Analyzing this comment can begin by asking:  to whom are positive studies "of little interest" unless there are prescriptive implications?  Is it to the marketing manager?  Are all positive studies "barren" unless they provide guidance as to how the marketing manager can make better decisions?  This appears to be the "meaningfulness" criterion that Robin is proposing.

No one would dispute that much of the positive study in marketing has managerial implications.  In my original article, I noted that "explanation and prediction [from positive studies] frequently serve as useful guides for developing normative decision rules and normative models" [2, p. 27].  However, to state that all positive studies are "meaningless" unless they assist the marketing manager is exactly the kind of narrow perception of the scope of marketing that has for so long caused so much mischief in our discipline.  Just as the entire discipline of psychology does not exist solely to help the clinical psychologist, the entire discipline of marketing does not exist solely and exclusively to serve the needs of the marketing manager.  Research and other scholarly inquiry in marketing have many functions.

The prime directive for scholarly research in marketing is the same as for all sciences:  to seek knowledge.  The knowledge must be intersubjectively certifiable [2, p. 44] and capable of describing, explaining, and predicting phenomena.  Sometimes the knowledge will assist marketing managers in making decisions.  Other times the knowledge will guide legislators in drafting laws to regulate marketing activities.  At still other times, the knowledge may assist the general public in understanding the functions that marketing activities provide society.  Finally, at the risk of "waxing philosophical," the knowledge may simply assist marketing scholars in knowing-- not an inconsequential objective.  Thus, Robin's observation that the positive/normative dichotomy is "meaningless" seems ill advised.

## CONCLUSION

The space limitations of this brief overview prevent the evaluation of the other issues.  However, evaluations will appear in the complete version of the paper at the conference and a listing of the issues that will be discussed is as follows:

1.  The positive/normative dichotomy is "unnecessary" for considering the "Is marketing a science?" controversy because "using scientific explanation in marketing simply requires that the normative statements be used as antecedent conditions" [3, p. 136].

2.  "The positive/normative dichotomy is a false dichotomy because we cannot escape from our own value systems."

3.  "The positive/normative dichotomy is dangerous because it may lead people to downgrade the importance of micro/normative marketing."

4.  "There is no difference between marketing in the profit sector and in the nonprofit sector.  Therefore, the profit sector/nonprofit sector dichotomy is simply excess baggage."

5.  The micro/macro dichotomy is ambiguous.  There appears to be no clear criterion for separating "micro" from "macro."

## REFERENCES

1.  Hunt, Shelby D.  "The Nature and Scope of Marketing," Journal of Marketing, 40 (July 1976), pp. 17-28.

2.  Popper, Karl R.  The Logic of Scientific Discovery. New York:  Harper and Row, 1959.

3.  Robin, Donald P.  "Comment on the Nature and Scope of Marketing," Journal of Marketing, 41 (January 1977), pp. 136-138.

# THE BOUNDARIES OF MARKETING

Donald P. Robin, Mississippi State University

## INTRODUCTION

This paper briefly analyzes the boundary issue in defining the scope of marketing and the benefits and problems of overlapping with other areas. In addition, an appeal is made to define marketing so as to allow flexible fringe areas to exist.

## THE BOUNDARY ISSUE IN DEFINING THE SCOPE OF MARKETING

Whenever a discussion arises about the nature and scope of marketing, the problem of conflicts from overlapping with boundary disciplines always seems to arise. The Kotler/Luck controversy is now well known but there have also been numerous other important opinions. For example, Bagozzi suggests "The (marketers) do not usurp the authority of specialists in areas such as social work, but rather they aid and complement the efforts of these social scientists. It is not so much the fact that the subject matter of marketing overlaps with that of other disciplines as it is that the problems of marketing are universal." [1, p.39] Blair took issue with Bagozzi's article commenting "Under Bagozzi's definition (of marketing), marketing loses its identity unless social psychologists are willing to be annexed under the marketing banner -- an unlikely possibility, to say the least...Bagozzi's response to these border skirmishes is rather imperialistic. Marketers should be able to accommodate expansion of their profession without annexing all of the social sciences." [2]

Other writers suggested that marketing should be defined with distinct and clear boundaries so as to "be both properly inclusive and exclusive." [3, p.19] The impression is left after reading the works of many authors on the subject that marketing must be defined so that distinct boundaries exist and that no one must trespass from the domain of one discipline to the domain of another. The discussion sometimes takes on warlike phrases like "border skirmishes" [2] to emphasize the idea that the territorial imperative of the discipline will be protected.

Marketers may choose to follow Bagozzi's definitional statement that "Marketing is a general function of universal applicability. It is the discipline of exchange behavior, and it deals with problems related to this behavior." [1, p.39] Or, they may choose to follow Luck's literal quid pro quo interpretation of Kotler's generic concept of marketing which states that "The core concept of marketing is the transaction. A transaction is the exchange of values between two parties." [5, p.71] [4, p.48] Or, marketers may choose some middle ground. In any instance, the question of border problems with other disciplines arises and marketers must deal with it.

## THE NATURE OF FRINGE AREAS

In dealing with the question of overlap with disciplines on the fringes of marketing, marketers should realize that definitive borders are not absolutely necessary. If the objective of science and scientists is knowledge, then what difference can it possibly make if someone that considers himself to be in the field of marketing spends time on problems traditionally thought to be part of social psychology. Similarly, if a social psychologist spends time working on problems that are considered to be part of marketing, or can be of assistance to marketers, so much the better for marketing. Marketing has often made use of knowledge and methodology developed or popularized in other fields. It is usually true that such information and methodology is applicable because of the similarity of problems in the areas involved, but it does not mean that marketing is invading the homeland of another discipline. It simply means that the problems of these other disciplines are also common to marketing, and that the problems of marketing are common to other disciplines.

Once marketers accept the idea of flexible fringe areas, a wealth of advantages accrue to them. Probably the biggest advantage is that the feedback of ideas from the fringe can suggest new ideas in the center. The problems of researching ideas in the fringe areas often require the individual to break away from the conventional wisdom of the center. The result of such new thinking can be beneficial to all concerned. The fringe areas and the overlaps with other disciplines are also likely to be the breeding grounds for new methodologies that can be useful to marketers. It would be extremely unfortunate if marketers defined their discipline so narrowly as to eliminate these advantages.

## THE DEFINITION OF MARKETING

The definition of marketing is not a fact to be discovered by some scientific test of hypothesis. Instead, the definition of marketing, like all definitions, is both normative and tautological. Definitions are useful because they are abstractions of things and events and thereby allow people to communicate with more understanding. The only thing necessary for a definition to be useful is agreement between the parties attempting to communicate, and they may define the thing or event in any way they choose. Thus, marketers have a free hand in determining what they mean when they use the term "marketing." Moreover, if at any time they wish to change the meaning of the label, they may agree to do so.

The overwhelming tide of opinion seems to be in favor of defining "marketing" in terms of the exchange process. The major arguments at this time relate to what types of exchanges will be included in the definition. It would be extremely unfortunate if marketers chose a definition that was highly restrictive. The fact that we haven't solved the problems of the center is no reason for ignoring the problems of the fringe areas, and information from these fringe areas may help us solve the problems of the core.

## REFERENCES

1. Bagozzi, Richard P. "Marketing as Exchange," Journal of Marketing, 39 (October, 1975), 32-39.

2. Blair, Ed. Journal of Marketing, 41 (January, 1977), 134.

3. Hunt, Shelley D. "The Nature and Scope of Marketing," Journal of Marketing, 40 (July, 1976), 17-28.

4. Kotler, Philip. "A Generic Concept of Marketing," Journal of Marketing, 36 (April, 1972), 46-54.

5. Luck, David J. "Social Marketing: Confusion Compounded," Journal of Marketing, 38 (October, 1974), 70-72.

# GENERAL THEORY OF MARKETING

Robert Bartels, The Ohio State University

## ABSTRACT

Explicit or implicit, general theory of marketing is, at a time, the broadest statement of what marketing is all about. As the concept of marketing broadens, so does the general theory of marketing. Whether in absolute or relative context, marketing theory needs to be better written and better taught.

## INTRODUCTION

Although the practice of marketing has ancient roots, development of it as a scientific discipline has occurred since 1900. Interest in its theoretical character surfaced during the 1930s, and what was probably the first AMA conference session devoted to marketing theory was held in 1946. Since then, much has been thought and written about both the form and content of marketing theory. A review of that thought leads one to four generalizations.

### MARKETING THOUGHT HAS EVOLVED IN A SUCCESSION OF GENERAL THEORIES OF MARKETING

A continuing interest to marketing theorists centers on the subject of a general theory of marketing: whether there is a general theory; whether such a theory can be formulated; whether there are several or one general theory of marketing. Any light which can be shed on this subject may bring into better perspective the recurring debates about it.

What may be called "general theory" is related to the tendency in scholarship to synthesize, generalize, and bring closure to a body of knowledge. Thus, in form, general theory is inclusive, encompassing. Its dimensions are determined by the implications of the definition of the subject. As related to marketing, general theory is delimited by the perceived scope of marketing and nature of its problems. It relates to and is intended to explain the broader nature of marketing. Although it may have operational implications and subset theories, its principal concern is the question of what marketing in general is all about.

Throughout 75 years, many theories of marketing have been expressed, but overriding them has been the scholarly impulse to define and to synthesize what marketing is. This articulation at any point in time has constituted a general theory of marketing. It may, at that time, even have been the general theory of marketing, being then the most comprehensive extant statement about marketing.

There have been a number of general theories of marketing, each expressive of the circumstances and viewpoints of their respective periods, each in succession different from and broader than its predecessors. Each was the product of someone pushing the frontiers of marketing thought into a broader integration of the subject. These successive statements constituted a series of rising plateaus in marketing thought from which additional lesser theories were formulated. There is, therefore, no reason to think that any currently creditable general theory is the last to be formulated. Others will follow as other concepts of marketing emerge.

The general theories of marketing have been stated in various terms, and for different audiences:

1. In the original "principles" of functions-institutions-commodities, to a world of early 20th century business awakening to consciousness of marketing,

2. In variables of the Four Ps and of the Marketing Mix, to professional marketers needing refinement of their decision making,

3. In sets of roles and systems, both economic and social, to administrators of increasingly complex and interacting elements,

4. In relationships of dependence and independence between marketing and its environment, to societies increasingly concerned with their means and ends,

5. In theories of macromarketing, for public administration of micro systems in the best interests of society at large.

Although not always perceived as "general theories," these theories have constituted the broad interpretations of marketing. They have evoked controversy among adherents of divergent viewpoints. They have elicited demand for precision of logic, research, and expression.

Whatever controversy exists today concerning the structural outline of any comprehensive interpretation of marketing, it should be viewed in the context of the continuing efford to define what marketing is.

### ALTHOUGH THE SUCCESSION OF GENERAL MARKETING THEORIES HAS HAD A REPETITIOUS PATTERN, IT HAS ALSO BEEN PROGRESSIVE

Periodic changes in marketing theory have resulted not so much from changing market conditions as from changing concepts of marketing held by practitioner, scholars, and society at large. The progressive character of these concepts is that they have been of an ever broadening nature. The original general theory of marketing presented an overall but narrow interpretation of marketing as an integration of functions involved in distribution. Later these were brought into focus as managerial marketing, not on the level of sales management but management of the entire micromarketing process, even in relation to other functions of the firm. Afterwards, the concept was enlarged to include behavioral as well as economic considerations for managers, orientation to the external environment, and, ultimately, responsibility thereto. Still other extensions of the concept of marketing have included reintegration of the physical and negotiatory aspects of distribution, association of domestic with international and foreign marketing, and recognition of marketing management in the public as well as in the private sector.

The progressiveness of this development has been of two types. First, each successive view of marketing has required a larger conceptual framework and more comprehensive intellectual capacity for interpreting it. Second, as one theory has been superceded by the next, it has also been subsumed by it, implicitly or explicitly included in it. In theory development, this relationship has not always been explicated, for it has required a breadth of perception and a dedication to generalization often believed to be professionally unprofitable. Nevertheless, the consistency and integrity of marketing thought must be

demonstrated, and a few theorists have attempted to provide a structure of theory and of metatheory which suggests these qualities, if only in outline.

In answer to the question:  Is such an effort useful, is
it practical?, one may say:  To the corner grocer, probably not; to the large domestic or multinational corporation,
probably yes; to the public administrator, yes; and to the
scholar and teacher of marketing, definitely yes.

### ANOMALIES OF STRUCTURE AND AMBIGUITY OF TERMINOLOGY HAVE MADE MARKETING THEORY LESS COHERENT THAN IT MIGHT BE

No one, individually or collectively, has set out intentionally to outline the complete structure of marketing or
the body of marketing though -- neither the scholars of
earlier years, nor more recent generalists, nor critics of
those who proposed a general theory framework.  Instead,
the discipline of marketing has just grown, somewhat like
Topsey -- here a little, there a little, often dependent
upon personal interests and qualifications.  Moreover, as
new concepts developed, many individuals coined terms and
phrases to express them.  Consequently, the structure of
marketing thought is no nicely developed whole, and the
task of constructing a general theory by integration of
its loosely related components is a difficult one.

Several instances illustrate this proposition.

1.  Although marketing was originally concerned with both
    the physical and negotiatory functions, they became
    separated as social and behavioral elements gained as-
    cendency in the negotiatory area, and as logistical
    and quantitative elements were introduced into physical
    distribution.  They must be reunited if general theo-
    ry is to be comprehensive.

2.  Although wholesaling and retailing have been treated
    as _institutional_ topics, their respective literatures
    warrant considering whether they should not be dealt
    with for their _functional_ differences, rather than
    for their management similarities.

3.  The functions of marketing have been listed as though
    their identification was a semantical question or a
    matter of literary license.  Yet as marketing is con-
    ceived, there are implicit functions to which little
    attention is given, as, for example, the function of
    availability.

4.  Because of absence of responsibility for accuracy and
    uniformity in definition, the AMA Committee on Defini-
    tions notwithstanding, some terms are used with dif-
    ferent meanings and to some meanings different terms
    are given.  The term "social marketing," for example,
    has several meanings in the literature.  Others un-
    clearly defined are "metamarketing," "metatheory,"
    "possession utility," and "macromarketing."

Macromarketing is deserving of attention, for as a new
concept it is used to represent such different ideas as
systems of micromarketing institutions, marketing in its
social context, social responsibility of marketing, and
theory concerned with the overall marketing institution.
Before the literature gets cluttered with personal definitions of the term, attention should be given to establishing the idea to which it is best fitted.

### ALONG WITH CONTINUING NEED TO WRITE BETTER MARKETING THEORY, THERE IS EQUALLY GREAT NEED TO TEACH IT

It is not uncommon for both undergraduate and graduate
students of marketing when challenged to identify and apply marketing theory, as in case courses, to claim that
they know no marketing theory.  This results from teachers'
presentation of marketing as a practice or process rather
than as a system of thought, from their belief that theory
is impractical, or from their own lack of an integrated
concentual framework for marketing.  These deficiencies
result also from the untheoretical nature of the marketing
literature.  Authors do not conceptualize their subject
nor define it so as to bare their concepts and underlying
assumptions.  They follow traditional classifications, and
they leave inherent principles, laws, and relationships to
the inference of the student.  In case courses, some of
the worst offenses against theory are committed as precedent, rules of thumb, and conventional micromanagement
policies, rather than objective, scientific marketing
theory, are employed to solve marketing problems.  If students are to be educated to cope with problems of the next
ten or twenty years, this can be done best as they are
taught to think scientifically, to recognize and appreciate
theory when they see it, and to know that a sound theoretical framework will be applicable to future problems as
well as to those of today.

The challenge to marketing educators and to the marketing
profession, therefore, is to build and to critique theoretical verbalization of what marketing means today, to
integrate this meaning with what it has meant at other
times and in other circumstances, to strengthen and to
clarify its terminology and structure, and to implant
theory in both percept and precept.

THE AMA COLLEGIATE CHAPTER FACULTY ADVISOR
AND THE MARKETING CONCEPT:
PROBLEMS AND SUGGESTIONS

Donald W. Eckrich, Illinois State University
James R. Moore, Southern Illinois University

## INTRODUCTION

Among the foremost challenges currently facing the AMA
Collegiate Chapter Faculty Advisor is the need for constant adaptation of the member organization to meet the
rapidly changing needs and wants of its typically diverse
student membership. As Enis and Smith [4] have so aptly
described it, the key to successful adaptation is rooted
in the marketing concept itself. It should be a simple
matter--undertaking to orient and adapt the organization
to the needs and wants of the student membership. This
paper seeks to identify and examine several of the problems associated with the management and operations of an
AMA Collegiate Chapter for the purpose of developing the
role of the marketing concept in chapter operations.

## SORTING THROUGH THE OBSTACLES

For the novice and enterprising faculty advisor the cliché
of "what worked in the past" provides little practical
guidance. Establishing a Collegiate Chapter's objectives,
or even aiding in their establishment dictates that an advisor resort to some comparative basis for guidance. For
the already successful chapter the adaptation problem is
usually considered minimal--continuity and experience often provide the necessary cues. The foundling chapter
(and its advisor), on the other hand, must diligently pre-
plan and anticipate successful activities.

Consider the assistance available through the AMA National
Headquarters. Each faculty advisor receives an Operation
Manual designed to aid in the efficient operation of the
local chapter. Among the guiding principles are: a membership quota before national affiliation and recognition
will be granted, a statement of the advisor's role in establishing Collegiate Chapter objectives, a sales-orient-
ed approach to organizational maintenance, and a modest
set of success criteria--hardly an exemplification of the
marketing concept!

The affiliation of the "marketing club" with the national
organization and its impact on the student membership are
by no means the sole contributing factors to the adaptation problem. Figure 1 illustrates the linkages of three
additional factors with the Collegiate Chapter.

FIGURE 1

FACTORS INFLUENCING THE OPERATIONS AND
MANAGEMENT OF A COLLEGIATE CHAPTER

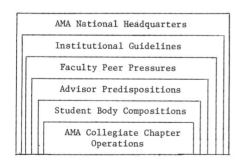

## DISCUSSION

It is indeed interesting that practically all AMA Collegiate Chapter "success stories" are based on extreme membership growth (evidence the January 1977 issue of the "Collegiate Communicator," AMA). In most cases it would appear that the sales concept has vast priority over the
marketing concept. If, in fact, the AMA Collegiate Chapter
program is designed to provide the opportunity for students
to develop both personally and professionally (the foremost
objectives stated by the AMA), then one has to seriously
question the motives underlying both the growth and continuity objectives (also stated by the AMA). While it is
understood that chapter growth and continuity may indeed
represent viable objectives for a particular Collegiate
Chapter, they may also be quite independent of the student development objective.

The prime issue in a chapter's struggle to adopt the marketing concept is identifying the appropriate measures of
success. Since most, if not all, AMA Collegiate Chapters
already possess the key--an extremely interested, enlightened, dedicated faculty advisor--it becomes a matter of
determining exactly how "successful" a chapter can be in
terms of individual student development and establishing
chapter objectives along these lines with the majority of
input coming directly from the students. In this way, the
AMA Collegiate Chapter becomes a major vehicle--not an end
--for student development.

Thus, it is conceivable--if not a reality--that a highly
successful, marketing concept-oriented Collegiate Chapter
of the AMA may stray far from the guidelines originally
designed and formulated by the AMA precisely for such chapters (in terms of size, longevity, and function). As long
as chapter success continues to be viewed in terms of head
counts, elaborate organizational-maintenance programs,
guideline conformity (whether institutional or other),
faculty-advisor peer values, and/or advisor goals, the marketing concept will remain just that--a concept--useful
only to those who pay it lip-service. However, implementation of the concept can be extremely rewarding to the
chapter and all its members.

## REFERENCES

1. Collegiate Chapter Operation Manual, American Marketing
   Association, September, 1976.

2. Collegiate Communicator, American Marketing Association,
   January, 1977.

3. Enis, Ben M. and Sam V. Smith, "The Marketing Curriculum of the Seventies: Period of the Pendulum or New
   Plane of Performance," in Marketing: 1776-1976 and Beyond, ed. by Kenneth L. Bernhardt, Chicago: American
   Marketing Association, 1976.

# POSITIONING: A KEY TO POTENTIAL SUCCESS OF A MARKETING CLUB

Paul C. Thistlethwaite, Western Illinois University
Terry T. Ball, Western Illinois University

## INTRODUCTION

The theories of marketing are applicable to the growth of a student marketing club. Trout and Ries in their 1972 article heralded a new era in marketing strategy, "the Era of Positioning." [3] The proper positioning of the marketing club may be a major factor in the success of the organization. Success will be defined as a continued commitment of a large proportion of the student members and the progressive expansion of the percentage of potential members actively involved in the organization's on-going programs. This success can be achieved through a positioning strategy.

## FOUNDATIONS OF POSITIONING

Proper positioning depends upon the accurate identification of target markets. Positioning appears to center on the qualities of the product that will be unique from its competitors. Maggard [2, p. 64] indicates that positioning may be more related to promotion and advertising than to the physical characteristics of the product.

Two major problems arise when positioning is applied to the marketing club. First, the nature of the competition is difficult to define and quantify. Second, the unique qualities of the marketing club that will attract students may be difficult to isolate. This paper considers four specific foundations of positioning.

1. What is the nature of the competition?
2. What is or who should be the club's target market(s)?
3. What are the appropriate attributes a club must possess in order to attract prospective members?
4. What are the qualities inherent in the club that will motivate the members to active participation?

### Competition Defined

The most apparent form of competition for the marketing club is the myriad of clubs found on most university campuses. For many a difficulty exists in distinquishing between similar organizations. Another competitive force facing the marketing club is the limited amount of time available to students for such activities. Consequently, an implicit ranking of various activities into some priority construct must be accomplished. The goal for the club is to have a top priority position for a majority of its members. This paper develops a student commitment continuum that appears to reflect this variation of student positioning.

### Identification of the Target Market(s)

Most students can be placed on a commitment continuum ranging from a very low commitment (potential club member: low priority) to a very high commitment (club member: top priority). Those students in the low commitment range will have some interest in the area of marketing but have not developed a strong identification with the field. Juniors who plan to major in marketing would fit into this category.

The senior marketing major who has participated in the club in the past may be a good example of the potential club member with a high priority for membership. The extent of commitment this student may possess after initially joining will depend upon the attractiveness of the offerings of the club and the relevancy of these offerings to the student's goals.

At the next level in the continuum is the uncommitted club member. Those students not establishing a priority list are at this level. These individuals may not be aware of the objectives of the club. As Berelson and Steiner suggest [1, p. 335], the objectives of the club are important in developing commitment to the group.

The top category, committed club members, set the patterns for the entire membership. Students in the lower position of this category have a strong identification with the club, even though they have other commitments. The students at the top of the continuum are the most actively involved. These are the top committee heads and officers. This group provides the leadership.

## APPLICATION OF POSITIONING

The success of the student chapter of the marketing club in positioning itself in the most favorable location will depend upon several factors. First, the degree of differentiation it can achieve as compared with similar clubs will be important. Second, it depends upon the variety of opportunities for the club members to become active participants. If the members are not afforded the opportunity of saying "yes," then the likelihood of them moving up the commitment scale is low. Third, the club can attract a mixture of target markets. This attraction will depend upon the scope and depth of the program.

If the programs are of interest to only a small select group, then most potential and marginal members will avoid involvement. When excessive emphasis is placed on specific areas of marketing, students having interest in other areas may become disinterested club members.

## EVALUATION OF THE PROGRAM

Qualitative success is difficult to measure. Quantitative success has been experienced in the club where appropriate positioning was attempted. Even with the fees set at $20, (a yearly increase of 25%), membership increased by over 25%. Of the 150+ members, over 130 were active during the school year. The definition of active must continually be reexamined.

## REFERENCES

1. Berelson, Bernard and Gary A. Steiner, Human Behavior, New York: Harcourt, Brace and World, Inc., 1964.

2. Maggard, John P., "Position Revisited," Journal of Marketing, Vol. 40, (1976), 63-66.

3. Trout, Jack and Al Ries, "Positioning Era Cometh," Advertising Age, (1972)

THE COLLEGIATE CHAPTER: A FRAMEWORK FOR
MARKETING STUDENTS JOB TALENTS - PUBLISHER
OF THE "RESUME BOOKLET."

Ronald S. Rubin, Florida Technological University

## INTRODUCTION

In the Fall quarter of 1973, during our country's recession, our students were experiencing difficulty obtaining job offers. Our student placement center had numerous cancellations by company recruiters. The decline of recruiters visiting our campus was most discouraging to the students. Also, our area's basic industry is tourism, and the recession in full swing, jobs were just not available.

At one of our weekly collegiate chapter meetings, noticing the despair of our students, I suggested that if the recruiters were not going to come to us, we shall go to them. The students in attendance were all marketing majors, and having learned how to market products and services throughout their classroom studies, I suggested turning all the knowledge they learned to their advantage and market themselves - - their knowledge, skills, and experiences.

I tried to explain to them that many sound companies, particularly smaller firms, do not have extensive college recruiting programs; or that the students may have missed the opportunity to interview a company of their choice when its recruiter was on campus. In such cases, the student should initiate a mail campaign as part of their employment search. Given this background, I suggested that the chapter include a new, potentially ongoing, project to assist members seeking jobs. They should consider becoming a publisher of a "Resume Booklet" that would summarize the students qualifications.

## DESCRIPTION OF THE PROGRAM

The chapters executive committee, after a lengthy discussion, decided that a project of this nature would be in the interest of its members and the college; and therefore, approved the "Resume Booklet" project. What follows is an abstract of the operations of the project which would help those interested in instituting it at their college.

The faculty acts as a source of job information in the sense that, as a group they pool their knowledge and develop a list of those companies within the United States who are the most appropriate prospects for the students. Taken into consideration are the type of jobs available, where the students live and want to work, and the demand in their field. The college placement center is asked to provide a list of those companies who have indicated an interest in our students. And finally, the students themselves submit a list of those companies they wish to have the publication sent to. From all these inputs, a subjective list is formed.

A flow chart was developed encompassing the activities and the approximate times necessary to accomplish the activities. This chart has been revised to eliminate those areas in which problems have arisen in the past. To date this process has proven effective.

An initial meeting, before the start of the project each year, with the faculty advisor is called to alert the students to the objective of the project and to tell them of the success of the past projects. It basically is a "motivation" session to instill enthusiasm within the students toward this undertaking.

The planning session embarks in the assigning of those interested students (this has been in the past 3/4's of the chapters members) to the committees necessary for accomplishing the completed publication. The committees established are:

Instructions and Data Form Committee, Typing Committee, Cover Design Committee, Printing Committee, Production Committee, and the Mailing Committee.

The cost of this project has been kept to a minimum, yet with professional results. The cost to the student, for the last four years of publication, has been $5.00 each, assuming that approximately 20 students participate. This price enables the chapter to print around 130 copies in which 90 are sent to various companies throughout the country, each student receives an individual copy, and the ones left over are distributed to the placement center, faculty, appropriate administrators, and when calls from recruiters ask for a copy, we more than oblige.

## CONCLUSION

The thought I would like to leave with you is that job-hunting requires the same intensity of preparation as a final examination in any of the student's college courses. Adequate planning will help assure the student of landing a job where he can make his maximum contribution and realize the most satisfaction. But such can only be the case when the student is taught to market himself. The collegiate chapter has the organizational framework in which the students can apply themselves to the task of marketing their skills. At our University, the Resume publication has become a yearly event, and the students look forward with enthusiasm to the publishing of the next edition. This project has become an experiential learning process at the same time, for they are applying the marketing concepts and techniques to a product that becomes self-seeking. The success of this project can be measured by the response received by the students from the various companies. Many of the students have received correspondence from companies seeking additional information. Company's personnel directors have called my office seeking a copy of the publication. Word of mouth has increased the recognition of the publication. In two words, to summarize the progress of our project, highly successful.

# JOURNAL AWARENESS AND QUALITY
## A STUDY OF ACADEMICIANS' VIEW OF JOURNALS

William G. Browne, Oregon State University
Boris W. Becker, Oregon State University

### ABSTRACT

The principal purpose of this study is the identification of
the prestige of journals which publish papers in marketing,
as seen by department chairmen or other administrators in
charge of marketing faculty.

### INTRODUCTION

There have been previous reports on evaluation of business
publications in general. However, there has not as yet
appeared a study dealing specifically with marketing papers
and publications. Marketing academicians have a particularly wide range of journals in which to publish their research
findings or speculative ruminations. The research question
is: What is the relative status of the numerous publication
vehicles available to marketing academicians?

This study was motivated by two reasons, the first of which
is admittedly somewhat crass. The publication of papers
plays an important effect on all our lives. Research productivity, however defined, allegedly affects decisions on
tenure, promotion and pay. If publication is an important
criterion in evaluation of marketing faculty and if, there
is a difference in the rewards to "excellent" papers and
papers in mediocre journals, then evaluation of journals by
administrators is a useful piece of information to use in
clarifying "the rules of the game."

The second reason motivating this study is simple intellectual curiosity. Paul Samuelson said, in his presidential
address to the American Economics Association, that we play
to the applause of our peers. If this is true, which it
probably is, then our administrators may give us some consensus as to where to publish a paper to get the most
applause, the most admiration, from our colleagues.

There are some other important, albeit subordinate, purposes to this study. First, do all marketing departments
evaluate journals similarly, or is there some systematic
variation in the prestige accorded these publications?
Second, to what extent has publication traditionally been
an important criterion in the evaluation of marketing faculty? Does publication appear to be growing or diminishing
in importance as an element in the marketing academician's
evaluation? Finally, does the importance of publication
vary across schools, as might the evaluation of journals?

### METHODOLOGY

The first step in the research was identification of the
relevant set of journals for evaluation. Journals selected
were those which were commonly referenced in the Journal of
Marketing, both in published articles and in the "Marketing
Abstract" section, and in widely used marketing texts.

A simple four-level rating scale was developed for evaluating the journals. The levels of the scale are: I - Highest quality; II - high quality; III - good quality; IV -
low quality. Of course, too much should not be read into
this instrument. The data are ordinally, rather than intervally scaled. A journal with an average rating of 1.7,
therefore, is not necessarily exactly twice as prestigious
as a journal rated 3.4. The instrument, nonetheless, does
allow the rank ordering of journals as to their quality,
which is the modest objective of this research.

Besides evaluations of the journals, data were also collected on the characteristics of responding departments and
schools and their views of publication. This was done to
assess representativeness of respondents and to see if any
systematic differences in journal evaluations could be
attributed to differences between schools.

The subjects for this research, in reality, constituted the
entire universe under consideration, rather than a sample.
The universe was defined as all those marketing departments which meet both of two criteria. First, at least two
members of the marketing faculty are AMA members. Second,
the school is a member of the American Association of Collegiate School of Business (AACSB). The questionnaire was
sent to 235 marketing departments which met the two criteria specified above. These included schools in the United
States and Canada, plus a small number of foreign institutions. The envelope was addressed to the chairman of the
marketing department. Together with the questionnaire was
mailed a cover letter, explaining the purpose of the study
and stressing the confidential nature of all responses.

### RESULTS

A total of 151 departments, 64% of the universe, responded
to the questionnaire. The respondents appear to be reasonably representative of the universe on a number of
dimensions: region; school size; curriculum type. Seventy-
one larger schools responded and 80 small schools.

Familiarity and quality indexes were compared for large
and small schools. Large business schools were defined as
those with 60 or more faculty members; small schools were
those with less than 60 faculty. There is clearly no difference between the familiartiy rankings for large and
small schools. The rank order correlation coefficient for
familiarity, across large and small schools, is 0.97!
Comparison of quality indexes yields a similar result. The
rank order correlation for mean quality, as between large
and small schools, is 0.91. There is undeniably a similarity between small and large business schools both as to
familiarity with marketing journals and the evaluation of
these journals as to quality.

Approximately one half of the smaller schools have had a
majority of their marketing staff publish during the past
year, while two-thirds of the larger schools have had a
majority of their faculty publish journal articles. The
historical importance of publishing in faculty evaluation
also differs between the large and smaller schools. Half
of the smaller have traditionally attributed importance to
publishing, while two-thirds of the large schools indicated
that publishing has previously been important in faculty
evaluation.

The influence of publication on faculty evaluation is becoming more important in schools of every size. Seventy-
two percent of the smaller schools and eighty percent of
the larger schools indicated that publication was becoming
even more important. Fifty percent of the smaller schools
indicated that the evaluation process differentiated between "peer" and "practitioner" publications, while seventy-
one percent of the larger schools indicated that the differentiation exists and/or occurs.

# WHEN MARKETING SCHOLARS CONGREGATE:
## CROSS-NATIONAL STUDY OF COMMUNICATIONS BEHAVIOR OF SCIENTIFIC OPINION LEADERS

Johan Arndt, University of Missoury - St. Louis
Kjell Grønhaug, Norwegian School of Economics and Business Administration
Oddvar Holmer, Norwegian School of Economics and Business Administration
Torger Reve, Northwestern University
Sigurd V. Troye, Norwegian School of Economics and Business Administration

## ABSTRACT

This study is concerned with the information-exchange behavior of a sample of European marketing scholars. Opinion leaders were more differentiated by evaluation of sources of information than by competence or strategic location. At an annual convention, scientific opinion leaders were more active in formal and informal channels.

## INTRODUCTION

A common goal of scientists is to produce knowledge, communicate the findings to the community of colleagues, and to add to the cumulative body of knowledge of their discipline. Scientists are not only motivated to communicate, but also to seek information and to utilize it. Therefore, communication among scientists serves a double function: it is a major input to and, at the same time, the ultimate objective of scientific endeavor.

In view of the wide recognition of the information function in marketing, it is somewhat surprising that the communication among marketing researchers has been almost completely neglected. The study to be reported in this paper is an attempt to rectify the matter.

## CONCEPTUAL FOUNDATIONS OF THE STUDY

In the conceptual framework underlying the study, the variable Opinion leadership is hypothesized to be related to a group of antecedent variables, and to be causally related to dimensions of conference behavior.

In the terms of Katz [1], influentials are characterized by competence (what one knows) and by strategic social location (whom one knows). In this case, competence was believed to be documented in scientific production and manifested in occupational achievement. To exert opinion leadership, influentials must have a central position in the personal networks. First, they must be accessible to their followers. Second, they must have contacts with more demanding cosmopolite personal and impersonal sources. On the basis of the profile of opinion leaders, they were expected to be more active at conferences both in presenting formal papers and being involved in informal person-to-person channels.

## METHOD

The conceptual framework requires measuring antecedent variables and opinion leadership prior to conference behavior of the population sampled.

The approach chosen was to make a two-step study of university-affiliated European researchers in marketing. The population in the first step was all members of the European Academy for Advanced Research in Marketing (EAARM) plus all non-members attending the Fourth Annual Conference in the Spring of 1975. In January/February 1976, a structured questionnaire (requesting information regarding indicators of competence, strategic location and evaluation of sources of information) was sent to the 158 persons included in the population. After two waves of mailings, supplemented with telephone calls, 88 respondents completed or partially completed the questionnaires.

The second population was the 105 participants at the Fifth Annual Conference conducted in April 1976. In all, 80 participants turned in a completed or partially completed questionnaire, either at the conference or by mail subsequently. The second questionnaire contained items relating to conference behavior such as participation in formal and informal channels.

Opinion leadership was measured in Step One by the sociometric method as each respondent was asked to name persons to whom he or she would turn for exchange of information. In all, only 28 persons received one or more choices (our operational definition of opinion leadership when viewed as a dichotomous trait).

## RESULTS

In order to assess the importance of the various antecedent variables with respect to opinion leadership, stepwise multiple regression was conducted.

The 15 variables entered explained about 40 per cent of the variance. The seven most important variables, as measured by the Beta coefficient, were all informational variables. These variables accounted for 73 per cent of the variance explained, as compared to 21 per cent for the competence indicators and 6 per cent for the strategic location variables.

The variables uncovered in the regression analysis were next used as predictors in a stepwise discriminant analysis. Since 18 out of the 88 persons reached in Step One were opinion leaders, the expected proportion of correct classifications by chance would be: .67.

The multiple discriminant function classified correctly 69 respondents, or 78 per cent.

As regards conference behavior of the opinion leaders, 67 per cent of the leaders included in the Step One population were present at the conference, as compared to 28 per cent for the non-leaders (p < .01).

The correlation between opinion leadership and number of informal contacts at the conference was r= +.46 (p<.01).

The leaders were also more active in the formal channels at the conference, such as presenting papers.

## REFERENCES

1. Katz, Elihu. "The Two-Step Flow of Communication: An Up-to-Date Report on an Hypothesis", Public Opinion Quarterly, 21 (Spring 1957), 61-78.

543
532

817132